Mathematics for Elementary School Teachers

A Problem-Solving Approach

Mathematics for Elementary School Teachers

A Problem-Solving Approach

JOSEPH NEWMARK

The College of Staten Island
City University of New York

ADDISON-WESLEY PUBLISHING COMPANY

Reading, Massachusetts • Menlo Park, California
New York • Don Mills, Ontario • Wokingham, England
Amsterdam • Bonn • Sydney • Singapore • Tokyo
Madrid • San Juan • Milan • Paris

Library of Congress Cataloging–in–Publication Data

Newmark, Joseph.
  Mathematics for elementary teachers : a problem solving approach/
by Joseph Newmark.
      p.   cm.
  Includes bibliographies and index.
  ISBN 0–201–19123–7
  1. Mathemathics—Study and teaching (Elementary)   2. Problem
solving.   I. Title.
QA135.5.N48 1991
372.7--dc20   89–35517
                                                                    CIP

ABCDEFGHIJ–DO–9594939291

To Trudy, Sharon, Rochelle,
Stephen, and Cindy

PREFACE

The goal of teaching mathematics is not only to drill students to master routine mechanical or computational procedures but also to facilitate problem solving. In 1989, The National Council of The Teachers of Mathematics (NCTM) published its *Curriculum and Evaluation Standards of School Mathematics* in which it recommended that "prospective teachers must be taught in a way similar to how they are to teach." This book was written with this recommendation as the guiding principle.

Additionally, this text follows the suggestions of the Committee on the Undergraduate Program in Mathematics as contained in *Recommendations on the Mathematics Preparation of Teachers*. Our guidelines have been to introduce mathematical concepts in an understandable and correct manner so as to progress from simple situations to more challenging ideas once the student gains confidence. We emphasize problem-solving skills so that the student can think, read, write, and speak the "language of mathematics."

We believe that this book is an improvement on the existing texts in the market in a number of important ways;

NCTM Guidelines   Each chapter opens with direct quotations from the NCTM guidelines that tie the chapter material to what the NCTM believes students should eventually be able to teach.

Organization   The topics are covered in the same sequential order as they are normally developed in the elementary school curriculum.

There is sufficient material in this book for either a one-semester or two-semester course, as indicated in the suggested course outline for both one- and two-semester courses.

SUGGESTED COURSE OUTLINE	
One-semester Course Suggested Chapters:	1, 2 (skip § 2.3), 3, 4 (skip § 4.5–4.7), 5, 6, 7 (skip § 7.2–7.3), 8, 9 (skip § 9.5–9.6), 10, 13 (skip all references to LOGO)
Two-semester Courses First Semester Suggested Chapters:	1, 2, 3, 4 (skip § 4.5–4.7), 5, 6, 7 (skip § 7.2–7.3), 8, 9, include all material on BASIC
Second Semester Suggested Chapters:	10, 11, 12, 13, 14, Appendices, include all material on BASIC and LOGO

Problem-Solving Approach   Throughout the book, Polya's four-step problem-solving approach is emphasized. Numerous strategies are developed that can be used for the examples or exercises. The depth of problem-solving coverage can be adjusted by the instructor depending upon the exercises assigned.

Examples and exercises   All of the applied examples and exercises have been selected to maintain student interest. The exercises (which are arranged from easy to more challenging) are grouped into three categories. The first group are routine and they help build skills and understanding of the concepts. The second group are of the problem-solving type for which Polya's four-step problem-solving technique is appropriate. The third group called brain-teasers are somewhat more challenging.

Typical Classroom Questions   Each chapter contains a section that presents questions that are often asked in class. The objective is to alert teachers to such questions and also to prepare them to answer these questions.

Coverage of Algebra and Probability and Statistics   This book offers more extensive coverage of Algebra and Probability and Statistics that can be found in other available texts. This is in line with the greater emphasis currently being placed on these topics.

Approach to Geometry The four chapters on geometry emphasize the five-level Van Hiele model of children's development in geometry.

LOGO The computer-oriented LOGO graphics program utilizing a turtle is integrated throughout the geometry chapters, as appropriate.

Calculator or Computer As suggested by the NCTM, the use of calculators or computers is highly recommended. In Chapter 1, we introduce the calculator as a problem-solving tool. Throughout the book, some of the examples and exercises are specifically designed to be worked out using a hand-held calculator. Such exercises are designated by the ▦ symbol. In addition to the BASIC programs that appear in Chapter 14, many BASIC programs appear throughout the book where they can be applied.

Real-Life Relevance Each chapter contains at least one newspaper article illustrating how the ideas discussed in the chapter occur in everyday life. Moreover, there are numerous magazine clippings and pictures throughout the book to further enhance the material. These show the student how the chapter's concepts can be applied in real-life situations.

Historical notes Most chapters contain brief historical notes about mathematicians who contributed to the ideas discussed within the chapter. These should help to humanize mathematics.

Pedagogical Aids

Chapter Objectives. Each chapter opens with chapter objectives that highlight the key ideas to be discussed.

Introduction. Each chapter's introductory section sets the stage for the ideas contained in the chapter.

Comments. In numerous places, "Comments" are included covering ideas that students often miss or find confusing.

Summary. Each chapter concludes with Study Guide, Key Words, and Formulas to Remember. The Key Words lists the significant new terms introduced in each section of the chapter. The Study Guide highlights the main point of the chapter (along with page numbers). Past experience indicates that students find these extremely useful in studying and preparing for exams.

Chapter Review Exercises. Each chapter concludes with a comprehensive review set of exercises that can be used as a student self-test.

Answers. Answers are provided at the end of the book for selected exercises as well as for all the Typical Classroom Questions and all the Chapter Review Exercises.

Supplementary Material A *Solutions Manual,* which provides detailed line-by-line solutions to *all* the exercises, is available from the publisher.

ACKNOWLEDGEMENTS

I am grateful to the many colleagues and former students for their valuable suggestions and constructive criticism of *Mathematics As A Second Language*. I continue to welcome any comments concerning material in this text.

I also wish to thank the following people who reviewed the manuscript and who made valuable suggestions for its improvement:

Carol J. Achs
Mesa Community College

Peter G. Braunfeld
University of Illinois

Donald J, Dessart
University of Tennessee, Knoxville

Annalisa Ebanks
Jefferson Community College

Herbert E. Kasube
Bradley University

Finally, and most importantly, I wish to thank my family for their understanding and continued encouragement as they patiently endured the enormous strain associated with such an undertaking.

Brooklyn, New York   Joseph Newmark

To The Student

Congratulations to you upon selecting teaching as a profession. As future teachers, you will often encounter students who ask "Why should I study mathematics? I'm never going to use it. It has no practical applications for me." In this text, we hope to show how mathematics affects almost every aspects of one's life. Regardless of one's objective in life, both career and recreational, a knowledge of mathematics is essential.

A special effort has been made in this text to make the ideas of mathematics available to students who are not prepared for elaborate symbolisms or complex arithmetic. Although the mathematical content is complete and correct, the language is rather elementary and understandable. Mathematical rigor has not been sacrificed. This makes the text comprehensible to students of varying backgrounds. We have tried to introduce complicated ideas at understandable levels. Words, phrases, and any modes of expression that students find difficult to comprehend have been avoided.

To facilitate your understanding and learning of the material the following student-oriented features have been included in this book.

Chapter objectives   Each chapter opens with chapter objectives that highlight the ideas to be discussed.

Newspaper article or magazine clipping   Each chapter contains at least one article representing ideas discussed in the chapter.

Moreover, there are numerous magazine clippings and pictures throughout the book to further enhance the material. These show you how the chapter's concepts can be applied in real-life situations.

Introduction   Each chapter's introductory section sets the stage for the ideas contained in the chapter.

Student-oriented comments   In numerous places, "Comments" are included, covering ideas that students often miss or find confusing.

Historical notes   Most chapters contain brief historical notes about mathematicians who contributed to the ideas discussed within the chapter. These should help to humanize mathematics.

Student aids   Each chapter concludes with Study Guide, Key Words, and Formulas to Remember. The Key Words lists the significant new terms introduced in each section of the chapter. The Study Guide highlights the main point of the chapter (along with page numbers). Past experience indicates that students find these extremely useful in studying and preparing for exams.

Boldface type, italics, and boxes   Certain words or ideas are set in italics for emphasis; key terms are set in boldface type as well as in color in the margin. Also, formulas and rules are highlighted by boxes.

Examples and exercises   All of the applied examples and exercises have been selected to maintain your interest. The exercises (which are arranged from easy to more challenging) are grouped into three categories. The first group are routine and they should help build your skill and understanding of the concepts. The second group are of the problem-solving type for which you should use Polya's four-step problem-solving technique. The third group called brain-teasers are somewhat more challenging.

Chapter Review Exercises   Each chapter concludes with a comprehensive review set of exercises that can be used to test your knowledge and understanding of the ideas covered within the chapter.

Answers   Answers are provided at the end of the book for the odd-numbered exercises as well as for all the Typical Classroom Questions and all the Chapter Review Exercises.

Suggested further reading   Each chapter concludes with a bibliography for articles or additional information.

We hope that you will find reading and using this book an enjoyable experience and that it will prove helpful to prepare you to become the best possible teacher that you could be.

Contents

Number System

CHAPTER 1

Using Mathematics for Problem Solving

CHAPTER OBJECTIVES

☐ **To discuss** Polya's four-point guidelines to be used for problem solving. (*Section 1.1*)

☐ **To introduce** inductive reasoning where we arrive at a general conclusion on the basis of special cases. (*Section 1.2*)

☐ **To indicate** that conjectures are claims believed to be true on the basis of specific cases. (*Section 1.2*)

☐ **To point** out that conjectures are not 100% true unless they are proven beyond any doubt. (*Section 1.2*)

☐ **To study** some specific conjectures. (*Section 1.2*)

☐ **To analyze** some mathematical patterns and how we use inductive reasoning to generalize. (*Section 1.2*)

☐ **To learn** about magic squares and their properties. (*Section 1.3*)

☐ **To describe** the different types of calculators available, how they work, and how they can be used in the problem-solving process. (*Section 1.4*)

☐ **To apply** the problem-solving technique to some examples. (*Throughout chapter*)

NCTM GUIDELINES

In its March 1989 *Curriculum And Evaluation Standards For School Mathematics* (p. 23), The National Council Of Teachers Of Mathematics recommends that the study of mathematics should emphasize problem solving as a method of inquiry and application so that students can:

❑ use problem-solving approaches to investigate and understand mathematical content,

❑ formulate problems for everyday and mathematical situations,

❑ develop and apply a variety of strategies to solve problems, with emphasis on multistep and nonroutine problems,

❑ verify and interpret results with respect to the original problem situation,

❑ generalize solutions and strategies to new problem situations,

❑ recognize patterns,

❑ acquire confidence in using mathematics meaningfully.

It should be noted that problem solving is not a distinct topic, but rather a process that should permeate the entire mathematics program and provide the context in which concepts and skills can be learned. It is for this reason that in this chapter we will study Polya's strategies for problem solving. These strategies will be used throughout the book.

Introduction

The goal of teaching mathematics is not only to drill students to master routine mechanical or computational procedures, but also to facilitate problem solving. As a matter of fact, a recent report by the National Council of Teachers of Mathematics asserted that the kind of problems most often encountered in the workplace and in real life are not as routine as they are laid out to be in traditional mathematics textbooks. The report further stated that it was more important for students to develop cognitive skills—among them, **investigation**, **estimation**, and **reasoning**—to build their confidence that they can solve whatever problems they meet.

The report concluded that while students should continue to learn mechanical mathematical skills, the current curriculum should emphasize the development of "**problem-solving skills**" to enable students to think, read, write, and speak the "language of mathematics."

These are the objectives that we will emphasize throughout this book. Toward this end, in this chapter we will discuss a problem-solving process that will aid you in solving problems.

1.1

USING THE PROBLEM-SOLVING PROCESS

One of the beauties of mathematics lies in our ability to use it to solve many real-life problems. In this book we will examine how the ideas of mathematics can be used in everyday settings to build your problem—solving abilities. Generally speaking, we often seek out a relationship in simpler cases; that is, we try to discover patterns. This is a very important strategy in problem solving. (The patterns may or may not be helpful in providing a solution.) Only when a pattern is discovered should one try to generalize any result. Different people may discover different patterns in the same set of data and form different conclusions.

Before attempting to solve any mathematical problems, we must develop techniques that can be used to solve them. It should be realized that some mathematical exercises are merely computational in nature. To arrive at solutions for such exercises, we must perform certain routine procedures. On the other hand, there are other problems that require careful thought, since we must apply our previously acquired knowledge to new and unfamiliar situations. What may seem like a problem for one person may actually be an exercise or a mathematical fact for another person. Thus, to a young child, finding $2 + 3$ and finding $3 + 2$ might appear to be two different problems, whereas to you they appear to be simple exercises or mathematical facts.

A well-known mathematician and teacher, George Polya, studied the strategy for solving problems. In his widely read book, *How To Solve It*,

four-step process to be used in problem solving

Polya developed a four-step process to be used in problem solving. It should be noted that these are merely guidelines; they will not provide us with the exact steps that will "work" in every problem. When you encounter a problem that *seems* beyond your capabilities, do not get discouraged. Take the time to reread the problem a second time (and perhaps a third or fourth time) slowly.

Polya's guide lines appear on the following page.

HISTORICAL NOTE

George Polya (1887–1985) was born in Hungary and attended the Universities of Budapest, Vienna, Göttingen, and Paris. After coming to the United States he accepted a teaching position at Stanford University. In 1945 he wrote his world-renowned book *How To Solve It*. This book, published by Princeton University Press, has been translated into 15 different languages. It explores and outlines techniques to be used in problem solving.

SO YOU THINK YOU'RE SMART

Each of the following problems represents a succession of letters, numbers, or diagrams. Each sequence is arranged according to a different pattern. After you discover the pattern, determine the next item in the sequence. Allow yourself 15 minutes to answer all the questions.

1. 27, 26, 24, 21, 17, 12, ...
2. A, E, I, M, ...
3. 4, 13, 28, 49, 76, ...
4. 2, 12, 36, 80, ...

5. A, B, D, G, K, ...
6. 1, 2, 6, 24, 120, ...
7. 4, 5, 6, 5, 6, 7, 6, 7, 8, ..., ... Which two numbers should come next? **a)** 9 and 10 **b)** 9 and 8 **c)** 7 and 6 **d)** 6 and 7 **e)** 7 and 8
8. What is the next diagram in the following sequence? — $\wedge$ $\triangledown$

a) $\square$ **b)** $\bigcirc$ **c)** $+$ **d)** $\vee$ **e)** $\triangleright$

Often we see brainteaser questions similar to the ones shown here in popular magazines. Obviously, in order to find the next item in the sequence, we must first analyze the sequence and determine the pattern illustrated. How do we discover patterns and solve these problems?

For the benefit of the curious, the answers to the above brainteasers are

1. 6
2. Q
3. 109 (This represents the sequence $3x^2 + 1$)
4. 150 (This represents the sequence $x^2 + x^3$)
5. P
6. 720 (This represents the sequence $x!$)
7. Choice (e)
8. Choice (a)

Polya's Four-step Process for Problem Solving

1. **Understanding the problem**

   a) Read the problem so that you understand it. Reread it a second (and perhaps a third and fourth) time. Can you restate the problem in your own words?

   b) Can you determine what you are looking for; that is, what is the unknown?

   c) What facts are given; that is, what information is supplied in the problem? Is the given information sufficient to solve the problem? Is it redundant or contradictory? Is any information missing? Possibly make a table or draw a diagram (introducing the appropriate notation) to illustrate the problem.

   d) What condition(s) must be satisfied?

2. **Devising a plan**

   a) Have you ever before seen this problem or one substantially similar to it? Can you find a pattern or relationship that exists in the problem?

   b) Do you know of a related problem? Is there a theorem or technique that could be useful to solve even a simpler or special case of the problem?

   c) Try to think of a familiar or simple problem you can solve that will help you solve the given problem.

   d) Can you write an equation that connects the unknown quantity with the known quantities? (Some problems may require several equations.)

   e) Can you guess the answer? Does it check out? Can you work backwards?

   f) Can you restate the problem differently so as to gain some additional insight?

3. **Carrying out the plan**

   Carry out the plan developed in part 2 to solve the problem. Perform the necessary computations and check each step as you proceed. Can you see clearly (and prove) that each step is correct?

4. **Looking back**

   a) Examine the solution obtained and interpret the results in terms of the original problem.

   b) Can you check your results? This means going back to the original statement of the problem and checking the results.

   c) Can you derive the result differently? Is there another method for finding the solution?

   d) Can you generalize your results; that is, can you use the result or method to solve other problems?

Throughout this book we will use Polya's approach. Some of the problems and exercises will be specifically designated as problem solving and will be labeled as such. However, we will combine steps 2 and 3 into one step. Thus we will have the following three parts to any problem-solving example.

1. Understanding the problem
2. A plan to solve the problem
3. Checking our solution.

It should be noted that some students often believe that they can do mathematics but cannot do word problems. To overcome this fear of word problems, greater emphasis should be placed on problem solving and on understanding a problem. To develop confidence, students should try to solve as many problems as possible. Although many problems can be solved in a variety of ways, students need find only one solution to be successful. Remember, experience in problem solving is very valuable. It is for this reason that students today are being introduced to a five-step checklist technique as can be seen in the exerpt from *Addison-Wesley Mathematics*, 1987, Grade 8, p. 138 on the next page.

In the following examples we will apply Polya's problem-solving technique. Furthermore, we will indicate which problem-solving technique we are using.

EXAMPLE 1

Problem-Solving Strategy 1—Making a Table
A postal carrier with an unusual mathematical curiosity notices that Mary Lou McDermitt and Jason Andrews both live on the same block and that the houses on that block have house numbers from 200 to 300. Both of their house numbers are exactly divisible by 23. Mary Lou's house number is as small as it can be whereas Jason's house number is as large as it can be. Find the house number of each person.

SOLUTION

Understanding the Problem
Mary Lou and Jason live on the same block. The houses on that block have numbers from 200 to 300. Based upon the given information, both of their house numbers are exactly divisible by 23. Also, Mary Lou's house number is as small as it can be, whereas Jason's is as large as it can be. We must find the house number of each person.

A Plan to Solve the Problem
As mentioned earlier, sometimes we can make up a list or table to help us see a pattern and solve a problem. Thus, since the house numbers are

PROBLEM SOLVING: Using the 5-Point Checklist

QUESTION
DATA
PLAN
ANSWER
CHECK

To Solve a Problem

1. Understand the QUESTION   4. Find the ANSWER

2. Find the needed DATA   5. CHECK back

3. PLAN what to do

Rhett ate a cheddar cheese sandwich and drank a glass of milk. The sandwich and the milk had a total of 505 calories. The milk had 180 calories. How many calories were there in the sandwich?

You can use the 5-Point Checklist as you write and solve an equation for the problem above.

1. Understand the QUESTION
You need to find the number of calories in the sandwich.

Choose a variable for the unknown number.

Let c = the number of calories in the sandwich.

2. Find the needed DATA
The total was 505 calories.
The milk had 180 calories.

$$\begin{array}{ccc} c & 180 & 505 \\ \uparrow & \uparrow & \uparrow \\ \text{Sandwich} & \text{Milk} & \text{Total} \end{array}$$

3. PLAN what to do
Write an equation.

$$c + 180 = 505$$

4. Find the ANSWER
Solve the equation.

$$c + 180 = 505$$
$$c + 180 - 180 = 505 - 180$$
$$c = 325$$

5. CHECK back
Substitute 325 for c.

$$325 + 180 = 505 \quad \text{It checks.}$$

The sandwich had 325 calories.

exactly divisible by 23 they must be multiples of 23. The multiples of 23 are 23, 46, 69, 92, 115, 138, 161, 184, 207, 230, 253, 276, 299, . . . The multiples of 23 between 200 and 300 are

$$207, 230, 253, 276, \text{ and } 299$$

Since Mary Lou's house number is as small as it can be, it must be 207. Also, as Jason's house number is as large as it can be it must be 299.

Checking Our Solution

The smallest multiple of 23 between 200 and 300 is 207 and the largest multiple is 299. Both of these numbers are exactly divisible by 23. No number between 200 and 300 that is smaller than 203 or larger than 299 is exactly divisible by 23. Thus Mary Lou's house number is 207 and Jason's house number is 299.

Problem-Solving Strategy 2—Making a List and/or Using Equations

EXAMPLE 2

Using equations. In order to graduate, many colleges and universities require that students demonstrate mathematical proficiency. Tom McCabe took a mathematics proficiency exam which consisted of 15 arithmetic questions each worth three points and 15 algebra questions each worth five points. Tom correctly answered 22 questions and scored 86 points on the exam. How many questions of each type did he answer correctly?

SOLUTION

Understanding the Problem

We are told that Tom scored 86 points on the exam that consisted of 30 questions. The 15 arithmetic questions were worth three points each and the 15 algebra questions were worth five points each. We are interested in determining the number of questions of each type that Tom answered correctly.

A Plan to Solve the Problem

There are several ways to solve the problem. We could make up a table listing all the possible ways that the 30 questions could be answered and the corresponding point values. This rather inefficient method would produce the following results:

Number of Correctly Answered		Point Value of Each		Total Points From		
Arithmetic Questions	Algebra Questions	Arithmetic Question	Algebra Question	Arithmetic Questions	Algebra Questions	Total Points
0	0	3	5	0	0	0
1	1	3	5	3	5	8
2	1	3	5	6	5	11
⋮	⋮	⋮	⋮	⋮	⋮	⋮
12	10	3	5	36	50	86
⋮	⋮	⋮	⋮	⋮	⋮	⋮
15	15	3	5	45	75	120

After an exhaustive list, we would arrive at the desired results. Tom correctly answered 12 arithmetic and 10 algebra questions.

A more efficient method for solving this problem involves getting an equation. Thus, let x represent the number of arithmetic questions correctly answered and let y represent the number of algebra questions correctly answered. Since each arithmetic question correctly answered counts 3 points, if Tom correctly answered x of these questions, he will have 3 times x or $3x$ points from the arithmetic questions. Similarly, since each correctly answered algebra question counts five points, Tom will have $5x$ points from the algebra questions. We are told that Tom answered 22 questions. Thus we must have $x + y = 22$. Also, his total point value was 86, so that $3x + 5y = 86$. Therefore we have two equations that we must solve. These are

$$x + y = 22$$
$$3x + 5y = 86$$

As we shall see later, the solution to this set of equations is $x = 12$ and $y = 10$. Thus Tom correctly answered 12 arithmetic and 10 algebra questions.

Checking Our Solution
We can check our results by returning to the original problem. Since Tom correctly answered 12 arithmetic and 10 algebra questions, he answered a total of 22 questions. Now, each correctly answered arithmetic question is worth three points, so 12 questions are worth 36 points. Also, each correctly answered algebra question is worth 5 points, so 10 questions are worth 50 points. Thus Tom received a total of $36 + 50$ points, or 86 points. No other combination of 22 correctly answered questions would yield a total of 86 points. ■

EXAMPLE 3

Problem-Solving Strategy 3—Working Backwards
In an attempt to conceal his true age, an actor states his birth year as follows. He claims that if 237 is subtracted from his birth year divided by 3, and if this number is now divided by 5, then the result is 83. In what year was the actor really born?

SOLUTION

Understanding the Problem
We must find the year in which the actor was born. First he tells us to divide his birth year by 3. Then we must subtract 237 from the result obtained. Then we must divide this answer by 5. The final result is 83.

A Plan to Solve the Problem

In this case several operations are involved and we are given the final result. If we let x represent the actor's birth year, then the information given in the problem can be written (in the order given) as

$$\boxed{x} \rightarrow \boxed{\div 3} \rightarrow \boxed{-237} \rightarrow \boxed{\div 5} \rightarrow \boxed{83}$$

We can solve for x by working backwards and using the numbers in reverse order. Thus we get

$$\boxed{83} \rightarrow \boxed{\times 5} \rightarrow \boxed{+237} \rightarrow \boxed{\times 3} \rightarrow \boxed{x}$$

$$
\begin{array}{ccc}
83 & 415 & 652 \\
\times 5 & +237 & \times 3 \\
\hline
415 & 652 & 1956
\end{array}
$$

Thus the actor was born in 1956.

Checking Our Solution

We can easily check our solution by referring back to the original problem. If the actor was born in 1956, then 1956 divided by 3 is 652. If we subtract 237 from 652 we get $652 - 237$, or 415. Finally, 415 divided by 5 gives 83. Thus our answer is indeed correct. ▬

The previous three examples were given merely to point out how Polya's problem-solving technique can be used. Throughout this book we will apply this technique to solve more complicated problems. However, since recognizing patterns plays a very important role in the problem-solving approach, in the next section we will indicate how inductive reasoning can be used for this purpose.

The following list summarizes different strategies that you should use when dealing with problem-solving examples.

1. Make a table
2. Look for simpler case
3. Look for subgoal
4. Look for patterns
5. Work backwards
6. Write an equation
7. Draw a diagram
8. Guess and check

These strategies (and others) will be used throughout this book.

1.2

NUMBERS AND PATTERNS OF MATHEMATICS

In our daily lives we must solve problems and arrive at conclusions on the basis of numerous observations. Often these decisions are based on analyzing similar situations and studying patterns. This type of reasoning—that is, arriving at a general conclusion on the basis of specific observations or examples—is called inductive reasoning.

Inductive reasoning

> **Definition 1.1   Inductive reasoning** is the process by which we arrive at a general conclusion on the basis of specific cases.

conjecture

When a mathematician or researcher makes a prediction that he or she believes to be true on the basis of specific cases, it is called a **conjecture**. While such conjectures are probably true, we must realize that we cannot be 100% sure that they are until they have been *proven* true beyond any doubt. Inductive reasoning is often used by mathematicians to *suggest* new conjectures, that is, in discovering new truths. However, as we shall see in Chapter 2, deductive reasoning is needed to prove these truths.

Over the years, many conjectures have been suggested by mathematicians. For example, consider the following:

Problem-Solving Strategy 4—Looking for a Pattern

EXAMPLE 1

Goldbach's conjecture

prime number

Goldbach's conjecture. A **prime number** is any whole number larger than 1 that can be evenly divided *only* by itself and 1 (assuming that we divide only by positive numbers). Some of the prime numbers are 2, 3, 5, 7, 11, 13, 17, 19, ... Note that

$$6 = 3 + 3$$
$$8 = 5 + 3$$
$$10 = 7 + 3 \quad \text{or} \quad 5 + 5$$
$$12 = 5 + 7$$
$$14 = 7 + 7 \quad \text{or} \quad 3 + 11$$
$$16 = 11 + 5$$
$$18 = 11 + 7 \quad \text{or} \quad 13 + 5$$
$$\vdots \qquad \vdots$$

Observe that all the numbers on the right of the equals sign are prime numbers. All the numbers on the left are *even* numbers larger than four.

The mathematician Goldbach, reasoning *inductively*, claimed that *any* even number larger than four can be written as the sum of two odd prime numbers. Although it seems reasonable, as yet no one has been able to prove this *deductively*. Do you agree with Goldbach's claim?   ▄

Problem-Solving Strategy 5—Draw a Picture

EXAMPLE 2

The four-color problem

The four-color problem. For many years a famous problem of mathematics was concerned with map coloring. When we color maps drawn on flat surfaces (planes), such as sheets of paper, two countries having a common border must be colored with different colors. If two countries meet at only one point, they can have the same color. Some examples of maps are shown in Fig. 1.1. No one was ever able to draw a map, no matter how complicated, that required more than four colors. Therefore, by inductive reasoning, it seemed probable that *every* map can be colored in *at most* four colors.

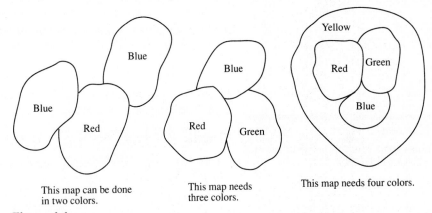

This map can be done in two colors.

This map needs three colors.

This map needs four colors.

Figure 1.1

In 1878, Arthur Cayley told the London Mathematical Society that he had tried to prove the theorem and could not. In 1889 an apparent proof was published, but the following year a mistake was found in the proof. In 1976, Kenneth Appel and Wolfgang Haken of the University of Illinois, using a combination of logic, ingenuity, and modern computer technology, succeeded in proving the theorem. The proof would have been impossible without a computer, since it would have been almost impossible to do a graph-by-graph checking using only human labor. As it was, Appel and Haken needed some 1200 hours of computer time to produce the proof.[1]   ▄

---

1. For a detailed discussion of the proof, see *Science*, 13 August 1976, 564, and *Bulletin of the American Mathetical Society*, September 1976.

Not only is inductive reasoning used in mathematics, but it is also often used in real-world situations. This may be seen in the following example, which presents several questions taken from a popular test of mental ability.

EXAMPLE 3

1. ⊙ is to ⊙ as ° | is to **a)** ◯ **b)** |° **c)** ☐ **d)** ⚊° **e)** ⚊°

2. △ is to ▷ as ⊼ is to **a)** ◁ **b)** Z **c)** M **d)** P **e)** ⟋|

3. ◯ is to D as △ is to **a)** ⟨| **b)** ☐ **c)** ☐ **d)** ▽ **e)** ◣

4. ⊖ is to ⊖ as ⊞ is to **a)** ⊟ **b)** ◇ **c)** ☐ **d)** ⊖ **e)** ⊞

5. 🜋 is to △ as ⊠ is to **a)** ▭ **b)** ⊔ **c)** 🜋 **d)** ⊠ **e)** ☐

SOLUTION
1. choice (**b**); **2.** choice (**b**); **3.** choice (**e**); **4.** choice (**c**); **5.** choice (**e**). ∎

Sometimes we can arrive at a conclusion inductively by finding a pattern. This can be seen in the following examples.

Problem Solving Strategy 6—Solving a Simpler Problem and Looking for Patterns

EXAMPLE 4

a) How many squares can you find in each of the following figures?

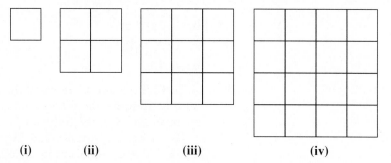

(i)   (ii)   (iii)   (iv)

b) How many different squares are there in a 7×7 checkerboard? In a checkerboard that is $n \times n$?

SOLUTION

a) We can solve the problem by carefully analyzing the above diagrams and observing certain facts. It is often helpful to record the results in a table. Thus we have the following:

Square Size	Total Number of Different Squares
1×1	1^2 or 1
2×2	$1^2 + 2^2$ or 5
3×3	$1^2 + 2^2 + 3^2$ or 14
4×4	$1^2 + 2^2 + 3^2 + 4^2$ or 30

b) The table reveals a pattern that is very useful for counting the total number of different squares for larger checkerboard sizes. Based upon the results of part (a) we would conclude that a 7×7 checkerboard has $1^2 + 2^2 + 3^2 + 4^2 + 5^2 + 6^2 + 7^2$, or 140 different squares. More generally, it would seem *inductively* that the total number of different squares in an $n \times n$ checkerboard is $1^2 + 2^2 + 3^2 + 4^2 + 5^2 + 6^2 + \cdots + n^2$. This observation does not constitute a proof. Such a proof (which involves deductive reasoning) is beyond the scope of this book.

Comment   Whenever we arrive at any conclusion using inductive reasoning, we must make sure to test it with several special cases to make sure that it is correct. If we can find any counterexample which disproves our conjecture, then obviously our conjecture is incorrect. If we cannot find any counterexample, then the conjecture is neither proven nor disproven.

EXAMPLE 5

Find the pattern in each of the following sequences of integers and then give the next three integers in the sequence.

a) 1, 1, 2, 3, 5, 8, 13, . . .

b) 1, 2, 4, 8, . . .

c) 15, 11, 7, 3, – 1, . . .

d) 4, – 4, 7, – 7, 10, – 10, . . .

SOLUTION

a) The next three numbers in the sequence are 21, 34, and 55. As seen below, each successive term represents the sum of the two previous numbers.

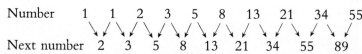

Number   1   1   2   3   5   8   13   21   34   55

Next number   2   3   5   8   13   21   34   55   89

b) The next three numbers in the sequence are 16, 32, and 64. Each successive term is obtained by multipying the previous number by 2.

c) The next three numbers in the sequence are – 5, – 9, and – 13. Each successive term is obtained by subtracting 4 from the previous number.

d) The next three numbers in the sequence are 13, -13, and 16. Can you see why?

sequence
terms

Any list of numbers having a first number, a second number, a third number, and so on, is called a **sequence**. The numbers in a sequence are called the **terms** of the sequence. In an arithmetic sequence, each term after the first is found by adding the same number to the preceding term. For example,

$$5, 8, 11, 14, \ldots$$

arithmetic sequence
arithmetic progression
common difference

is an **arithmetic sequence** or **arithmetic progression**. Each term after the first is found by adding 3 to the preceding term. The number 3 is called the **common difference**. To find the common difference for an arithmetic progression, choose any term except the first and subtract the preceding term from it.

EXAMPLE 6

Find the common differences in each of the following arithmetic progressions:

a) 17, 23, 29, 35, . . .

b) 5, -2, -9, -16, . . .

SOLUTION

a) We choose any term and subtract the term coming just before it. Thus, if we choose 23 and 29, we get common difference $= 29 - 23 = 6$

b) Common difference $= -9 - (-2) = -7$

In the previous example, let us denote the first term of the sequence by a_1 (read a sub one) so that in part (a) of Example 6, $a_1 = 17$. The common difference is 6. If we denote the second term of the sequence by a_2, then

$$a_2 = a_1 + 6 = 17 + 6 \quad \text{or} \quad 23$$

We can obtain the next few terms of the sequence as follows:

$$a_3 = a_2 + 6 = (a_1 + 6) + 6 = a_1 + 2 \cdot 6$$
$$a_4 = a_3 + 6 = (a_2 + 6) + 6 = (a_1 + 6) + 6 + 6 = a_1 + 3 \cdot 6$$
$$a_5 = a_4 + 6 = a_1 + 4 \cdot 6$$

You will notice that each subscript on the left side is one more than the number that is multiplied by 6, the common difference, on the right side.

This result suggests the following: If a_1 is the first term of an arithmetic progression, and if d is the common difference for the sequence, then the nth term of the progression, a_n is

$$a_n = a_1 + (n - 1) \cdot d$$

In the above example, the twentieth term is (here $n = 20$)

$$a_{20} = 17 + (20 - 1) \cdot 6$$
$$= 17 + (19) \cdot 6$$
$$= 17 + 114$$
$$a_{20} = 131$$

In this example, you may want to use a table such as the one shown below to arrive at the same results or to help you discover the pattern.

Term	Value	Breakdown	Alternate form
a_1	17	a_1	$a_1 = a_1 + 0 \cdot 6$
a_2	23	$a_1 + 6$	$a_1 + 6 = a_1 + 1 \cdot 6$
a_3	29	$a_2 + 6$	$(a_1 + 6) + 6 = a_1 + 2 \cdot 6$
a_4	35	$a_3 + 6$	$(a_2 + 6) + 6 = a_1 + 3 \cdot 6$
a_5	41	$a_4 + 6$	$(a_3 + 6) + 6 = a_1 + 4 \cdot 6$
$\vdots$	$\vdots$	$\vdots$	$\vdots$
a_n		$a_{n-1} + 6$	$(a_{n-2} + 6) + 6 = a_1 + (n - 1)6$

PROBLEM-SOLVING EXERCISES FOR SECTION 1.2

The answers to some of the following exercises can be obtained by analyzing the patterns shown and then using inductive reasoning. Some are easy and some are more complicated. Don't get discouraged if you cannot find a solution to a problem immediately. Try analyzing it again.

1. Consider the following multiplication patterns:

Multiplication Problem	Alternative Way of Writing Problem	Answer
$2 \cdot 5$	$2^1 \cdot 5^1$	10
$4 \cdot 25$	$2^2 \cdot 5^2$	100
$8 \cdot 125$	$2^3 \cdot 5^3$	1000
$16 \cdot 625$	$2^4 \cdot 5^4$	10000
$32 \cdot 3125$	$2^5 \cdot 5^5$	100,000

On the basis of your observations given in the above chart, and using inductive reasoning, what is the product of $2^9 \cdot 5^9$? Can you generalize to the product of $2^n \cdot 5^n$?

2. Select any three-digit number where all the digits are different, say 289. Reverse the digits, getting the number 982. Subtract the smaller number from the larger, getting 693. Reverse the answer and add the result to the difference. We get

$$
\begin{array}{r}
982 \\
- 289 \\
\hline
693 \\
+ 396 \\
\hline
1089
\end{array}
$$

Try this with several other three-digit numbers. What can you conclude inductively?

3. Select any four-digit number, say 5694. Rearrange the digits of this number to form the largest and the smallest possible number. In our case, the largest number is 9654 and the smallest number is 4569.

Subtract the smallest from the largest. We get

$$\begin{array}{r} 9654 \\ -\,4569 \\ \hline 5085 \end{array}$$

Again rearrange the digits of 5085 to get a smallest and a largest number. Subtract the smallest from the largest. We get

$$\begin{array}{r} 8550 \\ -\,0558 \\ \hline 7992 \end{array}$$

Repeat this process numerous times and you will eventually arrive at the result 6174.

Try this result with several other four-digit numbers (not all the digits being the same). What can you conclude inductively?

4. The ancient Greeks called numbers like 1, 3, 6, 10 and 15 **triangular numbers** because of their geometric configurations, as shown here:

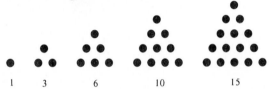

a) List all the triangular numbers up to 100.

b) Can you describe a procedure for finding the next few triangular numbers without drawing pictures?

c) Choose a triangular number. Add it to the next larger triangular number. What do you notice about the sum? Using inductive reasoning, can you generalize?

5. The ancient Greeks called numbers like 1, 4, 9, 16, and 25 **square numbers** because of their geometrical configurations, as shown below.

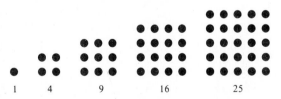

a) List all the square numbers up to 100.

b) Can you describe a procedure for finding the next few square numbers without drawing pictures?

6. **Palindromic numbers** are numbers that remain unchanged when their digits are written in reverse order. Find the smallest multiple of 13 and the next smallest multiple of 13, each of which is a palindromic number.

7. Using inductive reasoning, find the next two numbers or letters in each of the following sequences.

a) 32, 16, 8, 4, . . .

b) 4, 8, 16, 32, . . .

c) 4, 5, 6, 5, 6, 7, 6, 7, . . .

d) 8, 4, 2, 1, . . .

e) 27, 9, 3, 1, . . .

f) 1, 3, 9, 27, . . .

g) 7, 12, 17, 22, . . .

*h) 2, 8, 18, 32, . . .

* i) 5, 11, 21, 35, . . .

* j) T, N, E, S, S, F, F, T, . . .

8. To find the sum of the first n terms of an arithmetic progression, we can use a technique similar to the one used by the mathematician C.F. Gauss (1777–1855) when he was a child. According to legend, Gauss's teacher had asked the students in the class to find the sum of the first hundred natural numbers. While the other students were feverishly adding the numbers, it is reported that Gauss proceeded as follows. He first wrote the numbers to be added twice, once in the correct sequential order and once in reverse order as shown below.

$$\begin{array}{ccccccccccc} 1 & + & 2 & + & 3 & + & 4 & + & \ldots & + & 99 & + & 100 \\ 100 & + & 99 & + & 98 & + & 97 & + & \ldots & + & 2 & + & 1 \\ \hline 101 & + & 101 & + & 101 & + & 101 & + & \ldots & + & 101 & + & 101 \end{array}$$

He noticed that by adding vertically, each pair of numbers had a sum of 101. Thus the sum should be $100 \cdot 101$ or 10,100. However, since each of the numbers was added twice, the final result must be half of 10,100. Thus he concluded that

$$1 + 2 + 3 + 4 + \cdots + 99 + 100 = \frac{10{,}100}{2}$$
$$= 5{,}050$$

More generally,

$$1 + 2 + 3 + 4 + \cdots + n = \frac{n(n+1)}{2}$$

Using a method very similar to the above, can you find a formula for finding the sum of the first n terms of an arithmetic progression where the first term is a and the common difference is d?

9. In the following diagram, 18 sticks are needed to form six small squares. If two sticks are removed (with the remaining sticks used as part of a complete square), how many small squares of the same size will remain?

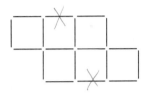

10. In the following diagram, the 16 sticks form five squares. If only three of the sticks are moved to new positions, show that just four squares are formed.

11. An escalator in a large office building has 48 visible steps. It takes 48 seconds to ride from the bottom to the top. A firefighter ran up the escalator steps, one at a time. The firefighter took 36 steps. Using inductive reasoning, determine how long it took the firefighter to get to the top.

 Brain-Teaser Problems

**12. The number 13031 is a palindromic number.

    a) Can you find another five-digit palindromic number which has 1 and 3 as its first two digits?

b) How many five-digit palindromic numbers are there which have 1 and 3 as their first two digits?

**13. Discover the pattern in the following ratios and then find the next three ratios.

    a) $\dfrac{1}{2}, \dfrac{3}{1}, \dfrac{4}{3}, \dfrac{7}{4}, \ldots$

    b) $\dfrac{3}{2}, \dfrac{7}{5}, \dfrac{17}{12}, \dfrac{41}{29}, \ldots$

**14. Two numbers are reciprocals of each other. One of them is nine times as large as the other. What are the numbers?

**15. How many different triangles are there in the following diagram? (*Hint*: Name the triangles by their vertices.)

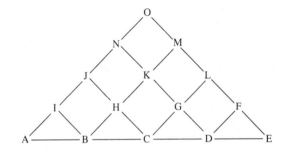

**16. How many straight line segments can be drawn connecting the nine dots shown below where each segment must be connected to an endpoint of at least one other segment?

**17. A book is opened. The product of the two facing-page numbers is 9506. What are the numbers of the pages?

**18. A book is opened. Can you prove that the product of the two facing-page numbers cannot be 2252?

1.3

MAGIC SQUARES

magic square

A **magic square** is an arrangement of numbers in the shape of a square in which the sum of each vertical column, each horizontal row, and each diagonal is the same. The number of rows and the number of columns must be the same, and this number is known as the **order of the magic square**. Some examples of magic squares are shown below:

order of a Magic Square

EXAMPLE 1

1

represents a magic square of order 1.   ■

EXAMPLE 2

4	9	2
3	5	7
8	1	6

represents a magic square of order 3. The sum of each row, each column, and along each diagonal is 15.   ■

EXAMPLE 3

4	14	15	1
9	7	6	12
5	11	10	8
16	2	3	13

represents a magic square of order 4. The sum of each row, each column, and along each diagonal is 34.   ■

Over the centuries, many mathematicians have been fascinated by the magic square problem. It is alleged that the first known example of a magic square was found on the back of a tortoise by the Chinese Emperor Yu around 2200 B.C. This form of Chinese magic is known as *lo-shu*. It appeared as an array of numerals indicated by knots in strings; black knots were used for even numbers, and white ones were used for odd numbers. In modern-day notation this represents a magic square whose order is 3. In this case, the **magic sum** or the sum along any row, any column, or any diagonal is 15. See Figs. 1.2 and 1.3.

magic sum

One of the methods used by the ancient Chinese mathematicians to solve the magic square problem involved pairs of integers. The ancient Chinese mathematician Yang Hui (1275) solved the magic square problem by a balancing technique. He interchanged elements of different sets of numbers and reordered them. To best understand his procedure, we begin with a definition.

> **Definition 1.2**   An interchange of a pair of numbers is called a **transposition.**

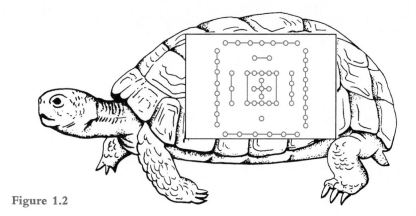

Figure 1.2

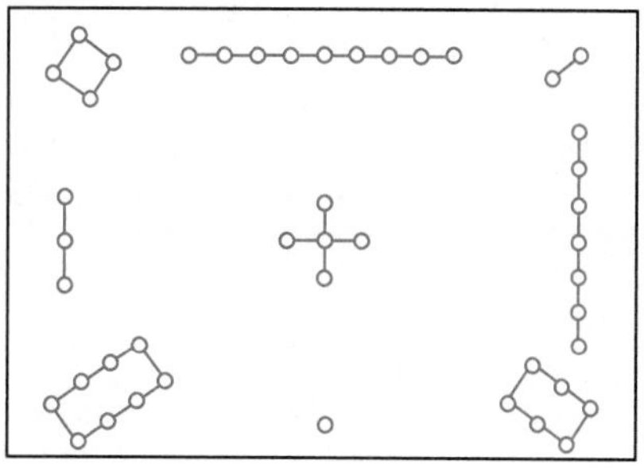

Figure 1.3
The *Lo-Shu*

To illustrate how the balancing technique was used by Yang Hui to solve the 3×3 magic square problem, let us arrange the integers $n = 1$ to $n = 9$ diagonally in their proper sequential order (from top to right) as shown in Fig. 1.4.

Now transpose the number in the top row and the number in the bottom row according to Definition 1.2, that is, interchange the 1 and the 9. This produces the scheme shown in Fig. 1.5.

Then transpose the 7 on the left with the 3 on the right. The result of this transposition is given in Fig. 1.6.

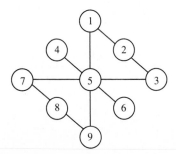

Figure 1.4

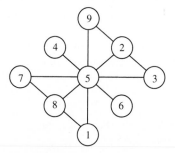

Figure 1.5

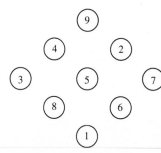

Figure 1.6

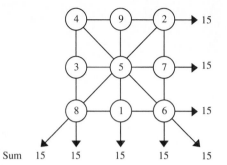

Figure 1.7

Sum   15   15   15   15   15

Finally, move the 2 and the 4 as well as the 8 and the 6 to corner positions. The result of all these moves, as given in Fig. 1.7, represents the solution to the 3×3 magic square problem.

The sum of each row, each column, and along each of the main diagonals is 15. Strictly speaking, the movement of numbers to corner positions is not a transposition as defined in Definition 1.2. Nevertheless, this procedure was used by Yang Hui to solve the 3×3 magic square problem.

To solve the 4×4 magic square problem, Yang Hui arranged the integers $n = 1$ to $n = 16$ horizontally and vertically in reverse order if read from top to bottom and right to left as shown in Fig. 1.8.

This arrangement is obviously not a solution to the 4×4 magic square problem, since the horizontal, vertical, and diagonal sums are not the same. The solution to this magic square problem begins with the transposition of the diagonally opposite corner numbers; that is, interchange the 1 and the 16 as well as the 4 and the 13. The results are given in Fig. 1.9.

If we now interchange the 6 with the 11 and the 7 with the 10, we arrive at the solution to the 4×4 magic square problem as shown in Fig. 1.10.

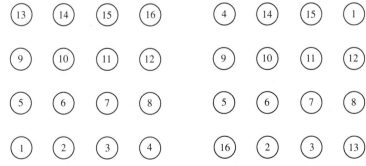

Figure 1.8   **Figure 1.9**

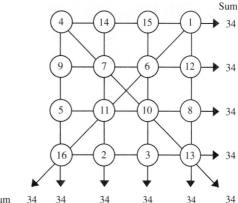

Figure 1.10   Sum   34   34   34   34   34   34

This process of rearranging a normal initial sequential ordering of numbers was also used by Yang Hui to solve the 5×5 and the 6×6 magic square problems.

Comment   If we know one magic square, we can construct other magic squares by using rotations, reflections, and/or other such techniques. However, our objective is merely to introduce you to magic squares. For further information the interested reader can consult the numerous articles that have been written about magic squares.

Students are often asked to discover (using inductive reasoning) number patterns within magic squares. This can be seen in the accompanying excerpt from *Addison-Wesley Mathematics*, 1987, Grade 6, p. 153.

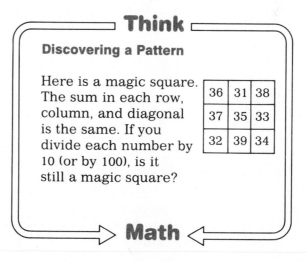

EXERCISES FOR SECTION 1.3

In Exercises 1–7, find the missing numbers so that the resulting arrangement will form a magic square. Verify that you have a magic square by finding the sum of each row, each column, and along the diagonals.

1.

6	1	8
7	5	3
2	9	4

2.

4	3	8
9	5	1
2	7	6

3.

8	1	6
3	5	7
4	9	2

4.

16	3	2	13
5	10	11	8
9	6	7	12
4	15	14	1

34

5.

17	24	1	8	15
23	5	7	14	16
4	6	13	20	22
10	12	19	21	3
11	18	25	2	9

6.

39	46	23	30	37
45	27	29	36	38
26	28	35	42	44
32	34	41	43	25
33	40	47	24	31

7.

6	2	34	33	35	1
	11	27	10	8	
19		16	15	20	18
13					24
12		9	28	26	7
36		3	4	5	31

8. Find two magic squares of order 4, one involving decimals and one involving fractions.

9. Make up a 7 × 7 magic square. *189 sum*

10. Read the article "An Art-Full Application Using Magic Squares" by Margaret J. Kenney, which appeared in the January 1982 issue of *The Mathematics Teacher* (pp. 83–89) for an interesting discussion of the numerous designs and artistic patterns that can be made from a magic square.

11. Read the article "The Billiard Ball Problem Solved by the Ancient Chinese Concept of Pairing" by Joseph Newmark and I-Chen Chang, which appeared in the March–April 1986 issue of *International Journal of Mathematical Education in Science and Technology* (Vol. 17, No. 2, pp. 169–178) for an interesting discussion of how the ancient Chinese concept of pairing (and balancing), which was used by Yang Hui to solve the magic squares problem, can also be applied to the modern-day billiard ball problem.

12. Complete the following magic square using the numbers 151–159 only.

152	157	156
159	155	151
154	153	158

465

13. In the following decimal magic square, the entries

	0.9	1.0
0.7	1.1	
1.2		0.8

consist of numbers with decimals. However, as with any magic square, each row, column, and diagonal must have the same sum.

  a) What is the magic sum for this magic square?

  b) Complete this magic square.

14. Create a magic square using the numbers 31, 32, 33, 34, 35, 36, 37, 38, and 39.

 Brain-Teaser Problems

**15. In the Chinese magic squares problem the objective is to obtain a rearrangement of the n^2 integers from 1 to n^2 in such a way that the sum of the numbers in all horizontal rows and vertical columns as well as both diagonals are the same. Find a formula for this sum.

**16. A student was asked to arrange the integers 1 through 9 in the form of a 3 × 3 magic square so that the sum of each row, each column, and each diagonal is the same. Using the problem-solving approach (making a diagram and a list), the student reasoned as follows:

Understanding the Problem. We are being asked to arrange the integers 1 through 9 in form of a 3 × 3 magic square so that the row, column, and diagonal sums are equal.

A Plan to Solve the Problem. How much should each row total, each column total, and each diagonal total? Let us guess 15, as the sum of the integers from 1 to 9 is 45. Since each row has three numbers, 45 ÷ 3 = 15. Now, each corner block is used three times as shown.

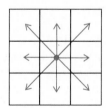

The center block is used four times as shown.

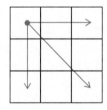

Each mid-side block is used two times as shown.

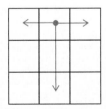

Starting with each of the numbers 1 through 9, let us see how many different ways there are of obtaining a sum of 15 without using the same numbers twice. Making a list of all of these possibilities produces the following:

Starting Number	Other Numbers			
1	9 + 5 and 8 + 6			
2	9 + 4 and 8 + 5	and 7 + 6		
3	8 + 4 and 7 + 5			
4	9 + 2 and 8 + 3	and 5 + 6		
5	9 + 1 and 8 + 2	and 7 + 3	and 6 + 4
6	8 + 1 and 7 + 2	and 5 + 4		
7	6 + 2 and 5 + 3			
8	6 + 1 and 5 + 2	and 4 + 3		
9	5 + 1 and 4 + 2			

After analyzing the above results, we conclude that:

the number 5 is used *four times*
the numbers 2, 4, 6, and 8 are used *three times*
the numbers 1, 3, 7, and 9 are used *two times*

We can now fill in the blanks in the magic square. The number 5 goes in the center, as it is used four times. The numbers 2, 4, 6, 8 go in the corners with 8 opposite 2 and with 6 opposite 4 to give a sum of 15 diagonally. Refer to the preceding list. Finally, the 1 goes with 8 + 6, the 3 with 8 + 4, the 7 with 6 + 2, and the 9 with 4 + 2. The completed magic square is shown here.

6	7	2
1	5	9
8	3	4

Do you agree with the student's procedure? If you do, can you find a similar procedure for arranging the integers 1 through 16 in the form of a 4 × 4 magic square?

1.4

USING A CALCULATOR IN THE PROBLEM-SOLVING PROCESS

In the past few years, sales of hand-held calculators have been phenomenal. When these calculators first came on the market in the early 1950s, they were extremely expensive. Nowadays, as a result of improved technology, you can buy a calculator for less than $5, and it seems that nearly everyone has.

The major advantage in using these calculators is the speed and accuracy of their calculations. Since so many different models are currently on the market, we will merely discuss some of the features common to all of them. Generally speaking, the price you pay for a calculator will reflect its capabilities.

The general-purpose calculators, which are the cheapest ones, are capable of performing only the four basic arithmetic operations of addition $\boxed{+}$, subtraction $\boxed{-}$, multiplication $\boxed{\times}$, and division $\boxed{\div}$. Some general-purpose calculators have a memory register in which partial calculations can be stored for later use. These memory registers are usually indicated by $\boxed{M+}$ or $\boxed{STO}$ or $\boxed{M}$ buttons.

The scientific calculators have features that make them especially useful to engineers and mathematicians. In addition to the functions already mentioned, scientific calculators have buttons that enable them to perform special calculations such as square root $\boxed{\sqrt{}}$, trigonometric functions $\boxed{SIN}$, $\boxed{COS}$, and $\boxed{TAN}$, as well as logarithmic functions $\boxed{LOG}$. Most also have square $\boxed{x^2}$ and exponent $\boxed{y^x}$ buttons.

The programmable calculators allow the user to insert cards that have special programs on them, enabling the calculators to perform complicated calculations for specific situations. There are also some special-purpose calculators currently on the market that are used primarily in business, medicine, and statistics. Graphics calculators can graph functions easily, and are currently being used in many college algebra courses. The teaching and learning of traditional topics in algebra can be improved with modern technologies. Some calculators today can add, subtract, multiply and divide fractions without finding the lowest common denominator. This is accomplished by pushing special keys.

All the calculators consist of two parts, the keyboard and the display panel. The keyboard has separate buttons for each of the numbers from 0 to 9 and buttons for the four basic operations $\boxed{+}$, $\boxed{-}$, $\boxed{\times}$, and $\boxed{\div}$. In addition there are $\boxed{CE}$ and $\boxed{C}$ buttons, the purpose of which

Figure 1.11

arithmetic logic

algebraic logic

Reverse Polish Notation

we will explain shortly. A typical calculator is shown in Fig. 1.11. The more expensive calculators have additional buttons that are designed to perform special calculations.

Your calculator may use either **arithmetic logic**, **algebraic logic**, or **Reverse Polish Notation** (RPN) logic. This will determine how you enter numbers.

Suppose we wish to evaluate $5 + 6 \times 7$ with a hand-held calculator. We notice that we have to perform the operations of addition and multiplication. In mathematics, we have certain rules which specify the proper order of performing multiplication, division, addition, and subtraction of real numbers. We also have rules for dealing with exponents. Most scientific calculators are programmed so that they will automatically perform the operations in the order stated in these rules.

If you have a calculator that uses arithmetic logic, then you will need to be careful about the order of operations. A calculator using the RPN logic requires you to push the $\boxed{\text{ENTER}}$ and $\boxed{\text{SAVE}}$ buttons. Such calculators do not have an equal $\boxed{=}$ button. Instead the operation symbols are entered after the numbers have been entered. Since most calculators use algebraic logic, that is the system that we will use in the rest of this book.

The following examples show many calculations (using the algebraic logic system). We suggest that you turn on your calculator and push the appropriate buttons as you read on. We will assume that you are familiar with the keyboard of the calculator.

EXAMPLE 1

SOLUTION

Using a calculator, add 23 and 62.

What you do	What appears on display panel
1. Turn on/off button to on.	0.
2. Push 2 button.	2.
3. Push 3 button.	23.
4. Push + button.	23.
5. Push 6 button.	6.
6. Push 2 button.	62.
7. Push = button.	85.

Comment   If you make a mistake while entering a number, push the CE (clear error) button. This will remove *only* the last entries and leave everything else. To clear the calculator completely of *everything* in it, push the C (clear) button.

EXAMPLE 2

SOLUTION

Using a calculator, calculate 20,412 ÷ 28.

What you do	What appears on display panel
1. Turn on/off button to on.	0.
2. In order, push the 2, 0, 4, 1, and 2 buttons.	20412.
3. Push ÷ button.	20412.
4. Push 2 and 8 buttons in order.	28.
5. Push = button.	729.

EXAMPLE 3

SOLUTION

Using a calculator, calculate 20,413 ÷ 28.

What you do	What appears on display panel
1. Turn on/off button to on.	0.
2. In order, push the 2, 0, 4, 1, and 3 buttons.	20413.
3. Push ÷ button.	20413.
4. Push, in order, the 2 and 8 buttons.	28.
5. Push = button.	

fixed decimal point

floating decimal point

   Notice that in the last step of Example 3 we have not indicated what will appear on the display panel. That is because the display will depend on the particular calculator being used. Some calculators are programmed with a **fixed decimal point**. For example, a machine that has a fixed decimal point with two decimal places will give the answer to Example 3 as 729.04. The decimal point has been programmed to be in this "fixed" position and cannot be moved. All answers are rounded off to two decimal places. On the other hand, if the calculator has a **floating decimal point**, then the decimal point will "float" and appear where it belongs when calculations are performed. If Example 3 were done with a floating point calculator, the display panel would show 729.0357143 at the last step. (We are assuming here that the display panel has room for 10 digits.)

EXAMPLE 4

SOLUTION

Using a calculator, find $3 \times 4 + 5 \times 6$.

In mathematics it is agreed that multiplications and divisions are always done before additions and subtractions. Thus this problem means: Multiply 3×4, getting 12. Then multiply 5×6, getting 30. Finally, add the results 12 and 30 to get 42. The scientific calculators are programmed to always perform multiplication and division before addition and subtraction. Therefore such calculators would treat this problem as if it were written as $(3 \times 4) + (5 \times 6)$.

Calculators that are not programmed this way (usually the general-purpose models) will perform the calculations exactly as they are entered. This is shown below.

What you do	What appears on display panel when using	
	scientific calculator programmed to do multiplication and division first	general-purpose calculator programmed to perform calculations as they are entered
Turn on/off button to on.	0	0.
Push 3 button	3	3.
Push × button	3.	3.
Push 4 button	4	4.
Push + button	12.	12.
Push 5 button	5	5.
Push × button	5.	17.
Push 6 button	6	6.
Push = button	42.	102.

Comment   To do the calculation above as $(3 \times 4) + (5 \times 6)$ on a general-purpose calculator, you would have to first compute 3×4 and record the result, which is 12. Then you would compute 5×6, getting 30. Finally, you would add 12 to the 30 to get 42.

Depending upon the logic used by your calculator, the problem discussed at the beginning of this section, $5 + 6 \times 7$, would be done as follows:

For calculators using					
Arithmetic Logic		Algebraic Logic		RPN Logic	
Turn on/off button to on	on/off	Turn on/off button to on	on/off	Turn on/off button to on	on/off
Push the 6 button	6	Push the 5 button	5	Push the 5 button	5
Push the × button	×	Push the + button	+	Push the enter button	ENTER
Push the 7 button	7	Push the 6 button	6	Push the 6 button	6
Push the = button	=	Push the × button	×	Push the enter button	ENTER
Push the + button	+	Push the 7 button	7	Push the 7 button	7
Push the 5 button	5	Push the = button	=	Push the × button	×
Push the = button	=			Push the + button	+
Result 47		Result 47		Result 47	

EXAMPLE 5

Using a scientific calculator, evaluate 7×9^2.

SOLUTION

What you do	What appears on display panel
Turn on/off button to on	0.
Push the 7 button	7.
Push the $\times$ button	7.
Push the 9 button	9.
Push the x^2 button	81.
Push the = button	567.

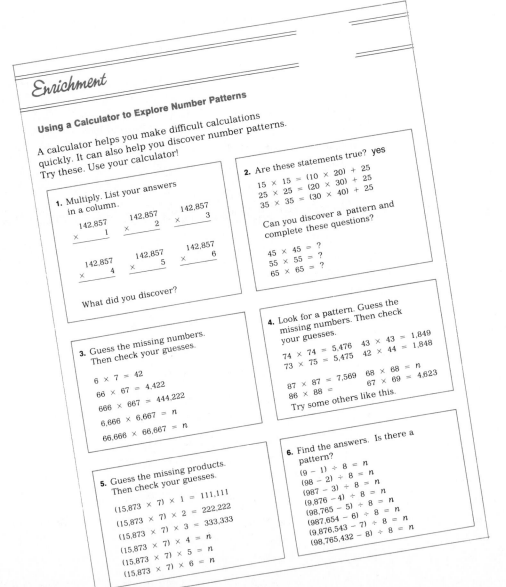

Enrichment

Using a Calculator to Explore Number Patterns

A calculator helps you make difficult calculations quickly. It can also help you discover number patterns. Try these. Use your calculator!

1. Multiply. List your answers in a column.

$$142,857 \times 1 \qquad 142,857 \times 2 \qquad 142,857 \times 3$$

$$142,857 \times 4 \qquad 142,857 \times 5 \qquad 142,857 \times 6$$

What did you discover?

2. Are these statements true? yes

$$15 \times 15 = (10 \times 20) + 25$$
$$25 \times 25 = (20 \times 30) + 25$$
$$35 \times 35 = (30 \times 40) + 25$$

Can you discover a pattern and complete these questions?

$$45 \times 45 = ?$$
$$55 \times 55 = ?$$
$$65 \times 65 = ?$$

3. Guess the missing numbers. Then check your guesses.

$$6 \times 7 = 42$$
$$66 \times 67 = 4,422$$
$$666 \times 667 = 444,222$$
$$6,666 \times 6,667 = n$$
$$66,666 \times 66,667 = n$$

4. Look for a pattern. Guess the missing numbers. Then check your guesses.

$$74 \times 74 = 5,476 \qquad 43 \times 43 = 1,849$$
$$73 \times 75 = 5,475 \qquad 42 \times 44 = 1,848$$

$$87 \times 87 = 7,569 \qquad 68 \times 68 = n$$
$$86 \times 88 = \qquad 67 \times 69 = 4,623$$

Try some others like this.

5. Guess the missing products. Then check your guesses.

$$(15,873 \times 7) \times 1 = 111,111$$
$$(15,873 \times 7) \times 2 = 222,222$$
$$(15,873 \times 7) \times 3 = 333,333$$
$$(15,873 \times 7) \times 4 = n$$
$$(15,873 \times 7) \times 5 = n$$
$$(15,873 \times 7) \times 6 = n$$

6. Find the answers. Is there a pattern?

$$(9 - 1) \div 8 = n$$
$$(98 - 2) \div 8 = n$$
$$(987 - 3) \div 8 = n$$
$$(9,876 - 4) \div 8 = n$$
$$(98,765 - 5) \div 8 = n$$
$$(987,654 - 6) \div 8 = n$$
$$(9,876,543 - 7) \div 8 = n$$
$$(98,765,432 - 8) \div 8 = n$$

| | EXAMPLE 6 | Using a scientific calculator, evaluate 8^3. |

SOLUTION

What you do	What appears on display panel
Turn on/off button to on	0.
Push the 8 button	8.
Push the y^x button	8.
Push the 3 button	3.
Push the = button	512.

Before deciding which particular calculator to buy, you should consider exactly what you will be using it for. In many cases the general-purpose model may be quite adequate. Buy a scientific model only if your work requires it.

Throughout this text, calculator exercises are marked with the calculator symbol ▦ . Calculators can also be an invaluable tool in the problem-solving process. Since calculators can perform computations quickly and accurately, they can be used to help discover patterns. This use of calculators can be seen in the examples on the facing page taken from *Addison-Wesley Mathematics*, 1987, Grade 6, p. 319.

EXERCISES FOR SECTION 1.4

Explain how you can use a general-purpose hand-held calculator to obtain the correct answer to each of the calculations given in Exercises 1–8. Actually perform the calculations using any kind of calculator.

1. $(5 + 7)^3 - 3 \times 4^2$

2. $\dfrac{700}{400 + 30 + 70}$

3. $7^3 + 8^3$

4. $\dfrac{7^2}{5^2 + 6^2}$

5. $9^3 + 10^2$

6. $\dfrac{7 \times 9^2}{8^2 - 4}$

7. $\dfrac{56 \times 81}{73 \times 69 \times 45}$

8. $(7 + 8 \times 3)^5$

9. Try to perform the calculation $\dfrac{3}{0}$ on your calculator. What happens?

10. Try to perform the calculation $\sqrt{-4}$ on your calculator. What happens?

In Exercises 11–20, perform each of the calculations on a calculator and then round your answer to the nearest hundredth.

11. $78 - 61.63$

12. 567.123×723.791

13. $0.00723 \div 53.72$

14. 0.5791×0.6423

15. $5693.721 + 71.6 + 39.54763$

16. $7239.23 \div 41.61795$

17. $723.39 \times 71.38 \div 73.002$

18. $642.73 \times 8.002 \div 61.732$

19. $\dfrac{68.93 \times 53.987 \times 0.793}{18.3 \times 0.0079 \times 6.93}$

20. $\dfrac{19.83 \times 71.82 \times 0.0073}{51.76 \times 0.5863 \times 0.0078}$

567

21. Using a calculator, evaluate 7×9^3. Use the $\boxed{y^x}$ button. (Be careful!)

22. Using a calculator, evaluate $(-3)^4$. Can you use the $\boxed{y^x}$ button? Be careful.

23. Using a calculator, evaluate 52^0.

24. Enter the number 7734 into your calculator. Now turn the machine upside down. What do you get?

25. Enter the number 57738 into your calculator. Now turn the machine upside down. What do you get?

26. Convert the fraction $732\frac{17}{23}$ to decimals.

27. Pick any three-digit number. Make a six-digit number by repeating the digits again. Divide the six-digit number by 7. Divide the result by 11. Divide the new result by 13. What is your answer? Repeat this process for three different numbers.

28. How many times does a person's heart beat in a month if the normal heart rate is 70 beats per minute?

TYPICAL CLASSROOM QUESTIONS

1. Using a calculator which has a $\boxed{y^x}$ key, a student attempts to evaluate 0^{10}. What happens and why does this happen?

2. Using a calculator, a student divides 6 by 0. The display panel shows $\boxed{\text{E} \qquad 0.}$. Why does the panel display a 0?

3. A student divides 2 by 3 on a calculator. The display panel shows $\boxed{0.6666666}$. Why doesn't the display show 0.6666667?

STUDY GUIDE

1 Guess + Test
2 Use a variable
3. Look for pattern
4. Solving a simpler problem 1st

Make a table

The following is a chapter outline in capsule form. You should now be able to demonstrate your knowledge of the ideas mentioned by giving definitions or specific examples. Page references are given in parentheses.

George Polya studied the strategy for solving problems. He established four **Guidelines For Problem Solving**. An important part of problem solving involves looking for **patterns**. (p. 6)

Inductive reasoning is the process by which we arrive at a general conclusion on the basis of specific cases. When a mathematician makes a prediction that he or she believes—on the basis of specific cases—to be true, it is called a **conjecture**. Such conjectures are probably true (unless a counterexample can be found), but they are not 100% true until proven so by deductive reasoning. (p. 12)

A **prime number** is any whole number larger than 1 that can be evenly divided only by itself and 1. (p. 12)

For many years a famous problem of mathematics was the **four-color problem**, which was concerned with the number of different colors needed to draw a map. It was finally established, using deductive reasoning, that no map (no matter how complicated) required more than four colors. (p. 13)

Any list of numbers having a first number, a second number, a third number, and so on, is called a **sequence**. The numbers in a sequence are called the **terms** of the sequence. (p. 16)

In an **arithmetic sequence** or **arithmetic progression**, each term after the first is found by adding the same number to the preceding term. This number is called the **common difference** for the arithmetic progression. (p. 16)

Palindromic numbers are numbers that remain unchanged when their digits are written in reverse order. (p. 18)

A **magic square** is an arrangement of numbers in the shape of a square in which the sum of each vertical column, each horizontal row, and each diagonal is the same. This sum is called the **magic sum.** The number of rows and the number of columns must be the same, and this number is known as the **order** of the magic square. (p. 20)

An interchange of a pair of numbers (in a magic square) is called a **transposition**. (p. 20)

Most calculators have special-purpose keys, including $\boxed{\text{M} +}$ or $\boxed{\text{STO}}$ or $\boxed{\text{M}}$ buttons which are used as memory registers as well as a $\boxed{\text{CE}}$ (clear error) button. There are many other special-purpose keys. (p. 26)

Calculators can use either **arithmetic logic, algebraic logic,** or **Reverse Polish Notation (RPN) logic.** The type of logic used determines how numbers must be entered. (p. 27)

Some calculators are programmed with a **fixed decimal point**. Others have a **floating decimal point**; i.e., the decimal point "floats" and appears where it belongs when calculations are performed. (p. 28)

KEY TERMS

Following is a list of key terms introduced in each section of this chapter.

1.1 **Polya's four-step process for problem solving**

1.2 **inductive reasoning**
conjecture
four-color problem
sequence
arithmetic sequence
common difference
palindromic numbers

1.3 **magic squares**
order
magic sum
transposition

1.4 **arithmetic logic**
algebraic logic
reverse Polish notation (RPN)
fixed-point decimals
floating-point decimals

FORMULAS TO REMEMBER

The following list summarizes all the formulas discussed in this chapter.

Polya's four-point guidelines for solving problems include the following:

a) Understanding the Problem
b) Devising a Plan
c) Carrying Out the Plan
d) Looking Back

The nth term of an arithmetic progression is

$$a_n = a_1 + (n - 1) \cdot d$$

where a_1 is the first term and d is the common difference for the sequence.

CHAPTER REVIEW EXERCISES

1. Consider the following additions involving fractions:

Addition problem	Sum in simplest form
$\dfrac{1}{1 \times 2} + \dfrac{1}{2 \times 3}$	$\dfrac{2}{3}$
$\dfrac{1}{1 \times 2} + \dfrac{1}{2 \times 3} + \dfrac{1}{3 \times 4}$	$\dfrac{3}{4}$
$\dfrac{1}{1 \times 2} + \dfrac{1}{2 \times 3} + \dfrac{1}{3 \times 4} + \dfrac{1}{4 \times 5}$	$\dfrac{4}{5}$

By analyzing the pattern obtained for successive sums, find the sum of

$$\frac{1}{1 \times 2} + \frac{1}{2 \times 3} + \cdots + \frac{1}{49 \times 50}$$

2. Find the next three numbers in the following sequence.

$$2, 7, 8, 12, 14, 17, \ldots \quad 20, 22, 26$$

3. Consider the number 84. The number with the digits reversed is 48. Add the original number and the number with its digits reversed. We get 132. Adding this sum, 132, to its reverse gives the palindrome number 363 as shown.

Original number	84
Reversed number	+ 48
Sum	132
Reverse of sum	+ 231
Palindrome number	363

Remember, a palindrome number is any number that reads the same whether you start at the right or at the left. How many additions will it take to find a palindrome for the following numbers?

a) 78   b) 148   c) 379

4. Find the next three numbers in the following sequence:

$$2, \quad 4, \quad 7, \quad 11, \quad 16, \quad 22, \ldots$$

5. Consider the following triangle of numbers.

$$1$$
$$2 \quad 4$$
$$3 \quad 6 \quad 9$$
$$4 \quad 8 \quad 12 \quad 16$$
$$5 \quad 10 \quad 15 \quad 20 \quad 25$$

By analyzing the pattern and using inductive reasoning,

a) find the next row of numbers,

b) can you determine what the last number in the 50th row would be?

6. Complete the following magic square by changing each of the decimals into fractions.

1.4	0.9	
	1.1	
		0.8

7. If you take three eggs from a dozen of eggs, how many do you have?

8. Find the next two numbers in the following sequence:

−6, +4

$$13, \quad 7, \quad 11, \quad 5, \quad 9, \quad 3, \quad 7, \ 1,5, -1 \ 3$$

9. Consider the following problems:

Problem	Answer
$1 + 1 \times 8$	9
$2 + 12 \times 8$	98
$3 + 123 \times 8$	987
$4 + 1234 \times 8$	9876
$5 + 12345 \times 8$	98765

a) What is the next problem in the sequence?

b) Without actually multiplying the numbers, what is your answer?

10. Consider the following problems:

Problem	Answer
$9 \times 1 - 1$	8
$9 \times 21 - 1$	188
$9 \times 321 - 1$	2888
$9 \times 4321 - 1$	38888

a) What is the next problem in this sequence?

b) Without actually multiplying the numbers, what is your answer?

c) Using inductive reasoning, can you predict the answer to the multiplication problem $9 \times 87654321 - 1$?

11. By arranging the odd numbers in a triangular form, as shown below, discover the pattern and use inductive reasoning to find the next two rows of this triangle as well as the sum.

	Sum of Numbers	Alternate Form For Sum
1	$1 = 1$	1^3
3 5	$3 + 5 = 8$	2^3
7 9 11	$7 + 9 + 11 = 27$	3^3
13 15 17 19	$13 + 15 + 17 + 19 = 64$	4^3

12. Find the next two numbers in the following sequence:

$$50, \quad 42, \quad 40, \quad 32, \quad 30, \quad 22, \ldots$$

13. Complete the following multiplication chart. Describe the pattern demonstrated.

Problem	Answer
1×1	
11×11	
111×111	
1111×1111	
11111×11111	
111111×111111	

14. Complete the following:

$\top$ is to $\llcorner$ as $\uparrow$ is to

a) $\swarrow$ **b)** $\urcorner$ **c)** $\searrow$ **d)** $\perp$ **e)** $\leftrightarrow$

15. What is the next diagram in the following sequence?

$\oplus$ is to $\ominus$ as $\diamondsuit$ is to

a)   **b)**   **c)**   **d)**   **e)**

16. Find the next two letters in the following sequence:

A, M, B, O, C, Q, D, S, E, F

17. Find the next two ratios in the following sequence.

$$\frac{5}{7}, \quad \frac{12}{5}, \quad \frac{17}{12}, \quad \frac{29}{17}, \quad \frac{46}{29}, \quad \frac{75}{46} \quad \frac{121}{75} \quad \frac{196}{121}$$

18. Complete the following magic square:

4.5	2.5	5.3
4.9	4.1	3.3
2.9	5.7	3.7

12.3

19. Find the next two ratios in the following sequence.

$$\frac{4}{5}, \quad \frac{14}{9}, \quad \frac{32}{23}, \quad \frac{78}{55}, \quad \frac{188}{133}, \quad \cdots$$

SUGGESTED FURTHER READING

Bartalo, D., "Calculators and Problem-Solving Instruction: They Were Made for Each Other," in *The Arithmetic Teacher* **30** (January 1983), p 18–21.

Benson, W.H., and Oswald Jacoby, *New Recreations with Magic Squares*. New York; Dover Publications, 1976.

Bruni, J., "Problem Solving For the Primary Grades," in *The Arithmetic Teacher* **29** (February 1982), 10–15.

Gathany, T., "Involving Students in Problem Solving," in *The Mathematics Teacher* **72** (November 1979), 617–621.

Kenney, M.J., "An Art-Full Application Using Magic Squares," in *The Mathematics Teacher* **75** (January 1982), 83–89.

Lappan, G., et al., "Powers and Patterns: Problem Solving With Calculators," in *The Arithmetic Teacher* **30** (October 1982), 42–44.

Newmark, J., and I-Chen Chang, "The Billiard Ball Problem Solved By The Ancient Chinese Concept Of Pairing," in *The International Journal of Mathematical Education in Science and Technology* **17**, 2 (May–June 1986), 169–178.

Newmark, J., "The Ancient Chinese Concept of Pairing Applied to the Fifteen Puzzle," in *The International Journal of Mathematical Education in Science and Technology* **19**, 5 (1988), 711–717.

Polya, G., *How To Solve It*. Princeton, N.J.: Princeton University Press, 1957.

Schaaf, O., "Teaching Problem-Solving Skills," in *The Mathematics Teacher* **77** (December 1984), 694–699.

Slesnick, T., "Problem Solving: Some Thoughts and Activities," in *The Arithmetic Teacher* **31** (March 1984), 41–43.

Whitin, D., "Patterns with Square Numbers," in *The Arithmetic Teacher* **27** (December 1979), 38–39.

CHAPTER 2

Sets and Logic

NCTM GUIDELINES

In its March 1989 *Curriculum And Evaluation Standards For School Mathematics* (p. 81), the National Council of Teachers of Mathematics recommends that reasoning should permeate the mathematics curriculum so students can:

☐ recognize and apply inductive and deductive reasoning,
☐ make and evaluate mathematical conjectures and arguments,
☐ validate their own thinking,
☐ appreciate the pervasive use and power of reasoning as a part of mathematics.

Logical reasoning is fundamental to the knowing and doing of mathematics. While the development of logical reasoning is tied to a child's intellectual and verbal development, many young students are capable not only of perceiving regularities and relationships, but also of more formal reasoning and abstraction.

The seeds of logical thinking are planted as students learn to describe objects or processes accurately and to elaborate on their properties. Thus, after introducing some of the important ideas of sets that we will use in later chapters, we will introduce logic—that is, inductive and deductive reasoning.

Introduction

In this chapter we introduce the theory in mathematics dealing with sets. Sets play an important role in mathematics today, as evidenced by the fact that many of the concepts of sets are being taught to elementary school children. Thus it is important that you have a thorough knowledge of sets, the notation used for them, the operations that can be performed with them, their pictorial representation, and, finally, their varied applications.

After thoroughly analyzing the different kinds of sets, the notations used for them, and the operations that can be performed with them, we will apply the ideas to voting coalitions. By means of Venn diagrams we will also be able to apply sets to different kinds of survey problems using a problem-solving approach.

Historically, in the last half of the nineteeth century, mathematicians started to look very carefully at the basic ideas and methods of their subject, at the "foundations" of mathematics. They began to ask such questions as: What is a number? What is infinity? How do we know that our methods of reasoning are correct? Moreover, general philosophic questions were considered, questions such as: What is mathematics? Is mathematics part of science? What is the relationship between mathematics and the "real world"? Do mathematical concepts like "number," "point," and "circle" really exist?

One of the outstanding people involved in these investigations was a German mathematician, Georg Cantor (1845–1918). His theory of sets provided a basis for explaining many of the questions raised at that time. His theory also provided a new way of looking at old ideas such as numbers, addition, and multiplication. So important was this theory that it has been said that it has "largely transformed most branches of mathematics."

Basic to Cantor's work is the idea of a set. The word "set" in mathematics has exactly the same meaning as it does in everyday English usage. It is just any collection of things.

In our daily lives we come across sets all the time. Think of all your friends and relatives; they form a set. The pages in this book form a set. If you own a phonograph, your collection of records forms a set. Empty your pockets; the contents form a set.

In what follows, we will see how the ideas of sets are easy to understand and interesting to apply.

2.1

THE DIFFERENT KINDS OF SETS

set

Since the idea of a set is so important in mathematics, we will state again what we mean by it. **A set** is any collection of objects.

HISTORICAL NOTE

Georg Cantor was a German mathematician involved in the study of sets. Born in 1845 in St. Petersburg (now Leningrad), he spent most of his life in Germany. He decided at an early age that he wanted to be a mathematician, but his father was determined that Georg should go into engineering, which he believed to be a better-paying profession. Being an obedient son, Cantor did study engineering as his father wished; however, he was so miserable that when he was seventeen, his father finally allowed him to pursue a career in mathematics.

Cantor became a great mathematician. However, his work was so different and controversial that it was vigorously attacked by the mathematical community.

It is not hard to understand why Cantor's work met with such resistance, since many of his results were startling. For example, suppose that you could draw a line from your house to the moon. Now look at the horizontal line shown here:

$$\longleftrightarrow$$

Which line has more points on it? Did you say the line to the moon? Then you are wrong. Cantor showed that both lines contain the same number of points. Even Cantor himself found some of his results hard to accept. In a letter to another mathematician he wrote of one result, "I see it, but I don't believe it."

Cantor's theory of sets and its implications led to a prolonged and unpleasant dispute with one of his former teachers, Leopold Kronecker (1823–1891), himself an important mathematician. Possibly as a result of the hostility and criticism directed at this work, Cantor was never able to get a teaching position at the University of Berlin, which was his ambition, but taught all his life at a third-rate university. Unable to cope with the attacks and the disappointments, Cantor suffered several mental breakdowns. He died in 1918 in an insane asylum at the age of seventy-three.

The French mathematician Henri Poincaré stated that later generations would think of Cantor's work as a "disease from which one has recovered." It should be noted, however, that not all mathematicians were bitterly critical of Cantor's work. The German mathematician David Hilbert asserted that "No one shall expel us from the paradise which Cantor has created for us."

EXAMPLE 1

a) The set of all letters of the English alphabet.

b) The set of all American Indians.

c) The set of all people over 22 ft tall.

d) The set of all months with fewer than 30 days.

e) The set of all numbers larger than 1.

elements or **members**

> **Definition 2.1**   The objects in the set are called either **elements** or **members** of the set.

In Example 1a above, the elements are $a, b, c, d, e, f, g, h, i, j, k, l, m, n, o, p, q, r, s, t, u, v, w, x, y,$ and z. In Example 1b, some of the elements are Pocahontas, Jim Thorpe, Geronimo, and Sitting Bull. In Example 1d, there is only one element, February. How many elements are there in the set of Example 1c? of Example 1e?

Instead of writing out the words "the set of all letters of the English alphabet," we can write the same thing in shortened form as {all letters of the English alphabet}. Similarly, Example 1b can be written as {all American Indians}. The braces (curly brackets) stand for the set containing whatever is written inside them.

Very often we must refer to a set whose elements we do not know or do not wish to write down. We then denote the set by the capital letter A, or B, or C, etc. We denote the elements of such a set by small letters of the alphabet, a, b, c, etc.

In Example 1a above, we notice that "g" is an element of the set. If we denote this set by the letter A, we write $g \in A$. This means "g is an element of set A," since the symbol $\in$ stands for the words "is an element of." Similarly, $a \in A$, $b \in A$, $c \in A$, $\ldots$, $z \in A$. Observe that Geronimo is not an element of set A. We symbolize this by writing Geronimo $\notin A$; $\notin$ stands for "is not an element of." If B denotes the set of Example 1b, then Geronimo $\in B$.

Notice that in Example 1a we have merely described the elements of the set without actually naming them. For someone not familiar with the English language, it would not be immediately obvious which elements are in the set. It would then be advisable to actually list the elements of the set, and write it as

$$A = \{a, b, c, d, e, f, g, h, i, j, k, l, m, n, o, p, q, r, s, t, u, v, w, x, y, z\}.$$

This set can also be written in an abbreviated form as $\{a, b, c, d, \ldots, z\}$, where the three dots stand for the letters between d and z. This notation assumes that the reader *is* familiar with the letters of the English alphabet. In the set $\{1, 2, 3, 4, \ldots\}$, the three dots stand for 5, 6, 7, 8, and so on.

roster method

descriptive method

set-builder notation

When we list the elements of a set, we refer to the process as the **roster method**, as opposed to the **descriptive method** in which we *describe* the elements of a set rather than list them. Similarly, the set in part (d) of Example 1 can be written in the roster method as {February}.

There is still another way of describing a set by using a method called **set-builder notation**. Suppose we are interested in the set of all whole numbers between 1 and 10. Using set-builder notation, we would write this as

$$\{X \mid X \text{ is a whole number between 1 and 10}\}.$$

This is read as the set of all elements X such that X is a whole number between 1 and 10. The vertical line stands for the words "such that." In this notation, X (or whatever letter is used) is called a *variable*, since it represents any element of a given set of numbers. (Variables will be discussed in greater detail in a later chapter.)

Some other examples of sets described by set-builder notation are

$$M = \{Y \mid Y \text{ is a state in the United States}\}.$$
$$N = \{a \mid a \text{ is a letter in the word mathematics}\}.$$

If we actually tabulate the elements in these sets, we find that set M has 50 elements and set N has 8 different elements. The elements of set N are

$$N = \{m, a, t, h, e, i, c, s\}.$$

In a West Coast town the local Clear-Air Committee and the Pure-Water activists decide to merge into one antipollution group. A list is drawn up of the membership of the new group. This list will, of course, contain the names of all those in either of the original groups. Mr. I.M. Covington belongs to both of the original groups. We write his name only *once* on the combined mailing list.

Consider the set $M = \{$all great baseball players$\}$. Is Reggie Jackson an element of that set or not? Some people may say yes; others may say no. There is no way of determining who is right. Such a set is said to be **not well-defined**.

not well-defined

---

well-defined

> **Definition 2.2**   If there is a way of determining for sure whether an object belongs to a set or not, we say that the set is **well-defined**.

EXAMPLE 2

a) The set of all cute children.

b) The set of all tall men.

c) The set of all ripe apples.

d) The set of all two-door automobiles.

e) The set of all planets on which water can be found.

Examples 2a and 2b are *not* well-defined because one may disagree as to whether Anton is cute or not, or as to whether Tyron, who is 5 ft 8 in., is tall or not. Is Example 2c well-defined or not? Example 2d *is* well-defined. Example 2e *is* well-defined also, because there is a way of determining which planets are to be included in this set (even though, at present, technology has not advanced far enough for us to know). In mathematics we use only well-defined sets.

Consider the set $\{$all months with less than 30 days$\}$. This set has but one element, namely, February. Such a set is called a **unit** set.

unit set

> **Definition 2.3**   Any set that has only one element in it is called a **unit set**.

Now, how many elements are there in the set {all people who weigh a ton} or the set {all people over 30 feet tall}? Your answer, of course, will be "none." Such a set is called a **null** set.

null or empty set

> **Definition 2.4**   Any set that has no elements in it is called a **null** or **empty set**. We denote such a set by the symbol $\varnothing$ or { }.

We will show shortly that there is only one null set.

Let us look again at Example 1a–e. Example 1a has 26 elements in it. Example 1b has a specific number of elements in it, although we may not know the number offhand. (The latest U.S. census figures show that there are about 1,000,000 American Indians.) Example 1c has no elements and is thus a null set. Example 1d has only one element and is thus a unit set.

finite sets
infinite set

All of these are examples of **finite sets**. How many elements are there in Example 1e? Example 1e is called an **infinite set**. Another example of an infinite set is the set of all fractions. Do you think that the set of all grains of sand on the beaches of Florida is a finite or an infinite set?

John and Ann were asked to think of a set. John thought of the set of all the vowels in the English alphabet. Ann thought of the set {a, e, i, o, u}. Are they thinking of different sets? Of course not. Both sets obviously have the same elements.

> **Definition 2.5**   Two sets that have exactly the same elements are called **equal sets**.

Mabel thought of the set {e, o, a, u, i}. Leon thought of the set {t, o, a, u, i}. Notice that Mabel's set is the same as Ann's and John's set, even though the elements are presented in a different order. *The order in which the elements of a set are written is not important.* What about Leon's set? Is it equal to the others? You probably answered that Leon's set was not equal to the others. However, it has the same number of elements as the others. Let us investigate this further.

Imagine that we have a set of three students: Maurice, Ben, and Arline. We also have a set of three chairs: a red chair, a blue chair, and a green chair. Each of the three students sits down on a chair. Obviously, each chair will be occupied, and each student will be seated. There will be no vacant chair and no standing student. We have matched each student with a chair and each chair with a student. Such a matching is called a one-to-one correspondence. More generally, the following holds.

one-to-one
correspondence

> **Definition 2.6**   Set A and set B can be put in **one-to-one (1–1) correspondence** if each element of set A can be paired with exactly one element of set B and every element of set B can be paired with exactly one element of set A.

EXAMPLE 3

Let

$$A = \{a, e, i, o, u\}$$
$$B = \{t, o, a, u, i\}$$

Sets A and B can be put in 1–1 correspondence in many different ways. One way is

$$A = \{a, \quad e, \quad i, \quad o, \quad u\}$$
$$\updownarrow \quad \updownarrow \quad \updownarrow \quad \updownarrow \quad \updownarrow$$
$$B = \{t, \quad o, \quad a, \quad u, \quad i\}$$

Another possible way is the following:

$$A = \{a, \quad e, \quad i, \quad o, \quad u\}$$
$$B = \{t, \quad o, \quad a, \quad u, \quad i\}$$

How many possible ways can you find of putting set A and set B in 1–1 correspondence?

EXAMPLE 4

Problem-Solving Example—Using a Diagram
Let

$$C = \{\triangle, \square, 0, \text{⚦}\},$$
$$D = \{a, b, c, d, e\}$$

Can sets C and D be put in one-to-one correspondence?

SOLUTION

Understanding the Problem
We must determine if each element of set C can be paired with exactly one element of set D and if every element of set D can be paired with exactly one element of set C.

A Plan to Solve the Problem

Let us draw a diagram and actually attempt to put these sets in 1–1 correspondence. If we attempt to put these sets in 1–1 correspondence, we find that it cannot be done. One element of set D is always left out of any pairing. For example,

$$C = \{\triangle, \square, 0, \unicode{x1F9CD}\},$$

$$\updownarrow \quad \updownarrow \quad \updownarrow \quad \updownarrow$$

$$D = \{a, \quad b, \quad c, \quad d, \quad e\}$$

Thus, sets C and D cannot be put in 1–1 correspondence.

Checking our Solution

We can easily check our solution by observing that element e is not matched with any element of set C. If we try to match e with any element of set C, we will be forced to leave out another element of set D. Thus sets C and D cannot be put into 1–1 correspondence. ▬

In Example 3 above, set A and set B are not equal, but they can be put in 1–1 correspondence. We say that they are **equivalent**.

equivalent

> **Definition 2.7**   Sets A and B are said to be **equivalent** if they can be put into 1–1 correspondence.

In everyday English, "equal" and "equivalent" mean the same thing. In our discussion of sets, equal sets and equivalent sets are not the same thing.

How many elements are there in set A and set B of Example 3? What about set C and set D of Example 4? In Example 3, both sets A and B have five elements. On the other hand, in Example 4, set C has four elements, whereas set D has five elements. This leads us to the following definition.

cardinal number

> **Definition 2.8**   The **cardinal number** of any set A is defined as the number of elements in set A. This is denoted by the symbol $n(A)$, read as "the number of elements in set A."

EXAMPLE 5

a) The set $T = \{x, y, z\}$ has cardinal number 3, that is, $n(T) = 3$.

b) The set $W = \{\unicode{x1F9CD}, \square, \triangle, \star, m, 1, \text{Joe}\}$ has cardinal number 7; that is, $n(W) = 7$.

c) The set $M = \{\text{all letters of the English alphabet}\}$ has 26 elements; $n(M) = 26$.

EXAMPLE 6

If $D = \{1, 2, 3, \ldots, 10\}$, what is $n(D)$?

In view of Definition 2.8 we could have defined "equivalent sets" as "sets that have the same cardinal number."

Comment   The following statements all say the same thing.

1. Sets A and B can be put into 1–1 correspondence.

2. Sets A and B are equivalent.

3. Sets A and B have the same cardinal number.

Comment   Any two null sets have the same elements, namely, *none.* Thus any two null sets are equal. This means that essentially there is only one null set. Therefore we speak of *the* null set.

Comment   The set $\{0\}$ is not an empty set, since this set contains the element 0.

Consider the set B = {all teachers at this school} and set A = {all math teachers at this school}. We notice that every member of set A is also a member of set B, that is, set A is part of set B. We then say that set A is a subset of set B.

subset

> **Definition 2.9**   Set A is said to be a **subset** of set B if every element of set A is an element of set B. We denote this by $A \subseteq B$. This symbol is read as "A is a subset of B" or "A is contained in B."

EXAMPLE 7

a) {all basketball players in this school} is a subset of {all athletes in this school}.

b) $\{a, b, c\}$ is a subset of $\{a, b, c, d\}$.

c) { Judas Priest, the Rolling Stones, the Go-Go's, the Talking Heads} $\subseteq$ {all singing groups}.

d) {Moe, Larry, Curly} $\subseteq$ {Curly, Moe, Larry}.

Dr. Chang, who teaches math at this school, is a member of the set A = {all math teachers at this school}. He is also a member of set B = {all teachers at this school}. Professor Rivera, who teaches history, is a member of set B, but not of set A. We say that A is a proper subset of B.

proper subset

> **Definition 2.10** Set X is said to be a **proper subset** of set Y if every element of set X is an element of set Y, and also set Y has at least one other element that is not in X. We denote this by $X \subset Y$. This symbol is read as "X is a proper subset of Y."

improper subset

> **Definition 2.11** Set X is said to be an **improper subset** of set Y if every element of set X is an element of set Y, but Y does not have any other elements that are not in X. This really means X equals Y, and we denote this as $X = Y$.

Comment If we know definitely that A is a proper subset of B, then we write $A \subset B$. If we know only that A is a subset of B but we do not know if it is proper or improper, then we write $A \subseteq B$.

EXAMPLE 8

a) {Moe, Larry, Curly} is an improper subset of {Larry, Curly, Moe}, and thus we usually write this as {Moe, Larry, Curly} = {Larry, Curly, Moe}.

b) $\{a, e, u, w\}$ is an improper subset of $\{a, e, u, w\}$. We write $\{a, e, u, w\} = \{a, e, u, w\}$. ∎

EXAMPLE 9

a) $\{a, e, u, w\}$ is a proper subset of $\{a, e, u, w, t\}$. We write $\{a, e, u, w\} \subset \{a, e, u, w, t\}$.

b) $\{a, e, u, w\}$ is also a proper subset of {all letters of the English alphabet}. ∎

Comment The null set is assumed to be a subset of *every* set. Can you see why?

Suppose in a journalism class we are discussing newspaper editorials. We might then consider the *New York Times*, the *Washington Post*, the *Atlanta Constitution*, the *San Francisco Examiner*, etc. It would not be appropriate for someone to introduce into the discussion an editorial heard on NBC News. The discussion is limited to newspapers only. We call the set of all newspapers the universal set for this discussion.

universal set

> **Definition 2.12** If all sets in a given discussion are to be subsets of a fixed overall set U, then this set U is called the **universal set**.

EXAMPLE 10

a) If we want to talk about the set of math teachers at this school, the set of English teachers at this school, etc., then a suitable universal set would be {all teachers at this school}.

b) If we are going to discuss positive numbers, negative numbers, fractions, etc., we might choose as our universal set {all numbers}.

c) Suppose we are considering Reggie Jackson, Tom Seaver, Willie Mays, etc. We could use {all baseball players} as our universal set. If we consider them as amateur golfers or tennis players as well as baseball players, then a more appropriate universal set would be {all athletes}.

Comment   The universal set may vary from discussion to discussion.

Comment   Every set is a subset of itself. Would you say that it is a proper or improper subset of itself?

EXERCISES FOR SECTION 2.1

In Exercises 1–8, describe each of the indicated sets in words.

1. {January, June, July} *all months*

2. {4, 8, 12, 16, 20, 24, 28}

3. {2, 3, 5, 7, 11, 13, 17, 19}

4. {1, 8, 27, 64, 125}

5. {Tuesday, Thursday}

6. {3, 6, 9, . . . , 999}

7. {IBM, Atari, Apple, Compaq, Commodore}

8. {2, 4, 6, 8, 10, . . .}

In Exercises 9–18, list the elements of the set that is described.

9. The set of different letters in the word MISSISSIPPI.

10. The set of months with fewer than 31 days.

11. The set of U.S. Presidents since Franklin D. Roosevelt.

12. The set of all whole numbers less than 80 that are squares of whole numbers.

13. The set of all even integers greater than 12 and less than 19.

14. $\{X \mid X$ is an even number between 11 and 12$\}$.

15. The set of all states in the United States that have executed criminals since 1980.

16. The set of all countries in the world in which capital punishment has been outlawed.

17. The set of all odd numbers less than 50 that are divisible by 2.

18. The set of all females who have been or are currently president of the United States.

In Exercises 19–24, determine whether the set is well-defined or not.

19. The set of all expensive math books.

20. The set of all popular folk music singing groups.

21. The set of all college students with a high grade point average (GPA) on their college transcripts.

22. The set of all good comedians.

23. The set of all days with 30 hours.

24. The set of all large corporations that use Federal Express delivery service or Purolator delivery service when shipping urgent packages.

In Exercises 25–34, state whether the set is a finite nonempty set, an infinite set, a unit set, or a null set.

25. The set of all women who are 150 centimeters tall.

26. The set of all women who are 150 feet tall.

27. The set of U.S. astronauts who have died while participating in the space exploration program.

28. The set of polluted lakes (or rivers) to which fish have returned as a result of cleanup campaigns by environmentalists.

29. The set of all people who weigh a ton.

30. The set of all prime numbers.

31. The set of all animals in the world.

32. The set of all countries where women are assigned to combat units in the armed forces.

33. The set of all triangles having two and only two sides.

34. The set of all points that are on a straight line.

In Exercises 35–42, tell whether the statement is true or false.

35. The set {0} and the null set are equal sets.

36. $4 \in$ {all even numbers}.

37. $\{m\} = m$.

38. Tomato $\in$ {all fruits}.

39. $A \in \{a, b, c, d\}$.

40. $\varnothing = 0$.

41. {all male senators} and {all female senators} are equivalent sets.

42. $10 \in \{X \mid X \text{ is an odd number}\}$.

43. Are equal sets equivalent? Explain.

44. Are equivalent sets equal? Explain.

In Exercises 45–53, determine which of the pairs of sets are equivalent, equal, both, or neither.

45. $\{12, 10, 8, 6\}$ and $\{6, 8, 10, 12\}$.

46. $\{a, b, c\}$ and $\{1, 2, 3, 4\}$.

47. {Tom, Dick, Harry} and {Mary Ruth, Jane}.

48. {letters in the word LARGE} and {letters in the word GLARE}.

49. $\{1, 4, 7\}$ and $\{1, 4, 7, 8\}$.

50. {all fish that can program a computer} and {all elephants that can cook}.

51. $\{X \mid X \text{ is an odd number between 18 and 24}\}$ and $\{Y \mid Y \text{ is a multiple of 3 that is larger than 4 but less than 13}\}$.

52. {Spring, Summer, Fall, Winter} and {four seasons of the year}.

53. {all male senators} and {all female senators}.

54. Determine several 1–1 correspondences between each of the following pairs of sets:

    a) $A = \{x, q, John, b\}$,
        $B = \{\triangle, \square, \alpha, c\}$.

    b) $C = \{Heather, Jason, Marlene\}$,
        $D = \{Marlene, Joe, Bill\}$.

In Exercises 55–59, find the cardinal number of the indicated sets.

55. {Professional football leagues in the U.S.}.

56. { }.

57. {Females who have been nominated as candidates for President or Vice President of the U.S. since 1930}.

58. {The states of the U.S. beginning with the letter Q}.

59. {All prime numbers less than 30}.

60. Find two different subsets of each of the following sets.

    a) {Reagan}

    b) {True, false}

    c) {All U.S. senators}

    d) {All vowels in the English language}

    e) $\{1, 2, \alpha, \beta\}$

    f) {Environmental problems that are of concern to environmentalists}

    g) {Hamburgers, beefburgers}

    h) {Foreign import subcompact cars}

61. Find an appropriate universal set for a discussion involving the following objects.

    a) Bell Atlantic, NYNEX, Pacific Telesis Group, US West, Southwestern Bell, Ameritech.

    b) Martina Navratilova, Chris Evert Lloyd, Andrea Jaeger, Tracy Austin, Sylvia Hanika.

    c) Wordstar, Visicalc, Lotus, Symphony, dBase III.

    d) Datsun, Honda, Volvo, Ferrari, Mecedes, Audi, Peugeot.

e) Federal Express, United Parcel Service, Purolator, Emery.

f) Catfish, trout, bass, salmon, whitefish, eel, whale, bluefish, snapper.

g) Apollo, Columbia.

h) Pepsi, Coca Cola, Seven-Up, Sprite.

62. In each of the following, state whether set A is a proper or an improper subset of set B or neither.

a) $A = $ {all even numbers}, $B = $ {all odd numbers}.

b) $A = $ {all even numbers divisible by 3}, $B = $ {all even numbers}.

c) $A = $ {Bill, Mary, George}, $B = $ {George, Mary, Bill}.

d) $A = $ {sperm whales}, $B = $ {mammals}.

e) $A = $ {musical instruments}, $B = $ {compact disc players}.

f) $A = $ {Pluto, Mercury, Mars, Earth, Venus}, $B = $ {planets}.

g) $A = $ {people with three heads}, $B = $ {people with six eyes}.

h) $A = $ {#, &, @}, $B = $ {#, &, ^, @}.

63. Let $A = $ {9, 11, 12}.

a) Find all the subsets of A that contain one element.

b) Find all the subsets of A that contain two elements.

c) Find all the subsets of A that contain three elements.

d) Find all the subsets of A that contain no elements.

64. List all the subsets of the indicated sets. (Be sure you do not leave any out.)

a) { }

b) $\{a\}$

c) $\{a, b\}$

d) $\{a, b, c\}$

e) $\{a, b, c, d\}$

f) $\{a, b, c, d, e\}$

65. Classify each of the following statements as either true or false. Justify your answer.

a) {Sue, Joan} is a subset of {Maria, Joan, Sue}.

b) $\varnothing$ is a subset of {5, 8, 12}.

c) $\{D, R, U, G, S\} \subseteq \{S, G, R, U, D\}$.

d) $\{7\} \subset \{n \mid n$ is an odd number$\}$.

e) {5, 7, 9, 11} is a subset of {5, 9, 11}.

f) $\{7\} \subset \{y \mid y$ is an even number$\}$.

g) $B \subseteq B$.

h) {fish} $\subset$ {salmon}.

i) {all airplanes over 200 years old} $\subset$ {all flying machines}.

PROBLEM-SOLVING EXERCISES

66. If set A has 3 elements and set B has 4 elements, can set A and set B be put into 1–1 correspondence? Explain.

67. If set $A = \{a, b\}$ and set $B = \{1, 9\}$, how many distinct 1–1 correspondences can be made between the elements of these sets?

68. How many different committees of people can be formed from each of the following sets.

a) {Ronald}

b) {Joanna, Jill}

c) {Steve, Kim, Juan}

d) {Smitty, Margaret, Cathy, Beth}

69. On the basis of your answers to Exercises 64 and 68, complete the following chart:

Number of elements in set	Number of possible sets
0	1
1	2
2	4
3	8
4	16
5	32
6	?
10	?
100	?
n	?

70. Put each of the pairs of sets given below into 1–1 correspondence. Give a "matching rule" in each case.

a) $\{3, 6, 9, 12, \ldots\}$ and $\{6, 12, 18, 24, \ldots\}$

b) {7, 14, 21, 28, . . .} and {8, 16, 24, 32, . . .}

c) {1, 8, 27, 64, . . .} and {1, 1/8, 1/27, 1/64, . . .}

d) {1, 8, 27, 64, . . .} and {1, 16, 81, 256, . . .}

e) {4, 8, 12, 16, . . .} and {4, 16, 64, 256, . . .}

▶ Brain-Teaser Problems ◀

**71. Is the null set a well-defined set? Explain your answer.

**72. Find the cardinal number of the set {all dots on a line 7 centimeters long}.

**73. If two sets A and B are equivalent, then the number of distinct 1–1 correspondences that can be made between the elements of these sets is shown in the following table:

If the number of elements in sets A and B is	then the total number of distinct 1–1 correspondences that can be made is
1	1
2	2
3	6
4	24
5	120

Write a formula for determining the total number of distinct one-to-one correspondences that can be made if each of the equivalent sets has n elements.

**74. *Cantor's Hotel* A famous mathematician arrives at a hotel and asks for a room. The hotel is full, but the hotel manager, who would like to please the mathematician, is determined to find a room for her. The manager does it by moving the guest who is in room 1 to room 2, the guest who is in room 2 to room 3, and so on. In this manner, the manager is able to provide a room for the mathematician and for each of the original guests. Doubling up is not allowed. How many rooms does Canton's hotel have?

**75. Figure 2.1 shows a circle within a square. Set up a 1–1 correspondence between the points on the circle and the points on the square.

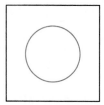

Figure 2.1

**76. For each of the diagrams in Figs. 2.2 and 2.3, set up a 1–1 correspondence between the points on the inner figure and the points on the outer figure.

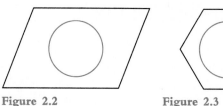

Figure 2.2   **Figure 2.3**

2.2

SET OPERATIONS

Suppose we wanted to distribute a questionnaire to all students in Math 1 and all students in English 1 at our school. We would have to compile a mailing list of all students in both classes. Some students may be in both

---

**Exercises preceded by ** require careful thought and consideration.

classes, but of course we would not list them twice. If we denote the set of students in Math 1 by A and the set of students in English 1 by B, our list would be an example of what is meant by the union of A and B.

union

> **Definition 2.13**   The **union** of two sets A and B, which is denoted as $A \cup B$ (read as "A union B"), means the set of all elements that are either in A or in B or both.

EXAMPLE 1

a) If $A = \{1,\ x,\ \triangle\}$ and $B = \{y,\ \text{☆}\}$, then $A \cup B = \{1,\ x,\ \triangle,\ y,\ \text{☆}\}$.

b)

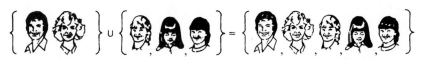

c) If $A = \{m,\ \text{John, Bob},\ y\}$ and $B = \{\text{Bob, Alice},\ x\}$, then $A \cup B = \{m,\ \text{John, Bob},\ y,\ \text{Alice},\ x\}$.

Observe that even though Bob is in both sets, we list him *only once* in $A \cup B$.

EXAMPLE 2

If $M = \{\text{all months of the year with only 6 days}\}$ and $N = \{\text{all months of the year with 30 days}\}$, then what is $M \cup N$?

Let us consider again our questionnaire project. If we want to send the questionnaire only to students in *both* classes (if there are any), then this set of students is called the intersection of sets A and B (remember $A = \{\text{Math 1 students}\}$ and $B = \{\text{English 1 students}\}$).

intersection

> **Definition 2.14**   The **intersection** of two sets A and B, denoted as $A \cap B$ (read as "A intersect B"), means the set of all elements that are in both sets A and B at the same time (if there are any).

disjoint sets

> **Definition 2.15** If sets A and B have no members in common, then sets A and B are called **disjoint sets**. This means that if A and B are disjoint, then $A \cap B = \varnothing$.

EXAMPLE 3

a) If $X = \{a, e, \text{☃}, \triangle\}$ and $Y = \{\text{☃}, \triangle, b, 1, \text{Joe}\}$, then $X \cap Y = \{\text{☃}, \triangle\}$.

b) If $M = \{$all convertibles$\}$ and $N = \{$all green cars$\}$, then $M \cap N = \{$all green convertible cars$\}$.

c) If $A = \{$all members of this school's baseball team$\}$ and $C = \{$all members of this school's baseketball team$\}$, then $A \cap C = \{$all members of this school who are on both the basketball and baseball teams$\}$.

d) If $M = \{$all men who have blond hair$\}$ and $N = \{$all women who have blond hair$\}$, then $M \cap N = \varnothing$. In this case, sets M and N are disjoint, since there are no elements common to both sets. ∎

Comment Note that the intersection is not {blond hair}. Having blond hair is a property of all the elements of each set. Blond hair itself is not an element of either set.

EXAMPLE 4

a) If $A = \{$all guitar players$\}$ and $B = \{$all musicians$\}$, then $A \cap B = \{$all guitar players$\}$.

b) If $X = \{$all Volkswagens with air conditioning$\}$ and $Y = \{$all Fords with air conditioning$\}$, what is $X \cap Y$? Note that $X \cap Y$ is not {air-conditioned cars}. Why? ∎

Imagine that we are sponsoring a school dance this Friday at 8:00 P.M. Let A be the set of students who have already bought tickets. Being on the dance committee, we would obviously be interested in the students who have not yet purchased tickets. If our universal set is the set of all students at this college, then we call the set of all students who have not yet purchased tickets the complement of set A.

complement

> **Definition 2.16**   The **complement** of set A, denoted by A' read as "A prime" or "A complement"), is the set of all elements in the universal set that are not also in A.

EXAMPLE 5

a) If the universal set = {1, 2, 3, 4, 5, 6, 7, 8, 9, 10} and A = {1, 4, 6, 8, 9}, then A' = {2, 3, 5, 7, 10}.

b) If the universal set = {all men} and X = {men who are bald}, then X' = {all men who have hair on their heads}.

c) If the universal set = {all American-made cars} and G = {all American—made cars with air conditioning}, then G' = {all American-made cars without air conditioning}.

d) If U = {all humans} and P = {all males}, then P' = {all females}.

e) If the universal set = {all vowels in the English language} and A = {a, e, i, o, u}, then what is A'?

Let A = {all students in this class} and B = {all students who read *Time*}. The set of all students in this class who do not read *Time* is called the difference between sets A and B.

difference between sets

> **Definition 2.17**   The **difference** between sets A and B, denoted as $A - B$ (read as "A minus B"), means the set of all elements that belong to set A but not to set B.

EXAMPLE 6

a) If M = {piano, guitar, drums, clarinet} and N = {piano, saxophone, organ, clarinet}, then $M - N$ = {guitar, drums}. Note that saxophone and organ are not part of the difference, since they are not in set M.

b) If H = {3, 6, 9, 12} and J = {3, 6, 9}, then $H - J$ = {12}. What is $J - H$? If your answer is {12}, you are wrong. (Look at the definition again.) The answer is $\varnothing$.

c) If V = {Milton, Bob, Carl} and F = {Bob, Carl, Milton}, then $V - F = \varnothing$. What is $F - V$? The answer is $\varnothing$.

d) If R = {all Mickey Mouse sweatshirts} and Q = {all triangles with two sides}, then $R - Q = R$, since Q is obviously the null set. What is $Q - R$? It is $\varnothing$.

e) If S = {9} and T = {3}, then $S - T$ = {9} and $T - S$ = {3}.

Bob and Rita are discussing their date for this Friday night. Their friends have recommended the following three restaurants: The China Palace, Tony's Grotto, and Esther's Soul Food. After eating, they plan to go to a discotheque or to a movie. Thus they can spend the evening in one of the following six ways.

Eat at	After eating, go to
1. The China Palace	a discotheque
2. The China Palace	a movie
3. Tony's Grotto	a discotheque
4. Tony's Grotto	a movie
5. Esther's Soul Food	a discotheque
6. Esther's Soul Food	a movie

ordered pair

This assumes that they plan to eat first. Let A = {The China Palace, Tony's Grotto, Esther's Soul Food} and B = {a discotheque, a movie}. Then each possibility can be thought of as an **ordered pair** of elements *where the first element comes from set A and the second element comes from set B*. For example, possibility (4) can be considered as an ordered pair where the first element is Tony's Grotto (from set A) and the second element is a movie (from set B). We write this as (Tony's Grotto, a movie).

> **Definition 2.18** An **ordered pair** of elements is any two elements written in a specific order. If the elements are a and b, we denote this by (a, b).

Since the order is important, the ordered pair (b, a) is different from the ordered pair (a, b).

EXAMPLE 7

The ordered pair (The China Palace, a movie) is different from (a movie, The China Palace). In the ordered pair (The China Palace, a movie), Bob and Rita eat first and then go out. In the ordered pair (a movie, The China Palace), they go out first and then eat. (As we all know, if you are hungry, it makes a big difference which you do first!)

cross product of two sets

> **Definition 2.19** The **cross product** of two sets A and B is the set of **all ordered pairs** that can be formed by taking the first element from set A and the second element from set B. We denote this by $A \times B$. (We read this as "A cross B.")

EXAMPLE 8

a) If A = {The China Palace, Tony's Grotto, Esther's Soul Food} and B = {a discotheque, a movie}, then $A \times B$ = {(The China Palace, a discotheque), (The China Palace, a movie), (Tony's Grotto, a discotheque), (Tony's Grotto, a movie), (Esther's Soul Food, a discotheque), (Esther's Soul Food, a movie)}. These correspond to the six possibilities listed above.

b) If A and B are the same as in part (a), then $B \times A$ = {(a movie, The China Palace), (a movie, Tony's Grotto), (a movie, Esther's Soul Food), (a discotheque, The China Palace), (a discotheque, Tony's Grotto), (a discotheque, Esther's Soul Food)}. This represents all the possibilities if they want to eat later in the evening.

c) If C = {6, 8, 9} and D = {x, y, z}, then $C \times D$ = {(6, x), (6, y), (6, z), (8, x), (8, y), (8, z), (9, x), (9, y), (9, z)}. Also $D \times C$ = {(x, 6), (x, 8), (x, 9), (y, 6), (y, 8), (y, 9), (z, 6), (z, 8), (z, 9)}.

d) If M = {□, △} then $M \times M$ = {(□, △), (□, □), (△, □), (△, △)}.

Cartesian product

Sometimes the cross product is called the **Cartesian product**. Look at Examples 8*a* and 8*b*. Observe that $A \times B$ is not the same as $B \times A$. This is usually the case.

Comment We have already mentioned (in Section 2.1) that, when listing the elements of a set, the order in which they are written is not important. For example, the set {a, 2} is the same as the set {2, a}. When writing an **ordered pair**, the order *is* important. For example, (a, 2) is not the same as (2, a). This idea of ordered pairs will be applied in Chapter 11, when we study graphs and functions.

The importance of ordered pairs and of cross products can be seen in everyday experiences. Imagine that Mr. Jones is planning a trip from New York to Paris in the spring. His travel agent has notified him that in the New York metropolitan area there are three airports from which he may depart: Kennedy, La Guardia, and Newark. In Paris he may land at either Le Bourget or Orly airport. Let the first element of an ordered pair represent the airport from which he leaves and the second element the airport at which he arrives. The ordered pair (Newark, Orly) means that he leaves from Newark airport and arrives at Orly. If A = {Kennedy, Newark, La Guardia} and B = {Orly, Le Bourget}, then $A \times B$ = {(Kennedy, Orly), (Kennedy, Le Bourget), (Newark, Orly), (Newark, Le Bourget), (La Guardia, Orly), (La Guardia, Le Bourget)}. This represents all the different ways that Mr. Jones can travel from New York to Paris.

In this example $B \times A$ would represent all the different ways that Mr. Jones can go from Paris to New York. These are:

$$B \times A = \{(\text{Orly, Kennedy}), (\text{Orly, La Guardia}), (\text{Orly, Newark}),$$
$$(\text{Le Bourget, Kennedy}), (\text{Le Bourget, La Guardia}),$$
$$(\text{Le Bourget, Newark})\}.$$

Students are introduced to the concept of an ordered pair of numbers at an early age. By a proper understanding of its meaning, we are able to solve the riddle puzzle from *Addison-Wesley Mathematics*, 1987, Grade 5, p. 293.

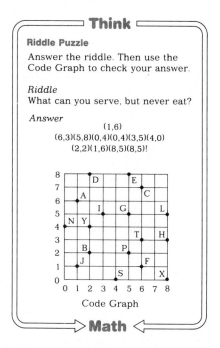

EXERCISES FOR SECTION 2.2

1. Let the universal set $U = \{a, b, c, d, e, f, g, h, i\}$, let $A = \{a, d, f, g\}$, $B = \{b, c, e, f, g, i\}$, and $C = \{b, f, i\}$. Find each of the following:

a) $A \cup B$

b) $A \cap B$

c) A'

d) $A' \cup B$

e) $A - B$

f) $B - A$

g) $C - B$

h) $A - C$

i) $A \times C$

j) $C \times A$

k) $(A' \cap B) \cup C$

l) $(A \cup B)' \cap C$

m) $A' \cap B' \cap C'$

n) $(A' \cap B') \cup C'$

2. Let the universal set $U = \{a, b, c, d, e, f, g, h\}$ and let $A = \{a, b, e, g\}$. Find each of the following:

a) A'

b) $A \cup A$

c) $A \cup A'$

d) $A \cup \varnothing$

e) $A \cap \varnothing$

f) $A - \varnothing$

g) $A \cup U'$

h) $A \cap A'$

i) $A \cap U$

j) $A - U$

k) $U - A$

l) $\varnothing - A$

3. a) If $A \cap B = A$, how are A and B related?

   b) If $A \cup B = A$, how are A and B related?

   c) If $A \cap B = B$, how are A and B related?

   d) If $A \cup B = B$, how are A and B related?

4. Let $A = \{x \mid x$ is a number between 1 and 20 inclusive$\}$, let $B = \{x \mid x$ is a number between 60 and 80 inclusive$\}$, and let $C = \{x \mid x$ is a number between 20 and 80 inclusive$\}$. Find each of the following:

   a) $A \cup B$ **b)** $A \cap C$

   c) $A \cap B$ **d)** $A \cup C$

   e) $B \cup C$ **f)** $B \cap C$

5. If $A \cup A = \varnothing$, what can be said about A?

6. Is it ever possible for $A \times B$ to equal $B \times A$? Explain.

7. Let the universal set $U = \{a, b, c, d\}$, $A = \{a, b\}$, $B = \{a, b, d\}$, $C = \{d\}$, and $D = \{c, d\}$. Indicate the answer to each of the following set operations by writing the capital letter that names the resulting set. (For example, $A \cap B = A$.)

   a) $A \cup C$ **b)** $A \cap C$

   c) $B \cup C$ **d)** $B \cap C$

   e) $B \cap D$ **f)** $A' \cap D$

   g) $D' \cup B$ **h)** $B \cap U$

   i) $B \cup U$

8. Recently, a nationwide survey by the Brown Associates of used car buyers in different age groups was conducted to determine which feature in a used car was of utmost concern to the buyer. The following results were obtained:

Age of buyer (in years)	Economy of operation (E)	Styling (S)	Size (Z)	Color (C)
Under 30 (U)	262	392	301	361
30–50yrs (T)	427	309	296	203
Over 50 (O)	522	283	371	152

Using the letters indicated, find the number of people in each of the following sets.

   a) T **b)** $O \cap E$

   c) $U - S$ **d)** $S \cap T$

   e) $U \cup C$ **f)** $E - T$

   g) $E - S$ **h)** $(O \cap E) \cup (O \cap S)$

   i) $Z \cup (E \cap O)$ **j)** $(C \cup U) \cap Z$

9. Refer to the newspaper article given below. Using the letters given in the article, find the number of people in the following sets.

   a) $(M \cap S) \cup N$ **b)** $D - (I \cup N)$

   c) $F \cap (N \cup S)$ **d)** $O \cup (M \cap S)$

Tighter Security at Airports

WASHINGTON—As a direct result of the recent bomb explosion aboard Pan American Flight 103, government officials have announced a series of security checks at airports of all international travelers and their luggage to thwart any possible terrorist attacks. Yesterday, the Tribune conducted a random survey of travelers at the nation's airports to determine whether they were satisfied with the new security arrangements and the resulting delays. The results are summarized below:

	Supports the checks enthusiastically despite delays (S)	Supports the checks moderately (D)	Is opposed to the checks because of delays (O)
Male			
Frequent traveler (M)	43	67	21
Infrequent traveler (I)	79	99	32
Female			
Frequent traveler (F)	48	58	17
Infrequent traveler (N)	69	95	27

Springfield Tribune, Feb. 5, 1989

10. A recent survey obtained by the Acme Insurance Company of 300 cars equipped with some anti-theft device revealed the information given below:

Type of anti-theft device

Type of car	Ignition shutoff (G)	Steering wheel lock (S)	Burglar alarm (B)
Compact (C)	48	27	53
Intermediate car (I)	32	19	46
Large size (L)	17	22	36

Determine the number of cars in each of the following categories:

a) $C \cap G \cap S'$ **b)** C

c) $C \cap G' \cap S$ **d)** C'

e) I **f)** $I \cap B$

g) $(I \cap S) \cup B$ **h)** $G \cup (S \cap L)$

i) $B \cup (I - G)$

11. If $A = \{a, b\}$ and $B = \{c, d, e\}$, find

a) $n(A)$ **b)** $n(B)$ **c)** $n(A \times B)$

12. If $n(A) = p$ and $n(B) = q$, how many elements are there in $n(A \times B)$?

13. A certain house can be purchased with or without a finished basement and with a choice of three possible sources of heat (solar, oil, or gas). List all the possible combinations of features that can be purchased with the house.

IIII ► **Brain-Teaser Problems** **◄ IIII**

**14. Suppose that Mr. Smith is a small-town barber who shaves all the men and only those men in his town who do not shave themselves. (Everyone in the town is shaved or shaves daily.) Let $A = \{$all men in the town who shave themselves$\}$, and let $B = \{$all men in the town who do not shave themselves$\}$.

a) Is Mr. Smith a member of set A?

b) Is Mr. Smith a member of set B?

c) What is $A \cup B$?

d) Is Mr. Smith a member of $A \cup B$?

2.3

USING VENN DIAGRAMS TO UNDERSTAND SETS

Venn diagrams

The universal set U

	U

Figure 2.4

In your experience with mathematics you have probably found that a diagram is often a useful device. In working with sets, diagrams can also be very helpful. Such diagrams are called **Venn diagrams**.

The universal set is pictured as a rectangle as shown in Fig. 2.4.

All other sets are drawn as circles within the rectangle. We shade the part that is in set A, as shown in Fig. 2.5.

It is easy to see how to picture A'. This time we shade the part that is in set A'. This is shown in Fig. 2.6.

If A is a *proper subset* of B (see Definition 2.10), we draw the circle for A completely inside the circle of B, as shown in Fig. 2.7. We do not shade anything here, since we are picturing a *relationship* between two sets. We shade the diagram only when we want to emphasize the set that we are picturing, rather than a relationship between two or more sets.

Set A

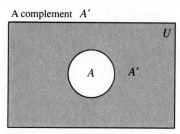

Figure 2.5

A complement A'

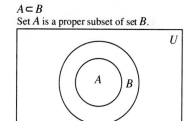

Figure 2.6

A ⊂ B
Set A is a proper subset of set B.

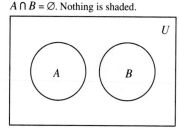

Figure 2.7

A = B
Set A is an improper subset of B.

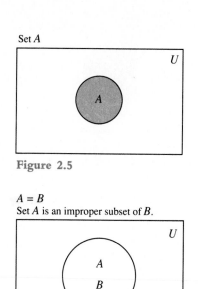

Figure 2.8

A ∩ B is not the null set.

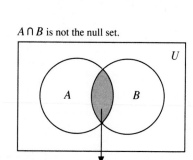

A ∩ B

Figure 2.9

A ∩ B = ∅. Nothing is shaded.

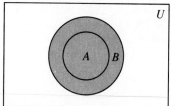

Figure 2.10

U = union set

must have equal sets   A = B

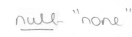
null "none"

A ∩ B when A is a proper subset of B.

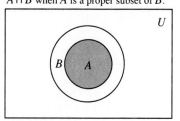

Figure 2.11

If A is an *improper subset* of B (remember, this means A = B), we draw only one circle and label it as both A and B, as shown in Fig. 2.8.

We picture A ∩ B as shown in Figs. 2.9 and 2.10 depending on whether A ∩ B ≠ ∅ or A ∩ B = ∅.

If A is a proper subset of B, we picture A ∩ B as shown in Fig. 2.11.

We picture A ∪ B as shown in Figs. 2.12, 2.13, and 2.14, depending on the relationship between A and B.

The Venn diagram for A – B or B – A is shown in Figs. 2.15, and 2.16 on the following page (if A ∩ B ≠ ∅).

A ∪ B when A and B are not disjoint.

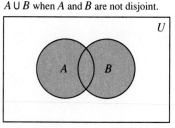

Figure 2.12

A ∪ B when A and B are disjoint.

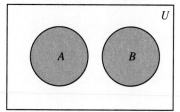

Figure 2.13

A ∪ B when A is a proper subset of B.

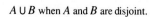

Figure 2.14

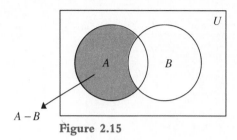

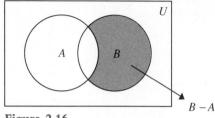

$A - B$

Figure 2.15

$B - A$

Figure 2.16

EXAMPLE 1

Let U = {all people}, A = {all men with blonde hair}, B = {all women with blonde hair}, and C = {all women with blue eyes}. The relationship between these sets is shown in Fig. 2.17.

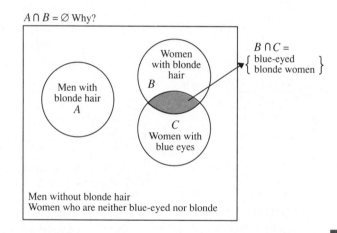

Figure 2.17

EXAMPLE 2

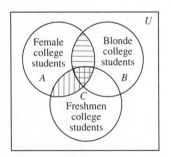

Figure 2.18

If U = {all college students}, A = {all female college students}, B = {all blonde college students}, and C = {all freshmen college students}, then we picture these sets as shown in Fig. 2.18.

The part that has been shaded horizontally represents $A \cap B$. This is the set of all female blonde college students.

The part that has been shaded vertically represents $A \cap C$. This is the set of all female freshmen college students.

Note that in the center part the shading overlaps. This represents $A \cap B \cap C$. How would you describe this set in words?

EXAMPLE 3

SOLUTION

(A∩B)′ is shaded |||||

Figure 2.19

A′∪B′

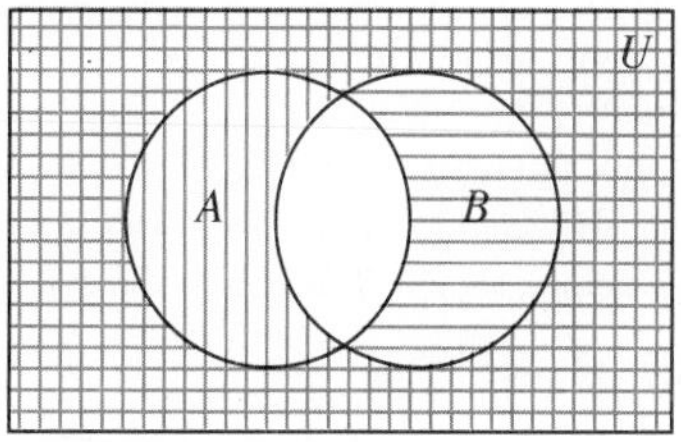

A′ is shaded =====
B′ is shaded |||||||
Figure 2.20

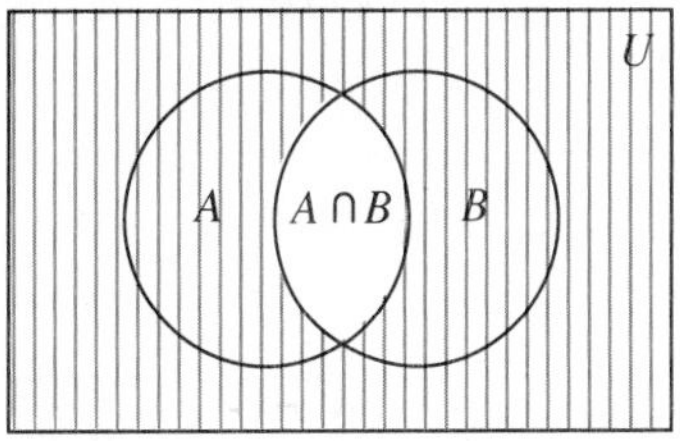

De Morgan's laws

Using Venn diagrams, show that $(A \cap B)' = A' \cup B'$.

We make two diagrams, one to represent $(A \cap B)'$ and one to represent $A' \cup B'$. To draw the diagram for $(A \cap B)'$, we first draw $A \cap B$ and then shade everything *outside* $A \cap B$. This is shown in Fig. 2.19.

To draw the diagram for $A' \cup B'$, we first shade horizontally everything outside A. This gives us A'. We then shade vertically everything outside B. This gives us B'. The part that has *any* shading is $A' \cup B'$. This is shown in Fig. 2.20.

Observe that in both diagrams the same regions have been shaded. This means that $(A \cap B)'$ and $A' \cup B'$ are equal. ∎

Comment The previous results, along with the fact that $(A \cup B)' = A' \cap B'$, are known as **De Morgan's laws** in honor of the famous mathematician Augustus De Morgan, who lived during the nineteenth century. Such formulas enable us to transform statements and formulas into alternative and often more useful forms.

Read the newspaper clipping below. On the basis of the data collected by Representative Smith's staff it would seem that the money should be spent on revamping the criminal justice system and hiring more police. Nevertheless, the governor's office claimed that the data are inconsistent. Is there a way to determine whether the data are consistent or not?

Surplus Budget Presenting Problems

SAYERVILLE—Ever since the governor announced that there would be an unexpected 358.4 million-dollar budget surplus, many of the state's legislators have been engaged in a heated debate over how the state should spend its huge surplus. Many suggestions have been put forth. The lastest survey of 2000 constituents conducted by Representative Ali Smith's staff indicates that 1354 believe the money should be spent on revamping the criminal justice system and hiring more police, 608 believe the money should be spent on building new roads and schools, 618 believe the money should be spent on combating the illicit drug business and establishing drug rehabilitation centers, 278 believe the money should be spent on both police and roads, 200 believe the money should be spent on building roads and combating illicit drugs, 178 believe the money should be spent on more police and combating illicit drugs, and 62 believe the money should be spent on all three proposals.

The governor's office refused to accept the report, claiming that the data were inconsistent. Representative Smith was unavailable for comment.

Middletown News, March 12, 1988

We will now discuss two important applications of sets: survey problems and voting coalitions.

Survey Problems

The first application of sets is to analyze **survey problems**. This is illustrated in the following examples.

EXAMPLE 4

Problem-Solving Example: Using a Diagram

Consider the newpaper article shown below.

> # Americans Love New Gadgets
>
> LOS ANGELES—A recent survey of 600 families revealed that 348 of them had a video cassette recorder (VCR), 198 had a microwave oven, and 75 had both a VCR and a microwave oven. Americans seem to be fascinated with any new technology.
>
> *Portland Star, June 3, 1989*

Based upon the information contained in the article,

a) how many families had neither a VCR nor a microwave oven?

b) how many families had only a VCR?

c) how many families had only a microwave oven?

SOLUTION

Understanding the Problem

We are given a newspaper article containing some information on the number of people who owned a VCR and/or a microwave oven and are asked to use that information to answer other questions.

A Plan to Solve the Problem

Let

$$U = \{\text{families involved in the survey}\},$$
$$V = \{\text{families who own a VCR}\},$$
$$M = \{\text{families who own a microwave oven}\}.$$

The article provides us with the following information:

1. The number of families surveyed, that is, $n(U) = 600$.
2. The number of families who own a VCR, that is, $n(V) = 348$.
3. The number of families who own a microwave oven, that is, $n(M) = 198$.

4. The number of families who own both a VCR and a microwave oven, that is, $n(V \cap M) = 75$.

We can illustrate this information with a Venn diagram as shown in Fig. 2.21. From the previous section we known that $V \cap M$ represents the region that is common to both circles. This represents region II in Fig. 2.21. Since $n(V \cap M) = 75$, we write 75 in this region. Since we are told that 348 families own a VCR, this means that $n(V) = 348$ or that the total number of families in regions I and II together is 348. However, we already know that region II contains 75 families, so region I contains 348 – 75 or 273. We indicate this on the diagram. Also, we are told that 198 families own a microwave oven. This means that the total number of families in regions II and III is 198. Again, we already know that region II contains 75, so region III contains 198 – 75 = 123. Finally, we have accounted for 273 + 75 + 123 in regions I, II, and III, respectively. This gives 471. Since the survey involved 600 families, we must have 600 families in regions I, II, III, and IV together. Thus we have 600 – 471 or 129 for region IV alone.

a) How many families had neither a VCR nor a microwave oven? This is represented by region IV in the diagram. The number of families in region IV is 129.

b) How many families had only a VCR? This is represented by region I in the diagram. The number of families in region I is 273.

c) How many families had only a microwave oven? This is represented by region III in the diagram. The number of families in region III is 123.

Checking Our Solution
We can easily verify that our solution is indeed correct by referring to Fig. 2.21. Since $n(U) = 600$, then the sum of all the numbers in the diagram must be 600. This is true as 273 + 75 + 123 + 129 = 600. Also, the diagram shows us that 273 families owned only a VCR, 75 families owned both a VCR and a microwave oven, and 123 owned only a microwave oven. Again this agrees with the given information as $n(V \cap M) = 75$, $n(V) = 273 + 75 = 348$, and $n(M) = 75 + 123 = 198$.   ▄

The following is another problem-solving example. However, we have not indicated the three parts: Understanding the problem, A plan to solve the problem, and Checking our solution. Can you insert them in their appropriate places as you read the problem?

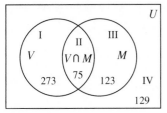

Figure 2.21

EXAMPLE 5

The student government at State University recently conducted a survey to gather more information on the high school backgrounds of entering freshmen. There were 100 students interviewed and the following data were collected:

28 took physics,
31 took biology,
42 took geometry,
9 took physics and biology,
10 took physics and geometry,
6 took biology and geometry, and
4 took all three subjects.

On the basis of these figures,

1. How many students took none of the three subjects?

2. How many students took physics but not biology or geometry?

3. How many students took biology and physics but not geometry?

SOLUTION

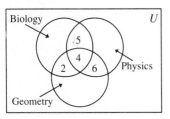

Figure 2.22

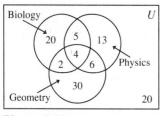

Figure 2.23

This problem can be solved easily by means of Venn diagrams. Three circles are used to represent the students taking each of the subjects.

In Fig. 2.22 we first put in the number of students who took all three subjects. This was given to be 4. Since we know that 6 altogether took biology and geometry, we must have 6 – 4, or 2, who took biology and geometry *but not* physics. We enter this in Fig. 2.22. Similarly, we know that 10 took physics and geometry. Therefore we must have 10 – 4, or 6, who took physics and geometry *but not* biology. We fill this in on the diagram. Also we know that 9 took physics and biology. Therefore we must have 5 who took physics and biology *but not* geometry. We fill this in on the diagram.

According to the data, 42 took geometry. If we look at the geometry circle, we see that we have accounted for 6 + 4 + 2, or 12. This leaves 42 – 12, or 30 students to be put in the remainder of the geometry circle. We then have the diagram shown in Fig. 2.23.

Now, 31 took biology. In Fig. 2.22, we have accounted for 5 + 4 + 2, or 11 students. This leaves 31 – 11, or 20 students to be put in the remaining portion of the biology circle. In a similar manner, there are 28 – 15, or 13 students for the remainder of the physics circle.

We now add together all the numbers appearing in the diagram: 20 + 5 + 4 + 2 + 6 + 13 + 30. This sum is 80. Since the survey involved 100 students, we are left with 100 – 80, or 20 students who did not take any of these subjects. This answers question 1. The answer to question 2 can be read from Fig. 2.23. It is obviously 13. The diagram also answers question 3. Five took biology and physics, but not geometry.

Another interesting application of sets is to voting coalitions.

Voting Coalitions*

Recently, the student government at State College appointed a committee consisting of Mike, Richard, Helen, Bess, and David to consider a proposal to establish a drug clinic on campus. There is some disagreement on this committee as to whether they should accept or reject the proposal. Each member has one vote. Richard, Mike, and Helen agree with the proposal, whereas David and Bess oppose it. The committee operates under majority rule. Since Richard, Mike, and Helen agree, we call them a **winning coalition**. Since David and Bess have only two votes between them, they form a **losing coalition**.

winning coalition

losing coalition

Let the universal set U be some voting body such as the committee above, or the United States Senate, etc. Assume that there are no abstentions or absentees. We then have the following definitions.

Definition 2.20   Any combination of people (that is, a subset of U) that can carry a proposal is called a **winning coalition.**

Definition 2.21   A combination of people (that is, a subset of U) is called a **losing coalition** if a proposal will pass even though they vote against it.

EXAMPLE 6

In the committee example above, the subset {Richard, Mike, Helen} is a winning coalition. The subset {David, Bess} is a losing coalition.   ■

EXAMPLE 7

a) Suppose a committee consists of three people whom we shall call p, q, r, so that $U = \{p, q, r\}$. If the committee operates under majority rule, then the winning coalitions are $\{p, q\}$, $\{p, r\}$, $\{q, r\}$, and $\{p, q, r\}$. The losing coalitions are $\{p\}$, $\{q\}$, and $\{r\}$.

b) Suppose the committee in part (a) elects p as its chairperson and gives her two votes. Everyone else has only one vote. Then the winning coalitions are $\{p, q, r\}$, $\{p, q\}$, and $\{p, r\}$. The coalition $\{q, r\}$ is no longer a winning coalition because p alone has two votes and can block q and r together. The losing coalitions are $\{q\}$ and $\{r\}$. Why is $\{p\}$ no longer a losing coalition?   ■

---

*The remainder of this section can be omitted without affecting the continuity of the text.

In the last example, assume that p votes against a proposal and q and r each vote for it. What happens? The proposal will neither win nor lose. It is **blocked**. We call $\{p\}$ and $\{q, r\}$ **blocking coalitions**. ▪

blocking coalition

> **Definition 2.22**   A coalition is called a **blocking coalition** if it can prevent any proposal from winning, but it cannot win by itself.

EXAMPLE 8

a) In Example 6 above, there are *no* blocking coalitions.

b) The U.C. Corporation of America has six members on its board of directors, each with one vote. Any coalition containing exactly three members is a blocking coalition. ▪

dictator

block

veto power

dummy

In some voting bodies (for example, fascist states), there is one person who has the power to pass any measure on his or her vote alone (even if no one else votes for it). Such a person is called a **dictator**. A somewhat less powerful person is someone who is not a dictator, but who can **block** any proposal with his or her single vote alone. Such a person is said to have **veto power**. There may also be someone who has little power. Any winning coalition to which he or she belongs would be a winning coalition even without him or her. Such a person is called a **dummy**.

> **Definition 2.23**   A **dictator** is someone who can pass any proposal with only his or her own vote. He or she needs no other votes.

> **Definition 2.24**   A member of a voting body has **veto power** if his or her vote alone is enough to **block** any proposal. (He or she cannot win alone.)

> **Definition 2.25**   A member of a voting body is called a **dummy** if any winning coalition of which he or she is a member will be a winning coalition even without him or her.

EXAMPLE 9

In ancient Greece the ostrakon
was used in elections to ensure
one vote for one person. (*Printed
by permission of the American School of
Classical Studies: Agora Excavations.*)

a) The City Council of Atlantis consists of four members with the
following voting strengths.

Mayor	5 votes
Treasurer	2 votes
County clerk	1 vote
Council president	1 vote

A simple majority, that is, more than half of the votes cast, is needed
to pass any proposal. The mayor is obviously the dictator.

    The treasurer, the county clerk, and the council president are each
dummies. Why?

b) In a neighboring town, the city council consists of four members with
voting strength as follows:

Mayor	3 votes with veto power
Treasurer	3 votes
Sheriff	2 votes
Council president	1 vote

A simple majority is needed to pass any proposal. If M denotes mayor,
T denotes treasurer, S denotes sheriff, and C denotes council president,
then M has veto power. The winning coalitions are $\{M, T, S, C\}$,
$\{M, T, S\}$, $\{M, T, C\}$, $\{M, S, C\}$, $\{M, S\}$, and $\{M, T\}$.

    The losing coalitions are $\{C\}$, $\{S\}$, $\{T\}$, $\{S, C\}$, and $\{T, C\}$.

    The council president C is the dummy. Are there any other
dummies? Why is $\{T, S, C\}$ not a winning coalition?

Look back at the last example. One of the winning coalitions was
$\{M, T, S\}$. Another was $\{M, S\}$. Coalition $\{M, T, S\}$ would still have been
winning, even if T or S (but not both) had voted against it. On the other
hand, in $\{M, S\}$, all votes are essential. Similarly, in $\{M, T\}$ all votes are
essential. Observe that $\{M, T\}$ and $\{M, S\}$ are proper subsets of $\{M, T, S\}$.
(Refer back to Definition 2.10.) Thus $\{M, T, S\}$ has proper subsets that are
also winning coalitions. On the other hand, $\{M, T\}$ and $\{M, S\}$ have no
subsets that are winning coalitions. This leads us to the following
definition.

minimal winning coalition

> **Definition 2.26** A **minimal winning coalition** is any winning
> coalition that has no proper subset that is a winning coalition (that
> is, each member's vote is essential or the proposal will not pass).

EXAMPLE 10

a) In Part (b) of Example 9 above, the minimal winning coalitions are $\{M, S\}$ and $\{M, T\}$.

b) A committee has six members $\{a, b, c, d, e, f\}$, each with one vote. A two-thirds vote is needed to carry any proposal. Any coalition with exactly four members in it is a minimal winning coalition. ▬

EXERCISES FOR SECTION 2.3

1. In each part, draw a Venn diagram similar to the diagram shown in Fig. 2.24 and shade in the area indicated

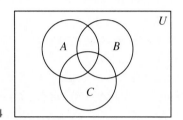

Figure 2.24

a) $A \cap B \cap C$ **b)** $A \cup B \cup C$

c) $(A \cap B \cap C)'$ **d)** $A \cup (B \cap C)$

e) $A \cap (B \cup C')$ **f)** $A' \cup (B \cap C)$

g) $[(A \cap B) \cup C]'$

2. Refer to Fig. 2.25. Let $T = \{\text{tall people}\}$, $I = \{\text{intelligent people}\}$, and $P = \{\text{pleasant people}\}$. Describe in words the set represented by each of the indicated symbols.

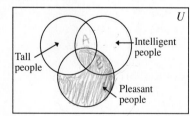

Figure 2.25

a) $T \cap I \cap P'$ **b)** $(T \cup I) \cap P$

c) $T \cap (I' \cup P)$ **d)** $T' \cup (I \cap P)$

e) $(T' \cup I) \cap P$ **f)** $(T \cap I) - P$

3. For each part, use Fig. 2.26 to find the value of the indicated expression.

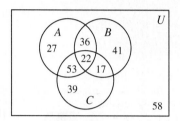

Figure 2.26

a) $n(A \cup B \cup C)$ **b)** $n(A \cap B \cap C)$

c) $n(B')$ **d)** $n[(A \cap B)']$

e) $n[(A \cup B') \cap C']$ **f)** $n[(A \cap B') \cup C']$

4. For each part, use Fig. 2.27 to find the number of people in each category.

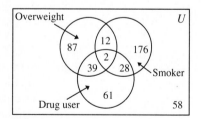

Figure 2.27

a) Overweight, nonsmoker, but drug user.

b) Overweight, smoker, but not drug user.

c) Not overweight but smoker and drug user.

d) Not overweight, not smoker, nor drug user.

e) Only drug user.

f) Overweight, smoker, and drug user.

g) Drug user, smoker, but not overweight.

5. In Fig. 2.28, the different parts of the circles are numbered from 1 to 8. For example, region 1 corresponds to the set $(A \cup B \cup C)'$. In a similar manner, describe symbolically the set that corresponds to each of the regions 2, 3, 4, 5, 6, 7, and 8.

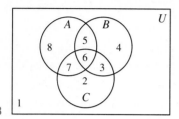

Figure 2.28

6. Using Venn diagrams, verify *De Morgan's law*, $(A \cup B)' = A' \cap B'$.

7. Use set notation to describe the shaded portion of the following diagrams.

a)

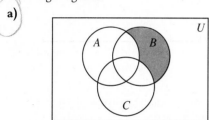

Figure 2.29

d)

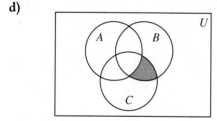

Figure 2.30

c)

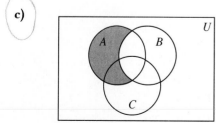

Figure 2.31

b)

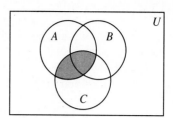

Figure 2.32

8. By using Venn diagrams, determine which of the following statements are true for all sets.

a) $A' \cup B' = A \cap B$

b) $(A \cup B)' = A' \cap B$

c) $A \cup (B \cap C) = (A \cup B) \cap C$

d) $A' \cup B' = A' \cap B$

e) $A' \cup (B \cap C) = A \cap (B \cup C)'$

f) $A \cap (B \cup C) = (A \cup B) \cap (A \cup C)$

g) $A \cap (B \cup C) = (A \cap B) \cup (A \cap C)$

h) $A \cap (B \cup C)' = A \cap (B' \cup C')$

9. Draw a Venn diagram to represent each of the following:

a) $A \subset B$

b) $A \cup \varnothing$

c) $A \cap U$

d) $A \cup B$ when $A \cap B = \varnothing$

e) $(A' \cup B)'$ when A and B are disjoint

f) $A \cup B$ when $A = B$

g) $A \cap B = B$

h) $A \cup B = A$

i) $(A \cup B)'$ when $A \cap B = \varnothing$

10. Use De Morgan's laws to simplify each of the following:

a) $A' \cup (A \cap B)'$

b) $A \cap (A \cup B)'$

c) $(A' \cup B)'$

d) $(A' \cap B')'$

e) $B \cup (A \cap B)'$

f) $(A' \cap B)' \cup A$

11. A total of 427 students were admitted to the business program at Technical University. Of these, 246 had taken intermediate algebra in high school, 159 had taken trigonometry, and 57 had taken both intermediate algebra and trigonometry.

   a) How many students took trigonometry but not intermediate algebra?

   b) How many students took intermediate algebra but not trigonometry?

   c) How many students did not take either subject in high school?

12. A survey of 600 farmers in the Midwest revealed that 382 of them raised hogs, 335 of them raised chickens, and 179 of them raised both hogs and chickens.

   a) How many of the farmers raised only chickens?

   b) How many of the farmers raised only hogs?

   c) How many farmers raised neither hogs nor chickens?

13. The following results were reported by researchers at the Kingston Medical Center. Of the 100 people in a control group who were suffering from arthritis, 75 were given a new drug. The remaining patients were given a placebo. Sixty of the patients showed improvement; 54 of these people actually received the drug.

   a) How many patients receiving the drug showed no improvement?

   b) How many patients not receiving the drug showed no improvement?

14. A survey of the 200 workers at the Printex Corporation revealed that 115 of the workers were union members, 53 of the workers were satisfied with the working conditions, and 27 of the workers were union members who were satisfied with the working conditions.

   a) How many union members were not satisfied with the working conditions?

   b) How many workers were satisfied with the working conditions but were not union members?

   c) How many workers were not satisfied with the working conditions and were not union members?

15. The 200 workers of the Printex Corporation have just negotiated a new contract with management whereby additional funds will be contributed to employee benefit programs. The employees were polled as to how the funds should be spent. The survey showed that

   94   wanted better pension benefits,

   99   wanted better health benefits,

   113   wanted better dental insurance,

   32   wanted better pension and health benefits,

   41   wanted better dental insurance and health benefits,

   47   wanted better pension and dental plans, and

   14   wanted better pension, health, and dental plans.

   a) How many employees wanted only a better pension plan?

   b) How many employees wanted only a better dental plan?

   c) How many employees wanted a better health and dental plan but were not interested in a pension plan?

   d) How many employees wanted a better health and pension plan only?

   e) How many employees were not interested in any of these programs?

16. In a recent survey of 400 business executives, the following information was obtained:

   190   read *Fortune*,

   230   read *Time*,

   110   read *Newsweek*,

   60   read *Fortune* and *Time*,

   50   read *Fortune* and *Newsweek*,

   70   read *Time* and *Newsweek*, and

   20   read all three.

   a) How many did not read any of the magazines?

   b) How many read *Fortune* but not *Time* or *Newsweek*?

   c) How many read only *Newsweek* but not *Time* or *Fortune*?

d) How many read *Time* and *Newsweek* but not *Fortune*?

e) How many read *Newsweek* and *Fortune* but not *Time*?

17. A survey conducted by Bradley and Robbins of 700 Americans who exercise regularly to maintain their physical fitness disclosed the following:

> 350 jog,
> 279 swim,
> 321 cycle,
> 133 jog and swim,
> 86 swim and cycle,
> 105 jog and cycle,
> 47 jog, swim, and cycle.

a) How many of the people surveyed only jog?

b) How many of the people surveyed only swim?

c) How many of the people surveyed only cycle?

d) How many of the people surveyed jog and swim but do not cycle?

e) How many of the people surveyed jog and cycle but do not swim?

f) How many of the people surveyed do not participate in any of the activities mentioned?

*18. A committee consists of six members: Bob, Sue, Jo, Ann, Tom, and Ron, each with one vote. Four votes are needed to carry any proposal.

a) Find all the winning coalitions.
b) Find all the losing coalitions.
c) Find all the minimal winning coalitions.
d) Are there any blocking coalitions? If so, find them.

*19. Refer back to the previous exercise. Assume that, if there is a tie, then Ann has an additional vote to break the tie.

a) Find all the winning coalitions.
b) Find all the losing coalitions.
c) Find all the minimal winning coalitions.

d) Are there any blocking coalitions? If so, find them.

*20. Can a voting power ever have two dictators?

*21. If a voting power has a dictator, can it also have a dummy?

*22. The Board of Directors of the Carle Corporation has eight members. The votes are distributed as follows:

Thomas Meringolo, Chairperson	4 votes
Lisa Palm, President	4 votes
Gary Yhap, Treasurer	4 votes
Judith Ramos	2 votes
Felix Sosa	2 votes
Kimberly Juliano	2 votes
Patrick Butler	2 votes
Robert Zimmer	2 votes

A simple majority carries an issue.

Find six minimal winning coalitions.

Find six blocking coalitions.

*23. The United Nations Security Council has fifteen member nations: the "Big Five" and ten smaller members. Each member of the Big Five has veto power. If nine votes are needed to pass any proposal, find the minimal winning, losing, and blocking coalitions.

PROBLEM-SOLVING EXERCISES

24. All customers returning Christmas gifts at Rochelle's Department Store must complete the questionnaire shown below:

Why are you returning the gift?	
Wrong size	☐
Wrong color	☐
Already have it	☐

A clerk tallied the results and submitted the following report on 100 returned items. (It was known that each customer had checked at least one box.)

---

*Exercises preceded by * correspond to material found in an optional section.

30   already have it,

23   wrong size,

50   wrong color,

20   wrong size and color,

8   already have it and wrong color,

5   already have it, wrong size, and wrong color.

The clerk was fired. Why?

25. Refer to the newspaper clipping that appears on page 63. By analyzing the data, determine whether or not the governor's office is justified in refusing to accept the report.

Brain-Teaser Problems

**26. Anita, Mary, and Heather are analyzing this Sunday's baseball schedule. The following teams are scheduled to play baseball games: Mets, Dodgers, Pirates, Cubs, Phillies, Giants, Astros, and Cardinals. Anita predicts that the winners will be the Mets, Dodgers, Pirates, and Phillies. Mary believes that the winners will be the Cubs, Pirates, Giants, and Mets. Heather believes that the winners will be the Phillies, Mets, Cardinals, and Giants. No one believes that the Astros will win. By means of Venn diagrams, determine which teams are scheduled to play each other.

**27. A small town has a population of 3600 and only one movie house. During the week of December 1–7 the film *Star Trek* was shown, and 2800 people from the town saw it. The following week the film *E.T.* was shown and 1420 people saw it.

a) Find the largest number of people who could have seen both movies.

b) Find the smallest number of people who could have seen both movies.

2.4

LOGIC: INDUCTIVE AND DEDUCTIVE REASONING

People's ability to reason distinguishes them from lower animals. Logic is not just a tool of the mathematician or logician; it is used by each of us every day in almost every aspect of our lives. As soon as we wake up in the morning, we must decide what to wear. In making our decision we consider the weather, the season, the activities planned for the day, what we wore yesterday, and so on. What we ultimately decide to wear is determined by a logical process. As the day progresses, we continually make decisions that involve logical thinking. Psychologists tell us that even though our dreams seem to be disconnected, there is actually a logical thought process connecting them. In mathematics, logic is an especially important tool, as you probably found in your high school studies.

Let us consider Dr. Smith, who recently announced that a new serum for a certain disease has been developed. Over a period of ten years, the doctor has administered the serum in varying dosages to 6341 patients. All those receiving this medicine recovered shortly thereafter. Dr. Smith therefore claims that the serum is a cure for this dreadful disease. Do you believe the doctor's claim?

You would probably say yes. Let us analyze the claim more carefully. Suppose on the 6342nd patient the serum fails. However, on the next 5000 patients it works. Does this one failure constitute a disproof of Dr. Smith's claim? Not really. We would not expect the serum to work in every case. It should work in *almost* every case. This is how we interpret the doctor's claim. In other words, we expect that anyone who gets the serum will *probably* recover.

Now consider a traffic light at the intersection of Main Street and Broadway. A taxi pulls up just as the light turns red. On the basis of past experience, the driver knows that the light changes every 30 seconds; consequently, at the end of 30 seconds the driver begins to move through the intersection. Since, in the past, the light has changed every 30 seconds, the driver assumes that the light will again change after 30 seconds and that one can proceed safely. In most cases this conclusion is correct. However, occasionally the light may be broken and will not change as anticipated. Although the driver's decision is probably justified, there still is a possibility that the light will not change.

Both of the above examples are illustrations of inductive reasoning.

HISTORICAL NOTE

Historically, the study of logic can be traced back to the ancient Greeks, specifically to Aristotle (384–322 B.C.). He is generally considered to be the "father" of logic. The logic of Aristotle was based on a formal kind of argument, called a *syllogism*. For example:

1. All men are mortal.
2. Socrates is a man

   Therefore Socrates is mortal.

It can be shown that the statement "Socrates is mortal" follows logically from the first two sentences. Much of Aristotle's logic was devoted to a detailed study of such syllogisms. For many centuries, Aristotle was considered to be the ultimate authority on logic. In fact, it has been said that further developments in the study of logic were delayed for centuries because of the unquestioning faith that logicians had placed in Aristotle's work.

inductive reasoning

> **Definition 2.27** In **inductive reasoning** we arrive at conclusions on the basis of a number of observations of specific instances. The conclusion is probably, but not necessarily, true.

Inductive reasoning is widely used in science. It is also the kind of reasoning we all use daily in making decisions. In inductive reasoning we assume that the present or future will resemble the past and we act or reason accordingly. The following examples illustrate these ideas.

EXAMPLE 1

Figure 2.33 The metal figure shown here is made up of unrelated components (e.g., an auto for its head). Is the whole greater than the sum of its parts? Does the unrelatedness affect the logic of the composition? (Picasso, Pablo. *Baboon and Young.* 1951. Bronze [cast 1955], after found objects, 21″ high, base $13\frac{1}{4} \times 6\frac{7}{8}$″. Collection, The Museum of Modern Art, New York. Mrs. Simon Guggenheim Fund.)

The Nature and Patterns of Inductive Logic

EXAMPLE 2

a) Before leaving the house in the morning, Alice looks out the window. The skies are overcast. She has heard the weather forecaster predict rain. She decides to take her umbrella. In making this decision, Alice is reasoning inductively. It *probably* will rain and Alice will need her umbrella. There is also a slim chance that it will clear up.

b) Johnny is crying. His father has just told him that they are going to the dentist. His past visits to the dentist were quite painful, so he concludes that the present visit will be painful. Although his fears are *probably* justified, he may find that the visit will turn out otherwise.

c) In 1866 the Austrian monk Gregor Mendel published a major work on the theory of heredity. In experiments with garden peas, Mendel noticed that certain characteristics appeared in peas according to a recognizable pattern. For example, when he crossbred green and yellow peas, he found that out of every four peas produced, approximately three were green and one was yellow. On the basis of these experiments, Mendel was able to state general "laws" of heredity, not only for plants but also for humans. These enabled him to predict such things as eye color and hair color.

d) In recent years, doctors in the United States have been experimenting with the drug lithium in the treatment of mentally depressed people. Approximately 80 percent of all such patients treated with lithium have reported feeling better. As a result, doctors are concluding that lithium may be a remedy for the symptoms of chronic depression. Their reasoning is inductive. There is no guarantee that a patient who takes lithium will feel better, but it is probable that he or she will. ∎

> If we were to analyze many of the arguments that exist in print or many of the speeches that are made by politicians, we would find that a good number of them are inconsistent. How do we determine whether something is logical or not? Would you consider the situation shown in Fig. 2.33 to be logical?

Not only is inductive reasoning used in everyday decision making, it is also used in mathematical situations, as can be seen in the following examples.

Suppose you are given the following sequence of numbers: 1, 4, 7, 10, 13, ... What is the next number in this sequence? Your answer is 16. How did you arrive at this answer? Are you 100 percent sure that you are right? Is there any possibility that there may be a different answer? ∎

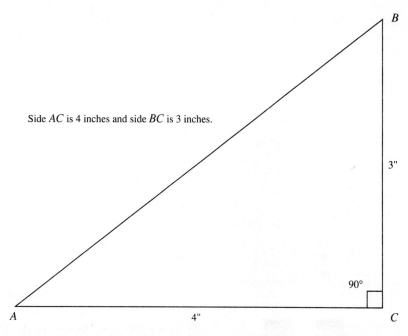

Side *AC* is 4 inches and side *BC* is 3 inches.

Figure 2.34

Now look at the triangle shown in Fig. 2.34. Side *AC* is 4 in. and side *BC* is 3 in. Measure side *AB*. How many inches did you get? You should get 5 in. If you didn't, try again. Notice that

$$(3 \times 3) + (4 \times 4) = 5 \times 5$$

In mathematics, 3×3 is abbreviated as 3^2. Similarly, 4×4 is abbreviated as 4^2. The same is true for 5×5, which is written as 5^2. Using this notation, we have

$$3^2 + 4^2 = 5^2$$

This is a special case of a well-known theorem in geometry known as the *Pythagorean theorem*. It states the following: *In a right triangle (that is, a triangle with a 90° angle)* such as the one in Fig. 2.35 *the sides are related by the formula* $a^2 + b^2 = c^2$.

The Pythagorean theorem is named for the Greek mathematician Pythagoras, who lived in the sixth century B.C. Actually, the theorem was known much earlier. According to some historians, the ancient Egyptians knew of at least one special case of the theorem. Tablets from the Babylonian era show that the Babylonians also knew of at least one special case of this theorem. In fact, one historian claims that they "did indeed make use of this theorem in its full generality."[1] In measuring land for tax

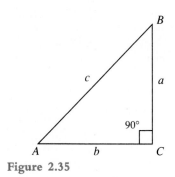

Figure 2.35

---

1. Asger Aaboe, *Episodes from the Early History of Mathematics*, p. 26. New York: Random House, 1964.

assessment and in building, some of the basic ideas of geometry were developed. It seems reasonable to assume that in measuring areas that were in the form of right triangles, the Babylonians observed this important relationship between the sides.

The Pythagorean theorem was discovered inductively by observing special cases of right triangles. But inductive reasoning can tell us only that it is *probably* true. In order to *know* that it is *always* true, it must be *proved deductively*. As we shall see shortly, in deductive reasoning, the conclusion *must* be true (if the hypotheses are true and the reasoning is valid). The proof of this theorem, which you may have studied in high school geometry, was given by Euclid about 200 years after Pythagoras. It is not known when it was *first* proved. The proof involves deductive reasoning.

We see, then, that both inductive and deductive reasoning have a place in mathematics, the former in *discovering* new truths and the latter in *proving* these truths.

EXAMPLE 3

prime number

Goldbach's conjecture. A **prime number** is any whole number larger than 1 that can be evenly divided *only* by itself and 1 (assuming that we divide only by positive numbers). Some of the prime numbers are 2, 3, 5, 7, 11, 13, 17, 19, ... Note that

$$6 = 3 + 3 \qquad\qquad 16 = 11 + 5$$
$$8 = 5 + 3 \qquad\qquad 18 = 11 + 7 \text{ or } 13 + 5$$
$$10 = 7 + 3 \text{ or } 5 + 5 \qquad\qquad \vdots \qquad \vdots$$
$$12 = 5 + 7$$
$$14 = 7 + 7 \text{ or } 11 + 3$$

Observe that all the numbers on the right of the equals signs are prime numbers. All the numbers on the left are *even* numbers larger than four. The mathematician Goldbach, reasoning *inductively*, claimed that *any* even number larger than four can be written as the sum of two odd prime numbers. Although it seems reasonable, as yet no one has been able to prove this *deductively*. Do you agree with his claim? ■

EXAMPLE 4

Consider the following arrangement of numbers.

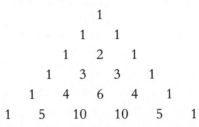

```
            1
          1   1
        1   2   1
      1   3   3   1
    1   4   6   4   1
  1   5  10  10   5   1
```

Pascal's triangle

Can you find the next row of numbers? This arrangement of numbers is called **Pascal's triangle**. Although studied by Pascal (1623–1662), it was known to the Chinese much earlier. Among other things, this triangle has applications in the theory of probability, as we shall see later.

EXAMPLE 5

Consider the following chart.

Numbers added	Sum	Another way of writing sum
$1 + 2$	3	$\dfrac{2 \times 3}{2}$
$1 + 2 + 3$	6	$\dfrac{3 \times 4}{2}$
$1 + 2 + 3 + 4$	10	$\dfrac{4 \times 5}{2}$
$1 + 2 + 3 + 4 + 5$	15	$\dfrac{5 \times 6}{2}$
$1 + 2 + 3 + 4 + 5 + 6$	21	$\dfrac{6 \times 7}{2}$
$1 + 2 + 3 + 4 + 5 + 6 + 7$	28	
$1 + 2 + 3 + 4 + 5 + 6 + 7 + 8$	36	
$1 + 2 + 3 + \cdots + 20$	210	
$1 + 2 + 3 + \cdots + n$		

Can you complete the third column? If you get the last entry in the last column right, you will have obtained a useful mathematical formula that gives the sum of the first n counting numbers, where n is any counting number. Your answer was obtained by observing the pattern in the last column. You reasoned inductively. This result can be proved deductively.

Deductive Reasoning

Until now we have been discussing inductive reasoning. Since in mathematics we prove statements using only deductive reasoning, in the remainder of this section we will analyze how this is done.

To get us started, consider the following argument:

1. All musicians have beards.

2. Jake is a musician.

3. Therefore Jake has a beard.

deductive reasoning

In this example we are using a different kind of reasoning called **deductive reasoning**. If you agree that statements (1) and (2) are true, then you *must* agree that statement (3) is also true. The three statements together make up an *argument*. Statements (1) and (2) are called the *hypotheses* or *premises* of the argument. Statement (3) is called the *conclusion* of the argument. It is important to note that this argument does not say that the statements (1) and (2) *are* true. It just says that *if* they are true, then so is (3).

deductive argument

> **Definition 2.28** If we are given a series of statements with the claim that one must follow from the others, then this is called a **deductive argument**.

conclusion

hypotheses or premises

The statement that follows from the others is called the **conclusion**. The other statements are called the **hypotheses**, or **premises**.

valid argument

invalid argument

> **Definition 2.29** If the conclusion of a deductive argument does follow logically from the hypotheses, then we say that the argument is **valid**. If the conclusion does not necessarily follow logically from the hypotheses, then the argument is **invalid.**

Comment In inductive reasoning, the conclusion is never more than probably true. In deductive reasoning, if the hypotheses are accepted as true, then the conclusion is *inescapable*.

Let us consider the following hypotheses and conclusions:

EXAMPLE 6

a) *Hypotheses:* 1. All Brooklynites live in New York State.
   2. All people who live in New York State pay high taxes.

   Conclusion: All Brooklynites pay high taxes.

b) *Hypotheses:* 1. All cats are dogs.
   2. All dogs meow.

   Conclusion: All cats meow.

c) *Hypotheses:* 1. All college students are nuts.
   2. All nuts talk to themselves.

   Conclusion: All college students talk to themselves.

d) *Hypotheses:* 1. All men are women.
   2. All women are mammals.

   Conclusion: All men are mammals.

e) *Hypotheses:* 1. All cattle are Texans.
2. All Texans are U.S. residents.

Conclusion: All cattle are U.S. residents.

In part (a) of Example 6, both the hypotheses and the conclusion are true. In part (b), both of the hypotheses are false, but the conclusion is true. In part (c), both the hypotheses and conclusion are false. In part (d), the first hypothesis is false, but the second hypothesis is true. The conclusion is true. What can you say about the truth or falsity of the hypotheses and conclusion of part (e)? All of the above arguments are *valid*.

Comment The above examples show that an argument may be valid even if one or more of the statements in it (that is, hypotheses or conclusion) is false. In everyday English we often use the words "true" and "valid" interchangeably. In logic they have different meanings. A **statement** is either true or false. An **argument** is either valid or invalid.

In inductive reasoning, the conclusion is never more than *probably true*. In deductive reasoning, if the hypotheses are accepted as true and the argument is valid, then the conclusion is *inescapable*.

Testing Validity— The Standard Diagram

standard diagram

There is an interesting way of using Venn diagrams to test the validity of arguments. This is by using the **standard diagram**. The standard diagram shows all possibilities in one diagram. It has the advantage that when using it, you need only one diagram and no more. However, you may find the diagram a little more difficult to work with than other Venn diagrams.

We will illustrate the standard diagram by using it to test some examples.

EXAMPLE 7

Hypotheses: 1. All cats are felines.
2. All felines are mammals.

Conclusion: All cats are mammals.

Let *C* stand for cats, *F* for felines, and *M* for mammals. We draw three intersecting circles to represent *C*, *F*, and *M*, as in Fig. 2.36.

Hypothesis (1) tells us that all *C*'s are inside the *F* circle. And there are *no C's outside the F* circle. We indicate this by putting a "∅" (the null set) in *all* parts of the *C* that are *outside* the *F* circle. This is shown in Fig. 2.37.

Hypothesis (2) tells us that there are no *F*'s outside the *M*'s. We represent this by putting ∅ in *all* parts of the *F*'s that are outside the *M* circle. We add this to the diagram, obtaining the result shown in Fig. 2.38.

The conclusion says that there are *no C*'s outside the *M* circle. This *does* follow from the final diagram (Fig. 2.38).

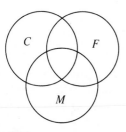

Figure 2.36

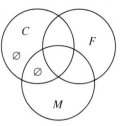
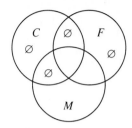

Figure 2.37   Figure 2.38

EXAMPLE 8

Hypotheses: 1. All gentle people are Republicans.
            2. Some dentists are gentle.

Conclusion: Some dentists are Republicans.

Let G stand for gentle people, R for Republicans, and D for dentists. Hypothesis (1) is pictured in Fig. 2.39.

To picture hypothesis (2), we must put an x where D and G overlap. The x in the diagram represents the one dentist that we know is definitely gentle. There may be many other gentle dentists. There are two parts where D and G overlap. Since one of these already has $\varnothing$ in it, we know that the x can't go there. (The $\varnothing$ tells us that there is *nothing* there.) Thus the x must go in the other part. This is shown in Fig. 2.40.

The conclusion says that there is an x where D and R overlap. The diagram confirms this. Thus the argument is valid.

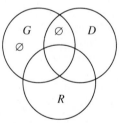
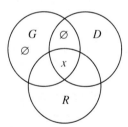

Figure 2.39   Figure 2.40

EXAMPLE 9

Hypotheses: 1. No children are nuisances.
            2. Some children are lovable.

Conclusion: No nuisances are lovable.

Let C stand for children. N for nuisances, and L for lovable.

Hypothesis (1) says that there is no one who is both a child and a nuisance. Thus we put $\varnothing$ in each part where C and N overlap, as in Fig. 2.41.

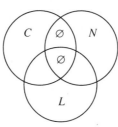
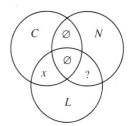

Figure 2.41   Figure 2.42

Since hypothesis (2) tells us that some children are lovable, we know that we must put an *x* in one of the two parts where *C* and *L* overlap. One of these parts already has a ∅ in it. Thus we must put the *x* in the other part. This is shown in Fig. 2.42.   The conclusion says there is nothing in the overlap of *N* and *L*. In our diagram the overlap of *N* and *L* has two parts. One of these definitely has a ∅ in it. The other part we know nothing about. In Fig. 2.42 we indicate this by a "?" The ? tells us that we do not know whether anything is there or not (from the given hypotheses). Thus the conclusion does not follow, and the argument is *not* valid.   ▆

EXAMPLE 10

Hypotheses: 1. Some men are angels.
                     2. Some angels sing.

Conclusion: Some men sing.

Let *M* stand for men, *A* for angels, and *S* for singers.
Hypothesis (1) tells us that there is an *x* in one of the two parts where *M* and *A* overlap, but it does not tell us which. Thus we put it on the border between the two parts, as shown in Fig. 2.43.
Hypothesis (2) tells us that there is a *y* in one of the two parts where *A* and *S* overlap, but again it does not tell us in which of the two parts to put it. Therefore we again put it on the borderline between *A* and *S* as shown in Fig. 2.44.

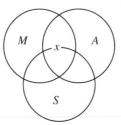
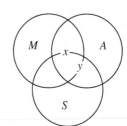

Figure 2.43   Figure 2.44

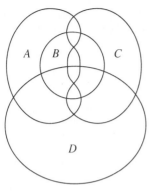

Figure 2.45

The conclusion says that there is *one* x or y that is in *both* M and S at the same time. In the diagram there is no such x or y, since the y is on the border between M and S. It may be in the part where M and S overlap, but, on the other hand, it may be in the part where they do not overlap. We do not know which situation is correct. The same is true for the x. Thus the conclusion is not necessarily true, and therefore the argument is invalid.

The standard diagram can also be applied when there are more than three letters. If there are four letters, then the diagram looks like the one in Fig. 2.45. This diagram cannot be made by drawing four circles for A, B, C, and D. In order to get all the possibilities, we have to "wiggle" the A and C, as shown.

EXERCISES FOR SECTION 2.4

In Exercises 1–4, determine whether the reasoning used is inductive or deductive.

1. Since the Arctic Ocean has had icebergs for thousands of years, it will continue to have them in the foreseeable future.

2. All cats are afraid of water. All things that are afraid of water never take a shower. Therefore all cats never take a shower.

3. Alan is trying to get his television set to work. He plugs it into every outlet in the house, and the television set still does not work. He concludes that there is an electrical blackout.

4. All students receiving financial aid from the state while attending college are residents of the state. Melissa is a resident of the state attending college. Therefore she is receiving financial aid.

5. Assume that you are offered two equally attractive jobs, each with a starting salary of $40,000. However, one job offers annual raises of $4000, while the other job promises a semiannual raise of $2000. Which job would you take and why?

6. What is the next picture in the following sequence?

7. What is the next number or letter in the indicated sequence?

   a) 1, 4, 9, 16, . . .
   b) 2, 4, 6, 4, 6, 8, 6, . . .
   c) 0, 1, 1, 2, 3, 5, 8, 13, . . .
   d) 1, 3, 1, 6, 1, 9, . . .
   e) 2, 3, 5, 7, 11, 13, . . .
   f) O, T, T, F, F, S, S, E, N, . . .
   g) 2, 5, 10, 17, 26, 37, . . .
   h) 8, 5, 4, 9, 1, 7, 6, . . .
   i) 1/4, 2/5, 3/6, 4/7, 5/8, . . .

PROBLEM-SOLVING EXERCISES

8. A circle separates a plane into two regions, the inside and outside of the circle. Two circles separate a plane into three regions if they do not intersect and four regions if they do.

   a) What is the maximum number of regions into which three circles divide a plane?

   b) What is the maximum number of regions into which four circles divide a plane?

   c) What is the maximum number of regions into which five circles divide a plane?

   d) Can you make a general statement relating the number of circles and the number of regions?

9. Draw a circle. If we mark off one point on the circle (as shown below), then there is only *one* region inside the circle. If we mark off two points on the circle and connect them with a straight line, then the line divides the circle into two regions (as shown below). If we mark off three points on the circle and connect them, then there are three lines and four regions. Complete the following table.

Number of points on the circle	Picture	Number of regions
1		1
2		2
3		4
4		8
5		?
6		?
7		?
8		?

10. The Pythagorean theorem states that in a right triangle, labeled as shown in Fig. 2.35 (p. 77)

$$a^2 + b^2 = c^2$$

One solution of this equation is $a = 3$, $b = 4$, and $c = 5$, since

$$3^2 + 4^2 = 5^2$$

or

$$9 + 16 = 25$$

Another solution of this equation is $a = 5$, $b = 12$, and $c = 13$. (Verify this.) Now consider the equation

$$a^3 + b^3 = c^3$$

Try to find values (natural numbers) for a, b, and c that are solutions to this equation. The seventeenth century mathematician Pierre Fermat claimed that no

solution exists. However, no proof was ever found among his papers. More generally, he claimed that if the equation is of the form

$$x^n + y^n = z^n \quad \text{(where } n \text{ is greater than 2),}$$

then no natural numbers can ever be found that would be solutions to this equation. Can you find any natural numbers that are solutions to this equation?

11. It has been suggested that the cube of every natural number larger than 1 can be written as the difference between the squares of two natural numbers. Thus

$$2^3 = 3^2 - 1^2,$$
$$3^3 = 6^2 - 3^2,$$
$$4^3 = 10^2 - 6^2$$

Can you express 5^3 and 6^3 as the difference between the squares of two natural numbers?

12. Consider the following facts:

$$1^3 = 1,$$
$$2^3 = 3 + 5,$$
$$3^3 = 7 + 9 + 11,$$
$$4^3 = 13 + 15 + 17 + 19$$

Adding the numbers on each side of the equation gives

$$1^3 + 2^3 + 3^3 + 4^3$$
$$= 1 + (3 + 5) + (7 + 9 + 11)$$
$$+ (13 + 15 + 17 + 19)$$
$$= 100$$
$$= 10^2$$

Thus

$$1^3 + 2^3 + 3^3 + 4^3 = 10^2 = (1 + 2 + 3 + 4)^2$$

Can you generalize the relationship demonstrated?

13. Refer back to the Pascal triangle, which was given in Example 4 and is reproduced here (see Fig. 2.46 on next page). Notice that we have numbered the rows for easy reference. We first observe that each row begins with and ends with a 1. Also each row is found by adding the two previous numbers as shown by the arrows.

[2.] Irving M. Copi, *Introduction to Logic*, pp. 16–17. New York: MacMillan, 1961. Reprinted by permission.

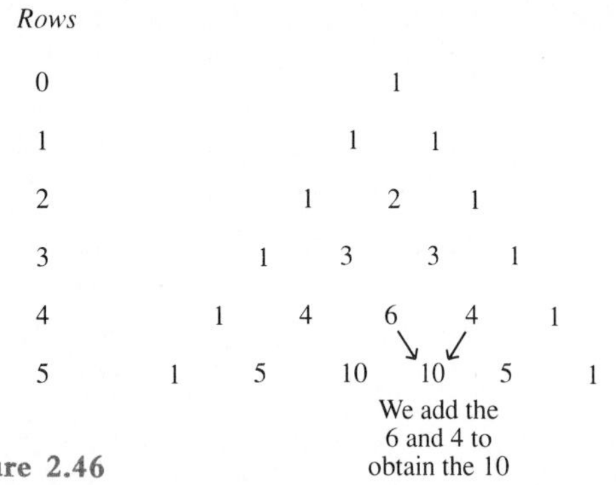

Rows

0	1
1	1 1
2	1 2 1
3	1 3 3 1
4	1 4 6 4 1
5	1 5 10 10 5 1

We add the
6 and 4 to
obtain the 10

Figure 2.46

a) Write down the next two rows of the Pascal triangle shown above.

b) What is the sum of the numbers in row 1 of Pascal's triangle?

c) What is the sum of the numbers in row 2 of Pascal's triangle?

d) What is the sum of the numbers in row 3 of Pascal's triangle?

e) What is the sum of the numbers in row 4 of Pascal's triangle?

f) Can you generalize about the sum of the numbers in row n of Pascal's triangle?

In Exercises 14–25, use the standard diagrams to test the validity of the indicated arguments.

14. *Hypotheses:* (1) Some senior citizens over 65 years of age need a hearing aid.
(2) Ernest Smith is a senior citizen over 65 years of age.

Conclusion: Ernest Smith needs a hearing aid.

15. *Hypotheses:* (a) Some senior citizen centers distribute U.S.D.A. surplus food.
(b) Some senior centers distributing U.S.D.A. surplus food are privately owned.

Conclusion: Some senior citizen centers are privately owned.

16. *Hypotheses:* (a) All low-calorie soft drinks are artificially sweetened.
(b) Some artificial sweeteners are dangerous to your health.

Conclusion: All low-calorie soft drinks are dangerous to your health.

17. *Hypotheses:* (a) All eyeglasses sold in the United States must have shatterproof lenses.
(b) All plastic lenses are shatterproof.

Conclusion: All eyeglasses sold in the United States must have plastic lenses.

18. *Hypotheses:* (a) All cattle in the United States are fed with food that contains antibiotics.
(b) Some antibiotics are harmful to humans when eaten.

Conclusion: Some cattle in the United States are harmful to humans when eaten.

19. *Hypotheses:* (a) Some cans of tuna fish contain large amounts of sodium.
(b) Some cans of sardines contain large amounts of sodium.

Conclusion: Some cans of tuna fish contain sardines.

20. *Hypotheses:* (a) Some professional athletes are married.
(b) Some professional athletes drive sports cars.

Conclusion: Some professional athletes who are married drive sports cars.

21. *Hypotheses:* (a) All houses built during the 1970s by the Ace Construction Company are extremely well insulated.
(b) No houses that are extremely well insulated allow any naturally occurring accumulated radon gas to escape.

Conclusion: Some houses built during the 1970s by the Ace Construction Company allow naturally occurring accumulated radon gas to escape.

22. *Hypotheses:* (a) All people over 60 years of age with a family history of colon cancer should have an annual medical examination.
(b) Some people who have an annual medical examination often discover that they have high blood pressure.

Conclusion: Some people over 60 years of age with a family history of colon cancer often discover that they have high blood pressure.

23. *Hypotheses:* (a) No nuclear electricity generating stations operating in the United States are older than 50 years.

(b) Some nuclear electricity generating stations operating in the United States are searching for new dumping sites for their nuclear waste material.

Conclusion: Some nuclear electricity generating stations operating in the United States that are searching for new dumping sites for their nuclear waste material are older than 50 years.

24. *Hypotheses:* (a) No cats can swim.
(b) No birds can swim.

Conclusion: No cats are birds.

25. *Hypotheses:* (a) No obstetricians are professional athletes.
(b) All major league baseball players are professional athletes.

Conclusion: No obstetricians are major league baseball players.

▮▮▮▮▶ ◀ **Brain-Teaser Problems** ▶ ◀▮▮▮▮

**26. *The missing two dollars:* The Smith's are analyzing how they spent the $100 that was budgeted for food during the month of February. They spent the money as follows:

Week of	Amount spent for food	Balance
Feb. 1--7	$ 40	$ 60
Feb. 8–14	30	30
Feb. 15–21	18	12
Feb. 22–28	12	0
	$100	$102

Adding, we find that the Smith's spent $100 for food. Yet the total of the balances is $102. What happened to the extra two dollars?

**27. Explain how Fig. 2.47 "proves" the Pythagorean theorem for isosceles triangles. (An *isosceles triangle* is a triangle with two sides equal.) [*Hint:* It is as easy as 2 + 2.]

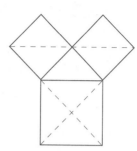

Figure 2.47

**28. James Garfield, our twentieth president, discovered a new proof of the Pythagorean theorem while he was a congressman. His proof was based on the fact that the area of a whole object equals the sum of the areas of its parts and on the formula for the area of a trapezoid. Explain how his diagram (see Fig. 2.48) can be used to prove that $a^2 + b^2 = c^2$. [*Hint:* The area of a trapezoid (see Fig. 2.49) equals the average of the height times the width or area equals $\frac{1}{2}(a + b) \cdot w$.]

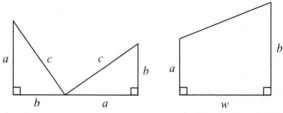

Figure 2.48   **Figure 2.49**

**29. An interesting proof of the Pythagorean theorem was given by the Indian mathematician Bhaskara. Look at the triangle in Fig. 2.50 and draw squares on each of the three sides as shown in Fig. 2.51. The Pythagorean theorem says that (the area of square 1) = (the area of square 2) + (the area of square 3).

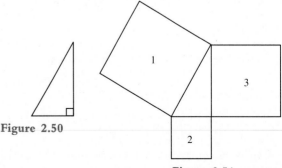

Figure 2.50

Figure 2.51

Unlike the proofs of the theorem that are usually given in high school geometry books, Bhaskara's proof consists only of cutting up square 1 and rearranging it as shown in Fig. 2.52. His only explanation was the word "Behold!"

Can you explain how this diagram "proves" the Pythagorean theorem? (*Hint:* Copy the diagram on a piece of paper, cut it up, and rearrange the pieces.)

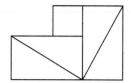

Figure 2.52

Some of the following problems can be solved by using the techniques we have discussed throughout this chapter. Others can be solved by using informal but correct reasoning. Try to solve as many as you can. Have fun!

**30. Suppose that Mr. Smith is a small-town barber who shaves those men and only those men of the town who do not shave themselves. Which of the following statements are true? (Everyone in the town is shaved or shaves himself.)

> Mr. Smith shaves himself.
>
> Mr. Smith does not shave himself.

**31. A travel agent has just booked flights for three of her clients, Bill Holland, Pat Canada, and Debbie England. One of them is going to Holland, one is going to Canada, and one is going to England. Bill is not going to Holland, Pat is not going to Canada, and Debbie is not going to England. If Pat is not going to England either, to which country is each going?

**32. There were three prisoners, one of whom was blind. Their jailor offered to free them all if any one could succeed in the following game. The jailor produced three white hats and two red hats and, in a dark room, placed a hat on each prisoner. Then the prisoners were taken into the light where, except for the blind one, they could see one another. (None could see the hat on his own head.) The game was for any prisoner to state correctly what color hat he himself was wearing. The jailor asked one of those who could see if he knew, and the man answered no. Then the jailor asked the other prisoner who could see, and he answered no. The blind prisoner at this point correctly stated the color of his own hat, winning the game for all three. How did he know?[2]

**33. The six employees of the Southshore Loan Company are Bill Black, Jane Coffee, Arlene McCarthy, George Kelly, Phil White, and Phyllis Pagano. The positions they occupy (not necessarily in order) are manager, assistant manager, cashier, stenographer, teller, and computer programmer. The assistant manager is the manager's grandson; the cashier is the stenographer's son-in-law; Bill Black is a bachelor; Phil White is 22 years old; Arlene McCarthy is the teller's stepsister; and George Kelly is the manager's neighbor. Which position does each person occupy?

**34. *Should I do my Homework Assignment?* Professor Gertrude Hoffman teaches mathematics at a midwestern university. The class meets five days a week (Monday through Friday). Homework assignments, which are very lengthy and require at least three hours of intensive work, are assigned daily. Professor Hoffman has found that many students have not been doing their homework assignments. She announces to the class that she will send students to the blackboard to do the homework assignments on one of the days of the following week. (Students will be graded on this work.) She does not specify on which day of the week this will occur, since that would encourage last minute cramming. However, she does promise that she will cancel the assignment completely if any student figures out, in advance (not necessarily before the week begins), the actual day on which students will be sent to the board (the "event").

Hilda Lichtenfeld is a student in the class. She boldly claims that under the conditions mentioned, the event can never occur. She reasons as follows: First, Friday is excluded as a possible day, since if no one is called to the board by Thursday, then everyone would know that Friday is the designated day. Professor Hoffman would thus be forced to cancel the assignment. Second, Thursday is excluded. Since Friday has already been eliminated, students will be able to recognize Thursday plans as soon as Wednesday ends without students being sent to the board. Professor Hoffman would thus be forced to cancel the assignment. In a similar manner, Wednesday, Tuesday, and Monday are successively eliminated as days on which Professor Hoffman will send students to the board. Do you agree with Hilda's reasoning? Explain your answer.

**35. A father wished to leave his fortune to the most intelligent of his three sons. He said to them, "I shall presently take each one of you away separately and paint either a white or a blue mark on each of your foreheads, and none of you will have any chance to know the color of the mark on his own head. Then I shall bring you together again, and anybody who is able to see two blue marks on the heads of his companions is to laugh. The first of you to figure out his own color is to raise his hand, and on convincing me that his solution is correct, will become my heir." After all three had agreed to the conditions, the father took them apart and painted a white mark on each forehead. When they met again, there was silence for some time, at the end of which the youngest brother raised his hand, saying: "I'm white." How was he able to deduce the color of the mark on his forehead?[3]

[3.] Max Black, *Critical Thinking*, 2nd ed., p. 12. New York: Prentice-Hall, 1952. Reprinted by permission.

**36. Three golfers, Tom, Dick, and Harry, are walking to the clubhouse. Tom always tells the truth, Dick sometimes tells the truth, and Harry never tells the truth. The three golfers are lined up from left to right. The golfer on the left says, "That guy in the middle is Tom." However, the golfer in the middle claims that he's Dick. Furthermore, the golfer on the right says, "No, the guy in the middle is Harry." Find out who is on the left, who is in the middle, and who is on the right. (*Hint:* First try to determine which one is Tom.)

**37. Four bank employees have been arrested for embezzling funds from the bank. It is known that one of these employees definitely embezzled the funds. In interviews with the bank investigators, Arthur claimed that Mike was the embezzler, Mike said that it was Georgina, Heather denied embezzling the funds, and Georgina declared that Mike had lied when he said that she was the embezzler. Each of these employees is then given a polygraph (lie detector) test. Assume that the results of the polygraph test are accurate. If the results of the polygraph tests show that only one of these employees is

a) lying, who is the guilty one?

b) telling the truth, who is the guilty one?

**38. Fingers Nelson was shot dead in a recent gang war, and his body was dumped into an unused mine shaft. After a lengthy investigation the sheriff arrested five men and charged them with the crime. Each man claimed that he was innocent. Nevertheless, each made three statements to the sheriff, two of which were true and one of which was false.

Rocky said: "I did not kill Fingers. I never owned a gun. Lucky did it."

Ricky said: "I am innocent. I never saw Rico before. Lucky did it."

Lucky said: "I am innocent. Rico is the guilty man. Rocky lied when he said I did it."

Rico said: "I did not kill Fingers. Fats is the guilty man. Ricky and I are old buddies."

Fats said: "I did not kill Fingers. I never owned a gun. The other guys are all passing the buck."

After analyzing their statements the sheriff was able to determine who was guilty. Who murdered Fingers Nelson?

**39. Mrs. Ada Gusher, wife of the oil billionaire Tex Gusher, was found murdered. Rock Head, the dashing private eye, was called in to solve the mystery. He discovered the following clues.

> The Gushers' maid, Sarah, was not home when the crime was committed.
>
> Either Sarah was home or the Gushers' son Rodney was out.
>
> If the stereo was on, Rodney was home.
>
> If the stereo was not on, Mr. Gusher did it. Rock Head solved the crime the same day. How? And who did it?

**40. Of two tribes inhabiting a tropical island, members of one tribe always tell the truth and members of the other always lie. A math teacher vacationing on the island comes to a fork in the road and has to ask a native bystander which branch she should take to reach the nearest village. She doesn't know whether the native is a truth-teller or a liar, but she nevertheless manages to ask only one true-false question so cleverly phrased that she will know from the reply which road to take. What question could she ask?

**41. In a certain mythical community, politicians always lie, and nonpoliticans always tell the truth. A stranger meets three natives and asks the first of them if he is a politician. The first native answers the question. The second native then reports that the first native denied being a politician. Then the third native asserts that the first native is really a politician. How many of these three natives are politicians?[4]

[4.] Copi, op. cit., p. 16.

**42. Mabel tells her friends, "I always lie; I never tell the truth." Is Mabel lying or telling the truth? Explain your answer.

**43. Frank has a cube that is three meters on each side. He wishes to cut it up into 27 one-meter cubes. There are several ways in which this can be done. One way is to make a series of six cuts through the cube while keeping it together in one block. Can you find another way to do this in which *fewer than* six cuts are needed? (*Hint:* The pieces may be rearranged after each cut.)

**44. There are three boxes of marbles on a table. It is known that one box has two red marbles, one box has one red and one white marble, and the third box has two white marbles. Three boxes have been labeled red–red, red–white, and white–white. However, the wrong labels were attached to each box. Thus a box that has the label red–white does not really have a red and a white marble in it. A volunteer is removing one marble at a time from a box. Find the *minimum* number of marbles that must be removed before she knows what is in a particular box.

45. Imagine that you have a checkerboard that has 64 squares. Since each domino can cover 2 squares, you would need 32 dominoes to cover the whole board. Imagine that we now cut off the 2 squares from opposite ends of the checkerboard. Can the checkerboard now be covered with only 31 dominoes? Explain your answer by using logic.

TYPICAL CLASSROOM QUESTIONS

1. Is there any difference between the symbols "⊂" and "∈"?
(**Clue** Do not confuse the symbol "⊂" which stands for "is a proper subset of," with "∈," which means "is an element of." For example, Sting ∈ {all singers} and Diana Ross ∈ {all singers}. However, {Sting, Diana Ross} is a proper subset of the set of all singers, i.e., {Sting, Diana Ross} ⊂ {all singers}).

2. Why is the null set assumed to be a subset of every set?
(**Clue** Let **A** be any set. Since the empty set has no elements, can there be any element in the empty set that is not in **A**?)

3. Can the sets **A** and **B** used in forming **A** × **B** (the cross product of the sets) ever be the same sets?
(**Clue**   If **A** = {1, 3} and **B** = {3, 1}, what is **A** × **B** and **B** × **A**?)

4. In the modern approach to teaching arithmetic, children are taught to add by the following method. Suppose you wish to add 3 + 4. First you take a set C with three elements, say {a, b, c}. Then you take a set D with four elements, say {m, n, o, p}. It is essential that sets C and D be disjoint, that is, have no elements in common. Now we form $C \cup D$, which is {a, b, c, m, n, o, p}. Then 3 + 4 is called the cardinal number of $C \cup D$, which is 7.

   a) In this scheme, why is it important that $C \cap D = \varnothing$?

   b) Use this technique to compute 5 + 3.

   c) Use this technique to compute 8 + 7.

   d) Use this technique to compute 6 + 0.

5. If deductive reasoning is used in math, then why bother to study inductive reasoning?

STUDY GUIDE

The following is a chapter outline in capsule form. You should now be able to demonstrate your knowledge of the ideas mentioned by giving definitions, descriptions, or specific examples. Page references are given in parentheses.

Basic Ideas

1. A **set** can be thought of as any collection of objects. (p. 40)

2. An **element** is any member of a set. (p. 41)

3. The **set-notation** for elements of a set is ∈; For example, $x \in \{x, y, z\}$ (p. 41)

4. Sets can be specified by listing all the elements of the set (the **roster method**), by describing in words the elements of the set (the **descriptive method**), or by using **set-builder notation**. (p. 42)

5. Sets should be **well-defined**; that is, we must know for sure whether any object does or does not belong to the set. (p. 43)

6. Sets are pictured by means of **Venn diagrams**. (p. 60)

Kinds of Sets

1. A **unit set** is a set with only one element. (p. 44)

2. The **null set** or **empty set**, denoted as $\varnothing$, is a set which contains no elements. (p. 44)

3. A set is **finite** if the number of elements in the set is zero or a natural number. (p. 44)

4. An **infinite set** is a set that is not finite. It contains an endless number of elements. (p. 44)

5. The **cardinal number** of a set A indicates the number of elements in set A. This is written as $n(A)$. (p. 46)

6. The **universal set** denoted as U, contains all elements being discussed. (p. 48)

7. If two sets have no elements in common, they are called **disjoint sets**. (p. 54)

Relations Between Sets

1. Two sets are **equal** if and only if they both have exactly the same elements. We write set A equals set B as $A = B$. (p. 44)

2. Two sets A and B are said to be in **one-to-one correspondence** if and only if every element of set A can be matched with exactly one element of set B and every element of set B can be matched with exactly one element of set A. (p. 45)

3. **Equivalent sets** are sets which can be put into 1–1 correspondence. We write this as $A \sim B$. (p. 46). Equivalent sets have the same cardinal number. (p. 46)

4. Set A is a **subset** of set B (written as $A \subseteq B$) if and only if every element of set A is also an element of set B. (p. 47)

5. Set A is a **proper subset** of set B if and only if every element of set A is an element of B and there is at least one other element of set B that is not in A. We write this as $A \subset B$. (p. 48)

6. Set A is an **improper subset** of set B if and only if every element of set A is an element of set B but B does not have any other elements that are not in A. We write this as $A = B$. (p. 48)

Set Operations

1. The **union** of two sets A and B is the set of all elements in A, in B, or in both A and B. We write this as $A \cup B$. (p. 53)

2. The **intersection** of two sets A and B is the set of all elements that are in both A and B. We write this as $A \cap B$. (p. 53)

3. The **complement** of set A is the set of all elements in the universal set that are not in A. We write this as A' or $\overline{A}$. (p. 55)

4. The **difference** between sets A and B is the set of all elements that belong to set A but not to set B. We write this as $A - B$. (p. 55)

5. The **Cartesian-product** or **Cross-Product** between sets A and B is the set of all ordered pairs where the first element of each pair is an element of A and the second element of each pair is an element of B. We write this as $A \times B$. (p. 56)

Applications of Sets

1. Sets can be applied to **survey problems** to help us analyze information obtained from surveys. (p. 64)

2. Sets can be applied to **voting coalitions** where a group of people will vote on a proposal. (p. 67)

Other Important Ideas

1. Any combination of people that can carry a proposal is called a **winning coalition**. (p. 67)

2. Any combination of people is called a **losing coalition** if a proposal will pass even though they vote against it. (p. 67)

3. Any coalition is called a **blocking coalition** if it can prevent any proposal from winning, but it cannot win by itself. (p. 68)

4. A **dictator** is someone who can pass any proposal with only his or her own vote. (p. 68)

5. A member of a voting body has **veto power** if his or her vote alone is enough to block any proposal. (p. 68)

6. A member of a voting body is called a **dummy** if any winning coalition of which he or she is a member will be a winning coalition even without his or her vote. (p. 68)

7. A **minimal winning coalition** is any winning coalition that has no proper subset that is a winning coalition. Each member's vote is essential or the proposal will not pass. (p. 69)

Reasoning

1. In **inductive reasoning** we arrive at a conclusion on the basis of a number of observations or specific instances. The conclusion is probably, but not necessarily, true. (p. 75)

2. If we are given a series of statements with the claim that one *must* follow from the others, then this is called a **deductive argument**. (p. 80)

3. In a deductive argument, the statement that follows from the others is called the **conclusion**. The other statements are called the **hypotheses** or **premises**. (p. 80)

4. If the conclusion of a deductive argument does follow logically from the hypotheses, then we say that the argument is **valid**. Otherwise, it is **invalid**. (p. 80)

5. The validity of an argument can be determined by using **the standard diagram**. We draw only one diagram and we show all of the possibilities in it. (p. 81)

KEY TERMS

Following is a list of key terms introduced in each section of this chapter.

2.1

elements	infinite set
members	equal sets
roster method	1–1 correspondence
descriptive method	equivalent sets
set-builder notation	cardinal number
well-defined	subset
unit set	proper subset
null or empty set	improper subset
finite set	universal set

FORMULAS TO REMEMBER

The following list summarizes all the formulas discussed in this chapter.

i) De Morgan's Laws: For all sets A and B,

$$(A \cap B)' = A' \cup B' \qquad \text{and}$$
$$(A \cup B)' = A' \cap B'$$

ii) When analyzing survey problems by means of Venn diagrams, be sure to first use the data about all three categories.

iii) A set that has n elements has 2^n possible subsets.

The standard diagram for testing validity (when three categories are involved) is shown here as Fig. 2.53.

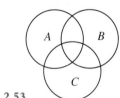

Figure 2.53

CHAPTER REVIEW EXERCISES

1. How many possible subsets does the set $\{a, b, c, d, e\}$ have?

a) 5   **b)** 10   **c)** 16   **d)** 32   **e)** none of these?

2. Figure 2.54 illustrates

a) $A - B$ **b)** $B - A$

c) $A \cap B$ **d)** $U \cap A$

e) none of these

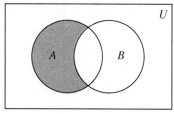

Figure 2.54

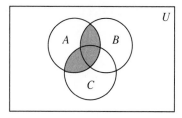

Figure 2.55

3. Figure 2.55 illustrates
   a) $A \cup (B \cap C)$
   b) $(A \cap B) \cup (A \cap C)$
   c) $A \cap B' \cap C'$
   d) $(A \cup B) \cap (A \cup C)$
   e) none of these

4. The cardinal number of the set $\{1, 2, 4, 5, 6\}$ is
   a) 4   **b)** 5   **c)** 6   **d)** 3   **e)** none of these

5. In a survey of 200 people the following information was obtained: 70 drank Coke, 55 drank Seven-Up, 60 drank Pepsi, 40 drank Coke and Pepsi, 35 drank Seven-Up and Pepsi, 50 drank Seven-Up and Coke, and 30 drank all three. How many drank only Coke?
   a) 10   **b)** 70   **c)** 90   **d)** 110   **e)** none of these

6. Refer back to Exercise 5. How many drank none of the three drinks mentioned?
   a) 90   **b)** 110   **c)** 30   **d)** 80   **e)** none of these

For questions 7–11, let $U = \{1, 2, 3, 4, 5, 6, 7, 8, 9, 10\}$, $A = \{2, 4, 6, 8\}$, $B = \{2, 3, 6, 9\}$, $C = \{4, 2, 6, 8\}$, and $D = \{3, 9\}$.

7. $A \cup B =$
   a) $\{2, 6\}$ **b)** $\{2, 4, 6, 8\}$ **c)** $\varnothing$
   d) $\{2, 3, 4, 6, 8, 9\}$ **e)** none of these

8. $A \cap B =$
   a) $\varnothing$ **b)** U **c)** $\{2, 3, 4, 6, 8, 9\}$ **d)** $\{2, 6\}$ **e)** none of these

9. $A' =$
   a) B **b)** $\varnothing$ **c)** C **d)** $B \cap C'$ **e)** none of these

10. $(A \cup B)' =$
   a) $\varnothing$ **b)** U **c)** A **d)** $A' \cap B'$ **e)** none of these

11. $n(D) =$
   a) 10   **b)** 0   **c)** 4   **d)** 2   **e)** none of these

12. Which of the following sets is not well-defined?
   a) All females over 67 feet tall

b) All disagreeable children

c) All math books that cost under one dollar

d) All curable cancers   **e)** none of these

13. Which of the following statements is false?

   a) Every set is a subset of itself.

   b) Equal sets are equivalent sets.

   c) All equivalent sets are equal.

   d) If $A \cap B = \varnothing$, then A and B are disjoint.

   e) none of these

14. Ellen, Jennifer, Jason, and Dominique form a committee. Ellen has 4 votes, Jennifer has 3 votes, Jason has 2 votes, and Dominique has 1 vote. Jennifer also has veto power. Then {Ellen, Jennifer, Dominique} forms

   a) a winning coalition   **b)** a blocking coalition

   c) a minimal winning coalition   **d)** a losing coalition

   e) none of these

15. In the committee given in Exercise 14, {Jennifer, Dominique} forms

   a) a winning coalition   **b)** a blocking coalition

   c) a minimal winning coalition   **d)** a losing coalition

   e) none of these

16. Set A is equal to set B if and only if

   a) they have exactly the same elements

   b) they have the same number of elements

   c) A is a subset of B

   d) B is a proper subset of A

   e) none of these

17. The set equal to $\varnothing$ is

   a) {0}   **b)** 0   **c)** { }   **d)** {$\varnothing$}   **e)** none of these

18. A is a subset of B if

   a) every element in A is an element in B

   b) every element in B is an element in A

   c) there are elements in A and B that are the same

   d) there are no elements in A and B that are the same

   e) none of these

19. If $A = \{1, 2, 3\}$ and $B = \{a, b\}$, then $A \times B$ is

   a) {(1, a), (1, b), (2, a), (2, b), (3, a), (3, b)}

   b) {(a, 1), (a, 2), (a, 3), (b, 1), (b, 2), (b, 3)}

   c) $B \times A$ **d)** {1, 2, 3, a, b}   **e)** none   of   these

20. Let B be any set. Then $B \cap \varnothing =$

   a) U **b)** B **c)** $\varnothing$ **d)** B' **e)** none of these

21. A survey of the residents living along Park Avenue revealed that 200 of them owned a home computer, 400 of them owned an exercise bike, and 70 of them owned both. How many residents own at least one of the items mentioned?

Use Fig. 2.56 to answer questions 22–26.

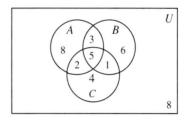

Figure 2.56

22. $n(A \cup B) =$
   a) 29   **b)** 14   **c)** 25   **d)** 8   **e)** none of these
23. Find $n(A \cap B')$
   a) 6   **b)** 18   **c)** 10   **d)** 8   **e)** none of these
24. Find $n(A \cap C)$
   a) 7   **b)** 5   **c)** 21   **d)** 8   **e)** none of these
25. Find $n(A \cup B \cup C)$
   a) 24   **b)** 37   **c)** 29   **d)** 5   **e)** none of these
26. Find $n(A \cap B' \cap C')$
   a) 3   **b)** 8   **c)** 5   **d)** 10   **e)** none of these
27. If $n(C) = 5$, $n(D) = 4$, and $n(C \cap D) = 2$, find $n(C \cup D)$.
28. Using De Morgan's laws, simplify the expression $(A \cup B')'$.
29. Five roads lead from Springfield to Madison, and three roads lead from Madison to Endicott. In how many different ways can a person travel from Springfield to Endicott by way of Madison?
30. The business department of a small midwestern college is analyzing the status of its majors. It discovers that 54 of the majors are juniors, 162 are sophomores, and 162 are freshmen. No seniors are currently majoring in business. Furthermore, 171 females are majoring in business, and twice as many sophomore females as sophomore males are business majors. For the juniors the ratio is reversed. On the basis of this information, how many female freshmen are business majors?
31. A man drinks 6 scotches and 6 sodas on Monday and gets drunk. On Tuesday he drinks 6 vodkas and 6 sodas and gets drunk. On Wednesday, he drinks 6 bourbons and 6 sodas and gets drunk. On Thursday, he drinks 6 brandies and 6 sodas and gets drunk. He concludes that the soda is making him drunk. This is an example of
   a) inductive reasoning   **b)** deductive reasoning
   c) illogical reasoning   **d)** conductive reasoning   **e)** none of these

32. Five hundred doctors in the metropolitan area were asked to recommend a sugarless gum. Since 50 percent of them recommended Tishman's gum, it was concluded that 50 percent of *all* doctors advise their patients to chew Tishman's gum. This is an example of

    a) deductive reasoning   b) inductive reasoning
    c) reductive reasoning   d) an indirect proof   e) none of these.

33. Test the following conclusion for validity by using the standard diagram:
    Hypotheses: (a) All things injected with growth hormones are unhealthy.
    (b) Some chickens are not injected with growth hormones.

    Conclusion: Some chickens are unhealthy.

    a) valid   b) invalid   c) not enough information given

34. Test the following for validity:
    Hypotheses: (a) All college graduates get good-paying jobs.
    (b) Some women get good-paying jobs.

    Conclusion: Some women are college graduates.

    a) valid   b) invalid   c) not enough information given

35. In inductive reasoning, the conclusion of an argument is

    a) probably true   b) probably false   c) definitely false
    d) none of these

SUGGESTED FURTHER READING

On Sets

Bell, E.T., *Men of Mathematics*, New York: Simon & Schuster, 1961. Chapter 29 contains a biography of G. Cantor.

Blomgre, G., "What's in the Box—Subsets!" in *The Arithmetic Teacher* **17** (March 1970), 272.

Dinkines, F., *Elementary Theory of Sets*. New York: Appleton-Century-Crofts, 1964. Contains a basic but thorough discussion of sets with applications.

Geddes, D., and S. Lipsey, "The Hazards of Sets," in *The Mathematics Teacher* **62** (October 1969), 454.

Mathematics in the Modern World (Readings from *Scientific American*). San Francisco: W.H. Freeman, 1968. Article 28 discusses paradoxes, and Article 30 discusses a set theory different from Cantor's.

Schoen, H., "Some Difficulty in the Language of Sets," in *The Arithmetic Teacher* **21** (March 1974), 236–237.

Stoll, R., *Sets, Logic, and the Axiomatic Method*. San Francisco: W.H. Freeman, 1974. A good discussion of set theory.

Vilenkin, N., *Stories about Sets*. New York and London: Academic Press, 1969.

On Logic

Copi, I.M., *Introduction to Logic*. New York: Macmillan, 1961. This text contains a clear discussion of inductive and deductive logic and use of inductive logic in science.

Cruikshank, D., "Sorting, Classifying, and Logic," in *The Arithmetic Teacher* **21** (November 1974), 590–591.

May, I.O., "The Origin of the Four-Color Problem," in *Isis* **56**, 1965, 346–348.

McGinty, R., and J. Van Beynen, "Deductive and Analytical Thinking," in *The Mathematics Teacher* **78** (March 1985), 188–194.

Scharf, William, *A biography of Recreational Mathematics*, Washington, D.C., National Council of Teachers of Mathematics, 1970.

Vance, J., "The Large-Blue-Triangle; A Matter of Logic," in *The Arithmetic Teacher* **22** (March 1975), 237–240.

Warman, M., "Fun with Logical Reasoning," in *The Arithmetic Teacher* **29** (May 1982), 26–30.

CHAPTER 3

Different Numeration Systems and the Whole Numbers

CHAPTER OBJECTIVES

- ❑ **To study** and **analyze** many different number systems including the Babylonian, Egyptian, Tamil, Mayan, and Roman systems. (*Section 3.1*)

- ❑ **To compare** calculations performed in these systems with the calculations performed in the Hindu-Arabic decimal system. (*Section 3.2*)

- ❑ **To discuss** different number bases and how the four basic operations are performed in these other bases. (*Section 3.3*)

- ❑ **To indicate** how to convert numbers from base 10 into some other base and how to convert numbers from some other base back into base 10. (*Section 3.4*)

- ❑ **To apply** the idea of different number bases to computers and to the game of *Nim*. (*Section 3.5*)

- ❑ **To review** the natural number system and the whole number system. (*Section 3.6*)

- ❑ **To specify** some of the properties that each of these systems must satisfy. (*Section 3.6*)

- ❑ **To describe** several algorithms for performing the four basic operations. (*Section 3.7*)

- ❑ **To use** scientific notation when working with very large numbers or very small numbers. (*Section 3.8*)

NCTM GUIDELINES

In its March 1989 *Curriculum And Evaluation Standards For School Mathematics* (p. 38), The National Council of Teachers of Mathematics recommends that the mathematics curriculum should include whole number concepts and skills as well as whole number computations so that students can:

❑ construct number meanings through real-world experiences and the use of physical materials,

❑ understand our numeration system by relating counting, grouping, and place-value concepts,

❑ develop number senses,

❑ interpret the multiple uses of numbers encountered in the real world,

❑ model, explain, and develop reasonable proficiency with basic facts and algorithms,

❑ select and use computation techniques appropriate to specific problems and determine whether the results are reasonable.

The purpose of computation is to solve problems. Thus, although computation is important in mathematics and in our daily life, our technological age requires us to rethink how computation is done today. It is for this reason that in this chapter we will discuss different numeration systems and how computations are performed in these systems.

Introduction

Humans learned how to count early in their development. Tally marks have been found on cave walls that indicate that even while still living in caves, people knew how to count and had progressed to the point at which they could record their results. Over the years, various bones have been dug up that have notches on them to represent different numbers. Some of these date back as far as 30,000 years.

However, it seems likely that the human ability to count dates back even farther than is indicated by any records that have been found. Counting appears to be a rather basic activity that does not require advanced mental development. It has been demonstrated that even some animals and birds (for example, crows) have the ability to distinguish between groups of up to four objects.[1] You may have seen, on television or in the circus, dogs and horses that can count small quantities.

In Section 3.1 we will examine one early number system. Then we will examine the decimal system, with which we all count today. We will also discuss other numeration systems and their applications.

HISTORICAL NOTE

Originally, early humans distinguished only between the numbers one and two. Everything else was just many. Thus if Ug had three children and his brother Og had ten children, each would say that he had "many" children. Even today there are some primitive tribes that still count this way.

As soon as people learned how to distinguish between larger numbers, they found it more convenient to count by groups of 10 than by ones. Today we count in groups of 10. Historically, counting has been done using groups of 2's, 3's, 5's, 10's, and other numbers. Groupings by 2's and 3's were widely used earlier in time. However, these were almost always replaced by groupings of 5's and 10's. From this came our present decimal system (from the Latin *decem*, meaning "ten").

Often, piles of stones were used in counting. For example, six stones represented the number "six." Because piles of stones can easily be disturbed, numbers were sometimes recorded by carving notches in rocks, bones, and sticks. In the nineteenth century a wolf bone was found in Czechoslovakia with 55 notches in it, arranged in groups of 5.

In some cultures, groups of 20 were used. These systems, based on 20, are still to be found in various parts of the world. The French word for 80 is *quatre-vingts*, which means "four 20's." This suggests that at some time in the past, counting in some parts of France was done in groups of 20.

It is easy to see how systems developed based on 2, 5, 10, and 20 (remember, cave people did not wear shoes). However, it is surprising to find evidence that some cultures may have counted in groups of four or eight. The Latin word for "nine" is *novem*, which may be connected with the Latin word *novus* meaning "new." This suggests that nine was the start of a new group.

---

[1] See Levi Conant, "The Number Concept: Its Origin and Development," 1923. In James R. Newman, ed., *The World of Mathematics*, pp. 432–441. New York: Simon and Schuster, 1956. Cf. H. Kalmus, "Animals as Mathematicians," *Nature* 202:1156–1160 (1964).

3.1

THE BABYLONIAN NUMERATION SYSTEM

The ancient Babylonians counted in groups of 60. Although it might seem strange that such a large number was used, we will see shortly that it has many advantages. In the late nineteenth century, tablets were found, most of which date back to around 1700 B.C. From these tablets we have been able to learn much about Babylonian mathematics.

In the Babylonian numeration system, two basic symbols were used: a vertical wedge Y and a corner wedge ◁. The vertical wedge represented the number 1, and the corner wedge represented the number 10. For example, the symbol YYY meant the number 3, the symbol ◁YY meant the number 12, and the symbol ◁YYY̶Y meant the number 14. The Babylonians wrote all the numbers 1, 2, 3, . . . , 59 in this manner. When they got to 60, they moved over one place to the left, as we do in our decimal system when we get to 10. Thus the number 72 would be written as Y ◁ YY. The first Y symbol represents not "1," but one "60," because of its position. The last two Y's (on the right) represent two "1's" because of their position.

The number 146 would be written as

$$\underbrace{YY}_{\text{Two 60's}} \quad \underbrace{\text{◁◁}}_{\text{Two 10's}} \quad \underbrace{\substack{YYY \\ YYY}}_{\text{Six 1's}}$$

The first two YY symbols represent two 60's, or 120. The two ◁◁ symbols mean two 10's, and the YYY̶YYY symbols mean 6. Thus we have 120 + 20 + 6 or 146.

When the Babylonians got to 60 × 60, or 3600, they moved over two places to the left as we do in our decimal system when we get to 10 × 10, or 100. Thus the number 4331 would be written as

$$\underbrace{Y}_{\text{One 3600}} \quad \underbrace{\text{◁YY}}_{\text{Twelve 60's}} \quad \underbrace{\text{◁Y}}_{\text{Eleven 1's}}$$

The first Y means one 60 × 60, or one 3600. The symbols ◁YY mean twelve 60's, or 720. Finally the symbol ◁Y on the right of the number means eleven 1's. This gives 3600 + 720 + 11 = 4331.

You will notice that in this system the value of a symbol is determined by its position. The same is true in our decimal system, as we will see later in this chapter.

An early system of writing, in Mesopotamia, was made up of small, simple drawings called pictograms. Each pictogram stood for an object or idea, or sometimes for several words. For numerals, astronomers used a base of 60, repeating number signs up to nine times.

One important difference between the Babylonian system and our decimal system is that the Babylonians never really had a symbol for zero as we use it today. Thus the symbol ⋎ might stand for 1, 60, 60 × 60, etc. In later texts they did use a sign that looked like this ⌃ to indicate the empty spaces if they occurred *inside* numbers. Thus this symbol acted as a placeholder, much as our number 0 does. However, the Babylonians never used this symbol at the end of a number. So, as we have said, the symbol ⋎ could stand for 1, 60, 60 × 60, etc.

To reemphasize the point, the importance of the Babylonian system was that the value of a number was determined by its position. This idea of **positional notation** is fundamental in our own decimal system, as we shall see in Section 3.2.

The Babylonians used 60 as a grouping number for several reasons. One reason was that 60 can be evenly divided by many numbers. For example, 60 can be divided by 2, 3, 4, 5, ... This made division and work with fractions much easier. The choice of 60 may also have been due to the Babylonian interest in astronomy. As a matter of fact, the Babylonian year was divided into 12 months of 30 days each, with an additional 5 feast days (12 times 30 equals 360, which can be evenly divided by 60). It has also been suggested by some historians that 60 was used as a natural combination of two earlier systems, one using 10 and the other using 6.

The Babylonian system was taken over by the Greek astronomers. In fact, it was used for many mathematical and practically all astronomical calculations as late as the seventeenth century. Many traces are to be found even today. For example, hours are divided into 60 minutes, and minutes are divided into 60 seconds. In geometry, angles are divided into degrees. Each degree is divided into 60 minutes.

EXERCISES FOR SECTION 3.1

The Egyptian Numeration System

The early Egyptians used the following symbols to represent numbers (the order or position of symbols was not important).

Number	1	2	3	4	5	6	7
Symbol	I	II	III	IIII	III II	III III	IIII III

Number	8	9	10	11	12	13
Symbol	IIII IIII	III III III	∩	I∩	II∩	III∩

Number	14	15	16	17	18
Symbol	IIII II ∩	III II ∩	III III ∩	IIII III ∩	IIII IIII ∩

Number	19	20	100	1000	10,000
Symbol	III III III ∩	∩∩	ꝯ	⧚	⌒

For example, the symbol ꝯꝯꝯ∩∩III would represent the number 322. The symbol ꝯ III∩ would represent the number 119. The number 21,318 could have been written by the Egyptians as

𓍢𓍢 𓍦 𓏺𓏺𓏺𓏺 𓈖
𓂝𓂝𓂝

1. What does each of the following symbols, written in the **Egyptian system**, represent in our system?

   a) 𓂝𓂝𓂝 ||| 𓈖𓈖𓈖

   b) 𓍢𓍢 𓍦 𓍦 𓈖𓈖𓈖 ||| 𓂝

   c) 𓍦 𓈖𓈖𓈖𓈖 𓂝𓂝 ||||

   d) 𓍢 𓍦 𓍦 𓂝𓂝𓂝𓂝 𓈖𓈖𓈖 ||||

   e) 𓍦 ||| 𓈖 𓂝

   f) 𓍢 ||| 𓂝𓂝 𓍦 𓈖𓈖 |||

2. Translate each of the following numbers into the Egyptian system.

a) 376	**b)** 4237
c) 98	**d)** 27,695
e) 5432	**f)** 6002
g) 10019	**h)** 11111

Addition and Subtraction in the Egyptian System

Addition and subtraction of numbers was not difficult in the Egyptian system. For example, 1231 and 3412 would be added as follows:

Plus 𓍦 𓂝𓂝 𓈖𓈖𓈖 |
         𓍦𓍦𓍦 𓂝𓂝𓂝𓂝 || 𓈖
———————————————
𓍦𓍦𓍦𓍦 𓂝𓂝𓂝𓂝𓂝𓂝 𓈖𓈖𓈖 |||

Sometimes regrouping (or "carrying") is needed when we obtain more than nine strokes | | | | | | | | | | . We just replace ten of these strokes (or heelbones) by the symbol ∩. Thus we have the following:

Plus 𓂝 𓈖𓈖 |||
                |||
      𓂝𓂝 𓈖𓈖𓈖𓈖𓈖𓈖𓈖 ||||
———————————————
𓂝𓂝𓂝 𓈖𓈖𓈖𓈖𓈖𓈖𓈖𓈖𓈖 ||| |||

More simply, the sum is 𓂝𓂝𓂝𓂝 || 𓈖

3. For each of the following, perform the indicated operations in the Egyptian system and check your answer by converting the numbers to our decimal system.

   a)

   Plus 𓍦𓍦𓍦 ||| 𓂝𓂝𓂝 𓈖𓈖
          ||| 𓍦𓍦 ||| 𓂝𓂝𓂝𓂝 𓈖𓈖𓈖 ||||
          |||

HISTORICAL NOTE

Much of our knowledge of the Egyptian numeration system comes from two sources; one is the Moscow Papyrus, which was written in about 1850 B.C. and contains 25 mathematical problems, and the other is the Rhind Papyrus. While vacationing in Egypt, Henry Rhind bought the papyrus in Luxor. It had been located in a small building near the Ramesseum. Evidently, around 1575 B.C., an ancient scribe named Ahmose copied (and possibly edited) an older manuscript. The papyrus, which consists of 85 mathematical problems, indicates how the Egyptians performed their calculations.

b)

Plus

$$\text{𝄞𝄞 ‖‖ ⌇⌇ 99999∩∩}$$
$$\text{𝄞 ⌇⌇99∩∩999∩∩‖‖}$$

_____

c)

Minus

$$\text{99999‖‖ ∩∩}$$
$$\text{999 ‖‖ ∩}$$

_____

d)

Minus

$$\text{𝄞⌇ 99999∩∩∩‖‖}$$
$$\text{⌇⌇⌇99999∩∩∩∩‖‖}$$

_____

4. Explain why the Egyptian system had no need for a symbol for zero.

Tamil Numeration System

In the Tamil numeration system (south India) the following symbols were used to represent numbers. (In this case the order or position of symbols was important.)

Number	1	2	3	4	5	6
Symbol	𝈹	2	𝍖	𝈴	𝈇	𝈰
Number	7	8	9	10	100	1000
Symbol	6	2	𝈳	ω	𝑚	𝈵

For example, the number 3456 would be written as

$$\text{𝍖 𝈵 𝈴 𝑚 𝈇 ω 𝈰}$$

5. Translate each of the following numbers into the Tamil system.

a) 47   **b)** 83   **c)** 398   **d)** 476
e) 987   **f)** 654   **g)** 8765   **h)** 4321

6. Each of the following symbols represents a number written in the Egyptian system. Translate each of them into the Tamil system and then into the Babylonian system.

a) ∩∩‖‖

b) ⌇⌇99∩‖‖

c) ∩999‖‖

d) ∩∩99999⌇‖‖

e) 𝄞⌇⌇99∩∩‖‖

f) 𝄞⌇⌇⌇999∩∩∩‖‖

g) 999∩∩∩∩∩⌇‖‖

h) 𝄞∩‖‖∩99⌇

The Mayan Numeration System

In the Mayan numeration system, dots and dashes were used to represent numbers. The dots were grouped horizontally above the dashes, and the dashes were stacked vertically. Thus the Mayan numeration system was a vertical system, quite different from the Egyptian system and our Hindu-Arabic system. In the Mayan system the following symbols were used to represent the numbers 1 through 19:

Number	1	2	3	4	5	6	7	8	9	10
Symbol	•	••	•••	••••	—	•̲	••̲	•••̲	••••̲	═

Number	11	12	13	14	15	16	17	18	19
Symbol	•̳	••̳	•••̳	••••̳	≡	•̿	••̿	•••̿	••••̿

For any number greater than 20 they used vertical groupings. Thus the Mayan number $\overset{\bullet\bullet\bullet}{\underset{\bullet\bullet}{}}$ consists of two groups of dots and dashes. The top group represents 8, and the bottom group represents 12 as shown below.

$$\left.\begin{array}{c}\bullet\bullet\bullet\\ \rule{0pt}{0pt}\end{array}\right\} \text{This represents 8}$$

$$\left.\begin{array}{c}\bullet\bullet\\ \rule{0pt}{0pt}\end{array}\right\} \text{This represents 12}$$

The numeral in the bottom group represents the number of ones or units in the number, and the numeral in the top group represents the number of 20's in the number. So we have

$$\left.\begin{array}{c}\bullet\bullet\bullet\\ \rule{0pt}{0pt}\end{array}\right\} \text{This represents } 8 \times 20 = 160$$

$$\left.\begin{array}{c}\bullet\bullet\\ \rule{0pt}{0pt}\end{array}\right\} \text{This represents } 12 \times 1 = \underline{\quad 12}$$

$$172$$

Thus the Mayan number represents 172. When three vertical groupings of dots and dashes appear, then the bottom group denotes 1's, the middle group denotes 20's, and the top group denotes 360's.

Thus the Mayan number would be 2392 in our system.

$$\left.\begin{array}{c}\bullet\\ \rule{0pt}{0pt}\end{array}\right\} \text{This represents } 6 \times 360 = 2160$$

$$\left.\begin{array}{c}\bullet\\ \rule{0pt}{0pt}\end{array}\right\} \text{This represents } 11 \times 20 = 220$$

$$\left.\begin{array}{c}\bullet\bullet\\ \rule{0pt}{0pt}\end{array}\right\} \text{This represents } 12 \times 1 = \underline{12}$$

$$2392$$

7. Translate each of the following numbers into the Mayan system.

a) 31   b) 57   c) 317
d) 1207   e) 1234   f) 2576

||||▶ **Brain-Teaser Problems** ◀||||

**8. What does the following Mayan symbol represent in our system?

$$\overset{\bullet\bullet\bullet}{\underline{\bullet}}$$

(*Hint:* You might be tempted to say that this represents 9, since there are 4 dots and 1 dash. However, this is wrong, since the four dots are not arranged horizontally.)

**9. The Mayan symbol for 20 is not ☰. What is the symbol for 20? (*Hint:* In the Mayan system a string of dots cannot have more than four, and a pile of dashes cannot have more than three.)

**10. What is the Mayan symbol for 360?

HISTORICAL NOTE

The Mayas, a group of related Indian tribes of the Mayan linguistic stock, lived in what are now the Mexican states of Veracruz, Yucatán, the whole Yucatán peninsula, Guatemala, and parts of British Honduras. Historical records dating back to about 200 A.D. indicate that their civilization was quite advanced. Their highly complex calendar was the most accurate until the introduction of the Gregorian calendar. The year began on July 16 and consisted of 365 days; 364 of the days were divided into 28 weeks of 13 days each. The new year began on the 365th day. Additionally, 360 days of the year were divided into 18 months of 20 days each. The series of weeks and months ran both consecutively and independently of each other.

3.2

THE BASE 10 NUMBER SYSTEM

In this section we will discuss the decimal system that is commonly used throughout the world today. We will start by looking at the Roman numeral system. In this system the following symbols are used:

I stands for 1,
V stands for 5,
X stands for 10,
L stands for 50,
C stands for 100,
D stands for 500,
M stands for 1000,

and so forth.

The number 43 is written as XLIII.
The number 63 is written as LXIII.

The position of the numerals is important. In 43, the X goes before the L to indicate that it is 10 less than 50. In 63, X goes after the L. This means that 10 is to be added to 50. As we will see shortly, in our number system the position of the digits 0, 1, 2, 3, 4, 5, 6, 7, 8, 9 is even more important than in the Roman system. For example, the number 31 is different from the number 13 even though both numbers contain the same digits, 1 and 3. It is the use of **position** or **place** that makes our system so convenient to work with. Note that the use of position in the Roman system is different from our use of position.

To better appreciate *our* system (which is known as the **Hindu-Arabic system**), try to add the numbers 43 and 63 *using Roman numerals*.

position

place

Hindu-Arabic system

$$\begin{array}{r} \text{XLIII} \\ + \text{LXIII} \\ \hline \end{array}$$

What is your answer? It should be CVI. If you did get this answer, was it by adding the Roman numerals? Or did you add 43 and 63 in our system and convert the answer to Roman numerals? If you did, it is understandable, since doing arithmetic in the Roman system is quite complicated. As we look at our system in detail, we will see exactly why it makes arithmetic so much easier.

To get started, consider the number 4683. This means

Bruce Anderson

$$4(\text{thousands}) + 6(\text{hundreds}) + 8(\text{tens}) + 3(\text{ones})$$

This can be restated as

$$4(1000) \quad + 6(100) \quad + 8(10) \quad + 3(1)$$

Notice something interesting about this:

$$1000 = 10 \times 10 \times 10$$

This is usually abbreviated as 10^3, which means 10 multiplied by itself 3 times. Similarly, $100 = 10 \times 10$. This is abbreviated as 10^2, which means 10 multiplied by itself. Moreover, 10 can be written as 10^1.

We can now write the number 4683 as $4(10^3) + 6(10^2) + 8(10^1) + 3$. This can be neatly summarized in the following chart.

10^3	10^2	10^1	1's
4	6	8	3

digits

In each of these columns, one of ten possible **digits** can appear. These digits are 0, 1, 2, 3, 4, 5, 6, 7, 8, 9. Every number can be expressed as some combination of these digits. Why are these ten sufficient? Why don't we need more?

Comment   In this system of writing numbers, the *place* of the number determines its value. In the example above, the *place* of the 4 tells us it stands not for 4 ones, 4 tens, or 4 hundreds, but for 4 thousands. Similarly, the place of the 8 tells us it stands for 8 tens, and so on.

As another example, consider the number 20,694. This stands for 2(ten-thousands) + 0(thousands) + 6(hundreds) + 9(tens) + 4(ones), or $2(10^4) + 0(10^3) + 6(10^2) + 9(10^1) + 4$. This can be written as

10^4	10^3	10^2	10^1	1's
2	0	6	9	4

placeholder

The zero that appears in the 10^3 column is very important. If we leave it out, the number would read 2694, and that is not the number we want. The zero is called a **placeholder**.

Now let us see how we add these two numbers. For convenience we put them in one chart.

	10^4	10^3	10^2	10^1	1's
		4	6	8	3
+	2	0	6	9	4
Sum	2	5	3	7	7

In the 1's column we add 3 and 4 and get 7 1's.

In the 10^1 column we add 8 and 9 and get 17. This means that we have 17 tens, or $10(\text{tens}) + 7(\text{tens})$. We know that $10(\text{tens})$ is 10×10, or 10^2. Thus we have $1(10^2)$ and $7(10^1)$. So the 1 must be **carried over** to the 10^2 column where it belongs. The 7 remains in the 10^1 column.

In the 10^2 column we add 6 and 6 and the 1 that was carried. This gives $13(10^2)$, which equals $10(10^2) + 3(10^2)$. Now $10(10^2)$ is $10 \times 10 \times 10$, which equals 10^3. Thus $13(10^2)$ equals $1(10^3) + 3(10^2)$. The 3 is left in the 10^2 column, and the 1 is **carried over** to the 10^3 column.

This procedure is repeated for each column until we are finished. We can summarize this procedure as follows:

1. In each column, the only digits allowed are 0, 1, 2, 3, 4, 5, 6, 7, 8, 9.

2. In any column, when the sum is more than 9, we carry everything over 9 to the next column.

regrouping

carrying

trading

The concept of "**regrouping**" and "**carrying**" that we have just described is taught to children at an early age. However, this process is often referred to as one of "**trading**". For example, consider how the concept of trading is used in the excerpted student page from *Addison-Wesley Mathematics*, 1987, Grade 2, p. 269, shown on the facing page.

This convenient method of addition works because of the way in which numbers are written in the Hindu-Arabic system. It will not work for the Roman system. In the Hindu-Arabic system the value of each digit depends on its *place*. For example, 53 means 5 tens plus 3, whereas 35 means 3 tens plus 5.

In doing multiplication we use a similar technique. For example,

$$
\begin{array}{r}
23 \\
\times\,45 \\
\hline
115 \\
92 \\
\hline
1035
\end{array}
$$

In doing this multiplication we first multiply the 23 by 5, giving 115. Then we multiply the 23 by 4. This gives 92. We write the 92 under the 115 as shown. We then add and get 1035 as our final answer. Why did we move the 92 one place to the left?

Division and subtraction are done similarly.

decimal system

The system we have just described is also called the **decimal system**. The decimal system was not widely accepted until the late Middle Ages. It took a long time for this system to be put into everyday use. In fact, in the late thirteenth century the city of Florence in Italy passed laws against the use of the Hindu-Arabic numerals. This was done to protect its citizens

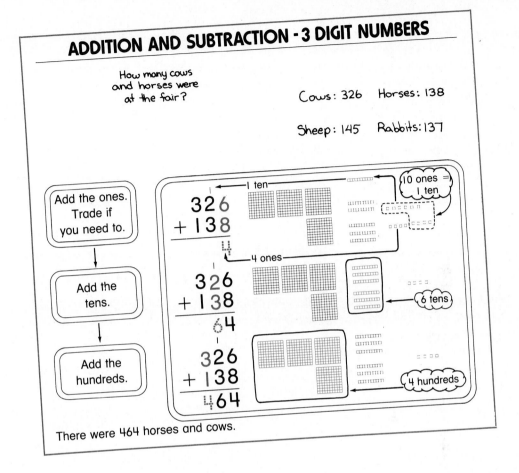

from the dishonest persons who did such things as interchange the numbers 0, 6, and 9.

Because the decimal system uses groupings of 10's, we refer to it as a **base 10 number system**.

base 10 number system

Comment   Although all of us are familiar with how the 10 digits are written in the decimal system, it should be noted that the digits that appear on the bottom of bank checks are often written in a slightly different form, as shown below:

EXERCISES FOR SECTION 3.2

1. Translate each of the following numbers into the Roman numeration system.

    a) 59   **b)** 94

    c) 69   **d)** 1234

2. Translate each of the following numbers from the Roman numeration system into the Hindu-Arabic system.

    a) LXXXIV   **b)** CCIX

    c) MCXLIX   **d)** MDCCCXXII

In Exercises 3–4, try to perform the indicated operations in the Roman numeration system.

3.   CXIX   **4.**   MDCCCLXXII
    + MDXLI   –   DCVI

5. Our number system is known as the Hindu-Arabic system because it originated in India and was spread by the Arabs. Look up the Hindu-Arabic numeration system in encyclopedias and books on the history of mathematics to determine exactly how the number system originated in India and how it was spread by the Arabs to Egypt.

3.3

OTHER BASES

We mentioned earlier that some primitive people counted in groupings of five. Suppose we had continued this method today and still counted by groupings of five. What would numbers look like in such a system? The setup is the same as that for the base 10 system. The only difference is that now we work with groupings of five. We will have only five digits. These are 0, 1, 2, 3, 4.

base 5 system

Let us consider the number written as 324 in the **base 5 system**.

5^2	5^1	1's
3	2	4

This means that we have $3(5^2) + 2(5^1) + 4(1\text{'s})$.

To indicate that we are working in base 5, we write this as $324_{(\text{five})}$. This is read as "three-two-four" and not as "three hundred and twenty-four." The words "thousand," "hundred," "twenty," "tens," etc., are words that are used only in the base 10 system.

In base 10, when we write 324, we mean

10^2	10^1	1's
3	2	4

This would mean $3(10^2) + 2(10^1) + 4(1\text{'s})$. This, of course, we read as "three hundred and twenty-four."

number

numeral

Comment   Although we use the same symbol 324 in both bases, they have different meanings; 324 in base 5 represents a different quantity than 324 in base 10. The symbol 324 is a *numeral* that represents different *numbers* in different bases. A **number** is a quantity, whereas a **numeral** is a symbol used to represent it.

To better understand the difference between number and numeral, consider the *number* seven. We can represent it by any of the following numerals:

$$\text{VII, \quad 7, \quad 7, \quad ||||||| \quad (Egyptian).}$$

As another example of a number written in a different base, consider 3203 in base 5, written as $3203_{(five)}$. This means

5^3	5^2	5^1	1's
3	2	0	3

$$3(5^3) + 2(5^2) + 0(5^1) + 3(1\text{'s}).$$

Let us now add $324_{(five)}$ and $3203_{(five)}$ in base 5.

	5^3	5^2	5^1	1's
	3	2	0	3
+		3	2	4
Numbers carried	1		1	
Answer	4	0	3	2

This procedure is exactly the same as in base 10, except that we are now working with groupings of five.

First we add 3 and 4. This gives 7, which is the same as 5 plus 2 or $1(5^1) + 2(1\text{'s})$. The $1(5^1)$ must be "carried" to the next column, which is the 5^1 column. The 2 remains in the 1's column.

Next we add 2 and 0 and the 1 we carried in the 5^1 column. This gives 3. No carrying is needed. We then add 2 and 3 in the 5^2 column. This gives $5(5^2)$ or $1(5^3)$. We put down 0 in the 5^2 column and carry a 1 into the 5^3 column.

Finally, we have in the 5^3 column a 3 and the 1 carried, which gives 4. Our final answer is $4032_{(five)}$.

We can summarize the procedure as follows.

1. In each column the only digits allowed are 0, 1, 2, 3, and 4.

2. In any column, when the sum is more than 4, we carry everything over 4 to the next column.

Compare this to the technique used in base 10, summarized earlier.

To further illustrate base 5 arithmetic, we give several other examples.

EXAMPLE 1

a) Add $1204_{(five)}$

$$\begin{array}{r} 1204_{(five)} \\ +\ \ 332_{(five)} \\ \hline 2041_{(five)} \end{array}$$

SOLUTION

In the 1's column, $2 + 4$ gives 6, which is $1(5^1) + 1$. We carry a 1 and leave 1. In the 5^1 column, $0 + 3 +$ the 1 carried gives 4. Since there is no carrying needed, we just leave 4. In the 5^2 column, $3 + 2$ gives 5, which is $5(5^2)$ or $1(5^3)$. We carry a 1 and leave 0. In the 5^3 column we have a 1 and the 1 carried, which gives 2. There is nothing to carry to the next column. Our answer is $2041_{(five)}$.

b) Multiply

$$\begin{array}{r} 23_{(five)} \\ \times\ 34_{(five)} \\ \hline 202 \\ 124\ \ \\ \hline 1442_{(five)} \end{array}$$

SOLUTION

First we multiply 3 by 4, which gives 12. We have $2(5^1)$ to carry and $2(1\text{'s})$ left over. Next we multiply 4 by 2, which is 8. Adding the carried 2, we have 10 altogether. This gives $2(5^1)$ to carry and 0 left over. So on the first line we have 202. Now we multiply the 23 by the 3. This gives 124. Notice that we move the 124 one space to the left. Compare this to the procedure we use for base 10. Why do we move one space to the left?
     Finally, we add and get $1442_{(five)}$.

c) Subtract

$$\begin{array}{r} 123_{(five)} \\ -\ 104_{(five)} \\ \hline 14_{(five)} \end{array}$$

SOLUTION

We cannot subtract 4 from 3, so we have to borrow. Since we are working in base 5, we borrow a 5. (Compare this to what we do in base 10. See the accompanying comment.) Now we have 4 from $3 +$ the borrowed 5, or 8. This leaves 4. The 2 in the second column is now a 1. (Why?) 1 minus 0 is 1. Finally, we have 1 minus 1 in the last column, which gives 0. Our final answer is $14_{(five)}$. (As in base 10, a zero at the beginning of a number is not written down.)

"borrowing"

"trading"

Comment   Students often refer to our concept of "**borrowing**" as one of "**trading**," similar to what is done by addition. This is illustrated on the facing page in the excerpt from *Addison-Wesley Mathematics*, 1987, Grade 4, p. 64.

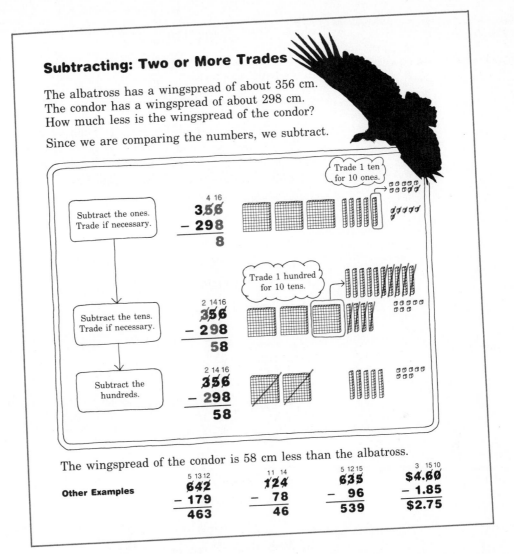

Subtracting: Two or More Trades

The albatross has a wingspread of about 356 cm.
The condor has a wingspread of about 298 cm.
How much less is the wingspread of the condor?

Since we are comparing the numbers, we subtract.

Trade 1 ten
for 10 ones.

Subtract the ones.
Trade if necessary.

$$\begin{array}{r} \overset{4\;16}{3\cancel{5}\cancel{6}} \\ -\,298 \\ \hline 8 \end{array}$$

Trade 1 hundred
for 10 tens.

Subtract the tens.
Trade if necessary.

$$\begin{array}{r} \overset{2\;14\,16}{\cancel{3}\cancel{5}\cancel{6}} \\ -\,298 \\ \hline 58 \end{array}$$

Subtract the
hundreds.

$$\begin{array}{r} \overset{2\;14\,16}{\cancel{3}\cancel{5}\cancel{6}} \\ -\,298 \\ \hline 58 \end{array}$$

The wingspread of the condor is 58 cm less than the albatross.

Other Examples

$$\begin{array}{r} \overset{5\;13\,12}{6\cancel{4}\cancel{2}} \\ -\,179 \\ \hline 463 \end{array} \qquad \begin{array}{r} \overset{11\;\;14}{1\cancel{2}\cancel{4}} \\ -\;\;78 \\ \hline 46 \end{array} \qquad \begin{array}{r} \overset{5\;12\,15}{6\cancel{3}\cancel{5}} \\ -\;\;96 \\ \hline 539 \end{array} \qquad \begin{array}{r} \overset{3\;\;15\,10}{\$4.\cancel{6}\cancel{0}} \\ -\,1.85 \\ \hline \$2.75 \end{array}$$

base 2 or

binary system

Many civilizations have only two numbers. Such a system is called a **base 2** or **binary system**. Let the two digits be 0 and 1. How would we do arithmetic in the binary system? Remember that we will use groupings of two. Let us consider the number 110110 in the base 2 system. We can represent it in a chart as

2^5	2^4	2^3	2^2	2^1	1's
1	1	0	1	1	0

This means that we have $1(2^5) + 1(2^4) + 0(2^3) + 1(2^2) + 1(2^1) + 0(1\text{'s})$.

EXAMPLE 2

SOLUTION

a) Add $101_{(two)}$ and $110_{(two)}$.

$$101_{(two)}$$
$$+\ 110_{(two)}$$
$$\overline{1011_{(two)}}$$

First we add 1 and 0, which gives 1. Then we add 0 and 1, which gives 1. Finally, we add 1 and 1, which gives 2. We carry this "2" (as a 1) to the next column and leave behind 0. Our final answer is $1011_{(two)}$. (Since the only digits are 0 and 1, we cannot have 2 in any column.)

b) Multiply

$$110_{(two)}$$
$$\times\ 11_{(two)}$$
$$\overline{110}$$
$$110$$
$$\overline{10010_{(two)}}$$

c) Subtract

$$1101_{(two)}$$
$$-\ 111_{(two)}$$
$$\overline{110_{(two)}}$$

It is possible to use any number larger than 1 as a base. The following examples illustrate some of these other bases.

EXAMPLE 3

a) Add

$$456_{(seven)}$$
$$+\ 324_{(seven)}$$
$$\overline{1113_{(seven)}}$$

b) Multiply

$$357_{(eight)}$$
$$\times\ 65_{(eight)}$$
$$\overline{2253}$$
$$2632$$
$$\overline{30573_{(eight)}}$$

c) Subtract

$$3101_{(four)}$$
$$-\ 233_{(four)}$$
$$\overline{2202_{(four)}}$$

d) Multiply $468_{(nine)}$
$\underline{\times\,57_{(nine)}}$

3632
$\underline{2574}$
$30472_{(nine)}$

In a base 12 system we need 12 digits. (Why?)

EXAMPLE 4

a) Let the digits of a base 12 system be 0, 1, 2, 3, 4, 5, 6, 7, 8, 9, t, and e. We have created two new symbols: t, which equals $9 + 1$, and e, which equals $9 + 2$. Let us add $12e_{(twelve)}$ and $t1_{(twelve)}$.

SOLUTION

$12e_{(twelve)}$
$\underline{+\,t1_{(twelve)}}$
$210_{(twelve)}$

b) Multiply $12e_{(twelve)}$
$\underline{\times\,t1_{(twelve)}}$

$12e$
$\underline{1052}$
$1064e_{(twelve)}$

EXAMPLE 5

SOLUTION

In some base b, $57_{(b)}$ equals 52 in base 10. Find b.

We know that

$$57_{(b)} \quad \text{means} \quad 5(b^1) + 7(1\text{'s}).$$

Therefore if $57_{(b)} = 52_{(ten)}$, we have

$$57_{(b)} = 5 \cdot b + 7 = 52$$

By trial and error you find that $b = 9$. (If you are familiar with algebra, you can solve it directly.)

Comment   Why should we study numbers written in bases other than 10? After all, the decimal (base 10) system is used throughout the world today. There are several reasons. As we shall see in Section 3.5, all modern computers work in base 2, 8, or 16. So if you ever work much with computers, you will need this background. We will also see how some popular games, many of them thousands of years old, can be analyzed mathematically by using base 2. Furthermore, as we have already seen, the difficulties we have in doing arithmetic in other bases are similar to those a beginner has in base 10. So if you ever teach a child arithmetic, either as a parent or a teacher, you will understand his or her struggles and be better able to help. We are so familiar with base 10 that we really have to study other bases to get a better understanding of base 10.

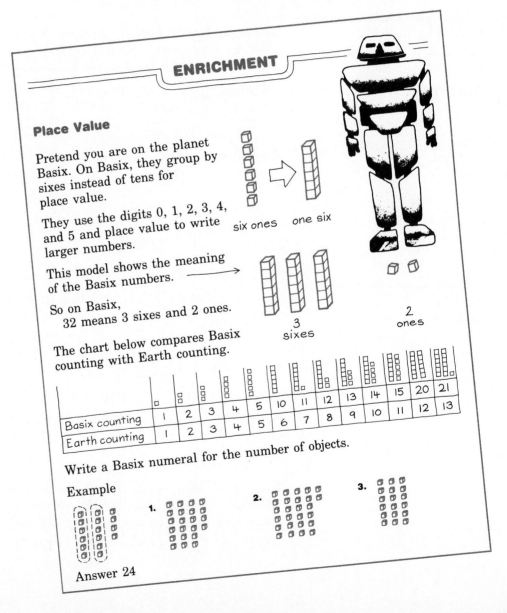

ENRICHMENT

Place Value

Pretend you are on the planet Basix. On Basix, they group by sixes instead of tens for place value.

They use the digits 0, 1, 2, 3, 4, and 5 and place value to write larger numbers.

This model shows the meaning of the Basix numbers. →

So on Basix, 32 means 3 sixes and 2 ones.

The chart below compares Basix counting with Earth counting.

six ones   one six

3 sixes   2 ones

| Basix counting | 1 | 2 | 3 | 4 | 5 | 10 | 11 | 12 | 13 | 14 | 15 | 20 | 21 |
| Earth counting | 1 | 2 | 3 | 4 | 5 | 6 | 7 | 8 | 9 | 10 | 11 | 12 | 13 |

Write a Basix numeral for the number of objects.

Example

1.

2.

3.

Answer 24

By studying groupings for place values in different number bases at an early age, students begin to appreciate groupings in base 10. This is shown on the facing page in the excerpt from *Addison-Wesley Mathematics*, 1987, Grade 4, p. 47.

Division in other bases is performed in exactly the same way that we do division in base 10. This is because division is thought of as the opposite of multiplication. For example, in the decimal system, $18 \div 6 = 3$, since $6 \cdot 3 = 18$. To illustrate the procedure for dividing in base 5, consider the following.

EXAMPLE 6

a) Divide $1434_{\text{(five)}}$ by $4_{\text{(five)}}$

SOLUTION

We set up the division problem as in base 10. We have

$$
\begin{array}{r}
221 \\
4\overline{)1434} \\
13 \\
\overline{13} \\
13 \\
\overline{4} \\
4 \\
\overline{0}
\end{array}
\qquad \text{(In base 5, we know that } 4 \times 2 = 13)
$$

Thus our answer is $221_{\text{(five)}}$.

b) Divide $21104_{\text{(five)}}$ by $413_{\text{(five)}}$

SOLUTION

Again we set up the problem as in base 10. We have

$$
\begin{array}{r}
23 \\
413\overline{)21104} \\
1331 \\
\overline{2244} \\
2244 \\
\overline{0}
\end{array}
$$

Thus our answer is $23_{\text{(five)}}$.

Comment We can verify that our answer is correct by multiplying $23_{\text{(five)}}$ with $413_{\text{(five)}}$. Our answer is indeed $21104_{\text{(five)}}$.

EXERCISES FOR SECTION 3.3

In Exercises 1–15, perform the indicated operations in the given base.

1. $11101_{(two)}$
 $+ 11111_{(two)}$

2. $21022_{(three)}$
 $+ 1102_{(three)}$

3. $6834_{(nine)}$
 $- 4565_{(nine)}$

4. $14te_{(twelve)}$
 $+ te1_{(twelve)}$

5. $1232_{(four)}$
 $+ 232_{(four)}$

6. $2012_{(seven)}$
 $- 1236_{(seven)}$

7. $4764_{(eight)}$
 $- 2175_{(eight)}$

8. $23232_{(eleven)}$
 $- 2323_{(eleven)}$

9. $354_{(six)}$
 $- 245_{(six)}$

10. $425_{(six)}$
 $\times 34_{(six)}$

11. $543_{(seven)}$
 $\times 65_{(seven)}$

12. $et5_{(twelve)}$
 $\times 2te_{(twelve)}$

13. $22122_{(three)}$
 $\times 2221_{(three)}$

14. $878_{(nine)}$
 $\times 57_{(nine)}$

15. $534_{(nine)}$
 $678_{(nine)}$
 $+ 837_{(nine)}$

In Exercises 16–20, divide the first number by the second number in the indicated base and check your answer.

16. Divide $13332_{(five)}$ by $23_{(five)}$

17. Divide $25454_{(six)}$ by $34_{(six)}$

18. Divide $101010101_{(two)}$ by $1011_{(two)}$

19. Divide $133t6t_{(twelve)}$ by $te1_{(twelve)}$

20. Divide $30230_{(four)}$ by $32_{(four)}$

In Exercises 21–24, find the base b in which the numbers are written.

21. $56_{(b)} = 51$

22. $35_{(b)} = 32$

23. $77_{(b)} = 70$

*24. $345_{(b)} = 137$

25. Why must the base of a number system be greater than 1?

26. What is wrong with the following calculation?

$$7563_{(nine)}$$
$$- 2315_{(nine)}$$
$$\overline{5248_{(nine)}}$$

In Exercises 27–30, a computation was performed in a base other than 10. Can you find the base?

27. $\begin{array}{r} 324 \\ + 513 \\ \hline 1140 \end{array}$

28. $\begin{array}{r} 543 \\ - 256 \\ \hline 265 \end{array}$

29. $\begin{array}{r} 245 \\ \times 32 \\ \hline 10302 \end{array}$

30. $\begin{array}{r} 527 \\ \times 32 \\ \hline 14822 \end{array}$

PROBLEM SOLVING EXERCISES

31. The following is an addition problem in base 3. However, instead of using the digits 0, 1, and 2, we have used the letters A, D, and M. Each letter stands for the same digit every time it is used. Determine which of the digits 0, 1, and 2 is represented by each letter.

$$\begin{array}{r} M\,A\,M\,A \\ + \quad D\,A\,D\,A \\ \hline M\,A\,M\,A\,A \end{array}$$

32. The following is an addition problem in base 4. However, instead of using the digits 0, 1, 2, and 3, we have used the letters A, D, M, and P. Each letter used represents the same digit every time it is used. Determine which of the digits 0, 1, 2, and 3 is represented by each letter.

$$\begin{array}{r} M\,A\,M\,A \\ + D\,A\,D\,A \\ \hline P\,A\,P\,A \end{array}$$

 Brain-Teaser Problems

**33. In base 10 the number 32 is even. Are there any bases in which this number is odd? Explain your answer.

**34. The following is an addition problem in base 10. However, instead of using the digits 0, 1, 2, 3, 4, 5, 6, 7, 8, and 9, we have used letters. Each letter used represents the same digit every time it is used. Determine which of the digits 0, 1, 2, . . . , 9 is represented by each letter.

$$\begin{array}{r} T\,W\,O \\ T\,H\,R\,E\,E \\ + S\,E\,V\,E\,N \\ \hline T\,W\,E\,L\,V\,E \end{array}$$

3.4

CONVERTING FROM BASE 10 TO OTHER BASES AND FROM OTHER BASES TO BASE 10

Imagine one person working in base 10 and another person working in base 5. To communicate with each other, they would need a method for changing a base 10 number to a base 5 number and vice versa. In this section we will first discuss how we convert a base 10 number to any other base, and then we will discuss the reverse procedure.

We will illustrate the technique by an example. Let us convert 258 written in base 10, to base 5. We write down 258 and divide it by 5. We get 51 with a remainder of 3. This is written as shown.

$$
\begin{array}{r|cc}
 & & \textit{Remainder} \\
5 & 258 & 3 \\
5 & 51 & 1 \\
5 & 10 & 0 \\
5 & 2 & 2 \\
 & 0 & \\
\end{array}
$$

Then we divide the 51 by 5. This gives 10 with a remainder of 1. We write the 1 under the 3 (as shown) in the remainder column. Now we divide 10 by 5. This gives 2 with a remainder of 0. The remainder of 0 is written under the 1 in the remainder column. Finally, we divide the 2 by 5. Since 5 does not "go" into 2, we write down 0 with 2 in the remainder column. We now read off the answer *from bottom to top in the remainder column.* Our answer is 2013. Therefore

$$258_{(ten)} = 2013_{(five)}$$

This technique will work for conversion from base 10 to *any* other base.

EXAMPLE 1

SOLUTION

a) Convert $152_{(ten)}$ to base 5.

$$
\begin{array}{r|cc}
 & & \textit{Remainder} \\
5 & 152 & 2 \\
5 & 30 & 0 \\
5 & 6 & 1 \\
5 & 1 & 1 \\
 & 0 & \\
\end{array}
$$

Our answer: $152_{(ten)} = 1102_{(five)}$.

b) Convert $167_{(ten)}$ to base 2.

SOLUTION

		Remainder
2	167	1
2	83	1
2	41	1
2	20	0
2	10	0
2	5	1
2	2	0
2	1	1
	0	

Our answer: $167_{(ten)} = 10100111_{(two)}$.

c) Convert $138_{(ten)}$ to base 3.

SOLUTION

		Remainder
3	138	0
3	46	1
3	15	0
3	5	2
3	1	1
	0	

Our answer: $138_{(ten)} = 12010_{(three)}$.

d) Convert $428_{(ten)}$ to base 9.

SOLUTION

		Remainder
9	428	5
9	47	2
9	5	5
	0	

Our answer: $428_{(ten)} = 525_{(nine)}$.

e) Convert $134_{(ten)}$ to base 12.

SOLUTION

$$\text{Remainder}$$

$$12\ |\ \underline{134} \qquad 2$$
$$12\ |\ \underline{11} \qquad e$$
$$0$$

Our answer: $134_{(ten)} = e2_{(twelve)}$.

Beware For this method to work you must read *up* the remainder column. If you read down the remainder column, your answer will be wrong.

In the preceding paragraphs we learned how to convert a number from base 10 to any other base. Now we will show how to convert a number written in any other base back into base 10.

Remember what 123 in base 5 really means. To refresh your memory, we will write it in the following form:

5^2	5^1	1's
1	2	3

This means that we have $1(5^2) + 2(5^1) + 3(1\text{'s})$.
Since $5^2 = 5 \times 5 = 25$, we then have

$$1(25) + 2(5^1) + 3(1\text{'s})$$
$$25 + 10 + 3$$
$$38$$

Therefore $123_{(five)} = 38_{(ten)}$.
Some further examples will be helpful.

EXAMPLE 2

a) Convert $314_{(six)}$ to base 10.

SOLUTION

We rewrite 314 in base 6 in the following form:

6^2	6^1	1's
3	1	4

This means that we have $3(6^2) + 1(6^1) + 4(1\text{'s})$.
Since $6^2 = 6 \times 6 = 36$, we have

$$3(36) + 1(6) + 4(1\text{'s})$$
$$108 + 6 + 4$$
$$118$$

Our answer: $314_{(six)} = 118_{(ten)}$.

b) Convert $111011_{(two)}$ to base 10.

SOLUTION

We write $111011_{(two)}$ as follows:

2^5	2^4	2^3	2^2	2^1	1's
1	1	1	0	1	1

Since

$$2^5 = 2 \times 2 \times 2 \times 2 \times 2 = 32$$
$$2^4 = 2 \times 2 \times 2 \times 2 \quad = 16$$
$$2^3 = 2 \times 2 \times 2 \qquad\quad = 8 \qquad \text{and}$$
$$2^2 = 2 \times 2 \qquad\qquad\quad = 4$$

we then have

$$1(32) + 1(16) + 1(8) + 0(4) + 1(2) + 1(1\text{'s})$$
$$32 + 16 + 8 + 0 + 2 + 1$$
$$59$$

Our answer: $111011_{(two)} = 59_{(ten)}$.

c) Convert $673_{(eight)}$ to base 10.

SOLUTION

Rewrite $673_{(eight)}$ as follows:

8^2	8^1	1's
6	7	3

Again $8^2 = 8 \times 8 = 64$, so we have

$$6(64) + 7(8^1) + 3(1\text{'s})$$
$$384 + 56 + 3$$
$$443$$

Our answer: $673_{(eight)} = 443_{(ten)}$.

d) Convert $158_{(twelve)}$ to base 10.

SOLUTION

Rewrite $158_{(twelve)}$ as follows:

12^2	12^1	1's
1	5	8

$$\text{Since } 12^2 = 12 \times 12 = 144, \text{ we get}$$

$$1(144) + 5(12^1) + 8(1\text{'s})$$

$$144 + 60 + 8$$

$$212$$

$$\text{Our answer: } 158_{(\text{twelve})} = 212_{(\text{ten})}.$$

EXERCISES FOR SECTION 3.4

1. Convert each of the following base 10 numbers to the indicated base

a) 423 to base 4	**b)** 178 to base 5
c) 129 to base 3	**d)** 426 to base 8
e) 546 to base 9	**f)** 478 to base 7
g) 386 to base 6	**h)** 329 to base 12
i) 278 to base 16	**j)** 288 to base 5
k) 84 to base 2	**l)** 193 to base 7
m) 129 to base 2	**n)** 278 to base 12
o) 627 to base 8	**p)** 4600 to base 12

2. Why does the technique discussed in this section work?

3. Write the number $217_{(\text{ten})}$ first in base 2 and then in base 8. Now do the same thing for the number 301. By examining your answers, can you find any relationship between base 2 and base 8?

4. What are some advantages to having a small-number base instead of a large-number base? What are some of the disadvantages?

5. Since base 2 involves only the digits 0 and 1, we can count in base 2 on our fingers. This can be done as follows. Keep all fingers down to represent 0 and a finger up to represent a 1. The position of the "up" finger denotes the position of the "1" in the base 2 representation. Thus we can represent the first six counting numbers as shown below.

$00001_{(\text{two})}$
The number 1

$00010_{(\text{two})}$
The number 2

$00011_{(\text{two})}$
The number 3

$00100_{(\text{two})}$
The number 4

$00101_{(\text{two})}$
The number 5

$00110_{(\text{two})}$
The number 6

Using a similar procedure, show how we can represent the numbers 17 through 31 on one hand.

6. Convert each of the following numbers from the indicated base to a base 10 number.

a) $12132_{(\text{four})}$	**b)** $1111011_{(\text{two})}$
c) $54321_{(\text{six})}$	**d)** $tee_{(\text{twelve})}$
e) $3231_{(\text{seven})}$	**f)** $4144_{(\text{five})}$
g) $86t2_{(\text{twelve})}$	**h)** $5486_{(\text{nine})}$
i) $1427_{(\text{eight})}$	**j)** $3114_{(\text{five})}$
k) $7481_{(\text{nine})}$	**l)** $12102_{(\text{three})}$
m) $210111_{(\text{three})}$	**n)** $1231_{(\text{eleven})}$
o) $12321_{(\text{five})}$	**p)** $21te1_{(\text{twelve})}$

7. Perform the following division: $13585_{(\text{nine})} \div et_{(\text{twelve})}$. Express your answer in base 5.

PROBLEM SOLVING EXERCISES

8. *Social Security.* Joanne Pucci is at a Social Security office applying for retirement benefits. She says that her age is $12_{(\text{sixty-four})}$ years old. The clerk believes that she is much too young. Is Joanne really as young as the clerk believes? Explain.

9. Three friends, who have not seen each other since they graduated from college, meet at a class reunion. Each friend is trying to impress the other by claiming

ner salary is quite high. The actual salaries
ollows:

Person	Salary (in dollars)
Arlene Anderson	$264563_{(seven)}$
Tom McDermott	$42782_{(nine)}$
Bill Sommers	$30213_{(twelve)}$

Which of the three friends has the highest salary?

Brain-Teaser Problems

**10. Mysterio the magician holds up four cards marked as shown below. He asks someone in the audience to think of a number from 1 through 15 and to tell him on which of the cards it appears. The first person tells him that the number he is thinking of is on cards 1, 3, and 4. Mysterio then correctly tells him that the number is 13. The second person then tells him that he is thinking of a number that appears only on cards 1 and 2. Mysterio tells him that his number is 3.

a) How does Mysterio do it?

b) Why does the trick work? (*Hint:* Write all the numbers 1 through 15 in the binary system.)

Card 1		Card 2		Card 3		Card 4	
1	9	2	10	4	12	8	12
3	11	3	11	5	13	9	13
5	13	6	14	6	14	10	14
7	15	7	15	7	15	11	15

3.5

APPLICATIONS TO THE COMPUTER AND TO THE GAME OF *NIM*

It has been said that we live in the computer age. Computers are involved in almost every aspect of our lives. Let us look at a day in the life of John Doe.

He wakes up in the morning and turns on the light. Nothing happens. Because of a computer error in processing his electric bill, his electricity has been turned off. On the way to work he uses his credit card to buy gas, for which the computer will bill him at the end of the month. Unfortunately, stopping for gas has made him late. Speeding to work, he is stopped by a police officer, who asks to see his computerized driver's license. He is then issued a computerized summons. At work he "punches in" on a computerized card. At the end of the day he receives his paycheck, but the computer made a mistake and underpaid him five dollars.

John decides to register with a computer dating service, and at lunchtime he mails them a check. (All checks are processed by computer.) After work, John registers for an evening course at City College. Of course, the entire registration process is computerized. When John gets home, he finds a letter from the Internal Revenue Service stating that the computer has found an error in his income tax return.

Although we are all affected by computers, many of us are unaware of what a computer really is, how it works, and what it can and cannot do.

Bruce Read

In 1804, Joseph Marie Jacquard made a loom for weaving intricate patterns. It used punched cards, pressed against a bank of needles, for each pass of the shuttle. Certain needles were pushed back by the card; others stayed in place because of holes in the card. This use of punched cards foreshadowed our present-day computers.

A computer can do *nothing* that a human could not do if given enough time. The usefulness of computers is in their tremendous speed and accuracy. Computer errors occur only where there is a mechanical failure or when the human operator makes a mistake.

How does a computer do things so quickly? It works on electrical impulse, and electricity travels at the speed of light (which is about as fast as you can get).

Most computers work in base 2 because of its simplicity. (Remember, in base 2 there are only two digits, 0 and 1.) Furthermore, the fact that there are only two digits makes it easy to represent numbers on the computer in many different ways.

In the modern-day computer, information is fed in by using base 10 (this is usually done by means of optical scanners, tapes, or typewriter). Words are also converted into base 10 numerals. The information is then converted into base 2 and stored for future use in the computer's memory. Some computers store information in base 8 or 16 to save space. A small computer with 100,000 "spaces" uses about 80,000 of these spaces for memory, that is, storage of information. Only about 20,000 spaces are actually used for computations.

To use the computer, we must feed information into the memory and then give precise instructions as to the computations to be performed with this information. We must also tell the machine how to write down the result. This is the job of the computer programmer.

All information and instructions must be given to the computer in specific form. If even a comma is left out, the computer will not be able to understand what to do. The computer *cannot think* on its own. It merely follows human-given directions.

Suppose on an exam you were given the problem: "Dvide 6 by 2." You of course would know that the word "divide" is misspelled. This would not stop you from doing the problem. Since a computer cannot reason, it would not understand what "dvide" meant. It would stop and await further instructions.

Computers cannot do our thinking for us. However, their ability to do computations accurately at lightning speed does relieve us of many of the time-consuming and boring calculations associated with mathematical and scientific projects. Many mathematical problems have been solved with the help of computers doing the "dirty work."

In Chapter 14 we will discuss computers in more detail.

The Game of *Nim*

Nim is a game that has been played in different forms for many centuries. Some time ago, a mechanical version for children was marketed in which the child played against a plastic mechanical computer. The word "Nim" comes from the German word "nehmen" meaning "to take." We will learn how to play the simplest version of the game.

We start with several piles of matches. Each pile can have any number of matches, and each pile can have a different number of matches. For example, we may have five piles with 4, 7, 3, 2, and 2 matches. The rules of the game are as follows.

1. There are two players who take alternate turns.
2. Each player in turn takes as many matches as he or she wants from *one and only one* pile. The player must take at least one match and may take them all. On the player's next turn he or she may select the same pile or a different pile.
3. The person who takes the last match wins.

To illustrate how *Nim* works, consider the following game between Joe and Frances. There are three piles with 4, 2, and 7 matches, as shown in Fig. 3.1. We now illustrate the situation that results after each move.

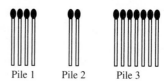

Pile 1   Pile 2   Pile 3

Figure 3.1

Move	Situation after move		
	Pile 1	**Pile 2**	**Pile 3**
Start of game	4 matches	2 matches	7 matches
Frances takes 2 matches from pile 3.	4 matches	2 matches	5 matches
Joe takes all the matches in pile 1.		2 matches	5 matches
Frances takes 1 match from pile 2.		1 match	5 matches
Joe takes 1 match from pile 3.		1 match	4 matches
Frances takes 1 match from pile 2.			4 matches
Joe takes the 4 matches from pile 3 and wins.			

It may seem to you that winning the game is a matter of skill. However, this is not entirely so. Someone who knows the secret of the game can win, no matter how clever his or her opponent is, provided he or she is allowed to choose who goes first. Gamblers who know this secret have won a lot of money from innocent "suckers."

How to Win at *Nim*

The explanation is lengthy but not difficult. It is given in three parts. Read each of parts I, II, and III carefully before going on to the next part.

Part I

Write the number of matches in each pile in the binary system. In our sample game this would be 100, 10, and 111. We write these numbers in a column and then add them *as if they were in base 10:*

$$
\begin{array}{r}
100 \\
10 \\
111 \\
\hline
221
\end{array}
$$

bad combination

good combination

If the result has all even digits, then we call it a **bad combination**. Otherwise, we call it a **good combination**.

EXAMPLE 1

a) If there are 3, 5, 8, and 4 matches, these numbers converted to base 2 and added are

$$
\begin{array}{r}
11 \\
101 \\
1000 \\
100 \\
\hline
1212
\end{array}
$$

This is a good combination.

b) If there are 10, 13, 2, 9, and 6 matches, these numbers converted to base 2 and added are

$$
\begin{array}{r}
1010 \\
1101 \\
10 \\
1001 \\
110 \\
\hline
3232
\end{array}
$$

Again this is a good combination.

c) If there are 11, 13, and 6 matches, these numbers converted to base 2 and added are

$$
\begin{array}{r}
1011 \\
1101 \\
110 \\
\hline
2222
\end{array}
$$

This is a bad combination.

Part II

Notice that just before the final winning play is made, there is only one pile. This means that there is only one number (written in base 2) in the sum of part I. Thus the total will consist just of this one number. Since numbers in base 2 contain only the digits 0 and 1, this total will also contain only the digits 0 and 1. Thus we must have a *good combination* (since it contains an odd number, 1). In our sample game, before Joe makes the last move, there are four matches in pile 3. Remember that 4 in base 10 is 100 in base 2 so we have the following:

Pile 1   0
Pile 2   0
Pile 3   100
———
Sum   100

This is a good combination.

Summarizing   *The final winning move can only be made from a good combination.*

Part III

Therefore our strategy is to keep our opponent from ever getting a good combination and to make sure at the end that we ourselves get one. This can be accomplished in the following way.

1. *A play from a bad combination will always leave a good combination.* The reason for this is that in any given move you can change only one number in the sum (since you can take only from one pile). Thus in each column of the sum you can change only one digit (and you must change at least one digit). The only digit change can be from 0 to 1 or from 1 to 0 (because we are in base 2, these are the only digits we have). Since the sum contained all even digits to begin with, this change will make some of them odd. This will result in a good combination. To see how this works, consider the bad combination of 11, 13, and 6 matches given in part (c) of Example 1 above. This combination was

1011
1101
110
———
2222

Suppose we take 7 matches from pile 1. This changes the first number to 100, leaving

100
1101
110
———
1311

This is a good combination. Try making the following plays on the original combination and verify that you always get a good combination.

a) Take 2 from pile 3.

b) Take 8 from pile 2.

c) Take all of pile 1.

2. *A play from a good combination can always be made into a bad combination.* We do this as follows: Go to the first odd column from the left of the sum in the good combination. Pick any number that has a 1 in this column. Circle this 1. Now go to the next odd column. Circle the digit on the same line in this column. Repeat this for all odd columns and only odd columns. Now change all the circled digits. Since we are working in base 2, we can only change 0's to 1's and 1's to 0's. Change *only* circled digits. After we change this number, we play to *leave* this amount of matches in this pile.

Comment   We will not explain here why this strategy works. It is given as an exercise.

EXAMPLE 2

Suppose we are playing the good combination of Example 1(a).

$$
\begin{array}{c c c c}
 & & 1 & 1 \\
 & 1 & 0 & 1 \\
 ① & 0 & ⓪ & 0 \\
 & 1 & 0 & 0 \\
 \hline
 1 & 2 & 1 & 2
\end{array}
$$

The first and third columns from the left (in the sum) are odd. There is only one number with a 1 in the first column. We must use it. We circle it. In column 3 we circle the digit on the same line. We change these and get 0010 which is 2 in base 10. Thus we take all but 2 in pile 3. Notice that after we play, we leave

$$
\begin{array}{c}
 11 \\
 101 \\
 10 \\
 100 \\
 \hline
 222
\end{array}
$$

This is a bad combination.

Summary

1. Determine whether the original combination is good or bad.

2. If the original is good, choose to go first. Otherwise, let your opponent go first.

3. Whenever you move, use the strategy discussed to leave your opponent with a bad combination.

4. No matter what your opponent does, he or she must leave you a good combination.

EXERCISES FOR SECTION 3.5

1. Determine which of the following are good combinations and which are bad combinations

   a) 8, 7, 2   **b)** 3, 3, 4, 5   **c)** 9, 13, 4

   d) 15, 9, 6, 4   **e)** 8, 7, 9, 11, 5

2. Using the strategy discussed in this section, change each of the following good combinations to bad combinations.

   a) 17, 9, 5   **b)** 8, 13, 11, 7   **c)** 5, 10, 1

3. Play the game of *Nim* with an opponent, using the following combinations.

   a) 5, 8, 11   **b)** 4, 8, 6, 10

   c) 5, 11, 3, 7, 6   **d)** 4, 2, 7, 5, 3, 8

   e) 5, 8, 6, 1, 3, 9

4. *Nim: Alternative version.* Suppose we change our rules slightly by allowing a player whose turn it is to pick up at least one stick, but that this can be done by selecting as many sticks as the player wants from at most x piles. How does this affect the game?

5. Rework the game discussed between Joe and Frances but use the rules given in Exercise 4. Who wins now?

6. Another interesting game involving base 2 is the *Tower of Brahma* or *Tower of Hanoi*. This game was invented by Edouard Lucas in 1883 and involves transferring discs from one needle to another in a minimum number of moves. By going to your library, try to discover how to play the *Tower of Hanoi* game.

7. Read one of the articles 44–50 in *Mathematics in the Modern World* (Readings from *Scientific American*). San Francisco: Freeman, 1968.

Brain-Teaser Problems

**8. Suppose you have just dropped on the floor 1000 cards numbered 0 to 999. You must pick them up and put them back into numerical order. It will be a long, tedious job, although a computer could do it in a fraction of a second. Surprisingly, by imitating the computer's technique you too could do the job, not as fast as the machine, but in a fairly short time. We will illustrate the method, not on 1000 cards, but on 32 cards numbered 0 to 31. First write the number of each card in base 2. Next cut holes in each card as shown in Fig. 3.2. A "closed" hole does not go through to the top of the card as does an "open" hole. A closed hole represents 1; an open hole represents 0. (See Fig. 3.3.)

Each card will have 6 holes. Now take a long, thin object like a knitting needle, pass it through the

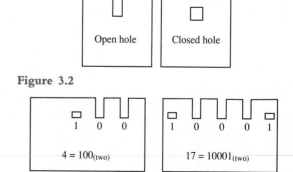

Figure 3.2

Figure 3.3

first hole on the right, and lift it up. The cards with closed holes in that place will be lifted with it. Place these behind the other cards. Repeat this on the second hole, then the third, fourth, fifth, and sixth. When you are finished, the cards will be sorted in numerical order from 0 to 31. The sorting takes only 6 "passes" through the pile.

a) Make a set of cards and perform this experiment.

b) Why does each card have 6 holes?

c) Explain why this procedure works.

d) How many passes would be needed if there were only 16 cards? (*Hint:* How many holes would each card have?)

e) How many passes are needed for 100 cards?

3.6

THE WHOLE NUMBERS AND THE OPERATIONS OF ADDITION, SUBTRACTION, MULTIPLICATION, AND DIVISION

The Natural Numbers

Humans must have invented natural numbers shortly after they learned how to count. At first they had only the numbers 1 and 2. A few more talented societies also had the number 3. Everything else was "many." Later, as society became more complex, it became necessary to count accurately larger quantities. At this point, numbers larger than 2 and 3 were introduced. Thus the natural numbers were born. Because they are used in counting, the natural numbers are also called the counting numbers.

natural (counting) numbers

Start w/ 1

> **Definition 3.1**   The **natural numbers**, or **counting numbers**, are the numbers 1, 2, 3, 4, 5, 6, 7, 8, 9, 10, 11, ...

Addition

addition

sum

Let us go back 25,000 years in history. Zaftig, the caveman, has 3 sheep. His brother has just given him 2 sheep. Zaftig now counts his sheep and discovers that he has 5 altogether. Zaftig, who is the "brain" of the tribe, sees that if you have 3 things and you then get 2 more, your total will *always* be 5 things. This is an example of what we call addition. Roughly speaking, by **addition** we mean that we combine *two numbers* to obtain a third number called the **sum**. This sum must be *unique*. (This means that there is *only one* answer. There can never be more than one answer.) For example,

$$4 + 7 = 11 \text{ (11 is the only answer), and}$$
$$5 + 8 = 13 \text{ (13 is the only answer).}$$

Do the following simple addition problem:

$$7$$
$$8$$
$$9$$
$$\overline{}$$
$$24$$

Your answer is 24, of course. How did you get it? You could add from bottom to top as follows: 9 + 8 equals 17, and then 17 + 7 equals 24. You could also add from top to bottom as follows: 7 + 8 equals 15, and then 15 + 9 equals 24.

Notice that no matter which way we add, *we can only add two numbers at a time*. To add three numbers, we first add any two, and then add the third to the sum. Addition is an example of a **binary operation**.

binary operation

> **Definition 3.2**   A **binary operation** on numbers is a process by which **two** numbers are combined to obtain a **unique** third number.

Suppose you were to ask a small child who is just learning arithmetic how much 2 + 3 is. The child would first put up 2 fingers and then 3 fingers and would count the total, getting 5. If you now ask the child to add 3 + 2, he or she would put up 3 fingers and then 2 more, again getting 5. The child soon discovers that

$$3 + 2 = 2 + 3$$

commutative law of addition

This is known as the **commutative law of addition**. What this tells you is that the *order* in which you add two numbers does not matter. Your answer is always the same. We state this formally as the following law.

> **Commutative law of addition**   If a and b stand for any natural numbers, then $a + b = b + a$.

order doesn't matter

This law may seem rather obvious to you. You may even feel that it does not say much. However, the commutative law is not always true for operations different from addition. For example, subtraction is not commutative:

$$5 - 3 \quad \text{is not equal to} \quad 3 - 5$$

When you add a column of numbers, you may add from the top down (or vice versa). The usual way of checking is to add again in reverse order. You know that if your addition is correct, the answer should be the same in both cases. You are using the commutative law of addition, which says that the order in which numbers are added is not important.

In everyday life situations the order in which we do things may or may not make a difference. For example, combing your hair and brushing your teeth in the morning is commutative. On the other hand, putting on your shoes and putting on your socks is not commutative.

Ask a chemist whether mixing water and sulfuric acid is commutative. That is, does it make a difference if we pour water into sulfuric acid or sulfuric acid into water?

In a certain town there are two schools, a two-story high school and a six-story elementary school. Recently the following headline appeared in the local newspaper: "High School Building Burns Down." Which one was it? The meaning is unclear, since we do not know whether the word "school" goes with "high" or with "building." If "school" is grouped with "high," then obviously the high school (two-story building) burned down. In other words, the grouping will make a big difference in the meaning. In English, to avoid this confusion, we can put a hyphen between the words "high" and "school" when we mean the two-story building.

Now consider Mr. Jones who has decided to buy a Volkswagen. Since the local bank is advertising "small car loans," he applies to the bank for a $2000 loan. The bank officer tells him that their maximum car loan is $300. Mr. Jones protests that they are advertising loans to buy small cars and that you cannot buy any small car for $300. The bank official responds that Mr. Jones is misinterpreting the advertisement, which offers small loans to buy cars. Who is right? In this case the disagreement is also about grouping. Mr. Jones is grouping "car" with "small." The bank official is grouping "car" with "loan."

In these two examples grouping made a difference in the meaning. This is not always the case. In the phrase "my friend Klunk the mechanic" it does not make any difference whether we group the word "Klunk" with "friend" or with "the mechanic."

In mathematics, grouping may or may not be important. Suppose we are asked to add

$$2 + 3 + 4$$

without changing the order of the numbers. Since we can add only two numbers at a time, this can be done in two ways. We have either

$(2 + 3) + 4$ (We always do what is in the parentheses
   $5 + 4$ first. In this case we first add the $2 + 3$.)
     9

Water into
Acid = Danger

or

$$2 + (3 + 4) \quad \text{(This time we first add the } 3 + 4.\text{)}$$
$$2 + 7$$
$$9$$

Note that in both cases our answer is the same, that is,

$$(2 + 3) + 4 = 2 + (3 + 4)$$

In other words, it makes no difference whether we group the 3 with the 2 or with the 4. This is called the **associative law of addition**. We state it here.

associative law of addition

grouping

> **Associative Law of Addition** If a, b and c are any natural numbers, then $(a + b) + c = a + (b + c)$.

Comment Since the position of the parentheses does not matter in doing addition, we usually leave them out and write, for example,

$$2 + 3 + 4$$

instead of $(2 + 3) + 4$ or $2 + (3 + 4)$.

Beware Do not confuse the associative law for addition with the commutative law for addition. The associative law keeps the numbers in the same order but merely groups them differently. The commutative law involves changing the order of the numbers.

Although the associative law holds for addition, it does not work for all the binary operations. In particular, the associative law does not hold for subtraction. For example, $(15 - 4) - 3$ is not equal to $15 - (4 - 3)$. This is so because

$$(15 - 4) - 3 = 11 - 3 = 8$$

Remember, we do what is in the parentheses first. On the other hand,

$$15 - (4 - 3) = 15 - 1 = 14$$

Thus $(15 - 4) - 3$ is not equal to $15 - (4 - 3)$.

Suppose you were restricted for some reason to using *only* the odd numbers 1, 3, 5, 7, 9, 11, etc. Then it would be impossible to add. If you add any two odd numbers, you will always get an *even* number. Since we are limited to *only* the odd numbers, this answer is not acceptable.

Consider now *all* the natural numbers. If we add any two natural numbers, our result will also be a natural number. This is called the

closure property for addition of natural numbers. We say that the natural numbers are closed under addition. The odd numbers are not closed under addition.

law of closure for addition

> **Law of closure for addition** If a and b are any natural numbers, then the sum, $a + b$, is also a natural number.

EXAMPLE 1

a) If we are restricted to the set of numbers {1, 2, 3}, then this set is *not* closed under the operation of addition. The numbers 2 and 3 are in the set, but their sum, which is 5, is not in the set.

b) Let S = {all even numbers}. Then S is closed under the operation of addition, since when we add two even numbers, the sum is *also* an even number.

c) Let A = {1}. A is not closed under addition since $1 + 1$ equals 2, and 2 is not in A.

Comment Are the natural numbers closed under the operation of subtraction? That is, if we subtract one natural number from another natural number, is our answer also a natural number?

Multiplication

Let us return to our friend Zaftig, the caveman. He now has a herd of cattle. Each day he takes them out to pasture, walking them 5 abreast.

As they return from pasture, Zaftig counts them to make sure that they are all there. Instead of counting them one by one, he discovers that it is easier to count them in groups of 5's. He has three groups of 5 each, that is, he has

$$5 + 5 + 5$$

3 groups of 5

multiplication

This means that Zaftig has 15 cattle. A convenient way of expressing this is to invent a new operation called **multiplication**, which is symbolized in one of the following ways: $3 \cdot 5$, $3(5)$, 3×5, or $(3)(5)$. Any one of these means

$$5 + 5 + 5$$

Similarly, $7 \cdot 4$, 7×4, $7(4)$, or $(7)(4)$ means

$$4 + 4 + 4 + 4 + 4 + 4 + 4$$

In general, $a \cdot b$ [also written as ab, $a(b)$, $a \times b$, or $(a)(b)$] means

$$\underbrace{b + b + b + \cdots + b}_{a \text{ of them}}$$

Note that since we can multiply only two numbers at a time, **multiplication is also a binary operation.**

According to our definition of multiplication, $2 \cdot 3$ means 2 groups of 3 things each. This can be pictured as in Fig. 3.4. On the other hand, $3 \cdot 2$ means 3 groups of 2 things each. This we picture as in Fig. 3.5. In both cases we have 6 things altogether. Therefore

$$2 \cdot 3 = 3 \cdot 2$$

This is an example of the commutative law of multiplication.

Figure 3.4

Figure 3.5

commutative law of multiplication

> **Commutative Law of Multiplication**   If a and b are any natural numbers, then $a \cdot b = b \cdot a$.

Multiplication of natural numbers is also associative. If you multiply $2 \times 4 \times 5$, this can be done in two ways (without changing the *order* of the numbers). One way is

$$2 \times (4 \times 5) \qquad \text{4 is grouped with 5}$$
$$2 \times 20$$
$$40$$

Another way is

$$(2 \times 4) \times 5 \qquad \text{4 is grouped with 2}$$
$$8 \times 5$$
$$40$$

In both cases our answer is, of course, the same. This shows that the grouping does not matter and that

$$2 \times (4 \times 5) = (2 \times 4) \times 5$$

In general terms, we have the following law.

associative law of multiplication

> **Associative Law of Multiplication** If a, b, and c are any natural numbers, then $a(bc) = (ab)c$.

Students are introduced to the concepts of the associative law of multiplication when they are asked to multiply three numbers. In the accompanying student page from *Addison-Wesley Mathematics*, 1987, Grade 3, p. 190, students are told that "the ( ) symbols tell which multiplication to do first." This is indeed the associative law of multiplication, although no mention is made of this name.

Multiplying Three Numbers

There are 3 tennis balls in each can. There are 2 cans in each box. There are 4 boxes. How many tennis balls are there in all?

$$(3 \times 2) \times 4$$
$$6 \times 4 = 24$$

Tennis balls in each box — Boxes — Tennis balls in all

$$3 \times (2 \times 4)$$
$$3 \times 8 = 24$$

Tennis balls in each can — Cans — Tennis balls in all

These symbols ( ) tell which multiplication to do first.

Find these products.

1. $(2 \times 4) \times 1 = \underline{8}$
2. $2 \times (4 \times 1) = \underline{8}$
3. $(4 \times 1) \times 5 = \underline{20}$
4. $4 \times (1 \times 5) = \underline{20}$
5. $(4 \times 2) \times 4 = \underline{32}$
6. $4 \times (2 \times 4) = \underline{32}$

> When you multiply, you can change the grouping and get the same product.

Comment   As with addition, since the parentheses do not matter, it is customary to leave them out and write abc instead of $a(bc)$ or $(ab)c$.

If we multiply any two natural numbers, our result will also be a natural number, that is, the natural numbers are closed under multiplication. This we state as the following law.

law of closure for multiplication

> **Law of Closure for Multiplication**   If a and b are any natural numbers, then ab is also a natural number.

How would you perform the following calculation?

$$(36 \times 57) + (36 \times 43)$$

Most likely, you would multiply 36×57, getting 2052, and then multiply 36×43, getting 1548. So you would have

$$(36 \times 57) + (36 \times 43)$$
$$= 2052 \ + 1548$$
$$= 3600$$

This calculation takes some time. It can be done more easily if you know the distributive law of multiplication over addition. Notice that 36 appears in both multiplications. We can "factor out" the 36 (put the 36 outside in front of the parentheses), getting $36(57 + 43)$. We can now add $57 + 43$, getting 100. Thus we have

$$(36 \times 57) + (36 \times 43)$$
$$= 36(57 + 43) \qquad \text{We factor the 36.}$$
$$= 36(100)$$
$$= 3600$$

Formally stated, we have the following law.

distributive law of multiplication over addition

> **Distributive Law of Multiplication over Addition**   If a, b, and c are natural numbers, then $a(b + c) = ab + ac$. Also $(b + c)a = ba + ca$.

Comment   This law says that whether we add $b + c$ first and then multiply by a or multiply by a first and then add, our result is the same.

EXAMPLE 2

SOLUTION

a) Multiply $(63 \times 51) + (63 \times 49)$, using the distributive law.

$$(63 \times 51) + (63 \times 49)$$
$$= 63(51 + 49) \qquad \text{We factor the 63.}$$
$$= 63(100)$$
$$= 6300$$

b) Multiply 80×23, using the distributive law.

SOLUTION

$$80 \times 23$$
$$= 80(23)$$
$$= 80(20 + 3)$$
$$= (80 \times 20) + (80 \times 3) \qquad \text{This is where we use the distributive law.}$$
$$= 1600 + 240$$
$$= 1840$$

Subtraction

Up to now we have mentioned subtraction without considering precisely what it means. If you spend \$3 in a store and give the salesclerk a \$10 bill, you will usually get your change as follows: The clerk says "three" and then, handing you the money, counts out the change, "four, five, six, seven, eight, nine, ten dollars." The clerk has to subtract 3 from 10 and does this by starting with 3. The clerk then figures how much change must be added to 3 to make 10. Thus the subtraction

$$10 - 3 = \text{change}$$

becomes

$$3 + \text{change} = 10$$

subtraction

In other words, the change is the amount that must be added to 3 to make 10. This procedure shows us what **subtraction** really is.

> **Definition 3.3** If a and b are natural numbers, then $a - b$ (read as "a minus b") means the number that must be added to b to obtain a (if such a number exists). If we call this number x, we have $a - b = x$, if $b + x = a$.

EXAMPLE 3

a) $4 - 1$ means some number x that must be added to 1 to make 4. Thus $1 + x = 4$. Therefore, $x = 3$. Then we have $4 - 1 = 3$.

b) $17 - 6$ means the number x that must be added to 6 to make 17. Thus $6 + x = 17$. And $x = 11$. So $17 - 6 = 11$.

Comment Subtraction is also a **binary operation**, since it involves *two* numbers, the number that we are subtracting and the number from which we are subtracting.

We have already pointed out that subtraction of natural numbers is *not* closed, commutative, or associative. The following examples should emphasize these facts.

EXAMPLE 4

a) $5 - 3 = 2$. However, $3 - 5$ is *not* equal to 2; $3 - 5$ equals a *negative* number, -2, which we will discuss further in the next chapter. Thus

$$5 - 3 \quad \text{is } not \text{ equal to} \quad 3 - 5$$

which shows that the operation of subtraction is *not* commutative.

b) In the above example we saw that $3 - 5 = -2$, which is *not* a natural number. Thus subtraction of natural numbers is *not closed*. (This means that when you subtract one natural number from another, the result is not always a natural number.)

c) $9 - (6 - 4) \quad$ equals
$9 - 2 \quad$ (remember, do what is in parentheses first)

which equals

7

On the other hand,

$(9 - 6) - 4 \quad$ equals
$3 - 4 \quad$ which equals
-1

Therefore $9 - (6 - 4)$ is *not* equal to $(9 - 6) - 4$, so subtraction of natural numbers is *not* an associative operation. ▪

Division

The final binary operation that we will consider is **division**. If you were asked to divide 6 by 2, you would immediately give the answer 3. How do you get this answer? Undoubtedly you would ask yourself, "What number multiplied by 2 will give 6?" With this in mind, we define division in general as follows.

> **Definition 3.4** If a and b are natural numbers, then $a \div b$, also denoted as $\dfrac{a}{b}$ (read as "a divided by b"), means the natural number x, such that $b \cdot x = a$.

EXAMPLE 5

a) $39 \div 13$ means a natural number x such that $13 \cdot x = 39$. Thus $x = 3$. We have, then, $39 \div 13 = 3$.

b) $24 \div 6$ means a natural number x, such that $6 \cdot x = 24$. Thus $x = 4$. Therefore $24 \div 6 = 4$.

c) $\frac{100}{20}$ means a natural number x, such that $20 \cdot x = 100$. Thus $x = 5$. Therefore, $\frac{100}{20} = 5$. ▪

It can easily be seen that division of natural numbers is not closed, commutative, or associative. This is illustrated by the following examples.

EXAMPLE 6

a) $3 \div 6$ equals $\frac{1}{2}$. This is not a natural number. Thus we see that when we divide one natural number by another, the result is *not* always a natural number. This shows that division of natural numbers is not closed.

b) We know that $6 \div 3 = 2$. However, $3 \div 6$ is not equal to 2. Thus $6 \div 3$ is *not* equal to $3 \div 6$, which shows that division is *not* commutative.

c) $24 \div (6 \div 2)$ equals
      $24 \div 3$ which equals
        8

However,

$$(24 \div 6) \div 2 \quad \text{equals}$$
$$4 \div 2 \quad \text{which equals}$$
$$2$$

Thus we see that $24 \div (6 \div 2)$ is *not* equal to $(24 \div 6) \div 2$, which shows that division is *not* associative.

Comment We have seen that subtraction and division are not associative operations. Therefore when we subtract or divide more than two numbers, we *must* insert parentheses to show which numbers are to be subtracted or divided first. For example, we must not write $24 \div 6 \div 2$, since (as we saw in part (c) of Example 6) this can have two different answers, depending on where the parentheses are inserted.

The Whole Numbers

If ever a number was misunderstood, then zero is it. Ask any five people (nonmathematicians, of course) what zero means to them. When we did this, some of the responses we got were the following.

1. Zero is nothing.

2. Zero is not just plain nothing; it is a something nothing.

3. Zero is not a number at all.

4. Zero is the absence of anything.

5. Zero is the null set.

6. Zero is either the beginning or end of something.

Despite beliefs to the contrary, zero is a number just like any other number. However, it has certain properties that other numbers do not have. Let us discuss some of these properties.

One source of confusion is the fact that zero plays different roles in different situations. In the number 405, zero acts as a "place holder." If you say sadly, "My bank balance is zero," then zero is used as a quantity indicating that there is nothing left.

Zero probably appeared first as a place holder. The Babylonians, who used a base 60 number system, at first had no symbol to represent empty places. Later in their history, they used the symbol **⌐** as a place holder. This is probably the first appearance of any symbol for zero. The Mayans also had invented zero symbols. Some of these were

Later, the Greeks invented their own symbol for zero and developed the *concept* of zero to represent nothingness.

Earlier civilizations do not appear to have used zero as a *number*. Later, the Hindus developed the concept of and a symbol for zero. Present evidence indicates that zero was used in India from the ninth century on and possibly earlier. The Hindus appear to have used zero not merely as a place holder or as a concept for nothing, but also as a *number*. India was invaded by the Arabs around 700 A.D. The Arabs later introduced the Hindu numerals to Europe. In the Western world, zero was not completely accepted and used as a number until much later, probably around the sixteenth century.

Let us investigate the role of zero as a number. We first have the following definition.

whole number

> **Definition 3.5**   The **whole numbers** are the natural numbers together with the number 0. Using set notation, this would be {0, 1, 2, 3, 4, . . .}.

Comment   The only difference between the set of natural numbers and the set of whole numbers is the number 0.

What can we say about 0? Perhaps the most important property that zero has is that when zero is added to any number, it does not do anything to that number. For example,

$$5 + 0 = 5,$$
$$0 + 4 = 4,$$
$$117 + 0 = 117, \quad \text{and}$$
$$0 + 0 = 0$$

In general, if a is any number, then $a + 0 = a$ and $0 + a = a$.

identity

A "do nothing" number of this type is called an **identity**. Thus *zero is the identity for addition*. Would you say that zero is the "do-nothing" number for multiplication? Obviously not. Consider $5 \cdot 0$. This means

$$\underbrace{0 + 0 + 0 + 0 + 0}_{5 \text{ of them}}$$

Thus, we have $5 \cdot 0 = 0$. Generally, if a is *any* number, then $a \cdot 0 = 0$ and $0 \cdot a = 0$.

division involving zero

How about division? What can we say about division that involves zero? Very often, division by zero and division into zero are confused. To help us understand the difference, suppose your Uncle Sam dies and leaves a will dividing his money equally among 20 people. Upon investigation it is found that his entire fortune is in Confederate money and is therefore worthless. So there is really nothing to divide. How much money do these 20 people get? Obviously, nothing. Thus

$$\frac{0}{20} = 0$$

To look at it another way, let us say that 0 divided by 20 is "something." So

$$\frac{0}{20} = \text{something}$$

Now what could this something be? Remember what division means.

$$\frac{0}{20} = \text{something}$$

means

$$0 = 20 \cdot \text{something}$$

If the something is 1, then $0 = 20 \cdot 1$, which is obviously wrong. If the something is 2, the $0 = 20 \cdot 2$, which is again wrong. If the something is 3, then $0 = 20 \cdot 3$, which is clearly wrong. Obviously, if the something is anything other than 0, the statement

$$0 = 20 \cdot \text{something}$$

cannot be true. We conclude that the something must be zero.

In other words, we can say that if x is any nonzero number, then x divided into 0 is 0, that is,

$$\frac{0}{x} = 0$$

On the other hand, what would we mean by $\frac{20}{0}$? In a mathematics class recently, students were asked this question. Various answers were given.

Some said that the answer was zero. Others believed that the answer was 20. Still others claimed that the answer was 1. Some even thought that the answer was "infinity."

To see who is right, let us check each of the suggested answers. If we claim that $\frac{6}{3} = 2$, then we can easily check this answer, since $6 = 3 \cdot 2$, so $\frac{6}{3} = 2$ is true.

For those who claimed that $\frac{20}{0} = 0$, is it true that

$$20 = 0 \cdot 0?$$

Obviously not, since we know that 0 times anything is 0 and not 20.

For those who claimed that $\frac{20}{0} = 20$, again this doesn't work, since it must follow that $20 = 0 \cdot 20$. But $0 \cdot 20$ is not 20.

What about those who thought that $\frac{20}{0} = 1$? Were they right? Again no, since 20 is not equal to $0 \cdot 1$.

For those who believed the answer to be infinity, we point out here only that the answer to a division problem (if an answer exists) must be a specific number. "Infinity" (usually denoted by ∞) is *not* a number.[2]

In fact, *it is not possible to divide by 0 at all.* Why? Suppose it were possible. There are two cases:

Case 1. A nonzero number divided by 0.
Case 2. Zero divided by 0.

For case 1, just to be specific, let the nonzero number be 20. Then as we have seen earlier, this is not possible. It would be the same had we used any other nonzero number besides 20. Try it to convince yourself.

For case 2, suppose 0 divided by 0 equals something. Thus

$$\frac{0}{0} = \text{something} .$$

This means $0 = 0 \cdot$ "something" (from our definition of division). What could this something be? Any number will do. For example, $0 = 0 \cdot 5$, or $0 \cdot 17$, or $0 = 0 \cdot 141$. Thus the something is not specific. The answer to a division problem *must* be a specific number.

Teachers often encounter students who confuse divisions involving 0. In the accompanying page from *Addison-Wesley Mathematics*, 1987, Grade 3, p. 260 (see next page), the difference between division by 0 and division into 0 is introduced at an early stage of learning arithmetic. It is explained in terms of a familiar example so as to avoid confusion.

---

[2] For those who want to know more about ∞, we suggest that you consult any elementary calculus text or your teacher. The discussion of this symbol is beyond the scope of this book.

More about Division

Kirk planned to give all the fish he caught to 2 friends. But Kirk did not catch any fish. How many fish did his friends get?

Joni caught 6 fish. She gave 0 fish to each of her friends. How many friends could she give 0 fish to?

THINK
? × 2 = 0

THINK
? × 0 = 6

0 ÷ 2 = 0

6 ÷ 0 = ___

His friends got 0 fish.

This does not make sense!

Zero divided by any number (not 0) is zero.

Never divide by zero.

Summarizing

We can summarize division involving 0 as follows.

1. Division into 0 always gives 0 (assuming we are not dividing by 0).

2. Division by zero is not possible.

It is interesting to find that the question of dividing by zero was actually considered by Aristotle more than 2000 years ago. He concluded that division by zero was impossible. This is surprising because it is so much like the modern approach to the problem. Division by zero was also considered by the Indian mathematician Bhaskara. He believed that when you divided by zero the result was an "unchangeable infinity" that was almost religious in nature. In fact, he compared this infinity with the unchanging nature of God.

It is important to understand the concept of divisions involving 0. To further understand the idea, do the following: Using any hand-held calculator try dividing 0 by 20 or by any other nonzero number. Your answer will always be 0. Now try dividing any number (possibly even zero) by 0. The display panel will indicate some error message such as Error, an E, a blinking 0, etc.

In the next chapter we will have more to say about zero and its properties.

EXERCISES FOR SECTION 3.6

1. In each of the following, state the property for natural numbers that justifies the computation being performed:

   a) $12 + 8 = 8 + 12$ *Communitive of Add.*

   b) $(6 \cdot 5)8 = 6(5 \cdot 8)$

   c) $5(8 + 12) = 5 \cdot 8 + 5 \cdot 12$ *Asso.*

   d) $9 + 8$ is a natural number

   e) $5 + (3 + 9) = (5 + 3) + 9$ *Asso*

   f) $5 + (3 + 9) = 5 + (9 + 3)$

   g) $6 \times 9 = 9 \times 6$ *comm. of Mult.*

   h) $5(9 \cdot 8) = (5 \cdot 9)8$

   i) $(7 + 8)2 = 7 \cdot 2 + 8 \cdot 2$ *Asso*

   j) $7 \cdot 6 = 42$

2. Perform the following calculations by using the distributive law.   *16(91+9)*

   a) $17 \times 102 = 1734$ **b)** $(16 \times 91) + (16 \times 9)$

   c) 103×38 **d)** $(76 \times 21) + (24 \times 21)$

   21(76+24)

3. Determine whether each of the given set of numbers is closed under the indicated operation.

Numbers	Operation
a) {2, 4, 6}	addition
b) {0}	multiplication
c) {even numbers}	multiplication
d) {odd numbers}	multiplication
e) {5, 10, 15, ...}	addition
f) {natural numbers less than 17}	multiplication
g) {0, 1}	multiplication

4. Which of the activities given below are commutative and which are not?

   a) Taking a picture with a camera and putting film in the camera.

   b) Applying for admission to college and taking the Scholastic Aptitude Test (SAT).

   c) Getting on a plane and paying the fare.

   d) Tuning up your car and rotating the tires.

   e) Drinking alcohol and driving a car.

   f) Learning computer programming and buying a computer.

   g) Getting undressed and taking a shower.

5. Consider an operation that we shall call | given by the following table:

$(x|y)|z = x|(y|z)$

$y|z = x|z$

$z = z$

x	x	y	z
x	x	y	z
y	y	y	z
z	z	z	z

$\bigcirc$ $2|x = 2$
$\square$ $y|z = 2$
$\triangle$ $x|y = y$

   a) Is | a closed operation?   *Yes*

   b) Is | a commutative operation?   *Yes*

   c) Is | an associative operation?   *Yes*

6. Consider an operation that we shall call ↑ given by the following table:

↑	x	y	z
x	x	z	z
y	y	x	z
z	z	z	x

Row → entry   *Table entry*

   a) Is ↑ a closed operation?   *Yes*

   b) Is ↑ a commutative operation?

   c) Is ↑ an associative operation?

\$19(6) + \$19(17)
\$19(6+17)
\$19(23) \$367

7. Explain how the distributive law can be applied in the following situation: Willy Martin is the manager of a Little League baseball team. Baseball gloves for a player on the team cost $19 apiece. On Wednesday, Willy orders 6 gloves, and on Thursday he orders 17 gloves. What is the total cost for all the gloves?

8. An operation called # is given by the rule

$$a \# b = a + b + 2$$

In other words, $a \# b$ is obtained by first adding a and b and then adding 2 to the results. For example, if a and b are 5 and 7, respectively, then

$$a \# b = 5 + 7 + 2 = 14$$

If a and b are 9 and 12 respectively, then

$$a \# b = 9 + 12 + 2 = 23$$

9-13

HISTORICAL NOTE

The four operations of addition, multiplication, subtraction, and division make up what is today called **arithmetic**. It is an important part of present-day elementary and secondary school education. The earliest recorded handbook of arithmetic is the papyrus of Ahmes, an Egyptian scribe of about the seventeenth century B.C. Ahmes copied his work from earlier records believed to date back to about 3000 B.C. Ahmes's papyrus entitled

"Directions for Obtaining the Knowledge of All Dark Things" indicates that the Egyptians had knowledge of the basic arithmetic operations.

Little or no arithmetic was taught in the Middle Ages. The first printed arithmetic was published in Treviso, Italy, in 1478. The first arithmetic textbook to originate in America (in 1729) was written by Isaac Greenwood, a professor of mathematics at Harvard College.

---

a) Is the operation # commutative?

b) Is the operation # associative?

9. The distributive law can be generalized as follows:

$$a(b + c + d + \ldots) = ab + ac + ad + \ldots$$

Use the generalized distributive law to evaluate each of the following computations.

a) $(19 \times 62) + (19 \times 12) + (19 \times 26)$ $19(62+12+26)$

b) $(42 \times 93) + (27 \times 93) + (31 \times 93)$ $93(42+27+31)$

c) 9×126

10. Recall that when we discussed sets in Chapter 2, we had several operations involving two sets. Specifically, these were $\cup$, $\cap$, and $\times$. Although we did not state it at the time, these are, of course, binary operations.

a) Which of these operations are commutative?

b) Which of these operations are closed?

c) Which of these operations are associative?

11. Is there an identity for multiplication? If yes, what is it? If no, why not? Yes, 1

12. Is zero the identity for subtraction? No

13. Is one the identity for division? Explain your answer. No

14. On p. 146 we showed that if a is any number, then $a \cdot 0 = 0$. We also stated that $0 \cdot a = 0$ without justifying it. Explain why $0 \cdot a = 0$.

15. Explain how the number 0 is used in our decimal system.

16. Suppose we define a new operation $\circ$ on the set of whole numbers as follows:

$$a \circ b = 0 \text{ if either } a \text{ or } b \text{ or both are odd}$$

$$a \circ b = 1 \text{ if } a \text{ and } b \text{ are both even}$$

where a and b are any whole numbers.

a) Is $\circ$ a commutative operation?

b) Is $\circ$ an associative operation?

PROBLEM-SOLVING EXERCISES

17. A **magic triangle** is an arrangement of natural numbers in the form of a triangle where the sum of the numbers on each of the sides (called the **magic sum**) is always the same. The amount of numbers on each side is called the **order**. For example,

represents a magic triangle whose order is 3 and whose magic sum is 11. Find a magic triangle of order 3 whose magic sum is 23.

18. The Pythagoreans investigated a special group of natural numbers known as **triangular numbers**. The numbers that have geometric forms that look like triangles are called triangular numbers. The first few triangular numbers are 1, 3, 6, 10, and 15, as can be seen from the diagram below:

Natural number   1   3   6   10   15

Determine the next three triangular numbers.

Brain-Teaser Problems

**19. What is wrong with the following?
Given: $a = b$ Multiply both sides by b:

$$ab = b^2$$

Subtract a^2 from both sides:

$$ab - a^2 = b^2 - a^2$$

Factor $ab - a^2$ as $a(b - a)$.
Factor $b^2 - a^2$ as $(b + a)(b - a)$, so that

$$a(b - a) = (b + a)(b - a)$$

Divide both sides by $b - a$:

$$\frac{a(b - a)}{b - a} = \frac{(b + a)(b - a)}{b - a}$$

We then have $a = b + a$.
Since we know $a = b$, we then have $a = a + a$ or that $a = 2a$.
Divide both sides by a, and we have

$$\frac{a}{a} = \frac{2a}{a}$$

or that $1 = 2$.

**20. What is wrong with the following?
Let a be any number but 1.
Also let $a = b$.
Add 1 to both sides:

$$a + 1 = b + 1$$

Multiply both sides by $a - 1$ so that

$$(a + 1)(a - 1) = (b + 1)(a - 1).$$

Simplifying, this gives

$$a^2 - 1 = ab - b + a - 1$$

Adding $+1$ to both sides and simplifying, we get

$$a^2 = ab - b + a$$

This can be further simplified by subtracting ab from both sides. We get

$$a^2 - ab = a - b$$

Factoring, we have

$$a(a - b) = a - b$$

Divide both sides by $a - b$. We get $a = 1$.
This contradicts the assumption that a was any number but 1.

3.7

ALGORITHMS FOR WHOLE-NUMBER ADDITION, SUBTRACTION, MULTIPLICATION, AND DIVISION

algorithm

An **algorithm** is a step-by-step procedure that can be used to accomplish a mathematical operation. For prospective mathematics teachers it is important to be familiar with several algorithms for performing the various operations. In this section we present some algorithms which might appeal to different students.

Algorithms for Addition

The use of concrete teaching aids is always invaluable. Thus the concept of "regrouping" or "carrying" in which students trade by regrouping, as discussed in Section 3.2, is easily illustrated in terms of base-ten blocks. This leads to the regrouping schemes discussed on p. 110 where a number can be represented in as few blocks as possible. Thus 64, for example, can be represented as 6 groups of ten each and 4 groups of ones, or 64 =

scratch addition

6 (tens) + 4 (ones). This concept of trading can be used to form an algorithm for whole-number addition. See the examples on p. 110.

Another algorithm for addition, called **scratch addition**, is illustrated in the following examples.

EXAMPLE 1

Add   59
      47
      25
      ──

SOLUTION

Step 1. Starting at the top and moving down we add the numbers in the units column. When a sum of 10 or more is obtained, scratch a line through the last number and write the number of units next to the scratched number. In our example, $9 + 7 = 16$ so we scratch the 7 and write a 6 next to the scratched number as shown below.

$$
\begin{array}{l}
59 \\
4\not{7}_6 \\
25 \\
\hline
\end{array}
$$

Step 2. Now we continue adding the units. Each time we get a sum which is 10 or more, we repeat (as often as needed) the process described in Step 1. In our case, we have

$$
\begin{array}{l}
59 \\
4\not{7}_6 \\
2\not{5}_1 \\
\hline
\end{array}
$$

Step 3. When we complete all the additions in the units column, we write down the number of units below the addition line. We then count up the number of scratches and add that number to the next column. In our case, we had 2 scratches, so we add the 2 to the next column as shown.

$$
\begin{array}{l}
{}^{2}\\
59 \\
4\not{7}_6 \\
2\not{5}_1 \\
\hline
1
\end{array}
$$

Step 4. Repeat the same procedure for each column (moving from right to left). In our case, we get

$$
\begin{array}{l}
{}^{2}\\
5\,9 \\
4_1\not{7}_6 \\
2\,\not{5}_1 \\
\hline
1\,3\,1
\end{array}
$$

EXAMPLE 2

Compute the following additions using the scratch method.

a)   426
    384
  + 503
  ‾‾‾‾‾
   1313

b)   1234
    5678
    9014
  + 3982
  ‾‾‾‾‾

SOLUTION

a)   1 1
    4 2 6
    3 8 4 0
    5 0 3
  ‾‾‾‾‾‾
    1 3 1 3

b)   1 2 1
    1 2 3 4
    5 6 7 8 2
    9 0 1 4
    3 9 8 2
  ‾‾‾‾‾‾‾
    1 9 9 0 8

Algorithms for Subtraction

As with addition, subtraction can be explained in terms of base-ten blocks and the idea of "trading." See the discussion on p. 110. Subtraction can also be defined a bit more formally, as was done in Definition 3.3. Thus $a - b = c$ is true if and only if $a = b + c$, that is, subtraction is defined in terms of addition. Another algorithm for subtraction involves **complements**.

complements

The **complement** of a digit x is $9 - x$. Thus the complement of 5 is 4. The complement of 7 is 2. The complement of 0 is 9. The method of subtraction by complements involves finding the complement of each digit in the subtrahend. The resulting numerals are then added to the minuend. The answer to the original subtraction problem is now found by deducting 1 from the left digit and adding 1 to the right digit. To illustrate, let us subtract 4356 from 8967. We have

      8967   Minuend
    − 4356   Subtrahend
    ‾‾‾‾‾‾

The complement of the digits in the subtrahend is

     9   9   9   9
   − 4   − 3   − 5   − 6
   ‾‾‾   ‾‾‾   ‾‾‾   ‾‾‾
     5   6   4   3

or 5643. This number is now added to 8967, yielding

      8967
    + 5643
    ‾‾‾‾‾‾
     14610

Subtracting 1 from the extreme left digit and adding 1 to the extreme right digit gives

$$\begin{array}{r} 14610 \\ -1 \quad +1 \\ \hline 4611 \end{array}$$

Thus our answer to the original subtraction problem is

$$\begin{array}{r} 8967 \\ -4356 \\ \hline 4611 \end{array} \quad \text{or} \quad 4611.$$

(You should verify that 4611 is indeed the answer.)

Algorithms for Multiplication

Multiplying two single digits is easy to understand. See the discussion on p. 139. After the single-digit multiplication facts are learned, then we can proceed to computations with two-digit factors. The distributive property of multiplication over addition is essential for an understanding of how this is done. See the discussion on p. 141. Other algorithms for multiplication are as follows:

Egyptian Duplation

The Egyptians multiplied by a process we call **duplation**. This method of multiplication is based on the fact that any number can be expressed as the sum of powers of 2. Thus 19 can be expressed as $19 = 1 + 2 + 16$. The product of two numbers is obtained by multiplying any one number by the different powers of 2 needed to get the other number. The partial products are added to obtain our answer. For example, let us multiply 19 by 58. We know that $19 = 1 + 2 + 16$, so we set up the following chart:

Powers of 2	×	Original Number	=	Product
①	×	58	=	㊳
②	×	58	=	⑯⑯
4	×	58	=	232
8	×	58	=	464
⑯	×	58	=	⑨㉘
19				1102

Adding the circled numbers gives 19 on the left side and 1102 on the right. Using the Egyptian numerals given in Section 3.1, we can multiply 19×7 as follows:

Powers of 2 × Original Number = Product

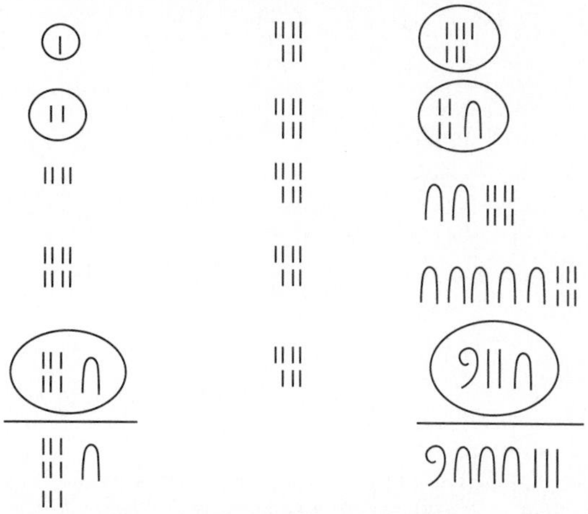

Russian Peasant Method

An unusual way of doing multiplication, which was used by the ancient Egyptians and until recently by the Russian peasants, is known as the **Russian peasant method**. To use it, you need only know how to multiply and divide by 2. We illustrate the technique by multiplying 67×18. This is shown in Fig. 3.6.

67	18
33	36
16	~~72~~
8	~~144~~
4	~~288~~
2	~~576~~
1	1152
	1206

Figure 3.6

What we did is the following. In the left column of the figure we divide 67 by 2, *disregarding the remainder*. This gives 33. Then we divide 33 by 2, disregarding the remainder. This gives 16. We repeat the same procedure until we get 1 on the left. On the right, we double 18 and get 36. Then we double 36 and get 72, etc.

Finally, we cross off the numbers on the right that are opposite *even* numbers on the left. We add what remains in the right column. The sum, 1206, is our answer. Check the answer by using ordinary multiplication.

The magazine clipping on page 156 indicates that there is more than one way of performing the four basic operations (some of these are either already in use or are constantly being tried). How do these approaches differ from our familiar way of performing calculations in the decimal system? Are these other approaches more efficient? Do these alternative approaches instill in youngsters a real sense of the *meaning* of numbers?

Chisanbop to Replace the Pocket Calculator

NEW YORK—In a day and age when schoolchildren are performing various calculations using pocket calculators instead of their brains, it is a pleasure to report on a new method of performing the four basic mathematical functions rather proficiently. The method is known as **Chisanbop** and was invented 20 years ago by Sung Jin Pai, an expert Korean mathematician. In this "finger calculation" method, which is based on our familiar decimal system, children can do any form of addition, multiplication, division, or subtraction. The fingers on the hand replace the calculator. The functions of accumulating data and computing answers are done by the fingers and not the mind. To accomplish this, the fingers are assigned different values as shown in the figure at right. The method is currently being tested in several schools in New York City.

TRENDS IN EDUCATION, March 27, 1980

The ten fingers are marked with the values that are assigned to them in the Chisanbop system.

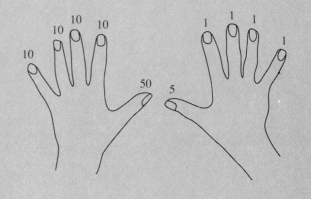

Finger Multiplication

Pick a number from 1 to 9. You can multiply it by 9 using **finger multiplication** (see Fig. 3.7). Suppose you are multiplying 4 by 9. Hold up your hands.

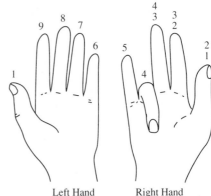

Figure 3.7

Left Hand Right Hand

Count off, in succession, 9 fingers and then 4 fingers (after you get to the tenth finger start again) going from right to left. When you finish counting, bend down the next finger.

You can now read off your answer. The first digit is the number of fingers to the right of the bent finger. This is 3. The second digit is the number of fingers to the left of the bent finger. This is 6. Our answer then is 36.

Comment This finger multiplication method works only when multiplying by 9. Can you explain why?

Galley or Gelosia Multiplication

Another way of doing multiplication is by the so-called **Gelosia method**. It works as follows: Suppose we want to multiply the two numbers, 257 and 49. We set it up as shown:

First we multiply 7 by 4. This gives 28, which is placed as shown below:

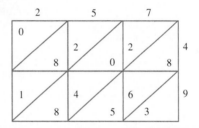

Then we multiply 9 by 7. This gives 63. We put this in as shown (second line, right column). Now we multiply 5 by 4. This gives 20, which we write in (first line, middle column). We complete the diagram in this manner. Note that 2 times 4 is entered as 08 (first line, left column). Now we add along the diagonals starting from the lower right corner, carrying where necessary. This gives the following:

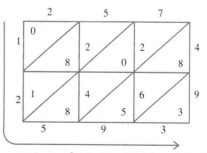

The first diagonal contains only 3. So 3 is its sum. The next diagonal contains 5, 6, and 8, which add to 19. We put the 9 down and carry the 1. The next diagonal contains 8, 4, 0, 2, and the 1 we carried. These add to 15, so we put down 5 and carry the 1. We continue, in a similar manner, until finished. Our answer is then read off as 12,593.

You can check the answer to the above problem by using regular multiplication.

Napier's Bones

The English mathematician John Napier (1550–1617) used the Gelosia system of multiplication to construct what we would today call a computing machine. His gadget is referred to as **Napier's rods** or **Napier's bones** (see Fig. 3.8). We can construct a variation of Napier's bones using 10 popsicle sticks and numbering them as shown in Fig. 3.9. The first stick is called the index and lists all the digits from 1 through 9.

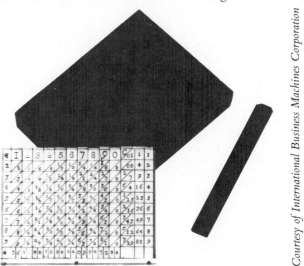

Courtesy of International Business Machines Corporation

Figure 3.8 Napier's bones

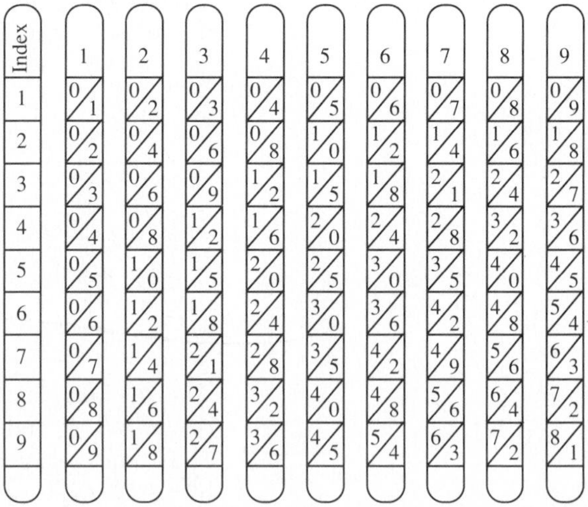

Figure 3.9

Index	4	3	5
1	0/4	0/3	0/5
2	0/8	0/6	1/0
3	1/2	0/9	1/5
4	1/6	1/2	2/0
5	2/0	1/5	2/5
6	2/4	1/8	3/0
7	2/8	2/1	3/5
8	3/2	2/4	4/0
9	3/6	2/7	4/5

Figure 3.10

On top of each of the other sticks we write one of the digits 1 through 9. Each stick gives the product of an index number with the number on the stick. The ones and tens of each product are separated by a diagonal line as in Gelosia multiplication. The different products are separated by horizontal lines.

To see how we can use these sticks to multiply two numbers, let us multiply 435 × 8. We place the index alongside the sticks headed by the digits 4, 3, and 5 as shown in Fig 3.10. Next we locate the row of numbers that are on the same line as 8 on the index:

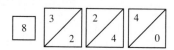

Finally, we add along the diagonals as we do in Gelosia multiplication:

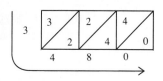

Our answer is 3480. Thus 435 × 8 = 3480.

Using a similar procedure, we find that the product of 435 and 9 is 3915.

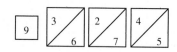

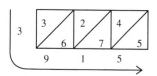

Thus 435 × 9 = 3915.

We can combine the two previous results to obtain the product 435 × 89. We have

$$
\begin{array}{r}
435 \\
\times\ 89 \\
\hline
\end{array}
\qquad
\begin{array}{l}
9 \times 435 = 3{,}915 \\
80 \times 435 = 34{,}800 \\
\hline
89 \times 435 = 38{,}715
\end{array}
$$

Thus 435 × 89 = 38,715.

Algorithm for Division

One popular algorithm for division involves using **repeated subtraction**. To illustrate the procedure, consider the following. *A farmer has 1452 eggs which have to be packaged in cartons that hold 12 eggs each. How many cartons are needed?*

We might reason that since one carton holds 12 eggs, then 10 cartons will hold 120 eggs and 100 cartons will hold 1200 eggs. Thus if 100 cartons are filled there will be

$1452 - 100 \cdot 12$, or 252 eggs remaining. If 10 more cartons are filled, then there will be

$252 - 10 \cdot 12$ or 132 eggs remaining. If 10 more cartons are filled, then there will be

$132 - 10 \cdot 12$ or 12 eggs remaining. Finally, these remaining 12 eggs will fill one carton, so that

$100 + 10 + 10 + 1$ or 121 cartons are needed. This procedure is summarized below:

a)
```
12 ⟌ 1452
    - 1200     100 cartons
    ──────
      252
    - 120      10 cartons
    ──────
      132
    - 120      10 cartons
    ──────
       12
    -  12       1 carton
    ──────
        0     121 cartons
```

The same division problem can be performed somewhat more efficiently as follows:

b)
```
12 ⟌ 1452
    - 1200     100 cartons
    ──────
      252
    - 240       20 cartons
    ──────
       12
    -  12        1 carton
    ──────
        0      121 cartons
```

In most elementary school texts, the above is written as

$$\left.\begin{array}{r}1\\20\\100\end{array}\right\}121$$

c) $12\overline{\smash)1452}$ or as   **d)** $12\overline{\smash)1452}$
-1200 -12
$\overline{252}$ $\overline{25}$
-240 -24
$\overline{12}$ $\overline{12}$
-12 -12
$\overline{0}$ $\overline{0}$

EXERCISES FOR SECTION 3.7

1. Using the scratch method for addition, find each of the following sums.

a) 427
    3696
    + 223
    ‾‾‾‾‾
    1019

b) 507
    627
    + 849
    ‾‾‾‾‾

c) 21783
    8643
    98795
    + 6325
    ‾‾‾‾‾
    26630

d) 4869
    2837
    7526
    + 1848
    ‾‾‾‾‾

2. Using the method of subtraction by complements, find each of the following differences.

a) 7961
    − 4358
    ‾‾‾‾‾

b) 6901
    − 4653
    ‾‾‾‾‾

Complements

c) 7654
    − 2976
    ‾‾‾‾‾

d) 6900
    − 4276
    ‾‾‾‾‾

2624

e) 623
    − 599
    ‾‾‾‾‾

3. Using the Egyptian system of duplation, multiply each of the following numbers.

a) 35×53 **b)** 18×37 **c)** 46×59

d) ∩||| × ||| ∩∩∩∩
                 |||

e) ∩∩∩∩ ||| × ∩∩∩ |||
     ∩∩∩ ||| ∩∩ |||

4. Using the Russian peasant multiplication technique, multiply the following numbers.

a)   53   **b)**   425
    × 32   × 38

c) 228   **d)**   574
    × 57   × 86

e) 243   **f)**   138
    × 94   × 36

g) 387   **h)**   291
    × 86   × 65

i) 862   **j)**   457
    × 194   × 179

k) 298
    × 791

5. How does the Russian peasant multiplication technique compare with the Egyptian method of duplation?

6. Using finger multiplication, multiply
    a) 7×9 **b)** 5×9 **c)** 8×9 **d)** 6×9

7. Using popsicle sticks, make up a set of Napier rods as described in this section and use them to find the following products.
    a) 53×8 **b)** 65×9 **c)** 374×64
    d) 586×76 **e)** 639×57 **f)** 768×54
    g) 395×563

8. Multiply each of the following numbers by using the Gelosia multiplication technique.

(a) 26
    × 68

(b) 428
    × 54

(c) 495
    × 68

d) 1897
   × 352

(e) 6926
    × 539

f) 9762
   × 536

9. Perform each of the following divisions by using the repeated-subtraction technique.

a) 35029 ÷ 23

b) 13510 ÷ 14

c) 16146 ÷ 26

d) 9414 ÷ 18

e) 18590 ÷ 29

 Brain-Teaser Problems

**10. Can you explain why the method of finger multiplication works?

**11. Can you explain why Gelosia multiplication works?

3.8

LARGE AND SMALL NUMBERS—SCIENTIFIC NOTATION

Very few of us ever need to use extremely large or extremely small numbers in our daily lives, but we often encounter them in news reports. It can be mind boggling just to think of such numbers. For example, the deficit in the U.S. budget is measured in billions of dollars. Just how large is a billion? How long would it take for us to count (starting at 1) to a billion? What is the difference between a billion and a trillion?

Now consider a medical researcher who finds that the size of a certain virus is 0.000000008 millimeters. Just how small is this?

Recall that in the Hindu-Arabic system all numbers are written as powers of 10. Hence the name decimal system. Thus the number 365 really means

$$3(\text{hundreds}) + 6(\text{tens}) + 5(\text{ones}) \quad \text{or}$$
$$= 3 \times 100 \quad + 6 \times 10 \ + 5 \times 1$$
$$= 3 \times 10^2 \quad + 6 \times 10^1 + 5 \times 10^0$$

Here we have used exponents according to the following.

exponents

Definition 3.6 **Exponents** For any nonzero number b and any natural number n,

$$b^n = \underbrace{b \times b \times b \times \cdots \times b}_{n \text{ of them}}$$

$$b^0 = 1 \quad \text{and} \quad b^{-n} = \frac{1}{b^n}$$

The number b is called the **base** and n is called the **exponent**.

---

base

Notation   In base 10 the following alternate forms of various numbers with exponents given in Table 3.1 are true.

TABLE 3.1	
Positive powers of ten	Negative powers of ten
$10^0 = 1$	$10^{-1} = \dfrac{1}{10^1} = 0.1$
$10^1 = 10$	$10^{-2} = \dfrac{1}{10^2} = 0.01$
$10^2 = 10 \times 10 = 100$	$10^{-3} = \dfrac{1}{10^3} = 0.001$
$10^3 = 10 \times 10 \times 10 = 1000$	$10^{-4} = \dfrac{1}{10^4} = 0.0001$
$10^4 = 10,000$	$10^{-5} = \dfrac{1}{10^5} = 0.00001$
$10^5 = 100,000$	$10^{-6} = \dfrac{1}{10^6} = 0.000001$
$10^6 = 1,000,000$	$10^{-7} = \dfrac{1}{10^7} = 0.0000001$
$10^7 = 10,000,000$	$10^{-8} = \dfrac{1}{10^8} = 0.00000001$
$10^8 = 100,000,000$	

Comment   When working with positive exponents (powers of 10), the number of zeros following the 1 in the value of a power of 10 is the same as the exponent of 10. Thus in $10^4 = 10,000$ the exponent is 4, and there are 4 zeros after the 1 in 10,000.

Comment   When working with negative exponents (powers of 10), the number of places to the right of the decimal point is equal to the exponent itself when we disregard the minus sign. Thus in $10^{-6} = 0.000001$ there are 6 places to the right of the decimal point. This is the same as the exponent when we disregard the minus sign.

decimal point

Comment   Often we use a **decimal point** in the decimal system to separate the whole part of a number from the fraction.

EXAMPLE 1

Write 456.789 in expanded notation using exponents.

SOLUTION

The number 456.789 can be written with exponents as

4(hundreds + 5(tens) + 6(ones) + 7(tenths) + 8(hundredths) + 9(thousandths)
$= (4 \times 10^2) + (5 \times 10^1) + (6 \times 10^0) + (7 \times 10^{-1}) + (8 \times 10^{-2}) + (9 \times 10^{-3})$

When working with numbers that are very large or very small, we can express them in a more convenient form called scientific notation.

scientific notation of a number

Definition 3.7 **Scientific Notation of a Number** A number written in *scientific notation* is expressed as a product of two quantities: the first is a number equal to or greater than 1 but less than 10, and the second is a power of 10.

Let us see what this definition really says.

EXAMPLE 2

The population of the United States in 1983 was approximately 225 million. Write this number in scientific notation.

SOLUTION

We first write 225 million as 225,000,000. Now we apply Definition 3.7. We first express 225,000,000 as a product of two numbers where one of the numbers must be between 1 and 10. We have

$$225,000,000 = 2.25 \times 100,000,000$$

Now we express the second number as a power of 10 using Table 3.1 so that

$$225,000,000 = 2.25 \times 10^8$$

EXAMPLE 3

The distance from the earth to the moon is approximately 2.4×10^5 miles. Write this number in ordinary decimal notation.

SOLUTION

Using Table 3.1, we know that $10^5 = 100,000$. Thus we first determine the value of the power of 10. We then multiply the results with the first number. This gives

$$2.4 \times 10^5 = 2.4 \times 100,000$$
$$= 240,000 \text{ miles}$$

Comment In Example 3 we could have obtained our answer quickly by moving the decimal point in 2.4 five places to the right.

EXAMPLE 4

A scientist measured the diameter of a certain cell and found it to be 0.00003 inches. Express this number in scientific notation.

SOLUTION

We first write 0.00003 as a product of two numbers where one of the numbers must be between 1 and 10. We have

$$0.00003 = 3 \times 0.00001$$

Now we express the second number as a power of 10 using Table 3.1 so that

$$0.00003 = 3 \times 10^{-5}$$

◼

EXAMPLE 5

In the metric system, 1 millimeter is equal to 1×10^{-5} km. Rewrite this in ordinary decimal notation.

SOLUTION

We first determine the value of 10^{-5} (using Table 3.1). We have $10^{-5} = 0.00001$. We then multiply this result with the first number. This gives

$$1 \times 10^{-5} = 1 \times 0.00001$$
$$= 0.00001$$

◼

Comment In Example 5 we could have obtained our answer quickly by moving the decimal point in 1 (understood to be at the end of the number) five places to the left.

Comment In a later chapter, when we discuss hand-held calculators, we will indicate how the various operations are performed when numbers are expressed in scientific notation.

EXERCISES FOR SECTION 3.8

1. Rewrite each of the following numbers into expanded notation using exponents.

   a) 78.1   **b)** 316.01   **c)** 412.37

   d) 51.001   **e)** 619.823   **f)** 3472.13

   g) 4609.182   **h)** 3247.193   **i)** 453.0258

2. Write each of the following numbers in scientific notation.

   a) 400   **b)** 7000   **c)** 0.003

   d) 0.0005   **e)** 17,000,000   **f)** 8,000,000

   g) 0.00000078 **h)** 0.0000000879

   i) 7654.32   **j)** 0.44

   k) 0.0006123

In Exercises 3–12, find the number that can replace the question mark so that the resulting statement is true.

3. $0.029 = 2.9 \times 10^{?}$

4. $125 = 1.25 \times 10^{?}$

5. $691,000 = 6.91 \times 10^{?}$

6. $3,810,000 = 3.81 \times 10^{?}$

7. $4290 = 4.29 \times 10^{?}$

8. $0.000000000012 = 1.2 \times 10^?$

9. $0.00001111 = 1.111 \times 10^?$

10. $423.60 = 4.236 \times 10^?$

11. $0.0000000001 = 1.0 \times 10^?$ -10

12. $40,000,000,000 = 4 \times 10^?$

In Exercises 13–22, write the number in ordinary decimal notation.

13. A ton is approximately 9.07×10^2 kilograms.

14. The sun weighs approximately 1.8×10^{27} tons.

15. The velocity of light in a vacuum is approximately 3×10^{10} cm/sec.

16. The distance between the earth and its nearest star (other than the sun), Alpha Centauri, is 2.6×10^{13} miles.

17. The age of the earth's crust is approximately 5×10^9 years.

18. The mass of the earth is 1.32×10^{25} pounds or 5.99×10^{24} kilograms.

19. The diameter of the orbit of an electron of a certain atom is 5.4×10^{-6} millimeters.

20. The distance from the earth to the sun is 9.3×10^7 miles.

21. The total area of the continental United States is 3.022387×10^6 square miles.

22. The volume of a certain neuron is about 4.37×10^{-9} cubic centimeters.

In Exercises 23–32, express the number in each statement in scientific notation.

23. A light year is the distance light travels in a year. A light year is approximately 9,500,000,000,000 kilometers.

24. The diameter of the universe is about 2,000,000,000 light years.

25. The diameter of a red blood corpuscle is 0.00075 centimeters.

26. The diameter of the smallest particle visible to the naked eye is about 0.01016 centimeters.

27. The number of atoms in a gram of hydrogen is about 600,000,000,000,000,000,000,000.

28. The population of the world was approximately 3,600,000,000 in 1984.

29. In one year there are about 31,557,600 seconds.

30. A spaceship travels at the rate of 18,000 miles per hour in space.

31. The planet Uranus is about 2,000,000,000 miles from the sun.

32. The first-stage thrust of a rocket's engine launched into space is about 9,000,000 lb just prior to burnout.

IIII ► **Brain-Teaser Problems** ◄ IIII

**33. A computer has been programmed to print all the counting numbers between 1 and 100,000 inclusive. The numbers will be separated by commas as they are printed by the printer. In executing this task, how many times will the digit zero be printed?

TYPICAL CLASSROOM QUESTIONS

1. In the Roman numeration system, what does the symbol IXC represent, 91 or 89?

2. In Section 3.5 we discussed the strategy of changing a good combination to a bad combination in playing the game of *Nim*. Why does this strategy work?

3. Let us calculate the following:

$$3 + 5 \cdot 6$$
$$3 + 30$$
$$33$$

Now compute

$$3(5 + 6)$$
$$3 \cdot 11$$
$$33$$

Thus $3 + 5 \cdot 6 = 3(5 + 6)$. From this we can conclude that if a, b, and c are natural numbers, then

$$a + bc = a(b + c)?$$

Explain.

4. Is 0 the identity for subtraction?

STUDY GUIDE

The following is a chapter outline in capsule form. You should now be able to demonstrate your knowledge of the ideas mentioned by giving definitions, descriptions, or specific examples. Page references are given in parentheses.

Basic Ideas

1. The **Babylonian numeration system** and its emphasis on **positional notation** where the position of a numeral determines which number is intended. (p. 103)

2. The **Egyptian numeration system** and the **Tamil numeration system** are examples of other numeration systems, one where position is not important and the other where position is important. (p. 104, 106)

3. The **Mayan numeration system** uses dots and dashes stacked vertically. This is an example of a **vertical numeration system**. (p. 106)

4. Zero is often used as a **place-holder**. (p. 109)

5. When adding numbers in any base, we must often "**carry**" numbers. (p. 110)

6. The **base 10**, which is also known as the **decimal** or **Hindu-Arabic system,** is the one that we use today to perform the various calculations. (p. 110)

7. The ability to perform the four basic operations in other number bases, as well as to **convert from base 10 into another base or vice versa**, is very important. (p. 121)

8. Studying different number bases enables one to study the computer and to analyze the game of **Nim** more effectively. (p. 126)

9. When playing the game of Nim, convert the number of matches in each pile into **binary system** numbers. Then add them as if they were in base 10. If the sum has all even digits, then we call it a **bad combination**. (p. 130) Otherwise, it is called a **good combination**. (p. 130)

10. The **natural numbers** or **counting numbers** are the numbers 1, 2, 3, 4, ... (p. 134)

11. The **whole numbers** are the numbers 0, 1, 2, 3, ... (p. 145)

Operations

The four basic operations for whole numbers are addition, subtraction, multiplication, and division.

1. **Addition** Two numbers a and b, known as **addends**, can be combined to obtain a third number $a + b$, called the **sum**. In terms of sets, if $n(A) = a$ and $n(B) = b$ where A and B are disjoint, then $a + b = n(A \cup B)$. (p. 134)
2. **Subtraction** If a and b are any whole numbers, then $a - b$ is the unique whole number c such that $a = b + c$ (if such a number exists). The number a is called the **minuend**, b is the **subtrahend** and c is the **difference**. (p. 142)
3. **Multiplication** If a and b are any whole numbers, then

$$a \cdot b \text{ (also written as } ab, a(b), a \times b \text{ or } (a)(b)) \text{ means}$$
$$a \cdot b = \underbrace{b + b + b + \cdots + b}_{a \text{ of them.}} \quad \text{(p. 139)}$$

4. **Division** If a and b are any whole numbers with $b \neq 0$, then $a \div b$ is the unique whole number c (if such a number exists), such that $a = b \cdot c$ (p. 143)

Rules for Addition and Multiplication of Whole Numbers

1. **Closure property** If a and b are any whole numbers, then $a + b$ is a whole number and also $a \cdot b$ is a whole number. (p. 138, 141)
2. **Commutative law** If a and b are any whole numbers, then $a + b = b + a$ and $a \cdot b = b \cdot a$. (p. 135, 139)
3. **Associative law** If a, b, and c are any whole numbers, then $a + (b + c) = (a + b) + c$ and $a(b \cdot c) = (a \cdot b)c$. (p. 137, 140)
4. **Distributive law of multiplication over addition** If a, b, and c are any whole numbers, then $a(b + c) = ab + ac$ or $(b + c)a = ba + ca$. (p. 141)
5. **Identity** 0 is the unique identity element for addition, and 1 is the unique identity for multiplication as $a + 0 = a = 0 + a$ and $a \cdot 1 = 1 = 1 \cdot a$ for any whole number a. (p. 145)

KEY TERMS

Following is a list of key terms introduced in each section of this chapter.

3.6   natural (counting) numbers
addition
sum
binary operation
commutative law of addition
associative law of addition
closure property for addition
multiplication
commutative law of multiplication
associative law of multiplication
closure property for multiplication
distributive law
subtraction
division
whole numbers

identity
division involving zero

3.7   algorithm
scratch addition
complements
Egyptian duplication
Russian Peasant method
finger multiplication
galley (Gelosia) multiplication
Napier's bones
repeated subtraction

3.8   exponents
base
decimal point
scientific notation

FORMULAS TO REMEMBER

In this chapter, different numeration systems were discussed. You should review the symbols used in each of these systems. In addition, we discussed the following algorithms (step-by-step procedures that can be used to accomplish a mathematical operation).

Technique	Used for
Scratch addition (p. 152)	addition
Complements (p. 153)	subtraction
Egyptian duplation (p. 154)	multiplication
Russian Peasant method (p. 155)	multiplication
Finger multiplication (p. 156)	multiplication
Gelosia multiplication (p. 157)	multiplication
Napier's bones (p. 158)	multiplication
Repeated subtraction (p. 160)	division
Scientific notation (p. 164)	simplifying large or small numbers

Additionally, divisions involving zero are often confused. Remember, division by any natural number into zero is permissible and results in 0 as an answer. On the other hand, division by 0 is not defined.

Exponents For any whole number n and any nonzero number b, we have

$$b^n = \underbrace{b \times b \times b \times \cdots \times b}_{n \text{ of them}}$$

$$b^0 = 1$$

and $$b^{-1} = \frac{1}{b}$$

where b is called the **base** and n is called the **exponent**.

Table 3.1 on p. 163 presents alternate forms of various numbers with exponents.

CHAPTER REVIEW EXERCISES

1. If $42_{(B)} = 26_{(ten)}$ then $B = ?$
   a) 4 b) 6 c) 7 d) 2 e) none of these

2. $\quad 1tee_{(twelve)}$
   $+ \quad te_{(twelve)}$
   _____

   a) $11071_{(twelve)}$ b) $1ett_{(twelve)}$ c) $1teete_{(twelve)}$
   d) $eeete_{(twelve)}$ e) none of these

3. $301_{(ten)} = ?$
   a) $100101101_{(two)}$ b) $101101001_{(two)}$ c) $10101101_{(two)}$
   d) $10010101_{(two)}$ e) none of these

4. The following is part of a Russian peasant multiplication problem. What is the value of the question mark?

   $$\begin{array}{cc} 21 & 17 \\ 10 & 34 \\ 5 & ? \\ 2 & 136 \\ 1 & 272 \end{array}$$

   a) 61 b) 68 c) 21 d) 17 e) none of these

5. Refer to question 4. What is the answer to the multiplication problem?
   a) 357 b) 170 c) 340 d) 289 e) none of these

6. Which of the following is true?
   a) $212_{(six)}$ is greater than $66_{(twelve)}$ b) $212_{(six)}$ is equal to $66_{(twelve)}$
   c) $212_{(six)}$ is less than $66_{(twelve)}$ d) none of these

7. Mary is $25_{(eight)}$ years old, and Christopher is $1012_{(three)}$ years old. By how many years is Christopher older than Mary?
   a) 27 b) 32 c) 21 d) 11 e) none of these

8. Add: $11011_{(two)}$
$\qquad 1011_{(two)}$
$\qquad 1101_{(two)}$

a) $110011_{(two)}$ **b)** $100011_{(two)}$ **c)** $11011_{(two)}$ **d)** $101111_{(two)}$
e) none of these

9. If the number 0.0000173 is written in the form 1.73×10^{n}, what is the value of n?
a) -4 **b)** -5 **c)** -6 **d)** -3 **e)** none of these

10. The following chart illustrates Gelosia multiplication. Which two numbers are being multiplied?
a) 368 and 16   **b)** 368 and 45   **c)** 16 and 560   **d)** 560 and 45
e) none of these

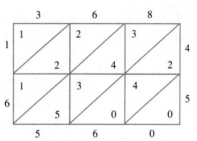

11. Refer to question 10. What is the answer to the multiplication problem?
a) 36845   **b)** 56045   **c)** 16560   **d)** 61368   **e)** none of these

12. In the Egyptian numeration system, what number is represented by
$9 \cap \begin{smallmatrix} | \, | \, | \\ | \, | \, | \end{smallmatrix}$?

a) 116   **b)** 916   **c)** 812   **d)** 423   **e)** none of these

13. Multiply: $te1_{(twelve)}$
$\qquad \times\ e6_{(twelve)}$

14. Subtract: $156_{(nine)}$
$\qquad -\ 78_{(nine)}$

15. Perform the following division: $13232_{(four)} \div 212_{(four)}$.

16. Convert $624_{(seven)}$ to a base 8 number.

17. In what base is the following computation being performed?

$\qquad 123$
$\qquad + 231$
$\qquad \overline{404}$

a) 2   **b)** 3   **c)** 4   **d)** 5   **e)** none of these

18. When playing the game of *Nim*, the combination of 5, 7, 11, and 14 is
   a) a good combination   b) a bad combination
   c) a neutral combination   d) a reverse combination
   e) none of these

19. Write the number 4.23×10^6 in ordinary decimal notation.

20. $518_{(ten)}$ equals what number in base 4?
   a) 20012   b) 21002   c) 1221   d) 10221   e) none of these

21. Write 451.623 in expanded notation using exponents.

22. Write the number 143,000,000,000 in scientific notation.

23. Perform the division $11270_{(twelve)} \div 1t_{(twelve)}$.

24. In what base is the following computation being performed?

$$25_{(B)} = 37$$

25. Perform the following subtraction:

$$\begin{array}{r} 241_{(six)} \\ -\ 42_{(six)} \\ \hline \end{array}$$

26. Convert $56_{(eight)}$ to a base 2 number.

27. Which computation illustrates the associative law of addition?
   a) $4 + (3 + 2) = (4 + 3) + 2$ b) $4 + (3 + 2) = 4 + (2 + 3)$
   c) $4(3 + 2) = 4 \cdot 3 + 4 \cdot 2$ d) $4(3 \cdot 2) = (4 \cdot 3)2$

28. Perform the following calculation by using the distributive law.

$$68 \times 102$$

29. Add by the scratch method:
$$\begin{array}{r} 54 \\ 228 \\ 694 \\ 723 \\ \hline \end{array}$$

30. Subtract by using complements:
$$\begin{array}{r} 2478 \\ -\ 1989 \\ \hline \end{array}$$

SUGGESTED FURTHER READING

Asboe, A.S., *Episodes From the Early History of Mathematics*. New York: Random House, 1964. Chapter 1 discusses the Babylonian number system.

Balin, F., "Finger Multiplication" in *The Arithmetic Teacher* **26** (March 1979) 34–37.

Beard, E., and R. Posis, "Subtraction Facts with Pattern Explorations," in *The Arithmetic Teacher* **29** (December 1981) 6–9.

Bergamini, D., et al., *Life Mathematics* (Life Science Library). New York: Time-Life Books, 1970.

Boyer, Carl, *A History of Mathematics*, New York: Wiley, 1968. This book contains a complete history of mathematics from ancient to modern times.

Boykin, W., "The Russian-Peasant Algorithm: Rediscovered and Extension," in *The Arithmetic Teacher* **20** (January 1973), 29–32.

Colton, B., "Subtraction without Borrowing," in *The Mathematics Teacher* **73** (March 1980), 196.

Computers and Computation (Readings from *Scientific American*) San Francisco: W.H. Freeman, 1971.

Dunkels, A., "More Popsicle-Stick Multiplication," in *The Arithmetic Teacher* **29** (March 1982), 20–21.

Gillings, R.J., *Mathematics in The Time of the Pharaohs*. Cambridge, Mass: MIT Press, 1962.

Kulm, G., "Multiplication and Division Algorithms in German Schools," in *The Arithmetic Teacher* **27** (May 1980), 26–27.

Robold, A., "Grid Arrays for Multiplication" in *The Arithmetic Teacher* **30** (January 1983), 14–17.

Schultz, J., "Using a Calculator to Do Arithmetic in Bases other than Ten," in *The Arithmetic Teacher* **26** (September 1978), 25–27.

Suydam, M., "Improving Multiplication Skills," in *The Arithmetic Teacher* **32** (March 1985), 52.

Young, J., "Uncovering the Algorithms," in *The Arithmetic Teacher* **32** (November 1984), 20.

CHAPTER 4

The Integers

NCTM GUIDELINES

In its March 1989 *Curriculum and Evaluation Standards for School Mathematics* (p. 87), The National Council of Teachers of Mathematics recommends that the mathematics curriculum should include the development of number and number relationships so that students can:

❑ understand, represent, and use numbers in a variety of equivalent forms (integer, fraction, decimal, percent, and scientific notation),

❑ develop number sense for whole numbers, fractions, decimals, integers, and rational numbers,

❑ represent and describe mathematical relationships,

❑ explore the use of variables to express relationships.

The report further asserts that as children work on basic facts, they should be encouraged to look for patterns and relationships. The following sequence of numbers is an excellent example of such an activity:

$$9, 18, 27, 36, 45, 54, 63, 72, 81, 90$$

Children will usually recognize that each number is nine more than the number before it. Each element should also be recognized as a multiple of 9 and represented as $9 \times n$. Replacing n with the numbers from 1 to 10 to generate the original set of numbers validates the symbolic representation of the pattern and reinforces multiplication facts. It also illustrates the concept of a variable. It is for this reason that in this chapter we will first study the integers and then explore the use of variables to represent, express, and solve mathematical relationships.

Introduction

The accompanying newspaper article lists the New York Stock Exchange transactions on the day of the big crash. Negative numbers show the extent of the disaster.

As the newspaper article indicates, negative numbers are very important in our everyday lives. Not only are they used to report losses on the stock market, but they are also used to describe such things as distances above and below sea level, temperatures above and below zero, etc.

Furthermore, if we had only the natural numbers available, then subtraction would not always be possible. For example, using only the

negative integer

natural numbers 7–5 would be possible but 5–7 would not be possible. In order to perform such operations, a new number was invented. This new number was called a **negative integer**.

In this chapter, we will discuss the properties of the integers and the various operations that can be performed with these integers. We will then apply these ideas to solving equations.

4.1

ADDITION, SUBTRACTION, MULTIPLICATION AND DIVISION OF INTEGERS

positive integers

The natural numbers that we introduced in the last chapter are also known as the **positive integers**. They are sometimes written as

$$+1, \ +2, \ +3, \ +4, \ +5, \ldots$$

instead of

$$1, 2, 3, 4, 5, \ldots.$$

Are the positive integers and 0 sufficient for all our everyday needs? Definitely not! To see why, recall that in Section 3.6 we showed that subtraction of natural numbers is not a closed operation. This means that when we subtract one natural number from another natural number, our answer is not always a natural number. For example, 5 – 2 is the natural number 3. On the other hand, 2 – 5 is *not* a natural number. Thus if we had only the natural numbers to work with, we would not always be able to subtract one number from another.

This situation is very inconvenient, and we can remedy it by introducing new numbers, which are called **negative integers**. This can be done as follows: Consider a building that has many floors both above and below street level. (The ones below street level are the basement and subbasements.)

The street level floor is labeled 0 (see Fig. 4.1). Floors above street level will be labeled + 1, + 2, + 3, etc. Floors below street level will be labeled – 1, – 2, – 3, and so on. If you get in on the street level floor and push the + 5 button, you will go 5 floors up; if you push the – 5 floor button, you will go 5 floors in the *opposite* direction, down.

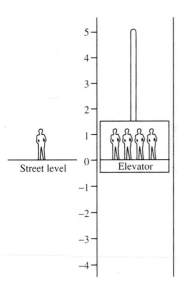

Figure 4.1

> **Definition 4.1** The **negative integers** are the numbers
>
> $$-1, \ -2, \ -3, \ -4, \ -5, \ldots.$$

This leads us to the following definition of integers.

integers

> **Definition 4.2** The set of **integers** consists of the whole numbers and the negative integers, that is, the set of integers is
>
> $$\{\ldots, \ -5, \ -4, \ -3, \ -2, \ -1, \ 0, \ +1, \ +2, \ +3, \ldots\}$$

HISTORICAL NOTE

Negative numbers can be traced back to the ancient Chinese who used red rods for positive numbers and black rods for negative numbers in their computations. At first, many mathematicians were reluctant to use negative numbers. Even respectable mathematicians such as René Descartes and Girolamo Cardano thought of the negative numbers as "false numbers." With the passage of time, however, the advantages of using negative numbers in algebra became evident.

Although negative numbers have become widely accepted and used since around the 17th century, different symbols have been used for them. The dash has not always been used to symbolize a negative number and for the operation of subtraction. Even today, students initially are taught to use a raised minus sign for a negative number (for example, we write minus 5 as $^-5$) rather than the ordinary minus sign which is used for subtraction.

Addition

We already know how to add positive integers (since these are just the natural numbers). How do we add negative numbers?

Let us go back to our elevator (see Fig. 4.2). Renée gets in on the tenth floor. She takes the elevator down two floors, picks up her paycheck there, and then goes down another eight floors to the street floor.

We can represent Renée's trip using negative numbers; (-2) stands for going down two floors. Similarly, (-8) represents going down eight floors. The total descent was (-10). Thus we see that $(-2) + (-8) = (-10)$.

Note that $2 + 8$ is 10, so that

$$-(2 + 8) \text{ is } (-10)$$

Therefore

$$(-2) + (-8) = -(2 + 8)$$

To further illustrate the idea, consider Frances, who works on the twentieth floor. She first takes the elevator down to the seventh floor where she meets her friend Leo. Together they go down to the cafeteria on the fifth floor. Her descent was (-13) and then (-2), or a total of (-15). Another way of saying this is

$$(-13) + (-2) = (-15)$$

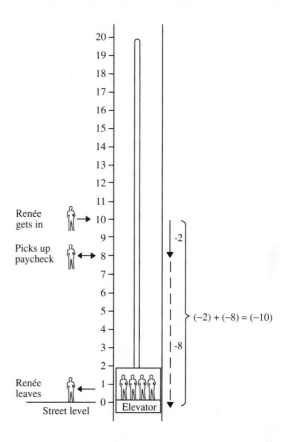

Figure 4.2

Note again that $13 + 2$ equals 15, so that $-(13 + 2)$ equals (-15). This gives

$$(-13) + (-2) = -(13 + 2)$$

This shows us how to add two negative integers.

Rule 4.1   If $(-a)$ and $(-b)$ represent two negative integers, then

$$(-a) + (-b) = -(a + b)$$

How do we add a positive and a negative integer? To answer this, again consider Frances (who works on the twentieth floor). She goes down to visit her friend Leo on the seventh floor. They have an argument, and Frances goes up to the tenth floor to consult her friend Renée. Her trip from the twentieth floor to the seventh floor can be represented by (-13).

Her trip from the seventh floor to the tenth floor can be represented by $(+3)$.

Now Frances starts on the twentieth floor and ends up on the tenth floor. The end result of her trip is (-10). Thus we see that

$$(-13) + (+3) = (-10)$$

While Frances is consulting with Renée, Leo goes looking for her. Since he goes from the seventh floor to the twentieth floor, this trip is $(+13)$. Upon hearing that Frances is with Renée, he goes down to the tenth floor. This trip is (-10). Since he starts from the seventh floor and ends up on the tenth floor, the end result of his trip is $(+3)$. Thus we see that

$$(+13) + (-10) = (+3)$$

We now give a general rule for adding a positive and a negative integer.

Rule 4.2 Consider the numbers without their signs and

　i): Select the larger.
　ii): Subtract the smaller from the larger.
　iii): Put the sign of the larger of step (i) in front of the answer of step (ii).

EXAMPLE 1

a) Add $(+2)$ and (-5).

SOLUTION

The numbers without their signs are 2 and 5.
Step (i): The larger is 5.
Step (ii): $5 - 2 = 3$.
Step (iii): Since the sign of the larger is $-$, our answer is (-3). Thus

$$(+2) + (-5) = (-3)$$

b) Add $(-23) + (+50)$.

SOLUTION

The numbers without their signs are 23 and 50.
Step (i): The larger is 50.
Step (ii): $50 - 23 = 27$.
Step (iii): Since the sign of the larger is $+$, our answer is $(+27)$. Thus

$$(-23) + (+50) = (+27)$$ ■

How much is $(+15)$ and (-15)? If we try to apply the rule, we notice that when we consider the numbers without their signs, neither is larger. What do we do now? To answer this question, we go back to the elevator. Dave gets in, goes up fifteen floors, and then goes down fifteen floors. This is represented by $(+15)+(-15)$. Since he returns to his starting point, the result of his trip is 0. Thus we have

$$(+15)+(-15)=0$$

In general, if b is any number, then $(+b)+(-b)=0$.
We call (-15) the additive inverse of $(+15)$.

additive inverse

> **Definition 4.3**   The **additive inverse** of a number b is the number which when added to b gives 0. This is $(-b)$.

EXAMPLE 2

a) The additive inverse of $(+7)$ is (-7), since $(+7)+(-7)=0$.

b) The additive inverse of (-10) is $(+10)$, since $(-10)+(+10)=0$.

c) We mentioned that (-15) is the additive inverse of $(+15)$. Is $(+15)$ the additive inverse of (-15)?   ▬

Subtraction

What do we mean by $2-5$? We can answer this by going back to our elevator. In this situation, one would normally interpret this to mean "go up 2 floors and then go down 5 floors." You would end up 3 floors below where you started, or (-3). Thus $2-5=(-3)$.

If you look back at Example 1a, you will notice that $(+2)+(-5)$ is also (-3). In other words, $2-5=(+2)+(-5)$.

This suggests the following definition.

a - b
is the
same as
a + (-b)

> **Definition 4.4**   If a and b are any integers, then
>
> $$a-b \quad \text{means} \quad a+(-b)$$
>
> In other words, $a-b$ means "a plus the additive inverse of b."

EXAMPLE 3

a) $4-7$ means $4+(-7)$. Using the rule for addition, we get

$$4+(-7)=(-3)$$

Thus

$$4-7=(-3)$$

b) $5-(-3)$ means $5+(+3)$. (Remember, $+3$ is the additive inverse of -3). Our result is $+8$. Therefore

$$5-(-3)=(+8)$$ ▬

Comment   In the previous example, we have 5 – (– 3). Although there are two minus signs, they have different meanings. The first minus represents subtraction. The second minus represents a negative integer.

Multiplication

Since positive integers are really natural numbers, multiplication of positive integers is exactly the same as multiplication of natural numbers. For example, $(+3)\cdot(+5)$ is the same as $3\cdot5$. Thus we really have $(+5)+(+5)+(+5)$. This sum is obviously $(+15)$.

Similarly, $(+7)\cdot(+4)$ means

$$(+4)+(+4)+(+4)+(+4)+(+4)+(+4)+(+4)$$

which equals $(+28)$.

Now what could we mean by $(+3)\cdot(-5)$? It seems reasonable to interpret this in a similar manner. Thus we say that $(+3)\cdot(-5)$ means

$$\underbrace{(-5)+(-5)+(-5)}$$
$$3 \text{ groups of } (-5)$$

which equals (-15).

Notice that $(+3)\cdot(-5) = -(3\cdot5)$.

Similarly, $(+4)\cdot(-6)$ means

$$\underbrace{(-6)+(-6)+(-6)+(-6)}$$
$$4 \text{ groups of } (-6)$$

which equals (-24).

Again notice that $(+4)\cdot(-6) = -(4\cdot6)$. This we can generalize as:

If $(+a)$ is a positive integer and $(-b)$ is a negative integer, then the product is

$$(+a)\cdot(-b) = -(a\cdot b)$$

What about $(-5)\cdot(+3)$? We would certainly like the commutative law to hold for multiplication. Thus, we want $(-5)\cdot(+3)$ to equal $(+3)\cdot(-5)$. Since $(+3)\cdot(-5)$ equals $-(3\cdot5)$, we have $(-5)\cdot(+3)$ equals $-(3\cdot5)$ or $-(5\cdot3)$. In both cases our answer is (-15).

In another example, $(-6)\cdot(+4)$ should equal $(+4)\cdot(-6)$. We therefore have

$$(-6)\cdot(+4) \;=\; -(6\cdot4) \;=(-24)$$

In general, if $(-a)$ is a negative integer, and $(+b)$ is a positive integer, then the product is

$$(-a)\cdot(+b) = -(a\cdot b)$$

We can summarize our discussion as the following rule.

product

> **Rule 4.3**   The **product** of a negative integer and a positive integer is found by multiplying the numbers without their signs and putting a minus sign in front of the answer.

A formal justification of this rule will be given in the exercises.

Finally, we must consider how to multiply two negative numbers. For example, what would $(-10) \cdot (-6)$ be? The answer is $(+60)$. To see why, consider Margaret, who has withdrawn from her bank account $10 a week for the past six weeks. Obviously, six weeks ago she was $60 richer.

Let $+1$ represent a deposit of $1.

Let -1 represent a withdrawal of $1.

Let $+1$ represent a week from now.

Let -1 represent a week ago.

Then (-10) represents Margaret's weekly withdrawal, and (-6) represents six weeks ago. Since six weeks ago she had $60 more, this situation can be written as $(-10) \cdot (-6) = (+60)$.

Now let us look at Rosalie, who has been on a diet for several weeks and has been steadily losing two pounds a week. If we let -4 represent four weeks ago and -2 represent a weight loss of two pounds, then four weeks ago she weighed $(-2) \cdot (-4)$ or $+8$ pounds more than she does now.

This leads us to the following rule.

> **Rule 4.4**   If $(-a)$ and $(-b)$ are negative integers, then the **product** is $(-a) \cdot (-b) = +(a \cdot b)$.

EXAMPLE 4

a) The product of $(-5) \cdot (-4)$ is $+(5 \cdot 4)$, which equals $(+20)$.

b) The product of $(-20) \cdot (-3)$ is $+(20 \cdot 3)$. This equals $(+60)$.   ▪

We can picture the set of integers $\{\ldots, -4, -3, -2, -1, 0, +1, +2, +3, \ldots\}$ on a horizontal number line as shown in Fig. 4.3.

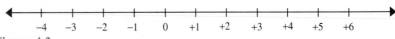

Figure 4.3

order the integers

This number line can then be used to **order the integers** as well as to add them. In Fig. 4.3 we see that $(+6) > (+2)$ since 6 is to the right of 2. Also $(-4) < (-2)$ since -4 is to the left of -2.

The number line in Fig. 4.4 shows how we add the two positive integers $(+3)$ and $(+2)$. Starting at zero we proceed three units to the right to $+3$. Then, since we are adding $+2$, we proceed 2 additional units to the right. This brings us to $+5$, as shown.

Whatever is to the right is greater than...

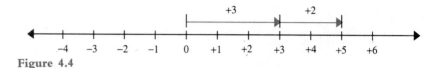

Figure 4.4

Similarly, to add $(+5)$ and (-4) we start at the origin and move 5 units to the right and then, from that point, we move 4 units to the left. We end up at $+1$, as shown in Fig. 4.5.

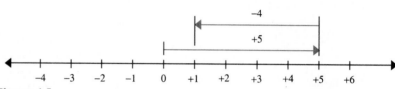

Figure 4.5

number line

The **number line** that we mentioned earlier can also be used to clarify the rules for multiplication of integers. The excerpt on the next page from *Addison-Wesley Mathematics*, 1987, Grade 7, p. 380, indicates how students are taught to use the number line to help them understand multiplication of integers.

Division

Division of integers is defined in a manner similar to division of whole numbers. In Definition 3.4 we stated that $a \div b$ (where $b \neq 0$) means the unique whole number c such that $a = b \cdot c$. If such a whole number does not exist, then $a \div b$ is not possible.

This leads us to the following definition for division involving integers.

Definition 4.5   If a and b are any integers where $b \neq 0$, then $a \div b$ $\left(\text{or } \dfrac{a}{b}\right)$ is the unique integer c, if it exists, such that $a = b \cdot c$.

Let us apply Definition 4.5.

Multiplying Integers

We can use the number line to help understand the rules we
use for multiplication of integers.

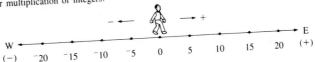

You are now at 0 walking
east at 5 km/h. Where will
you be **3 h from now**?

5 (Walking east at 5 km/h) $\times$ 3 (3 h from now) $=$ 15 (15 km east of 0)

You are now at 0 walking
east at 5 km/h. Where were
you **2 h ago**?

5 (Walking east at 5 km/h) $\times$ $^-2$ (2 h ago) $=$ $^-10$ (10 km west of 0)

You are now at 0 walking
west at 5 km/h. Where will
you be **4 h from now**?

$^-5$ (Walking west at 5 km/h) $\times$ 4 (4 h from now) $=$ $^-20$ (20 km west of 0)

You are now at 0 walking
west at 5 km/h. Where were
you **3 h ago**?

$^-5$ (Walking west at 5 km/h) $\times$ $^-3$ (3 h ago) $=$ 15 (15 km east of 0)

The product of a positive integer and a negative integer
is a negative integer.

The product of two positive integers or two negative integers
is a positive integer.

EXAMPLE 5

Evaluate each of the following:

a) $(+6) \div (-3)$ **b)** $(-6) \div (+3)$ **c)** $(-6) \div (-3)$ **d)** $(-6) \div 4$

SOLUTION

a) $(+6) \div (-3)$ means we are looking for an integer c such that $(+6) = (-3) \cdot c$. Using the rules for multiplication of integers, we have $c = -2$.

b) $(-6) \div (+3)$ means we are looking for an integer c such that $(-6) = (+3) \cdot c$. Using the rules for multiplication of integers, we have $c = -2$.

c) $(-6) \div (-3)$ means we are looking for an integer c such that $(-6) = (-3) \cdot c$. Again using the rules for multiplication of integers, we have $c = +2$.

d) $(-6) \div 4$ means that we are looking for an integer c such that $(-6) = 4 \cdot c$. We *cannot* find any integer satisfying this equation. Thus $(-6) \div 4$ is not possible using only integers. ▪

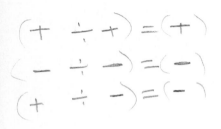

We can summarize our discussion for division involving integers in the following rule:

> **Rule 4.5** If a and b are both positive integers with $b \neq 0$, or if a and b are both negative integers, then the quotient (if it exists) will be a positive integer c such that $a = b \cdot c$. If a and b are integers with opposite signs, then the quotient (if it exists) will be a negative integer c such that $a = b \cdot c$.

EXERCISES FOR SECTION 4.1

1. In each of the following, calculate the answer to the indicated problem.

a) $(+15) + (+9)$ **b)** $(-4) + (-7)$

c) $(+8) + (-3)$ **d)** $(-6) + (+7)$

e) $(-9) + (+4)$ **f)** $(-3) - (-2)$

g) $(-4) + (+9)$ **h)** $0 - (-8)$

i) $(-9) + (+8)$ **j)** $(-8)(+3)$

k) $(-8)(-3)$ **l)** $(+8)(-3)$

m) $(-7) - 0$ **n)** $(-7) \cdot 0$

o) $(+7) + (+7)$ **p)** $(+18) \div (-2)$

q) $(-18) \div (+9)$ **r)** $(-8) \div (-2)$

s) $0 \div (-4)$ **t)** $(-4) \div 0$

2. Perform each of the following:

a) $7 - 9$ **b)** $-3 - 4$

c) $-6 + (4 - 7)$ **d)** $-3 - (4 - 7)$

e) $5 - 4 - 9$ **f)** $-3 - 6 + 4$

3. What is the identity for addition of integers?

4. Are the integers closed under division? Explain your answer.

5. The commutative, associative, and closure laws hold for addition and multiplication of integers. For example, the commutative law for addition states:

If x and y are any integers, then $x + y = y + x$.

State, in symbols, each of the other laws.

6. For every signed number a and every signed number b, is $a + b$ a unique signed number?

7. The **distributive law of multiplication over addition** states that if a, b, and c are any integers, then

$$a(b + c) = ab + ac$$

For example,

$$5(4 + 3) = 5 \cdot 4 + 5 \cdot 3$$
$$5(7) = 20 + 15$$
$$35 = 35$$

Is it also true that $(a + b)c = ac + bc$? Give examples to support your answer.

8. The rule for multiplying a positive integer and a negative integer can be justified with the following argument. We will show that $(+4) \cdot (-16)$ must equal (-64):

$$4[16 + (-16)]$$
$$= 4(16) + 4(-16) \quad \text{(Distributive law)}$$
$$= 64 + 4(-16) \quad\quad\quad\quad\quad (1)$$

On the other hand, we know that

$4[16 + (-16)] = 4(0)$ because $16 + (-16) = 0$

Therefore $4[16 + (-16)] = 0$. So $64 + 4(-16) = 0$ in view of (1). From this it follows that $4(-16)$ is the additive inverse of 64. We already know that the additive inverse of 64 is -64. Thus

$$4(-16) = (-64)$$

Construct a similar argument showing that $(-a)(-b) = +(ab)$.

9. Which law justifies each of the following computations? Do each also!

   a) $(+8) + (+6) = (+6) + (+8)$ Comm

   b) $(-5)[(-8) + (-3)] = (-5)(-8) + (-5)(-3)$

   c) $(+6) + [(-7) + (-9)] = [(+6) + (-7)] + (-9)$

   d) $(-5)(-7)$ is an integer

   e) $(-7)[(-8)(-9)] = [(-7)(-8)](-9)$

   f) $(-6)[8 + 2] = (-6)(8) + (-6)(2)$

   g) $(-11)(0) = 0$

   h) $(-5) + (+5) = 0$

   i) $(+8)(-3) = (-3)(+8)$

10. Use the distributive law to find the value of each of the following computations.

   a) $(-16) \cdot (+94) + (-16) \cdot (+6)$

   b) $(-9) \cdot (+72) + (-9)(+21) + (-9)(+7)$

   c) $(-19)(-24) + (-19)(-76)$

11. Show that $(-1) \cdot x = -x$.

12. The symbol a^n stands for

$$a^n = \underbrace{a \cdot a \cdot a \cdot a \cdots a}$$

   a multiplied by itself n times

where n is a positive integer.
If a is a negative integer, will a^n be positive or negative when:

   a) n is even? Explain.

   b) n is odd? Explain.

13. An archaeologist discovered an ancient relic that dates back to the year 426 B.C. How old was the relic in the year 1988?

14. Aristotle was born in 384 B.C. and Euclid was born in 365 B.C. Who was born first?

For Exercises 15 and 16, let I represent the set of integers, W the set of whole numbers, and N the set of natural numbers.

15. Write a set relationship (using subsets) connecting each of the following:

   a) W and I **b)** W and N **c)** N and I

16. Find each of the following:

   a) $N \cup W$ **b)** $N \cap W$ **c)** $I \cap N$

   d) $W \cap I$ **e)** $W \cup I$ **f)** $N \cup I$

The **absolute value** of an integer is defined as the undirected distance of that integer from zero on a number line. For example, the absolute value of -9 is 9. The absolute value of $+9$ is 9. The symbol for absolute value is $|\ |$. Thus $|-9|$ is read as "the absolute value of -9." The undirected distance (direction does not count) between 0 and -9 on a number line is 9.

17. Evaluate each of the following absolute values.

   a) $|+11|$ **b)** $|-8|$

   c) $|3 - 10|$ **d)** $|0|$

   e) $|+9 - 9|$ **f)** $|9 - 5|$

   g) $|(7 - 6) - 4|$ **h)** $|7 - (6 - 4)|$

   i) $|12 - 12|$

18. Calculators which have a $\boxed{+/-}$ key can be used to perform the various operations involving integers. For example, to find $(-4) + (-2)$ on a calculator, we first enter 4. Then we press $\boxed{+/-}$, then $\boxed{+}$, then $\boxed{2}$ then $\boxed{+/-}$, then $\boxed{=}$. Your results should be -6.

Using a calculator, find the following:

   a) $(-6) + (+3)$ **b)** $(+80) + (+16)$

   c) $(+10) + (-7)$ **d)** $(-12) + (-3)$

   e) $(+5) \times (-3)$ **f)** $(-9) - (-5)$

   g) $(-16) \div (+8)$ **h)** $(-6) \times (-4)$

   i) $(-10) - (+12)$ **j)** $-12 - 5$

   k) $5 - (-3)$ **l)** $-11 + 6$

   m) $(-60) \div (-15)$ **n)** $(+10) \div (-2)$

   o) $(-12) \div 0$

||||▶   Brain-Teaser Problems   ◀||||

**19. The rule for addition of a positive signed number and a negative signed number can be stated formally as follows: If a is a positive signed number and if b is a negative signed number, then

$$\text{if } |a| \geq |b| \text{ then } a + b = |a| - |b|$$

and

$$\text{if } |b| > |a| \text{ then } a + b = -(|b| - |a|).$$

Illustrate this rule by selecting different values for *a* and *b* and calculating *a* + *b*. Check your answer by using the rule given on page 180.

∗∗20. *Triangular numbers*   Replace the question marks with numbers selected from the set $\{-4, -3, -2, -1, 0, 1, 2, 3, 4\}$ so that the magic sum (sum of the integers along each side of the triangle) is 0.

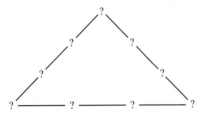

Figure 4.6

∗∗21. Discover the pattern for each of the following sequences of integers and use these results to find the next integer in the sequence.

a) 5, − 10, 20 − 40, . . .

b) 20, 14, 8, 2, − 4, . . .
c) 4, − 12, 36, − 108, . . .
d) 10, 6, 2, − 2, − 6, . . .

∗∗22. One of Goldbach's conjectures is that any odd number greater than 7 can be expressed as the sum of three odd primes (for example, $9 = 3 + 3 + 3$). Show that this conjecture is true for all positive integers from 11 to 25.

∗∗23. Classify each of the following as true or false. If your answer is false, give a counterexample.

a) $|x| = |-x|$ **b)** $|x - y| = |x| - |y|$

c) $|a - b| = |b - a|$

∗∗24. An integer is *even* if it can be expressed as 2 times another integer, that is, an even integer can be expressed as $2n$ where *n* represents some integer. If an integer is not even, it must be *odd*. Prove that the product of two even integers is an even integer.

∗∗25. Prove that the sum of an even integer and an odd integer is an odd integer.

∗∗26. Is the product of an even integer and an odd integer even or odd? Prove your result.

4.2

FUNCTIONS AND FUNCTION NOTATION

Let us consider the charts of numbers given in the following examples.

EXAMPLE 1

a) A neighborhood movie theater owner finds that the number of people coming to the movies per evening is dependent on the charge for admission, as shown in this table.

Admission charge	$3.50	$3.75	$4.00	$5.00	$6.00	$7.00	$8.00
Number of people attending per evening	3000	2700	2500	2000	1700	1200	600

b) A baseball team owner finds that the attendance at baseball games at home depends on who the opposing team is, as shown in this table.

Opposing team	Team A	Team B	Team C	Team D	Team E	Team F
Attendance at game	10,000	25,000	30,000	37,000	46,000	55,000

c) A homeowner finds that the number of gallons of oil used in heating the house for the entire winter season depends on the setting of the thermostat, as shown in this table.

Thermostat (°Fahrenheit)	74°	72°	70°	68°	66°	64°
Number of gallons of oil needed to heat house	2600	2300	2000	1700	1400	1100

In each of the above examples we notice that there is a correspondence between the entries in the top row and the entries in the bottom row. Thus in Example 1(a) we see that when the admission charge is $3.50, then 3000 people will attend the movie, and when the admission charge is $8.00, only 600 people will attend the movie. We note that to each number in the top row we associate one and only one number. Mathematicians say that the number of people attending the movie is a **function of** or **depends on** the admission charge.

function

> **Definition 4.6**   A **function** is a rule that assigns to each number in a set of numbers a unique second number. If the two members of the set are x and y, then we can say that a function is a relationship between the two variables x and y (any letters may be used) such that for each value substituted for x, there is obtained a unique value of y.

Since we will be studying functions a great deal, we introduce some special notation.

Notation

Notation   We abbreviate the words "y is a function of x" as $y = f(x)$. This is read "y equals f of x."

EXAMPLE 2

a) The equation $y = x^2$ represents a function. If we replace x by 1, we get $y = 1$. If we replace x by -2, we get $y = 4$, etc. For each value of x we get a unique value of y. In this case, y is a function of x, and we write $y = f(x) = x^2$.

b) The equation $y = 3x + 2$ represents a function, since if we replace x by any number, we get a unique value of y. We write $y = f(x) = 3x + 2$.

c) The equation $y = \dfrac{1}{x}$ represents a function, and we write $y = f(x) = \dfrac{1}{x}$, provided that $x \neq 0$. ∎

EXAMPLE 3

a) The equation $y = \pm\sqrt{x}$ (which means y equals either the positive or negative square root of x) cannot represent a function. The reason for this is that if we replace x by any number, we *do not* get a unique value for y. Thus if x is 4, we get $y = 2$ and $y = -2$.

b) The equation $y = -\sqrt{x}$ represents a function, since now there *is* a unique value of y for each value of x. Thus if x is 4, y can have only the value -2. ∎

A function is like a coin-operated machine: Each time you put in a coin, you get an item out. We put x-values into the "function machine." For each x-value we put in, we get a unique y-value out of the machine.

Like any coin-operated machine, the function will "accept" some values of x, but may reject others. For example, in the function $y = 1/x$, we cannot put in the value $x = 0$. (Why not?) This leads us to the following definition.

Definition 4.7   When using the function notation, the set of all values of x that can be substituted in the function is called the **domain** of the function. The set of all values of y that these substitutions create is called the **range** of the function.

domain

range

EXAMPLE 4

a) In the function $y = 1/x$ we can put in any value for x except 0. So the domain of this function is all real numbers except 0.

b) In the function $y = -\sqrt{x}$ we can put in any positive number or 0 for x. We cannot put in negative values for x because these would give us complex numbers. Thus the domain of this function is $x \geq 0$.

c) In the function $y = 2x - 3$ we can put in *any* value for x. So the domain is all real numbers. ∎

EXAMPLE 5

a) In the function $y = -\sqrt{x}$, only negative values of y or 0 come out, so the range is $y \leq 0$.

b) In the function $y = x^2$, only positive values of y or 0 come out, so the range is $y \geq 0$.

c) In the function $y = |x|$ (y is the absolute value of x), only positive values of y or 0 come out, so the range is $y \geq 0$. ▰

Notation   If we have a function $y = f(x)$, then the symbol $f(a)$ means the value of the function when $x = a$.

EXAMPLE 6

For the function $y = 2x - 3$, $f(1) = 2(1) - 3$ or -1.
For the function $y = 2x - 3$, $f(0) = 2(0) - 3$ or -3.
For the function $y = 2x - 3$, $f(-1) = 2(-1) - 3$ or -5.
For the function $y = 2x - 3$, $f(a) = 2a - 3$. ▰

EXAMPLE 7

For the function $y = x^2$, $f(3) = 3^2$ or 9.
For the function $y = x^2$, $f(1) = 1^2$ or 1.
For the function $y = x^2$, $f(t) = t^2$. ▰

EXAMPLE 8

For the function $\dfrac{3x - 4}{5}$, $f(2) = \dfrac{3(2) - 4}{5}$ or $\dfrac{2}{5}$

For the function $\dfrac{3x - 4}{5}$, $f(-6) = \dfrac{3(-6) - 4}{5}$ or $\dfrac{-22}{5}$

For the function $\dfrac{3x - 4}{5}$, $f(0) = \dfrac{3(0) - 4}{5}$ or $\dfrac{-4}{5}$ ▰

EXERCISES FOR SECTION 4.2

For each of the situations described in Exercises 1–2, determine whether y is a function of x. If not, explain why.

1.

Weight of an envelope, x	Postage required (in 1989), y
Up to 1 ounce	25¢
Between 1 and 2 ounces	45¢
Between 2 and 3 ounces	65¢
Between 3 and 4 ounces	85¢
Between 4 and 5 ounces	105¢

2.

Number of college credits being taken this semester, x	Student fee payable, y
More than 0 and up to and including 3 credits	$12
More than 3 and up to and including 6 credits	$17
More than 6 and up to and including 9 credits	$25
More than 9 and up to and including 12 credits	$32
More than 12 credits	$44

3. For each of the following functions find $f(1)$, $f(0)$, $f(-3)$, $f(a)$, and $f(x+h)$
   a) $f(x) = 4x - 3$
   b) $f(x) = 3x + 2$
   c) $f(x) = x^2 + 3$
   d) $f(x) = 3x^2$
   e) $f(x) = (2 - x)(7 + x)$
   f) $f(x) = x^2 + 7x + 6$
   g) $f(x) = 2x^3 + 3x^2 + 7x + 5$

PROBLEM-SOLVING EXERCISES

4. The Brookhaven Camp provides door-to-door luggage pickup service for its campers. The charges are as follows: $15 for a camp trunk and one duffel bag. There is a $6 charge for each additional duffel bag. Thus if a camper has x duffel bags, the cost is y dollars.
   a) Is y a function of x?
   b) If y is a function of x, can you find an equation expressing this relationship?
   c) If Linda has 4 duffel bags altogether (in addition to the trunk), what is the cost for the luggage pickup service?

5. A lottery dealer makes a profit of 6¢ on each state lottery ticket that she sells. Furthermore, if she sells more than 25,000 tickets in a month, the state gives her a rebate, which results in an extra 2¢ on each ticket over 25,000 sold. If she sells x tickets, her profit is y dollars.

a) Is y a function of x?
b) If y is a function of x, can you find an equation expressing this relationship?
c) For each of the months shown in the table, find the dealer's profit.

Month	Number of lottery tickets sold
January	24,228
February	17,368
March	26,014
April	28,132
May	29,485
June	38,692

6. Melissa's monthly rent is $428. She has signed a long-term lease with her landlord whereby her rent will be raised 1% every six months. Thus x months from now, her monthly rent will be y dollars.
   a) Is y a function of x?
   **b) If y is a function of x, can you find an equation expressing this relationship?
   c) Find her monthly rent five years from now.

7. Find the domain and range of each of the following functions.

   a) $f(x) = 2x^2 + 5$
   *b) $f(x) = \sqrt{7x + 2}$
   *c) $f(x) = \dfrac{4x - 3}{2x + 1}$
   d) $f(x) = |2x + 2|$

4.3

SOLVING LINEAR EQUATIONS AND INEQUALITIES

Linear Equations in One Variable and Their Application

mathematical models
equations

Much of the beauty of mathematics lies in the fact that many real-world situations can be translated into mathematical equations. Such mathematical descriptions of real-world situations are called **mathematical models**. These mathematical models are often given in the form of **equations**, which may be simple or complicated.

Equations and Their Solution

Basically, an equation is a mathematical statement that consists of two expressions joined together by an equal sign. It specifies that the expression on the left side of the equality sign is equal to the expression on the right variable

solution

side. Any unknown in an equation is represented by a letter and is known as a **variable**. A **solution** to an equation is a number which when substituted for the variable results in a true statement.

EXAMPLE 1

The following are examples of equations:

a) $5x = 20$ is an equation.

b) $9x + 3 = 6x + 8$ is an equation.

c) $8x^2 + 3x + 9 = 0$ is an equation.

d) $8x + 27 - 3 = 0$ is an equation.

e) $4x + 1$ is *not* an equation. Can you see why?   ▬

linear equation

Any equation containing x (the unknown) raised only to the exponent 1 and to no higher or lower exponent is called a **linear equation** in x.

EXAMPLE 2

a) $7x - 3 = 18$ is a linear equation in x.

b) $5x^2 - 3x + 7 = 0$ is *not* a linear equation in x because it contains an x^2 term.

c) $7x - 3y + 8z^2 = 10$ is a linear equation in x. It is also a linear equation in y. It is *not* a linear equation in z.   ▬

solve an equation

To **solve an equation** in x means to find a value of x that makes the equation true.

EXAMPLE 3

a) The equation $5x = 45$ has as its solution $x = 9$, since $5(9) = 45$ is true.

b) $x^2 - 16 = 0$ has as its solutions $x = 4$ and $x = -4$, since $4^2 - 16 = 0$ is true and $(-4)^2 - 16 = 0$ is true.

c) $x + 8 = x$ has no solution, since there is no value of x that will make the equation true.   ▬

To solve an equation for x, we must get the equation into the form "$x = $ some expression." To do this, we use the following rules.

> **Rules for Solving Linear Equations**
>
> **1.** Any number may be added to or subtracted from both sides of an equation.
>
> **2.** Both sides of an equation may be multiplied or divided by the same number (except that we cannot divide by 0).

The following examples illustrate the use of these rules.

EXAMPLE 4

Solve the equation $8x = 12x - 8$ for x.

SOLUTION

Subtract $12x$ from both sides of the equation. This gives

$$
\begin{array}{rl}
8x = & 12x - 8 \\
-12x = & -12x \\
\hline
\end{array}
$$

We get

$$-4x = -8$$

Now we divide both sides of the equation by -4.

$$\frac{-4x}{-4} = \frac{-8}{-4}$$

So the solution is $x = 2$.

EXAMPLE 5

Solve the equation $8x - 5 = 3x + 10$ for x.

SOLUTION

Add 5 to both sides of the equation.

$$
\begin{array}{rl}
8x - 5 = & 3x + 10 \\
+5 & +5 \\
\hline
8x = & 3x + 15
\end{array}
$$

Subtract $3x$ from both sides of the equation.

$$
\begin{array}{rl}
8x = & 3x + 15 \\
-3x & -3x \\
\hline
5x = & 15
\end{array}
$$

Divide both sides of the equation by 5.

$$\frac{\cancel{5}x}{\cancel{5}} = \frac{15}{5}$$

So the solution is $x = 3$.

EXAMPLE 6

Solve the equation $2ax - 5 + 3z = 7z$ for x.

SOLUTION

Add $5 - 3z$ to both sides of the equation.

$$
\begin{array}{rl}
2ax - 5 + 3z = & 7z \\
+5 - 3z & 5 - 3z \\
\hline
\end{array}
$$

We get

$$2ax = 5 + 4z$$

Divide both sides of the equation by $2a$.

$$\frac{\cancel{2a}x}{\cancel{2a}} = \frac{5 + 4z}{2a}$$

Therefore

$$x = \frac{5 + 4z}{2a}$$

EXAMPLE 7

SOLUTION

Solve the equation $2ax - 5 + 3z = 7z$ for z.

Subtract $2ax$ from both sides of the equation.

$$
\begin{array}{r}
2ax - 5 + 3z = 7z \\
- 2ax \qquad\qquad - 2ax \\
\hline
- 5 + 3z = 7z - 2ax
\end{array}
$$

Add 5 to both sides of the equation.

$$
\begin{array}{r}
- 5 + 3z = 7z - 2ax \\
+ 5 \qquad\qquad + 5 \\
\hline
3z = 7z - 2ax + 5
\end{array}
$$

Subtract $7z$ from both sides of the equation.

$$
\begin{array}{r}
3z = \quad 7z - 2ax + 5 \\
- 7z \quad - 7z \\
\hline
- 4z = \; - 2ax + 5
\end{array}
$$

Divide both sides of the equation by -4.

$$\frac{-\cancel{4}z}{-\cancel{4}} = \frac{-2ax + 5}{-4}$$

Therefore

$$z = \frac{-2ax + 5}{-4}$$

Comment We could have also obtained the same answer for the previous example if we had first subtracted $3z$ from both sides of the equation, getting $2ax - 5 = 4z$, and then divided both sides of the equation by 4. Our answer would then be $z = \dfrac{2ax - 5}{4}$. Is this the same answer that we obtained previously?

Forming Algebraic Equations

Since we must often form an equation that is an adequate model of some real-world situation, it is important to practice the formation of such equations. This is always the first step in building such mathematical models. Naturally, students need to develop the proficiency in forming mathematical models and the skill needed to solve *simple* word problems before attempting more complicated problems. Polya's problem-solving process, as mentioned in Chapter 1, is appropriate for the solution of word problems. For our situations, this involves the following: In the *Understanding the Problem* part, identify the given information and then determine what is to be found. In the *A Plan to Solve the Problem* part, assign letters to the unknown quantities, translate the given information into a mathematical equation or inequality, and proceed to solve it. In the *Checking Our Solution* part, we check our solution to make sure that we have answered the question. This procedure is illustrated in the following examples and also in the remainder of the chapter. The reader should analyze each example carefully.

EXAMPLE 8

Problem-Solving Example—Using an Equation

The cost of a certain computer and its software programs is $36,000. The computer costs 8 times as much as the software programs. Find the cost of each.

SOLUTION

Understanding the Problem

We are told that the computer costs eight times as much as the software programs. We must then find an equation which represents the cost of the computer and its software programs.

A Plan to Solve the Problem

Let $x =$ the cost of the software programs; then $8x =$ the cost of the computer. We then have the following equation based upon the given information.

$$8x + x = 36,000$$

Now we solve for x:

$$8x + x = 36,000$$

We combine terms:

$$9x = 36,000 \qquad \text{(Remember that } x = 1x.\text{)}$$

We divide both sides of the equation by 9, getting

$$\frac{9x}{9} = \frac{36,000}{9}$$

so that

$$x = 4000$$

Thus the software programs cost $4000, and the computer costs $32,000.

Checking Our Solution
We can easily check our solution. The computer costs $32,000, which is eight times as much as the software program. The total cost is $32,000 + $4,000 or $36,000.

EXAMPLE 9

Problem-Solving Example—Using an Equation
Evelyn and Margaret are stockbrokers. One week, they opened 89 new customer accounts. Evelyn opened 1 more than 3 times the number of new accounts opened by Margaret. Find the number of new customer accounts opened by each.

SOLUTION

Understanding the Problem
Since Evelyn and Margaret did not open the same number of new customer accounts, we must find an equation which represents the number of accounts opened by each.

A Plan to Solve the Problem
Let x = the number of new customer accounts opened by Margaret. Then $3x + 1$ = the number of new customer accounts opened by Evelyn. Since Evelyn and Margaret opened 89 new accounts, we have

$$x + 3x + 1 = 89$$

so that

$$4x + 1 = 89$$

We subtract 1 from both sides of the equation, getting

$$
\begin{array}{rcl}
4x + 1 & = & 89 \\
-1 & & -1 \\
\hline
4x & = & 88
\end{array}
$$

Now we divide both sides of the equation by 4. This gives

$$\frac{4x}{4} = \frac{88}{4}$$

so that

$$x = 22$$

Thus, Margaret opened 22 new customer accounts, and Evelyn opened 67 new customer accounts.

Checking Our Solution
Evelyn opened 67 new customer accounts. This represents 1 more than 3 times the number of new accounts opened by Margaret. Margaret opened 22 accounts. Together they opened 89 accounts.   ▬

EXAMPLE 10

Problem-Solving Example—Using an Equation
A supermarket has just received a shipment of 65 cases of corn flakes. The supermarket wishes to divide the 65 cases so that they can be stored in two different warehouses, with the larger warehouse getting more than the smaller warehouse. If 3 times the number of cases that the larger warehouse will receive is 6 more than 6 times the number of cases that the smaller warehouse will receive, how many cases will each warehouse receive?

SOLUTION

Understanding the Problem
Each warehouse will receive different numbers of cases. We must determine the number of cases to be received by each under the conditions specified.

A Plan to Solve the Problem
Let $x =$ the number of cases assigned to the larger warehouse. Then $65 - x =$ the number of cases to be stored in the smaller warehouse. On the basis of the given information, we have

$$3x = 6(65 - x) + 6$$

or

$$3x = 390 - 6x + 6$$

so that

$$3x = 396 - 6x$$

Add $6x$ to both sides of the equation. We get

$$
\begin{array}{r}
3x = 396 - 6x \\
+\,6x \qquad +\,6x \\
\hline
9x = 396
\end{array}
$$

Now we divide both sides of the equation by 9. This gives

$$\frac{9x}{9} = \frac{396}{9}$$

or

$$x = 44$$

Thus the larger warehouse should receive 44 cases, and the smaller warehouse should receive $65 - 44$ or 21 cases.

Checking Our Solution
If the larger warehouse receives 44 cases, then 3 times this amount, or 132, is 6 more than 6 times the number of cases that the smaller warehouse will

receive. Since the smaller warehouse will receive 21 cases, then 6 more than 6 times this amount, or $6 \times 21 + 6$, is 132. ▪

Solving Verbal Problems By Using Linear Inequalities

inequalities

Until now we have been dealing with equations. Of course, on many occasions we must deal with mathematical expressions in which one expression is not equal to another expression. Such statements are known as **inequalities**. When dealing with inequalities the following symbols of inequality are used.

Symbol	Meaning
$x < y$	x is less than y
$x \leq y$	x is less than or equal to y
$x > y$	x is greater than y
$x \geq y$	x is greater than or equal to y

As with equations, we can have linear inequalities in one variable or in many variables.

EXAMPLE 11

The following are examples of linear inequalities.
a) $3x > 12$ is a linear inequality in x.
b) $9x + 6 \leq 4x + 3$ is a linear inequality in x.
c) $4x + 5y > 3$ is a linear inequality in x and y.

Let us solve the inequality $2x > 10$ algebraically, where x is an integer. We can find the solution to an inequality in much the same way that we solve equations. However, there are some exceptions. We may add or subtract the same number to both sides of an inequality, a procedure that is similar to what we did with equalities. When we multiply or divide both sides of an inequality by the same number, we must be careful. When both sides of an inequality are multiplied or divided by a positive number, then this is allowed, as we do when we work with equalities. On the other hand, when both sides of an inequality are multiplied or divided by a negative number, then the order of the inequality is reversed. Thus if $2x > 10$ and we divide both sides of this inequality by 2 (a positive number), we get $x > 5$. On the other hand, if $-2x > +8$ and we divide both sides of this inequality by -2 (a negative number), we get $x < -4$. The order of the inequality sign is reversed.

EXAMPLE 12

Find and graph the solution set of the inequality

$$x - 8 > 1$$

SOLUTION

We add 8 to both sides of the inequality. This will leave us with x alone on one side of the inequality. We get

$$
\begin{array}{rcl}
x - 8 & > & 1 \\
+8 & & +8 \\
\hline
x & > & 9
\end{array}
$$

The graph of the solution set is shown in Fig. 4.7. Note that 9 is not included in the graph.

Figure 4.7

EXAMPLE 13

Find and graph the solution set of the inequality

$$3x + 2 \leq 12 - 2x$$

SOLUTION

We first add $+2x$ to both sides of the inequality. We get

$$
\begin{array}{rcl}
3x + 2 & \leq & 12 - 2x \\
+2x & & +2x \\
\hline
5x + 2 & \leq & 12
\end{array}
$$

Now we subtract 2 from both sides of the inequality. This gives

$$
\begin{array}{rcl}
5x + 2 & \leq & 12 \\
-2 & & -2 \\
\hline
5x & \leq & 10
\end{array}
$$

Finally, we divide both sides of this inequality by 5 (a positive number). Our result is

$$\frac{\cancel{5}x}{\cancel{5}} \leq \frac{10}{5} \quad or \quad x \leq 2$$

The graph of the solution set is shown in Fig. 4.8. Note that 2 is included in the graph.

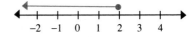

Figure 4.8

EXAMPLE 14

Find and graph the solution set of the inequality

$$4(2x - 3) - 12x \leq 0$$

SOLUTION

Using the distributive law, we remove parentheses.

$$4(2x - 3) - 12x \leq 0$$
$$8x - 12 - 12x \leq 0$$
$$-4x - 12 \quad\quad \leq 0$$

$$\begin{array}{rcl} & +12 & +12 \\ \hline \dfrac{-4x}{-4} & \leq & \dfrac{12}{-4} \\ x & \geq & -3 \end{array}$$

(We add $+12$ to both sides.)
(We divide both sides by -4, a negative number. The sense of the inequality is reversed.)

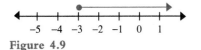

Figure 4.9

The graph of the solution set is shown in Fig. 4.9. Note that -3 is included in the graph. ∎

EXAMPLE 15

Problem-Solving Example

Christopher needs $80 to fix his car. His boss has agreed to pay him $6 an hour for shoveling snow in addition to his regular part-time salary of $50. What is the minimum number of hours that Christopher must work to earn the $80 to fix his car?

SOLUTION

Let x = the number of hours that Christopher must work shoveling snow. Since he earns $6 an hour, his total extra money earned from shoveling the snow for x hours is $6x$. His weekly part-time salary is $50. Since he needs at least $80, we have

$$6x + 50 \geq 80$$

Now we solve this inequality for x:

$$\begin{array}{rcl} 6x + 50 & \geq & 80 \\ -50 & & -50 \end{array}$$ (We subtract 50 from both sides.)

$$\dfrac{6x}{6} \geq \dfrac{30}{6}$$ (We divide both sides by 6, a positive number.)

$$x \geq 5$$

Thus Christopher must work at least 5 hours shoveling snow. ∎

EXAMPLE 16

Problem-Solving Example

Allison received grades of 98, 83, 84, and 86 on her first four math exams. What grade must she receive on the next exam so that her average will be at least 90% for all five exams?

SOLUTION

Let x = the fifth exam grade. An average is found by adding the grades together and dividing the sum by the number of exams. Thus her average is

$$\dfrac{98 + 83 + 84 + 86 + x}{5}$$

Since this must be at least 90%, we must have

$$\frac{98 + 83 + 84 + 86 + x}{5} \geq 90$$

or

$$\frac{351 + x}{5} \geq 90$$

$$5\left(\frac{351 + x}{5}\right) \quad \geq \quad 90(5) \qquad \text{(We multiply both sides by 5, a positive number.)}$$

$$\begin{array}{rcl} 351 + x & \geq & 450 \\ -351 & & -351 \\ \hline x & \geq & 99 \end{array} \qquad \text{(We subtract 351 from both sides.)}$$

Thus Allison must receive at least a 99 on her next exam for her to have at least 90% average on all five exams. ▬

EXERCISES FOR SECTION 4.3

1. Solve each of the following equations for x.

a) $8x = 24$

b) $-6x = 24$

c) $10x + 4x = 28$

d) $9x + 3 = 21$

e) $4x + 3x - 8 = 62$

f) $7x - 14 - 3x = -38$

g) $9x + 7 = 5x + 47$

h) $9x - 2 = 3x - 14$

i) $\dfrac{x}{3} = 7$

j) $\dfrac{4}{7}x = \dfrac{16}{49}$

k) $8x - 4 + 7 = 6x + x + 9$

l) $6x - 12 - x = 9x + 53$

m) $5(3x - 2) = 5$

n) $15x - 3(x + 6) = 6$

o) $2 - 7(x - 1) = 3(x - 2) - 5(x + 3)$

p) $2(x - 3) - 17 = 13 - 3(x + 2)$

q) $bx - 5 = c$

r) $m^2x - 3m^2 = 12m^2$

s) $a = bx + 6$

t) $8bx - 6b^2 = 4bx + 12b^2$

u) $2ax = 10a^2 - 3ax$

v) $22x - 3(5x + 4) = 16$

w) $3x + (2x - 5) = 13 - 2(x + 2)$

x) $15x - 8(x + 6) = 14x + 3$

y) $\dfrac{7x + 5}{8} - \dfrac{3x + 15}{10} = 2$

z) $\dfrac{3}{2}(2x + 1) - \dfrac{1}{3}(4x - 1) = -3\dfrac{1}{6}$

2. Find and graph the solution set for each of the following inequalities.

a) $x - 5 > 7$

b) $x + 2 > 10$

c) $x - 2.5 \leq 3.5$

d) $x + 4 < 6$

e) $12 < x + 3$

f) $16 \geq 4y$

g) $-6x \leq 24$

h) $-10x \geq -30$

i) $\dfrac{x}{2} \leq 3$

j) $\dfrac{x}{3} \geq -4$

k) $\dfrac{2}{3}x \leq 30$

l) $\dfrac{-4}{9}x \geq -36$

m) $3x + 1 \geq -31$

n) $6x + 1 \geq -17$

o) $14x - 8 < 12 + 4x$

p) $12x + 4 - 16x < 28$

q) $24x - 6(2x + 3) \geq 0$

r) $-3(2x + 4) - 2 \geq -5(x - 3)$

3. Let n represent a number. Then match each of the sentences given in column A with an equation that represents it from column B.

Column A	Column B
a) Four times a number is 64.	**i.** $7 - 5n = 58$
b) A number increased by 7 is 28.	**ii.** $8n = 72$
c) One number is $\frac{1}{5}$ of another, and the difference is 58.	**iii.** $\frac{1}{8}n - 7 = 58$
d) One-eighth of a number decreased by 7 is 58.	**iv.** $5n - 7 = 58$
e) One number is $\frac{1}{5}$ of another, and their sum is 103.	**v.** $n + \frac{1}{5}n = 103$
f) The product of 8 and a number is 72.	**vi.** $n - \frac{1}{5}n = 58$
g) When 7 is subtracted from 5 times a number, the result is 58.	**vii.** $\frac{1}{5}n - n = 58$
h) When 5 times a number is subtracted from 7, the result is 58.	**viii.** $4n = 64$
	ix. $n + 7 = 28$

PROBLEM-SOLVING EXERCISES

Use an algebraic equation to solve each of Exercises 4–22.

4. A merchant sold a home video system for $450, which was 25% above its cost to him. What was the cost of the home video system to the merchant?

5. During a sale, the cost of a television set was decreased from $99 to $66. What was the percent decrease in price?

6. One evening, a movie theater sold 450 tickets and received $1650 in proceeds for the performance. Children's tickets were $3.00, and adult tickets were $4.00. How many children's and how many adult tickets were sold?

7. Marilyn deposited $160 in her bank. The number of $5 bills she deposited was 3 more than the number of $10 bills she deposited, and the number of $1 bills she deposited was 30 more than the number of $5 bills she deposited. How many bills of each type did Marilyn deposit?

8. Phyllis and Madeline are account executives for a large Wall Street brokerage company. During the first two business days of January, they completed 162 transactions. If the number of transactions completed by Phyllis is 2 more than 3 times the number completed by Madeline, find the number completed by each.

9. Gail is analyzing the number of credit card sales completed. On Tuesday the number of credit card sales completed was 2 more than Monday's number of credit card sales completed. Twice as many credit card sales were completed on Wednesday as on Monday. The total number of credit card sales completed on Monday and Wednesday exceeds the number of credit card sales completed on Tuesday by 2. How many credit card sales were completed on each day?

10. George purchased a new car for $8784 and paid $724.68 as sales tax. What is the percent of the sales tax?

11. Mark receives a shipment of transistor parts. The bill is $47,392.68. The shipper allows a discount of $3\frac{1}{2}\%$ if the total bill is paid C.O.D. If Mark decides to pay C.O.D., how much does he have to pay?

12. Kay Parsons invests a sum of money in municipal bonds paying 6% annual interest. She then decides to invest $500 more than the sum originally invested in a real estate venture paying 10% annual interest. Her total annual income from both investments is $210. How much did she invest in each venture?

13. The personnel director of the Calyn Company is analyzing the age of the president of the company and the age of her secretary. This is being studied so that a new pension plan can be started. The director finds that the president is 3 times as old as her secretary. Eight years from now, the president's age will exceed twice her secretary's age at that time by 14 years. How old is each one now?

14. Steve saves $18 a week from his salary. He already has accumulated $324. In how many weeks will Steve accumulate at least $468?

15. Mary has at least 6 times as many cassette tapes as does her sister Stephanie. If together, Mary and Stephanie have at least 98 tapes, find the least number of cassette tapes that each girl has.

16. Suzanne has joined a weight watchers' club and has agreed to lose at least 54 pounds in equal amounts per week over a 9-week period. What is the minimum amount that she must lose each week to accomplish this goal?

17. Hector has been told by his supplier that his franchise will be canceled unless he sells at least 90,000 gallons of gas over a 4-month period. During the first month, Hector sold 21,000 gallons of gas. At least how many

inequality problem

gallons of gas must Hector sell in each of the remaining 3 months (assuming equal monthly sales) so that his franchise will not be canceled?

18. Gina purchased 4 computer discs and handed the clerk a $20 bill. She received less than $8 change. What is the minimum cost of a disc?

19. Lester purchased a set of tires for his car. The tires are guaranteed to provide at least 30,000 miles of driving (under normal conditions). Lester plans to drive from the East Coast to the West Coast and back, a total distance of at most 6000 miles. Assuming that he makes the trip, what is the minimum number of miles remaining for the tires to be guaranteed?

20. Cecile Robinson is a guest speaker. For each lecture delivered she receives at least $175 in compensation. Last year she earned a minimum of $2000 from her speaking engagements. What is the least number of guest lectures that she delivered?

Brain-Teaser Problems

**21. The photocopying machine on the eighth floor of a large office building is situated on a platform whose length is 8 feet more than its width. If the length of the platform is increased by 4 feet and the width is decreased by 1 foot, the area will remain unchanged. Find the dimensions of the platform.

**22. Bill, Mag, and Chris have each sent out résumés to numerous companies seeking employment. The number of résumés sent out by Mag is 1 less than the number sent out by Bill. The number of résumés sent out by Chris is 5 less than twice the number sent out by Mag. If the number of résumés sent out by Chris exceeds the number sent out by Bill by 12, find the number of résumés sent out by each.

4.4

ALGEBRAIC SOLUTION OF A SYSTEM OF SIMULTANEOUS LINEAR EQUATIONS

system of simultaneous linear equations

Let us consider Michael, who knows that he has 12 coins in his piggy bank, which amount to 80¢. He also knows that there are only nickels and dimes in the piggy bank. How many coins of each kind does Michael have? Do we have enough information to solve the problem?

Let n = the number of nickels in the piggy bank and let d = the number of dimes in the piggy bank. Since there are 12 coins in the bank altogether, we must have $n + d = 12$. Also, each nickel is worth 5 cents, so n nickels are worth $5n$ cents. Similarly, each dime is worth 10 cents, so d dimes are worth $10d$ cents. The value of all the coins together is 80 cents. Thus $5n + 10d = 80$. Here the two equations $n + d = 12$ and $5n + 10d = 80$ impose two conditions on the variables at the same time. We call the two equations a **system of simultaneous linear equations**.

To **solve** such a system, that is, to find a **solution** of a system of simultaneous linear equations in two variables, means that we are looking for a pair of numbers that satisfies both equations. While there are numerous techniques for solving such a system, at this point we will merely discuss an algebraic solution. A system of linear equations may have exactly one solution, no solution, or infinitely many solutions.

EXAMPLE 1

Solve the following system of equations:

$$n + d = 12 \qquad \text{[A]}$$
$$5n + 10d = 80 \qquad \text{[B]}$$

SOLUTION

Let us multiply both sides of equation [A] by -5. This yields an equivalent equation [C], in which the number in front of n is exactly the same as the number in front of n in equation [B] but is of the opposite sign. We get

	Original equation	*New equation*	
[A]	$n + d = 12$	$-5n - 5d = -60$	[C]
[B]	$5n + 10d = 80$	$5n + 10d = 80$	[B]

Now we add the corresponding members of equations [B] and [C] to eliminate the variable n. We get

$$5d = 20$$

We now solve for the value of d by dividing both sides of the resulting equation by 5, getting

$$d = 4$$

We then replace d by its value in any equation involving both variables and solve for n. We get

$$n + d = 12$$
$$n + 4 = 12$$
$$n = 8$$

Thus we have $n = 8$ and $d = 4$. Referring back to the problem given at the beginning of this section, we conclude that Michael has 8 nickels and 4 dimes in his piggy bank.   ▪

Comment   We can easily check that 8 nickels and 4 dimes is indeed the solution, since 8 nickels are worth 40¢ and 4 dimes are also worth 40¢. The total value of the 12 coins is 80¢.

EXAMPLE 2

Solve the following system of equations:

$$3x - 7 = 7y \qquad \text{[A]}$$
$$4x = 3y + 22 \qquad \text{[B]}$$

SOLUTION

We will first transform each of the given equations [A] and [B] into two equivalent equations [C] and [D], in which the terms containing the variables appear on one side and the constant appears on the other side of the equation.

We get

$$3x - 7y = 7 \qquad \text{[C]}$$
$$4x - 3y = 22 \qquad \text{[D]}$$

Now we eliminate one of the variables, say y, from both equations. To accomplish this, let us multiply both sides of equation [C] by 3 and both sides of equation [D] by -7. This gives

$$9x - 21y = 21 \qquad \text{[E]}$$
$$-28x + 21y = -154 \qquad \text{[F]}$$

We notice that in both of the equations [E] and [F] the numbers in front of y have the same numerical value but are of opposite sign. Adding these two equations eliminates the variable y. We get

$$-19x = -133$$

Dividing both sides of this last equation by -19 gives

$$x = 7$$

Replacing x by its value in any equation containing both variables gives

$$3x - 7y = 7$$
$$3(7) - 7y = 7$$
$$21 - 7y = 7$$
$$-7y = -14 \qquad \text{(We subtract 21 from both sides of the equation.)}$$
$$y = 2 \qquad \text{(We divide both sides of the equation by } -7.)$$

Our answer is $x = 7$ and $y = 2$. The reader should check that these values satisfy *both* equations. ∎

EXAMPLE 3

Problem-Solving Example

Yogi is the manager of a Little League baseball team. Yesterday he purchased 8 bats and 4 gloves for the team. The total cost was $156. Today he purchased at the same prices an additional 3 bats and 7 gloves. The total cost was $108. Find the cost of a bat and the cost of a glove.

SOLUTION

Let b = the cost of a bat, and let g = the cost of a glove. On the basis of the information given in the problem, 8 bats and 4 gloves cost $156. This means $8b + 4g = 156$. Also, 3 bats and 7 gloves cost $108, or $3b + 7g = 108$. Thus we must solve the following set of equations:

$$8b + 4g = 156$$
$$3b + 7g = 108$$

Multiply both sides of the first equation by 7 and both sides of the second equation by -4. We get

$$56b + 28g = 1092$$
$$\underline{-12b - 28g = -432}$$

Adding these two equations will eliminate the variable g. Our result is

$$44b = 660$$

Dividing both sides of this equation by 44 gives $b = 15$. Replacing b by its value in any equation containing both variables gives

$$8b + 4g = 156$$
$$8(15) + 4g = 156$$
$$120 + 4g = 156$$
$$4g = 36$$
$$g = 9$$

Thus $b = 15$ and $g = 9$. This means that a bat costs \$15 and a glove costs \$9.   ■

EXERCISES FOR SECTION 4.4

Use the techniques of this section to solve each of the sets of equations given in Exercises 1–13.

1. $4x + 3y = 29$
   $2x - 3y = 1$

2. $4x + 5y = -7$
   $2x - 3y = 13$

3. $3x + 4y = -5$
   $4x + 5y = -7$

4. $y = x + 12$
   $10y + 5x = 360$

5. $3x + 7y = 33$
   $2x + 5y = 23$

6. $3x - y = 3$
   $x + 3y = 11$

7. $4x + 5y = 22$
   $-4x + 3y = -6$

8. $3x + 2y = 41$
   $4x - y = 40$

9. $4y - 6x = -26$
   $6y - 4x = -24$

10. $3x + 2y = 6$
   $x + y = 1$

11. $6x + 10y = 7$
   $15x - 4y = 3$

12. $x - y = 11$
   $3x + 2y = 3$

13. $3x + 6y = 15$
   $-x - 2y = 12$

PROBLEM-SOLVING EXERCISES

14. *Admission Charges*   A family of 2 adults and 5 children paid \$34 for admission to the Animal Town Amusement Park. Another family of 3 adults and 2 children paid \$29 for admission. (The admission price includes all rides.) Find the admission price for an adult and the price for a child.

15. *Check Cashing*   Jessica is a bank teller. Yesterday she cashed a \$200 check and gave the customer 25 bills in \$10 and \$5 bills. How many \$5 bills and how many \$10 bills did she give the customer?

16. *Stamp Collecting*   Ken is a stamp collector. In one group of 75 stamps he has only 20¢ and 25¢ stamps with a total face value of \$17.50. How many stamps of each kind does he have?

17. *Little League Baseball*   The coach of a Little League baseball team purchased 6 balls and 4 bats for the team at a cost of \$72. The following day the coach purchased at the same prices 8 additional balls and 6 additional bats at a cost of \$104. Find the cost of a bat and the cost of a ball.

18. *Wage Discrimination*   A farmer in the West has been accused of paying female sharecroppers lower wages than male sharecroppers for identical jobs. Records show that during one week the farmer paid out $550 in wages for a work force consisting of four men and five women. In another week the farmer paid out $1150 for a work force consisting of ten men and eight women. Find the weekly wages paid by the farmer for a male sharecropper and for a female sharecropper.

19. *College Admissions*. A large southern university received 6000 applications for admission to the premedical or the prelaw program. The number of applications for the premedical program was three times the number of applications for the prelaw program. How many students applied to the premedical program and how many applied to the prelaw program?

20. The Outboard Amusement Company rents out motorboats and rowboats for the afternoon. The rental fee received for 7 rowboats and 6 motorboats is $63. The rental fee for 4 rowboats and 3 motorboats is $33. Find the rental fee for a motorboat and for a rowboat.

Brain-Teaser Problems

**21. *Anthropology*. In 1953, anthropologists discovered a group of 2200 people living on a small island in the Pacific. Of these 2200 people, 400 were considered functionally illiterate. This represented 20% of the male population and 16% of the female population. How many males and how many females were in the group?

**22. The owners of the White Lake Recreation Area wish to spray the shores of the lake with a chemical to kill the mosquitoes, which bother the sunbathers. Local environmental regulations require that the chemical spray contain only 20% Dursban. The owners have two chemical solutions, one that contains 4% Dursban and one that contains 40% Dursban. How many gallons of each should the owners use to produce 36 gallons of a solution that contains 20% Dursban?

**23. Alexis is on a special diet. Her doctor has told her to limit her daily intake of calcium and vitamin C to 800.08 and 65.395 milligrams, respectively. (These are the minimum daily requirements.) Medical research indicates that each cup of skim milk contains 284 milligrams of calcium and 1.25 milligrams of vitamin C. A cup of orange juice contains 22 milligrams of calcium and 129 milligrams of vitamin C. How much of each of these foods should Alexis consume to maintain her special diet?

4.5

MATRICES, DEFINITION AND NOTATION

matrix (plural, matrices)

The **matrix** (plural, **matrices**) is a powerful tool of mathematics and the sciences. It has its beginnings in the work of the remarkable Irish genius William Rowan Hamilton (1804–1865). By the age of thirteen he knew thirteen different languages, among them Greek, Latin, Hebrew, Sanskrit, Arabic, and Persian. When he was seventeen, he had already begun his first great work in mathematical physics.

quaternions

Hamilton's theory of **quaternions** led to the theory of matrices, which was developed by Arthur Cayley (1821–1895) and James Joseph Sylvester (1814–1897). Cayley and Sylvester were lifelong friends, although their personalities were quite different. Sylvester was hot-tempered, whereas Cayley was calm and rarely lost his temper. Each

HISTORICAL NOTE

Cayley and Sylvester were both victims of some form of religious prejudice. Cayley received a teaching position at Cambridge University. At the time, all teachers at Cambridge were required to take religious vows. Although Cayley was a member of the Church of England, he refused to take holy orders just to keep his position. As a result, his teaching position was not renewed. Since he could not work as a mathematics professor because of his refusal to take these religious vows, he became a lawyer. After fourteen years as a successful lawyer he was again offered a professorship at Cambridge, which he accepted.

James Joseph Sylvester was born in London in 1814 to an orthodox Jewish family. He attended the University of London at the young age of fourteen, where he studied under the famous mathematician Augustus DeMorgan. At the age of fifteen he entered the Royal Institution of Liverpool. Here he was subject to religious persecution and at one point ran away to Dublin. At seventeen he entered

Cambridge, where he was unable to compete in certain mathematical contests because he was not a Christian. In fact, Cambridge would not even grant him his degree because he refused to accept the religious beliefs of the Church of England. In 1871, when the religious requirements were removed, Sylvester finally received his degree. This was forty years after he first entered Cambridge.

Sylvester held many jobs including various teaching positions, two of them in the United States. He taught at the University of Virginia, where he resigned his position when the university refused to discipline a student who had insulted him. He also taught at Johns Hopkins University. In London he worked for an insurance company as an actuary, preparing statistical charts. While working as an actuary, he gave private lessons in mathematics. One of his students was the famous nurse Florence Nightingale.

demonstrated his exceptional mathematical talent as a child, and each continued his mathematical activities until practically the day of his death.

Cayley and Sylvester continued the work begun by Hamilton. Although Hamilton's work was concerned with geometric situations, it has been found that the theory of matrices can be applied to almost all areas of mathematics and physics. As we shall see, it has many interesting applications in business and economics. Of course, matrices are also used extensively in pure mathematics.

You are probably wondering what a matrix is. It is just any list (or array) of numbers, such as the following:

$$\begin{pmatrix} 1 & 7 \\ 6 & 3 \end{pmatrix} \quad \begin{pmatrix} 1 & 7 & 6 \\ 0 & -2 & 4 \\ 4 & 7 & 9 \\ 1 & 3 & 3 \end{pmatrix} \quad \begin{pmatrix} 1 \\ 4 \\ 3 \\ -7 \end{pmatrix} \quad (3 \quad 2 \quad 9 \quad 10)$$

We enclose each matrix within parentheses, as shown.

The concept of a matrix can arise in familiar nonmathematical situations. Suppose the student council of Zeesa University is sponsoring a music concert, the proceeds of which are to go to the local drug rehabilitation clinic. There are two performances, one on Friday and one on Saturday. Seat prices are as follows:

$3.00 Front orchestra
 2.50 Back orchestra
 2.00 Mezzanine
 1.50 Lower balcony
 1.00 Upper balcony

The table below shows the number of tickets sold and the amount of money collected on Friday.

Type of seat	Number of seats		Price per seat	Total collected
Front orchestra	250	×	$3.00	$ 750.00
Back orchestra	120	×	2.50	300.00
Mezzanine	73	×	2.00	146.00
Lower balcony	208	×	1.50	312.00
Upper balcony	124	×	1.00	124.00
				$1632.00

On Saturday night the numbers of seats sold were: 300 front orchestra, 110 back orchestra, 78 mezzanine, 220 lower balcony, and 113 upper balcony.

The treasurer wants to figure out how much money has been collected altogether for the two concerts. He can do this in two ways.

1. He can calculate the amount collected on Saturday by setting up a table similar to the one above. He would get $1774.00. He would now add the totals together, getting $1632.00 plus $1774.00, or $3406.00

2. He can also calculate the total number of each kind of ticket sold for both nights, multiply each total by the price of that ticket, and then add. Such a calculation would look like this:

Type of seat	Seats sold Friday	Seats sold Saturday	Total seats sold		Price per seat	Total collected
Front orchestra	250	300	550	×	3.00	$1650.00
Back orchestra	120	110	230	×	2.50	575.00
Mezzanine	73	78	151	×	2.00	302.00
Lower balcony	208	220	428	×	1.50	642.00
Upper balcony	124	113	237	×	1.00	237.00
						$3406.00

In performing these calculations, we have taken lists of objects (seats) and prices, and added and multiplied them in various ways. When we work with matrices, we do the same thing in similar ways, as we shall see. The difference is that, with matrices, we use only the **numbers** involved. We do not consider the **type** of objects involved in the lists.

We begin our discussion with a formal definition of a matrix.

Definition 4.8 A **matrix** is a rectangular array (table) of numbers. We enclose the matrix within parentheses.

Some examples of matrices are as follows:

a) $\begin{pmatrix} 1 & 2 \\ 4 & -7 \end{pmatrix}$ b) $\begin{pmatrix} -1 & 0 & 3 \\ 5 & 0 & -9 \\ 1 & 3 & 8 \end{pmatrix}$ c) $\begin{pmatrix} 1 & 0 \\ 0 & 1 \end{pmatrix}$

d) $(0 \ 0 \ 0)$ e) $\begin{pmatrix} 1 \\ 2 \\ -5 \\ 7 \end{pmatrix}$ f) $\begin{pmatrix} 1 & 7 & 8 \\ -2 & -1 & -3 \\ 1 & -4 & 9 \\ -8 & 0 & 1 \end{pmatrix}$

g) (4)

The matrix of (a) has 2 rows and 2 columns. We call it a 2×2 matrix. The matrix of (b) has 3 rows and 3 columns. We call it a 3×3 matrix. The matrix of (f) has 4 rows and 3 columns. We call it a 4×3 matrix. The

Much information that is put into a computer can be fed in and processed in matrix form. Computers do addition and subtraction, as well as multiplication, of matrices. The computer can also provide results in matrix form, as shown here in a section of a printout.

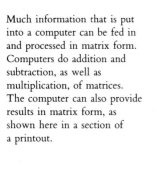
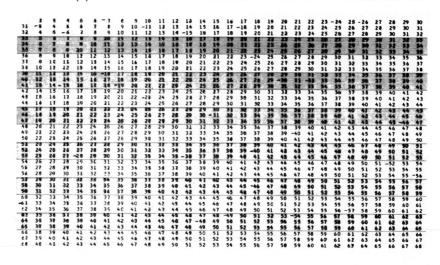

matrix of (c) is a 2×2 matrix; (d) is a 1×3 matrix; (e) is a 4×1 matrix; and (g) is a 1×1 matrix.

dimension of the matrix

In general, *a matrix that has m rows and n columns is called an m × n matrix*, read as "*m* by *n* matrix." We say that the **dimension** of the matrix is $m \times n$.

square matrix

If a matrix has the same number of rows and columns, we call it a **square matrix**. Both (a) and (c) above are 2×2 square matrices, and (b) is a 3×3 square matrix. On the other hand, (d), (e), and (f) are not square matrices. Is (g) a square matrix?

In our discussion, we will denote matrices by capital letters, such as A, B, C, ...

4.6

ADDITION, SUBTRACTION, AND MULTIPLICATION OF MATRICES

Adding two matrices

Adding two matrices is a simple procedure. We just add corresponding elements. Let $A = \begin{pmatrix} 1 & 3 \\ -2 & 0 \end{pmatrix}$, and let $B = \begin{pmatrix} 5 & 4 \\ 1 & -7 \end{pmatrix}$. Then $A + B$ is

$$\begin{pmatrix} 1 & 3 \\ -2 & 0 \end{pmatrix} + \begin{pmatrix} 5 & 4 \\ 1 & -7 \end{pmatrix} = \begin{pmatrix} 1+5 & 3+4 \\ -2+1 & 0+(-7) \end{pmatrix} = \begin{pmatrix} 6 & 7 \\ -1 & -7 \end{pmatrix}$$

EXAMPLE 1

Add the matrices $\begin{pmatrix} 2 & 4 \\ -1 & 0 \\ 6 & 6 \end{pmatrix}$ and $\begin{pmatrix} 1 & 1 \\ 10 & 8 \\ 12 & -3 \end{pmatrix}$

SOLUTION

$$\begin{pmatrix} 2 & 4 \\ -1 & 0 \\ 6 & 6 \end{pmatrix} + \begin{pmatrix} 1 & 1 \\ 10 & 8 \\ 12 & -3 \end{pmatrix} = \begin{pmatrix} 2+1 & 4+1 \\ -1+10 & 0+8 \\ 6+12 & 6+(-3) \end{pmatrix} = \begin{pmatrix} 3 & 5 \\ 9 & 8 \\ 18 & 3 \end{pmatrix}$$ ◼

EXAMPLE 2

Add the matrices $(1 \quad 7 \quad 9)$ and $(2 \quad -3 \quad 0)$

SOLUTION

$$(1 \quad 7 \quad 9) + (2 \quad -3 \quad 0) = (1+2 \quad 7+(-3) \quad 9+0)$$
$$= (3 \quad 4 \quad 9)$$ ◼

EXAMPLE 3

Add the matrices $\begin{pmatrix} 1 & -2 & 4 \\ 8 & 0 & -1 \\ 0 & 3 & 4 \end{pmatrix}$ and $\begin{pmatrix} 7 & 7 & -7 \\ -5 & 2 & 1 \\ 4 & 3 & 4 \end{pmatrix}$

SOLUTION

$$\begin{pmatrix} 1 & -2 & 4 \\ 8 & 0 & -1 \\ 0 & 3 & 4 \end{pmatrix} + \begin{pmatrix} 7 & 7 & -7 \\ -5 & 2 & 1 \\ 4 & 3 & 4 \end{pmatrix}$$

$$= \begin{pmatrix} 1+7 & -2+7 & 4+(-7) \\ 8+(-5) & 0+2 & -1+1 \\ 0+4 & 3+3 & 4+4 \end{pmatrix} = \begin{pmatrix} 8 & 5 & -3 \\ 3 & 2 & 0 \\ 4 & 6 & 8 \end{pmatrix}$$ ▬

Notice that you can add together two matrices *only* if they are of the same *dimension*. This means that the number of rows in each is the same, and the number of columns in each is the same.

EXAMPLE 4

The matrices $\begin{pmatrix} 1 & 4 \\ -3 & 9 \end{pmatrix}$ and $\begin{pmatrix} 4 & 9 & -3 \\ -2 & 0 & 1 \end{pmatrix}$ *cannot* be added because the first matrix has 2 columns and the second matrix has 3 columns. ▬

Subtraction of matrices

Subtraction of matrices is similar to addition. If the matrices are of the same dimension, we subtract the corresponding elements, as the following examples illustrate.

EXAMPLE 5

Subtract the matrix $\begin{pmatrix} 2 & 0 \\ -3 & -5 \end{pmatrix}$ from $\begin{pmatrix} 4 & 8 \\ -3 & 5 \end{pmatrix}$

SOLUTION

$$\begin{pmatrix} 4 & 8 \\ -3 & 5 \end{pmatrix} - \begin{pmatrix} 2 & 0 \\ -3 & -5 \end{pmatrix} = \begin{pmatrix} 4-2 & 8-0 \\ -3-(-3) & 5-(-5) \end{pmatrix} = \begin{pmatrix} 2 & 8 \\ 0 & 10 \end{pmatrix}$$ ▬

EXAMPLE 6

Perform the subtraction $\begin{pmatrix} 4 & 1 & 1 \\ -2 & 0 & -8 \end{pmatrix} - \begin{pmatrix} 1 & 5 & 9 \\ 8 & 3 & -5 \end{pmatrix}$

SOLUTION

$$\begin{pmatrix} 4 & 1 & 1 \\ -2 & 0 & -8 \end{pmatrix} - \begin{pmatrix} 1 & 5 & 9 \\ 8 & 3 & -5 \end{pmatrix}$$

$$= \begin{pmatrix} 4-1 & 1-5 & 1-9 \\ -2-8 & 0-3 & -8-(-5) \end{pmatrix} = \begin{pmatrix} 3 & -4 & -8 \\ -10 & -3 & -3 \end{pmatrix}$$

Comment Wherever addition is possible, the commutative and associative laws hold. This means that if A, B, and C are matrices of the same dimension, then

$$A + B = B + A \qquad \text{(Commutative law)}$$
$$A + (B + C) = (A + B) + C \qquad \text{(Associative law)}$$

equal matrices

> **Definition 4.9** Two matrices are said to be **equal** if they are of the same dimension and if their corresponding entries are equal. When matrices A and B are equal, we write this as $A = B$.

EXAMPLE 7

If $A = \begin{pmatrix} 9 & 3 \\ 2 & 7 \end{pmatrix}$ and $B = \begin{pmatrix} 9 & 3 \\ 2 & 7 \end{pmatrix}$, then $A = B$.

EXAMPLE 8

If $A = \begin{pmatrix} 8 & 2 \\ 16 & 4 \end{pmatrix}$ and $B = \begin{pmatrix} x & y \\ 16 & 4 \end{pmatrix}$, then $A = B$ only if $x = 8$ and $y = 2$. Otherwise, matrix $A \neq$ matrix B.

EXAMPLE 9

If $A = \begin{pmatrix} 5x + 7y \\ 3x - 2y \end{pmatrix}$ and $B = \begin{pmatrix} 22 \\ 5 \end{pmatrix}$, then $A = B$ only if $5x + 7y = 22$ and $3x - 2y = 5$. This represents the pair of simultaneous equations

$$\begin{Bmatrix} 5x + 7y = 22 \\ 3x - 2y = 5 \end{Bmatrix}$$

that must be solved for values of x and y.

EXAMPLE 10

If $A = \begin{pmatrix} -3 & 2 \\ 9 & 4 \end{pmatrix}$ and $B = \begin{pmatrix} -3 & 2 & 1 \\ 9 & 4 & 5 \end{pmatrix}$, then $A \neq B$ because A and B are not of the same dimension.

Multiplication of Matrices

It may seem that multiplication of matrices should be done in a manner similar to that of addition of matrices. However, if multiplication is done this way, then the range of applications is extremely limited. Since our main interest in matrices is in their applications, we will multiply matrices in a way that turns out to be useful. The procedure for multiplication will at first appear strange and unnecessarily complicated. However, you will find after working with it that it is very useful.

row matrix

column matrix

To best understand the procedure, let us start with a row matrix A and a column matrix B, that is, let A be the **row matrix** $A = (a_1\ a_2\ a_3\ \ldots\ a_n)$ and let B be the **column matrix**

$$B = \begin{pmatrix} b_1 \\ b_2 \\ \vdots \\ b_n \end{pmatrix}$$

Then the product $A \cdot B$ is the 1×1 matrix (written in parentheses) whose entries are calculated by multiplying corresponding entries of A and B and forming the sum; that is,

$$A \cdot B = \begin{pmatrix} a_1 & a_2 & a_3 \ldots a_n \end{pmatrix} \cdot \begin{pmatrix} b_1 \\ b_2 \\ b_3 \\ \vdots \\ b_n \end{pmatrix}$$

$$= (a_1 b_1 + a_2 b_2 + a_3 b_3 + \cdots + a_n b_n)$$

Thus if $A = (8\ \ 5\ \ 6)$ and $B = \begin{pmatrix} 4 \\ 1 \\ 2 \end{pmatrix}$, then

$$A \cdot B = (8 \cdot 4 + 5 \cdot 1 + 6 \cdot 2) = (49)$$

The above procedure works nicely since matrix A is 1×3 and matrix B is 3×1. Notice that the number of columns of the left matrix equals the number of rows of the right matrix. How would we multiply the following matrices?

$$\begin{pmatrix} 1 & 2 \\ 3 & 5 \end{pmatrix} \cdot \begin{pmatrix} 2 & 7 \\ 3 & 4 \end{pmatrix}$$

In this case we first multiply the rows of the left matrix by the columns of the right matrix. We must be careful to write the rows or columns as they appear in the original matrices. Thus we initially multiply the first row of the left matrix $(1 \quad 2)$ with the first column of the right matrix $\begin{pmatrix} 2 \\ 3 \end{pmatrix}$. We get

$$(1 \ 2) \cdot \begin{pmatrix} 2 \\ 3 \end{pmatrix} = (1 \cdot 2 + 2 \cdot 3) = (8)$$

This will be the entry in the first row, first column of the product matrix. Thus we have

$$\begin{pmatrix} 1 & 2 \\ 3 & 5 \end{pmatrix} \cdot \begin{pmatrix} 2 & 7 \\ 3 & 4 \end{pmatrix} = \begin{pmatrix} 8 & \\ & \end{pmatrix}$$

Then we multiply the first row of the left matrix by the second column of the right matrix. We get

$$(1 \ 2) \cdot \begin{pmatrix} 7 \\ 4 \end{pmatrix} = (1 \cdot 7 + 2 \cdot 4) = (15)$$

This will be the entry in the first row, second column of the product matrix. So we now have

$$\begin{pmatrix} 1 & 2 \\ 3 & 5 \end{pmatrix} \cdot \begin{pmatrix} 2 & 7 \\ 3 & 4 \end{pmatrix} = \begin{pmatrix} 8 & 15 \\ & \end{pmatrix}$$

Now we multiply the second row of the left matrix by the first column of the right matrix. We get

$$(3 \ 5) \cdot \begin{pmatrix} 2 \\ 3 \end{pmatrix} = (3 \cdot 2 + 5 \cdot 3) = (21)$$

Therefore

$$\begin{pmatrix} 1 & 2 \\ 3 & 5 \end{pmatrix} \cdot \begin{pmatrix} 2 & 7 \\ 3 & 4 \end{pmatrix} = \begin{pmatrix} 8 & 15 \\ 21 & \end{pmatrix}$$

Finally, we multiply the second row of the left matrix by the second column of the right matrix. This gives

$$(3 \ 5) \cdot \begin{pmatrix} 7 \\ 4 \end{pmatrix} = (3 \cdot 7 + 5 \cdot 4) = (41)$$

Our final answer is

$$\begin{pmatrix} 1 & 2 \\ 3 & 5 \end{pmatrix} \cdot \begin{pmatrix} 2 & 7 \\ 3 & 4 \end{pmatrix} = \begin{pmatrix} 8 & 15 \\ 21 & 41 \end{pmatrix}$$

Since every row of the left matrix has been multiplied by every column of the right matrix we are finished.

More generally, let us multiply the two matrices

$$\begin{pmatrix} 2 & 4 \\ 3 & -2 \\ 9 & 0 \end{pmatrix} \cdot \begin{pmatrix} 3 & 0 & 2 & 7 \\ 2 & 4 & -1 & 2 \end{pmatrix}$$

The first matrix has 3 rows and 2 columns. It is a 3×2 matrix. The second matrix is 2×4. Notice that to multiply matrices, it is *not* necessary that they have the same dimension. *What is necessary is that the number of columns of the first matrix be exactly the same as the number of rows of the second matrix.* In our case this number is 2. Our answer will be a 3×4 matrix.

The following diagram illustrates the relationship between the number of rows and columns of the matrices to be multiplied and the answer.

$$3 \times ②\text{ and }②\times 4$$
Do they match?
If yes, our answer is
$$3 \times 4$$

Now how do we obtain the numbers for the 3×4 matrix that is our answer? Let us rewrite the problem with blanks in the answer.

$$\begin{pmatrix} 2 & 4 \\ 3 & -2 \\ 9 & 0 \end{pmatrix} \cdot \begin{pmatrix} 3 & 0 & 2 & 7 \\ 2 & 4 & -1 & 2 \end{pmatrix} = \begin{pmatrix} ? & ? & ? & ? \\ ? & ? & ? & ? \\ ? & ? & ? & ? \end{pmatrix}$$

To find out what belongs in the first row, first column (the circled one), we multiply each element of row 1 of the first matrix by the *corresponding* elements of column 1 of the second matrix, and then add. This gives

$$2 \cdot 3 + 4 \cdot 2 = 6 + 8$$
$$= 14$$

To find what belongs in the third row, fourth column we multiply row 3 of the first matrix by corresponding elements of column 4 of the second matrix, and then add. This gives

$$9 \cdot 7 + 0 \cdot 2 = 63 + 0$$
$$= 63$$

In a similar manner we find the number that belongs in the second row, third column. We multiply row 2 of the first matrix by column 3 of the second matrix. We get

$$3 \cdot 2 + (-2)(-1) = 6 + 2$$
$$= 8$$

Proceeding in the same way for all the other blanks, we get

$$\begin{pmatrix} 2 & 4 \\ 3 & -2 \\ 9 & 0 \end{pmatrix} \cdot \begin{pmatrix} 3 & 0 & 2 & 7 \\ 2 & 4 & -1 & 2 \end{pmatrix}$$

$$= \begin{pmatrix} 2\cdot3+4\cdot2 & 2\cdot0+4\cdot4 & 2\cdot2+4(-1) & 2\cdot7+4\cdot2 \\ 3\cdot3+(-2)2 & 3\cdot0+(-2)4 & 3\cdot2+(-2)(-1) & 3\cdot7+(-2)(2) \\ 9\cdot3+0\cdot2 & 9\cdot0+0\cdot4 & 9\cdot2+0(-1) & 9\cdot7+0\cdot2 \end{pmatrix}$$

$$= \begin{pmatrix} 14 & 16 & 0 & 22 \\ 5 & -8 & 8 & 17 \\ 27 & 0 & 18 & 63 \end{pmatrix}$$

Notice that if we try to multiply

$$\begin{pmatrix} 3 & 0 & 2 & 7 \\ 2 & 4 & -1 & 2 \end{pmatrix} \cdot \begin{pmatrix} 2 & 4 \\ 3 & -2 \\ 9 & 0 \end{pmatrix}$$

it cannot be done, since the first matrix is 2×4 and the second matrix is 3×2. The number of columns of the first matrix is *not* the same as the number of rows of the second.

EXAMPLE 11

Multiply $\begin{pmatrix} 1 & 4 \\ 3 & -2 \end{pmatrix}$ by $\begin{pmatrix} 1 & 0 & 2 \\ -1 & 3 & 5 \end{pmatrix}$

SOLUTION

The matrices are 2×2 and 2×3, respectively. We draw a diagram.

$$2 \times \textcircled{2} \text{ and } \textcircled{2} \times 3$$
Do they match?
Yes!
Our answer is 2×3

Computing the entries for the 2×3 matrix, we get

$$\begin{pmatrix} 1 & 4 \\ 3 & -2 \end{pmatrix} \cdot \begin{pmatrix} 1 & 0 & 2 \\ -1 & 3 & 5 \end{pmatrix}$$

$$= \begin{pmatrix} 1\cdot1+4(-1) & 1\cdot0+4\cdot3 & 1\cdot2+4\cdot5 \\ 3\cdot1+(-2)(-1) & 3\cdot0+(-2)3 & 3\cdot2+(-2)5 \end{pmatrix}$$

$$= \begin{pmatrix} -3 & 12 & 22 \\ 5 & -6 & -4 \end{pmatrix}$$

EXAMPLE 12

Multiply $(1 \quad 3 \quad -1)$ by $\begin{pmatrix} 7 \\ -8 \\ 0 \end{pmatrix}$

SOLUTION

The matrices are

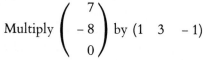

$$1 \times \boxed{3} \text{ and } \boxed{3} \times 1$$
Do they match?
Yes!
Our answer is 1×1

Computing the answer, we get

$$\left(1 \cdot 7 + 3 \cdot (-8) + (-1) \cdot 0\right) = \left(-17\right)$$

It would be wrong to write the answer as -17. Since the answer is a matrix, the parentheses are necessary.

EXAMPLE 13

Multiply $\begin{pmatrix} 7 \\ -8 \\ 0 \end{pmatrix}$ by $(1 \quad 3 \quad -1)$

SOLUTION

The matrices are

$$3 \times \boxed{1} \text{ and } \boxed{1} \times 3$$
Do they match?
Yes!
Our answer is 3×3

Computing the answer, we have

$$\begin{pmatrix} 7 \\ -8 \\ 0 \end{pmatrix} \cdot (1 \quad 3 \quad -1) = \begin{pmatrix} 7 \cdot 1 & 7 \cdot 3 & 7(-1) \\ (-8)1 & (-8)3 & (-8) \cdot (-1) \\ 0 \cdot 1 & 0 \cdot 3 & 0 \cdot (-1) \end{pmatrix}$$

$$= \begin{pmatrix} 7 & 21 & -7 \\ -8 & -24 & 8 \\ 0 & 0 & 0 \end{pmatrix}$$

William Rowan Hamilton

Compare this problem with Example 12. What does it tell us about the commutative law for multiplication of matrices? We can obviously conclude that the commutative law does not hold. When Hamilton discovered this, he was so excited about it that he scratched the result on a bridge in Dublin, where he happened to be walking at the time.

EXAMPLE 14

Multiply $\begin{pmatrix} 5 & 7 \\ -3 & 2 \end{pmatrix}$ by $\begin{pmatrix} 4 & 3 & 8 \\ -2 & 5 & 9 \\ 1 & 0 & 1 \end{pmatrix}$

SOLUTION

The matrices are

$$2 \times ② \text{ and } ③ \times 3$$
Do they match?
No!

Since they do not match, this multiplication is impossible.

EXAMPLE 15

Multiply $\begin{pmatrix} 5 & 7 \\ -3 & 2 \end{pmatrix}$ by $\begin{pmatrix} 1 & 0 \\ 0 & 1 \end{pmatrix}$

SOLUTION

The matrices are

$$2 \times ② \text{ and } ② \times 2$$
Do they match?
Yes!
Our answer is 2×2

The product is

$$\begin{pmatrix} 5 & 7 \\ -3 & 2 \end{pmatrix} \cdot \begin{pmatrix} 1 & 0 \\ 0 & 1 \end{pmatrix} = \begin{pmatrix} 5 \cdot 1 + 7 \cdot 0 & 5 \cdot 0 + 7 \cdot 1 \\ (-3)1 + 2 \cdot 0 & (-3)0 + 2 \cdot 1 \end{pmatrix}$$

$$= \begin{pmatrix} 5 & 7 \\ -3 & 2 \end{pmatrix}$$

In the last example the answer was the same matrix as the one we started with. Multiplying by $\begin{pmatrix} 1 & 0 \\ 0 & 1 \end{pmatrix}$ did nothing. If you multiply $\begin{pmatrix} 1 & 0 \\ 0 & 1 \end{pmatrix}$ by $\begin{pmatrix} 5 & 7 \\ -3 & 2 \end{pmatrix}$, you will find that the answer is also $\begin{pmatrix} 5 & 7 \\ -3 & 2 \end{pmatrix}$. Verify this. We say that $\begin{pmatrix} 1 & 0 \\ 0 & 1 \end{pmatrix}$ is the **identity for multiplication** of 2×2 matrices. Multiplying any 2×2 matrix by the matrix $\begin{pmatrix} 1 & 0 \\ 0 & 1 \end{pmatrix}$ does not change anything.

EXAMPLE 16

a) Multiply $\begin{pmatrix} 4 & 3 \\ 5 & 7 \\ -1 & 0 \end{pmatrix} \cdot \begin{pmatrix} 1 & 0 \\ 0 & 1 \end{pmatrix}$

b) Multiply $\begin{pmatrix} 1 & 0 \\ 0 & 1 \end{pmatrix} \cdot \begin{pmatrix} 4 & 3 \\ 5 & 7 \\ -1 & 0 \end{pmatrix}$

SOLUTION

a) $\begin{pmatrix} 4 & 3 \\ 5 & 7 \\ -1 & 0 \end{pmatrix} \cdot \begin{pmatrix} 1 & 0 \\ 0 & 1 \end{pmatrix} = \begin{pmatrix} 4 & 3 \\ 5 & 7 \\ -1 & 0 \end{pmatrix}$

b) This multiplication cannot be done. Why not?

In Example 15, $\begin{pmatrix} 1 & 0 \\ 0 & 1 \end{pmatrix}$ was the identity matrix because no matter which way we performed the multiplication, our answer was always $\begin{pmatrix} 5 & 7 \\ -3 & 2 \end{pmatrix}$. In Example 16, $\begin{pmatrix} 1 & 0 \\ 0 & 1 \end{pmatrix}$ is *not* the identity matrix, since we can multiply only from one side. Thus we define an identity matrix for multiplication in the following way.

identity matrix for multiplication

> **Definition 4.10** An **identity matrix for multiplication** is a square matrix that, when multiplied by another square matrix A on the left side or on the right side, leaves the matrix A unchanged. Thus $\begin{pmatrix} 1 & 0 \\ 0 & 1 \end{pmatrix}$ is the 2×2 identity matrix, and it can be shown that
>
> $$\begin{pmatrix} 1 & 0 & 0 \\ 0 & 1 & 0 \\ 0 & 0 & 1 \end{pmatrix}$$
>
> is the 3×3 identity matrix.

Sometimes we want to multiply a matrix by an ordinary number. For example, suppose we want to multiply the matrix $\begin{pmatrix} 3 & 5 \\ -1 & 7 \end{pmatrix}$ by the number 4. This is done by multiplying each entry of the matrix by 4. Thus we have the following.

$$4\begin{pmatrix} 3 & 5 \\ -1 & 7 \end{pmatrix} = \begin{pmatrix} 4\cdot 3 & 4\cdot 5 \\ 4(-1) & 4(7) \end{pmatrix} = \begin{pmatrix} 12 & 20 \\ -4 & 28 \end{pmatrix}$$

In general terms, if k is any number and A is any matrix, then kA means another matrix whose elements are obtained by multiplying each element of matrix A by the number k.

EXAMPLE 17

a) $3\begin{pmatrix} 4 & 7 \\ 2 & -2 \\ 7 & 4 \end{pmatrix} = \begin{pmatrix} 3\cdot 4 & 3\cdot 7 \\ 3\cdot 2 & 3(-2) \\ 3\cdot 7 & 3\cdot 4 \end{pmatrix} = \begin{pmatrix} 12 & 21 \\ 6 & -6 \\ 21 & 12 \end{pmatrix}$

b) $-2\begin{pmatrix} 5 \\ 0 \\ -4 \\ 9 \end{pmatrix} = \begin{pmatrix} (-2)5 \\ (-2)0 \\ (-2)(-4) \\ (-2)9 \end{pmatrix} = \begin{pmatrix} -10 \\ 0 \\ +8 \\ -18 \end{pmatrix}$

Perhaps you are wondering why matrix multiplication is defined in such a complicated fashion, especially since multiplication is not commutative. As we indicated earlier, it is the applications for matrices that lead us to define multiplication in such an unusual way. The following problem illustrates one simple application. In Section 4.7 we will give many other applications.

Suppose Mary is in a supermarket comparing the prices of several cans of vegetables. She obtains the following information on the cost per can of several nationally advertised brand name items: beans 49¢, corn 59¢, beets 55¢. This information can be written in a 1×3 matrix as

$$(49 \quad 59 \quad 55)$$

If Mary decides to purchase 7 cans of beans, 5 cans of corn, and 6 cans of beets, then we can arrange this information as a 3×1 column matrix

$$\begin{pmatrix} 7 \\ 5 \\ 6 \end{pmatrix}$$

The product of these two matrices represents the total cost. Thus,

$$(49 \quad 59 \quad 55)\cdot\begin{pmatrix} 7 \\ 5 \\ 6 \end{pmatrix} = (49\cdot 7 + 59\cdot 5 + 55\cdot 6) = (968)$$

Mary would spend a total of 968¢ or $9.68 for these items.

The supermarket also carries a no-name label (generic label) for these items. The prices for these items along with the brand name ones can be arranged in matrix form as shown.

$$
\begin{array}{c}
\begin{array}{ccc}
\text{Beans} & \text{Corn} & \text{Beets}
\end{array}\\
\begin{array}{l}
\text{Nationally advertised}\\
\text{brand name}\\
\text{No-name generic label}
\end{array}
\left(\begin{array}{ccc}
49 & 59 & 55\\[10pt]
41 & 53 & 47
\end{array}\right) = A
\end{array}
$$

Since Mary is not sure about the quality of the no-name generic-labeled cans, she decides to purchase several cans of each as indicated in matrix B.

$$
\begin{array}{c}
\begin{array}{cc}
\begin{array}{c}\text{Nationally advertised}\\ \text{brand name}\end{array} & \begin{array}{c}\text{No-name}\\ \text{generic label}\end{array}
\end{array}\\
\begin{array}{l}
\text{Beans}\\
\text{Corn}\\
\text{Beets}
\end{array}
\left(\begin{array}{cc}
4 & 3\\
3 & 2\\
4 & 2
\end{array}\right) = B
\end{array}
$$

Let us now perform the multiplication $A \cdot B$

$$
A \cdot B = \begin{pmatrix} 49 & 59 & 55 \\ 41 & 53 & 47 \end{pmatrix} \cdot \begin{pmatrix} 4 & 3 \\ 3 & 2 \\ 4 & 2 \end{pmatrix}
$$

$$
= \begin{pmatrix} 49(4) + 59(3) + 55(4) & 49(3) + 59(2) + 55(2) \\ 41(4) + 53(3) + 47(4) & 41(3) + 53(2) + 47(2) \end{pmatrix} = \begin{pmatrix} 593 & 375 \\ 511 & 323 \end{pmatrix}
$$

Can you interpret these results? The 593, for example, means that she spent $5.93 on the nationally advertised brand name items, and the 323 means that she spent $3.23 on the no-name generic-labeled items. What interpretation can you find for the 375 and the 511?

We can also perform the multiplication $B \cdot A$

$$
B \cdot A = \begin{pmatrix} 4 & 3 \\ 3 & 2 \\ 4 & 2 \end{pmatrix} \cdot \begin{pmatrix} 49 & 59 & 55 \\ 41 & 53 & 47 \end{pmatrix}
$$

$3 \times ②$ and $② \times 3$

Do they match?

Yes. The answer is

of dimension

3×3

We have

$$B \cdot A = \begin{pmatrix} 4(49) + 3(41) & 4(59) + 3(53) & 4(55) + 3(47) \\ 3(49) + 2(41) & 3(59) + 2(53) & 3(55) + 2(47) \\ 4(49) + 2(41) & 4(59) + 2(53) & 4(55) + 2(47) \end{pmatrix}$$

$$= \begin{pmatrix} 319 & 395 & 361 \\ 229 & 283 & 259 \\ 278 & 342 & 314 \end{pmatrix}$$

In this matrix the 319 means that Mary spent \$3.19 for beans, the 283 means that she spent \$2.83 for corn, and the 314 means that she spent \$3.14 for beets. Can you interpret the other numbers?

Comment The preceding problem illustrates that even when two matrices are compatible for multiplication on both sides, the results and the corresponding interpretations are completely different.

In Section 4.7 we will discuss further applications of matrices.

EXERCISES FOR SECTION 4.6

Find the dimension of each of the matrices given in Exercises 1–8.

1. $\begin{pmatrix} 1 & 7 & 6 \\ 3 & -2 & 1 \\ -9 & 7 & 8 \\ 4 & 0 & 2 \end{pmatrix}$
2. $\begin{pmatrix} 3 & 9 & 2 \\ 1 & 0 & -7 \end{pmatrix}$

3. $\begin{pmatrix} 9 & 2 \\ 5 & -3 \\ -6 & 1 \\ 8 & 2 \end{pmatrix}$
4. $(7 \quad 9 \quad 3 \quad 8)$

5. (9)
6. $\begin{pmatrix} 1 & 0 & 0 & 0 \\ 0 & 1 & 0 & 0 \\ 0 & 0 & 1 & 0 \\ 0 & 0 & 0 & 1 \end{pmatrix}$

7. $\begin{pmatrix} 3 & 7 & 6 \\ -4 & -2 & 9 \\ 8 & 3 & 1 \end{pmatrix}$
8. $\begin{pmatrix} 5 \\ 0 \\ -2 \\ -3 \\ 1 \end{pmatrix}$

9. Which (if any) of the matrices given in Exercises 1–8 are square matrices?

10. Are the following matrices equal? Explain your answer.

$$\begin{pmatrix} 5 & 3 & 2 & 7 \\ 4 & 9 & 0 & -1 \end{pmatrix} \qquad \begin{pmatrix} 5 & 4 \\ 3 & 9 \\ 2 & 0 \\ 7 & -1 \end{pmatrix}$$

In Exercises 11–16, find a value for the variable(s) so that matrices A and B will be equal. If this is not possible, explain why.

11. $A = \begin{pmatrix} 7 & 3 \\ 4 & x \end{pmatrix}$ $B = \begin{pmatrix} 7 & 3 \\ 4 & 9 \end{pmatrix}$

12. $A = \begin{pmatrix} -3 & 9 \\ -14 & 2y \end{pmatrix}$ $B = \begin{pmatrix} -3 & 9 \\ -14 & 20 \end{pmatrix}$

13. $A = \begin{pmatrix} 10 & 17 \\ 16 & -5y \\ 4 & -9 \end{pmatrix}$ $B = \begin{pmatrix} 10 & 17 \\ 2x & 25 \\ 4 & -9 \end{pmatrix}$

14. $A = \begin{pmatrix} 11 & 7 & 2x \\ 6 & 4 & 5y \\ 2 & 9 & 3z \end{pmatrix}$ $B = \begin{pmatrix} 11 & 7 & 10 \\ 6 & 4 & 0 \\ 2 & 9 & 10 \end{pmatrix}$

15. $A = \begin{pmatrix} 1 & 7 & x \\ 6 & 2 & 3 \end{pmatrix}$ $B = \begin{pmatrix} 1 & 7 & 8 & 3 \\ 6 & 2 & 3 & 9 \end{pmatrix}$

16. $A = \begin{pmatrix} 4 & 2x+7 & 9 \\ 3 & 5z-3 & 7 \end{pmatrix}$ $B = \begin{pmatrix} 4 & 4x-1 & 9 \\ 3 & 3z+7 & 2y \end{pmatrix}$

In each of the Exercises 17–42, perform the indicated operations or indicate why the operation cannot be performed.

17. $\begin{pmatrix} 1 & 7 \\ -3 & 4 \end{pmatrix} + \begin{pmatrix} 2 & 0 \\ -8 & 9 \end{pmatrix}$

18. $\begin{pmatrix} 1 \\ 7 \\ 9 \end{pmatrix} + \begin{pmatrix} 3 \\ 0 \\ -2 \end{pmatrix}$

19. $\begin{pmatrix} 4 & 1 & 9 \\ 10 & -3 & 7 \end{pmatrix} + \begin{pmatrix} 0 & -2 & -5 \\ 3 & 8 & 4 \end{pmatrix}$

20. $\begin{pmatrix} 7 & 8 & -3 \end{pmatrix} - \begin{pmatrix} -4 & -2 & 9 \end{pmatrix}$

21. $\begin{pmatrix} -4 & -2 \\ 8 & 3 \end{pmatrix} + \begin{pmatrix} 2 & 7 & 8 \\ 1 & 6 & 0 \end{pmatrix}$

22. $\begin{pmatrix} 1 & 8 & 3 \\ 9 & 10 & -12 \end{pmatrix} - \begin{pmatrix} 8 & 0 & 11 \\ 6 & -2 & 7 \\ 3 & 5 & 4 \end{pmatrix}$

23. $\begin{pmatrix} 8 & 1 & 10 \\ 11 & -2 & -\frac{1}{2} \\ 3 & 7 & -4 \end{pmatrix} - \begin{pmatrix} 5 & -3 & -4 \\ 2 & 0 & \frac{3}{2} \\ 2 & -8 & 9 \end{pmatrix}$

24. $\begin{pmatrix} 7 & -1 & 8 \\ 10 & 12 & -7 \end{pmatrix} - \begin{pmatrix} 0 & -6 & -5 \\ -2 & 3 & 8 \end{pmatrix}$

25. $\begin{pmatrix} 5 & 3 & 2 \\ 1 & 4 & 7 \\ 0 & 2 & 9 \end{pmatrix} + \begin{pmatrix} 0 & 0 & 0 \\ 0 & 0 & 0 \\ 0 & 0 & 0 \end{pmatrix}$

26. $\begin{pmatrix} 4 & 7 \\ x & y \end{pmatrix} + \begin{pmatrix} 0 & 0 \\ 0 & 0 \end{pmatrix}$

27. $\begin{pmatrix} 0 & 0 \\ 0 & 0 \end{pmatrix} + \begin{pmatrix} 4 & 7 \\ x & y \end{pmatrix}$

28. $\begin{pmatrix} 2 & 7 \\ -3 & 6 \end{pmatrix} \cdot \begin{pmatrix} 4 & -1 \\ -2 & 9 \end{pmatrix}$

29. $\begin{pmatrix} 1 & 7 \\ 0 & 2 \end{pmatrix} \cdot \begin{pmatrix} 8 & -3 \\ -9 & 6 \end{pmatrix}$

30. $\begin{pmatrix} 1 & 7 & 6 \\ 2 & -3 & 1 \\ 4 & 8 & 3 \end{pmatrix} \cdot \begin{pmatrix} 1 & 0 \\ -3 & -7 \\ 2 & 9 \end{pmatrix}$

31. $\begin{pmatrix} 3 & -8 & 2 \\ 6 & -9 & 1 \end{pmatrix} \cdot \begin{pmatrix} -2 & 7 \\ 6 & -1 \\ 0 & 9 \end{pmatrix}$

32. $\begin{pmatrix} 1 & -8 \\ -3 & 7 \\ 6 & 5 \end{pmatrix} \cdot \begin{pmatrix} 2 & -3 & 5 \\ -4 & 8 & 1 \end{pmatrix}$

33. $\begin{pmatrix} 1 & 3 & 7 & 10 \end{pmatrix} \cdot \begin{pmatrix} 2 \\ -1 \\ -6 \\ -9 \end{pmatrix}$

34. $\begin{pmatrix} 2 \\ -1 \\ 6 \\ 9 \end{pmatrix} \cdot \begin{pmatrix} 1 & 3 & 7 & 10 \end{pmatrix}$

35. $\begin{pmatrix} 4 & -5 & 3 \\ 8 & 1 & 0 \end{pmatrix} \cdot \begin{pmatrix} 21 & 6 & 8 \\ 10 & -2 & 5 \\ -11 & 12 & 0 \end{pmatrix}$

36. $-3 \begin{pmatrix} 5 & -1 & 6 \\ 2 & -1 & 8 \\ 7 & 0 & 9 \end{pmatrix}$

37. $-6\begin{pmatrix} 0 & 2 & 5 \\ 1 & 7 & 2 \\ 6 & 6 & 3 \\ 5 & 8 & -7 \end{pmatrix}$

38. $4\begin{pmatrix} 7 & -1 & 10 \\ 3 & -6 & 2 \\ 5 & 1 & 3 \end{pmatrix} \cdot \begin{pmatrix} 8 & 2 & 6 \\ -1 & -4 & -2 \\ 0 & 3 & 5 \end{pmatrix}$

39. $5\begin{pmatrix} 3 & 7 \\ 1 & 6 \end{pmatrix} + 3\begin{pmatrix} 8 & 2 \\ 0 & 3 \end{pmatrix}$ **40.** $8\begin{pmatrix} 2 & 1 \\ 6 & 9 \end{pmatrix} - 4\begin{pmatrix} 3 & 8 \\ 4 & 2 \end{pmatrix}$

41. $3\begin{pmatrix} -1 & 4 & 7 \\ 6 & -9 & 3 \\ 1 & -4 & 5 \end{pmatrix} - 4\begin{pmatrix} -3 & 4 & -7 \\ 6 & 1 & 0 \\ 2 & 5 & -3 \end{pmatrix}$

42. $-3\begin{pmatrix} 9 & 6 \\ 4 & 2 \\ 0 & 1 \end{pmatrix} \cdot \begin{pmatrix} -2 & -9 \\ 3 & 4 \end{pmatrix}$

43. Find x and y such that
$$\begin{pmatrix} 2 & 7 \\ 9 & x \end{pmatrix} + \begin{pmatrix} y & -3 \\ 6 & -5 \end{pmatrix} = \begin{pmatrix} 8 & 4 \\ 15 & 10 \end{pmatrix}$$

44. If
$$A = \begin{pmatrix} 4 & 3 & 7 \\ 6 & -2 & 0 \\ 1 & 9 & 8 \end{pmatrix}, \quad B = \begin{pmatrix} 1 & -8 & 2 \\ -3 & 9 & 10 \\ 5 & 1 & 8 \end{pmatrix},$$

$$C = \begin{pmatrix} -1 & 7 & 9 \\ 2 & 8 & 4 \\ 6 & 0 & 5 \end{pmatrix},$$

verify that the associative law for addition, $A + (B + C) = (A + B) + C$, holds for these matrices.

45. Refer back to the previous exercise. Verify that the commutative law for addition, $A + B = B + A$, holds for these matrices.

46. The president of the Back Corporation is analyzing the number of hours that each of the company's 5 computer programmers spends on the computer terminals. On Monday the programmers Bill, Cindy, Gail, Jake, and Jason spent 6, 4, 5, 3, and 9 hours, respectively, on the terminals. On Tuesday they spent 8, 6, 5, 7, and 2 hours, respectively, and on Wednes-

day they spent 9, 6, 8, 3, and 7 hours, respectively.

a) Rewrite this information in matrix form.

b) Find the total amount of time spent by each of these programmers on the terminals over the three days.

c) What is the total number of hours spent by these employees on the terminals over the three day period?

47. *Inflation.* The accompanying chart indicates how the average prices for several auto repair items have changed from the previous years in each of two years for three cities. In these charts a plus sign indicates an increase in price, whereas a minus sign indicates a decrease in price (*Note*: All price changes are in dollars.)

	Engine tune-up	Transmission tune-up	1988 Exhaust system repair	Charging air conditioning system	New tires
City A	+6	+7	+13	+1	+8
City B	+8	+3	+8	-2	0
City C	+5	0	-1	-3	0

	Engine tune-up	Transmission tune-up	1989 Exhaust system repair	Charging air conditioning system	New tires
City A	+8	+2	0	+1	-1
City B	+5	+8	+4	+3	0
City C	-1	-3	+6	0	+7

a) Find the net effect of inflation over the two-year period by adding the matrices.

b) Which item's price increased the most and in which city?

c) Which item's price increased the least or decreased the most and in which city?

48. *Inventory Control.* A large supermarket chain has four warehouses from which it ships various items to its stores located within the city. It keeps accurate records on the inventories at each of these warehouses as shown in the accompanying charts:

a) How many items were removed from the inventory during June?

b) Which warehouse shipped the most merchandise in June?

c) Which warehouse shipped the least merchandise in June?

		June 1 Inventory				July 1 Inventory			
		Warehouse location				**Warehouse location**			
		Main St.	West St.	Beck St.	Ave. L	Main St.	West St.	Beck St.	Ave. L
Item	Coffee	1258	373	984	262	375	250	225	130
	Detergent	1728	841	636	954	870	726	432	298
	Sugar	894	1381	1292	651	695	977	973	179
	Oil	1523	1281	990	657	603	527	408	199

 Brain-Teaser Problems

**49. Find a 2×2 matrix A such that

$$A^2 = A \cdot A = \begin{pmatrix} 1 & 0 \\ 0 & 1 \end{pmatrix}$$

(Assume that A is not the identity matrix.)

**50. Consider any matrix

$$A = \begin{pmatrix} x & y \\ z & w \end{pmatrix}$$

Under what conditions will it be true that

$$A^2 = A \cdot A = \begin{pmatrix} 1 & 0 \\ 0 & 1 \end{pmatrix}$$

**51. Let $\quad A = \begin{pmatrix} x & y \\ z & w \end{pmatrix} \quad$ and $\quad B = \begin{pmatrix} 1 & 1 \\ -1 & 1 \end{pmatrix}$

where A is not the 2×2 identity matrix. Under what circumstances will it be true that $A \cdot B = B \cdot A$?

**52. Can you find two 2×2 matrices A and B such that

$$A \neq \begin{pmatrix} 0 & 0 \\ 0 & 0 \end{pmatrix} \quad B \neq \begin{pmatrix} 0 & 0 \\ 0 & 0 \end{pmatrix} \quad \text{and}$$

$$A \cdot B = \begin{pmatrix} 0 & 0 \\ 0 & 0 \end{pmatrix}$$

**53. Can you find a 2×2 matrix A such that $A \cdot A = A$? Assume that

$$A \neq \begin{pmatrix} 0 & 0 \\ 0 & 0 \end{pmatrix}$$

4.7

APPLICATIONS OF MATRICES

Matrices can be very useful in analyzing such business problems as determining cost, profit, and amounts of materials needed. The following examples illustrate how this can be done.

A drug and cosmetics company markets the following products: Eagle hair tonic, Victor toothpaste, and Laury deodorant. The following table indicates the number of cases of each product ordered by four different supermarkets.

	Hair tonic	Toothpaste	Deodorant
Market I	5	4	7
Market II	8	0	1
Market III	13	3	9
Market IV	2	6	3

The hair tonic costs \$12 per case, the toothpaste costs \$9 a case, and the deodorant costs \$15 a case.

There are many things that may be of interest to both the manufacturer and store managers. Each of these can be expressed by some combination of matrices. Suppose the manufacturer wants to know the total income from each supermarket and also the total income from all supermarkets together.

From market I the income is $5(12) + 4(9) + 7(15) = \$201$.

From market II the income is $8(12) + 0(9) + 1(15) = \$111$.

From market III the income is $13(12) + 3(9) + 9(15) = \$318$.

From market IV the income is $2(12) + 6(9) + 3(15) = \$123$.

We can put the final result in matrix form as

$$\begin{pmatrix} 201 \\ 111 \\ 318 \\ 123 \end{pmatrix}$$

The entire computation can be done in a much more efficient way using matrices as follows.

Let A represent the amounts ordered of each product. We then have

$$A = \begin{pmatrix} 5 & 4 & 7 \\ 8 & 0 & 1 \\ 13 & 3 & 9 \\ 2 & 6 & 3 \end{pmatrix}$$

Let C represent the cost of each item. Then

$$C = \begin{pmatrix} 12 \\ 9 \\ 15 \end{pmatrix}$$

and

$$A \cdot C = \begin{pmatrix} 5 & 4 & 7 \\ 8 & 0 & 1 \\ 13 & 3 & 9 \\ 2 & 6 & 3 \end{pmatrix} \cdot \begin{pmatrix} 12 \\ 9 \\ 15 \end{pmatrix} = \begin{pmatrix} 5(12) + 4(9) + 7(15) \\ 8(12) + 0(9) + 1(15) \\ 13(12) + 3(9) + 9(15) \\ 2(12) + 6(9) + 3(15) \end{pmatrix} = \begin{pmatrix} 201 \\ 111 \\ 318 \\ 123 \end{pmatrix}$$

The matrix AC represents the total income from each supermarket. Market I paid \$201 for all three products; \$111 is the total income from market II. Similarly, \$318 and \$123 are the incomes from markets III and IV, respectively.

The total income from all the supermarkets is obtained by adding the numbers down. This gives \$753.

Some further examples illustrate how matrices can be used in business problems.

EXAMPLE 1

Let us refer back to the concerts discussed on p. 210. The computations performed there can be done in matrix form as follows: Let the matrix A represent the number of tickets sold on Friday night. Let the matrix B stand for the number of tickets sold on Saturday. Let C be the cost matrix. Then

$$A = \begin{pmatrix} 250 \\ 120 \\ 73 \\ 208 \\ 124 \end{pmatrix} \quad B = \begin{pmatrix} 300 \\ 110 \\ 78 \\ 220 \\ 113 \end{pmatrix} \quad C = (3.00 \quad 2.50 \quad 2.00 \quad 1.50 \quad 1.00)$$

$$A + B = \begin{pmatrix} 250 + 300 \\ 120 + 110 \\ 73 + 78 \\ 208 + 220 \\ 124 + 113 \end{pmatrix} = \begin{pmatrix} 550 \\ 230 \\ 151 \\ 428 \\ 237 \end{pmatrix} = \begin{matrix} \text{Total seats sold} \\ \text{of each type} \\ \text{Friday and} \\ \text{Saturday,} \end{matrix}$$

$$C \cdot (A + B) = (3.00 \quad 2.50 \quad 2.00 \quad 1.50 \quad 1.00) \cdot \begin{pmatrix} 550 \\ 230 \\ 151 \\ 428 \\ 237 \end{pmatrix} = (3406)$$

This represents the total income from both performances.

EXAMPLE 2

The following table lists the number of summonses issued for various traffic violations for the first three months of 1989 in one midwestern town.

	Speeding	Illegal U-turn	Double parking	Drunken driving
January	2064	210	5314	206
February	3018	342	3709	421
March	1997	78	4112	308

Furthermore, the fines for these offenses are $50, $10, $20, and $30, respectively.

Mayor Peters wants to know how much money the town can expect from these summonses. She may also be interested in determining how much money will be collected each month. Using matrices she can proceed in the following way.

Let the matrix A represent the number of summonses, and let the matrix C be the fine for each offense. We have

$$A = \begin{pmatrix} 2064 & 210 & 5314 & 206 \\ 3018 & 342 & 3709 & 421 \\ 1997 & 78 & 4112 & 308 \end{pmatrix} \quad C = \begin{pmatrix} 50 \\ 10 \\ 20 \\ 30 \end{pmatrix}$$

$$A \cdot C = \begin{pmatrix} 217{,}760 \\ 241{,}130 \\ 192{,}110 \end{pmatrix} \begin{matrix} \leftarrow \text{amount collected in January.} \\ \leftarrow \text{amount collected in February.} \\ \leftarrow \text{amount collected in March.} \end{matrix}$$

The total amount collected for all three months is found by adding the monthly totals together. It is $651,000. ■

EXAMPLE 3

Three salesmen for a dress manufacturer submit the following orders for the month of January. The results are coded in the form of matrices where the rows stand for the dress sizes: 8, 10, 12, and 14. The columns represent the colors; black, red, green, and beige.

Salesman 1

$$\begin{pmatrix} 12 & 10 & 5 & 1 \\ 8 & 2 & 8 & 5 \\ 7 & 0 & 17 & 9 \\ 5 & 4 & 19 & 0 \end{pmatrix}$$

Salesman 2

$$\begin{pmatrix} 2 & 3 & 4 & 1 \\ 5 & 0 & 9 & 6 \\ 3 & 14 & 17 & 8 \\ 10 & 7 & 3 & 2 \end{pmatrix}$$

Salesman 3

$$\begin{pmatrix} 0 & 4 & 8 & 12 \\ 5 & 4 & 3 & 9 \\ 8 & 7 & 12 & 6 \\ 0 & 1 & 5 & 0 \end{pmatrix}$$

From these reports the manufacturer can obtain much information. Some of these results are summarized below. In each case, you should verify the results given.

108 size 12 dresses were sold,

59 beige dresses were sold,

65 black dresses were sold,

84 dresses were sold by salesman 3,

290 dresses were sold altogether.

Comment In doing these examples it may be possible to write a matrix in two different ways. For instance, in Example 2 the matrix C was written as a 4×1 matrix,

$$C = \begin{pmatrix} 50 \\ 10 \\ 20 \\ 30 \end{pmatrix}$$

We could have written it as a 1×4 matrix: $(50 \quad 10 \quad 20 \quad 30)$. However, note that if we had written it as a 1×4, it would not have been possible to multiply it by A. (Why not?) We would then have been unable to solve this problem using matrices. Care is needed in deciding which matrices are to be used and how they are to be written. You must consider what is to be done with the matrix when making these decisions.

Perhaps you are wondering why we use matrices to solve these problems when general arithmetic would work just as well. One reason is that the same type of problem may have to be solved many times with different numbers. For example, a salesman may send in monthly sales reports, all of which have different figures and all of which have to be analyzed by the same procedure. Matrices provide a *mechanical* procedure for doing this. All we have to do is "plug in" the new numbers each time and work out the answer mechanically. We do not have to rethink the method each time.

Another reason for using matrices is that the lists may be very long. There may be many different things that we want to analyze. In such situations we could use a computer to help us with the calculations. Matrix operations can be very easily performed by a computer, and there are many software programs prepared to do such operations.

Applications to Systems of Equations

If we are asked to solve the system of equations

$$\left\{ \begin{array}{l} 2x + 3y = 11 \\ 7x + 5y = 33 \end{array} \right\}$$

for x and y, then we are looking for one value of x and one value of y that satisfy both equations. The solution for these equations is $x = 4$ and $y = 1$. This can be verified by substituting $x = 4$ and $y = 1$ into each of the equations. This answer can be obtained using matrices in the following way.

We first write the numbers on the left-hand side, in matrix form. Call this matrix A. It consists of the numbers in front of the letters. If no number is indicated, it is understood to be 1. In our case we have

$$A = \begin{pmatrix} 2 & 3 \\ 7 & 5 \end{pmatrix}$$

The numbers on the right-hand side of the equation can be written as a matrix C:

$$C = \begin{pmatrix} 11 \\ 33 \end{pmatrix}$$

The unknowns x and y can be written as a matrix M:

$$M = \begin{pmatrix} x \\ y \end{pmatrix}$$

If we multiply matrices A and M (by matrix multiplication), we get

$$AM = \begin{pmatrix} 2 & 3 \\ 7 & 5 \end{pmatrix} \cdot \begin{pmatrix} x \\ y \end{pmatrix} = \begin{pmatrix} 2x + 3y \\ 7x + 5y \end{pmatrix}$$

Notice that the result is the same as C, since $2x + 3y = 11$ and $7x + 5y = 33$. Therefore

$$AM = C$$

inverse of matrix

It can be shown that a 2×2 matrix, such as A, may have an **inverse**. This means that there may exist another matrix which when multiplied by A will give the identity matrix (see Definition 4.10). Such an inverse will be denoted by A^{-1}. We can verify (see Example 6 p. 235) by direct matrix multiplication that if matrix $T = \begin{pmatrix} a & b \\ c & d \end{pmatrix}$, then the inverse, T^{-1}, is $\begin{pmatrix} d & -b \\ -c & a \end{pmatrix}$ multiplied by the number $\dfrac{1}{ad - bc}$, provided that $ad - bc$ is not 0.[1] Using this result, we find that the inverse of $A = \begin{pmatrix} 2 & 3 \\ 7 & 5 \end{pmatrix}$ is $A^{-1} =$

---

[1] If $ad - bc = 0$, then the number $1/(ad - bc)$ would be $1/0$. This, of course, is undefined.

$\begin{pmatrix} 5 & -3 \\ -7 & 2 \end{pmatrix}$ multiplied by $\dfrac{1}{2(5) - 3(7)}$, or $A^{-1} = \begin{pmatrix} 5 & -3 \\ -7 & 2 \end{pmatrix}$ multi-

plied by $-\dfrac{1}{11}$. This gives

$$A^{-1} = \begin{pmatrix} \dfrac{-5}{11} & \dfrac{+3}{11} \\ \dfrac{+7}{11} & \dfrac{-2}{11} \end{pmatrix}$$

(If you have forgotten how this type of multiplication is performed, see p. 222). You should verify that this is the inverse by multiplying it with A. You should get

$$\begin{pmatrix} 2 & 3 \\ 7 & 5 \end{pmatrix} \cdot \begin{pmatrix} \dfrac{-5}{11} & \dfrac{+3}{11} \\ \dfrac{+7}{11} & \dfrac{-2}{11} \end{pmatrix} = \begin{pmatrix} 1 & 0 \\ 0 & 1 \end{pmatrix}$$

Let us go back to our equation $AM = C$. Multiplying both sides by A^{-1} gives us

$$A^{-1}(AM) = A^{-1}C$$
$$(A^{-1}A)M = A^{-1}C \qquad \text{(by the associative law)}$$

Since $A^{-1}A$ is the 2×2 identity matrix, and the identity matrix (Definition 4.10) does not change anything when you multiply with it, we get

$$M = A^{-1}C$$

(Be careful! $A^{-1}C$ may not equal CA^{-1}, since matrix multiplication is not always commutative.)

This means that

$$\begin{pmatrix} x \\ y \end{pmatrix} = \begin{pmatrix} \dfrac{-5}{11} & \dfrac{+3}{11} \\ \dfrac{+7}{11} & \dfrac{-2}{11} \end{pmatrix} \cdot \begin{pmatrix} 11 \\ 13 \end{pmatrix}$$

$$= \begin{pmatrix} \dfrac{-5}{11} \cdot (11) + \dfrac{+3}{11} \cdot (33) \\ \dfrac{+7}{11} \cdot (11) + \dfrac{-2}{11} \cdot (33) \end{pmatrix} = \begin{pmatrix} -5 + 9 \\ 7 - 6 \end{pmatrix} = \begin{pmatrix} 4 \\ 1 \end{pmatrix}$$

Thus we have $x = 4$ and $y = 1$.

EXAMPLE 4

Solve $\begin{Bmatrix} 3x - 2y = 0 \\ 2x + y = 7 \end{Bmatrix}$ for x and y.

SOLUTION

We have

$$A = \begin{pmatrix} 3 & -2 \\ 2 & 1 \end{pmatrix} \quad M = \begin{pmatrix} x \\ y \end{pmatrix} \quad C = \begin{pmatrix} 0 \\ 7 \end{pmatrix}$$

$$A^{-1} = \begin{pmatrix} 1 & 2 \\ -2 & 3 \end{pmatrix} \quad \text{multiplied by} \quad \frac{1}{3 \cdot (1) - (-2)2}$$

$$A^{-1} = \begin{pmatrix} 1 & 2 \\ -2 & 3 \end{pmatrix} \quad \text{multiplied by} \quad \frac{1}{+7}$$

Therefore

$$A^{-1} = \begin{pmatrix} \dfrac{1}{7} & \dfrac{2}{7} \\ \dfrac{-2}{7} & \dfrac{3}{7} \end{pmatrix}$$

Our answer is then

$$M = A^{-1}C$$

$$\begin{pmatrix} x \\ y \end{pmatrix} = \begin{pmatrix} \dfrac{1}{7} & \dfrac{2}{7} \\ \dfrac{-2}{7} & \dfrac{3}{7} \end{pmatrix} \cdot \begin{pmatrix} 0 \\ 7 \end{pmatrix} = \begin{pmatrix} \dfrac{1}{7} \cdot (0) + \dfrac{2}{7} \cdot (7) \\ \dfrac{-2}{7} \cdot (0) + \dfrac{3}{7} \cdot (7) \end{pmatrix}$$

$$= \begin{pmatrix} 0 + 2 \\ 0 + 3 \end{pmatrix} = \begin{pmatrix} 2 \\ 3 \end{pmatrix}$$

Finally, we have $x = 2$ and $y = 3$. (You should check these answers by substituting $x = 2$ and $y = 3$ into the original equations.) ■

This technique can be extended to solve a system with any number of equations and the same number of unknowns.

EXAMPLE 5

Solve $\begin{Bmatrix} 4x - 3y = 5 \\ x + 2y = 4 \end{Bmatrix}$ for x and y.

SOLUTION

We have

$$A = \begin{pmatrix} 4 & -3 \\ 1 & 2 \end{pmatrix} \quad M = \begin{pmatrix} x \\ y \end{pmatrix} \quad C = \begin{pmatrix} 5 \\ 4 \end{pmatrix}$$

$$A^{-1} = \begin{pmatrix} 2 & 3 \\ -1 & 4 \end{pmatrix} \quad \text{multiplied by} \quad \frac{1}{4(2)-(-3)(1)}$$

$$A^{-1} = \begin{pmatrix} 2 & 3 \\ -1 & 4 \end{pmatrix} \quad \text{multiplied by} \quad \frac{1}{11}$$

Therefore

$$A^{-1} = \begin{pmatrix} \dfrac{2}{11} & \dfrac{3}{11} \\ \dfrac{-1}{11} & \dfrac{4}{11} \end{pmatrix}$$

Our answer is then

$$M = A^{-1}C$$

$$\begin{pmatrix} x \\ y \end{pmatrix} = \begin{pmatrix} \dfrac{2}{11} & \dfrac{3}{11} \\ \dfrac{-1}{11} & \dfrac{4}{11} \end{pmatrix} \cdot \begin{pmatrix} 5 \\ 4 \end{pmatrix} = \begin{pmatrix} \dfrac{2}{11} \cdot (5) + \dfrac{3}{11} \cdot (4) \\ \dfrac{-1}{11} \cdot (5) + \dfrac{4}{11} \cdot (4) \end{pmatrix}$$

$$= \begin{pmatrix} \dfrac{10}{11} + \dfrac{12}{11} \\ \dfrac{-5}{11} + \dfrac{16}{11} \end{pmatrix}$$

$$= \begin{pmatrix} \dfrac{22}{11} \\ \dfrac{11}{11} \end{pmatrix} = \begin{pmatrix} 2 \\ 1 \end{pmatrix}$$

Thus we have $x = 2$ and $y = 1$. (Again you should check these answers by substituting $x = 2$ and $y = 1$ into the original equations.) ▄▄

EXAMPLE 6

Verify, by matrix multiplication, that if matrix

$$T = \begin{pmatrix} a & b \\ c & d \end{pmatrix}$$

then its inverse is

$$\begin{pmatrix} d & -b \\ -c & a \end{pmatrix} \quad \text{multiplied by} \quad \frac{1}{ad - bc}$$

(We will assume that $ad - bc$ is not equal to 0. Otherwise the inverse does not exist.)

SOLUTION

We first multiply $\begin{pmatrix} a & b \\ c & d \end{pmatrix}$ by $\begin{pmatrix} d & -b \\ -c & a \end{pmatrix}$, getting

$$\begin{pmatrix} a & b \\ c & d \end{pmatrix} \cdot \begin{pmatrix} d & -b \\ -c & a \end{pmatrix} = \begin{pmatrix} ad + b(-c) & a(-b) + ba \\ cd + d(-c) & c(-b) + da \end{pmatrix}$$

$$= \begin{pmatrix} ad - bc & -ab + ba \\ cd - dc & -bc + da \end{pmatrix}$$

$$= \begin{pmatrix} ad - bc & 0 \\ 0 & ad - bc \end{pmatrix}$$

Finally, multiplying this matrix by $\dfrac{1}{ad - bc}$ gives

$$\begin{pmatrix} \dfrac{ad - bc}{ad - bc} & \dfrac{0}{ad - bc} \\ \dfrac{0}{ad - bc} & \dfrac{ad - bc}{ad - bc} \end{pmatrix} = \begin{pmatrix} 1 & 0 \\ 0 & 1 \end{pmatrix}$$

which is the 2×2 identity matrix. Also

$$\begin{pmatrix} d & -b \\ -c & a \end{pmatrix} \cdot \begin{pmatrix} a & b \\ c & d \end{pmatrix} = \begin{pmatrix} da - bc & 0 \\ 0 & -cb + ad \end{pmatrix}$$

Multiplying this matrix by $\dfrac{1}{ad - bc}$ gives $\begin{pmatrix} 1 & 0 \\ 0 & 1 \end{pmatrix}$. Thus the inverse of $\begin{pmatrix} a & b \\ c & d \end{pmatrix}$ is $\begin{pmatrix} d & -b \\ -c & a \end{pmatrix}$ multiplied by $\dfrac{1}{ad - bc}$ ◼

*Elementary Row Operations

We can also solve a system of equations by performing what are known as **elementary row operations**. These are defined as follows.

> **Definition 4.11** An **elementary row operation** on any matrix consists of any one of the following three operations:
>
> 1. Interchanging any two rows.
> 2. Multiplying all elements of any row by a given nonzero number.
> 3. Multiplying each element of a row by a number and then adding the results to the corresponding elements of another row.

---

* The remainder of this section can be skipped without affecting the continuity.

EXAMPLE 7

a) The matrix $\begin{pmatrix} 3 & 7 \\ 9 & 4 \end{pmatrix}$ can be transformed into the matrix $\begin{pmatrix} 9 & 4 \\ 3 & 7 \end{pmatrix}$ by interchanging the first and the second rows.

b) The matrix $\begin{pmatrix} 4 & 8 \\ 6 & 9 \end{pmatrix}$ can be transformed into the matrix $\begin{pmatrix} 2 & 4 \\ 2 & 3 \end{pmatrix}$ by multiplying each element of row 1 by $\frac{1}{2}$ and each element of row 2 by $\frac{1}{3}$.   ▬

Comment   The elementary row operations correspond to operations that we can perform with a system of equations without changing the solution to the equations. For example, we may interchange any two equations, or we may multiply both sides of an equation by a number and then add it to the other equation.

Let us solve the system of equations

$$\begin{cases} 4x - 3y = 5 \\ x + 2y = 4 \end{cases}$$

for x and y by using elementary row operations. (These equations were already solved in Example 5.) We already know that

$$A = \begin{pmatrix} 4 & -3 \\ 1 & 2 \end{pmatrix} \quad \text{and} \quad C = \begin{pmatrix} 5 \\ 4 \end{pmatrix}$$

augmented matrix

We combine these two matrices into an **augmented matrix** using a dashed line to separate them:

$$\begin{pmatrix} 4 & -3 & \vdots & 5 \\ 1 & 2 & \vdots & 4 \end{pmatrix}$$

Now we perform a series of elementary row operations on the augmented matrix to arrive at the answer. We indicate the operations applied to the equations and to the augmented matrix so that you can see the correspondence.

Equation	*Matrix*
$4x - 3y = 5$ $x + 2y = 4$	Our objective is to apply elementary row operations to the augmented matrix so that we get the identity matrix to the left of the dashed line. Thus we try to get a 1 in the row 1, column 1 position, and then a 0 in the row 2, column 1 position. To

$$x + 2y = 4$$
$$4x - 3y = 5$$

$$x + 2y = 4$$
$$4x - 4x - 3y - 8y = 5 - 16$$

or

$$x + 2y = 4$$
$$0x - 11y = -11$$

accomplish this, we interchange row 2 and row 1. This results in

$$\begin{pmatrix} 1 & 2 & | & 4 \\ 4 & -3 & | & 5 \end{pmatrix}$$

Now we multiply each element of row 1 by -4 and add the results to row 2. We get

$$\begin{pmatrix} 1 & 2 & | & 4 \\ 0 & -11 & | & -11 \end{pmatrix}$$

(Note that row 1 remains unchanged)

Next we want to get a 1 in the row 2, column 2 position. To accomplish this, we multiply each element of row 2 by $\dfrac{-1}{11}$.
This gives us

$$x + 2y = 4$$
$$0x + y = 1$$

$$\begin{pmatrix} 1 & 2 & | & 4 \\ 0 & 1 & | & 1 \end{pmatrix}$$

Finally, we want to have a 0 in the row 1, column 2 position. To accomplish this, we multiply each element of row 2 by -2 and add the results to row 1. We get

$$x + 0y = 2$$
$$0x + y = 1$$

$$\begin{pmatrix} 1 & 0 & | & 2 \\ 0 & 1 & | & 1 \end{pmatrix}$$

The final augmented matrix gives us the solution to the problem. We have

Thus $x = 2$,
$y = 1$

$$1x + 0y = 2$$
$$0x + 1y = 1$$

or simply

$$x = 2, \quad y = 1$$

This is exactly the same answer that we obtained using matrix inverses.

Gauss-Jordan method

This new technique, which is called the **Gauss-Jordan method** in honor of the two famous mathematicians Carl F. Gauss (1777–1855) and Camille Jordan (1833–1922), is illustrated in Example 8.

EXAMPLE 8

Using matrix methods, solve the following system of equations for x and y:

$$\begin{cases} 5x + 3y = -1 \\ 3x - 4y = 11 \end{cases}$$

SOLUTION

Again we will indicate the operations applied to the equations and to the augmented matrix so that you can see the correspondence.

Equation	*Matrix*

Matrix

We first form the augmented matrix

$$\begin{pmatrix} 5 & 3 & | & -1 \\ 3 & -4 & | & 11 \end{pmatrix}$$

Then we perform several elementary row operations so that the numbers to the left of the dashed line will make up an identity matrix. To get started, we try to get a 1 in the row 1, column 1 position. This can be accomplished by multiplying each element of row 1 by $\frac{1}{5}$. This gives us

Equation

$$5x + 3y = -1$$
$$3x - 4y = 11$$

Then we perform several operations so that one of the variables drops out. We divide the first equation by 5 to get

$$x + \frac{3}{5}y = -\frac{1}{5}$$
$$3x - 4y = 11$$

$$\begin{pmatrix} 1 & \frac{3}{5} & | & \frac{-1}{5} \\ 3 & -4 & | & 11 \end{pmatrix}$$

Now we try to get a 0 in the row 2, column 1 position. To accomplish this, we multiply each element of row 1 by -3 and add the result to row 2, getting

We multiply the first equation by -3 and add the result to the second equation, getting

$$x + \frac{3}{5}y = -\frac{1}{5}$$
$$0x - \frac{29}{5}y = \frac{58}{5}$$

$$\begin{pmatrix} 1 & \frac{3}{5} & | & \frac{-1}{5} \\ 0 & \frac{-29}{5} & | & \frac{58}{5} \end{pmatrix}$$

Now we try to get a 1 in the row 2, column 2 position. We multiply each element of row 2 by $\frac{-5}{29}$. Our result is

We multiply the second equation by $\frac{-5}{29}$. We get

$$x + \frac{3}{5}y = -\frac{1}{5}$$
$$0x + \quad y = -2$$

$$\begin{pmatrix} 1 & \frac{3}{5} & | & \frac{-1}{5} \\ 0 & 1 & | & -2 \end{pmatrix}$$

We multiply the second equation by $\dfrac{-3}{5}$ and add the result to the first equation, getting

$$x + 0y = 1$$
$$0x + y = -2$$

Finally we try to get a 0 in the row 1, column 2 position. To accomplish this, we multiply each element of row 2 by $\dfrac{-3}{5}$ and add the results to row 1. This gives us

$$\begin{pmatrix} 1 & 0 & \vdots & 1 \\ 0 & 1 & \vdots & -2 \end{pmatrix}$$

We notice that we have an identity matrix to the left of the dashed line. We can now read our answer from the extreme right column:

$$1x + 0y = 1$$
$$0x + 1y = -2$$

Our answer is

$$x = 1, \quad y = -2$$

or

$$x = 1, \quad y = -2 \quad \blacksquare$$

Comment   As we indicated earlier, after we obtain the augmented matrix, our main objective is to change the numbers to the left of the dashed line into the identity matrix so that the numbers to the right of this line will become solutions for x and y.

We summarize the above procedure as follows:

To solve a system of equations using row reduction, you must:

1. Form the augmented matrix.
2. Perform the row operations necessary to get a 1 in the upper left-hand corner of the matrix.
3. Perform row operations to get an identity matrix to the left of the dashed line if this matrix is a square matrix. (If the matrix is not square, then 1's must be gotten along the main diagonal, and all other entries must be zero.)
4. Read the solutions on the right of the dashed line.

cryptography

code theory

Another important application of matrices and their inverses is in **cryptography**, or **code theory**. Secret codes are used by governments when sending messages. There are many specialists who are experts at breaking codes. Yet secret codes are quite difficult to break when they are written in matrix form. They can be decoded by using matrix inverses.

One way of coding messages is to associate each letter of the alphabet with some other letter or with some number. Such codes are rather easy to break since certain letters of the alphabet occur more frequently than others. Nevertheless, this is done quite often. When this system is used, we associate a different coding symbol with each letter to avoid confusion.

EXAMPLE 9

Coding. Use the following coding scheme to code the message DESTROY.

A B C D E F G H I J K L M N O P Q R S T U V W X Y Z
↓ ↓
F H Q S A T J B N W C U I O V D L X E Y R G Z M P K

SOLUTION

Using the coding scheme, the message DESTROY would be transmitted as SAEYXVP.

EXAMPLE 10

Coding—Alternate Scheme. Use the following coding scheme to code the message DESTROY.

A B C D E F G H I J K L M N O P Q R S T U V W X Y Z
↓ ↓
8 2 9 13 20 1 10 17 5 18 22 3 15 19 11 26 21 25 4 24 12 23 7 14 16 6

SOLUTION

The message DESTROY would be transmited as

13 20 4 24 25 11 16.

EXAMPLE 11

Use the coding scheme given in Example 9 to decode the following message: SV-OVY-JNGA-RD.

SOLUTION

The message SV-OVY-JNGA-RD is DO NOT GIVE UP.

Messages can also be coded by using matrices. We must decide in advance whether the message is to be grouped in pairs of letters, triplets of letters, or some other pattern. This determines the dimension of the matrix that has to be used. For example, suppose we wish to send the message

THE DEAL IS OFF

We would rewrite this message in groups of two letters as

TH ED EA LI SO FF

With the code given in Example 10 this message can be written in matrix form as

$$\binom{24}{17}\binom{20}{13}\binom{20}{8}\binom{3}{5}\binom{4}{11}\binom{1}{1}$$

Now we select any 2×2 matrix that has an inverse and contains no fractions. One such matrix is

$$A = \begin{pmatrix} 2 & 3 \\ 1 & 2 \end{pmatrix}$$

Its inverse is

$$A^{-1} = \begin{pmatrix} 2 & -3 \\ -1 & 2 \end{pmatrix}$$

The product of A and each of the code matrices is

$$\begin{pmatrix} 2 & 3 \\ 1 & 2 \end{pmatrix} \cdot \begin{pmatrix} 24 \\ 17 \end{pmatrix} \quad \begin{pmatrix} 2 & 3 \\ 1 & 2 \end{pmatrix} \cdot \begin{pmatrix} 20 \\ 13 \end{pmatrix} \quad \begin{pmatrix} 2 & 3 \\ 1 & 2 \end{pmatrix} \cdot \begin{pmatrix} 20 \\ 8 \end{pmatrix}$$

$$\begin{pmatrix} 2 & 3 \\ 1 & 2 \end{pmatrix} \cdot \begin{pmatrix} 3 \\ 5 \end{pmatrix} \quad \begin{pmatrix} 2 & 3 \\ 1 & 2 \end{pmatrix} \cdot \begin{pmatrix} 4 \\ 11 \end{pmatrix} \quad \begin{pmatrix} 2 & 3 \\ 1 & 2 \end{pmatrix} \cdot \begin{pmatrix} 1 \\ 1 \end{pmatrix}$$

The coded message then is transmitted as

$$99, \quad 58, \quad 79, \quad 46, \quad 64, \quad 36 \ldots$$

encoding

decode

The process of translating a message into a matrix is called *encoding*. To *decode*, we simply regroup the numbers into a matrix and then multiply by the matrix A^{-1}. For the above example we have

$$A^{-1} = \begin{pmatrix} 2 & -3 \\ -1 & 2 \end{pmatrix}$$

so that

$$\begin{pmatrix} 2 & -3 \\ -1 & 2 \end{pmatrix} \begin{pmatrix} 99 \\ 58 \end{pmatrix} = \begin{pmatrix} 24 \\ 17 \end{pmatrix}$$

$$\begin{pmatrix} 2 & -3 \\ -1 & 2 \end{pmatrix} \begin{pmatrix} 79 \\ 46 \end{pmatrix} = \begin{pmatrix} 20 \\ 13 \end{pmatrix}$$

$$\begin{pmatrix} 2 & -3 \\ -1 & 2 \end{pmatrix} \begin{pmatrix} 64 \\ 36 \end{pmatrix} = \begin{pmatrix} 20 \\ 8 \end{pmatrix}$$

$$\vdots$$

etc.

The message in coded matrix form then is

$$\begin{pmatrix} 24 \\ 17 \end{pmatrix} \begin{pmatrix} 20 \\ 13 \end{pmatrix} \begin{pmatrix} 20 \\ 8 \end{pmatrix} \cdots$$

To finish the decoding process, we use the code given in Example 10.

EXERCISES FOR SECTION 4.7

1. *Long Distance.* Marjorie has made several long-distance calls for her boss as shown in the table at the top of the next page.

a) Write the number of minutes as a row matrix for these items.

Country to which call was made	Number of minutes	Cost per minute
France	7	$3.21
Brazil	8	2.69
Egypt	4	4.92
Sweden	6	6.52
Holland	9	5.02

b) Write the cost as a column matrix for these items.

c) Using matrix multiplication, find the total cost for these long distance calls.

2. *Watching Your Calories.* Glen is celebrating his twentieth wedding anniversary and is in a restaurant where he has just ordered a 14-ounce steak, 3 pieces of garlic bread, $\frac{2}{3}$ cup of vegetables, 2 scoops of mashed potatoes, 3 slices of apple pie, and 2 drinks of liquor. The number of calories in each of these items is as follows:

Item	Calories
Steak	105 per ounce
Garlic bread	115 per piece
Vegetables	72 per cup
Mashed potatoes	110 per scoop
Apple pie	350 per slice
Liquor	100 per drink

a) Write the quantity ordered of each item as a row matrix.

b) Write the calorie content of each item as a column matrix.

c) Using matrix multiplication, find the total number of calories in the dinner.

3. The AZE Publishing Company publishes books and magazines that must be processed by each of its three factories. The following matrix indicates the hourly production by each factory for a shipment of magazines and a shipment of books:

$$\begin{array}{c} \\ \text{Books} \\ \text{Magazines} \end{array} \begin{array}{ccc} \text{Factory I} & \text{Factory II} & \text{Factory III} \end{array}$$

$$\begin{pmatrix} 8 & 6 & 5 \\ 10 & 3 & 4 \end{pmatrix} = A$$

$$\text{Let} \qquad B = \begin{pmatrix} 8 \\ 9 \\ 7 \end{pmatrix}$$

be the number of hours per day that each factory operates. Compute $A \cdot B$ and interpret the results.

Gov't to Prosecute Bilo for Illegal Dumping

MARLBERG—Officials of the state's Environmental Protection Agency announced yesterday that they would begin prosecuting the Bilo Chemical Corp. for illegally dumping chemical wastes from its Patchaw plant into neighboring lakes and streams. Said a spokesperson for the agency, Bilo has callously disregarded the environmental impact of such dumping. The adverse effects are beginning to show up. Last week, many dead fish were washed up on the shoreline.

Bilo claims that it already has installed antipolluting devices.

THE GLOBE, August 26, 1989

4. Consider the newspaper article above. It is known that the Bilo Chemical Corp. manufactures five different items. Furthermore, the amount and kind of pollution generated in the production of each of these items are shown in the following matrix:

	Pollutant I	Pollutant II	Pollutant III	
Item I	9	5	3	
Item II	6	11	4	
Item III	10	8	2	$= A$
Item IV	6	9	8	
Item V	7	3	11	

The company claims that its costs per unit associated with removing these pollutants after installing the antipolluting devices are $12,000, $36,000, and $20,000, respectively.

a) Write the cost as a column matrix for these antipolluting devices. Call it B.

b) Compute the product of the two matrices $A \cdot B$ and interpret the results.

5. The Mark School operates two day-care centers, one in Newton and one in Baylif. Each of the centers

operates independently of the other. On February 1 the food manager of the Newton center purchased 112 cans of peaches, 48 pounds of beef, and 23 pounds of vegetables, while the food manager of the Baylif center purchased 84 cans of peaches, 53 pounds of beef, and 51 pounds of vegetables. A can of peaches costs 59¢, a pound of beef costs $1.32, and a pound of vegetables costs 32¢. Using matrix multiplication, find the amount of money spent by the Mark School in purchasing the food for these two day-care centers.

6. *Cost Averaging.* Refer back to Exercise 5. In order to cost average, the food managers of the two day-care centers order the same quantities of food on February 25. However, the prices are now different. A can of peaches costs 62¢, a pound of beef costs $1.29, and a pound of vegetables costs 49¢.

   a) Using matrix multiplication, find the amount of money spent by both centers on these food items.

   b) How much money was spent by the Mark School on food for these two orders? (Use matrix techniques.)

In each of Exercises 7–19, find the appropriate elementary row operation(s) that can be used to transform matrix A into matrix B.

7. $A = \begin{pmatrix} 4 & 1 \\ 3 & 8 \end{pmatrix}$ $B = \begin{pmatrix} -12 & -3 \\ -9 & -24 \end{pmatrix}$

8. $A = \begin{pmatrix} 5 & 7 & 8 & 14 \\ 3 & 0 & 2 & -6 \end{pmatrix}$

   $B = \begin{pmatrix} -10 & -14 & -16 & -28 \\ -6 & 0 & -4 & 12 \end{pmatrix}$

9. $A = \begin{pmatrix} 15 & 18 \\ 12 & 9 \\ 27 & 21 \end{pmatrix}$ $B = \begin{pmatrix} 10 & 12 \\ 8 & 6 \\ 18 & 14 \end{pmatrix}$

10. $A = \begin{pmatrix} 1 & 4 & 7 \\ 3 & 9 & 2 \\ -2 & 1 & 7 \end{pmatrix}$ $B = \begin{pmatrix} 1 & 4 & 7 \\ 0 & -3 & -19 \\ 0 & 9 & 21 \end{pmatrix}$

11. $A = \begin{pmatrix} 2 & 3 & 9 \\ 1 & 0 & 1 \\ -3 & 0 & 4 \end{pmatrix}$ $B = \begin{pmatrix} 0 & 3 & 7 \\ 1 & 0 & 1 \\ 0 & 0 & 7 \end{pmatrix}$

12. $A = \begin{pmatrix} 7 & 3 & 2 \\ 1 & 2 & 1 \\ 5 & 2 & 0 \end{pmatrix}$ $B = \begin{pmatrix} 1 & 2 & 1 \\ 0 & -11 & -5 \\ 0 & -8 & -5 \end{pmatrix}$

**13. $A = \begin{pmatrix} 5 & 3 & 8 \\ -2 & 7 & 5 \\ 1 & 0 & 2 \end{pmatrix}$ $B = \begin{pmatrix} 1 & 0 & 0 \\ 0 & 1 & 0 \\ 0 & 0 & 1 \end{pmatrix}$

**14. $A = \begin{pmatrix} 4 & 12 & 70 \\ 6 & -9 & 1 \\ 3 & 2 & 4 \end{pmatrix}$ $B = \begin{pmatrix} 1 & 0 & 0 \\ 0 & 1 & 0 \\ 0 & 0 & 1 \end{pmatrix}$

Write the augmented matrix for each set of equations in Exercises 15–25. Do not attempt to solve them.

15. $\begin{cases} 7x + 3y = 11 \\ 5x - 2y = 19 \end{cases}$ 16. $\begin{cases} 12x - 2y = 13 \\ 5x + 9y = 23 \end{cases}$

17. $\begin{cases} 2x - 3y = 5 \\ 7x + 12y = 19 \end{cases}$ 18. $\begin{cases} 5x - 3y = 15 \\ 4x + 3y = -12 \end{cases}$

19. $\begin{cases} 2x + 3y - 5z = 10 \\ 3x - 7y + 8z = -15 \end{cases}$ 20. $\begin{cases} 2x + 3y - 4z = 24 \\ 8x - 4y + 7z = 16 \end{cases}$

21. $\begin{cases} 3x - 5y + 8z = 12 \\ 2x + 3y = 12 \end{cases}$ 22. $\begin{cases} 7x + 8y = 27 \\ 2x - 9y = 18 \end{cases}$

23. $\begin{cases} x = 7 \\ y - 3z = 10 \\ x - 8z = 23 \end{cases}$ 24. $\begin{cases} 4x + y = 10 \\ 3y - z = 17 \\ 2x + 7z = 15 \end{cases}$

25. $\begin{cases} 2x + 3y + 5z - 8w = 7 \\ 3x - 2y - 4z + 7w = 0 \\ 4x + 7y - 3z - 4w = -3 \\ 2x + 3z - w = 1 \end{cases}$

26. Write a linear system to correspond to each of the following augmented matrices.

   a) $\begin{pmatrix} 5 & 7 & | & 10 \\ 3 & 9 & | & 14 \end{pmatrix}$ b) $\begin{pmatrix} 8 & 7 & | & 24 \\ 9 & 5 & | & 45 \end{pmatrix}$

   c) $\begin{pmatrix} 2 & 3 & -7 & 6 & | & 10 \\ 5 & 4 & 8 & 1 & | & 0 \end{pmatrix}$

   d) $\begin{pmatrix} 2 & 9 & 6 & | & 1 \\ 5 & -4 & -7 & | & 0 \\ 3 & -2 & 9 & | & 10 \end{pmatrix}$

e) $\begin{pmatrix} 2 & 5 & 1 & 2 & | & 8 \\ 1 & 3 & 0 & 3 & | & 10 \\ 9 & 2 & 7 & 4 & | & 14 \end{pmatrix}$

In Exercises 27–38, use matrix operations to find solutions (if they exist) for the set of equations.

27. $\begin{Bmatrix} 5x + 3y = 13 \\ 2x - 5y = -1 \end{Bmatrix}$ **28.** $\begin{Bmatrix} 4x - y = 13 \\ 2x + 3y = 3 \end{Bmatrix}$

29. $\begin{Bmatrix} 8x + 5y = -28 \\ 4x - 6y = 20 \end{Bmatrix}$ **30.** $\begin{Bmatrix} 5x - 3y = 26 \\ x + 8y = 31 \end{Bmatrix}$

31. $\begin{Bmatrix} 6x + 8y = 48 \\ 3x - 5y = 24 \end{Bmatrix}$ **32.** $\begin{Bmatrix} 4x - 16y = 14 \\ 10x + 4y = 2 \end{Bmatrix}$

33. $\begin{Bmatrix} 7x - 3y = 16 \\ x + 2y = -5 \end{Bmatrix}$ **34.** $\begin{Bmatrix} 2x + 3y = 800 \\ 0.06x + 0.04y = 140 \end{Bmatrix}$

35. $\begin{Bmatrix} 3x - y = 7 \\ 6x + 2y = 22 \end{Bmatrix}$ **36.** $\begin{Bmatrix} 2x + 3y = -4 \\ x - 2y = 19 \end{Bmatrix}$

37. $\begin{Bmatrix} 2x - 7y = 26 \\ 3x + 4y = -19 \end{Bmatrix}$ **38.** $\begin{Bmatrix} 7x + 9y = 35 \\ 5x - 3y = 25 \end{Bmatrix}$

39. Use the code given in Example 9 to encode the message

JONES-IS-AN-ENEMY-AGENT

40. Use the coding scheme given in Example 10 to encode the message given in the previous exercise.

41. Use the coding scheme given in Example 10 to decode the following message

4, 5, 19, 22, 24, 17, 20, 4, 17, 5, 26

|||| ➤ Brain-Teaser Problems ◀ ||||

**42. Arrange the following message into groups of two letters:

BILL-IS-YOUR-CONTACT-MAN

Find an appropriate 2×2 matrix and indicate how the coded message can be transmitted.

**43. Verify that the inverse of matrix $\begin{pmatrix} a & b \\ c & d \end{pmatrix}$ is $\begin{pmatrix} d & -b \\ -c & a \end{pmatrix}$ multiplied by $\dfrac{1}{ad - bc}$ by using the following procedure. Consider

$$\begin{pmatrix} a & b \\ c & d \end{pmatrix} \cdot \begin{pmatrix} w & x \\ y & z \end{pmatrix} = \begin{pmatrix} 1 & 0 \\ 0 & 1 \end{pmatrix}$$

Using multiplication on the left-hand side, we get

$$\begin{pmatrix} aw + by & ax + bz \\ cw + dy & cx + dz \end{pmatrix} = \begin{pmatrix} 1 & 0 \\ 0 & 1 \end{pmatrix}$$

This means that

$$aw + by = 1$$
$$ax + bz = 0$$
$$cw + dy = 0$$
$$cx + dz = 1$$

Solve the first two equations and the last two equations in pairs for w, x, y, and z. You should get

$$w = \frac{d}{ad - bc}$$
$$x = \frac{-b}{ad - bc}$$
$$y = \frac{-c}{ad - bc}$$
$$z = \frac{a}{ad - bc}$$

Compare this with the answer we got. They are the same.

**44. *Counterespionage.* An enemy agent transmits the following message,

187 65 409 143 361 126 77 26 66 23 113 39,

which has been coded with $\begin{pmatrix} 3 & 17 \\ 1 & 6 \end{pmatrix}$ as the coding matrix. Use matrix inverses to decode the message.

TYPICAL CLASSROOM QUESTIONS

1. A student claims that if $x < y$, then $x^2 < y^2$ where x and y are integers. Do you agree?

2. A student claims that $|x + y| = |x| + |y|$ where x and y are any integers. Do you agree?

3. Do you agree with the following "proof" that $(-1)(-1) = +1$? There are two possibilities: Either $(-1)(-1) = +1$ or $(-1)(-1) = -1$. Let us try the second possibility. We already know that $1(-1) = -1$. Thus $(-1)(-1)$ has to be equal to $+1$, or that the product of two negative integers is a positive integer.

4. Refer back to the previous exercise. A second student offers the following "proof" that $(-1)(-1) = +1$. Again there are two possibilities: Either $(-1)(-1) = +1$ or $(-1)(-1) = -1$. Let us try the second possibility. We know that $-1 = (-1) \cdot 1$. Thus, $(-1)(-1) = -1$ can be rewritten as $(-1) \cdot 1 = (-1)(-1)$ (by substitution). Dividing both sides by -1 gives the erroneous conclusion that $1 = -1$. By the idea of a proof by contradiction, our assumption that $(-1)(-1) = -1$ leads to a contradiction. Therefore, we must conclude that $(-1)(-1) = +1$. Do you agree with this proof?

STUDY GUIDE

The following is a chapter outline in capsule form. You should now be able to demonstrate your knowledge of the ideas mentioned by giving definitions, or specific examples. Page references are given in parentheses.

The **positive integers** are the numbers $+1, +2, +3, +4, \ldots$ (p. 177)

The **negative integers** are the numbers $-1, -2, -3, -4, \ldots$ (p. 177)

The set of **integers** consists of the whole numbers and the negative integers, that is, the set of integers is $\{\ldots -5, -4, -3, -2, -1, 0, +1, +2, +3, +4, \ldots\}$. (p. 178)

Addition If A and B are any disjoint sets with $n(A) = a$ and $n(B) = b$ where a and b are integers, then $a + b = n(A \cup B)$. (p. 178)

If $(-a)$ and $(-b)$ represent two negative integers, then

$$(-a) + (-b) = -(a + b) \qquad \text{(p. 179)}$$

To **add** a positive integer and a negative integer, consider the integers without their signs and (i) select the larger, (ii) subtract the smaller from the larger, (iii) put the sign of the larger of step (i) in front of the answer of step (ii). (p. 180)

The **additive inverse** of a number b is the number which when added to b gives 0. This is $(-b)$. (p. 181)

Subtraction If a and b are any integers, then $a - b$ means $a + (-b)$. (p. 181)

In other words, $a - b$ means "a plus the additive inverse of b." Thus, $a - b = n$ if and only if $a = b + n$. (p. 181)

Multiplication Since positive integers are really natural numbers, multiplication of positive integers is exactly the same as multiplication of natural numbers. (p. 182)

If $(+a)$ is a positive integer and $(-b)$ is a negative integer, then the **product** is $(+a) \cdot (-b) = -(a \cdot b)$. Similarly, if $(-a)$ is a negative integer, and $(+b)$ is a positive integer, then the product is $(-a) \cdot (+b) = -(a \cdot b)$. The product of a negative integer and a positive integer is found by multiplying the numbers without their signs and putting a minus sign in front of the answer. (p. 183)

Division If a and b are any integers where $b \neq 0$, then $a \div b$ or $\dfrac{a}{b}$ or a/b is the unique integer c (if it exists) such that $a = b \cdot c$. (p. 184)

The set of integers can be pictured on a **number line** which then can be used to **order** the integers as well as to add them. (p. 184)

The rules for dividing integers are exactly the same as the rules for multiplication of integers (p. 186)

The integers are **closed** under the operations of addition and multiplication. The **commutative** and **associative** laws are valid for addition and multiplication of integers. The **identity for addition** is 0 and the **identity for multiplication** is 1. Every integer has an additive inverse. The **distributive law of multiplication over addition** states that if a, b, and c are any integers, then $a(b + c) = ab + ac$. (p. 186)

The **absolute value** of an integer is the undirected distance of that integer from zero on a number line. (p. 187)

An integer is **even** if it can be expressed as two times another integer.

If an integer is not even it must be **odd.** (p. 188)

A **function** is a rule that assigns to each number a unique second number. If the two numbers of the set are x and y, then we say that a function is a relationship between the two variables x and y such that for each value substituted for x, there is obtained a **unique** value of y. We write $y = f(x)$. (p. 189)

The set of all values that can be substituted in the function is called the **domain** of the function. The set of all values of y that these substitutions create is called the **range** of the function. (p. 190)

An **equation** is a mathematical statement that consists of two expressions joined together by an equal sign. Any unknown in an equation is represented by a letter and is known as a **variable**. A **solution** to an equation is a number which when substituted for the variable results in a true statement. (p. 192)

Any equation containing x raised to the exponent of 1 and to no higher or lower exponent is called a **linear equation** in x. (p. 193)

To **solve** an equation in x means to find a value of x that makes the equation true. (p. 193)

An **inequality** is a mathematical statement that says that one thing is not equal to something else. (p. 199)

A **system of simultaneous linear equations** in two variables means that we have two equations involving two unknowns. Solving such a system means that we are looking for a pair of numbers that satisfies both equations. (p. 204)

A **matrix** is a rectangular array (table) of numbers. We enclose the matrix within parentheses. A matrix is of **dimension** $m \times n$ if it has m rows and n columns. (p. 211, 212)

If a matrix has the same number of rows and columns, it is a **square** matrix. (p. 212)

Two matrices are said to be **equal** if they are of the same dimension and if their corresponding entries are equal. (p. 214)

An **identity matrix** for multiplication is a square matrix that, when multiplied by another square matrix A on the left side or on the right side, leaves the matrix A unchanged. (p. 221)

The **inverse** of matrix A is another matrix denoted as A^{-1} (if it exists) such that when multiplied by matrix A on either side results in the identity matrix. (p. 232)

An **elementary row operation** on any matrix consists of any one of the following three operations:

1. Interchanging any two rows.
2. Multiplying all elements of any row by a given nonzero number.
3. Multiplying each element of a row by a number and then adding the results to the corresponding elements of another row. (p. 236)

An **augmented matrix** is a matrix whose entries are those of two other matrices where we usually use a dashed line to separate the entries. (p. 237)

An important application of matrices is in **cryptography** or the study of codes. (p. 240)

KEY TERMS

Following is a list of key terms introduced in each section of this chapter.

4.1	positive integers	4.2	function
	negative integers		function notation
	integers		domain
	addition		range
	additive inverse		
	subtraction	4.3	mathematical models
	multiplication		equations
	division		variable
	number line		solution
	ordering the integers		linear equation
	distributive law		solving an equation
	absolute value		inequalities

FORMULAS TO REMEMBER

The following list summarizes all the formulas discussed in this chapter.

The rules for solving linear equations as given on p. 193.

The procedure for solving word problems involves the following:

In the **Understanding the Problem** part, identify the given information and then determine what is to be found. In the **A Plan to Solve the Problem** part, assign letters to the unknown quantities and translate the given information into a mathematical equation or inequality and proceed to solve it. In the **Checking Our Solution** part, we check our solution to make sure that we have answered the question.

Properties of inequalities are as follows:

Addition property If $a > b$ and c is any integer, then $a + c > b + c$.

Multiplication property If $a > b$ and $c > 0$, then $ac > bc$.
If $a > b$ and $c < 0$, then $ac < bc$.

When adding matrices they must be of the same dimension.

When multiplying a matrix that is $m \times n$ with a matrix that is $n \times p$, the resulting matrix will be $m \times p$. To find the entries see pp. 215–217.

The inverse of the matrix $A = \begin{pmatrix} a & b \\ c & d \end{pmatrix}$ is $\begin{pmatrix} d & -b \\ -c & a \end{pmatrix}$ multiplied by the number $\dfrac{1}{ad - bc}$, provided that $ad - bc \neq 0$.

CHAPTER 4 REVIEW EXERCISES

1. Place the correct symbol ($<$, $>$, or $=$) between the numbers -4 and -6.

    a) $-4 < -6$ **b)** $-4 > -6$ **c)** $-4 = -6$

    d) $0 < -6$ **e)** none of these

2. Evaluate $-|-5|-|-7|$
   a) -12 b) -2 c) $+2$ d) $+12$ e) none of these

3. Add: $-5+(-3)+(-11)$
   a) -19 b) -9 c) -3 d) $+19$ e) none of these

4. Subtract: $-14-18-(-21)$
   a) -43 b) -11 c) $+11$ d) $+43$ e) none of these

5. Multiply: $-3(-4)(-5)(2)$
   a) $+120$ b) -120 c) -60 d) $+60$ e) none of these

6. Divide: $-240 \div (-12)$
   a) -20 b) $+20$ c) $+12$ d) -18 e) none of these

7. On January 1, the temperature in a city dropped from $+7°F$ to $-10°F$. Find the change in temperature.
   a) $-3°$ b) $-17°$ c) $+3°$ d) $+17°$ e) none of these

8. An archaeologist discovered an ancient relic that dates back to the year 793 B.C. How old was the relic in the year 1989?

9. Simplify: $\dfrac{7(-2)-4(-8)}{2(-1)-(-6-3)}$

10. When simplified, $(-4)[(-7)-(-8)]$ becomes
    a) $+4$ b) -4 c) $+60$ d) -60 e) none of these

11. In the temperature formula $F = \dfrac{9}{5} C + 32$, at what temperature is $F = C$?
    a) $+8°$ b) $-8°$ c) $+40°$
    d) $-40°$ e) none of these

12. Solve the following inequality for x: $-2x+7(3x-1) > -4(9x+3)$

13. Solve the following inequality for x: $7x-3 \geq 10x+21$

14. A concrete mixture requires 2 parts of gravel, 3 parts of cement, and 4 parts of sand by weight. How many pounds of cement are required for $4\frac{1}{2}$ tons of this mixture? (1 ton = 2000 pounds)
    a) 2000   b) 1000   c) 3000   d) 4000   e) none of these

15. A mechanic's hourly wage is 4 times her helper's. They were paid a total of $78 for a job on which the mechanic worked 5 hours and the helper worked 6 hours. Find the hourly wage of the helper.

16. A soda vending machine in the student cafeteria contains 20 coins. Some of the coins are nickels, and the rest are quarters. If the value of the coins is $4.40, find the number of coins of each kind. (Solve by algebraic techniques only.)

17. Working alone, Maria can draw architectural plans for a building in 10 hours, and Adolf can draw the plans in 12 hours. How long will it take them to do the job if they work together?

18. One bricklayer takes twice as long as a second bricklayer to build a certain wall. Together they can build the wall in 6 hours. How long will it take each bricklayer to build the wall alone?

19. Jennifer invested $5000, part at 6% and the remainder at 8%. The annual income from the 8% investment is $260 greater than the annual income from the 6% investment. Find the amount of money invested at each rate.

20. If $A = \begin{pmatrix} 1 & 7 \\ 6 & 9 \\ 3 & -2 \end{pmatrix}$ and $B = \begin{pmatrix} 1 & 0 \\ 0 & 1 \end{pmatrix}$, find $A \cdot B$.

21. If $\begin{pmatrix} 25 & 16 \\ 18 & 40 \end{pmatrix} = \begin{pmatrix} 5x + 10 & 16 \\ 2y + 5 & 40 \end{pmatrix}$, find x and y.

22. If $A = \begin{pmatrix} 4 & 7 \\ 3 & -9 \end{pmatrix}$ find A^{-1}.

23. For the system of equations $\begin{cases} 4x + 3y = 17 \\ 2x - 9y = 12 \end{cases}$ find the augmented matrix.

24. If $A = \begin{pmatrix} 3 & 9 & -2 \\ 7 & -6 & 1 \\ 4 & 0 & 5 \end{pmatrix}$ and $B = \begin{pmatrix} 9 & -3 & 5 \\ 0 & 2 & 6 \\ 7 & 1 & -4 \end{pmatrix}$ find $3A - 4B$.

25. Write a linear system to correspond to the following matrix:

$$\begin{pmatrix} 7 & 12 & \vdots & 5 \\ 3 & -4 & \vdots & 11 \end{pmatrix}$$

26. If $A = \begin{pmatrix} 1 & 7 \\ 1 & 7 \end{pmatrix}$ find A^{-1}.

27. If $A = \begin{pmatrix} 5 & 3 \\ -9 & 7 \end{pmatrix}$ find A^2.

28. If $A = \begin{pmatrix} 4 & 6 \\ -3 & 5 \end{pmatrix}$, find

a) A^{-1}

b) $(A^{-1})^{-1}$. What can you conclude?

29. If $A = \begin{pmatrix} 5 & -9 \\ 6 & 1 \end{pmatrix}$, $B = \begin{pmatrix} -1 & 6 \\ 4 & 3 \end{pmatrix}$, and $C = \begin{pmatrix} 0 & 8 \\ 9 & -7 \end{pmatrix}$, verify that the

distributive law, $A(B + C) = A \cdot B + A \cdot C$, holds for these matrices.

30. *Construction Costs.* A construction firm hired 7 plumbers and 8 helpers for a day to do a certain job. The total cost was $1190. At the same rate of pay, the construction firm hired 5 plumbers and 9 helpers for a day and paid $1080. How much does a plumber and how much does a helper earn each day? (Use only matrix techniques to solve the problem.)

31. An insurance salesperson is analyzing the marital status of the 450 females of the George Corporation. Some information about them is summarized in the accompanying matrix.

$$
\text{Age (in years)}
\begin{array}{c}
19\text{--}25 \\
26\text{--}34 \\
35\text{--}44 \\
45\text{--}60
\end{array}
\begin{pmatrix}
27 & 36 & 7 \\
31 & 38 & 27 \\
16 & 81 & 43 \\
21 & 65 & 58
\end{pmatrix}
$$

Marital status: Single Divorced Widowed

If the salesperson wishes to sell life insurance to only single women, how many women does the salesperson have to interview?

32. Dr. Jones and Dr. Smith are both surgeons. During 1989, they performed the following operations:

$$
\begin{array}{c}
\text{Dr. Jones} \\
\text{Dr. Smith}
\end{array}
\begin{pmatrix}
84 & 63 \\
58 & 73
\end{pmatrix} = A
$$

Appendectomy Hernia

Furthermore, the charge for each operation was

$$
\begin{array}{c}
\text{Appendectomy} \\
\text{Hernia}
\end{array}
\begin{pmatrix}
\$1600 \\
1000
\end{pmatrix} = B
$$

Cost for operation

Find $A \cdot B$ and intepret the results.

33. Using the coding scheme given in Example 9 of Section 4.7, code the following message:

THE-MICROFILM-IS-IN-THE-CAMERA.

34. *Women's Gains.* Consider the following table[2] listing the number of elective jobs held by women.

Job	1974	1978
Members of Congress	16	20
Governors	0	2
Lieutenant governors	0	3
Secretaries of state	7	11
State treasurers	8	8
State legislators	466	702
Mayors	566	735
County commissioners	456	660
Municipal council members	5365	6961

[2] *Source:* Center for the American Woman and Politics.

a) Rewrite the information in matrix form.

b) Compute the total number of elective jobs held by women in 1974 and in 1978. Compare the figures and comment.

35. *Legal Costs*. Valerie is a lawyer. Over a four month period she reported handling the number of cases shown in the accompanying matrix. Furthermore, Valerie charged $175 for each uncontested divorce, $85 for writing a will, $475 for a simple house closing, and $125 for each personal bankruptcy.

	Uncontested divorces	Writing wills	House closings	Personal bankruptcy
Month 1	3	6	5	1
Month 2	2	7	3	0
Month 3	7	4	2	2
Month 4	4	6	4	1

Using matrix multiplication, find Valerie's income for each month. What is Valerie's total income for this period?

SUGGESTED FURTHER READING

Battista, M., "A Complete Model for Operations on Integers," in *The Arithmetic Teacher* **30** (May 1983), 26–31.

Campbell, H., *An Introduction to Matrices, Vectors, and Linear Programming*, 2nd edition. New York: Appleton-Century-Crofts, 1971. (An excellent introduction to matrix theory.)

Charles R., "Get the Most Out of Word Problems," in *The Arithmetic Teacher* **29** (November 1981), 39–40.

Johnson, J. "Working with Integers" in *The Mathematics Teacher* **71** (January 1978), 31.

Kemeny, J., L. Snell, and J. Thompson, *Introduction to Finite Mathematics*, 3rd edition. Englewood Cliffs, N.J.: Prentice-Hall, 1974. (Chapter 4 discusses matrices and their applications.)

Newmark, J., *Using Finite Mathematics*. New York: Harper & Row, 1982 (See Chapter 11.)

Peterson, J., "Fourteen Different Strategies for Multiplication of Integers, or Why $(-1)(-1) = 1$," in *The Arithmetic Teacher* **19** (May 1972), 396–403.

Richardson, L., "The Role of Strategies for Teaching Pupils to Solve Verbal Problems," in *The Arithmetic Teacher* **22** (May 1975) 414–421.

Sawyer, W.W., *Prelude to Mathematics*. Baltimore: Penguin Books, 1959. (Chapter 8 discusses matrix algebra.)

Zlot, W., and R. Roberts, "The Multiplication of Signed Numbers," in *The Mathematics Teacher* **75** (April 1982), 302–304.

CHAPTER 5

Number Theory

CHAPTER OBJECTIVES

☐ **To learn** some rules of divisibility, that is, under what conditions one number divides another. (*Section 6.1*)

☐ **To analyze** some interesting numbers such as Fibonacci sequences or perfect numbers. (*Section 6.2*)

☐ **To indicate** how to find prime numbers. (*Section 6.3*)

☐ **To show** that every number is either a prime number or can be expressed as a product of prime numbers. (*Section 6.3*)

☐ **To present** techniques for finding the greater common divisor and least common multiple of numbers (*Section 5.4*)

☐ **To describe** what is meant by clock arithmetic and how to add using different clocks. (*Section 5.5*)

☐ **To discuss** modular arithmetics, which deal with the remainders that are obtained when we divide. (*Section 5.5*)

☐ **To study** how we can check the answers for addition, multiplication, and subtraction problems by casting out 9's and by casting out 11's. (*Section 5.6*)

NCTM GUIDELINES

In its March 1989 *Curriculum and Evaluation Standards for School Mathematics* (p. 91), the National Council of Teachers of Mathematics recommends that the mathematics curriculum include the study of number systems and number theory so that students can

❑ understand and appreciate the need for numbers beyond the whole numbers,

❑ understand how the basic arithmetic operations are related to one another,

❑ develop and apply number theory concepts (e.g., primes, factors, and multiples) in real-world and mathematical problem situations.

Furthermore, the report continues, great emphasis should be placed on number theory, as number theory offers many rich opportunities for explorations that are interesting, enjoyable, and useful. Moreover, these explorations have payoffs in problem solving, in understanding and developing other mathematical concepts, in illustrating the beauty of mathematics, and in understanding the human aspects of the historical development of the number. It is for this reason that in this chapter we will study number theory in detail.

Introduction

The elementary **theory of numbers** usually deals with only the numbers 0, 1, 2, 3, 4, ... These numbers are called **whole numbers**. Since these numbers are so simple, you may think that this area of mathematics is especially easy in comparison to other areas. However, this is not the case. There are problems in number theory that have been handed down to us by the ancient Greeks and, after 2500 years, still remain unsolved.

Whatever the reason, number theory has attracted, and still attracts, the attention of many first-rate mathematicians. The great German mathematician Gauss once said, "Mathematics is the queen of the sciences, and number theory is the queen of mathematics."

One of the reasons that the numbers are so fascinating is that in working with them we discover many surprising and interesting patterns.

EXAMPLE 1

Let us examine the following number facts carefully to discover a method for finding the square of a number.

$$1^2 = 1$$
$$2^2 = 1 + 2 + 1 = 4$$
$$3^2 = 1 + 2 + 3 + 2 + 1 = 9$$
$$4^2 = 1 + 2 + 3 + 4 + 3 + 2 + 1 = 16$$
$$5^2 = 1 + 2 + 3 + 4 + 5 + 4 + 3 + 2 + 1 = 25$$
$$6^2 = 1 + 2 + 3 + 4 + 5 + 6 + 5 + 4 + 3 + 2 + 1 = 36$$
$$7^2 = 1 + 2 + 3 + 4 + 5 + 6 + 7 + 6 + 5 + 4 + 3 + 2 + 1 = 49$$

From the above patterns it is obvious that to find the square of a number, we start with 1 and keep adding 1 until we get to our number. Then we go down by 1's until we get back to 1 again. Thus to find 8^2, we have

$$1 + 2 + 3 + 4 + 5 + 6 + 7 + 8 + 7 + 6 + 5 + 4 + 3 + 2 + 1,$$

which equals 64. Therefore $8^2 = 64$. We can generalize this to obtain the square of any number n. We have

$$1 + 2 + 3 + \cdots + (n - 1) + n + (n - 1) + \cdots + 3 + 2 + 1$$

When we add these, we get n^2.   ▄

EXAMPLE 2

The mathematician Nichomachus of Gerasa (about 100 A.D.) noticed that if you write the odd numbers in the pattern

1   3, 5   7, 9, 11   13, 15, 17, 19   21, 23, 25, 27, 29 . . .

then the sums of the above groupings in order are

HISTORICAL NOTE

We know that the Greeks, especially the Pythagoreans, were fascinated by number theory. It is likely that even before them the Babylonians studied it. Why should this subject arouse so much interest? There are several answers.

In the first place, as we have already pointed out, this branch of mathematics deals with rather simple numbers. This makes it easy, even for the nonmathematician, to state and understand many number theory problems. (Solving them is quite a different story.)

Another reason for the Greeks' interest in number theory was their belief that numbers had certain magical powers. Some of these superstitions survive even today. We consider 7 lucky, except if you break a mirror, in which case you get seven years of bad luck. We also think of 11 as being a lucky number. The number 13 is unlucky to many people, and some tall buildings have no thirteenth floor because it cannot be rented easily. How do you feel about taking an exam on Friday the thirteenth? The number 3 is usually considered lucky, but there are some smokers who will not light three cigarettes with one match.

The Pythagoreans went even further. They believed that the entire universe could be explained in terms of the numbers 0, 1, 2, 3, ... According to their beliefs, the number 1 gave rise to all other numbers, and they considered it the "number of reason." They called 2 the first female number (all other even numbers were also female). On the other hand, 3 was the first male number (all other odd numbers were also male). We do not care to comment on their belief that 2 was the "number of opinion" and 3 the "number of harmony." They believed that 5 was the "number of marriage" (can you see why?) and that 6 was the "number of creation" (remember, the Bible tells us that God created the world in six days).

The Pythagoreans believed that 10 was the holiest number. It was the number of the universe and the symbol of health and harmony. Because they believed that 10 was the perfect number, they believed that there were 10 heavenly bodies. At the center of the universe there was a fire. Around this fire the sun, earth, moon, and the five known planets revolved. Since this totaled only 9 heavenly bodies, they invented a tenth one called a "counterearth."

Finally, some of the ideas of number theory are closely related to geometry. This may not seem like much of an attraction to you, but the study of geometry was itself of major concern to both the Babylonians and the Greeks.

$$
\begin{aligned}
1 &= 1 = 1^3 \\
3 + 5 &= 8 = 2^3 \\
7 + 9 + 11 &= 27 = 3^3 \\
13 + 15 + 17 + 19 &= 64 = 4^3 \\
&\vdots
\end{aligned}
$$

Thus we see that these successive sums are the cubes of integers.

EXAMPLE 3

The odd numbers are the numbers 1, 3, 5, 7, 9, 11, ... We see that

$$
\begin{aligned}
1 &= 1 \text{ which is the same as } 1^2 \\
1 + 3 &= 4 \text{ which is the same as } 2^2 \\
1 + 3 + 5 &= 9 \text{ which is the same as } 3^2 \\
1 + 3 + 5 + 7 &= 16 \text{ which is the same as } 4^2 \\
1 + 3 + 5 + 7 + 9 &= 25 \text{ which is the same as } 5^2 \\
1 + 3 + 5 + 7 + 9 + 11 &= 36 \text{ which is the same as } 6^2
\end{aligned}
$$

There is a relationship between the number of odd numbers we are adding and the sum. The relationship can be seen when we rewrite the above list as follows:

Sum of first odd number equals 1, which is 1^2;

Sum of first two odd numbers equals 4, which is 2^2;

Sum of first three odd numbers equals 9, which is 3^2;

In general, the sum of the first n odd numbers equals n^2.

Thus, for example, the sum of the first ten odd numbers $(1 + 3 + 5 + 7 + 9 + 11 + 13 + 15 + 17 + 19)$ is 100 or 10^2. Compare this result with Example 1. What do you notice?

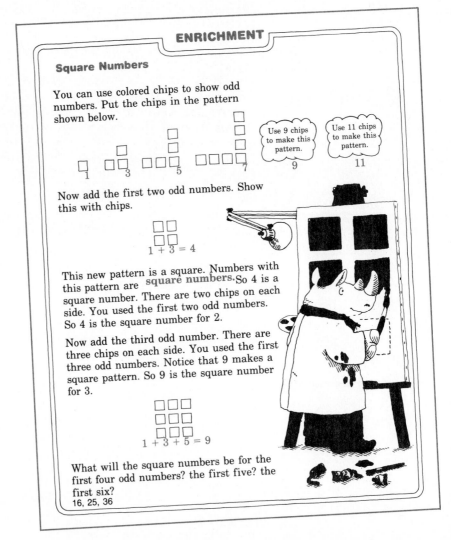

ENRICHMENT

Square Numbers

You can use colored chips to show odd numbers. Put the chips in the pattern shown below.

1   3   5   7   9   11

Use 9 chips to make this pattern.

Use 11 chips to make this pattern.

Now add the first two odd numbers. Show this with chips.

$1 + 3 = 4$

This new pattern is a square. Numbers with this pattern are **square numbers.** So 4 is a square number. There are two chips on each side. You used the first two odd numbers. So 4 is the square number for 2.

Now add the third odd number. There are three chips on each side. You used the first three odd numbers. Notice that 9 makes a square pattern. So 9 is the square number for 3.

$1 + 3 + 5 = 9$

What will the square numbers be for the first four odd numbers? the first five? the first six?

16, 25, 36

An Interesting Number

by Sam Hoffman

The following interesting number was brought to my attention by one of my students. It is the number 142857. The number has six digits, and no digit is repeated. Furthermore, it has no zeroes, three, sixes, or nines. When this number is multiplied by two, the same six digits appear in the product. When this number is multiplied by three, four, five, or six, the product always maintains the same order of the digits as in the original number. The only difference is in the first and last digit.

However, a strange thing happens when the original number is multiplied by seven. Try it and see what happens.

The Island Teacher

Ever since the various number systems were invented to count and do computations, people have been fascinated by the properties that some numbers have and others do not have.

It is with questions of this nature that mathematicians concern themselves. In this chapter, we will analyze some interesting **number patterns**. Even at an early age, children are urged to discover number patterns for themselves. This can be seen from student page 217 from *Addison-Wesley Mathematics*, 1987, Grade 4, on the facing page.

5.1

DIVISIBILITY

divisibility

A basic idea of number theory is that of one number dividing another number evenly. For example, 4 divides 12 evenly, but 4 does *not* divide 11 evenly. We therefore begin with a discussion of what we mean by **divisibility**.

We say that 4 divides 12 evenly because 12 consists of the sum of exactly three 4's. To put it another way, $4 \cdot 3 = 12$.

Similarly, we know that 4 does not divide 11 because 11 does not consist exactly of a whole number of 4's. In other words, there is no whole number m such that $4 \cdot m = 11$. This leads us to the following definition.

divisor

> **Definition 5.1** We say that x **divides** y whenever there is a whole number m such that $x \cdot m = y$. If no such number m exists, then we say that x does not divide y. If x divides y, then we call x a **divisor** of y.

Comment   In this definition we *never* let $x = 0$. Remember, you cannot divide by 0. However, y *can* equal 0.

EXAMPLE 1

7 divides 21 because $7 \cdot 3 = 21$.
9 does *not* divide 21, because there is no whole number m such that $9 \cdot m = 21$.
8 divides 200, because $8 \cdot 25 = 200$.
8 does *not* divide 100, because there is no whole number m such that $8 \cdot m = 100$. ∎

Comment   The following statements are equivalent: (a) 7 divides 21; (b) 21 is divisible by 7; (c) 7 is a divisor of 21; (d) 21 is a multiple of 7; and (e) 7 is a factor of 21. We often use the notation $7|21$ to stand for "7 divides 21".

EXAMPLE 2

The divisors of 18 are 1, 2, 3, 6, 9, and 18 itself, since each of these divides 18. ∎

EXAMPLE 3

5 divides 50 and 5 also divides 15. Let us now add 50 and 15. We get 65. How about 65? It is obvious that 5 divides 65 also, since $5 \cdot 13 = 65$. This leads us to the following useful statement about divisibility. ∎

Statement 1   Suppose x divides y and x also divides z. Then x divides $y + z$.

This just says that if x divides each of two numbers, then it also divides their sum.

Proof of Statement 1

If x divides y, this means that there is a whole number m such that

$$y = x \cdot m \tag{1}$$

Similarly, if x divides z, this means that there is a whole number n such that

$$z = x \cdot n \tag{2}$$

If we now add (1) and (2) together, we see that

$$y + z = x \cdot m + x \cdot n$$
$$= x(m + n) \qquad \text{(by the distributive law).}$$

Now $(m + n)$ is the sum of two whole numbers and is therefore itself a whole number. Why? Let us call it M. Thus $M = m + n$. Then

$$y + z = x(m + n)$$

or

$$y + z = xM \qquad\qquad (1)$$

This last line (3) says that there is a number M such that $x \cdot M = y + z$. By Definition 5.1, we therefore have that x divides $y + z$.

EXAMPLE 4

a) 4 divides 8, and 4 also divides 20. Statement 1 tells us that 4 divides $8 + 20$, or that 4 divides 28.

b) 6 divides 30 and 6 divides 12. Statement 1 tells us that 6 divides $30 + 12$, or that 6 divides 42.

c) 3 divides 12; 3 does not divide 5. Does 3 divide $12 + 5$, or 17? Obviously not!

The last example leads us to another useful statement.

Statement 2 If x divides y, and x does not divide z, then x does not divide $y + z$.

This just says that if x divides one part of a sum and x does not divide the second part, then it cannot divide the entire sum.

Proof of Statement 2

This proof is a proof by contradiction, so you should review this technique before reading further.

There are two possibilities

a) x does divide $y + z$, or

b) x does not divide $y + z$.

Either (a) or (b) *must* be true.

Let us try possibility (a) and suppose that it is true. Then x divides $y + z$. By Definition 5.1 this means that there is a number m such that $x \cdot m = y + z$. Since we are given that x divides y, then this means that there is a number n such that $x \cdot n = y$. Now

$$x \cdot m = y + z$$
$$x \cdot m = (x \cdot n) + z \qquad \text{(We just substitute for } y.)$$

Let us subtract $x \cdot n$ from both sides of this equation. We get

$$(x \cdot m) - (x \cdot n) = (x \cdot n) + z - (x \cdot n)$$

$(x \cdot m) - (x \cdot n) = z$ (The $x \cdot n$'s on the right side cancel out.)

$x(m - n) = z$ (Here we used the distributive law on the left side of the equation.)

Now $m - n$ is the difference of two whole numbers, and m is larger than n. (Why?) Thus $m - n$ is also a whole number. Let us call it M. We then have

$$x(m - n) = z$$

$x \cdot M = z$ (We substituted M for $m - n$.)

But this last line says that there is a number M that, when multiplied by x, will give z. By Definition 5.1. this means that x *divides* z.

However, since we were told that x *does not divide* z, we therefore have a *contradiction*. This means that possibility (a) is wrong. Since possibility (a) cannot be correct, then we conclude that possibility (b), which says that x does *not* divide $y + z$, is correct.

EXAMPLE 5

6 divides 12. However, 6 does not divide 13. What about the sum of 12 and 13? Clearly, 6 does not divide $12 + 13$, or 25. ▪

Tests for Divisibility

There are many situations in which we want to know whether one number divides another evenly. Take the following example. In a certain town the sanitation department employs 291 people. The department works in crews of 3. Can these 291 people be evenly divided into crews of 3? You can answer this question by actually dividing 3 into 291. If you do, you find that 3 goes into 291 exactly 97 times. However, sometimes we do not want to spend the time required to do this. It turns out that we can often answer such questions without actually doing the division, but divisibility tests   by using the following **divisibility tests**.

Test for Divisibility by 2

A number is divisible by 2 when the ones digit is 0, 2, 4, 6, or 8.

EXAMPLE 6

The number 4308 is divisible by 2, since the ones digit is 8.

The number 23456 is divisible by 2, since the ones digit is 6.

The number 51694 is divisible by 2, since the ones digit is 4. ▪

Test for Divisibility by 3

A number is divisible by 3 when the sum of its digits is divisible by 3.

EXAMPLE 7

The number 52341 is divisible by 3, since the sum of its digits is $5 + 2 + 3 + 4 + 1$, or 15, and 15 is divisible by 3.

The number 291 is divisible by 3, since the sum of its digit is $2 + 9 + 1$, or 12, and 12 is divisible by 3. ▪

Test for Divisibility by 4

A number is divisible by 4 when the number formed by the last two digits is divisible by 4.

EXAMPLE 8

The number 5344 is divisible by 4, since the last two digits form the number 44, and 44 is divisible by 4.

The number 6213 is *not* divisible by 4, since the last two digits form the number 13, and 13 is not divisible by 4. ▪

Test for Divisibility by 5

A number is divisible by 5 when the ones digit is 0 or 5.

EXAMPLE 9

The number 42805 is divisible by 5, since the ones digit is 5.

The number 28130 is divisible by 5, since the ones digit is 0. ▪

Test for Divisibility by 9

A number is divisible by 9 if the sum of its digits is divisible by 9.

EXAMPLE 10

The number 5346 is divisible by 9, since the sum of its digits is $5 + 3 + 4 + 6$, or 18, and 18 is divisible by 9.

The number 3289 is *not* divisible by 9, since the sum of its digits is $3 + 2 + 8 + 9$, or 22, and 22 is not divisible by 9. ▪

A very useful application of these divisibility tests is in reducing fractions to lowest terms. For example, the fraction $\frac{1470}{21657}$ can be reduced. The divisibility test for 3 shows us that both the numerator and the denominator can be divided by 3. We get $\frac{1470}{21657} = \frac{3 \cdot 490}{3 \cdot 7219} = \frac{490}{7219}$. Can the fraction be reduced by any other number?

We can easily verify the tests for divisibility by 2, 4, and 5 by using statements 1 and 2 given earlier. We will give a proof of the divisibility test by 2 for any arbitrary three-digit number. (A similar proof holds for any number of digits.) Suppose we let n be any three-digit number. Then we can write it as $n = a \cdot 10^2 + b \cdot 10 + c$. Notice that

$$a \cdot 10^2 + b \cdot 10 = 10(a \cdot 10 + b)$$

Obviously, 2 divides 10, so that for any digit values of a and b, 2 divides $10(a \cdot 10 + b)$ or 2 divides $(a \cdot 10^2 + b \cdot 10)$. Therefore, if 2 divides c where c is the ones digit, then 2 must also divide $(10(a \cdot 10 + b) + c)$, so that 2 divides $(a \cdot 10^2 + b \cdot 10 + c)$. Thus 2 divides n.

Conversely, let 2 divide $(a \cdot 10^2 + b \cdot 10 + c)$. Then since 2 divides $(a \cdot 10^2 + b \cdot 10)$ we must have that 2 divides

$$[(a \cdot 10^2 + b \cdot 10 + c) - (a \cdot 10^2 + b \cdot 10)]$$

or that 2 divides c. This shows that 2 divides a number if and only if 2 divides that number's ones digit. A similar reasoning can be used to verify the tests for divisibility by 4 and 5.

We can also easily verify the test for divisibility of a three-digit number by 3 as follows. (Again a similar test holds for any number of digits.) Let $n = a \cdot 10^2 + b \cdot 10 + c$ be any three-digit number. We can rewrite n as follows:

$$n = a \cdot (99 + 1) + b \cdot (9 + 1) + c$$
$$= a \cdot 99 + a \cdot 1 + b \cdot 9 + b \cdot 1 + c$$
$$= (a \cdot 11 + b)9 + a + b + c$$

Thus since 3 divides 9 it also divides $(a \cdot 11 + b)9$. Therefore if 3 divides $(a + b + c)$, the sum of the digits of n, then 3 must divide n, as 3 divides $[(a \cdot 11 + b)9 + (a + b + c)]$. Conversely, if 3 divides n, then 3 divides $(a + b + c)$, since 3 divides $[n - (a \cdot 11 + b) \, 9]$ and $n - (a \cdot 11 + b)9 = a + b + c$. A similar reasoning can be used to justify the test for divisibility by 9.

Divisibility Tests for Other Numbers

Often we can combine two divisibility tests simultaneously to come up with new divisibility tests. For example, we can combine the divisibility test for 2 and the divisibility test for 5 to come up with a divisibility test for 10 as follows. The divisibility test for 2 tells us that a number is divisible by 2 when the ones digit is 0, 2, 4, 6, or 8. Similarly, the test for 5 tells us that a number is divisible by 5 when the ones digit is 0 or 5. If we combine these two tests, we find that a number is divisible by 10 if and only if the ones digit is 0. We can combine any two divisibility tests to test any number in general. For example, if Mary owes $3542 on a used car, we can use the divisibility tests for 3 and 4 to determine that this *cannot* be paid in 12 *equal* monthly installments.

For the benefit of the reader, we summarize some of the divisibility tests in the following chart:

DIVISIBILITY TESTS

A number is divisible by	when
2	the ones digit is 0, 2, 4, 6, or 8.
3	the sum of its digits is divisible by 3.
4	the number formed by the last two digits is divisible by 4.
5	the ones digit is 0 or 5.
8	the number formed by the last three digits is divisible by 8.
9	the sum of its digits is divisible by 9.
10	the ones digit is 0.

EXAMPLE 11

Problem-Solving Example

The police force of a city consists of 14,378 officers. To facilitate random drug testing, the mayor of the city announces that the entire force will be divided into two groups, some of which will contain six officers each and the remaining groups will contain nine officers each. After analyzing the plan, the police commissioner claims that this cannot be done mathematically. Is the police commissioner's claim correct?

SOLUTION

Understanding the Problem

Assuming that each group will contain either six officers or nine officers, the problem is to determine whether the police commissioner's claim is correct.

A Plan to Solve the Problem

We must determine whether 14,378 is divisible by 6 and/or by 9. It can be shown that a number is divisible by 6 if and only if the number is divisible by both 2 and 3. The number 14,378 is divisible by 2 since the ones digit is 8. However, the number 14,378 is not divisible by 3 nor by 9 since the sum of the digits is $1 + 4 + 3 + 7 + 8$, or 23, and 23 is not divisible by 3 nor 9. Thus the police commissioner's claim that this cannot be done mathematically is correct.

Checking the Solution

If the mayor's plan is valid, then we should be able to find whole numbers m and n such that $6m + 9n = 14{,}378$, as all 6 police officers and 9 police officer groups must contain a total of $6m$ and $9n$ police officers respectively. Using a computer program, we can actually determine all whole-number values for m and n. With such a list, one would find that the police commissioner's claim is correct. No whole-number values exist for m and n for which

$$6m + 9n = 14{,}378$$

EXERCISES FOR SECTION 5.1

1. Find all the divisors of each of the following numbers.

a) 56   b) 86   c) 98   d) 62
e) 132   f) 160   g) 149   h) 482
i) 376   j) 558

2. Find all the divisors of 0.

3. Test each of the following numbers to see whether it is divisible by 2, 3, 4, 5, or 6.

a) 324   b) 436   c) 864   d) 685
e) 293   f) 456   g) 890   h) 3402
i) 5678   j) 1396

4. a) Make up a test to determine whether a number is divisible by 6.

b) Use this test to determine which of the numbers given in Exercise 3 are divisible by 6.

5. Determine which of the numbers given in Exercise 3 are divisible by 8.

6. Can you find a five-digit number that is divisible by 4, 5, 8, and 9?

7. Can you find a six-digit number that is divisible by 5, 6, 7, and 9?

8. Can you find a six-digit number that is divisible by 5 and 7 and not by 4, 6, or 9?

9. Find a rule for determining when a number is divisible by 50.

10. A leap year is a year whose date is divisible by 4. However, century years (that is, years that end in two zeros) are leap years only when their dates are divisible by 400. Which of the following years are leap years?

   a) 1984   **b)** 1623   **c)** 1492   **d)** 1900
   e) 1400   **f)** 1424   **g)** 1776   **h)** 1943

11. If the sum of the divisors of a number, excluding the number itself, is equal to another number, and *vice versa*, then we say that the numbers are **amicable** or **friendly**. Show that 220 and 284 are friendly numbers.

12. Complete each of the following computations. Can you generalize?

   a) $1 \cdot 9 + 2 = ?$
   $12 \cdot 9 + 3 = ?$
   $123 \cdot 9 + 4 = ?$
   etc.

   b) $9 \cdot 9 + 7 = ?$
   $98 \cdot 9 + 6 = ?$
   $987 \cdot 9 + 5 = ?$
   etc.

   c) $1 \cdot 8 + 1 = ?$
   $12 \cdot 8 + 2 = ?$
   $123 \cdot 8 + 3 = ?$
   etc.

   d) $3 \cdot 37 = 111$ and $1 + 1 + 1 = 3$
   $6 \cdot 37 = ?$ and   ?
   $9 \cdot 37 = ?$ and   ?
   etc.

   e) $1 \cdot \ \ 1 = ?$
   $11 \cdot \ \ 11 = ?$
   $111 \cdot 111 = ?$
   etc.

   f) $7 \cdot \ \ 7 = ?$
   $67 \cdot \ \ 67 = ?$
   $667 \cdot 667 = ?$
   etc.

   g) $7 \cdot 15873 = ?$
   $14 \cdot 15873 = ?$
   $21 \cdot 15873 = ?$
   etc.

13. Use the results of Example 2 in the introduction to this chapter to find the sum of the indicated numbers.

   a) $1 + 3 + 5 + \ldots + 29$
   b) $1 + 3 + 5 + \ldots + 71$
   c) $13 + 15 + 17 + \ldots + 89$

14. A **magic triangle** is any arrangement of the natural numbers in the form of a triangle where the sum of the numbers on each of the sides (called the **magic sum**) is always the same. The amount of numbers on each side is called the order. For example,

represents a magic triangle whose order is 3 and whose sum is 11. Find a magic triangle of order 3 whose sum is 23.

15. The Pythagoreans investigated a special group of natural numbers known as **triangular numbers**. The numbers that have geometric forms that look like triangles are called triangular numbers. The first few triangular numbers are 1, 3, 6, 10, and 15, as can be seen from the diagram below:

Natural number   1   3   6   10   15

Determine the next three triangular numbers.

▶ Brain-Teaser Problems ◀

**16. Can you find a 3-digit number that is divisible by the product of its digits?

**17. a) Multiply the numbers 5, 6, and 7 together. Divide the results by 6.

   b) Multiply the numbers 13, 14, and 15 together. Divide the results by 6.

   c) Multiply the numbers 25, 26, and 27 together. Divide the results by 6.

   d) On the basis of the results obtained in parts (a), (b), and (c), can you generalize about the product of any three numbers?

   e) What statement can be made about the product of any four numbers?

**18. Determine whether the following statement is true: A number is divisible by 8 if and only if the difference between the sum of the digits in the odd places and the sum of the digits in the even places is divisible by 11.

**19. Pick a 3-digit number, such as 273. Write the digits again in the same order to make the 6-digit number 273273. Divide 273273 by 13 and you will see that there is no remainder. Now pick another 3-digit number, rewrite the digits again to make a 6-digit number, and divide the result by 13. Again you will

get no remainder.

a) Generalize this result.

b) Try to explain why this happens.

**20. Follow the same procedure as in Exercise 19, except divide by 7 instead of 13. What happens? Can you generalize this result? Can you explain why this happens?

**21. Determine whether the following statement is true: A number is divisible by 6 if and only if it is divisible by both 2 and 3.

5.2

SOME INTERESTING NUMBERS

In this section we will discuss some special types of numbers that have fascinated mathematicians over the years because of their unusual properties. We will start with the Fibonacci numbers.

Fibonacci Numbers

Suppose we have decided to breed rabbits. Obviously, we must start with a pair, whom we shall call Jack Rabbit and Bunny Rabbit. We will assume the following.

1. Jack and Bunny are newborn when we start.

2. Rabbits begin to reproduce exactly two months after their own birth.

3. Thereafter, every month a pair of rabbits will produce exactly *one* other pair (a male and a female).

4. None of the rabbits dies.

Let us see how fast the number of pairs of rabbits increases.

The first pair, Jack and Bunny Rabbit, will have their first pair of children after two months. This gives us two pairs of rabbits.

After three months, Jack and Bunny will have another pair. We now have three pairs. After four months, Jack and Bunny will again have another pair. Also, their first pair of children will have *their* first pair. This brings the total to five pairs.

This process will continue. Figure 5.1 (see next page) shows the number of rabbits at the end of each month through the first six months. The total number of pairs of rabbits for the first twelve months is shown in Table 5.1.

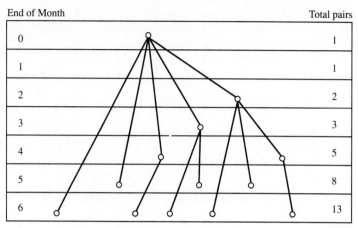

Figure 5.1

TABLE 5.1	
Number of months passed	Total number of pairs of rabbits
0	1
1	1
2	2
3	3
4	5
5	8
6	13
7	21
8	34
9	55
10	89
11	144
12	233

Figure 5.2 What connection does this picture have with Fibonacci numbers?

We see that at the end of the first year there will be 233 pairs of rabbits! If we were to continue this process beyond 12 months, we would get more and more pairs of rabbits.

Now let us examine the numbers in the second column of the table. They are 1, 1, 2, 3, 5, 8, 13, 21, 34, 55, 89, 144, 233. There is something especially interesting about these numbers (even to mathematicians who don't like rabbits). If we look at them carefully, we see that when we add the first two numbers, we get $1 + 1 = 2$. This is the next number. Then $1 + 2 = 3$. This is the next number. And $2 + 3 = 5$. This again is the next number.

In general, we see that if we add any two consecutive numbers, we always get the next number in the list. The list of numbers 1, 1, 2, 3, 5, 8, 13, 21, 34, 55, 89, 144, 233, . . . is called a **Fibonacci sequence** in honor of its discoverer. He was Leonardo of Pisa, a remarkable Italian mathematician who lived in the last part of the twelfth century and the early thirteenth century. His father's name was Bonaccus, and Leonardo was nicknamed Filius Bonacci (which is Latin for "son of Bonaccus"). This nickname was shortened to Fibonacci.

Fibonacci sequence

Another entertaining application of Fibonacci numbers is to the game of *Fibonacci Nim.* This game is played by two players. There is one pile of matches. The first player takes one or more matches, but cannot take the whole pile. The next player can take up to twice the number of matches his or her opponent took, but no more. The first player can now also take up to twice the number of matches his or her opponent took on the last play, but no more. The play continues in this way. For example, if one player takes 4 matches on any play, the other may take as many as 8 matches on the next play, but no more. The game continues until all the matches are gone. The player who takes the last match wins.

Fibonacci Nim

It can be shown that if the number of matches in the original pile is a Fibonacci number, then the second player can *always* win if he or she plays correctly. If the number of matches in the original pile is not a Fibonacci number, then the first player can *always* win if he or she plays correctly. Play this game with a friend and figure out the winning strategy.

Fibonacci numbers can also be applied to the situation shown in Fig. 5.3. Suppose the bee wants to go to cell 3. The bee must *always move to the right* and always to a cell right next to it. In how many different ways can the bee get to cell 3?

Figure 5.3

One possible way is for the bee first to go to cell 1 and then to cell 3. We write this as

$$1 \rightarrow 3$$

Another possible path is

$$0 \rightarrow 2 \rightarrow 3$$

The other possible paths are

$$0 \rightarrow 1 \rightarrow 2 \rightarrow 3$$
$$1 \rightarrow 2 \rightarrow 3$$
$$0 \rightarrow 1 \rightarrow 3$$

Thus the bee has five possible paths by which to get to cell 3. If you also calculate the number of possible paths by which the bee can get to cells 0, 1, 2, and 4, you get the results shown in Table 5.2. Notice that the number of possible paths form a Fibonacci sequence (except for the first term).

	TABLE 5.2

Cell	Number of possible paths
0	1
1	2
2	3
3	5
4	8

The Fibonacci sequence has many other interesting properties and applications. If you are interested, you can find some of these in the suggested further readings for this chapter.

Perfect Numbers

The numbers that divide 6 evenly, excluding 6 itself, are 1, 2, and 3. Notice that $1 + 2 + 3 = 6$. We call a number **perfect** if it equals the sum of all the numbers that divide it and if these numbers are smaller than the number itself.

EXAMPLE 1

The number 12 is *not* a perfect number, since the numbers that divide it (that are less than 12) are 1, 2, 3, 4, and 6. We find that

$$1 + 2 + 3 + 4 + 6 = 16$$

So 12 is *not* equal to the sum of these numbers.

Figure 5.4

The number 15 is *not* perfect, since the numbers that divide it (that are less than 15) are 1, 3, and 5. If we add these numbers, we get $1 + 3 + 5$, which equals 9. Thus 15 is *not* equal to the sum of these numbers.

The number 28 *is* perfect, since the numbers less than 28 that divide it are 1, 2, 4, 7, and 14. Adding these, we get $1 + 2 + 4 + 7 + 14 = 28$.

It was once believed that perfect numbers had magical properties. In fact, it was believed that God created the world in 6 days because 6 is the smallest perfect number.

The first four perfect numbers are 6, 28, 496, and 8128. No one knows how many perfect numbers there are, although it is likely that there are infinitely many. All the known perfect numbers are even, for no one has yet discovered an odd one. However, there may be odd perfect numbers. It *is* known that every even perfect number ends in either 6 or 8.

There is a formula that will give all the even perfect numbers. It is

$$2^{P-1}(2^P - 1),$$

where P is a prime number and where $2^P - 1$ is also a prime number.

EXERCISES FOR SECTION 5.2

1. We have given the first twelve numbers in the Fibonacci sequence. Write the next eight.

2. **a)** Add the first three numbers of the Fibonacci sequence. You get $1 + 1 + 2 = 4$. This is one less than the fifth number, which is 5. Now add the first four numbers. How does this sum compare to the sixth number?

b) Add the first five numbers of the Fibonacci sequence. How does this sum compare to the seventh number?

c) Without actually adding them, can you say what would be the sum of the first six numbers in the Fibonacci sequence?

3. Divide each number of the Fibonacci sequence by 4 and write down the remainders. Do this for the first thirty numbers. Do you notice any pattern?

4. Consider the ratios of successive terms of the Fibonacci sequence, that is, divide any term of the Fibonacci sequence by the next term. We get the results shown in the table at the top of the next column. Note that this sequence oscillates and is approximately equal to 1.618. This number is called the **golden ratio**. It occurs frequently in mathematics. Select any two nonzero numbers. Add them together to obtain a

Ratio	Value	Ratio	Value
$\frac{1}{1}$	= 1.000	$\frac{13}{8}$	= 1.625
$\frac{2}{1}$	= 2.000	$\frac{21}{13}$	≈1.615
$\frac{3}{2}$	= 1.500	$\frac{34}{21}$	≈1.619
$\frac{5}{3}$	≈1.667	$\frac{55}{34}$	≈1.618
$\frac{8}{5}$	= 1.600	$\frac{89}{55}$	≈1.618

third number. Form a sequence of numbers by adding the two previous terms to obtain the next term, much the same way that we obtained the numbers in the Fibonacci sequence. Verify that if you form the ratios of successive terms, then after a while the values oscillate around the golden ratio.

5. In the application of Fibonacci numbers to the bee's path, find all the possible paths by which it can get to cells 5, 6, and 7.

5.3
Pg. 269

6. Closely related to the Fibonacci numbers are the **Lucas numbers**, named after the nineteenth century French mathematician Edouard Lucas (1842–1891). The Lucas numbers are generated in the same way as the Fibonacci sequence but start differently. The first six Lucas numbers are 1, 3, 4, 7, 11, 18. Find the next six Lucas numbers.

*7. Can you locate the Fibonacci numbers embedded in Pascal's triangle?

8. Show that 10 is not a perfect number.

*9. Write each of the four perfect numbers 6, 28, 496, and 8128 in binary notation. Do you notice any pattern?

Consider the sequence of numbers 1, 4, 7, 10, 13, ... Each number is 3 more than the one before it. Such a sequence is called an **arithmetic progression**. We can find the 100th term in this sequence without actually listing all the numbers by rewriting them as follows.

Number of term in sequence	Number	Rewritten form
1	1	1
2	4	$1 + (1 \cdot 3)$
3	7	$1 + (2 \cdot 3)$
4	10	$1 + (3 \cdot 3)$
5	13	$1 + (4 \cdot 3)$
6	16	$1 + (5 \cdot 3)$
7	19	$1 + (6 \cdot 3)$
⋮	⋮	⋮
In general, we have n	?	$1 + (n - 1)3$

Thus to find the 100th term, we take $n = 100$ and get

$$1 + (n - 1)3 = 1 + (100 - 1)3$$
$$= 1 + (99)3$$
$$= 298$$

Therefore the 100th term in the above sequence is 298. To convince yourself that this is true, write out the first 100 numbers in the sequence.

Using a similar method, find the indicated term of each of the arithmetic progressions in Exercises 10–14.

10. 3, 6, 9, . . . the 40th term

11. 1, 9, 17, . . . the 17th term

12. 4, 15, 26, . . . the 23rd term

13. 68, 62, 56, . . . the 11th term

14. 103, 100, 97, . . . the 17th term

15. Consider the sequence 1, 2, 4, 8, 16, 32, ... In this sequence, each number is twice the one before it. Such a sequence is called a **geometric progression**. We can find the tenth term in this progression without actually listing all the numbers by rewriting them as follows.

Number of term in sequence	Number	Rewritten form
1	1	1 (also written as 2^0)
2	2	2^1
3	4	2^2
4	8	2^3
5	16	2^4
⋮	⋮	⋮
In general, we have n	?	2^{n-1}

Thus to find the 10th term, we take $n = 10$ and get

$$2^{n-1} = 2^{10-1} = 2^9 = 512$$

Therefore the tenth term in the sequence is 512. Using a similar procedure, find the ninth term in the sequence 1, 5, 25, 125, ...

Classify the sequences given in Exercises 16–20 as arithmetic, geometric, both, or neither.

16. 1, 5, 9, 13, . . .

17. 1, 4, 16, 64, . . .

18. 1, 4, 7, 10, . . .

19. 96, 90, 84, 78, . . .

20. 100, 50, 25, 12.5, . . .

IIII ▶ **Brain-Teaser Problems** ◀ IIII

21. The president of Geometric Progressions of America, Inc. is paid a monthly salary (31 days) of $25,000. The stockholders believe that she is overpaid. Being familiar with geometric progressions, she agrees to take an immediate drastic salary cut. She offers to be

paid according to the following schedule:

      1¢ first day of month,

      2¢ second day of month,

      4¢ third day of month,

      8¢ fourth day of month,

that is, each day's salary is double the previous day's salary. The stockholders eagerly agree to this proposal. Is the stockholder's decision a wise one? Explain your answer.

5.3

PRIME NUMBERS AND PRIME FACTORIZATION

prime number

composite

You will recall that a **prime number** is any number larger than 1 that is divisible by only itself and 1, assuming we divide only by positive numbers. The first few prime numbers are 2, 3, 5, 7, 11, 13, ... A number that is *not* prime is called **composite**.

EXAMPLE 1

The number 4 is not a prime number, since it can be divided by 2 as well as by itself and 1. It is a composite number. We know that 17 is a prime number, since the only numbers that divide it are 17 and 1. But 12 is not a prime number. It can be divided by 2, 3, 4, and 6. It is a composite number.

How can we determine whether a number is prime or not? One method was developed by the Greek mathematician Eratosthenes (approximately 276–194 B.C.). His procedure, called the **sieve of Eratosthenes**, enables us to find all primes less than a given number.

sieve of Eratosthenes

We will illustrate the technique by finding all the primes up to 50. We write down all the numbers from 1 to 50 as shown below.

$$
\begin{array}{cccccccccc}
\cancel{1} & ② & ③ & \cancel{4} & ⑤ & \cancel{6} & ⑦ & \cancel{8} & \cancel{9} & \cancel{10} \\
⑪ & \cancel{12} & ⑬ & \cancel{14} & \cancel{15} & \cancel{16} & ⑰ & \cancel{18} & ⑲ & \cancel{20} \\
\cancel{21} & \cancel{22} & ㉓ & \cancel{24} & \cancel{25} & \cancel{26} & \cancel{27} & \cancel{28} & ㉙ & \cancel{30} \\
㉛ & \cancel{32} & \cancel{33} & \cancel{34} & \cancel{35} & \cancel{36} & ㊲ & \cancel{38} & \cancel{39} & \cancel{40} \\
㊶ & \cancel{42} & ㊳ & \cancel{44} & \cancel{45} & \cancel{46} & ㊼ & \cancel{48} & \cancel{49} & \cancel{50}
\end{array}
$$

First cross out 1, which is not a prime. Circle 2, which is a prime, and cross out every *second* number after it. Now circle the next uncrossed number, 3, which is a prime, and cross out every *third* number after it. (Some of these will already have been crossed out.) Circle the next uncrossed number, 5, which is a prime, and cross off every fifth number after it.

Continuing in this manner, we find all the prime numbers up to 50. We find that all the prime numbers have been circled and all nonprime numbers have been crossed off. Using the same technique, we can find all the prime numbers less than any given number. Of course, if the given number is fairly large, this process may become very long and tiresome.

Prime Factorization

Now that we know how to find prime numbers, let us look at a nonprime number, such as 12. It can be written as 6×2. Notice that 2 is a prime, but 6 is not. However, 6 can be written as 2×3, and 2 and 3 are both primes. Thus we can write 12 as

$$12 = 2 \times 3 \times 2$$

which is a product of prime numbers.

Can 12 be written as a product of primes in a different way from $2 \times 3 \times 2$? The answer is obviously yes. It can also be written as

$$12 = 2 \times 2 \times 3$$

or

$$12 = 3 \times 2 \times 2$$

However, these are really the same as the original one, $2 \times 3 \times 2$, except for the order. We see, then, that 12 can be written as a product of primes in exactly *one* way if order is not considered.

Similarly, 20 can be written as a product of primes in only one way (except for order) as $2 \times 2 \times 5$. And 15 can be written as a product of primes in only one way, 3×5.

factor tree

The procedure for finding the prime factors can be organized using a model called a **factor tree**. This is shown below, where the last branches of the tree display the prime factors of 12 and 20.

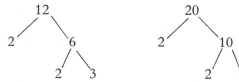

fundamental theorem of arithmetic

Actually, every integer greater than 1 (that is, 2, 3, 4, etc.) is either a prime number or can be written as a product of primes in exactly one way if order does not count. This fact is called the **fundamental theorem of arithmetic**, and we restate it formally in the following way.

Fundamental Theorem of Arithmetic   Any integer greater than 1 is either a prime number or can be written as a product of primes in only one way, except for order.

---

order doesn't matter

EXAMPLE 2

The number 21 can be written as 3×7, which is a product of primes.

The number 18 can be written as $2 \times 3 \times 3$, which is also a product of primes.

The number 100 can be written as $2 \times 2 \times 5 \times 5$, which is also a product of primes.

The number 385 can be written as $5 \times 7 \times 11$, which is also a product of primes.

Many interesting questions can be asked about prime numbers. For example, we may ask: How many prime numbers are there? Is there a formula that tells us which numbers are primes and which are not? In the remainder of this section we will attempt to answer some of these questions.

Let us begin with the first question: How many prime numbers are there? This was answered over 2000 years ago by Euclid, who *proved* that there are infinitely many prime numbers. He used the method of proof called **proof by contradiction**.

proof by contradiction

Euclid's Proof That the Number of Primes Is Infinite

There are two possibilities:

Possibility A.   There are only a finite (specific) number of primes.
Possibility B.   There are infinitely many primes.

Suppose possibility A is true. Then (if we have enough time), we can list *all* the primes. We let P_1 stand for 2, which is the first prime; P_2 will stand for 3, which is the second prime; P_3 will stand for 5, which is the third prime. Similarly, P_4 will denote the next prime, P_5 the prime after that, and so on. Eventually, we will come to the last prime, which we call P_n. (We must come to a last prime if Possibility A is true, since there is only a finite number of them.)

Let us now multiply all these primes together. We get

$$P_1 \times P_2 \times P_3 \times P_4 \times \cdots \times P_n$$

(The dots stand for the primes between P_4 and P_n.)

Let Q be the number we get by adding 1 to this product. Thus

$$Q = P_1 \cdot P_2 \cdot P_3 \cdot P_4 \cdots P_n + 1$$

What type of number is Q, prime or composite? If Q is *not* a prime number, then it must have divisors, and some of these are primes. (Why?) Let P denote one of these divisors that is a prime. Since P is prime, it is one of the primes $P_1, P_2, P_3, \ldots, P_n$ (since these are all the primes that there are). Therefore P *must* divide the product $P_1 \times P_2 \times \cdots \times P_n$. However, we know that P cannot divide 1. (Why?)

Thus we have that *P divides* $P_1 \times P_2 \times \cdots \times P_n$ and *P* does not divide 1. As we saw in Statement 2 of Section 5.1, *P cannot* divide the sum

$$P_1 \times P_2 \times P_3 \times \cdots \times P_n + 1$$

Since this sum is just *Q*, we conclude that *P does not divide Q*. But this contradicts our earlier statement that *Q* was divisible by the prime *P*.

The contradiction means that possibility A is wrong. This leaves us with possibility B, which must be correct. Thus we see that the number of primes is infinite.

Euclid's proof also answers the next question: Is there a *largest* prime number? Clearly, the answer must be no. Why? The largest number that is definitely known to be prime (at least, up to the time that this book was written) is the number $2^{132,049} - 1$. This means it is the number we get when multiplying 2 by itself 132,049 times and then subtracting 1 from the result. If you do not believe that this is a prime number, why don't you try to multiply 2 by itself 132,049 times and subtract 1 from the result. If you survive this, you may want to convince yourself that this number is prime by trying to find a number that divides it other than itself and 1. (Don't spend too much time on this!)

Obviously, Euclid's proof shows us that this is definitely *not* the largest prime that exists. There is no such number. The number $2^{132,049} - 1$ is just the largest number that is known for sure to be a prime.

There is another question that has puzzled mathematicians for a long time and that has not yet been answered: Is there a formula that tells us which numbers are prime and which are not; a formula that, when numbers are substituted into it, will produce only prime numbers? Many attempts have been made to find such a formula, but none have been successful.

The mathematician Pierre Fermat (1601–1665) believed that he had succeeded in finding such a formula. He thought that the formula $2^{2^n} + 1$ would give only prime numbers, no matter what was substituted for *n*. Let us try it and see what happens!

If $n = 0$, the formula becomes

$$2^{2^0} + 1 = 2^1 + 1 \quad \text{(remember } 2^0 = 1\text{)}$$
$$= 2 + 1 \quad \text{(since } 2^1 = 2\text{)}$$
$$= 3, \quad \text{which is prime.}$$

If $n = 1$, the formula

$$2^{2^1} + 1 = 2^2 + 1 \quad \text{(since } 2^1 = 2\text{)}$$
$$= 4 + 1 \quad \text{(since } 2^2 = 4\text{)}$$
$$= 5 \quad \text{which is prime.}$$

Pierre Fermat (1601–1665).

If $n = 2$, the formula gives

$$2^{2^2} + 1 = 2^4 + 1 \quad \text{(since } 2^2 = 4\text{)}$$
$$= 16 + 1 \quad \text{(since } 2^4 = 16\text{)}$$
$$= 17 \qquad \text{which is prime.}$$

If $n = 3$, we get from the formula

$$2^{2^3} + 1 = 2^8 + 1 \quad \text{(since } 2^3 = 8\text{)}$$
$$= 256 + 1 \quad \text{(since } 2^8 = 256\text{)}$$
$$= 257 \qquad \text{and this is prime.}$$

If $n = 4$, the formula yields

$$2^{2^4} + 1 = 2^{16} + 1 \quad \text{(since } 2^4 = 16\text{)}$$
$$= 65536 + 1 \quad \text{(since } 2^{16} = 65{,}536\text{)}$$
$$= 65537 \qquad \text{and this too can be shown to be prime.}$$

So far, things look good. However, the next "Fermat number" is

$$2^{2^5} + 1 = 2^{32} + 1 \qquad \text{(since } 2^5 = 32\text{)}$$
$$= 4{,}294{,}967{,}297$$

and it has been shown that this number is *not* prime. In fact, it is divisible by 641. Try it!

It has also been shown that Fermat was wrong when $n = 6$. If $n = 6$, then $2^{2^6} + 1$ is a composite number.

Another attempt to produce a "prime-number-generating" formula was made by the Swiss mathematician Leonhard Euler (1707–1783). In addition to being a great mathematician, Euler had an amazing ability to perform calculations in his head. For the last 17 years of his life he was blind. Yet he was able to do accurate calculations to 50 decimal places. His formula was

$$n^2 - n + 41.$$

If we let $n = 1$ in this formula, we get

$$1^2 - 1 + 41 = 1 - 1 + 41 = 41,$$

which is prime. If $n = 2$, we get

$$2^2 - 2 + 41 = 4 - 2 + 41 = 43,$$

which is prime. If $n = 3$, we get

$$3^2 - 3 + 41 = 9 - 3 + 41 = 47,$$

which is prime.

Leonhard Euler. (Although unable to produce a prime generating formula, Euler did produce a prime number of children, thirteen.)

This formula also gives primes if $n = 3$, 4, 5, and up to $n = 40$. But if $n = 41$, we get

$$41^2 - 41 + 41 = 41^2,$$

which is *not* prime, since it equals $41 \cdot 41$, and thus has 41 as a divisor, in addition to itself and 1.

Euler knew that his formula would not give primes *all* the time. However, he found that it seemed to give primes for about half of the possible values of n. No one has been able to prove for certain whether this percentage of primes remains the same as more and more values of n are tried.

Up to the present, no formula has been found that will give *only* prime numbers, and no one has come up with a formula that will give *all* the prime numbers.

The following two BASIC computer programs will prove to be very useful when working with prime numbers. These programs assume some knowledge of the BASIC computer language. If you are unfamiliar with language you may want to read the material on computers in Chapter 14 first. The first computer program can help us determine whether a given integer larger than 1 is prime or composite, and the second computer program can be used to find the prime factorization of any integer larger than 1.

```
10   REM     THIS COMPUTER PROGRAM WILL DETERMINE WHETHER AN
             INTEGER LARGER THAN 1 IS PRIME
20   REM     ENTER NUMBER
30   PRINT   "IF YOU WANT TO DETERMINE WHETHER AN INTEGER
             LARGER THAN 1"
35   PRINT   "IS PRIME OR NOT, AFTER THE QUESTION MARK TYPE THE"
40   PRINT   "POSITIVE INTEGER."
45   INPUT N
50   IF N = 2 THEN GOTO 100
60   REM     TEST TO FIND THE POSSIBLE FACTORS
70   FOR X = 2 TO INT ( SQR (N) )
80   IF N / X = INT ( N / X ) THEN GOTO 120
90   NEXT X
100  PRINT N; "IS A PRIME."
110  GOTO 130
120  PRINT N; "IS NOT A PRIME NUMBER. IT IS A COMPOSITE NUMBER."
130  END
     RUN
IF YOU WANT TO DETERMINE WHETHER AN INTEGER LARGER THAN 1 IS
PRIME OR NOT, AFTER THE QUESTION MARK TYPE THE POSITIVE INTEGER.
?147
147  IS NOT A PRIME NUMBER. IT IS A COMPOSITE NUMBER.
```

```
10    REM      THIS COMPUTER PROGRAM WILL FIND THE PRIME
               FACTORIZATION OF ANY INTEGER LARGER THAN 1
20    REM      ENTER VALUE
30    PRINT "TO FIND THE PRIME FACTORIZATION OF ANY INTEGER LARGER
      THAN"
35    PRINT "1, AFTER THE QUESTION MARK TYPE THE POSITIVE INTEGER."
40    INPUT N
50    PRINT N; " = " ;
60    REM      INITIALIZE LOOP
70    LET X = 1
80    REM INCREMENT LOOP
90    LET X = X + 1
100   REM      TEST TO FIND POSSIBLE FACTORS
110   IF N / X < > INT (N / X) THEN GOTO 90
120   PRINT X;
130   LET N = N / X
140   IF N = 1 THEN GOTO 170
150   PRINT " * ";
160   GOTO 110
170   END
      RUN
TO FIND THE PRIME FACTORIZATION OF ANY INTEGER LARGER THAN 1,
AFTER THE QUESTION MARK TYPE THE POSITIVE INTEGER.
?120
120 = 2 * 2 * 2 * 3 * 5
```

→ write sieve to 100

EXERCISES FOR SECTION 5.3

1. Write down the first nineteen prime numbers.

2. Find two consecutive numbers, both of which are prime.

3. Find three consecutive numbers, none of which is prime.

4. Find four consecutive numbers, none of which is prime.

5. Using the sieve of Eratosthenes, find all the prime numbers up to 100.

6. Write each of the following numbers as a product of primes.

   a) 72 **b)** 49 **c)** 1000 **d)** 525

   e) 602 **f)** 327 **g)** 400 **h)** 780

   i) 925 **j)** 1100

7. Can a prime number ever end in the digit 6? In 5?

8. The prime number 13 can be written as $4 \cdot 3 + 1$. Can you find three other primes that can be written in the form $4n + 1$, where n is any whole number?

9. The prime number 7 can be written as $4 \cdot 1 + 3$. Can you find three other primes that can be written as $4n + 3$, where n is any whole number?

10. Find three prime numbers that can be written in the form $2^P - 1$, where P is itself a prime number.

11. **a)** Find two values of n for which the formula $n! + 1$ gives primes. (See p. 421 for the meaning of $n!$)

    b) Find two values of n for which the formula $n! + 1$ gives composite numbers.

12. Two prime numbers that differ by 2 are called **twin primes**. For example, 3 and 5 are twin primes. Find three other pairs of twin primes.

13. Find a set of three prime numbers that differ from each other by 2. Can you find another such set?

14. Can a prime number ever be perfect?

15. **a)** List all the prime numbers that are less than 50. How many are there?

   b) List all the prime numbers that are less than 100. How many are there?

16. Pick a number—say, 100. Double it to get 200. There is at least one prime number between 100 and 200. One such prime number is 101. It has been proved that given any number n and its double $2n$, there is always at least one prime number between these two numbers.

   a) Find a prime number between 18 and 39.

   b) Find a prime number between 250 and 290.

   c) Find a prime number between 2000 and 3000

17. **a)** Complete the following chart.

Prime number	Prime number + 1	Prime number − 1
5	6	4
7	8	6
11		
13		
17		
19		

   b) Divide each of the numbers in the second and third columns by 6 and consider their remainders (if any).

   **c) Examine the results of part (b). Make a general statement about prime numbers larger than 3. (*Hint:* It involves division by 6.)

18. Using numbers that are part of twin primes, write 18 as a sum in two distinct ways.

19. *Goldbach's Conjecture.* As we mentioned in Chapter 2, the famous mathematician Christian Goldbach stated that "Every even number greater than 2 can be expressed as the sum of *two* prime numbers." Show that Goldbach's conjecture is true for all even numbers (except 2), up to and including 36. The first few numbers are

$$4 = 2 + 2$$
$$6 = 3 + 3$$
$$8 = 3 + 5$$

20. *Another Goldbach Conjecture.* One of Goldbach's conjectures is that every odd number larger than 5 can be expressed as the sum of three primes. For example, 7 can be written as $2 + 2 + 3$; also $9 = 2 + 2 + 5$; and $11 = 7 + 2 + 2$. Verify that this conjecture is true by writing each of the odd numbers between 19 and 39 as the sum of three primes.

21. Several prime numbers can be expressed as 1 more than the square of a natural number, whereas others can be written as 1 less than the square of a natural number. For example, the prime number 5 can be written as $2^2 + 1$, whereas the prime number 3 can be written as $2^2 - 1$.

   a) Find three prime numbers that can be written as 1 more than the square of a number.

   b) Find two prime numbers that can be written as 1 less than the square of a number.

22. A formula that often yields prime numbers is $n^2 - n + 41$. For each of the following, determine whether this formula yields primes, using the indicated value of n.

   a) 60   **b)** 65   **c)** 70

   d) 73   **e)** 81

Brain-Teaser Problems

**23. There are 168 prime numbers that are less than 1000. There are 303 prime numbers that are less than 2000. There are 430 prime numbers that are less than 3000. How many prime numbers are there that are less than 1,000,000? As of now, the only way to answer this question is to write down the primes and count them. (Good luck!) No one has yet discovered a formula that will tell you how many primes there are that are less than a given number.

**24. There are seven prime number years in the period 1950–2000. Can you find three of them?

5.4

GREATEST COMMON FACTOR AND LEAST COMMON MULTIPLE

Greatest Common Factor

greatest common factor (GCF)
greatest common divisor

Often, we are given a fraction which we must reduce to lowest terms. The concept of greatest common divisor, which is used in the next chapter, will prove very useful in simplifying fractions. The **greatest common factor (GCF)** or **greatest common divisor** of two (or more) nonzero whole numbers is the largest whole number that is a factor or divisor that is common to both (or all) of the numbers. The greatest common factor of the whole numbers a and b is denoted as GCF (a, b).

set-intersection method

There are several techniques that we can use to find the greatest common factor of two numbers. One of these is known as the **set-intersection method**. For example, suppose we wanted to find the GCF of 30 and 48. We first write down all the divisors of 30 and of 48. We get

$$\text{Set of divisors of } 30 = \{1, 2, 3, 5, 6, 10, 15, 30\}$$
$$\text{Set of divisors of } 48 = \{1, 2, 3, 4, 6, 8, 12, 16, 24, 48\}$$

The intersection of both sets is

$$\{\text{divisors of } 30\} \cap \{\text{divisors of } 48\} = \{1, 2, 3, 6\}$$

The largest number in this set is 6. This number represents the GCF of 30 and 48. Symbolically, GCF $(30, 48) = 6$.

Comment   The above method also can be used to find the greatest common factor of more than two numbers.

prime–factorization method

A second and more efficient technique that can be used to find the GCF of two (or more) numbers involves finding the prime factorization of each number and is known as the **prime–factorization method**. To use this method, we first find the prime factorization of each of the numbers, and then take each common prime factor of the given numbers. The GCF is the product of these common factors, each raised to the lowest power of that prime that occurs in either of the prime factorizations.

Applying this technique to the numbers 30 and 48 produces the following: The prime factorization of 30 and of 48 is

$$30 = 2 \cdot 3 \cdot 5 \quad \text{and} \quad 48 = 2 \cdot 2 \cdot 2 \cdot 2 \cdot 3 \quad \text{or} \quad 2^4 \cdot 3$$

The common factors are 2 and 3, so that the greatest common factors are $2 \cdot 3$, or 6. Thus GCF $(30, 48) = 6$.

We illustrate the techniques with several examples.

EXAMPLE 1

Find the GCF of 40 and 60 in two different ways.

SOLUTION

Method 1: Set-intersection technique The divisors of 40 and 60 are

set of divisors of 40 = {1, 2, 4, 5, 8, 10, 20, 40}
set of divisors of 60 = {1, 2, 3, 4, 5, 6, 10, 12, 15, 20, 60}

The intersection of both sets is

{divisors of 40} ∩ {divisors of 60} = {1, 2, 4, 5, 10, 20}

The largest number in this set is 20, so that GCF (40, 60) = 20.

Method 2: Prime factorization technique The prime factorization of 40 and of 60 is

$$40 = 2 \cdot 2 \cdot 2 \cdot 5 \quad \text{or} \quad 2^3 \cdot 5 \quad \text{and} \quad 60 = 2 \cdot 2 \cdot 3 \cdot 5 \quad \text{or} \quad 2^2 \cdot 3 \cdot 5$$

Thus the GCF (40, 60) = $2^2 \cdot 5$, or $4 \cdot 5 = 20$.

EXAMPLE 2

Find the GCF of 12, 30 and 56 in two different ways.

SOLUTION

Method 1: Set-intersection technique The divisors of 12, 30 and 56 are

Set of divisors of 12 = {1, 2, 3, 4, 6, 12}
Set of divisors of 30 are = {1, 2, 3, 5, 6, 10, 15, 30}
Set of divisors of 56 = {1, 2, 4, 7, 8, 14, 28, 56}

The intersection of all three sets is

{divisors of 12} ∩ {divisors of 30} ∩ {divisors of 56} = {1, 2}

The largest number in this set is 2, so GCF (12, 30, 56) = 2.

Method 2: Prime factorization technique The prime factorization of 12, 30, and 56 is

$$12 = 2 \cdot 2 \cdot 3 \quad \text{or} \quad 2^2 \cdot 3 \quad \text{and} \quad 30 = 2 \cdot 3 \cdot 5 \quad \text{and} \quad 56 = 2 \cdot 2 \cdot 2 \cdot 7 \quad \text{or} \quad 2^3 \cdot 7$$

Thus the GCF (12, 30, 48) = 2.

Euclidean Algorithm

There is a third technique for finding the greatest common factor of two nonzero whole numbers which is known as the **Euclidean Algorithm**. This algorithm will be discussed in the exercises for this section.

Least Common Multiple

least common multiple (LCM)

Another important idea in number theory involves the least common multiple of two (or more) integers. It is especially useful when adding or subtracting two fractions. The **least common multiple (LCM)** of two (or more) nonzero whole numbers is the least positive multiple that the two numbers have in common. Both the set-intersection technique and the prime-factorization technique can be used to find the LCM. When using the second method, first find the prime factorization of each of the numbers. Then take each of the primes that are factors of either of the given numbers. The LCM will be the product of these primes, each raised to the greatest power of the prime that occurs in either of the prime factorizations.

We illustrate both methods for finding the LCM in the following examples.

EXAMPLE 3

Find the LCM of 30 and 48 in two different ways.

SOLUTION

Method 1: Set-intersection technique   The set of nonzero multiples of 30 are

$$\{30, 60, 90, 120, 150, 180, 210, 240, 270, 300, \ldots\}$$

The set of nonzero multiples of 48 are

$$\{48, 96, 144, 192, 240, 288, 336, \ldots\}$$

The intersection of these two sets is

$$\{\text{nonzero multiples of 30}\} \cap \{\text{nonzero multiples of 48}\} = \{240, 480, \ldots\}$$

The smallest number in the set of common multiples is 240.
Thus LCM (30, 48) = 240.

Method 2: Prime Factorization technique   The prime factorization of 30 and 48 is

$$30 = 2 \cdot 3 \cdot 5 \qquad \text{and} \qquad 48 = 2 \cdot 2 \cdot 2 \cdot 2 \cdot 3 \quad \text{or} \quad 2^4 \cdot 3$$

The LCM will be a number of the form $2^x \cdot 3^y \cdot 5^z$, where x is the larger of the exponents of the 2's, y is the larger of the exponents of the 3's, and z is the larger of the exponents of the 5's. Between $30 = 2 \cdot 3 \cdot 5$ and $48 = 2^4 \cdot 3$, we have that 4 is the largest exponent of the 2's so that $x = 4$. Also 1 is the largest exponent of the 3's so that $y = 1$, and 1 is the largest exponent of the 5's so that $z = 1$. Thus

$$\text{LCM } (30, 48) = 2^4 \cdot 3^1 \cdot 5^1 \text{ or } 240$$

(Note that all primes from either number are used when finding the LCM.)

There is an important connection between the GCF and the LCM of two numbers. This is illustrated in the next example.

EXAMPLE 4

SOLUTION

Find the GCF and LCM of 18 and 24.

The prime factorization of 18 and 24 is as follows:

$$18 = 2 \cdot 3 \cdot 3 = 2 \cdot 3^2 \quad \text{and} \quad 24 = 2 \cdot 2 \cdot 2 \cdot 3 = 2^3 \cdot 3$$
$$\text{The GCF of } 18 = 2 \cdot 3^2 \quad \text{and} \quad 24 = 2^3 \cdot 3 \text{ is } 2 \cdot 3 \text{ or } 6.$$

The multiples of 18 and 24 are

Set of multiples of 18 = {18, 36, 54, 72, 90, 108, 126, . . .}
Set of multiples of 24 = {24, 48, 72, 96, 120, . . .}

Thus the LCM (18, 24) = 72.
Summarizing, GCF (18, 24) = 6 and LCM (18, 24) = 72.

Notice that in the previous example

$$\begin{aligned} \text{GCF } (18, 24) \times \text{LCM } (18, 24) &= 6 \times 72 \\ &= 432 \\ &= 18 \times 24 \end{aligned}$$

More generally, the connection between the GCF and LCM of any two natural numbers is given in the following important relation.

$$\text{GCF } (a, b) \times \text{LCM } (a, b) = ab$$

Comment   The above result is often useful in finding the LCM of two natural numbers a and b when their prime factorizations are difficult to find. Thus

$$\text{LCM}(a, b) = \frac{ab}{\text{GCF}(a, b)}$$

Comment   The connection discussed above, between the GCF and the LCM, is valid for two numbers only.

When the prime factorization of numbers is difficult to find, we can use the following computer BASIC program to find the GCF of a pair of numbers.

```
10    REM   FIND THE GREATEST COMMON FACTOR OF A PAIR OF
      NATURAL NUMBERS
20    PRINT "IF YOU WANT TO FIND THE GCF OF TWO NATURAL
      NUMBERS, AFTER"
25    PRINT "THE QUESTION MARK TYPE THE TWO NUMBERS (THE
      SMALLER ONE"
30    PRINT "FIRST)."
35    REM    ENTER VALUES
40    INPUT X
50    INPUT Y
60    REM   FIND POSSIBLE FACTORS
70    FOR A = X TO 1 STEP – 1
80    IF X / A < > INT ( X / A) THEN GOTO 100
90    IF Y / A = INT ( Y / A ) THEN GOTO 110
100   NEXT A
110   PRINT "THE GCF OF ";X;" AND ";Y;" is ";A
120   END
      RUN
IF YOU WANT TO FIND THE GCF OF TWO NATURAL NUMBERS, AFTER THE
QUESTION MARK TYPE THE TWO NUMBERS (THE SMALLER ONE FIRST).
?   18
??   24
THE GCF OF 18 AND 24 IS 6
```

EXERCISES FOR SECTION 5.4

1. Find the greatest common factor and least common multiple of the following numbers using the set-intersection technique.

a) 15 and 18 **b)** 14 and 72 **c)** 18, 24 and 60
d) 72 and 88 **e)** 144 and 200 **f)** 96, 156, and 175

2. Find the greatest common factor and least common multiple of the following numbers using the prime-factorization technique.

a) 50 and 80 **b)** 36 and 120 **c)** 24, 40, and 60
d) 64 and 84 **e)** 144 and 316 **f)** 18, 144, and 128

3. Find the LCM of each of the following numbers using any technique.

a) 144 and 220 **b)** 44, 68, and 84
c) 104, 220, 360

4. Find each of the following by using any technique.

a) GCF (96, 120) **b)** LCM (48, 55)
c) LCM (75, 120) **d)** GCF (2424, 3000)
e) GCF (380, 490, 760)

*5. Another technique for finding the greatest common factor of two natural numbers is known as the **Euclidean Algorithm**. It is based upon the following: if a and b are any two whole numbers with $a \geq b$, then GCF (a, b) = GCF (r, b) where r is the remainder when a is divided by b. Let us apply this algorithm to find GCF (34, 96). We have

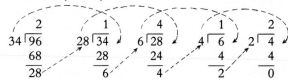

The last nonzero remainder of 2 represents the greatest common factor. Thus GCF (34, 96) = 2

Using the Euclidean algorithm, find the GCF of the following numbers:

a) 56 and 78 **b)** 12 and 75 **c)** 18 and 120

PROBLEM-SOLVING EXERCISES

6. Roz and Enjo work on an assembly line. Their job is to inspect the VCR's before packaging. Roz inspects the electronic circuitry of every 24th VCR, whereas Enjo inspects the paint finish of every 36th VCR. If they both start working at the same time, how many VCR's must each inspect before they both inspect the same item?

7. Jeanine and Jennifer are jogging along a circular path in a park. Jeanine completes one round in 8 minutes, whereas Jennifer completes one round in 14 minutes. If both joggers start at the same time and same place and jog in the same direction, after how many minutes will they meet each other at the start line?

Brain-Teaser Problems

**8. We already know that if a and b are any natural numbers, then GCF $(a, b) \times$ LCM$(a, b) = ab$. If a, b, and c are any natural numbers, is it true that GCF $(a, b, c) \times$ LCM $(a, b, c) = abc$? Explain your answer.

**9. Using the computer program given in this section, find the GCF of the following numbers.

a) 3456 and 5678 **b)** 9682 and 8594

**10. Assume that a and b are natural numbers. If GCF $(a, b) = 1$, find LCM (a, b)

11. By finding the greatest common factors of 204 and 2508, reduce the fraction $\frac{204}{2508}$ to lowest terms.

12. Show that the numbers 1540 and 1989 are relatively prime. (*Hint:* Show that GCF (1540, 1989) = 1.)

5.5

CLOCK ARITHMETIC AND MODULAR ARITHMETIC

Let us consider a clock that has only four numbers on it, as shown in Fig. 5.5.

Starting at 0, the clock hand will point to 1, 2, and 3 in order, and then return to 0. This cycle repeats itself over and over. Let $\oplus$ represent the turning of the hand of the clock in the direction of the arrow. Then $2 \oplus 3$ means that the clock is at the 2 position and then moves through 3 positions. It stops at the 1 position, so we say that

$$2 \oplus 3 = 1$$

Similarly, $1 \oplus 2$ would mean that the clock is first in the 1 position and then moves 2 more places, ending up in the 3 position. Thus we have

$$1 \oplus 2 = 3$$

We can make up a table showing all possible starting positions and all possible ending positions (Table 5.3).

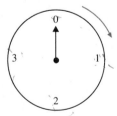

Figure 5.5

TABLE 5.3				
$\oplus$	0	1	↓2	3
0	0	1	2	3
1	1	2	3	0
2	2	3	0	1
→ 3	3	0	(1)	2

This chart is read as follows: To find $3 \oplus 2$, for example, go to row 3 then over to column 2. We have indicated this by means of arrows in Table 5.3. We find the answer to be 1. Thus

$$3 \oplus 2 = 1$$

In a similar manner we read from the table that

$$3 \oplus 3 = 2$$

Top Fruit to Install New Computer Sales

SPRINGFIELD: In an effort to make sure that the consumer is not being cheated, the management of the Top Fruit Chain Stores has announced that it would begin replacing the scales in all of its 100 stores by new computer scales. The new scales print out on a display panel the weight of an object correct to the nearest hundredth. This should eliminate the numerous complaints received by the Consumer Fraud Department that the clerks at several of the stores were cheating customers by reading the scales incorrectly.

The total cost to the company was estimated to be $100,000.

THE CHRONICLE, April 17, 1988

All of us have seen an old-fashioned scale such as the one discussed in the accompanying newspaper article. When using such a scale, we must determine two things: where the pointer stops and how many times the pointer passes the 0. Although the Top Fruit Store Chain mentioned in the article is replacing such scales with the more modern computer scales, these older scales do illustrate the ideas of clock and modular arithmetics discussed in this section.

We can think of the different positions of this clock as a set G, whose members are 0, 1, 2, and 3. So,

$$G = \{0, 1, 2, 3\}$$

binary operation

The operation of turning the hand, which we denoted by $\oplus$, can be considered a **binary operation**. (Recall that a binary operation involves combining any two elements of a set to get a third element.)

We can observe a number of interesting things about this system. First of all, Table 5.3 indicates that no matter where we start, we will always end up at one of the four positions 0, 1, 2, or 3. This means that the operation $\oplus$ is **closed**. (Remember, an operation is closed if, when we perform the operation, the result is always within the set we started with.)

closed

Now notice the following:

$$0 \oplus 0 = 0 \qquad 0 \oplus 0 = 0$$
$$0 \oplus 1 = 1 \qquad 1 \oplus 0 = 1$$
$$0 \oplus 2 = 2 \qquad 2 \oplus 0 = 2$$
$$0 \oplus 3 = 3 \qquad 3 \oplus 0 = 3$$

identity element

Thus when we perform the operation $\oplus$ with 0 on any element, the element remains unchanged. Here 0 is the **identity element** (see page 145) for the operation $\oplus$.

Now suppose we are at any position on the clock. Can we always get back to 0 by the operation $\oplus$? The answer is clearly yes, as the following results indicate:

$$0 \oplus 0 = 0$$
$$1 \oplus 3 = 0$$
$$2 \oplus 2 = 0$$
$$3 \oplus 1 = 0$$

inverse

We call 3 the **inverse** of 1 for the operation $\oplus$ because when we perform $3 \oplus 1$, we get 0. Similarly, 2 is the inverse of 2 for the operation $\oplus$, 1 is the inverse of 3, and 0 is its own inverse.

Every element of this system has an inverse. In other words, we can always get back to 0.

Now consider the expression $2 \oplus 3 \oplus 1$. This can be interpreted in two different ways. One way is to first do $2 \oplus 3$, getting 1. Then do $1 \oplus 1$, getting 2. In other words,

$$(2 \oplus 3) \oplus 1 = 1 \oplus 1 = 2$$

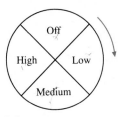

Figure 5.6

Another way is to first do $3 \oplus 1$, getting 0. Then do $2 \oplus 0$, which gives 2. That is,

$$2 \oplus (3 \oplus 1) = 2 \oplus 0 = 2$$

In both cases our answer is 2. We conclude that $(2 \oplus 3) \oplus 1 = 2 \oplus (3 \oplus 1)$. This shows that the associative law holds for these three numbers. In a similar manner we can show that *the associative law holds for any three numbers in this system.*

This clock is called a **mod 4 clock** because of its four positions.

Next, let us look at a familiar object, a three-way switch on a table lamp. Such a switch can be pictured as shown in Fig. 5.6. We turn the switch in a clockwise direction as indicated by the arrow. If the switch is in the "off" position, turning it once puts it in "low." Another turn moves it to "medium." Still another turn moves it to "high." The next turn moves it to the off position again. If the switch is in the low position, turning it twice moves it to the high position. Turning it three times puts it in the off position. This cycle can be repeated as often as we like.

If we start at the off position, then we need 0 turns to get to the off position, 1 turn to get to low, 2 turns to medium, and 3 turns to high. Thus we let

0 stand for the off position,

1 stand for the low position,

2 stand for the medium position,

3 stand for the high position, and

$\oplus$ stand for turning the switch clockwise.

Table 5.4 shows the final position of the switch, depending on where you start and the number of turns you make.

TABLE 5.4				
$\oplus$	0	1	2	3
0	0	1	2	3
1	1	2	3	0
2	2	3	0	1
3	3	0	1	2

Compare this table with the table for the mod 4 clock (Table 5.3). It is exactly the same. What this means is that both situations have the same mathematical structure, although they appear to be completely different.

EXAMPLE 1

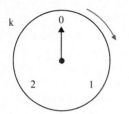

Figure 5.7

Let us construct a table for a mod 3 clock (that is, a clock with 3 positions). The clock is shown in Fig. 5.7. As before, let $\oplus$ represent turning the clock. We then have the results shown in Table 5.5.

TABLE 5.5			
$\oplus$	0	1	2
0	0	1	2
1	1	2	0
2	2	0	1

EXAMPLE 2
SOLUTION

What would $6 \oplus 5$ be in a mod 10 clock? in a mod 8 clock?

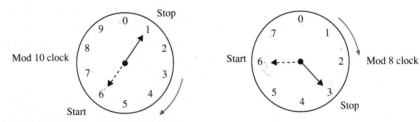

Figure 5.8

We draw both clocks as shown in Fig. 5.8. We start at 6 and move through 5 additional positions. In the mod 10 clock we stop at 1 as indicated in the diagram. Thus

$$6 \oplus 5 = 1 \text{ in mod } 10$$

In the mod 8 clock we stop at 3, again as indicated in Fig. 5.8. Thus

$$6 \oplus 5 = 3 \text{ in mod } 8$$

EXAMPLE 3
SOLUTION

In what clock is $4 \oplus 3 = 1$?

The number 4 shows us that the clock must be *at least* a mod 5 clock. (Why?) Let us try mod 5. A quick check (which the reader should verify by actually drawing such a clock) will show that

$$4 \oplus 3 = 2 \text{ in mod } 5$$

So mod 5 is wrong. Next we try mod 6. This works. (Try it, to convince yourself.)

$$4 \oplus 3 = 1 \text{ in mod } 6$$

EXAMPLE 4

Let us define "subtraction" on a clock as "turning the clock backwards." We will denote this as $\ominus$. Let us find $3 \ominus 5$ in a mod 8 clock. (See the mod 8 clock in Fig. 5.8.) We start at 3 and move back 5 positions, stopping at 6. Thus

$$3 \ominus 5 = 6 \text{ in mod } 8$$

Comment Some readers may say that $3 \ominus 5 = -2$. However, there is no -2 on the clock. Nevertheless, if we interpret -2 to mean "start at 0 and go back 2," then, of course, we stop at 6. We will always give our answer as 6 rather than as -2.

EXAMPLE 5

SOLUTION

In a mod 7 clock, $4 \ominus x = 6$. Find x.

We start at 4 and move back x places until we get to 6. From the clock in Fig. 5.9 we find that

$$4 \ominus 5 = 6$$

Thus $x = 5$.

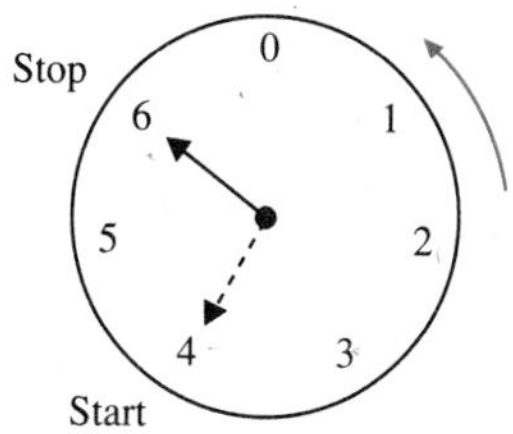

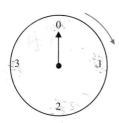

Figure 5.9

Comment We define "multiplication" on a clock as moving the hands of the clock through an appropriate number of positions. We will denote this as $\otimes$. Thus $4 \otimes 3$ on a mod 5 clock means that we move through 12 positions. Of course, we stop at the 2 position. Thus,

$$4 \otimes 3 = 2 \text{ in mod } 5$$

This idea will be further illustrated in the exercises for this section.

Let us look again at the mod 4 clock discussed earlier, which is shown in Fig. 5.10.

Suppose we were to start at 0 and move through 11 places. We would make 2 complete turns and then stop at 3. Notice that if you divide 11 by 4, you get a remainder of 3. This is no coincidence. Every time we make a complete turn on the clock, we go through 4 positions. Thus the number of complete turns is the number of times that 4 goes into 11 (that is, 2). We then have to go through the remaining 3 positions. This is the remainder when 11 is divided by 4.

Similarly, if we start at 0 and move through 18 positions, we would stop at 2. If we divide 18 by 4, the remainder would also be 2.

In other words, each position on the clock represents the remainder that we get when we divide a number by 4. This gives us a new way of looking at this clock. We can think of it as just the remainders we get when we divide by 4. From this point of view this system is called a **modulo 4 arithmetic**. The number 4 is called the **modulus**.

Figure 5.10

modulo 4 arithmetic
modulus.

EXAMPLE 6

In a modulo 5 arithmetic the numbers would be the remainders we get when we divide by 5. These are 0, 1, 2, 3, 4. In this system the modulus is 5. In a mod 5 clock, moving through 17 positions, starting at 0, leaves us at 2. We get the same result if we divide 17 by 5.

In a modulo 4 arithmetic, suppose we were to add $3 + 2$. We know that $3 + 2 = 5$. However, we are only interested in the remainder when we divide by 4, so our answer would be 1. We write this answer as $3 + 2 \equiv 1$ in modulo 4 arithmetic. The three-lined equals sign indicates that we are working only with remainders. This corresponds to $3 \oplus 2 = 1$ of the table for the mod 4 clock (see Table 5.4). ▪

Notation Instead of writing out the words "in modulo arithmetic" for the previous example, we abbreviate this as "(mod 4)." We write the answer as $3 + 2 \equiv 1$ (mod 4). This is read as

$$3 \text{ plus } 2 \text{ is } \textbf{congruent} \text{ to } 1 \text{ modulo } 4$$

EXAMPLE 7

SOLUTION

a) Add $4 + 5$ (mod 6).

$4 + 5$ is 9. If we divide 9 by 6, our remainder will be 3. Therefore

$$4 + 5 \equiv 3 \text{ (mod 6)}$$

b) Add $7 + 9$ (mod 10).

SOLUTION

$7 + 9 = 16$. Dividing 16 by 10, we get a remainder of 6. Therefore

$$7 + 9 \equiv 6 \text{ (mod 10)}$$

c) Add $5 + 5$ (mod 7).

SOLUTION

$5 + 5 = 10$. Dividing 10 by 7, the remainder is 3. Our answer is

$$5 + 5 \equiv 3 \text{ (mod 7)}$$ ▪

EXAMPLE 8

SOLUTION

a) Multiply $7 \cdot 3$ (mod 5).

$7 \cdot 3 = 21$. If we divide 21 by 5 we get a remainder of 1. Thus

$$7 \cdot 3 \equiv 1 \text{ (mod 5)}$$

On a mod 5 clock this means that we move through 21 positions, stopping at the 1 position.

b) Multiply $5 \cdot 9$ (mod 15).

SOLUTION

$5 \cdot 9 = 45$. Dividing 45 by 15, we get a remainder of 0. Thus

$$5 \cdot 9 \equiv 0 \text{ (mod 15)}$$ ▪

EXAMPLE 9

SOLUTION

a) Subtract 5 – 2 (mod 6).

5 – 2 = 3. Dividing 3 by 6, we get a remainder of 3. Therefore

$$5 - 2 \equiv 3 \ (\text{mod } 6)$$

b) Subtract 3 – 6 (mod 9).

SOLUTION

To do this problem, we look at a mod 9 clock (see Fig. 5.11). We start at 3 and go back 6, stopping at 6. Thus

$$3 - 6 \equiv 6 \ (\text{mod } 9)$$

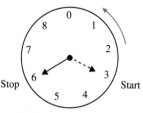

Figure 5.11

In a modular arithmetic a number corresponds to its remainder when divided by the modulus. Thus in a mod 5 system the number 38 corresponds to 3, since 38 divided by 5 gives a remainder of 3. We write this as $38 \equiv 3 \ (\text{mod } 5)$.

Notice that 38 – 3 is exactly divisible by 5. This leads us to a useful way of rephrasing the idea of modular arithmetics.

congruent modulo *m*

> **Definition 5.2** **We say that two integers** *a* **and** *b* **are congruent modulo** *m* if $a - b$ can be divided exactly by *m* (*m* is a natural number). We write this as
>
> $$a \equiv b \ (\text{mod } m).$$

EXAMPLE 10

$7 \equiv 3 \ (\text{mod } 2)$ means 7 is congruent to 3 modulo 2. This is true because 7 – 3 can be divided exactly by 2.

Note that if we divide 7 by 2, the remainder is 1, and if we divide 3 by 2, the remainder is also 1. *If any two numbers are congruent mod m, then their remainders when divided by m are the same.*

EXAMPLE 11

a) $10 \equiv 15 \ (\text{mod } 5)$ because 10 – 15, which is – 5, is exactly divisible by 5.

b) $12 \equiv 7 \ (\text{mod } 3)$ is *not* true because 12 – 7, which is 5, cannot be exactly divided by 3.

c) $25 \equiv 7 \ (\text{mod } 9)$ is true because 25 – 7, which equals 18, is divisible by 9.

d) $38 \equiv 5 \ (\text{mod } 11)$ is true because 38 – 5 = 33, and 33 is exactly divisible by 11.

e) $-5 \equiv 6 \pmod{11}$ is true because $-5 - 6$, which is -11, can be divided exactly by 11.

f) $5 \equiv -13 \pmod 9$ because $5 - (-13)$, which equals $5 + 13$ or 18, is exactly divisible by 9. ▄

We wish to emphasize a comment made in Example 10. We pointed out that if $a \equiv b \pmod m$, then when we divide a by m or b by m, the remainder is the same in both cases. Thus whether two numbers are congruent modulo m depends on whether they have the same remainders when we divide them by m. To put it another way, if $a \equiv b \pmod m$, the positions of a and b on the mod m clock are the same.

EXAMPLE 12

If New Year's Day is Thursday, on what day of the week will February 1 fall?

SOLUTION

January has 31 days. Since there are 7 days in a week, we can consider this as a modulo 7 system, where Sunday is 0, Monday is 1, and so forth. If we now divide 31 by 7, our remainder is 3. Thus from January 1 until February 1 there are exactly 4 weeks and 3 days. Therefore, February 1 will occur three days after a Thursday. It will occur on a Sunday. ▄

EXERCISES FOR SECTION 5.5

1. Make up a table for the operation $\oplus$ on the following clocks:

a) mod 7   b) mod 8
c) mod 2   d) mod 5

2. Make up a table for the operation $\ominus$ on the following clocks:

a) mod 5   b) mod 9

3. Determine the answer to each of the following calculations.

a) $4 \oplus 6$ in mod 9   b) $2 \oplus 3$ in mod 5
c) $5 \ominus 9$ in mod 10   d) $4 \ominus 7$ in mod 11
e) $4 \oplus 4$ in mod 6   f) $4 \oplus 4$ in mod 7
g) $8 \ominus 8$ in mod 15   h) $7 \ominus 11$ in mod 13
i) $5 \otimes 4$ in mod 6   j) $6 \otimes 7$ in mod 8
k) $9 \otimes 0$ in mod 10   l) $3 \ominus 14$ in mod 9

4. For each of the following, find the value of x.

a) $2 \oplus x = 7$ in mod 8   b) $2 \ominus x = 4$ in mod 5
c) $3 \oplus x = 1$ in mod 4   d) $x \ominus 5 = 4$ in mod 9

e) $4 \oplus x = 2$ in mod 7   f) $1 \ominus x = 3$ in mod 12

5. In what clock are the following calculations being performed?

a) $4 \oplus 5 = 3$ b) $2 \ominus 5 = 4$
c) $3 \oplus 3 = 1$ d) $4 \ominus 5 = 6$
e) $7 \oplus 8 = 3$ f) $3 \ominus 4 = 7$

6. In a mod 6 clock, name the inverse of each element.

7. In a mod 9 clock, name the inverse of each element.

8. Make up a table for the operation $\oplus$ on a mod 5 clock, and determine whether the associative law

$$a \oplus (b \oplus c) = (a \oplus b) \oplus c$$

is valid

9. Each of the following equations is valid for a mod 11 clock. Solve for x.

a) $4 \otimes 5 = x$ b) $5 \ominus x = 9$
c) $4 \otimes (5 \oplus x) = 3$ d) $\dfrac{x}{3} = 5$
e) $x \otimes (2 \oplus 5) = 3$ f) $5 \otimes 5 = x$

g) $9 \oplus x = 3$ **h)** $3 \otimes x = 4$

10. In each of the following, perform the indicated operations in the specified modular arithmetics.

a) $4 + 8$ (mod 3) **b)** $6 + 9$ (mod 9)
c) $5 \cdot 6$ (mod 11) **d)** $8 \cdot 3$ (mod 7)
e) $5 - 8$ (mod 3) **f)** $1 - 6$ (mod 8)
g) $0 - 5$ (mod 5) **h)** $-4 \cdot 3$ (mod 7)
i) $-8 \cdot 5$ (mod 7) **j)** $-4 \cdot 8$ (mod 9)

11. Which of the following statements are true?

a) $18 \equiv 3$ (mod 5) **b)** $16 \equiv 2$ (mod 7)
c) $14 \equiv -1$ (mod 5) **d)** $-6 \equiv 14$ (mod 10)
e) $8 \cdot 7 \equiv 6$ (mod 9) **f)** $15 \equiv 11$ (mod 8)
g) $10 \equiv 10$ (mod 3) **h)** $-8 \equiv -5$ (mod 3)
i) $18 \equiv 20$ (mod 2) **j)** $6 \cdot 8 \equiv -2$ (mod 5)

12. In each of the following, find one possible replacement for x, so that the resulting statement will be true. (More than one answer may be possible.)

a) $x \equiv 3$ (mod 5) **b)** $2x \equiv 1$ (mod 7)
c) $x \equiv 3$ (mod 4) **d)** $x + 5 \equiv 2$ (mod 6)
e) $4 - x \equiv 7$ (mod 11) **f)** $x - 4 \equiv 7$ (mod 8)
g) $x + 6 \equiv 3$ (mod 12) **h)** $7x + 2 \equiv 1$ (mod 15)
i) $3x \equiv 6$ (mod 5) **j)** $4x \equiv 2$ (mod 10)

13. In each of the following, find one possible replacement for m, so that the resulting statement will be true. (More than one answer may be possible.)

a) $8 \equiv 3$ (mod m) **b)** $2 \equiv -9$ (mod m)
c) $13 \equiv 3$ (mod m) **d)** $-5 \equiv -5$ (mod m)
e) $-6 \equiv -8$ (mod m) **f)** $4 \equiv -6$ (mod m)
g) $8 \equiv -6$ (mod m) **h)** $-3 \equiv -7$ (mod m)
i) $12 \equiv -8$ (mod m) **j)** $-5 \equiv 20$ (mod m)

14. In a certain year, April 15 falls on a Saturday. In that same year, on what day of the week will July 4 fall?

15. August 15, 1989, fell on a Tuesday. On what day of the week will August 15, 1996, fall?

16. If George Washington's birthday (February 22) falls on a Tuesday this year, on what day of the week will Independence Day (July 4) fall?

17. A computer programmer is rearranging his computer discs. He knows that he has fewer than 100 discs in his collection. When he arranges the discs in piles of 5 each, he has 4 left over. When he arranges the discs in piles of 7 each, he has 5 left over. When he arranges the discs in piles of 4 each, he has 1 left over. How many discs does the programmer have?

18. A caterer has to launder identical soiled tablecloths. She knows that there are fewer than 100. However, she does not know exactly how many tablecloths there are. In an effort to determine how many there are, she piles the tablecloths into stacks of 10 each. When she does this, she has 8 left over. When she arranges the tablecloths in piles of 7 each, she has 1 left over. When she arranges the tablecloths in piles of 4 each, she has 2 tablecloths left over. How many soiled tablecloths does the caterer have?

19. For an interesting discussion on how modular arithmetic can be used to create interesting patterns, read the article "Using Mathematical Structures to Generate Artistic Designs" by Sonia Forseth and Andria Price Troutman in *The Mathematics Teacher* (May 1984, pp. 393–398).

Brain-Teaser Problems

**20. July 4, 1985, occurred on a Thursday. On what day of the week was the Declaration of Independence (July 4, 1776) signed?

**21. *Friday, the thirteenth.* Thomas Jefferson, the third president of the United States, is the only president who was born on the 13th of the month. His birthday was April 13, 1743. Was he born on Friday the 13th?

**22. *Tiles.* In designing tiles we can often use the addition or multiplication tables of the various clock arithmetics to obtain different patterns. Thus, in mod 3 we have the following addition and multiplication tables:

$\oplus$	0	1	2		$\oplus$	0	1	2
0	0	1	2		0	0	0	0
1	1	2	0		1	0	1	2
2	2	0	1		2	0	2	1

If we represent the number 0 as , the number 1 as a box with three vertical lines in it ⊔⊔⊔ , and the number 2 as a box with two semicircles in it

, then we get the following tile design based on the addition table.

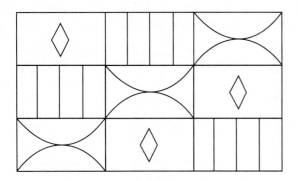

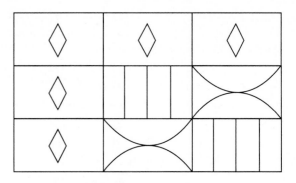

Using the addition and multiplication tables for the mod 5 and 6 clocks, construct tiles with appropriate designs based on these tables.

A design based on the multiplication table might be pictured as follows (using the same representations).

5.6

CASTING OUT 9'S AND CASTING OUT 11'S

casting out 9's

Whenever we perform a computation, we like to check our answer. One way of doing this is by **casting out 9's**. It works this way.

$$\text{Add:} \quad \begin{array}{r} 476 \\ + 237 \\ \hline 713 \end{array}$$

We check this by adding the digits in each number as shown. Thus we have

$$476 \rightarrow 4 + 7 + 6 = 17 \rightarrow 1 + 7 = 8$$
$$+237 \rightarrow 2 + 3 + 7 = 12 \rightarrow 1 + 2 = 3 \Big\} \text{We add these.}$$
$$11 \rightarrow 1 + 1 = ②$$
$$713 \rightarrow 7 + 1 + 3 = 11 \rightarrow 1 + 1 = ②$$

Let us examine this procedure. We first add the digits in 476. This gives 17. Now we add the digits in 17. This gives 8.

We repeat the process on 237. First we get 12. Then adding the digits of 12, we get 3.

Next we *add* the results 8 and 3, getting 11. Finally, adding the digits of 11, we get 2.

Now we do the same thing to the total 713. Again we end up with 2.

Since in both cases the result is 2, our answer is *probably* correct. There is a *slight* possibility that the answer is wrong.

If the results are not the same, then we know definitely that we have made a computational error. To illustrate this, suppose we add 2437 and 5617 and obtain the incorrect answer 8044. Let us check.

$$2437 \rightarrow 2+4+3+7 = 16 \rightarrow 1+6 = \qquad\qquad 7$$
$$+ \, 5617 \rightarrow 5+6+1+7 = 19 \rightarrow 1+9 = 10 \rightarrow 1+0 = \; 1 \left.\right\} \text{We add these.}$$
$$\textcircled{8}$$

$$8044 \rightarrow 8+0+4+4 = 16 \rightarrow 1+6 = \textcircled{7}$$

The fact that one result is 8 and the other is 7 tells us that we made a mistake. Find the error.

EXAMPLE 1

SOLUTION

Add 368, 47, and 5928, and check by casting out 9's.

$$368 \rightarrow 3+6+8 \quad = 17 \rightarrow 1+7 = \; 8$$
$$47 \rightarrow 4+7 \qquad\quad = 11 \rightarrow 1+1 = \; 2 \left.\right\} \quad \text{We add these.}$$
$$+ \, 5928 \rightarrow 5+9+2+8 = 24 \rightarrow 2+4 = \; 6$$
$$16 \rightarrow 1+6 = \textcircled{7}$$

$$6343 \rightarrow 6+3+4+3 = 16 \rightarrow 1+6 = \textcircled{7}$$

Since we get 7 in both cases, the addition is *probably* correct.

EXAMPLE 2

SOLUTION

Multiply 731 by 26 and check by casting out 9's.

$$731 \rightarrow 7+3+1 = 11 \rightarrow 1+1 = \; 2$$
$$\times \;\; 26 \rightarrow 2+6 = \qquad\qquad = \; 8 \left.\right\} \quad \text{We multiply these.}$$
$$\overline{4386} \qquad\qquad\qquad 16 \rightarrow 1+6 = \textcircled{7}$$
$$\underline{1462}$$
$$\overline{19006} \rightarrow 1+9+0+0+6 = 16 \rightarrow 1+6 = \textcircled{7}$$

This time, because it is a multiplication problem, we multiply the 2 and the 8, as we indicated. Since the result in both cases is 7, our answer is *probably* correct.

EXAMPLE 3

SOLUTION

Multiply 68 by 281 and check by casting out 9's.

$$68 \rightarrow 6+8 \quad\;\; = 14 \rightarrow 1+4 = \; 5$$
$$\times \, 281 \rightarrow 2+8+1 = 11 \rightarrow 1+1 = \; 2 \left.\right\} \quad \text{We multiply these.}$$
$$\overline{68} \qquad\qquad\qquad\quad 10 \rightarrow 1+0 = \textcircled{1}$$
$$564$$
$$\underline{136}$$
$$\overline{19308} \rightarrow 1+9+3+0+8 = 21 \rightarrow 2+1 = \textcircled{3}$$

The difference in the results tells us that we have made a mistake. Can you find it? ■

EXAMPLE 4

a) Subtract 256 from 468 and check by casting out 9's.

SOLUTION

$$468 \rightarrow 4 + 6 + 8 = 18 \rightarrow 1 + 8 = 9$$
$$-256 \rightarrow 2 + 5 + 6 = 13 \rightarrow 1 + 3 = 4 \Bigg\} \text{ We subtract.}$$
$$\text{⑤}$$
$$212 \rightarrow 2 + 1 + 2 = ⑤ \longleftarrow$$

b) Subtract 273 from 465 and check by casting out 9's.

SOLUTION

$$465 \rightarrow 4 + 6 + 5 = 15 \rightarrow 1 + 5 = 6$$
$$-273 \rightarrow 2 + 7 + 3 = 12 \rightarrow 1 + 2 = 3 \Bigg\} \text{ We subtract.}$$
$$\text{③}$$
$$192 \rightarrow 1 + 9 + 2 = 12 \rightarrow 1 + 2 = ③$$

c) Subtract 213 from 778 and check by casting out 9's.

SOLUTION

$$778 \rightarrow 7 + 7 + 8 = 22 \rightarrow 2 + 2 = 4$$
$$-213 \rightarrow 2 + 1 + 3 \qquad\qquad = 6 \Bigg\} \text{ We subtract.}$$
$$\text{(-2)}$$
$$565 \rightarrow 5 + 6 + 5 = 16 \rightarrow 1 + 6 = \quad ⑦$$

On first thought it would appear that our answer is incorrect. However, note that 7 is congruent to $-2 \pmod 9$ because $7 - (-2) = 7 + 2 = 9$ is exactly divisible by 9. Thus in mod 9 arithmetic, -2 and 7 are really the same, so that our answer is *probably* right. ■

You are probably wondering why this mysterious procedure works. The secret will now be revealed.

Consider the number 3221, which can be written as

$$3(\text{thousands}) + 2(\text{hundreds}) + 2(\text{tens}) + 1$$
$$3(1000) \qquad + 2(100) \qquad + 2(10) \quad + 1$$

If you divide 1000 by 9, the remainder is 1. Thus if you divide $3(1000)$ by 9, the remainder is $3(1)$, or 3.

Similarly, if we divide 100 by 9, the remainder is 1. Therefore if we divide $2(100)$ by 9, the remainder is $2(1) = 2$.

Also if we divide 10 by 9, the remainder is 1. So if you divide $2(10)$ by 9, the remainder is $2(1)$, which is 2.

But 1 divided by 9 doesn't go. We just have a remainder of 1.

Putting this all together, if we divide 3221 by 9, we will get a total remainder of $3 + 2 + 2 + 1$, or 8. (You should verify this by actually dividing 3221 by 9). Notice that the remainder is exactly the sum of the digits.

In general, if we divide any number by 9, the remainder will be the sum of the digits. (If the sum of the digits is greater than 9, repeat the procedure.)

Now let us look at an example of casting out 9's.

$$436 \rightarrow 4 + 3 + 6 = 13 \rightarrow 1 + 3 = \left.\begin{array}{l} 4 \\ \end{array}\right\}$$
$$\underline{+\ 237} \rightarrow 2 + 3 + 7 = 12 \rightarrow 1 + 2 = \left.\begin{array}{l} 3 \end{array}\right\} \text{ We add.}$$
$$ \textcircled{7}$$
$$673 \rightarrow 6 + 7 + 3 = 16 \rightarrow 1 + 6 = \textcircled{7}$$

The numbers 4 and 3 are the remainders we get when we divide 436 and 237, respectively, by 9. If the addition is correct, then the sum of these remainders should equal the remainder we get when we divide 673 by 9. It is the same in this case, so we are *probably* correct.

Comment We stated that if the remainders check, then our answer is *probably* correct. You cannot be 100% sure that your answer is correct because if you make a mistake that is a multiple of 9, then the remainders will not be affected by the error. The remainders will still check.

casting out 11's

Another method commonly used to check computations is **casting out 11's**. In this method, for each number, *we start at the right* and move to the left. We put a + in front of the first digit, then a − in front of the second digit, and continue alternating the signs. We add the results. This is illustrated below.

$$2741 \rightarrow +1 - 4 + 7 - 2 = 2$$
$$5673 \rightarrow +3 - 7 + 6 - 5 = -3$$
$$781 \rightarrow +1 - 8 + 7 = 0$$

From here on, the procedure is the same as that for casting out 9's.

EXAMPLE 5

SOLUTION

a) Add 2741 and 781 and check the result by casting out 11's.

$$2741 \rightarrow +1 - 4 + 7 - 2 = \left.\begin{array}{l} 2 \\ \end{array}\right\}$$
$$\underline{+\ 781} \rightarrow +1 - 8 + 7 = \left.\begin{array}{l} 0 \end{array}\right\} \text{ We add.}$$
$$ \textcircled{2}$$
$$3522 \rightarrow +2 - 2 + 5 - 3 = \textcircled{2}$$

Since in both cases we get 2, our answer is probably correct.

b) Add 142936 and 782225 and check the result by casting out 11's.

SOLUTION

$$142936 \rightarrow +6 - 3 + 9 - 2 + 4 - 1 = 13 \rightarrow +3 - 1 = \; 2$$
$$+782225 \rightarrow +5 - 2 + 2 - 2 + 8 - 7 = \qquad\qquad\quad 4$$

We add.

⑥

$$925161 \rightarrow +1 - 6 + 1 - 5 + 2 - 9 = \boxed{-16}$$

-16 is congruent to 6 (mod 11) because $-16 - 6$, which is -22, is exactly divisible by 11. Hence our answer is probably correct.   ▬

EXAMPLE 6

SOLUTION

Multiply 321 and 68 and check by casting out 11's.

$$321 \rightarrow +1 - 2 + 3 \qquad\quad = \; 2$$
$$\times \; 68 \rightarrow +8 - 6 \qquad\qquad = \; 2$$

We multiply.

④

$$\underline{2568}$$
$$\underline{1926}$$
$$21828 \rightarrow +8 - 2 + 8 - 1 + 2 = 15 \rightarrow +5 - 1 = ④$$

Hence our answer is probably correct.   ▬

EXERCISES FOR SECTION 5.6

In Exercises 1–12, perform the indicated operations and check your result by casting out 9's.

1. 768
     + 423

2. 7893
     5329
     + 6458

3. 582
     − 293

4. 56834
     − 37945

5. 4567
     − 3672

6. 327
     × 645

7. 231
     × 68

8. 6038
     × 246

9. 5138
     6257
     + 1894

10. 5462
      − 2837

11. 2234
      × 5683

12. 1234
      × 1234

In Exercises 12–24 perform the indicated operations and check your results by casting out 11's.

13. 278
      + 587

14. 394
      + 685

15. 4642
      + 8975

16. 6832
      7614
      + 8329

17. 321
      − 263

18. 7123
      − 3567

19. 8234
      − 1762

20. 23
      × 69

21. 523
      × 65

22. 823
      × 746

23. 6942
      × 837

24. 7432
      × 6578

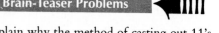

Brain-Teaser Problems

**25. Can you explain why the method of casting out 11's works?

**26. Several students were asked to multiply 69 and 73. One answer given was 5048. Check by casting out 9's and by casting out 11's. What happens? Can you explain why this happens?

**27. Perform each of the following calculations in the indicated base.

a) $212_{(eight)}$
$+ 627_{(eight)}$

b) $27_{(eight)}$
$\times 45_{(eight)}$

c) $376_{(eight)}$
$\times 127_{(eight)}$

d) Check each of the answers obtained in parts (a), (b), and (c) by casting out by a number one less than the base. (This method is similar to the method of casting out 9's.)

TYPICAL CLASSROOM QUESTIONS

1. A teacher making up an arithmetic exam accidentally wrote the problem

$$2357 \quad \text{as} \quad 2537$$
$$+ 1245 \qquad\quad + 1245$$

She has prepared an answer sheet in advance and decides to check by casting out 9's. She does not find her error. Why?

2. What does casting out 9's have to do with congruence and modular arithmetic?

3. Is there any way to tell whether a number is divisible by 9 (without actually dividing by 9)?

4. By looking at the last digit only, can we tell whether a number is divisible by 9?

5. In base 3 the method of checking by casting out 9's will *not* work, since there are no 9's. Can you think of a method similar to that of casting out 9's that would work for base 3?

6. Consider the reversed number products example which is shown on the student page below from *Addison-Wesley Mathematics*, 1987, Grade 8, p. 17. Why are the pairs of products the same?

THINK MATH

Reversed Number Products

$$12 \times 84 = 1{,}008$$
$$21 \times 48 = 1{,}008$$

Why are the pairs of products the same? Find more pairs like these.

Find each pair of products.

1. $36 \times 42 =$
$63 \times 24 =$

2. $62 \times 39 =$
$26 \times 93 =$

3. $96 \times 46 =$
$69 \times 64 =$

4. $39 \times 31 =$
$93 \times 13 =$

7. A claim is made that a number is divisible by 7 if and only if the number represented without its units digit minus twice the units digit of the original number is exactly divisible by 7. Do you agree?

8. A claim is made that a number is divisible by 11 if and only if the sum of the digits in the places that are even powers of 10 minus the sum of the digits in the places that are odd places of 10 is exactly divisible by 11. Do you agree?

STUDY GUIDE

The following is a chapter outline in capsule form. You should now be able to demonstrate your knowledge of the ideas mentioned by giving definitions, descriptions, or specific examples. Page references are given in parentheses.

Divisibility

We say that x divides y whenever there is a whole number m such that $x \cdot m = y$. If x divides y, then we call x a **divisor** of y. (p. 259)

Divisibility facts and tests

i) If x divides y and also divides z, then x divides $y + z$. (p. 260)

ii) If x divides y and x does not divide z, then x does not divide $y + z$. (p. 261)

iii) A number is divisible by 2 when the ones digit is 0, 2, 4, 6, or 8. (p. 262)

iv) A number is divisible by 3 when the sum of its digits is divisible by 3. (p. 262)

v) A number is divisible by 4 when the number formed by the last two digits is divisible by 4. (p. 263)

vi) A number is divisible by 5 when the ones digit is 0 or 5. (p. 263)

vii) A number is divisible by 8 when the number formed by the last three digits is divisible by 8. (p. 264)

viii) A number is divisible by 9 if the sum of its digits is divisible by 9. (p. 263)

ix) A number is divisible by 10 when the ones digit is 0. (p. 264)

The set of numbers {1, 1, 2, 3, 5, 8, 12, 21, 34, . . .}, obtained by adding any two consecutive numbers to obtain the next number in the set, is called a **Fibonacci sequence**. (p. 269)

A number is called a **perfect number** if it equals the sum of all the numbers that divide it and if these numbers are smaller than the number itself. (p. 270)

The **Lucas numbers** are generated in the same way as the Fibonacci sequence but start off differently. The first few Lucas numbers are 1, 3, 4, 7, 11, 18, . . . (p. 272)

An **arithmetic progression** is a sequence in which each term after the first is the sum of the preceding term and a constant. (p. 272)

A **geometric progression** is a sequence in which each term after the first is the product of the preceding term and a constant. (p. 272)

Any positive integer larger than 1 that is divisible only by itself and 1 is called a **prime number**. A number that is not prime is called a **composite number**. (p. 273)

The **Sieve of Eratosthenes** is a technique that enables us to find all the primes less than a given number. (p. 273)

The **Fundamental Theorem of Arithmetic** states that any integer greater than 1 is either a prime number or can be written as a product of primes in one way, except for order. (p. 274)

A method of proof called **proof by contradiction** can be used to prove that the number of primes is infinite. (p. 275)

Two prime numbers that differ by 2 are called **twin primes**. (p. 279)

The **greatest common factor (GCF)** or **greatest common divisor** of two (or more) natural numbers is the largest whole number that is a factor or divisor common to both (or all) of the numbers. (p. 281)

The **least common multiple (LCM)** of two (or more) nonzero whole numbers is the least positive multiple that the two numbers have in common. (p. 283)

The **set-intersection technique**, the **prime factorization technique**, and the **Euclidean algorithm** can be used to find the GCF of two numbers. (p. 281, 285)

Clock and modular arithmetic

For any two integers a and b, a **is congruent to** b **modulo** m if $a - b$ can be divided exactly by m (m is a natural number). We write this as $a \equiv b \pmod{m}$. (p. 293)

If any two integers are congruent modulo m, then their remainders when divided by m are the same. (p. 293)

The accuracy of computations can be checked by casting out 9's and/or by casting out 11's. (p. 296, 299)

KEY TERMS

Following is a list of key terms introduced in each section of this chapter.

5.1 divisibility
divisor
divisibility tests
amicable (friendly) numbers

5.2 Fibonacci numbers
Fibonacci Nim
perfect numbers
golden ratio
Lucas numbers
arithmetic progression

prime factor tree
geometric progression

5.3 prime numbers
composite numbers
sieve of Eratosthenes
factor tree
fundamental theorem
of arithmetic
proof by contradiction
twin primes

5.4   **greatest common factor**   **binary operation**
     greatest common divisor   **closed operation**
     set-intersection method   **inverse**
     prime-factorization   **identity**
       method   **modular arithmetic**
     Euclidean algorithm   **modulus**
       method   **congruent**
     least common multiple
                               5.6   **casting out 9's**
5.5   **clock arithmetic**   **casting out 11's**

FORMULAS TO REMEMBER

The following list summarizes all the formulas discussed in this chapter.

1. Various divisibility tests as given on p. 264.

2. The Fibonacci numbers are 1, 1, 2, 3, 5, 8, 13, 21, 34, . . .

3. The Sieve of Eratosthenes for finding prime numbers less than any given number.

4. GCF $(a,b) \times$ LCM $(a,b) = ab$

5. LCM $(a,b) = \dfrac{ab}{\text{GCF } (a,b)}$

6. To find the GCF or the LCM of two natural numbers, use one of the following:

   a) set-intersection technique

   b) prime-factorization technique

   c) Euclidean algorithm

7. $a \equiv b$ (mod m) means that $a - b$ is exactly divisible by m.

CHAPTER REVIEW EXERCISES

1. Refer back to the magazine clipping on p. 259. Multiply 142857 by 7. What happens?

2. Find all the divisors of 1492.

3. If $x \equiv 4$(mod 6), then one replacement for x is

   a) 0   **b)** 4   **c)** 2   **d)** 7   **e)** none of these

4. $2 \oplus 3$ (mod 5) = ?

   a) 0   **b)** 1   **c)** 2   **d)** 3   **e)** none of these

5. $4 \otimes 3$ (mod 6) = ?

   a) 0   **b)** 12   **c)** 3   **d)** 5   **e)** none of these

6. Let $G = \{0, 1, 2, 3, 4, 5\}$ under addition modulo 6. If $4 \oplus x = 3$, then $x = ?$

   a) 5   **b)** 1   **c)** 2   **d)** 4   **e)** none of these

7. If $9 \equiv 6 \pmod{m}$ is true, then one possible value of m is

    a) 0   **b)** 2   **c)** 6   **d)** 3   **e)** none of these

8. If Washington's Birthday (February 22) is on a Friday, on what day of the week will July 4th occur? (Assume no leap year.)

    a) Sunday   **b)** Monday   **c)** Wednesday   **d)** Thursday

    e) none of these

9. If $x \oplus 4 \equiv 0 \pmod 9$, then $x = ?$

    a) 3   **b)** 4   **c)** 5   **d)** 7   **e)** none of these

10. Find the GCF of 144 and 160. (Use the set-intersection technique.)

11. Find the GCF of 108 and 144. (Use the prime-factorization technique.)

12. Find the GCF of 82 and 96. (Use the Euclidean-algorithm technique.)

13. Find the GCF of 824 and 960. (Use any technique.)

14. What is the LCM of 124 and 160?

15. Find the GCF of 88, 120, and 160.

16. What is the LCM of 28, 36, and 48?

17. A math teacher is rearranging the test papers from one of her lecture classes to make it easier for her to grade them. She knows that there are fewer than 100 students in the class. When she arranges the papers in piles of 5 each, she has 1 left over. When she arranges the papers in piles of 7 each, she has 6 left over, and when she arranges the papers in piles of 4 each, she has 0 left over. How many test papers does the teacher have to grade?

18. Perform each of the indicated operations and check your results by casting out 9's and 11's.

    a) $\begin{array}{r} 368 \\ + 527 \\ \hline \end{array}$ **b)** $\begin{array}{r} 872 \\ - 583 \\ \hline \end{array}$ **c)** $\begin{array}{r} 732 \\ \times 346 \\ \hline \end{array}$

19. In what clock is $4 \ominus 6 \equiv 8$ true?

    a) mod 7   **b)** mod 8   **c)** mod 9   **d)** mod 10   **e)** none of these

20. August 20, 1985, occurred on a Tuesday. In that same year, on what day of the week did November 25 occur?

21. A coin box contains only nickels. Leslie knows that there are fewer than 100 nickels in the box. However, she does not know exactly how many there are. When she arranges the coins in piles of 8, she has 4 left. When she arranges them in piles of 9 each, she also has 2 left. When she arranges them in piles of 12 each, she again has 8 left. How many coins does Leslie have?

22. **a)** Multiply 39×31

    b) Multiply 93×13

    c) Explain how the answers in parts (a) and (b) compare? Explain your answer.

23. Is 2024 a leap year?

24. If $-5 \equiv -8 \pmod{x}$, then $x = ?$

    a) -3 **b)** 3   **c)** 8   **d)** 5   **e)** none of these

25. If $5 \ominus x \equiv 2 \pmod 8$, find x.

    a) 2   **b)** 3   **c)** 4   **d)** 5   **e)** none of these

26. The number 6 has four divisors, 1, 2, 3, and 6. The number 16 has five divisors 1, 2, 4, 8, and 16. We can construct the following chart listing the total number of possible divisors that various numbers have.

	Numbers
0	
1	1
2	2, 3
3	
4	6
5	
6	16
7	
8 or more	

Number of divisors that number has

a) Determine the number of divisors that each of the numbers 2 through 40 has by completing the above chart.

b) The numbers in the third row represent those numbers that have exactly two divisors, namely, 1 and themselves. What do you notice about these entries?

SUGGESTED FURTHER READING

Bezuska, S., "Even Perfect Numbers – An Update," in *The Mathematics Teacher* **74** (September 1981), 460–461.

Engle, J., "A Rediscovered Test for Divisibility by Eleven," in *The Mathematics Teacher* **69** (December 1976), 669.

Forseth, S., and A.P. Troutman, "Using Mathematical Structures to Generate Artistic Design," in *The Mathematics Teacher* **77** (May 1984), 393–398.

Kennedy, R., "Divisibility for Integers Ending in 1, 3, 7, or 9," in *The Mathematics Teacher* **64** (February 1971), 137–138.

Lappan, G., and M. Winter, "Prime Factorizations," in *The Arithmetic Teacher* **27** (March 1980), 24–27.

Mann, N. III, "Modulo System. One More Step," in *The Mathematics Teacher* **65** (March 1972), 207–209.

Singer, R., "Modular Arithmetic and Divisibility Criteria," in *The Mathematics Teacher* **63** (December 1970), 653–656.

Smith, L., "A General Test for Divisibility," in *The Mathematics Teacher* **71** (November 1978), 668–669.

White, P., "An Application of Clock Arithmetic" in *The Mathematics Teacher* **66** (November 1973), 645–647.

CHAPTER 6

The Rational Numbers

NCTM GUIDELINES

In its March 1989 *Curriculum And Evaluation Standards For School Mathematics* (p. 57), The National Council Of Teachers Of Mathematics recommends that the mathematics curriculum should include fractions so that students can

☐ develop concepts of fractions and mixed numbers,

☐ develop number sense for fractions,

☐ use models to relate fractions to decimals and to find equivalent fractions,

☐ use models to explore operations on fractions,

☐ apply fractions to problem situations.

The report further states that an understanding of fractions broadens students' awareness of the usefulness and power of numbers and extends their knowledge of the number system. An awareness of the relative size of fractions fosters number sense and enhances basic understandings. It is for this reason that in this chapter we will study the rational number system, the operations that can be performed within this system, the ordering of the rational numbers as well as their application to ratio and proportion.

Introduction

fraction

People often refer to rational numbers as fractions. Actually, a **fraction** is a number of the form $\frac{a}{b}$ where a and b ($b \neq 0$) are any numbers and not necessarily integers. Thus it is possible for us to have fractions that are not rational numbers. For example, $\frac{\sqrt{3}}{2}$ represents a fraction that is not a rational number. We will discuss this in detail in the next chapter.

Fractions are used in mathematics in a variety of ways. Some of these uses are the following:

a) To express part of a whole. This use of fractions can be seen from the accompanying student page from *Addison-Wesley Mathematics*, Grade 6, 1987, p. 194.

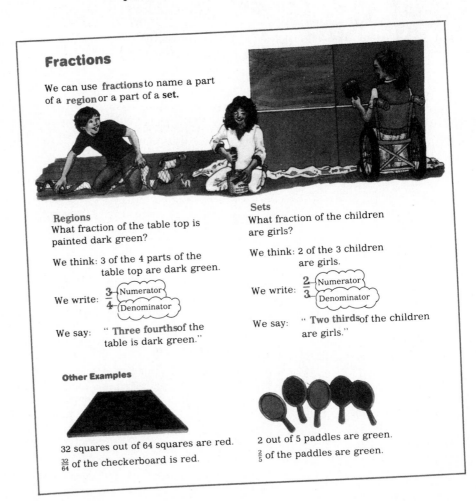

Fractions

We can use **fractions** to name a part of a **region** or a part of a **set**.

Regions

What fraction of the table top is painted dark green?

We think: 3 of the 4 parts of the table top are dark green.

We write: $\frac{3}{4}$ (Numerator) (Denominator)

We say: " **Three fourths** of the table is dark green."

Sets

What fraction of the children are girls?

We think: 2 of the 3 children are girls.

We write: $\frac{2}{3}$ (Numerator) (Denominator)

We say: " **Two thirds** of the children are girls."

Other Examples

32 squares out of 64 squares are red.
$\frac{32}{64}$ of the checkerboard is red.

2 out of 5 paddles are green.
$\frac{2}{5}$ of the paddles are green.

b) To solve algebraic equations as in the solution to $3x = 7$ or $x = \frac{7}{3}$.

c) To form a ratio as in "the ratio of peanuts to cashew nuts in a certain can of mixed nuts is seven to four."

As we shall see, rational numbers are special types of fractions. In this chapter we will analyze rational numbers in detail, and the various operations that can be performed with rational numbers. Then we shall see how they can be applied.

HISTORICAL NOTE

The concept of a fraction arose during the Bronze Age, but it was not fully developed for some time. As late as the year 1650 B.C.[1], the Egyptians, who were rather good mathematicians, did not use fractions as we use them today. They used mostly unit fractions, that is, fractions whose numerators are 1, such as $\frac{1}{2}$, $\frac{1}{3}$, $\frac{1}{4}$, etc., and the fraction $\frac{2}{3}$. Other fractions were written as combinations of unit fractions. For example, $\frac{7}{12} = \frac{1}{3} + \frac{1}{4}$.

6.1

ADDITION AND SUBTRACTION OF RATIONAL NUMBERS

Division is not always possible if one has only the integers. For example, try to divide 2 by 7. The answer is $\frac{2}{7}$ which, of course, is not an integer. To overcome this difficulty, the rational numbers were invented. We define these as follows:

rational number

numerator

denominator

> **Definition 6.1** A **rational number** is any number that can be written as $\frac{a}{b}$ where a and b are integers and b is not zero. Here a (the number on top) is called the **numerator**, and b (the number on the bottom) is called the **denominator**. The rational number $\frac{a}{b}$ may also be represented as a/b or $a \div b$.

Note that in this definition we stated that the denominator cannot be zero. Why?

---

[1] Our knowledge of Egyptian mathematics is derived from the Rhind Papyrus which dates from approximately 1650 B.C.

EXAMPLE 1

The following are examples of rational numbers:

$$\frac{2}{3}, \quad \frac{+5}{-3}, \quad \frac{-5}{+3}, \quad \frac{8}{2}, \quad \frac{-13}{1}$$

The integer 4 is a rational number since it can be written as $\frac{4}{1}$. Similarly, -17 is a rational number. It can be written as $\frac{-17}{1}$. Also, 0 is a rational number. Why?

As a matter of fact, all the integers (and therefore all the natural numbers also) are rational numbers, since we can write them as

$$\frac{\text{integer}}{1}$$

ratio

Comment The rational numbers are so named not because they are in better mental health than other numbers, but because they can be written as the **ratio** of two integers.

Comment As we mentioned earlier, rational numbers are often referred to as fractions. Thus the properties to be developed for rational numbers in this chapter will also hold for fractions.

Equal Rational Numbers

If you have two quarters and your friend has a half-dollar, then clearly you both have the same amount of money. This means that $\frac{2}{4}$ represents the same quantity as $\frac{1}{2}$ (the half-dollar). Consequently,

$$\frac{2}{4} = \frac{1}{2}$$

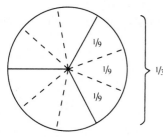

Figure 6.1

The rational numbers $\frac{3}{9}$ and $\frac{1}{3}$ are also equal. To see this, consider a pie divided into nine equal parts (Fig. 6.1). Clearly $\frac{3}{9}$ of the pie is a third of the entire pie. $\frac{3}{9}$ and $\frac{1}{3}$ are called **equivalent**. We have

---

Definition 6.2 Two fractions that name the same part of a set or the same part of a region are called **equivalent fractions**.

Referring back to the fractions $\frac{1}{3}$ and $\frac{3}{9}$, we can multiply the numerator and denominator of $\frac{1}{3}$ by 3. We then have $\frac{1 \times 3}{3 \times 3} = \frac{3}{9}$, so that $\frac{1}{3} = \frac{3}{9}$.

Comment Strictly speaking, $\frac{1}{3}$ and $\frac{3}{9}$ are equivalent fractions. However, as we saw in Fig. 6.1, they both represent equal amounts of the pie. Thus we write $\frac{1}{3} = \frac{3}{9}$ and say that "$\frac{1}{3}$ equals $\frac{3}{9}$." The process of generating fractions equivalent to a given fraction is known as the **fundamental law of fractions**, which can be stated formally as follows:

fundamental law of fractions

Fundamental Law of Fractions For any rational number $\frac{a}{b}$ and any nonzero integer c,

$$\frac{a}{b} = \frac{ac}{bc} \qquad (b, c \neq 0)$$

In words, this law states that the value of a fraction does not change if both the numerator and denominator of the fraction are multiplied by the same nonzero number. A justification of this rule will be given shortly.

Consider the statement $\frac{2}{4} = \frac{1}{2}$. Notice that if we "cross multiply"

$$\frac{2}{4} \bowtie \frac{1}{2}$$

we have $2 \cdot 2 = 4 \cdot 1$. Similarly, in the statement $\frac{3}{9} = \frac{1}{3}$, if we cross multiply

$$\frac{3}{9} \bowtie \frac{1}{3}$$

we get $3 \cdot 3 = 9 \cdot 1$

In general, we have the following rule,

Rule 6.1 The rational numbers $\frac{a}{b}$ and $\frac{c}{d}$ are equal if, when we cross multiply

$$\frac{a}{b} \bowtie \frac{c}{d}$$

we get $ad = bc$.

EXAMPLE 2

The rational numbers $\frac{3}{8}$ and $\frac{12}{32}$ are equal, since when we cross multiply

$$\frac{12}{32} \bowtie \frac{3}{8}$$

we get

$$12 \cdot 8 = 32 \cdot 3$$
$$96 = 96$$

EXAMPLE 3

$\frac{5}{11}$ is *not* equal to $\frac{4}{9}$, since if we cross multiply

$$\frac{5}{11} \bcancel{\times} \frac{4}{9}$$

we get $5 \cdot 9$, which is 45. This is not equal to $11 \cdot 4$, which is 44.   ▬

It is easy to see that $\frac{2}{3} = \frac{8}{12}$, since $2 \cdot 12 = 3 \cdot 8$. Let us look more closely at the rational number $\frac{8}{12}$. It can be written as $\frac{2 \cdot 4}{3 \cdot 4}$. Since 4 appears in the numerator and in the denominator, we can "**cancel**" out (divide the numerator and denominator by) the 4. As a result we have

cancellation

$$\frac{2 \cdot \cancel{4}}{3 \cdot \cancel{4}} = \frac{2}{3}$$

In general, if a, b, and c are any integers (with b and c not zero), then the fundamental law of fractions states that

$$\frac{ac}{bc} = \frac{a}{b} \qquad \text{and} \qquad \frac{ca}{cb} = \frac{a}{b}$$

To justify this, apply the definition of equal rational numbers. We cross multiply $\frac{ac}{bc} = \frac{a}{b}$, getting $(ac)b = (bc)a$. By using the commutative, associative, and closure laws for multiplication of integers, it can be shown that $(ac)b$ does equal $(bc)a$, so the rational numbers $\frac{ac}{bc}$ and $\frac{a}{b}$ are equal. Similarly, we can show that $\frac{ca}{cb}$ and $\frac{a}{b}$ are equal. Another justification of this cancellation principle will be given after we discuss multiplication of rational numbers.

The rational number

$$\frac{8}{12} \text{ can be written as } \frac{4 \cdot 2}{6 \cdot 2}$$

If we cancel the 2, we are left with $\frac{4}{6}$. So we have another rational number $\frac{4}{6}$, which is equal to $\frac{8}{12}$. Also, $\frac{8}{12}$ can be written as $\frac{2}{3}$, as we saw above. The rational numbers $\frac{8}{12}$, $\frac{4}{6}$, and $\frac{2}{3}$ are all equal. However, $\frac{2}{3}$ is different from the others because it is not possible to cancel any more numbers from its numerator and denominator. When $\frac{8}{12}$ is written as $\frac{2}{3}$, we say that it has

reduced to lowest terms

been **reduced to lowest terms**.

greatest common factor

The idea of the **greatest common factor** of two numbers is very helpful in reducing fractions to lowest terms. For example, to reduce the fraction $\frac{24}{36}$ to the lowest terms, we first find the factors of 24. These are 1, 2, 3, 4, 6, 8, 12, and 24. Now we find the factors of 36. These are 1, 2,

3, 4, 6, 9, 12, 18, and 36. The common factors of 24 and 36 are 1, 2, 3, 4, 6, and 12. The greatest common factor is 12, so we divide both the numerator and denominator by 12. We get

$$\frac{24 \div 12}{36 \div 12} = \frac{2}{3}$$

Generally, to reduce a fraction to lowest terms:

Divide the numerator and the denominator by the greatest common factor (GCF) to find the lowest-terms fraction, or

Divide the numerator and the denominator by any common factor and continue to divide until you find the lowest-terms fraction.

lowest terms

relatively prime

> **Definition 6.3**   A fraction $\frac{a}{b}$ is in its **lowest terms** when the greatest common factor of the numerator and denominator is 1. We then say that a and b are **relatively prime**.

EXAMPLE 4

a) Reduce $\frac{15}{20}$ to lowest terms.

SOLUTION

$$\frac{15}{20} = \frac{3 \cdot 5}{4 \cdot 5} = \frac{3}{4}$$

b) Reduce $\frac{-18}{21}$ to lowest terms.

SOLUTION

$$\frac{-18}{21} = \frac{(-6)(+3)}{(+7)(+3)} = \frac{-6}{7}$$

EXAMPLE 5

a) A student was asked to reduce $\frac{360}{240}$ to lowest terms. He wrote

$$\frac{360}{240} = \frac{36 \cdot \cancel{10}}{24 \cdot \cancel{10}} = \frac{36}{24}$$

What is wrong?

SOLUTION

We see that this has not been reduced to lowest terms, since we can further reduce $\frac{36}{24}$ as

$$\frac{36}{24} = \frac{3 \cdot \cancel{12}}{2 \cdot \cancel{12}} = \frac{3}{2}$$

Therefore $\frac{360}{240}$ reduced to lowest terms is $\frac{3}{2}$.

b) $\dfrac{7}{7} = \dfrac{1 \cdot \cancel{7}}{1 \cdot \cancel{7}} = \dfrac{1}{1}$. This is written as 1.   ◼

compare (or order) fractions

The idea of rewriting fractions into equivalent fractions with a common denominator enables us to **compare (or order) fractions**. Once the denominators of the fractions are the same, we compare the numerators. The fractions will then compare the same way that the numerators compare. For example, to determine if $\frac{4}{5}$ and $\frac{5}{6}$ are the same (or if not, which is larger) we proceed as follows:

$$\frac{4}{5} = \frac{24}{30}$$
$$\frac{5}{6} = \frac{25}{30}$$

common denominator
(the same)

Since 25 is larger than 24, we have that $\frac{25}{30}$ is larger than $\frac{24}{30}$, or that $\frac{5}{6}$ is greater than $\frac{4}{5}$.

Addition and Subtraction

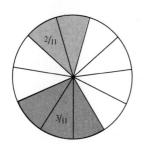

Figure 6.2

How do we add $\frac{3}{11}$ and $\frac{2}{11}$? Look at the pie in Fig. 6.2, which has been divided into eleven equal parts. Clearly $\frac{2}{11} + \frac{3}{11}$ equals $\frac{5}{11}$. Both denominators are the same. Since $2 + 3 = 5$, then we have

$$\frac{2}{11} + \frac{3}{11} = \frac{2+3}{11} = \frac{5}{11}$$

In general terms, we have the following rule.

Rule 6.2   If $\dfrac{a}{b}$ and $\dfrac{c}{b}$ are rational numbers, then $\dfrac{a}{b} + \dfrac{c}{b} = \dfrac{a+c}{b}$.

Now let us subtract $\frac{2}{11}$ from $\frac{3}{11}$, that is, $\frac{3}{11} - \frac{2}{11}$. Again referring back to the pie, we find that $\frac{3}{11} - \frac{2}{11} = \frac{1}{11}$. Since the denominators are the same and $3 - 2 = 1$, we have

$$\frac{3}{11} - \frac{2}{11} = \frac{3-2}{11} = \frac{1}{11}$$

which suggests the following rule.

Rule 6.3   If $\dfrac{a}{b}$ and $\dfrac{c}{b}$ are rational numbers, then $\dfrac{a}{b} - \dfrac{c}{b} = \dfrac{a-c}{b}$.

EXAMPLE 6

a) $\dfrac{3}{10} + \dfrac{4}{10} = \dfrac{3+4}{10} = \dfrac{7}{10}$

b) $\dfrac{3}{14} + \dfrac{5}{14} = \dfrac{3+5}{14} = \dfrac{8}{14}$. Since $\dfrac{8}{14}$ can be written as $\dfrac{4 \cdot 2}{7 \cdot 2}$, we can

cancel the 2's, getting $\dfrac{4}{7}$. Thus $\dfrac{3}{14} + \dfrac{5}{14} = \dfrac{4}{7}$

c) $\dfrac{2}{5} - \dfrac{3}{5} = \dfrac{2-3}{5} = \dfrac{-1}{5}$

Now let us add $\frac{2}{3}$ and $\frac{4}{5}$. Since they do not have the same denominators, the previous rule does not appear to apply. You may think (or wish) that these numbers cannot be added. However, we have a way out of this difficulty.

$$\frac{2}{3} \text{ is the same as } \frac{2 \cdot 5}{3 \cdot 5} = \frac{10}{15} \qquad \text{(cancellation principle)}$$

$$\frac{4}{5} \text{ is the same as } \frac{4 \cdot 3}{5 \cdot 3} = \frac{12}{15} \qquad \text{(cancellation principle)}$$

Therefore

$$\frac{2}{3} + \frac{4}{5} \text{ is the same as } \frac{10}{15} + \frac{12}{15}$$

Now we can use our rule:

$$\frac{10}{15} + \frac{12}{15} = \frac{10+12}{15} = \frac{22}{15}$$

We conclude that $\dfrac{2}{3} + \dfrac{4}{5} = \dfrac{22}{15}$

Our procedure is generalized in the following rule.

Rule 6.4   To add two rational numbers $\dfrac{a}{b}$ and $\dfrac{c}{d}$ that have different denominators,

1. rewrite each number so that they have the same denominator, and
2. add the resulting rational numbers by the rule on p. 316.

Subtraction is done by a similar procedure.

EXAMPLE 7

a) Add $\dfrac{5}{6} + \dfrac{3}{4}$

SOLUTION

$$\frac{5}{6} = \frac{5 \cdot 4}{6 \cdot 4} = \frac{20}{24} \quad \text{and} \quad \frac{3}{4} = \frac{3 \cdot 6}{4 \cdot 6} = \frac{18}{24}$$

Therefore

$$\frac{5}{6} + \frac{3}{4} = \frac{20}{24} + \frac{18}{24} = \frac{20 + 18}{24}$$

$$= \frac{38}{24}$$

which can be reduced as

$$\frac{38}{24} = \frac{19 \cdot 2}{12 \cdot 2} = \frac{19}{12}$$

We have $\dfrac{5}{6} + \dfrac{3}{4} = \dfrac{19}{12}$

b) Add $\dfrac{2}{3} + \dfrac{1}{9}$

SOLUTION

$$\frac{2}{3} = \frac{2 \cdot 3}{3 \cdot 3} = \frac{6}{9}$$

We do not have to do anything to $\frac{1}{9}$, since the denominator is already 9. Thus we have the following:

$$\frac{2}{3} + \frac{1}{9} = \frac{6}{9} + \frac{1}{9}$$

$$= \frac{6 + 1}{9} = \frac{7}{9}$$

Our answer is $\dfrac{2}{3} + \dfrac{1}{9} = \dfrac{7}{9}$

EXAMPLE 8

Subtract $\dfrac{5}{7} - \dfrac{1}{2}$

SOLUTION

$$\frac{5}{7} = \frac{5 \cdot 2}{7 \cdot 2} = \frac{10}{14} \quad \text{and} \quad \frac{1}{2} = \frac{1 \cdot 7}{2 \cdot 7} = \frac{7}{14}$$

Therefore

$$\frac{5}{7} - \frac{1}{2} = \frac{10}{14} - \frac{7}{14}$$

$$= \frac{10 - 7}{14} = \frac{3}{14}$$

Thus

$$\frac{5}{7} - \frac{1}{2} = \frac{3}{14}$$

Mixed Numbers

mixed number

If we form the sum of an integer and a rational number, our answer is often written as a **mixed number**. For example, the sum of 2 and $\frac{3}{7}$ is usually written as $2\frac{3}{7}$. This does not represent 2 times $\frac{3}{7}$ similar to ab which means a times b. Instead $2\frac{3}{7}$ stands for $2 + \frac{3}{7}$. When working with the mixed number $2\frac{3}{7}$, we note the following:

$$2\frac{3}{7} = 2 + \frac{3}{7} = \frac{2}{1} + \frac{3}{7}$$

$$= \frac{2 \cdot 7}{1 \cdot 7} + \frac{3}{7}$$

$$= \frac{14}{7} + \frac{3}{7}$$

$$= \frac{17}{7}$$

improper fraction

Thus $2\frac{3}{7}$ is equivalent to $\frac{17}{7}$. Since the numerator of $\frac{17}{7}$ is greater than the denominator, we call $\frac{17}{7}$ an **improper fraction** as opposed to $2\frac{3}{7}$, which is called a **mixed number**.

EXAMPLE 9

SOLUTION

a) Find a mixed number for $\frac{25}{8}$

We divide the numerator by the denominator. We then write the quotient as the whole number part and the remainder over the divisor as the fraction part. In our case we have

$$\frac{25}{8} \quad or \quad 8\overline{)25} \quad \overset{3 \leftarrow \text{whole number}}{\underset{\underset{1 \nwarrow}{24}}{}}$$

$$\text{remainder}$$

Thus $\frac{25}{8} = 3 + \frac{1}{8} = 3\frac{1}{8}$.

b) Find an improper fraction for $5\frac{2}{3}$

SOLUTION

We multiply the whole number by the denominator, and then add the numerator to the product. Finally, we write the sum over the denominator. In our case, we have

$$5\frac{2}{3} = \frac{5 \cdot 3 + 2}{3} = \frac{15 + 2}{3} = \frac{17}{3}$$

EXAMPLE 10

SOLUTION

Add $2\frac{3}{5} + 4\frac{5}{7}$

Method 1

We change each mixed number into an improper fraction and then add. We have

$$2\frac{3}{5} = \frac{2 \cdot 5 + 3}{5} = \frac{13}{5}$$

$$4\frac{5}{7} = \frac{4 \cdot 7 + 5}{7} = \frac{33}{7}$$

Now we add $\frac{13}{5} + \frac{33}{7}$. We get

$$\frac{13}{5} + \frac{33}{7} = \frac{13 \cdot 7 + 5 \cdot 33}{5 \cdot 7}$$

$$= \frac{91 + 165}{35}$$

$$= \frac{256}{35} = 7\frac{11}{35}$$

Method 2

We add the fractional parts and the integer parts of the mixed numbers separately. We have

$$2\frac{3}{5} = 2\frac{21}{35}$$

$$+ 4\frac{5}{7} = 4\frac{25}{35}$$

$$\overline{\qquad 6\frac{46}{35}}$$

However, $\frac{46}{35} = 1\frac{11}{35}$ so that

$$6\frac{46}{35} = 6 + \frac{46}{35}$$

$$= 6 + 1\frac{11}{35} = 7\frac{11}{35}$$

Using either method we conclude that $2\frac{3}{5} + 4\frac{5}{7} = 7\frac{11}{35}$.

EXERCISES FOR SECTION 6.1

1. Reduce each of the following fractions to lowest terms.

a) $\dfrac{70}{72}$ b) $\dfrac{-130}{180}$ c) $\dfrac{24}{144}$ d) $\dfrac{17}{153}$

e) $\dfrac{76}{38}$ f) $\dfrac{-12}{12}$ g) $\dfrac{15}{3}$ h) $\dfrac{30}{-25}$

2. Which of the following pairs of rational numbers are equal?

a) $\dfrac{5}{7}, \dfrac{15}{21}$ b) $\dfrac{12}{14}, \dfrac{5}{7}$ c) $\dfrac{13}{17}, \dfrac{91}{119}$

d) $\dfrac{8}{20}, \dfrac{56}{140}$ e) $\dfrac{9}{13}, \dfrac{8}{117}$ f) $\dfrac{9}{7}, \dfrac{4}{3}$

g) $\dfrac{6}{7}, \dfrac{7}{8}$ h) $\dfrac{8}{12}, \dfrac{12}{18}$

3. Write each of the following rational numbers in two different ways.

a) $\dfrac{8}{9}$ b) $\dfrac{4}{13}$ c) $\dfrac{5}{7}$ d) $\dfrac{4}{11}$

4. Perform the indicated operations and simplify the results.

a) $\dfrac{3}{4} + \dfrac{9}{4}$ b) $\dfrac{8}{9} - \dfrac{3}{9}$

c) $\dfrac{2}{9} + \dfrac{4}{3}$ d) $\dfrac{7}{12} + \dfrac{8}{16}$

e) $\dfrac{8}{9} - \dfrac{5}{7}$ f) $\dfrac{2}{3} - 4$

g) $12\dfrac{1}{4} - 5\dfrac{3}{4}$ h) $8\dfrac{1}{4} + 2\dfrac{2}{3}$

i) $4\dfrac{7}{8} + 3\dfrac{3}{4}$ j) $5\dfrac{2}{7} - 3\dfrac{1}{8}$

k) $12 - \left(\dfrac{3}{4} + \dfrac{12}{13}\right)$ l) $\dfrac{2}{3} - \left(2\dfrac{1}{9} - 4\dfrac{3}{7}\right)$

5. Convert each of the following mixed numbers to improper fractions.

a) $7\dfrac{3}{5}$ b) $2\dfrac{3}{7}$ c) $-3\dfrac{2}{9}$ d) $-8\dfrac{4}{7}$

6. Convert each of the following improper fractions to mixed numbers.

a) $\dfrac{47}{3}$ b) $\dfrac{12}{5}$ c) $\dfrac{-37}{7}$ d) $\dfrac{-58}{9}$

7. Compare each of the following pairs of numbers and then replace the question mark with a > (greater than) or < (less than) symbol or = (equal) symbol.

a) $\dfrac{4}{32} ? \dfrac{5}{40}$ b) $\dfrac{12}{15} ? \dfrac{16}{20}$ c) $\dfrac{15}{18} ? \dfrac{25}{30}$

d) $14\dfrac{1}{3} ? 14\dfrac{6}{16}$ e) $\dfrac{3}{4} ? \dfrac{4}{5}$ f) $\dfrac{9}{15} ? \dfrac{18}{30}$

8. Mary works at a fast-food restaurant which is $2\dfrac{5}{8}$ miles from her home. Her brother Bill commutes daily to work a distance of $3\dfrac{5}{9}$ miles each way. How much further does Bill have to commute to work than Mary?

9. Bob purchased $\dfrac{5}{8}$ of a pound of walnuts for the party. George purchased 10 ounces of walnuts for the party. Who purchased more walnuts for the party?

10. One week, Jim worked $11\dfrac{6}{7}$ hours overtime. The following week, he worked $12\dfrac{1}{3}$ hours overtime. By how many hours did his overtime hours during the second week increase over his overtime hours during the first week?

11. One fraction in each of the following groups is *not* in lowest terms. Find this fraction.

a) $\dfrac{8}{15}, \dfrac{10}{27}, \dfrac{15}{33}$ b) $\dfrac{13}{16}, \dfrac{13}{39}, \dfrac{13}{27}$

c) $\dfrac{42}{51}, \dfrac{21}{32}, \dfrac{10}{33}$

12. Joe purchased 100 shares of stock of the ABC company. During the first week the stock rose $\dfrac{5}{8}$ of a point on the first day, dropped $\dfrac{3}{4}$ of a point on the second day, dropped $\dfrac{9}{16}$ of a point on the third day, and rose $1\dfrac{7}{32}$ on the last day of the week. What was the net gain in the value of the stock?

13. The following is a series of steps that can be used to show that the commutative law of addition,

$$\dfrac{a}{b} + \dfrac{c}{d} = \dfrac{c}{d} + \dfrac{a}{b},$$

is valid for rational numbers. State the reason for each of these steps.

a) $\dfrac{a}{b} + \dfrac{c}{d} = \dfrac{ad + bc}{bd}$ b) $\dfrac{a}{b} + \dfrac{c}{d} = \dfrac{da + cb}{db}$

c) $\dfrac{a}{b}+\dfrac{c}{d}=\dfrac{cb+da}{db}$ **d)** $\dfrac{a}{b}+\dfrac{c}{d}=\dfrac{c}{d}+\dfrac{a}{b}$

e) $\dfrac{112}{119}-\dfrac{31}{17}$ **f)** $\dfrac{69}{332}+\dfrac{14}{119}$

14. We can add or subtract rational numbers on a calculator without using decimals provided that the calculator has a memory button. To add or subtract two fractions we use Rules 6.2 and 6.3 in the following way:

$$\text{Add}\qquad \frac{2}{3}+\frac{5}{7}$$

Here $a = 2$, $b = 3$, $c = 5$ and $d = 7$. Now we proceed as follows:

ENTER	PRESS	DISPLAY
2×7	$\boxed{=}$ $\boxed{M+}$	14.
3×5	$\boxed{+}$ $\boxed{MR}$ $\boxed{=}$	29.←Numerator
3×7	$\boxed{=}$	21←Denominator

$$\text{Thus}\qquad \frac{2}{3}+\frac{5}{7}=\frac{29}{21}$$

To find the difference, we follow the above steps exactly except that we change $\boxed{+}$ to $\boxed{-}$

$$\text{Thus}\qquad \frac{2}{3}-\frac{5}{7}=\frac{-1}{21}$$

Using a calculator, add or subtract the following rational numbers.

a) $\dfrac{5}{8}+\dfrac{3}{10}$ **b)** $\dfrac{2}{9}+\dfrac{7}{11}$

c) $\dfrac{29}{37}+\dfrac{16}{19}$ **d)** $\dfrac{9}{29}-\dfrac{18}{23}$

Brain-Teaser Problems

**15. We mentioned earlier that the Egyptians used unit fractions, that is, fractions whose numerators were 1.

   a) Express $\frac{1}{3}$ as a sum of 2 unit fractions.

   b) Express $\frac{1}{4}$ as a sum of 2 unit fractions.

   c) Express $\dfrac{1}{n}$ as a sum of 2 unit fractions.

**16. Prove that $\dfrac{-a}{-b}=\dfrac{a}{b}$ (*Hint:* Use the definition of equal rational numbers.)

**17. Prove each of the following:

   a) $\dfrac{-a}{b}=\dfrac{a}{-b}$ **b)** $\dfrac{-a}{b}=-\dfrac{a}{b}$

   (*Hint:* Use the definition of equal rational numbers.)

**18. Consider the two rational numbers $\dfrac{a}{b}$ and $\dfrac{c}{d}$. Find values of a, b, c, and d for which:

   a) $\dfrac{a}{b}+\dfrac{c}{d}=\dfrac{a+c}{b+d}$

   b) $\dfrac{a}{b}+\dfrac{c}{d}\neq\dfrac{a+c}{b+b}$

**19. Discover the pattern and then find the missing fraction or mixed numbers.

   a) $2\dfrac{3}{5}$, $4\dfrac{1}{5}$, $5\dfrac{4}{5}$, ?, 9

   b) 12, $10\dfrac{1}{3}$, $8\dfrac{2}{3}$, ?, $5\dfrac{1}{3}$

6.2

MULTIPLICATION AND DIVISION OF RATIONAL NUMBERS

Multiplication

The area of a rectangle may be calculated by multiplying the length times the width. The following two diagrams illustrate this.

3 | Area is $3\cdot5 = 15$
5

4 | Area is $4\cdot6 = 24$
6

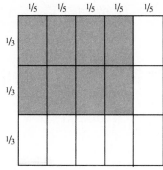

Figure 6.3

Now consider a rectangle measuring 1 by 1 that has been broken up into fifteen smaller rectangles of the same size, as shown in Fig. 6.3.

Each little rectangle measures $\frac{1}{3}$ by $\frac{1}{5}$. Suppose we wanted to find the area represented by the shaded portion of the diagram. From the area formula this would be $\frac{2}{3} \cdot \frac{4}{5}$. On the other hand, the shaded portion contains 8 little rectangles. Since there are 15 altogether, the area is $\frac{8}{15}$ of the total area. Thus we see that

$$\frac{2}{3} \cdot \frac{4}{5} = \frac{8}{15}$$

Notice that $2 \cdot 4 = 8$, and $3 \cdot 5 = 15$. So we have

$$\frac{2}{3} \cdot \frac{4}{5} = \frac{2 \cdot 4}{3 \cdot 5}$$

$$= \frac{8}{15}$$

What we have done is to multiply the numerators and also the denominators to get the product. This gives us the following rule.

Rule 6.5 If $\frac{a}{b}$ and $\frac{c}{d}$ are rational numbers, then the product is

$$\frac{a}{b} \cdot \frac{c}{d} = \frac{ac}{bd}$$

EXAMPLE 1

a) Multiply $\frac{3}{7} \cdot \frac{5}{8}$

SOLUTION

$$\frac{3}{7} \cdot \frac{5}{8} = \frac{3 \cdot 5}{7 \cdot 8} = \frac{15}{56}$$

b) Multiply $\frac{-10}{3} \cdot \frac{5}{9}$

SOLUTION

$$\frac{-10}{3} \cdot \frac{5}{9} = \frac{(-10) \cdot 5}{3 \cdot 9}$$

$$= \frac{-50}{27}$$

c) Multiply $4 \cdot \frac{6}{7}$

SOLUTION

Since 4 is the same as $\dfrac{4}{1}$, we have

$$\frac{4}{1}\cdot\frac{6}{7}=\frac{4\cdot6}{1\cdot7}=\frac{24}{7}$$

Comment   We now have another way of justifying the cancellation principle introduced earlier.

$$\frac{ac}{bc}=\frac{a\cdot c}{b\cdot c}\qquad(b\text{ and }c\text{ are not zero})$$

$$=\frac{a}{b}\cdot\frac{c}{c}=\frac{a}{b}\cdot1=\frac{a}{b}$$

Therefore $\dfrac{ac}{bc}=\dfrac{a}{b}$

which means that we can cancel the c's.

Division

In your previous mathematical studies you learned a rather peculiar procedure for dividing one rational number by another. It can be stated as follows.

Rule 6.6   If $\dfrac{a}{b}$ and $\dfrac{c}{d}$ are rational numbers, then $\dfrac{a}{b}\div\dfrac{c}{d}=\dfrac{a}{b}\cdot\dfrac{d}{c}$.

In words, this says that you invert $\dfrac{c}{d}$ to get $\dfrac{d}{c}$ and multiply $\dfrac{d}{c}$ by $\dfrac{a}{b}$.

EXAMPLE 2

a) Divide $\dfrac{4}{7}$ by $\dfrac{3}{5}$

SOLUTION

$$\frac{4}{7}\div\frac{3}{5}=\frac{4}{7}\cdot\frac{5}{3}=\frac{4\cdot5}{7\cdot3}=\frac{20}{21}$$

b) Divide $\dfrac{-2}{3}$ by $\dfrac{8}{9}$

SOLUTION

$$\frac{-2}{3}\div\frac{8}{9}=\frac{-2}{3}\cdot\frac{9}{8}=\frac{(-2)\cdot9}{3\cdot8}$$

$$=\frac{-18}{24}\quad\text{which can be reduced as}$$

$$=\frac{-3\cdot\cancel{6}}{4\cdot\cancel{6}}=\frac{-3}{4}$$

c) Divide $\frac{2}{5}$ by 3

SOLUTION

$$\frac{2}{5} \div 3 = \frac{2}{5} \div \frac{3}{1} = \frac{2}{5} \cdot \frac{1}{3} = \frac{2 \cdot 1}{5 \cdot 3} = \frac{2}{15}$$

If you are like most students (including the author), this rule probably seemed very mysterious when you first saw it. It was something you learned to humor the teacher, without really understanding why it works. The mystery will now be unraveled.

Remember that $6 \div 3 = 2$ means $6 = 3 \cdot 2$. This says that $6 \div 3$ is a number (namely 2) that when multiplied by 3 results in 6.

Similarly, $\frac{4}{7} \div \frac{3}{5}$ means a rational number that when multiplied by $\frac{3}{5}$ will give $\frac{4}{7}$. We claim that this number is $\frac{4}{7} \cdot \frac{5}{3}$, or $\frac{20}{21}$. So we want to multiply $\frac{3}{5}$ by some number and come up with an answer of $\frac{4}{7}$. This can be accomplished by first multiplying $\frac{3}{5}$ by $\frac{5}{3}$. This yields

$$\frac{3}{5} \cdot \frac{5}{3} = \frac{3 \cdot 5}{5 \cdot 3} = \frac{15}{15} = 1$$

Now if we multiply the 1 by $\frac{4}{7}$, we get

$$1 \cdot \frac{4}{7} = \frac{1}{1} \cdot \frac{4}{7} = \frac{1 \cdot 4}{1 \cdot 7} = \frac{4}{7}$$

Therefore to get from $\frac{3}{5}$ to $\frac{4}{7}$, we multiply by $\frac{5}{3}$ and then by $\frac{4}{7}$ or by $\left(\frac{5}{3} \cdot \frac{4}{7}\right)$. To check that we are right, we have

$$\frac{4}{7} = \frac{3}{5} \cdot \left(\frac{4}{7} \cdot \frac{5}{3}\right) = \frac{3}{5} \cdot \left(\frac{4 \cdot 5}{7 \cdot 3}\right) = \frac{3}{5} \cdot \frac{20}{21} = \frac{3 \cdot 20}{5 \cdot 21} = \frac{60}{105} = \frac{4 \cdot 15}{7 \cdot 15} = \frac{4}{7}$$

Comment The commutative, associative, and distributive laws hold for addition and multiplication of rational numbers.

identity for multiplication

The number 1 is the **identity for multiplication** of rational numbers, since it is the unique number such that for any rational number $\frac{a}{b}$ we have

$$1 \cdot \left(\frac{a}{b}\right) = \frac{a}{b} = \left(\frac{a}{b}\right) \cdot 1$$

identity for addition

The number 0 is the **identity for addition** of rational numbers, since it is the unique number such that for any rational number $\frac{a}{b}$ we have

$$0 + \frac{a}{b} = \frac{a}{b} + 0 = \frac{a}{b}$$

multiplicative inverse

reciprocal

For every nonzero rational number $\frac{a}{b}$ there exists a unique rational number $\frac{b}{a}$ called the **multiplicative inverse** or **reciprocal** of $\frac{a}{b}$ such that

$$\frac{a}{b} \cdot \frac{b}{a} = \frac{b}{a} \cdot \frac{a}{b} = 1$$

For any nonzero rational number $\frac{a}{b}$, we have

$$\frac{a}{b} \cdot 0 = 0 = 0 \cdot \frac{a}{b}$$

multiplication property of zero

This is known as the **multiplication property of zero** for rational numbers.

Reciprocals can be used to solve some multiplication equations that contain fractions. For example, suppose we want to solve the equation $\frac{5}{8}x = \frac{9}{17}$. We proceed as follows.

$$\frac{5}{8}x = \frac{9}{17}$$

$$\frac{8}{5} \cdot \frac{5}{8}x = \frac{9}{17} \cdot \frac{8}{5} \qquad \text{We multiply each side by } \frac{8}{5}, \text{ the reciprocal of } \frac{5}{8}$$

$$1 \cdot x = \frac{72}{85} \qquad \text{We simplify each side}$$

$$x = \frac{72}{85} \qquad \text{Multiplication Property of 1}$$

denseness property

The set of rational numbers has a special property which neither the set of integers nor the set of whole numbers has. This is the **denseness property**, which says that given any two rational numbers a and c, there exists another rational number between these two. We can always find a fraction between any two fractions by finding the average of these fractions. For example, to find a fraction between $\frac{2}{3}$ and $\frac{4}{5}$ we divide the sum of these two fractions, $\frac{2}{3} + \frac{4}{5} = \frac{22}{15}$, by 2. We get $\frac{22}{15} \div \frac{2}{1} = \frac{22}{15} \cdot \frac{1}{2} = \frac{11}{15}$. Thus $\frac{11}{15}$ is a fraction between $\frac{2}{3}$ and $\frac{4}{5}$.

There is an alternate approach for dividing one rational number by another. This is illustrated in the following: Suppose we wish to divide $\frac{64}{15}$ by $\frac{32}{15}$. First we note that the denominators of both rational numbers are the same. If we divide the numerator of the first fraction by the numerator of the second fraction, we get $64 \div 32 = 2$. This is indeed the answer we get when we divide $\frac{64}{15}$ by $\frac{32}{15}$ using Rule 6.6.

If we wish to divide two rational numbers which have different denominators, we must first rename the fractions so that the denominators are equal. For example, to divide $\frac{a}{b}$ by $\frac{c}{d}$, we can proceed as follows:

$$\frac{a}{b} \div \frac{c}{d} = \frac{ad}{bd} \div \frac{bc}{bd} = ad \div bc = \frac{ad}{bc}$$

Ordering Rational Numbers

We can compare rational numbers in much the same way that we compare fractions or integers. Thus, if one child has 75 cents, then that child has $\frac{3}{4}$ of a dollar. If a second child has only 25 cents, then the second child has only $\frac{1}{4}$ of a dollar. Obviously, $\frac{3}{4} > \frac{1}{4}$, since 75 cents is more than 25 cents. Thus if we are given two fractions with the same positive denominator, then we can order the fractions by comparing the numerators. The fraction with the greater numerator is the larger fraction. This method of comparing fractions is called the **common-positive-denominator approach**. Symbolically, if a, b, and c are integers and $b > 0$, then $\frac{a}{b} > \frac{c}{b}$ if and only if $a > c$.

common-positive-denominator approach for ordering rational numbers

---

EXAMPLE 3

Order the following rational numbers:

a) $\frac{8}{7}$ and $\frac{12}{7}$ **b)** $\frac{-2}{7}$ and $\frac{-5}{7}$

SOLUTION

a) As the denominators of these two rational numbers are both positive and equal, we can compare numerators. Since $12 > 8$, we have $\frac{12}{7} > \frac{8}{7}$.

b) Again, the denominators of these two rational numbers are both positive and equal. Comparing numerators, we find that $-5 < -2$, so $\frac{-5}{7} < \frac{-2}{7}$.

This common-positive-denominator approach can also be used to determine which of two rational numbers is larger even when the denominators are different. To see how this is done, assume that $\frac{a}{b} > \frac{c}{d}$ where b and d are both nonzero positive integers. Then we know that

$$\frac{a}{b} = \frac{ad}{bd}$$

and

$$\frac{c}{d} = \frac{bc}{bd}$$

so that $\frac{ad}{bd} > \frac{bc}{bd}$ since bd is positive. (Why?) We can then conclude that $ad > bc$.

Alternately, if $ad > bc$ where b and d are both nonzero positive integers, then

$$\frac{ad}{bd} > \frac{bc}{bd}$$

so that

$$\frac{a}{b} > \frac{c}{d}$$

This leads us to the following:

Rule 6.7 If $\dfrac{a}{b}$ and $\dfrac{c}{d}$ are two rational numbers where b and d are both nonzero positive integers, then $\dfrac{a}{b} > \dfrac{c}{d}$ if and only if $ad > bc$.

EXAMPLE 4

Determine if $\frac{5}{9} > \frac{8}{15}$ is a valid inequality.

SOLUTION

As the denominators of both rational numbers are positive, we can apply Rule 6.7. We have $\frac{5}{9} > \frac{8}{15}$ if and only if $5(15) > 9(8)$. Since $75 > 72$, we conclude that the inequality $\frac{5}{9} > \frac{8}{15}$ is valid. ∎

number-line approach

We can also compare (or order) rational numbers by noting their position on a number line. We can state this **number-line approach** as follows: $\dfrac{a}{b} > \dfrac{c}{d}$ if and only if $\dfrac{a}{b}$ is to the right of $\dfrac{c}{d}$ on the rational number line.

addition approach for ordering rational numbers

There is a third way of comparing (or ordering) two rational numbers. This involves the definition of greater-than and less-than for rational numbers which is comparable to the definition for integers. We have the following **addition approach for ordering rational numbers**:

Rule 6.8 If $\dfrac{a}{b}$ and $\dfrac{c}{d}$ are rational numbers, then $\dfrac{a}{b} > \dfrac{c}{d}$ if and only if there is a positive rational number $\dfrac{p}{q}$ such that $\dfrac{c}{d} + \dfrac{p}{q} = \dfrac{a}{b}$. Alternatively, $\dfrac{a}{b} > \dfrac{c}{d}$ if and only if $\dfrac{a}{b} - \dfrac{c}{d}$ is positive.

EXAMPLE 5

Determine if $\frac{-4}{7} > \frac{-2}{3}$ is a valid inequality.

SOLUTION

Using Rule 6.8, we have $\frac{-4}{7} - \left(\frac{-2}{3}\right) = \frac{-4}{7} + \frac{2}{3} = \frac{-12}{21} + \frac{14}{21} = \frac{2}{21}$, which is positive. Therefore, $\frac{-4}{7} > \frac{-2}{3}$ is a valid inequality. If we use a number line we find that $\frac{-4}{7}$ is to the right of $\frac{-2}{3}$ so that $\frac{-4}{7} > \frac{-2}{3}$ is indeed a valid inequality.

The following is a list of some of the properties of rational numbers involving greater-than and less-than. Most of these properties are similar to those of the integers. The proofs of these is left to the student as an exercise.

Properties of Rational Numbers

Let $\frac{a}{b}, \frac{c}{d}$, and $\frac{e}{f}$ be any rational numbers.

Transitive property of greater than: If $\frac{a}{b} > \frac{c}{d}$ and $\frac{c}{d} > \frac{e}{f}$, then $\frac{a}{b} > \frac{e}{f}$.

Addition property of greater than: If $\frac{a}{b} > \frac{c}{d}$, then $\frac{a}{b} + \frac{e}{f} > \frac{c}{d} + \frac{e}{f}$.

Multiplication property of greater than involving a positive number: If $\frac{a}{b} > \frac{c}{d}$ and $\frac{e}{f} > 0$, then $\left(\frac{a}{b}\right)\left(\frac{e}{f}\right) > \left(\frac{c}{d}\right)\left(\frac{e}{f}\right)$

Multiplication property of greater than involving a negative number: If $\frac{a}{b} > \frac{c}{d}$ and $\frac{e}{f} < 0$, then $\left(\frac{a}{e}\right)\left(\frac{e}{f}\right) < \left(\frac{c}{d}\right)\left(\frac{e}{f}\right)$.

The above properties can be used to solve algebraic inequalities.

EXAMPLE 6

Solve for x:

a) $\frac{2}{3}x \geq \frac{-4}{7}$ b) $\frac{-4}{9}x \geq 3$

SOLUTION

a) We multiply both sides of the inequality by $\frac{3}{2}$ the reciprocal of $\frac{2}{3}$. Since $\frac{3}{2}$ is a positive number, the sense of the inequality does not change, so that

$$\left(\frac{3}{2}\right) \cdot \left(\frac{2}{3}x\right) \geq \left(\frac{3}{2}\right)\left(\frac{-4}{7}\right)$$

$$\left(\frac{3}{2} \cdot \frac{2}{3}\right)x \geq \frac{-12}{14}$$

$$x \geq \frac{-12}{14} \quad \text{or} \quad \frac{-6}{7}$$

b) We multiply both sides of the inequality by $\frac{-9}{4}$, the reciprocal of $\frac{-4}{9}$. Since $\frac{-9}{4}$ is a negative number, the sense of the inequality is reversed, so that

$$\left(\frac{-9}{4}\right)\left(\frac{-4}{9}x\right) \leq \left(\frac{-9}{4}\right)3$$

$$\left(\frac{-9}{4} \cdot \frac{-4}{9}\right)x \leq \left(\frac{-9}{4}\right)3$$

$$x \leq \frac{-27}{4}$$

EXAMPLE 7

Solve for x: $\frac{1}{3}x + \frac{1}{7} \geq \frac{3}{5}x - \frac{4}{9}$

SOLUTION

It is usually easier to work with inequalities that do not involve fractions. To accomplish this we will multiply both sides of the inequality by the least common multiple (LCM) of all the denominators. The LCM of the denominators 3, 7, 5, and 9 is 315. Multiplying both sides of the inequality by the positive number 315 gives

$$315\left(\frac{1}{3}x + \frac{1}{7}\right) \geq 315\left(\frac{3}{5}x - \frac{4}{9}\right)$$

$105x + 45 \geq 189x - 140$ (Distributive law)

$-84x \geq -185$ (Combining terms)

$x \leq \frac{185}{84}$ (The sense of the inequality is reversed as we divided by the negative number -84.)

Estimation for problems involving inequalities and rational numbers can often be quite useful. In the following student page, from *Addison-Wesley Mathematics*, 1987, Grade 5, p. 252, we see how estimation can be used as a problem-solving tool when working with inequalities and rational numbers.

Problem Solving: Using Estimation

You can estimate with mixed numbers by rounding each mixed number to the nearest whole number. Here are the rules for rounding fractions.

For the problems on this page, find the best estimate by rounding. Then find the exact answer.

Rules

- Round **down** if the fraction part is less than $\frac{1}{2}$. $5\frac{2}{5} \rightarrow 5$
- Round **up** if the fraction part is greater than or equal to $\frac{1}{2}$. $5\frac{3}{5} \rightarrow 6$

Example

Lisa jogged $4\frac{3}{4}$ miles on Saturday and $6\frac{1}{10}$ miles on Sunday. How far did she jog over the weekend?

A 10 miles
B 11 miles
C 12 miles

Estimate:

$4\frac{3}{4}$ is about 5.
$6\frac{1}{10}$ is about 6.
$5 + 6 = 11$, so
B is the best estimate.

Exact:

$$4\frac{3}{4} = 4\frac{15}{20}$$
$$+ 6\frac{1}{10} = 6\frac{2}{20}$$
$$\overline{\phantom{+ 6\frac{1}{10} = } 10\frac{17}{20}\text{ miles}}$$

1. Earl jogs from home to school and back home. The school is $3\frac{1}{8}$ miles from his home. How far does he jog?
   A 6 miles   **B** 7 miles   **C** 8 miles

2. Jackie rode her bike $12\frac{1}{10}$ miles Friday and $22\frac{4}{5}$ miles Saturday. How far did she ride those two days?
   A 34 miles   **B** 35 miles   **C** 36 miles

3. Inga rides her bike $7\frac{5}{8}$ miles to her school. Her younger brother rides $4\frac{1}{2}$ miles to his school. How much farther does Inga ride?
   A 3 miles   **B** 4 miles   **C** 5 miles

4. Susan jogged $7\frac{1}{4}$ miles Monday and $9\frac{3}{5}$ miles Tuesday. How far did she jog in all on those days?
   A 15 miles   **B** 16 miles   **C** 17 miles

5. Dick jogged $8\frac{3}{4}$ laps around the track before school. He jogged $12\frac{7}{8}$ laps after school. How many more laps did he jog after school than before school?
   A 3   **B** 4   **C** 5

6. **Strategy Practice** On Monday there was 1 person jogging on the track. On Tuesday 3 more people began jogging, for a total of 4. On Wednesday 5 more people began jogging, and on Thursday 7 more began. If the pattern continued, how many people were jogging on Sunday?

EXERCISES FOR SECTION 6.2

1. Perform the indicated operations and simplify the results.

a) $\frac{4}{3} \times \frac{1}{2}$

b) $\frac{5}{11} \cdot \frac{55}{12}$

c) $\frac{4}{9} \cdot \frac{27}{17}$

d) $\frac{-8}{11} \cdot \frac{13}{17}$

e) $\left(\frac{-8}{11}\right)\left(\frac{-11}{8}\right)$

f) $\left(\frac{4}{3}\right) \div \left(\frac{5}{7}\right)$

g) $16 \div 8$

h) $\frac{7}{9}\left(\frac{1}{2} - \frac{1}{3}\right)$

i) $\frac{5}{8}\left(\frac{2}{3} - 4\right)$

j) $\frac{5}{8} \times \left(\frac{2}{3} \times \frac{12}{5}\right)$

2. Perform the following multiplications.

a) $1\frac{2}{3} \times 2\frac{1}{2}$

b) $2\frac{1}{8} \times 1\frac{3}{4}$

c) $\left(9\frac{7}{10} \times 3\right) - 29\frac{1}{4}$

d) $\left(3 \times \frac{1}{4}\right) + \left(6 \times \frac{1}{4}\right)$

3. Perform the following divisions.

a) $4\frac{1}{2} \div 2\frac{3}{4}$

b) $6\frac{1}{2} \div 2\frac{2}{3}$

c) $16 \div 1\frac{7}{9}$

d) $\left(6 - 4\frac{2}{3}\right) \div 1\frac{2}{5}$

4. Find the multiplicative inverse of each of the following:

a) $\frac{-2}{5}$

b) $\frac{4}{7}$

c) $\frac{12}{6}$

d) $4\frac{1}{9}$

e) $\frac{4}{-5}$

f) -8

5. Find the value of x in each of the following: (*Hint:* Think about reciprocals.)

a) $\frac{4}{7}x = 1$

b) $\frac{1}{4}x = 1$

c) $3\frac{1}{4}x = 1$

d) $\frac{5}{3} \times \frac{3}{5} = x$

e) $\left(\frac{1}{4} + \frac{1}{5}\right)x = 1$

f) $\left(\frac{1}{3} \cdot \frac{2}{7}\right)x = 1$

g) $\left(2\frac{3}{7} - 1\frac{5}{8}\right)x = 1$

6. Order the following rational numbers:

a) $\frac{5}{7}$ and $\frac{8}{11}$

b) $\frac{-3}{7}$ and $\frac{-4}{9}$

c) $\frac{-3}{7}, \frac{-5}{8}, \frac{-6}{11}$

7. Find the value of x in each of the following:

a) $\frac{2}{3}x > \frac{8}{5}$

b) $\frac{3}{4}x - 1 \le 7$

c) $\frac{-3}{5}x > \frac{7}{8}$

d) $\frac{-2}{5}x + 5 < 9$

e) $\frac{4}{7}x + \frac{5}{9} \le \frac{2}{13}$

f) $\frac{-2}{9}(x + 1) \ge \frac{5}{11}$

g) $\frac{2}{11}x - \frac{8}{7} \ge \frac{4}{9}x - \frac{3}{5}$

h) $\frac{4}{11}\left(\frac{2}{3}x - \frac{9}{5}\right) \le \frac{5}{7}(2x - 3) + \frac{5}{6}$

8. Show that the following inequalities are true by finding the positive rational number $\frac{p}{q}$ in the addition approach:

a) $\frac{2}{5} \le \frac{5}{7}$

b) $\frac{-5}{6} \ge \frac{-2}{5}$

c) $\frac{-3}{11} \ge \frac{-5}{6}$

9. Verify each of the properties of inequalities for rational numbers given on p. 329.

10. A broken hose leaks 1 gallon of water every $\frac{3}{4}$ hour. How many gallons of water will it leak in $3\frac{3}{4}$ hours?

11. A florist needs $3\frac{1}{4}$ yards of rope to make a hanger for a plant. If the florist has $55\frac{1}{4}$ yards of rope available, how many hangers for plants can be made?

12. Marguretta received $\frac{2}{3}$ of her uncle's estate when he died. If his estate was worth $2\frac{1}{4}$ million dollars, how much did Marguretta receive?

13. A dressmaker finds that it takes $2\frac{7}{8}$ yards of material to make a dress and $\frac{3}{4}$ yd of the material to make a jacket. How many yards of the material are needed to make 9 dress-and-jacket outfits?

14. Solve each of the following equations for x:

a) $1\frac{4}{5}x = 9$

b) $2\frac{8}{9}x = \frac{3}{4}$

c) $4\frac{1}{3}x = 7\frac{1}{4}$

d) $2\frac{1}{7}x = 3\frac{1}{3}$

 Brain-Teaser Problems

**15. José is analyzing his college transcript. Of his credits, $\frac{1}{2}$ are in the social sciences and $\frac{1}{3}$ are in the sciences. Additionally, he has 4 credits in physical education. How many credits has José completed until now?

**16. Can you find a fraction such that if you double $\frac{1}{8}$ of it and multiply the result by the original fraction, the answer will be $\frac{1}{9}$?

6.3

RATIO AND PROPORTION

Often we find ourselves comparing different quantities. Thus a business major may find that 30 credits out of the 128 credits required for a bachelor's degree must be in business courses. The student may be interested in determining what part of the degree consists of business courses. Ratios are used to make such comparisons.

ratio

terms of the ratio

> **Definition 6.3**   A **ratio** of one number to another (nonzero) number is the quotient of the first number divided by the second number. The ratio of a to b can be expressed as $\frac{a}{b}$ or $a \div b$ or $a : b$. The numbers a and b are called the **terms** of the ratio.

For example, the ratio of 12 to 6 is $12 \div 6$ or $\frac{12}{6}$. The quotient $\frac{12}{6}$ is equivalent to $\frac{2}{1}$ or 2. If the ratio between the number of computers and printers in an office is 2 : 1, then for every 2 computers in the office there is 1 printer.

A ratio is expressed in **simplest form** when both terms of the ratio are whole numbers and when there is no number (other than 1) that divides exactly into these terms.

In the example discussed earlier the ratio of the number of business courses to the total number of credits required for a degree is

$$\frac{30}{128} \quad \text{or} \quad \frac{15}{64}$$

EXAMPLE 1

A certain cookie recipe calls for $1\frac{1}{3}$ cups of water to $1\frac{5}{6}$ cups of flour. What is the ratio of the number of cups of water to the number of cups of flour?

SOLUTION

The ratio of cups of water to the number of cups of flour is

$$\frac{1\frac{1}{3}}{1\frac{5}{6}} = \frac{\frac{4}{3}}{\frac{11}{6}} = \frac{4}{3} \div \frac{11}{6} = \frac{4}{3} \cdot \frac{6}{11} = \frac{8}{11}$$

unit pricing

As shoppers in supermarkets, we often find similar items with different prices. Since the similar items may be packaged differently, **unit pricing** allows us to compare the costs and get the best buy. Students are taught about unit pricing in terms of a ratio, as can be seen from the student page

Dover (Nov 12): As a result of numerous complaints, the Consumer Affairs Department announced yesterday that effective January 1, 1989, all large supermarkets doing business in the city will be required to prominently display the unit price of an item on the shelf alongside of the item. This course of action is a direct outgrowth of numerous complaints received by the Bureau. Under unit pricing, consumers will be able to see the actual unit cost of an item. This will enable the consumer to shop wisely by brand comparison or by considering different size packages of the same item.

Dover News—November 20, 1988

Based upon the article, it would seem that unit pricing is definitely beneficial to the consumer. How do we determine the unit cost of an item which would facilitate comparisons?

246 from *Addison-Wesley Mathematics*, 1987, Grade 8, shown on the facing page. The following examples show how this can be done.

EXAMPLE 2

A student sees an advertisement for a computer magazine. The advertised rates are $22.00 for 24 issues and $17.00 for 18 issues. Which rate is a better deal?

SOLUTION
unit cost

We set up a ratio representing the unit cost of the magazine under each of the possible rates. If the student orders 24 issues, then the **unit cost** per issue is

$$\frac{\text{cost}}{\text{number of issues}} = \frac{\$22.00}{24} \approx \$0.92, \quad \text{or about 92 cents an issue.}$$

If the student orders 18 issues, then the unit cost per issue is

$$\frac{\text{cost}}{\text{number of issues}} = \frac{\$17.00}{18} \approx \$0.94, \quad \text{or about 94 cents an issue.}$$

Obviously, the 24-month rate is cheaper, but not by much.

EXAMPLE 3

Kim is in a supermarket comparing the prices of several brands of rice krispies. The national brand contains 567 grams and sells for $2.09. The store brand contains 539 grams and sells for $1.69. Which brand has the lower cost per gram?

SOLUTION

To determine which brand has the lower cost per gram, we set up a ratio between the cost of the item and the number of units in the package. This will give us the **unit cost** for each brand. In our case we have

The price for *one* unit of an item is called the

UNIT PRICE:
?

APPLE JUICE

1.40 L

UNIT PRICE:
?

APPLE JUICE

1.80 L

What is the unit price of each bottle of apple juice? Which bottle costs less per unit?

Write a ratio of the price to the number of units.	Divide the price by the number of units.	Write the unit price.
$\dfrac{\$1.26}{1.4\ \text{L}}$	$\$1.26 \div 1.4 = \$0.90$	$\$0.90/\text{L}$
$\dfrac{\$1.53}{1.8\ \text{L}}$	$\$1.53 \div 1.8 = \$0.85$	$\$0.85/\text{L}$

The 1.8-liter bottle costs less per unit.

Grapefruit: **4** for **$1.08**

Unit price $= \dfrac{\$1.08}{4} = \$0.27/\text{grapefruit}$

Fresh grapes: **$1.35** for **0.45** kg

Unit price $= \dfrac{\$1.35}{0.45\ \text{kg}} = \$3/\text{kg}$

Give the unit price.

1. 1.5 L for $3.30

2. $2.17 for 0.7 kg

3. 24 cans for $23.28

4. 0.6 kg for $1.40

5. 24 packages for $16.32

6. 2.5 L for $9.95

	National brand		Store brand	
$\dfrac{\text{cost}}{\text{number of units}}$	$= \dfrac{\$2.09}{567\ \text{grams}}$	$= \dfrac{209\ \text{cents}}{567\ \text{grams}}$	$\dfrac{\$1.69}{539\ \text{grams}}$	$= \dfrac{169\ \text{cents}}{539\ \text{grams}}$
		$= 0.37\ \text{cents/gram}$		$= 0.31\ \text{cents/gram}$

Thus the store brand is 0.37 – 0.31 or 0.06 cents per gram cheaper. ■

EXAMPLE 4

Will Rogers runs 400 meters in 35 seconds. His brother Gill runs 1500 meters in 129 seconds. Which runner is faster?

SOLUTION

To determine which runner is faster, we set up a ratio between the distance and the time. We get

Will	Gill
$\dfrac{400 \text{ meters}}{35 \text{ seconds}}$ = 11.43 meters/second	$\dfrac{1500 \text{ meters}}{129 \text{ seconds}}$ = 11.63 meters/second

Thus Gill is the faster runner. ▪

EXAMPLE 5

During a baseball season the ratio of the number of times that Daryl got a hit to the official number of times he was at bat is 4 : 11. If Daryl had 440 official times at bat that season, how many hits did Daryl get?

SOLUTION

The ratio 4 : 11 tells us that $\frac{4}{11}$ of Daryl's official times at bat resulted in a hit. Since Daryl was at bat 440 times, we know that $\frac{4}{11}$ of these times he got a hit. Thus Daryl got $\frac{4}{11} \times 440$ or 160 hits that season. ▪

Consider the ratio $\frac{3}{12}$ and the ratio $\frac{1}{4}$. We notice that $\frac{3}{12} = \frac{1}{4}$. The equation $\frac{3}{12} = \frac{1}{4}$ is called a proportion.

proportion

> **Definition 6.4**   A **proportion** is an equation stating that two ratios are equal.

In the previous example the proportion $\frac{3}{12} = \frac{1}{4}$ can also be written as 3 : 12 = 1 : 4. In both cases we read this as "3 is to 12 as 1 is to 4."

More generally, if we have the proportion $\frac{a}{b} = \frac{c}{d}$, then the first and

extremes

means

fourth terms are called the **extremes**, and the second and third terms are called the **means** of the proportion.

Notice that in the proportion 3 : 12 = 1 : 4, the product of the means

12×1 is equal to the product of the extreme 3×4. In both cases the answer is 12.

In Rule 6.1 we indicated that two rational numbers $\frac{a}{b}$ and $\frac{c}{d}$ are equal if when we cross-multiply

$$\frac{a}{b} \times \frac{c}{d}$$

we get $ad = bc$.

We can now state this in words as follows.

Formula 6.1   In the proportion $\frac{a}{b} = \frac{c}{d}$, the product of the means is equal to the product of the extremes: that is, $ad = bc$.

Let us apply Formula 6.1

EXAMPLE 6

Tell whether $\frac{2}{3} = \frac{10}{15}$ is a valid proportion.

SOLUTION

In the equation $\frac{2}{3} = \frac{10}{15}$ the product of the means (second and third terms) is 3×10 or 30. The product of the extremes (first and fourth terms) is 2×15 or 30. Since the answer is the same for both, we conclude that $\frac{2}{3} = \frac{10}{15}$ is a valid proportion.

EXAMPLE 7

Solve for x in the proportion $\dfrac{3}{5} = \dfrac{24}{x}$

SOLUTION

We apply Formula 6.1

$$\frac{3}{5} = \frac{24}{x}$$

$$3x = 24 \times 5$$

$$3x = 120$$

$$x = \frac{120}{3} \quad \text{(We divide both sides of the equation by 3.)}$$

$$x = 40$$

Problem-Solving Example

EXAMPLE 8

The real estate tax in Culver City in 1989 was $8.60 for every $100 of assessed value. If a house is assessed at $9000, what is the real estate tax?

SOLUTION

Understanding the Problem
We are told that the real estate tax rate is $8.60 for every $100 of assessed value and are asked to find the real estate tax for a house assessed at $9000.

A Plan to Solve the Problem
We can solve this problem by setting up a proportion as follows:

$$\frac{\text{Real estate tax}}{\text{Assessed value}} = \frac{\$8.60}{\$100} = \frac{\text{Real estate tax}}{\$9000}$$

Since we wish to find the real estate tax for a house assessed at $9000, let us call this quantity x. The proportion then becomes

$$\frac{8.60}{100} = \frac{x}{9000}$$

We must now solve for x. Applying Formula 6.1 gives

$$100x = 8.60 \times 9000$$

$$100x = 77400$$

$$x = \frac{77400}{100} \quad \text{(We divide both sides of the equation by 100.)}$$

$$x = 774$$

The real estate tax on a house assessed at $9000 is $774.

SOLUTION

Checking the solution
We can easily check our solution. The real estate tax is $8.60 for every $100 or $86 for every $1000 of assessed value. Thus the real estate tax for a house assessed at $9 \times \$1000$ or $9000 is $9 \times \$86$ or $774.   ▬

EXAMPLE 9

The United States is gradually converting from the English system to the metric system of measurement. In most states today the posted speed limit is 55 miles per hour. What will the posted speed limit be in kilometers per hou. when the conversion is completed? (Assume that 1 kilometer is approximately 0.62 miles.)

SOLUTION

We can write a proportion to compare kilometers to miles. Let $x =$ the number of kilometers in 55 miles. We then have

$$\frac{1 \text{ km}}{0.62 \text{ miles}} = \frac{x \text{ km}}{55 \text{ miles}}$$

We now apply Formula 6.1

$$0.62x = 1 \times 55$$
$$0.62x = 55$$

$$x = \frac{55}{0.62} \quad \text{(We divide both sides of the equation by 0.62)}$$

$$x = 88.71$$

Thus the posted speed limit will be 89 kilometers per hour.

EXERCISES FOR SECTION 6.3

Express each of the ratios given in Exercises 1–6 in simplest form.

1. 80 meters to 45 meters

2. 16 cm to 64 cm

3. $60 to $80

4. $6 to 50 cents

5. 14 ounces to 2 pounds $\frac{14}{32} = \frac{7}{16}$

6. 4 hours to 12 minutes

7. If 14 cars can be serviced by 7 mechanics in one day, how many cars can be serviced by 8 mechanics in one day?

8. Mark typed 1400 words in 35 minutes. Arlene typed 1200 words in 30 minutes. Who is the faster typist?

9. Howie replaced 3 of the 8 spark plugs in his car. What is the ratio of the number of spark plugs replaced to the number of spark plugs not replaced?

10. An obstetrician delivered 30 boys and 20 girls during the month of July. For every 3 boys delivered, how many girls were delivered?

11. In a supermarket a package containing 6 bars of soap sells for $1.39. At the same time, a package containing 10 bars of the same soap sells for $2.25. Which is the better buy?

12. Doug's monthly income is $1000. Doug spends this money on rent, food, education, entertainment and miscellaneous items in the ratio of $6 : 5 : 3 : 2 : 4$. How much does Doug spend on each item?

13. A painter needs 25 gallons of a paint mixture. This mixture is obtained by mixing white paint and blue paint in the ratio of $3 : 2$. How many gallons of each kind must the painter use?

14. In a magazine containing 192 pages the ratio of the number of pages devoted to advertisements to the number of pages devoted to articles is 13 to 3. How many pages of each are contained in the magazine?

15. In a certain bag of mixed fruit the ratio of the number of dried apricots to the number of dried apples is $8 : 7$. If the bag contains 300 pieces of fruit, how many of them are apricots?

In Exercises 16–21, tell whether the given ratios form a valid proportion.

16. $\dfrac{5}{4} = \dfrac{15}{12}$

17. $\dfrac{8}{7} = \dfrac{15}{14}$

18. $\dfrac{7}{8} = \dfrac{8}{7}$

19. $\dfrac{7}{1} = \dfrac{14}{2}$

20. $\dfrac{120}{15} = \dfrac{16}{2}$

21. $\dfrac{18}{4} = \dfrac{27}{6}$

Solve for x in each of the proportions given in Exercises 22–27.

22. $\dfrac{x}{15} = \dfrac{3}{5}$

23. $\dfrac{10}{3} = \dfrac{x}{12}$

24. $\dfrac{20}{3x} = \dfrac{30}{4.5}$

25. $\dfrac{18}{x} = \dfrac{12}{9}$

26. $\dfrac{2}{16} = \dfrac{2x}{40}$

27. $\dfrac{7}{x} = \dfrac{28}{16}$

PROBLEM-SOLVING EXERCISES

28. Refer back to Example 7. What is the real estate tax on a house that is assessed for $12,500?

29. If the posted speed limit on a highway is 40 miles per hour, what is the speed limit in kilometers per hour?

30. In a sporting-goods store, 7 bats cost $56. At the same rate, what is the cost of 12 bats?

31. Leo drove 300 miles while using 14.5 gallons of gas. Assuming the same driving conditions, how many gallons of gas are needed to drive 425 miles?

32. Three ounces of a certain food contain 95 calories. How many calories are contained in 7 ounces of the food?

33. Spencer owns 15 shares of stock of the Back Corp. He receives $4.95 in dividends. How much would he receive in dividends if he owned 25 shares of the stock?

34. Harley Smith made 234 photocopies of a poster and paid $14.04. At the same rate, what would 185 photocopies of the poster cost?

35. Gary stayed in the hospital for 8 days. The bill came to $1968. Assuming the same daily charges, what would be the cost of a 10-day stay at the hospital?

36. George drove 40 miles in 50 minutes. How many miles would he be able to drive in 80 minutes, if he drives at a constant rate?

37. On a map, $\frac{1}{4}$ inch represents 8 miles. If two cities are $4\frac{1}{2}$ inches apart on this map, what is the actual distance between them?

38. Sharon drove about 132 km on 11 liter of gasoline. She is planning a trip of 430 km. About how many liters of gasoline will she use?

Brain-Teaser Problems

**39. Dividing a number by 2 is the same as taking $\frac{1}{2}$ of the number. Do you agree? Explain your answer.

**40. At a certain factory, 5 auto mechanics can assemble 7 cars in 8 days. How long would it take 9 auto mechanics to assemble 10 cars, assuming that all work is done at the same rate?

6.4

EXPONENTS REVISITED

You will recall that when working with exponents, if x, m and n are natural numbers then we have the following properties.

PROPERTIES FOR EXPONENTS

Name	Property
1. Definition of exponent	1. $x^n = \underbrace{x \cdot x \cdot x \cdots x}_{n \text{ of them}}$
2. Multiplication rule	2. $x^m \cdot x^n = x^{m+n}$
3. Division rule	3. $x^m \div x^n = x^{m-n}$ (where $m > n$)
4. Zero exponent	4. $x^0 = 1$
5. Power of a power	5. $(x^m)^n = x^{mn}$

There is no reason to require that x be a natural number only. Thus, if x is any nonzero rational number, then the above properties also apply.

EXAMPLE 1

a) $\left(\dfrac{1}{2}\right)^5$ means $\left(\dfrac{1}{2}\right)\left(\dfrac{1}{2}\right)\left(\dfrac{1}{2}\right)\left(\dfrac{1}{2}\right)\left(\dfrac{1}{2}\right)$ or $\dfrac{1}{32}$

b) $\left(\dfrac{8}{11}\right)^3 \cdot \left(\dfrac{8}{11}\right)^4 = \left(\dfrac{8}{11} \cdot \dfrac{8}{11} \cdot \dfrac{8}{11}\right) \cdot \left(\dfrac{8}{11} \cdot \dfrac{8}{11} \cdot \dfrac{8}{11} \cdot \dfrac{8}{11}\right)$

$= \left(\dfrac{8}{11}\right)^{3+4} = \left(\dfrac{8}{11}\right)^7$

c) $\left(\dfrac{5}{7}\right)^5 \div \left(\dfrac{5}{7}\right)^3 = \left(\dfrac{5}{7}\right)^{5-3} = \left(\dfrac{5}{7}\right)^2$ or $\dfrac{25}{49}$

d) $\left(\dfrac{5}{7}\right)^0 = 1$

e) $\left[\left(\dfrac{5}{7}\right)^2\right]^3 = \left[\dfrac{5}{7} \cdot \dfrac{5}{7}\right]^3 = \left(\dfrac{5}{7} \cdot \dfrac{5}{7}\right)\left(\dfrac{5}{7} \cdot \dfrac{5}{7}\right)\left(\dfrac{5}{7} \cdot \dfrac{5}{7}\right) = \left(\dfrac{5}{7}\right)^{2 \cdot 3} = \left(\dfrac{5}{7}\right)^6$

Exponents can be negative integers also. We first define

$$x^{-n} \quad \text{as} \quad \dfrac{1}{x^n}$$

This can be deduced from the following. Suppose we apply the division rule to $\dfrac{x^3}{x^5}$. We would get $\dfrac{x^3}{x^5} = x^{3-5} = x^{-2}$. On the other hand, by the definition of exponents we know that

$$\dfrac{x^3}{x^5} = \dfrac{\cancel{x} \cdot \cancel{x} \cdot \cancel{x}}{\cancel{x} \cdot \cancel{x} \cdot \cancel{x} \cdot x \cdot x}$$

$$= \dfrac{1}{x \cdot x} \qquad \text{By cancellation}$$

$$= \dfrac{1}{x^2} \qquad \text{By definition of exponents}$$

Thus we define x^{-2} as $\dfrac{1}{x^2}$, or more generally that $x^{-n} = \dfrac{1}{x^n}$. Another way to explain this definition is as follows: The multiplication property says that $x^m \cdot x^n = x^{m+n}$ for all integral exponents. In particular, if $m = -n$, then the multiplication rule would say that $x^m \cdot x^n = x^{-n} \cdot x^n = x^{-n+n} = x^0 = 1$. Thus x^{-n} has to be the multiplicative inverse of x^n, or that $x^{-n} = \dfrac{1}{x^n}$.

EXAMPLE 2

a) $\left(\dfrac{2}{3}\right)^5\left(\dfrac{2}{3}\right)^{-3} = \left(\dfrac{2}{3}\right)^5 \cdot \dfrac{1}{\left(\dfrac{2}{3}\right)^3} = \dfrac{\left(\dfrac{2}{3}\right)^5}{\left(\dfrac{2}{3}\right)^3} = \dfrac{\left(\dfrac{2}{3}\right)^2\left(\dfrac{2}{3}\right)^3}{\left(\dfrac{2}{3}\right)^3} = \left(\dfrac{2}{3}\right)^2$

b) $\left(\dfrac{2}{3}\right)^{-5}\left(\dfrac{2}{3}\right)^3 = \left(\dfrac{2}{3}\right)^{-5+3} = \left(\dfrac{2}{3}\right)^{-2}$

Comment The properties of exponents presented above when x is a natural number can be extended and are valid when x is any rational number.

How would we evaluate $\left(\dfrac{2}{3}\right)^5$? By the definition of exponents we have

$$\left(\dfrac{2}{3}\right)^5 = \left(\dfrac{2}{3}\right)\left(\dfrac{2}{3}\right)\left(\dfrac{2}{3}\right)\left(\dfrac{2}{3}\right)\left(\dfrac{2}{3}\right)$$

Using the rule for multiplication of rational numbers, this equals

$$\dfrac{2 \cdot 2 \cdot 2 \cdot 2 \cdot 2}{3 \cdot 3 \cdot 3 \cdot 3 \cdot 3} \quad \text{or} \quad \dfrac{2^5}{3^5}$$

This last example suggests that for any nonzero rational number $\dfrac{x}{y}$ and any integer m, we have

$$\left(\dfrac{x}{y}\right)^m = \dfrac{x^m}{y^m} \quad \text{Power of quotient property}$$

Using this rule, and the definition of negative integers along with the rule for division of rational numbers (Rule 6.6), we have

$$\left(\dfrac{x}{y}\right)^{-m} = \dfrac{1}{\left(\dfrac{x}{y}\right)^m} = \dfrac{1}{\left(\dfrac{x^m}{y^m}\right)} = \dfrac{y^m}{x^m} = \left(\dfrac{y}{x}\right)^m$$

or that

$$\left(\dfrac{x}{y}\right)^{-m} = \dfrac{y^m}{x^m} \quad \text{Negative power of quotient property}$$

We illustrate all of the properties of rational numbers with exponents with another example.

EXAMPLE 3

Simplify each of the following:

a) $\left(\dfrac{3}{5}\right)^{4} \div \left(\dfrac{3}{5}\right)^{4}$ b) $\left(\dfrac{3}{5}\right)^{-6} \div \left(\dfrac{3}{5}\right)^{-4}$ c) $(x^{-2} + y^{-3})^{-1}$ d) $27^{3} \cdot 9^{-4}$

SOLUTION

a) We apply the quotient rule. We get

$$\left(\frac{3}{4}\right)^{4} \div \left(\frac{3}{4}\right)^{4} = \left(\frac{3}{4}\right)^{4-4} = \left(\frac{3}{4}\right)^{0} = 1$$

b) Again using the quotient rule, we have

$$\left(\frac{3}{5}\right)^{-6} \div \left(\frac{3}{5}\right)^{-4} = \left(\frac{3}{5}\right)^{-6-(-4)} = \left(\frac{3}{5}\right)^{-6+4} = \left(\frac{3}{5}\right)^{-2} \text{ or } \left(\frac{5}{3}\right)^{2} = \frac{25}{9}$$

c) Since we have negative exponents, we must first rewrite each rational number so that it has a positive exponent. We have

$$(x^{-2} + y^{-3})^{-1} = \left(\frac{1}{x^{2}} + \frac{1}{y^{3}}\right)^{-1} = \left(\frac{y^{3} + x^{2}}{x^{2}y^{3}}\right)^{-1} = \frac{x^{2}y^{3}}{y^{3} + x^{2}}$$

d) To evaluate expressions which have exponents, we must make sure that the bases are the same. (The properties given earlier assume this.) Thus we have

$$27^{3} = (27)^{3} = (3^{3})^{3} = 3^{9}$$

and

$$9^{-4} = (9)^{-4} = (3^{2})^{-4} = 3^{-8}$$

Therefore

$$27^{3} \cdot 9^{-4} = (3^{9}) \cdot (3^{-8}) = 3^{9+(-8)} = 3^{1} \quad \text{or} \quad 3 \qquad ▬$$

EXAMPLE 4

Using a calculator, evaluate $\left(\dfrac{3}{5}\right)^{-4}$

SOLUTION

In order to evaluate this on a calculator, we must first change $\frac{3}{5}$ into a decimal. To accomplish this, we enter 3 and then push the $\boxed{\div}$ button. Then we enter 5 and push the $\boxed{=}$ button. The display panel should show 0.6. Now we push the $\boxed{y^{x}}$ button. We then enter 4 and push the $\boxed{+/-}$ button. Finally, we push the $\boxed{=}$ button. Our final answer is 7.71604938.

EXERCISES FOR SECTION 6.4

1. Perform the indicated operations and express your answer in simplest form (with positive exponents).

a) $\left(\dfrac{1}{2}\right)^5 \cdot \left(\dfrac{1}{2}\right)^3$

b) $\left(\dfrac{2}{3}\right)^5 \div \left(\dfrac{2}{3}\right)^2$

c) $\left(\dfrac{1}{2}\right)^3 \cdot \left(\dfrac{2}{3}\right)^4$

d) $\left(\dfrac{5}{9}\right)^5 \div \left(\dfrac{5}{9}\right)^5$

e) $\left(\dfrac{5}{9}\right)^4 \div \left(\dfrac{5}{9}\right)^7$

f) $\left[\left(\dfrac{2}{3}\right)^4\right]^5$

g) $\left(\dfrac{5}{7}\right)^{-4} \div \left(\dfrac{7}{5}\right)^2$

h) $4^{-2} + 4^{-3}$

i) $3^{-2} + 2^{-3}$

j) $(2^{-4} + 4^{-2})^{-1}$

k) $8^{-2} \cdot 16^3$

l) $10^3 \div 5^2$

2. Solve each of the following for the value of the integer x.

a) $3^x = 27$

b) $3^x = \dfrac{1}{9}$

c) $\left(\dfrac{1}{3}\right)^x = 9$

3. For each of the following pairs of fractions select the larger fraction.

a) $\left(\dfrac{1}{3}\right)^5$ or $\left(\dfrac{1}{3}\right)^6$

b) $\left(\dfrac{2}{3}\right)^4$ or $\left(\dfrac{2}{3}\right)^2$

c) $\left(\dfrac{5}{9}\right)^{10}$ or $\left(\dfrac{4}{5}\right)^{10}$

TYPICAL CLASSROOM QUESTIONS

1. The fundamental law of fractions says that the value of a fraction does not change if its numerator and denominator are multiplied by the same nonzero number. If we add the same nonzero number to both the numerator and denominator of a fraction, will the resulting fraction be equivalent to the original fraction? Explain your answer.

2. What, if anything, is wrong, with each of the following?

a) $\dfrac{5}{8} = \dfrac{5 \cdot 0}{8 \cdot 0} = 0$ and $\dfrac{9}{10} = \dfrac{9 \cdot 0}{10 \cdot 0} = 0$

since $\dfrac{5}{8}$ and $\dfrac{9}{10}$ are both equal to 0, they are equal to each other, that is, $\dfrac{5}{8} = \dfrac{9}{10}$.

b) $3 = \dfrac{6+3}{3} = \dfrac{6}{3} + 3 = 2 + 3 = 5$

c) $2 = \dfrac{16}{8} = \dfrac{16}{4+4} = \dfrac{16}{4} + \dfrac{16}{4} = 4 + 4 = 8$

3. Is it ever true that $\dfrac{1}{a} + \dfrac{1}{b} = \dfrac{1}{a+b}$? Explain your answer.

4. A student reduced $\dfrac{16}{64} = \dfrac{1}{4}$ by canceling the 6's. Is there anything wrong?

STUDY GUIDE

The following is a chapter outline in capsule form. You should now be able to demonstrate your knowledge of the ideas mentioned by giving definitions, descriptions, or specific examples. Page references are given in parentheses.

Rational numbers are numbers that can be written in the form $\frac{a}{b}$ where $b \neq 0$ and a and b are integers. (p. 311)

Rational numbers can be used to express part of a whole, to solve algebraic equations, and also to form a ratio. (p. 311)

In the rational number $\frac{a}{b}$, the number on top, a, is called the **numerator** and the number on the bottom, b, is called the **denominator**. (p. 311)

Two fractions that name the same part of a set or the same part of a region are called **equivalent fractions**. (p. 312)

For any rational number $\frac{a}{b}$ and any nonzero integer c, the **fundamental law of fractions** states that $\frac{a}{b} = \frac{ac}{bc}$ ($b \neq 0$). (p. 313)

Two rational numbers $\frac{a}{b}$ and $\frac{c}{d}$ are **equal** if and only if $ad = bc$. (p. 313)

By canceling, we can generate fractions equal to a given fraction. (p. 314)

A fraction $\frac{a}{b}$ is in its **lowest terms** when the greatest common factor of the numerator and denominator is 1. We then say that a and b are **relatively prime.** (p. 315)

If the denominators of two fractions are the same, then we can **compare** (or **order**) the fractions by comparing the numerators. (p. 316)

**Operations on
Rationally Numbers**

1. $\frac{a}{b} + \frac{c}{b} = \frac{a+c}{b}$ Addition of two fractions when the denominators are the same. (Rule 6.2 on p. 316)

2. $\frac{a}{b} - \frac{c}{b} = \frac{a-c}{b}$ Subtraction of two fractions when denominators are the same. (Rule 6.3 on p. 316)

3. $\frac{a}{b} + \frac{c}{d} = \frac{ad+bc}{bd}$ Addition of two fractions when denominators are different. (Rule 6.4 on p. 317)

4. $\frac{a}{b} \cdot \frac{c}{d} = \frac{ac}{bd}$ Multiplication of two fractions. (Rule 6.5 on p. 323)

5. $\frac{a}{b} \div \frac{c}{d} = \frac{a}{b} \cdot \frac{d}{c} = \frac{ad}{bc}$ b, c, and $d \neq 0$ Division of two fractions. (Rule 6.6 on p. 324)

The sum of an integer and a rational number is called a **mixed number**. (p. 319)

An **improper fraction** is a fraction whose numerator is greater than its denominator. To change an improper fraction to a mixed number, divide the numerator by the denominator, and then write the quotient as the whole-number part and the remainder over the divisor as the fraction part. (p. 319).

The number 1 is the **identity for multiplication** of rational numbers. (p. 325)

The number 0 is the **identity for addition** of rational numbers. (p. 325)

For any nonzero rational number $\frac{a}{b}$ there exists a unique rational number $\frac{b}{a}$ called the **multiplicative inverse**, or **reciprocal** of $\frac{a}{b}$, such that $\frac{a}{b} \cdot \frac{b}{a} = \frac{b}{a} \cdot \frac{a}{b} = 1$. (p. 326)

For any nonzero rational number $\frac{a}{b}$, the **multiplication property of zero** states that $\frac{a}{b} \cdot 0 = 0 \cdot \frac{a}{b} = 0$. (p. 326)

The **denseness property** states that between any two rational numbers there exists another rational number. (p. 326)

We can **order** the rational numbers by using

a) the common positive denominator approach,

b) the number line approach, or

c) the addition approach. (p. 327-328)

A **ratio** of one number to another number is the quotient of the first number divided by the second number. The ratio of a to b is written as $\frac{a}{b}$ or $a \div b$ or $a : b$. The numbers a and b are called the **terms** of the ratio. (p. 333)

By writing ratios in simplest form, **unit pricing** allows us to compare costs and to get the best buy. (p. 333)

A **proportion** is an equation stating that two ratios are equal. (p. 336)

In the proportion $a : b = c : d$, the first and fourth terms are called the **extremes** and second and third terms are called the **means** of the proportion. (p. 336)

In a proportion, the product of the means is equal to the product of the extremes. Symbolically if $\frac{a}{b} = \frac{c}{d}$, then $ad = bc$. (p. 337)

KEYS TERMS

The following list presents the key terms introduced in this chapter.

6.1 rational number
numerator
denominator
ratio
equivalent fractions
fundamental law of fractions
cancelling
reducing to lowest terms
greatest common factor
relatively prime
comparing (ordering) fractions
mixed number
improper fraction

6.2 identity for multiplication
identity for addition
multiplicative inverse
reciprocal
multiplication property of zero
denseness property
ordering rational numbers
common-positive-denominator approach
number-line approach
addition approach for ordering rational numbers

FORMULAS TO REMEMBER

The following list summarizes the various properties for exponents involving rational numbers.

Properties for Exponents

Definition of exponents: $x^n = \underbrace{x \cdot x \cdots x}_{n \text{ of them}}$ n is an integer and x is any non-zero rational number.

Multiplication rule $x^m \cdot x^n = x^{m+n}$
Division rule $x^m \div x^n = x^{m-n}$

Negative exponent $x^{-n} = \dfrac{1}{x^n}$ where $x \neq 0$

Power of a power $\left(x^m\right)^n = x^{mn}$

Power of a quotient $\left(\dfrac{x}{y}\right)^m = \dfrac{x^m}{y^m}$

Negative property $\left(\dfrac{x}{y}\right)^{-m} = \dfrac{y^m}{x^m}$

Zero exponent $x^0 = 1$

Properties of Rational Numbers

Let $\dfrac{a}{b}, \dfrac{c}{d}$ and $\dfrac{e}{f}$ be any rational numbers.

Transitive property of greater than:

$$\text{If } \frac{a}{b} > \frac{c}{d} \text{ and } \frac{c}{d} > \frac{e}{f}, \text{ then } \frac{a}{b} > \frac{e}{f}$$

Addition Property of Greater Than:

$$\text{If } \frac{a}{b} > \frac{c}{d}, \text{ then } \frac{a}{b} + \frac{e}{f} > \frac{c}{d} + \frac{e}{f}$$

Multiplication Property of Greater Than Involving a Positive Number:

$$\text{If } \frac{a}{b} > \frac{c}{d} \text{ and } \frac{e}{f} > 0, \text{ then } \left(\frac{a}{b}\right)\left(\frac{e}{f}\right) > \left(\frac{c}{d}\right)\left(\frac{e}{f}\right)$$

Multiplication Property of Greater Than Involving a Negative Number:

$$\text{If } \frac{a}{b} > \frac{c}{d} \text{ and } \frac{e}{f} < 0, \text{ then } \left(\frac{a}{b}\right)\left(\frac{e}{f}\right) < \left(\frac{c}{d}\right)\left(\frac{e}{f}\right)$$

CHAPTER REVIEW EXERCISES

1. Add $2\frac{3}{4} + 5\frac{5}{9}$

2. Multiply $\left(+5\frac{2}{3}\right)\left(-2\frac{7}{8}\right)$

3. Divide: $\left(\frac{-18}{19}\right) \div \left(\frac{-7}{6}\right)$

4. Divide: $\left(-12\frac{1}{4}\right) \div \left(-2\frac{3}{5}\right)$

5. Solve for x: $\frac{5}{7}x = 8$

6. Evaluate: $\left(\dfrac{8}{27}\right)^{-2}$

7. Solve for x: $2\frac{5}{9}x = 8\frac{3}{4}$

8. Solve for x: $\left(1\frac{5}{7} + 2\frac{2}{9}\right)x = 3\frac{1}{4}$

9. Which of the following pairs of rational numbers are equal?

    a) $\frac{4}{5}, \frac{20}{25}$ **b)** $\frac{5}{6}, \frac{2}{3}$ **c)** $\frac{8}{12}, \frac{3}{5}$ **d)** $4\frac{1}{4}, 3\frac{5}{4}$

10. A share of stock rose $1\frac{5}{8}$ of a point on Monday, dropped $2\frac{1}{3}$ points on Tuesday, rose $1\frac{5}{7}$ points on Wednesday and dropped $1\frac{1}{4}$ points on Thursday. What was the net change over the 4-day period?

11. What is the next fraction or mixed number in the following?

$$8\tfrac{1}{4}, \ 6\tfrac{3}{4}, \ 5\tfrac{1}{4}, \ \ldots$$

12. Combine: $\dfrac{3}{5x} + \dfrac{1}{x^2}$

13. Simplify: $\left[\left(\dfrac{1}{2}\right)^3 \left(\dfrac{4}{3}\right)^5\right]^{-2}$

14. Evaluate: $16^2 \cdot 2^{-5}$

15. Simplify: $(x^{-2} + y^{-2})^{-2}$

16. Is the following a valid proportion? $\frac{9}{1} = \frac{81}{2}$

17. Three ounces of a certain chemical cost \$1.95. At the same rate, how much would 7 ounces of the chemical cost?

18. In the following proportion, solve for x: $\dfrac{8}{3x} = \dfrac{9}{216}$.

19. A certain recipe calls for flour and oil in the ratio of $3\frac{1}{4}$ cups of flour to $1\frac{1}{3}$ cups of oil. How much oil will be needed when 14 cups of flour are used?

20. The real estate tax rate on a residence in a certain city is $9.40 for every $100 of assessed value. If a house is assessed at $12,500, what is the real estate tax?

21. Bill ran 420 meters in 29 seconds. His wife Joan ran 280 meters in 19 seconds. Which runner is faster?

22. In a supermarket, a jar of apple juice containing 28 ounces sells for 69 cents. At the same time, another jar of apple juice, containing 18 ounces, sells for 42 cents. Which is a better buy?

23. If 18 cars can be serviced by 5 mechanics in 3 days, how many cars can be serviced by 4 mechanics in 5 days?

24. Mark can type 1200 words in 20 minutes. At the same rate, how long will it take him to type 1400 words?

25. Evaluate $\left| \frac{2}{3} - \frac{5}{7} \right|$

26. Order the following rational numbers: $\frac{5}{8}, \frac{2}{3}, \frac{6}{11}$

27. Solve for x: $\frac{5}{9} x \geq \frac{7}{15}$

28. Solve for x: $\frac{-2}{7} x + 5 \leq 15$

29. Solve for x: $\frac{-5}{11} (x - 3) \geq \frac{7}{9} (x - 5)$

30. Solve for x: $\frac{4}{7} x + \frac{3}{8} \geq \frac{-2}{5} \left(\frac{3}{4} x + \frac{5}{9} \right)$

SUGGESTED FURTHER READING

Etline, J., "A Uniform Approach to Fractions," in *The Arithmetic Teacher* **32** (March 1985), 42–43.

Feinberg, M., "Is It Necessary to Invest?" in *The Arithmetic Teacher* **27** (January 1980), 50–52.

Hollis, L., "Teaching Rational Numbers—Primary Grades," in *The Arithmetic Teacher* **31** (February 1984), 36–39.

Kiernen, T., "One Point of View: Helping Children Understand Rational Numbers," in *The Arithmetic Teacher* **31** (February 1984), 3.

Lester, F., "Teacher Education: Preparing Teachers to Teach Rational Numbers," in *The Arithmetic Teacher* **31** (February 1984), 54–56.

Scott, W., "Fractions Taught by Folding Paper Strips," in *The Arithmetic Teacher* **28** (January 1981), 18–21.

Skypek, D., "Special Characteristics of Rational Numbers," in *The Arithmetic Teacher* **31** (February 1984), 10–12.

Sweetland, R., "Understanding Multiplication of Fractions," in *The Arithmetic Teacher* **32** (September 1984), 48–52.

Trafton, P., and J.S. Zawojewski, "Teaching Rational Number Division: A Special Problem," in *The Arithmetic Teacher* **31** (February 1984), 20–22.

CHAPTER 7

Decimals and the Real Numbers

NCTM GUIDELINES

In its March 1989 *Curriculum and Evaluation Standards for School Mathematics* (p. 87), The National Council of Teachers of Mathematics recommends that the mathematics curriculum should include decimals and real numbers so that students can

❑ understand, represent, and use numbers in a variety of equivalent forms (fraction, decimal, percent, exponential, and scientific) in real-world and mathematical problem illustrations,

❑ develop number sense for decimals,

❑ understand and apply ratios, proportions, and percents in a wide variety of situations,

❑ investigate relationships among fractions, decimals, and percents.

The report further states that to provide students with a lasting sense of number and number relationships, students should learn to identify equivalent forms of a number and understand why a particular representation is useful in a given setting. It is for this reason that in this chapter we will discuss how we convert decimals to fractions and vice versa, percents, the operations that we can perform with decimals, and numerous applications of this information. Of course, this will lead to a discussion of the real number system.

Introduction

Let us look in on Evelyn, who is analyzing the bills she just received in the mail. Among these are

> her life insurance premium bill,
> her mortgage payment bill,
> her credit card bill, on which a new revolving interest charge appears, and her real estate tax bill announcing that the assessed value of her house has been increased by 8%.

On the way to the bank to withdraw the interest from her savings account, Evelyn stops off at a local supermarket to buy food. With her calculator in hand, she is able to determine the unit costs of various items so that she gets the most for her money. Most of her computations invariably will involve decimals. The word **decimal** is derived from the Latin word *decem,* meaning ten.

decimal

decimal point

If Evelyn determines that the unit cost of an item is $2.43, then the dot in $2.43 is the **decimal point**. It separates the integer part of the number (which is to the left of the decimal point) from the other numbers that are to the right of it. The latter represent the sum of rational numbers whose numerator are the given digits and whose denominators are successive powers of 10, that is 10^1, 10^2. . . . (See the discussion given earlier in Section 3.8.) Thus the number 2.43 represents

$$2 + \frac{4}{10^1} + \frac{3}{10^2} \quad \text{or} \quad 2\frac{43}{100}$$

Similarly, 54.3678 represents

$$54 + \frac{3}{10^1} + \frac{6}{10^2} + \frac{7}{10^3} + \frac{8}{10^4} \quad \text{or} \quad 54\frac{3678}{10000}$$

When discussing interest, whether you are interested in obtaining a loan for your college tuition or need to make a down payment on your car, a knowledge of percents and interest calculations is vital. In such computations, decimals play an ever-increasing role. In this chapter we will discuss rules for working with and applying decimals.

7.1

OPERATIONS WITH DECIMALS: PERCENTS

Decimals

We know that the rational number $\frac{1}{2}$ can be written as 0.5 in **decimal form.** Similarly, 0.3333. . . is the decimal representation of the rational number $\frac{1}{3}$. The three dots indicate that there are infinitely many 3's following. Here the 3 forms a pattern that repeats forever. More generally,

decimal form

HISTORICAL NOTE

Interest on money borrowed has had an unusual and often tainted history. Over the years, scoundrels have charged enormous interest rates for the use of their money. There also have been "legitimate businesses that purposely disguised the true amount or percentage of interest charged. An interest charge of 6% may have been an actual rate of 18%.

In 1969 the U.S. Congress passed the Truth in Lending Law for the benefit of consumers who use credit. Under the provisions of the law, full disclosure must be made of any interest charged (finance charges) and of the method used to calculate the interest. Interest must be expressed as an annual percentage rate on the monthly statement received. Although these actual charges vary from state to state, great progress has been made in making the ideas of interest understandable by the everyday person. It should be noted, however, that the Truth in Lending Law is a consumer protection act and does not apply to business loans.

a decimal is a number written with a **decimal point**, such as 67.32, 8.1245, 0.5, or 0.33333. . . . Each digit to the right or left of the decimal point has a place value as shown below:

| thousands | hundreds | tens | ones | · | tenths | hundredths | thousandths |

Thus the number 563.482 is read as five hundred sixty-three and four hundred eight-two thousandths, and the number 3.21 is read as three and twenty-one hundredths.

The decimal 0.5 is called a **terminating** decimal, since it ends after a specific number of places.

The decimal 0.3333. . . is called a **repeating** decimal. It does not end after a specific number of places. The same number repeats itself endlessly.

The decimal 0.434343. . . is also a repeating decimal. In this case the repeating pattern consists of the two numbers 43, which repeat themselves endlessly.

terminating decimal

repeating decimal

nonterminating and
nonrepeating decimal

> **Definition 7.1**   A **terminating decimal** is one that ends after a specific number of places. A **repeating decimal** is one in which (after a certain point) the same pattern of numbers repeats itself endlessly. A **nonterminating and nonrepeating decimal** is one that continues endlessly without the same group of numbers reappearing again in the same pattern.

EXAMPLE 1

0.25 is a terminating decimal.
0.76914 is a terminating decimal.
0.484848. . . is a repeating decimal.

0.592592. . . is a repeating decimal.
0.1434343. . . is a repeating decimal.
0.12345678910111213. . . is a nonterminating and nonrepeating decimal.
(What would the next few places be?)
0.43794162. . . (where the numbers are chosen at random) is a nonterminating and nonrepeating decimal.

Often when dealing with numbers, we find it necessary to round. For example, if you live on the East Coast and your sister lives on the West Coast, 3003 miles away, you would probably say that she lives 3000 miles away. In this case you rounded 3003 to 3000. The same is true for decimals. We often round to the nearest tenth, hundredth, thousandth, etc., as specified. To round decimals, we use the following rule.

rounding decimals

Rule 7.1—Rounding Decimals

1. Underline the digit that appears in the position to which the number is to be rounded.
2. Examine the first digit to the right of the underlined position.
   a) If the digit is 0, 1, 2, 3, or 4, replace all digits to the right of the underlined position by zeros.
   b) If the digit is 5, 6, 7, 8, or 9, add 1 to the digit in the underlined position and replace all digits to the right of the underlined position by zeros.
3. If any of these zeros (from step 2) are to the right of the decimal point, omit them.

Let us see how this rule is used.

EXAMPLE 2

SOLUTION

a) Round 61.379 to the nearest hundredth.

We underline the digit that appears in the position to which the number is to be rounded.

$$61.3\underline{7}9$$

Since the digit to the right of the underlined position is 5 or more, we add 1 to the digit in the underlined position. Thus 61.379 rounded to the nearest hundredth is 61.38.

b) 0.0792 rounded to the nearest thousandth is 0.079

c) 36.746 rounded to the nearest whole number is 37

It can be shown that every rational number can be written as either a terminating decimal or a repeating decimal. It is also true that repeating decimals and terminating decimals represent rational numbers.

To change a rational number to a decimal, simply divide the denominator of the fraction into the numerator.

EXAMPLE 3

a) The fraction $\frac{3}{5}$ can be converted to decimal form by the following procedure. We divide 5 into 3, getting

$$\begin{array}{r} 0.6 \\ 5\overline{)3.0} \\ 3.0 \\ \hline \end{array}$$

Therefore $\frac{3}{5} = 0.6$

b) The fraction $\frac{1}{7}$ can be converted to decimal form by dividing 7 into 1:

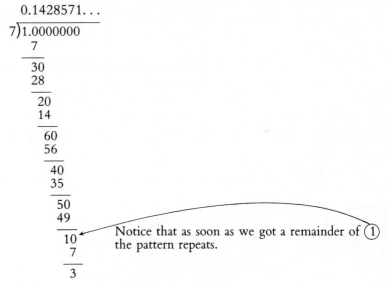

$$\begin{array}{r} 0.1428571\ldots \\ 7\overline{)1.0000000} \\ 7 \\ \hline 30 \\ 28 \\ \hline 20 \\ 14 \\ \hline 60 \\ 56 \\ \hline 40 \\ 35 \\ \hline 50 \\ 49 \\ \hline 10 \\ 7 \\ \hline 3 \end{array}$$

Notice that as soon as we got a remainder of ① the pattern repeats.

Thus, $\frac{1}{7} = 0.1428571\ldots$ is a repeating decimal.

Similarly, we can convert terminating decimals to rational numbers.

EXAMPLE 4

SOLUTION

a) Convert 0.25 to a rational number.

The decimal 0.25 stands for $\frac{25}{100}$ or $\frac{1}{4}$

b) Convert 3.45 to a rational number.

SOLUTION

3.45 means $3\frac{45}{100}$ or

$$3 + \frac{45}{100} = \frac{300}{100} + \frac{45}{100} = \frac{345}{100}$$

Of course, this reduces to $\frac{69}{20}$

c) Convert 0.0059 to a rational number.

SOLUTION

0.0059 means $\frac{59}{10,000}$

operations with decimals

Decimals can be added and subtracted in much the same way that we add and subtract whole numbers. The only exception is that we require that the decimal points be aligned. For example, to add 16.38 with 7.581 and 9.1, we first align the decimal points as shown:

$$
\begin{array}{r}
16.38 \\
7.581 \\
9.1 \\
\hline
33.061
\end{array}
$$

Most people prefer to add additional zeros to the right so that all the numbers contain the same number of decimal places. Thus the above problem could be rewritten as

$$
\begin{array}{r}
16.380 \quad \leftarrow 1 \text{ zero added} \\
7.581 \\
9.100 \quad \leftarrow 2 \text{ zeros added} \\
\hline
33.061
\end{array}
$$

EXAMPLE 5

SOLUTION

a) Subtract 3.32 from 8.761

We first rewrite the problem with the decimals lined up and zeros added. We get

$$
\begin{array}{r}
8.761 \\
-3.320 \quad \leftarrow 1 \text{ zero added} \\
\hline
5.441
\end{array}
$$

b) Subtract 3.946 from 5

SOLUTION

We have

$$
\begin{array}{r}
5.000 \quad \leftarrow 3 \text{ zeros added} \\
-3.946 \\
\hline
1.054
\end{array}
$$

Multiplying decimals is very much like multiplying whole numbers. *We simply multiply the numbers as if they were whole numbers and then locate the decimal point in the answer by **adding** the number of decimal places in each number being multiplied.*

EXAMPLE 6

a) Multiply 1.073 by 68.21

SOLUTION

$$
\begin{array}{r}
1.073 \leftarrow 3 \text{ decimal places} \\
\times\, 68.21 \leftarrow 2 \text{ decimal places} \\
\hline
1073 \\
2146 \\
8584 \\
6438 \\
\hline
73.18933 \leftarrow 3 + 2 = 5 \text{ decimal places}
\end{array}
$$

b) Multiply 4.1 by 0.0029

SOLUTION

$$
\begin{array}{r}
4.1 \leftarrow 1 \text{ decimal place} \\
\times\, 0.0029 \leftarrow 4 \text{ decimal places} \\
\hline
369 \\
82 \\
\hline
0.01189 \leftarrow 1 + 4 = 5 \text{ decimal places}
\end{array}
$$

Comment   In the preceding example it was necessary to place a zero to the left of one so that the decimal point could be placed in the correct position.

Division involving decimals is similar to division involving whole numbers. We just have to be sure that we are dividing by a whole number.

EXAMPLE 7

Divide 8.05 by 2.3

SOLUTION

If we rewrite, we have $\dfrac{8.05}{2.3}$. We first move the decimal one place to the right in the numerator and the denominator as shown:

$$
\frac{8.05}{2.3} = \frac{80.5}{23}
$$

(This is actually accomplished by multiplying both the numerator and denominator by 10.) Now that the decimal point in the denominator has been repositioned, we can divide as usual. We have

$$
\begin{array}{r}
3.5 \\
23{\overline{\smash{\big)}\,80.5}} \\
\underline{69} \\
115 \\
\underline{115} \\
00
\end{array}
$$

The decimal point in the answer is placed straight above where it was in the dividend. Thus 8.05 divided by 2.3 is 3.5.

Although the Hindu-Arabic numeration system (as discussed in Chapter 3) was developed much earlier, the first formal rules concerning decimals were given by Simon Stevin (1548–1620). In his book *La Disme,* which was published in 1584, Stevin presented complete rules for performing computations with decimals.

Percents

We often read newspaper articles such as the one shown below or are involved in discussions in which the word "percent" is used. Actually, the word is derived from the Latin word *per centum* meaning "per hundred." A **percent** can be considered as the ratio of a number to 100. For example, 9%, which means $\frac{9}{100}$, is the ratio of 9 to 100. Similarly, 5.5% means $\frac{5.5}{100}$, which is the ratio of 5.5 to 100. Also, $x\%$ means $\frac{x}{100}$.

percent

Higher Phone Bills

DOVER: The Public Service Commission yesterday authorized the telephone company to raise its rates by 3%. This represents the third increase in less than 5 years. Last year the telephone company raised its rates by 5.5%.

Business News, August 5, 1989

Percents are usually written with the percent symbol, as in the above examples. However, since they are often written in fraction form (where the denominator is 100) or in decimal form, let us pause for a moment to indicate how we change fractions to percents and vice versa.

EXAMPLE 8

Change $\frac{3}{5}$ to a percent.

SOLUTION

Since percent means the ratio of a number to 100, we can change $\frac{3}{5}$ to a percent by setting up the following proportion:

$$\frac{3}{5} = \frac{x}{100} \quad \text{(This is a proportion because it consists of two equal ratios.)}$$

$$5x = 300 \quad \text{(In a proportion the product of the means equals the product of the extremes.)}$$

$$x = \frac{300}{5} \quad \text{(We divide both sides of the equation by 5.)}$$

$$x = 60$$

Thus $\frac{3}{5} = \frac{60}{100}$ or 60%.

We can also change $\frac{3}{5}$ to a percent by dividing 5 (the denominator) into 3 (the numerator), then multiplying the quotient by 100 and adding a percent symbol. Thus in our case we get

$$\frac{3}{5} = 0.6 \quad \text{(First we divide 5 into 3.)}$$

$$0.6 \times 100 = 60 \quad \text{(We multiply the quotient by 100.)}$$

Therefore $\frac{3}{5} = 60\%$. We add the percent symbol.

Comment   If you are using a calculator, the second method of changing a fraction to a percent is much easier.

EXAMPLE 9

Convert $\frac{1}{3}$ to a percent.

SOLUTION

We first change $\frac{1}{3}$ from a fraction into a decimal. What we get is $\frac{1}{3} = 0.3333\ldots$, a nonterminating but repeating decimal. Now we multiply by 100 and add the percent symbol. We get $\frac{1}{3} = 33.33\%$. You will notice that we have rounded our answer to 2 decimal places. In the remainder of this section we will *round* all our answers to 2 decimal places.

If a number is already written in decimal form, then we change it to a percent by multiplying by 100 and then adding the percent symbol. Since multiplication by 100 is equivalent to moving the decimal point two places to the right, we can change a number from decimal form to a percent form very quickly by moving the decimal point two places to the right and then adding the percent symbol.

> Consider the clipping on the top of the next page from the side panel of a popular brand of cereal. You will notice the use of percentages and percents. How do we interpret percents?

> # Percentages of U.S. Recommended Daily Allowances (U.S. RDA)
>
> | | | |
> |---|---|---|
> | Protein | 2% | 8% |
> | Vitamin A | 25% | 30% |
> | Vitamin C | * | * |
> | Thiamine | 25% | 30% |
> | Riboflavin | 25% | 35% |
> | Niacin | 25% | 25% |
> | Calcium | * | 15% |
> | Iron | 15% | 15% |
> | Vitamin D | 10% | 25% |
> | Vitamin B_6 | 25% | 30% |
> | Folic Acid | 25% | 25% |
> | Vitamin B_{12} | 25% | 30% |
> | Phosphorus | 2% | 15% |
> | Magnesium | 2% | 6% |
> | Zinc | 10% | 15% |
> | Copper | 2% | 2% |
>
> *Contains less than 2% of the U.S. RDA of these nutrients*

EXAMPLE 10

SOLUTION

Change 0.792 to a percent.

We can change 0.792 to a percent by first multiplying it by 100. Then we add the percent symbol. Thus $0.792 \times 100 = 79.2\%$.

Alternatively, we move the decimal point in 0.792 two places to the right and add the percent symbol as shown:

$$0.792 = 79.2\%$$

converting percents to decimals

Finally, to convert a number written with a percent symbol to a decimal equivalent, we drop the percent symbol and divide the number by 100. This is really an application of the definition of percent, which means the ratio of a number to 100.

EXAMPLE 11

SOLUTION

Convert 94% to a decimal.

To convert 94% to a decimal, we drop the percent symbol and then divide the number by 100. We get

$$94\% = \frac{94}{100} = 0.94$$

Thus $94\% = 0.94$

Comment   Since division by 100 is equivalent to moving the decimal point two places to the left, we can change a number from percent form to decimal form very quickly by moving the decimal point two places to the left.

EXAMPLE 12

Many banks pay $5\frac{1}{4}\%$ interest on savings accounts. Express this percent as a decimal.

SOLUTION

$5\frac{1}{4}\%$ is the same as 5.25% since $\frac{1}{4} = 0.25$. Then we move the decimal point two places to the left and drop the percent symbol. Thus 5.25% = 0.0525.

Notice that we have to add an extra zero. Why?   ▅

EXAMPLE 13

Of the 780 graduates of Stoneyville College receiving their bachelor's degree this year, 663 said that they would continue their education and go on to the master's degree. What percent of the graduates will continue their education?

SOLUTION

The percent of the graduates who will continue their education is the ratio of the number who will continue to the total number of graduates. Thus we divide the number who will continue by the total number of graduates and multiply the result by 100. At the end we add a percent symbol. In our case we get

$$\frac{663}{780} \times 100 = 0.85 \times 100 = 85\%$$

Therefore 85% of the graduates will continue their education.   ▅

EXAMPLE 14

In the previous example, 40% of the graduates have a grade point average (GPA) above 3.3. How many students have a GPA above 3.3?

SOLUTION

We first write 40% in decimal form as

$$40\% = \frac{40}{100} = 0.40$$

Since there are 780 graduates, 40% of whom had a GPA above 3.3, this means that there are 780×0.40 or 312 students with a GPA above 3.3.   ▅

EXAMPLE 15

Vicky purchased a new car for $7850. She made a down payment of 14% of the price of the car when she bought it. How much was her down payment?

SOLUTION

We first write 14% in decimal form as

$$14\% = \frac{14}{100} = 0.14$$

Since the down payment was 14%, this means that it was

$$0.14 \times 7850 \text{ or } \$1099$$

EXAMPLE 16

Mr. Jaskel, who earns $300 per week in wages, has just been informed by his boss that his salary will be increased to $375. Find the percent of increase in his salary.

SOLUTION

percent increase

To determine the **percent increase** in his salary, we first find the actual increase. We then divide this by the original salary. Finally, we multiply our answer by 100 and add the percent symbol. Since Mr. Jaskel's salary went from $300 to $375, his actual increase was $75. His original salary was $300. Thus the percent increase is

$$\frac{375 - 300}{300} \times 100 = \frac{75}{300} \times 100$$
$$= 0.25 \times 100$$
$$= 25\%$$

Often when working with decimals or percents, one wishes to estimate an answer. This can be done by rounding off as can be seen from the accompanying student page from *Addison-Wesley Mathematics,* 1987, Grade 7, p. 129, shown on the facing page.

Problem-Solving Example

EXAMPLE 17

An electronics store advertised a VCR at a 10% discount, for a savings of $40. A month later, the store advertised the same VCR at 35% off the original price. What is the current selling price of the VCR?

SOLUTION

Understanding the Problem

We are told that when the VCR was discounted 10%, then the customer saved $40. We can use this information to determine the original selling price. Then we can find the current selling price.

A Plan to Solve the Problem

As stated earlier, a good strategy in solving any verbal problem is to write an equation. Thus, let x = the original selling price. Since 10% of x

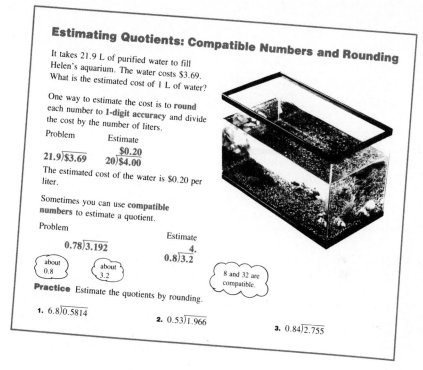

Estimating Quotients: Compatible Numbers and Rounding

It takes 21.9 L of purified water to fill Helen's aquarium. The water costs $3.69. What is the estimated cost of 1 L of water?

One way to estimate the cost is to **round** each number to **1-digit accuracy** and divide the cost by the number of liters.

Problem   Estimate

$$21.9\overline{)\$3.69} \qquad \frac{\$0.20}{20\overline{)\$4.00}}$$

The estimated cost of the water is $0.20 per liter.

Sometimes you can use **compatible numbers** to estimate a quotient.

Problem   Estimate

$$0.78\overline{)3.192} \qquad \frac{4.}{0.8\overline{)3.2}}$$

about 0.8   about 3.2   8 and 32 are compatible.

Practice Estimate the quotients by rounding.

1. $6.8\overline{)0.5814}$ **2.** $0.53\overline{)1.966}$ **3.** $0.84\overline{)2.755}$

amounts to $40, we have

$$10\% \cdot x = 40$$
$$0.10x = 40$$

or that

$$x = 400$$

Thus the VCR originally sold for $400. To find the amount of the current discount, we must find 35% of $400. We have $0.35 \times 400 = \$140$. Thus the current selling price of the VCR is $400 – $140, or $260.

Checking the solution

We can easily check our solution as follows: If a 10% discount off the original price of the VCR amounts to $40, then a 35% discount should amount to 3.5 times 40, or $140. This savings is then subtracted from the original price to obtain $260. ▪

Often we must determine whether one decimal number is greater than or less than another number. This can easily be done if both numbers are arranged so that both decimal points are lined up. The numbers can then be compared in much the same way that we compare integers. This can be seen on the following page from *Addison-Wesley Mathematics*, 1987, Grade 5, p. 82.

Comparing and Ordering Decimals

Sandra asked this trivia question about baseball history: "Who had the higher batting average, Ty Cobb in 1917 or Rogers Hornsby in 1923?"

Compare the two averages to see which is greater.

Batting Averages of Some Great Hitters of the Past		
1917	Ty Cobb	0.383
1923	Rogers Hornsby	0.384
1924	Babe Ruth	0.378
1934	Lou Gehrig	0.363

Line up the decimal points. Start at the left. Find the first place where the digits are different. $\longrightarrow$ Compare these digits. Which digit is greater? $\longrightarrow$ The numbers compare the same way the digits compare.

0.383
0.384

4 is greater than 3.
4 > 3

is greater than
0.384 > 0.383

is less than
0.383 < 0.384

Rogers Hornsby's average was greater.

Order the averages shown in the table by listing them from greatest to least. Do this by comparing them two at a time.

0.384 ← greatest
0.383
0.378
0.363 ← least

Warm Up Write >, <, or = for each ●.

1. 4.6 ● 4.8
2. 1.336 ● 1.431
3. 9.05 ● 9.01
4. 0.039 ● 0.390
5. 1.7 ● 1.70
6. 0.90 ● 0.89
7. 37.73 ● 36.73
8. 0.008 ● 0.100
9. 4.96 ● 5.02
10. 0.002 ● 0.020
11. 9.3 ● 9.30
12. 1.686 ● 1.868

13. Order from greatest to least: 3.549; 3.594; 3.459; 3.954; 4.345

14. Order from least to greatest: 7.089; 7.421; 6.984; 7.500; 6.099

EXERCISES FOR SECTION 7.1

1. Identify each of the following decimals as either terminating, nonterminating but repeating, or nonterminating and nonrepeating.

a) 0.123
b) 0.878787...
c) 0.191919
d) 0.893893
e) 0.81828384...
f) 0.040040004...
g) 0.132134136138

2. Convert each of the following rational numbers into decimals.

a) $\frac{5}{8}$
b) $\frac{2}{9}$
c) $\frac{9}{14}$
d) $\frac{15}{12}$

e) $\frac{11}{13}$
f) $\frac{12}{7}$
g) $\frac{9}{11}$
h) $\frac{8}{24}$
i) $\frac{3}{27}$

3. Convert each of the following decimals into rational

numbers.

a) 0.83   **b)** 0.2

c) 58.321   **d)** 0.00000029

4. For each of the following, perform the indicated operations and round off all answers to the nearest hundredth.

a) Subtract 6.69 from 9.723

b) Subtract 5.432 from 8

c) Multiply 2.096 by 79.37

d) Multiply 8.532 by 0.0039

e) Divide 7.32 by 4.5

f) Divide 6.81 by 0.23

5. The repeating decimal 0.838383... can be converted to a rational number as follows: Let N stand for the number:

Thus $N = 0.838383...$

Multiply by 100. We get

$100N = 100(0.838383...)$ or

$100N = 83.8383...$

Subtract N: $N = 0.8383...$

$99N = 83$

Dividing both sides by 99, we obtain

$N = \dfrac{83}{99}$ or that $\dfrac{83}{99} = 0.838383...$

By a similar procedure, convert each of the following repeating decimals to rational numbers.

a) 0.282828...   **b)** 0.898989...

c) 0.191919...   **d)** 0.356356...

e) 0.847847...   **f)** 5.232323...

g) 7.535353...   **h)** 5.21373737...

6. Convert each of the following fractions or numbers into percents.

a) $\dfrac{4}{5}$ **b)** $\dfrac{1}{4}$ **c)** $\dfrac{2}{3}$ **d)** $\dfrac{5}{7}$

e) 2   **f)** 3   **g)** $1\dfrac{2}{5}$ **h)** $2\dfrac{1}{3}$

i) $1\dfrac{2}{3}$ **j)** $\dfrac{53}{200}$

7. Convert each of the following decimals into percents.

a) 0.12   **b)** 0.567   **c)** 0.01   **d)** 0.002

e) 5.1   **f)** 6.23   **g)** 1.01   **h)** 1.00

8. Convert each of the following percents into decimals.

a) $5\dfrac{1}{2}\%$ **b)** $2\dfrac{1}{2}\%$ **c)** $6\dfrac{2}{3}\%$

d) $12\dfrac{1}{2}\%$ **e)** 18%   **f)** $1\dfrac{1}{2}\%$

g) 10.1%   **h)** 16.23%   **i)** $\dfrac{7}{8}\%$

9. What is 7% of 95?

10. What is 12% of 426?

11. What is 8.2% of 578?

12. What is $9\dfrac{1}{4}\%$ of 360?

13. One hundred is 125% of what number?

14. Eleven is $5\dfrac{1}{2}\%$ of what number?

15. Gwendolyn just purchased a new dress for $49.95. The sales tax is $8\dfrac{1}{4}\%$. How much tax does Gwendolyn have to pay?

16. Bob just bought a new set of radial tires for $198. Sales tax is $7\dfrac{1}{2}\%$. What is the total cost of the tires (including tax)?

17. When Madeline started on her car trip, the odometer of the car read 41632.8. At the end of the trip it read 42591.2. For the entire trip she used 46.8 gallons of gas. How many miles per gallon (to the nearest hundredth) did the car average? (*Hint:* Divide the total number of miles traveled by the number of gallons of gas used.)

18. The electric meter on Don's house read 1453.6 kilowatt hours at the beginning of the month. At the end of the month it read 1710.4 kilowatt hours. What is Don's electric bill for that month if electricity in his area costs 12.38 cents per kilowatt hour?

PROBLEM-SOLVING EXERCISES

19. The general sales tax in a certain state is 7% of gross sales. One week a department store collected $36,820 in sales tax. What were the gross sales for the week?

20. Catherine rented a car for a week at a cost of $79 (car only). The sales tax was $4.59 extra. What is the percent of the sales tax?

21. *Cash or Charge.* Many gas stations give customers a discount on cash purchases for gasoline. At one gas station, credit card customers pay $1.119 per gallon of gas, whereas cash customers receive a discount of 6 cents per gallon of gas. What is the percent of discount for cash-paying customers?

22. At a recent sale a 35-mm camera, which costs the dealer $89.98 and usually lists for $124.49, was selling for $104.98.

   a) Find the regular percent markup.

   b) Find the percent decrease of the sale price.

23. After taking a 3% discount for early payment, Marty paid his credit card company bill with a check in the amount of $163.93. What was the original amount of the bill?

24. Alexis purchased a new car for $7800. At the end of the year, the value of the car had depreciated by $1560. By what percent did the value of the car decrease?

25. As a result of a new union contract, Joanne's annual salary will be increased from $42,000 to $45,500. Find the percent increase in her salary.

26. The police force of Ardsley consists of 78 police officers, 27 of whom are from minority groups. What percent of the police force is from minority groups?

27. A doctor tested 476 samples of blood and found that 6 of these samples had a certain virus in them. What percent of the blood samples had the virus in them?

28. Ninety-eight percent of all people with a certain form of skin cancer (when detected early) will be cured after appropriate medical treatment. If 412 new cases were reported in Shawnee last year, how many of these patients will be cured after appropriate medical treatment?

▌▌▌▌▶ **Brain-Teaser Problems** ◀▐▐▐▐

**29. The owner of a pet store paid $220 for a rare bird to sell in his store. He wishes to price it so that he can offer a 15% discount and still make a 25% profit of

the price that he paid for it. At what price should the bird be marked?

**30. To generate sales, a dealer reduced the price of a camera by $67.25 for a week. This represented a discount of 25% of the original price. On the last day of the sale the camera was further discounted to sell for 60% of its original price. What was the final selling price of the camera?

**31. At a recent sale, the price of an attaché case was reduced from $60 to $40. What was the percent decrease in price?

**32. It can be proved that any rational number $\frac{a}{b}$ which is in simplest form can be written as a terminating decimal if and only if the prime factorization of the denominator contains no primes other than 2 or 5.

   Use this fact to determine which of the following fractions can be written as terminating decimals.

   a) $\frac{5}{12}$ b) $\frac{8}{28}$ c) $\frac{3}{35}$ d) $\frac{5}{40}$

**33. A certain sales person earns a 7% monthly commission if the monthly sales are under $10,000 and an additional 5% monthly commission when the monthly sales are over $10,000. Last month, the sales person earned $2944 in commission. What was the total value of the monthly sales?

**34. a) Enter the decimal 45.986 into a calculator. By using just one operation, can you make the calculator show the decimal with the 8 changed to a 0?

   b) Using only one operation, change the 4 in 26.487 into a 0.

   c) Using only one operation, change the 9 in 43.789 into a 1.

**35. Without performing any calculations, explain how we know that $\frac{1}{123456789}$ will have a repeating but non-terminating decimal representation.

7.2

SIMPLE AND COMPOUND INTEREST

At one time or another in our lives we must either borrow money or lend money. We may borrow money to help pay for college tuition, to help finance a car, or to buy a house that sells for $225,000 when we have only $30,000 for the down payment. In these situations we need money and are willing to pay **interest** to someone or some business for the use of the money.

On the other hand, we may lend money to someone or to some business or government agency. In this case the business or governmental agency may sell bonds, which in essence promise to repay the loan at a specified date. In the meantime, interest will be paid, usually at six-month intervals, for the use of the money.

Many of us have department store credit cards or general bank credit cards such as Master Card, Visa, and American Express. When we do not repay the monthly charges by the date specified, we are charged interest. This is usually labeled **finance charges** on the monthly statement that we receive.

As a matter of fact, a large part of the U.S. economy is based on borrowing and interest. It is for this reason that a knowledge of interest, whether on money borrowed or on money saved, is a valuable tool.[1]

Interest is the money paid for the use of money. The amount of money borrowed when an individual applies for a loan from a bank or when an individual lends money to a bank in the form of a savings account or to a governmental agency in the form of a bond is called **principal.**

When money is borrowed, the borrower agrees to pay the lender interest at a specified rate over a period of time — for example, 6% over 3 years or 10% over 4 years. In each case the rate of interest is specified as a percentage, either by using the % symbol or by writing it in decimal form. Thus we can write an interest rate of 18 percent as 18% or as 0.18 and an interest rate of five percent as 5% or as 0.05.

Comment   Many savings banks pay $5\frac{1}{4}$% interest on savings accounts. This is written in decimal form as 0.0525 and *not* as 0.525. The latter represents 52.5%, a rather high interest rate.

The interest charged on a loan may be simple or compound. **Simple interest** is generally used for short-term loans of a year or less and is computed on the whole amount of money borrowed for the entire period of the loan. On the other hand, when a loan is for a longer period of time or for interest paid by a bank, the interest is added to the original loan at specified times (quarterly, semiannually, monthly, etc.), thereby increasing the amount of interest paid. This is known as **compound interest** and will be discussed later in this section.

margin terms:
- finance charges
- interest
- principal
- simple interest
- compound interest

Simple Interest

Suppose $6000 is borrowed for 1 year. If the rate of interest is 8% per year, then the interest is 8% of $6000, or

$$0.08 \times \$6000 = \$480$$

---

[1] It is strongly suggested that the reader use a calculator to work through many of the examples and exercises in this section.

If the money is borrowed for 2 years, then the total interest paid is

$$0.08 \times \$6000 \times 2 = \$960$$

where 0.08 is the rate of interest, $6000 is the amount of money borrowed (the principal), and 2 is the time period.

More generally, we have the following simple-interest formula.

simple-interest formula

Formula 7.1   Simple-Interest Formula The total simple interest, I, in dollars on a loan of P dollars for n years, where the annual interest rate is r, is given by

$$I = P \cdot r \cdot n.$$

EXAMPLE 1

Find the simple interest on a loan of $900 for 4 years, given that the rate of interest is 6% per year.

SOLUTION

We use the simple-interest formula. Here $P = 900$, $r = 0.06$, and $n = 4$. Then

$$
\begin{aligned}
I &= P \cdot r \cdot n \\
&= 900(0.06)(4) \\
&= \$216
\end{aligned}
$$

Thus the total simple interest is $216. ▬

When working with the simple-interest formula, you must express both r (rate) and n (time) in the same unit of time — for example, days, months, years. If this is not the case, then one of them must be converted so that they are both in the same unit of time, as illustrated in the following examples.

EXAMPLE 2

Friendly loans. Bill arranges to borrow $800 from his friend for 9 months. The simple interest rate is 30% per year. How much money does Bill have to repay to his friend?

SOLUTION

We use the simple-interest formual (Formula 7.1). Here $P = 800$ and $r = 0.30$. Since the loan is for only 9 months, we must express this as a fraction of the year. Thus $n = 9$ months $= \frac{9}{12}$ year (n is usually expressed in years). Then

$$I = P \cdot r \cdot n$$

$$= 800(0.30)\left(\frac{9}{12}\right) = \$180$$

Thus the interest is $180. Since the loan was for $800, Bill must repay $980 to his friend.

EXAMPLE 3

Off-track betting (OTB). Harry is in the OTB office in New York when he receives a tip on a particular horse. He borrows $940 from a friend and agrees to repay $1000 to his friend in two months. Find the annual rate of interest.

SOLUTION

Again we will use the simple-interest formula. Here $P = 940$ and $n = 2$ months $= \frac{2}{12}$ year. Since Harry borrowed $940 and will repay $1000, the interest is $1000 - $940 = $60. Then

$$I = P \cdot r \cdot n$$

$$60 = 940 \cdot r \cdot \left(\frac{2}{12}\right)$$

Solving this equation for r gives us

$$r = \frac{18}{47} \quad \text{or} \quad 0.3830$$

Thus the annual rate of interest is 38.30%.

EXAMPLE 4

Short-term loan. Marie Cartright arranges for a short-term loan at an annual interest rate of 15%. The total interest charged is $300. If Marie repays the loan in 3 months, then how much money did she borrow?

SOLUTION

We are interested in finding the amount of money borrowed, so we must find the value of P. We use Formula 7.1 with $r = 0.15$, $n = 3$ months $= \frac{3}{12}$ year, and $I = 300$. We have

$$I = P \cdot r \cdot n$$

$$300 = P(0.15)\left(\frac{3}{12}\right)$$

$$300 = 0.0375P$$

Now we divide both sides of this equation by 0.0375. We get

$$\frac{300}{0.0375} = \frac{0.0375P}{0.0375}$$

$$8000 = P$$

Thus Marie borrowed $8000.

Compound Interest

Suppose a person has some money to deposit in a savings bank that pays compound interest. Since some banks in the United States now pay interest **compounded continuously,** let us analyze what is meant by **compound interest.**

Suppose we deposit $1000 (called the principal) in a bank that pays 6% interest per year compounded annually. Then at the end of one year we would have $1060. This amount represents the $1000 principal plus the 1000(0.06), or $60, interest earned on the money.

During the second year the bank will pay 6% interest on $1060, so we will earn $1060(0.06), or an additional $63.60, in interest. Thus at the end of the second year we would have a total accumulation of $1123.60. The same thing will happen in succeeding years. Table 7.1 indicates the amount of money accumulated after several years, assuming the bank pays 6% interest compounded annually.

TABLE 7.1

Amount of money accumulated after six years, assuming a 6% interest rate compounded annually

Year	Amount of money on deposit at beginning of year	Interest earned during year	Amount of money on deposit at end of year	Simplified form
1	$1000	1000(0.06)	$1000 + 1000(0.06)$ $= 1000(1 + 0.06)$	$1060
2	$1060	1060(0.06)	$1060 + 1060(0.06)$ $= 1000(1 + 0.06)^2$	$1123.60
3	$1123.60	1123.60(0.06)	$1123.60 + 1123.60(0.06)$ $= 1000(1 + 0.06)^3$	$1191.02
4	$1191.02	1191.02(0.06)	$1191.02 + 1191.02(0.06)$ $= 1000(1 + 0.06)^4$	$1262.48
5	$1262.48	1262.48(0.06)	$1262.48 + 1262.48(0.06)$ $= 1000(1 + 0.06)^5$	$1338.23
6	$1338.23	1338.23(0.06)	$1338.23 + 1338.23(0.06)$ $= 1000(1 + 0.06)^6$	$1418.52

On the other hand, if the bank pays 6% interest compounded semiannually, then it is really paying only 3% interest for each six-month period. Similarly, when the bank pays 6% interest compounded quarterly, it is really paying only 1.5% interest for every three-month period. What happens when the bank pays 6% interest compounded continuously? Table 7.2 gives the amount of money that can be accumulated when different compounding periods are used. The values given in this table were obtained by using the **compound-interest formula,** to be discussed shortly.

Tables 7.1 and 7.2 suggest that as the number of compounding periods increases, the amount of money that we accumulate also increases. Yet the amount of money that we accumulate does not increase without bounds

	TABLE 7.2				
	Amount of money accumulated after one year at 6% interest using different compounding periods				
Principal	Compounded annually	Compounded semiannually	Compounded quarterly	Compounded monthly	Compounded continuously
$1000	$1060	$1060.90	$1061.36	$1061.68	$1061.84
$5000	$5300	$5304.50	$5306.82	$5308.39	$5309.18

(unfortunately!). There is a limit. To find this limit, we can use the compound-interest formula, which follows directly from the fourth column of Table 7.1. We have the following.

compound-interest formula

> **Formula 7.2—Compound-Interest Formula** The compound amount A (principal + interest) that results when P dollars (the principal) is invested at a rate of r per period for n periods is given by the formula
>
> $$A = P(1 + r)^n$$

When the money is compounded continuously, we have the following.

compounded continuously

> **Formula 7.3**—If P dollars is invested in a bank that pays interest at the rate of r per year **compounded continuously,** the amount of money accumulated, A, after n years is
>
> $$A = Pe^{rn}$$
>
> where the values of e to the appropriate power can be determined from Table A1 in the Appendix.

letter e

Comment The letter e given in Formula 7.3 is used often in mathematics to represent a number whose value is approximately 2.71828. . . . The values of e to the appropriate power can be determined from Table A1 in the Appendix.

EXAMPLE 5

John has $4000 that he can deposit in one of three banks, all of which pay 9% yearly interest. However, one bank compounds the interest annually, one compounds it quarterly, and one compounds it continuously.

Compute the different amounts of interest that can be earned in each of these banks in 3 years.

SOLUTION

We will use the compound-interest formula, $A = P(1 + r)^n$. For the bank that compounds its interest annually, there will be 3 paying periods (one for each year), so that $n = 3$. Then

$$A = \$4000(1 + 0.09)^3$$
$$= 4000(1.09)^3$$
$$= \$5180.12$$

For the bank that compounds its interest quarterly there will be 12 paying periods (4 for each year), so that $n = 12$. Also the rate of interest is 9% per year or $\frac{9\%}{4}$ = 2.25% per paying period. Then

$$A = \$4000(1 + 0.0225)^{12}$$
$$= 4000(1.0225)^{12}$$
$$= \$5224.20$$

For the bank that compounds its interest continuously, we use Formula 7.3 which is $A = Pe^{rn}$. The money will remain in the bank for 3 years, so that $n = 3$. (When using Formula 7.3, we express n in years. The same is true for the interest rate, r.) Then

$$A = 4000e^{0.27}$$
$$= 4000(1.30996)$$
$$= \$5239.84$$

In this problem the difference between compounding continuously and compounding annually amounts to $5239.84 - $5180.12, or $59.72. ■

Many banks now quote interest rates with the expression "effective interest rate." Using the above notation, we have the following.

effective annual interest rate

Formula 7.4   The **effective annual interest rate** corresponding to an interest rate of r compounded continuously is given by $e^r - 1$.

Thus if a bank pays 6% interest compounded continuously, the effective annual interest rate is

$$e^{0.06} - 1 = 1.06184 - 1$$
$$= 0.06184, \text{ or } 6.184\%$$

This means that a 6% interest rate compounded continuously will yield the same amount of money to the depositor as a 6.184% interest rate compounded annually.

EXAMPLE 6

What is the effective annu
continuously?

SOLUTION

We will use Formula 7.4.

$$e^r - 1$$

Thus the effective annual i

Comment If your calcula
obtain these values from Ta

Handwritten note: #2, 3, 5 simple interest $I = Prt$

EXERCISES FOR SECTION 7.2

1. Find the simple interest on a loan of $8000 that is borrowed for 3 years at an 18% annual interest rate.

2. Find the simple interest on a loan of $8800 that is borrowed for 20 months at an 18% annual interest rate.

3. Leslie borrowed $4800 from his friend and repaid $5578 to his friend in six months. What was the (simple) annual rate of interest?

4. Jennifer borrowed $4000 from a finance company. She repaid the loan in 5 months and was charged $450 as interest. What was the annual rate of interest?

5. Heather borrowed $6000 from a cousin and repaid her $6560. The interest was 24% per year. How long did it take Heather to repay the loan?

6. If $3000 is deposited in a bank that pays 8% annual interest compounded quarterly, how much money will accumulate in 6 years?

7. What is the effective annual interest rate of a 7% interest rate compounded continuously?

8. What is the effective annual interest rate of a $6\frac{1}{4}$% interest rate compounded continuously?

9. Marlene deposits $5000 in a time deposit account of a bank that pays 10% interest compounded annually. If Marlene plans to leave the money in the bank for 11 years, how much money will she have in the account?

10. *Financing a college education.* Charlotte deposits $3000 in a bank that pays 8% annual interest compounded

quarterly. She plans to leave the money in the bank for 15 years, at which time she will use it to finance her son's college education. How much money will Charlotte have then?

11. *Individual retirement accounts (IRA).* Judy opens an Individual Retirement Account by making an initial deposit of $2000. Judy is $39\frac{1}{2}$ years old. According to government regulations, Judy may not withdraw any of the money until she reaches $59\frac{1}{2}$ years. If Judy makes no other deposits and the bank pays 9% interest compounded quarterly, how much money will she have when she reaches $59\frac{1}{2}$ years of age?

12. Loretta is about to deposit $8000 in a bank that pays 7% annual interest. If the money will be kept in the bank for 9 years, then find the total amount that will accumulate if the bank compounds its interest (a) annually; (b) quarterly; (c) daily; (d) continuously.

13. Scott borrowed some money from a finance company that charged him $480 interest. The loan was for 8 months. If the finance company charges simple interest at the rate of 22% per year, then how much money did Scott borrow from the company?

14. Richard bought a used car from a dealer who charges interest at the rate of 24% compounded per year. Richard repaid the loan in 8 months and was charged $320 interest. How much money did Richard borrow from the dealer?

15. Miguel invests $2000 in a bank that pays $8\frac{3}{4}\%$ annual interest compounded quarterly. Julia invests $2000 in a bank that pays 8.85% annual interest compounded semiannually. After one year who will have more money?

16. Is it wiser to invest money in a bank that pays $6\frac{3}{4}\%$ annual interest compounded quarterly or in a bank that pays 7% annual interest compounded semiannually?

17. George deposits $1000 in a bank certificate of deposit (CD) that pays interest at the rate of $8\frac{1}{4}\%$ per year. How much money will accumulate after one year, if the interest is compounded.

a) annually   **b)** semiannually

c) quarterly   **d)** monthly

e) continuously

7.3

INSTALLMENT BUYING AND MORTGAGES

installment plan

down payment

Often people buy things on an installment plan. For example, suppose Matthew wishes to buy a television set that costs $500. Furthermore, suppose he has only $100 available. The store may agree to sell Matthew the television set on the **installment plan.** Under this plan, Matthew will pay $100 **down** (as a **down payment)** plus an additional charge in a series of regular payments (usually monthly). If the monthly charge is $36 and these payments are spread over a 20-month period, then the total cost of the television set can be found by multiplying the monthly charge by the number of payments and then adding the down payment. In our case we have

$$\$36 \times 20 = \$720 \quad \text{Total amount of monthly payments}$$
$$+\ \$100 \quad \text{Down payment}$$
$$\overline{\$820} \quad \text{Total cost of television set.}$$

Thus Matthew is paying $500 for the television and $820–$500, or $320, as interest.

EXAMPLE 1

Martha has just purchased a $1500 piano. She has agreed to make a down payment of $200 and to pay the balance on the installment plan by making 15 monthly payments of $110. What is the total cost of the piano (including interest)?

SOLUTION

Martha will make 15 monthly payments of $110 each. Thus her monthly payments will amount to $1650. To this we must add the initial down payment of $200. Thus the total cost of the piano is $1650 + 200 = 1850. Of this amount, $1500 is for the piano and $350 is for interest.

EXAMPLE 2

Bill has just purchased a used car for $1500. He pays $500 as a down payment and agrees to pay the $1000 balance in 5 monthly installments. Interest is $1\frac{1}{2}\%$ per month on any unpaid balance. What is the total cost of the car including interest?

SOLUTION

The first monthly payment is for the $1000 balance. Since the interest is $1\frac{1}{2}\%$ per month on any unpaid balance, the interest is

$$1000 \times 0.015 = \$15$$

so Bill owes $1015. If Bill makes a payment of $215, the next bill will be for $1015 − $215, or $800. The interest charge for the second month is $1\frac{1}{2}\%$ per month on the unpaid balance of $800, or

$$800 \times 0.015 = \$12$$

so Bill owes $812. If Bill makes a payment of $215, the next bill will be for $812 − $215, or $597. The interest charge for the third month is $1\frac{1}{2}\%$ per month on the unpaid balance of $597, or

$$597 \times 0.015 = \$8.96$$

so Bill owes $605.96. If Bill again makes a payment of $215, the next bill will be for $605.96 − $215 = $390.96. The interest charge for the fourth month is $1\frac{1}{2}\%$ per month on the unpaid balance of $390.96, or

$$390.96 \times 0.015 = \$5.86$$

so Bill owes $396.82. If Bill makes a payment of $215, the next bill will be for $396.82 − $215 = $181.82. The interest charge for the fifth month is $1\frac{1}{2}\%$ per month on the unpaid balance of $181.82, or

$$181.82 \times 0.015 = \$2.73$$

so Bill owes $184.55. Bill pays this completely. Bill has paid a total of $500 + $215 + $215 + $215 + $215 + $184.55, or $1544.55. Of this amount, $1500 is for the car and $44.55 is for interest.   ◼

Comment   Most banks and finance companies use a scheme similar to the one outlined in the preceding examples to compute the interest charges.

mortgage

Usually an individual who wishes to buy a home does not have enough money to pay for the house entirely. He or she then arranges for a long-term **mortgage** from a bank and agrees to repay the mortgage by making equal periodic payments to the bank. In this case, each periodic payment includes partial repayment on the principal plus interest payments on the declining balance of the principal. The process of making payments

amortization

under these conditions is called **amortization**.

It should be noted that although each periodic payment is the same, the percentage of the periodic payments that is used to pay for the interest charge and the percentage of the amount that is used to repay the principal will change. Thus in the early years of a mortgage, most of the periodic payments are used to pay off the interest for the loan over the entire period, and relatively little is used to repay the principal. However, in the later years, almost all of each periodic payment is used to repay the principal. This fact is clearly illustrated in Table A2 in the Appendix, in which we have given the amortization schedule for a mortgage loan of $130,000 at a 9.5% rate of interest to be paid over a 15-year period.

How do we determine the periodic payments necessary to amortize (pay off under the conditions described) a loan? Fortunately, mathematicians have compiled many charts that simplify the computations considerably. One such chart is given in Table A3 in the Appendix. We illustrate the use of this chart with several examples.

EXAMPLE 3

Paying a Mortgage. Martha Galzen arranged for a 15-year mortgage for $34,000 with the Second National City Bank. She decided to amortize the loan by making equal payments to the bank every 3 months. Interest is 8% a year compounded quarterly. How much money will Martha have to pay the bank every 3 months?

SOLUTION

Since the mortgage is to run for 15 years and there are to be 4 payments per year, there will be a total of 15×4, or 60, payment periods. Interest is 8% a year compounded quarterly, or $\frac{8\%}{4} = 2\%$ per payment period. Now we use Table A3 with 60 payment periods and an interest rate of 2%. The chart value is 0.028768. We multiply the chart value by the amount of the mortgage, getting

$$34000(0.028768) = 978.11$$

Thus Martha will have to pay the bank $978.11 every 3 months.

EXAMPLE 4

Buying a television on installment. Mack Jones bought a color TV for $489. He made a down payment of $89 and agreed to pay the $400 balance in equal monthly payments over a 3-year period. Interest is 18% a year compounded monthly. How much money must Mack pay monthly in order to amortize the loan over the 3-year period?

SOLUTION

Since Mack will repay the loan over a 3-year period, there will be 3×12, or 36, payment periods. The interest rate is 18% a year, or $\frac{18\%}{12} = 1.5\%$ a month. Now we use Table A3. The chart value for 36 payment periods and a $1\frac{1}{2}$% rate of interest is 0.036152. We multiply the chart value by the amount of the balance, getting

$$400(0.036152) = 14.46 \text{ (rounded off)}.$$

Thus his monthly payment is $14.46. Over the 3 years, Mack will pay $36 \times \$14.46$, or $520.56. The original loan was for $400. Therefore he will pay $120.56 in interest. ◼

EXAMPLE 5	To combat the rise in shoplifting, the Rochelle Department Store purchased $400,000 worth of closed-circuit television monitors for its several stores. The department store chain agreed to pay for the equipment by making equal monthly payments to the manufacturer over a 5-year period. Interest is 9% a year, compounded monthly. What are the monthly payments?
SOLUTION	Since the loan will be repaid over a 5-year period, there will be a total of 12×5, or 60, payment periods. The interest rate is $\frac{9\%}{12}$, or $\frac{3}{4}$% per month. Now we use Table A3. The chart value is 0.020758. Since the loan was for $400,000, the monthly payments will be

$$400,000(0.020758) = \$8303.20 \qquad ◼$$

conventional loans or conventional mortgages

All of the loans and mortgages discussed up to this point are referred to as **conventional loans** or **conventional mortgages.** The money is borrowed from a commercial bank or a savings and loan association.

Over the last few years, as money has become very "tight," interest rates for home mortgage loans have risen dramatically. Many prospective home buyers, particularly younger people, have become discouraged from buying homes because of the high interest rates. To promote more home mortgage loans, lending institutions have developed several alternative forms of mortgages to suit the home buyer's pocketbook. Among some of these alternatives are the following.

Adjustable Rate Mortgages (ARM)

In this type of mortgage loan, the rate of interest is adjusted up or down at a specific interval (usually every six months). The adjusted rate depends upon the yield of one-year U.S. treasury bills. The initial interest rate is much less than that of regular (conventional) mortgages. However, the rates can be raised at every adjustment period. Some adjustable rate mortgages have special clauses that place a cap on the maximum rate of interest over the life of the mortgage.

Variable Rate Mortgage

In this type of mortgage the rate of interest is adjustable up or down and is based upon an index that reflects the cost of funds to the bank.

Points

Many lending institutions now require the prospective home buyer to pay one or more points when the house is bought, that is, at closing time. **One**

point equals 1% of the amount of the mortgage. Thus the monthly mortgage payments will be lower, since the rate of interest on the mortgage will be lower.

Since there are so many different types of mortgages available, the prospective home buyer should shop around carefully before signing on the dotted line.

On the basis of what we have seen until now, we notice that when the interest charges are added to any item purchased on the installment plan, the true interest rate may be considerably higher than what it is initially specified by the seller. To make it easier for the consumer to determine the true interest rate, Congress passed the Truth in Lending Act in 1969. This law requires *all* lenders to accurately state the **annual percentage rate (APR).** Each lender must specify the APR, whether the lender is a local merchant, a bank, or a credit card issuer.

annual percentage rate (APR)

Are You Still Stuck With A 14% Mortgage?
Cut Down to Today's Low Fixed Rates!

NOW 11$\frac{1}{2}$%

11.81% A.P.R.

NO INCOME VERIFICATION AVAILABLE

Yes, you can get rid of those higher payments by **REFINANCING YOUR HOME**

If you look closely at this newspaper advertisement, you will notice the 11.81% A.P.R. in small print. What does A.P.R. stand for? Shouldn't an $11\frac{1}{2}$% mortgage be an $11\frac{1}{2}$% mortgage?

Lengthy and extensive tables have been computed by the Federal Reserve System for determining the APR. In Table A4 in the Appendix we present part of the APR table. We use the numbers in this table as follows.

> **Rule 7.2   Rule for Finding the Annual Percentage Rate** To find the actual APR, we first divide the actual interest charge (or finance charge) by the amount borrowed. We then multiply the result by 100. This gives us the interest (finance) charge per $100 of the amount being financed. Using this number, look in Table A4 to find the actual APR for the appropriate number of payments.

EXAMPLE 6

Hugh Carson purchased a $7000 car with a down payment of $1200. The balance is being financed by the dealer. Hugh has agreed to make 48 monthly payments of $168.86 each. What is the APR?

SOLUTION

Since Hugh made a down payment of $1200, the amount borrowed is $7000 – $1200 or $5800. He has agreed to make 48 monthly payments of $168.86 each. This amounts to 48 × $168.86 or $8105.28. Since only $5800 was borrowed, the total finance charge is

$$\$8105.28 - \$5800 = \$2305.28$$

The actual interest (finance charge) is $2305.28, and the amount borrowed is $5800, so

$$\frac{\text{Actual interest}}{\text{Amount borrowed}} \times 100 = \frac{2305.28}{5800} \times 100$$
$$= \$39.75$$

Thus Hugh is paying $39.75 for every $100 borrowed. We now look in Table A4. We look for 48 in the number of payments row. Then we move down this column until we find the number closest to 39.75. In this case, we find that 39.75 is listed exactly in this table. We look in the left column and find that the APR is 17.50%.

EXAMPLE 7

Yolanda purchased a stereophonic cable-ready video cassette recorder for $945. She made a down payment of $150 and paid the balance in 18 equal installments of $49.70 each. What was the APR?

SOLUTION

The actual amount borrowed is $945 – $150 or $795. Yolanda made 18 installment payments of $49.70 each. This amounts to 18 × 49.70 or $894.60. Since only $795 was borrowed, the actual interest charge is $99.60. Thus

$$\frac{\text{Actual interest}}{\text{Amount borrowed}} \times 100 = \frac{99.60}{795} \times 100$$
$$= \$12.53$$

Thus Yolanda is paying $12.53 for every $100 borrowed. Now we look in Table A4. We look for 18 in the number of payments row. Then we move down this column until we find the number closest to 12.53. This number is between 12.50 and 12.72 but closer to 12.50. Thus the APR was approximately 15.25%. ▄▄▄

EXERCISES FOR SECTION 7.3

1. Kathy wishes to purchase some stereo equipment that costs $1800. She agrees to pay $800 down and to pay the $1000 balance over a 15-month period by making monthly payments of $90. How much is Kathy really paying for the stereo equipment?

2. Steve works in a jewelry store. He wishes to buy a $3000 engagement ring for his fiancée. His boss agrees to sell him the ring by deducting $35 from Steve's weekly paycheck over a two-year period. No down payment is required. How much does the ring really cost Steve?

3. Jack has an outstanding balance of $385 with a major credit card company that charges $1\frac{1}{2}\%$ interest per month on any unpaid balance. Jack will repay the credit card company by making monthly payments of $45 until the balance is completely paid. How many months does it take Jack to repay the loan?

4. In Exercise 3, how much money does Jack end up paying the company?

5. Bruce can repay a $600 loan by making monthly payments of $60 each, where the interest is 3% per month on any unpaid balance, or by making monthly payments of $80 each, where interest is 2% per month on any unpaid balance. Which of the two methods results in a lower total interest charge?

6. Trudy joined a health club that charges $385 annual membership dues. Trudy decides to pay the $385 on the installment plan by making monthly payments of $50. Interest is $3\frac{1}{2}\%$ on any unpaid balance. How much does Trudy end up paying for the membership dues?

7. Al Jordan arranged for a 8-year conventional mortgage for $35,000 with a bank that charges 12% annual interest compounded monthly. Al agrees to amortize the loan by making equal monthly payments to the bank. What are Al's monthly payments?

8. What are the quarterly payments for a $25,000 conventional mortgage from a bank that charges 10% annual interest compounded quarterly, given that the loan is for 6 years?

9. Michael has just renovated his house. To accomplish this, he borrowed $5000 from a bank that charges interest at an annual rate of 14% compounded quarterly. Michael wants to repay the loan by making equal quarterly payments over a 5-year period. What are his quarterly payments?

10. What are the monthly payments for a $45,000 conventional mortgage from a bank that charges 12% annual interest compounded monthly given that the loan is to run for 6 years?

11. In Exercise 10, what are the periodic payments if they are to be made every month and the loan is to run for 8 years?

12. David borrowed $3000 from a finance company that charges 18% annual interest compounded monthly. David agrees to repay the loan over a 30-month period. What are his monthly payments?

13. Juan Rodrigues arranges with his college to pay for his $1400 tuition bill by making monthly payments over a 4-month period. The college will not allow Juan to register next semester until this semester's bills are paid completely. Furthermore, the college charges 9% annual interest compounded monthly. What are Juan's monthly payments?

14. Bridget Connors purchased a complete home computer system for $1600. She made a down payment of $400 and paid the balance over a 12-month period in 12 equal installments of $107.32 each. What was the APR?

15. *Paying your tuition can be costly.* Jerry Bates paid $\frac{1}{8}$ of his $2400 college tuition bill at registration and agreed to

pay the balance in 6 equal installments of $364.95 each.

a) What was the finance charge?

b) What was the APR?

16. *Bad credit rating.* Connie Johnson had a very bad credit rating and had to borrow $2000 from a local finance company. She repaid the loan in 12 equal installments of $200 each. What was the APR?

17. Pedro arranged for a $50,000 mortgage from a bank. The annual rate of interest is 0.14 on the *entire* amount, and the interest is payable monthly. What is the monthly interest charge?

7.4

THE REAL NUMBERS: ORDER OF OPERATIONS

Irrational Numbers

In the first sections of this chapter we pointed out that there are three different kinds of decimals:

1. terminating decimals,

2. repeating decimals, and

3. nonrepeating and nonterminating decimals.

The first two kinds represent rational numbers. On the other hand, *numbers that can be written as nonrepeating and nonterminating decimals are called* **irrational numbers.** The fact that they are called irrational does not mean that they do not make sense. They are as meaningful as any other numbers. We do not introduce them merely to make our discussion of decimals complete. They are important and interesting in themselves, and mathematicians could not work without them.

irrational numbers

Some examples of irrational numbers are π (which you will remember if you have studied geometry), $\sqrt{2}$, $\sqrt{3}$, etc.[2]

The story of the discovery of irrational numbers is one of the more interesting chapters in the history of mathematics. Irrational numbers were first discovered around the sixth century B.C. by the Pythagoreans, a school of Greek mathematicians. This school was named after its founder, Pythagoras, a philosopher, mathematician, and mystic. We know nothing certain about him except that he was born in Samos in Greece and is believed to have traveled widely, as far as Egypt, Babylon, and even India. When Pythagoras returned from his travels, he settled at Croton in southern Italy. There he founded a school for the study of religion, philosophy, mathematics, and science. An interesting story is told about

---

[2] Read $\sqrt{2}$ as "the square root of 2." It means a number that when multiplied by itself gives 2. For example, $\sqrt{4} = 2$, since $2 \cdot 2 = 4$; and $\sqrt{9} = 3$, since $3 \cdot 3 = 9$.

Pythagoras's attempt to get students for his school. He found a poor workman and offered to pay him to learn geometry. Pythagoras promised to give him a coin for each theorem that he learned. The workman happily accepted the challenge and earned many coins. Gradually, the workman became so interested in geometry that he wanted Pythagoras to teach him more and more. To persuade him, the workman now offered Pythagoras a coin for each theorem that he taught him. In the end, Pythagoras got back all his money.

The Pythagorean school was also a secret society. This society was in some ways like a modern commune. Men and women were equal, all property was common, and activities were communal. Even mathematical and scientific achievements were considered work of the entire community.

Many of the Pythagoreans' religious beliefs seem somewhat strange to us. They believed in the transmigration of souls and would not eat meat, being afraid that they might be dining off some departed friend. Among the things they considered sinful were

eating beans,
picking up anything that had fallen (a belief shared by many small children today),
eating from a whole loaf,
walking on highways (apparently Croton traffic was an earlier version of the Los Angeles Freeway),
letting swallows sit on one's roof.

When they were not worrying about these matters, the Pythagoreans passed the time studying philosophy and mathematics. Pythagoras said, "All is number," which meant that the form of all things in the world can be explained in terms of numbers. The mathematical basis of music was one of his important discoveries.

Probably the greatest accomplishment of his school was its investigation of what is today known as the Pythagorean theorem. This theorem says: In a right triangle (labeled as shown in Fig. 7.1),

$$a^2 + b^2 = c^2$$

It is said that Pythagoras was so pleased by this theorem that he sacrificed an ox to celebrate its discovery. Actually, various special cases of the theorem had been known for centuries before the Pythagoreans.

Unfortunately, this achievement led to the downfall of the society and its philosophy. Remember that they believed that the universe could be explained entirely in terms of *numbers,* which for them meant rational numbers. Now consider the right triangle shown in Fig. 7.2.

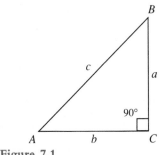

Figure 7.1

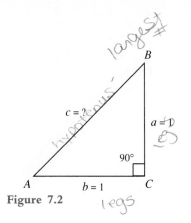

largest #

hypotenuse

$c = ?$

$a = 1$

$90°$

A $b = 1$ C

Figure 7.2

legs

Pythagorean triple

3, 4, 5

$3^2 + 4^2 = 5^2$

The Pythagorean theorem says

$$a^2 + b^2 = c^2$$
$$1^2 + 1^2 = c^2$$
$$1 + 1 = c^2$$
$$2 = c^2$$
$$2 = c \cdot c$$

$b^2 = c^2 - a^2$
to find
one side

Thus c is a number that when multiplied by itself gives 2. Symbolically (see the footnote on p. 381), $c = \sqrt{2}$. It was discovered by a Pythagorean named Hippasus (at least so the story goes) that $\sqrt{2}$ *is not a rational number.* Thus we have a physical thing, that is, the longest side of our triangle (the hypotenuse), that is *not* a rational number. This, of course, upset the whole Pythagorean philosophy.

The discovery that $\sqrt{2}$ is not a rational number was a terrible shock to Pythagoreans. According to one report, they drowned Hippasus to prevent him from spreading the "bad" news. (This is one way to solve a mathematical dispute.) Another version states that Hippasus was shipwrecked by the gods for his wickedness. However, nothing the Pythagoreans could do was able to change mathematical fact: $\sqrt{2}$ was not, and is not, rational. It is irrational.

It turns out that $\sqrt{2}$ is not the only irrational number. There are infinitely many of them. Another important irrational number that you might have come across in other mathematics courses is π (pronounced "pie"). In the Bible (I Kings 7:23 and II Chronicles 4:22), calculations indicate that 3 was used as the value of π. In recent years, π has been computed accurately to 500,000 places. The value of π correct to 14 places is 3.14159265358979. In the nineteenth century the legislature of Indiana attempted to pass a law establishing a fixed decimal value for π. They gave up when the idea was ridiculed in the press.

Fact $\sqrt{2}$ was, and is, not rational. It is irrational.

Let us see why. In order to prove this, we need a few simple definitions and facts.

integer

even

2n

even #

Definition 7.2   An integer is **even** if it can be divided exactly (no remainder) by 2. Thus every even number can be written as

$$2 \cdot (integer)$$

If you try to divide any number by 2, then either there is no remainder or the remainder is one. If there is no remainder, then the number is even. If the remainder is 1, then we have the following definition.

odd

[handwritten: 2n+1 odd]

Definition 7.3   An integer is said to be **odd** if it can be written as

$$2 \cdot (integer) + 1$$

EXAMPLE 1

The integer 16 is even, since we can write it as

$$16 = 2 \cdot 8$$

EXAMPLE 2

The integer 17 is odd, since we can write it as

$$17 = 2 \cdot 8 + 1$$

[handwritten: odd # is ✓ it still is odd]

Now consider the following:

The number 9 is an odd number. If we multiply it by itself, we get 9×9, or 9^2, which is 81. Notice that 81 is also an odd number.

Similarly, 7 is an odd number. And 7 multiplied by itself, or 7^2, gives 49 which is also an odd number.

In general, we have the following two statements:

Statement 1   *If a number, n, is odd, then n multiplied by itself is odd, or **if n is odd, then n^2 is odd.***

[handwritten: even # is ✓ it still is even]

Now look at the number 4, which is even: 4 is 2^2, and 2 is also even.

Similarly, 100 is also an even number; 100 is 10^2, and 10 is also even. This leads to the next statement.

Statement 2   *If the square of a number is even, then the number itself is even, or **if n^2 is even, then n is even.***

We will now prove these two statements. The proof of statement 1 requires a little algebra, so if you have had *no* algebra, go on to Example 3 below.

Proof of Statement 1   We are given an odd number, *n*.

We want to show that n^2 is also odd.

Since *n* is odd, we can write *n* as

$$2 \cdot (integer) + 1$$

Let us call the integer *k*. Then

$$n = 2k + 1$$

Therefore
$$n^2 = n \cdot n$$
$$= (2k + 1) \cdot (2k + 1)$$
$$= 4k^2 + 4k + 1 \qquad \text{(since the product } (2k + 1)(2k + 1)$$
$$\text{equals } 4k^2 + 4k + 1)$$
$$= (4k^2 + 4k) + 1 \qquad \text{(Here we use the associative law to group}$$
$$4k^2 + 4k \text{ together.)}$$
$$= 2(2k^2 + 2k) + 1 \qquad \text{(The distributive law is used here to}$$
$$\text{factor out the 2.)}$$

Now by the closure laws for integers $(2k^2 + 2k)$ is an integer also. Let us call it c. Then we have

$$n^2 = 2c + 1$$

That is,

$$n^2 = 2 \cdot (\text{integer}) + 1$$

This means that n^2 is an odd number, and our statement is proved.

Let us illustrate Statement 1 with some examples.

EXAMPLE 3

a) 3 is odd. Therefore 3^2, which is 9, is also odd.

b) 5 is odd. Thus 5^2, which equals 25, is also odd.   ▬

proof by contradiction

Before we prove statement 2 we first need to review the idea of a **proof by contradiction.** Suppose you were invited to a party at a certain address. When you arrive there, you discover that the house has two apartments, A and B, and you do not know which of them is the right one. You would pick one apartment, say A, and ring the bell. If the occupants of apartment A said that the party was not there, you would then know that it was in apartment B.

The reasoning process you would use in the above situation is the same as the reasoning in a proof by contradiction. We can summarize it as follows.

1. You know that either possibility A or B must be true.

2. You try possibility A and find that it is wrong.

3. You conclude that possibility B is correct.

This method will be used in our proof of Statement 2.

Proof of Statement 2

We are given an even number n^2 and asked to prove that n is also even. We know that *either n is odd* (possibility A) *or n is even* (possibility B).

Let us consider whether possibility A can be right. Possibility A says that n is odd.

If n is odd, then Statement 1 tells us that n^2 is also odd.
But we are given that n^2 is even.
Thus n *cannot be odd.*
We conclude that possibility A is wrong. It then follows that possibility B is right. This means that n must be even. Thus Statement 2 is proved.

EXAMPLE 4

a) 64, which is 8^2, is even. Therefore 8 is also even.

b) 36, which is the same as 6^2, is even. Thus 6 is also even.

Now we are ready to prove that $\sqrt{2}$ is not rational. The proof is again a proof by contradiction and uses a little algebra. If you have *never* studied algebra, omit it.

Proof that $\sqrt{2}$ is not rational
Either $\sqrt{2}$ is rational (possibility A) or $\sqrt{2}$ is not rational (possibility B.)

Suppose A is correct, so that $\sqrt{2}$ is rational. Then, by our definition of rational number, $\sqrt{2}$ can be written as $\frac{a}{b}$, where a and b are integers and b is not 0.

Now we know that every rational number can be reduced to lowest terms. So we can assume that

$$\sqrt{2} = \frac{a}{b} \qquad \text{where } a \text{ and } b \text{ have no common divisors (that is, } \frac{a}{b} \text{ is reduced to lowest terms.)}$$

Square both sides of this equation. We get

$$(\sqrt{2})^2 = \left(\frac{a}{b}\right)^2$$

$$2 = \frac{a^2}{b^2}$$

Multiply both sides by b^2. We get

$$2b^2 = \frac{a^2}{b^2} \cdot b^2$$

or upon simplifying,

$$2b^2 = a^2$$

We see that

$$a^2 = 2 \cdot b^2 = 2 \cdot (\text{integer}) \tag{1}$$

which means that a^2 is even.

Since a^2 is even, Statement 2 tells us that a must be even.
Now that we know a is even, we can write it as

$$a = 2 \cdot (\text{integer})$$

If we call this integer p, we have

$$a = 2p$$

Squaring both sides, we have

$$a^2 = (2p)^2 = 4p^2$$

If we substitute $4p^2$ for the a^2 in equation (1) above, we will get $4p^2 = 2b^2$. Dividing both sides by 2, we get

$$2p^2 = b^2$$

or

$$2 \cdot (\text{integer}) = b^2$$

This means that b^2 is even. Since b^2 is even, Statement 2 tells us that b is even. Thus we can write b as

$$b = 2 \cdot (\text{integer})$$

Now we have

$$a = 2 \cdot (\text{integer})$$
$$b = 2 \cdot (\text{integer})$$

So *a and b have a common divisor of 2.* But when we started out, *a and b had no common divisors.* This is obviously a **contradiction.** We must conclude that possibility A ($\sqrt{2}$ is rational) is wrong. Since A is wrong, B (which says that $\sqrt{2}$ is not rational) must be correct.

Finally, we conclude that $\sqrt{2}$ *is not rational.*

The Real Numbers

In Chapter 3, we started the discussion of our number system with the natural numbers. However, subtraction was not always possible using only the natural numbers, so we needed the integers. Although this made subtraction a closed operation, we still found that division was not always possible. To remedy this situation, we introduced the rational numbers. Then, we discovered that there exist certain numbers such as $\sqrt{2}$, $\sqrt{3}$, etc., that are not rational numbers but do occur frequently in mathematics. These we called the irrational numbers. All of these numbers together make up what we call the **real numbers.** These are the numbers used in most of elementary mathematics and in everyday situations. They are defined as follows.

real number

> **Definition 7.4   A real number** is any number that is either a rational number or an irrational number. In the notation of sets we have
>
> {real numbers} = {rational numbers} ∪ {irrational numbers}.

We can draw a diagram illustrating the relationship among the different kinds of numbers:

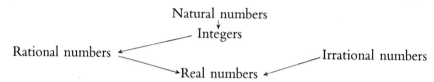

Another way of picturing the relationships between numbers is by means of a Venn diagram, as shown in Fig. 7.3.

Anything not a perfect square, is an irrational #

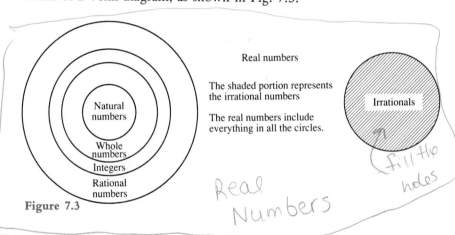

Figure 7.3

Real Numbers

(fill the holes

EXAMPLE 5

Let R = {real numbers}, I = {integers}, Q = {rational numbers}, and T = {irrationals}.

a) Find $R \cap Q$ **b)** Find $I \cap T$ **c)** Is $T \subset I$ true?

SOLUTION

a) $R \cap Q = Q$, since the diagram shows that the only elements that are in both sets are the rational numbers.

b) $I \cap T = \varnothing$, since the diagram shows that there is no number that is both an integer and an irrational number.

c) If $T \subset I$ were true, then the circle for the irrationals would be inside the circle for the integers. Since it is not true, then the statement $T \subset I$ cannot be true.

The commutative, associative, distributive, and closure laws hold for addition and multiplication. Subtraction and division are closed for real numbers (with the exception of division by 0 which, of course, is not possible).

The identity for addition is 0.
The identity for multiplication is 1.
Thus we see that the real-number system is a very complete system.

Picturing Real Numbers

real-number line

A very important property of the real numbers is that every real number is either positive, negative, or zero. A convenient way of picturing the real numbers is by means of a **real-number line.** Such a line is shown in Fig. 7.4.

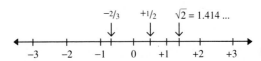

Figure 7.4

We pick a point on the line and label it 0. Then we pick another point to the right of 0 and label it $+1$. Next, we take a point to the right of $+1$ that is the same distance from $+1$ as $+1$ is from 0. We label this point $+2$. Similarly, we mark off $+3$, $+4$, $+5$, etc., ... Points to the left of 0 are labeled -1, -2, -3, etc.

Fractions are points between these numbers. (For example, see $+\frac{1}{2}$ and $-\frac{2}{3}$ in Fig. 7.4.)

Can we find a number like $\sqrt{2}$ on the number line? Look at the right triangle shown in Fig. 7.5. On p. 383 we showed that side c has length equal to $\sqrt{2}$. Now suppose we take this triangle and place point M at 0 on the number line, and place side c along the number line as shown in Fig. 7.6. Then N will be exactly $\sqrt{2}$ units to the right of 0. Thus the point on the number line that N touches is $\sqrt{2}$. It can be shown that $\sqrt{2}$ is approximately equal to 1.414. The number $\sqrt{2}$ cannot be represented exactly by a repeating or terminating decimal.

Every point on the line represents a real number. Similarly, every real number can be represented by a point on the line.

Pick any two numbers on the line. To be specific, let us take $+3$ and -2. The number $+3$ is to the right of -2. We say that $+3$ is larger than or greater than -2. This is symbolized by writing $(+3) > (-2)$. The symbol ">" stands for "is greater than."

We also see that -2 is to the left of $+3$. In this case we say that -2 is less than or smaller than $+3$. This is symbolized as $(-2) < (+3)$. The symbol "<" stands for "is less than."

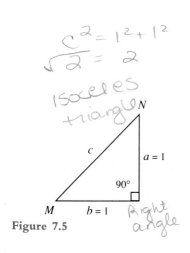

$$c^2 = 1^2 + 1^2$$
$$\sqrt{2} = 2$$

isoceles triangle

Figure 7.5

Right angle

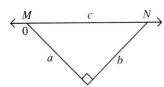

Figure 7.6

Sometimes we know that one number is either less than another number or equal to it. But we do not know which one is the case. In this situation we use the symbol "≤," which is read as "equal to or less than."

Similarly, the symbol "≥" means "equal to or greater than."

We can summarize our discussion in the following definition.

Definition 7.5   If a and b are any real numbers on a number line, then:

$a < b$ means a is to the left of b,

$a > b$ means a is to the right of b,

$a \leq b$ means a is to the left of b or a is the same as b, and

$a \geq b$ means a is the right of b or a is the same as b.

Comment   Given any two numbers a and b, then *one and only one* of the following must be true:

i) $a = b$

ii) $a > b$ or

iii) $a < b$

$$a = , >, < \; b$$

law of trichotomy

This is sometimes called the **law of trichotomy**.

EXAMPLE 6

a) $2 < 3$ means 2 is to the left of 3, as shown below.

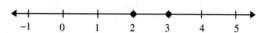

b) $5 > -3$ means 5 is to the right of -3, as shown below.

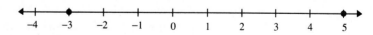

c) $10 \leq b$ means 10 is to the left of point b or the same as point b.   ▪

Order of Operations

Suppose we are asked to evaluate $2 + 3 \times 4$. There are two ways to approach this problem, as follows:

One person might multiply first and then add, getting	Another person might add first and then multiply, getting
$2 + 3 \times 4 = 2 + 12$	$2 + 3 \times 4 = 5 \times 4$
$= 14$	$= 20$

Obviously, the answers are not the same. Which is right?

Often when working with expressions involving two or more operations, we must decide which operation is to be performed first. Mathematicians have agreed upon procedures that specify the exact order to follow. We have

order of operations

> **Rule 7.3   Order of Operations** When simplifying expressions involving several operations,
> 1. do all the multiplications and divisions first, performing them in order from left to right,
> 2. then do all the additions and subtractions, performing them in order from left to right.

Applying Rule 7.3, we see that the value of $2 + 3 \times 4$ is 14, since we first multiply 3×4, getting 12, and then add $2 + 12$, getting 14.

EXAMPLE 7

Evaluate $8 \times 4 + 3 \times 5$

We do all the multiplications first and then add. Thus

$$8 \times 4 + 3 \times 5 = 32 + 15$$
$$= 47$$

EXAMPLE 8

Evaluate $18 + 0 \div 9 - 5 \times 0.2$

We first do all the multiplications and divisions from left to right and then add. Thus

$$18 + 0 \div 9 - 5 \times 0.2 = 18 + 0 - 1$$
$$= 17$$

Let us refer back to the example $2 + 3 \times 4$ given earlier. Rule 7.3 tells us that the answer is 14. Suppose we wanted to add the 2 and 3 together before multiplying by 4. In this case we would enclose the sum $2 + 3$ in parentheses and write this example as $(2 + 3) \times 4$. When written in this manner, we find the sum before doing the multiplication. Thus

$$(2 + 3) \times 4 = 5 \times 4 = 20$$

When $(2 + 3) \times 4$ is written with parentheses, then we do not follow Rule 7.3 as $(2 + 3) \times 4$ is *not* the same as $2 + 3 \times 4$. Thus when simplifying any expression involving parentheses (which act as a grouping symbol), we always perform the operations indicated on the numbers within the parentheses first.

Comment   Parentheses are not the only symbols used to indicate grouping. Brackets [ ] and braces { } are also used and have the same meaning as parentheses.

Comment   If an expression contains two or more grouping symbols, then we perform the operations on the numbers within the innermost symbols first.

We can now expand our rule for order of operations. We have

Rule 7.4   Order of Operations When Working with Parentheses

To simplify an expression involving parentheses (or any other grouping symbol) and several operations,

1. first perform the operations within the parentheses starting with the innermost group,
2. then do all the multiplications and divisions, performing them in order from left to right, and
3. finally do all the additions and subtractions, performing them in order from left to right.

EXAMPLE 9

SOLUTION

Simplify the expression $4 + 5[8 + (4 - 2) \times 3]$.

We start with the innermost parentheses first:

$$4 + 5[8 + (4 - 2) \times 3] = 4 + 5[8 + 2 \times 3]$$
$$= 4 + 5[8 + 6] \quad \text{(Inside the brackets we do multiplication first.)}$$
$$= 4 + 5(14) \quad \text{(We evaluate the numbers inside the parentheses.)}$$
$$= 4 + 70 \quad \text{(We multiply first.)}$$
$$= 74$$

When simplifying expressions containing powers (exponents), we first evaluate the exponent and then follow the usual order for the other operations. Thus

$$2 \times 5^2 = 2 \times 25 \quad \text{(since } 5^2 = 5 \times 5 = 25\text{)}$$
$$= 50$$

Our answer is 50 and *not* 100, which is obtained by first multiplying 2×5, getting 10, and then squaring. Exponents are evaluated first.

We summarize our discussions with the following general rule.

> **Rule 7.5   Order of Operations (General Case)** To simplify an expression involving exponents, parentheses, and several operations,
>
> 1. simplify any expressions that are within parentheses (or any other grouping symbol), starting with the innermost grouping symbol,
>
> 2. evaluate any powers or roots,
>
> 3. do all multiplications and divisions, performing them in order from left to right,
>
> 4. do all additions and subtractions, performing them in order from left to right.

EXAMPLE 10

SOLUTION

Evaluate $5(7 - 3)^2 - 2$.

$$5(7 - 3)^2 - 2 = 5(4)^2 - 2 \qquad \text{(We first simplify the expression within parentheses.)}$$
$$= 5(16) - 2 \qquad \text{(We evaluate the exponent.)}$$
$$= 80 - 2 \qquad \text{(We do the multiplication.)}$$
$$= 78 \qquad \text{(We do the subtraction.)}$$

Comment When using hand-held calculators, note that scientific calculators perform calculations according to Rule 7.5, but nonscientific calculators perform the various operations in the order in which they are written.

Calculators provide us with an easy way of estimating products and quotients involving decimals, as can be seen on student page 322 from *Addison-Wesley Mathematics*, 1987, Grade 5, which is shown on the next page.

Imaginary Numbers

You may have the impression that there can be no numbers other than real numbers. This is not true. To see this, consider the innocent-looking $\sqrt{-1}$ (the square root of -1). What does this symbol really mean? The symbol $\sqrt{-1}$ means some number which when multiplied by itself gives -1. Let us call this number i. Then $i^2 = -1$. Now what kind of number is i? Is it negative, positive, or zero?

If i is negative, then i^2 would have to be positive (since a negative number times a negative number is a positive number). But i^2 is -1, which is negative. Therefore i cannot be negative.

If i is positive, then i^2 would have to be positive (since a positive number times a positive number is a positive number). Since i^2 is -1, i cannot be positive.

If i is zero, then i^2 is 0 (since 0 times 0 is 0). This definitely is not -1.

< less than
left of a #

> greater than
right of a #

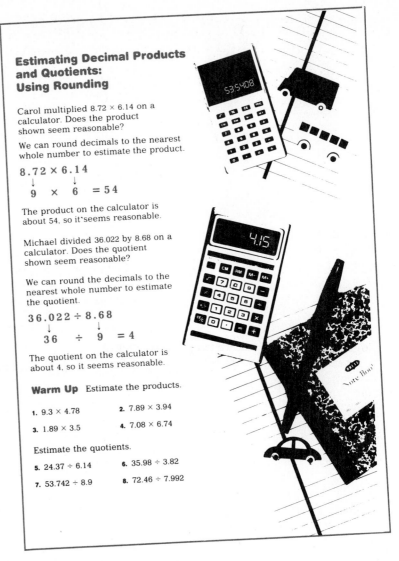

Estimating Decimal Products and Quotients: Using Rounding

Carol multiplied 8.72×6.14 on a calculator. Does the product shown seem reasonable?

We can round decimals to the nearest whole number to estimate the product.

$$8.72 \times 6.14$$
$$\downarrow \qquad \downarrow$$
$$9 \quad \times \quad 6 \quad = 54$$

The product on the calculator is about 54, so it seems reasonable.

Michael divided 36.022 by 8.68 on a calculator. Does the quotient shown seem reasonable?

We can round the decimals to the nearest whole number to estimate the quotient.

$$36.022 \div 8.68$$
$$\downarrow \qquad \downarrow$$
$$36 \quad \div \quad 9 \quad = 4$$

The quotient on the calculator is about 4, so it seems reasonable.

Warm Up   Estimate the products.

1. 9.3×4.78 2. 7.89×3.94

3. 1.89×3.5 4. 7.08×6.74

Estimate the quotients.

5. $24.37 \div 6.14$ 6. $35.98 \div 3.82$

7. $53.742 \div 8.9$ 8. $72.46 \div 7.992$

imaginary

complex numbers

So here we have a number, i (that is, $\sqrt{-1}$), that is neither negative, positive, nor zero. It follows that i cannot be a real number. (Remember that every real number is either negative, positive, or zero.)

Numbers like i are called **imaginary** or **complex numbers**. They play an important role in mathematics, physics, and technology. In particular, they are used in many branches of engineering, such as electrical engineering, heat conduction, elasticity, and aeronautical engineering. The suggestions for further reading at the end of this chapter contain some references to further discussions of imaginary numbers.

EXERCISES FOR SECTION 7.4

Solve Exercises 1 and 2 by using the Pythagorean theorem.

1. A 17-foot ladder leans against a building so that the base of the ladder is 15 feet away from the building, as shown. How high up the building does the ladder reach?

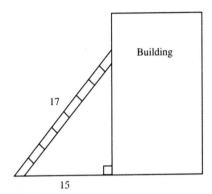

Building

17

15

2. A 24-foot telephone pole is to be anchored by a 26-foot long guy wire attached to a peg in the ground as shown. How far away from the base of the pole is the peg?

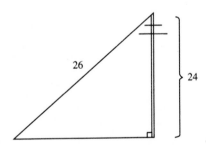

26

24

3. Let R = {real numbers}, I = {integers}, Q = {rational numbers}, and W = {irrational numbers}. Find each of the following:

a) $R \cap I$ b) $I \cap Q$ c) $W \cap I$
d) $R \cup Q$ e) $Q \cup W$ f) $W \cap R$
g) $W \cup R$ h) $I \cup Q$ i) $I \cap (Q \cup W)$

4. Using the notation of Exercise 3, which of the following statements are true?

a) $Q \subset R$ b) $Q \subset I$ c) $I \subset Q$
d) $R \subset W$ e) $W \subset R$ f) $I \subset (Q \cup W)$

5. Represent each of the following numbers on a number line.

a) 8   b) -9 c) $+\dfrac{1}{4}$

d) -0.7 e) 8.6   f) $\sqrt{7}$

6. Using a number line, determine which is the correct symbol ($>$, $=$, $<$) for each of the following pairs of numbers

a) 4.5, 4.6   b) $+5$, -6

c) -7, -8 d) $\dfrac{1}{4}$, $\dfrac{1}{5}$

e) 4, 4   f) $\dfrac{1}{8}$, 0.125

g) $\sqrt{3}$, 1.7   h) $\dfrac{1}{6}$, 0.166...

7. If x is any real number, then $x > 3$ means x is to the right of 3 on the number line. We can picture this as shown below:

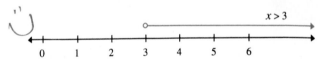

$x > 3$

0   1   2   3   4   5   6

Similarly, $x \leq -1$ can be pictured as

$x \leq -1$

-4 -3 -2 -1 0   1

Picture each of the following, using a number line.

a) $x \leq 4$ b) $x > -6$ c) $x < \dfrac{3}{4}$

d) $x \geq -8$ e) $x < -3$ f) $x \geq 5$

g) $x > -\dfrac{3}{5}$ h) $x \leq 0.8$

8. Let a, b, and x be any real numbers. Using the properties of real numbers, prove that if

$$a + x = b + x,$$

then

$$a = b.$$

This is called **cancellation law of addition.**

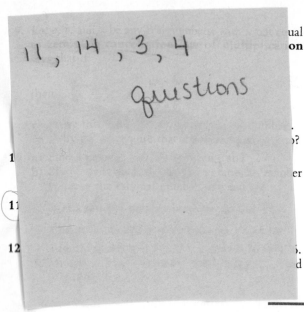

11, 14, 3, 4

questions

13. Evaluate each of the following expressions.

a) $40 + \frac{1}{2} \times 20$ **b)** $16 - 4 \div \frac{1}{2}$

c) $5 \times 9 - 3 \times 8$ **d)** $40 + 40 \div 5 + 3$

e) $4(5 - 9) - 4$ **f)** $6 + 7(9 - 5)$

g) $8 + 3[7 + (6 - 2) \times 5]$

h) $5 + 9[8 + (6 - 3) \times 2]$

i) $(2^4)\left(\frac{1}{2}\right)^5$ **j)** $6^2 + 7^2$

k) $5(6^2) - 36$ **l)** $(12 + 6)^2$

m) $14 - 3(4 - 2)^3$ **n)** $9(4^2 - 3^2)$

o) $2 + (10^2 - 9^2)(8^2 + 7^2) - 7$

14. Complete the following chart.

Number	Natural number	Whole number	Integer	Rational number	Irrational number	Real number
-5	no	no	yes	yes	no	yes
$\sqrt{13}$	no	no	no	no	yes	yes
5						
$-\frac{1}{8}$						
$3.021021\ldots$						
7.1						
0						
$6\sqrt{3}$						
$2.13587\ldots$						
$\frac{2}{\sqrt{3}}$						

15. Prove: If n is not divisible by 3, then n^2 is not divisible by 3.

16. Use Exercise 15 to prove: If n^2 is divisible by 3, then n is also divisible by 3.

17. Use Exercise 16 to prove that $\sqrt{3}$ is not rational.

18. Write a statement similar to that of Exercise 15 using 5 instead of 3.

19. Write a statement similar to that of Exercise 16 using 5 instead of 3.

20. Use Exercise 19 to prove that $\sqrt{5}$ is not rational.

21. Where, in our proof of the fact that $\sqrt{2}$ is not rational, did we use Statement 1?

22. We know that 1 is rational and $\sqrt{2}$ is not rational. Prove that the sum $1 + \sqrt{2}$ is not rational. (*Hint:* Use proof by contradiction.)

**23. Two examples of irrational numbers are $5\sqrt{3}$ and $4\sqrt{3}$.
a) Is their product irrational? Explain. **b)** Is their quotient irrational? Explain. **c)** Is their sum irrational? Explain.

**24. Show, by examples, that the product of two irrational numbers may be rational or may be irrational.

**25. Construct a line segment which measures $\sqrt{5}$ inches long. (*Hint:* Use the Pythagorean theorem for triangles.)

26. A **Pythagorean triple is a set of three nonzero whole numbers $\{a, b, c\}$ such that $a^2 + b^2 = c^2$. For example, $\{3, 4, 5\}$ is a Pythagorean triple. Find at least three other sets of Pythagorean triples where none is a multiple of the others.

27. One particular Pythagorean triple $\{3, 4, 5\}$ is called a **primitive Pythagorean triple since the numbers 3, 4, and 5, have 1 as their only common prime factor. On the other hand the Pythagorean triple $\{6, 8, 10\}$

is not a primitive Pythagorean triple as these numbers do not have 1 as their *only* common factor. It can be shown that for any primitive Pythagorean triple $\{a, b, c\}$ we must have $a = 2uv$, $b = u^2 - v^2$, and $c = u^2 + v^2$ where u and v are relatively prime, $u > v$, and either u or v is even with the other being odd. Using these equations, find at least three other sets of primitive Pythagorean triples.

**28. Consider the following decimal equations.

$$0.1089 \times 9 = x$$
$$0.10989 \times 9 = x$$
$$0.109989 \times 9 = x$$

Can you find the next two decimal equations in the above pattern?

**29. Using a number line that has decimals on it (as shown below), find

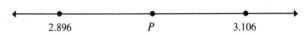

| 2.896 | P | 3.106 |

the decimal representation of point P, which is halfway between 2.896 and 3.106.

7.5

THE REAL NUMBERS: RATIONAL NUMBERS AS EXPONENTS

Throughout the remainder of this book we will be studying the real number system. Let us then pause for a moment to review some of its properties that we will use in analyzing the nature of algebra.

When working with real numbers, we must often deal with exponents. Although these were briefly discussed in Section 6.4, here we will expand our discussion to include rational numbers as exponents. First we have

---

Definition 7.5   If x is a real nonzero number and n is any integer, then

$$x^n = \underbrace{x \cdot x \cdot x \cdots x}_{n \text{ of them}}$$

exponent

base

x is called the **base**, and n is called the **exponent**.

For example, x^3 represents $x \cdot x \cdot x$, and 5^4 represents $5 \cdot 5 \cdot 5 \cdot 5$. If $n = 0$, then the value of x^n is defined to be 1. Thus $5^0 = 1$. Also, $x^{-n} = \dfrac{1}{x^n}$. For example,

$$x^{-7} = \frac{1}{x^7} \quad \text{and} \quad 7^{-3} = \frac{1}{7^3}$$

Similarly, $(100{,}000)^0 = 1$.

If your calculator has a $\boxed{y^x}$ button, then you can evaluate any expression involving exponents quite simply. For example, to evaluate 7^3 using a calculator, we proceed as follows:

What you do	What appears on display panel
Turn on machine	0.
Push 7 button	7.
Push y^x button	7.
Push 3 button	3.
Push = button	343.

Comment On most calculators the base must be a positive number when using the $\boxed{y^x}$ button. Otherwise you will get an error message.

Comment Great care must be exercised when using the $\boxed{y^x}$ button on the calculator. Try to evaluate 2×5^3 using the $\boxed{y^x}$ button. What happens?

When dealing with expressions involving exponents, we use certain properties. Since our discussion is intended only as a review, we will merely present the rules. A complete discussion and justification can be found in any algebra book.

Multiplication Rule $x^a \cdot x^b = x^{a+b}$ (We simply add the exponents.)

Power Rule $(x^a)^b = x^{ab}$ (We simply multiply the exponents.)

Quotient Rule $\dfrac{x^a}{x^b} = x^{a-b}$ $(x \neq 0)$ (We simply subtract the exponents.)

EXAMPLE 1

a) $x^7 \cdot x^5 = x^{7+5} = x^{12}$

b) $3^5 \cdot 3^9 = 3^{5+9} = 3^{14}$ (We do *not* multiply the 3's. We only add the exponents.)

c) $(5^7)^4 = 5^{7 \cdot 4} = 5^{28}$

d) $\dfrac{x^{15}}{x^5} = x^{15-5} = x^{10}$ (We do *not* divide the exponents.)

e) $\dfrac{10^5}{10^2} = 10^{5-2} = 10^3$ (We do *not* divide the 10's. We only subtract the exponents.) ▪

EXAMPLE 2

$\dfrac{16^2}{4^3}$ cannot be evaluated in its present form by using the quotient rule. The reason is that the bases are not the same. Of course, we can evaluate 16^2, getting 256, and evaluate 4^3, getting 64. We then divide 256 by 64. Our answer is 4. ▪

EXAMPLE 3

Refer back to Example 2. We notice that $16 = 4^2$. Thus

$$\frac{16^2}{4^3} = \frac{(16)^2}{4^3}$$

$$= \frac{(4^2)^2}{4^3}$$

$$= \frac{4^{2 \cdot 2}}{4^3} \qquad \text{(by the power rule)}$$

$$= \frac{4^4}{4^3}$$

$$= 4^1 \qquad \text{(by the quotient rule)} \qquad ▪$$

Comment   If the exponent of a number is 1, it is customary to omit it. Thus 4^1 will be written as 4.

Until now we have assumed that the exponent was an integer. Of course, exponents need not necessarily be integers. A number can have a rational number as an exponent also. Thus if x is a positive number, $x^{1/2}$ defined as $\sqrt{x}$, and $x^{1/3}$ is defined as $\sqrt[3]{x}$. Similarly, $x^{1/4}$ is defined as $\sqrt[4]{x}$. Thus $25^{1/2} = \sqrt{25}$ or the square root of 25. This means we are looking for a number that when multiplied by itself gives 25. One answer is 5, so that $25^{1/2} = 5$. Also, $8^{1/3} = \sqrt[3]{8}$ or the cube root of 8. This means that we are looking for a number that when multiplied by itself 3 times gives 8. One answer is 2, so that $8^{1/3} = 2$.

More generally, $x^{1/n} = \sqrt[n]{x}$, where $n \neq 0$. (If x is a negative number, then n may be an odd integer only.) This means that we are looking for a number that when multiplied by itself n times gives x. Applying this definition gives $\sqrt[n]{x^m} = (x^m)^{1/n} = x^{m/n}$. Also, $(\sqrt[n]{x})^m = (x^{1/n})^m = x^{m/n}$. Therefore

---

RULE 7.6 $x^{m/n} = \sqrt[n]{x^m}$ or $x^{m/n} = (\sqrt[n]{x})^m$ *where* $n \neq 0$ *and* $x > 0$.

The above rule is easy to use, as the following examples will illustrate.

EXAMPLE 4

a) $27^{2/3}$ means $(\sqrt[3]{27})^2$. Since $\sqrt[3]{27}$ represents the cube root of 27, or 3, we must evaluate 3^2. This, of course, equals 9. Thus $27^{2/3} = 9$.

b) $32^{3/5}$ means $(\sqrt[5]{32})^3$. Since $\sqrt[5]{32}$ means that we are looking for a number that when multiplied by itself 5 times gives 32, its value must be 2. Thus we must evaluate 2^3. This, of course, equals 8. Therefore $32^{3/5} = 8$.

EXAMPLE 5   Evaluate $8^{-2/3}$

SOLUTION   We first eliminate the negative exponent by rewriting

$$8^{-2/3} \quad \text{as} \quad \frac{1}{8^{2/3}}$$

Then we apply the above rule. We get

$$8^{-2/3} = \frac{1}{8^{2/3}} \qquad \text{(definition of negative exponents)}$$

$$= \frac{1}{(\sqrt[3]{8})^2} \qquad \text{(rule for fractional exponents)}$$

$$= \frac{1}{2^2}$$

$$= \frac{1}{4}$$

The rules for exponents can be used to simplify the square root (or more generally the nth root) of many numbers. The procedure is illustrated in the following examples.

EXAMPLE 6

Simplify each of the following:

a) $\sqrt{32}$ **b)** $\sqrt{27}$ **c)** $\sqrt[3]{250}$ **d)** $\sqrt{50} \cdot \sqrt{6}$

SOLUTION

a) $\sqrt{32} = \sqrt{16 \cdot 2} = \sqrt{16} \cdot \sqrt{2} = 4\sqrt{2}$
b) $\sqrt{27} = \sqrt{9 \cdot 3} = \sqrt{9}\sqrt{3} = 3\sqrt{3}$
c) $\sqrt[3]{250} = \sqrt[3]{125 \cdot 2} = \sqrt[3]{125} \cdot \sqrt[3]{2} = 5\sqrt[3]{2}$
d) $\sqrt{50} \cdot \sqrt{6} = \sqrt{50 \cdot 6} = \sqrt{300} = \sqrt{100 \cdot 3} = \sqrt{100} \cdot \sqrt{3} = 10\sqrt{3}$ ■

Expressions involving addition and subtraction of radicals can be combined when they are simplified.

EXAMPLE 7

Simplify $\sqrt{12} + \sqrt{48} - \sqrt{75}$

SOLUTION

We first note that $\sqrt{12} = \sqrt{4 \cdot 3} = \sqrt{4} \cdot \sqrt{3} = 2\sqrt{3}$

and that
$$\sqrt{48} = \sqrt{16 \cdot 3} = \sqrt{16} \cdot \sqrt{3} = 4\sqrt{3}.$$

Also
$$\sqrt{75} = \sqrt{25 \cdot 3} = \sqrt{25} \cdot \sqrt{3} = 5\sqrt{3}$$

so that
$$\sqrt{12} + \sqrt{48} - \sqrt{75} = 2\sqrt{3} + 4\sqrt{3} - 5\sqrt{3} = \sqrt{3}$$

We can summarize our discussion of exponents in the following table:

Notation	Name
$b^x = \underbrace{b \cdot b \cdot b \cdots b}_{x \text{ of them}}$ where x is an integer	Definition of exponents
$b^x \cdot b^y = b^{x+y}$	Multiplication rule
$(b^x)^y = b^{xy}$	Power rule
$b^{-x} = \dfrac{1}{b^x}$ $\quad (b \neq 0)$	Negative exponents
$b^0 = 1$	Zero exponents
$\dfrac{b^x}{b^y} = b^{x-y}$ $\quad (b \neq 0)$	Quotient rule
$b^{x/y} = (\sqrt[y]{b})^x = \sqrt[y]{b^x}$ $\quad (b > 0)$	Fractional exponents

EXERCISES FOR SECTION 7.5

1. Simplify each of the following expressions which involve exponents;

a) $16^{2/3}$ **b)** $64^{3/2}$ **c)** $-85^{5/3}$

d) $4^{-\frac{1}{2}}$ **e)** $\left(\dfrac{1}{2}\right)^{-3}$ **f)** $(5^2)^3$

g) 10^0 **h)** $4^{3/2} \cdot 4^{7/2}$ **i)** $\dfrac{16^4}{16^3}$

j) $(2^3)(2^2)(2^7)$ **k)** $49^{-3/2}$

l) $2 \cdot 3^2$ **m)** $(2^3 \cdot 3^3)^3$

2. Evaluate $25^{1/2}$, using a calculator.

3. Evaluate $5 \cdot 4^3$, using a calculator.

4. Evaluate $16^{-3/4}$, using a calculator.

5. Write each of the following square roots in simplest form:

a) $\sqrt{288}$ **b)** $\sqrt{18}$

c) $\sqrt{\dfrac{12}{27}}$ **d)** $\sqrt{\dfrac{32}{25}}$

6. Simplify each of the following:

a) $\sqrt[3]{-64}$ **b)** $\sqrt[3]{27}$

c) $\sqrt[4]{96}$ **d)** $\sqrt[3]{500}$

7. Combine each of the following:

a) $\sqrt{32} - \sqrt{8} + \sqrt{50}$

b) $\sqrt{27x^2} + \sqrt{75x^2} - 2x\sqrt{12}$

c) $\sqrt[3]{24} + \sqrt[3]{3}$

d) $\sqrt{20} + \sqrt{45}$

e) $\sqrt{28} - \sqrt{63}$

8. Simplify each of the following:

a) $16^{3/4} \cdot 4^{5/2}$ **b)** $125^{2/3} \cdot 8^{-4/3}$

9. Using a scientific calculator, approximate each of the following:

a) $(\sqrt{2})^{3/2}$ **b)** $(\sqrt{2})^{\sqrt{3}}$

c) $(\sqrt{5})^{\sqrt{5}}$ **d)** $16^{0.42}$

▶ Brain-Teaser Problems ◀

10. **a) Is $\sqrt{x^2 + y^2} = x + y$ for *all* values of x and y?

b) Is $\sqrt{x^2 + y^2} = x + y$ for *any* values of x and y?

11. The numbers 25 and 49 are examples of numbers that are called **perfect squares since they are squares of rational numbers. For example, 25 is a perfect square as, $\sqrt{25} = 5$ and 5 is a rational number. Similarly, $\frac{49}{81}$ is a perfect square as $\sqrt{\frac{49}{81}} = \frac{7}{9}$ and $\frac{7}{9}$ is a rational number. What about a number that is not a perfect square, for example, $\sqrt{2}$. We know that $\sqrt{2}$ is irrational. Using a calculator we can find an approximation to the value of $\sqrt{2}$ as follows. Since $1 \times 1 = 1$ and $2 \times 2 = 4$, then $\sqrt{2}$ must be between 1 and 2. Thus $1 < \sqrt{2} < 2$. Since $1.4 \times 1.4 = 1.96$ and $1.5 \times 1.5 = 2.25$, then $\sqrt{2}$ must be between 1.4 and 1.5. Therefore, $1.4 < \sqrt{2} < 1.5$. Continuing in this manner, we note that $1.41 \times 1.41 = 1.9881$ and $1.42 \times 1.42 = 2.0164$, so that $\sqrt{2}$ must be between 1.41 and 1.42, or that $1.41 < \sqrt{2} < 1.42$. Regardless of how far we continue this **squeezing process,** we will never reach a point where we can express $\sqrt{2}$ as a terminating or as a repeating decimal. We are merely finding approximations for $\sqrt{2}$. Using this squeezing process, approximate the square root of the following numbers to the nearest hundredth:

a) 5   **b)** 15.7   **c)** 0.029

**TYPICAL CLASSROOM
QUESTIONS**

1. When you add two repeating decimals, will your answer be a repeating decimal? Explain.

2. When you add two nonrepeating and nonterminating decimals, will your answer be a nonrepeating and nonterminating decimal? Explain.

3. In its January 2, 1967 issue, *Newsweek* reported on page 10 that Mao-Tse Tung cut the salaries of certain Chinese government officials by 300%. Is it possible for a salary to be cut by 300%? Explain your answer.

4. We know that $\sqrt{x^2} = x$. Can we conclude that $\sqrt{(-9)^2} = -9$? Explain your answer.

5. A student claims that since $\sqrt{a}\sqrt{b} = \sqrt{ab}$, then $\sqrt{-3}\sqrt{-3} = \sqrt{(-3)(-3)} = \sqrt{9} = +3$. Do you agree? Explain your answer.

6. The following multiplication problem appears on an arithmetic examination: Multiply (4.5) (6.5). Two students attempt to do the problem. One student converts the decimals to fractions and then multiplies the mixed numbers. The other student multiplies the numbers with their decimals. The students' computations are shown below:

Student 1	*Student 2*
4.5	$4.5 = 4\frac{1}{2}$
$\times\, 6.5$	$\times\, 6.5 = 6\frac{1}{2}$
$\overline{}$	
225	$2\frac{1}{4}$ (since $\frac{1}{2}$ times $4\frac{1}{2} = 2\frac{1}{4}$)
270	24 (since $6 \cdot 4 = 24$)
$\overline{29.25}$	$\overline{26\frac{1}{4}}$

Which student is correct? Explain your answer.

STUDY GUIDE

The following is a chapter outline in capsule form. You should now be able to demonstrate your knowledge of the ideas mentioned by giving definitions, or specific examples. Page references are given in parentheses.

A **terminating decimal** is one that ends after a specific number of places to the right of the decimal point. All terminating decimals are rational numbers. (p. 353)

A **repeating decimal** is one in which (after a certain point) the same pattern of numbers repeats itself endlessly. The technique for converting repeating decimals to rational numbers is given on p. 365.

A **nonterminating and nonrepeating decimal** is one that goes on forever without the same group of numbers repeating over and over in the same pattern. (p. 353)

Rule 7.1 presents guidelines for **rounding decimals** to the nearest tenth, hundredth. (p. 354)

A **percent** can be considered as the ratio of a number to 100. Thus, percent means per hundred. $x\%$ means $\dfrac{x}{100}$ (p. 358)

Interest is the money paid for the use of money. The amount of money borrrowed or the amount of money involved when an individual lends money to someone is called the **principal.** When we borrow money and do not repay the monthly charges by the date specified, we are charged a **finance charge** (interest). (p. 367)

Simple interest is generally used for short-term loans and is computed on the whole amount of money borrowed for the entire period of the loan. When interest is added to the original loan so that interest is earned (or paid) on interest in addition to the principal, thereby increasing the amount of interest paid, we have **compound interest.** (p. 367)

A person buying a house may arrange for a long-term **mortgage** from a bank and agree to repay the mortgage by making equal periodic payments to the bank. These periodic payments consist of partial repayment of the principal plus interest payments on the declining balance of the principal. A payment made under these conditions is called **amortization. (**p. 375)

When the rate of interest on a loan is adjusted up or down at a specified interval, and when the rate depends on the yield of one-year U.S. treasury bills or the cost of funds to the bank, we have **Adjustable Rate Mortgages (ARM)** or **Variable Rate Mortgages.** Many banks charge points on mortgage loans. One **point** equals 1% of the amount of the mortgage. (p. 377)

The **Annual Percentage Rate (APR)** represents the true interest rate on a loan. (p. 378).

Numbers that can be written as nonrepeating and nonterminating decimals are called **irrational numbers.** (p. 381)

An integer is **even** if it can be divided exactly (no remainder) by 2. (p. 383)

An integer is said to be **odd** if it can be written as $2 \cdot (\text{integer}) + 1$. (p. 384)

A **proof by contradiction** can be used when we have two possibilities, A or B, that must be true. We try possibility A and find that it is wrong. We then conclude that possibility B is correct. (p. 385)

A **real number** is any number that is either a rational number or an irrational number. (p. 388)

The real numbers are often pictured on a **real-number line.** (p. 389)

The **law of trichotomy** states that for any two real numbers a and b, one and only one of the following must be true: (i) $a = b$ (ii) $a > b$ or (iii) $a < b$. (p. 390)

When performing computations involving real numbers, the **order of operations** rule specifies which operation is performed first. (p. 393)

Numbers involving square roots of negative numbers are called **imaginary** or **complex numbers** and involve i where $i = \sqrt{-1}$. (p. 393)

We define real numbers involving **fractional exponents** as $x^{m/n} = \sqrt[n]{x^m}$ or $x^{m/n} = (\sqrt[n]{x})^m$. (p. 400)

KEY TERMS

The following list presents the key terms introduced in this chapter.

7.1 decimal
 decimal point
 decimal form
 terminating decimal
 repeating decimal
 nonterminating and
   nonrepeating decimal
 rounding decimals
 operations with decimals
 percent
 percent increase
 converting percents to decimals

7.2 interest
 finance charges
 principal and interest
 compound interest
 simple interest formula
 compound interest formula
 compounded continuously
 the number e
 effective annual interest rate

7.3 installment plan
 down payment
 mortgage
 amortization
 conventional loans (mortgages)

 adjustable rate mortgages
   (ARM)
 variable rate mortgages
 points
 annual percentage rate
   (APR)

7.4 irrational numbers
 proof by contradiction
 real numbers
 real number line
 law of trichotomy
 order of operations
 imaginary (complex)
   numbers
 cancellation law of
   addition
 cancellation law of
   multiplication
 Pythagorean triples
 primitive Pythagorean
   triples

7.5 base
 exponent
 fractional exponent
 perfect squares
 squeezing process

FORMULAS TO REMEMBER

The following list summarizes all the formulas discussed in this chapter.

To **round decimals** use Rule 7.1 given on page 354.

Simple-Interest Formula The total simple interest, I, in dollars on a loan of P dollars, where the annual interest rate is r, is given by $I = P \cdot r \cdot n$

Compound-Interest Formula The compound amount A (principal + interest) that results when P dollars are invested at a rate of r per period for n periods is $A = P(1 + r)^n$

If P dollars are invested in a bank that pays interest at the rate of r per year **compounded continuously,** the amount of money accumulated, A, after n years is $A = Pe^{rn}$.

The **effective annual interest rate** corresponding to an interest rate of r compounded continuously is $e^r - 1$.

To determine the **periodic payments under an amortization payment plan**, multiply the amount of the mortgage by the appropriate value obtained from Table A3.

To find the actual **Annual Percentage Rate** (APR), first divide the actual interest charge by the amount borrowed. Then multiply the result by 100. This gives the interest charge per $100 borrowed. Using this number find the actual APR from Table A4.

The **order of operations** rules as given on p. 391.

When working with real numbers, the following apply:

a) To change a rational number to a decimal, divide the denominator of the fraction into the numerator.

b) To convert a number written with a percent symbol to a decimal equivalent, drop the percent symbol and divide the number by 100 or drop the percent symbol and move the decimal point two places to the left.

c) To change a number from decimal form to a percent form, multiply by 100 and add the percent symbol or move the decimal point two places to the right and add the percent symbol.

d) To convert a nonterminating but repeating decimal to a rational number, use the procedure outlined in Exercise 5 on p. 365.

The rules for exponents are summarized on p. 401. Additionally, we have $x^{m/n} = \sqrt[n]{x^m}$ or $x^{m/n} = (\sqrt[n]{x})^m$ where $n \neq 0$ and $x > 0$.

CHAPTER REVIEW EXERCISES

1. Convert $\frac{8}{9}$ to a percent.

2. Convert 0.532 into a percent.

3. Change $2\frac{3}{4}\%$ into decimals.

4. What is $4\frac{1}{2}\%$ of 360?

5. Nine is $7\frac{1}{2}\%$ of what number?

6. Perform the indicated operations and round off all answers to the nearest hundredth:

   a) Subtract 5.39 from 8.143

b) Subtract 7.618 from 11

c) Multiply 3.712 by 81.58

d) Multiply 5.163 by 0.0078

e) Divide 8.41 by 3.6

f) Divide 16.032 by 0.0023

7. The electric meter on Jan's house read 4376.2 kilowatt hours at the beginning of the month. At the end of the month it read 4628.4 kilowatt hours. What is Jan's electric bill for this month if electricity in her area costs 13.89 cents per kilowatt hour?

8. Express 0.191919... as a rational number.

9. Is it true or false that $(-5) < (-3)$?

10. Nonterminating but repeating decimals are

   a) rational numbers

   b) integers

   c) irrational numbers

   d) whole numbers

   e) none of these

11. Simplify: $9 \times 8 - 2^4$.

12. Evaluate $[(-50) \div (-5)^2] \div [(-2)^3 + 4]$

13. Find a real number such that if you quadruple $\frac{1}{8}$ of it and multiply the result by the original number, the answer will be $\frac{32}{25}$.

14. At a sale Bill purchased a calculator for $15.60. At this price, Bill saved 35% of the original price. What was the original price of the calculator?

15. A teacher announces that 22 of the 27 students who took a CLEP examination passed. What percentage of the students passed?

16. Mary owns a $5000 municipal bond. She receives a check every 6 months (representing interest payments for the 6-month period) in the amount of $237.50. What is the annual rate of interest?

17. Evaluate $6 \cdot 2^{-3}$ using a calculator.

18. Write $\sqrt{72}$ in simplest form.

19. Combine: $5\sqrt{12} + 2\sqrt{48}$

20. Simplify: $\sqrt[3]{-8} + \sqrt[3]{-27} + \sqrt[3]{-64} + \sqrt[3]{-125}$

21. Find the simple interest on a loan of $7500 for $2\frac{1}{2}$ years given that the rate of interest is 9% per year.

22. Alan borrows $1500 from his friend for 8 months. The simple interest rate is 25% per year. How much money does Alan have to repay to his friend?

23. Zelda borrows $525 from her boss and agrees to repay $600 to her boss in three months. What is the annual simple rate of interest?

24. Gazelle arranges for a short term loan with the mechanic to repair her car. The annual rate of interest is 15%. If the total interest charged is $25 and Gazelle repays the loan in 2 months, how much money did she borrow?

25. What is the effective annual interest yield of a 9% annual interest rate compounded continuously?

26. Gregory invests his son's gifts from his first birthday, which amount to $743.00, in a certificate of deposit that pays interest at an annual rate of 12% compounded quarterly. How much will this money be worth when Gregory's son starts college at age 18?

27. Helen, who is $45\frac{1}{2}$ years old, opens an Individual Retirement Account (IRA) by depositing $2000. If Helen makes no other deposits and the bank pays 10% interest a year compounded quarterly, how much money will Helen have when she reaches $59\frac{1}{2}$ years of age and is eligible to withdraw the money?

28. In a certain state, the personal income tax rate is $825 plus $12\frac{1}{4}$% for any earnings over $38,000. If Jane Rodgers earns $43,712 a year, what is her personal tax liability in her state?

29. Karen has just purchased a used car for $3000. She makes a down payment of 20% and agrees to pay the balance on the installment plan by making 40 weekly payments of $80. What is the total cost of the car (including interest)?

30. Reggie has just renovated his house at a cost of $10,000. He paid the contractor $4000 as a down payment and agreed to pay the $6000 balance in 6 monthly installments with a minimum payment of $1000 per month. Interest is $1\frac{1}{2}$ % per month on any unpaid balance. Reggie wishes to pay the minimum amount. What is the total cost of the renovations including interest?

31. Rich Jones bought a complete home entertainment center for $1289. He made a down payment of $200 and agreed to pay the $1089 balance in equal monthly payments over a 2-year period. Interest is 18% a year compounded monthly. How much money must Rich pay monthly in order to amortize the loan over the 2-year period?

32. Terry Raskin arranged for a $65,000 conventional mortgage from a bank that charges 12% annual interest compounded quarterly. The loan is to run for 11 years. What are Terry's quarterly payments?

SUGGESTED FURTHER READING

Boling, B., "A Different Method for Solving Percentage Problems," in *The Mathematics Teacher* **78** (October 1985), 523–524.

Cole, B., and H. Weissenfluh, "An Analysis of Teaching Percentages," in *The Arithmetic Teacher* **21** (March 1974), 226–228.

Dewar, Jk., "Another Look at the Teaching of Percent," in *The Arithmetic Teacher* **31** (March 1984), 48–49.

Dressler, I., and B. Rich, *Algebra Two and Trigonometry*. New York: Amsco School Publications, 1972.

Glatzer, D., "Teaching Percentage: Ideas and Suggestions," in *The Arithmetic Teacher* **31** (February 1984), 24–26.

Grossman, A., "Decimal Notation: An Important Research Finding," in *The Arithmetic Teacher* **30** (May 1983), 32–33.

Jacobs, J., and E. Herbert, "Making $\sqrt{2}$ Seem 'Real'," in *The Arithmetic Teacher* **21** (February 1974), 133–136.

Keenan E., and A. Gantert, *Integrated Math-Course III*. New York: Amsco School Publications, 1982.

Newmark, J., *Using Finite Mathematics*. New York: Harper and Row, 1982.

Robidoux, D., and N. Montefusco, "An Easy Way to Change Repeating Decimals to Fractions—Nick's Method," in *The Arithmetic Teacher* **24** (January 1977), 81–82.

Wagner, S., "Fun with Repeating Decimals," in *The Mathematics Teacher* **26** (January 1979), 18–20.

CHAPTER 8

Probability

CHAPTER OBJECTIVES

- ☐ **To discuss** a counting principle and tree diagrams that can be used to find the number of possible outcomes of an experiment. (*Section 8.1*)

- ☐ **To distinguish** between permutations and combinations which are arrangements of objects in which order does and does not count, respectively. (*Section 8.2*)

- ☐ **To study** formulas for calculating the number of possible permutations, $_nP_r$, and the number of possible combinations, $_nC_r$, by using factorial notation (a shorthand notation for multiplication) or by using Pascal's triangle. (*Section 8.2*)

- ☐ **To define** what is meant by probability. (*Section 8.3*)

- ☐ **To look at** a procedure for obtaining random numbers. (*Section 8.3*)

- ☐ **To indicate** that mutually exclusive events are events that cannot occur at the same time. (*Section 8.4*)

- ☐ **To analyze** independent events in which the occurrence of one event does not affect the occurrence of a second event. (*Section 8.5*)

- ☐ **To use** probability to determine the odds in favor of or the odds against some event. (*Section 8.6*)

- ☐ **To apply** probability and to determine the amount of money to be won or lost in the long run (mathematical expectation). (*Section 8.6*)

NCTM GUIDELINES

In its March 1989 *Curriculum And Evaluation Standards For School Mathematics* (p. 109), The National Council Of Teachers Of Mathematics recommends that the mathematics curriculum should include explorations of probability in real-world settings so that students can

❑ model situations by devising and carrying out experiments or simulations to determine probabilities,

❑ model situations by constructing a sample space to determine probabilities,

❑ appreciate the power of using a probability model by comparing experimental results with mathematical expectations,

❑ make predictions that are based on experimental or theoretical probabilities,

❑ develop an appreciation for the pervasive use of probability in the real world.

Probability, the measure of the likelihood of an event, can be determined theoretically or experimentally. An understanding of probability and the related area of statistics is essential to being an informed citizen. Since the study of probability develops concepts and methods for investigating the fairness and the chances of winning games, in this chapter we will study the concepts of probability. We will especially emphasize the above points.

Introduction

Many people start the day by listening to the weather forecast. The announcer may say: "There is a 90% *probability* of rain today." What is meant by this statement? Either it will rain or it won't rain.

We also frequently hear expressions such as "I'll *probably* get an A in this course." or "I'll *probably* call her for a date," or "In all *probability*, you are right."

Even children are taught to use probability for making predictions. This can be seen from the accompanying student page from *Addison-Wesley Mathematics*, 1987, Grade 8, p. 336.

Predicting with Probability

Based on weather records, a meteorologist said, "The probability of a tornado in a Southwest region of the United States on any day is about $\frac{1}{7}$.

About how many tornadoes would be expected in this region in a year?

Since $P(\text{tornado}) = \frac{1}{7}$, this means we can expect the area to have a tornado on about $\frac{1}{7}$ of the days in a year.

Expected tornadoes = $P(\text{tornado}) \times$ number of days

Expected tornadoes $= \frac{1}{7} \times 365 = 52\frac{1}{7}$

About 52 tornadoes would be expected in the Southwest region each year.

Other Examples

Toss a coin 100 times.
Predict the number of heads.

$P(\text{H}) = \frac{1}{2}$

Expected number of heads $= \frac{1}{2} \times 100 = 50$

Toss two dice 120 times. Predict the number of times the sum will be 7.

$P(\text{sum of } 7) = \frac{1}{6}$

Expected sums of 7 $= \frac{1}{6} \times 120 = 20$

Warm Up

Give the probability of each event. Then predict the number of times the event will occur.

1. Spin the spinner 60 times.

$P(\text{red}) = $
Expected number red =

2. Toss two pennies 80 times.

$P(\text{H,H}) = $
Expected number (H,H) =

HISTORICAL NOTE

The mathematical study of probability can be traced back to the mathematician Jerome Cardan (1501–1576). The illegitimate child of a distinguished lawyer, Cardan became a famous doctor, who treated many prominent people throughout Europe. On various occasions he was also a professor of medicine at several Italian universities. While practicing as a doctor, he also studied, taught, and wrote mathematics.

Although he was extremely talented, Cardan's personality and personal life appear to have been less than perfect. He was very hot-tempered. In fact, he is said to have cut off one of his son's ears in a fit of rage. (His sons seem to have followed their father's example. One of them poisoned his own wife.)

Cardan was also an astrologer. There is a legend that claims that he predicted the date of his death astrologically and, to guarantee its accuracy, he drank poison on that day. That's one way of being right!

Cardan suffered from many illnesses that prevented him from enjoying life. To forget his troubles, he gambled daily for many years. His intense interest in gambling led him to write a book on the subject. This work, called *The Book on Games of Chance*, is really a textbook for gamblers, complete with tips on how to succeed in cheating. In this book we find the beginnings of the study of probability.

The development of mathematical probability was further helped along its way by the Chevalier de Méré. Like Cardan, he was a gambler. He was also an amateur mathematician and was interested in the following prob-

Jerome Cardan (1501–1576).

lem: Suppose a gambling game must be interrupted before it is finished. How should the players divide up the money that is on the table? He sent the problem to his friend, the mathematical genius Blaise Pascal (1623–1662).

When Pascal received the Chevalier de Méré's gambling problem, he sent it to his friend, the great amateur mathematician Pierre Fermat (1602–1665). The two men wrote to each other on this subject. This correspondence was the starting point for the modern theory of probability. Many other gifted mathematicians were attracted by the work that Pascal and Fermat had begun.

Historically, probability theory had its beginnings in the gambling halls and was used by gamblers to succeed in cheating. However, as the subject of statistics developed, it was discovered that a knowledge of probability is also essential to the statistician. Today, the use of probability in gambling is just one of its minor applications. The importance of probability lies in its wide range of application to such nonmathematical fields as medicine, psychology, economics, and business, to name a few.

In this chapter we will be discussing the meaning of probability and how it is used.

8.1

COUNTING PROBLEMS

Suppose we toss two coins. What are the possible outcomes? There are four possibilities.

Coin 1	Coin 2
Head	Head
Head	Tail
Tail	Head
Tail	Tail

If we let H stand for head and T stand for tail, then the set of these outcomes can be written as {HH, HT, TH, and TT}.

If we were to flip a coin three times, then we would have eight possible outcomes. These form the set {HHH, HHT, HTH, HTT, THH, THT, TTH, and TTT}.

In these two examples, and in other similar problems, it is rather simple to list and count all the possible outcomes. In other situations there may be so many possible outcomes that it may be impractical or impossible to list all the possibilities. For problems like that, we will introduce an easy rule that can be used. The following examples will illustrate the above ideas.

EXAMPLE 1

a) A die (the plural is dice) is tossed once. The possible outcomes are 1, 2, 3, 4, 5, and 6.

b) If two dice are tossed, then there are 36 possible outcomes. These are

1, 1	1, 2	1, 3	1, 4	1, 5	1, 6
2, 1	2, 2	2, 3	2, 4	2, 5	2, 6
3, 1	3, 2	3, 3	3, 4	3, 5	3, 6
4, 1	4, 2	4, 3	4, 4	4, 5	4, 6
5, 1	5, 2	5, 3	5, 4	5, 5	5, 6
6, 1	6, 2	6, 3	6, 4	6, 5	6, 6

EXAMPLE 2

Four men and five women have signed up for mixed doubles at the Norfolk Tennis Club. (In mixed doubles two teams compete against each other, and each team consists of one man and one woman.) The men are Stu, Drew, Lou, and Hugh. The women are Nell, Adele, Anabel, Clarabel, and Maybelle. How many different teams can be arranged?

SOLUTION

There are 20 possible teams. These are listed below.

Men	Women	Men	Women
Stu	Nell	Lou	Nell
Stu	Adele	Lou	Adele
Stu	Anabel	Lou	Anabel
Stu	Clarabel	Lou	Clarabel
Stu	Maybelle	Lou	Maybelle
Drew	Nell	Hugh	Nell
Drew	Adele	Hugh	Adele
Drew	Anabel	Hugh	Anabel
Drew	Clarabel	Hugh	Clarabel
Drew	Maybelle	Hugh	Maybelle

There are four men and five women. Norfolk can select either Stu, Drew, Lou, or Hugh as the man for any team. If they select Stu, then they can select any one of the five women to be his partner. Thus there are five possible teams on which Stu can be the male partner. Similarly, there are five teams on which Drew can be the male partner, five teams for Lou, and five for Hugh. This makes a total of 4×5, or 20, teams. If there were 5 men and 6 women, then each of the 5 men would have 6 possible partners, and there would be 5×6, or 30, possible teams.

This leads us to the following useful rule.

Rule 8.1 If one thing can be done in m ways, and if, after this is done, something else can be done in n ways, then there are a total of $m \cdot n$ possible ways of doing both things (in the stated order).

Fundamental Principle of Counting

Comment This rule is often known as **The Fundamental Principle of Counting**.

EXAMPLE 3

Sally is planning to go away for a week and is taking with her three blouses and four skirts. Sally will wear any of the blouses with any of the skirts. How many different outfits will Sally have if the colors of the clothes are as shown below?

Blouses	Skirts
Beige	Beige
White	Blue denim
Black	Gray
	Red

SOLUTION

For each outfit, Sally can select any one of three blouses and any one of four skirts. This gives her a total of 3×4, or 12, possible outfits.   ■

EXAMPLE 4

Assume that we have a deck of cards that consists of only four aces, four kings, four queens, and four jacks. We first select one card from this deck and then, without replacing it, select another. How many different outcomes are there?

SOLUTION

On the first draw, any one of 16 cards may be selected. There are now only 15 cards left for the second draw. This gives us a total of

$$16 \times 15 = 240 \text{ possible outcomes}$$ ■

EXAMPLE 5

How many different three-digit numbers can be formed by using only the numbers 5, 7, 8, or 9, if

a) repetitions are allowed?

b) repetitions are not allowed?

c) you can't start with 5, but repetitions are allowed?

SOLUTION

a) The first digit can be 5, 7, 8, or 9; that is, it can be chosen in four different ways. Similarly (since repetition is permitted), the second digit can be chosen in four different ways. The same is true for the third digit. This gives us four possibilities for the first digit, four possibilities for the second digit, and four possibilities for the third digit, so that we have

$$4 \times 4 \times 4 = 64$$

possible three-digit numbers. Notice that we are using the same rule as given above, but we have extended it to three possible things. The same rule can obviously be extended to any number of possible things.

b) Again there are four different ways of selecting the first digit. Once we select a digit (whatever it is), it can no longer be used. Thus for the second digit we have only *three* choices. For the last digit there are only *two* choices. Why? Therefore we have a total of

$$4 \times 3 \times 2 = 24 \text{ possible three-digit numbers}$$

c) Since 5 cannot be used as the first digit, there are *three* choices for the first digit. However, *any* number, including 5, may be used for both the second and third digits. Thus for each of these there are four possible choices. This gives us a total of

$$3 \times 4 \times 4 = 48 \text{ possible three-digit numbers}$$

EXAMPLE 6

In Example 3 Sally could choose any one of three blouses and any one of four skirts. The solution to this problem can be pictured in a diagram as shown in Fig. 8.1.

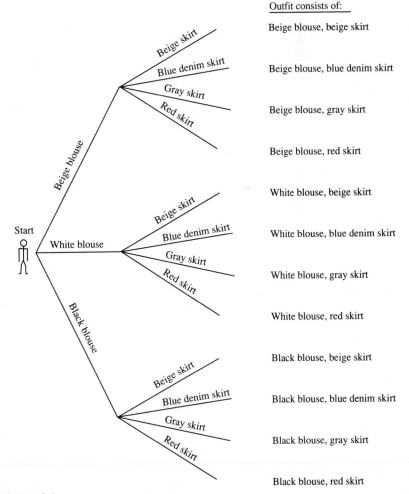

Outfit consists of:

Beige blouse, beige skirt

Beige blouse, blue denim skirt

Beige blouse, gray skirt

Beige blouse, red skirt

White blouse, beige skirt

White blouse, blue denim skirt

White blouse, gray skirt

White blouse, red skirt

Black blouse, beige skirt

Black blouse, blue denim skirt

Black blouse, gray skirt

Black blouse, red skirt

Figure 8.1

tree diagram

This diagram shows each blouse paired with all possible skirts. Such a diagram is called a **tree diagram.** We construct it as follows.
We draw a branch for each blouse. Each branch then breaks up into four smaller branches corresponding to the four skirts. The number of possible outcomes is obtained by counting the total number of smaller branches on the right.

EXAMPLE 7

A coin is tossed four times. Using a tree diagram, find the total number of possible outcomes.

SOLUTION

There are 16 little branches on the right of the diagram as shown in Fig. 8.2. So there is a total of 16 possible outcomes.

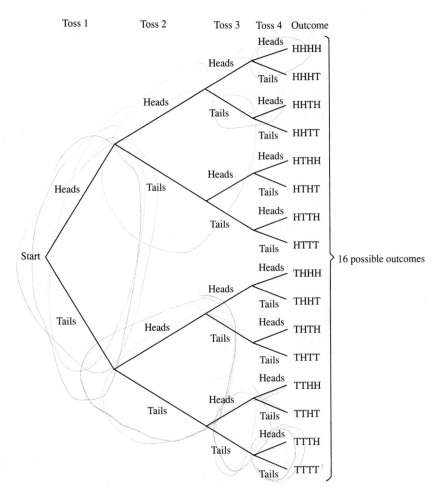

Figure 8.2

EXERCISES FOR SECTION 8.1

1. A television network has the following list of possible shows: four quiz shows, three variety shows, three movies, and two newscasts. In how many different ways can it schedule these shows, assuming that any other factors can be neglected and assuming that order counts?

2. A restaurant offers the following menu:

Main course	Dessert	Beverage
Shrimp	Tapioca	Soda
Lamb chop	Rice pudding	Tea
Ham	Ice cream	Coffee
Steak	Jelly tart	
Fish and chips		
Chicken		

In how many different ways can a meal be ordered?

3. In the first row of a jury box there are 6 vacant seats. In how many different ways can 6 jurors be seated in this row of 6 seats?

4. In a certain state all domestic animals (dogs and cats) must have a coded identification tag around their neck. These identification tags are of the following type: The first place of each identification code must be a 3, the second and third places must be letters, and the fourth and fifth places can be any numbers with repetition allowed. How many different identification tags can be made?

5. Seven people are waiting at a motor vehicle office to have their photos taken for new driver's licenses. In how many different ways can they stand in line?

6. Consider the article at the right. Eight depositors are anxiously standing in line waiting to withdraw their money. In how many different ways can they stand in line?

7. A jewelry salesman carries all of his samples in his attaché case. There is a combination lock on either side of the case. Each lock has three dials that have to be rotated independently so that any number from 0 to 9 inclusive shows on each dial. Both locks can be opened only if the correct number shows on each dial displayed. How many combinations does a thief have to try before the locks open and the thief can steal the sample jewels from the attaché case?

8. How many different three-digit numbers larger than 700 can be formed from the digits 5, 6, 7, 9 if

a) repetition is allowed?

b) repetition is not allowed?

9. There are 9 approach roads leading to an airport. Because of heavy traffic, a taxi driver decides to go to the airport by one road and to leave by another road. In how many different ways can this be done?

10. How many different numbers greater than 2000 can be formed with the digits 1, 3, 4, and 7 if no repetitions are allowed?

11. The *New York Daily News* has as a daily feature a five-letter or a six-letter word that the reader has to unscramble to make a meaningful word. In how many different ways can the letters of the word "MODERN" be arranged? (*Note:* Each arrangement does not necessarily have to form a word.)

*12. In the base 5 number system of counting, how many different three-digit numbers are there? (*Note:* A three-digit number cannot have zeros as the first digit or the first two digits. Thus 001 is not a three-digit number.)

Police Quell Depositor Unrest

NEW YORK: Local police had to be called in yesterday to restore order at the Golden Pacific Bank following the announcement by state banking officials that the bank was insolvent and that depositors would be allowed to withdraw only $100 per person pending further action by the Federal Deposit Insurance Corporation.

THE LOCAL TIMES, June 10, 1985

13. In how many different ways can the letters of each of the following words be arranged?

a) GOAL $\quad 4 \cdot 3 \cdot 2 \cdot 1 = 24$

b) GREAT $\quad 5 \cdot 4 \cdot 3 \cdot 2 \cdot 1 = 120$

c) DESTROY $\quad 7 \cdot 6 \cdot 5 \cdot 4 \cdot 3 \cdot 2 \cdot 1 = 5040$

(*Note:* Each arrangement does not necessarily have to form an English word.)

14. *Environmental Protection.* In an effort to protect the environment, the Nuclear Regulatory Commission of a certain state requires that all nuclear or chemical wastes be placed in special drums. These drums must then be stamped with numbers or letters as follows:

a) The company number as assigned by the commission; there are 6 companies within the state.

b) The plant location within the state; the state is divided into 8 geographical areas labeled A, B, C, D, E, F, G, or H.

c) The date of sealing: month and last two digits of the year.

For example, a drum with the code 3A0784 stamped on it means that it was sealed by company 3 located in area A during July 1984. Using the above scheme, how many different codes are possible for drums sealed during the years 1980–1986?

15. Using tree diagrams, determine the total number of possible ways that a family can consist of four children.

  Brain-Teaser Problems

**16. An amateur auto mechanic is repairing his car and accidentally disconnects 3 cables as shown in the accompanying diagram. A qualified mechanic arrives and must reconnect the cables exactly as they were originally. In how many different ways can the cables be reconnected?

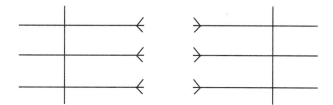

**17. There are 7 members on the Board of Directors of the GAP Corp. as follows: John Robertson, Jeremy Johnson, Susan Blakely, Jennifer Pacifico, Juanita Gonzalez, Patricia Washington, and Gustave Riccio. At any stockholder's meeting, these members are seated at a (straight) head table. If Jennifer Pacifico and Gustave Riccio are bitter enemies and cannot be seated together, how many different seating arrangements are possible?

**18. In the baseball world series, two teams play against each other in a series of up to 7 games. The first team that wins 4 games is the winner. Assume that the two teams are labeled A and B. Make a tree diagram showing all the possible ways in which the world series can end.

8.2

PERMUTATIONS AND COMBINATIONS

In some of the exercises of the previous section, order was important, whereas in others it was not. For example, in Exercise 6, order *was* important. On the other hand, in Exercise 2, order was not important. This leads us to the useful idea of **permutations**. We state this as a definition.

permutation

> **Definition 3.1**   A **permutation** is any arrangement of objects **in a certain order**.

EXAMPLE 1

SOLUTION

How many permutations are there of the letters in the word "cat"?

There are 6. They are {cat, cta, act, atc, tca, tac}.

EXAMPLE 2

SOLUTION

How many different three-letter permutations can be formed by using the letters of the word "drug"?

There are 24. They are

drg	dgu	grd	gud	rug	rdg	urg	udr
dgr	dru	gdr	gru	rgu	rdu	ugr	ugd
dug	dur	gdu	gur	rgd	rud	urd	udg

In Example 2 we were interested in the number of possible permutations of 3 things that can be formed out of a possible 4 things. The symbol we use for this is $_4P_3$. We read this as "the number of permutations of 4 things taken 3 at a time."

If we were interested in the number of possible permutations of 2 things that can be formed out of a possible 4 things, then we would write this as $_4P_2$. More generally, we have the following.

$_nP_r$

$_nP_n$

Notation   The symbol $_nP_r$ means the number of permutations of n things taken r at a time. The symbol $_nP_n$ means the number of permutations of n things taken n at a time. This, of course, simply represents the number of different ways of arranging these n things.

There is a simple formula that allows us to calculate $_nP_r$ for any values of n and r. Before giving this formula we introduce the symbolism $n!$, read as "n factorial."

n factorial

For example, 4!, read as "4 factorial," means $4 \cdot 3 \cdot 2 \cdot 1$. Thus

$$4! = 4 \cdot 3 \cdot 2 \cdot 1 = 24$$

Also,

$$5! = 5 \cdot 4 \cdot 3 \cdot 2 \cdot 1 = 120$$

and

$$7! = 7 \cdot 6 \cdot 5 \cdot 4 \cdot 3 \cdot 2 \cdot 1 = 5040$$
$$1! = 1$$

The symbol 0! is taken to be equal to 1.

Now we are ready for the formula for the number of permutations of n things taken r at a time.

Formula 8.1 $_nP_r = \dfrac{n!}{(n-r)!}$

EXAMPLE 3

Find $_5P_3$

SOLUTION

The symbol $_5P_3$ means the number of permutations of 5 things taken 3 at a time. Using the above formula, we have $n = 5$ and $r = 3$, so that we get

$$_5P_3 = \frac{5!}{(5-3)!} = \frac{5!}{2!} = \frac{5 \cdot 4 \cdot 3 \cdot 2 \cdot 1}{2 \cdot 1}$$

$$= \frac{5 \cdot 4 \cdot 3 \cdot \cancel{2} \cdot \cancel{1}}{\cancel{2} \cdot \cancel{1}} = 5 \cdot 4 \cdot 3 = 60$$

Thus $_5P_3 = 60$.

EXAMPLE 4

Find $_6P_2$

SOLUTION

The symbol $_6P_2$ means the number of permutations of 6 things taken 2 at a time. Using Formula 8.1, we see that $n = 6$ and $r = 2$. Thus

$$_6P_2 = \frac{6!}{(6-2)!}$$

$$= \frac{6!}{4!} = \frac{6 \cdot 5 \cdot 4 \cdot 3 \cdot 2 \cdot 1}{4 \cdot 3 \cdot 2 \cdot 1}$$

$$= \frac{6 \cdot 5 \cdot \cancel{4} \cdot \cancel{3} \cdot \cancel{2} \cdot \cancel{1}}{\cancel{4} \cdot \cancel{3} \cdot \cancel{2} \cdot \cancel{1}} = 6 \cdot 5 = 30$$

Therefore $_6P_2 = 30$.

EXAMPLE 5

In Example 2 we found all the three-letter permutations of the four-letter word "drug." There were 24 of them. We could have used Formula 8.1 to obtain this answer. Since we have 4 letters to start with, $n = 4$. We are selecting three-letter permutations, so $r = 3$. Thus we want $_4P_3$, which equals

$$\frac{4!}{(4-3)!} = \frac{4!}{1!} = \frac{4 \cdot 3 \cdot 2 \cdot 1}{1} = 24$$

This confirms our previous answer, which we found by listing the permutations.

EXAMPLE 6

Philip has just typed 5 letters and 5 envelopes. Before he can insert the letters into the envelopes, he drops them on the floor and they get all mixed up. When Philip picks them up, he inserts the letters into the envelopes without looking at them. In how many different ways can this be done?

SOLUTION

Since the problem involves the ordering of envelopes, it is a permutation problem. When Philip picks up a letter, he has to select 1 out of 5 envelopes into which to put it. Thus $n = 5$ and $r = 5$. The total number of different ways that he can do this is

$$_5P_5 = \frac{5!}{0!} = \frac{5 \cdot 4 \cdot 3 \cdot 2 \cdot 1}{1} \qquad \text{(Remember that } 0! = 1\text{)}$$

$$= 120$$

Philip can then insert the letters into the envelopes in 120 different ways.

Next we consider a slightly different permutation problem. How many different four-letter words can be formed from the word "GURU"? Since there are two U's and we cannot tell them apart, Formula 8.1 has to be changed somewhat. Let us first list all the possible permutations. There are twelve of them, as shown.

GURU	UURG
GRUU	UUGR
GUUR	URGU
UGRU	RGUU
URUG	RUGU
UGUR	RUUG

Had we used Formula 8.1, we would have obtained

$$_4P_4 = \frac{4!}{(4-4)!} = \frac{4!}{0!}$$

$$= \frac{4 \cdot 3 \cdot 2 \cdot 1}{1} \qquad \text{(Remember that } 0! = 1)$$

$$= 24$$

Why did we get only 12 when Formula 8.1 gives 24? A little thought shows us that since we cannot tell the two U's apart, half of the 24 permutations of the formula will be repetitions. We therefore do not count them. So we end up with half of 24, or 12, different permutations. For example, if we label the two U's as U_1 and U_2, then two possible permutations given by Formula 8.1 are U_1U_2GR and U_2U_1GR. However, we cannot tell these apart (since when writing these, we do not really label the U's with 1 and 2). Thus we count these two possibilities as just one permutation.

This example leads us to the following formula for the number of permutations of n things, when some of them are alike.

Formula 8.2   Suppose we have n things of which p are alike, q are alike, r are alike, etc. Then the number of different permutations is

$$\frac{n!}{p!\, q!\, r! \cdots}$$

(It is understood that $p + q + r + \cdots = n$)

EXAMPLE 7

SOLUTION

How many different permutations are there of the letters of the word (a) coffee? (b) Tennessee?

a) Since "coffee" has 6 letters, then $n = 6$. The "f" is repeated twice, and so is the "e." So $p = 2$ and $q = 2$. Formula 8.2 then tells us that the number of permutations is

$$\frac{6!}{2!\, 2!\, 1!\, 1!} = \frac{6 \cdot 5 \cdot 4 \cdot 3 \cdot 2 \cdot 1}{2 \cdot 1 \cdot 2 \cdot 1 \cdot 1 \cdot 1}$$

$$= \frac{6 \cdot 5 \cdot {}^2\!\!\!\not{4} \cdot 3 \cdot \not{2} \cdot \not{1}}{\not{2} \cdot \not{1} \cdot \not{2} \cdot \not{1} \cdot \not{1} \cdot \not{1}} = 180$$

There are 180 permutations.

b) "Tennessee" has nine letters, so n is 9. There are 4 e's, 2 n's, and 2 s's, so p is 4, q is 2, and r is 2. Formula 8.2 tells us that the number of permutations is

$$\frac{9!}{4!\,2!\,2!\,1!} = \frac{9\cdot8\cdot7\cdot6\cdot5\cdot4\cdot3\cdot2\cdot1}{4\cdot3\cdot2\cdot1\cdot2\cdot1\cdot2\cdot1\cdot1}$$

$$= \frac{9\cdot\overset{2}{\cancel{8}}\cdot7\cdot6\cdot5\cdot\cancel{4}\cdot\cancel{3}\cdot\cancel{2}\cdot\cancel{1}}{\cancel{4}\cdot\cancel{3}\cdot\cancel{2}\cdot1\cdot\cancel{2}\cdot1\cdot\cancel{2}\cdot\cancel{1}\cdot1} = 3780$$

So there are 3780 permutations.   ▄

Combinations

Suppose that Mike is in a record shop. He has enough money to buy only 3 records by the latest popular singing group, the Rockheads. The store has 5 different records by this group. In how many ways can Mike make his selection?

In this situation we are again interested in selecting 3 out of 5 things. However, this time we are *not* interested in the order in which the selection is made. We call a selection of this kind a **combination**.

combination

> **Definition 8.2** A **combination** is any selection of things where the order is not important.

notation $\binom{n}{r}$ $_nC_r$

Notation The number of combinations of n things taken r at a time will be denoted as $_nC_r$ (some books use the notation $\binom{n}{r}$ instead of $_nC_r$).

Let us go back to Mike in the record shop. He must select 3 out of 5 records. This can be done in $_5C_3$ ways. We want to calculate $_5C_3$. If the records are labeled as A, B, C, D, and E and if order counts, then there are $_5P_3$ possible ways of selecting 3 records out of a total of 5. This gives

$$_5P_3 = \frac{5!}{(5-3)!} = \frac{5!}{2!} = 60$$

This figure takes order into account, since it is the number of permutations. In our case we do not care about the order. Thus if he selects records A, B, and C, then all of the following permutations represent the same purchase: ABC, CAB, ACB, BAC, BCA, CBA. These six permutations are thus considered *one* combination. The same is true for any other combination of 3 records. Therefore to get the correct number of combinations, we divide the 60 by 6 and obtain 10. Notice that 6 is 3!. Thus $_5C_3$ is

$$\frac{_5P_3}{3!} = \frac{5!}{(5-3)!\,3!} = 10$$

Thus we have the following formula.

Formula 8.3 $\quad _nC_r = \dfrac{n!}{(n-r)!\,r!}$

The following examples illustrate how the formula is used.

EXAMPLE 8

Eight workers at the Excelsior Music Corporation are unhappy about their working conditions. They wish to complain to the management. If management will listen to a committee of only 3 people, in how many ways can such a committee be formed?

SOLUTION

Since the order of selecting people for the committee is not important, the answer is the number combinations of 8 things taken 3 at a time. We thus want $_8C_3$, which is

$$_8C_3 = \binom{8}{3} = \frac{8!}{(8-3)!\,3!} = \frac{8!}{5!\,3!} = \frac{8\cdot7\cdot6\cdot5\cdot4\cdot3\cdot2\cdot1}{5\cdot4\cdot3\cdot2\cdot1\cdot3\cdot2\cdot1} = 56$$

Thus 56 different committees can be formed.

EXAMPLE 9

Tom is going to the supermarket to buy 4 pints of ice cream. The store sells 28 different flavors of ice cream, and the smallest amount they will sell of any one flavor is one pint. Tom wants to try as many different flavors as he can. In how many different ways can he buy 4 different flavors?

SOLUTION

Since order is not important, we want $_{28}C_4$. Formula 8.3 tells us that this is

$$\frac{28!}{(28-4)!\cdot4!} = \frac{28!}{24!\cdot4!} = 20{,}475$$

Thus Tom can select the 4 different flavors in 20,475 ways.

EXAMPLE 10

In Playland Amusement Park there is a game that consists of throwing 3 balls into 6 baskets. You win if you get 1 ball each into 3 different baskets. In how many different ways can someone win?

SOLUTION

Since order is not important, we are interested in $_6C_3$. Formula 8.3 tells us that this is

$$\frac{6!}{(6-3)!\,3!} = \frac{6!}{3!\,3!} = 20$$

There are 20 winning combinations.

EXAMPLE 11

In how many different ways can a committee of 3 men and 4 women be formed from a group of 8 men and 6 women?

SOLUTION

We must select any 3 men from a possible 8, and order does not matter. This can be done in $_8C_3$ ways.

Then we must select any 4 women from a possible 6, again where order does not count. This is $_6C_4$.

Since any group of men can be combined with any group of women to form the entire committee, then by the Fundamental Principle of Counting rule given in Section 8.1 (page 415) we have a total of

$$_8C_3 \cdot {_6C_4} = \frac{8!}{(8-3)!\,3!} \cdot \frac{6!}{(6-4)!\,4!}$$

$$= \frac{8!}{5!\,3!} \cdot \frac{6!}{2!\,4!}$$

$$= 56 \cdot 15 = 840$$

Thus 840 committees can be formed.

Pascal's Triangle

Another useful technique for computing the number of possible combinations is by means of **Pascal's triangle**. The triangle is shown in Fig. 8.3. It is not hard to see how this triangle is constructed.

Figure 8.3

Each row has a 1 on either end. All the other entries are obtained by adding the numbers immediately above it directly to the right and left as shown by the arrows in Fig. 8.4. Thus to get the entries for the sixth row, we add 1 and 5 to get 6. Then we add 5 and 10 to get 15. We next add 10 and 10 to get 20, and so on. To complete the row, we add 1's on each end. The numbers must be lined up exactly as shown in the diagram.

Pascal's triangle

A triangle of numbers such as this is called Pascal's triangle. It can have as many rows as you want. This triangle was known to the Chinese for several centuries before Pascal's time. However, it is named for Pascal because of the many interesting applications he found for it. (See Fig. 8.5.)

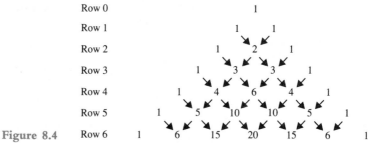

Row 0
Row 1
Row 2
Row 3
Row 4
Row 5

Figure 8.4 Row 6

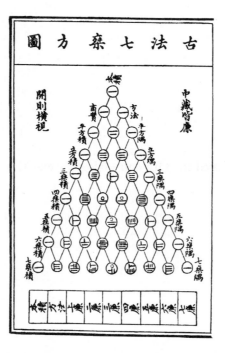

Figure 8.5 The Pascal triangle as depicted in 1303 at the front of Chu Shih-Chieh's *Ssu Yuan Yii Chien*. It is entitled "The Old Method Chart of the Seven Multiplying Squares" and tabulates the binomial coefficients up to the eighth power. *Reproduced with permission from Joseph Needham,* Science and Civilization in China, III, 135 (*New York: Cambridge University Press*)

HISTORICAL NOTE

Blaise Pascal had demonstrated his mathematical talent at an early age. He proved a very important theorem in geometry when he was only 16 years old. His interest in mathematics was not limited to geometry. When he was about 18 years old, he built the first successful computing machine. He also did valuable work in physics, notably confirming the fact that air has weight.

Throughout his life, Pascal suffered from severe illness, and hardly a day passed without pain. He was deeply religious, and when he was almost killed by a runaway horse in 1654, he regarded his narrow escape as a sign from God. As a result, he devoted himself even more than ever to religious meditation and writing. His great work is *Pensées*, which deals largely with philosophy and religion. Pascal died in 1662 at the age of only 39. He is famous both as a mathematician and philosopher.

Let us now see how Pascal's triangle can be used to solve problems in combinations.

EXAMPLE 12

In a recent mining accident a volunteer rescue squad consisting of 3 people was needed. Seven people volunteered. In how many different ways could a rescue squad be formed?

SOLUTION

Since order is not important, we want $_7C_3$. First let us evaluate $_7C_3$ by using Formula 8.3. We have

$$\binom{7}{3} = {_7C_3} = \frac{7!}{(7-3)!\,3!} = 35$$

Thus there are 35 possible rescue squads that can be formed.

Now let us evaluate $_7C_3$ by using Pascal's triangle. We have 7 people to select from, so we write the first 7 rows of Pascal's triangle as shown in Fig. 8.6. Look at Row 7. Since we must select 3 people, we go to the third entry (from the left) *after* the end 1. This entry is 35, and this is our answer. Thus again we see that $_7C_3$ is 35. We used the third entry (after the end 1) in row 7 because we wanted $_7C_3$. If we had wanted $_7C_5$, we would have used the fifth entry (after the end 1) in row 7. This entry is 21. Thus $_7C_5$ is 21.

Row 0							1							
Row 1						1		1						
Row 2					1		2		1					
Row 3				1		3		3		1				
Row 4			1		4		6		4		1			
Row 5		1		5		10		10		5		1		
Row 6	1		6		15		20		15		6		1	
Row 7	1	7		21		35		35		21		7		1

Figure 8.6   ▬

In general, to find the value of $_nC_r$, we go to row n. Then we select the rth number (after the end 1) from the left. This entry is $_nC_r$. In this procedure *we always label the first row as row 0*.

EXAMPLE 13

Using Pascal's triangle, find (a) $_6C_4$; (b) $_6C_0$; and (c) $_5C_5$.

SOLUTION

We will use the Pascal triangle shown in Fig. 8.6.

a) To find $_6C_4$, go to row 6. Then go across to the fourth entry from the left (after the end 1). This entry is 15. Thus $_6C_4 = 15$.

b) To find $_6C_0$, go to row 6. Then go across to the "0'th entry" from the left (after the end 1). This means that we must remain at the 1. Thus $_6C_0 = 1$.

c) To find $_5C_5$, we go to row 5. Then we go across to the fifth entry from the left (after the end 1). This entry is 1. Thus $_5C_5 = 1$. ▄

Although we have used Pascal's triangle to evaluate $_nC_r$, there are many other interesting and important applications of this triangle. Consult the suggested further readings given for such applications.

EXERCISES FOR SECTION 8.2

1. Evaluate each of the following symbols.

a) $\dfrac{5!}{3!}$ **b)** $\dfrac{7!}{5!}$ **c)** $\dfrac{8!}{8!}$ **d)** $\dfrac{0!}{7}$

e) $_8P_6$ **f)** $_7P_7$ **g)** $_6P_4$ **h)** $_{11}P_8$

i) $_6P_6$ **j)** $_6P_0$ **k)** $_9P_4$ **l)** $_0P_0$

m) $_7C_3$ **n)** $_8C_5$ **o)** $_6C_5$ **p)** $_6P_5$

q) $_9C_9$ **r)** $_8C_7$ **s)** $_8C_1$ **t)** $_{10}C_9$

u) $_{10}C_1$ **v)** $_7C_0$ **w)** $_8C_8$ **x)** $_9C_4$

y) $_{10}C_{11}$ **z)** $_0C_0$

2. How many different permutations are there of the letters of the following words?

a) DIFFERENCES **b)** FLAMMABLE

c) SUCCESSION **d)** MISSISSIPPI

3. A cosmetics company has 10 members on its board of directors. In how many different ways can it elect a president, vice-president, secretary, and treasurer?

4. In how many different ways can a police department arrange suspects in a police lineup if each lineup consists of 7 people?

5. A movie critic is asked to list, in order of preference, the ten worst movies that she had seen in 1989. If she saw 20 movies during the year, in how many ways can she select the 10 worst movies?

6. In how many different ways can a jury of 12 people be selected from a panel of 18 prospective jurors?

7. A drill sergeant enters the barracks, where there are 12 soldiers playing cards. He needs four "volunteers": one to mop the floor, one to peel potatoes, one to scrub the walls, and one to wash dishes. In how many different ways can he get his group of volunteers? (Assume order counts.)

8. A stock clerk is arranging four cases of corn flakes, three cases of toilet tissue, and two cases of paper towels on a loading platform. In how many different ways can these cases be arranged if

a) the cases can be arranged in any order?

*b) the corn flakes are to be placed together, the toilet tissue together, and the paper towels together?

9. How many committees of seven people from a group of eight Blacks and nine Asian-Americans can be formed to investigate discrimination charges if each committee must have

a) four Blacks?

*b) at least four Blacks?

10. How many different seven-card rummy hands can be formed from a deck of 52 cards?

11. A television network president is arranging next month's schedule of shows. In how many different ways can eight shows be arranged for one evening's telecast if

a) the news special (which is one of the eight shows) must be the last show?

b) any show can be telecast at any time?

12. At a baseball game the commissioner and six other guests are to be seated in seven box seats along the third base line. In how many different ways can this be done if

a) anyone can sit anywhere?

b) the commissioner must sit in the middle?

c) the commissioner must sit in the middle and his press secretary must sit at the extreme left to answer reporters' questions?

13. A jewelry designer is making a necklace out of precious stones. She has 11 pearls, 8 rubies, and 5 emeralds. The necklace is to contain 4 pearls, 5 rubies, and 2 emeralds. In how many different ways can she select the jewels for the necklace? (Assume that the order in which the jewels appear on the necklace is not important.)

14. Dr. Bergen, a medical researcher, needs 5 human volunteers to test the effectiveness of a new pain-relieving arthritis drug. If 17 people have volunteered, in how many different ways can Dr. Bergen select the 5 volunteers to test the effectiveness of the new drug?

15. The Federal Savings Bank employs 16 full-time and 9 part-time bank tellers. As an economy move, the management decides to lay off 2 part-time and 3 full-time bank tellers. Neglecting seniority and any other considerations, in how many different ways can the workers to be laid off be selected?

16. Each day, a sample of 5 of the 12 microwave ovens produced on production line A are checked for radiation leakage before being shipped to the consumer.

a) In how many different ways can the 5 microwave ovens selected to be checked be chosen?

b) In how many different ways can the 7 microwave ovens selected *not* to be checked be chosen?

c) How do the answers in parts (a) and (b) compare? Explain your answer.

17. Look at the diagonals in the Pascal's triangle shown in Fig. 8.7.

a) Find the entry in diagonal 1.

b) Add the entries in diagonal 2.

c) Add the entries in diagonal 3.

d) Add the numbers in diagonal 4, and so on throughout.

e) What do you notice about the results?

**18. The number of different ways in which *n* distinct objects can be arranged in a circle is $(n - 1)!$

a) Explain why this formula is valid.

b) In how many different ways can a florist display

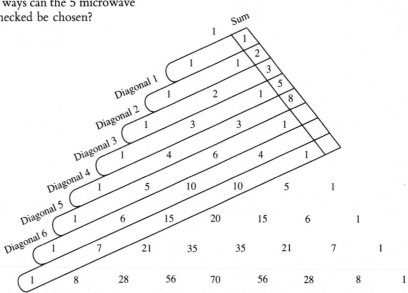

Figure 8.7

five different flowers in a circular arrangement on a shelf?

c) Five people are seated in a bar at a circular table. They decide to change seats. In how many different ways can these people rearrange themselves?

**19. A committee of four is to be set up to investigate charges of incompetence at a major airline company. The members of the committee are to be selected from 7 pilots, 4 mechanics, 3 flight attendants and 2 baggage handlers on the company payroll.

In how many different ways can the committee be selected, if

a) one member must be from each of the above mentioned categories?

b) at least one pilot and one flight attendant must be on the committee.

**20. As mentioned, many books use the notation $\binom{n}{r}$ instead of $_nC_r$. Using Pascal's triangle, show that $\binom{n}{r} = \binom{n}{n-r}$, that is, numbers in a particular row read from left to right are the same as read from right to left.

**21. Explain how the identity

$$\binom{n+1}{r} = \binom{n}{r} + \binom{n}{r-1}$$

enables us to construct Pascal's triangle. (*Hint:* First verify the identity.)

8.3

DEFINITION OF PROBABILITY

We are now ready to define what is meant by the concept of probability.

Suppose we toss an honest coin many times and observe the number of heads that appear. The results of several such experiments are summarized in the chart below.

Number of heads appearing	4	26	49	250	498	5,001
Number of tosses	10	50	100	500	1,000	10,000

We see that in each case the number of heads appearing is approximately $\frac{1}{2}$ the number of tosses. If we flip the coin one million times, we would expect to get approximately 500,000 heads. If we now toss a coin once, we would say that *the probability of getting a head is $\frac{1}{2}$*.

Note that when we flip the coin, there are two possible outcomes, heads and tails, both of which are equally likely. We are interested in only one of these outcomes—namely, heads. If heads occurs, we will call this a **favorable** outcome. The probability in this case is the number of favorable outcomes divided by the total number of possible outcomes, that is, it is 1 divided by 2, or $\frac{1}{2}$.

favorable outcome

Suppose we were now to roll a die once. What is the probability of getting a 4? There are six possible outcomes, all of which are equally likely. These are 1, 2, 3, 4, 5, and 6. Assuming that the die is fair, we would expect to get a 4 approximately $\frac{1}{6}$ of the time, since there are 6 possible outcomes and only 1 of these, namely the 4, is favorable. We would then say that *the probability of getting a 4 is $\frac{1}{6}$*.

We can now make this concept of probability more specific. Before doing so, however, we will give a definition that makes it easier to talk about probability.

sample space

event

> **Definition 8.3**   The set of all possible outcomes of an experiment is called the **sample space**. We will usually not be concerned with the entire sample space but rather with only some of these outcomes. Such a collection will be referred to as an **event**. (In other words, an event is a subset of the sample space.)

EXAMPLE 1

If we toss a coin once, then the possible outcomes are H and T. Thus the sample space is {H, T}.

If we were to toss the coin twice, then the sample space would be {HT, TH, HH, TT}. The event "no heads" would be {TT}.   ■

Comment   A sample space is not unique, that is, there could be more than one sample space. If we toss the coin twice, then another sample space could be {0, 1, 2} where 0, 1, 2 refers to the number of heads (or tails). It all depends on what we are interested in.

EXAMPLE 2

If a die is tossed once, then the sample space is {1, 2, 3, 4, 5, 6}.

The event "even number" is {2, 4, 6}.

The event "odd number" is {1, 3, 5}.

The event "number greater than 4" is {5, 6}.

The event "number divisible by 3" is {3, 6}.   ■

We are now ready to define probability.

probability

> **Definition 8.4**   If an event can occur in any one of n equally likely ways and if f of these are considered as favorable outcomes, then the **probability** of getting a favorable outcome is
>
> $$\frac{\text{number of favorable outcomes}}{\text{total number of outcomes}} = \frac{f}{n}$$
>
> Symbolically, we write
>
> $$p(\text{favorable event}) = \frac{f}{n}$$

EXAMPLE 3

A card is drawn from a 52-card deck. What is the probability of getting **a)** a heart? **b)** a black card? **c)** an ace? **d)** the ace of spades?

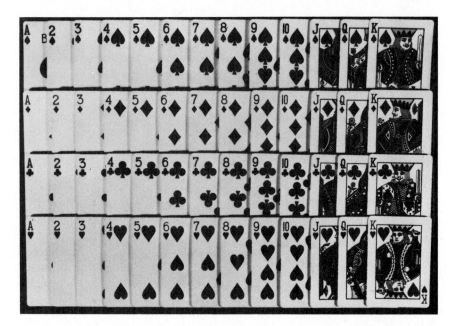

SOLUTION

Since there are 52 cards in the deck, the total number of outcomes is 52.

a) There are 13 hearts in a deck, so there are 13 favorable outcomes. Using Definition 8.4, we get

$$p(\text{hearts}) = \frac{13}{52} = \frac{1}{4}$$

b) Half of the deck consists of black cards, so there are 26 favorable outcomes. Hence

$$p(\text{black card}) = \frac{26}{52} = \frac{1}{2}$$

c) There are 4 aces in a deck, so there are 4 favorable outcomes. We then have

$$p(\text{ace}) = \frac{4}{52} = \frac{1}{13}$$

d) There is only one ace of spades in a deck. We therefore have only one favorable outcome. Thus

$$p(\text{ace of spades}) = \frac{1}{52}$$

EXAMPLE 4

A fair die is tossed once. What is the probability of getting

a) an odd number larger than 1?

b) a number larger than 3?

c) a prime number? (Remember, a prime number is any number larger than 1 that is exactly divisible only by itself and 1.)

d) a number larger than 6?

SOLUTION

There are six possible outcomes. These are 1, 2, 3, 4, 5, and 6.

a) We know that 1, 3, and 5 are the possible odd numbers; 3 and 5 are larger than 1. So there are two possible favorable outcomes. Hence

$$p(\text{odd number larger than 1}) = \frac{2}{6} = \frac{1}{3}$$

b) There are three favorable outcomes 4, 5, and 6, so that

$$p(\text{number larger than 3}) = \frac{3}{6} = \frac{1}{2}$$

c) The prime numbers between 1 and 6 are 2, 3, and 5. There are three of them. Thus

$$p(\text{prime number}) = \frac{3}{6} = \frac{1}{2}$$

d) Since there are no numbers larger than 6 on a die, the number of favorable outcomes is 0. So

$$p(\text{number larger than 6}) = \frac{0}{6} = 0$$

EXAMPLE 5

In a state lottery, each ticket has 5 numbers. If you get all 5 numbers right, you win $50,000. If you get the last 4 numbers in the correct order, you win $10,000. If you get the last 3 numbers in the correct order, you win $5000. If you get the last 2 numbers in the correct order, you win $1000. What is the probability of winning

a) $50,000?   **b)** $10,000?   **c)** $5000?

SOLUTION

Since there are 5 numbers on each ticket, ranging from 00001 to 99,999, there is a total of 99,999 possible outcomes.

a) Only 1 ticket has the winning number, so there is just 1 favorable outcome. Thus

$$p(\text{winning } \$50,000) = \frac{1}{99,999}$$

b) To win $10,000, we must calculate how many tickets have the last 4 numbers in the correct order. We do not care about the first number. So the first number could be any one of 10 possible numbers. Hence there are 10 tickets that have the last 4 digits in the correct order. However, one of these (the one with the correct first number) is the big winner. So we don't count it. Thus there are only 9 favorable outcomes. Since there are 99,999 total possible outcomes we get

$$p(\text{winning } \$10,000) = \frac{9}{99,999} = \frac{1}{11,111}$$

c) To win $5000, we must calculate how many tickets have the last 3 numbers in the correct order. This time we don't care about the first 2 numbers. The first place can be filled in 10 ways, and so can the second. So there is a total of 10×10, or 100, possible tickets with the last 3 digits correct. We must disregard 10 of these since 1 is the big winner and 9 are $10,000 winners. This then leaves us with 90 favorable outcomes out of a total of 99,999 possible outcomes. Thus

$$p(\text{winning } \$5,000) = \frac{90}{99,999} = \frac{10}{11,111}$$ ▬

Now consider the newspaper clipping. Despite beliefs to the contrary, the probability of a bank failure in the United States is not zero. As the article indicates, the number of bank failures has been increasing over the past few years. In 1988, there were 217 bank failures.

Bank Failure Sets Record

ROSWELL, N.M.: Moncor Bank of Roswell today became the 80th American bank to fail this year, eclipsing the record 79 bank failures in 1984, a Federal Deposit Insurance Corporation official said.

The bank, closed after being declared insolvent by the Deputy United States Comptroller of the Currency, Michael Patriarca, was the second Moncor bank in southeastern New Mexico to fail in the last two weeks. Moncor Bank of Hobbs was closed Aug. 30. The Roswell bank was the last of six banks held by Moncor Inc., which filed for reorganization under Chapter 11.

Mr. Patriarca said the F.D.I.C. was appointed receiver of the Roswell bank.

BUSINESS NEWS, September 12, 1985.

EXAMPLE 6

Greg, Rita, William, Frank, Yolando, and Dawn are six students who are enrolled in a math honors course at State University. The departmental policy is to award a $100 prize to each of the top two students. What is the probability that Dawn and William will receive the prize?

SOLUTION

We first find the total number of different ways in which the two winners can be selected. This is $_6C_2$ (the number of ways of selecting two out of six people where order does not count). Using Formula 8.3 given in Section 8.2, we get

$$_6C_2 = \frac{6!}{(6-2)! \; 2!} = \frac{6!}{4! \; 2!} = 15$$

Of these 15 ways of selecting the two winners, only one consists of Dawn and William. Thus

$$p(\text{Dawn and William win prize}) = \frac{1}{15}$$

■

EXAMPLE 7

SOLUTION

What is the probability that your math teacher will be fired on April 31?

Since April has exactly 30 days, your math teacher cannot be fired on April 31. There are no favorable outcomes. Thus

$$p(\text{your math teacher gets fired on April 31}) = 0$$

■

null event	Something that can never happen is called the **null** event. Its probability is 0.

EXAMPLE 8

SOLUTION

Mary has just been admitted to the maternity ward at a hospital to have a baby. What is the probability that the baby is a boy or a girl?

There are only two possible outcomes (boy or girl), so that $n = 2$. Both of these are favorable, so $f = 2$. Thus

$$p(\text{boy or girl}) = \frac{2}{2} = 1$$

It is obvious that a favorable outcome *must* occur in this case. ■

definite event	Something that is certain to occur is called the **definite** event. Its probability is 1.

Comment An event may never occur, in which case its probability is 0. An event may occur for certain, in which case its probability is 1. There are events that may or may not occur, and these will have probability between 0 and 1. Thus *the probability of any event is always somewhere between 0 and 1 and possibly including 0 or 1.*

Now that we have computed the probability of several different events, we can go back to the question we raised earlier: "What do we mean by probability?"

Let us analyze the weather forecaster's prediction that the probability of rain is 90%. We first point out that 90% can also be written as $\frac{90}{100}$. The weather forecaster means that, in the past, when the clouds and winds have been as they are today, then it has rained 90 times out of 100. In other words, on 100 days, when conditions have been as they are today, the event of rain has occurred on 90 of these days. Thus on the basis of past experience, he or she predicts rain for today with a probability of $\frac{90}{100}$, or 90%.

In a similar manner, when the doctor tells you that you have a 50–50 chance of surviving an operation, it means that on the basis of past experience, out of every 100 patients that the doctor has operated on, 50 pulled through and 50 didn't. Thus the probability of surviving is 50 out of 100, or $\frac{1}{2}$.

In general, if the probability of any event is $\frac{f}{n}$, this means that, in the long run, out of every n trials there will be f favorable outcomes. Thus probability represents the percentage of the time that the event will happen in the long run. This is sometimes called the **relative frequency** of the event.

relative frequency

This definition of probability is based on the number of favorable events occurring in many repeated trials. Obviously, this involves collecting statistical data about the number of events. For this reason this approach is often called **statistical probability**. Some books use another approach and define probability using axioms. This approach is often called **axiomatic probability**. The interested reader can consult any standard text on probability for a more detailed discussion of axiomatic probability.

statistical probability

axiomatic probability

Problem-Solving Example

EXAMPLE 9

Two fair dice are rolled at the same time and the number of dots appearing on both dice is counted. Find the probability that this sum is an odd number larger than 6.

SOLUTION

Understanding the Problem

When two fair dice are rolled at the same time, the sum of the number of dots appearing on both dice may be an even number or an odd number. We must determine the possible sums that can be obtained and also the probability that this sum is an odd number larger than 6.

A Plan to Solve the Problem

When two dice are rolled there are 36 possible outcomes, that is, the sample space has 36 possibilities. These are shown below.

Die 1	Die 2	Die 1	Die 2	Die 1	Die 2
1	1	3	1	5	1
1	2	3	2	5	2
1	3	3	3	5	3
1	4	3	4	5	4
1	5	3	5	5	5
1	6	3	6	5	6
2	1	4	1	6	1
2	2	4	2	6	2
2	3	4	3	6	3
2	4	4	4	6	4
2	5	4	5	6	5
2	6	4	6	6	6

The statement "a sum that is an odd number larger than 6" means a sum of 7, a sum of 9, or a sum of 11. A sum of 7 on both dice together can happen in 6 ways. Similarly, a sum of 9 on both dice together can happen in 4 ways, and a sum of 11 can happen in 2 ways. There are then 12 favorable outcomes out of 36 possibilities. Thus, the probability that the sum is an odd number larger than $6 = \frac{12}{36} = \frac{1}{3}$.

Checking Our Solution

By listing all the possible outcomes and counting the number of favorable outcomes, we can be rather certain that our answer is correct.   ■

Comment   In the earlier grades, children are taught to solve such problems by using an ordered pair approach on a 6×6 grid. This can be seen on the following page which is a student page from *Addison-Wesley Mathematics*, 1987, Grade 7, p. 348.

We mentioned earlier that probability can be thought of as the fraction of times that an outcome will occur in a long series of experiments. Suppose we were to write each of the ten digits 0, 1, 2, . . . , 9 on a separate piece of paper, one for each digit, and place all of the papers in a bowl. Now let us select a paper from the bowl and note its number. Replace the paper and thoroughly mix the papers in the bowl. If we repeat this procedure 1000 times then we would expect each of the digits to come up approximately 100 times. However, the sequences in which these digits occur should be random. To see why this is important, let us consider the following.

Ordered Pairs in Probability

Using a red die and a green die from a game of backgammon, what is the probability of rolling a sum of 10?

Each outcome is an **ordered pair** of numbers: the number on the red die first and the number on the green die second.

We must find the total number of outcomes *and* the number of outcomes which have a sum of 10.

The grid shows there are 36 ordered-pair outcomes.

Only 3 of the outcomes have a sum of 10.

$$P(\text{sum of } 10) = \frac{3}{36} = \frac{1}{12}$$

There are 3 chances in 36 or 1 chance in 12 of rolling a sum of 10. The probability is $\frac{1}{12}$.

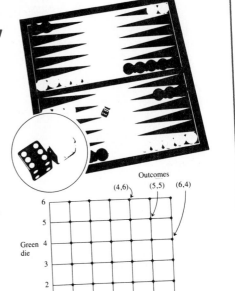

Other Examples

$P(2,4) = \frac{1}{36}$ $P(\text{sum of } 11) = \frac{2}{36} = \frac{1}{18}$ $P(\text{sum} < 5) = \frac{6}{36} = \frac{1}{6}$

The outcomes are **(5,6)** and **(6,5)**

The outcomes are **(1,1),(1,2),(2,1), (3,1),(2,2),(1,3)**

Random Numbers

In a large city the social services department has decided to make a detailed study of 100 welfare cases. These 100 cases are to be chosen completely *at random* from among the 20,000 families currently receiving aid. It is important to the department that each family have an equal chance of being selected for the study. How can the department select the families for the study? There are several ways in which this can be done.

1. Write each family name on a piece of paper and put the names in a box. After mixing the contents thoroughly, select 100 names from the box. While this approach might seem sensible, it is unlikely that we would obtain a truly random mix. For one thing, most people would not stick their hand in to the bottom of the box to make a selection. Thus the names on the bottom are less likely to be selected than the

names on top. Moreover, if you do not replace each name after a selection, then the 100th name drawn has a greater likelihood of being selected than the first name drawn. (Can you see why this is so?) Even if we correct these difficulties, which clearly can be done, this method is obviously inefficient.

2. Arrange all the names alphabetically and number them from 1 to 20,000. Then select every 200th name. Again this does not give a truly random selection. By selecting every 200th name we are actually making sure that those families with numbers 1–199, 201–399, etc., never have a chance of being selected.

random numbers

3. Assign a 5-digit case number to each family, starting with the number 00001. Then use a spinner like one shown here, to generate *random numbers* as follows. Use the spinner 5 times to obtain 5 digits in order. The 5-digit number obtained by this process is the first case number to be selected. We continue in this way until we get the 100 case numbers that we want.

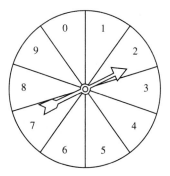

It is unlikely that this method will generate completely random numbers either. Can you find some reasons why it will not? Basically, this last method is good. That is, generating random numbers and using the families whose numbers have been selected is reasonable. The difficulties arise because we generate the random numbers using the spinner. We can overcome this difficulty by using a different technique to generate the random numbers. There are various ways of doing this, most of which use computers. Random numbers generated in this manner are often listed in *Tables of Random Digits*.

Table of Random Digits

Therefore the best way for the social services department to select the families for the study is to use such a table to generate random case numbers, and then use the families whose numbers come up in this way.

On page 442 we give a table of random digits. To use the table, we can start at any column and on any line. Thus if we use column 1 and read off the numbers, we get 10480, 22368, 24130, and so forth. Since the

TABLE 8.1

Table of Random Digits

Col. Line	(1)	(2)	(3)	(4)	(5)	(6)	(7)	(8)	(9)	(10)	(11)	(12)	(13)	(14)
1	10480	15011	01536	02011	81647	91646	69179	14194	62590	36207	20969	99570	91291	90700
2	22368	46573	25595	85393	30995	89198	27982	53402	93965	34095	52666	19174	39615	99505
3	24130	48360	22527	97265	76393	64809	15179	24830	49340	32081	30680	19655	63348	58629
4	42167	93093	06243	61680	07856	16376	39440	53537	71341	57004	00849	74917	97758	16379
5	37570	39975	81837	16656	06121	91782	60468	81305	49684	60672	14110	06927	01263	54613
6	77921	06907	11008	42751	27756	53498	18602	70659	90655	15053	21916	81825	44394	42880
7	99562	72905	56420	69994	98872	31016	71194	18738	44013	48840	63213	21069	10634	12952
8	96301	91977	05463	07972	18876	20922	94595	56869	69014	60045	18425	84903	42508	32307
9	89579	14342	63661	10281	17453	18103	57740	84378	25331	12566	58678	44947	05585	56941
10	85475	36857	53342	53988	53060	59533	38867	62300	08158	17983	16439	11458	18593	64952
11	28918	69578	88231	33276	70997	79936	56865	05859	90106	31595	01547	85590	91610	78188
12	63553	40961	48235	03427	49626	69445	18663	72695	52180	20847	12234	90511	33703	90322
13	09429	93969	52636	92737	88974	33488	36320	17617	30015	08272	84115	27156	30613	74952
14	10365	61129	87529	85869	48237	52267	67689	93394	01511	26358	85104	20285	29975	89868
15	07119	97336	71048	08178	77233	13916	47564	81056	97735	85977	29372	74461	28551	90707
16	51085	12765	51821	51259	77452	16308	60756	92144	49442	53900	70960	63990	75601	40719
17	02368	21382	52404	60268	89368	19885	55322	44819	01188	65255	64835	44919	05944	55157
18	01011	54092	33362	94904	31273	04146	18594	29852	71585	85030	51132	01915	92947	64951
19	52162	53916	46369	58586	23216	14513	83149	98736	23495	64350	94738	17752	35156	35749
20	07056	97628	33787	09998	42698	06691	76988	13602	51851	46104	88916	19509	25625	58104
21	48663	91245	85828	14346	09172	30168	90229	04734	59193	22178	30421	61666	99904	32812
22	54164	58492	22421	74103	47070	25306	76468	26384	58151	06646	21524	15227	96909	44592
23	32639	32363	05597	24200	13363	38005	94342	28728	35806	06912	17012	64161	18296	22851
24	29334	27001	87637	87308	58731	00256	45834	15398	46557	41135	10367	07684	36188	18510
25	02488	33062	28834	07351	19731	92420	60952	61280	50001	67658	32586	86679	50720	94953
26	81525	72295	04839	96423	24878	82651	66566	14778	76797	14780	13300	87074	79666	95725
27	29676	20591	68086	26432	46901	20849	89768	81536	86645	12659	92259	57102	80428	25280
28	00742	57392	39064	66432	84673	40027	32832	61362	98947	96067	64760	64584	96096	98253
29	05366	04213	25669	26422	44407	44048	37937	63904	45766	66134	75470	66520	34693	90449
30	91921	26418	64117	94305	26766	25940	39972	22209	71500	64568	91402	42416	07844	69618
31	00582	04711	87917	77341	42206	35126	74087	99547	81817	42607	43808	76655	62028	76630
32	00725	69884	62797	56170	86324	88072	76222	36086	84637	93161	76038	65855	77919	88006
33	69011	65795	95876	55293	18988	27354	26575	08625	40801	59920	29841	80150	12777	48501
34	25976	57948	29888	88604	67917	48708	18912	82271	65424	69774	33611	54262	85963	03547
35	09763	83473	73577	12908	30883	18317	28290	35797	05998	41688	34952	37888	38917	88050
36	91567	42595	27958	30134	04024	86385	29880	99730	55536	84855	29080	09250	79656	73211
37	17955	56439	90999	49127	20044	59931	06115	20542	18059	02008	73708	83517	36103	42791
38	46503	18584	18845	49618	02304	51038	20655	58727	28168	15475	56942	53389	20562	87338
39	92157	89634	94824	78171	84610	82834	09922	25417	44137	48413	25555	21246	35509	20468
40	14577	62765	35605	81263	39667	47358	56873	56307	61607	49518	89686	20103	77490	18062
41	98427	07523	33362	64270	06138	92477	66969	98420	04880	45585	46565	04102	46880	45709
42	34914	63976	88720	82765	34476	17032	87589	40836	32427	70002	70663	88863	77775	69348
43	70060	28277	39475	46373	23219	53416	94970	25832	69975	94884	19661	72828	00102	66794
44	53976	54914	06990	67245	68360	82948	11398	42878	80287	88267	47363	46634	06541	97809
45	76072	29515	40980	07391	58745	25774	22987	80059	39911	96189	41151	14222	60697	59583
46	90725	52210	83974	29992	65831	38857	50490	83765	55657	14361	31720	57375	56228	41546
47	64364	67412	33339	31926	14883	24413	59744	92351	97473	89286	35931	04110	23726	51900
48	08962	00358	31662	25388	61642	34072	81249	35648	56891	69352	48373	45578	78547	81788
49	95012	68379	93526	70765	10592	04542	76463	54328	02349	17247	28865	14777	62730	92277
50	15664	10493	20492	38391	91132	21999	59516	81652	27195	48223	46751	22923	32261	85653

Page 1 of *Table of 105,000 Random Digits*, Statement No. 4914, May 1949, File No. 261-A-1, State Commerce Commission, Washington, D.C.

families have numbers only up to 20,000, we skip those numbers that are over 20,000. Therefore we skip the number 22368. The same is true of the number 24130. The next number that we accept is on line 13; it is 09429, then 10365, and so forth. Proceeding in this manner, we can obtain a random sample by selecting those families whose numbers are 10480, 09429, 10365, 07119, 02368, 01011, 07056. . . . When we get to the bottom of column 1, we go to column 2 and follow the same procedure. We stop when we get the 100 numbers that we need.

EXAMPLE 10

During 1988 a large auto manufacturer received 350 complaints from customers about the quality of the service performed by one particular dealer. The company decides to investigate some of these complaints by selecting a random sample of 18 of these complaints and thoroughly investigating them. By using column 4 of Table 8.1, which customers will we select?

SOLUTION

We first number the customers' complaint letters from 1 to 350. Then we use column 4 of the table of random digits. Although the table gives 5-digit numbers, we simply use the first 3 digits of the column. Thus we select the numbers 20, 166, 79, 102, 332, 34, 81, 99, 143, 242, 73, 264, 129, 301, 73, 299, 319, and 253. Therefore the customers with these numbers will have their complaints investigated.   ■

EXAMPLE 11

Sixty students have registered for a statistics course. The chairperson of the department wishes to start a new section. She asks for 15 volunteers, but no one volunteers to transfer to the new section. She decides to randomly select 15 students. By using column 5 of Table 8.1, how can this be done?

SOLUTION

She should first assign each student a number from 1 to 60. Then she should use the first 2 digits of the numbers in column 5. Thus she should select those students whose numbers are 30, 7, 6, 27, 18, 17, 53, 49, 48, 31, 23, 42, 9, 47, and 13.   ■

EXERCISES FOR SECTION 8.3

1. Two dice are rolled. What is the probability
  a) of getting a sum of 1?
  b) that the same number appears on both dice?
  c) that the sum of the number of dots appearing on both dice is larger than 9?
  d) that the sum of the number of dots appearing on both dice is an even number?
  e) that two ones appear?

2. A card is drawn from an ordinary deck of 52 cards. What is the probability that it is
  a) a club?
  b) a two?
  c) a picture card?
  d) a card higher than 7? (Aces are considered to be 1's.)

3. A man and a woman who do not know each other

board a plane in Paris that is bound for St. Louis, with stopoffs in London, New York, and Chicago. What is the probability that they both get off at the same airport?

4. A coin box has 9 nickels, 8 pennies, 6 dimes, and 4 quarters in it. A young child shakes the box, and a coin falls out. What is the probability that the coin that falls out is

a) a penny?

b) a nickel?

c) a dime?

d) a quarter?

5. The following information is available on the 418 members of the Beach Resort Health Club:

		Sex	
		Male	Female
Age	Under 30 years	126	109
	30 years and over	89	94

What is the probability that a club member selected at random

a) will be a female under 30 years of age?

b) will be a female?

c) will be under 30 years of age?

6. A computer programmer prepares 3 different computer discs (with different programs on each) and 3 different identifying labels. Before attaching each label to the appropriate disc, she drops everything on the floor. If she picks up all the discs and labels, and randomly attaches a label to a disc, what is the probability that each disc will be labeled correctly?

7. Which of the following numbers cannot be the probability of some event?

a) $-\dfrac{3}{4}$

b) 1.47

c) $\dfrac{11}{12}$

d) 0

e) 1

f) 0.99

8. The following is a breakdown of the different types of credit card sales of a large department store for a particular day.

	Type of credit card used			
Amount of purchase	Master Card	VISA	American Express	Store Card
under $25	78	82	32	53
between $25 and $75	62	53	18	28
over $75	37	29	11	17

What is the probability that a credit card sale selected at random will be

a) a Master Card sale?

b) under $25?

c) a Master Card sale that is under $25?

9. *Mercy Killing.* A random survey[1] of 1000 adults in California was taken. Each person was asked to indicate his or her opinion on mercy killing of terminally ill patients. The following results were obtained:

	Were in favor of mercy killing	Were opposed to mercy killing	Had no opinion
Male	326	212	37
Female	207	199	19

What is the probability that an individual selected at random from this group

a) is a male who had no opinion?

b) is opposed to mercy killing?

c) is a female?

d) is a female who is in favor of mercy killing?

10. A local blood bank reports that 223 pints of blood were collected at a shopping center on Monday. After analysis it is determined that 7 of these pints are contaminated. The bottles are not labeled. A nurse selects a bottle at random. What is the probability that the bottle selected is *not* contaminated?

11. A computer company manufactured 1000 computer chip boards during one week, each numbered with a number from 1 to 1000. A few months later the company decides to recall those chip boards whose

---

1. *Source:* Crescent and Bowes, Los Angeles, California.

last digit is 9. Anton Jones owns one of the chip boards. What is the probability that he owns one of the chip boards that is being recalled?

12. A slot machine in a gambling casino has three wheels, and each wheel has a picture of a lemon, a cherry, and an apple on it. When the appropriate amount of money is inserted and the button is pushed, each wheel will rotate and then display a picture of one of the items mentioned. Each wheel operates independently of the other. When all three wheels show the same item, then the player wins $5000.

    a) List all the possible outcomes for this machine.

    b) Find the probability of a player winning $5000 when playing this slot machine.

13. In a certain state, license plates have 5 digits. The state motor vehicle department is intereseted in knowing how many of these cars are equipped with radial tires. It decides to send a letter to 100 randomly selected car owners. If columns 1 and 2 of Table 8.1 are used, which car owners will be selected to receive this letter?

14. A new drug is being tested for its ability to overcome drowsiness. Two hundred people have volunteered to take this drug to test its effectiveness Each person is given a number from 1 to 200. For experimental purposes, only 15 people will receive the new drug. The remaining 185 will be given a sugar pill. If columns 2 and 3 of Table 8.1 are used, which of the volunteers will be selected to receive the new drug?

15. During 1988 a manufacturer produced 9000 stereo sets, each with a serial number from 1 to 9000. The company decides to send a questionnaire to 30 owners of these sets. Using the seventh column of Table 8.1, to which owners should the company send the questionnaire?

16. A new movie has just been seen by 4000 people. The producer wants to know how the people reacted to a particular horror scene. Since each person already has a ticket stub with a number from 1 to 4000 on it, the producer decides to select a random sample of 25 people. If columns 9 and 10 of Table 8.1 are used, which ticket holder will be selected?

17. There are 328 licensed restaurants in Newville. The health department has decided to investigate the sanitary conditions of these restaurants by randomly selecting 20 of these restaurants. The licenses are numbered consecutively from 1 to 328. If columns 8 and 9 of Table 8.1 are used, which restaurants should be investigated?

18. An excellent article on random numbers can be found in *Science,* Volume 231, No. 4742, March 7, 1986. Read this article.

Brain-Teaser Problems

19. *Friday, the Thirteenth*. Many people believe that 13 is an unlucky number. There are numerous hotels that do not have a thirteenth floor. Furthermore, some people believe that when the thirteenth day of a month falls on a Friday, this represents an unlucky event. Furthermore, they believe that this does not occur too often. To check the truth of this belief, let us consider the following facts. The calendar changes every year. By this we mean that if your birthday falls on a Monday this year, then next year it will fall on a Tuesday or Wednesday (depending on whether it is a leap year or not). However, our calendar repeats itself every 400 years. There are 4800 months during this period. The thirteenth day of the month in each of these 4800 months occurs on the different days of the week according to the following chart.

Day of week	Sun.	Mon.	Tues.	Wed.
How often the 13th day of month occurs on this day	687	685	685	687

Thurs	Fri.	Sat.
684	688	684

    a) Using the above chart, find the probability that the thirteenth day of the month will occur on a Friday.

    b) Is this probability greater than, less than, or equal to the probability of its falling on any other day of the week?

    c) How do you explain this phenomenon?

8.4

RULES OF PROBABILITY

mutually exclusive

Consider the following problem. A card is selected from an ordinary deck of 52 cards. What is the probability that it is either a heart *or* a black card? Obviously, a card cannot be both a heart and a black card at the same time. We say that the events of drawing a heart and of drawing a black card are **mutually exclusive**. If A represents the event of drawing a heart and if B represents the event of drawing a black card, then $A \cap B = \varnothing$.

The probability of getting a heart is $\frac{13}{52}$, or $\frac{1}{4}$, since there are 13 hearts out of a possible 52 cards.

The probability of getting a black card is $\frac{26}{52}$, or $\frac{1}{2}$. Since there are 13 hearts and 26 black cards, this gives us a total of 39 favorable outcomes. As there are 52 cards in the deck, our answer is

$$p(\text{heart or black card}) = \frac{39}{52} = \frac{3}{4}$$

Note that if we add the probability of a heart and the probability of a black card, we get the following:

$$p(\text{heart}) + p(\text{black card}) = \frac{1}{4} + \frac{1}{2}$$

$$= \frac{3}{4}$$

Thus we see that

$$p(\text{heart or black card}) = p(\text{heart}) + p(\text{black card})$$

This leads us to the following.

Definition 8.5 Two events, A and B, are said to be **mutually exclusive** if both A and B cannot occur at the same time. In terms of sets this means $A \cap B = \varnothing$.

Addition Rule I

Addition Rule I—Formula 8.4 If A and B are mutually exclusive events, then

$$p(A \text{ or } B) = p(A) + p(B)$$

Before using this formula, we must be certain that we have mutually exclusive events. The events "scoring above 100 on an IQ test" and "scoring below 100" are mutually exclusive events. Similarly, the events "being a registered democrat" and "being a registered Republican" are mutually exclusive events. On the other hand, the events "being a woman" and "being a medical doctor" are not mutually exclusive events.

EXAMPLE 1

A card is drawn from a deck of 52 cards. What is the probability of getting a 7 or a picture card?

SOLUTION

The events "getting a 7" and "getting a picture card" are mutually exclusive. We can therefore use Formula 8.4. We first calculate p(getting a 7). Since there are four 7's out of a total of 52 cards,

$$p(7) = \frac{4}{52} = \frac{1}{13}$$

Also, we know that there are 12 picture cards in a 52-card deck. Thus

$$p(\text{picture card}) = \frac{12}{52} = \frac{3}{13}$$

By Formula 8.4 we get

$$p(7 \text{ or picture card}) = p(7) + p(\text{picture card})$$

$$= \frac{1}{13} + \frac{3}{13} = \frac{4}{13}$$

EXAMPLE 2

At the Fresh Air Fund Charity Bazaar, there is a table at which 30 unmarked surprise packages are being sold. Six of the packages contain cameras, 3 contain perfume, 10 contain wallets, 5 contain ashtrays, and 6 contain shavers. No package contains more than one item, and all the packages are wrapped identically. What is the probability that Ann, who buys the first package, gets either a camera or perfume?

SOLUTION

Since Ann is buying only one package, the events "getting a camera" and "getting perfume" are mutually exclusive. Thus Formula 8.4 can be applied. Since there are 30 packages altogether, 6 of which are cameras and 3 of which are perfume, then

$$p(\text{gets a camera}) = \frac{6}{30}$$

and

$$p(\text{gets perfume}) = \frac{3}{30}$$

Therefore

$$p(\text{gets a camera or gets perfume}) = p(\text{gets a camera}) + p(\text{gets perfume})$$
$$= \frac{6}{30} + \frac{3}{30} = \frac{9}{30} = \frac{3}{10}$$

Therefore the probability that Ann gets a camera or perfume is $\frac{3}{10}$. ■

EXAMPLE 3

A mailman cannot read the address on a letter. He is not sure but thinks that the address is either 390 Main Street or 890 Main Street. The probability that he will deliver it to 390 Main Street is $\frac{1}{3}$, and the probability that he will deliver it to 890 Main Street is $\frac{2}{5}$. What is the probability that he will deliver the letter to 890 Main Street or 390 Main Street?

SOLUTION

Since the mailman cannot deliver the letter to both addresses (at the same time) we are dealing with mutually exclusive events. Formula 8.4 can be used. Therefore

$$p(390 \text{ or } 890 \text{ Main St.}) = p(390) + p(890)$$
$$= \frac{1}{3} + \frac{2}{5} = \frac{5}{15} + \frac{6}{15} = \frac{11}{15}$$

The probability that he delivers it to one of these addresses is $\frac{11}{15}$. ■

EXAMPLE 4

John drives his car over a nail. If the probability that he gets a flat tire is $\frac{4}{7}$, what is the probability that he does not get a flat tire?

SOLUTION

Since the events "getting a flat" and "not getting a flat" are mutually exclusive, we can use Formula 8.4. Clearly, one of these events *must* happen. Thus the event "flat or not flat" is the certain event and has probability of 1. By Formula 8.4 we then have

$$p(\text{flat or not flat}) = p(\text{flat}) + p(\text{no flat})$$

$$1 = \frac{4}{7} + p(\text{no flat})$$

Subtracting $\frac{4}{7}$ from both sides, we get

$$1 - \frac{4}{7} = p(\text{no flat})$$

$$\frac{3}{7} = p(\text{no flat})$$

Therefore John's chance of not getting a flat is $\frac{3}{7}$. ■

Events That Are Not Mutually Exclusive

Now let us consider the following problem. What is the probability of drawing from a deck of cards an ace *or* a spade? We first notice that the events "drawing an ace" and "drawing a spade" are *not* mutually exclusive, since the ace of spades is both an ace and a spade. If we let A stand for the event of drawing an ace and let B stand for the event of drawing a spade, then $A \cap B \neq \varnothing$. Thus Formula 8.4 cannot be used. For situations of this type, we introduce the following.

Addition Rule II

Addition Rule II—Formula 8.5   If A and B are any events, then

$$p(A \text{ or } B) = p(A) + p(B) - p(A \text{ and } B)$$

Let us apply this formula to the above problem. We know that

$$p(A) = \frac{4}{52} \quad \text{and} \quad p(B) = \frac{13}{52}$$

We now calculate $p(A \text{ and } B)$. This event occurs only when the card drawn is an ace of spades. This had already been calculated on p. 434. Thus $p(A \text{ and } B) = \frac{1}{52}$. Using Formula 8.5, we get

$$p(A \text{ or } B) = p(A) + p(B) - p(A \text{ and } B)$$

$$= \frac{4}{52} + \frac{13}{52} - \frac{1}{52} = \frac{16}{52} = \frac{4}{13}$$

The probability of drawing an ace or a spade is $\frac{4}{13}$. ∎

EXAMPLE 5

Sarah has just bought a new car. The probability that the body of the car will rust within six months is $\frac{1}{6}$. The probability that the oil will leak is $\frac{3}{8}$. The probability of both of these disasters happening is $\frac{1}{16}$. (We are assuming that these events are not mutually exclusive.) What is the probability that the body will rust *or* that the oil will leak?

$$p(\text{rust or oil leak}) = p(\text{rust}) + p(\text{oil leak}) - p(\text{rust and oil leak})$$

$$= \frac{1}{6} + \frac{3}{8} - \frac{1}{16} = \frac{8}{48} + \frac{18}{48} - \frac{3}{48} = \frac{23}{48}$$

Thus the probability that Sarah's car will rust or have an oil leak is $\frac{23}{48}$.

EXAMPLE 6

Betty is anxious to know her grades in two courses, History 2.3 and Math 1.6. The probabilities of her getting an A in these courses are $\frac{1}{3}$ and $\frac{2}{9}$, respectively. Furthermore the probability of her getting an A in both courses is $\frac{1}{27}$. What is the probability that Betty will get an A in either course?

SOLUTION

Applying Formula 8.5 (since the events are not mutually exclusive), we get

$$p(\text{A in history or in math}) = p(\text{A in history}) + p(\text{A in math}) - p(\text{A in both})$$

$$= \frac{1}{3} + \frac{2}{9} - \frac{1}{27} = \frac{9}{27} + \frac{6}{27} - \frac{1}{27} = \frac{14}{27}$$

The chance of Betty getting an A in either course is $\frac{14}{27}$. ◼

EXAMPLE 7

On a certain day the probability of rain is $\frac{3}{5}$, the probability of thunder is $\frac{2}{5}$, and the probability of both is $\frac{1}{5}$. What is the probability that it will rain *or* thunder?

SOLUTION

We use Formula 8.5,

$$p(\text{rain or thunder}) = p(\text{rain}) + p(\text{thunder}) - p(\text{rain and thunder})$$

$$= \frac{3}{5} + \frac{2}{5} - \frac{1}{5} = \frac{4}{5}$$

The chances of it raining or thundering are $\frac{4}{5}$. ◼

Comment Formula 8.4 is just a special case of Formula 8.5, Formula 8.5 applies to *any* events A and B. If these events happen to be mutually exclusive, then A and B cannot happen together. Thus $p(A \text{ and } B)$ is 0. In this case, Formula 8.5 becomes

$$p(A \text{ or } B) = p(A) + p(B) - p(A \text{ and } B),$$
$$p(A \text{ or } B) = p(A) + p(B) - 0$$
$$p(A \text{ or } B) = p(A) + p(B)$$

This is exactly the same as Formula 8.4.

EXERCISES FOR SECTION 8.4

Determine which of the events given in Exercises 1–6 are mutually exclusive and which are not.

1. Catching a cold and getting a headache.

2. Getting a 3 and a 6 on one throw of a die.

3. Heating a home with gas heat and heating a home with oil heat.

4. Going on a skiing vacation in the Swiss Alps and going on a skiing vacation in Denver during the winter intersession period.

5. Smoking cigarettes and chewing tobacco.

6. Subscribing to the *Wall Street Journal* and subscribing to the *New York Times*.

7. A random survey of the members of the Lucky Health Club disclosed the following: the probability that a member uses the whirlpool is $\frac{3}{8}$, and the probability that a member uses the sauna is $\frac{1}{4}$. What is the probability that a member uses the whirlpool or the sauna if the probability that the member uses both is $\frac{1}{32}$?

8. According to local auto club officials, the probability that a gas station in the city has a functioning air pump is $\frac{2}{11}$, and the probability that the gas station attendant will check your oil is $\frac{5}{13}$. If the probability both that the gas station has a functioning air pump and that the attendant will check your oil is $\frac{2}{143}$, what is the probability of either event happening?

9. Insurance company statistics indicate that the probability that a married man in Rego Park has major medical insurance is 0.87 and the probability that he has disability insurance is 0.21. If the probability that he has both forms of insurance is 0.16, what is the probability that he has at least one of those forms of insurance?

10. How many credit cards are you carrying? A recent survey by a group of banks found that the probability that a person in Boulton has a Master Card issued in his or her name is 0.67 and the probability that the person has a VISA credit card is 0.71. Furthermore, the probability that the person has either of these credit cards is 0.92. What is the probability that a person has *both* a Master Card and a VISA credit card issued in his or her name in Boulton?

11. A computer club found that 59% of the people who own home computers use it for word processing, 31% of the owners use it for entertainment (games), and 27% of the owners use it for both word processing and entertainment. What is the probability that a home computer owner will use it either for word processing or for entertainment?

12. Willie walks into a bank. The probability that a teller is a part-time employee is $\frac{9}{17}$, and the probability that the teller is a male is $\frac{9}{34}$. If the probability of finding either a male teller or a part-time teller is $\frac{53}{68}$, what is the probability of finding a part-time male teller at the bank?

13. Motor vehicle records indicate that the probability that an applicant for a driver's license can pass the written exam on the first attempt is $\frac{2}{3}$. Furthermore,

the probability is $\frac{2}{7}$ that the applicant can pass the road test on the first attempt, and the probability is $\frac{2}{21}$ that the applicant can pass both the written test and the road test on the first attempt. What is the probability that the applicant can pass either test on the first attempt?

14. Pete is in charge of the mail room of a stock brokerage office. The probability that he will send an important package by Federal Express is $\frac{5}{9}$, and the probability that he will send it by Purolator is $\frac{2}{9}$. What is the probability that he will *not* send an important package by Federal Express or Purolator?

15. Professor Gonzales teaches different types of computing courses. The probability that he will teach Computing 106 (Introduction to BASIC) next semester is 0.59, and the probability that he will teach Computing 327 (Data Base Management) next semester is 0.62. If the probability that he will teach either of these courses is 0.86, what is the probability that he will teach both of these courses next semester?

16. Government records indicate that 40% of all mothers in San Pedro work (at least part-time) to supplement their family income, and 65% of all mothers in San Pedro send their young children to nursery school. If 14% of all working mothers send their children to nursery school, what is the probability that a mother will work or send her child to nursery school?

For any three events A, B, and C the probability of A or B or C is given by

$$p(A \text{ or } B \text{ or } C) = p(A) + p(B) + p(C)$$
$$- p(A \text{ and } B)$$
$$- p(A \text{ and } C)$$
$$- p(B \text{ and } C)$$
$$+ p(A \text{ and } B \text{ and } C)$$

Use this formula to solve the following problems:

17. Dave is planning on a going-away party for Sherry. He will definitely buy and serve potato chips, pretzels, or taco chips. The probability that he serves potato chips is $\frac{4}{9}$, the probability that he serves pretzels is $\frac{1}{2}$, the probability that he serves taco chips is $\frac{2}{5}$, the probability that he serves potato chips and pretzels is $\frac{1}{7}$, the probability that he serves potato chips and taco chips is $\frac{1}{6}$, and the probability that he serves pretzels and taco chips is $\frac{1}{8}$. Find the probability that he serves all three items mentioned.

18. Marilyn is the manager of a local fast-food restaurant. Over the past few years she has determined the following probabilities on the items that a customer will order:

Item(s)	Probability
Steak sandwich	$\frac{4}{7}$
French fries	$\frac{1}{2}$
Malted	$\frac{5}{11}$
Steak sandwich and French fries	$\frac{2}{9}$
French fries and malted	$\frac{1}{7}$
Steak sandwich, and malted	$\frac{1}{4}$
Steak sandwich, French fries, and malted	$\frac{1}{44}$

What is the probability that a customer will order either a steak sandwich, French fries, or a malted?

19. A recent survey[1] of numerous obstetricians specializing in high risk pregnancies revealed the following facts about their patients and their recent deliveries. These doctors determined the following probabilities for their patients.

Fact	Probability
Mother over 35 years of age	0.27
First child for mother	0.22
Mother had a well-paying career job	0.42
First child for mother and over 35 years of age	0.17
First child for mother and mother had a well-paying career job	0.09
Mother over 35 years of age and had a well-paying career job	0.16
First child for mother and mother over 35 years of age who had a well-paying career job	0.07

What is the probability that a randomly selected mother in this group is either over 35 years of age or had a well-paying career job or that the child is a first child for the mother?

---

1. Johnson and Baker, New York, 1989.

8.5

CONDITIONAL PROBABILITY

In the last section we considered problems in which more than one event occurred. The formulas given there do not apply to all situations, as the following examples illustrate.

EXAMPLE 1   Joan is at a stand in an amusement park where there are three identical boxes, two of which contain one red marble each. The third box has a white marble in it. To win, Joan must guess the color of the marble in each box. She has guessed that the first box has a red marble, and she is right. Joan claims that the marble in the second box is red. What is the probability that she is correct?

SOLUTION

From the information given, we know that there is a red marble in box 1. This means that only one red marble and one white marble remain. Since either of them can be in box 2, the probability that she is correct if she guesses a red marble is $\frac{1}{2}$. ■

EXAMPLE 2

Bob has drawn a card from a 52-card deck. What is the probability that it is a jack if we know that it is a picture card?

SOLUTION

There are 12 picture cards: 4 jacks, 4 queens, and 4 kings and thus 12 outcomes, of which 4 are favorable. Thus the probability that the card is a jack, given that it is a picture card, is $\frac{4}{12}$, or $\frac{1}{3}$. ■

EXAMPLE 3

Bill is getting dressed. He reaches into a drawer where he has 3 black and 2 gray socks (these are not pairs, but individual socks). He selects one sock and then, without replacing it, selects another. What is the probability that both are black?

SOLUTION

An easy way to solve this problem is to list all the possible outcomes and then to count all the favorable ones. To do this, we label the black socks as b_1, b_2, b_3 and the gray socks as g_1, g_2.
   The possible outcomes are:

$\mathbf{b_1, b_2}$	$\mathbf{b_2, b_3}$	b_3, g_1	g_1, g_2
$\mathbf{b_1, b_3}$	b_2, g_1	b_3, g_2	g_2, b_1
b_1, g_1	b_2, g_2	g_1, b_1	g_2, b_2
b_1, g_2	$\mathbf{b_3, b_1}$	g_1, b_2	g_2, b_3
$\mathbf{b_2, b_1}$	$\mathbf{b_3, b_2}$	g_1, b_3	g_2, g_1

Out of the 20 possible outcomes, 6 are favorable. These are the ones in boldface. They represent a pair of matching black socks. Thus the probability that both are black is $\frac{6}{20}$. ■

EXAMPLE 4

In the previous example, what is the probability that the second sock selected is black if we know that the first sock is black?

SOLUTION

There are two ways to do this problem. One way is to list all possible outcomes and then count the favorable ones. There are 12 possible outcomes, 6 of which are favorable. These are in boldface as shown here:

$\mathbf{b_1, b_2}$	$\mathbf{b_2, b_3}$	b_1, g_1	b_2, g_2
$\mathbf{b_1, b_3}$	$\mathbf{b_3, b_1}$	b_1, g_2	b_3, g_1
$\mathbf{b_2, b_1}$	$\mathbf{b_3, b_2}$	b_2, g_1	b_3, g_2

Thus the probability that the second sock is black, if we know that the first sock is black, is $\frac{6}{12}$, or $\frac{1}{2}$. ▪

Comment Compare this answer with the answer to Example 3. It is not the same because in Example 3 we were considering only the probability of selecting a pair of black socks out of *all* possible ways of selecting a pair of socks. In Example 4, we considered the probability of selecting a second black sock *after* we know that the first sock is already a black one.

conditional probability

The situation of Example 4 is called a **conditional probability** because we are interested in the probability of getting a black sock, given that (or conditional on the fact that) the first sock was black. We use a special symbol for this. We write

$$p(\text{second sock is black} \mid \text{first sock is black})$$

The vertical line "⎮" stands for the words "given that" or "if we know that." Using this notation, we have

$$p(\text{second sock is black} \mid \text{first sock is black}) = \frac{1}{2}$$

conditional probability formula

A second way of approaching this problem involves a formula called the **conditional probability formula**.

Formula 8.6 If A and B are any events, then

$$p(A \mid B) = \frac{p(A \text{ and } B)}{p(B)}$$

Applying this formula to our problem, we have

$p(\text{second sock is black} \mid \text{first sock is black})$

$$= \frac{p(\text{second sock is black and first sock is black})}{p(\text{first sock is black})}$$

This simplifies to

$$\frac{p(\text{both socks are black})}{p(\text{first sock is black})}$$

Both of these numbers are easily calculated. As a matter of fact, the top part of the fraction was calculated in Example 3. It is $\frac{6}{20}$. The bottom part of the fraction is found by calculating the number of outcomes in which the first sock is black. This gives 12 out of a possible 20 outcomes. (Verify that there are actually 12 by counting them.)

Thus Formula 8.6 gives

$$p(\text{second sock is black} \mid \text{first sock is black}) = \frac{6/20}{12/20} = \frac{6}{20} \div \frac{12}{20}$$

$$= \frac{6}{20} \cdot \frac{20}{12} = \frac{6}{12} = \frac{1}{2}$$

EXAMPLE 5

SOLUTION

We will redo Example 2 on p. 453 using Formula 8.6.

We want $p(\text{jack} \mid \text{picture card})$. Using Formula 8.6, we get

$$p(\text{jack} \mid \text{picture card}) = \frac{p(\text{jack and picture card})}{p(\text{picture card})}$$

For a card to be both a jack and a picture card it must be a jack. We therefore have that the probability that a card is a jack *and* a picture card is $\frac{4}{52}$. Since there are 12 picture cards, the probability of a picture card is $\frac{12}{52}$.

Putting these into the formula, we get

$$p(\text{jack} \mid \text{picture card}) = \frac{4/52}{12/52} = \frac{4}{52} \div \frac{12}{52} = \frac{4}{52} \cdot \frac{52}{12} = \frac{4}{12} = \frac{1}{3}$$

Of course this is the same answer as the one we got before.

EXAMPLE 6

An absentminded professor often forgets to put money in the meter when he parks. The probability that he will forget to put money in the meter is $\frac{7}{10}$. If the probability that he gets a ticket when he forgets to put money in the meter is $\frac{3}{7}$, what is the probability that he will forget to put money in the meter and that he will get a ticket?

SOLUTION

We will use Formula 8.6:

$$p(\text{gets ticket} \mid \text{forgets money}) = \frac{p(\text{forgets money and gets ticket})}{p(\text{forgets money})}$$

Using the given information, we have

$$\frac{3}{7} = \frac{p(\text{forgets money and gets ticket})}{7/10}$$

We multiply both sides by $\frac{7}{10}$ getting

$$\frac{7}{10} \cdot \frac{3}{7} = \frac{7}{10} \cdot \frac{p(\text{forgets money and gets ticket})}{7/10}$$

$$\frac{3}{10} = p(\text{forgets money and gets ticket})$$

Therefore the probability that he will forget to put money in the meter *and* that he will get a ticket is $\frac{3}{10}$. ▬

Independent Events

independent events

In many cases it turns out that whether or not one event happens does not affect whether or not another will happen. For example, if a coin is tossed and if a die is rolled, the outcome of the coin toss has nothing to do with the outcome of rolling the die. Also, if two coins are tossed, then the outcome for the first coin has nothing to do with the outcome for the second coin. Such events are called **independent events**.

For independent events, Formula 8.6 can be simplified, as the following example shows.

EXAMPLE 7

If a die is rolled once and if a coin is tossed once, what is the probability that the die will show a 3 and that the coin will come up heads?

SOLUTION

We will solve the problem in two ways. One is by counting. The other way is by the formula for independent events.

To do it by counting, we will list all the possible outcomes. There are 12 of them. These are:

1 H	**3 H**	5 H
1 T	3 T	5 T
2 H	4 H	6 H
2 T	4 T	6 T

Among the 12 possible outcomes, only one of them is favorable. This is the boldface one, **3 H**. Therefore the probability of getting a 3 and a head is $\frac{1}{12}$. ▬

Now we will do the problem by using the following formula.

Formula 8.7 If A and B are independent events, then

$$p(A \text{ and } B) = p(A) \cdot p(B)$$

If we let A represent the event of getting a 3 when we throw a die and let B stand for the event of getting a head, then we are looking for

$$p(A \text{ and } B)$$

By the formula this is $p(A) \cdot p(B)$. We know that $p(A) = \frac{1}{6}$ and that $p(B) = \frac{1}{2}$. Thus

$$p(A \text{ and } B) = p(A) \cdot p(B) = \frac{1}{6} \cdot \frac{1}{2} = \frac{1}{12}$$

Comment   Formula 8.7 may look like a new formula to be learned. This is not so. It is really a simplified case of Formula 8.6. Let us see why. Formula 8.6 says that for *any* events A and B

$$p(A \mid B) = \frac{p(A \text{ and } B)}{p(B)}$$

If A is independent of B, then $p(A \mid B)$ is the same as $p(A)$. Why? Therefore for independent events, Formula 8.6 becomes

$$p(A) = \frac{p(A \text{ and } B)}{p(B)}$$

If we now multiply both sides by $p(B)$, we get

$$p(A) \cdot p(B) = p(A \text{ and } B)$$

This is exactly the same as Formula 8.7.

EXERCISES FOR SECTION 8.5

1. Thirty-eight percent of the employees of Apex Consulting Company are male *and* are systems analysts. Fifty-four percent of the Apex Consulting Company employees are male. If a male employee of the Apex Consulting Company is randomly selected, what is the probability that he is a systems analyst?

2. Jack McAllister owns and operates a huge farm in California. The probability that an employee is a migrant worker is 0.95, and the probability that the worker is a migrant worker *and* an illegal alien is 0.24. If a migrant worker is randomly selected, what is the probability that the worker is an illegal alien?

3. A recent study found that the probability that a person in Bakersville has a checking account is 0.82 and the probability that the person has a checking account as well as overdraft privileges is 0.31. (Overdraft privileges allow customers to write checks for amounts that exceed their current balance.) If a customer who has a checking account is randomly selected, what is the probability that the customer has overdraft privileges?

4. *Legalizing Drugs.* A newspaper reporter[2] conducted a nationwide survey of 1638 people to find out what

they thought about legalizing drug use. The results of the survey are shown in the accompanying table:

Region of country in which respondent lives	In favor of proposal	Against proposal
East	164	204
Midwest	110	358
South	128	276
Far West	146	252

Find the probability that a randomly selected individual in the group

   a) lives in the East given that he or she is against the proposal.

   b) is against the proposal given that he or she lives in the East.

   c) is against the proposal.

5. Consider the newspaper article on top of next page. The probability of a motorist having a mechanical breakdown on the city's highways is 0.03. What is the probability that a motorist's car will break down and that the motorist will *not* be able to summon help because of a call box that is not functioning properly?

---

2. Dave Hamel, Los Angeles, 1989.

Majority of Police Call Boxes Not Functioning

NEW YORK: A random survey by reporters for the local auto club found that 57% of the emergency call boxes on the city's highways were not functioning properly because of vandalism or were missing telephones completely. The phones in these strategically placed call boxes allow a motorist to summon help in the event of a mechanical breakdown.

Daily Press, May 17, 1988

6. Roberto is having trouble with the disc drive of his computer. He is also using cheap discs, which often are defective. The probability that the disc drive is not operating properly is $\frac{3}{11}$. The probability that the disc drive is not operating properly *and* that the cheap discs are defective is $\frac{2}{33}$. If it is known that the disc drive is not operating properly, find the probability that the cheap discs are defective.

7. Government records indicate that 17% of all residents in a certain city are senior citizens and have had some sort of trouble in the past with the Social Security system. Moreover, in this city, 51% of the population are senior citizens. If a senior citizen is selected at random, what is the probability that the individual has never had any sort of trouble in the past with the Social Security system?

8. The Bruce Mechanical Corporation owns two photocopying machines, which often do not operate properly. The probability that the first machine will produce unacceptable copies is 0.23, and the probability that the second machine will produce unacceptable copies is 0.16. What is the probability that on a given day both machines will produce copies that are acceptable?

9. Beth McGuire, Nancy Peters, and Joy Richards have applied to a bank for auto loans. The probability that Beth McGuire's application will be approved is 0.82. The probability that Nancy Peter's application will be approved is 0.73 and the probability that Joy Richard's application will be approved is 0.67. Assuming independence, what is the probability that all three applications will be approved?

10. Refer back to the previous question. What is the probability that only Nancy Peter's application will be approved?

11. In a certain mining town the following statistics have been accumulated. The probability that a miner has black lung disease is 0.53, and the probability that a miner has arthritis is 0.21. Assuming independence, what is the probability that a randomly selected miner does not have black lung disease but has arthritis?

12. Heather has just parked her car by a parking meter. She notices that someone has placed a paper bag over the meter and scribbled the words "meter out of order" on it. Is this an accurate description of the meter? Should she deposit her quarter? The probability that the parking meter is out of order is $\frac{5}{12}$. The probability that the parking meter is out of order *and* that she loses her quarter is $\frac{2}{9}$. If the parking meter is actually out of order, what is the probability that she does *not* lose her quarter?

13. *Law.* In June 1964 an elderly woman was mugged in San Pedro, California. In the vicinity of the crime a bearded, black man sat waiting in a yellow car. Shortly after the crime was committed, a young white woman, wearing her blonde hair in a ponytail, was seen running from the scene of the crime and getting into the car, which sped off. The police broadcast a description of the suspected muggers. Soon afterward a couple fitting the description was arrested and convicted of the crime. Although the evidence in the case was largely circumstantial, the prosecutor based his case on probability and the unlikelihood of another couple having such characteristics. He assumed the probabilities shown in the table at the top of the next page.

The prosecutor then multiplied the individual probabilities:

$$\left(\frac{1}{10}\right)\left(\frac{1}{1000}\right)\left(\frac{1}{3}\right)\left(\frac{1}{10}\right)\left(\frac{1}{4}\right)\left(\frac{1}{10}\right)=\frac{1}{12,000,000}.$$

He claimed that the probability is 1/12,000,000 that another couple has such characteristics. The jury agreed and convicted the couple. The conviction was overturned by the California Supreme Court in 1968. The defense attorneys got some professional advice on probability. Serious errors were found in the prosecutor's probability calculations. Some of these involved assumptions about independent events. As a matter of

Characteristic	Assumed probability
Drives yellow car	$\frac{1}{10}$
Black-white couple	$\frac{1}{1000}$
Black man	$\frac{1}{3}$
Man with beard	$\frac{1}{10}$
Blonde woman	$\frac{1}{4}$
Woman with ponytail	$\frac{1}{10}$

fact, it was demonstrated that the probability is 0.41 that another couple with the same characteristics existed in the area once it was known that there was at least one such couple. For a complete discussion of this probability case, read "Trial by Mathematics" in *Time* (January 8, 1965, p. 42; and April 26, 1968, p. 41).

14. *Shuttle safety:* In its February 2, 1987 article on NASA, *U.S. News & World Report* stated that there are 748 "critically 1" items needed for a successful shuttle launch. If one analyzes this article we can conclude that while a perfectly reliable shuttle is unachievable, it is not surprising that mission No. 25 did indeed fail. If each of the 748 "critically 1" items meet NASA's "four nines" reliability standard of 99.99%, the reliability for all these critical items taken together is 0.9999 raised to the 748th power. Using a calculator with a $\boxed{y^x}$ button, this number is approximately 93%. Thus we can conclude that there is a 7% chance that at least one "critically 1" item will fail. Do you think that our space shuttle program is statistically reliable?

8.6

ODDS AND MATHEMATICAL EXPECTATION

Gamblers are always interested in the odds of a game or a race. They are also interested in the amount of money to be won. In this section we will investigate the meaning of these ideas and learn how to calculate odds.

To best understand these ideas, let us consider a man at Aqueduct Raceway. Nine horses have been entered in the big race. Our man places $10 on the horse Liverwurst. We will assume that each horse has an equal chance of winning. Therefore the probability that the man will win is $\frac{1}{9}$.

odds

Gamblers prefer to speak in term of **odds**. They would say that the odds in favor of winning are 1 to 8 and the odds against his winning are 8 to 1. The 8 represents the eight chances of losing. Thus we have the following definitions.

odds in favor

> **Definition 8.6** The **odds in favor** of an event occurring are *p* to *q*, where *p* is "the number of favorable outcomes" and *q* is the "the number of unfavorable outcomes."

odds against

> **Definition 8.7** The **odds against** an event occurring are q to p, where q and p are the same as in Definition 8.6.

We illustrate these definitions with several examples.

EXAMPLE 1

What are the odds in favor of drawing an ace from a full deck of 52 cards on one draw?

SOLUTION

Since there are 4 aces and 48 non-aces, Definition 8.6 tells us that the odds in favor of drawing an ace are 4 to 48, or 1 to 12.

EXAMPLE 2

What are the odds in favor of winning at the Hopeless Wheel of Fortune, which is divided into 10 equal parts, each with a different color, if someone bets the colors red and blue and only one color wins?

SOLUTION

Since there are 2 favorable and 8 unfavorable outcomes, Definition 8.6 tells us that the odds in favor of winning are 2 to 8, or 1 to 4.

EXAMPLE 3

What are the odds *against* throwing a 2 or a 12 in throwing a pair of dice?

SOLUTION

When a pair of dice is thrown, there are 36 possible outcomes (p. 439). Two are favorable, and 34 are unfavorable. Thus Definition 8.7 tells us that the odds against getting a 2 or a 12 are 34 to 2, or 17 to 1.

When gambling (as well as in business situations), the amount of money to be won in the long run is called the **mathematical expectation**. It is defined as follows.

mathematical expectation

> **Definition 8.8** Suppose an event has several possible outcomes with probabilities p_1, p_2, p_3, and so on. Suppose on the first event the payoff is m_1, on the second event the payoff is m_2, on the third event the payoff is m_3, etc. Then the **mathematical expectation** of the event is
> $$m_1p_1 + m_2p_2 + m_3p_3 + \cdots.$$

The following examples show how this definition is applied.

EXAMPLE 4

A die is tossed once. If a 1 comes up, then Joe will win $10; and if a 4 comes up, he will win $7. What is his mathematical expectation?

SOLUTION

When a die is tossed once, then the probability of getting a 1 is $\frac{1}{6}$. Similarly, the probability of getting a 4 is $\frac{1}{6}$. Using Definition 8.8, we find that the mathematical expectation is

$$10\left(\frac{1}{6}\right) + 7\left(\frac{1}{6}\right) = \frac{17}{6} = \$2.83 \quad \text{(when rounded)} \quad \blacksquare$$

EXAMPLE 5

The local chapter of the American Cancer Society is planning to hold a bazaar to raise funds. If the bazaar is held outdoors, $100,000 is expected to be raised. If the bazaar is held indoors, then $75,000 is expected to be raised. The probability that it will rain, forcing the bazaar to be held indoors, is $\frac{3}{5}$ and the probability that the weather will be suitable for an outdoor bazaar is $\frac{2}{5}$. How much money can they expect to raise?

SOLUTION

We will use Definition 8.8. We have

$$100,000\left(\frac{2}{5}\right) + 75,000\left(\frac{3}{5}\right) = 40,000 + 45,000 = 85,000$$

Thus they can expect to raise $85,000. $\blacksquare$

> Consider the lottery ticket. Does a person really have a "reasonable" chance (or probability) of winning when buying such a ticket? If a person buys many such tickets or plays the lottery on a regular basis, will this affect the person's expected amount of money to be won?

EXAMPLE 6

A wheel of fortune at an amusement park is divided into 4 colors: red, blue, yellow, and green. The probabilities of the spinner's landing in any of these colors are $\frac{3}{10}$, $\frac{4}{10}$, $\frac{2}{10}$, and $\frac{1}{10}$, respectively. A player can win $4 if the spinner stops on red and $2 if it stops on green, and lose $2 if it stops on blue and $3 if it stops on yellow. Trudy has decided to try her luck at the wheel. What is her mathematical expectation?

SOLUTION

We indicate the possible outcomes and the corresponding probabilities by the chart below.

Outcome	Probability	Amount of money won or lost
Red	$\dfrac{3}{10}$	$+4$
Blue	$\dfrac{4}{10}$	-2
Yellow	$\dfrac{2}{10}$	-3
Green	$\dfrac{1}{10}$	$+2$

Thus her mathematical expectation is

$$(4)\left(\frac{3}{10}\right) + (-2)\left(\frac{4}{10}\right) + (-3)\left(\frac{2}{10}\right) + (2)\left(\frac{1}{10}\right) = \frac{12}{10} - \frac{8}{10} - \frac{6}{10} + \frac{2}{10} = 0$$

Her mathematical expectation is 0. What does this 0 mean? We interpret this to mean that in the long run she will win 0 dollars or break even. ■

Comment Some gamblers base their decision whether or not to play a particular game solely on the game's mathematical expectation. Obviously, if the game has a negative mathematical expectation, a gambler should not play, since he or she will lose money in the long run. There would be little point in playing a game whose mathematical expectation is 0, since in the long run the amount of money that can be won is 0.

Mathematical expectation can also be applied to nonmoney situations, as the following example will illustrate.

EXAMPLE 7

An observer for an energy conservation group has collected the following statistics on the number of occupants per car that pass through a certain tollgate.

Number of passengers in car (including driver)	1	2	3	4	5	6
Probability	0.37	0.29	0.18		0.05	0.02

What is the expected number of occupants per car?

SOLUTION

We apply Definition 8.8 and multiply each of the possible outcomes by its probability. We get

$$1(0.37) + 2(0.29) + 3(0.18) + 4(0.09) + 5(0.05) + 6(0.02)$$

which equals 2.22. Thus the expected number of occupants per car is 2.22.

Pascal used mathematical expectation to make a "wager with God." As we have said, Pascal was extremely religious. He reasoned that leading a religious life will result in eternal happiness. The value of eternal happiness is infinite. Therefore the expectation is

$$m \cdot p = \left(\begin{array}{c} \text{value of eternal} \\ \text{happiness} \end{array} \right) \left(\begin{array}{c} \text{probability of obtaining} \\ \text{eternal happiness} \end{array} \right)$$

Since the value of eternal happiness is infinite, the product $m \cdot p$ is also infinite, even if the probability of obtaining eternal happiness is small. Thus it pays to lead a religious life, since the expectation is infinite.

Application to Genetics

genetics

One very interesting application of probability is in the science of **genetics**. This science is concerned with which traits can be inherited. The pioneer in this field was Gregor Mendel. As we mentioned in Chapter 2, Mendel performed many experiments with garden peas. As a result of his experiments, Mendel was able to state the basic laws of heredity.

Specifically, Mendel crossbred plants from wrinkled seeds with plants from smooth seeds. The resulting plants all had smooth seeds. However, when he crossbred these new plants with one another, a strange thing happened. Three-fourths of the plants had smooth seeds, and one-fourth had wrinkled seeds (See Fig. 8.8).

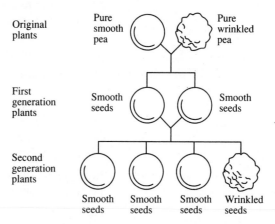

Figure 8.8

dominant genes

recessive genes

He concluded that certain *genes* are *dominant*. When a gene is dominant, then the trait that it represents will always appear, no matter which gene it is paired with. Such was the case for smooth seeds. On the other hand, there are other genes that are *recessive.* If a trait is recessive, it must be matched with the same type of gene for that trait to appear. Wrinkled seeds are recessive. This explains why when wrinkled seeds are matched with smooth seeds, the resulting plants all had smooth seeds. The smooth-seed gene "dominated" the wrinkled-seed one. On the other hand, in the second generation, "mixed" plants that now had both wrinkled and smooth genes were matched with each other. Those that contained any smooth-seed genes produced smooth-seed plants, and those that contained *only* wrinkled-seed genes produced wrinkled seeds as shown below.

	Smooth seeds	Wrinkled seeds
Smooth Seeds	Offspring have smooth seeds	Offspring have smooth seeds
Wrinkled Seeds	Offspring have smooth seeds	Offspring have wrinkled seeds

The same analysis was used by Mendel to explain why different flowers of the same kind of plant have different colors. For example, when a red-flowered four o'clock plant carrying a gene R for red was crossbred with another four o'clock plant carrying R, the offspring was RR and always had red flowers. Similarly, when a white-flowered four o'clock plant carrying a gene W for white was crossbred with another four o'clock plant carrying W, the offspring was WW and always had white flowers. On the other hand, when a plant carrying R was crossbred with a plant carrying W, a strange thing happened. The offspring contained the genes RW and was therefore pink, P. Mendel continued with these experiments and recorded the numerical percentages with which characteristics were inherited as shown in the following table.

		Genes of one plant		
		Red (RR) Offspring will be	White (WW) Offspring will be	Pink (RW) Offspring will be
Genes of other plant	Red (RR)	RR offspring— all red	RW offspring— all pink	RR—50% red RW—50% pink
	White (WW)	RW offspring— all pink	WW offspring— all white	RW—50% pink WW—50% white
	Pink (RW)	RR—50% red RW—50% pink	RW—50% pink WW—50% white	RR—25% red RW—50% pink WW—25% white

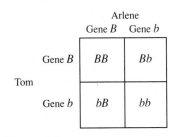

Arlene
Gene *B*   Gene *b*

Tom

	Gene *B*	Gene *b*
Gene *B*	*BB*	*Bb*
Gene *b*	*bB*	*bb*

Figure 8.9

From his observations on the peas and flowers, Mendel concluded that certain characteristics (or traits) were determined by a single pair of genes (one for each parent). The same is true of human beings. For example, it is known that a baby's eye color is determined by certain genes, one obtained from each parent. There are other inherited traits that are determined by several genes from each parent. In this section we concern ourselves only with those characteristics that are determined by a single pair of genes.

Let us analyze several such traits, such as eye color and the blood factor Rh.

EXAMPLE 8

It is known that in human eyes, the color brown is dominant and the color blue is recessive. Let B represent a gene for brown eyes and let b represent a gene for blue eyes. Thus a person who has BB genes (that is, brown from each parent) or Bb genes (brown from one parent and blue from the other) will have brown eyes, since brown is dominant. On the other hand, a person who has bb genes (blue from both parents) will have blue eyes. Arlene, who is known to have Bb genes, marries Tom, who is also known to have Bb genes. What is the probability that their child will have blue eyes?

SOLUTION

We set up a chart indicating how the genes can be matched and the resulting child's eye color (Fig. 8.9). In this chart, every time B is paired with any other gene, the child will have brown eyes. Only the pairing bb will result in blue eyes for the baby. Out of the 4 possible outcomes BB, Bb, bB, and bb, only 1 is favorable. Thus the probability that the child will have blue eyes is $\frac{1}{4}$.

EXAMPLE 9

Another inherited trait that is known to be determined by a single gene from each parent is the Rh blood factor. When a person has this factor in his or her blood, we say that he or she is Rh positive. Otherwise he or she is Rh negative. Eighty-five percent of American Caucasians and 93 percent of Blacks are born with this inherited substance. Thus if the parents of the husband and of the wife are pure Rh positive, then all the children will be Rh positive. On the other hand, if both husband and wife had one Rh-positive and one Rh-negative parent, then such a couple would produce, in every 4 children, one child who is pure Rh positive, 2 children who are partial Rh positive, and one child who is Rh negative.

In a recent court suit, Jane, who was known to be Rh negative, claimed that Bill, who was also Rh negative, was the father of her Rh-positive baby. Find the probability that Bill actually was the father.

SOLUTION

Since Jane is known to be Rh negative, it is impossible for Bill to be the father, since he is also Rh negative. Two Rh-negative parents can produce only an Rh-negative child. Thus the probability that Bill is the father of Jane's child is 0.   ■

Comment   Certain traits in human beings are known to be determined by the genes received from each parent. For example, albinism (no skin color, eye color, or hair color), muscular atrophy, Tay-Sach's disease, hemophilia, and sickle-cell anemia are known to be determined by genes. With appropriate medical care and advice the probability of these occurring can be reduced.

EXERCISES FOR SECTION 8.6

1. A card is drawn from an ordinary deck of cards. What are the odds in favor of getting a picture card?

2. A clothing store receives 100 pairs of "designer" jeans. Ninety-five of these are authentic, and 5 are cheap imitations. Maureen buys a pair of these jeans. What are the odds against her getting the designer jeans?

3. Jerry parks his car by a meter. He needs to put a quarter into the meter, but he has no change. There are 15 people standing nearby. Jerry decides to ask *only* one person to give him change for a dollar. If 6 of the people actually have change, what are the odds against his getting the change?

4. Consider the newspaper article below. Bill Sadowski invested a considerable amount of money in an abusive tax shelter. What are the odds in favor of his tax return being audited?

IRS To Investigate Abusive Tax Shelters

WASHINGTON: Officials of the Internal Revenue Service announced yesterday that they would carefully scrutinize all abusive tax shelters. Furthermore, an official said that an individual who invests in such shelters has a 95% chance of having his or her tax return audited.

THE TIMES, May 10, 1988

---

5. Barbara purchased 100 shares of stock of a company. The probability that there will be a stock split is $\frac{4}{9}$. What are the odds in favor of there being a stock split?

6. The town of Rockville is planning a flea market sale with profit going to the volunteer ambulance corps. If the weather is nice, then the flea market will be held outdoors in the baseball field. It is expected that $10,000 can then be raised. If it rains, then the flea market will be held indoors in the high school gym. If this occurs, then only $5500 can be raised, since many people do not like the tight spaces of the gym. If it snows, then the flea market sale will be canceled completely, and no money will be raised. The weather forecast is as follows:

Weather forecast	Probability
Nice weather	$\frac{5}{9}$
Rain	$\frac{3}{9}$
Snow storm	$\frac{1}{9}$

How much money can the town expect to raise?

7. A manufacturer has just introduced a new laundry detergent and would like to promote it by advertising on television, radio, in magazines, and by distributing free samples. Market research indicates the following

sales to be generated from each advertisement medium and the associated probability:

Advertisement medium	Potential sales	Probability
Television	$70,000	0.37
Radio	$37,000	0.56
Magazine	$45,000	0.49
Distributing free samples	$50,000	0.42

Find the expected sales from each medium.

8. Refer back to the previous exercise. If the manufacturer wishes to use only one of these advertisement media, which one should be selected? Explain your answer.

9. A man has just taken out a life insurance policy that will pay his beneficiaries $10,000 in the event of his death. The premium for this insurance coverage is $300. If the probability of the man dying is 0.07, what is the insurance company's mathematical expectation?

10. A clerk in the police department has compiled the following list on the number of requests for gun permits by individual citizens per day.

Number of requests	Probability
0	0.07
1	0.13
2	0.25
3	0.14
4	0.13
5	0.10
6	0.15
7	0.03

What is the expected number of requests for gun permits per day?

11. Jake purchased 100 tickets for this week's state lottery. The cost per ticket was $1. There will be one grand prize and ten second prizes as follows:

Prize amount	Probability of any one ticket winning
Grand prize: $10,000 (only 1 winner)	0.0003
Second prize: $1000 (for each winning ticket)	0.0009

What is Jake's mathematical expectation?

12. Casey is considering opening up a fast-food restaurant at one of two amusement parks. In park I he must invest $20,000, and he can expect an annual income of $100,000 with a probability of $\frac{5}{9}$ if successful. In park II he must invest $5000, and he can expect an annual income of $37,000 with a probability of $\frac{7}{9}$ if successful.

a) What is his mathematical expectation from each park?

b) On the basis of mathematical expectation only, in which park should Casey open his fast-food restaurant? Explain your answer.

13. Jim is told to roll a pair of dice. He can either win or lose money, depending upon the sum of the number of dots shown on both dice together. The amount of money won or lost is as follows:

Sum of the number of dots shown	Amount of money won or lost
2 or 4	win $12
5 or 8 or 9	lose $7
3 or 6	win $9
10 or 12	lose $10
7 or 11	win $15

What is the amount of money that Jim could expect to win (or lose)?

For Exercises 14–16, use the following information: An important human characteristic that is known to be transmitted by genes is albinism, in which a child is born with no skin color, no eye color, and no hair color. It is known that albinism is a recessive trait. Thus if N is the normal gene and a is a gene for albinism, then a person with Na genes will have normal color, and a child with aa genes will be an albino.

14. Mr. Gelespie has *Na* genes, and Mrs. Gelespie has *Na* genes. Find the probability that their child will have normal color.

15. Mr. Jones has *NN* genes, and Mrs. Jones has *Na* genes. Find the probability that their child will

  a) be an albino.

  b) have normal color.

16. Mrs. Smith has just given birth to an albino child. Furthermore, it is known that Mrs. Smith has *aa* genes. What type of genes can Mr. Smith have for him to be the father?

17. A botanist is experimenting with flowers that have a certain trait *T* or *t*. She crossbreeds a plant that has *Tt* genes with a plant that has *TT* genes. Find the probability that the offspring will be:

  a) *TT*   **b)** *Tt*   **c)** *tt*

18. A researcher in a laboratory is splicing genes. She crossbreeds an organism that has a certain characteristic *T* (it has *Tt* genes) with another organism that lacks the trait (it has *tt* genes). Find the probability that the offspring will be:

  a) *TT*   **b)** *tt*   **c)** *Tt*

TYPICAL CLASSROOM QUESTIONS

1. Bill Johnson has just had a massive heart attack. He reasons that since there are two possibilities, live or die, then the probability that he will survive the heart attack is $\frac{1}{2}$. Do you agree with his reasoning? Explain your answer.

2. A student claims that a combination lock is really not a combination lock but a permutation lock. Do you agree?

3. Jill Stevens, who already has six boys, is pregnant with her seventh child. She reasons that according to averages the probability that the next child is a girl is greater than the probability that it is a boy. Do you agree?

4. Scientists have determined that the number of possible genetic makeups that a child of one couple can have is 2^{48}. Little Billy claims that his "identical" twin brother is exactly like him in *all* respects. Is it likely that Billy is correct? (*Hint*: Find the probability that both boys have the same genetic makeup.)

5. What, if anything, is wrong with the following? The probability that Tracy plays a guitar is 0.82 and the probability that she plays a clarinet is 0.71. Therefore, the probability that she plays a guitar or a clarinet is $0.82 + 0.71 = 1.53$.

6. Debby Robinson was born on February 29. Her teacher asks everyone to write their birthdates on a little piece of paper. The teacher then places these papers in a bowl and randomly selects a birthdate. Debby reasons that since there are 365 days in a year, and that a leap year occurs every fourth year, then the probability of her birthdate coming up is $\left(\frac{1}{365}\right) \cdot \left(\frac{1}{4}\right)$. Do you agree?

7. A secretary types three letters and addresses three envelopes. Before the letters are inserted into their appropriate envelopes, they all fall on the floor. The secretary picks up all three letters and envelopes and randomly (without looking) inserts a letter into an envelope. The secretary reasons that the probability that each letter will be inserted in its correct envelope is $\frac{1}{3}$, since there are three envelopes available. Do you agree?

8. So convinced that a particular event will *never* occur, a student concludes that the probability of the event occurring is -1. Do you agree?

9. A family is known to have two children. A student claims that the probability that both children are boys is $\frac{1}{3}$, since there are three possible outcomes: two boys, one boy and one girl, or two girls. Do you agree?

STUDY GUIDE

The following is a chapter outline in capsule form. You should now be able to demonstrate your knowledge of the ideas mentioned by giving definitions, or specific examples. Page references are given in parentheses.

I Counting Principles

The fundamental principle of counting states that if one thing can be done in m ways, and if, after this is done, something else can be done in n ways, then there are $m \cdot n$ possible ways of doing both things (in the stated order). (p. 415)

The branches of a **tree diagram** enable us to determine the number of possible outcomes of an experiment. (p. 418)

A **permutation** is any arrangement of objects in a certain order. The symbol $_nP_r$ means the number of permutations of n things taken r at a time. (p. 421)

n factorial, represented by the symbol $n!$, represents the product of all the natural numbers less than or equal to n, that is,

$$n! = n \cdot (n-1) \cdot (n-2) \cdots 1$$

Also, $0! = 1$. (p. 422)

A **combination** is any selection of things in which the order is not important. The symbol $_nC_r$ or $\binom{n}{r}$ means the number of combinations of n things taken r at a time. (p. 425)

Pascal's triangle enables us to compute the value of $_nC_r$, that is, the number of possible combinations. (p. 427)

II Probability

The set of all possible outcomes of an experiment is called the **sample space**. (p. 433)

An **event** is a subset of the sample space. (p. 433)

Outcomes are **equally likely** if each outcome is as likely to occur as any other. (p. 433)

If an event can occur in any one of n equally likely ways, and if f of these are considered as favorable outcomes, then the **probability** of getting a **favorable outcome** is

$$\frac{\text{number of favorable outcomes}}{\text{total number of outcomes}} = \frac{f}{n} \qquad \text{(p. 433)}$$

Something that can never happen is called the **null event**. Its probability is 0. (p. 437)

Something that is certain to occur is called the **definite event**. Its probability is 1. (p. 437)

The probability of any event must be between 0 and 1 and possibly including 0 or 1. (p. 438)

Probability represents the percentage of the time that an event will happen in the long run. This is called the **relative frequency** of the event. (p. 438)

A **table of random digits** lists numbers that have been generated randomly where each digit has an equally likely chance of being selected. (p. 441)

Two events, A and B, are said to be **mutually exclusive** if both A and B cannot occur at the same time. In terms of sets this means $A \cap B = \emptyset$. (p. 446)

III Conditional Probability and Independent Events

If A and B are events in a sample space, and if B is not the null event, then the **conditional probability** of A, given B, denoted by $p(A \mid B)$, is given by

$$p(A \mid B) = \frac{p(A \text{ and } B)}{p(B)} \qquad \text{(p. 454)}$$

The **multiplication rule for probability** states that for any events A and B we have $p(A \text{ and } B) = p(A \mid B) \cdot p(B)$. (p. 455)

Two events A and B are **independent** if it turns out that whether or not one event happens does not affect whether or not another will happen. For independent events, $p(A \mid B) = p(A)$. (p. 456)

If $p(A \mid B) \neq p(A)$, then events A and B are **dependent**. (p. 456)

IV Odds, Expectation, and Genetics

The **odds in favor** of an event occurring are p to q where p is "the number of favorable outcomes" and q is "the number of unfavorable outcomes." (p. 459)

The **odds against** an event occurring are q to p where q and p are defined as in the previous sentence. (p. 460)

If an event has several possible outcomes with probabilities $p_1, p_2, p_3 \ldots$ and so on, and if on the first event the payoff is m_1, on the second event the payoff is m_2, on the third event the payoff is m_3, etc., then the **mathematical expectation** of the event is

$$m_1 p_1 + m_2 p_2 + m_3 p_3 + \cdots \qquad \text{(p. 460)}$$

Genetics is the science concerned with which traits can be inherited. (p. 463)

When a **gene** is **dominant**, then the trait that it represents will always appear. (p. 464)

If a **trait** is **recessive**, then it must be matched with the same type of gene for that trait to appear. (p. 464)

KEY TERMS

The following list presents the key terms introduced in this chapter.

8.1 **fundamental principle of counting**
tree diagram

8.2 **permutation**
$_nP_r$ and $_nP_n$
factorial notation

combination

$_nC_r$ or $\binom{n}{r}$

Pascal's triangle

8.3   favorable outcome
sample space
event
probability
null event
definite event
relative frequency
statistical probability
axiomatic probability
random number
table of random digits

8.4   addition rule I

mutually exclusive events
addition rule II
nonmutually exclusive
events

8.5   conditional probability
conditional probability
formula
independent events

8.6   odds
odds in favor
odds against
mathematical expectation
genetics
genes (recessive and
dominant)

FORMULAS TO REMEMBER

The following list summarizes all the formulas given in this chapter

1. Probability of an event $= \dfrac{\text{number of favorable outcomes}}{\text{number of possible outcomes}}$

2. The number of permutations of n things taken r at a time is

$$_nP_r = \frac{n!}{(n-r)!}$$

3. The number of permutations of n things when p are alike, q are alike, r are alike, etc., is

$$\frac{n!}{p!\,q!\,r!} \qquad (\text{where } p + q + r + \ldots = n)$$

4. The number of combinations of n things taken r at a time is

$$\binom{n}{r} = {_nC_r} = \frac{n!}{r!\,(n-r)!}$$

5. $p(A \text{ or } B) = p(A) + p(B)$ if A and B are mutually exclusive.

6. $p(A \text{ or } B) = p(A) + p(B) - p(A \text{ and } B)$ for any events.

7. $p(A \text{ or } B \text{ or } C) = p(A) + p(B) + p(C) - p(A \text{ and } B) - p(A \text{ and } C)$
$\qquad - p(B \text{ and } C) + p(A \text{ and } B \text{ and } C)$

8. $p(A \mid B) = \dfrac{p(A \text{ and } B)}{p(B)}$

9. $p(A \text{ and } B) = p(A \mid B) \cdot p(B)$

10. $p(A \text{ and } B) = p(A) \cdot p(B)$ for independent events

11. The mathematical expectation of an event is

$$m_1p_1 + m_2p_2 + m_3p_3 + \ldots$$

12. Odds in favor of an event are p to q where p = the number of favorable outcomes and q = the number of unfavorable outcomes.

13. Odds against an event are q to p where p and q are defined as in preceding Formula 12.

CHAPTER REVIEW EXERCISES

1. Which of the following *cannot* be the probability of some event?

a) 0.003   **b)** $\dfrac{7}{9}$ **c)** $\dfrac{99}{100}$ **d)** -0.001 **e)** 0.27

2. One hundred people are being held by rioting prisoners as hostages. It is decided that 10 of these hostages will be selected to negotiate with authorities. In how many different ways can the negotiators be selected?

a) $\dfrac{100!}{90!}$ **b)** $_{100}P_{10}$ **c)** $\dfrac{100!}{10!}$ **d)** $\dfrac{100!}{90!10!}$ **e)** none of these

3. Two people who do not know each other, Cory and Steve, board a train at the same station. The train will make 5 stops before going out of service. What is the probability that they both get off at the same stop?

a) $\dfrac{1}{5}$ **b)** $\dfrac{1}{2}$ **c)** $\dfrac{2}{5}$ **d)** $\dfrac{1}{25}$ **e)** none of these

4. Given the numbers 5, 6, 7, 8, and 9. How many 3-digit numbers larger than 700 can be formed from these digits if repetition is *not* allowed?

a) 18   **b)** 36   **c)** 125   **d)** 60   **e)** none of these

5. A tax agent finds that 1 out of every 10 income tax filers in a certain city has claimed more than 7 dependents. If an income tax return is randomly selected from this group, what are the odds against the filer claiming more than 7 dependents?

a) 1 to 10   **b)** 1 to 9   **c)** 10 to 1   **d)** 9 to 1   **e)** none of these

6. There are 7 smokers and 8 nonsmokers at a city council meeting. A committee of 3 smokers and 3 nonsmokers is to be chosen from this group to study new ordinances governing smoking in restaurants. In how many different ways can they be chosen?

7. In how many different ways can the letters of the word "CALCULUS" be arranged?

a) 8!   **b)** $\dfrac{8!}{2!}$ **c)** $\dfrac{8!}{2!\,2!}$ **d)** $\dfrac{8!}{2!\,2!\,2!}$ **e)** none of these

For questions 8–10, use the following information. A taste test was given to 900 people at a shopping mall to determine which brand of vanilla ice cream they preferred. The results were:

	Brand A	Brand B	Brand C	Brand D
Male	128	131	118	101
Female	123	116	109	74

8. What is the probability that a person in the survey preferred brand A?

9. What is the probability that a person preferred brand A given that the person is a female?

10. What is the probability that the person is a female given that the person preferred brand A?

11. Twenty-one percent of all students at Whipple University are dormitory students and have a credit card. Twenty-six percent of the students are dormitory students. If a student who is a dormitory student is selected at random, what is the probability that the student has a credit card?

12. A biologist is experimenting with plants that have a particular trait A or a. If a plant that has Aa genes is crossbred with another plant that has Aa genes, find the probability that the offspring will be

a) AA **b)** aa **c)** Aa

13. *Fertilizer.* The Balken Chemical Company manufactures nine different kinds of fertilizer, each containing different concentrations of nitrogen as follows:

$$4–6–3$$
$$4–6–2$$
$$4–4–1$$
$$4–4–2$$
$$4–2–3$$
$$4–8–5$$
$$12–6–1$$
$$9–3–2$$

Earl and Helen Weaver are farmers who use the fertilizers produced by this company. They discover a bag of fertilizer in their barn. Unfortunately, only the first digit that indicates the nitrogen content is legible. If the first digit is a 4, find the probability that the bag contains a 4–8–5 mixture.

14. Mathew Priofsky is in a gambling casino and observes a card dealer selecting 3 cards (without replacement) from a deck of 52 cards. In how many different ways can the 3 cards be selected?

15. Each calculator manufactured by the Texas Calculator Co. is inscribed with a six-digit serial number preceded *and* followed by a letter. Using this serial number scheme, how many different codes are possible?

16. A chemist has mixed five different solutions together and created a new plastic compound. Unfortunately, she does not remember the order in which the chemicals were introduced into the solutions. She decides to repeat the experiment. How many possibilities are there?

17. Charlie drives up to a parking meter and notices a piece of paper on the ground that says "Meter out of order—No parking." Is this an old sign? Should he deposit money in the meter and park there? The probability that the meter is out of order is $\frac{4}{9}$. The probability that the meter is out of order *and* that he will get a ticket for parking there is $\frac{2}{13}$. If the meter is actually out of order, what is the probability that he will get a ticket?

18. To reverse its past discriminatory practices, the Hasting Corp. plans to hire 5 Asians and 6 Hispanics. If 12 Asians and 18 Hispanics qualify for the job, find the number of ways in which the vacancies can be filled.

19. The Geary Supermarket chain employs 16 part-time and 10 full-time clerks at one of its stores. As an economy move, the company plans to lay off 2 full-time and 2 part-time workers. In how many different ways can this be done?

20. Each year, readers of a certain magazine are asked to rank the top three best-dressed men from among a list of 12 candidates. In how many different ways can this be done?

21. There are 6 vacant conference rooms in an office building. The Bordeaux Corp. is planning 6 meetings for which it will need the 6 conference rooms. In how many different ways can these meetings be assigned to the conference rooms?

22. The Argavon Corp. believes that it is in the company's best interest to maintain the physical fitness of its 40 employees. It recently purchased 6 exercise machines to be used by the employees during their lunch break or after work. In how many different ways can 6 of the 40 employees be assigned to the different machines?

23. Matthew Valentine is the keynote speaker at tomorrow's board of directors' meeting. He can select any one of 5 pairs of trousers, 8 shirts, 8 ties, and 6 pairs of shoes to wear for the meeting. How many different outfits are possible?

24. A farmer has 5 different kinds of vegetables, 6 different kinds of fruits, and 3 different dairy products. In how many different ways can the farmer select one item from each of these categories?

25. In how many different ways can a circus operator arrange 10 different performances, that is, in how many different ways may the 10 performances be ordered?

26. A contestant on a network variety show must select one of three doors behind which there are different items, as shown below:

Door	Value of item(s)
1	$3 magazine
2	$7000 car
3	$2700 home entertainment center

If the contestant is likely to select any door with equal probability, find the contestant's expected amount of money to be won.

27. A visitor traveling in Europe stops at an airport in Italy. The visitor stops a guard and asks for directions. The probability that the guard speaks French

is 0.22, and the probability that the guard speaks German is 0.33. What is the probability that the guard speaks either language if the probability that the guard speaks both is 0.17?

28. A Japanese camera manufacturer ships 125 cameras to an American store. Owing to a packer's error, 20 of these cameras were packed with operating instructions in Japanese only. A customer (who does not read or understand Japanese) buys one of these cameras. What are the odds against getting one of the cameras with operating instructions in Japanese only?

29. Caroline has been having trouble with her car. The probability that she turns on the air conditioning system and that the car overheats is 0.32. Furthermore, the probability that she turns on the air conditioning system is 0.68. If Caroline is observed driving the car with the air conditioning system on, what is the probability that the car will overheat?

30. Twenty-eight female and 25 male college graduates have applied for a computer training program. For various reasons, the program can accept only 22 female and 16 male applicants. In how many different ways can these applicants be selected?

SUGGESTED FURTHER READING

Adler, I., *Probability and Statistics for Everyman.* New York: New America Library, 1966.

Bergamini, D., and eds. *Life Mathematics* (Life-Science Library). New York Time-Life Books, 1970. Pages 126 to 147 discuss figuring the odds in an uncertain world.

Burns, M., "Put Some Probability in Your Classroom," in *The Arithmetic Teacher* **30** (March 1983), 21–22.

Chaote, S., "Activities in Applying Probability Ideas," in *The Arithmetic Teacher* **26** (February 1979), 40–42.

Epstein, R.A., *Theory of Gambling and Statistical Logic.* New York: Academic Press, 1967. Contains an interesting discussion on the fairness of coins.

Heiny, R., "Gambling, Casinos and Game Simulation," in *The Mathematics Teacher* **74** (February 1981), 139–143.

Travers, K., and K. Gray, "The Monte Carlo Method: A Fresh Approach to Teaching Probabilistic Concepts," in *The Mathematics Teacher* **74** (May 1981), 327–334.

Woodward, E., "An Interesting Probability Problem," in *The Mathematics Teacher* **75** (December 1982), 765–768.

CHAPTER 9

Statistics

NCTM GUIDELINES

In its March 1989 *Curriculum and Evaluation Standards For School Mathematics* (p. 187), The National Council of Teachers of Mathematics recommends that the mathematics curriculum should include the study of data analysis and statistics so that all students can

☐ construct and draw inferences from charts, tables, and graphs that summarize data from real-world situations,

☐ use curve fitting to predict from the data

☐ understand and apply measures of central tendency, variability, and correlation,

☐ understand sampling and recognize its role in statistical claims

☐ transform data to aid interpretation and prediction.

Collecting, representing, and processing data are activities of major importance to contemporary society. In the natural and social sciences, data are also summarized, analyzed, and transformed. These activities involve simulations and/or sampling, fitting curves, testing hypotheses, and drawing inferences. To enhance their social awareness and career opportunities, students should learn to apply these techniques in solving problems and in evaluating the myriad statistical claims they encounter in their daily lives. It is for these reasons that in this chapter we will study some of the basic ideas of both descriptive and inferential statistics.

Introduction

statistics

data

Most of us have heard of, and have some idea of what is meant by, the word **statistics.** We usually think of statistics as having something to do with tables or charts of numbers. Mathematicians, however, usually use this word in a more general sense. To the mathematician the subject of statistics is concerned with how to collect numerical facts, called **data,** how to organize and analyze them, and finally how to interpret the data.

The subject of statistics has been applied to many different areas, including medicine, insurance, electronics, advertising, television audiences, population growth, and student enrollment in schools. Some knowledge of statistics is fast becoming an important tool for everyone. The following examples of the use of statistics should be quite familiar.

1. Statistics show that male drivers under the age of 25 have more accidents than other drivers. On the basis of this information, insurance companies charge higher premiums for these drivers.

2. On election-day television newscasts, computers are used to "project" the winners on the basis of only very early returns. Samples from representative districts are collected, and the predictions are based on these statistics.

3. The latest statistics released by the FBI indicate that serious crime in a large northeastern city increased by 38% during the year 1988.

4. Statistics indicate that because of the extremely high tax rate in New York City, many citizens and businesses are moving out of the city into neighboring states. Consequently, the statistics show that an increase in taxes will result in an exodus of people and businesses from the city.

5. When the Social Security system was first put into effect, the rate of contribution was determined by statistics that predicted how long a person would live. Statistics show that people have been living longer in recent years. As a result, the rate of contribution has been steadily increasing.

6. The Nielsen television ratings show that one network has 20% more viewers than another between the hours of 7:00 P.M. and 8:00 P.M. on Monday night.

What mathematical knowledge is needed to understand and use statistics? The collection and organization of the data requires little or no mathematical background. On the other hand, the interpretation of the data is another story. The statistician should have some mathematical knowledge if he or she is to interpret the data in a meaningful way.

If the data are not interpreted properly, very wrong and sometimes ridiculous conclusions can be drawn from them. As an example of how data can be misinterpreted, consider the following statistics. During 1988 in a southern state there were 1246 accidents involving drunken pedestrians. There were 723 accidents involving drunken drivers. You could conclude that it is more dangerous to be a drunken pedestrian than a drunken driver. Do you agree that this is a reasonable way of interpreting the data; that is, do you agree with the conclusion?

In this chapter we will discuss how statistical data can be organized and tabulated so that meaningful results can be drawn from them.

HISTORICAL NOTE

The study of statistics was really begun by an Englishman, John Graunt (1620–1674). Graunt studied death records in various cities and noticed that the percentages of deaths from different causes were about the same and did not change much from year to year. Graunt was also the first to discover (using statistics) that there were more boys born than girls. Because, at the time, men were more subject to death from occupational accidents and diseases and from war, it turned out that at the age suitable for marriage the number of men and women was about equal. Graunt believed that this was a natural way of guaranteeing monogamy.

In 1662, Graunt published *Natural and Political Observations . . . upon the Bills of Mortality*, which has been said to have founded the science of statistics.

The work begun by Graunt was continued by others, who wanted to make the social sciences more "quantitative," that is, based more on mathematics. In the late seventeenth century, life insurance companies were formed, and they, of course, were also interested in the information to be obtained from statistics, such as death rates and life expectancy. The Industrial Revolution increased interest in statistics even further. Government agencies and social reformers wanted statistics on births and deaths, national and individual incomes, unemployment, occurrence of disease, etc. By the nineteenth century, statistics was also accepted as an important tool in the physical sciences.

9.1

SAMPLING; RANDOM NUMBERS

sample

Suppose a producer is interested in knowing what percentage of the television audience enjoys watching a new show. He or she obviously will not (or cannot) ask every individual who watches television for a reaction to the new show. What he or she will do is take a **sample**. A relatively small group of TV viewers will be selected and asked for their reactions. From their comments, a generalization will be made for *all* television viewers.

Before indicating some of the difficulties involved in taking a sample, we first state formally what we mean by a sample.

population

> **Definition 9.1** A **sample** is a small group of individuals (or objects) selected to stand for a larger group, usually called the **population**.

In taking a sample, a number of problems can arise. The first problem is that of sample size. If a sample is too small, then the individuals used may not be truly typical (or representative) of the population. A sample that is too large is usually very costly. A good sample should be large enough to be typical of the population it represents, but not so large that its cost is ridiculously expensive. How large a sample to select varies from situation to situation. Only by applying statistical procedures can one be reasonably confident of the correct sample size.

random sample

The most important requirement in taking a sample is that it be a **random** one. This means that each individual in the population should have an equally likely chance (or probability) of being selected. Unless the sample is a random one, it may not give a true picture of the population it represents.

In 1948 the pollsters predicted that Harry Truman would lose the presidential election. This prediction was based on a sample of the population. It turned out that the pollsters were wrong. This was because their sample was not random and was not truly representative of the population.

Similarly, on April 6, 1976, both ABC and NBC television networks projected that Morris Udall would win the Democratic primary in Wisconsin. Their projections were based on samples from selected precincts and did not take certain districts into consideration. When all the rural votes were counted, Jimmy Carter came out on top. Many newspapers were so confident of their predictions that they printed, erroneously, the morning editions of their newspapers with the headline "CARTER UPSET BY UDALL"

Sometimes in a statistics class a student will suggest that one could get a random sample by opening a telephone book and selecting every hundredth name appearing. But this technique does not result in a random sample because not every name has an equal chance of being selected. (Why not?) Statisticians have devised techniques for conducting a random sample. Although the *table of random digits* technique discussed in the last chapter is the simplest way of obtaining a random sample, there are other techniques that can be used. A discussion of these is beyond the scope of this text.

In this chapter we will assume that all data have been collected from random samples.

9.2

MEASURES OF CENTRAL TENDENCY; PERCENTILES

In this section we shall be concerned with several methods of interpreting data. To understand what we mean by this, consider a used car dealer, who, because of economic conditions, has decided to fire one of two salesmen, Crazy Eddie or Mad Mike. Obviously, the dealer wants to keep the better salesman. To help him decide which employee to fire, he has made a chart as shown below, indicating the number of cars sold by each man over the last seven weeks.

	Crazy Eddie	Mad Mike
Week 1	8	10
Week 2	6	12
Week 3	12	12
Week 4	8	11
Week 5	6	12
Week 6	38	12
Week 7	6	8
Total	84	77

At first glance, one would claim that Crazy Eddie is a better salesman, since he sold a total of 84 cars, whereas Mad Mike sold only 77 cars. However, let us analyze the situation a bit more carefully. Notice that Mad Mike sold more cars than, or the same number of cars as, Crazy Eddie during every week but the sixth.

Let us compute the average number of cars sold by both salesmen by dividing each total by the number of weeks (which is 7). We get

$$\text{Crazy Eddie's average: } \frac{84}{7} = 12$$

$$\text{Mad Mike's average: } \frac{77}{7} = 11$$

Thus Crazy Eddie sold 12 cars on the average, whereas Mad Mike sold only 11 on the average. It would again appear that Crazy Eddie is a better salesman.

Another look at the data, however, shows that Mad Mike sold 12 cars most often (on 4 weeks). Crazy Eddie sold 12 cars only once. Crazy Eddie sold 6 cars most often. One might now say that Mad Mike is a better salesman in terms of consistent performance.

Suppose we were to arrange the number of cars sold by each (per week) in order from smallest to largest. We get the following table.

Crazy Eddie	Mad Mike
6	8
6	10
6	11
⑧	⑫
8	12
12	12
38	12

Note that two numbers have been circled. These are the numbers that are in the middle. For Mad Mike this number is 12, and for Crazy Eddie this number is 8. This example leads us to the following definitions.

mean
average

> **Definition 9.2**   The **mean** or **average** of a set of numbers is found by adding them together and dividing the total by the number of numbers added.

mode

> **Definition 9.3**   The **mode** of a set of numbers is the number that occurs most often. If every number occurs only once, then we say that there is no mode. A set of numbers may have more than one mode.

median

> **Definition 9.4**   If a set of numbers is arranged in order (from smallest to largest), then the number that is in the middle is called the **median**. This is only when there is an odd number of numbers. If there is an even number of them, then the **median** is the average of the middle two numbers (when arranged in order).

Let us now apply these definitions to our two salesmen. We have the following:

	Crazy Eddie	Mad Mike
Mean	12	11
Median	8	12
Mode	6	12

Who is a better salesman, Crazy Eddie or Mad Mike? One would probably say Mad Mike, even though his mean (or average) is less than Crazy

Eddie's. Eddie's average is 12 only because of the sixth-week sales, when he sold 38 cars. Mike, on the other hand, consistently sold 11 or 12 cars. In this case the mean does not tell us as much about the salesmen as does the median or the mode.

The above ideas will be illustrated further by several examples.

EXAMPLE 1

A professor recently gave a test to her statistics class of eleven students. The following results (grades) were obtained: 78, 53, 100, 27, 94, 88, 98, 93, 98, 91, and 89. Find the mean, median, and mode for this class.

SOLUTION

We first arrange the grades in order from lowest to highest. We get 27, 53, 78, 88, 89, 91, 93, 94, 98, 98, and 100.

The grade that occurred most often is 98. Thus the mode is 98.

The grade that is in the middle (now that we have arranged them in order) is 91, so the median is 91.

To find the mean, we first add all the numbers. The sum is 909. We then divide 909 by the total number of grades (which is 11), getting $909/11 = 82.64$ (rounded off to two decimal places). The mean is then 82.64.

Which is a better indication of class performance in this particular example, the mean, median, or mode?

EXAMPLE 2

The mathematics department at a state university consists of eight members whose salaries are given in the following chart.

Rank	Salary
Dave, chairman	$41,000
Arthur, professor	39,000
Roger, assoc. professor	38,500
Betsy, assoc. professor	37,000
Nancy, assist. professor	36,000
Alice, assist. professor	35,810
Bob, instructor	33,120
Jim, lecturer	32,810

Find the mean, median, and modal salary for the members of the mathematics department at this particular university.

SOLUTION

We notice that the salaries are already arranged in order, from highest to lowest. We can then read up the list.

To find the median, we look for the number that is in the middle. In this case there is an even number of salaries, so that no number is in the middle. The median is somewhere between $36,000 and $37,000. Definition 9.4 tells us that the median is the average of these two numbers, or that the median is

$$\frac{36{,}000 + 37{,}000}{2} = \frac{73{,}000}{2} = \$36{,}500$$

What about the mode? Notice that no salary occurred more than once. Definition 9.3 tells us that there is no mode.

To find the mean, we first add all the salaries. The total is $293,240. We now divide the total by 8, getting

$$\frac{293{,}240}{8} = \$36{,}655$$

For the salaries in the mathematics department of this university we have

Mean $36,655   Median $36,500   Mode   none

Which is a better indication of the teachers' salary, the mean or the median?   ▪

measures of central tendency

Comment   The mean, median, and mode are called **measures of central tendency.** The reason for this name should be obvious. Each of these (mean, median, or mode) measures some central or general trend of the data. Depending on the situation, one will usually prove to be more meaningful than the others.

Comment   The word "average" is often used in newspaper or magazine articles. Note the use of the word *average* in the article at the top of the following page. Has the "average" SAT score increased or decreased over the years?

summation notation

We can rewrite Definition 9.2 by using **summation notation**. In this notation the Greek letter Σ, read as sigma, stands for the operation of adding a sequence of numbers. Thus suppose that we have a group of numbers x_1, x_2, x_3, ..., x_n, where n is the total number in the group. Then we have Formula 9.1

$$\text{Formula 9.1} \quad \mu = \frac{\Sigma x}{n} = \frac{x_1 + x_2 + x_3 + \cdots + x_n}{n}$$

grouped data

Often we are given **grouped data,** where the data are grouped according to different categories or classifications. The following example illustrates

SAT Score Averages 1963–1983

Score averages from 1963 to 1966 represent all SAT candidates.

From 1967 to 1983 the figures represent the average scores of college-bound seniors only, which are released each year by the College Board in its national report on College-Bound Seniors.

	Verbal	Mathematics			Verbal	Mathematics
1963	478	502		1974	444	480
1964	475	498		1975	434	472
1965	473	496		1976	431	472
1966	471	496		1977	429	470
1967	466	492		1978	429	468
1968	466	492		1979	427	467
1969	463	493		1980	424	466
1970	460	488		1981	424	466
1971	455	488		1982	426	467
1972	453	484		1983	427	468
1973	445	481				

how we calculate the various measures of central tendency for such a situation.

EXAMPLE 3

There are 19 employees in the sportswear department of Bert's Department store. Their salaries are determined by their title as shown in the table. What are the mean, median, and modal annual salaries of these employees?

Title	Number of people with this title	Annual salary
Chief buyer	2	$35,000
Assistant buyer	7	28,600
Full-time sales person	4	23,500
Part-time sales person	2	19,400
Stock clerk	3	16,100
Maintenance	1	10,305

SOLUTION

To find the mean, we must find the sum of the salaries of all 19 employees. Since the data have been grouped according to job titles, we must multiply the number of employees in the various job titles by their respective annual salaries. We get

Number of employees	Annual Salary	Total payment
2	$35,000	$70,000
7	28,600	200,200
4	23,500	94,000
2	19,400	38,800
3	16,100	48,300
1	10,305	10,305
		$461,605

Thus, the mean annual salary is

$$\mu = \frac{\Sigma x}{n} = \frac{\$461,605}{19} = \$24,295$$

The modal annual salary is $28,600, and the median annual salary is $23,500. Can you see why?

Comment   In Example 3 the mean annual salary is $24,295 even though nobody actually earns that amount.

Comment   Instead of grouping the numbers, children are often taught to use random samples to find sample means. This can be seen from the accompanying student page 371 from *Addison-Wesley Mathematics*, 1987, Grade 8, shown on page 487.

Percentiles

In the preceding paragraphs, we discussed different ways of analyzing data. Quite often, one is interested in knowing the position of a score in a list of numbers. Thus if Mary Ruth got a score of 83 on a civil service exam that she has just taken, she undoubtedly would be interested in knowing how this score compares with the scores of others who have taken the exam. In such a situation she would probably be more interested in her **percentile rank** than in the mean, median, or mode.

Let us analyze the results of the civil service exam that Mary Ruth took. The exam was given to 200 people, including Mary Ruth. She finds that 70% of the people who took the exam got below 83, 10% of the people got 83, and the remaining 20% scored above 83. Since 70% of the people scored below 83 and 20% scored above 83, her percentile rank should be between 70 and 80. (Why?) We use 75, which is halfway between 70 and 80. What we have done is find the percentage of scores that are below her score and add one-half of the percentage of scores that are the same as her score. The result is her percentile rank. In our case, Mary Ruth's percentile rank is 75. This means that *approximately 25%* of the people who took the exam scored higher than she did and 75% of the

Finding a Sample Mean

What is the mean number of letters per word used in the article of 100 words at the right?

Instead of counting the letters in each word, you can take a 10-word **random sample** and compute the mean number of letters per word in the sample.

The words in the sample are chosen by finding the number of the word that corresponds to the **random numbers** in the first row of the table.

The social and economic problems of large cities are undeniable, and as yet they are largely unsolved. Some economists feel that the basic problem of the cities is a problem of scale. A large city offers considerable economies of scale in the provision of goods and services for its residents. Bus rides, kilowatt hours of electricity, and chemically purified drinking water can all be purchased at lower cost in big cities because of the large demand for these goods and services and the accompanying economies of scale in mass production. But in the last several decades, prices for such services . . .

Random Numbers

Random number	Word	Number of letters
23	basic	5
77	for	3
30	problem	7
9	are	3
11	and	3
78	these	5
40	scale	5
29	a	1
96	decades	7
85	economies	9
	Total	48

Computer-Generated Random Numbers 1 to 100

23	77	30	9	11	78	40	29	96	85
56	75	75	51	72	45	76	87	61	74
18	57	49	8	76	20	41	32	66	80
4	59	11	17	99	60	26	31	10	81
38	94	22	35	27	62	34	77	18	57
70	21	81	23	93	62	27	4	69	45
43	74	93	29	67	99	21	62	42	15
92	47	30	4	60	97	81	35	5	69
40	38	68	62	33	71	32	50	70	10
66	28	35	2	61	3	74	72	66	81

Mean number of letters per word $= \dfrac{48}{10} = 4.8$

1. Use the second row of numbers in the Random Number table to make a 10-word sample. What is the mean of this sample?

2. What is your estimate of the actual mean number of letters per word in the complete article?

people scored lower than she did. (Why is it only approximate?) Most civil service tests are graded by using such a procedure.

This leads us to the following.

percentile rank

Definition 9.5 The **percentile rank** of a score is found by adding the percentage of scores below it to one-half of the percentage of scores equal to it.

Although this definition enables us to find the percentile rank of an individual score, in practice we can use a convenient formula. Let X be a given score, let B represent the *number* of scores below the given score X, and let E represent the *number* of scores equal to the given score X. If the total number of scores is n, then the percentile rank of the given score can be found by the following formula.

$$\text{Formula 9.2} \quad \text{Percentile rank of } X = \frac{B + \frac{1}{2}E}{n} \cdot 100$$

Let us illustrate the use of Formula 9.2 with an example.

EXAMPLE 4

There are 23 students in a statistics class. On the midterm exam the grades of the students were 79, 63, 94, 100, 83, 92, 78, 62, 53, 84, 76, 22, 17, 52, 57, 66, 83, 72, 81, 70, 69, 46 and 97. Douglas got an 83 on the exam. Find his percentile rank.

SOLUTION

Since 23 people took the exam, $n = 23$. Analyzing the individual scores, we find that 16 scores are below 83 and exactly 2 scores (including Douglas's) are equal to 83. Thus $B = 16$ and $E = 2$. We now apply Formula 9.2 to find Douglas's percentile rank. We have

$$\text{Douglas's percentile rank} = \frac{B + \frac{1}{2}E}{n} \cdot 100 = \frac{16 + \frac{1}{2}(2)}{23} \cdot 100$$

$$= \frac{16 + 1}{23} \cdot 100 = \frac{17}{23} \cdot 100$$

$$= 73.91$$

Therefore Douglas's percentile rank is 73.91. This means that Douglas did better than approximately 73.91% of the students and that only about 26.09% of the students did better than Douglas.

Comment   In the example above, Douglas's percentile rank was 73.91. We sometimes say that Douglas was in the 73.91st percentile.

Statisticians have special names for certain percentiles. The 25th percentile is called the *lower or first quartile*. The 50th percentile is called the *median or middle quartile*. The 75th percentile is called the *upper or third quartile*.

lower or first quartile

median or middle quartile

upper or third quartile

We mentioned earlier that the median divides the data into two equal parts. Similarly, the **quartiles** denoted by $Q_1, Q_2,$ *and* Q_3 divide the ranked data into four equal parts. Roughly speaking, the lowest quartile, Q_1, divides the ranked scores into a bottom 25% and a top 75%. Also the middle quartile, Q_2, which is the median, separates the bottom 50% from the top 50% of the ranked scores. The upper quartile, Q_3, separates the bottom 75% of the ranked scores from the top 25%. It should be noted that if Q_1 is the lower quartile, then approximately 25% of the scores will be less than or equal to Q_1 and approximately 75% of the scores will be greater than or equal to Q_1. Corresponding comments can be made for Q_2 and Q_3.

deciles

percentiles

There are nine **deciles,** denoted as $D_1, D_2, D_3, \ldots D_9$. They separate the data into 10 groups with approximately 10% of the scores falling within each group. Similarly, the 99 **percentiles** separate the data into 100 groups, with each group containing approximately 1% of the scores. Although we do not give any formulas for finding the cutoff numbers needed to determine percentiles, quartiles, and deciles, they are used extensively in reporting the results of tests in education.

Comment   If a student takes a special aptitude exam and is ranked in the 95th percentile, then this does not mean that he or she received a grade of 95% on the exam. It means that this student scored higher than approximately 95% of the other people who took the exam and that approximately 5% of those other people who took the exam scored higher than this student.

EXERCISES FOR SECTION 9.2

1. *Funeral Costs*. Consider the accompanying newspaper article. During the week of November 4-8 the Jefferson Funeral Chapels performed six funerals. The charges for these funerals were $1480, $1700, $1370, $1510, $1625, and $1430. Find the mean, median, and modal prices for the charge of a funeral performed by the Jefferson Funeral Chapels.

State to Investigate Funeral Charges

MARLINGTON—Commissioner White of the State Investigatory Commission announced yesterday that he would launch an immediate investigation into the funeral costs charged by the Jefferson Funeral Chapels, Inc. Commissioner White revealed that his agency had received numerous complaints about overcharges and unexplained charges that bereaved families have been forced to pay. Most of the complaints centered around the Jefferson funeral Chapels, Inc.

MARLINGTON NEWS, November 5, 1988

2. An insurance company executive is analyzing the sales records of 12 brokers who work for the company. The executive has the following information for one business day.

Salesperson	Number of new policies sold
Philip	4
Cheryl	2
Ellen	8
Frank	3
Martin	4
Peter	16
Evens	6
Kim	1
Anthony	7
Evelyn	2
Patrick	3
Daniel	4

Find the mean, median, and mode for the number of new policies sold.

3. The Porterville Savings Bank employs 75 people at its downtown branch office. The salary of these employees is dependent upon the title of the worker as shown in the accompanying chart.

Category	Number of workers in this category	Annual salary
Vice-President	4	$36,000 144
Teller (full-time)	17	16,000 272
Teller (part-time)	23	7,000 161
Supervisor	6	25,000 150
Secretarial	9	10,000 90
Security guard	4	14,000 56
Other	12 75	9,000 108

981,000

Find the mean, median, and modal salaries.

4. A taxi driver claims that the average tip that she receives is $1.25. To which average is she probably referring: the mean, median, or mode?

5. *Cost Averaging.* For the past seven weeks, Jackie Zweigh has purchased shares of ABC stock at the prevailing price each Monday morning as shown below:

Number of shares purchased	Price per share
120	$33
150	29
80	31
90	30
110	28
60	35
170	25

Jackie wishes to cost average and has directed her broker to purchase 100 shares of the stock the following Monday. At what price should these be purchased so that the price for all the shares purchased will be $29 a share?

6. There are 19 mechanics on the payroll of Mel's Automatic Transmission Repair Shop. The mean weekly salary is $382, the median weekly salary is $326, and the modal weekly salary is $345. Find the total weekly payroll.

7. Refer back to Exercise 1. Officials of the Jefferson

Funeral Chapels have announced that as of January 1, the cost for each of the funerals mentioned will be increased by 10%. How are the mean, median, and mode affected by the proposed price changes?

8. The union representing 812 textile workers is negotiating a new labor contract with the company. The union claims that the *average* hourly rate of pay is $5.11, which is much lower than the pay of workers in competing companies. Management claims that the *average* hourly rate of pay is $8.69, which is much higher than the pay of workers in competing companies. A labor negotiator believes that both the union claim and the management claim are accurate. How can this be? Explain your answer.

9. Seven people were hospitalized at Brookhaven Hospital last year because of a particular disease. The length of stay in the hospital is shown below. You will notice that the average length of stay at the hospital for these patients is 25 days, which is longer than the length of stay of all but one person. What can you conclude?

Patient	Length of stay in hospital
John Bender	19 days
Grace Ahl	20 days
David Browne	4 days
Andrew Digiacomo	2 days
Pat Elsayed	13 days
George Grigoli	16 days
Chris Hardy	101 days

10. Owing to numerous boiler breakdowns, a new heating system was recently installed in Skytown Towers. Several tenants are still complaining that it is now too warm, whereas others are complaining that it is now too cold. In an attempt to satisfy everyone, management has decided to install an energy-saving thermostat and to poll each of the residents as to what temperature it should be set at. When this is done the following data are obtained.

Mean 71°   Median 70°   Mode 69°

At what temperature should the thermostat be set so as to satisfy as many residents as possible?

11. A certain set of numbers has mean 25. What happens to the mean if each number in the set is

a) increased by 3   b) decreased by 4

c) multiplied by 7   **d)** divided by 5

12. The weights (in pounds) of the 20 members of a soccer team are

Tim: 180	Stu: 220	Stan: 206
John: 169	Jose: 210	Maurice: 180
Joe: 198	George: 229	Cornell: 184
Bill: 176	Bob: 204	Catfish: 192
Hal: 199	Jack: 213	Sigmund: 208
Jasper: 210	Allen: 216	Roger: 186
Mike: 237	Al: 239	

Find the percentile rank of Maurice.

13. The following are the test results for an advanced calculus final:

72	77	84	71	67	61	67
53	81	55	87	68	60	78
45	68	79	92	100	68	77
72	97	80	77	90	53	53
82	71	47	58	99	49	
67	63	93	79	88	61	

What is the percentile rank of the student(s) who scored 79 on the exam?

14. In Maureen's psychology class there are 40 students. On a midterm exam, 24 students got lower grades than she did, and 10 students got higher grades. What is Maureen's percentile rank?

15. Refer back to Exercise 14. If the teacher decides to curve the exam by adding six points to everyone's grade, how is Maureen's percentile rank affected?

Brain-Teaser Problems

****16.** Consider the set of numbers 1, 6, 8, 4, 9, 13, 14, 11, 12, and 10. Find

a) Σx **b)** μ
c) $\Sigma (x - \mu)$ **d)** $\Sigma (x - \mu)^2$

****17.** For the numbers given in Exercise 16, compute

a) Σx^2 **b)** $(\Sigma x)^2$
c) Are the answers the same? Explain why or why not.

9.3

MEASURES OF VARIATION

It is very hard to find two things of any type that are identical. Two people of the same age and sex may differ a great deal in height, weight, etc. Every cook knows that the same recipe may not always result in the same quality of cake. Even things that are mass-produced are not really exactly the same. There is some variation or difference among them. In this section we will discuss some of the methods used to measure variation.

To get us started, let us consider the following. A state consumers' group is investigating the milk prices charged by two large supermarket chains in various parts of the city. Both chains claim that their average milk price is 50¢ a quart. Investigators find that the prices charged by these chains in five different neighborhoods of the city are as follows.

Chain A	Chain B
53¢	52¢
48	50
61	48
47	49
41	51

Note that the average (mean) price for a quart of milk at each chain is 50¢. Yet for chain A the price of a quart of milk varies from 41 to 61 cents. This gives a *range* of 61–41, or 20 cents. For chain B the prices vary from 48 to 52 cents. Their range is 52–48, or 4 cents.

This leads us to the following definition.

range

Definition 9.6   The **range** of a set of numbers is found by subtracting the smallest number from the largest.

Comment   No matter how many numbers are in the original data, only two of them (the smallest and the largest) are needed to compute the range.

Unfortunately, the range does not tell us anything about how the other numbers vary. For this reason we need another measure of variation called the **standard deviation.** This tells us how "spread out" the numbers are. Finding the standard deviation for each of the supermarket chains above is a relatively simple procedure. We first find the mean. In our case we already know that it is 50¢. We then subtract the mean from each price and square the result. We then find the average of these squares. Finally, we take the square root of this average. The result is called the standard deviation.

standard deviation

We will now calculate the standard deviation for each supermarket chain.

Supermarket chain A

Price (in cents)	Difference from mean	Square of difference
53	53 – 50 = 3	(3)(3) = + 9
48	48 – 50 = – 2	(– 2)(– 2) = + 4
61	61 – 50 = 11	(11)(11) = + 121
47	47 – 50 = – 3	(– 3)(– 3) = + 9
41	41 – 50 = – 9	(– 9)(– 9) = + 81
Total 250		Total 224
Mean = $\dfrac{250}{5}$ = 50		Average = $\dfrac{224}{5}$ = 44.8

Thus the standard deviation for supermarket chain A is $\sqrt{44.8}$ or approximately 6.69.[1] The standard deviation is a measure of how spread out the data are.

---

1. A knowledge of how to compute square roots is not assumed. These values can be obtained by using a calculator.

What about supermarket chain B? Let us compute its standard deviation.

Supermarket chain B

Price (in cents)	Difference from mean	Square of difference
52	52 – 50 = 2	(2)(2) = +4
50	50 – 50 = 0	(0)(0) = 0
48	48 – 50 = – 2	(– 2)(– 2) = +4
49	49 – 50 = – 1	(– 1)(– 1) = +1
51	51 – 50 = +1	(1)(1) = +1
Total $\overline{250}$		Total $\overline{10}$
Mean = $\dfrac{250}{5}$ = 50		Average = $\dfrac{10}{5}$ = 2

Therefore for supermarket chain B the standard deviation is $\sqrt{2}$, or approximately 1.41.

We can summarize the procedure to be used in finding the standard deviation by the following rule.

Rule 9.1 The **(population) standard deviation** of a set of numbers is the result obtained by finding (in order)

a) the mean (or average) of the numbers,
b) the difference between each number and the mean,
c) the squares of each of these differences,
d) the average of these squares,
e) the square root of the average of these squares.

We will illustrate this rule further with another example.

EXAMPLE 1

A large city in the south requires that its police officers be at least 5 ft 7 in. tall (67 in.) Seven police officers are selected and their heights recorded. What is the standard deviation if their heights are 69, 72, 74, 67, 68, 70, and 70 in.?

SOLUTION

We arrange their heights in order as shown in the table on the next page and then calculate the standard deviation. The standard deviation of their heights is thus $\sqrt{4.857}$, or approximately 2.2.

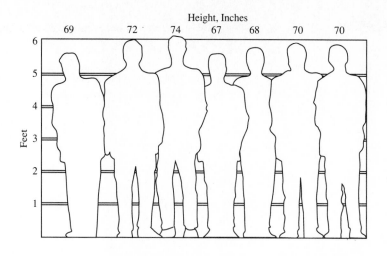

Height, Inches

| 69 | 72 | 74 | 67 | 68 | 70 | 70 |

Height	Differen~~ce f~~	~~Square of difference~~
	~~7~~0 = − 3	(− 3)(− 3) = + 9
68	68 − 70 = − 2	(− 2)(− 2) = 4
69	69 − 70 = − 1	(− 1)(− 1) = 1
70	70 − 70 = 0	(0)(0) = 0
70	70 − 70 = 0	(0)(0) = 0
72	72 − 70 = 2	(2)(2) = 4
74	74 − 70 = 4	(4)(4) = 16
$\overline{490}$		$\overline{34}$

$$\text{Mean} = \frac{490}{7} = 70 \qquad\qquad \text{Variance} = \frac{34}{7} \approx 4.857$$

Comment You may feel that the standard deviation is a rather complicated number to calculate, so why bother. However, it is an extremely important and useful number to the mathematician. A detailed discussion of how it is used is beyond the scope of this text.

variance

Another measure of variation that is often used is the **variance.** It is computed in a manner similar to that for the standard deviation, with one difference. We omit step (e) of the rule on p. 493. Thus for Example 1 the standard deviation is $\sqrt{4.857}$, and the variance is 4.857.

EXAMPLE 2

A researcher is interested in determining the number of full-time women professors in the mathematics departments of several Western colleges. The researcher has obtained the following information on 9 such colleges. For every 100 faculty members, these schools employed 21, 7, 10, 2, 43, 15, 22, 14, and 1 women. Find the standard deviation and the variance.

SOLUTION

We arrange the numbers as shown in the following table and then calculate the variance and standard deviation.

Number of female employees	Difference from mean	Square of difference	
21	$21 - 15 = 6$	$(6)(6)$	$= 36$
7	$7 - 15 = -8$	$(-8)(-8)$	$= 64$
10	$10 - 15 = -5$	$(-5)(-5)$	$= 25$
2	$2 - 15 = -13$	$(-13)(-13)$	$= 169$
43	$43 - 15 = 28$	$(28)(28)$	$= 784$
15	$15 - 15 = 0$	$(0)(0)$	$= 0$
22	$22 - 15 = 7$	$(7)(7)$	$= 49$
14	$14 - 15 = -1$	$(-1)(-1)$	$= 1$
1	$1 - 15 = -14$	$(-14)(-14)$	$= 196$
Total 135		Total	1324

$$\text{Mean} = \frac{135}{9} = 15$$

$$\text{Variance} = \frac{1324}{9} = 147.11$$

Thus the variance is 147.11, and the standard deviation is $\sqrt{147.11}$, or approximately 12.13.

average deviation

Another measure of variation that is often used is the **average deviation.** It is computed in a manner similar to that for the standard deviation, with one major exception. Instead of squaring the differences from the mean, we simply take the absolute value (neglect any negative signs) of the differences and find the average of these absolute values. No square roots are involved.

We illustrate the procedure with the following example.

EXAMPLE 3

Find the average deviation of the numbers 7, 11, 20, 5, 3, 4, 6, 12, 19, and 3.

SOLUTION

We arrange the numbers in a chart form and proceed as indicated by the chart on the following page. Thus the average deviation is 5.2.

Notation We denote the population standard deviation of set of numbers by the Greek symbol σ (read as sigma). Thus, in symbols, we have

$$\sigma = \sqrt{\frac{\Sigma(x - \mu)^2}{n}}$$

Number	Difference from mean	Absolute value of difference from mean
3	$3 - 9 = -6$	6
3	$3 - 9 = -6$	6
4	$4 - 9 = -5$	5
5	$5 - 9 = -4$	4
6	$6 - 9 = -3$	3
7	$7 - 9 = -2$	2
11	$11 - 9 = +2$	2
12	$12 - 9 = 3$	3
19	$19 - 9 = 10$	10
$\underline{20}$	$20 - 9 = 11$	$\underline{11}$
90		52

Mean $= \dfrac{90}{10} = 9$ Average deviation $\dfrac{52}{10} = 5.2$

Comment   The standard deviation measures how spread out the numbers are around the mean, whereas the range measures only the difference between the larger and smaller numbers. Thus the standard deviation does more than the range in measuring the spread of the data.

The following example illustrates how the standard deviation provides us with more information than the range.

EXAMPLE 4

Find the standard deviation and range for the following scores:

a) $-2, \ -2, \ 0, \ 0, \ 0, \ 2, \ 2$ **b)** $-2, \ -2, \ -2, \ 0, \ 2, \ 2, \ 2$

SOLUTION

a) We can think of the scores as one-pound weights placed on a ruler, as shown in the following line plot.

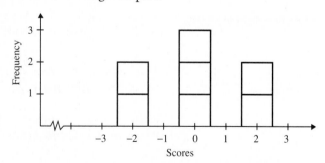

For these scores we have

         mean $= 0$ standard deviation $= 1.5119$

        median $= 0$ range $= 2 - (-2) = 4$

b) Again we can think of the scores as one-pound weights placed on a ruler, as shown in the following line plot.

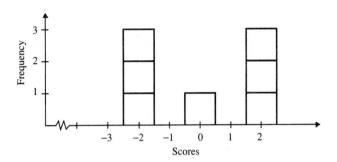

For these scores, we have

$$\text{mean} = 0 \qquad \text{standard deviation} = 1.8516$$

$$\text{median} = 0 \qquad \text{range} = 2 - (-2) = 4$$

Comment   The previous example illustrates that although both sets of scores in parts (a) and (b) have the same range, the standard deviation is different. This is because the standard deviation measures how far the scores are away from the mean.

EXERCISES FOR SECTION 9.3

1. The number of arrests for drunken driving on the Washington Turnpike during the first 10 days of 1989 was as follows:

Day	Number of arrests
Jan. 1	32
Jan. 2	26
Jan. 3	17
Jan. 4	19
Jan. 5	22
Jan. 6	12
Jan. 7	18
Jan. 8	16
Jan. 9	14
Jan. 10	20

Find the range and standard deviation for the number of arrests.

2. The number of stock transactions executed by Jan Segal over a two-week period is as follows:

Day	No. of stock transactions executed
Mon.	123
Tues.	112
Wed.	96
Thurs.	142
Fri.	53
Mon.	88
Tues.	76
Wed.	89
Thurs.	91
Fri.	108

Find the range and standard deviation for the number of stock transactions executed.

3. The price of a share of stock of the Bil Corporation on a daily basis was as follows: $23, $26, $19, $24, $23, $27, $20, and $25. Find the range and standard deviation for the price of a share of stock of this company over this period.

4. *Home Heating Needs.* The number of degree days used in determining home heating oil needs on a daily basis over a two-week period for a northeastern city was as follows: 23, 58, 62, 29, 32, 41, 84, 99, 121, and 109. Find the range and standard deviation for the number of degree days.

5. *Car Insurance.* On June 10, 1988, Joe Frapacci called 6 different insurance companies to obtain price quotes for car insurance for his 1986 Honda. The prices quoted for the same coverages were $812, $690, $750, $902, $784, and $848. Find the mean and standard deviation of the price for car insurance.

6. *Inflation.* Refer back to Exercise 5. A year later, Joe Frapacci calls the same 6 insurance companies to obtain price quotes for car insurance. Each company informs Joe that because of inflation the rates have been increased by 10%.

   a) Calculate the mean and standard deviation for the new rates for car insurance.

   b) How do the answers compare with the answers obtained in Exercise 5?

7. *Arson.* The average cost of fire insurance for a 200-square-ft two-story loft in a certain city is $3000 annually with a standard deviation of $310. Due to the high incidence of arson in the city, the rates will be doubled next year. What will the new mean and standard deviation be?

8. *Money Market Fund.* Stacy is interested in investing some money in a money market fund. After analyzing the investment objectives of numerous companies, Stacy has narrowed down her choice to either Fund A or Fund B. For the past eight months the price of a unit share in either fund has been as follows:

| Date | Unit value of a share of | |
	Fund A	Fund B
Jan. 1	$16.12	$32.17
Feb. 1	17.03	33.19
Mar. 1	16.82	31.78
Apr. 1	17.08	32.14
May. 1	16.91	33.03
June 1	16.72	31.64
July 1	16.41	32.01
Aug. 1	15.93	31.45

a) Find the range and standard deviation of the unit value of a share of each fund.

b) Which fund performed more consistently?

Brain-Teaser Problems

**9. Consider a set of numbers $x_1, x_2, x_3, \ldots, x_n$. Add a constant amount c to each number, thereby forming a new set of numbers $x_1 + c, x_2 + c, x_3 + c, \ldots, x_n + c$. What effect does this operation have on the standard deviation? Explain your answer.

**10. In the previous question, what effect does adding a constant amount to each number have on the range?

**11. Consider a set of numbers $x_1, x_2, x_3, \ldots, x_n$. Multiply each number by a a constant, thereby forming a new set of numbers $cx_1, cx_2, cx_3, \cdots, cx_n$.

a) What effect does this operation have on the range?

b) What effect does this operation have on the standard deviation?

9.4

FREQUENCY DISTRIBUTION AND GRAPHS

There are many situations in which the data may be so numerous that it would be difficult (if not possible) to come up with any meaningful interpretation of them. To see how this can happen, consider Michael, who is late for work many times. His boss tells him that for the past six weeks he has been late the number of minutes per day shown below.

7	6	1	4	0	13
15	10	12	3	3	12
10	12	11	13	2	11
2	3	8	5	3	14
5	14	6	7	7	9

All one can say definitely at first glance is that he was on time only once and one day he was as much as 15 minutes late. Since the numbers are not arranged in order, it is somewhat difficult to conclude anything else from them. For this reason we use a frequency distribution to organize the data. First we have the following definition.

frequency distribution

frequency

> **Definition 9.7**   A **frequency distribution** is a convenient way of organizing data so that we may see what patterns they have. The word **frequency** will be interpreted to mean how often a number occurred.

A frequency distribution is made very easily. We first make a list of numbers from 0 to 15 in a column to show how many minutes Michael was late. Then we make a second column for tally marks. We go through the original numbers, and each time he was late we put a tally mark in the appropriate space. Finally, we add the tally marks per line and indicate this sum in the frequency column. When we apply this to our problem, we get the table shown below.

Minutes late to work	Tally	Frequency	Minutes late to work	Tally	Frequency
0	|	1	8	|	1
1	|	1	9	|	1
2	||	2	10	||	2
3	||||	4	11	||	2
4	|	1	12	|||	3
5	||	2	13	||	2
6	||	2	14	||	2
7	|||	3	15	|	1

Once we have done this, we can come up with meaningful interpretations. We see that most latenesses were 3-minute ones (there were four of them). Michael was also late more than 5 minutes 19 times. This would

Statistics are used in making all kinds of calculations. The graph shown here pictures the top 10 operations performed in 1988. How are such graphs constructed?

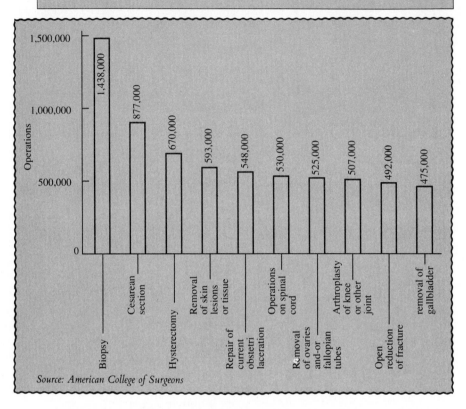

Source: American College of Surgeons

represent 19 out of 30 times, or approximately 60% of the time. Still other interpretations can be given to the data shown.

One may want to draw a **bar graph** for these numbers.

bar graph

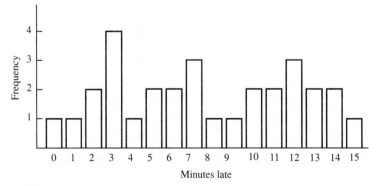

Figure 9.1

To construct the bar graph, we first draw two lines, one horizontal (across) and one vertical (up–down). The horizontal line we will label "Minutes late" and the vertical line we will label "Frequency."

Once we have the frequency distribution, we can draw the bar graph very easily. The height of each bar will represent the frequency. The bar graph will also tell us at a glance that the most latenesses were the 3-minute ones. See Fig. 9.1

We could shorten the above frequency distribution as shown in the following chart.

Minutes late	Tally	Frequency	Minutes late	Tally	Frequency
0–1	||	2	8–9	||	2
2–3	ＨＨ |	6	10–11	||||	4
4–5	|||	3	12–13	ＨＨ	5
6–7	ＨＨ	5	14–15	|||	3

This chart is more compact, *but* some of the information is lost in this version. For example, we can see that Michael is late 2–3 minutes 6 times. But we cannot tell exactly how often he is 2 minutes late or 3 minutes late.

When there are many numbers, listing them separately as we did in the first chart may make it difficult to look at the data and draw meaningful conclusions. If the data are grouped, as in the second chart, they may be easier to interpret.

To further illustrate the idea of a frequency distribution and a bar graph, consider the following example.

EXAMPLE 1

A large midwestern university is reviewing the performance of its star basketball player. During the past season he scored the following number of points per game.

27	16	19	24	18	23	24	18	24	25
23	16	23	24	19	22	17	25	19	27
19	29	24	25	24	18	32	23	21	30

Find the frequency distribution and draw the bar graph for the above numbers.

SOLUTION

We make three columns. The first column will contain the number of points scored, the second will have the tally, and the third will give the frequency.

Number of points	Tally	Frequency	Number of points	Tally	Frequency
16	||	2	25	|||	3
17	|	1	26		0
18	|||	3	27	||	2
19	||||	4	28		0
20		0	29	|	1
21	|	1	30	|	1
22	|	1	31		0
23	||||	4	32	|	1
24	⊬⊬ |	6			

The bar graph for this distribution is shown in Fig. 9.2. One thing should be immediately obvious. The player scored 24 points most often.

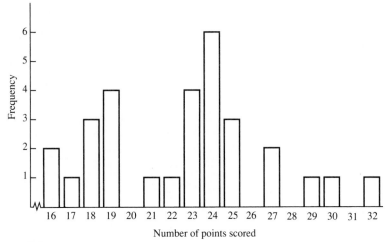

Figure 9.2

EXAMPLE 2

George is a maintenance man in a large office building. He has compiled the following list of numbers that indicate the life length (in hours) of 25 special light bulbs.

$$
\begin{array}{ccccc}
50 & 40 & 40 & 55 & 50 \\
45 & 55 & 50 & 60 & 45 \\
55 & 50 & 45 & 50 & 60 \\
60 & 45 & 55 & 45 & 55 \\
50 & 35 & 50 & 65 & 40
\end{array}
$$

Find the frequency distribution and draw the bar graph for these numbers.

SOLUTION

Again we make three columns. The first column is for the life length, the second for the tally, and the third for the frequency. We have the chart shown below.

Life length	Tally	Frequency
35	|	1
40	|||	3
45	ⵌ	5
50	ⵌ ||	7
55	ⵌ	5
60	|||	3
65	|	1

The bar graph for this distribution is shown in Fig. 9.3

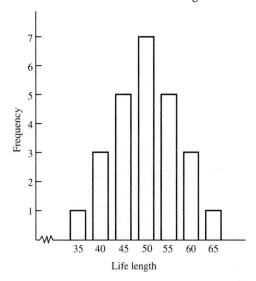

Figure 9.3

Statistics and probability can often be combined to obtain interesting results. Students are taught that if they keep accurate tallies, the statistics they gather can be used to estimate the value of π. This can been seen in exerpted page 365 from *Addison-Wesley Mathematics,* 1987, Grade 7, shown on page 504.

Until now we have seen how a bar graph can be used to picture information. In statistics we use not only bar graphs, but also other kinds of graphs to show all the information given in a situation. This is often of great help in arriving at meaningful conclusions.

The following examples illustrate how bar graphs and other kinds of graphs can be used.

================= **ENRICHMENT** =================

Probability

You can find an approximate value of $\pi = 3.14159\ldots$ by doing this experiment.

You will need a penny and a large grid of squares drawn on paper or posterboard.

Make the sides of each square of the grid the same length as the diameter of a penny (1.8 cm).

Toss a penny on the grid. The outcome is a "hit" if the penny covers a point of intersection on the grid. Otherwise, it is a "miss."

Toss a penny on the grid 100 times. Keep a tally of the number of hits and misses.

Tosses = hits + misses

Use this formula to compute an approximate value for π.

$$\pi \approx \frac{4 \times \textbf{number of hits}}{\textbf{number of tosses}}$$

Combine your numbers of hits and misses with those of several classmates. Use the formula for π again to see if the combined results are a better approximation of π.

EXAMPLE 3

The number of vehicles passing through a toll booth on a turnpike during a 24-hour period is given in the table at the top of page 505.

To be able to draw any meaningful conclusion from these data, we construct a bar graph that contains all the given information (Fig. 9.4). From this graph we can see that the greatest number of cars passed through

Time	Number of cars arriving
12 midnight–2 A.M.	120
2 A.M.–4 A.M..	640
4 A.M.–6 A.M.	1790
6 A.M.–8 A.M.	5780
8 A.M.–10. A.M.	3460
10 A.M.–12 noon	2010
12 noon–2 P.M.	1860
2 P.M.–4 P.M.	2000
4 P.M.–6 P.M.	4030
6 P.M.–8 P.M.	5640
8 P.M.–10 P.M.	2440
10 P.M.–12 midnight	560

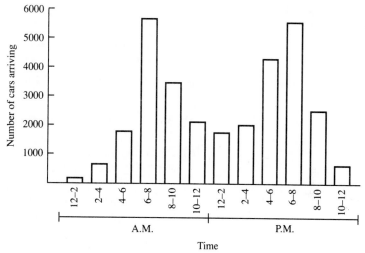

Figure 9.4

the toll booth during the hours of 6 to 8 A.M. Traffic then began dropping off until after 2 P.M., at which time the number of cars increased until about 8 P.M. and then dropped off again.

Information of this type is needed by the authorities to determine the number of toll collectors to hire and the hours to hire them for, so that motorists will not have to wait in long lines. It is easier to determine this information from a graph than from the table of numbers.   ■

EXAMPLE 4

The latest statistics showing the incidence of heart attacks among various age groups in a certain community in the southwest are pictured in the bar graph in Fig. 9.5.

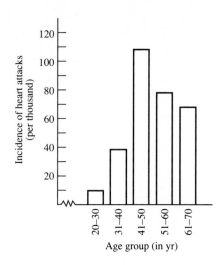

Figure 9.5

a) For this particular community, in what age group are there more than 60 heart attacks per thousand?

b) In what age group are there more than 100 heart attacks per thousand?

SOLUTION

a) We see from the graph that in the age groups between 41 and 70 yr there were more than 60 heart attacks per thousand people.

b) From the graph we see that only the age group of 41–50 yr had more than 100 heart attacks per thousand people. ▪

histogram

 Often data are displayed graphically in the form of a **histogram,** which is simply a bar graph in which the bars are placed next to each other. With the exception of any interval having a frequency of zero, there are no gaps between the bars drawn in a histogram. We bring the bars close together to illustrate that as one interval ends, the next interval begins. In essence, the bars of a histogram show us changes in the same item. For the data given in the previous example, we have the histogram at the top of the following page.

 In this histogram the first bar shows us that there were 10 incidences of heart attacks (per thousand) in the 20–30 year age group; 40 incidences of heart attacks in the 31–40 year age groups; 110 incidences of heart attacks in the 41–50 year age group; 80 incidences of heart attacks in the 51–60 year age group, and 70 incidences of heart attacks in the 61–70 year age group.

Comment As the histogram displays the frequency (or number) of scores that fall in each category (interval), it is sometimes known as a **frequency histogram**.

frequency histogram

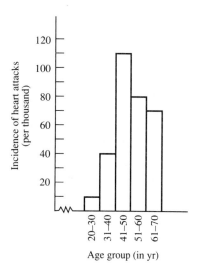

EXAMPLE 5

A large supermarket chain is interested in knowing which flavor of soda is in greatest demand and during which months. It needs this information so that it can adequately stock its warehouses in advance. For its three most popular flavors it has available last year's statistics, which have been recorded in the form of a bar graph (Fig. 9.6).

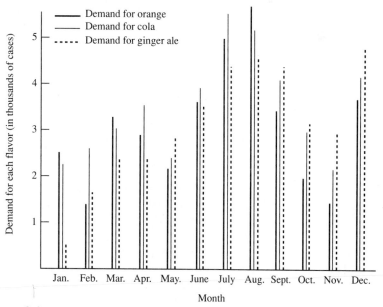

Figure 9.6

a) In which months is orange most popular?

b) Which flavor is most popular in December?

c) Which flavor is least popular in February?

EXAMPLE 6
circle graph

The budget of the student government at a particular university has just been approved. The **circle graph** in Fig. 9.7 indicates how the students plan to spend their money. If the college administration has granted them $100,000, how much money will be spent for:

a) club activities? **b)** drug information?

c) lounge furniture? **d)** student aid?

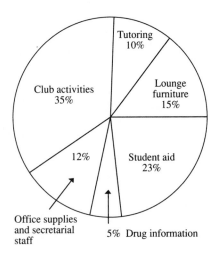

Figure 9.7

SOLUTION

a) Since 35% of $100,000 will be spent on club activities, we have

$$0.35 \times 100,000 = 35,000$$

Thus they will spend $35,000 on club activities. (We write 35% in decimal form as 0.35.)

b) They will spend 5% of $100,000 for drug information. (We write 5% as 0.05.) Thus they will spend

$$0.05 \times 100,000 = 5000$$

or $5000 for drug information.

c) They will spend

$$0.15 \times 100,000 = 15,000$$

or $15,000 for lounge furniture.

d) They will spend

$$0.23 \times 100{,}000 = 23{,}000$$

or $23,000 for student aid.

pie charts

Comment Circle graphs are also known as **pie charts.**

EXAMPLE 7

Problem-Solving Example

There are 450 doctors in the Brookview Medical Club. Their areas of specialization are as follows:

Area of specialization	Number of doctors in this area
Cardiology	92
Pediatrics	98
Internal medicine	118
Neurology	76
Urology	66
	Total = 450

Draw a circle graph to picture this information.

SOLUTION

Understanding the Problem

We are asked to draw a circle graph to picture the information. However, since we are not given the percent of doctors in each category we must first find these percentages and then use them to draw the graph.

A Plan to Solve the Problem

We first convert the numbers into percentages by dividing each by the total 450. Thus we have

Area of specialization	Number of doctors	Percentage of total
Cardiology	92	$\dfrac{92}{450} = 0.2044$, or 20.44%
Pediatrics	98	$\dfrac{98}{450} = 0.2178$, or 21.78%
Internal Medicine	118	$\dfrac{118}{450} = 0.2622$, or 26.22%
Neurology	76	$\dfrac{76}{450} = 0.1689$, or 16.89%
Urology	66	$\dfrac{66}{450} = 0.1467$, or 14.67%

Now we multiply each percentage by 360° (the number of degrees in a circle) to determine the number of degrees to assign to each part. We get

$0.2044 \times 360° = 73.58°$, or 74°, for cardiology

$0.2178 \times 360° = 78.41°$, or 78°, for pediatrics

$0.2622 \times 360° = 94.39°$, or 94°, for internal medicine

$0.1689 \times 360° = 60.80°$, or 61°, for neurology

$0.1467 \times 360° = 52.81°$, or 53°, for urology

Then we use a protractor and compass to draw each part, in order, using the appropriate number of degrees. In our case we obtain the circle graph represented in Fig. 9.8

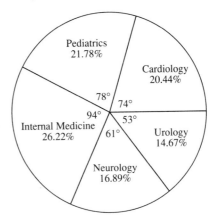

Figure 9.8

Checking our Solution

We can check our answer by multiplying the percentages given in each category by 450. Thus, for example, the circle graph indicates that 20.44% of the doctors are cardiologists. We then have 20.44% of 450, or $0.2044 \times 450 = 91.98$, or 92. The same procedure is used to check all of the categories.   ▬

Comment   The sum of the percentages may not necessarily be 100%. This discrepancy is due to the rounding off of numbers.

EXAMPLE 8

line graph

An electric company wants to know during which hours electrical supply is in greatest demand on a typical summer day. It needs this information so that it can prepare itself to satisfy consumer demands adequately. Information for one typical day has been gathered and is shown in the **line graph** in Fig. 9.9.

a) During which hour(s) is electricity in greatest demand?

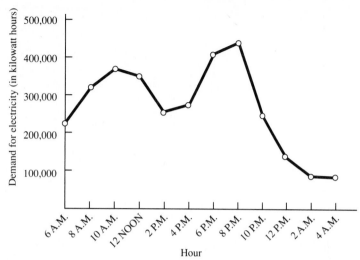

Figure 9.9

b) During which hours is the demand for electricity decreasing?

c) During which hour(s) is electricity in least demand?

line segment graphs

Elementary school children are often taught to use "line segment graphs" to make predictions. This can be seen in student page 358 from *Addison-Wesley Mathematics,* 1987, Grade 8, shown on page 512.

In recent years the bars of a bar graph have often been replaced by a series of equally spaced identical pictures, where each picture or symbol represents a specified quantity. Such graphs, which are called **pictographs** or **pictograms**, are used to catch the reader's eye and to make the graph more appealing.

pictograph
pictogram

EXAMPLE 9

The price of gas. The pictograph in Fig. 9.10 shows how the price of gas has changed over the past few years in one particular city.

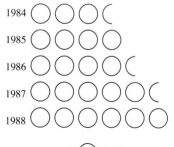

Figure 9.10
Average selling price of
a gallon of gasoline.

Line Segment Graphs

Joel Maxwell is a demographer. He uses population statistics. He found the data on life expectancy in a data bank.

To see how the different entries are related and to use them to make predictions, he made a **line segment graph**.

Present Age	Life Expectancy for Men and Women	
	Life Expectancy (Years)	
	Men	Women
At birth	70.6	78.3
20	52.3	59.3
40	34.0	40.3
50	25.2	31.1
65	14.3	18.7

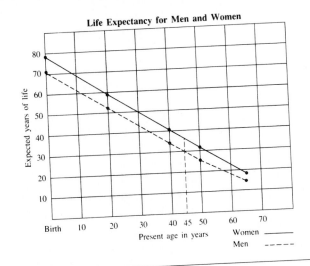

Life Expectancy for Men and Women

Warm Up

Use the line segment graph above for exercises 1–6.

1. What is the title of the graph?

2. What do the numbers on the horizontal axis show?

3. What do the numbers on the vertical axis show?

4. How is the data for women shown?

5. Estimate the life expectancy of a woman whose present age is 45.

6. Estimate the life expectancy of a man whose present age is 45.

EXAMPLE 10

Population changes. The pictograph in Fig. 9.11 indicates the population change of the United States from 1890 to 1980. (Each symbol represents ten million people.)

a) How many people were there in 1930?

b) By approximately how many people did the population of the United States change from 1920 to 1970?

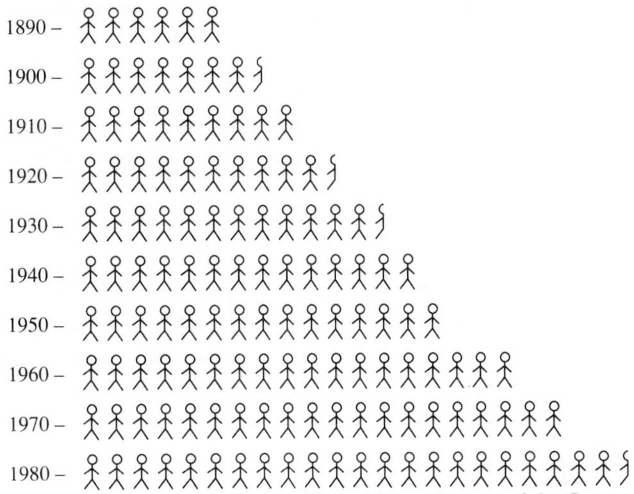

Source: United States Bureau of the Census

Figure 9.11

SOLUTION

a) In 1930 there were 125 million people in the United States.

b) The population of the United States increased from 105 million in 1920 to 200 million in 1970, or by 95 million people.

Stem-and-Leaf Diagrams

The graphical techniques discussed to this point are well-suited to handle most situations. In recent years, however, a new technique known as **stem-and-leaf diagrams** has become very popular. It represents a combination of sorting techniques often used by computers and a graphical technique.

To see how this new method works let us analyze some information on the weights of students in a math class. The following is the weight (in pounds) of all the students in the class:

120	112	117	111	119	147
135	148	122	137	103	116
147	162	117	149	108	123
110	123	176	182	133	148
101	135	138	155	118	142
103	159	131	137	156	149

Using stem-and-leaf diagrams we can group the data and at the same time obtain a display that looks like a bar graph. This is done as follows: The first number on the list is 120. We designate the first two leading digits (12) as its **stem.** We call the last (or trailing) digit its **leaf,** as illustrated at the top of page 514.

stem

leaf

Stem (First or leading digits)	Leaf (Last or trailing digit)
12	0

The stem and leaf of the number 135 are 13 and 5, respectively. Also, the stem and leaf of the number 147 are 14 and 7, respectively.

To form a stem-and-leaf display for the above data, we first list all stem possibilities in a column starting with the smallest stem, 10 (which corresponds to the number 101), and ending with the largest stem, 18 (which corresponds to the number 182). Then we place the leaf of each number from the original data in the row of the display corresponding to the number's stem. This is accomplished by placing the last (or trailing) digit on the right side of the vertical line opposite its corresponding leading digit or stem. For example, our first data value is 120. The leaf 0 is placed in the stem row 12. Similarly, for the number 135, the leaf 5 is placed in the stem row 13. We continue in this manner until each of the leaves is placed in the appropriate stem rows. The completed stem-and-leaf display will appear as shown in Fig. 9.12.

Stem	Leaves
10	1 3 3 8
11	0 2 7 7 1 9 8 6
12	0 3 2 3
13	5 5 8 1 7 7 3
14	7 8 9 7 8 2 9
15	9 5 6
16	2
17	6
18	2

Figure 9.12

The stem-and-leaf diagram arranges the data in a convenient form since we can now count the number of leaves for each stem. We then obtain the frequency distribution. From this it is very easy to draw the bar graph. If we turn the above stem-and-leaf display on its side we obtain the

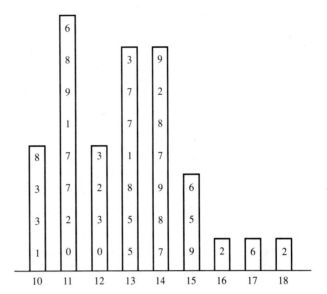

Figure 9.13

same type of bar graph provided by the frequency distribution. This is shown in Fig. 9.13.

Comment   One major advantage of a stem-and-leaf diagram over a frequency distribution is that the original data are preserved. The stem-and-leaf diagram displays the value of each individual score as well as the size of each data class. This is not possible with a bar graph.

Comment   A stem-and-leaf diagram presents the data in a more convenient form. This will make it possible to perform various arithmetic calculations to be studied later in this chapter.

We summarize the procedure to be used in constructing stem-and-leaf diagrams in the following rule.

Rule 9.2   To construct a stem-and-leaf diagram, proceed as follows:
1. Determine how the stems and the leaves will be identified.
2. Arrange the stems in order in a vertical column, starting with the smallest stem and ending with the largest.
3. Go through the original data and place a leaf for each observation in the appropriate stem row.
4. If the display looks too cramped and narrow, we can stretch the display by using two lines (or more) per stem so that we can place leaf digits 0, 1, 2, 3, and 4 on one line of the stem and leaf digits 5, 6, 7, 8, and 9 on the other line of the stem.

Let us illustrate the preceding with another example.

EXAMPLE 11

The number of new housing permits issued for each of the days of February in Boyertown is as follows:

$$
\begin{array}{cccccc}
17 & 32 & 46 & 64 & 81 & 27 \\
56 & 49 & 21 & 62 & 68 & 39 \\
24 & 19 & 18 & 53 & 66 & 16 \\
29 & 18 & 16 & 37 & 22 & 33 \\
18 & 38 & 29 & 49 & 34 &
\end{array}
$$

Draw a stem-and-leaf diagram for the above data.

SOLUTION

Let us use the first digit of each of the numbers as the stem and the second digit as the leaf. Then we arrange the stems in order in a vertical column. Although they can be arranged horizontally, the stems are usually arranged vertically. We get

Stem	
1	
2	
3	
4	
5	
6	
7	
8	

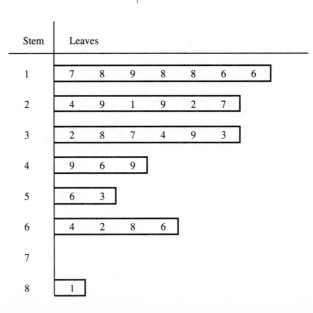

Stem	Leaves
1	7 8 9 8 8 6 6
2	4 9 1 9 2 7
3	2 8 7 4 9 3
4	9 6 9
5	6 3
6	4 2 8 6
7	
8	1

Figure 9.14

Now we go through the original data and place a leaf for each observation in the appropriate stem row. The stem-and-leaf diagram is shown in Fig. 9.14.

EXERCISES FOR SECTION 9.4

1. *Jogging.* The ages of the 40 runners who have registered to run in this year's 26-mile marathon are as follows:

```
31  36  34  29  18  21  18
32  24  32  34  25  19  30
19  34  32  22  17  31  33
20  21  28  29  27  17  28
24  36  31  16  34  29
18  26  18  18  25  22
```

Construct the frequency distribution for these data and then draw its bar graph.

2. The number of flights scheduled to depart daily from Republic Airport for the month of January is as follows:

```
27  17  20  17  16  19  21
26  33  35  23  26  20
25  27  25  19  27  40
27  15  20  26  18  24
23  32  22  21  18  35
```

Construct the frequency distribution for these data and then draw its bar graph.

3. Each of the 38 students in a statistics class were asked to indicate the number of children in their families. The results are as follows:

```
7  8  2  6  6  1  4  3
3  5  4  2  1  9  1  2
7  9  4  5  3  2  3  2
8  1  7  4  1  2  2
3  5  5  4  2  1  5
```

Construct the frequency distribution for the data and then draw its bar graph.

4. The number of new housing permits issued during a particular 6 week period on a daily basis in Sequa Valley is as follows:

```
21   5  38  14  21   8
 5   8  16  40   5  17
12  16  12  28  12   9
15  13  15  31  15
10  12  10  16  21
```

Construct the frequency distribution for the data and then draw its bar graph.

5. The Printex Corporation employs 823 people. Recently, management decided to change the life insurance coverage that it provides for its workers. The company analyzed the ages of its workers so that it could apply to another insurance company. The ages of the workers are as follows:

Age	Male	Female
Under 30 yrs	103	203
Between 30 and 40 yrs	91	127
Between 40 and 55 yrs	106	82
Over 55 yrs	62	49

Draw a circle graph (pie chart) to picture the above information.

6. The Hakewa Clothing Corporation sells its products throughout the world as shown in the accompanying circle graph. (Fig. 9.15)

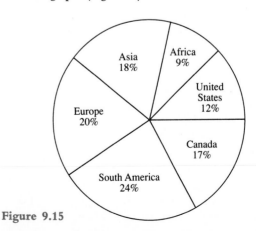

Figure 9.15

If the Hakewa Company had sales of $7,823,100 during 1989, find the sales figures for each region mentioned.

7. The graph in Fig. 9.16 shows the number of murders in a large southeastern city for the years 1983–1988.

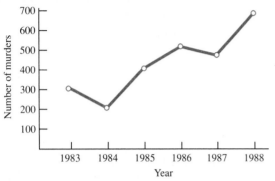

Figure 9.16

a) In 1985, how many murders were there?

b) In 1986, how many murders were there?

c) What was the increase between 1983 and 1988?

8. The graph in Fig. 9.17 shows the number of businesses filing for Chapter 11 bankruptcy during 1989 in District 6.

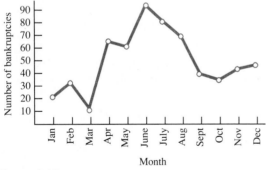

Figure 9.17

a) During which month(s) were there the greatest number of bankruptcies?

b) How many bankruptcies were there during the entire year of 1989?

9. Refer to the accompanying newspaper article. The data following it are available from the survey. Draw a bar graph to picture the information.

Unemployment Seen as Top Problem

BOSTON (Dec. 9)—The results of a national Gallup Poll of nearly half of the U.S. voters—both Democratic and Republican—disclosed unemployment as the most important problem facing their congressional districts. The survey was taken during the third week of September, much before the staggering 10.1 per cent unemployment figures were released.

Forty-seven percent of the people polled indicated that unemployment was their main concern. Furthermore, when asked which party they thought would be better able to deal with this problem, the Democratic Party won handily over the GOP, 45 percent when compared with 20 percent.

Other problems named by the respondents ranked far behind unemployment. Some of these other problems of concern to voters include the following: inflation (11 percent), the economy (9 percent), local problems (8 percent), taxes (7 percent), crime (7 percent), and high interest rates (3 percent).

SAN FRANCISCO GLOBE, DECEMBER 9, 1982

Problem of concern to you

	Democrat	Republican
Unemployment	352	118
Inflation	82	28
The economy	68	22
Local problems	62	20

10. The Jones spend their $26,000 family income as follows:

Food	$4500
Clothing	$5000
Rent	$6000
Education	$2700
Entertainment	$2400
Travel	$3200
Miscellaneous	$2200
	$26,000

Draw a circle graph to picture this information.

11. *Real Estate Taxes.* Real estate taxes per $1000 of assessed evaluation on residential property in Charleston have changed over the past 8 years as shown in the accompanying chart. Draw a line graph to picture this information.

Year	1982	1983	1984	1985
Real estate taxes	$84	$88	$97	$105

Year	1986	1987	1988	1989
Real estate taxes	$116	$132	$157	$194

Construct a stem-and leaf diagram for the following:

12. The following list gives the weight, in pounds, of each student in a physical education class.

87	119	143	123	145	160	116
113	132	158	129	126	108	132
141	120	99	133	142	112	153
127	105	162	139	158	135	141
138	139	151	150	163	121	

13. The following list gives the total number of inches of rainfall that fell in the Yucahu rain forest over a 30 month period.

39.7	33.9	31.7	37.6	36.1	39.0
31.4	31.7	32.9	38.1	35.3	35.6
40.2	39.5	38.2	37.6	38.6	36.4
33.2	34.7	36.1	38.3	35.4	38.8
36.2	37.7	34.5	35.9	36.1	37.3

Brain-Teaser Problems

**14. The student government at Loden University is interested in purchasing new furniture and musical equipment for the student lounge. They have placed ads in the local newspapers and have obtained the following bids for the specified items:

$4000	$4100	$3850	$4298	$4198	$4005
3996	3890	4498	4489	4305	4398
3974	3998	3952	3801	3805	3895
4098	4298	4008	4300	4096	3998
4290	4400	3976	3895	4402	4000

Group the numbers so that 50 values could fall on each line. Thus the stems will be $3800–3849, $3850–3899, and so on.

**15. Thirty students in a bowling class scored the following number of points.

186	132	127	212	215	175
173	123	187	272	225	161
149	131	193	263	183	145
188	213	201	133	186	203
128	185	226	210	219	139

Group the numbers so that 20 values could fall on each line. Thus the stems will be 1 and 2 where each stem will have five lines. Values falling between 100–119 (inclusive) will be on the first leaf, values between 120 and 139 (inclusive) falling on the second leaf, etc.

9.5

THE NORMAL DISTRIBUTION

Recently, a survey was taken of the weights of the 800 students at Trixy College. After the data were arranged into a frequency distribution containing 14 intervals, the histogram shown in Fig. 9.18 was obtained. When the data were grouped into a frequency distribution containing 28

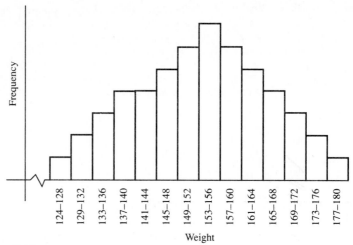

Figure 9.18

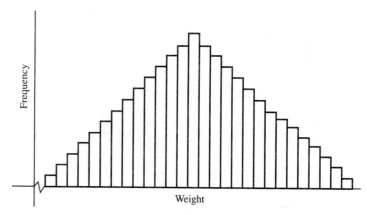

Figure 9.19

normal curve

normal distribution

Figure 9.20

intervals, the histogram shown in Fig. 9.19 was obtained. If we were to continue this process of adding additional intervals, the graph would tend to smooth out into a continuous curve similar to the one shown in Fig. 9.20. Such a curve is called a *normal curve,* and the distribution that gives rise to it is called a *normal distribution.*

Since the normal distribution has wide-ranging applications, we need a careful description of a normal curve and some of its properties. The graph of a normal distribution is a bell-shaped curve that extends in both directions. Although the curve gets closer and closer to the horizontal axis, it never really touches it, no matter how far it is extended.

The mean of the normal distribution is at the center of the curve, and the curve is symmetric about the mean. This tells that we can fold the

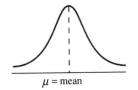

μ = mean

Figure 9.21

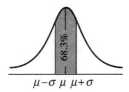

$\mu - \sigma \ \mu \ \mu + \sigma$

Figure 9.22

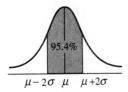

$\mu - 2\sigma \ \mu \ \mu + 2\sigma$

Figure 9.23

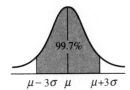

$\mu - 3\sigma \ \mu \ \mu + 3\sigma$

Figure 9.24

curve along the dotted line in Fig. 9.21 and either portion of the curve will correspond with the other portion.

For a normal distribution the mean, the median, and the mode are all equal. Remember that μ represents the mean and σ represents the population standard deviation.

The data that make up the normal distribution tend to cluster around the middle with very few values more than three standard deviations from the mean on either side. As a matter of fact, about 68.3% of the data will fall within one standard deviation of the mean on either side (see Fig. 9.22). Also, approximately 95.4% of the data will fall within two standard deviations of the mean on either side (see Fig. 9.23), and approximately 99.7% of the data will fall within three standard deviations of the mean on either side (see Fig. 9.24).

Thus in our case, if the weights of the college students are normally distributed with a mean of 150 pounds and a standard deviation of 10 pounds, then we would expect approximately 68.3% of the students to weigh between

$$\mu - \sigma \text{ and } \mu + \sigma$$
$$150 - 10 \text{ and } 150 + 10$$

or between 140 and 160 pounds. Similarly, we would expect approximately 95.4% of the students to weigh between

$$\mu - 2\sigma \text{ and } \mu + 2\sigma$$
$$150 - 2(10) \text{ and } 150 + 2(10)$$

or between 130 and 170 pounds. Also 99.7% of the students should weigh between

$$\mu - 3\sigma \text{ and } \mu + 3\sigma$$
$$150 - 3(10) \text{ and } 150 + 3(10)$$

or between 120 and 180 pounds.

A normal distribution is completely specified by its mean and standard deviation. Thus although all normal distributions are basically bell-shaped,

Figure 9.25
Different normal distributions

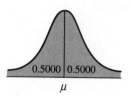

Figure 9.26

area under normal curve

different means and different standard deviations will describe different bell-shaped curves (see Fig. 9.25). It is possible, however, to convert each of these different normal distributions into one standard form. You may be wondering, why bother? The answer is rather simple as we shall see.

The total area under the normal curve is exactly one (one square unit). Since the normal curve is symmetric about the mean, we can immediately conclude that $\frac{1}{2}$ (or 0.5000) of *all* the area is to the right of the mean and $\frac{1}{2}$ (or 0.5000) of the area is to the left of the mean (see Fig. 9.26).

Area under the normal curve is associated with probability. Thus if a measurement x, the weights of college students in our case, is normally distributed, then the probability that x will fall between the values of a and b is equal to the **area** *under the normal curve between a and b.*

Since areas under a normal distribution are related to probability, we can use special normal distribution tables for calculating probabilities. Since the mean and the standard deviation can be any values, however, it would seem that we need an endless number of tables. Fortunately, this is not the case; we need only one standardized table. (See Table 9.1 p. 524.) Thus the area under the curve between 40 and 60 of a normal distribution with a mean of 50 and a standard deviation of 10 will be the same as the area between 70 and 80 of another normally distributed variable with mean 75 and standard deviation 5. They are both within one standard deviation unit from the mean. It is for this reason that statisticians use a standard normal distribution. See the diagram below.

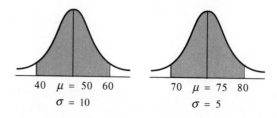

standard normal
distribution

> **Definition 9.8**   A **standard normal distribution** is a normal distribution with a mean of 0 and a standard deviation of 1.

Thus, what we attempt to do is to convert any normal curve with mean μ and standard deviation σ into a normal curve with mean 0 and standard deviation 1. For example, suppose we consider the weights of college students (discussed earlier) whose mean $\mu = 150$ and whose standard deviation $\sigma = 10$. From the original data, one standard deviation to the right of the mean corresponds to 150 + 10, or 160. On the standard normal curve this simply corresponds to + 1. Also, from the original data, two standard deviations to the right of the mean corresponds to 150 + 2(10), or 170. On the standard normal curve this simply corresponds to + 2. The corresponding value on the standard normal curve is usually expressed in units of z (see Fig. 9.27). Similarly, one standard deviation to the left of the mean corresponds to a weight of 150 – 10, or 140 pounds. On the standard normal curve this corresponds to a negative z-value of – 1. In a similar manner a weight of 151 pounds corresponds to $z = 0.1$, a weight of 152 corresponds to $z = 0.2$, and so on.

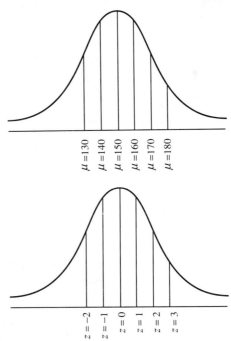

Figure 9.27
The correspondence between the original data (top) and the standard normal curve (bottom)

Table 9.1
Areas of a Standard Normal Distribution
An entry in the table is the proportion under the entire curve that is between $z = 0$ and a positive value of z. Areas for negative values of z are obtained by symmetry.

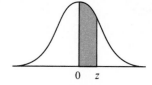

z	0.00	0.01	0.02	0.03	0.04	0.05	0.06	0.07	0.08	0.09
0.0	0.0000	0.0040	0.0080	0.0120	0.0160	0.0199	0.0239	0.0279	0.0319	0.0359
0.1	0.0398	0.0438	0.0478	0.0517	0.0557	0.0596	0.0636	0.0675	0.0714	0.0753
0.2	0.0793	0.0832	0.0871	0.0910	0.0948	0.0987	0.1026	0.1064	0.1103	0.1141
0.3	0.1179	0.1217	0.1255	0.1293	0.1331	0.1368	0.1406	0.1443	0.1480	0.1517
0.4	0.1554	0.1591	0.1628	0.1664	0.1700	0.1736	0.1772	0.1808	0.1844	0.1879
0.5	0.1915	0.1950	0.1985	0.2019	0.2054	0.2088	0.2123	0.2157	0.2190	0.2224
0.6	0.2257	0.2291	0.2324	0.2357	0.2389	0.2422	0.2454	0.2486	0.2517	0.2549
0.7	0.2580	0.2611	0.2642	0.2673	0.2704	0.2734	0.2764	0.2794	0.2823	0.2852
0.8	0.2881	0.2910	0.2939	0.2967	0.2995	0.3023	0.3051	0.3078	0.3106	0.3133
0.9	0.3159	0.3186	0.3212	0.3238	0.3264	0.3289	0.3315	0.3340	0.3365	0.3389
1.0	0.3413	0.3438	0.3461	0.3485	0.3508	0.3531	0.3554	0.3577	0.3599	0.3621
1.1	0.3643	0.3665	0.3686	0.3708	0.3729	0.3749	0.3770	0.3790	0.3810	0.3830
1.2	0.3849	0.3869	0.3888	0.3907	0.3925	0.3944	0.3962	0.3980	0.3997	0.4015
1.3	0.4032	0.4049	0.4066	0.4082	0.4099	0.4115	0.4131	0.4147	0.4162	0.4177
1.4	0.4192	0.4207	0.4222	0.4236	0.4251	0.4265	0.4279	0.4292	0.4306	0.4319
1.5	0.4332	0.4345	0.4357	0.4370	0.4382	0.4394	0.4406	0.4418	0.4429	0.4441
1.6	0.4452	0.4463	0.4474	0.4484	0.4495	0.4505	0.4515	0.4525	0.4535	0.4545
1.7	0.4554	0.4564	0.4573	0.4582	0.4591	0.4599	0.4608	0.4616	0.4625	0.4633
1.8	0.4641	0.4649	0.4656	0.4664	0.4671	0.4678	0.4686	0.4693	0.4699	0.4706
1.9	0.4713	0.4719	0.4726	0.4732	0.4738	0.4744	0.4750	0.4756	0.4761	0.4767
2.0	0.4772	0.4778	0.4783	0.4788	0.4793	0.4798	0.4803	0.4808	0.4812	0.4817
2.1	0.4821	0.4826	0.4830	0.4834	0.4838	0.4842	0.4846	0.4850	0.4854	0.4857
2.2	0.4861	0.4864	0.4868	0.4871	0.4875	0.4878	0.4881	0.4884	0.4887	0.4890
2.3	0.4893	0.4896	0.4898	0.4901	0.4904	0.4906	0.4909	0.4911	0.4913	0.4916
2.4	0.4918	0.4920	0.4922	0.4925	0.4927	0.4929	0.4931	0.4932	0.4934	0.4936
2.5	0.4938	0.4940	0.4941	0.4943	0.4945	0.4946	0.4948	0.4949	0.4951	0.4952
2.6	0.4953	0.4955	0.4956	0.4957	0.4959	0.4960	0.4961	0.4962	0.4963	0.4946
2.7	0.4965	0.4966	0.4967	0.4968	0.4969	0.4970	0.4971	0.4972	0.4973	0.4974
2.8	0.4974	0.4975	0.4976	0.4977	0.4977	0.4978	0.4979	0.4979	0.4980	0.4981
2.9	0.4981	0.4982	0.4982	0.4983	0.4984	0.4984	0.4985	0.4985	0.4986	0.4986
3.0	0.4987	0.4987	0.4987	0.4988	0.4988	0.4989	0.4989	0.4989	0.4990	0.4990

More generally, we can convert any raw score x into a z-score by using Formula 9.3

z-score
z-value

> **Formula 9.3**   The **z-score** or **z-value** of any number x in a normal distribution is given by
>
> $$z = \frac{x - \mu}{\sigma}$$
>
> where x = original score, μ = mean, and σ = standard deviation.

Comment   A z-score tells us how many standard deviation units a particular number is away from the mean as well as whether this number is above or below the mean.

EXAMPLE 1

A certain brand of flashlight battery has a mean life μ of 40 hours and a standard deviation σ of 5 hours. Find the z-score of a battery that lasts for
a) 50 hours   **b)** 35 hours   **c)** 40 hours

SOLUTION

Since $\mu = 40$ and $\sigma = 5$, we use Formula 9.3

a) The z-score of 50 is

$$z = \frac{x - \mu}{\sigma} = \frac{50 - 40}{5} = 2$$

Since the z-score is a positive number, we know that $x = 50$ lies to the right of the mean.

b) The z-score of 35 is

$$z = \frac{x - \mu}{\sigma} = \frac{35 - 40}{5} = -1$$

Since the z-score is a negative number, we know that $x = 35$ lies to the left of the mean.

c) The z-score of 40 is

$$z = \frac{40 - 40}{5} = \frac{0}{5} = 0$$

Since the z-score is 0, we know that $x = 40$ coincides with the mean.

Comment   Because σ is always a positive number, z will be a negative number whenever x is less that μ, as $x - \mu$ is then a negative number. A z-score of 0 implies that the term has the same value as the mean.

Let us now apply the idea of z-score to find the areas under a normal curve and thus probability calculations.

Table 9.1 on page 524 gives the areas of a standard normal distribution between $z = 0$ and $z = 3.09$. We read the table as follows: The first two digits of the z-score are under the column headed by z; the third digit heads the other columns. To find the area from $z = 0$ to $z = 2.59$, we first look under z to 2.5 and then across from $z = 2.5$ to the column headed by 0.09. The area is 0.4952 or 49.52%.

Similarly, to find the area from $z = 0$ to $z = 1.94$, we first look under $z = 1.9$ and then move across to the column headed by 0.04. The area is 0.4738.

EXAMPLE 2

SOLUTION

Find the area between $z = 0$ and $z = 1.13$ in a standard normal curve.

We first draw a sketch as shown in Fig. 9.28. Then using Table 9.1 for $z = 1.13$, we find that the area between $z = 0$ and $z = 1.13$ is 0.3708. This means that the probability of a score with this normal distribution falling between $z = 0$ and $z = 1.13$ is 0.3708. ◼

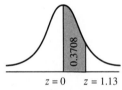

$z = 0$ $z = 1.13$

Figure 9.28

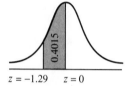

$z = -1.29$ $z = 0$

Figure 9.29

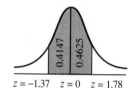

$z = -1.37$ $z = 0$ $z = 1.78$

Figure 9.30

EXAMPLE 3

SOLUTION

Find the area between $z = -1.29$ and $z = 0$ in a standard normal distribution.

We first draw a sketch as shown in Fig. 9.29. Then using Table 9.1, we look up the area between $z = 0$ and $z = 1.29$. The area is 0.4015, not -0.4015. A negative value of z tells us that the value of z is to the left of the mean. The area under the curve (and the resulting probability) is *always* a positive number. Thus the probability of getting a z-score between 0 and -1.29 is 0.4015. ◼

EXAMPLE 4

SOLUTION

Find the area between $z = -1.37$ and $z = 1.78$ in a standard normal distribution.

We draw the sketch as shown in Fig. 9.30. Since Table 9.1 gives the area only from $z = 0$ on, we first look under the normal curve from $z = 0$ to $z = 1.78$. We get 0.4625. Then we look up the area between $z = 0$ and $z = -1.37$. We get 0.4147. Finally, we add these two together and get $0.4625 + 0.4147 = 0.8772$. Thus the probability that a z-score is between $z = -1.37$ and $z = 1.78$ is 0.8772. ◼

By following a procedure similar to that used in Example 4, you should verify the following:

1. The probability that a z-score falls within one standard deviation of the mean on either side, that is, between $z = -1$ and $z = 1$, is approximately 68%.

2. The probability that a z-score falls within two standard deviations of the mean, that is, between $z = -2$ and $z = 2$, is approximately 95%.

3. The probability that a z-score falls within three standard deviations of the mean is 99.7%. Thus approximately 99.7% of the z-scores fall between $z = -3$ and $z = 3$.

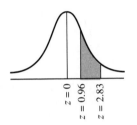

Figure 9.31

In many cases we have to find areas between two given values of z or areas to the right or left of some value of z. Finding these areas is an easy task provided that we remember that the area under the entire normal distribution is 1. Thus since the normal distribution is symmetrical about $z = 0$, we conclude that the area to the right of $z = 0$ and the area to the left of $z = 0$ are both equal to 0.5000.

EXAMPLE 5

Find the area between $z = 0.96$ and $z = 2.83$ in a standard normal distribution. (See Fig. 9.31)

SOLUTION

We cannot look this up directly, since the chart starts at 0, not at $z = 0.96$. However, we can look up the area between $z = 0$ and $z = 2.83$ and get 0.4977 and then the area between $z = 0$ and $z = 0.96$ and get 0.3315 (see Fig. 9.31). We then take the difference between the two and get 0.4977 − 0.3315 = 0.1662   ◼

EXAMPLE 6

Find the probability of getting a z-value that is less than 0.48 in a standard normal distribution. (See Fig. 9.32.)

SOLUTION

The probability of getting a z-value that is less than 0.48 really refers to the area under the curve to the left of $z = 0.48$. This represents the shaded portion of Fig. 9.32. We look up the area from $z = 0$ to $z = 0.48$ and get 0.1844. We add this to 0.5000, getting 0.1844 + 0.5000 = 0.6844. Thus the probability of getting a z-value less than 0.48 is 0.6844.   ◼

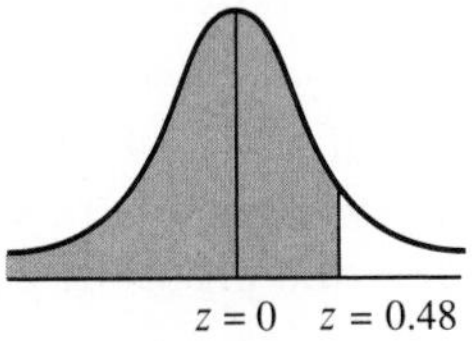

$z = 0$ $z = 0.48$

Figure 9.32

If we are given a normal distribution whose mean is different from 0 and whose standard deviation is different from 1, we can convert this normal distribution into a standard normal distribution by converting each of its scores into a standard score by using Formula 9.3.

Expressing the scores of a normal distribution as standard scores allows us to calculate different probabilities, as Example 7 shows.

EXAMPLE 7

In a normal distribution with $\mu = 40$ and $\sigma = 5$, find the probability of obtaining the following.

a) A value greater than 50

b) A value less than 25

SOLUTION

a) We use Formula 9.3. We have $\mu = 40$, $x = 50$, and $\sigma = 5$, so that

$$z = \frac{x - \mu}{\sigma} = \frac{50 - 40}{5} = \frac{10}{5} = 2$$

See Fig. 9.33. Thus we are really interested in the area to the right of $z = 2$ of a standard normal curve. The area from $z = 0$ to $z = 2$ is 0.4772. The area to the right of $z = 2$ is then $0.5000 - 0.4772 = 0.0228$. Therefore the probability of obtaining a value greater than 50 is 0.0228.

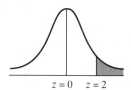

Figure 9.33

$z = 0$ $z = 2$

b) We use Formula 9.3. We have $\mu = 40$, $x = 25$, and $\sigma = 5$, so that

$$z = \frac{x - \mu}{\sigma} = \frac{25 - 40}{5} = -\frac{15}{5} = -3$$

See Fig. 9.34. Thus we are interested in the area to the left of $z = -3$. The area from $z = 0$ to $z = -3$ is 0.4987. Thus the area to the left of $z = -3$ is $0.5000 - 0.4987 = 0.0013$. The probability of obtaining a value less than 25 is therefore 0.0013.

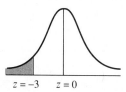

Figure 9.34

$z = -3$ $z = 0$

Let us now apply the normal distribution to some examples.

EXAMPLE 8

From past experience it has been found that the weight of a newborn at a maternity hospital is normally distributed with a mean of $6\frac{1}{2}$ pounds (104 ounces) and a standard deviation of 21 ounces. If a newborn baby is selected at random, find the probability that the baby weighs more than 8 pounds (128 ounces).

SOLUTION

We use Formula 9.3. Here $\mu = 104$, $\sigma = 21$, and $x = 128$, so that

$$z = \frac{x - \mu}{\sigma} = \frac{128 - 104}{21} = \frac{24}{21} = 1.14$$

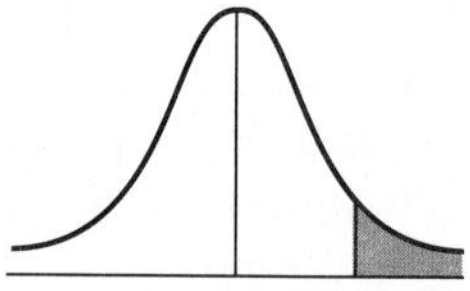

Thus, we are interested in the area to the right of $z = 1.14$. The area from $z = 0$ to $z = 1.14$ is 0.3729, so the area to the right of $z = 1.14$ is $0.5000 - 0.3729 = 0.1271$. See Fig. 9.35. Therefore the probability that a randomly selected baby weighs more than 8 pounds is 0.1271.

$\mu = 104$ $z = 1.14$
$z = 0$

Figure 9.35

EXAMPLE 9

In a recent study in a certain town it was found that the number of hours that a typical ten-year-old child watches television per week is normally distributed with a mean of 7 hours and a standard deviation of 0.83 hours.

Lester is a ten-year-old child in this town. What is the probability that he watches between 5 and 8 hours of television per week?

SOLUTION

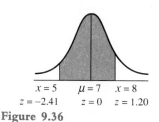

$x = 5$ $\mu = 7$ $x = 8$
$z = -2.41$ $z = 0$ $z = 1.20$

Figure 9.36

We first find the probability that Lester will watch television between 7 and 8 hours and add to this the probability that he will watch television between 5 and 7 hours per week. Using Formula 9.3, we get

$$z = \frac{x - \mu}{\sigma} = \frac{8 - 7}{0.83} = 1.20$$

The area between $z = 0$ and $z = 1.20$ is 0.3849. See Fig. 9.36.

Also,

$$z = \frac{x - \mu}{\sigma} = \frac{5 - 7}{0.83} = -2.41$$

The area between $z = 0$ and $z = -2.41$ is 0.4920. Adding these two probabilities, we get $0.4920 + 0.3849 = 0.8769$. Thus the probability[2] that Lester watches between 5 and 8 hours of television per week is 0.8769.

Comment   There is often a need to compare scores taken from separate populations with different means and standard deviations. The standard z score, which is a measure of the number of standard deviations above or below the mean, facilitates such comparisons. This will be illustrated in the exercises.

EXERCISES FOR SECTION 9.5

1. Which of the following would be likely to be normally distributed? (In each case, assume a random sample of size 5000.)

   a) height of statisticians

   b) useful life of a car

   c) age at which American men marry for the first time

   d) age at which Americans have their first heart attack

2. The distribution shown in Fig. 9.37 represents the number of accidents (per year) occurring in a factory

which employs 10,000 workers. (The mean is 10 and the standard deviation is 2.)

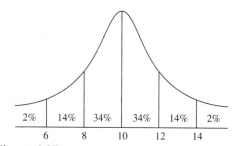

| 2% | 14% | 34% | 34% | 14% | 2% |

6   8   10   12   14

Figure 9.37

---

2. For a more detailed discussion of the applications and uses of the normal distribution, see *Statistics and Probability in Modern Life* by Joseph Newmark, 4th ed., chap. 8 (Philadelphia: Saunders College Publishing, 1988).

a) What percent of the employees had 8–12 accidents per year?

b) What percent of the employees had more than 8 accidents per year?

c) What percent of the employees had fewer than 8 accidents per year?

d) Approximately how many employees had between 6 and 14 accidents per year?

3. In a standard normal distribution, find the area

a) between $z = 0$ and $z = 2.78$

b) between $z = -0.91$ and $z = 0$

c) to the right of $z = 1.37$

d) to the left of $z = -1.98$

e) to the right of $z = 2.76$

f) between $z = -1.63$ and $z = 1.94$

g) between $z = -1.93$ and $z = 2.79$

h) between $z = -2.46$ and $z = 2.24$

4. Find the percentage of z-scores in a standard normal distribution that are

a) above $z = -1.69$

b) below $z = 2.83$

c) between $z = 0.89$ and $z = 3.01$

d) above $z = 2.01$

e) below $z = -2.86$

f) between $z = -2.27$ and $z = -1.49$

g) between $z = -2.08$ and $z = 2.81$

5. In a recent weight-lifting contest the average weight lifted was 215 lb with a standard deviation of 12 lb. Find the z-score of an individual who

a) lifted 227 lb   **b)** lifted 251 lb

c) lifted 191 lb   **d)** lifted 215 lb

6. Find the percentage of z-scores in a normal distribution with $\mu = 79$ and $\sigma = 4$ that are

a) between 75 and 83   **b)** between 81 and 84

c) less than 85   **d)** more than 76

7. In a recent experiment, numerous volunteers were given 5 different brands of beer and were asked to determine which beer maintained its head the longest. The volunteers rated the beers in terms of z-scores.

Brand	Rating
A	-1.12
B	3.72
C	1.59
D	0.18
E	-0.93

a) Rank these beers from highest to lowest.

b) Which brands were above average?

c) Which brands were below average?

8. A manufacturer claims that the outdoor paint being marketed by the company will require an average of 6 hours drying time with a standard deviation of 1.2 hours. Furthermore, the drying time is normally distributed. Find the probability that a house that is painted with this brand of paint will require more than 8 hours to dry.

9. According to medical officials, the number of hours elapsed before any reaction to a particular vaccination takes place is normally distributed with a mean of 36 hours and a standard deviation of 2.3 hours. Find the probability that a person who was given this vaccination will develop a reaction before 30 hours.

10. One brand of video game is manufactured by an automated process that gives the game an average useful life of 3000 hours with a standard deviation of 350 hours. The average useful life is known to be normally distributed. George buys one such video game. Find the probability that it will last between 2700 hours and 3500 hours.

11. Marjorie Johnson is the personnel director for the General's Department Store Chain. Each day she interviews prospective workers. It has been found that the number of minutes that she needs to interview an applicant is normally distributed with a mean of 20 minutes and a standard deviation of 4 minutes. What percentage of the time will it take Marjorie more than 25 minutes to interview an applicant?

12. Bank officials claim that the number of days required to process a mortgage application is normally distributed with a mean of 12 days and a standard deviation of 2.4 days. Martha has applied for a mortgage. Find the probability that it will be processed in at most 14 days.

Brain-Teaser Problems

**13. In a normal distribution with $\mu = 75$ and $\sigma = 11$, find the percentile rank of a score of

  a) 55   **b)** 61   **c)** 81   **d)** 70

**14. A certain normal distribution has mean $\mu = 40$ and unknown standard deviation σ. However, it is known that 30% of the area lies to the right of 50. Find σ.

**15. A certain normal distribution has an unknown mean, μ, with a standard deviation of 12.37. However, it is known that the probability that a score is less than 125 is 0.7123. Find μ.

**16. It is known that the lengths of sheets of a special kind of paper cut by a machine are normally distributed. Moreover, 8.08% of these papers are more than 15.948 inches in length and 18.67% of these papers are less than 15.2152 inches in length. Find the mean length and standard deviation of the length of a sheet of paper cut by this machine.

---

*9.6

LINEAR CORRELATION AND REGRESSION[3]

Many colleges require students to take a mathematics placement test before allowing them to enroll in any calculus courses. Presumably, a student who scores well on such a placement test is more likely to do better in a calculus course than a student who scores poorly on such an exam. College officials may be interested in determining the reliability of such tests. Furthermore, they may be interested in being able to predict a student's performance in the calculus course when his or her performance on the placement exam is known.

Similarly, many colleges administer vocational aptitude tests. The officials may be interested in knowing whether there is any relationship between the math aptitude score and the business aptitude score. Do students who score well on the math part of the aptitude exam also do well on the business part? If we know a student's math score, can we predict the student's business score? Questions of this nature frequently arise when we have many variables and are interested in determining relationships between them.

Sir Francis Galton, a cousin of Charles Darwin, undertook a detailed study of human characteristics. He was interested in determining whether a relationship exists between the heights of fathers and the heights of their sons. Do tall parents have tall children? Do intelligent parents or successful parents have intelligent or successful children? In *Natural Inheritance,* Galton introduced the idea that we today refer to as **correlation.** This mathematical idea allows us to measure the closeness of the relationship between two variables. Galton found that there exists a very close

correlation

---

3. Examples and exercises in this section should be solved with the aid of a hand-held calculator.

relationship between the heights of fathers and the heights of their sons. On the question of whether intelligent parents have intelligent children, it has been found that the correlation is 0.55. As we shall see, this means that it is not necessarily true that intelligent parents have intelligent children.

To understand what is meant by correlation, let us consider the different aptitude scores that were obtained by ten students at State Tech College as shown in the accompanying table. Is there any relationship between math aptitude scores and business aptitude scores? If a student scores well in math, will the student also score well in business or in language?

Student	Math score	Language score	Music score	Business score
A	44	75	20	40
B	70	31	9	72
C	32	22	50	31
D	49	11	17	50
E	51	19	24	49
F	63	67	13	59
G	28	31	54	24
H	26	48	57	27
I	49	53	23	49
J	52	26	22	48

scatter diagram
axes

We can analyze the situation pictorially by means of a **scatter diagram.** We simply draw two lines (called **axes**), one vertical and one horizontal. On one of these axes we indicate the math scores, and on the other we indicate the business scores. After both axes are labeled, we use a point to represent each student's score. The point is placed directly above the student's math score and directly to the right of the business score. Thus the point for student A's scores is placed directly above the 44 score on the math axis and to the right of 40 on the business axis. This is pictured in Fig. 9.38. In a similar manner we plot the other scores. You will notice that these points form an approximate straight line. When this happens, we say that there is a **linear correlation** between the two variables. Notice that the higher the math score, the higher is the business score. The line moves in a direction from lower left to upper right. When this happens, we say that there is a **positive correlation** between the math scores and the business scores. This means that a student with a higher math score will also have a higher business score.

linear correlation

positive correlation

Now let us draw the scatter diagram for the business aptitude scores and the music aptitude scores. It is given in Fig. 9.39. In this case you will

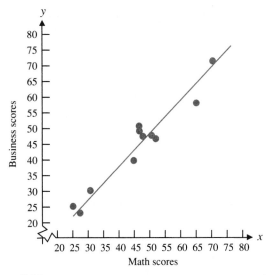

Figure 9.38
Scatter diagram for the math and business scores

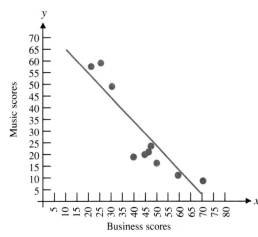

Figure 9.39
Scatter diagram for the business and music scores

notice that the higher the business score, the lower the music score. Again the points arrange themselves in the form of a line, but this time the line moves in a direction from upper left to lower right. When this happens, we say that there is a **negative correlation** between the business scores and the music scores. This means that a student with a high business score will have a low music score.

negative correlation

Now let us draw the scatter diagram for the language scores and the music scores. It is given in Figure 9.40. In this case the points do not form

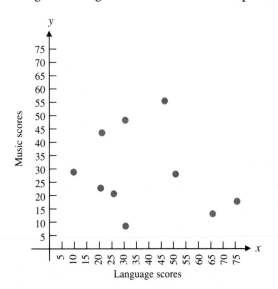

Figure 9.40
Scatter diagram for the language and music scores

zero correlation

a straight line. When this happens, we say that there is little or **zero correlation** between the language scores and the music scores.

Once we have determined that there is a linear correlation between two variables, we may be interested in determining the strength of the linear relationship. Karl Pearson developed a *coefficient of linear correlation,* which measures the strength of the relationship between two variables. The value of the coefficient of linear correlation is calculated by means of a formula.

coefficient of linear correlation

Formula 9.4   The **coefficient of linear correlation** is given by

$$r = \frac{n(\Sigma\, xy) - (\Sigma\, x)(\Sigma\, y)}{\sqrt{n(\Sigma\, x^2) - (\Sigma\, x)^2}\ \sqrt{n(\Sigma\, y^2) - (\Sigma\, y)^2}}$$

where

x = label for one of the variables,
y = label for the other variable,
n = number of pairs of scores.

When using Formula 9.4 the coefficient of correlation will always have a value between $+1$ and -1. A value of $+1$ means perfect positive correlation and corresponds to the situation in which all the dots lie exactly on a straight line. A value of -1 means perfect negative correlation and again corresponds to the situation in which all the points

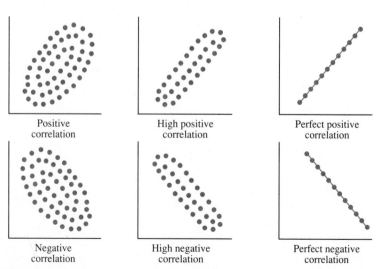

| Positive correlation | High positive correlation | Perfect positive correlation |
| Negative correlation | High negative correlation | Perfect negative correlation |

Figure 9.41

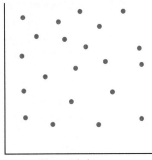

Figure 9.42   No correlation

lie exactly on a straight line. Correlation is considered high when it is close to $+1$ or -1 and low when it is close to 0. If the coefficient of linear correlation is 0, we say that there is no linear correlation. These possibilities are indicated in Figs. 9.41 and 9.42.

Although Formula 9.4 looks complicated, it is rather easy to use. The only new symbol that appears is $\Sigma\, xy$. This value is found by multiplying the corresponding values of x and y and then adding all the products. The following examples illustrate the procedure.

EXAMPLE 1

Find the coefficient of linear correlation between the business and music scores given here.

Business score	40	72	31	50	49	59	24	27	49	48
Music score	20	9	50	17	24	13	54	57	23	22

SOLUTION

We let x represent the business score and y the music score. Then we arrange the data in tabular form.

x	y	x^2	y^2	xy
40	20	1600	400	800
72	9	5184	81	648
31	50	961	2500	1550
50	17	2500	289	850
49	24	2401	576	1176
59	13	3481	169	767
24	54	576	2916	1296
27	57	729	3249	1539
49	23	2401	529	1127
48	22	2304	484	1056
$\Sigma x = 449$	$\Sigma y = 289$	$\Sigma x^2 = 22{,}137$	$\Sigma y^2 = 11{,}193$	$\Sigma xy = 10{,}809$

Now we use Formula 9.4. We have

$$r = \frac{n(\Sigma\, xy) - (\Sigma\, x)(\Sigma\, y)}{\sqrt{n(\Sigma\, x^2) - (\Sigma\, x)^2}\ \sqrt{n(\Sigma\, y^2) - (\Sigma\, y)^2}}$$

$$= \frac{10(10{,}809) - (449)(289)}{\sqrt{10(22{,}137) - 449^2}\ \sqrt{10(11{,}193) - 289^2}}$$

$$= \frac{-21{,}671}{\sqrt{19{,}769}\ \sqrt{28{,}409}} = \frac{-21{,}671}{(140.60)(168.55)}$$

$$= \frac{-21{,}671}{23{,}698.13} = -0.9145$$

Thus the coefficient of correlation is -0.9145. Since this value is close to -1, we say that there is a high degree of negative correlation. Fig. 9.39 also indicated this. ▪

EXAMPLE 2

A fire department official believes that as the temperature decreases, the number of fires increases. To support this claim, she has gathered the statistics shown in the table at the top of p. 537. Compute the coefficient of linear correlation and comment.

The fire official believes that as the temperature decreases the number of fires increases.

Temperature, x	40°	35°	30°	25°	20°	15°	10°	5°
Number of fires, y	33	37	40	44	56	60	61	71

SOLUTION

We arrange the data in tabular form.

x	y	x^2	y^2	xy
40	33	1600	1089	1320
35	37	1225	1369	1295
30	40	900	1600	1200
25	44	625	1936	1100
20	56	400	3136	1120
15	60	225	3600	900
10	61	100	3721	610
5	71	25	5041	355
$\Sigma x = 180$	$\Sigma y = 402$	$\Sigma x^2 = 5100$	$\Sigma y^2 = 21{,}492$	$\Sigma xy = 7900$

Now we use Formula 9.4. We have, with $n = 8$

$$r = \frac{n(\Sigma\, xy) - (\Sigma\, x)(\Sigma\, y)}{\sqrt{n(\Sigma\, x^2) - (\Sigma\, x)^2}\ \sqrt{n(\Sigma\, y^2) - (\Sigma\, y)^2}}$$

$$= \frac{8(7900) - (180)(402)}{\sqrt{8(5100) - 180^2}\ \sqrt{8(21{,}492) - 402^2}}$$

$$= \frac{-9160}{\sqrt{8400}\ \sqrt{10{,}332}} = \frac{-9160}{(91.65)(101.65)}$$

$$= -0.9832$$

Thus the coefficient of correlation is -0.9832, a rather high negative correlation. Therefore the data would seem to support the fire official's claim. ■

Although the coefficient of correlation is usually the first number that is calculated when we are given several sets of scores, great care must be used in interpreting the results. It can undoubtedly be said that among all the statistical measures discussed in this chapter the correlation coefficient is the one that is most misused. One reason for this is the assumption that because the two variables are related, a change in one will result in a change in the other. Frequently, two variables may appear to have a high correlation, even though they are not directly associated with each other. There many be a third variable that is highly correlated to these two variables.

Regression Lines

Once we determine that there is a correlation between two variables, we might be interested in finding the equation of the line that best fits the set of points. If a relationship in the form of an equation can be found between the two variables, we can use this equation to *predict* the value of one of the variables if the value of the other is known.

Students often use samples to make predictions. This is done in a somewhat less mathematical way. In the student page shown here from *Addison-Wesley Mathematics,* 1987, Grade 8, p. 362, students are asked to predict if there are enough acorns in the forest for the deer population. How accurate are such predictions?

APPLIED PROBLEM SOLVING

 There are about 150 deer who get much of their food from the acorns of an oak forest that they inhabit. You are helping a naturalist who needs to decide if there is enough food for the deer. To find the amount of acorns available, you take several samples from plots of one square meter and count the acorns in these samples.

Sample Plots (1 m²)	Number of Acorns
A	4
B	1
C	10
D	3
E	7
F	0
G	2
H	9

Some Things to Consider

- The oak forest covers about 4 km².
- About 450 kg of acorns are needed for each deer.
- Acorns weigh about 5 g each.
- The oak trees are fairly evenly distributed throughout the forest.

Some Questions to Answer

1. What is the number of square meters in the oak forest?

2. Which sample plot has the greatest number of acorns? Which sample plot has the least number of acorns?

3. Use sample plot D to estimate the number of acorns in the forest. Number of acorns = number in sample × area of forest in square meters.

4. Using sample plot D, about how many grams of acorns are there in the forest? How many deer would this feed?

5. What is the average number of acorns in all 8 samples?

What Is Your Decision?

Are there enough acorns in the forest for the deer population, or should some of the deer be resettled in other areas where there is a better supply of food?

Fitting a line to a set of numbers is by no means an easy task. Nevertheless, methods have been designed to handle such prediction problems. The **least squares method** determines the line in such a way that the sum of the squares of the y distances between the given points and the line is a minimum. Such a line is called a **regression line** of y on x.

least squares method

regression line

equation of the regression line

> **Formula 9.5** The **equation of the regression line** is given by
>
> $$y = mx + b$$
>
> where
>
> $$m = \frac{n(\Sigma\, xy) - (\Sigma\, x)(\Sigma\, y)}{n(\Sigma\, x^2) - (\Sigma\, x)^2}$$
>
> $$b = \frac{(\Sigma\, y)(\Sigma\, x^2) - (\Sigma\, x)(\Sigma\, xy)}{n(\Sigma\, x^2) - (\Sigma\, x)^2}$$
>
> and n is the number of pairs of scores.

Let us use Formula 9.5 in the next examples to find the regression equation connecting two variables. (There are many inexpensive calculators on the market today that accept entries of paired data and provide the values of m and b directly.)

EXAMPLE 3

Fifteen students have been receiving special instruction prior to taking a state civil service exam. In an effort to determine the effectiveness of the program, a comparison is made between the grade on the exam and the number of weeks each student received the special instruction. The results are given in the following table:

Number of weeks, x	0.50	0.75	1.00	1.25	1.50	1.75	2.00	2.25	2.50	2.75	3.00	3.25	3.50	3.75	4.00
Grade, y	57	64	59	68	74	76	79	83	85	86	88	89	90	94	96

a) Compute the correlation coefficient between x and y.

b) Find the regression equation that will predict a student's score if we know how many weeks of special instruction he or she received.

c) If a student receives 0.65 weeks of special instruction, what is the student's predicted score on the exam?

SOLUTION

We arrange the data in tabular form.

x	y	x^2	y^2	xy
0.50	57	0.2500	3249	28.50
0.75	64	0.5625	4096	48.00
1.00	59	1.0000	3481	59.00
1.25	68	1.5625	4624	85.00
1.50	74	2.2500	5476	111.00
1.75	76	3.0625	5776	133.00
2.00	79	4.0000	6241	158.00
2.25	83	5.0625	6889	186.75
2.50	85	6.2500	7225	212.50
2.75	86	7.5625	7396	236.50
3.00	88	9.0000	7744	264.00
3.25	89	10.5625	7921	289.25
3.50	90	12.2500	8100	315.00
3.75	94	14.0625	8836	352.50
4.00	96	16.0000	9216	384.00
$\Sigma x = 33.75$	$\Sigma y = 1188$	$\Sigma x^2 = 93.4375$	$\Sigma y^2 = 96{,}270$	$\Sigma xy = 2863.00$

a) To compute the coefficient of correlation, we use Formula 9.4;

$$r = \frac{n(\Sigma\, xy) - (\Sigma\, x)(\Sigma\, y)}{\sqrt{n(\Sigma\, x^2) - (\Sigma\, x)^2}\ \sqrt{n(\Sigma\, y^2) - (\Sigma\, y)^2}}$$

$$= \frac{15(2863) - (33.75)(1188)}{\sqrt{15(93.4375) - 33.75^2}\ \sqrt{15(96{,}270) - 1188^2}}$$

$$= \frac{2850}{\sqrt{262.5}\ \sqrt{32{,}706}} = \frac{2850}{(16.20)(180.85)}$$

$$= 0.9728$$

Thus the coefficient of correlation is 0.9728.

b) To find the regression equation, we must first calculate the values of m and b. We have

$$b = \frac{(\Sigma\, y)(\Sigma\, x^2) - (\Sigma\, x)(\Sigma\, xy)}{n(\Sigma\, x^2) - (\Sigma\, x)^2} = \frac{(1188)(93.4375) - (33.75)(2863.00)}{15(93.4375) - 33.75^2}$$

$$= \frac{14377.5}{262.5} = 54.77$$

$$m = \frac{n(\Sigma\, xy) - (\Sigma\, x)(\Sigma\, y)}{n(\Sigma\, x^2) - (\Sigma\, x)^2} = \frac{15(2863) - (33.75)(1188)}{15(93.4375) - 33.75^2} = \frac{2850}{262.5} = 10.86$$

Thus the regression equation predicting a student's score when we know how many weeks of special instruction he or she received is, using Formula 9.5,

$$y = mx + b$$
$$= 10.86x + 54.77$$

Therefore the regression equation is $y = 10.86x + 54.77$.

c) If the student receives 0.65 weeks of instruction, then $x = 0.65$. Substituting this value of x into the regression equation gives

$$y = 10.86x + 54.77$$
$$= 10.86(0.65) + 54.77$$
$$= 61.83$$

Thus the student's predicted score on the exam is 61.83.

EXAMPLE 4

As we indicated earlier, Galton believed that there exists a very close relationship between the heights of fathers and the heights of their sons. To test this claim, a scientist selects eight men at random and records their heights and the heights of their sons (in inches) as shown in the table.

Father, x	66	68	71	72	69	69	73	70
Son, y	63	66	70	74	70	68	73	70

a) Find the regression equation.

b) If a father is 74 inches tall, what is the predicted height of his son?

SOLUTION

We arrange the data in tabular form.

x	y	x^2	xy
66	63	4356	4158
68	66	4624	4488
71	70	5041	4970
72	74	5184	5328
69	70	4761	4830
69	68	4761	4692
73	73	5329	5329
70	70	4900	4900
$\Sigma\, x = 558$	$\Sigma\, y = 554$	$\Sigma\, x^2 = 38{,}956$	$\Sigma\, xy = 38{,}695$

a) To find the regression equation, we calculate the values of m and b. We have

$$b = \frac{(\Sigma\, y)(\Sigma\, x^2) - (\Sigma\, x)(\Sigma\, xy)}{n(\Sigma\, x^2) - (\Sigma\, x)^2} = \frac{(554)(38{,}956) - (558)(38{,}695)}{8(38{,}956) - 558^2}$$

$$= \frac{-10186}{284} = -35.87$$

$$m = \frac{n(\Sigma\, xy) - (\Sigma\, x)(\Sigma\, y)}{n(\Sigma\, x^2) - (\Sigma\, x)^2} = \frac{8(38{,}695) - (558)(554)}{8(38{,}956) - 558^2}$$

$$= \frac{428}{284} = 1.51$$

Thus the regression equation is

$$y = mx + b$$
$$= 1.51x - 35.87$$

b) If a father is 74 inches tall, then $x = 74$. Substituting this value of x into the regression equation gives

$$y = 1.51x - 35.87$$
$$= 1.51(74) - 35.87$$
$$= 75.87$$

Thus the predicted height of the son is 75.87 inches.   ■

After determining the least squares regression equation that predicts a value of y when x has a particular value, we may be interested in determining how the predicted value of y and the observed value of y compare. Quite often there may be large differences between the two.

Fortunately, statisticians have devised a method for measuring the differences between the predicted and the observed values. This is the **standard error of the estimate** and is given by the formula

standard error of the estimate

$$\sqrt{\frac{\Sigma(Y - Y_p)^2}{n - 2}}$$

where Y_p is the predicted value, Y is the observed value, and n is the number of pairs of scores.[4]

---

4. A complete discussion of this formula is beyond the scope of this book. The interested reader can find a detailed discussion in *Statistics and Probability in Modern Life* by Joseph Newmark, 4th ed., chap. 9 (Philadelphia: Saunders College Publishing, 1988).

Predicting with Sample Statistics

Jan wanted to find out what the 120 eighth-grade students in her school watched on TV.

Instead of asking every student, she took a **sample** of 30 students.

3 out of 30, or $\frac{1}{10}$, of the students in the sample watched the news special.

The same part of all the students would be expected to have watched the news special.

$$\frac{1}{10} \times 120 = 12$$

Sample   Total   Predicted
ratio   number   number

Jan can predict that about 12 students watched the news special.

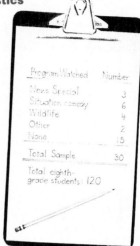

Program Watched	Number
News Special	3
Situation comedy	6
Wildlife	4
Other	2
None	15
Total Sample	30

Total eighth-grade students: 120

Other Examples

6 out of 30, or $\frac{1}{5}$, of the students in the sample watched a situation comedy.

$\frac{1}{5} \times 120 = 24$

About 24 out of 120 students would be predicted to have watched a situation comedy.

15 out of 30, or $\frac{1}{2}$, of the students in the sample did not watch TV.

$\frac{1}{2} \times 120 = 60$

About 60 out of 120 students would be predicted to have not watched TV.

Warm Up

Use the data in the sample above for exercises 1–4.

1. What fraction of the 30 students watched the wildlife program?

2. Predict the number of students out of 120 students that watched the wildlife program.

3. What fraction of the 30 students watched other programs?

4. Predict the number of students out of 120 students that watched other programs.

Children are taught to use statistics to make predictions, as can be seen above in the student page from *Addison-Wesley Mathematics*, 1987, Grade 7, p. 354.

> Statistics can also be used in making predictions and projections, as shown in the articles below. How are such projections made? Are they accurate?

Job Outlook For New Ph.D.s Very Bleak

WASHINGTON (Jan. 12)—Half of the people who obtained their doctorates though 1989 will be unable to get jobs suitable to their training, according to the latest projections released by the U.S. Bureau of Labor Statistics. This continues a trend that began with the end of the boom in the 1960s and reflects the continuing inability of our present economy to fully absorb these very highly educated people.

NATIONAL TIMES, January 12, 1989

	1950	1985	2020
POPULATION			
Ages 65-84 (in millions)	11.7	25.8	44.3
85 and over (in millions)	0.6	2.7	7.1
65 and over as % of total population	7.7%	12%	17.3%
LIFE EXPECTANCY			
Total	68.2	74.7	78.1
Male	65.5	71.2	74.2
Female	71.0	78.2	82.0
Black	60.7	69.5	75.5
White	69.0	75.3	78.5
FEDERAL SPENDING			
Pension and health-care payments as % of GNP	1.6%	9.3%	11.8%

EXERCISES FOR SECTION 9.6

1. *Advertising.* A cereal manufacturer has determined that sales of his cereals are influenced by the number of times per week that commercials advertising his product are seen on television as shown in the following table:

Number of times that commercial is seen, x	Sales of product, y (in millions of dollars)
7	85
10	87
11	92
12	93
14	95
17	98
19	100
25	110

a) Draw the scatter diagram for the data.
b) Compute the coefficient of correlation.
c) Find the regression equation.
d) If the commercial is televised 22 times per week, what is the predicted sales?

2. The City of Cornwall wishes to sell $175 million of 20-year bonds. The comptroller has approached several banks to act as underwriting syndicates. The comptroller has found that the number of banks expressing an interest in the bonds is dependent upon the annual rate of interest to be paid as shown in the accompanying table.

Interest rate, x	Number of banks, y
7%	8
8%	10
9%	12
10%	13
$10\frac{1}{2}$%	15
11%	16
$11\frac{1}{2}$%	17
12%	

a) Draw the scatter diagram for the data.
b) Compute the coefficient of correlation.

c) Find the regression equation.

d) If the annual interest rate is $9\frac{1}{2}\%$, what is the predicted number of banks that will participate in the underwriting?

3. *Height and Starting Salaries.* Numerous studies have shown that taller people land better jobs and make more money than shorter people. To investigate this claim further, Halsey and Cobb obtained the following data for numerous people who obtained identical jobs.

Height, x (in inches)	Average starting salary, y
65	$21,000
66	24,000
68	25,000
70	27,000
72	28,000
73	29,000
74	30,000

a) Draw the scatter diagram.

b) Compute the coefficient of correlation.

c) Find the regression equation.

d) What is the predicted starting salary of a person who is 69 inches tall?

4. Several scientists are experimenting with chemicals that generate heat as they are blended together. The temperature of the solution, y, measured in degrees Celsius is dependent upon the number of minutes elapsed, x, after the chemicals are mixed together as shown below:

Time, x	Temperature, y
1	80°
2	84°
4	85°
6	87°
9	90°
11	94°
12	95°
15	98°
17	100°

a) Compute the coefficient of correlation.

b) Find the regression equation.

c) What is the predicted temperature 10 minutes after the chemicals are mixed together?

5. *Age and Weight.* The following table shows the age and weights of boys in different age groups at the Carvano Elementary School.

Age, x (in years)	Weight, y (in lb)
5	55
6	58
7	63
8	67
9	69
10	75
11	79
12	85
13	90

a) Compute the coefficient of correlation.

b) Find the regression equation.

c) What is the predicted weight of a $10\frac{1}{2}$-year-old boy at this school?

6. Medical researchers at a hospital have found that the number of days required for post-operative convalescence in the hospital after undergoing a particular operation is directly related to the age of the patient as shown below:

Age of patients, x (in years)	Number of days, y
25	2
28	3
31	4
35	5
40	6
45	8
53	9
60	11
65	12

a) Compute the coefficient of correlation.

b) Find the regression equation.

c) What is the predicted number of days of convalescence for a patient who is 50 years old?

7. As a result of a new state bottling law, which requires that all soda bottles sold in the state be recycled, industry officials are uncertain as to how much deposit to charge for each bottle. Past experience in other states indicates that the percentage of bottles returned depends upon the amount of money required as a deposit as shown below:

Per bottle deposit charge, x (in cents)	Percentage of bottles returned, y
1	75
2	77
3	80
4	82
5	90
8	94
10	96

a) Compute the coefficient of correlation.

b) Find the regression equation.

c) What is the predicted percentage of bottles that will be returned if the per bottle deposit charge is 7¢?

8. According to city government officials, the number of new housing starts is dependent upon the prevailing mortgage rate of interest as shown below:

Prevailing mortgage rate of interest, x (in percent)	Monthly number of new housing starts in the city, y
8	112
9	109
10	103
11	94
12	79
13	60
14	48

a) Compute the coefficient of correlation.

b) Find the regression equation.

c) What is the predicted number of new housing starts if the mortgage rate of interest is $13\frac{1}{2}$%?

9. Local AAA records indicate that the number of calls for assistance depends upon the outside temperature and is greatest when the temperature is lowest as shown below:

Outside temperature (in °F), x	Average number of calls for assistance, y
40°	227
35°	240
30°	260
25°	290
20°	340
15°	400
10°	470
5°	550
0°	700

a) Compute the coefficient of correlation.

b) Find the regression equation.

c) If the outside temperature drops to 3°F, what is the predicted number of calls for assistance?

10. Health officials claim that as the quality of the air we breathe increases (on a scale from 1 to 10), then the reported number of cases of upper respiratory infections decreases as shown below:

Air quality, x	Number of reported cases, y
1	80
2	65
3	48
4	37
5	25
6	19
8	15
9	12
10	7

a) Find the regression equation.

b) If the air quality is 7, what is the predicted number of cases of upper respiratory infections that will be reported?

11. The accompanying table (based on data from *Official Used Car Prices*) lists the price of a particular used car and its age.

a) Find the regression equation.

b) If a car of this particular type is $4\frac{1}{2}$ years old, what is the predicted selling price of a car?

Age (in years), x	Suggested price, y
$\frac{1}{2}$	$8900
1	7975
$1\frac{1}{2}$	7400
2	6900
$2\frac{1}{2}$	6100
3	5600
$3\frac{1}{2}$	5000
4	4000
5	2800
$5\frac{1}{2}$	2100

9.7

MISUSES OF STATISTICS

Statistics can be very meaningful and useful when applied properly, but great care must be taken to make sure that we do not read too much into them. This is the job of the statistician. It is important to know the size and extent of the sample, whether it was selected randomly, the kinds of analysis used, and so on.

An interesting example of how statistics can be misused is the following: A university in Texas has three female faculty members in the mathematics department. Recently, one of them married one of her students. The student newspaper then printed an article under the following headline.

$33\frac{1}{3}$% OF OUR FEMALE MATHEMATICS FACULTY

MEMBERS MARRY THEIR STUDENTS

What, if anything, is wrong with this headline?

There are many other examples of how statistics can be misused. For example, consider the following argument. There were at least two automobile accidents for every driver per 10,000 miles driven during 1988. Also, there were two electrical storms during the year, but there were no airplane accidents during these storms. Can we conclude that it is safer to be in an airplane during an electrical storm than it is to drive a car at any time?

Sometimes statistics can lead to contradictory conclusions. For example, in 1970 the Nobel Prize winner Dr. Linus Pauling claimed, on the basis of statistical data that he had collected, that large doses of vitamin C

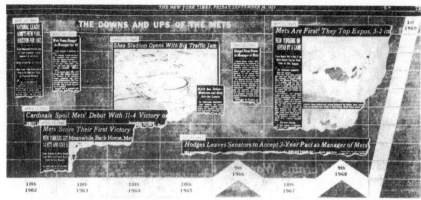

In April 1969 the *New York Times* stated that the Mets, who had finished tenth in the National League five times and ninth twice, were trying for third or fourth place that year but were not considered strong contenders. They won first place in 1969. Are statistics reliable information in making predictions?

are quite effective in preventing the occurrence of the common cold and also in reducing its severity. To test this claim, many other studies have been made. Specifically, several doctors at the University of Toronto's School of Hygiene conducted such a study during the winter of 1971–1972. They found that vitamin C had no significant effect in preventing colds but did seem to reduce the severity of colds. So in one respect the findings of the Toronto group contradicted those of Dr. Pauling, whereas in another respect they confirmed them.

Other studies have both supported and contradicted Dr. Pauling's results. Thus whether or not you believe that vitamin C is a "cure" for the common cold may depend on how you collect and interpret your statistics.

Different Horizontal and/or Vertical Scales

Consider the two graphs shown in Fig. 9.43. Both indicate how the crime rate has changed in a particular city over the past six years. One paints a more alarming picture than the other. Can you see why?

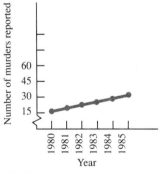

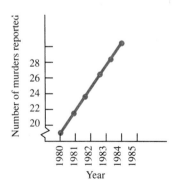

Figure 9.43

Correlation

Many people have applied a positive correlation to prove a cause-and-effect relationship that may not even exist. To illustrate the point, it has been shown that there is a high positive correlation between teachers' salaries and the use of drugs on campus. Does this mean that the more money a teacher earns, the more prevalent the use of drugs will be on campus?

Disregarding Unfavorable Data

Often statistics are used in the area of consumer products. For example, a drug manufacturer may be interested in claiming that 90% of the doctors surveyed recommend her particular product. She then has her advertising agent poll groups of 100 doctors until she finds a group in which the overwhelming majority use the product. The unfavorable results are then discarded.

Units Not Indicated

Consider the following headline that appeared in a local newspaper: "In 1984 Murder in Our City Increased by 100%." Upon careful analysis it was found that in 1983 there were four murders committed in a city of 5 million and in 1984 there were eight murders committed. Thus although the headline may be mathematically accurate, it definitely does give one the impression that crime is more widespread in the city than it actually is.

For further examples of how statistics can be misused or misinterpreted, see *How to Lie with Statistics* by Darrell Huff (New York: W. W. Norton, 1954).

TYPICAL CLASSROOM QUESTIONS

1. A company pays its workers the following salaries depending on title.

Title	Number of employees	Weekly salary
Manager	1	$500
Supervisor	3	300
Machinists	8	275
Other workers	14	200
Secretaries	4	150

Two students were asked to calculate the average. One student did as follows:

$$\mu = \frac{500 + 300 + 275 + 200 + 150}{5} = \frac{1425}{5} = \$285$$

This student then claimed that the average salary was $285 per week. A second student computed a **weighted arithmetic average** as follows:

$$\mu = \frac{1 \cdot 500 + 3 \cdot 300 + 8 \cdot 275 + 14 \cdot 200 + 4 \cdot 150}{30} = \frac{7000}{30} = \$233.33$$

He claimed that the average salary was $233.33. Which student is correct and why?

2. Two identical stereo components manufactured by two different companies were thoroughly tested to determine the useful life of each component. The following results were obtained.

	Average life	Standard deviation
Component manufactured by Company A	140 hours	7 hours
Component manufactured by Company B	135 hours	2 hours

Which stereo component would you buy? Explain your answer.

3. A worker reasons that the following statistics "prove" that there are only 60 working days in a year. What is wrong (if anything) with the proof?

$$
\begin{array}{rl}
365 \leftarrow & \text{days in a year} \\
- \ 60 \leftarrow & \text{two months vacation} \\
\hline
305 & \\
- \ 19 \leftarrow & \text{recognized national state holidays} \\
\hline
286 & \\
- 122 \leftarrow & \text{days sleeping (8 hours per day)} \\
\hline
164 & \\
- 104 \leftarrow & \text{52 weekends} \\
\hline
60 \leftarrow & \text{working days in a year}
\end{array}
$$

4. Professor Rogers teaches two sections of Math 21, a morning section and an afternoon section. Recently, Professor Rogers gave the same final examination to both classes. The following are the test results of the final examination.

	Morning section	Afternoon section
Average	75	85
Standard deviation	5	5
Number of students, n	60	58

Bill Southerly, who is in the morning section, and Jennifer Lockwood, who is in the afternoon section, both received grades of 90 on the final examination. A fellow student claims that since they both received the same grade of 90, then their performances are equal when compared to other students in their respective classes. Do you agree?

STUDY GUIDE

The following is a chapter outline in capsule form. You should now be able to demonstrate your knowledge of the ideas mentioned by giving definitions, descriptions, or specific examples. Page references are given in parentheses.

Descriptive statistics is the science of collecting, organizing, and summarizing numerical data. (p. 478)

A **sample** is a small group of individuals (or objects) selected to stand for a larger group, usually called the **population.** (p. 480)

For us to have a **random sample,** each individual in the population should have an equally likely chance of being selected. One way of accomplishing this is by using a **Table of Random Digits.** (p. 441)

Measures of Central Tendency (Numerical methods used to describe data)

The **mean** or **average** of a set of numbers is found by adding them together and dividing the total by the number of numbers added. (p. 482)

The **mode** of a set of numbers is the number (or numbers) that occurs most often. (p. 482)

If a set of numbers is arranged in order (from smallest to largest), then the number that is in the middle is called the **median.** If there is no middle number, then the median is the mean of the two middle numbers. (p. 482)

Summation notation is often used to find the mean. In this notation, Σ stands for the operation of adding a sequence of numbers. (p. 484)

If data are grouped according to different categories or classifications, then we have **grouped data.** (p. 484)

The **percentile rank** of a score is found by adding the percentages of scores below it to one-half of the percentage of scores equal to it. (p. 484)

The 25th percentile is called the **lower or first quartile.** (p. 488)

The 50th percentile is called the **median or middle quartile.** (p. 488)

The 75th percentile is called the **upper or third quartile.** (p. 488)

Measures of Variation

The **range** of a set of numbers is found by subtracting the smallest from the largest. (p. 492)

The **standard deviation** is equal to the square root of the variance. (p. 493)

The (population) **variance** is found by subtracting the mean from each value, squaring each of these differences, finding the sum of these squares, and dividing by $n,$ where n is the number of observations. (p. 494)

Instead of squaring the differences from the mean, we can take the absolute value of the differences and find the average of these absolute values. This gives the **Average Deviation.** (p. 495)

Data can be analyzed graphically. A **frequency distribution** is a convenient way of organizing data so that we may see what patterns they have. The word **frequency** is interpreted to mean how often a number occurs. (p. 499)

Different Graphs Discussed

1. **Bar graphs and histograms** (p. 506)
2. **Circle graphs, or pie charts** (p. 508)
3. **Line (segment) graphs** (p. 510)
4. **Pictograms or pictographs** (p. 511)
5. **Stem-and-leaf diagrams,** where the **stem** is the leading digit and the **leaf** is the trailing digit. (p. 513)
6. **The normal curve** and the **normal distribution**, where 68% of the values are within one standard deviation of the mean, 95.4% are within two standard deviations of the mean, and 99.7% are within three standard deviations of the mean. (p. 521) A **standard normal distribution** is a normal distribution with a mean of 0 and a standard deviation of 1. (p. 523)
7. **Scatter Diagrams** can be used to determine if there is any correlation (positive, negative, or zero) between two variables. (p. 532)

The **coefficient of linear correlation** can be used to measure the strength of the relationship between two variables. (p. 534)

The **least-squares method** determines a regression line in such a way that the sum of the squares of the y distances between the given points and the line is a minimum. (p. 539)

The differences between a predicted value and an observed value can be measured by computing the **standard error of the estimate.** (p. 542)

KEY TERMS

The following list presents the key terms introduced in this chapter.

9.1 sample
population
random
table of random digits

9.2 mean or average
median
mode
measures of central tendency
summation notation
grouped data
percentile
percentile rank
lower (first) quartile
middle quartile
upper (third) quartile
decile

9.3 range
standard deviation

variance
average deviation

9.4 frequency distribution
bar graph
histogram
circle graph
pie charts
line graph
line segment graphs
pictograph
pictograms
stem-and-leaf diagrams
stem (leading digits)
leaf (trailing digit)

9.5 normal curve
normal distribution
area under normal curve

standard normal distribution
z-score
z-value

9.6 correlation
scatter diagram
axes
linear correlation
positive correlation
negative correlation

zero correlation
coefficient of linear
correlation
least-squares method
regression line
equation of regression
line
standard error of the
estimate

FORMULAS TO REMEMBER

The following list summarizes the formulas given in this chapter.

Mean
Median
Mode
$\Bigg\}$ See pp. 482–484   Also $\mu = \dfrac{\Sigma x}{n}$

Percentile rank of $X = \dfrac{B + \frac{1}{2}E}{n} \cdot 100$

Standard deviation
Variance
Average deviation
$\Bigg\}$ See pp. 491–496

Range = largest number – smallest number.

z-score or z-value: $z = \dfrac{x - \mu}{\sigma}$

Coefficient of linear correlation:

$$r = \frac{n(\Sigma\, xy) - (\Sigma\, x)(\Sigma\, y)}{\sqrt{n(\Sigma\, x^2) - (\Sigma\, x)^2}\ \sqrt{n(\Sigma\, y^2) - (\Sigma\, y)^2}}$$

Regression equation: $y = mx + b$ where

$$b = \frac{(\Sigma\, y)(\Sigma\, x^2) - (\Sigma\, x)(\Sigma\, xy)}{n(\Sigma\, x^2) - (\Sigma\, x)^2}$$

$$m = \frac{n(\Sigma\, xy) - (\Sigma\, x)(\Sigma\, y)}{n(\Sigma\, x^2) - (\Sigma\, x)^2}$$

Standard error of the estimate: $\sqrt{\dfrac{\Sigma\,(Y - Y_p)^2}{n - 2}}$

CHAPTER REVIEW EXERCISES

1. The proportion of area under the normal curve from $z = 0.4$ to $z = 0.7$ is

   a) 0.1554   **b)** 0.2580   **c)** 0.4134   **d)** 0.1026   **e)** none of these

For questions 2–4, use the following information: Dr. James Conway is a cardiologist. The following chart shows the number of patients that Dr. Conway visited in the hospital and also the number of hours that Dr. Conway spent at the hospital.

Number of hours, x	Number of patients, y
4	15
5	20
8	25
10	30
11	31

2. Find the coefficient of correlation for this data.

3. Find the least squares prediction equation, that is, regression equation.

4. What is the predicted number of patients that Dr. Conway will see if he spends 9 hours at the hospital?

5. The area under a standardized normal curve below $z = 2.45$ is

   a) 0.0071   **b)** 0.4929   **c)** 0.9929   **d)** 0.4918   **e)** none of these

6. If $x_1 = 12$, $x_2 = 13$, $x_3 = 17$, $x_4 = 21$, and $x_5 = 25$, find

   a) Σx^2 **b)** $(\Sigma x)^2$

7. In a standard normal distribution, which z-score cuts off the top 13%?

8. A correlation coefficient of -0.15

   a) indicates a strong negative correlation

   b) indicates a weak negative correlation

   c) is impossible

   d) is insignificant

   e) none of these

9. What type of correlation exists between lung cancer and smoking?

   a) strong negative correlation

   b) zero correlation

   c) positive correlation

   d) depends upon the individual

   e) none of these

10. On a recent dancing skills test, the mean was 250 and the standard deviation was 25. What percent of the contestants scored *below* 225?

    a) 68.16%   **b)** 15.87%   **c)** 34.13%   **d)** 84.13%   **e)** none of these

11. Marianne is one of 50 players on a volleyball team. In one particular tournament she performs better than exactly 36 players on the team, and 12 players perform better than her. What is her percentile rank?

12. Consider the distribution 16, 12, 8, 4. The standard deviation of this distribution is

   a) 5   **b)** $\sqrt{5}$ **c)** 20   **d)** $\sqrt{20}$ **e)** none of these

13. Consider a distribution where $\mu = 10$ and $\sigma = 3$. The z-score of 10 is

   a) 0   **b)** 10   **c)** 3   **d)** 9   **e)** 1

14. In a normal distribution, the median is at

   a) $z = -1$ **b)** $z = 0$ **c)** $z = +1$ **d)** $z = 0.5$ **e)** none of these

15. In a certain health club the weights of the members are normally distributed with a mean of 160 lb and a standard deviation of 10 lb. The percentage of members whose weights are above 170 lb is approximately

   a) 16   **b)** 14   **c)** 34   **d)** 84   **e)** none of these

16. The number of births and the number of deaths for a small midwestern city during the first five days of February were as follows:

Number of births, x	Number of deaths, y
4	7
7	9
5	6
9	11
6	8

Find the coefficient of correlation for this data.

17. The circle graph shown here gives the breakdown of the 500 vehicles parked in a city-owned garage.

   a) How many vehicles are trucks?

   b) How many vehicles are subcompact cars?

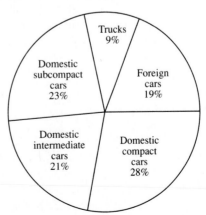

18. A new computer terminal is to be installed on the tenth floor of a large office building to serve the needs of the numerous offices located on the floor. In an effort to determine where the machine should be placed, a list is made of the distance from each office to one particular spot. The mean, median, and modal distances are then computed. Which of these *average* distances would be more helpful in deciding where the terminal should be placed? Explain your answer.

19. Consider the accompanying newspaper clipping. Explain why the median is used when discussing age, salary and number of years teaching experience.

New York State Public School Teachers

	1976–77	1981–82
Median	37	39
Median Salary	$17,150	$23,437
Median Number of Years	11	14
Total Education Experience	9	13
Local District Experience		
Percent with:	58%	65%
Master's Degree	85%	87%
Permanent Certification		
Percent:	59%	61%
Female	41%	39%
Male		
Number of teachers	173,975	168,516

Source: New York State Education Department, Bureau of Basic Educational Data System (BEDS)

20. *Birth and Death Rates.* The birth and death rates for several countries are given in the accompanying table. Draw the bar graph to picture this information.

Country	Birth rate	Death rate
Egypt	34.8	13.1
Israel	27.2	7.1
Japan	19.4	6.6
France	16.4	10.7
Philippines	24.8	7.3
Mexico	44.7	9.1
United States	15.0	9.4
USSR	17.7	8.7
Puerto Rico	24.1	6.7

21. *Natural Resources.* Although the United States had 6% of the world population, it consumes very high percentages of the world production of certain materials as shown in the accompanying table. Draw a bar graph to picture this information.

Material	Percentage
Natural gas	57
Silver	42
Aluminum	36
Petroleum	32
Tin	32
Nickel	30
Copper	27
Steel	19

22. *Interest Rates.* The following line graph shows the interest rates paid on short-term loans over the years. Is it true that interest rates are highest during a recession? Explain your answer.

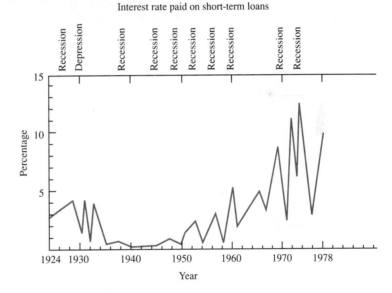

Source: Federal Reserve Board, U.S. Dept. of Commerce

23. *Stolen Cars.* The following pictograph indicates the number of cars that were reported stolen in a city over the past six years. By how many cars did the number of reported stolen cars in 1984 exceed the number of reported stolen cars in 1979?

1979	
1980	
1981	
1982	
1983	
1984	
1985	

Note: Each symbol represents 10,000 cars

24. *Stay in School.* According to one study, the average salary of an individual in a certain state is influenced by the number of years of schooling beyond high school that the individual has as shown below:

Number of years of schooling beyond high school, x	Average salary, y
0	$11,150
1	14,000
2	16,500
3	17,880
4	19,150
5	24,000
6	29,000

Find the regression equation.

25. Refer back to question 24. Find the predicted salary of an individual who has completed $4\frac{1}{2}$ years of schooling beyond high school.

SUGGESTED FURTHER READING

Bestgen, B., "Making and Interpreting Graphs and Tables: Results and Implications from National Assessment," in *The Arithmetic Teacher* **28** (December 1980), 26–29.

Book, S., *Statistics: Basic Techniques for Solving Applied Problems.* New York: McGraw-Hill, 1977.

Christopher, L., "Graphs Can Jazz Up The Mathematics Curriculum," in *The Arithmetic Teacher* **30** (September 1982), 28–30.

Collis, B., "Teaching Descriptive and Inferential Statistics Using a Classroom Microcomputer," in *The Mathematics Teacher* **76** (May 1983), 318–322.

Haylock, D., "A Simplified Approach to Correlation," in *The Mathematics Teacher* **76** (May 1983), 332–336.

Huff, D., *How To Lie With Statistics.* New York: W.W. Norton, 1954.

Jamski, W., "Introducing Standard Deviation," in *The Mathematics Teacher* **74** (March 1981), 197–198.

Johnson, E., "Bar Graphs for First Graders," in *The Arithmetic Teacher* **29** (December 1981), 30–31.

Kimberling, C., "Mean, Standard Deviation, and Stopping the Stars," in *The Mathematics Teacher* **77** (November 1984), 633–636.

MacDonald, A., "A Stem-Leaf Plot : An Approach to Statistics," in *The Mathematics Teacher* **75** (January 1982), 25, 27, 28.

Newmark, J., *Statistics and Probability in Modern Life, Fourth Edition,* New York: Saunders College Publishing Company, 1988.

Shuttle, A., "A Case for Statistics," in *The Arithmetic Teacher,* **26** (February 1979), 24.

Tanur, J.M., F. Mosteller, W. H. Kruskul, R. F. Link, R. S. Pieters, and G.R. Rising, *Statistics: A Guide to the Unknown.* San Francisco: Holden-Day, 1978.

Tukey, J. W., *Exploring Data Analysis.* Reading, MA: Addison-Wesley, 1977.

CHAPTER 10

Introduction to Geometry

NCTM GUIDELINES

In its March 1989 *Curriculum And Evaluation Standards For School Mathematics* (p. 112), The National Council Of Teachers Of Mathematics recommends that the mathematics curriculum should include the study of the geometry of one, two, and three dimensions in a variety of situations so that students can

- ☐ identify, describe, compare, and classify geometric figures,
- ☐ visualize and represent geometric figures with special attention to developing spatial sense,
- ☐ explore transformations of geometric figures,
- ☐ represent and solve problems using geometric models,
- ☐ understand and apply geometric properties and relationships,
- ☐ develop an appreciation of geometry as a means of describing the physical world.

The study of geometry helps students represent and make sense of the world. Since geometric skills and concepts are essential to the process of problem solving, a primary problem-solving strategy should be the drawing of a picture or a diagram, which is, in many situations, a geometric representation of the problem. The following three samples illustrate this point.

A dog is tied to a 5-meter rope at the middle of the side of a garage. The side of the garage is 10 meters long. Make a sketch and use centimeter grid paper to estimate the area and shape of the ground on which the dog can walk.

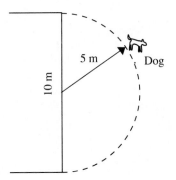

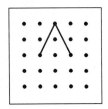

The diagram at the left (top) is part of a closed figure. Complete it so that it has two lines of symmetry.

Using the diagram at the left (bottom), make another shape that intersects this one to form a rectangle.

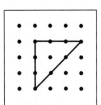

Students can explore what happens when they connect the midpoints of the sides of several quadrilaterals. Their discovery that a parallelogram is formed can prompt them to raise such questions as what quadrilateral they would start with so that the new figure is a square, or a rhombus. Computer software (such as LOGO) that allows students to construct geometric figures creates a rich environment for the investigation of geometrical properties and relationships.

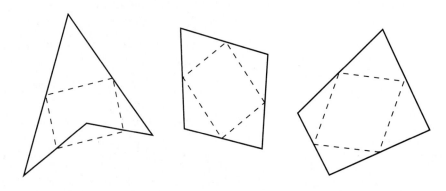

Experience with geometry should sensitize students to looking at the world around them in a more meaningful way. It is for this reason that in this chapter we study various geometrical ideas and the LOGO computer language.

Innovative Approaches in Geometry

March 1: We all know that the construction industry uses geometric ideas on a daily basis. However, with the widespread availability of microcomputers, students should find the task of studying geometry considerably easier. The abundance of computer graphics software today allows students to create and manipulate different geometrical figures and shapes.

Computer microworlds, such as the LOGO graphics, enable students to determine, for example, whether a polygon can be used to tile a plane. Such tiling, or more technically tessellations, can be used to create the Escher-type tessellations shown below.

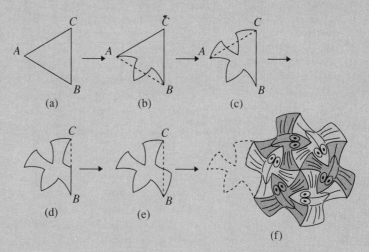

These advances in technology should increase the student's interest in geometry and provide an opportunity for them to experience the creative interplay between math and art, or more generally to discover the relevance of geometry in our world.

THE GREENVIEW EDUCATOR, March 7, 1989

The article above indicates that geometry has very important applications in our daily lives and that computer graphics enable us to study and accurately visualize many geometric figures and properties. The LOGO turtle plays an important role in this process. In this chapter, we will introduce the important LOGO graphics program.

Introduction

The importance of geometry can be seen in the wide-ranging and ever-growing application of its concepts. For example, when the U.S. Mint produces dimes, it tries to make them all the same size and shape. (This idea is known as **congruence**, and we will have more to say about

HISTORICAL NOTE

The Babylonians and Egyptians developed considerable skill in practical geometry, that is, in calculating areas, volumes, etc. They also knew such facts as certain special cases of the Pythagorean theorem. However, the geometric knowledge of the Babylonians and Egyptians was just a collection of facts accumulated through practical experience. The Greeks were the first people to undertake a formal study of geometry.

While there were many great Greek mathematicians, one of the best known was Euclid (about 300 B.C.). Although Euclid was a Greek, he was a mathematics professor at the University of Alexandria in Egypt. The story is told of a student who asked Euclid of what use it was to study geometry (a question quite familiar to all mathematics teachers). In reply, Euclid gave the student three pennies, since "he must make gain of what he learns."

Euclid's greatness lies not so much in his discovering new truths of geometry, but rather in his showing that all the known facts could be obtained from a few simple assumptions, using deductive logic. The modern high school geometry course is based on Euclid's *Elements*.

it later.) If you decide to carpet your home, you need some basic geometry in computing the number of square feet of carpet to buy. When railroad tracks are laid, we see geometry at work in the plan for them. It is necessary that they be the same distance apart everywhere. (When they are, they are then said to be **parallel**.)

Because geometry is so useful and necessary, it was one of the first branches of mathematics to be seriously studied. The science of geometry dates back at least to the ancient Babylonians and Egyptians, who needed it for the measurement of land for taxation purposes and for building. The precision with which the pyramids were built clearly indicates the Egyptians' skill with geometry. Geometry was also used in studying astronomy, which was, in turn, important in constructing calendars.

During the eighteenth century in the city of Königsberg (formerly in Prussia) there was an island surrounded by the river Pregel. This river was crossed by seven bridges as shown in Fig. 10.1. On pleasant afternoons the citizens of Königsberg would amuse themselves with the following problem. Could anyone walk across *all* seven bridges without crossing any of the bridges twice? No one had ever been able to do it. Whenever anyone attempted it, either one bridge was not crossed at all or else one bridge had to be crossed more than once. Eventually, the citizens of Königsberg came to believe that it was impossible to do this, but they did not know why. The Swiss mathematician Leonhard Euler heard about the problem. Not only did he solve it, but in doing so he laid the basis for a whole new branch of mathematics called **topology**. Today topology is an important and growing field of mathematics with wide-ranging applications.

In this chapter we will discuss some of the basic concepts of geometry, the work of Euclid, and also two other interesting geometries that differ from Euclid's in some of the basic assumptions. Also, we will examine the

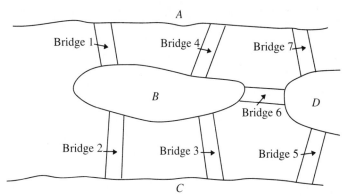

Figure 10.1

basic ideas of topolgy and discuss several interesting applications of these ideas, such as the Königsberg Bridge problem, the conveyor belt problem, and the Möbius strip.

10.1

POINTS, LINES, AND PLANES

The word **geometry** comes from the Greek *ge* meaning "earth" and *metria* meaning "measurement." Early humans observed that certain shapes, such as triangles, rectangles, circles, and surfaces, occurred frequently in nature. The study of geometry began with people's need to measure and understand the properties of these shapes.

Suppose you were asked "What is a triangle?" You would probably say that a triangle is a figure bounded by three straight lines. This definition depends on your knowing what a line is. What exactly is a line? Everyone, of course, has an idea of what a line is. You could draw one if asked to do so, but could you describe a line in words?

Line

A **line** is often said to be a collection of points. However, understanding such a definition depends on your knowing what a point is. Moreover, the definition does not distinguish between lines and other geometric figures that can be thought of as collections of points. For example, a plane (flat surface) is also a collection of points.

Another definition of a line that is often given is that it is the shortest distance between two points. Again this depends on your knowing what a point is. It also depends on what is meant by "distance" and how it is measured. This definition is "circular."

No matter how we try to define a line, we encounter similar problems. Therefore although we all know what a line is, we do not attempt to define it formally. We accept it as an *undefined term*.

Point

Now let us consider the term **point**. What is a point? The following definitions have been suggested.

1. A point is a dot.

2. A point is a location in space.

3. A point is something that has no length, breadth, or thickness.

If we analyze these definitions, we see that none of them is really satisfactory. Dots have varying thicknesses and can be measured with a precise instrument (and a magnifying glass). Thus when speaking of a point, we would have to specify what size dot we mean. This would involve measurement and length. Obviously, this is not what we want.

We can make similar objections to the other definitions. Therefore we accept point as another *undefined term*.

undefined terms

In mathematics, as in language in general, when we try to define a term, we find that the definition depends on other terms, which in turn must also be defined. Ultimately, we see that we must start with some basic terms that we do not define. These are called **undefined terms**. All other definitions are based on them. In geometry, point and line are undefined terms, as we have stated.

Mathematicians did not always recognize the need for undefined terms. In fact, the most famous geometry book of the ancient world, Euclid's *Elements*, opens with twenty-three definitions. Many of these definitions involve other terms that have not been defined. As a result, they do not really define anything. For example, Euclid defines "point" as "that which has no part." However, no definition of what is meant by "part" is given. The modern mathematician recognizes the fact that we cannot define everything, and so we must start with some undefined terms, such as "point" or "line."

Because pictures are so useful in mathematics, a *point* is represented by a dot. The smaller we make the dot, the better it will represent the mathematical idea of a point.

Although the term *line* (by line, we will always mean a straight line) is undefined, it has certain important properties, which we now state.

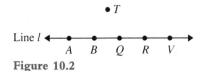

Line *l*

Figure 10.2

collinear

1. *A line is a set of points in space.* The points of the line are said to lie on the line, and the line is said to contain them or pass through them. Points that lie on the same line are said to be **collinear**. In Fig. 10.2 the line *l* is drawn with arrows pointing in both directions. This indicates that the line can be extended indefinitely in either direction. The points *A*, *B*, *Q*, *R*, and *V* all lie on the line *l*. They are collinear. Point *T* does not lie on the line *l*.

Notation   Lines will be denoted by lowercase letters such as *l*, *m*, *n*, ... Points are denoted by capital letters. A line passing through two points, say

P

Left half-line   Right half-line

Figure 10.3

half-line

end-point

ray

line segment

A and *B*, can be denoted as $\overleftrightarrow{AB}$. The line of Fig. 10.2 can be denoted as line *l*, $\overleftrightarrow{AB}$, $\overleftrightarrow{AQ}$, $\overleftrightarrow{QV}$, $\overleftrightarrow{AV}$, etc.

2. *Given any two different points in space, there is exactly one line passing through these two points.*

3. *Any point on a line divides a line into two parts.* Each of these parts is called a **half-line**. The dividing point is known as the **end-point** of the half-line. The dividing point is not included in either of the half-lines. (See Fig. 10.3.)

> **Definition 10.1**   A half-line, together with its dividing point, is known as a **ray**.

There will be many times when we will be interested in only certain finite parts of a line rather than either the whole line or the ray. For this reason we introduce the following definition.

> **Definition 10.2**   Any two points *A* and *B* on a line, together with all the points on the line that lie between them, are called a **line segment**. We denote it by $\overline{AB}$.

EXAMPLE 1

A computer-drawn geometric figure.

The different terms and notations are illustrated below.

Description	Picture	Symbol
Line *AB*	*A* *B*	$\overleftrightarrow{AB}$
Ray *AB*	*A* *B*	$\overrightarrow{AB}$
Ray *BA*	*A* *B*	$\overrightarrow{BA}$
Line segment *AB*	*A* *B*	$\overline{AB}$

A solid dot, •, means that the point is to be included. An open dot, ○, means that the point is not to be included.

Notice the difference between ray $\overrightarrow{AB}$ and ray $\overrightarrow{BA}$. Ray $\overrightarrow{AB}$ starts at point A and extends in the direction of point B. Ray $\overrightarrow{BA}$ starts at point B and extends in the direction of point A.   ▬

intersecting lines

Two different lines that contain the same point are said to **intersect** at the point. Lines l and m of Fig. 10.4 intersect at point P. Both lines contain this point.

Plane

A **plane** can be thought of as a flat surface, such as the page of this book or the floor in your room. Mathematically, the word *plane* is an undefined term. Planes also have certain important properties.

1. *A plane is a set of points.* We say that the points are on the plane and that the plane contains them. Points that are on the same plane are said to be **coplanar**.

coplanar points

2. *Any three noncollinear points determine one and only one plane.* The plane of Fig. 10.5 contains the three points A, P, and Q. This is the only plane that can contain these three points.

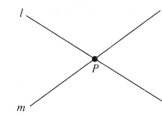

Figure 10.4

We have all seen four-legged tables that wobble because one of the legs is longer or shorter than the other three. This happens because the table can be steady only if all four feet are on the plane of the floor. When one leg is longer or shorter than the others, then the four feet do not lie in the same plane (the floor) and the table wobbles. A three-legged table is much more likely to be steady because it has only three feet and these three feet will always lie on some plane.

3. *If two points of a line are on a plane, then the whole line is on the plane.*

4. *A line on a plane divides the plane into two parts called **half-planes**.* The line does not belong to either of the half-planes. In Fig. 10.6, line l divides the plane into two half-planes.

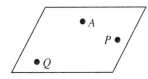

Figure 10.5

5. *If we are given two planes, then they either meet in a line or do not meet at all.* Planes that do not meet at all are called **parallel planes**.

half-planes

parallel planes

Figure 10.7 shows two planes intersecting in line l. Figure 10.8 shows two parallel (nonintersecting) planes. The ceiling and floor of your room are examples of parallel planes. The ceiling and walls of your room are examples of intersecting planes.

Parallel Lines

If we are given two lines in the same plane that *never* meet, then such lines are called **parallel lines**. Railroad tracks are an example of parallel lines. The edges of the pages of this book are another example of parallel lines. If line l and line m are parallel, we write this as $l \parallel m$; that is, the symbol "$\parallel$" stands for "is parallel to."

Parallel lines have played an important role in the development of geometry, as we shall see later.

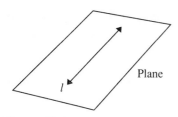

Figure 10.6

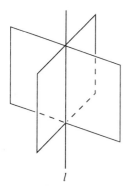

Figure 10.7

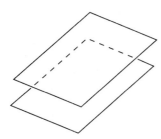

Figure 10.8

Some of the basic figures used in geometry today can be identified in everyday real-world situations. This can be seen in this student page from *Addison-Wesley Mathematics*, 1987, Grade 5, p. 272, where students are presented with several photos which suggest basic geometric ideas.

Points, Lines, and Segments

Leon's photography club had a photo contest. Prizes were given for the best pictures of "Geometry in Our World." Some of the photos are used below to suggest some basic geometric ideas.

A pin showing a location on a map suggests a **point**.
We write: P
We say: "point P"

The trail of a jet plane, which seems unending in both directions, suggests a **line**.
We write: $\overleftrightarrow{AB}$ or ℓ
We say:
"line AB" or "line ℓ"

The edge of a box suggests a part of a line called a **segment**.
We write: $\overline{AB}$
We say:
"segment AB"

The diagonal boards on a fence suggest **intersecting lines**.
We write:
ℓ intersects m
We say:
"Line ℓ intersects line m."

The railroad tracks suggest **parallel lines**.
We write: j ∥ k
We say:
"Line j is parallel to line k."

The two strings that form square corners suggest **perpendicular lines**
We write: r ⊥ s
We say:
"Line r is perpendicular to line s."

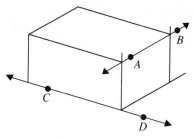

Figure 10.9

Two lines that do not lie in the same plane and that do intersect are called **skew lines**. In Fig. 10.9, lines $\overleftrightarrow{AB}$ and $\overleftrightarrow{CD}$ are skewed lines.

The **distance** between any two points A and B on a line is the nonnegative difference of the real numbers a and b on a real number line to which A and B correspond. In Fig. 10.10 the distance from A to B, written as AB or BA, is often expressed in terms of the numbers a and b. These numbers are known as the **coordinates** of A and B on $\overleftrightarrow{AB}$.

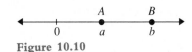

Figure 10.10

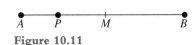

Figure 10.11
M is the midpoint of line segment $\overline{AB}$

skew lines
distance
coordinates
midpoint of line segment

In Fig. 10.11 point P is between points A and B. This means that the coordinates of P with reference to line segment $\overline{AB}$ are numerically between the coordinates of A and B. Point M is called the **midpoint** of line segment $\overline{AB}$ if it is equidistant from points A and B, that is if $AM = MB$.

EXERCISES FOR SECTION 10.1

For Exercises 1–8, refer to the line shown in Fig. 10.12 with the indicated points. Find each of the following:

1. $\overline{CA} \cap \overline{BC}$ **2.** $\overline{AD} \cap \overline{BC}$

3. $\overline{BC} \cup \overline{AB}$ **4.** $\overrightarrow{AB} \cap \overline{AD}$

5. $\overrightarrow{AB} \cap \overline{BC}$ **6.** $\overleftrightarrow{AB} \cup \overleftrightarrow{CD}$

7. $\overline{AD} \cup \overline{BC}$ **8.** $\overrightarrow{BC} \cup \overrightarrow{CD}$

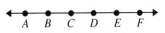

Figure 10.12

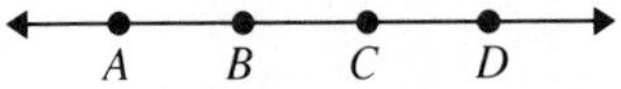

For Exercises 9–18, refer to the line shown in Fig. 10.13 with the indicated points. Find each of the following.

9. $\overline{AB} \cap \overline{BC}$ **10.** $\overline{AB} \cup \overline{BC}$

11. $\overrightarrow{AB} \cap \overline{CD}$ **12.** $\overrightarrow{DC} \cup \overrightarrow{DE}$

13. $\overrightarrow{DC} \cap \overrightarrow{DE}$ **14.** $\overleftrightarrow{AB} \cap \overline{CD}$

15. $\overrightarrow{FE} \cap \overrightarrow{EA}$ **16.** $\overline{EF} \cap \overline{AB}$

17. $\overline{BC} \cup \overline{DE}$ **18.** $\overrightarrow{BC} \cup \overline{EF}$

For Exercises 19–26, refer to Fig. 10.14 with the indicated points. Find each of the following:

19. $\overline{BC} \cup \overline{CD}$ **20.** $\overline{BC} \cup (\overline{CD} \cup \overline{BD})$

21. $\overline{BC} \cap \overline{CD}$ **22.** $\overrightarrow{BC} \cap \overrightarrow{AD}$

Figure 10.13

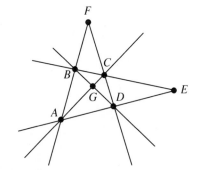

Figure 10.14

23. $(\overline{AB} \cup \overline{BC}) \cup (\overline{CD} \cup \overline{DA})$ **24.** $\overrightarrow{BC} \cap \overrightarrow{AC}$

25. $(\overline{AB} \cup \overline{BC}) \cap \overline{BD}$ **26.** $\overline{AD} \cup \overline{DC}$

27. How many different lines can be drawn connecting three different noncollinear points?

28. How many different lines can be drawn connecting four different noncollinear points that lie on the same plane?

29. If two parallel planes, plane 1 and plane 2, both intersect a third plane in two lines l and m, must lines l and m necessarily be parallel? Explain your answer.

PROBLEM-SOLVING EXERCISES

30. Using inductive reasoning, determine the greatest number of points in which n distinct lines can intersect.
(*Hint:* Consider the following facts.)

31. Consider any line l and a point A not on l. How many lines can be drawn that intersect line l and that pass through point A?

32. Suppose that we have two intersecting lines on plane 1 and that both lines are parallel to plane 2. Is plane 1 parallel to plane 2?

33. If two distinct lines are parallel to a third line in space, must the lines be parallel to each other?

34. Can the intersection of three planes ever be a single point? Explain your answer.

**35. Prove the following statements:

a) Two distinct lines that intersect form a plane.

Situation	Diagram	Greatest number of points of intersection
2 distinct lines		1
3 distinct lines		3
4 distinct lines		6
5 distinct lines		10

b) A line and a point not on the line determine a plane.
(*Hint:* Use property 2 about planes given on page 568.)

**36. How many different lines can be drawn connecting four different points that do not lie on the same plane if no three of the points are collinear?

**37. Is it possible to have two lines on the same plane that are not parallel and that do not intersect? Explain your answer. What if the lines are on different planes?

**38. If *l* is a line in plane *P*, *m* is a line in plane *Q*, and plane *P* is parallel to plane *Q*, then is line *l* parallel to line *m*?

**39. Suppose we are given four different points, *A*, *B*, *C*, and *D*, which do not all lie on the same plane. How many different planes can be drawn containing any three of the points if no three of the points are collinear?

10.2

ANGLES

What is an angle? We can all draw one as shown in Fig. 10.15. We can define an angle formally as follows.

angle

sides

vertex

> **Definition 10.3**   An **angle** is the union of two rays that have a common endpoint. The rays are called the **sides** of the angle, and the endpoint is called the **vertex** of the angle.

In Fig. 10.15 the angle is formed by the rays $\overrightarrow{AB}$ and $\overrightarrow{AC}$ and the vertex is *A*. We identify this angle in one of the following ways:

1. By writing ∠*A*. In this notation, ∠ stands for angle, and *A* represents the vertex.

2. By writing ∠*BAC* or ∠*CAB*. In this notation the vertex is in the middle, and the other two points are points on either side of the angle.

3. By inserting a "1," a "2," etc., and calling it ∠1 or ∠2, as we have done in Fig. 10.15.

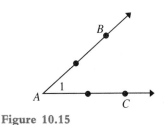

Figure 10.15

An angle divides the points of a plane that are not on the angle into two sets of points called **regions**. One region is called the **interior of the angle**, and the other is called the **exterior of the angle**. These are labeled in Fig. 10.16. The region that contains all points *P* is called the interior of the angle. All other points on the plane (except those in the angle itself) are called the exterior of the angle.

regions

interior of the angle

exterior of the angle

protractor

Angles are measured by an instrument called a **protractor**, such as the one shown in Fig. 10.17. Angles are usually measured in units called

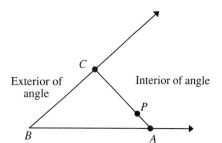

Figure 10.16

degrees

Figure 10.17

degrees, and these are denoted by the symbol °. The scale on the protractor is marked from 0 to 180 degrees as shown. To measure an angle, the point marked 0 on the protractor is placed at the vertex, and the 0° line is placed along one of the rays. The size of the angle is determined by the position of the second ray on the protractor. Thus $\angle AOB$ of Fig. 10.18 measures 40°. We denote this as $m(\angle AOB) = 40°$ where m stands for the "the measure of."

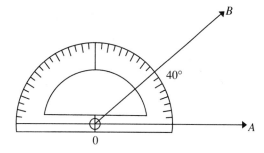

Figure 10.18

minutes

seconds

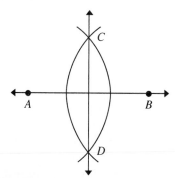

Figure 10.19

Each degree is divided into 60 smaller units known as **minutes**. The symbol for minute is ′. Thus 1° = 60′. Each minute is further divided into 60 smaller units known as **seconds**, which are denoted as ″. Therefore we have

$$1° = 60'$$

and

$$1' = 60''$$

This system of angular measurement can be traced back to the Babylonians, who used a base-60 number system (see Chapter 3).

Consider the following construction. Draw a straight line AB as shown in Fig. 10.19. Now take a compass, place the steel point on A, and draw an arc. Then put the steel point on B and, keeping the compass open the same amount, draw another arc that intersects the first arc in two places, C and D, as shown. (If they do not intersect, repeat the above procedure using larger compass settings.) Now join the two intersecting points.

Lines $\overleftrightarrow{CD}$ and $\overleftrightarrow{AB}$ form an angle. Measure it! It measures 90°. Such an angle is called a **right angle**, and the lines $\overleftrightarrow{AB}$ and $\overleftrightarrow{CD}$ that form the right angle are said to be **perpendicular**.

perpendicular

Definition 10.4   Two lines are said to be **perpendicular** if the angle at which they intersect is 90°, or a right angle.

We denote this by using the symbol "$\perp$". Thus if line $\overleftrightarrow{AB}$ is perpendicular to line $\overleftrightarrow{CD}$, we write $\overleftrightarrow{AB} \perp \overleftrightarrow{CD}$.

It is convenient to distinguish among the different kinds of angles, depending on their measure. We do this in the following definition.

right angle

straight angle

acute angle

obtuse angle

Definition 10.5   A **right angle** is an angle whose measure is 90°. A **straight angle** is an angle whose measure is 180°. An **acute angle** is an angle whose measure is between 0° and 90°. An **obtuse angle** is an angle whose measure is between 90° and 180°.

EXAMPLE 1

An angle of 35° is an acute angle.
An angle of 138° 12′ 16″ is an obtuse angle.   ▪

Comment   According to our definition, an angle is merely a set of points. It consists of the points on the two rays (and the vertex, of course).

Comment   The measurement of an angle as described above requires that the measure of any angle be between 0° and 180°. Why?

It is not always convenient to restrict the measure of an angle to between 0° and 180°.

To extend angular measure beyond the 0°–180° restriction, we can think of an angle as being formed in the following way. Draw any ray and call this the **initial side**. Keeping its endpoint fixed, rotate this side a certain amount and stop. The place where we stop is another ray, which we call the **terminal side**. Some angles formed in this manner are shown in Fig. 10.20. The arrow indicates the direction and amount of the rotation. In each case the vertex is at point A.

initial side of angle

terminal side of angle

In Fig. 10.20(a) the rotation is counterclockwise, and its measure is considered to be positive.

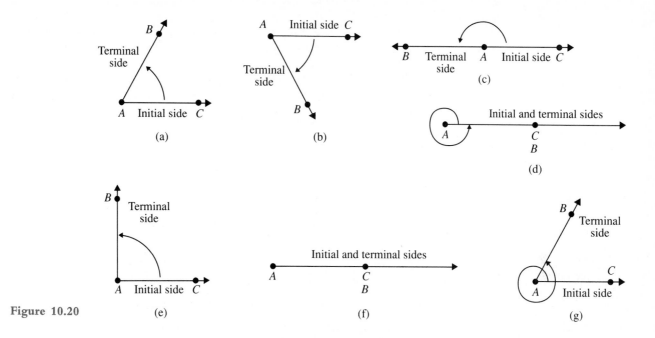

Figure 10.20

In Fig. 10.20(b) the rotation is clockwise, and its measure is thought of as being negative.

Notice that the angle of Fig. 10.20(d) represents one complete revolution, and therefore the terminal side is the same as the initial side. It is agreed that in one complete revolution there are 360 degrees, or 360°. This standard of measurement also comes from the Babylonians and was related to their studies in astronomy.

Notice that the angle of Fig. 10.20(c) contains one-half of a complete revolution, or measures 180°. This conforms to the method first discussed for measuring angles using protractors.

In Fig. 10.20(g), we have an angle whose measure is larger than 360°. Using rotations, we can have angles of any size, both positive and negative, as shown in Fig. 10.21 on the following page.

rotational angles

Such **rotational angles** frequently occur in everyday situations. For example, the rotational angles + 480° and − 600° have the same initial and terminal sides, as shown in Fig. 10.22. If we consider these angles in terms of the initial and terminal sides, Definition 10.3 tells us that the two angles are the same, since they are determined by the same rays and the same vertex. However, from the rotational point of view they are obviously different. Suppose your car is stuck near the edge of a cliff and someone is giving you directions on how to proceed safely. It makes a big difference whether he tells you to rotate the wheels of the car + 480° or − 600° (see Fig. 10.23).

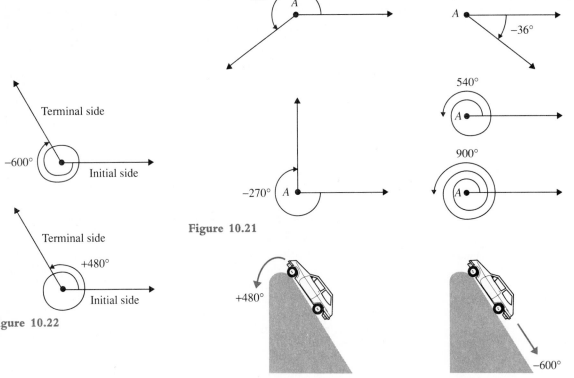

Figure 10.21

Figure 10.22

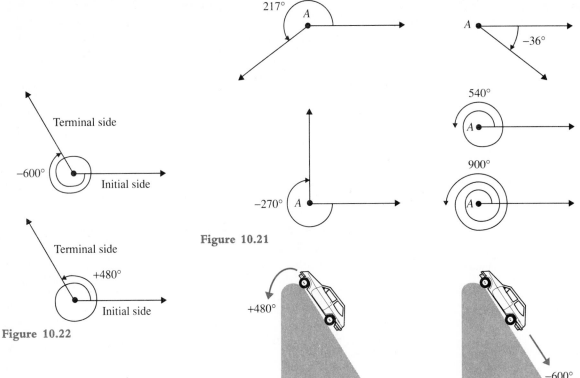

Figure 10.23

When any two lines intersect, four angles are formed, as shown in Fig. 10.24. Angles 1 and 2 have a common ray, $\overrightarrow{PC}$, and we call them **adjacent angles**. Similarly, angles 2 and 3 have a common ray, $\overrightarrow{PB}$, and they are also adjacent angles. There are two other pairs of adjacent angles in this diagram. Name them.

In the same illustration, angles 2 and 4 are nonadjacent. We call them **vertical angles**. Similarly, angles 1 and 3 are called vertical angles. This leads us to the following definitions.

Figure 10.24

adjacent angles

Definition 10.6 Two **angles** are said to be **adjacent** if they have a common ray and a common vertex but do not have any interior points in common.

---

vertical angles

Definition 10.7 When two lines intersect, the nonadjacent angles formed are said to be **vertical** angles.

Radian Measure

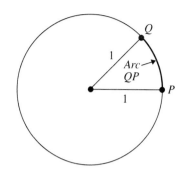

Figure 10.25

radian

radius

We know that we can measure something—for instance, the length of this piece of paper—with standard rulers of different units. The length can be given in either inches or centimeters. Similarly, weight can be measured in different units—in either pounds or grams. So far in this chapter, we have been using degrees as the unit of measurement for angles, but there is another unit that is often used in mathematics, science, and engineering. This is called the **radian**.

Consider a circle whose radius is 1 in. (a **radius** is any line segment drawn from the center of the circle to the circle). Draw a radius in this circle (see Fig. 10.25). Now take a piece of string 1 in. long and place it *along the circle* with one end at the point where the radius drawn meets the circle (point P). Put the other end of the string at point Q. Draw another radius from the center to point Q. The arc QP (portion of the circle between points P and Q) obviously has length equal to 1 in. The angle between the two radii (plural of radius) is assigned a measure of one **radian**.

We know that in one complete rotation there are 360°. How many radians are there in one complete rotation? Let us see. It can be shown that if a string were to be placed around the entire circle, it would measure 2π in. As you know, π is an irrational number that cannot be written exactly as a decimal. It is approximately equal to 3.1415.... An arc of 1 in. gives an angle of 1 radian. Therefore an arc of 2π in. (the whole circle) gives an angle of 2π radians.

Thus in one complete rotation there are 2π radians or 360°, depending on which unit you are using.

Formula 10.1 2π radians = 360°   (1)

Since 2π radians is 360°, we can find how many degrees there are in 1 radian by dividing by 2π. We get

$$\frac{2\pi}{2\pi} \text{ radians} = \frac{360°}{2\pi} \qquad \left(\frac{2\pi}{2\pi} \text{ equals } 1\right)$$

Formula 10.2 1 radian = $\dfrac{180°}{\pi}$ (2)

Similarly, if we divide (1) by 360, we get

$$\frac{2\pi}{360} \text{ radians} = \frac{360°}{360}$$

Formula 10.3 $\dfrac{\pi}{180}$ radians = 1 degree   (3)

If we use 3.14 as an approximation for π, we get

$$1 \text{ radian} = \frac{180°}{\pi} = \frac{180°}{3.14}$$

which is approximately 57°. Also,

$$1 \text{ degree} = \frac{\pi}{180} \text{ radians}$$

$$= \frac{3.14}{180} \text{ radians}$$

which is approximately 0.0174 radian. *Thus 1 radian is approximately 57 degrees, and 1 degree is approximately 0.0174 radian.*

Formulas 10.2 and 10.3 enable us to convert from degrees to radians and from radians to degrees, as shown in the following examples.

EXAMPLE 2

Convert $\dfrac{\pi}{4}$ radians to degree measure.

SOLUTION

We use Formula 10.2, which says that

$$1 \text{ radian} = \frac{180}{\pi} \text{ degrees}$$

We multiply both sides by $\dfrac{\pi}{4}$ and get

$$\frac{\pi}{4}(1 \text{ radian}) = \frac{\pi}{4}\left(\frac{180}{\pi} \text{ degrees}\right)$$

$$\frac{\pi}{4} \text{ radians} = \frac{180}{4} \text{ degrees}$$

$$\frac{\pi}{4} \text{ radians} = 45°$$

EXAMPLE 3

Convert 60° to radian measure.

SOLUTION

We use Formula 10.3, which says that

$$1 \text{ degree} = \frac{\pi}{180} \text{ radians}$$

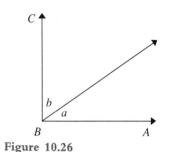

Figure 10.26

We multiply both sides by 60 and get

$$60(1 \text{ degree}) = 60\left(\frac{\pi}{180} \text{ radians}\right)$$

$$60 \text{ degrees} = \frac{60\pi}{180} \text{ radians}$$

$$60 \text{ degrees} = \frac{\pi}{3} \text{ radians}$$

Complementary and Supplementary Angles

Consider the following angle ABC (see Fig. 10.26). The measure of angle a is 35°, and the measure of angle b is 55°. The sum of the measures of these two angles is 90°. Angles a and b are said to be **complementary**, and each angle is the complement of the other. Formally, we have that *two angles are complementary angles if the sum of their measures is 90°*.

Now consider angle IJK shown in Fig. 10.27. The measure of angle c is 60°, and the measure of angle d is 120°. The sum of the measures of these two angles is 180°. Angles c and d are said to be **supplementary**, and each angle is the supplement of the other. Formally, we have that *two angles are supplementary angles if the sum of their measures is 180°*.

Comment We can represent the measure of the complement of an angle whose measure is x degrees by $(90 - x)°$, since $x + (90 - x) = 90$.

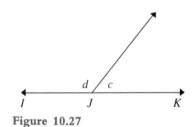

Figure 10.27

Comment We can represent the measure of the supplement of an angle whose measure is x degrees by $(180 - x)°$, since $x + (180 - x) = 180$.

EXAMPLE 4

SOLUTION

Problem-Solving Example

The measure of the complement of an angle is eight times the measure of the angle. Find the measure of the angle.

Understanding the Problem
We are dealing with an angle and its complement. We are told that the measure of its complement is eight times the measure of the angle.

A Plan to Solve the Problem
We will solve the problem by setting up an equation. Let $x =$ the measure of the angle. Then $8x =$ the measure of the complement of the angle. Since the angles are complementary, the sum of their measures is 90°, so

$$x + 8x = 90$$
$$9x = 90 \quad \text{(We combine the } x \text{ and the } 8x\text{)}$$
$$x = 10 \quad \text{(We divide both sides of the equation by 9)}$$

Thus the measure of the angle is 10°.

Checking our Solution
If the measure of the angle is 10°, then the measure of its complement is 90° – 10°, or 80°. This represents 8 times the angle.

Problem-Solving Example

EXAMPLE 5

Find the measure of an angle whose measure is 80° more than the measure of its supplement.

SOLUTION

Understanding the Problem
Here we are dealing with an angle and its supplement. We are told that the relationship between the angle and its supplement is that the measure of the angle is 80° more than the measure of its supplement.

A Plan to Solve the Problem
Again we will solve the problem by setting up an equation. Let x = the measure of the supplement of the angle. Then $x + 80°$ represents the measure of the angle. Since the angles are supplementary, the sum of their measures is 180°, so

$$x + x + 80 = 180$$
$$2x + 80 = 180 \quad \text{(combining terms)}$$
$$2x = 100 \quad \text{(We subtract 80 from both sides of the equation)}$$
$$x = 50$$

Thus the measure of the supplement is 50°, and the measure of the angle is 50° + 80°, or 130°.

Checking our Solution
If the measure of the angle is 130°, then the measure of its supplement is 180° – 130°, or 50°. The angle is indeed 80° more than its supplement.

Parallel Lines Cut by a Transversal

Often we are given two parallel lines that are cut by a transversal. A **transversal** is a line that intersects two other lines in two different points as shown in Fig. 10.28, where line $\overleftrightarrow{EF}$ is a transversal that intersects the two parallel lines $\overleftrightarrow{AB}$ and $\overleftrightarrow{CD}$. Angles 3, 4, 5, and 6 are called **interior angles**, and angles 1, 2, 7, and 8 are called **exterior angles**. Furthermore, angles 4 and 5 as well as angles 3 and 6 are called **alternate interior angles**. They are interior angles on opposite sides of the transversal and do not have the same vertex.

alternate interior angles

alternate exterior angles

Angles 1 and 8 are called **alternate exterior angles**. They are exterior angles on opposite sides of the transversal and do not have the same vertex. Can you find another pair of alternate exterior angles?

interior angles on the same
side of the transversal

corresponding angles

Angles 4 and 6 are called **interior angles on the same side of the transversal**. Can you find another pair of interior angles on the same side of the transversal?

Angles 1 and 5 are called **corresponding angles**. One is an exterior angle and the other is an interior angle, both being on the same side of the transversal. There are three other pairs of corresponding angles. Can you find them? One such pair is angles 2 and 6.

In the above parallel lines it can be shown that the alternate interior angles 3 and 6 have the same measure. The same is true for the alternate interior angles 4 and 5. More generally, if two lines cut by a transversal are parallel, then their alternate interior angles have the same measure.

Also in the above parallel lines the interior angles on the same side of the transversal, angles 4 and 6 as well as angles 3 and 5, are supplementary.

Finally, the corresponding angles 1 and 5 have the same measure. The same is true for the corresponding angles 2 and 6, the corresponding angles 3 and 7, and the corresponding angles 4 and 8. Whenever two parallel lines are cut by a transversal, their corresponding angles always have the same measure.

We can apply the alternate interior angles property to verify a very important theorem in geometry. This theorem says that *in any triangle the sum of the measures of its angles is 180°.* Consider the triangle shown in Fig. 10.29.

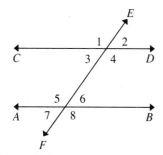

Figure 10.28

Let us draw a line *l* that passes through point *A* and that is parallel to line *m* as shown in Fig. 10.30. Then lines $\overleftrightarrow{AB}$ and $\overleftrightarrow{AC}$ are transversals for lines *l* and *m*. Therefore, ∠1 and ∠6 are alternate interior angles, so (by the alternate interior angle property mentioned above) they are equal in measure. Similarly, ∠3 and ∠5 are alternate interior angles that are equal in measure. Summarizing, we have the following.

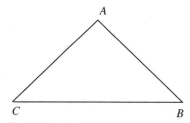

Figure 10.29
The sum of the measures of the angles of the triangle is 180°.

$$\text{measure } \angle 1 = \text{measure } \angle 6$$
$$\text{measure } \angle 3 = \text{measure } \angle 5$$
$$\text{measure } \angle 2 = \text{measure } \angle 2$$

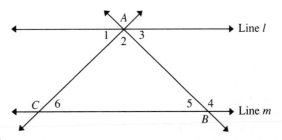

Figure 10.30

Since angles 1, 2, and 3 form a straight line, their sum must be 180°. Substituting what we obtained above gives

$$\text{measure } \angle 1 + \text{measure } \angle 2 + \text{measure } \angle 3 = 180°$$
$$\text{measure } \angle 6 + \text{measure } \angle 2 + \text{measure } \angle 5 = 180°$$

This last statement means that the sum of the measures of the angles of a triangle equals 180°. In view of this fact, we can conclude that a triangle can have at most one right angle and at most one obtuse angle.

We will have more to say about the angle sum in a triangle property later in this chapter.

Lines and Planes

If we are given any line and a plane, then one of the following must always be true:

a) The line and the plane have no points in common. In this case the line is parallel to the plane. (See Fig. 10.31.)

b) The line shares all of its points with the plane. This means that the line is on the plane. (See Fig. 10.32.)

c) The line intersects the plane but is not contained in the plane, that is, it intersects the plane in only one point. (See Fig. 10.33.)

It is possible for a line and a plane to intersect in such a way that they are perpendicular to each other. In Fig. 10.34, plane 1 and plane 2 represent two walls of a room which intersect along the line $\overleftrightarrow{AB}$. Notice that line $\overleftrightarrow{AB}$ is perpendicular to every line which is on the plane of the floor (plane 3) that passes through point B. Thus we can conclude that a line and a plane are perpendicular if and only if they intersect and the line is perpendicular to every line in the plane that passes through the point of intersection. On the other hand, two planes are perpendicular if and only if one plane contains a line perpendicular to the other plane. In Fig. 10.34, the plane containing the wall (plane 1) is perpendicular to the plane containing the floor (plane 3). Plane 1 contains line $\overleftrightarrow{AB}$ which is perpendicular to plane 3.

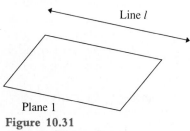

Line *l*

Plane 1

Figure 10.31
Line *l* is parallel to plane 1.

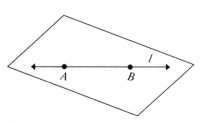

l

A　　*B*

Figure 10.32
Line *l* is on the plane.

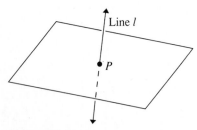

Line *l*

P

Figure 10.33
Line *l* intersects the plane at point *P* only.

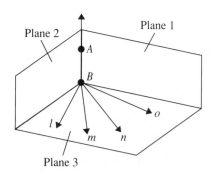

Plane 2　　　Plane 1

A

B

l　*m*　*n*　*o*

Plane 3

Figure 10.34

EXERCISES FOR SECTION 10.2

In Exercises 1–4, use a protractor to construct an angle having the indicated measures.

1. 50°   **2.** 65°   **3.** 130°   **4.** 95°

In Exercises 5–10, use a protractor to construct the following rotational angles.

5. 210°   **6.** 370°   **7.** 450°
8. – 190°   **9.** – 360°   **10.** – 780°

In Exercises 11–15, find all the adjacent and all the vertical angles for the indicated diagrams.

11.   **12.**

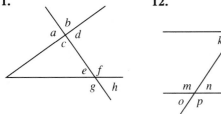

13.   **14.**

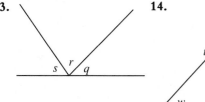

15.

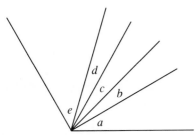

Each of the angles in Exercises 16–27 is given in degrees. Convert each to radians.

16. 10°   **17.** 210°   **18.** 315°   **19.** – 45°
20. 190°   **21.** – 720°   **22.** 1040°   **23.** – 570°
24. 900°   **25.** – 60°   **26.** – 330°   **27.** 1600°

Each of the angles in Exercises 28–36 is given in radian measure. Convert each to degree measure.

28. $\dfrac{3\pi}{4}$ **29.** $\dfrac{\pi}{2}$ **30.** $\dfrac{7\pi}{6}$

31. $\dfrac{11\pi}{12}$ **32.** $-\dfrac{8\pi}{9}$ **33.** $-\dfrac{12\pi}{5}$

34. 10   **35.** 5π **36.** $-\dfrac{7\pi}{15}$

For Exercises 37–40, refer to Fig. 10.35 and the indicated points. Find each of the following.

37. $\angle DAB \cap \angle BAC$ **38.** $\angle EAB \cap \angle DAE$
39. $\angle DAE \cap \angle BAC$ **40.** $\angle BAD \cap \angle CAE$

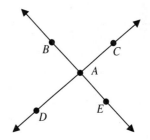

Figure 10.35

41. In Fig. 10.36, $\overleftrightarrow{AB} \parallel \overleftrightarrow{CD}$. Find the measure of
   a) angle 5 when the measure of angle 3 is 150°.
   b) angle 2 when the measure of angle 6 is 140°.
   c) angle 4 when the measure of angle 5 is 60°.
   d) angle 8 when the measure of angle 3 is 130°.

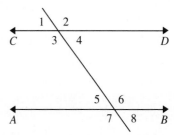

Figure 10.36

42. In Fig. 10.37 below, $\overleftrightarrow{AB} \parallel \overleftrightarrow{CD}$. If the measures of angles 7 and 8 are 60° and 70°, respectively, find the measures of the remaining angles in the figure.

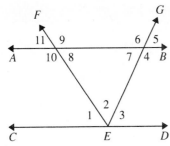

Figure 10.37

PROBLEM-SOLVING EXERCISES

43. Find the measure of an angle that is 36° more than the measure of its supplement.

44. Two angles are supplementary. The measure of the larger angle is twice the measure of the smaller angle. Find the measure of the smaller angle.

45. The measures of two complementary angles are in the ratio 7:2. Find the measure of each angle.

46. The measure of the supplement of an angle exceeds 4 times the measure of the angle by 30. Find the measure of the angle.

47. The measure of an angle is 40° less than the measure of its supplement. Find the measure of the supplement.

Brain-Teaser Problems

**48. Is it ever possible for a line to be perpendicular to one line within the plane and still not be perpendicular to the plane? Explain your answer.

**49. Is it ever possible for a line to be perpendicular to two distinct lines in a plane and still not be perpendicular to the plane?

50. In Fig. 10.38, angles ∠1 and ∠6 are known as **alternate exterior angles. Prove the following:

   a) If angles 1 and 6 have the same measure, then line l is parallel to line m.

   b) If line l is parallel to line m, then angles 1 and 6 have the same measure.

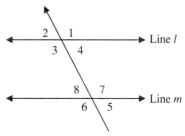

Figure 10.38

**51. Consider the set of nonparallel lines cut by a transversal shown in Fig. 10.39. Find the measure of angle x.

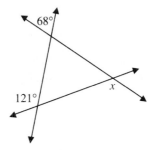

Figure 10.39

10.3

CURVES, TRIANGLES, AND POLYGONS

Using straight lines, we can construct figures in a plane that are known as **polygons**. Several examples of polygons are shown in Fig. 10.40.

To define a polygon formally, we first introduce the idea of a simple closed curve.

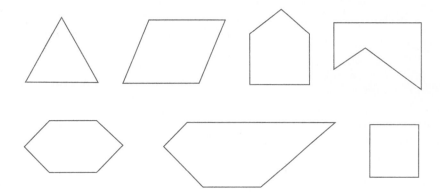

Figure 10.40

simple closed curve

> **Definition 10.8   A simple closed curve** is any curve that can be drawn without lifting the pencil (or other writing instrument) and that has the following properties:
>
> **1.** The drawing starts and stops at the same point.
>
> **2.** No point is touched twice (with the exception of the starting point).

The examples of Fig. 10.41 illustrate this definition. In Fig. 10.41, (a), (b), and (c) are simple closed curves. Figure (d) is not a simple closed curve because it does not start and stop at the same point. (It is not closed.) Figure (e) is not a simple closed curve because point P is touched twice in drawing the curve. (To see this, try to draw it.) Figures (f) and (g) are not simple closed curves. Why not?

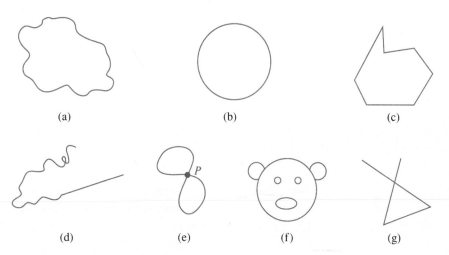

Figure 10.41   (d)   (e)   (f)   (g)

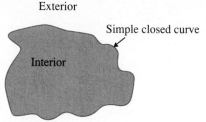

Figure 10.42

Jordan Curve Theorem

polygon

triangle

sides

vertex

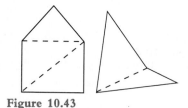

Figure 10.43

diagonal

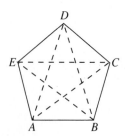

Figure 10.44

In all of the simple closed curves above, we note that the plane is divided into three mutually disjoint sets of points—the curve itself, the interior, and the exterior of the curve. These three sets of points are illustrated in Fig. 10.42. This property of simple closed curves is known as the **Jordan Curve Theorem**. The Jordan Curve Theorem is often stated in a slightly different (but equivalent) form. If any point in the interior of the curve is joined with a point in the exterior of the curve by a continuous path of points, then this path must intersect the curve itself.

We can now define what we mean by a polygon.

> **Definition 10.9**   A **polygon** is a simple closed curve consisting of straight-line segments such that no two segments with a common endpoint are collinear.

The simplest kind of polygon is a **triangle**, which consists of *three* lines called **sides**. Triangles are very important in the study of geometry, since any polygon can be broken up into triangles, such as the figures shown in Fig. 10.43. The Babylonians and Egyptians often used this idea in measuring land that was in the shape of a polygon. They divided the land into triangles and measured each part individually.

The straight line segments that form any general polygon are called its **sides**. The point where two sides meet is called a **vertex**.

Polygons are classified according to the number of sides (or vertices) that they have as shown below.

Polygon Name	Number of sides
Triangle	3
Quadrilateral	4
Pentagon	5
Hexagon	6
Heptagon	7
Octagon	8
Nonagon	9
Decagon	10
Dodecagon	12
Icosagon	20
n-gon	n

Any line segment connecting nonconsecutive vertices of a polygon is called a **diagonal**. In Fig. 10.44, the segments $\overline{AC}, \overline{BD}, \overline{BE}, \overline{AD}$, and $\overline{CE}$ represent the five diagonals of polygon $ABCDE$.

(a)

(b)

Geometric shapes in architecture: (a) Transamerica Building (courtesy of Transamerica Corporation); (b) the Pentagon (Courtesy of the U.S. Navy).

There are many different kinds of triangles. Three types that are important are equilateral, isosceles, and right triangles. These are defined as follows.

Definition 10.10 An **equilateral triangle** is a triangle with three sides whose measures are equal. An **isosceles triangle** is a triangle with two sides whose measures are equal. A **right triangle** is a triangle that contains a 90° angle.

It can be shown that if a triangle is equilateral, then all the angles are equal and each will measure exactly 60° (Fig. 10.45).

equilateral triangle

isosceles triangle

right triangle

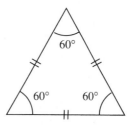

Figure 10.45

It can also be shown that if a triangle is isosceles, then the measures of the two angles opposite the equal sides are also equal (Fig. 10.46).

The Pythagorean theorem states that in a right triangle, such as the one in Fig. 10.47, $a^2 + b^2 = c^2$.

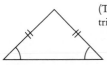

(The equal signs on the sides of the triangle mean that these sides are equal.)

Figure 10.46

(The right angle of this triangle is indicated by the symbol "⌐" in it. All right angles are similarly marked.)

Figure 10.47

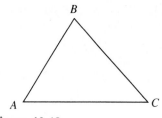

Figure 10.48

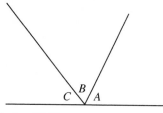

Figure 10.49

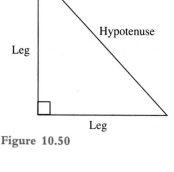

Figure 10.50

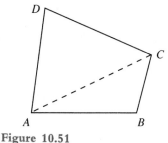

Figure 10.51

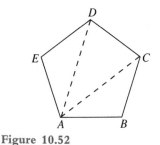

Figure 10.52

Consider the triangle shown in Fig. 10.48. Trace each of the angles on separate pieces of paper and cut them out. Now place the cutout angles with the vertices (plural of vertex) together and the sides adjacent to each other, as shown in Fig. 10.49.

Notice that the three angles together add up to a straight angle (180°). This will be true for any triangle. What this means is that the sum of the measures of the angles of any triangle is 180°. This is a basic idea in the geometry of Euclid. We will see later that it is not true in non-Euclidean geometries.

Comment   In discussing a right triangle the two sides that form the right angle are called the **legs** of the right triangle. The third side, which is opposite the right angle, is called the **hypotenuse**. These are shown in Fig. 10.50.

Now consider the quadrilateral shown in Fig. 10.51. If we draw diagonal $\overline{AC}$, two triangles are formed. Since the sum of the measures of the angles of each of these triangles is 180°, the sum of the measures of the angles of quadilateral $ABCD$ is $2 \cdot 180°$, or 360°.

What about any pentagon? If we draw the two diagonals $\overline{AC}$ and $\overline{AD}$ for the pentagon $ABCDE$ shown in Fig. 10.52, we note that the pentagon is divided into three triangles. Since the sum of the measures of the angles of each of these triangles is 180°, the sum of the measures of the angles of a pentagon is $3 \cdot 180°$, or 540°. We can generalize this procedure in the following:

Regular polygon consists of	Polygon can be divided into	Sum of the measures of the interior angles
3 sides	1 triangle	$1 \cdot (180°) = 180°$
4 sides	2 triangles	$2 \cdot (180°) = 360°$
5 sides	3 triangles	$3 \cdot (180°) = 540°$
6 sides	4 triangles	$4 \cdot (180°) = 720°$
⋮	⋮	⋮
n sides	$n - 2$ triangles	$180 (n - 2)$

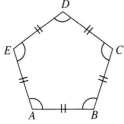

Figure 10.53

regular polygon

In Fig. 10.53, the polygon is both equilateral (since all the sides have the same measure) and equiangular (since all the angles have the same measure). Here pentagon *ABCDE* is a regular polygon. This leads us to the following:

Definition 10.11 A **regular polygon** is a polygon that is both equilateral and equiangular.

For regular polygons only, we can prove the following:

a) The sum of the measures of the interior angles of a polygon on *n* sides is $180°\,(n-2)$.

b) The sum of the measures of the exterior angles of a polygon is $360°$.

To illustrate these ideas, from the above chart we can conclude that the sum of the measures of an octagon (8-sided polygon) is $180°(8-2)$, or $1080°$. *The measure of each interior angle of a regular polygon can be found by dividing the sum of the measures of the interior angles by the number of angles.* In our case we have

$$\text{Measure of each interior angle of a regular octagon} = \frac{1080°}{8} = 135°$$

This leads us to the following definition.

convex polygon

Definition 10.12 A **convex polygon** is a polygon each of whose interior angles measures less than $180°$.

---

concave polygon

When a polygon has at least one interior angle measuring more than $180°$, we call this a **concave polygon**. Quadrilateral *ABCD* of Fig. 10.54 is an example of a concave polygon.

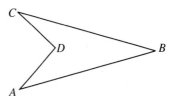

Figure 10.54 Concave polygon
The measure of the interior angle at vertex *D* is more than $180°$.

Since quadrilaterals (four-sided polygons) are studied extensively in geometry, we state the following characteristics about some special types of quadrilaterals. (Fig. 10.55–10.60)

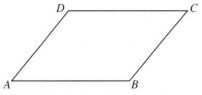

Figure 10.55 Parallelogram
Both pairs of opposite sides are parallel and are equal in length.

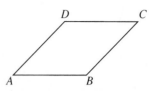

Figure 10.56 Rhombus
Both pairs of opposite sides are parallel. All sides are equal in length.

Figure 10.57 Rectangle
Both pairs of opposite sides are parallel. The four interior angles are right angles.

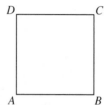

Figure 10.58 Square
Both pairs of opposite sides are parallel. All sides are equal in length. The four interior angles are right angles.

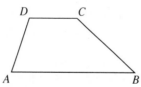

Figure 10.59 Trapezoid
Only two sides are parallel.

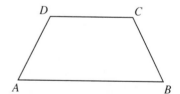

Figure 10.60 Isosceles Trapezoid
Only two sides are parallel. The two non-parallel sides are equal in length.

Often students are asked to determine which special types of quadrilaterals can be constructed and which cannot be constructed using some given information. In the accompanying student page from *Addison-Wesley Mathematics,* 1987, Grade 5, p. 280, students are asked to use the seven pieces of the famous Tangram puzzle for exactly such a task. This process is very useful in space perception and in recognizing the various properties of several geometric figures.

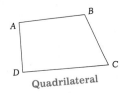

Quadrilaterals

A **quadrilateral** has four sides ($\overline{AB}$, $\overline{BC}$, $\overline{CD}$, and $\overline{AD}$) and four angles ($\angle A$, $\angle B$, $\angle C$, and $\angle D$).

Quadrilateral

Four types of quadrilaterals have been made below by putting together all seven pieces of the famous tangram puzzle. Another quadrilateral, called a rhombus, cannot be made with all the pieces. Study the properties of each quadrilateral.

Square

All sides the same length
All angles right angles

Rectangle

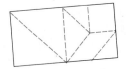

Two pairs of sides the same length
All right angles

Parallelogram

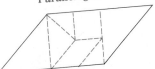

Two pairs of sides the same length
Two pairs of parallel sides

Trapezoid

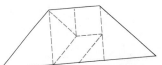

One pair of parallel sides

Rhombus

All sides the same length

EXERCISES FOR SECTION 10.3

Which of the figures given in Exercises 1–6 are simple closed curves?

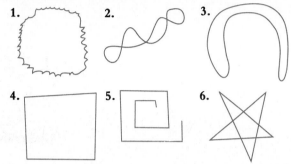

1.   **2.**   **3.**

4.   **5.**   **6.**

Which of the figures given in Exercises 7–12 are polygons?

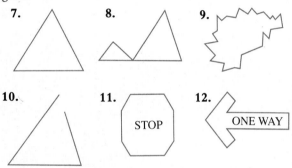

7.   **8.**   **9.**

10.   **11.** STOP   **12.** ONE WAY

13. Draw a triangle whose sides are 6 cm, 9 cm, and 12 cm. What happens?

14. Draw a triangle whose sides are 6 cm, 6 cm, and 12 cm. What happens?

15. Find the length of the hypotenuse of a right triangle *ABC* whose legs measure 16 and 30 cm as shown in Fig. 10.61.

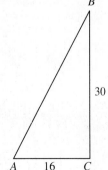

Figure 10.61   *A*   16   *C*

16. Find the length of the third side of a right triangle if the hypotenuse measures 34 cm and one of the legs measures 30 cm.

In Exercises 17–22, use the Pythagorean theorem to calculate the length of the missing side in each diagram.

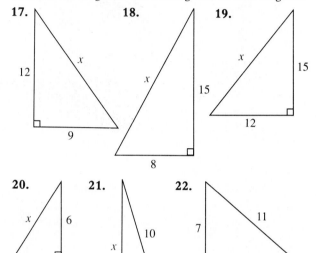

17.   **18.**   **19.**

20.   **21.**   **22.**

Use the Pythagorean theorem to solve Exercises 23 and 24.

23. As shown in Fig. 10.62 a 25-foot ladder leans against the side of a house. The base of the ladder is 12 feet from the house on level ground. Find, to the *nearest foot*, the distance from the top of the ladder to the ground.

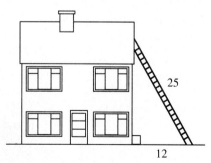

Figure 10.62

24. As shown in Fig. 10.63, a tree 45 feet high on level ground casts a shadow 81 feet long. Find, to the *nearest foot*, the distance from the top of the tree to the end of the shadow on the ground.

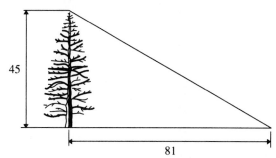

45

81

Figure 10.63

25. Draw a right triangle that is isosceles.

26. Draw an obtuse triangle that is isosceles.

27. Can a triangle have two right angles? Explain.

28. Can a triangle have a right angle and an obtuse angle? Explain.

29. Draw a triangle whose angles are 50°, 80°, and 45°. What happens?

30. Draw two triangles that intersect at exactly one point.

31. Draw two triangles that intersect at exactly two points.

32. Draw two triangles that intersect at exactly three points.

33. Is an angle a simple closed curve? Explain.

34. Draw a quadrilateral and a triangle such that the intersection is exactly

    a) one point   **b)** two points   **c)** three points

35. Classify each of the following as true or false.

    a) Every parallelogram is a square.

    b) Every trapezoid is a parallelogram.

    c) The sum of the angles of any quadrilateral is 180°.

    d) A square is a rhombus.

    e) A triangle can be drawn when the sides measure 17 cm, 18 cm, and 35 cm.

    f) If a triangle is equilateral, then it is equiangular.

    g) An obtuse triangle may have two obtuse angles.

PROBLEM-SOLVING EXERCISES

36. Find the sum of the measures of the interior angles of a polygon that has

    a) 7 sides   **b)** 9 sides   **c)** 10 sides

37. Find the sum of the measures of the interior angles of a(n)

    a) heptagon **b)** octagon **c)** nonagon **d)** decagon

38. Find the sum of the measures of the exterior angles of a(n)

    a) heptagon **b)** octagon **c)** nonagon **d)** decagon

39. How many sides does a *regular* polygon have if the sum of the measures of its interior angles is

    a) 900°   **b)** 1620°   **c)** 2160°   **d)** 2700°

40. The measure of each exterior angle of a regular polygon is three times as large as the measure of each interior angle. How many sides does the polygon have?

41. The angles of a quadrilateral are in the ratio of 4:5:6:9. Find the measure of the smallest angle of the quadrilateral.

42. The measure of the exterior angle at vertex C of the isosceles triangle ABC (Fig. 10.64) is represented by $4x + 20°$. Find x.

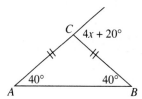

C $4x + 20°$

$40°$ $40°$

A B

Figure 10.64

43. In Fig. 10.65, lines $\overleftrightarrow{AB}$ and $\overleftrightarrow{CD}$ are parallel. Using the measures of the angles given in the diagram, find x.

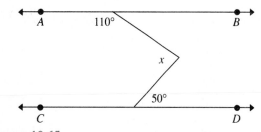

A $110°$ B

x

$50°$

C D

Figure 10.65

Brain-Teaser Problems

**44. How many triangles can you find in Fig. 10.66?

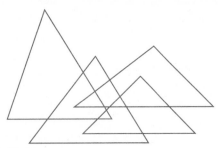

Figure 10.66

**45. How many squares can you find in Figs. 10.67 and 10.68?

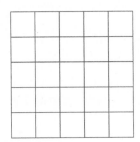

Figure 10.67   Figure 10.68

**46. The square shown in Fig. 10.69 has 2 diagonals. The pentagon shown in Fig. 10.70 has 5 diagonals. The hexagon shown in Fig. 10.71 has 9 diagonals, as shown. How many diagonals does a convex polygon of n sides have?

Figure 10.69   Figure 10.70

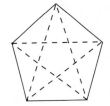

Figure 10.71

**47. Referring to the isosceles trapezoid shown in Fig. 10.72, which of the following are true?

a) The diagonals are equal in length and bisect each other.

b) The diagonals are perpendicular to each other.

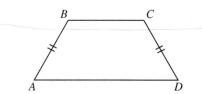

Figure 10.72

**48. The maximum number of points of intersection for a triangle and a square (where no two sides lie on the same straight line) is six, as can be seen in Fig. 10.73. Find the maximum number of points of intersection for

a) a triangle and a hexagon

b) a pentagon and a square

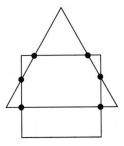

Figure 10.73

49. A **convex region is one in which a line segment joining any two points in the region must lie within the region. A region that is not convex is called **concave**. Which of the following are convex regions and which are concave regions?

a)   **b)**   **c)**

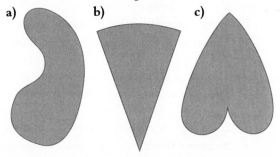

**50. Suppose we are given a pile of toothpicks, all of the same size. Using three toothpicks placed end to end in the same plane, we can form one equilateral triangle, as shown.

Using four toothpicks, no triangles can be formed. Using five toothpicks, we can form one isosceles triangle, as shown.

Using six toothpicks, one equilateral triangle can be formed, as shown.

Using seven toothpicks, two isosceles triangles can be formed, as shown.

We can organize our results in the following chart.

No. of toothpicks	3	4	5	6	7	...
Is triangle possible?	Yes	No	Yes	Yes	Yes	...
No. of triangles	1	0	1	1	2	...
Kind of triangle	equi-lateral		isos-celes	equi-lateral	isos-celes	

Can you generalize the above chart?

10.4

EUCLIDEAN AND NON-EUCLIDEAN GEOMETRY

Elements

Euclid's great work was his *Elements*, which was written around 300 B.C. It was a collection of all elementary mathematics, including geometry, and was actually an introductory textbook. When Euclid wrote the *Elements*, all the geometry in it was already known. His contribution consisted of organizing the available material into a mathematical system.

The *Elements* had an enormous influence on Western civilization. For 2000 years it was considered the best and most thorough example of mathematical reasoning. Early editions of the *Elements* were hand-copied in Greek, Latin, and Arabic, and the first printed version appeared in 1482. Since then, about 1000 different editions have been published. Most of our modern editions of Euclid are based on an edition of Euclid's *Elements* revised by Theon, a fourth century mathematican. Theon is also known as the father of the first important woman mathematician, Hypatia.

Euclid started (and so we have too) with certain basic terms such as *point* and *line.* However, unlike modern mathematicians, he did not see the need for undefined terms. He believed that it was possible to define all terms, and the *Elements* begins with twenty-three definitions. Unfortunately, these definitions are not adequate because they depend on other terms that have not been previously defined. For example, *point* is defined as "that which has no part." In order to understand this definition, you must first know what "part" is. Again *line* is defined as "breadthless length." To understand this, you have to know what "breadth" and "length" mean. These were never defined by Euclid. His definitions are circular in the sense discussed in Section 10.1. Apparently, Euclid did not see this, and he considered his definitions satisfactory.

Although Euclid did not see that there were certain terms that had to be undefined, he did recognize that there were certain statements that had to be accepted without proof. Euclid intended to give deductive proofs of known mathematical facts such as the Pythagorean theorem. These proofs depend on other facts, which in turn depend on still others, and so on. This can go on forever unless you agree to stop somewhere. Therefore it is necessary to start with certain statements that must be accepted without proof. These are called **postulates** or **axioms**, and Euclid assumed ten. They are sometimes thought of as statements that are self-evident, statements that must be true because they are obvious. There is some indication that Euclid may have regarded at least some of his postulates in this way.

postulates

axioms

However, it often turns out that "obvious" truths are false. A good example of this is that it was once obvious to almost everyone that the sun revolved around the earth; one could watch it moving through the sky from east to west as the day passed. Today we all know that this obvious truth is false. Furthermore, in recent years, scientists and philosophers have shown that it is very difficult to be certain about anything at all. Thus present-day mathematicians do not claim that the postulates they use are true. They merely say that these postulates are what they are assuming. Postulates are just a starting point. If they turn out to be true statements about the physical world, so much the better. If not, it is still interesting to see what follows logically from them.

Euclid's ten postulates[1] or axioms were the following.

1. A straight line may be drawn connecting any two points.

2. A line segment can be extended indefinitely to form a line.

---

1. See Carl Boyer, *A History of Mathematics*, pp. 116–117. New York: John Wiley, 1968.

3. A circle may be drawn with any center and any radius. (The *radius* of the circle is a line segment drawn from the center to the circle.)

4. All right angles are equal.

5. Given a line and a point not on the line, then only one line can be drawn parallel to the first line passing through the given point. (Remember, parallel lines are lines that do not intersect.) This version of Euclid's fifth postulate, which was popularized by John Playfair, is the one that appears in many high school geometry texts. There are other versions of this postulate.

6. Things equal to the same things are equal to each other.

7. If equals are added to equals, then the sums are equal.

8. If equals are subtracted from equals, then the differences are equal.

9. Things that coincide with one another are equal to one another.

10. The whole is greater than any of its parts.

theorems

Starting from these postulates, Euclid was able to prove deductively many important and interesting statements called **theorems**. Some of the important theorems are the following.

1. Vertical angles are equal.

2. The base angles of an isosceles triangle are equal.

3. If the base angles of a triangle are equal, then the triangle is isosceles. (This is the converse of Theorem 2.)

4. The sum of the measures of the angles of any triangle equals 180°.

5. The Pythagorean theorem.

David Hilbert (1862–1943).

Although, as we pointed out earlier, Euclid's work was long considered a perfect example of deductive reasoning, within the past century it has been discovered that his reasoning is often incomplete. These logical gaps occur because he makes certain unstated assumptions based on diagrams. These assumptions cannot always be justified logically. To fill in the logical gaps, additional postulates must be introduced. This can and has been done, notably by the German mathematician David Hilbert (1862–1943).

One example of the kind of gap that occurs in Euclid's reasoning is the following "proof" that there exists a triangle with two right angles. (Of course this is ridiculous in Euclidean geometry, since the sum of the three angles of a triangle must be 180°. If two angles of a triangle are each 90°, then their sum alone is 180°, and when we add the third angle, the total is more than 180°.)

Proof that there exists a triangle with two right angles

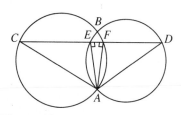

Figure 10.74

Take two circles that meet in points A and B as in Fig. 10.74. Let $\overline{AC}$ and $\overline{AD}$ be their diameters drawn from A. (A *diameter* is a line segment through

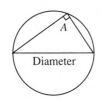

Figure 10.75

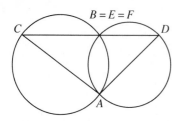

Figure 10.76

congruent figures

corresponding sides

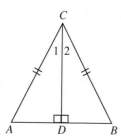

Figure 10.78

the center of the circle that bisects the circle.) Draw line segment $\overline{CD}$ meeting the circles at points E and F, as given. It can be shown in Euclidean geometry that $\angle AFC$ is a right angle. (Any angle inscribed in a semicircle is a right angle.)[2] Similarly, $\angle AED$ is a right angle (because it also is inscribed in a semicircle).

We now have triangle AEF with two right angles. What is wrong with this proof?

If you draw your own diagram very carefully, you will discover that $\overline{CD}$ passes through point B, as shown in Fig. 10.76. Thus we see that points E and F are exactly the same as point B. So triangle AEF does not even exist. The carelessly drawn diagram of Fig. 10.74 was misleading.

You may think that the above proof was rigged and that Euclid himself would never have made such an error. However, many of the proofs in the *Elements* and in high school geometry texts (which are based on Euclid) contain similar faults. The following proof is taken from a geometry text.

For the sake of the proof, we will use the following facts now and discuss them in greater detail later. **Congruent figures** are figures which have the same size and shape. In Fig. 10.77, if we cut out $\triangle LMN$[3] and place it on top of $\triangle ABC$ (with $\angle L$ falling on top of $\angle A$ and $\angle M$ falling on top of $\angle B$), then $\triangle LMN$ will fit *exactly* over $\triangle ABC$. Each triangle can be considered to be a carbon copy of the other. The symbol $\cong$ is read "is congruent to." Also, side $\overline{AB}$ is equal in length to its corresponding side $\overline{LM}$. These sides are called **corresponding sides**. In a similar way we say that two angles are congruent if they have the same measure.

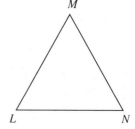

Figure 10.77

> **Theorem**   The base angles of an isosceles triangle (Fig. 10.78) are congruent.

---

2. "An angle inscribed in a semicircle" is an angle such as $\angle A$ shown in Fig. 10.75. Its vertex is on the circle, and its rays (sides) pass through the endpoints of a diameter.

3. The symbol "$\triangle LMN$" stands for "triangle LMN."

Given: $\triangle ABC$ with $\overline{AC} \cong \overline{BC}$

To prove: $\angle A \cong \angle B$

Proof

Statements	Reason
1. Draw the bisector of $\angle C$ (this is the line that divides $\angle C$ into two congruent angles).	1. Every angle has a bisector.
2. Extend the bisector of $\angle C$ to meet line segment $\overline{AB}$ at point D.	2. A line segment may be extended.
3. In $\triangle ACD$ and $\triangle BCD$, $\overline{AC} \cong \overline{BC}$	3. Given.
4. $\angle 1 \cong \angle 2$	4. An angle bisector divides the angle into two congruent angles.
5. $\overline{CD} \cong \overline{CD}$	5. Anything is congruent to itself.
6. $\triangle ACD$ is congruent to $\triangle BCD$	6. Two triangles are congruent when two sides and the included angle of one are equal, respectively, to two sides and the included angle of the other.
7. $\angle A \cong \angle B$	7. If two triangles are congruent, then the corresponding parts are congruent.

This proof contains an error similar to the error in the previous proof. What is wrong? The problem is in the second step. Our reason for this step is that a line may be extended. This is Postulate 2 (p. 596). However, this postulate does not tell us that when this line is actually extended, it will meet line segment $\overline{AB}$. The diagram certainly suggests that it does. But there is nothing that logically forces us to conclude that the bisector will meet $\overline{AB}$ at point D as shown. In Fig. 10.79 the bisector does *not* meet the line segment $\overline{AB}$.

You may say that straight lines simply do not behave like line $\overline{CD}$ of Fig. 10.79. But what do you mean by a straight line? If you mean a straight pencil mark on paper or a straight chalk mark on the blackboard, then you are right. However, we are not discussing chalk or pencil marks. We are discussing lines, which have only the properties assumed in the postulates and no others. It does not follow *logically* from the postulates that a line cannot behave as $\overline{CD}$ does in Fig. 10.79. Mathematicians are

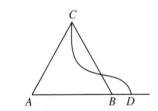

Figure 10.79

(a)

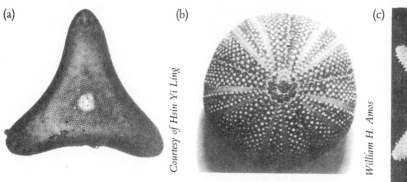

(b)

Courtesy of Hsin Yi Ling

(c)

William H. Amos

Lee H. Somers

Geometric shapes in nature: (a) Photomicrograph of a diatom; (b) sea urchin; (c) starfish.

concerned with what follows *logically* from the postulates and not with what *appears* to be true in a picture.

Some of Euclid's other proofs contain similar faults. However, by adding suitable postulates to Euclid's original ten, modern mathematicians have been able to correct the faults. Let us not underestimate the work of Euclid because of these gaps. It took 2000 years for critics to discover and correct them.

Euclid may have considered some of his postulates as obviously true. There is evidence, however, that Euclid was not entirely convinced of the truth of at least one postulate, namely, the fifth. This is called the parallel postulate[4] and it states:

Euclid's Parallel Postulate

> **Euclid's Parallel Postulate**   Given a line and a point not on the line, then only one line can be drawn parallel to the first line passing through the given point.

Euclid did not use the parallel postulate in proving theorems until he could not continue any further without it, and it is this apparent hesitation to use Postulate 5 that suggests that he was not completely satisfied with it. Why not? Well, let us look at the postulate closely (see Fig. 10.80).

The postulate states that it is possible to construct a line parallel to a given line. This means that the two lines will *never* meet, no matter how far they are extended. It is not humanly possible to go on extending lines forever. So how can we really know that these two lines will *never* meet

---

4. Euclid stated this postulate differently. The version given here is that of the English mathematician Playfair.

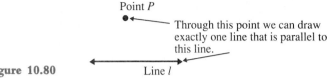

Figure 10.80

at some point? Perhaps they would meet billions and billions of miles away from the starting point.

Other mathematicians were also doubtful about the truth of the parallel postulate; for 2000 years after the *Elements* first appeared, several attempts were made to *prove* this postulate rather than accept it as an unproved statement. However, these attempts all involved other unproved assumptions that were actually the same as the parallel postulate but were stated differently.

In the seventeenth century an Italian monk named Girolamo Saccheri (1667–1733) approached the problem in a new way. He used the method called *proof by contradiction*. Saccheri wanted to prove that Euclid's parallel postulate was true. Obviously, there are only two possibilities.

Possibility 1. Euclid's parallel postulate is false.

Possibility 2. Euclid's parallel postulate is true.

He assumed that Euclid's parallel postulate was false (Possibility 1) and tried to arrive at a contradiction. Believing that he had actually reached the contradiction, he concluded that Possibility 2 is correct, that is, that the parallel postulate is true. He published his results in *Euclides Vindicatus*, which means "Euclid vindicated," or "Euclid proved true." Apparently, Saccheri had great faith in Euclid and was very anxious to show that the parallel postulate was true. In fact, Saccheri made an error and did not really obtain a contradiction at all. Thus he did not prove the parallel postulate as he thought he had.

Saccheri's work is of great interest because he actually proved many theorems in the non-Euclidean geometries developed in the next century by Bolyai and Lobachevsky. So, although he failed to prove Euclid's geometry true, he paved the way for a new and important approach to geometry.

Saccheri's approach, as we have said, was to assume that the parallel postulate was false. If it is indeed false, then one of the following two situations is possible.

Possibility 1. Given a line *l* and a point *P* not on *l*, *at least two lines* can be drawn parallel to it passing through the given point (see Fig. 10.81 on the next page).

Possibility 2. Given a line *l* and a point *P* not on *l*, *no* lines can be drawn parallel to *l* that pass through the given point.

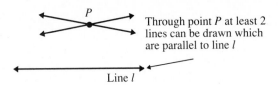

Figure 10.81

J. Bolyai (1802–1860), a Hungarian army officer, and N. I. Lobachevsky (1793–1856), a Russian mathematician, each independently developed a geometry based on Possibility 1. They used all the postulates of Euclid except the fifth, and in its place they substituted Possibility 1. This is known as the *Lobachevskian parallel postulate*. Then from this new set of postulates they proceeded to prove theorems. The geometry that they developed in this way is called *Lobachevskian geometry*, and it is different from Euclid's geometry in many startling ways. Some of the theorems of this geometry are as follows.

Lobachevskian parallel postulate

1. Given a line *l* and a point *P* not on *l*, then through point *P* many lines can be drawn parallel to it (compare this with the Euclidean parallel postulate).

2. The sum of the measures of the angles of any triangle is *less than* 180°.

3. Different triangles have different angle sums.

4. The sum of the measures of the angles of any quadrilateral is *less than* 360° (compare this with the value given on page 588).

5. There are no rectangles. (This follows from the last theorem. Why?)

6. If two triangles are similar, then they must also be congruent. (This means that if two figures have the same shape, then they must also have the same size. Thus in a Lobachevskian world, miniature or enlarged copies of objects would be impossible to produce without distortion. To be accurate, all photographs would have to be life-size!)

7. Parallel lines are not spaced an equal distance apart.

It is interesting to note that the great German mathematician K. F. Gauss (1777–1855) also developed a geometry that is based on the Lobachevskian parallel postulate, but he did not want to publish it at the time because the ideas of Euclid were so widely accepted.

In 1854, B. Riemann (1826–1866), a German mathematician, introduced a different non-Euclidean geometry. He replaced Euclid's parallel postulate by Possibility 2, which is now called the *Riemann parallel postulate*. When the parallel postulate is replaced by Possibility 2, it is also necessary to give up some of Euclid's other assumptions. There is actually a choice as to which assumptions can be abandoned. You can give up Postulate 1 (p. 596), or you can give up the principle, discussed in Section 10.1, that a line separates a plane into two half-planes.

Riemann parallel postulate

B. Riemann (1826–1866).

The theorems of Riemann's geometry are also surprising and interesting. Some of them are as follows.

1. Parallel lines do not exist.

2. The sum of the measures of the angles of any triangle is greater than 180°.

3. There are no rectangles.

4. If two triangles are similar, then they must also be congruent. (This means that if the two figures have the same shape, then they also have the same size.)

5. A line is not separated by a point into two half-lines.

6. Two different lines intersect in *two* points. (This theorem is true only if you make the choice to abandon Postulate 1.)

Geometries make statements about physical objects—figures, shapes, areas, distances, etc. Thus they can be used to explain the physical world in which we live. The theorems of Riemannian and Lobachevskian geometry seem very strange to us. On first seeing these theorems it is natural to think that they cannot possibly be true in the real world. In fact, some of them actually seem to contradict our own experiences. (For example, haven't we all seen rectangles with our own eyes? Yet these don't exist in either Riemannian or Lobachevskian geometry.) It was partly this feeling that convinced Saccheri that he had proved Euclid's geometry to be true.

However, it has been shown that if Euclid's geometry is *logically* correct, then so are Riemann's and Lobachevsky's. Thus none of these three has any "logical superiority." Nevertheless, for 2000 years, Euclid's geometry had been accepted as an absolutely accurate description of the physical world. So it was difficult for mathematicians and scientists to accept the possibility that it might not be correct and that one of the non-Euclidean geometries might describe the world more accurately. Thus, for a long time, most mathematicians believed that the non-Euclidean geometries were interesting logical works but could not have any application to the real world.

In this connection it is interesting to note that the great German mathematician Karl Friedrich Gauss (1777–1855) was actually the first to realize that Euclid's parallel postulate was not necessarily true. He created a non-Euclidean geometry. However, he did not publish his results, partly because he was afraid of being ridiculed.

Gauss tried to test the "truth" of his geometry in the following way. In Euclidean geometry the sum of the angles of a triangle is *exactly* 180°. In non-Euclidean geometry it is either less than or greater than 180°. (In Gauss's version it was less than 180°.) So he tried to measure the angle sums of triangles to see whether they would turn out to be exactly 180°

or less than 180°. Now if you draw a triangle on a piece of paper, measure the angles, and add them up, you will find that the angle sum seems to be 180° (if you do it carefully). But measurements are only approximate, no matter how carefully they are made. Even worse, in Gauss's geometry the smaller the triangle is, the closer the angle sum is to 180°. For example, in Gauss's geometry a small triangle such as the one in Fig. 10.82 might have angle sum equal to 179.99999999999999°. This is so close to 180° that it would be impossible to measure any difference between this triangle and one that was exactly 180°. Thus Gauss needed very large triangles. He got them by putting three people on three different mountains. Each one measured the angle between the lines of sight from himself to the other two observers, as shown in Fig. 10.83.

Figure 10.82

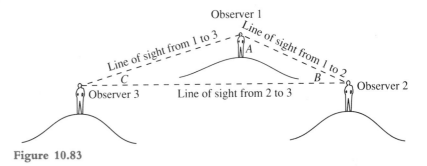

Figure 10.83

In this figure, observer 1 measured angle *A*, observer 2 measured angle *B*, and observer 3 measured angle *C*. The sum of these three angles turned out to be 179°59′58″. Did this mean that Gauss's geometry was correct because the result was less than 180°? No, the difference between his result and 180° was too small to be conclusive and might have been due to a measuring error. What was needed was an enormously large triangle, such as is found in astronomy.

In fact, the discoveries of twentieth century physics gave this kind of support to non-Euclidean geometry. In his work on relativity, Einstein used non-Euclidean geometry and obtained far better results than with Euclidean geometry. That is, predictions made on the basis of Einstein's theory agreed more closely with observed facts if non-Euclidean geometry was used. Then even the strongest supporters of Euclid had to acknowledge the applicability of non-Euclidean geometry to the real world.

Now the greater usefulness of non-Euclidean geometry in relativity theory is certainly a strong argument for its truth. But it does not *prove* that it *is* true.

Perhaps you are wondering why Euclidean geometry is still taught in all schools and used in engineering and practical applications if it is probably not true. The reason is simple—it works! Why does it work? As we have said with regard to Gauss's triangle experiment, in small areas there is no significant measurable difference between the results of Euclidean and non-Euclidean geometries. The earth is a very small region when compared to the whole universe. So on earth, Euclidean geometry is as "true" as any of the others for practical use. Since it is familiar and the easiest to use, we do so with perfectly good results.

The discovery and acceptance of non-Euclidean geometry has had an impact even outside mathematics. Most of science uses Euclidean geometry, and the doubt about its truth necessarily led to doubt about the truth of the scientific conclusions based on it. In fact, scientists began to doubt whether it was possible to ever find absolute scientific truths. The modern view is that such truths are not possible and that scientific "laws" are just approximate descriptions of the way we see the physical world. When the "absolutely true" geometry of Euclid turned out to be not as true as people had thought, scholars in other areas began to question their "truths." In fact, philosophers began to ask whether we can ever discover truths in general. This has led to a reexamination of what we can "know" in all areas of human knowledge—history, economics, law, ethics, etc. The debate about what we can know is still in progress. It will probably continue for many years to come.

10.5

THE KÖNIGSBERG BRIDGE PROBLEM AND THE CONVEYOR BELT PROBLEM

Our aim in this section is to "solve" the Königsberg Bridge problem mentioned at the beginning of this chapter. We will examine some of the basic facts needed for the solution (without proving them) and then show how these facts can be used to solve the problem.

network theory
vertices

The ideas needed have to do with **network theory**. A network begins with some points called **vertices**. Some of these may be connected with lines or curves that do not cross each other. (Arcs that meet at the same vertex are not considered to cross each other.) These connecting lines are called **simple arcs**. A **network** consists of these vertices and the connecting arcs. Some examples of networks are shown in Figs. 10.84–10.90 on the next page.

simple arcs
network

even vertex
odd vertex

In a network a vertex is **even** if it has an even number of arcs going to or from it. A vertex is **odd** if it has an odd number of arcs going to or from it. *For the purpose of determining whether a vertex is even or odd, a loop is counted twice.* In Figs. 10.84–10.90 some of the vertices are even and some are odd, as shown in Table 10.1 on the following page.

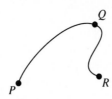

Figure 10.84 A network with two vertices, P and Q, and one arc.

Figure 10.85 A network with three vertices, P, Q, and R, and two arcs.

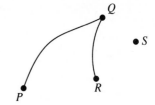

Figure 10.86 A network with four vertices, P, Q, R and S, and two arcs.

Figure 10.87 A network with two vertices, P and Q, and two arcs.

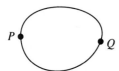

Figure 10.88 A network with one vertex, P. There is one arc that connects with point P twice. This arc is called a **loop**.

Figure 10.89 This is *not* a network, since the arc is not simple. It crosses itself.

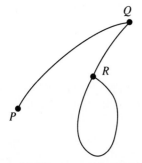

Figure 10.90 A network with three vertices, P, Q, and R, and three arcs.

	TABLE 10.1	
Figure number	Even vertices	Odd vertices
10.84	none	P, Q
10.85	Q	P, R
10.86	Q, S (0 is an even number)	P, R
10.87	P, Q	none
10.88	P (since the loop is counted twice)	none
10.90	Q	P, R

Königsberg Bridge problem

Now we are ready to solve the Königsberg Bridge problem. Look at the Königsberg bridges, which we have redrawn in Fig. 10.91. This picture can be thought of as a network by taking the locations A, B, C, and D as the vertices and by taking the bridges as arcs. This is shown in Fig. 10.92.

The picture can be further simplified as shown in Fig. 10.93.

We can now restate the Königsberg Bridge problem as follows: *Can we trace the complete network exactly once without going over any one point twice and without lifting the pencil from the paper?* Before reading further, see if you can do this.

Euler proved that this could be done only if the number of odd vertices is exactly 0 or 2. Look at Fig. 10.93 again. We see that A, B, C, and D

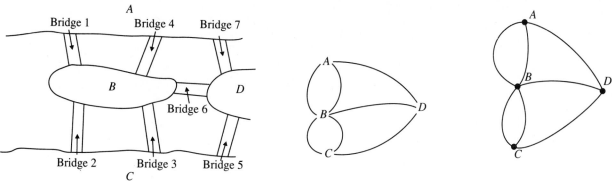

Figure 10.91   Figure 10.92   Figure 10.93

are *all* odd vertices. Thus there is a total of 4 odd vertices in this network. Since the total number of odd vertices is *not* 0 or 2, the bridges can never be crossed as required. This does not mean that it is difficult to cross the bridges as specified, but that it is *impossible*.

conveyor-belt problem

Another interesting problem that can be solved by using network theory is the **conveyor-belt problem**. Suppose that in a factory there are three different inspection stations and three different loading platforms, as shown in Fig. 10.94.

Figure 10.94

The manager wishes to connect each of the inspection stations to all three loading platforms by means of conveyor belts. For safety reasons, none of the belts may cross each other. Can this be done? If so, how? We suggest that the reader try to draw a diagram connecting the stations to the platforms under the given conditions before reading further.

connected network

This problem can be solved by using the idea of a **connected network**. *A network is said to be connected if every two of its vertices are connected by one or more arcs in succession.* In Fig. 10.95 the networks shown in parts (a), (b), (d), (f), (g), and (h) are connected. The network shown in part (c) is not connected because vertex *S* is not connected to any other arc. To put it another way, a network is connected if you can start at any vertex and

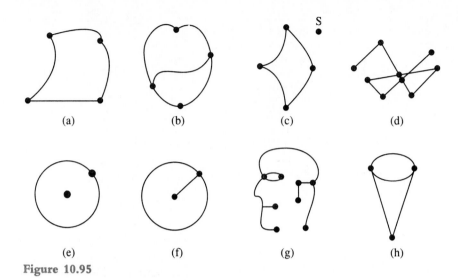

Figure 10.95

get to any other vertex by moving a pencil along arcs without lifting the pencil. Similarly, the network shown in part (e) is not connected.

In discussing connecting networks the following symbols are used.

V = the number of vertices,
E = the number of arcs, and
F = the number of regions into which the
network divides the page

Since this notation is important for the solution of the conveyor belt problem, we will illustrate it with some examples.

EXAMPLE 1

In Fig. 10.96 there are three vertices, A, B, and C. So $V = 3$. There are three arcs, so $E = 3$. The network divides the page into two parts, the inside (labeled I) and all of the outside (labeled II), so $F = 2$.   ■

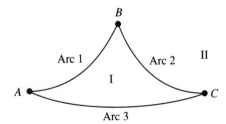

Figure 10.96

EXAMPLE 2

In Fig. 10.97 there are three vertices, so $V = 3$. There are four arcs, so $E = 4$. And we see there are three regions labeled I, II, and III, so $F = 3$.

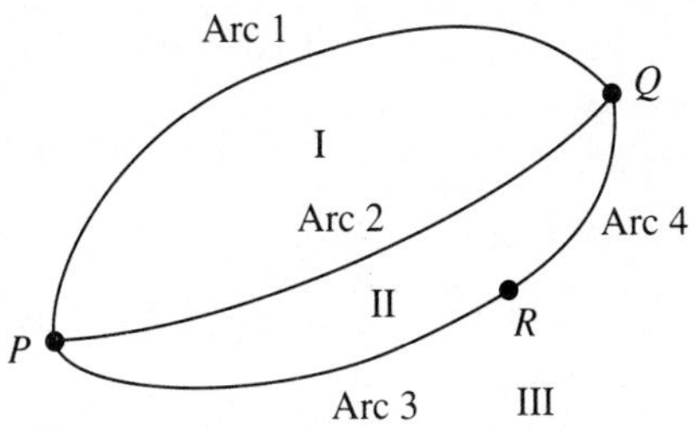

Arc 1

Q

I

Arc 2

Arc 4

II

R

P

Arc 3   III

Figure 10.97

Euler proved that for any connected network the following must always be true.

Euler's Formula

> **Euler's Formula** $V - E + F = 2$

Comment   In using Euler's formula a loop is considered to be *one* arc.

EXAMPLE 3

Verify Euler's formula for Example 1 above.

SOLUTION

In Example 1 we saw that $V = 3$, $E = 3$, and $F = 2$. Thus,

$$V - E + F = 3 - 3 + 2 = 2$$

Therefore $V - E + F = 2$, which is exactly what Euler's formula states.

EXAMPLE 4

Verify Euler's formula for Example 2 above.

SOLUTION

In Example 2 we saw that $V = 3$, $E = 4$, and $F = 3$. Thus

$$V - E + F = 3 - 4 + 3 = 2$$

so that again we have $V - E + F = 2$, which is what Euler's formula states.

EXAMPLE 5

Verify Euler's formula for the network shown in Fig. 10.98.

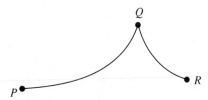

Q

R

P

Figure 10.98

SOLUTION

For this network, $V = 3$ and $E = 2$. How many regions are there for this network? From the diagram we see that the page is not divided into two or more parts by any of the arcs. Thus $F = 1$. Therefore

$$V - E + F = 3 - 2 + 1 = 2$$

Again, Euler's formula is true.

Let us now return to the conveyor belt problem described earlier. We will solve it by using a proof by contradiction. Suppose that the problem can be solved. That is, suppose that it *is* possible to connect the inspection stations with the loading platforms by belts that do not cross. In Fig. 10.99 we have drawn the three stations and the three platforms connected by belts. Pretend that the belts do not cross, even though in the diagram they appear to do so.

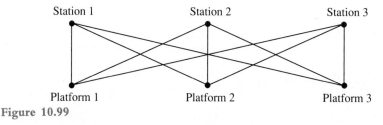

Figure 10.99

Let the inspection stations and loading platforms be vertices. There are six altogether. We can think of the belts as arcs. There are a total of nine such arcs. Since the problem specifies that the belts are not permitted to cross each other, these are actually simple arcs. This makes the diagram a network. Furthermore, it is a connected network. Therefore we can use Euler's formula. According to the formula, $V - E + F = 2$. Since $V = 6$ and $E = 9$, we have $6 - 9 + F = 2$. By trial and error, or by algebra, we find that $F = 5$. Remember that F represents the number of regions into which the network divides the page. Now look carefully at Fig. 10.99. There are no regions enclosed by exactly three arcs, like the ones shown in Figs. 10.100 and 10.101. Thus each separate region in the network must be enclosed by at least four arcs. Each individual arc borders on two regions, as shown in Fig. 10.102.

Now F (which is the number of regions) is five, and each of these has at least four arcs on its border. This gives us 5×4 or 20 arcs. However, since each arc is shared by two regions, we can divide the 20 in half, getting at least 10 arcs.

Thus the network must have at least 10 arcs. However, we previously saw that E (the number of arcs) is exactly 9 for this network. This is a contradiction, since E cannot be exactly 9 and, at the same time, at least 10.

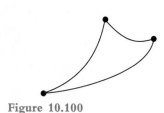

Figure 10.100

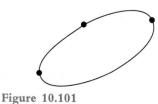

Figure 10.101

Figure 10.102 Arc A borders on both region I and region II.

Thus our assumption that it is possible to connect the stations to the platforms as specified leads to a contradiction. By the principle of the proof by contradiction our assumption is wrong. It follows that it is not possible to connect the stations with the platforms as specified.

EXERCISES FOR SECTION 10.5

1. Draw a network that has

   a) 3 vertices and 1 arc.

   b) 1 vertex and 4 arcs.

   c) 5 vertices and 2 arcs.

   d) 4 vertices and 4 arcs.

   e) 3 vertices and 3 arcs.

   f) 3 vertices and 5 arcs.

2. For each of the networks drawn in Exercise 1, state whether the vertices are even or odd.

Which of the networks given in Exercises 3–12 can be drawn without lifting the pencil from the paper and without drawing any line more than once? If possible, do it.

3.

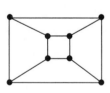

4.

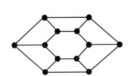

5.

6.

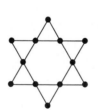

7.

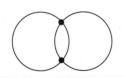

8.

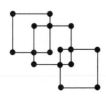

9.

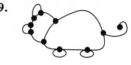

10.

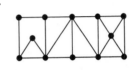

11.

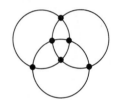

12.

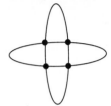

13. After Euler solved the Königsberg Bridge problem, an eighth bridge was built, as shown in Fig. 10.103. With this extra bridge added, can a person cross all eight bridges without crossing any one bridge twice?

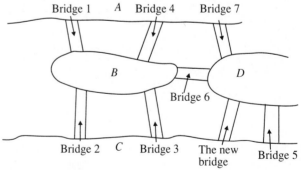

Figure 10.103

14. Figure 10.104 shows a map of part of the New York City area.

   a) Redraw the map as a network.

b) Is it possible to cross every bridge and tunnel once without crossing any one more than once?

Figure 10.104

15. Figure 10.105(a) is a floor plan of this authors' house.

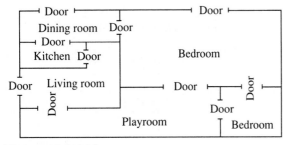

Figure 10.105(a)

A thief has just broken into the house and wants to ransack every room as quickly as possible. Can the thief go from one room to another without ever going through any door twice?

16. Having found nothing in the author's house, the thief has now broken into a neighbor's house. The floor plan for this house is shown in Fig. 10.105 (b)

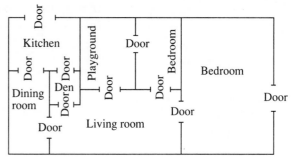

Figure 10.105(b)

For this house, can the thief go from one room to another without going through any one door twice?

17. In the nineteenth century the mathematician William Rowan Hamilton invented the following puzzle. Consider the picture shown in Fig. 10.106. Can we find a path along the edges of the picture that passes through each vertex once and yet returns to its starting point? (*Hint:* Not every arc has to be crossed.)

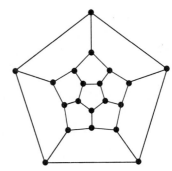

Figure 10.106
The Hamiltonian puzzle

18. A sanitation crew must collect garbage from every street in the territory shown in Fig. 10.107.

a) How can this be done so that no street is crossed twice?

b) A new road is being built between points *A* and *B*. When this road is built, will the sanitation crew still be able to collect the garbage from every street without covering any one street twice?

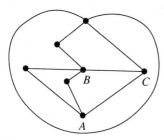

Figure 10.107

For each of the networks given in Exercises 19–27, determine whether the network is connected. If it is, find the values of V, E, and F, and verify Euler's formula.

19.

20.

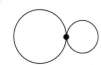

21.

22.

23.

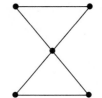

24.

25.

26.

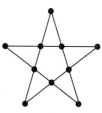

27.

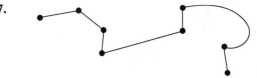

28. Suppose that one of the inspection stations in the conveyor belt problem has to be connected to only two of the loading platforms. All the other conditions remain the same. It is now possible to solve the problem. Draw a diagram showing how this can be done.

10.6

THE MÖBIUS STRIP

Consider the page you are now reading. It has two sides, one called page 613 and the other page 614. If you wish, you can paint one side blue and the other side red. The edge of the page separates the two sides.

Most surfaces have two sides. For example, take off one of your socks or stockings. There is an inside and an outside. If some paint fell on your sock while you were painting this page, you could turn it inside out, and the paint would not show because it would now be on the inside. Manufacturers of belts sometimes make use of this fact by making reversible belts. One side is one color, and the other side is another color.

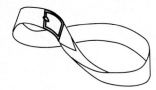

Figure 10.108

Figure 10.109

Figure 10.110
"Halving" a Möbius strip

Figure 10.111
A Möbius strip cut in thirds

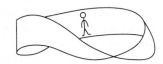

Figure 10.112

The German mathematician Augustus Ferdinand Möbius (1790–1868) was able to create a surface that had only one side! Actually, it is not difficult to make such a surface. You can make one by taking off your belt, giving it a half-twist and then fastening it, as shown in Fig. 10.108.

You now have a surface that is called a **Möbius strip**. If you do not have a belt, you can make a Möbius strip by taking a strip of paper, giving one end a half-twist, and then gluing the ends together, as shown in Fig. 10.109.

Now take a Möbius strip made out of paper and start painting or coloring one side. What happens should convince you that this surface has only one side! Now take another Möbius strip and cut it along the middle of the strip as shown in Fig. 10.110. What happens?

Next take another Möbius strip and cut it, this time one-third of the way in from an edge as shown in Fig. 10.111. What happens this time?

On a one-sided surface, such as a Möbius strip, many unusual things can happen. For example, imagine that we have a two-dimensional man who lives on this page, as shown in Fig. 10.112. This man lives entirely within this page and cannot come out. Suppose that a friend comes to visit him and walks up behind him. Our man wants to turn around to greet him. However, to do this, he must come out of the page, which he cannot do. If he tries to turn around to face his friend, he will end up standing on his head as shown in Fig. 10.113.

However, if our man lived in a Möbius strip, while he would still be a two-dimensional man, he would be able to face his friend without standing on his head. All he has to do is simply walk around the strip once. To see how he does this, see Fig. 10.114.

While Möbius strips are very entertaining, they are more than that. In recent years the Goodrich Rubber Company applied for a patent on a conveyer belt that was constructed as a Möbius strip. (See Fig. 10.115.) What would be the advantage of using such a conveyor belt?

Figure 10.113

Figure 10.114

Figure 10.115

EXERCISES FOR SECTION 10.6

1. Take a strip of paper and give it three half twists. Now glue the edges together. This is another type of Möbius strip.

   a) Cut it down the middle and see what happens.

   b) Cut it on a line one-third of the way from one edge. What happens?

2. Cut an ordinary Möbius strip one-fourth of the way from the edge. What happens?

3. Another interesting one-sided surface is the **Klein bottle**, shown at the right. The German mathematician Felix Klein (1849–1925) was the first to discover such a bottle. Consult the references in a library to find out all you can about Klein bottles.

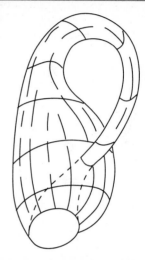

Figure 10.116
The bottle with
no inside

---

*10.7

INTRODUCING THE LOGO TURTLE : USING LOGO IN GEOMETRY

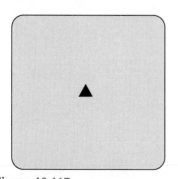

Figure 10.117

In this section we indicate how the computer language LOGO can be used as a problem solving tool in mathematics. LOGO enables us to draw pictures on a computer screen. Thus LOGO is especially suited for studying geometry. Although the material in this section is independent of any other material on LOGO that appears in this book, the reader is urged to first read the material on LOGO in Chapter 14 before proceeding further.

To draw any pictures on the display screen, we use a small triangle, ▲, called the **LOGO turtle**. (See Fig. 10.117.) This turtle is a powerful object in that it lets us draw any kinds of pictures. However, we must tell the turtle exactly what to do. We can think of the turtle as a mechanical robot that methodically follows our commands. The two most important

FORWARD
BACK
RIGHT
LEFT

types of LOGO commands at our disposal are those that make the turtle move in a straight line and those that make it turn. By using the correct combinations of these commands, we can make the turtle draw almost anything. The LOGO commands **FORWARD** and **BACK** are used to make the turtle draw lines. The commands **RIGHT** and **LEFT** are used to make the turtle turn.

The easiest figure to draw is a square. We first load the LOGO program. After we see both the turtle and the question mark with the text cursor next to it, we enter FORWARD 20. This moves the turtle 20 units, as shown in Fig. 10.118.

Next, we instruct the turtle to turn right 90 degrees. To accomplish this, we enter RIGHT 90. The results are shown in Fig. 10.119.

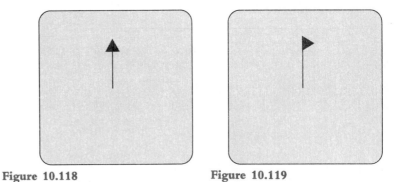

Figure 10.118   Figure 10.119

Next, we instruct the turtle to move forward 20 units. We enter FORWARD 20. (See Fig. 10.120.)

Now we tell the turtle to turn right 90 degrees. We enter RIGHT 90. Continuing in this manner we find that the turtle returns to its initial starting position and its starting orientation after following the commands FORWARD 20 and RIGHT 90 repeated four times. (See Fig. 10.121.)

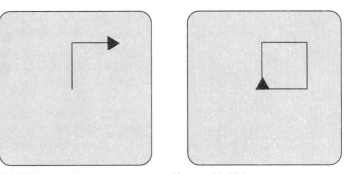

Figure 10.120   Figure 10.121

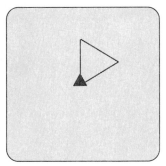

Figure 10.122

RIGHT 45 FORWARD 60
LEFT 135 FORWARD 40
LEFT 135 FORWARD 60

Figure 10.123

LOGO has a special command that makes it easy for us to write repeated expressions. To draw a square quickly, we enter

REPEAT 4 [FORWARD 20 RIGHT 90]

This command repeats the move inside the brackets four times. The turtle draws a square. Similarly, the command

REPEAT 3 [FORWARD 30 RIGHT 120]

tells the turtle to draw an equilateral triangle that is 30 units long on each side. (See Fig. 10.122.)

Notice that the amount of turning needed for the turtle to return to its original starting position and orientation is equal to the amount of turning in a complete circle. Actually, any convex polygon can be drawn with the total turtle turning being 360°. This result is known as **Total Turtle Trip Theorem**.

In each of the two previous examples, we sent the turtle around a perfectly closed path and back to its exact starting position. Such closed paths are called **state change invariant**. In Fig. 10.123 the turtle does not return to its initial starting position.

Suppose we wish to have the turtle draw a five-pointed star. If we enter FORWARD 30, we notice that to complete the star, the turtle draws a line 30 units in length, then must turn through some angle A and repeat the process four more times. (See Fig. 10.124.)

The command REPEAT 5 [FORWARD 30 RIGHT A] should accomplish this provided we can determine the value of A. In Fig. 10.125 we indicate several possible diagrams that result by using different values for A.

Figure 10.124

REPEAT 5 [FORWARD 30 RIGHT 140]

Figure 10.125

REPEAT 5 [FORWARD 30 RIGHT 150]

By a trial-and-error procedure, we find that angle A must be 144 degrees. We can indeed verify that this is the correct value of A by instructing the

Figure 10.126

turtle to execute REPEAT 20 [FORWARD 30 RIGHT 144]. The turtle draws the five-pointed star shown in Fig. 10.126 and repeats it numerous times.

EXERCISES FOR SECTION 10.7

1. Find the missing LOGO command in each of the following:

a)

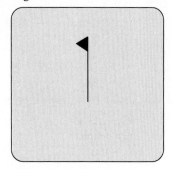

FORWARD 50 _____ 90

b)

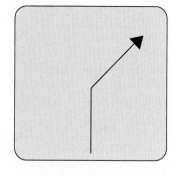

FORWARD 50 _____ 45
FORWARD 50

c)

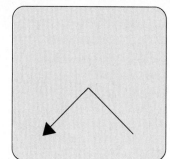

LEFT 45 FORWARD 50
_____ 90 FORWARD 50

d)

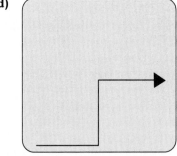

RIGHT 90 FORWARD 50
_____ 90 FORWARD 50
RIGHT 90 FORWARD 50

Draw a picture for the LOGO commands given in Exercises 2–4.

2. FORWARD 50 LEFT 90
   FORWARD 50 LEFT 90
   FORWARD 50

3. FORWARD 50 RIGHT 90
   FORWARD 50 RIGHT 90
   FORWARD 50 RIGHT 90
   FORWARD 50

4. REPEAT 12 [FORWARD 30 RIGHT 60]

5. Write LOGO commands to enable the turtle to draw the following pictures.

a)

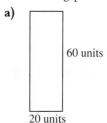

60 units

20 units

b)

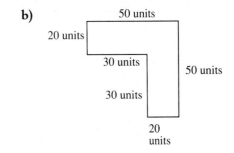

6. How many degrees must the turtle turn at each angle so as to complete

   a) a regular heptagon?
   b) a regular octagon?
   c) a regular decagon?
   d) a regular dodecagon?

TYPICAL CLASSROOM QUESTIONS

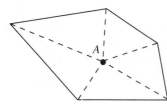

Figure 10.127

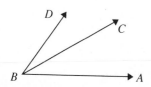

Figure 10.128

1. A student claims that it is possible for two skew lines to be coplanar. Do you agree?

2. A student claims that a line segment cannot contain an infinite set of points, since a line segment has a definite starting and a definite ending point. Do you agree?

3. The sum of the measures of the interior angles of a regular polygon of n sides is $180 (n - 2)$. A student wonders if this is true for only a regular polygon or if this is true for any convex polygon. What is your answer? Explain your answer.

4. A student claims that the sum of the measures of the interior angles of any convex pentagon can be found by selecting any interior point A and constructing triangles as shown in Fig. 10.127.
   Do you agree that this procedure will yield the same result that we obtained earlier, namely $180° (n - 2)$?

5. Can the procedure described in the previous question be used to find the sum of the measures of the angles of any convex polygon?

6. Is it true that if two lines do not intersect, then they must be parallel?

7. A student believes that angles ABC and ABD shown in Fig. 10.128 are adjacent angles. Do you agree?

8. Is it true that angles DBE and ABC, shown in Fig. 10.129, are vertical angles?

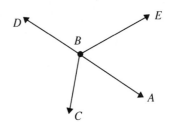

Figure 10.129

The following is a chapter outline in capsule form. You should now be able to demonstrate your knowledge of the ideas mentioned by giving definitions, descriptions, or specific examples. Page references are given in parentheses.

A. Some Basic Ideas

Point, **line**, and **plane** are **undefined terms**. (p. 566)

Points that lie on the same line are **collinear**. A point divides a line into two **half-lines**. (p. 567)

A half-line together with its dividing point is called a **ray**. (p. 567)

Any two points A and B, together with all the points on the line that lie between them, determine **line segment** $\overline{AB}$. (p. 567)

Two distinct lines that contain the same point are said to **intersect** at that point. If two distinct lines that are in the same plane do not contain a common point, then they are **parallel**. (p. 568)

Points that lie on the same plane are **coplanar**. (p. 568)

Two lines that do not lie on the same plane and that do not intersect are called **skew lines**. (p. 570)

The **distance** between any two points A and B on a line is the nonnegative difference of the real numbers a and b on a real number line to which A and B correspond. (p. 570)

Point M is called the **midpoint** of line segment $\overline{AB}$ if it is equidistant from points A and B; that is, if $\overline{AM} = \overline{MB}$. (p. 570)

B. Angles

An **angle** is the union of two rays that have a common endpoint. The rays are called the **sides** of the angle and the endpoint is called the **vertex** of the angle. (p. 572)

Two lines are said to be **perpendicular** if the angle at which they intersect is 90°, or a right angle. (p. 574)

A **right angle** is an angle whose measure is 90°. A **straight angle** is an angle whose measure is 180°. An **acute angle** is an angle whose measure is between 0° and 90°. An **obtuse angle** is an angle whose measure is between 90° and 180°. (p. 574)

Rotational angles can be drawn of any size. (p. 575)

The unit of angular measures is either **degrees** or **radians**. (p. 575)

Two angles are said to be **adjacent** if they have a common ray and a common vertex but do not have any interior points in common. (p. 576)

When two lines intersect, the nonadjacent angles formed are called **vertical angles**. (p. 576)

Two angles are **complementary** if the sum of their measures is 90°. (p. 579)

Two angles are **supplementary** if the sum of their measures is 180°. (p. 579)

C. Some Theorems Involving Angles

When two distinct lines intersect, the vertical angles formed are congruent. (p. 576)

If two distinct lines are cut by a **transversal** as shown in Fig. 10.130, then the following are true if and only if the lines are parallel:

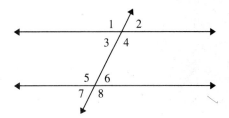

Figure 10.130

a) Pairs of corresponding angles (angles 2 and 6 or 4 and 8 or 1 and 5 or 3 and 7) are congruent.

b) Alternate interior angles (angles 3 and 6 or 4 and 5) are congruent.

c) Alternate exterior angles (angles 1 and 8 or 2 and 7) are congruent.

d) interior angles on the same side of the transversal (angles 4 and 6 or 3 and 5) are supplementary (pages 580–581).

D. Curves, Triangles and Polygons

A **simple closed curve** is any closed curve that can be drawn without lifting the pencil such that the drawing starts and stops at the same point and that no point is touched twice (with the exception of the starting point). (p. 585)

A simple closed curve separates the plane into three mutually disjoint sets of points — the curve itself, the interior of the curve, and the exterior of the curve. (The **Jordan Curve Theorem**) (p. 586)

A **polygon** is a simple closed curve consisting of straight line segments such that no two segments with a common endpoint are collinear. (p. 586)

The straight line segments that form any general polygon are called its **sides**. The point at which two sides meet is called a **vertex**. (p. 586)

Polygons are classified according to the number of sides (or vertices) they have. A **triangle** has three sides, a **quadrilateral** has four sides, a **pentagon** has five sides, a **hexagon** has six sides, etc. (p. 587)

Any line segment joining nonconsecutive vertices of a polygon is called a **diagonal**. (p. 587)

A **regular polygon** is a polygon that is both equilateral and equiangular. (p. 589)

Triangles can be **equilateral**, **isosceles**, **scalene**, or **right**. In a right triangle the side opposite the right angle is called the **hypotenuse.** The other sides are called the **legs** of the triangle. (p. 588)

A **convex polygon** is a polygon each of whose interior angles measures less than 180°. When at least one interior angle of a polygon measures more than 180°, we have a **concave polygon**. (p. 589)

Parallelograms, **rectangles**, **rhombuses**, **squares**, and **trapezoids** are all special types of quadrilaterals. (p. 590)

Congruent figures are figures with the same size and shape. (p. 598) Euclidean and non-Euclidean geometries differ in which postulates they assume. (p. 602)

E. Networks

A **network** is a collection of points called **vertices** and a collection of connecting lines called **simple arcs**. (p. 605)

In a network a vertex is **even** if it has an even number of arcs going to or from it. A vertex is **odd** if it has an odd number of arcs going to or from it. For the purpose of determining whether a vertex is even or odd, a **loop** is counted twice. (p. 605)

Euler proved that the **Königsberg Bridges** could never be crossed as required since the number of odd vertices is not exactly 0 or 2. (p. 607)

A network is said to be **connected** if every two of its vertices are connected by one or more arcs in succession. (p. 607).

Euler's formula shows that it is not possible to connect the stations with the platforms as specified in the **Conveyor-belt problem**. (p. 607)

A surface that has only one side is called a **Möbius strip**. (p. 614)

The **Klein bottle** is a bottle that has only one surface. (p. 615)

F. LOGO

LOGO is a computer graphics program that enables us to draw geometric pictures on a computer screen. We draw pictures by using a small triangle, ▲, called the **LOGO turtle**. (p. 615)

The LOGO commands **FORWARD** and **BACK** are used to make the turtle draw lines. The commands **RIGHT** and **LEFT** are used to make the turtle turn. (p. 616)

When the turtle travels along a perfectly closed path and returns to its exact starting point, then the closed path is called **state change invariant**. (p. 617)

Any convex polygon can be drawn with the turtle's turns totaling 360°. This result is known as **Total Turtle Trip Theorem**. (p. 617)

KEY TERMS

The following list presents the key terms introduced in this chapter.

10.1 line   half-line
         point   endpoint
         undefined term   ray
         collinear points   line segment

intersecting lines
plane
coplanar
half-plane
parallel planes
parallel lines
skew lines
distance between points
coordinates of points
midpoint of segment

10.2 angle
sides of an angle
vertex
regions
interior of an angle
exterior of an angle
protractor
degrees, minutes, seconds
perpendicular lines
right angle
straight angle
obtuse angle
rotational angles
adjacent angles
vertical angles
radian measure
complementary angles
supplementary angles
transversal
alternate interior angles
corresponding angles

10.3 simple closed curve
Jordan Curve Theorem
polygon
triangle
sides
vertex
diagonal
equilateral triangle
isosceles triangle
right triangle
hypotenuse

legs
regular polygon
interior and exterior
  angles
convex polygon
concave polygon
convex region

10.4 *Elements*
Euclid
Euclidean postulates
theorems
congruent figures
corresponding sides
Euclid's parallel
  postulate
Lobachevskian parallel
  postulate
Riemann parallel
  postulate

10.5 network theory
vertices
simple arcs
even vertex
odd vertex
loop
Königsberg bridge
  problem
conveyor-belt problem
connected network
Euler's formula

10.6 The Möbius strip
Klein bottle

10.7 The LOGO turtle
FORWARD
BACK
RIGHT
LEFT
Total turtle trip
  theorem
State change invariant

FORMULAS TO REMEMBER   The following list summarizes all of the formulas given in this chapter.

$$1 \text{ radian} = \frac{180°}{\pi} \quad \text{and} \quad \frac{\pi}{180} \text{ radians} = 1 \text{ degree}$$

One radian is approximately 57 degrees and one degree is approximately 0.0174 radians.

To convert from an angle measured in degrees to radian measure, multiply by $\dfrac{\pi}{180}$.

To convert from an angle measured in radians to degree measure, multiply by $\dfrac{180}{\pi}$.

The sum of the measures of the angles of a triangle is 180°.

The sum of the measures of the interior angles of any convex polygon of n sides is $180° \, (n - 2)$.

The sum of the measures of the exterior angles of any convex polygon is 360°.

The measure of each interior angle of a convex polygon of n sides is $\dfrac{180° \, (n - 2)}{n}$.

In a right triangle, the sum of the squares of the legs equals the square of the hypotenuse.

Euler's Formula. For any connected network $V - E + F = 2$,

where V = the number of vertices,
E = the number of arcs, and
F = the number of regions into which the network divides the page.

CHAPTER REVIEW EXERCISES

1. Given that the length of the hypotenuse of a right triangle is 13 and the length of one leg is 12, find the length of the other leg.

2. Two angles of a triangle are equal in measure and the third angle is 150°. Find the number of degrees in one of the two equal angles.

3. The perimeter of a regular pentagon is represented by $(15x - 20)$. Express in terms of x the length of one side of the pentagon.

4. An angle of 75° measures how many radians?

5. Convert $\dfrac{7\pi}{12}$ radians to degree measure.

6. The measures of the angles of a triangle are represented by x, $2x$, and $x + 20$. Find the number of degrees in the measure of the *largest* angle of the triangle.

7. The lengths of two legs of a right triangle are 3 and 5. Find, in radical form, the length of the hypotenuse.

8. Draw a network that has five vertices and three arcs.

9. Determine whether the network shown in Fig. 10.131 is connected.

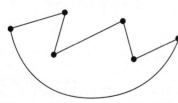

Figure 10.131

10. Find the number of sides that a regular polygon has if each of its exterior angles measures $20°$.

11. Find the number of sides that a regular polygon has if each of its interior angles measures $108°$.

12. Find the number of diagonals that a polygon has if the sum of the measures of its interior angles is $540°$.

13. The measure of the vertex angle of an isosceles triangle is $110°$. Find the measure of a base angle of the triangle.

14. In $\triangle ABC$, if the measures of angles A and B are $40°$ and $45°$, what is the measure of an exterior angle drawn to the triangle at vertex C?

For questions 15–18 refer to Fig. 10.132, where line $\overleftrightarrow{GH}$ is a transversal intersecting parallel lines $\overleftrightarrow{AB}$ and $\overleftrightarrow{CD}$ at points E and F respectively.

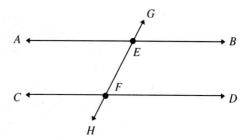

Figure 10.132

15. The measures of angles BEF and EFC are $7x - 30$ and $5x + 10$ respectively. Find x.

16. The measures of angles BEF and DFE are $4x + 20$ and $2x + 10$ respectively. Find x.

17. The measures of angles AEG and CFE are $6x + 15$ and $10x - 45$ respectively. Find x.

18. The measures of angles GEB and HFC are $2x + 19$ and $8x - 29$ respectively. Find x.

19. The measures of the angles of a quadrilateral are in the ratio $2:3:4:9$. Find the number of degrees in the measure of the smallest angle of the quadrilateral.

20. If the measures of the angles of a triangle are represented by m, n, and $m + n$, then the triangle must be

   a) isosceles   **b)** right   **c)** equilateral   **d)** obtuse

For questions 21–24 refer to Fig. 10.133 with the indicated points.

21. Find $\overline{AD} \cap \overline{GD}$

22. Find $\overline{BG} \cup \overline{FC}$

23. Find $(\overline{AD} \cup \overline{DC}) \cup (\overline{BC} \cup \overline{BA})$

24. Find $(\overline{GC} \cup \overline{CD}) \cap \overline{DG}$

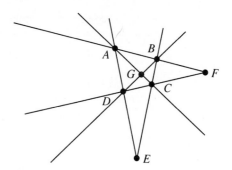

Figure 10.133

25. Two angles of a triangle are complementary. Find the number of degrees in the measure of the third angle of the triangle.

26. The sum of the measures of two angles is 120°. If the measure of one of the angles is five times that of the other, which statement must be true?

a) The angles are supplementary.

b) Both angles are acute angles.

c) The angles are complementary.

d) One angle is an acute angle and the other is an obtuse angle.

27. In Fig. 10.134, $\overleftrightarrow{AB} \parallel \overleftrightarrow{CD}$ and $\overleftrightarrow{EF}$ intersects $\overleftrightarrow{AB}$ at G and $\overleftrightarrow{CD}$ at H. The degree measure of $\angle AGH$ is $(3x - 10)$ and the degree measure of $\angle GHD$ is 80. Find the value of x.

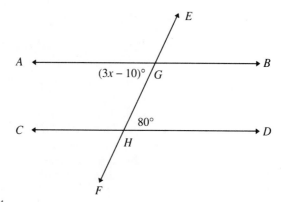

Figure 10.134

28. As shown in Fig. 10.135, $\overleftrightarrow{AB}$ and $\overleftrightarrow{CD}$ intersect at point E. The degree measures of vertical angles AED and CEB are represented by $(3x + 20)°$ and $(8x - 5)°$. Find the value of x.

29. In Fig. 10.136 $\angle BCD$ is an exterior angle of triangle ABC. The measure of $\angle A$ is 35° and the measure of $\angle B$ is 75°. Find the number of degrees in the measure of $\angle BCD$.

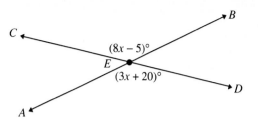

Figure 10.135

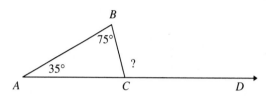

Figure 10.136

SUGGESTED FURTHER READING

Choquet, G., *Geometry in a Modern Setting*. Paris: Hermann, 1961. Section 57 deals with the definition of angles.

Cox, P., "Informal Geometry—More is Needed," in *The Mathematics Teacher* **78** (September 1985), 404–405.

Henderson, G., and C. Collier, "Geometric Activities for Later Childhood Education," in *The Arithmetic Teacher* **20** (October 1973), 444–453.

Jacobs, H.R., *Geometry*. San Francisco: W.H. Freeman, 1974.

Kline, M., *Mathematics: A Cultural Approach*. Reading, Mass: Addison-Wesley, 1962. Chapter 6 discusses the nature and uses of Euclidean geometry; Chapter 26 discusses non-Euclidean geometries and their significance.

Ross, J., "How to Make a Möbius Hat," in *The Mathematics Teacher* **78** (April 1985), 419–428.

Synge, J.L., *Science: Sense and Non-sense*. New York: W.W. Norton, 1950. Pages 26–30 contain an imaginary discussion between Euclid and a 12-year-old boy.

Toth, L., "Non-Euclidean Geometry Before Euclid," in *Scientific American* (November 1969). This article suggests that the ancient Greeks knew about non-Euclidean geometry.

Zaslavsky, C., "Network—New York Subways, A Piece of String and African Traditions," in *The Arithmetic Teacher* **29** (October 1981), 42–47.

CHAPTER 11

Coordinate Geometry

CHAPTER OBJECTIVES

☐ **To review** the rectangular coordinate system and how we plot points in this system. (*Section 11.1*)

☐ **To introduce** the distance and midpoint formulas which enable us to prove some basic theorems involving congruent lines. (*Section 11.2*)

☐ **To learn** how we draw the graph of a linear equation. (*Section 11.3*)

☐ **To indicate** how we find the x- and y-intercept of a line. (*Section 11.4*)

☐ **To understand** what is meant by the slope of a line. (*Section 11.4*)

☐ **To study** the different forms of an equation of a line. (*Section 11.4*)

☐ **To demonstrate** how we draw graphs involving linear inequalities. (*Section 11.5*)

☐ **To point out** how we can solve a system of linear equations and a system of linear inequalities graphically. (*Section 11.6*)

☐ **To use** the LOGO computer graphics program. (*Section 11.7*)

☐ **To apply** the ideas of coordinate geometry to many different geometric settings. (*Throughout this chapter*)

In its March 1989 *Curriculum and Evaluation Standards For School Mathematics* (p. 161), the National Council Of Teachers Of Mathematics recommends that the mathematics curriculum should include the study of the geometry of two and three dimensions from an algebraic point of view so that students can

☐ translate between synthetic and coordinate representations,
☐ deduce properties of figures using coordinates,
☐ apply coordinates in problem solving situations.

The interplay between geometry and algebra strengthens students' ability to formulate and analyze problems from situations both within and outside mathematics. Objects and relations in geometry correspond directly to objects and relations in algebra. For example, a point in geometry corresponds to an ordered pair (x, y) of numbers in algebra, a line to a set of ordered pairs satisfying an equation of the form $ax + by = c$, and the intersection of two lines to the set of ordered pairs that satisfy the corresponding equations. It is correspondences like these that allow translation between the two "languages" and permit concepts in one to clarify and reinforce concepts in the other. In fact, deducing properties of geometric figures using their coordinate representations is often easier for students than synthetic proofs are. For example, all students can calculate the coordinates of the midpoints of two sides of a triangle with given numerical coordinates and use the results to deduce that the segment

joining them is parallel to the third side of the triangle and equals half its length.

It is for this reason that in this chapter we analyze the basic ideas of coordinate geometry and indicate how these ideas can be extended to prove results in general.

When we drive in a car, we often encounter road signs such as the one shown at the left. This alerts us that we are heading for a downgrade that may be long, steep or sharply curved. Highway slopes are measured in percents with Interstate highways being restricted to a maximum slope of 6%. Thus a highway with a slope of 2% gains 2 feet in altitude for every 100 feet that the road travels hroizontally.

In this chapter we will discuss and apply the idea of slope.

Introduction

Most of us are familiar with the concept of a graph, although we might not use this name specifically. For example, consider the map of part of San Francisco shown in Fig. 11.1. Chinatown has a map location of approximately I7. To find it, we move across the bottom scale until we arrive at the I position. We draw a vertical line through this location. Next, we find 7 on the side of the map and draw a horizontal line through this point. The place where the horizontal and vertical lines meet (intersect) is the approximate location of Chinatown. What is the map location of Alcatraz? Alcatraz has a map location of N3. What is the map location of Fisherman's Wharf?

Since most of the functions that we discuss in this book are given by means of an equation, we often find it convenient to draw a "picture," called the **graph** of the equation. It is for this reason that in this chapter we study the rectangular coordinate system and graphs that can be drawn in this system.

graph

HISTORICAL NOTE

The idea of graphs can be traced back to the ancient Egyptians and Greeks. Many Greek mathematicians, including Euclid and Apollonius, studied graphs. *The Elements*, written by Euclid, contains a detailed treatment of figures formed by straight lines and circles. *Conic Sections*, written by Apollonius, presents a thorough discussion of the graphs of conic sections, which he named ellipses, parabolas, and hyperbolas. In the seventeenth century the French mathematician René Descartes (1596–1650) developed an algebraic method for analyzing curves. This is the basis of the coordinate geometry and graphs that we study in this chapter.

So successful was Descartes's work that he soon was invited to the courts of many kings and queens. He routinely declined most of these invitations. In 1649, however, he was invited to the court of Queen Christina of Sweden to give the queen instruction in philosophy. He accepted this invitation. Queen Christina preferred to work in the mornings in the unheated castle, whereas Descartes was accustomed to staying in bed until noon, when it warmed up a bit. Several months after arriving in Stockholm, Descartes contracted pneumonia. In 1650, Descartes died at the age of 54, apparently as a result of his inability to adapt to the rigors of the Swedish winter.

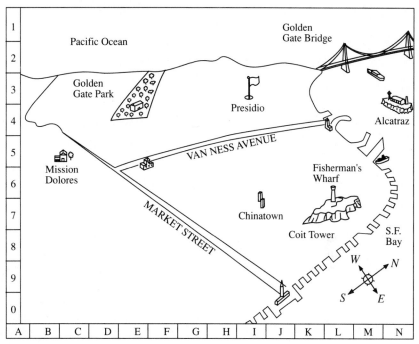

Figure 11.1

11.1

THE RECTANGULAR COORDINATE SYSTEM

number line

origin

positive direction

negative direction

coordinate

To get started, let us first discuss a convenient way of representing numbers, that is, by means of a **number line**. A horizontal line is drawn, and any point on it is selected as the starting point. This point is labeled 0 and is called the **origin** (see Fig. 11.2). Since a line can be extended indefinitely in either direction, we indicate this by putting arrows at the left and at the right.

Next we select any convenient unit of length and mark off points in succession both to the right and left of zero. When we move in a direction that is to the right of 0, we say that we are moving in the **positive direction**. When we move to the left, we say that we are moving in the **negative direction**. We label the points as shown in Fig. 11.3. The number that names a point is called the **coordinate** of the point.

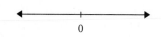

0

Figure 11.2

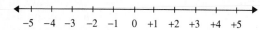

−5 −4 −3 −2 −1   0 +1 +2 +3 +4 +5

Figure 11.3 A horizontal number line

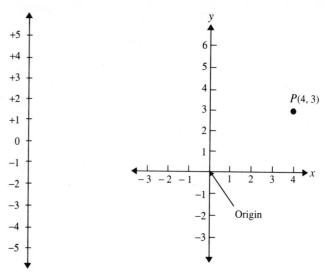

Figure 11.4 A vertical number line   **Figure 11.5**

Number lines do not necessarily have to be drawn horizontally. They may also be drawn vertically, as shown in Fig. 11.4.

In the rectangular coordinate system we draw two lines (one vertical and one horizontal) that are perpendicular to each other. The horizontal line is called the **x-axis**, and the vertical line is called the **y-axis**. The point where the x-axis and the y-axis meet is called the **origin**. Both of the axes are labeled with a **number scale**, as shown in Fig. 11.5. Starting at the origin, if we move to the right, we are going in the positive direction on the x-axis as opposed to moving to the left, which is the negative direction. Similarly, if we start at the origin and move up, we are going in the positive direction on the y-axis as opposed to moving down, which is the negative direction.

Look at Fig. 11.5. To get to point P, we start at the origin and move 4 units to the right and then, from that point, move up 3 units. We call 4 the **x-coordinate** or **abscissa** of the point and 3 the **y-coordinate** or **ordinate** of the point. We label the point as (4, 3), always being careful to write the x-coordinate first and then the y-coordinate. The numbers (4, 3) are called the **coordinates** of point P. We always enclose the x- and y-coordinates within parentheses and separate them by a comma.

In Fig. 11.6 the coordinates of point Q are (−3, 1). This means that we start at the origin, move 3 units to the left, and then, from that point, move up 1 unit.

The coordinates of point R are (−4, −2). We start at the origin, move 4 units to the left, and then, from that point, move down 2 units.

The coordinates of point S are (3, 0). We start at the origin, move 3 units to the right, and then move 0 units up or down.

x-axis

y-axis
origin

number scale

x-coordinate

abscissa

y-coordinate

ordinate

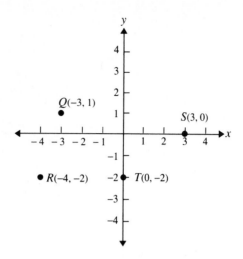

Figure 11.6

The coordinates of point T are $(0, -2)$. We start at the origin and move 0 units to the right or left. Then, from that point, we move down 2 units.

Notice that the x-axis and y-axis divide the plane (paper) into four regions. Each region is called a **quadrant**, and these are labeled counterclockwise as shown in Fig. 11.7. The values of x and y for any point may be positive or negative depending on the quadrant in which they are located. The different possibilities are summarized below.

quadrant

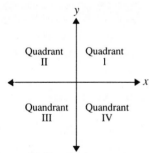

Figure 11.7   The four quadrants

If point is in quadrant	Then x is	Then y is
I	positive	positive
II	negative	positive
III	negative	negative
IV	positive	negative

What are the values of x and y when the point is on the line between the quadrants?

rectangular coordinate system

The system that we have just described, which was developed by René Descartes, is called a **rectangular coordinate system**. It is the one that is most commonly used in mathematics. It should be noted that other systems are possible. In this text we use only a rectangular coordinate system.

To stimulate interest, the rectangular coordinate system can be presented to children in the form of a ridde. This can be seen in the riddle on the top of the next page which is from *Addison-Wesley Mathematics*, 1987, Grade 5, p. 293.

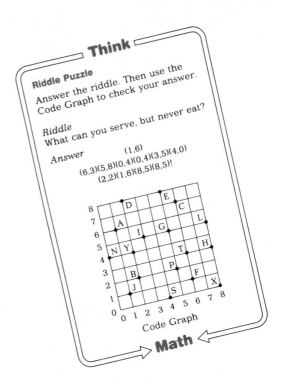

Think

Riddle Puzzle

Answer the riddle. Then use the Code Graph to check your answer.

Riddle
What can you serve, but never eat?

Answer
(1,6)
(6,3)(5,8)(0,4)(0,4)(3,5)(4,0)
(2,2)(1,6)(8,5)(8,5)!

Code Graph

Math

EXERCISES FOR SECTION 11.1

For Exercises 1–8, refer to the graph shown in Fig. 11.8. Find the coordinates of the points indicated.

1. Point A **2.** Point B **3.** Point C

4. Point D **5.** Point E **6.** Point F

7. Point G **8.** Point H

For Exercises 9–20, draw a pair of coordinate axes and graph the specified points.

9. $(7, 3)$ **10.** $(4, -3)$ **11.** $(-2, -7)$

12. $(3, 0)$ **13.** $(-4, 0)$ **14.** $(0, 3)$

15. $(0, -8)$ **16.** $(0, 0)$ **17.** $(|-3|, 7)$

18. $(|-4|, |-3|)$ **19.** $(-4, |-3|)$ **20.** $(|5|, |-3|)$

For Exercises 21–24, determine the quadrant in which the point lies.

21. $(3, -7)$ **22.** $(-2, -4)$

23. $(-7, 5)$ **24.** $(|-2|, |-1|)$

25. Graph the points $(1, -4)$ and $(4, 5)$. Join them together with a straight line. Where does this line cut the y-axis? In other words, find the y-value at this point.

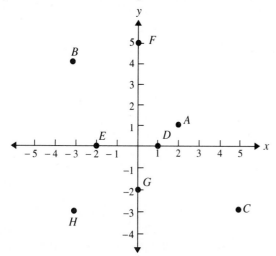

Figure 11.8

26. Graph the points (10, − 3) and (− 5, 6). Join them together with a straight line. Where does this line cut the *x*-axis? In other words, find the *x*-value at this point.

27. Locate several points on the *x*-axis. What is the *y*-value for every point on the *x*-axis?

28. Locate several points on the *y*-axis. What is the *x*-value for every point on the *y*-axis?

29. What are the coordinates of the origin?

30. Graph the points (3, 5) and (7, 9). Join them together with a straight line. What is the *y*-value of the point on this line when *x* = 6?

31. A teacher making out a seating chart for the following class decides to use ordered pairs to represent each student. For example the teacher records Bill Blakely in the grade book as (4, 1). How would the teacher record Manya Dubor and Cecile Delaney?

	1	2	3	4	5	6
5	Meyer Jorgano	Bob Hartman	David Palter	Arthur Ng	Cecile Delaney	Roger Jones
4	Joan Crawford	Manya Dubor	Chuck Peters	Mabel Shu	George Dressler	Cynthia Zuckerman
3	Louise Volpe	Emil Chi	Mary Gambling	Gwen Jackson	Hobart Garrison	Stephanie Udell
2	Mario Stephenson	Heather Meade	Bill Correll	Fran Malarkey	Arline Coffee	Harris Goldberg
1	Gladys Castro	Christine McDermit	Joe Gormley	Bill Blakely	Joel Merzer	Mohammed Yousel

Teacher's Desk

The rectangular coordinate system discussed until now can be generalized to a three-dimensional coordinate system as follows: We draw a *z*-axis perpendicular to both the *x*-axis and the *y*-axis at the origin as shown in Fig. 11.9. In this diagram, the axes, taken as pairs, determine three coordinate planes called the *xy*-plane, the *xz*-plane, and the *yz*-plane. These three coordinate planes separate three-space into eight **octants**. In the first octant all three coordinates are positive. Octants 2, 3, and 4 are found by moving counterclockwise through the other upper octants. Octant 5 is below octant 1. In this three dimensional system, a point *P* in space is determined by an ordered

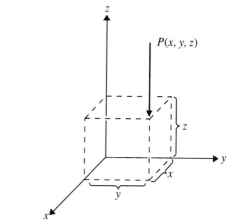

Figure 11.9

triple (*x*, *y*, *z*) where

x = directed distance from *yz*-plane to *P*
y = directed distance from *xz*-plane to *P*
z = directed distance from *xy*-plane to *P*

Several points are plotted in Fig. 11.10.

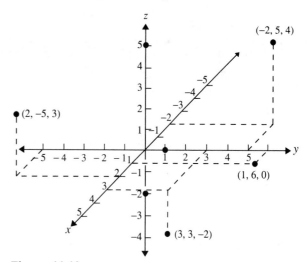

Figure 11.10

32. Plot the following points in a three-dimensional system.

  a) (1, 2, 3)   **b)** (− 3, 4, 5)   **c)** (4, − 3, − 2)

11.2

THE DISTANCE AND MIDPOINT FORMULAS

The Distance Formula

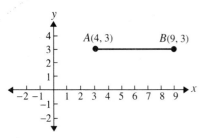

Figure 11.11

Consider points A and B shown in Fig. 11.11. Their coordinates are $(4, 3)$ and $(9, 3)$ respectively. The distance between these two points can be found by either counting the number of units contained in $\overline{AB}$ or by taking the absolute value of the difference between the abscissas of point A and B. Thus the absolute value of the difference of these abscissas is

$$|9 - 4| = |5| = 5 \quad \text{or} \quad |4 - 9| = |-5| = 5$$

Thus the distance between points A and B is 5.

More generally, if we select any two points A and B whose x-coordinates are x_1 and x_2, and which have the same ordinate y_1 (see Fig. 11.12), then the distance between A and B is the absolute value of the difference of their abscissas. We have

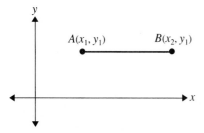

Figure 11.12

> **Definition 11.1** The **distance** between two points having the same ordinate is the absolute value of the difference of their abscissas. Symbolically, the distance between points $A(x_1, y_1)$ and $B(x_2, y_1)$ is given by
>
> $$AB = |x_2 - x_1| = |x_1 - x_2|$$

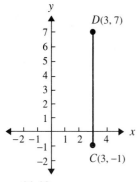

Figure 11.13

Now consider points $C(3, -1)$ and $D(3, 7)$ as shown in Fig. 11.13. These points both have the same abscissa, 3. Again the distance between points C and D can be found by either counting the number of units contained in $\overline{CD}$ or by taking the absolute value of the differences between the ordinates of points C and D. Thus the absolute value of the difference of these ordinates is

$$|-1 - 7| = |-8| = 8 \quad \text{and} \quad |7 - (-1)| = |7 + 1| = 8$$

More generally, if we select two points C and D which have the same abscissa and whose y-coordinates are y_1 and y_2 (see Fig. 11.14), then the distance between C and D is the absolute value of the difference of the ordinates. We have

> **Definition 11.2** The **distance** between two points having the same abscissa is the absolute value of the difference of their ordinates.

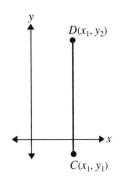

Figure 11.14

Symbolically, the distance between point $C(x_1, y_1)$ **and** $D(x_1, y_2)$ **is given by**

$$CD = |y_2 - y_1| = |y_1 - y_2|$$

Suppose we now want to find the distance between points $E(2, 4)$ and $F(5, 8)$, as shown in Fig. 11.15. Since these two points have different abscissas and ordinates, we cannot use the methods discussed until now. Instead, let us draw perpendiculars from points E and F to the x- and y-axes respectively, forming right triangle EFG. Angle FGE is a right angle and the coordinates of point G are $(5, 4)$. (Why?) Now

$$\text{distance } \overline{EG} = |5 - 2| = |3| = 3$$
$$\text{distance } \overline{FG} = |8 - 4| = |4| = 4$$

We can then use the Pythagorean theorem. Thus

$$\begin{aligned}(\overline{EF})^2 &= (\overline{EG})^2 + (\overline{GF})^2 \\ &= 3^2 \quad\ + 4^2 \\ &= 9 \quad\ + 16 \\ &= 25\end{aligned}$$

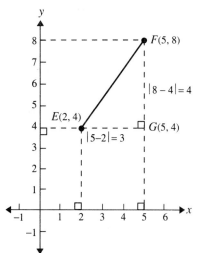

Figure 11.15

Therefore,

$$\overline{EF} = \sqrt{25} = 5$$

We can generalize this method to find the distance between any two points $P(x_1, y_1)$ and $Q(x_2, y_2)$. (See Fig. 11.16). First draw perpendiculars from points P and Q to the x- and y-axes respectively to form right triangle PQR. The coordinates of point R are (x_2, y_1). Then $\overline{PR} = |x_2 - x_1|$ and $\overline{QR} = |y_2 - y_1|$. Using the Pythagorean theorem

$$\begin{aligned}(\overline{PQ})^2 &= (\overline{PR})^2 + (\overline{QR})^2 \\ &= |x_2 - x_1|^2 + |y_2 - y_1|^2\end{aligned}$$

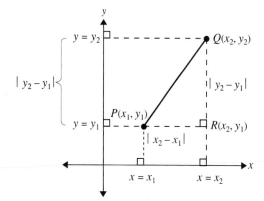

Figure 11.16

However,

$$|x_2 - x_1|^2 = (x_2 - x_1)^2$$

and

$$|y_2 - y_1|^2 = (y_2 - y_1)^2$$

so that

$$(\overline{PQ})^2 = (x_2 - x_1)^2 + (y_2 - y_1)^2$$

Taking the square root of each member of the equation gives

$$\overline{PQ} = \sqrt{(x_2 - x_1)^2 + (y_2 - y_1)^2}$$

This result is known as the distance formula.

Formula 11.1—The Distance Formula   The distance between points $P(x_1, y_1)$ and $Q(x_2, y_2)$ is given by

$$\overline{PQ} = \sqrt{(x_2 - x_1)^2 + (y_2 - y_1)^2}$$

Let us apply Formula 11.1 to several examples.

EXAMPLE 1

Find the distance between the points $P(3, 2)$ and $Q(5, 7)$.

SOLUTION

We use Formula 11.1 with $x_1 = 3$, $y_1 = 2$, $x_2 = 5$, and $y_2 = 7$. We have

$$\begin{aligned}
\text{distance} &= \sqrt{(x_2 - x_1)^2 + (y_2 - y_1)^2} \\
&= \sqrt{(5 - 3)^2 + (7 - 2)^2} \\
&= \sqrt{2^2 + 5^2} \\
&= \sqrt{4 + 25} \\
&= \sqrt{29}
\end{aligned}$$

Thus the distance between the points $(3, 2)$ and $(5, 7)$ is $\sqrt{29}$. (See Fig. 11.17.)

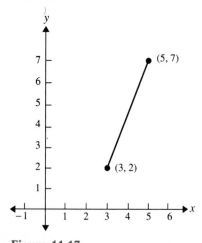

Figure 11.17

Comment   In the previous example, we get the same answer if we let $x_1 = 5$, $y_1 = 7$, $x_2 = 3$, and $y_2 = 2$. The reader should verify this.

EXAMPLE 2

SOLUTION

Find the distance between the points $(-3, -4)$ and $(-7, -8)$

We use Formula 11.1 with $x_1 = -3$, $y_1 = -4$, $x_2 = -7$, and $y_2 = -8$. We have

$$\text{distance} = \sqrt{[-7-(-3)]^2 + [-8-(-4)]^2}$$
$$= \sqrt{(-4)^2 + (-4)^2}$$
$$= \sqrt{16 + 16}$$
$$= \sqrt{32} = \sqrt{16} \cdot \sqrt{2} = 4\sqrt{2}$$

The distance between $(-3, -4)$ and $(-7, -8)$ is $4\sqrt{2}$. ▬

EXAMPLE 3

Find a relationship between x and y so that the distance between the point (x, y) and the point $(3, 5)$ is the same as the distance between (x, y) and the point $(-2, 7)$. (See Fig. 11.18).

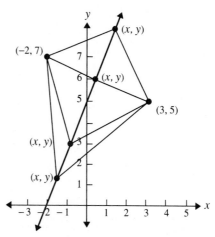

Figure 11.18   The distance from the point $(-2, 7)$ to any point (x, y) is the same as the distance from (x, y) to $(3, 5)$.

SOLUTION

In this case we apply Formula 11.1 twice. First we find the distance between (x, y) and $(3, 5)$. This distance is

$$\sqrt{(3-x)^2 + (5-y)^2}$$

Then we find the distance between (x, y) and $(-2, 7)$, which is

$$\sqrt{(-2-x)^2 + (7-y)^2}$$

Since these distances are to be equal, we have

$$\sqrt{(3-x)^2+(5-y)^2} = \sqrt{(-2-x)^2+(7-y)^2}$$

Squaring both sides gives

$$(3-x)^2+(5-y)^2 = (-2-x)^2+(7-y)^2$$

Simplifying, we find that

$$9-6x+x^2+25-10y+y^2 = 4+4x+x^2+49-14y+y^2$$

Combining like terms gives $4y - 10x - 19 = 0$. Thus the point (x, y) will be equidistant from the points $(3, 5)$ and $(-2, 7)$ if it satisfies the equation $4y - 10x - 19 = 0$. ■

EXAMPLE 4

Show that the points $(1, 0)$, $(5, 3)$, and $(4, -4)$ are the vertices of a right triangle.

SOLUTION

We first find the distance between the points $(1, 0)$ and $(5, 3)$. It is

$$\sqrt{(5-1)^2+(3-0)^2} = \sqrt{4^2+3^2} = 5$$

The distance between the points $(5, 3)$ and $(4, -4)$ is

$$\sqrt{(4-5)^2+(-4-3)^2} = \sqrt{(-1)^2+(-7)^2} = \sqrt{50}$$

The distance between the points $(1, 0)$ and $(4, -4)$ is

$$\sqrt{(4-1)^2+(-4-0)^2} = \sqrt{3^2+(-4)^2} = 5$$

Using the converse of the Pythagorean theorem, we find $5^2 + 5^2 = (\sqrt{50})^2$ is true, since $25 + 25 = 50$. Thus, we have a right triangle with the line segment joining points $(5, 3)$ and $(4, -4)$ as hypotenuse. ■

EXAMPLE 5

Quadrilateral *KLMN* has vertices $K(2, 3)$, $L(7, 3)$, $M(4, 7)$, and $N(-1, 7)$. (See Fig. 11.19.) Prove by means of coordinate geometry that *KLMN* is a rhombus.

SOLUTION

We use the distance formula.

Length of $\overline{KL}$ where $x_1 = 2$, $y_1 = 3$, $x_2 = 7$, and $y_2 = 3$,

$$= \sqrt{(7-2)^2+(3-3)^2}$$
$$= \sqrt{5^2+0^2} = \sqrt{25}$$
$$= 5$$

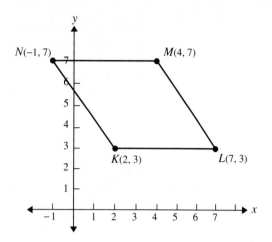

Figure 11.19

Length of $\overline{LM}$ where $x_1 = 7$, $y_1 = 3$, $x_2 = 4$, and $y_2 = 7$,

$$= \sqrt{(4-7)^2 + (7-3)^2}$$

$$= \sqrt{(-3)^2 + 4^2} = \sqrt{25}$$

$$= 5$$

Length of $\overline{MN}$ where $x_1 = 4$, $y_1 = 7$, $x_2 = -1$, and $y_2 = 7$,

$$= \sqrt{(-1-4)^2 + (7-7)^2}$$

$$= \sqrt{(-5)^2 + 0^2} = \sqrt{25}$$

$$= 5$$

Length of $\overline{NK}$ where $x_1 = -1$, $y_1 = 7$, $x_2 = 2$, and $y_2 = 3$,

$$= \sqrt{(2-[-1])^2 + (3-7)^2}$$

$$= \sqrt{(2+1)^2 + (-4)^2} = \sqrt{25}$$

$$= 5$$

Since $\overline{KL}$, $\overline{LM}$, $\overline{MN}$, and $\overline{NK}$ all equal 5, the quadrilateral is equilateral. An equilateral quadrilateral is a rhombus. ■

The Midpoint Formula

We know that a midpoint divides a line segment into two segments that are equal in length. We can apply the distance formula to find the midpoint of a line segment. To see how this can be done, suppose we want to find the midpoint of the line segment joining the points $A(3, 4)$ and $B(9, 4)$ in Fig. 11.20. We can count the number of units on the horizontal segment. The midpoint is at point M, whose abscissa is 6 since $\overline{AM} = \overline{MB} = 3$ units. The ordinate of point M is the same as the ordinate of points A and B. Thus the coordinates of point M are (6, 4). Note that

$$\text{abscissa of } M = \frac{9+3}{2} = \frac{12}{2} = 6$$

and

$$\text{ordinate of } M = \frac{4+4}{2} = \frac{8}{2} = 4$$

Thus the coordinates of point M represent the average of the abscissas and the ordinates of the line segment.

Similarly, the midpoint (point N) of the line segment joining point $C(1, -2)$ and point $D(1, 6)$ in Fig. 11.20 is

$$\text{abscissa of } N = \frac{1+1}{2} = \frac{2}{2} = 1$$

$$\text{ordinate of } N = \frac{-2+6}{2} = \frac{4}{2} = 2$$

Thus the coordinates of point N are (1, 2).

In general, to find the coordinates of the midpoint (point M) of the line segment joining points $P(x_1, y_1)$ and $Q(x_2, y_2)$ of Fig. 11.21 we can proceed as follows: Let us denote the abscissa of point M by $\bar{x}$. By the definition of midpoint, we must have

$$\bar{x} - x_1 = x_2 - \bar{x}$$

Rearranging this equation gives $2\bar{x} = x_1 + x_2$, or that

$$\bar{x} = \frac{x_1 + x_2}{2}$$

Similarly, let us denote the ordinate of point M by $\bar{y}$. By the definition of midpoint we must have $\bar{y} - y_1 = y_2 - \bar{y}$, so that $2\bar{y} = y_1 + y_2$, or that

$$\bar{y} = \frac{y_1 + y_2}{2}$$

This leads us to the following:

Formula 11.2—Midpoint Formula   If the coordinates of the endpoints of line segment $\overline{AB}$ are $A(x_1, y_1)$ and $B(x_2, y_2)$ and if M is the midpoint of $\overline{AB}$, then the coordinates of point M are

$$M = \left(\frac{x_1 + x_2}{2}, \frac{y_1 + y_2}{2} \right)$$

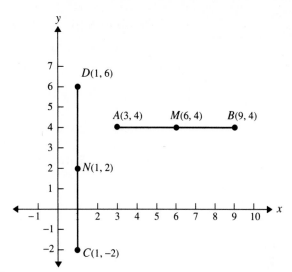

Figure 11.20

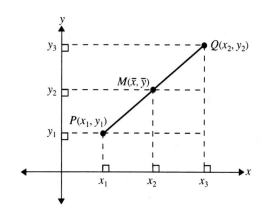

Figure 11.21

We illustrate the above formula with several examples.

EXAMPLE 6

Find the coordinates of the midpoint of the line segment whose endpoints are $(-4, 8)$ and $(2, 14)$.

SOLUTION

We use the midpoint formula with $x_1 = -4$, $y_1 = 8$, $x_2 = 2$, and $y_2 = 14$. We have that the coordinates of midpoint M are

$$M = \left(\frac{x_1 + x_2}{2}, \frac{y_1 + y_2}{2}\right) = \left(\frac{-4 + 2}{2}, \frac{8 + 14}{2}\right) = (-1, 11)$$

Thus the coordinates of the midpoint are $(-1, 11)$.

EXAMPLE 7

Problem-Solving Example

If the midpoint M of line segment $\overline{PQ}$ has coordinates (5, 3), and if the coordinates of P are (3, 1), what are the coordinates of Q?

SOLUTION

Understanding the Problem
We are given the coordinates of the midpoint and of one of the endpoints of a line segment. We wish to find the coordinates of the other endpoint.

A Plan to Solve the Problem
Let us denote the coordinates of point Q by (x_1, y_1). We can then apply the midpoint formula with $P = (x_2, y_2) = (3, 1)$. We have

$$\text{Midpoint } M = \left(\frac{x_1 + x_2}{2}, \frac{y_1 + y_2}{2} \right)$$

Substituting the above values gives

$$(5, 3) = \left(\frac{x_1 + 3}{2}, \frac{y_1 + 1}{2} \right)$$

We must now solve two equations, one involving abscissas and one involving ordinates:

$$5 = \frac{x_1 + 3}{2} \qquad 3 = \frac{y_1 + 1}{2}$$
$$10 = x_1 + 3 \qquad 6 = y_1 + 1$$
$$7 = x_1 \qquad 5 = y_1$$

Thus the coordinates of point Q are (7, 5).

Checking our Solution
We can easily check our solution by noting that if the coordinates of point Q are (7, 5), then by the midpoint formula the coordinates of the midpoint of line segment $\overline{PQ}$ are $\left(\frac{3+7}{2}, \frac{1+5}{2} \right)$ = (5, 3). This is indeed the value that given. ∎

EXAMPLE 8

Problem-Solving Example

A quadrilateral has vertices $A(-3, 3)$, $B(3, 4)$, $C(7, 6)$, and $D(1, 5)$. See Fig. 11.22. Show that $ABCD$ is a parallelogram.

SOLUTION

Understanding the Problem
We are given the coordinates of a quadrilateral and are asked to show that it is a parallelogram.

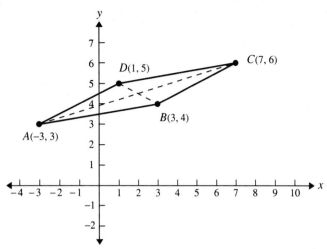

Figure 11.22

A Plan to Solve the Problem

To show that $ABCD$ is a parallelogram we will prove that its diagonals bisect each other. This can be accomplished by using the midpoint formula and showing that both diagonals have the same midpoint. The midpoint of diagonal $\overline{AC}$ is

$$\left(\frac{-3+7}{2}, \frac{3+6}{2}\right) = \left(\frac{4}{2}, \frac{9}{2}\right) = \left(2, \frac{9}{2}\right)$$

The midpoint of diagonal $\overline{BD}$ is

$$\left(\frac{3+1}{2}, \frac{4+5}{2}\right) = \left(\frac{4}{2}, \frac{9}{2}\right) = \left(2, \frac{9}{2}\right)$$

Since both diagonals have the same midpoint, they bisect each other. This tells us that $ABCD$ is a parallelogram.

Checking our Solution

We can verify that $ABCD$ is a parallelogram by using the distance formula and showing that $\overline{AB} = \overline{CD} = \sqrt{37}$ and that $\overline{BC} = \overline{DA} = \sqrt{20}$. Since both pairs of opposite sides are congruent, the quadrilateral is a parallelogram.

■

Equation of a Circle

radius

We can also apply the distance formula to find the equation of a circle. In Fig. 11.23 we have a circle whose center is at $C(3, 4)$ and whose radius is 5. To find the equation of this circle, let $P(x, y)$ be any point on the circle. Since the **radius**—the distance between any point P and the center $(3, 4)$—must be 5 (why?), we can apply the distance formula. We let $P(x, y) = (x_1, y_1)$ and $C(3, 4) = (x_2, y_2)$. We are told that the radius of the

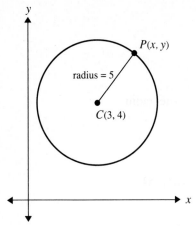

Figure 11.23

circle is 5, so $\overline{CP} = 5$. By the distance formula

$$\sqrt{(x_2 - x_1)^2 + (y_2 - y_1)^2} = \overline{CP}$$

By substitution

$$\sqrt{(x_1 - 3)^2 + (y_1 - 4)^2} = 5$$

Squaring both sides

$$(x_1 - 3)^2 + (y_1 - 4)^2 = 5^2$$

or

$$(x_1 - 3)^2 + (y_1 - 4)^2 = 25$$

Thus the coordinates of any point $P(x, y)$ on this circle must satisfy the equation $(x - 3)^2 + (y - 4)^2 = 25$.

In general, if we are given any circle whose center is at (a, b) and whose radius has a length of r, a procedure similar to what we did above will give us the following:

Formula 11.3—Equation of a Circle   The equation of a circle whose center is at (a, b) and whose radius has a length of r is given by

$$(x - a)^2 + (y - b)^2 = r^2$$

The above results are pictured in Fig. 11.24.

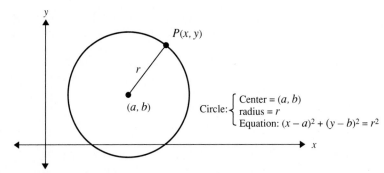

Figure 11.24

Let us apply Formula 11.3 in several examples.

EXAMPLE 9

Find the equation of a circle whose center is at

a) the origin and whose radius is 3

b) (7, 8) and whose radius is 4

SOLUTION

a) The coordinates of the origin are (0, 0). Since the center is at the origin we have $a = 0$ and $b = 0$. Also the radius is 3, so $r = 3$. We substitute these values into Formula 11.3. The equation of the circle then is

$$(x - a)^2 + (y - b)^2 = r^2$$

$$(x - 0)^2 + (y - 0)^2 = 3^2$$

or

$$x^2 + y^2 = 9$$

b) Since the center is at (7, 8) and the radius is 4, we have $a = 7$, $b = 8$, and $r = 4$. We substitute these values into Formula 11.3. The equation of the circle is $(x - 7)^2 + (y - 8)^2 = 4^2$, or $(x - 7)^2 + (y - 8)^2 = 16$. ■

EXAMPLE 10

Find the center and radius of a circle whose equation is

$$(x + 5)^2 + (y - 3)^2 = 9$$

SOLUTION

The equation of a circle whose center is at the point (a, b) and whose radius has length r is $(x - a)^2 + (y - b)^2 = r^2$. In our case, we are given that the equation of a circle is $(x + 5)^2 + (y - 3)^2 = 9$. If we compare the corresponding parts of the two equations, we get

$$
\begin{array}{ccc}
x - a = x + 5 & y - b = y - 3 & r^2 = 9 \\
-a = +5 & -b = -3 & r = \sqrt{9} \\
a = -5 & b = 3 & r = 3
\end{array}
$$

Thus the center of the circle is at $(-5, 3)$ and the radius is 3. ■

Studying geometry by using coordinates has many interesting and varying applications. Cartographers (map makers) use coordinates to draw maps of different sizes and shapes. This use of coordinates was illustrated in Fig. 11.1 at the beginning of this chapter. The student page shown here from *Addison-Wesley Mathematics*, 1987, Grade 6, p. 269, prompts students to use coordinates to help determine the shortest path to a point.

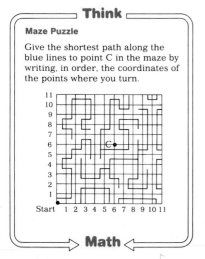

Think

Maze Puzzle

Give the shortest path along the blue lines to point C in the maze by writing, in order, the coordinates of the points where you turn.

Math

1. For each of the following, locate the pairs of points on a coordinate system and then find the distance between them and the coordinates of the midpoint of the line segment joining the points.

   a) (3, 5) and (4, 9)

   b) (6, 1) and (2, 0)

   c) (3, – 2) and (– 6, 5)

   d) (4, 3) and (0, – 3)

   e) (2, 5) and (– 3, – 4)

   f) (– 5, – 6) and (– 4, – 1)

   g) (– 1, 0) and (0, – 3)

   h) (5, 2) and (2, 5)

2. Determine whether or not the three given points are vertices of a right triangle.

   a) $A(0, 2)$, $B(3, 0)$, $C(4, 8)$

   b) $A(2, 4)$, $B(5, 2)$, $C(6, 0)$

   c) $A(0, 4)$, $B(0, 5)$, $C(12, 4)$

   d) $A(3, 2)$, $B(1, 1)$, $C(– 1, 5)$

3. Show that a triangle with vertices at $A(2, 3)$, $B(6, 2)$ and $C(3, – 1)$ is isosceles.

4. Show that the quadrilateral with vertices at $A(3, 2)$, $B(0, 5)$, $C(– 3, 2)$, and $D(0, – 1)$ is a square. (*Hint:* Find the length of each of the sides and then use the Pythagorean theorem.)

5. Find all values of x for which the distance between $(5, – 2)$ and $(x, 1)$ is 4.

6. Find a relationship between x and y if the distance from (x, y) to $(– 5, 4)$ is the same as the distance between (x, y) and $(7, – 2)$.

7. Find a relationship between x and y if the distance from (x, y) to $(– 3, – 4)$ is twice the distance between (x, y) and $(5, 6)$.

8. The vertices of $\triangle ABC$ are $A(5, 8)$. $B(1, – 2)$, and $C(7, 6)$. Points F and G are midpoints of sides $\overline{AB}$ and $\overline{AC}$ respectively. Show that $\overline{FG} = \frac{1}{2}(\overline{BC})$.

9. A **median** in a triangle is a line segment joining a vertex to the midpoint of the opposite side. In $\triangle ABC$, the vertices are $A(6, 10)$, $B(– 2, 8)$, and $C(0, – 2)$. Find the lengths of the medians $\overline{AM_1}$, $\overline{BM_2}$, and $\overline{CM_3}$ in this triangle.

10. Triangle ABC has vertices $A(– 2, 1)$, $B(5, 2)$, and $C(6, – 5)$. Show that $\triangle ABC$ is an isosceles right triangle.

11. Find the center and radius of the circle whose equation is

    a) $(x – 4)^2 + (y – 1)^2 = 49$

    b) $(x + 4)^2 + (y – 6)^2 = 65$

    c) $(x + 2)^2 + (y + 9)^2 = 12$

    d) $x^2 + (y + 2)^2 = 16$

12. Write the equation of a circle

    a) with center at $(1, 3)$ and radius = 4.

    b) with center at $(– 3, – 4)$ and radius = 2.

    c) with center at the origin and radius = $\sqrt{29}$.

    d) with center at $(– 5, 8)$ and which passes through the origin.

    e) which has a diameter whose endpoints are at $(– 2, 4)$ and $(6, 8)$.

    f) which has a diameter whose endpoints are at $(– 6, – 2)$ and $(– 8, 10)$.

    g) with center at $(7, 8)$ and which passes through the point $(3, 1)$.

    h) with center at $(– 5, 4)$ and which passes through the point $(4, 3)$.

13. Determine whether the specified point P lies on the circle whose equation is given.

Point	Equation
a) $P(– 4, 3)$	$x^2 + y^2 = 25$
b) $P(3, 2)$	$(x – 2)^2 + (y + 1)^2 = 10$
c) $P(2, – 7)$	$(x + 4)^2 + y^2 = 36$
d) $P(– 3, – 2)$	$(x + 1)^2 + (y – 7)^2 = 25$

PROBLEM-SOLVING EXERCISES

14. One circle has center at $(3, 4)$ and radius 5. A second circle has center at $(– 1, – 3)$ and radius 4. Do these circles intersect? (*Hint:* Draw both circles on the same set of axes or solve algebraically.)

15. The vertices of $\triangle ABC$ are $A(– 1, 2)$, $B(3, 8)$, and $C(5, – 2)$.

    a) Prove that $\triangle ABC$ is a right triangle.

b) Prove that point M, the midpoint of the hypotenuse, is equidistant from all three vertices of the triangle.

16. Refer back to Exercise 9. Prove that the three medians of $\triangle ABC$ intersect in a point x that divides each median in a ratio of 2:1. The point X is called the **centroid** of $\triangle ABC$.

17. Find the coordinates of the centroid of $\triangle ABC$ whose coordinates are $A(0, 2)$, $B(6, 4)$, and $C(8, 10)$.

18. Given the points $A(-6, 8)$, $B(4, 9)$ and $C(x, y)$. If B is the midpoint of line segment $\overline{AB}$, find the value of x and the value of y.

19. The vertices of quadrilateral $ABCD$ are $A(7, 2)$, $B(16, 5)$, $C(15, 8)$, and $D(6, 5)$.

a) Find the coordinates of the midpoint of $\overline{AC}$ and of $\overline{BD}$.

b) Find the length of diagonal $\overline{AC}$ and diagonal $\overline{BD}$.

c) Show that $ABCD$ is a parallelogram.

d) Show that $ABCD$ is a rectangle.

20. Point $C(3, 5)$ is the center of a circle and points P and Q are the endpoints of a diameter in this circle.

a) If the coordinates of Q are $(8, 5)$, find the coordinates of point P.

b) Find the length of a radius of this circle.

c) Show that the point $R(7, 2)$ is a point on this circle.

d) Show that $\triangle PQR$ is a right triangle.

21. Using the distance formula, show that points $A(2, 6)$, $B(5, 9)$, and $C(8, 12)$ are collinear.

IIII► Brain-Teaser Problems ◄IIII

**22. Three vertices of a parallelogram are given. Find the coordinates of the fourth vertex:

a) $(0, 0)$, $(5, 0)$, $(0, 8)$

b) $(-3, 5)$, $(4, 9)$, $(-1, -1)$

(*Hint:* More than one answer is possible. Find all possibilities.)

**23. Using the coordinates specified in Fig. 11.25, prove that the diagonals of a square are congruent.

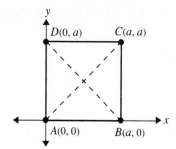

Figure 11.25

**24. Using the coordinates specified in Fig. 11.26, prove that the diagonals of a parallelogram bisect each other.

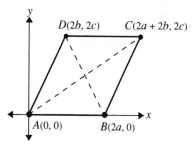

Figure 11.26

**25. Using the coordinates specified in Fig. 11.27, where points A, B, C, and D are the midpoints of any quadrilateral $PQRS$, prove that $ABCD$ is a parallelogram.

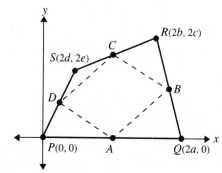

Figure 11.27

**26. Using the coordinates specified in Fig. 11.28, prove that the line segment joining the midpoints of two sides of a triangle is $\frac{1}{2}$ the length of the third side.

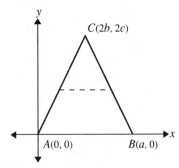

Figure 11.28

27. Using the coordinates specified in Fig. 11.29, where the two medians $\overline{AD}$ and $\overline{BE}$ are congruent, prove that the triangle is isosceles.

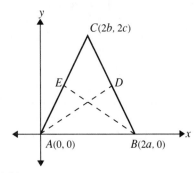

Figure 11.29

28. Using the coordinates specified in Fig. 11.30, prove that the diagonals of an isosceles trapezoid are congruent.

29. Many of the formulas discussed for the two-dimensional rectangular coordinate system can be extended to the three-dimensional system mentioned in the previous section. For example, to find the distance between two points in space, we apply the

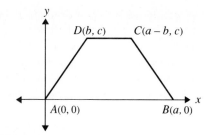

Figure 11.30

Pythagorean theorem twice, to obtain the following formula for the distance between points (x_1, y_1, z_1) and (x_2, y_2, z_2). See Fig. 11.31.

$$\text{Distance} = \sqrt{(x_2 - x_1)^2 + (y_2 - y_1)^2 + (z_2 - z_1)^2}$$

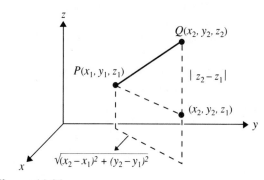

Figure 11.31

Similarly, the midpoint of the line segment joining the points (x_1, y_1, z_1) and (x_2, y_2, z_2) has coordinates

$$\left(\frac{x_1 + x_2}{2}, \frac{y_1 + y_2}{2}, \frac{z_1 + z_2}{2} \right)$$

Find the distance between the following points and the coordinates of the midpoint of the line segment joining these points:

a) $(2, -4, 5)$ and $(4, 6, 3)$

b) $(5, -7, 3)$ and $(1, -3, 1)$.

11.3

THE GRAPH OF A STRAIGHT LINE

Consider the equation $y = 2x + 1$. One solution of this equation is $x = 2$ and $y = 5$. We can write this solution in abbreviated form as $(2, 5)$. Another solution is $x = 1$ and $y = 3$, which we write as $(1, 3)$. Other solutions are $(3, 7)$, $(-1, -1)$, $(0, 1)$, and so on. Actually, there are infinitely many such pairs of values that are solutions for this equation. To find other solutions, we let x be any convenient number and solve for y as shown in the following table.

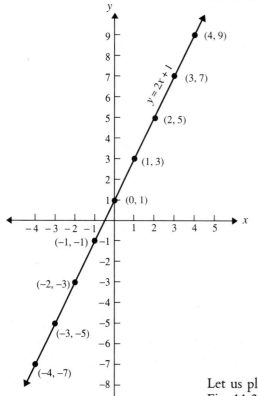

x	$y = 2x + 1$	y	Point
4	$2(4) + 1$	9	$(4, 9)$
3	$2(3) + 1$	7	$(3, 7)$
2	$2(2) + 1$	5	$(2, 5)$
1	$2(1) + 1$	3	$(1, 3)$
0	$2(0) + 1$	1	$(0, 1)$
-1	$2(-1) + 1$	-1	$(-1, -1)$
-2	$2(-2) + 1$	-3	$(-2, -3)$
-3	$2(-3) + 1$	-5	$(-3, -5)$
-4	$2(-4) + 1$	-7	$(-4, -7)$

Figure 11.32   Graph of $y = 2x + 1$

Let us plot these points on a rectangular coordinate system, as shown in Fig. 11.32. If we join these points, we get a straight line. This line is called the **graph** of the equation. Actually, the graph of the equation consists of *all* of the points (x, y) that are solutions of the equation.

EXAMPLE 1

Draw the graph of $y = 5x + 3$.

SOLUTION

We set up a table of values by finding several pairs of numbers that are solutions to the equation, as shown below. Then we plot the points and

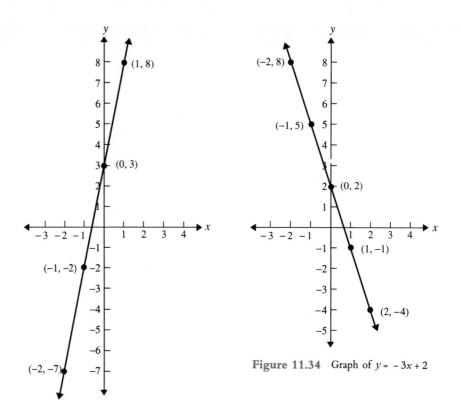

Figure 11.33   Graph of $y = 5x + 3$

Figure 11.34   Graph of $y = -3x + 2$

join them. The resulting straight line is the graph of $y = 5x + 3$. See Fig. 11.33.

x	$y = 5x + 3$	y
2	$5(2) + 3$	13
1	$5(1) + 3$	8
0	$5(0) + 3$	3
-1	$5(-1) + 3$	-2
-2	$5(-2) + 3$	-7

EXAMPLE 2

Draw the graph of $y = -3x + 2$.

SOLUTION

We set up a table of values by finding several pairs of numbers that are solutions to the equation. The graph is given in Fig. 11.34.

x	$y = -3x + 2$	y
2	$-3(2) + 2$	-4
1	$-3(1) + 2$	-1
0	$-3(0) + 2$	2
-1	$-3(-1) + 2$	5
-2	$-3(-2) + 2$	8

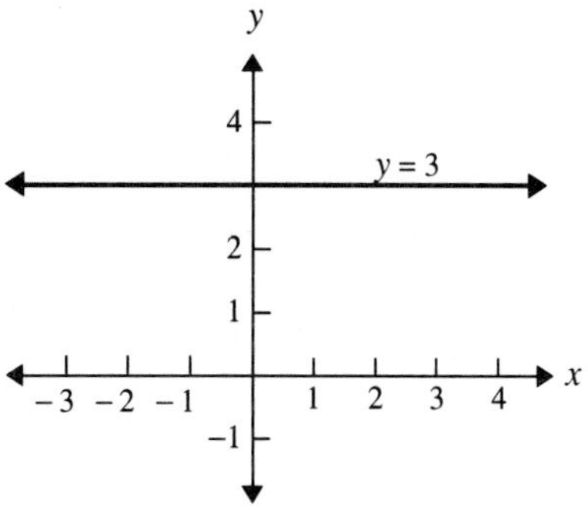

Figure 11.35

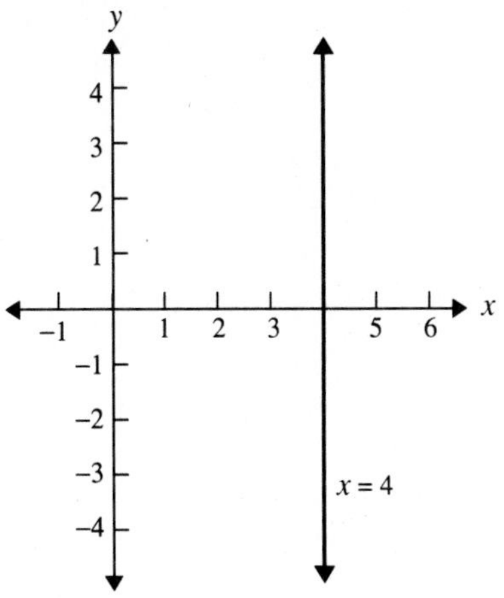

Figure 11.36

EXAMPLE 3

Draw the graph of $y = 3$.

SOLUTION

We set up a table of values as we did in the previous examples. In this case, we note that y must always be 3, no matter what value x has. The graph of $y = 3$ is given in Fig. 11.35. It is a line parallel to the x-axis.

x	y
2	3
1	3
0	3
-1	3
-2	3

EXAMPLE 4

Draw the graph of $x = 4$.

SOLUTION

We set up a table of values. In this case we note that x must always be 4, no matter what value y has. The graph of $x = 4$ is given in Fig. 11.36. It is a line parallel to the y-axis.

x	y
4	-2
4	-1
4	0
4	1
4	2

All of the graphs that we have drawn so far are straight lines. Actually, the graph of any equation of the form $Ax + By + C = 0$ (where A, B, and C are constants and A and B are not both 0) will be a straight line. An equation whose graph is a straight line is called a **linear equation**.

linear equation

The results of the previous examples can be summarized as follows:

Summary

1. The graph of $Ax + By + C = 0$ (where A, B, and C are constants and A and B are not both 0) is called a straight line.
2. The graph of $x = C$ is a straight line parallel to the y-axis.
3. The graph of $y = B$ is a straight line parallel to the x-axis.

EXAMPLE 5

Is the point (2, 3) on the graph of $3x + 5y = 21$?

SOLUTION

The point (2, 3) is on the graph of $3x + 5y = 21$ if and only if $x = 2$, $y = 3$ is a solution of the equation. Substituting, we find that $3(2) + 5(3) = 21$. Thus the point (2, 3) is on the graph of $3x + 5y = 21$. ■

Graphing Equations involving Absolute Values

Graphing equations involving absolute values is also done by using a table of values. Thus to draw the graph of $y = |x|$, we first find several solutions of $y = |x|$ by replacing x with several signed numbers and finding the corresponding y-values. Of course, y must always be a nonnegative number. We have the following table of values and its graph in Fig. 11.37.

x	y
-3	3
-2	2
-1	1
0	0
1	1
2	2
3	3

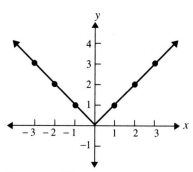

Figure 11.37   Graph of $y = |x|$

EXERCISES FOR SECTION 11.3

Draw the graph of each of the equations given in Exercises 1–11.

1. $y = 3x + 7$

2. $y = x + 4$

3. $y = -3x + 7$

4. $y = -5x + 3$

5. $y = -3x$

6. $4x = 8$

7. $5y = -15$

8. $4x + 3y = 12$

9. $5x + 3y = 15$

10. $y = \dfrac{x}{4} + 3$

11. $y = -\dfrac{x}{3} - 4$

 Brain-Teaser Problems

**12. Draw the graph of $y = |2x - 3|$.

**13. Draw the graph of $|x - 2| = 9$.

**14. Draw the graph of $|y - 3| = 6$.

**15. Draw the graph of $|x - y| = 3$.

**16. Draw the graph of $|x| - |y| = 3$.

**17. Draw the graph of $|y| - |x| = 3$.

**18. On the same set of axes draw the graphs of $y = 2x + 4$ and $y = -\dfrac{1}{2}x - 4$. How are the graphs related?

**19. Give the equation of the graph shown here.

a)

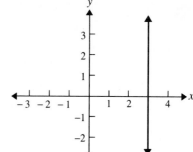

b)

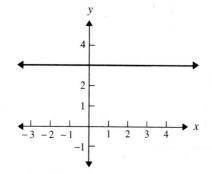

11.4

INTERCEPTS, SLOPE, AND EQUATION OF A STRAIGHT LINE

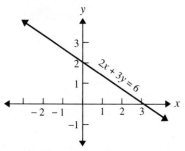

Figure 11.38   Graph of $2x + 3y = 6$

Consider the graph of $2x + 3y = 6$, which is given in Fig. 11.38. Notice that this graph crosses the x-axis at the point $(3, 0)$, and then crosses the y-axis at the point $(0, 2)$. Mathematicians refer to these crossing points as the x- intercept and the y-intercept, respectively.

Definition 11.3   The point at which a graph crosses the x-axis is called the **x-intercept**. To find the x-value of this point, set $y = 0$, and then solve for x.

> **Definition 11.4** The point at which a graph crosses the y-axis is called the **y-intercept**. To find the y-value of this point, set $x = 0$, and then solve for y.

EXAMPLE 1

Find the x-intercept and the y-intercept of the line $4x + 3y = 12$.

SOLUTION

We apply Definitions 11.3 and 11.4. To find the x-intercept, we let $y = 0$ and solve for x, getting

$$4x + 3(0) = 12$$
$$4x = 12$$
$$x = 3$$

Thus the x-intercept is at $(3, 0)$. To find the y-intercept, we let $x = 0$ and solve for y, getting

$$4(0) + 3y = 12$$
$$3y = 12$$
$$y = 4$$

Thus the y-intercept is at $(0, 4)$. The graph is given in Fig. 11.39. ∎

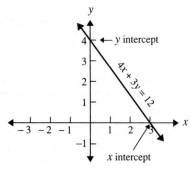

Figure 11.39 Graph of $4x + 3y = 12$

EXAMPLE 2

Draw the graph of a straight line whose x-intercept is at $(-3, 0)$ and whose y-intercept is at $(0, -2)$.

SOLUTION

Since we are told that the x-intercept is at $(-3, 0)$, we know that the graph crosses the x-axis at the point $(-3, 0)$. Also, since the y-intercept is at $(0, -2)$, the graph crosses the y-axis at the point $(0, -2)$. Thus we plot these two points on a coordinate axis and join them to get the straight line shown in Fig. 11.40. ∎

Another important number associated with the graph of a straight line is its **slope**. We define the slope of a line as the change in the vertical distance divided by the change in the horizontal distance. To understand this concept, consider the roof shown in Fig. 11.41. To climb to the top, a person would cover a horizontal distance of 365 centimeters and a vertical distance of 730 centimeters. Therefore in this case the slope of the roof is $\frac{730}{365}$ or 2. The slope of the roof shown in Fig. 11.42 is $\frac{365}{1095}$ or $\frac{1}{3}$. The first roof has a greater slope and hence is steeper.

Now consider the photograph shown in Fig. 11.43. On August 7, 1974, Philippe Petit walked across a guy wire connecting the twin towers of the World Trade Center in New York City. In accomplishing this feat the only change that occurred was the horizontal distance covered. There was no vertical distance covered. Such a line has zero slope.

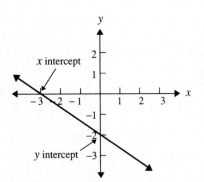

Figure 11.40 Graph of a line whose x intercept is at $(-3, 0)$ and whose y intercept is at $(0, -2)$

State to Reconstruct Highway 17

Marlboro: As a result of the numerous accidents and jackknifes occurring on a particular stretch of Highway 17, the State Highway Department announced yesterday that it will reconstruct the viaduct in the vicinity of Rodger's overpass. The reconstruction will raise the highway slope in the region to 5%. This will enable trucks, especially the larger ones, to negotiate the turns more safely.

Marlboro News April 27, 1989

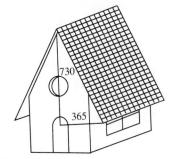

Figure 11.41

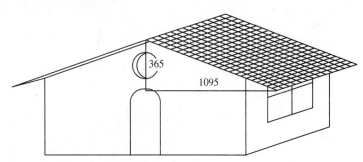

Figure 11.42

(Source: United Press International)

Figure 11.43

(Source: United Press International)

Figure 11.44

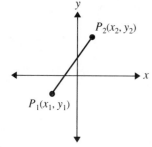

Figure 11.45

slope

On May 26, 1977, George Willig scaled the side of the World Trade Center in New York City. In his climb up the 110 floors the only change that occurred was the vertical distance. There was no horizontal distance covered. Such a line has no slope, since we would have to divide by zero. (See Fig. 11.44.)

More formally, suppose that we are given two distinct points, P_1 and P_2, in a rectangular coordinate plane as shown in Fig. 11.45. The subscripts are used merely to distinguish the points. Let the coordinates of these points be $P_1(x_1, y_1)$ and $P_2(x_2, y_2)$. These two points determine a unique number called the slope of the line.

Formula 11.4   The **slope** of the line passing through the points (x_1, y_1) and (x_2, y_2) is given by

$$\frac{y_2 - y_1}{x_2 - x_1}$$

provided that $x_2 \neq x_1$. If $x_2 = x_1$, then $x_2 - x_1 = 0$, and

$$\frac{y_2 - y_1}{x_2 - x_1}$$

does not exist.[1] We usually use the letter m to represent the slope.

---

[1] In mathematics, division by zero is not defined. For a detailed discussion of division involving zero, see pages 146–147.

Comment   Some people define slope as $\dfrac{\text{rise}}{\text{run}}$. Of course, this is the same as the one given in Formula 11.4.

EXAMPLE 3

SOLUTION

Find the slope of the line passing through the points (2, 5) and (7, 8).

We apply Formula 11.4. Let $x_1 = 2$, $y_1 = 5$, $x_2 = 7$, and $y_2 = 8$. Then

$$x_2 - x_1 = 7 - 2 = 5$$
$$y_2 - y_1 = 8 - 5 = 3$$

so that

$$\frac{y_2 - y_1}{x_2 - x_1} = \frac{3}{5}$$

Thus the slope of the line passing through the points (2, 5) and (7, 8) is $\frac{3}{5}$. ◼

Comment   In applying Formula 11.4 it makes no difference which point is called $P_1(x_1, y_1)$ and which point is called $P_2(x_2, y_2)$. In both cases we get the same answer. To illustrate, suppose that in Example 3 we let $x_1 = 7$, $y_1 = 8$, $x_2 = 2$, and $y_2 = 5$. Then the slope of the line is

$$\frac{y_2 - y_1}{x_2 - x_1} = \frac{5 - 8}{2 - 7} = \frac{-3}{-5} = \frac{3}{5}$$

This is exactly the same answer we obtained in Example 3.

EXAMPLE 4

Find the slope of the line passing through the points
  a) (3, 4) and (5, 1)
  b) (7, 6) and (9, 6)
  c) (4, 5) and (4, -2)

SOLUTION

We apply Formula 11.4.

a) $\dfrac{y_2 - y_1}{x_2 - x_1} = \dfrac{1 - 4}{5 - 3} = \dfrac{-3}{2} = -\dfrac{3}{2}$

b) $\dfrac{y_2 - y_1}{x_2 - x_1} = \dfrac{6 - 6}{9 - 7} = \dfrac{0}{2} = 0$

c) $\dfrac{y_2 - y_1}{x_2 - x_1} = \dfrac{-2 - 5}{4 - 4} = \dfrac{-7}{0}$ (This cannot be done. Therefore there is no slope; see footnote 1.) ◼

It can be shown that if the slope of a line is positive, then the line rises as we go from left to right. If the slope of a line is negative, then the line falls as we go from left to right. If the slope of a line is zero, then the line is parallel to the *x*-axis. If a line has no slope, then the line is parallel to the *y*-axis. Thus the slope of a line tells us the "direction" of the line. These possibilities are pictured in Figs. 11.46–11.49.

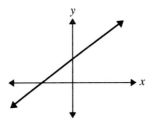

Figure 11.46　Positive slope (line rises as we move from left to right)

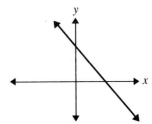

Figure 11.47　Negative slope (line falls as we move from left to right)

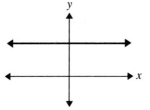

Figure 11.48　Zero slope (line is parallel to *x*-axis)

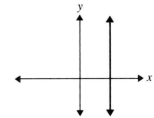

Figure 11.49　No slope (line is parallel to *y*-axis)

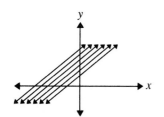

Figure 11.50　Parallel lines (all lines have the same slope)

Lines that are parallel have the same slope. Can you see why? (See Fig. 11.50.)

Let us again analyze the graph of $y = 3x + 2$. Several pairs of values that satisfy this equation are shown in the accompanying table.

x	y
2	8
1	5
0	2
-1	-1
-2	-4

The graph is given in Fig. 11.51. To calculate the slope of this line we pick any two points on the line, say *P* and *Q*, and find the slope of the line

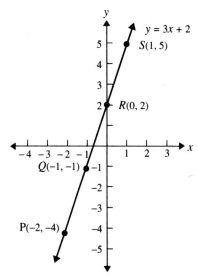

Figure 11.51   Graph of $y = 3x + 2$

passing through these points. We have

$$\text{Slope} = m = \frac{-4-(-1)}{-2-(-1)} = \frac{-4+1}{-2+1} = \frac{-3}{-1} = +3$$

If we had selected points R and S, the slope of the line would still be 3. In both cases we get the same value for the slope; it is 3. More generally, if we select any two points on this line, the slope will always be 3. We say that *the slope of a line is constant*. Notice that 3 is the coefficient of x in the equation $y = 3x + 2$. Next we observe that the line crosses the y-axis at $(0, 2)$. In the equation $y = 3x + 2$, the 2 is the number that stands alone. We generalize our results in the following formula.

Formula 11.5   The equation $y = mx + b$ represents a straight line whose slope is m and whose y-intercept is at $(0, b)$.

The accompanying table gives several examples of slope and y-intercept.

Equation	Slope	y-intercept at
$y = 2x + 5$	2	$(0, 5)$
$y = -3x + 4$	-3	$(0, 4)$
$y = 5x$	5	$(0, 0)$
$y = -x$	-1	$(0, 0)$
$y = 4$	0	$(0, 4)$
$y = x + 1$	1	$(0, 1)$
$x = 2$	Undefined	There is none

EXAMPLE 5

Find the equation of a line with a slope of 3 and whose y intercept is at $(0, 14)$.

SOLUTION

Using Formula 11.5, we find that the equation is $y = 3x + 14$.   ▪

EXAMPLE 6

Find the equation of a line that has a slope of -2 and passes through the origin.

SOLUTION

Since the line passes through the origin, its y-intercept is at $(0, 0)$. Thus by using Formula 11.5 the equation is $y = -2x + 0$, or $y = -2x$.   ▪

Since we will be interested in finding the equation of a line under many different conditions, we list several different forms of the equation, depending on the information given.

Name	Given Information	Equation
slope-intercept form	slope = m, y-intercept = $(0, b)$	$y = mx + b$
point-slope form	slope = m, point = (x_1, y_1)	$y - y_1 = m(x - x_1)$
two-point form	point = (x_1, y_1) point = (x_2, y_2)	$y - y_1 = \dfrac{y_2 - y_1}{x_2 - x_1}(x - x_1)$ $(x_1 \neq x_2)$
two-intercept form	x-intercept = $(a, 0)$ y-intercept = $(0, b)$	$\dfrac{x}{a} + \dfrac{y}{b} = 1$

EXAMPLE 7

Find the equation of a line whose slope is 3 and that passes through the point $(-1, -2)$.

SOLUTION

Since we are given the slope of the line and a point on the line, we use the point-slope form. We have $m = 3$ and $x_1 = -1$, $y_1 = -2$, so when we substitute into $y - y_1 = m(x - x_1)$, we get

$$y - (-2) = 3[x - (-1)]$$
$$y + 2 = 3(x + 1)$$
$$y = 3x + 1$$

The equation of the line then is $y = 3x + 1$.

EXAMPLE 8

Find the equation of the line that passes through the points $(3, 4)$ and $(6, 10)$.

SOLUTION

Since we are given two points, we use the two-point form. We let $x_1 = 3$, $y_1 = 4$, $x_2 = 6$, and $y_2 = 10$, so when we substitute these values into

$$y - y_1 = \frac{y_2 - y_1}{x_2 - x_1}(x - x_1)$$

we get

$$y - 4 = \frac{10 - 4}{6 - 3}(x - 3)$$

Simplifying, we get

$$y - 4 = 2(x - 3)$$
$$y = 2x - 2$$

Thus the equation of the line is $y = 2x - 2$.   ■

EXAMPLE 9

Find the equation of the line whose x-intercept is 4 and whose y-intercept is 12.

SOLUTION

Since we are given both the x-intercept and the y-intercept, we use the two-intercept form. We let $a = 4$ and $b = 12$, so on substitution we get

$$\frac{x}{a} + \frac{y}{b} = 1$$

$$\frac{x}{4} + \frac{y}{12} = 1$$

Simplifying this equation gives $3x + y = 12$. Therefore the equation of the line is $3x + y = 12$.   ■

EXAMPLE 10

Find the equation of the line that passes through the point $(1, 9)$ and that is parallel to the line whose equation is $y = 4x + 7$.

SOLUTION

The line that we are interested in is parallel to the line whose equation is $y = 4x + 7$. Therefore the slope of both lines is 4. A point on the line is $(1, 9)$. Now that we know the slope of the line and a point on the line, we use the point-slope form with $m = 4$ and $x_1 = 1$, $y_1 = 9$. We have

$$y - y_1 = m(x - x_1)$$
$$y - 9 = 4(x - 1)$$
$$y - 9 = 4x - 4$$
$$y = 4x + 5$$

Therefore the equation of the line is $y = 4x + 5$.   ■

Perpendicular Lines

Consider Fig. 11.52. Using the coordinates in the diagram, we find that

$$\text{slope of } \overleftrightarrow{AB} = \frac{y_2 - y_1}{x_2 - x_1} = \frac{6 - 1}{7 - 3} = \frac{5}{4}$$

$$\text{slope of } \overleftrightarrow{CD} = \frac{y_2 - y_1}{x_2 - x_1} = \frac{5 - 1}{1 - 6} = \frac{4}{-5}$$

In this case we notice that $\overleftrightarrow{AB} \perp \overleftrightarrow{CD}$, and that the product of the slopes of these two lines is -1, that is $\left(\frac{5}{4}\right)\left(\frac{4}{-5}\right) = -1$. The slope of one of the lines is the negative reciprocal of the slope of the other line. (One number is the **negative reciprocal** of a second number if the product of both numbers is -1.) Thus we have: *if two nonvertical lines are perpendicular, then the slope of one line is the negative reciprocal of the slope of the other line; and*

negative reciprocal

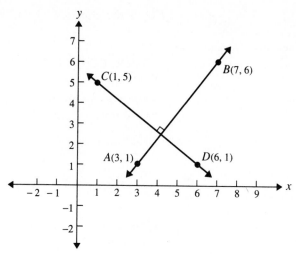

Figure 11.52

also, *if the slope of one line is the negative reciprocal of the slope of another line, then the lines are perpendicular.*

EXAMPLE 11

Find the equation of the line passing through the point $(-3, 1)$ and which is perpendicular to the line whose equation is $y = \frac{3}{2}x + 1$.

SOLUTION

The slope of the line $y = \frac{3}{2}x + 1$ is $\frac{3}{2}$. The slope of the line that is perpendicular to this line is $\frac{-2}{3}$, and a point on this line is $(-3, 1)$. Using the point slope form with $m = \frac{-2}{3}$, $x_1 = -3$, and $y_1 = 1$, we have

$$y - y_1 = m(x - x_1)$$

$$y - 1 = \frac{-2}{3}[x - (-3)]$$

$$3y - 3 = -2x - 6 \qquad \text{or that}$$

$$3y + 2x = -3$$

Therefore, the equation of the line is $3y + 2x = -3$.   ▬

EXAMPLE 12

Show by means of slopes that the triangle whose vertices are at $A(4, 1)$, $B(7, 4)$, and $C(5, 6)$ is a right triangle.

SOLUTION

Using the slope formula, we have

$$\text{slope } \overline{AB} = \frac{y_2 - y_1}{x_2 - x_1} = \frac{4 - 1}{7 - 4} = \frac{3}{3} = 1$$

$$\text{slope } \overline{BC} = \frac{y_2 - y_1}{x_2 - x_1} = \frac{6 - 4}{5 - 7} = \frac{2}{-2} = -1$$

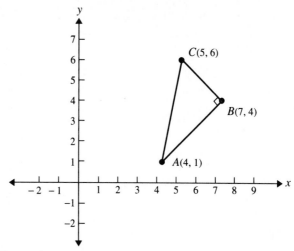

Figure 11.53

Since the slope of $\overline{AB}$ is the negative reciprocal of the slope of $\overline{BC}$, then $\overline{AB}$ is perpendicular to $\overline{BC}$ and $\triangle ABC$ is a right triangle with a right angle at B. (See Fig. 11.53.)   ▬

EXERCISES FOR SECTION 11.4

1. Find the slope of each of the following situations.

a)

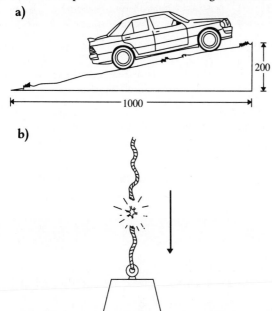

c)

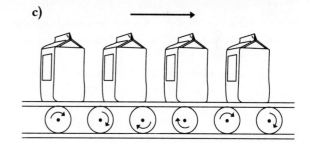

2. Find the slope of the line passing through the following points.

    a) $(3, 5)$ and $(5, 9)$

    b) $(6, 1)$ and $(3, 0)$

    c) $(3, -2)$ and $(-6, 5)$

    d) $(5, 3)$ and $(0, -4)$

    e) $(3, 9)$ and $(-3, -5)$

    f) $(-4, -5)$ and $(-3, -2)$

    g) $(-4, 0)$ and $(0, -5)$

    h) $(4, 3)$ and $(3, 4)$

b)

i) (4, 4) and (8, 9)   **j)** (5, 6) and (2, 6)

3. Find the slope and the y-intercept of the line whose equation is as follows.

a) $y = 3x - 1$ **b)** $y = \dfrac{x}{3} + 4$

c) $5y - 3x = 15$ **d)** $8x - 5y = 40$

e) $y = x$ **f)** $y = 7$

g) $x = 1$

4. Is the point $(-3, -2)$ on the graph of $5x - 3y = -21$?

5. Find the x-intercept and the y-intercept of the lines whose equations are as follows.

a) $4x - 3y = 12$ **b)** $-7x + 14y = 21$

c) $y = 3x$ **d)** $6x - 3y - 15 = 0$

e) $8x = 24$ **f)** $-3y = 14$

6. Find the equation of the lines satisfying the indicated conditions:

a) has slope -3 and y-intercept is at $(0, -8)$.

b) passes through the points $(4, 5)$ and $(8, 10)$.

c) has slope $-\dfrac{2}{3}$ and passes through the point $(5, 8)$.

d) passes through points $(-3, 7)$ and $(-2, -1)$.

e) has slope $-\dfrac{5}{7}$ and passes through the origin.

7. Find the equation of the line that passes through the point $(4, 2)$ and is parallel to the line whose equation is $y = 4x + 5$.

8. Write an equation of the line that is parallel to $y = 2x + 3$ and has the same y-intercept as $y + 5 = 4x$.

9. Write an equation of the line that is perpendicular to the line $x + 3y = 9$ and that passes through the origin.

10. Are the following sets of lines parallel?

a) $y = 3x + 1$ **b)** $y = -5x$
   $y = 3x - 8$ $3y + 15x = 11$

c) $4x = 8y - 3$
   $24y = 12x + 17$

11. The vertices of parallelogram $ABCD$ are at $A(-2, 4)$, $B(2, 6)$, $C(7, 2)$ and $D(x, 0)$.

a) Find the slope of line $\overline{AB}$

b) Express the slope of line $\overline{CD}$ in terms of x.

c) Using the results in answer to parts (a) and (b), find the value of x.

d) Write an equation of line $\overline{BD}$.

PROBLEM-SOLVING EXERCISES

12. The vertices of $\triangle ABC$ are $A(-2, 3)$, $B(0, -3)$, and $C(4, 1)$. Prove, by means of coordinate geometry, that

a) $\triangle ABC$ is isosceles.

b) the median to side $\overline{BC}$ is also the **altitude** to side $\overline{BC}$, that is, median to side $\overline{BC} \perp$ side $\overline{BC}$.

13. The points $A(-1, 4)$, $B(3, -2)$, $C(0, -4)$, and $D(-4, 2)$ form a quadrilateral. Using slopes, prove that $ABCD$ is a rectangle.

▷▷▷▷ **Brain-Teaser Problems** ◁◁◁◁

14. Find the equation of the circle that circumscribes the triangle whose vertices are at $A(2, 4)$, $B(6, 8)$, and $C(4, 12)$. (*Hint:* A circle that **circumscribes a triangle must pass through all three of its vertices.)

15. The three altitudes of any triangle intersect at a point called the **orthocenter of the triangle. Find the orthocenter of the triangle whose vertices are at $A(2, 4)$, $B(5, 9)$ and $C(7, 10)$.

11.5

LINEAR INEQUALITIES AND THEIR GRAPHS

Often we are concerned with **inequalities**. These are expressions such as

$$2x - y < 4, \qquad x + y > 5, \qquad 4x \geq 2, \qquad y + 3 \leq 4.$$

Inequalities contain "less than" ($<$) or "greater than" ($>$) signs instead of only the equals sign. In this chapter we will deal only with inequalities in which the sign in front of the y-term is positive. If this is not the case, we apply the rules for inequalities to change the sign in front of the y-term to a positive sign.

The graph of the type of inequality to be discussed in this chapter can easily be drawn by the following procedure:

a) Change the inequality sign to an equals sign.

b) Graph the line given by step (a).

c) If the inequality is "less than," shade in the area below the line. If the inequality is "greater than," shade in the area above the line.

d) If the inequality is "≤" or "≥," include the line. Otherwise do not include the line in the shaded area. This situation is usually indicated by a dashed line.

e) If the line is vertical and the inequality is "greater than," shade the area to the right of the line.

f) If the line is vertical and the inequality is "less than," shade the area to the left of the line.

EXAMPLE 1

Graph the inequality $x + y > 5$.

SOLUTION

We first change the ">" sign to an " = " sign, getting $x + y = 5$. We graph this line, using the table of values below.

x	y
0	5
2	3
5	0

Since the inequality is ">," we shade the area above the line. The line itself is not included. We indicate this by drawing it as a dashed line. (See Fig. 11.54.) The line is called a **plane divider**. The plane divider always divides the plane into two **half-planes**, one of which is shaded and the other which is not.

plane divider
half-plane

EXAMPLE 2

Graph the inequality $2x + 3y \leq 6$.

SOLUTION

We first change the "≤" sign to an " = " sign, getting $2x + 3y = 6$. We graph this line as shown in Fig. 11.55. Since the inequality is "≤," we shade in the area below the line and include the line as well. The half-plane below the line as well as the line itself represents the graph of $2x + 3y \leq 6$.

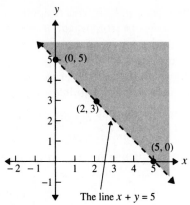

Figure 11.54

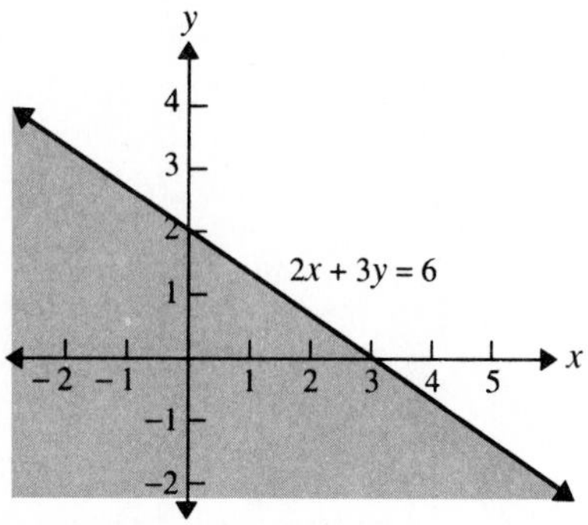

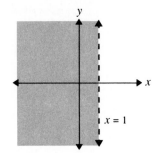

Figure 11.55

EXAMPLE 3

Draw the graphs of the following inequalities:

a) $x \geq 1$ **b)** $x < 1$ **c)** $y \geq 2$ **d)** $y < 2$

SOLUTION

The graphs of these inequalities are given in the Figs. 11.56–11.59.

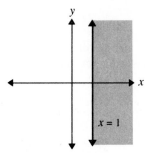

Figure 11.56

Figure 11.57

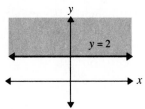

Figure 11.58

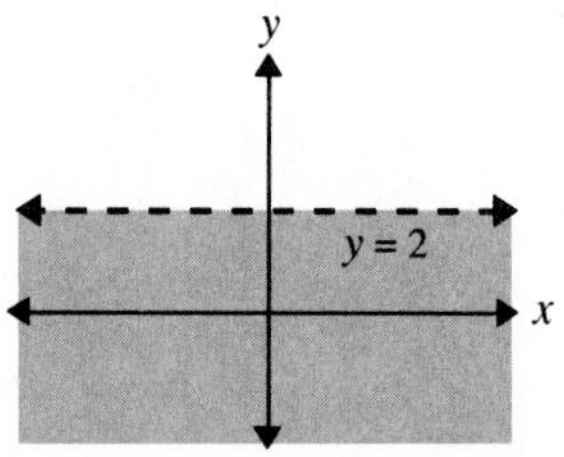

Figure 11.59

Notice that since the inequality is $\geq$ in parts (a) and (c), we shade in the area that is to the right of or above the line and include the line as well.

On the other hand, in parts (b) and (d) the inequality is "<." We shade in only the region that is to the left of or below the line. The line itself is not included. We indicate this by drawing it as a dashed line.

There is an alternative, and often more convenient, way of determining whether the region above or below a line or the region to the right of or left of a line should be shaded. We simply select any convenient point, and determine whether the coordinates of the point satisfy the inequality. If they do, then the region containing that point is shaded. Otherwise, the region containing the point is not shaded. This technique is illustrated in the following example.

EXAMPLE 4

Graph the inequality $3x + 4y \leq 12$.

SOLUTION

We first change the "$\leq$" sign to an "$=$" sign, getting $3x + 4y = 12$. We graph this line, using the table of values below.

x	y
4	0
0	3
8	-3

Now we must determine whether we shade the region above the line or below the line. Let us select $(0, 0)$ as a convenient point. Substituting $x = 0$ and $y = 0$ into the inequality $3x + 4y \leq 12$ gives

$$3(0) + 4(0) \leq 12$$

or $0 \leq 12$, which is a true statement. Thus $(0, 0)$ is a point in the solution set. We thus shade the region (half-plane) below the line. The line itself is also included as shown in Fig. 11.60.

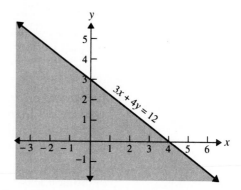

Figure 11.60

Comment When using this alternative technique for determining which region to shade, it is not necessary to make sure that the coefficient of y is positive or not.

Draw the graph of each of the inequalities given in Exercises 1–20.

1. $x > 3$

2. $x \leq -5$

3. $y \geq 5$

4. $y < -2$

5. $x \geq 0$

6. $y \leq -1$

7. $y > 3x$

8. $y > x + 1$

9. $2y - 3x > 12$

10. $2x + 5y \leq 10$

11. $2x + 3y > 6$

12. $2x - 3y \leq 6$

13. $y - x \leq -4$

14. $x - y \geq 2$

15. $x \leq -2y$

16. $3y - 6x \geq 9$

17. $2x + y - 3 \geq 0$

18. $7x - 3y \leq -21$

19. $5x - 4y \leq 20$

20. $15 \leq 3x - 5y$

Rearrange each of the inequalities given in Exercises 21–26 so that the number in front of the y-term is positive.

21. $5x - 6y \leq 12$

22. $7x - 3y \leq 8$

23. $x - y \leq 0$

24. $2x - y \geq 0$

25. $3x - 2y \geq -4$

26. $15x - 18y \leq -10$

11.6

GRAPHICAL SOLUTION OF A SYSTEM OF LINEAR EQUATIONS AND LINEAR INEQUALITIES IN TWO VARIABLES

In Section 5.8 we studied an algebraic technique for solving a system of two equations in two unknowns. Now that we have learned how to draw graphs, we can solve such a system graphically. To find the solution of a system of linear equations in two unknowns graphically, we simply draw the graphs of both equations on the same set of axes. The coordinates of the point of intersection represent the one common solution that satisfies both equations. The following situations may arise:

a) If a system of linear equations has *one* common solution, it is called a **system of consistent independent equations**. Graphically, this will occur when the two straight lines have unequal slopes and intersect in one point.

b) If a system of linear equations has *no* common solution, it is called a **system of inconsistent equations**. Graphically, this will occur when two straight lines have equal slopes but different y-intercepts and are thus parallel.

c) If a system of linear equations is of such a nature that every solution of either one of the equations is also a solution of the other, it is called a **system of consistent dependent equations**. Graphically, this will occur when two linear equations are graphed in a coordinate plane and turn out to be the same line.

We illustrate the above ideas with several examples.

EXAMPLE 1

Find the solution to the following system of linear equations graphically.

$$y + x = 6$$
$$2y - 3x = 2$$

SOLUTION

We first draw the graph of $y + x = 6$. Several pairs of values that satisfy this equation are shown here. The graph is given in Fig. 11.61.

Table of values for $y + x = 6$		Table of values for $2y - 3x = 2$	
x	y	x	y
3	3	4	7
5	1	0	1
6	0	-2	-2

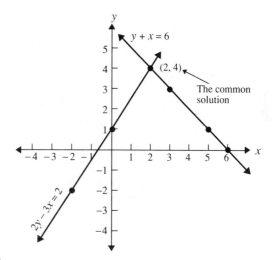

Figure 11.61

On the same set of axes we draw the graph of $2y - 3x = 2$. Several pairs of values that satisfy this equation are shown here. This graph is also given in Fig. 11.61. The coordinates of the point of intersection of the two lines is (2, 4). This represents the common solution. It is the *only* point that satisfies both equations. Thus our answer is $x = 2$ and $y = 4$. The system of equations is consistent.

EXAMPLE 2

Solve the following system of linear equations graphically.

$$y - x = 2$$
$$2y = 2x + 10$$

SOLUTION

We first draw the graph of $y - x = 2$ by finding several pairs of values that satisfy this equation. The graph is given in Fig. 11.62.

Table of values for $y - x = 2$

x	y
3	5
0	2
−1	1

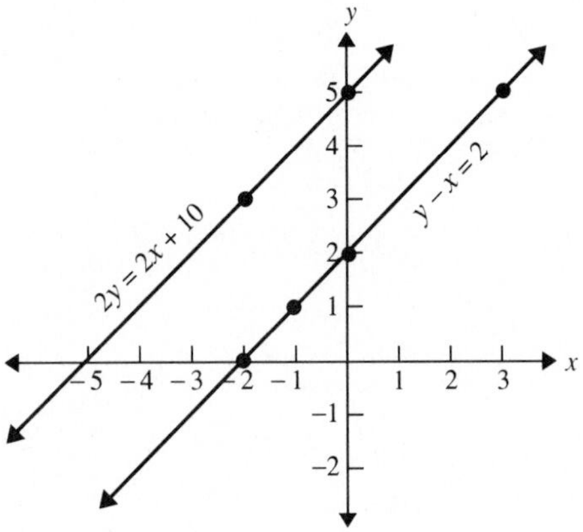

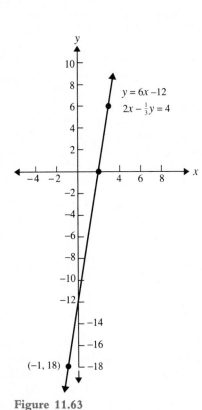

Figure 11.62

On the same set of axes we draw the graph of $2y = 2x + 10$ by finding several pairs of values that satisfy this equation.

Table of values for $2y = 2x + 10$

x	y
3	8
0	5
−2	3

We notice that the two lines do not intersect; they are parallel. Both lines have the same slope of 1. (Verify this.) There is no common solution, and the system is said to be inconsistent.

Figure 11.63

EXAMPLE 3

Solve the following system of linear equations graphically:

$$2x - \frac{1}{3}y = 4$$

$$y = 6x - 12$$

SOLUTION

We first draw the graph of $2x - \frac{1}{3}y = 4$ by finding several pairs of values that satisfy this equation. The graph is given in Fig. 11.63.

Table of values for $2x - \frac{1}{3}y = 4$

x	y
2	0
3	6
-1	-18

On the same set of axes we draw the graph of $y = 6x - 12$ by finding several pairs of values that satisfy this equation.

Table of values for $y = 6x - 12$

x	y
2	0
3	6
-1	-18

We notice that all the points lie on the same line. The two equations represent the same line, so any solution for one of the equations will also be the solution for the second equation. The system of equations is **dependent**. It has an infinite number of solutions.

Graphing Systems of Linear Inequalities

In Section 11.5 we indicated how to draw the graph of an inequality. Until now in this section we showed how we can solve a system of equations graphically. Now we will combine these ideas so that we will be able to solve a system of linear inequalities graphically.

   To solve a system of linear inequalities graphically, we simply draw the graphs of both inequalities on the same set of axes. We find the ordered pairs that satisfy all the inequalities. These are the solutions to the system. There may be an infinite number of such ordered pairs.

EXAMPLE 4

Graph the solution set for the following system of inequalities:

$$x < 3$$

$$y > -1$$

SOLUTION

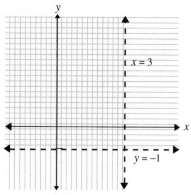

Figure 11.64
The region where the shading overlaps
represents the solution of both

We first draw the graph of $x < 3$ by drawing the plane divider $x = 3$ as indicated in Fig. 11.64. The line itself is drawn as a broken line. The half-plane to the left of this line represents the graph of the solution set of $x < 3$. This has vertical shading.

On the same set of axes we draw the graph of $y > -1$ by drawing the plane divider $y = -1$ as indicated in Fig. 11.64. Again, the line itself is drawn as a broken line. The half-plane above this line, which has been shaded horizontally, represents the graph of the solution set of $y > -1$. Notice that in one region the shading overlaps. This shaded region, which is the intersection of both of the graphs $y > -1$ and $x < 3$, is the graph of the solution set of these inequalities. The coordinates of any point in this region satisfy both inequalities. The coordinates of no other point can satisfy both inequalities.

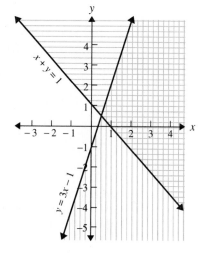

Figure 11.65
The region where the shading overlaps
represents the solution set of both
inequalities.

EXAMPLE 5

Graph the solution set for the following system of inequalities:

$$x + y \geq 1$$
$$y \leq 3x - 1$$

SOLUTION

We draw the graph of $x + y \geq 1$ by first graphing the plane divider $x + y = 1$. The half-plane *above* the line as well as the line itself form the graph of the solution set of $x + y \geq 1$. (See Fig. 11.65.) Using the same set of axes, we draw the graph of $y \leq 3x - 1$ by first graphing the plane divider $y = 3x - 1$. The half-plane *below* the line as well as the line itself form the graph of the solution set of $y \leq 3x - 1$. In the diagram, one region has been shaded twice. This region, which is the intersection of both graphs $x + y \geq 1$ and $y \leq 3x - 1$, is the graph of the solution set of these inequalities. Again, the coordinates of any point in this region satisfy both inequalities.

EXAMPLE 6

Graph the solution set for the following system of inequalities:

$$3x + 2y \geq 12$$
$$2x + 3y \leq 15$$
$$x \geq 0$$
$$y \geq 0$$

SOLUTION

We first draw the graph of $3x + 2y \geq 12$ by graphing the plane divider $3x + 2y = 12$. The half-plane above the line as well as the line itself form the graph of the solution set of $3x + 2y \geq 12$. On the same set of axes we draw the graph of $2x + 3y \leq 15$ by graphing the plane divider $2x + 3y = 15$. The half-plane below the line as well as the line itself form the graph of the solution set of $2x + 3y = 15$. (See Fig. 11.66.) On the same set of axes we draw the graphs of $x \geq 0$ and $y \geq 0$ by first drawing

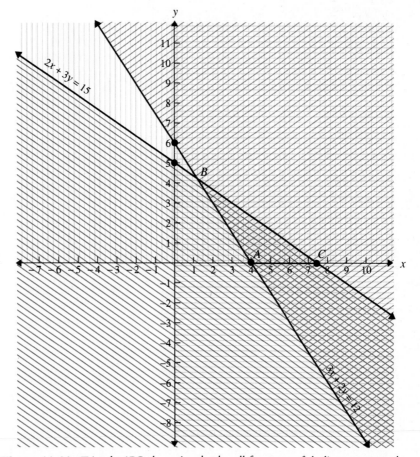

Figure 11.66 Triangle *ABC*, the region that has all four types of shading, represents the solution set of all four inequalities.

the plane dividers $x = 0$ and $y = 0$. The half-plane to the right of the line together with the line $x = 0$ forms the graph of the solution of $x \geq 0$. Similarly, the half-plane above the line together with the line $y = 0$ forms the graph of the solution of $y \geq 0$.

The region with all four types of shading is the graph of the solution set of the inequalities $3x + 2y \geq 12$, $2x + 3y \leq 15$, $x \geq 0$, and $y \geq 0$. This region includes all the points that are in the interior of triangle ABC as well as those points that are on $\overline{AB}$, $\overline{BC}$, and $\overline{AC}$, which are the sides of this triangle. Any point in this region satisfies all four inequalities. ▪

EXERCISES FOR SECTION 11.6

Solve the system of linear equations given in Exercises 1–14 graphically.

1. $\begin{cases} y = 4x \\ y = 2x + 6 \end{cases}$

2. $\begin{cases} y = x + 3 \\ y = 2x + 5 \end{cases}$

3. $\begin{cases} y = -2x + 1 \\ y = \dfrac{1}{2}x + 1 \end{cases}$

4. $\begin{cases} y = 2x \\ 3x - y = 3 \end{cases}$

5. $\begin{cases} 3x + y = 5 \\ 4x - y = 9 \end{cases}$

6. $\begin{cases} 5x - 3y = 11 \\ 2x + 3y = 17 \end{cases}$

7. $\begin{cases} x = 1 \\ y = 2 \end{cases}$

8. $\begin{cases} x = -3 \\ y = -1 \end{cases}$

9. $\begin{cases} 2x = y + 5 \\ 3x = 5y - 10 \end{cases}$

10. $\begin{cases} 2x + 3y = 11 \\ 3x - 2y = 10 \end{cases}$

11. $\begin{cases} x + y + 3 = 0 \\ 3x = -7y + 3 \end{cases}$

12. $\begin{cases} 5x - 4y = 5 \\ 2x - 3y = -5 \end{cases}$

13. $\begin{cases} 4x - 3y = -6 \\ 3x - 4y = -1 \end{cases}$

14. $\begin{cases} x = y + 2 \\ 3y = 5x - 8 \end{cases}$

In Exercises 15–20, determine whether the system is consistent, inconsistent, or dependent.

15. $7x - 2y = 20$
$4y = 14x + 6$

16. $3x - 2y = 12$
$2x - 3y = -6$

17. $2x - 5y = 10$
$y = \dfrac{2}{5}x - 2$

18. $x + 6y - 3 = 0$
$x = 3$

19. $y = 2x + 1$
$-6x = 3 - 3y$

20. $2x + 3y = 2$
$5x + 3y = 14$

In Exercises 21–36 graph the solution set of each system of inequalities.

21. $\begin{cases} x \geq 5 \\ y < 7 \end{cases}$

22. $\begin{cases} x \leq 3 \\ y \geq -1 \end{cases}$

23. $\begin{cases} x > 1 \\ y < 2 \end{cases}$

24. $\begin{cases} y \leq x \\ x < 4 \end{cases}$

25. $\begin{cases} x \geq 1 \\ y \leq 3x \end{cases}$

26. $\begin{cases} x + y > 5 \\ x - y < 8 \end{cases}$

27. $\begin{cases} 2x - y \leq -6 \\ x + y > 3 \end{cases}$

28. $\begin{cases} 3x + y \geq -6 \\ 2x - 3y < 6 \end{cases}$

29. $\begin{cases} 3x + 2y \leq 6 \\ x - y > 5 \end{cases}$

30. $\begin{cases} 4x - 7y \leq 28 \\ 2x - y > 1 \end{cases}$

31. $\begin{cases} x \geq 2 \\ y \leq 3 \\ x + y \geq 1 \end{cases}$

32. $\begin{cases} x + 3y \leq 6 \\ 2x > 5 \\ 3y < 8 \end{cases}$

33. $\begin{cases} 5x - 2y < 10 \\ 2x + 3y \geq -1 \\ x > 0 \end{cases}$

34. $\begin{cases} 4x - 3y \leq 12 \\ 2x + y \leq 7 \\ y < 10 \\ x > 3 \end{cases}$

35. $\begin{cases} 2x + y \leq 8 \\ 3x - 4y \leq 9 \\ x \geq 0 \\ y \geq 0 \end{cases}$

36. $\begin{cases} 3x + 4y \leq 12 \\ 2x + 3y \leq 6 \\ x + y < 1 \\ x \geq 0 \\ y \geq 0 \end{cases}$

11.7

USING LOGO IN COORDINATE GEOMETRY

HOME

SETX a

SETY b

The LOGO computer graphics program can easily be used to picture points on a coordinate system. This is because each point on the screen is associated with an ordered pair of numbers (x, y). The turtle's **HOME** position is the origin $(0, 0)$. The LOGO command **SETX** a moves the turtle horizontally to the point whose x-coordinate is a. For example, SETX 30 moves the turtle to the point whose x-coordinate is 30. The turtle's heading or orientation is not affected. Similarly, the LOGO command **SETY** b moves the turtle vertically to a point whose y-coordinate is b. Thus SETY 40 moves the turtle to the point whose y-coordinate is 40. If the values of a or of b are large, then the turtle will "wrap around" the screen, that is, it will go off the screen and reappear at the opposite edge.

To illustrate the use of SETX and SETY, suppose we start with the turtle at the home position and input the following LOGO commands:

	Position of turtle (in coordinate form)	
LOGO command	Before executing command	After executing command
SETX 30	(0, 0)	(30, 0)
SETY 40	(30, 0)	(30, 40)
SETX – 10	(30, 40)	(– 10, 40)
SETY 20	(– 10, 40)	(– 10, 20)

The turtle's complete path is shown in Fig. 11.67.

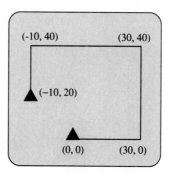

Figure 11.67

The LOGO command **SETXY** a b combines the SETX a and SETY b commands. It moves the turtle to the point whose coordinates are (a, b). For example, the command SETXY 20 30 moves the turtle to a position whose coordinates are (20, 30). This represents a combination of SETX 20 and SETY 30.

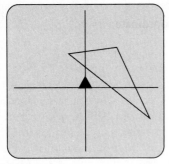

Figure 11.68

To draw a line segment connecting two points *A* and *B*, we must first pick up the pen (**PENUP** command), tell the turtle to move to the first point whose coordinates are specified, put down the pen (**PENDOWN** command), and then move to the second point. The following are the LOGO commands that must be followed to draw coordinate axes and then to plot a triangle whose vertices are at (25, 40), (−20, 30), and (50, −60). Figure 11.68 shows the turtle's path.

```
TO PLOT . POINTS
    HOME
    FORWARD 100
    BACK 200
    HOME
    RIGHT 90
    FORWARD 100
    BACK 200
    HOME
    PENUP
    SETXY 25   40
    PENDOWN
    SETXY −20   30
    SETXY 50   −60
    SETXY 25   40
    PENUP
    HOME
    END
```

EXAMPLE 1

Write the LOGO command that must be followed to draw the trapezoid whose coordinates are at *A*(10, 0), *B*(70, 0), *C*(60, 30), and *D*(20, 50).

SOLUTION

The necessary LOGO steps are as follows:

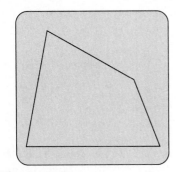

Figure 11.69

```
PENUP
SETXY 10   0
PENDOWN
SETXY 70   0
SETXY 60   30
SETXY 20   50
SETXY 10   0
PENUP
END
```

When executed, the turtle will draw the trapezoid shown in Fig. 11.69.

Comment The LOGO commands **XCOR** and **YCOR** tell us the turtle's current coordinates. If we type **PRINT XCOR** and press

RETURN, then the x-coordinate of the turtle will be displayed. Similarly, **PRINT YCOR** displays the y-coordinates of the turtle.

We can find the length of a line segment in LOGO by using the distance formula discussed earlier in this chapter. This is seen in the following example.

EXAMPLE 2

Write the LOGO procedure for finding the distance between the points $A(10, 20)$ and $B(15, 30)$.

SOLUTION

The necessary LOGO steps are as follows:

```
TO DISTANCE 10   20   15   30
    PRINT SQRT (15–10) * (15–10) + (30–20) * (30–20)
    END
```

When executed, the above program finds the distance between the points $(10, 20)$ and $(15, 30)$. The value of 11.1803 is displayed on the screen.

More generally the following procedure enables us to find the distance between the points (x_1, y_1) and (x_2, y_2).

```
TO DISTANCE :X1 :Y1 :X2 :Y2
    PRINT SQRT (:X2–:X1) * (:X2–:X1) + (:Y2–:Y1) * (:Y2–:Y1)
    END
```

Comment   In the above program, the notation (:X1, :Y1) is used to represent the x- and y-coordinates of a point.

LOGO can also be used to move the turtle to the midpoint of a line segment. This is especially useful when working with medians of a triangle. For example, to move the turtle to the midpoint of the line segment joining the points $(10, 50)$ and $(40, 60)$ we enter the following:

```
TO MIDPOINT 10   50   40   60
    SETXY  (10 + 40)/2   (50 + 60)/2
    END
```

When executed, the above program moves the turtle to the $(25, 55)$ position. More generally, the following procedure moves the turtle to the midpoint of the line segment determined by the points (x_1, y_1) and (x_2, y_2).

```
TO MIDPOINT :X1 :Y1 :X2 :Y2
    SETXY  (:X1 + :X2)/2   (:Y1 + :Y2)/2
    END
```

EXERCISES FOR SECTION 11.7

1. Write a LOGO procedure (that uses coordinate commands) for drawing the following figures.

   a) Triangle   b) Rectangle

   c) Square   d) Trapezoid

2. What, if anything, is wrong with each of the following LOGO commands?

   a) PU 30   b) DRAW RECTANGLE

   c) SETX 30   d) SETXY 40   30

3. Write a **LOGO** procedure for

   a) drawing the line segment joining the points (20, 60) and (30, 70).

   b) finding the coordinates of the midpoint of the line segment joining these points.

   c) finding the distance between these points.

4. Using the LOGO SETX, SETY, and SETXY commands, draw the largest rectangle that can be displayed on your computer video display screen.

 Brain-Teaser Problems

**5. A quadrilateral has coordinates (10, 70), (50, 30), (−20, −10), and (−20, 40). Write a LOGO procedure for drawing the parallelogram formed by joining the successive midpoints of the sides of this quadrilateral.

TYPICAL CLASSROOM QUESTIONS

1. A student claims that a horizontal line which has zero slope and a vertical line which has undefined slope are essentially the same, since zero slope and undefined slope are the same. Do you agree?

2. A student wonders why a system of linear inequalities can have an infinite number of solutions, but a system of linear equations can have at most one pair of values (unless both equations are dependent). How do you respond?

3. Is there any way of checking a solution to a system of linear inequalities?

4. Can the midpoint formula be used to find the midpoint of a *line*, not just a line segment? Explain your answer.

5. Does every line have an *x*-intercept? A *y*-intercept? Can a line have only a *y*-intercept or only an *x*-intercept or neither?

6. A student claims that the equation $(x - 2)^2 + (y - 3)^2 = -16$ represents the equation of a circle whose center is at (2, 3) and whose radius is −4. Do you agree? Explain.

7. A student claims the distance formula can be simplified by eliminating the squares and square root formula as shown below.

$$\text{Distance formula} \quad \sqrt{(x_2 - x_1)^2 + (y_2 - y_1)^2} = r$$

Remove squares and square root symbols $\quad (x_2 - x_1) + (y_2 - y_1) = r$ or that

$$|(x_2 - x_1)| + |(y_2 - y_1)| = r$$

Do you agree? Explain your answer.

STUDY GUIDE

The following is a chapter outline in capsule form. You should now be able to demonstrate your knowledge of the ideas mentioned by giving definitions, descriptions, or specific examples. Page references are given in parentheses.

In the **rectangular coordinate system** we start off with two mutually perpendicular lines, the x-axis and the y-axis. We write any point in the plane as an **ordered pair** of numbers (x, y). (p. 632)

The **x-coordinate** or **abscissa** is written first. This is followed by a comma and then the **y-coordinate** or **ordinate**, which is written second. We enclose both within parentheses. (p. 632)

The x-axis and the y-axis divide the plane into four **quadrants**. (p. 633)

In a three-dimensional coordinate system, the x-, y-, and z-axes taken as pairs determine three coordinate planes, the xy-plane, the xz-plane, and the yz-plane. The three coordinate planes divide three-space into eight **octants**. (p. 635)

The **distance formula** enables us to find the distance between any two points. (p. 638)

The **midpoint formula** enables us to find the coordinates of the midpoint of the line segment joining any two points. (p. 642)

A **circle** represents the set of all points that are a fixed distance away from a given point. The fixed point is called the **center** of the circle, and the fixed distance is called the **radius** of the circle. (p. 645)

A **median** in a triangle is a line segment joining any vertex to the midpoint of the opposite side. (p. 648)

The three medians of a triangle meet in a point called the **centroid** of the triangle. (p. 649)

The **graph** of an equation consists of all points (x, y) that are solutions to the equation. (p. 651)

The point at which a graph crosses the x-axis is called the **x-intercept**. At that point, $y = 0$. (p. 655)

The point at which a graph crosses the y-axis is called the **y-intercept**. At that point, $x = 0$. (p. 656)

The **slope** of a line is a measure of its steepness. A line with positive slope rises as we move from left to right. A line with negative slope falls as we move from left to right. A horizontal line (a line parallel to the x-axis) has zero slope. A vertical line (a line parallel to the y-axis) has undefined slope. (p. 660)

If **two lines are parallel**, they have the same slope. (p. 660)

The equation $y = mx + b$ represents a straight line whose slope is m and whose y-intercept is b. The equation of any horizontal line can be written in the form $y = b$. The equation of any vertical line can be written in the form $x = a$. (p. 661)

If **two lines are perpendicular**, then the slope of one line is the negative reciprocal of the slope of the other. (p. 663)

In a triangle, an **altitude** is a line from one vertex that is perpendicular to the opposite side to which it is drawn. (p. 666)

The three altitudes of any triangle intersect at a point called the **orthocenter** of the triangle. (p. 666)

Inequalities are expressions which contain $<$ or $>$ symbols instead of only the equals sign. (p. 666)

When drawing inequalities involving lines, any line (which is called a **plane divider**) divides the plane into two **half-planes**, one of which is shaded and the other which is not. (p. 667)

When solving a system of linear equations graphically, the following situations may occur:

a) If a system has no common solutions, it is called a **system of consistent independent equations**. Graphically, this will occur when the two straight lines have unequal slopes and intersect in one point. (p. 670)

b) If a system has no common solution, it is called a **system of inconsistent equations**. Graphically, this will occur when two straight lines have equal slopes but different y-intercepts and are thus parallel. (p. 670)

c) If a system is of such a nature that every solution of either one is also a solution of the other, it is called a **system of consistent dependent equations**. When graphed in a coordinate plane, they turn out to be the same line. (p. 670)

LOGO procedures can be used in coordinate geometry to have the turtle draw various geometric figures. The following commands can be used:

HOME   return turtle to origin (0, 0).
SETX a moves the turtle horizontally to the point whose x-coordinate is a.
SETY b moves the turtle vertically to the point whose y-coordinate is b.
SETXY a b moves the turtle to the point whose coordinates are (a, b).
XCOR   tells us the x-coordinate of the turtle.
YCOR   tells us the y-coordinate of the turtle.

KEY TERMS

The following list presents the key terms introduced in this chapter.

11.1   graph
       number line
       origin
       positive direction
       negative direction
       coordinates
       x- and y-axes

scale
x-coordinate (abscissa)
y-coordinate (ordinate)
quadrant
rectangular coordinate system
octant

FORMULAS TO REMEMBER

The following list summarizes all of the formulas discussed in this chapter.

THE DISTANCE FORMULA The distance between points $P(x_1, y_1)$ and $Q(x_2, y_2)$ is

$$PQ = \sqrt{(x_2 - x_1)^2 + (y_2 - y_1)^2}$$

MIDPOINT FORMULA The coordinates of the midpoint of the line segment joining (x_1, y_1) and (x_2, y_2) is

$$M = \left(\frac{x_1 + x_2}{2}, \frac{y_1 + y_2}{2} \right)$$

EQUATION OF A CIRCLE The equation of a circle whose center is at (a, b) and whose radius has a length of r is

$$\sqrt{(x - a)^2 + (y - b)^2} = r$$

x-INTERCEPT To find the *x*-intercept of a line, set $y = 0$ and solve for x.

y-INTERCEPT To find the *y*-intercept of a line, set $x = 0$ and solve for y.

SLOPE The slope of the line passing through the points (x_1, y_1) and (x_2, y_2) is

$$m = \frac{y_2 - y_1}{x_2 - x_1} \qquad (x_2 \neq x_1)$$

EQUATION OF A LINE

Name	Given information	Equation
Slope-intercept form	slope = m, y-intercept = b	$y = mx + b$
Point-slope form	slope = m, point = (x_1, y_1)	$y - y_1 = m(x - x_1)$
Two-point form	point = (x_1, y_1)	$y - y_1 = \dfrac{y_2 - y_1}{x_2 - x_1}(x - x_1)$
	point = (x_2, y_2)	where $(x_2 \neq x_1)$
Two-intercept form	x-intercept = $(a, 0)$	$\dfrac{x}{a} + \dfrac{y}{b} = 1$
	y-intercept = $(0, b)$	
Parallel to y-axis form	undefined slope x-intercept = a	$x = a$
Parallel to x-axis form	slope = 0, y-intercept = b	$y = b$

For proofs involving coordinate geometry use the following:

To prove that	Show that	Formula to use
Line segments are congruent	Line segments have same length	Distance formula
Line segments bisect each other	Lines have same midpoint	Midpoint formula
Lines intersect at a point	Equations of these lines have a common solution	Equation of a line $y = mx + b$
Lines are parallel	Both lines have same slope	$m_1 = m_2$ where m_1 = slope of line 1, m_2 = slope of line 2
Lines are perpendicular	Slope of one line is the negative reciprocal of the slope of the other	$m_1 = \dfrac{-1}{m_2}$ or $m_1 \cdot m_2 = -1$

CHAPTER REVIEW EXERCISES

1. Find, in radical form, the length of the line segment joining the points (1, 5) and (3, 9).

2. Find the slope of the line that passes through the points $A(4, 5)$ and $B(3, -4)$.

3. In parallelogram $ABCD$, the coordinates of A are (7, 3) and those of C are (5, −1). What are the coordinates of the intersection of the diagonals?

4. If the points (3, 5), (4, 2), and (5, k) lie on a straight line, the value of k is
   a) 1
   b) −1
   c) 0
   d) −2

5. Which pair of points will determine a line parallel to the y-axis?
   a) (2, 3) and (−1, 3)
   b) (3, 2) and (3, −1)
   c) (2, 2) and (−3, −3)
   d) (2, −2) and (−2, 2)

6. Which is an equation of the line that has a y-intercept of -2 and is parallel to the line whose equation is $4y = 3x + 7$?

   a) $y = \frac{3}{4}x - 2$ **b)** $y = \frac{4}{3}x - 2$

   c) $y = \frac{3}{4}x + 2$ **d)** $y = -\frac{4}{3}x - 2$

7. The graph of which equation is perpendicular to the graph of $y = \frac{1}{2}x + 3$?

   a) $y = -\frac{1}{2}x + 5$ **b)** $2y = x + 3$

   c) $y = 2x + 5$ **d)** $y = -2x + 3$

8. What are the coordinates of the center of a circle whose equation is $(x - 1)^2 + (y + 5)^2 = 7$?

9. If $\triangle ABC$ has vertices $A(0, 0)$, $B(0, 32)$, and $C(8, 6)$, and $\overline{MN}$ is drawn where M and N are the midpoints of $\overline{AB}$ and $\overline{BC}$ respectively, prove that $\overline{MN} \parallel \overline{AC}$.

10. Which is a point on the circle whose center is $(0, 0)$ and whose radius is 5?

    a) $(2, 3)$ **b)** $(3, 4)$

    c) $(4, 5)$ **d)** $(0, 0)$

11. Which is an equation of the line whose slope is 3 and which passes through the point $(10, 5)$?

    a) $y = -3x + 5$ **b)** $y = 3x - 5$

    c) $y = 3x + 25$ **d)** $y = 3x - 25$

12. In $\triangle ABC$, median $\overline{CD}$ intersects side $\overline{AB}$ at point D. The coordinates of point A are $(4, 8)$ and of point B are $(10, -2)$. Find the coordinates of point D.

13. Triangle ABC has vertices $A(-3, -4)$, $B(-1, 7)$, and $C(3, 5)$. Find the coordinates of the centroid of this triangle.

14. Write an equation of the line which passes through the points $(2, 1)$ and $(6, 3)$.

15. If $(x - 3)^2 + (y + 5)^2 = 20$ is an equation of a circle and the center is $(h, -5)$, find h.

16. The line that passes through the points $(-2, 3)$ and $(5, y)$ has slope of $\frac{4}{7}$. Find y.

17. In Fig. 11.70, point $S(-3, 4)$ lies on circle O with center $(0, 0)$. Line $\overleftrightarrow{AB}$ and radius $\overline{OS}$ are drawn.

    a) Find the length of $\overline{OS}$.

    b) Write an equation of circle O.

    c) If $\overleftrightarrow{AB} \perp \overline{OS}$, find the slope of $\overleftrightarrow{AB}$.

    d) Write an equation of line $\overleftrightarrow{AB}$.

    e) Find the coordinates of any point on $\overleftrightarrow{AB}$ other than S.

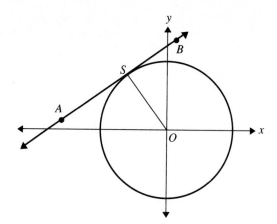

Figure 11.70

18. In $\triangle ABC$ the vertices are $A(-1, 2)$, $B(7, 0)$, and $C(1, -6)$. If $D(4, -3)$ is a point on $\overline{BC}$, prove that $\overline{AD}$ is the perpendicular bisector of $\overline{BC}$.

19. The slope of $\overleftrightarrow{AB}$ is $\dfrac{3}{5}$ and the slope of line $\overleftrightarrow{CD}$ is $\dfrac{9}{k}$. If $\overleftrightarrow{AB}$ is parallel to $\overleftrightarrow{CD}$, what is the value of k?

20. The vertices of triangle ABC are $A(1, 1)$, $B(10, 4)$, and $C(7, 7)$.

   a) Find the slope of $\overline{AB}$.

   b) If $D(7, k)$, is a point on $\overline{AB}$, find k.

   c) Write an equation for $\overleftrightarrow{AC}$

   d) If E is a point on $\overline{AC}$ such that $\overleftrightarrow{DE} \parallel \overleftrightarrow{BC}$, find the coordinates of E.

21. Solve the following system of equations graphically and check:
$$\begin{cases} 2x - y = -1 \\ x + 3y = 17 \end{cases}$$

22. Solve the following system of equations graphically and check:
$$\begin{cases} x + y = -3 \\ 2x - y = 6 \end{cases}$$

23. a) On the same set of coordinate axes, graph the following system of inequalities:
$$\begin{cases} y > -2x + 7 \\ y \le 3x - 3 \end{cases}$$

   b) Write the coordinates of a point in the solution set of this system.

24. a) On the same set of coordinate axes, graph the following system inequalities:
$$\begin{cases} y < 2x + 4 \\ x + y \le 7 \end{cases}$$

   b) Write the coordinates of a point in the solution set of this system.

25. $A(4, 5)$, $B(2, 3)$, $C(2, 0)$, and $D(7, 5)$ are the vertices of quadrilateral $ABCD$. Show that $ABCD$ is an isosceles trapezoid.

SUGGESTED FURTHER READING

Avery, J., "The Cartesian Classroom," in *The Mathematics Teacher* **76** (September 1983), 407–408.

Bell, W., "Cartesian Coordinates and Battleship," in *The Arithmetic Teacher* **21** (May 1974), 421–422.

Smith, R., "Coordinate Geometry for Third Graders," in *The Arithmetic Teacher* **33** (April 1986), 10.

Terc, M., "Coordinate Geometry—Art and Mathematics," in *The Arithmetic Teacher* **33** (October 1985), 22–24.

CHAPTER 12

Measurement

NCTM GUIDELINES

In its March 1989 *Curriculum and Evaluation Standards For School Mathematics* (p. 51), The National Council of Teachers Of Mathematics recommends that the mathematics curriculum should include measurements so that students can

- understand the attributes of length, capacity, weight, area, volume, and temperature;
- develop the process of measuring and concepts related to units of measurement;
- make and use estimates of measurement;
- make and use measurements in problem and everyday situations.

Measurement is of central importance to the curriculum because of its power to help children see that mathematics is useful in everyday life and to help them develop many mathematical concepts and skills. The process of measuring is identical for any attribute. We choose a unit, compare that unit to the object, and report the number of units. The number of units can be determined by counting, by using an instrument, or by using a formula. In the examples of Fig. 12.1, the number of area units is determined by counting and the number of length units is determined with a ruler.

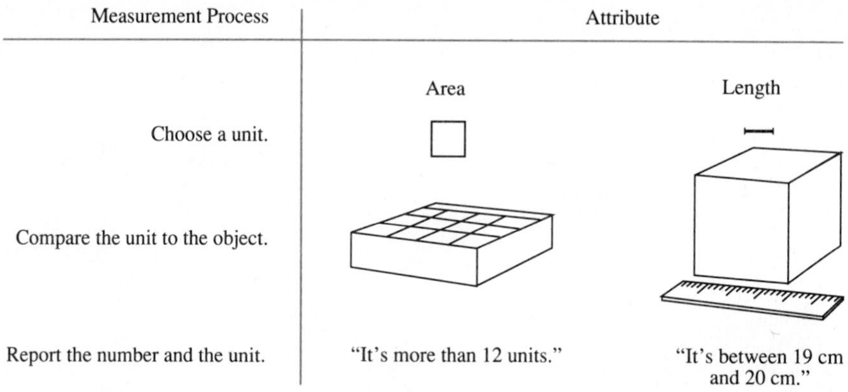

Measurement Process	Attribute	
	Area	Length
Choose a unit.		
Compare the unit to the object.		
Report the number and the unit.	"It's more than 12 units."	"It's between 19 cm and 20 cm."

Figure 12.1

Units of measure translate physical qualities into terms that are understandable and universally accepted; a meter is of a specific length everywhere on earth. And units of measure can be as precise as we need them to be.

The choice of a unit is arbitrary, but it must have the same attributes as that which is being measured. That is, a unit of area must be selected to measure area, a unit of weight to measure weight, and so forth. It is for this reason that in this chapter we will study the different units of measurement.

Introduction

In everyday life, people need to make many kinds of measurements to help them resolve common questions: About how long will it take? About how much do I need to buy? About how much will it hold? Often an estimate is sufficient. Of course, the ability to hold one's hands about a meter apart, to know the length of a foot or stride, or to know the width of a fingernail, all represent useful estimating tools. Good estimation, however, does require a judgment about an entity's approximate relationship to a standard.

In this chapter, we indicate how geometry and measurement are interconnected and how they support each other in many ways. For example, we use line segments and squares to determine the perimeter and area of irregular figures. The area of any geometric figure does not change if it is partitioned and rearranged. This enables us to find the areas of any polygon.

People encounter measurement ideas both in and out of school situations. By studying measurement, we learn about the usefulness and practical application of mathematics. Thus in this chapter we will study two precise systems of standard units, namely the English system that is used in the United States today and the more common metric system which almost all other countries use.

HISTORICAL NOTE

$$\pi = 3.14159265358979323846264338327950288419716 9\dots$$

When working with measurements involving circles, the symbol π (pronounced "pie") appears. Actually, this ancient Babylonian constant represents the ratio of the circumference of a circle to its diameter. The accurate calculation of its value has always fascinated mathematicians. In the Bible (*I Kings* 7:23 and *II Chronicles* 4:22), calculations indicate that 3 was used as the value of π.

In the nineteenth century, the legislature of Indiana attempted to pass a law establishing a fixed decimal value for π. They gave up when the idea was ridiculed in the press. Today we know that the value of π correct to 42 places is the number shown above.

In the 1950s the U.S. led the way, churning out estimates of pi accurate to thousands and tens of thousands of decimal places. Then the French took the lead. With the emergence of Japan's supercomputer industry in the 1980s, pi became an almost exclusive province of the Japanese. The last world record, 201 million digits, was set on a Japanese supercomputer in 1988. In June 1989, using U.S.-made supercomputers, two Columbia University mathematicians, Soviet emigré brothers David and Gregory Chudnovsky, computed the value of π to 480 million digits. This number, if printed out linearly, would extend 600 miles.

12.1

THE METRIC SYSTEM

With a ruler measure the line segment $\overline{AB}$ shown in Fig. 12.2. You should find that it is three inches long. In measuring the line segment you compared it to the markings on a ruler. How did the company that made the ruler know how to mark it? Obviously, they had some standard measure, but where did that come from? Units of measurement, whether of weight, volume, or other measure, have been determined in the following way.

_____
A   B

Figure 12.2

yard

Scientists agree on a basic unit of measurement for a particular quantity. For example, in the United States at present the standard unit of measurement of length is the **yard**. The standard yardstick is kept at the National Bureau of Standards in Washington, D.C. It is made of metal and is maintained at a constant temperature to prevent the metal from expanding. All other yardsticks are copies of this standard yardstick.

We're Going Metric

ALBANY: The New York State Thruway Authority announced yesterday that it would begin changing all of the destination marker signs and speed limit signs on the length of the New York Thruway to metric units in the spring. Not only will speed limit signs such as the one shown be changed, but signs indicating the distances between cities and towns will eventually be changed also. The cost of the changeover is expected to run into millions of dollars and will be accomplished gradually over a period of several years.

THE NEWS, February 20, 1985

The above article indicates that America is gradually changing over to the metric system. Industries will have to replace machinery and tools as well as maintain dual inventories during this transition period. Furthermore, the public will have to be reeducated in how to use this new system and how to convert measurements from our present system to the metric system. In this section we will explain how this is done.

metric system

foot-pound

British system

There are two standard systems of measurement in use today. One of these is known as the **metric system** and is used throughout most of the civilized world. The United States still uses the older **foot-pound**, or **British system** in which the standard unit of length is the yard.

Many industries in the United States are opposed to converting to the metric system because of the cost of a changeover. After much debate, the U.S. Congress passed the Metric Conversion Act of 1975. In effect, this established a board to oversee the "voluntary" conversion. Thus in due time, many of the standard measures with which we are familiar will become metric units. Indeed, we are already beginning to "think metric," since many companies are now packaging their items in metric units.

One major advantage of using the metric system is that all measurements are expressed in powers of 10 (that is, 10, 100, 1000, etc.). The same is not true in the British system. For example, in the British system there are 3 feet in a yard, 12 inches in a foot, 5280 feet in a mile, etc.

Standard prefixes (which are powers of 10) are added to the various metric units to indicate multiples or submultiples of the basic units. These are shown in Table 12.1.

A meter measures approximately 39.37 inches. Similar standard measures have been agreed on for other quantities such as weight and liquid measure.

TABLE 12.1		
Prefix	Symbol	Meaning
kilo-	k	one thousand times
hecto-	h	one hundred times
deka-	da	ten times
deci-	d	one tenth of
centi-	c	one hundredth of
milli-	m	one thousandth of

Metric Unit of Length

meter

In the metric system of measurement *the* **meter** *is accepted as the unit of length*. Originally, the meter was defined as one ten-millionth of the distance measured along a meridian through Paris from the North Pole to the equator. A standard meter bar was constructed, but in fact it differed slightly (about 0.023%) from its intended length. Copies of the standard meter are kept in the major cities of the world. In 1961 the General Conference of Weights and Measures defined the meter in terms of the wavelength of a particular isotope of krypton.

Some of the lengths used in the metric system, as well as their abbreviations, are shown in Table 12.2.

TABLE 12.2		
Metric unit	Commonly used abbreviation	How many meters?
Kilometer	km	1000
Hectometer	hm	100
Dekameter	dam	10
Meter	m	1
Decimeter	dm	1/10 or 0.1
Centimeter	cm	1/100 or 0.01
Millimeter	mm	1/1000 or 0.001

The following examples show how we convert from one unit to another in the metric system.

EXAMPLE 1

How many centimeters are there in 325 meters?

SOLUTION

Since 1 m equals 100 cm, we have 1 m = 100 cm. Therefore

$$325 \times 1 \text{ m} = 325 \times 100 \text{ cm}$$
$$325 \text{ m} = 32{,}500 \text{ cm}$$

Thus 325 m = 32,500 cm.

EXAMPLE 2

How many kilometers are there in 7342 millimeters?

SOLUTION

Since 1 mm equals 0.001 m, we have 1 mm = 0.001 m. Therefore

$$7342 \times 1 \text{ mm} = 7342 \times 0.001 \text{ m}$$
$$7342 \text{ mm} = 7.342 \text{ m}$$

Now

$$1 \text{ km} = 1000 \text{ m}$$

This means that

$$1 \text{ m} = 1/1000 \text{ km or } 0.001 \text{ km}$$

Thus

$$7.342 \times 1 \text{ m} = 7.342 \times 0.001 \text{ km} \quad \text{or} \quad 0.007342 \text{ km}$$

Therefore

$$7342 \text{ mm} = 0.007342 \text{ km}$$

Since both the metric and British systems are still widely used, we should know how to convert from one system to the other. Table 12.3 shows the approximate relationships between the two systems.

TABLE 12.3			
Converting from the metric system to the British system		Converting from the British system to the metric system	
1 millimeter	0.04 inch	1 inch	2.54 centimeters
1 centimeter	0.4 inch	1 foot	30.48 centimeters
1 meter	1.1 yards	1 yard	0.914 meter
1 kilometer	0.62 mile	1 mile	1.6 kilometers

Using the relationships given in Table 12.3, we can convert from the metric system to the British system and vice versa. This is illustrated in the following examples.

EXAMPLE 3

Convert 55 miles to kilometers.

SOLUTION

From Table 12.3 we see that 1 mile is 1.6 km. Therefore 55 miles = 55 × 1.6 km or 88 km.

EXAMPLE 4

Convert 75 centimeters to inches.

SOLUTION

From Table 12.3 we see that 1 centimeter is 0.4 inch. Therefore 75 cm = 75 × 0.4 inch or 30 inches.

EXAMPLE 5

The wheelbase of Bill's car measures 112 inches. How many centimeters does this measure?

SOLUTION

From Table 12.3 we know that each inch is equivalent to 2.54 centimeters. Thus 112 inches is equivalent to 112 × 2.54 or 284.48 centimeters.

EXAMPLE 6

Melissa's dining room is 12 feet by 9 feet. Express the measurement of her dining room in meters.

SOLUTION

From Table 12.3 we know that 1 foot is 30.48 centimeters, so that 12 feet = 12 × 30.48 or 365.76 centimeters; also 9 feet = 9 × 30.48 or 274.32 centimeters. Since each centimeter is 1/100 of a meter, we have

$$365.76 \text{ cm} = \frac{365.76}{100} \text{ m or } 3.6576 \text{ m}$$

and

$$274.32 \text{ cm} = \frac{274.32}{100} \text{ m or } 2.7432 \text{ meters.}$$

Thus Melissa's room measures 3.6576 by 2.7432 meters.

A convenient way to convert from one metric unit to another is as follows. Suppose we want to convert 0.023 km to centimeters. We can set up the following chart.

	km	hm	dam	m	dm	cm	mm
Step 1							
Step 2	0	2	3				
Step 3	0	2	3				
Step 4	0	2	3	0	0		

Step 1—Place decimal point on km line because we are starting with km.
Step 2—Place digits in columns.
Step 3—Move decimal point from km line to cm line.
Step 4—Fill in columns between 3 and decimal point with zeros

Our answer then is 0.023 km = 2300 cm.

Comment When using this procedure, we do not have to think whether to multiply or divide.

Metric Unit of Weight

Technically speaking, there is an important difference between the weight of an object which is affected by gravity and the mass of an object which is not affected by gravity. Thus when an astronaut travels through space in orbit above the earth, the astronaut's weight is different than on earth. The astronaut's mass, on the other hand, remains the same. However, in this book, we will not distinguish between weight and mass. We will use English units of weight and metric units of mass. Both of these units are used to weigh objects.

gram

In the metric system of measurement the standard unit of weight is the **gram**, as opposed to our pound. There are many abbreviations used when working with weights in the metric system. These are given in Table 12.4.

	TABLE 12.4	
Unit of weight	Commonly used abbreviation	How many grams?
Kilogram	kg	1000
Hectogram	hg	100
Dekagram	dag	10
Gram	gm	1
Decigram	dg	1/10 or 0.1
Centigram	cg	1/100 or 0.01
Milligram	mg	1/1000 or 0.001

To convert from the metric unit of weight to the British system or vice versa, we proceed as follows.

To convert from the metric unit of kilograms to the British unit of pounds, multiply by 2.2; that is, 1 kg ≈ 2.2 lb.

To convert from the British unit of pounds to the metric unit of kilograms, multiply by 0.45; that is, 1 lb ≈ 0.45 kg.

EXAMPLE 7

Convert 763 centigrams to kilograms.

SOLUTION

From Table 12.4 we find that 1 cg equals 0.01 gm. Therefore 1 cg = 0.01 gm, so that 763×1 cg = 763×0.01 gm, or 763 cg = 7.63 gm. Now we must convert 7.63 gm to kilograms. Since 1000 gm = 1 kg, we have 1 gm = $\frac{1}{1000}$ kg or 0.001 kg. Thus 7.63 gm = 7.63×0.001 kg or 0.00763 kg.

EXAMPLE 8

Convert 2133 pounds to kilograms.

SOLUTION

Using the above conversion rule, we find that 1 lb = 0.45 kg. Therefore 2133 pounds = 2133×0.45 kg, or 959.85 kg.

EXAMPLE 9

In a supermarket, Vera Nelson is examining a box of cookies that was manufactured in Europe. The label on the package reads "Net weight 355 grams." A similar box of cookies manufactured in the United States reads "Net weight 12 ounces." If both boxes of cookies sell for the same price, which box gives Vera the most for her money?

SOLUTION

In order to compare them we must express both weights in the same unit. We will convert grams to ounces. Using the conversion rule given above, the reader should verify that 1 gram equals approximately 0.035 ounce, so that 355 grams equals 355×0.035 or 12.425 ounces. Thus the box made in Europe gives Vera the most for her money.

Metric Unit of Volume

In the metric system the standard unit of liquid measure (volume) is the **liter**, as opposed to our quart. Some of the abbreviations commonly encountered when working with the metric system are shown in Table 12.5.

liter

	TABLE 12.5	
Unit of volume	Commonly used abbreviation	How many liters?
Kiloliter	kL	1000
Hectoliter	hL	100
Dekaliter	daL	10
Liter	L	1
Deciliter	dL	1/10 or 0.1
Centiliter	cL	1/100 or 0.01
Milliliter	mL	1/1000 or 0.001

To convert from one system to the other, we can use the relationships given in Table 12.6.

TABLE 12.6			
Converting from the metric system to the British system		Converting from the British system to the metric system	
1 liter	1.05 liquid quarts	1 liquid quart	0.95 liters
1 liter	0.91 dry quarts	1 dry quart	1.1 liters
1 kilogram	2.2 pounds	1 pound	0.45 kilograms

EXAMPLE 10

Convert 17.3 liters to liquid quarts.

SOLUTION

From Table 12.6 we find that 1 liter = 1.05 liquid quarts, so that 17.3 liters = 17.3 × 1.05 liquid quarts, or 17.3 liters = 18.165 liquid quarts. ▪

For the benefit of the reader we present in Table 12.7 a chart that makes it easier to convert from one system to the other (see next page).

EXAMPLE 11

Patrick Michaelson owns a car that has a 22-gallon gas tank. On a recent trip to Canada, Patrick stopped at a gas station to fill up. To his amazement, he was able to fill up his car with 47 liters. How many gallons of gas did Patrick actually purchase?

SOLUTION

We must convert 47 liters to gallons. From Table 12.7 we know that 1 liter equals 0.26 gallon, so that 47 liters equals 47 × 0.26 or 12.22 gallons. Thus Patrick purchased only 12.22 gallons of gas. ▪

Temperature

degrees Celsius

degrees Fahrenheit

In the metric system, temperature is measured in **degrees Celsius** after the Swedish astronomer, Anders Celsius, who created it in 1748. This scale was originally known as the "Centigrade" scale. On the Celsius scale, water freezes at 0° and boils at 100°, whereas on the Fahrenheit scale it freezes at 32° and boils at 212°. A formula for converting **degrees Fahrenheit** to degrees Celsius is

$$C = \frac{F - 32}{1.8}$$

where C and F are degrees Celsius and degrees Fahrenheit, respectively.

EXAMPLE 12

To conserve energy, government officials recommend a thermostat setting of 68°F during the heating season. What is this in degrees Celsius?

TABLE 12.7			
	To convert from	to	multiply by
Length	inches	millimeters	25
	inches	centimeters	2.54
	feet	centimeters	30.48
	feet	meters	0.3
	yards	meters	0.914
	miles	kilometers	1.6
	millimeters	inches	0.04
	centimeters	inches	0.4
	meters	feet	3.28
	meters	yards	1.1
	kilometers	miles	0.62
Weight	ounces	grams	28.3
	pounds	kilograms	0.45
	grams	ounces	0.035
	kilograms	pounds	2.2
Liquid Measure	ounces	milliliters	29.76
	pints	liters	0.476
	quarts	liters (liquid)	0.95
	gallons	liters	3.81
	milliliters	ounces	0.034
	liters	pints	2.1
	liters	quarts (liquid)	1.05
	liters	gallons	0.26

SOLUTION

We use the formula $C = \dfrac{F - 32}{1.8}$ with $F = 68°$. Thus a room temperature of 68°F is equivalent to

$$\frac{F - 32}{1.8} = \frac{68 - 32}{1.8} = 20°$$

EXAMPLE 13

Normal human body temperature is 37°C. What is this in degrees Fahrenheit?

SOLUTION

Solving the formula $C = \dfrac{F - 32}{1.8}$ for F gives $F = 1.8C + 32$, so that a body temperature of 37°C is equivalent to 1.8 (37) + 32, or 98.6 degrees Fahrenheit.

EXERCISES FOR SECTION 12.1

In Exercises 1–26, convert each measurement to the units indicated.

1. 9 yards to meters
2. 553 pounds to grams
3. 7 liters to liquid quarts
4. 2.3 kg to lb
5. 384 lb to cg
6. 3.7 L to cL
7. 12 ft to cm
8. 396 mm to inches
9. 1760 mL to gal
10. 77 km to cm
11. 275 kg to gm
12. 17.5 ft to m
13. 364 m to yd
14. 286 L to liquid quarts
15. 67 ft to mm
16. 83 mL to L
17. 54 kg to lb
18. 21 m to ft
19. 16 L to dry quarts
20. 62 dm to cm
21. 38 m, 4 dm to ft
22. 726 in. to mm
23. 354 dry quarts to L
24. 17 m, 5 cm to yd
25. 0.7 kg to cg
26. 138 m, 8 dm, 6 cm to miles
27. Consider the sign shown in Fig. 12.3. How would this sign read in the metric system?

SPEED
LIMIT
35

Figure 12.3

28. Consider the sign shown in Fig. 12.4. How would this sign read in the metric system?

BRIDGE
WEIGHT
LIMIT
7500 LB

Figure 12.4

29. A certain football player is 6′5″ tall, weighs 195 lbs, and has a waist of 38″. What are these measurements in the metric system?

30. A plane's normal cruising altitude is 10,000 meters. Express this altitude in feet.
31. Jason supplements his normal food intake with 1200 milligrams of vitamin C. Express this weight in ounces.
32. The oil tank in Heather's two-family house has a capacity of 275 gallons. Express the tank's capacity in liters.
33. On January 1, 1989, unleaded gasoline sold in New York City for $1.39 per gallon of premium gas. Find the cost of one liter.
34. At what temperature would you most likely go swimming?
    a) 40°C   b) 20°C   c) 5°C
35. The temperature on a cold winter day at the North Pole was –23°C. What was the temperature in degrees Fahrenheit?
36. The coldest temperature ever recorded was –126.9°F (recorded in the Antarctic). What is this temperature in degrees Celsius?

PROBLEM-SOLVING EXERCISES

37. The mathematics office in a school has a large sign painted on its door, as follows: Each letter in the words "MATHEMATICS DEPARTMENT" is 9 mm wide, the space between letters is 5 mm wide, and the space between words is 7 mm wide. How many centimeters long is the sign?
38. A particular car washing machine uses 185 L of water to thoroughly wash each car. How many kiloliters of water are needed to wash 32 cars a day for 1 month (31 days)?

Brain-Teaser Problems

**39. A particular shower uses 19.7 L of water per minute when used without a flow restrictor, and 12.4 L of water per minute when used with a flow restrictor. How much water (in gallons) can be saved in a month (31 days) by using the flow restrictor, if 7 people each take two 4-minute showers daily?

12.2

MEASURE AND AREA; USING THE METRIC SYSTEM

distance

unit distance

In the previous section we discussed different units of length. You will recall that when we studied the real-number line in Chapter 7 (and again in Chapter 11), we indicated that if we select any two points A and B on a real number line where A corresponds to a and B corresponds to b, then the **distance** from A to B is the real number obtained as the nonnegative difference between a and b. We denote this distance as AB. Of course, the distance from 0 to 1 on the number line is called the **unit distance**. Also, for all points A and B, we have $AB = BA$.

EXAMPLE 1

Suppose A, B, and C are points on a number line such that A corresponds to 1.371, B corresponds to 3.691, and C corresponds to 7.390 (see Fig. 12.5). Find AB, BC, and AC.

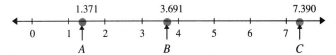

Figure 12.5

SOLUTION

In this case $a = 1.371$, $b = 3.691$, and $c = 7.390$, so that

$$AB = 3.691 - 1.371 = 2.32$$
$$BC = 7.390 - 3.691 = 3.699$$
$$AC = 7.390 - 1.371 = 6.019$$

We note that since B is between A and C, we have $AB + BC = AC$. ▪

triangular inequality

The results of the last example can be generalized as follows: For any three distinct points A, B, and C, the distance between A and B plus the distance between B and C is greater than or equal to the distance between A and C, that is, $AB + BC \geq AC$. This result is known as the **triangular inequality**. Of course, if A, B, and C are collinear, then $AB + BC = AC$.

Perimeter

The sum of the lengths of the sides of a polygon, that is, the "distance around" the polygon, is called the **perimeter** of the polygon. For example, the perimeter of several familiar geometric shapes is shown here:

Shape	Picture	Perimeter
Triangle		$a + b + c$
Parallelogram		$2a + 2b$
Rectangle		$2a + 2b$
Pentagon		$a + b + c + d + e$
Regular hexagon		$6s = 30$

Circumference

The perimeter of a circle, that is, the distance around the circle, is called its **circumference**. Thus circumference is a linear measure. Regardless of the size of the circle, its circumference is equal to $2\pi r$ where r is the radius of the circle or $C = \pi d$ where d is the diameter of the circle. The latter equation tells us that $\pi = \frac{C}{d}$. The ancient Greeks knew that if they divided the circumference of a circle by its diameter, they always obtained the same value, no matter what size circle was used. The number π is an irrational number whose value is 3.14159.... In most cases we use $\frac{22}{7}$, $3\frac{1}{7}$ or 3.14 as an approximation for π.

pi (π)

Area

Now let us consider area. In dealing with figures in a plane we often want to measure quantities other than just length of line segments. For example, we may want to measure the area of a polygon. We all have some idea of what is meant by area. If someone were to ask you to find the area of this page, you could do so with little difficulty. What do we mean by area? How do we measure it?

To answer these questions, imagine that we have a room that measures 9 m by 6 m, as shown in Fig. 12.6.

We wish to cover the floor with square tiles that measure 1 m by 1 m. It seems reasonable to say that each tile has unit area. If you are measuring length in meters, then the unit used for measuring area is square meters. Thus each of these tiles has area equal to 1 sq m.

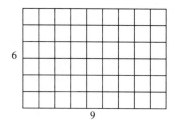

Figure 12.6

How many of the tiles will we need to cover the floor, assuming that no tiles will overlap? To answer this, we place 9 of these along the longer side of the floor and 6 along the shorter side of the floor, as shown. We continue to place tiles next to each other until the entire floor is covered. We see that it takes 54 tiles to completely cover the floor. Since one tile has an area of 1 sq m, it makes sense to say that the entire floor will have an area of 54 sq m. We note that $9 \times 6 = 54$, so we know that the area of the floor is its length times its width.

If we wanted to measure the area of any other rectangle (for example, a polygon with four sides and four right angles), then we could follow the same procedure. In each case it would lead us to the conclusion that the area is length times width. Thus for rectangles we agree that

$$\text{Area of rectangle} = \text{length} \times \text{width}$$

In symbols we have

$$A = l \cdot w$$

In our previous example we did not actually have to place tiles on the floor to determine its area. We could simply have multiplied the length by the width, getting 9×6, or 54, square meters.

Area of Right Triangle

How do we measure the area of a right triangle such as the one shown in Fig. 12.7? In this case we cannot place square tiles over the triangle and expect to cover it exactly. The unit squares will cover either too much or too little. Instead, we can use the following procedure. Take tracing paper, copy the triangle, and then cut it out. Place the cutout triangle (the dotted

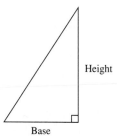

Height

Figure 12.7   Base

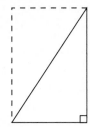

Figure 12.8

one) alongside the original triangle as shown in Fig. 12.8. We see that the two triangles together make a rectangle whose area we already know how to calculate by using the formula Area = length × width. Since our rectangle is two triangles, we see that the area of the original triangle is half the area of the rectangle. Thus

$$\text{Area of triangle} = \frac{1}{2} \text{ length} \times \text{width of rectangle}$$

Note that the length of the rectangle equals the base of the triangle and that the width of the rectangle equals the height of the triangle. Therefore the area of the triangle can be written as

$$\text{Area of triangle} = \frac{1}{2} \text{ base} \times \text{height}$$

In symbols,

$$A = \frac{1}{2} b \cdot h$$

Area of Any Triangle

Now suppose that we are given any triangle (not necessarily a right triangle) and we wish to measure its area. From one of the vertices we can draw a perpendicular to the opposite side, as shown in Fig. 12.9.

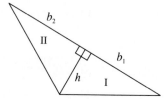

Figure 12.9

The resulting figure will consist of two right triangles whose area we already know how to calculate. In this case the area of triangle I is $\frac{1}{2}b_1 h$, and the area of triangle II is $\frac{1}{2}b_2 h$. Thus the total area is

$$\frac{1}{2} b_1 h + \frac{1}{2} b_2 h$$

$$= \frac{1}{2}(b_1 + b_2)h \qquad \text{(by the distributive property)}$$

$$= \frac{1}{2} \text{ (entire base) (height)}$$

$$= \frac{1}{2} b \cdot h$$

Therefore the area of *any* triangle is given by $A = \frac{1}{2}bh$, where h is the perpendicular drawn from a vertex to the opposite side, b (see Fig. 12.10).

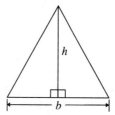

Figure 12.10

Area of Parallelogram

We can find the area of a parallelogram by drawing a diagonal so as to form two triangles which have the same height, as shown in Fig. 12.11.

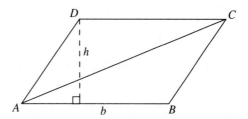

Figure 12.11

We observe that in $\triangle ABC$ the base is b, and the height (the distance between lines $\overline{AB}$ and $\overline{DC}$) is h. Thus the area of $\triangle ABC$ is $\frac{1}{2}bh$. Similarly, in $\triangle ACD$ if we use $\overline{DC}$ as a base, then $DC = AB = b$, as the opposite sides of any parallelogram have the same length. Also h is the corresponding height of this triangle. (Why?) Thus the area of $\triangle ACD$ is also $\frac{1}{2}bh$, so that

$$\text{Area of parallelogram } ABCD = \text{Area of } \triangle ABC + \text{Area of } \triangle ACD$$

$$= \frac{1}{2}bh + \frac{1}{2}bh$$

$$= bh$$

Summarizing   The area A of a parallelogram whose base is b and whose height is h is $A = bh$.

The area of a triangle can be used to find the area of a trapezoid as follows: Suppose we are given any trapezoid $ABCD$ whose bases have lengths a and b and whose height is h. (see Fig. 12.12.) The parallel sides are AB and CD. If we draw diagonal AC, the trapezoid is divided into two

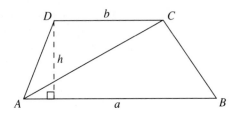

Figure 12.12

triangles. The area of $\triangle ABC$ is $\frac{1}{2}ah$ since its base has length a and its height has length h. Similarly, the area of $\triangle ACD$ is $\frac{1}{2}bh$ since its base has length b and its height has length h. Thus the area of the trapezoid $ABCD$ is the sum of the areas of both triangles, or

$$\text{Area of trapezoid } ABCD = \text{Area of } \triangle ABC + \text{Area of } \triangle ACD$$

$$= \tfrac{1}{2}ah + \tfrac{1}{2}bh$$

$$= \tfrac{1}{2}h(a + b)$$

Summarizing   The area A of any trapezoid whose parallel sides have lengths a and b and height h is $A = \frac{1}{2}h(a + b)$.

Area of Regular Polygons

Just as the area of a triangle can be used to find the area of a parallelogram and a trapezoid, it can also be used to find the area of any polygon. For example, to find the area of any regular hexagon, we can subdivide the hexagon into six congruent triangles, each of which has a vertex at the center of the hexagon, whose side is s, and whose height is a. (see Fig. 12.13.) (The height of such a triangle is called its **apothem**.) Since the area of each of the six triangles is $\frac{1}{2}as$, the area of the hexagon which consists of six such triangles is $6(\frac{1}{2}as)$. This formula can be written as $\frac{1}{2}a(6s)$. Observe that $6s$ represents the perimeter of the polygon. Thus the area A of any regular hexagon equals one-half the product of the apothem and the perimeter of the hexagon, or $A = \frac{1}{2}ap$ where a is the length of its apothem and p is its perimeter. The same procedure can be used to find the area of any polygon.

apothem

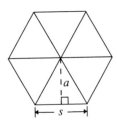

Figure 12.13

Area of a Circle

What about the area of a circle? If we inscribe a regular polygon of n sides inside a circle whose radius has length r (see Fig. 12.14), then the area of the n-gon can be used to approximate the area of the circle. As the number of sides of the polygon gets larger and larger, then the area of the polygon approaches the area of the circle. Also, the perimeter of the polygon will approach the circumference of the circle. Since the area of the polygon equals $\frac{1}{2}ap$, this will approximate $\frac{1}{2}r \cdot 2\pi r = \pi r^2$. This is actually the formula for the area of a circle.

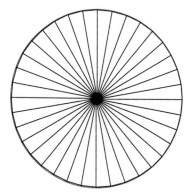

Figure 12.14

Summarizing   The area A of a circle whose radius is of length r is πr^2.

Early in their experiences with mathematical theorems and facts, students are asked to "justify" the reasonableness of the formula for the area of a circle. This can be seen in the accompanying student page from *Addison-Wesley Mathematics*, 1987, Grade 8, p. 308.

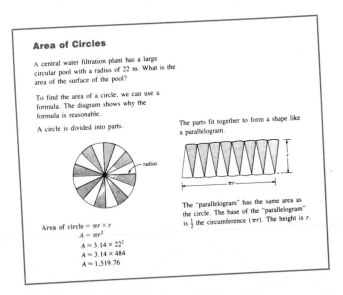

EXERCISES FOR SECTION 12.2

Find the perimeter of each of the geometric figures given in Exercises 1–5.

1.

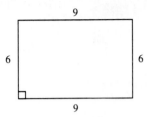

2.

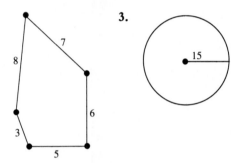

3.

4.

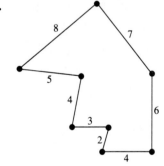

5.

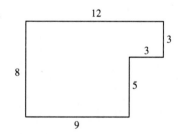

6.

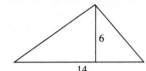

7.

8.

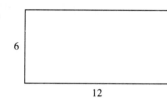

9.

10.

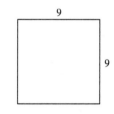

11.

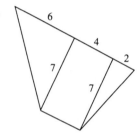

12.

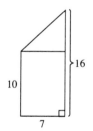

13.

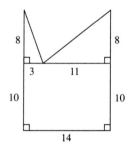

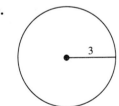

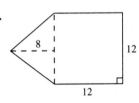

In Exercises 6–13, find the area of each of the indicated geometric figures.

14. Two rooms have area equal to 600 square feet. One room measures 20 ft in width, and the other measures 40 ft in length. Which room is wider and why?

In each of Exercises 15–25, find the area of the shaded portions.

15.

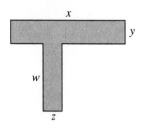

16.

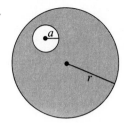

17.

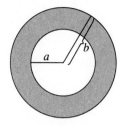

18.

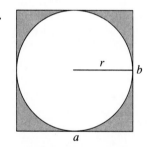

19.

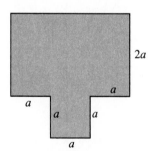

20.

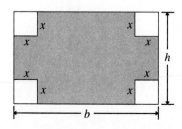

21.

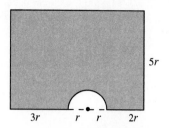

22.

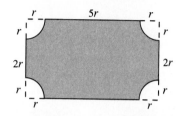

23.

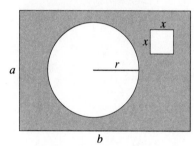

24.

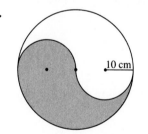

25.

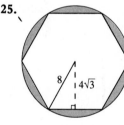

26. To find the area of a **sector** of a circle (a pie-shaped region of the circle determined by the central angle), we must keep it in mind that this area depends on the radius of the circle and the number of degrees in the measure of its central angle. For example, we know that the area of an entire circle whose radius measures 10 cm is 100π cm². Let's say we wish to find the area of a sector in this circle whose central angle measures $90°$. Since there are $360°$ in an entire circle, a sector of $90°$ represents $\frac{90}{360}$ or $\frac{1}{4}$ of the entire circle. Thus the area of such a sector must be $\frac{1}{4}$ of the area of the entire circle, that is, the area is $\frac{1}{4}$ (100π) or 25π. More generally a sector whose central angle has measure θ degrees has area $\frac{\theta}{360}(\pi r^2)$. Use this formula to find the area of the shaded portion in the following geometric figure.

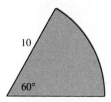

27. Find the area of the shaded portion in the following figure.

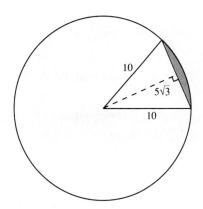

Area in Coordinate Geometry

We can use the area formulas developed until now to find the areas of polygons in coordinate geometry. For example, to find the area of a triangle whose vertices are $A(1, 3)$, $B(6, 3)$, and $C(4, 7)$ (see Fig. 12.15), we can reason as follows: Since one side of the triangle is parallel to the x-axis, we can use this side as the base where AB has a measure of 5. Now draw altitude CD. The measure of its length is 4, so for $\triangle ABC$ in Fig. 12.15.

$$\text{Area} = \tfrac{1}{2}(\text{base})(\text{height})$$
$$= \tfrac{1}{2}(5)(4) = 10$$

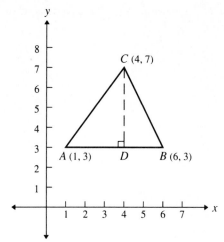

Figure 12.15

If no sides are parallel to either axis, we can complete a rectangle by drawing a series of lines parallel to each of the axes and then subtracting the areas of the regions that we are not interested in. For example, to find the area of the triangle whose vertices are at $A(1, 2)$, $B(-3, -1)$, and

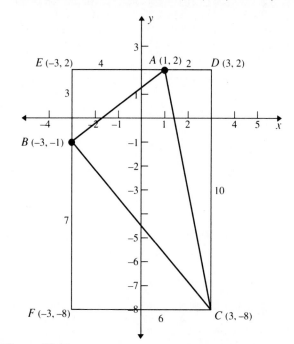

Figure 12.16

C (3, − 8), (see Fig. 12.16), we proceed as follows. Draw lines $\overleftrightarrow{FE}$ and $\overleftrightarrow{CD}$ parallel to the y-axis. These two lines pass through the points that are most to the left and most to the right of points B and C, respectively. Similarly, draw lines $\overleftrightarrow{ED}$ and $\overleftrightarrow{FC}$ parallel to the x-axis. These lines pass through the uppermost and lowermost points A and C, respectively. The length of the various sides can be found by counting the number of boxes as shown in the diagram. Thus

Area of $\triangle ABC$ = Area of rectangle $FCDE$ − Area of $\triangle CDA$ − Area of $\triangle AEB$ − Area of $\triangle BFC$

$$= 6(10) - \tfrac{1}{2}(2)(10) - \tfrac{1}{2}(4)(3) - \tfrac{1}{2}(7)(6)$$

$$= 23$$

Therefore, in Fig. 12.16 the area of triangle ABC = 23.

Use the ideas outlined above to solve the following problems.

28. Determine the area of $\triangle ABC$ whose vertices are $A(-4, -2)$, $B(2, 6)$, and $C(2, -2)$.

29. Find the area of $\triangle ABC$ whose vertices are $A(-1, 2)$, $B(3, 8)$, and $C(5, -2)$.

30. Triangle ABC has vertices $A(-3, -4)$, $B(-1, 7)$, and $C(3, 5)$. Find the area of $\triangle ABC$.

31. Quadrilateral $ABCD$ has vertices at $A(-4, -2)$, $B(0, 5)$, $C(9, 3)$, and $D(7, -4)$. Find the area of quadrilateral $ABCD$.

32. Quadrilateral $ABCD$ has vertices $A(-1, 0)$, $B(3, 3)$, $C(6, -1)$, and $D(2, -4)$. Find the area of quadrilateral $ABCD$.

33. Find the area of quadrilateral $ABCD$ with vertices $A(-1, 1)$, $B(3, 4)$, $C(8, 5)$, and $D(5, -3)$.

12.3

UNDERSTANDING AND USING THE PYTHAGOREAN RELATIONSHIP

hypotenuse

legs

One of the more important theorems in geometry is the Pythagorean relationship, which connects the lengths of the side of a right triangle (the **hypotenuse**) with the other two sides (called **legs**).

Consider Fig. 12.17. Let us find the areas of the squares on legs a, b, and hypotenuse c. We have

Area of square I + Area of square II = Area of square III
$$a^2 + b^2 = c^2$$

Rule of Pythagoras

This relationship was discovered by the Greek mathematician Pythagoras more than 2000 years ago and is often referred to as the **Rule of Pythagoras**. It states: In any right triangle, the sum of the areas of the squares on the legs is equal to the area of the square on the hypotenuse. The Pythagoreans affirmed geometric results on their observations of special cases. However, this result applies to any right triangle and is known as the **Pythagorean theorem**. We have: *In a right triangle, if the legs have lengths a and b, and if the hypotenuse has length c, then $a^2 + b^2 = c^2$.*

Pythagorean theorem

Today, there are hundreds of known proofs for the Pythagorean theorem, some of which have already been mentioned in earlier chapters.

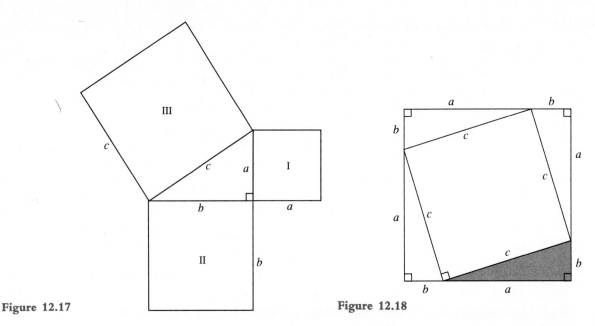

Figure 12.17

Figure 12.18

We can also prove the Pythagorean theorem using four right triangles surrounding a smaller square (see Fig. 12.18). In this diagram we note that the four triangles together with the inner smaller square form a large square. Using the area formulas given in the last section, we find that the area of the larger square is $(a + b)^2$. The area of each of the triangles equals $\frac{1}{2}$(base)·(height) or $\frac{1}{2}ab$, so that the area of all four triangles is $4(\frac{1}{2}ab) = 2ab$. Also the area of the smaller inner square is c^2. Thus

$$\text{Area of larger square} = \text{Area of 4 triangles} + \text{Area of smaller square}$$
$$(a + b)^2 = 2ab + c^2 \qquad \text{Simplifying gives}$$
$$(a + b)(a + b) = 2ab + c^2$$
$$a^2 + 2ab + b^2 = 2ab + c^2 \qquad \text{or that}$$
$$a^2 + b^2 = c^2$$

This proves the Pythagorean theorem.

If we are given any triangle whose sides have lengths a, b, and c satisfying the relationship $a^2 + b^2 = c^2$, must the triangle be a right triangle? The converse of the Pythagorean theorem must also be true, so that if we are given any triangle ABC with sides whose measure is a, b, and c satisfying the relationship $a^2 + b^2 = c^2$, then triangle ABC must be a right triangle with the right angle opposite the side whose length measures c.

EXAMPLE 1

Find the length of the hypotenuse of a right triangle whose legs measure 8 and 15. (Fig. 12.19)

SOLUTION

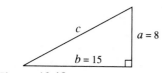

Figure 12.19

Using the Pythagorean theorem,

$$c^2 = a^2 + b^2$$
$$c^2 = 8^2 + 15^2$$
$$c^2 = 64 + 225$$
$$c^2 = 289$$
$$c = 17$$

Thus the length of the hypotenuse measures 17. ■

Pythagorean triple

When three integers are so related that the sum of the squares of two of them equals the square of the third, then the set of three integers is called a **Pythagorean triple**. For example, the integers 3, 4, and 5 form a Pythagorean triple because the integers 3, 4, and 5 satisfy the relationship $3^2 + 4^2 = 5^2$. Another example of a Pythagorean triple that occurs frequently is 5, 12, and 13, as is 8, 15, and 17.

Comment With a knowledge of Pythagorean triples, we can solve some right triangle problems, without writing out a lengthy algebraic solution.

EXAMPLE 2

In a certain triangle, the lengths of the sides measure 7, 8, and 10. Is this a right triangle?

SOLUTION

Let $c = 10$ be the longest side with $a = 7$ and $b = 8$. Then we must determine whether $c^2 = a^2 + b^2$. We have

$$10^2 = 7^2 + 8^2$$

Since $100 \neq 49 + 64$, or 113, this triangle *cannot* be a right triangle. ■

Problem-Solving Example

EXAMPLE 3

The length of a rectangle is 7 units more than its width. A diagonal of the rectangle measures 13 units. Find the length and width of the rectangle.

SOLUTION

Understanding the Problem
We are given a relationship between the length and width of a rectangle as well as the measure of its diagonal. We wish to find its dimensions.

A Plan to Solve the Problem
When we draw a diagonal in a rectangle, then two triangles are formed with the diagonal as the hypotenuse of each triangle. Thus we can use the Pythagorean theorem. We let $x =$ the width of the rectangle and $x + 7 =$ the height of the rectangle.

By the Pythagorean theorem

$$a^2 + b^2 = c^2$$
$$(x)^2 + (x + 7)^2 = 13^2$$
$$x^2 + x^2 + 14x + 49 = 169$$
$$2x^2 + 14x - 120 = 0$$

so that $x = 5$ or $x = -12$ (which we reject because it is a negative value). Therefore, the width is 5 units and the length is 12 units.

Checking Our Solution
We can easily check our solution since $5^2 + 12^2 = 13^2$, or $25 + 144 = 169$.

EXAMPLE 4

A guy wire is stretched 40 meters from the top of a radio antenna pole 30 meters high to a point on the ground. How far is the base of the pole from the point?

SOLUTION

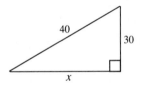

Let x be the distance from the point on the ground to the base of the pole. We assume that the pole is standing perpendicular to the ground. Thus we can apply the Pythagorean theorem with the guy wire as the hypotenuse. We have

$$(\text{guy wire})^2 = (\text{height of pole})^2 + (x)^2$$
$$40^2 = 30^2 + x^2$$
$$1600 = 900 + x^2$$
$$700 = x^2 \qquad \text{so that}$$
$$\sqrt{700} = x$$

Thus the base of the pole is $\sqrt{700}$ or approximately 26.46 meters from the point.

EXERCISES FOR SECTION 12.3

1. Using the Pythagorean theorem, solve for x.

a)

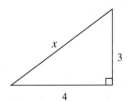

b)

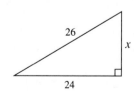

c)

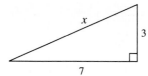

d)

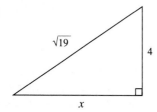

e)

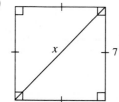

f)

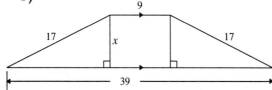

2. The lengths of three sides of a triangle are given. Is this triangle a right triangle or not?

   a) 8, 9, and 11

   b) 10, 15, and 20

   c) 15, 36, and 39

PROBLEM-SOLVING EXERCISES

3. The screen of a computer monitor is a square that is 25 cm on each side. What is the length of the diagonal of the screen?

4. Jodi rented a motorboat and traveled 55 km east from the rental dock, after which she traveled north. How far, along a straight line, did she travel north if she is now 75 km from the renting dock?

5. Boris has a skateboard that is 69 cm long and 7 cm wide. He wishes to place it in a rectangular box that is 62 cm long and 44 cm wide. Will the skateboard fit in the box?

Brain-Teaser Problems

**6. Find x in the following diagram.

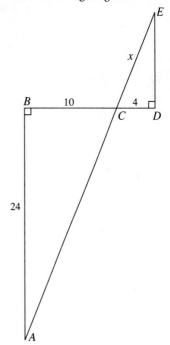

**7. One way of generating Pythagorean triples is to select any odd whole number x larger than 1. Then x, $\dfrac{x^2 - 1}{2}$ and $\dfrac{x^2 + 1}{2}$ will be a Pythagorean triple. Verify this. $\left[\textit{Hint:} \text{ Show that } x^2 + \left(\dfrac{x^2 - 1}{2} \right)^2 = \left(\dfrac{x^2 + 1}{2} \right)^2 \right]$

**8. If we select any two whole numbers a and b, where $a > b$, then $a^2 - b^2$, $2ab$ and $a^2 + b^2$ will form a Pythagorean triple. Verify this. [*Hint:* Show that $(a^2 - b^2)^2 + (2ab)^2 = (a^2 + b^2)^2$]

12.4

SURFACE AREA OF THREE-DIMENSIONAL FIGURES

surface area

The **surface area** of a three-dimensional figure is the total area of its external surfaces, that is, the surface area of a polyhedron is the sum of the areas of the faces of the polyhedron. When dealing with three-dimensional figures having bases, we have one of two possibilities.

lateral area

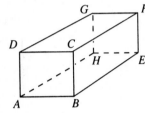

Figure 12.20

> **Definition 12.1** The **lateral area** of a three-dimensional figure having bases is the sum of the area of its lateral faces, that is, the lateral area is the total surface area minus the area of its bases.

> **Definition 12.2** The **(total) surface area** is the sum of the lateral area and the area of its bases.

For the right rectangular prism shown in Fig. 12.20, we have:

a) The lateral area is the sum of the areas of the four rectangular faces, or

$$\text{lateral area} = \text{area of } ABCD + \text{area of } BEFC + \text{area of } EFGH + \text{area of } HGDA$$

b) The total surface area is the sum of the lateral area and the areas of the two bases, or

$$\text{total surface area} = (\text{area of } ABCD + \text{area of } BEFC + \text{area of } EFGH + \text{area of } HGDA) + (\text{area of } FGDC + \text{area of } ABEH)$$

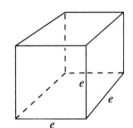

Figure 12.21

EXAMPLE 1

Find the (total) surface area of a cube whose edge measures e units (see Fig. 12.21).

SOLUTION

We are dealing with a cube, each of whose edges (sides) measure e units, so each face is a square with area e^2 units. Since there are six faces, the surface area of the cube is $6e^2$. On the other hand, the lateral area is only $4e^2$. Can you explain why? ▬

EXAMPLE 2

The total surface area of a cube is 216 cm^2. Find the length in the measure of an edge of the cube.

SOLUTION

From the previous example we know that the total surface area of a cube is $6e^2$. Since we are told that the total surface area is 216 cm^2, we have

$$6e^2 = 216$$
$$e^2 = 36$$
$$e = 6$$

Thus each edge of the cube measures 6 cm.

EXAMPLE 3

Find the surface area of the right octagonal prism shown in Fig. 12.22.

SOLUTION

In Fig. 12.23 we show how this prism looks when it is "disassembled." This cut-up version shows the top, the bottom, and the lateral faces. The lateral faces are stretched out flat. This stretched-out portion forms a rectangle whose length is $b_1 + b_2 + b_3 + \cdots + b_8$ and whose altitude is h. We already know that $b_1 + b_2 + \cdots + b_h$ represents the perimeter of the base of the prism, so the lateral area is $(b_1 + b_2 + \cdots + b_8) \cdot h$ or ph where p is the perimeter of the base of the prism. We have

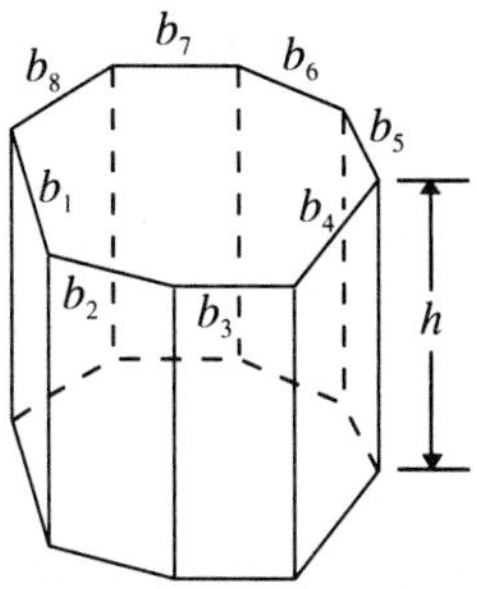

Figure 12.22

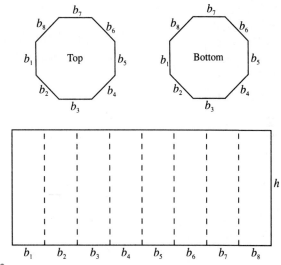

Figure 12.23

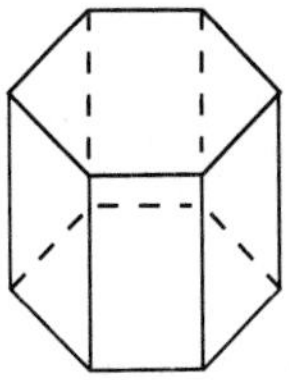

Figure 12.24

Formula 12.1   Lateral Area and Surface Area of a Right Prism   If the area of each of the bases of a right prism is represented by A (where p is the perimeter of each base) and if h is the height of prism (see Fig. 12.24), then lateral area $= ph$ and surface area $= 2A + ph$.

EXAMPLE 4

Find the lateral area and surface area of the following right prisms.

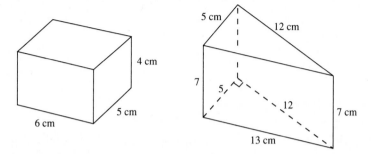

SOLUTION

a) The perimeter of the base is $6 + 5 + 6 + 5 = 22$ and the altitude of the prism is 4. Now we use Formula 12.1, where lateral area $= p \cdot h = 22 \cdot 4 = 88$ and area of base $= 6 \cdot 5 = 30$.
Thus the lateral area of the prism $= 88$ cm^2 and the surface area of the prism $= 2(30) + 88 = 148$ cm^2.

b) Each base is a right triangle whose perimeter is $5 + 12 + 13 = 30$ and whose area is $\frac{1}{2}(5) \cdot (12) = 30$. The height is 7. Using Formula 12.1 we have

$$\text{lateral area} = p \cdot h = 30(7) = 210 \text{ sq cm}$$
$$\text{surface area} = 2A + ph = 2(30) + 210 = 270 \text{ sq cm}$$

We can obtain a formula for the surface area of a cylinder by "disassembling" the cylinder. If we cut open a cylinder (see Fig. 12.25), a

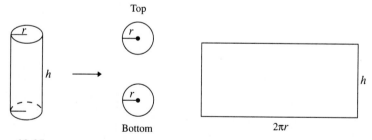

Figure 12.25

procedure similar to what we did earlier with the right prism, we obtain a rectangle plus two circular bases. The area of each circular base is πr^2, so the area of the two circular bases is $2\pi r^2$. The length of the rectangle is $2\pi r$ (as it is the circumference of the circle) and its height is h. Thus the area of the rectangle is $2\pi rh$. Therefore, the surface area of a right circular cylinder represents the sum of these two areas. We have

Figure 12.26

Formula 12.2 **Lateral Area and Surface Area of a Right Circular Cylinder** The lateral area of a right circular cylinder is equal to the product of the circumference of its base and the measure of its altitude.

The surface area S of a right circular cylinder whose base has radius r and whose height is h (see Fig. 12.26) is $S = 2\pi r^2 + 2\pi rh$.

EXAMPLE 5

Find the lateral area and surface area of a right circular cylinder the radius of whose base measures 8 cm and whose altitude measures 12 cm.

SOLUTION

Using Formula 12.2 with $r = 8$ and $h = 12$, we have

$$\text{lateral area of the cylinder} = 2\pi rh = 2\pi(8)(12) = 192\pi \text{ cm}^2$$
$$\text{surface area of the cylinder} = 2\pi r^2 + 2\pi rh$$
$$= 2\pi(8^2) + 2\pi(8)(12)$$
$$= 128\pi + 192\pi = 320\pi \text{ cm}^2$$

Comment "Disassembling" a three-dimensional figure so as to understand how we can find its surface area is a technique that students are exposed to when the topic of space figures is discussed. This can be seen in the accompanying student page from *Addison-Wesley Mathematics*, 1987, Grade 8, p. 312.

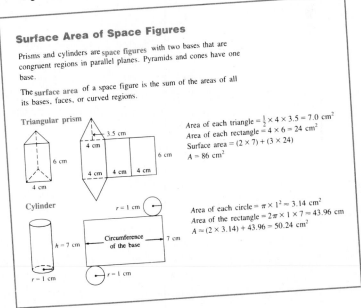

slant height

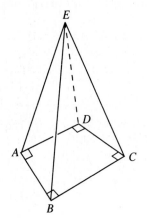

Figure 12.27

In any right regular pyramid, the height L of each triangular face is called its **slant height**. Thus the lateral area of a regular pyramid whose base has perimeter p and whose slant height has a measure of L is $\frac{1}{2}pL$. This follows from the fact that the measure of the slant height of each face is L and the measure of each base is $\frac{p}{n}$ where n is the number of sides in the base.

The sum of the area of the base and the lateral area gives us the surface area.

For the regular right square pyramid shown in Fig. 12.27, we have

$$\text{lateral area} = \text{area of } \triangle ABE + \text{area of } \triangle BCE + \text{Area of } \triangle CDE$$
$$+ \text{ area of } \triangle DAE$$

and

$$\text{surface area} = \text{lateral area} + \text{area of base (which is a square)}$$
$$= \text{area of } \triangle ABE + \text{area of } \triangle BCE + \text{area of } \triangle CDE$$
$$+ \text{ area of } \triangle DAE \; + \text{area of square } ABCD$$

Our previous discussion can be generalized as follows:

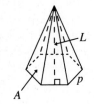

Figure 12.28

> **Formula 12.3** **Lateral and Surface Area of a Right Regular Pyramid** The lateral area of a right regular pyramid whose base has perimeter p and whose slant height is L (see Fig. 12.28) is $\frac{1}{2}p \cdot L$.
> The surface area S of a right regular pyramid with base area A, perimeter p, and slant height L (see Fig. 12.28) is $A + \frac{1}{2}p \cdot L$.

To derive a formula for the surface area of a right circular cone, we start off with a right pyramid and increase its number of sides as shown in Fig. 12.29. We already know that the surface area of each right pyramid is $\frac{1}{2}pL + A$ where p is the perimeter of the base, L is the slant height, and A is the area of the base. For the right circular cone shown in Fig. 12.30, where h is the height of the cone and r is the radius of the base, the slant height L is, using the Pythagorean theorem, $L = \sqrt{h^2 + r^2}$.

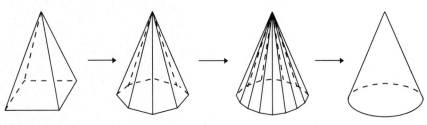

Figure 12.29

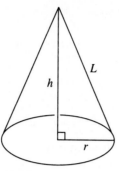
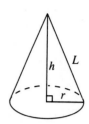

Figure 12.30   Figure 12.31

As we increase the number of sides in the bases of the pyramid, the perimeter of the bases will approach the circumference of the base of the cone. Thus we get

---

Formula 12.4   Lateral Area and Surface Area of a Right Circular Cone   The lateral area of a right circular cone whose base has radius r and whose height is h (see Fig. 12.31) is $\pi r \sqrt{h^2 + r^2}$ or $\pi r L$.

The surface area of a right circular cone whose base has radius r and whose height is h (see Figure 12.31) is $\pi r^2 + \pi r \sqrt{h^2 + r^2}$ or $\pi r^2 + \pi r L$, where L is the slant height.

EXAMPLE 6

Find the lateral area and surface area of a regular triangular pyramid, if each edge of a base measures 8 cm and each lateral edge of the pyramid measures 5 cm. (see Fig. 12.32.)

SOLUTION

We must find the slant height. We are told that the pyramid is a regular pyramid, so $\triangle ACD$ is an isosceles triangle where CE is the perpendicular bisector of DA. Thus $EA = 4$. Using the Pythagorean theorem, in right triangle ACE we have

$$(CE)^2 + (EA)^2 = (CA)^2$$
$$L^2 + 4^2 = 5^2$$
$$L^2 + 16 = 25$$
$$L^2 = 9$$
$$L = 3$$

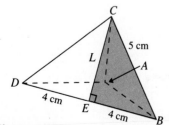

Figure 12.32

Now we apply Formula 12.3 where the perimeter of the base is 24 and

$L = 3$. We have

$$\text{lateral area of pyramid} = \frac{1}{2}pL$$

$$= \frac{1}{2}(24)(3) = 36 \text{ cm}^2$$

To find the area of the base triangle ABD, we realize that this triangle is equilateral. From our earlier work, the area of an equilateral triangle whose side has a measure of x is $\frac{x^2}{4}\sqrt{3}$, so that in our case

$$\text{area of base triangle} = \frac{8^2}{4}\sqrt{3} = 16\sqrt{3} \text{ cm}^2$$

Thus, surface area of pyramid = lateral area + area of base = $(36 + 16\sqrt{3}) \text{ cm}^2$

EXAMPLE 7

SOLUTION

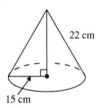

22 cm

15 cm

great circle

Find the lateral area and surface area of a right circular cone in which the radius of the base measures 15 cm and the slant height measures 22 cm.

We apply Formula 12.4 with $r = 15$ and $L = 22$. We have

$$\text{lateral area} = \pi r L$$
$$= \pi(15)(22) = 330\pi \text{ cm}^2$$
$$\text{surface area} = \pi r^2 + \pi r L$$
$$= \pi(15)^2 + \pi(15)(22) = 555\pi \text{ cm}^2$$

It can be shown that the surface area of a sphere is four times the area of its great circle. A **great circle** of a sphere is a circle whose radius is equal to the radius of the sphere (see Fig. 12.33). Thus we have

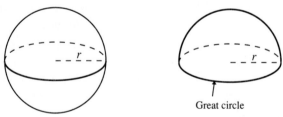

Great circle

Figure 12.33

Surface Area of a Sphere

Formula 12.5   Surface Area of a Sphere   The surface area S of a sphere of radius r is $S = 4\pi r^2$.

EXAMPLE 8

The surface area of a sphere is 400π in². Find the measure of the radius of the sphere.

SOLUTION

We use Formula 12.5. Since we are told that the area of the sphere is 400π in², we have

$$\text{surface area of sphere} = 4\pi r^2 = 400\pi$$
$$r^2 = 100$$
$$r = 10$$

Thus, the measure of the radius of this sphere is 10 in. ■

EXERCISES FOR SECTION 12.4

1. Find the lateral area and surface area of a cube whose edge measures 9 cm.

2. Find the lateral area and surface area of a right hexagonal prism if the base of the prism is a regular hexagon whose side measures 9 cm and whose altitude measures 12 cm.

3. Find the lateral area and surface area of a regular triangular pyramid if each edge of the base measures 12 cm and each lateral edge of the pyramid measures 16 cm.

4. Find the lateral area and surface area of a regular square pyramid if each side of the base measures 10 cm and the altitude of the pyramid measures 14 cm.

5. Find the lateral area and surface area of a right circular cylinder if the radius of the base of the cylinder measures 12 in. and the altitude of the cylinder measures 8 in.

6. The lateral area of a right circular cylinder is 64π sq ft and the altitude of the cylinder measures 4 ft. Find the surface area of the cylinder.

7. The lateral area of a right circular cone is 100π sq in. and the radius of its base measures 4 in. Find the measure of the slant height and the altitude of the cone.

8. A sphere has an area of 144π sq ft. Find the measure of the diameter of the sphere.

9. Find the surface area of each of the following:

a)

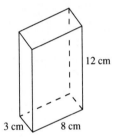

b)

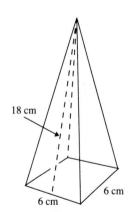

c)

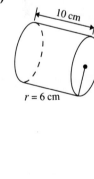

10. Two cubes have sides of length 10 cm and 12 cm respectively. What is the ratio between the surface areas?

11. If the length of each edge of a cube is tripled, what happens to its surface area?

12. If the slant height and the radius of the base of a right circular cone are each tripled, what happens to its lateral area?

PROBLEM-SOLVING EXERCISES

13. A fish aquarium (without a top) is in the form of a rectangular solid whose height, width, and length measure respectively 20 in., 18 in., and 24 in. Find the number of square inches of plate glass needed to make this tank.

14. How many square feet of wallpaper are needed to paper the four walls of a classroom that is 24 feet long, 18 feet wide, and 9 feet high? (Assume no windows, doors, or chalkboard.)

15. A large canvas tent in an amusement park is shaped in the form of a right circular cone. If the radius of the base of the tent is 50 feet and the altitude is 30 feet, how many square feet of canvas material are needed to construct this tent?

16. Estimate the number of gallons of paint that are needed to paint the walls of a room that is 10 feet wide, 22 feet long, and 8 feet high. (Assume that there are no windows or doors and that each gallon of paint will cover 400 sq. ft. of area.)

**17. A can manufacturer makes two kinds of closed cylindrical cans. One can has a base radius of 5 cm and a height which measures 10 cm. The second can has a base radius of 10 cm and a height which measures 5 cm. Which can requires more metal to manufacture? How much more?

**18. The planet Earth is basically a sphere. What is the total surface area of Earth? (*Hint:* The radius of Earth is approximately 6370 km.)

**19. A sphere is inscribed in a cylinder, as shown here. What is the relationship between the lateral area of the cylinder and the surface area of the sphere?

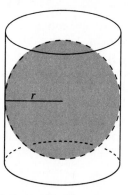

12.5

VOLUME

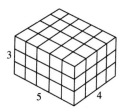

Figure 12.34

In the previous sections, we discussed *area* of three-dimensional or planar figures. In this section, we discuss *volume* of three-dimensional figures. **Volume** is a measure of the amount of space that a figure occupies. To find the volume of the right rectangular prism shown in Fig. 12.34, we must determine the number of cubes needed to build it. If we start with small cubes, each of them one unit in length, then we will need $5 \cdot 4$ or 20 unit cubes for the base. Since there are three such layers, we would need a total of $20 \cdot 3$ or 60 unit cubes. The volume of a cube that is one unit on each edge is **one cubic unit**. Thus the volume of the rectangular prism shown in Fig. 12.34 is 60 cubic units.

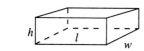

Figure 12.35

cubic foot

cubic centimeter

More generally, we have the following:

> **Formula 12.6   Volume of a Right Rectangular Prism**   The volume V of a right rectangular prism whose dimensions are l, w, and h (see Fig. 12.35), is $V = l \cdot w \cdot h$.

Comment   In using Formula 12.6, it is assumed that l, w, and h are measured in the same linear units. In the British system, the standard unit of volume is the **cubic foot**, where l, w, and h are each measured in feet.

In the metric system, if the length, width, and height of a right rectangular prism each measure 1 centimeter, then the volume is $1 \times 1 \times 1$ or 1 **cubic centimeter**. This is often denoted as 1 cm^3. Similarly, if the length, width, and height each measure 1 meter, then the volume is 1 **cubic meter**, denoted as 1 m^3.

Comment   In the metric system, each unit of length is 10 times as large as the next smaller unit. Hence, each metric unit of area is 100 times as great as the next smaller unit and each metric unit of volume is 1000 times as great as the next smaller unit. Thus, in the previous example, if we had used smaller cubes whose sides are only $\frac{1}{10}$ of a unit on each side, then we would need $10 \times 10 \times 10$ or 1000 of these tiny cubes to fill a unit cube.

It should be obvious from Formula 12.6 that if we are working with a cube where all the edges (sides) have the same measure, then the volume is e^3. We have

Figure 12.36

> **Formula 12.7   Volume of a Cube**   The volume V of a cube whose edge length measures e (see Fig. 12.36) is
> $$V = e^3$$

More generally, to find the volume of *any* prism we can reason as follows: Since the volume of a right rectangular prism whose length, width, and height are l, w, and h respectively, is $V = l \cdot w \cdot h$, we note that $l \times w$ is the area of the base of the prism. Therefore, we can write the volume formula as $V = A \cdot h$ where A is the area of the base of the prism. Thus we have

Area of
base is A

Figure 12.37

> **Formula 12.8   Volume of any Prism**   The volume V of any prism whose base has area A and whose height is h (see Fig. 12.37), is $V = A \cdot h$.

Comment When using Formula 12.8, it is assumed that all cross sections parallel to the base are congruent to the base.

We can obtain a formula for the volume of any cylinder in a manner similar to that we used earlier when discussing circles. We increase the number of sides in the bases of right regular prisms until we approximate a cylinder (see Fig. 12.38). Since the volume of each prism is the product of the area of its base and its height, we would expect the same to be true for a cylinder. We have

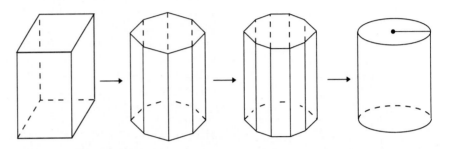

Figure 12.39

> **Formula 12.9** **Volume of a Cylinder** The volume V of a cylinder whose base has area A and whose height is h (see Fig. 12.39), is $V = A \cdot h$

If the base of the cylinder is a circle of radius r, then we have a right circular cylinder. Since the area of a circle is πr^2, we have

Figure 12.40

> **Formula 12.10** **Volume of a Right Circular Cylinder** The volume V of a right circular cylinder whose radius is r and whose height is h (see Fig. 12.40) is $V = \pi r^2 h$.

EXAMPLE 1

Find the volume of each of the following figures:

a)

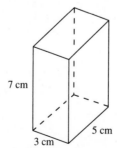

b)

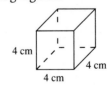

c)

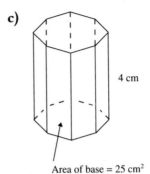

4 cm

Area of base = 25 cm²

d)

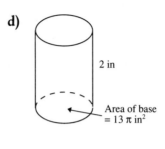

2 in

Area of base
= 13 π in²

e)

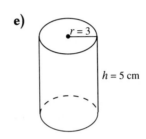

r = 3

h = 5 cm

SOLUTION

a) Here we have a right rectangular prism. Using Formula 12.6 we have $V = l \cdot w \cdot h = 3 \text{ cm} \times 5 \text{ cm} \times 7 \text{ cm} = 105 \text{ cm}^3$.

b) Here we have a cube whose edge measures 4 cm. Using Formula 12.7 we have $V = e^3 = (4 \text{ cm})^3 = 64 \text{ cm}^3$.

c) In this case the area of the base is given to be 25 cm², so that using Formula 12.8 we have $V = A \cdot h = 25 \text{ cm}^2 \times 4 \text{ cm} = 100 \text{ cm}^3$.

d) For this cylinder, the area of the base is 13π in² and the height h is 2 in., so that (using Formula 12.9) the volume is $V = A \cdot h = 13\pi \text{ in}^2 \times 2 \text{ in.} = 26\pi \text{ in}^3$.

e) Here we have a right circular cylinder whose radius measures 3 cm and whose height measures 5 cm. Using Formula 12.10 we have $V = \pi (3 \text{ cm})^2 \times 5 \text{ cm} = 45\pi \text{ cm}^3$. ■

Finding the volume of the right rectangular prism in part (a) of Example 1 suggests a procedure for finding the volume of any pyramid. In Fig. 12.41 we have a right triangular prism. However, suppose that the

Figure 12.41

triangle is an equilateral triangle. We can subdivide the prism into three pyramids whose bases have the same area and whose heights are the same as those of the prism. This is shown in the diagram. However, in this case, the volume of each right triangular pyramid is $\frac{1}{3}$ the volume of the triangular prism. Actually, the results hold for any pyramid with any base. We have

Figure 12.42

> **Formula 12.11 Volume of a Pyramid** The volume V of a pyramid whose base has area A and whose height measures h (see Fig. 12.42), is
>
> $$V = \frac{1}{3}A \cdot h$$

EXAMPLE 2

Find the volume of a regular square pyramid if each edge of the base measures 6 cm and the slant height of the pyramid measures 5 cm (see Fig. 12.43).

SOLUTION

Using the Pythagorean theorem, in right triangle ABC,

$$(BC)^2 + (AB)^2 = (AC)^2$$
$$h^2 + (3)^2 = (5)^2$$
$$h^2 + 9 = 25$$
$$h^2 = 16$$
$$h = 4$$

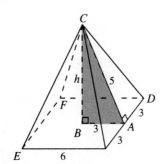

Figure 12.43

Now, area of the base of the pyramid $A = s^2 = (6)^2 = 36$, so that volume of the pyramid $V = \frac{1}{3}A \times h = \frac{1}{3}(36) \cdot (4) = 48$. Therefore, the volume of the pyramid is 48 cm^3. ∎

We can find the volume of a cone by starting off with a pyramid and then increasing the number of sides in the base. (See Fig. 12.44.)

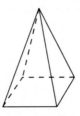
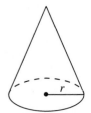

Figure 12.44

We already know that the volume of each pyramid is $\frac{1}{3}$ of the volume of the smallest prism containing it. Thus it seems reasonable that the volume of the cone should be $\frac{1}{3}$ of the volume of the smallest cylinder containing it. Indeed, this is the case. We have

Base area is A

Figure 12.45

Formula 12.12   Volume of a Cone   The volume V of a cone whose base has area A and whose height measures h (see Fig. 12.45), is

$$V = \frac{1}{3} A \cdot h$$

If the base of the cone is a circle of radius r, then we have a right circular cone. Since the area of a circle is πr^2 we have

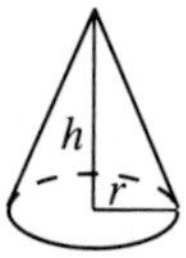

Figure 12.46

Formula 12.13   Volume of a Right Circular Cone   The volume V of a right circular cone whose base radius is r and whose height measures h (see Fig. 12.46), is $V = \frac{1}{3}\pi r^2 h$.

Let us illustrate the use of this formula with an example.

EXAMPLE 3

Find the volume of a right circular cone if the radius of its base measures 5 cm, and its altitude measures 12 cm. (see Fig. 12.47.)

SOLUTION

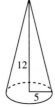

Figure 12.47

Using Formula 12.8 with $r = 5$ and $h = 12$, we have

$$V = \frac{1}{3}\pi r^2 h = \frac{1}{3}\pi(5)^2(12)$$

$$= \frac{1}{3}(25)(12) = 100\pi \text{ cm}^3$$

We can derive formulas for finding the volumes of many other three-dimensional figures from a principle stated by the Italian mathematician Bonaventure Cavalieri. His principle compares solids where cross sections have equal areas. We have

Cavalieri's principle

Cavalieri's Principle   Two three-dimensional solids will have the same volume if they are contained between two parallel planes where every plane parallel to the two given planes cuts cross-sections of the solids with equal areas.

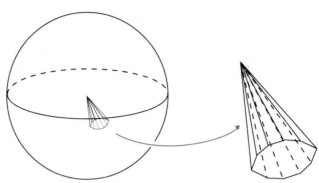

Figure 12.48

Comment Cavalieri's principle explains why two pyramids that have the same altitude and the same base must have the same volume. It also explains why the volume of a prism or a cylinder depends only on the base and height.

To find the volume of a sphere we can consider a sphere which consists of many pyramids with apexes at the center of the sphere. Assume also that the vertices of the sphere touch the sphere as shown in Fig. 12.48. We can select the pyramid in such a way so that the bases are very small. Then the height of each pyramid approximately equals the radius r. Using Formula 12.11 the volume of each pyramid is $\frac{1}{3}A \cdot h$ or $\frac{1}{3}A \cdot r$ where A is the area of the base. Since we have a total of n pyramids each with base area A, then the total volume of the pyramid is $V = \left(\frac{1}{3}A \cdot r\right) n$ or $V = \frac{1}{3}n \cdot A \cdot r$. We already know that $n \cdot A$ represents the total surface area of all the bases of the pyramid. We can then use this as an approximation for the total surface area of a sphere, $4\pi r^2$. We then have

Figure 12.49

Formula 12.14 Volume of a Sphere The volume V of a sphere whose radius has measure r (see Fig. 12.49), is $V = \frac{4}{3}\pi r^3$.

We illustrate the use of this formula with several examples.

EXAMPLE 4

Find, to the nearest cubic centimeter, the volume of a sphere whose radius measures 14 cm. (Use $\frac{22}{7}$ as an approximation for π.)

SOLUTION

We use Formula 12.14 with $r = 14$. We have

$$V = \frac{4}{3}\pi r^3$$

$$= \frac{4}{3}\left(\frac{22}{7}\right) \cdot (14) \cdot (14) \cdot (14) = 11,498.67$$

Thus the volume of the sphere is 11,499 cubic centimeters.

capacity

Although the metric units of volume discussed until now are usually used in very accurate scientific measurements, units of **capacity** are used in everyday measurements to specify the quantity that can be placed in cans or containers. The accompanying student page from *Addison-Wesley Mathematics*, 1987, Grade 7, p. 262, indicates this use of capacity.

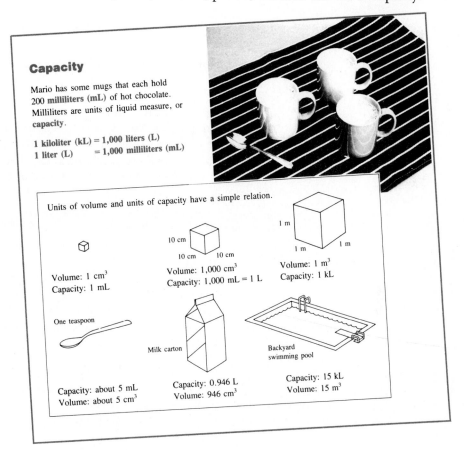

Capacity

Mario has some mugs that each hold 200 **milliliters** (mL) of hot chocolate. Milliliters are units of liquid measure, or **capacity**.

1 kiloliter (kL) = 1,000 liters (L)
1 liter (L)   = 1,000 milliliters (mL)

Units of volume and units of capacity have a simple relation.

Volume: 1 cm³
Capacity: 1 mL

10 cm
10 cm   10 cm
Volume: 1,000 cm³
Capacity: 1,000 mL = 1 L

1 m
1 m   1 m
Volume: 1 m³
Capacity: 1 kL

One teaspoon
Capacity: about 5 mL
Volume: about 5 cm³

Milk carton
Capacity: 0.946 L
Volume: 946 cm³

Backyard swimming pool
Capacity: 15 kL
Volume: 15 m³

Problem-Solving Example

EXAMPLE 5

The ratio of the measures of the radii of two spheres is 3:1. Find the ratio of the volumes of the spheres.

SOLUTION

Understanding the Problem

We are told that the ratio of the radii of two spheres is 3:1. This means that the radius of one sphere is three times as large as the radius of a second sphere. We are asked to find the ratio between the volumes of these spheres.

A Plan To Solve the Problem

Let r equal the radius of the smaller sphere and let $3r$ equal the radius of the larger sphere. By Formula 12.14, the volume of the smaller sphere is $\frac{4}{3}\pi r^3$ and the volume of the larger sphere is $\frac{4}{3}\pi(3r)^3$. The ratio of the volumes of these spheres is

$$\frac{\text{volume of smaller sphere} = \frac{4}{3}\pi r^3}{\text{volume of larger sphere} = \frac{4}{3}\pi(3r)^3}$$

This simplifies to $\frac{1}{27}$, so that the ratio between the volumes of these spheres is 1:27.

Checking Our Solution

We can easily check our solution by substituting specific values. Thus, the volume of a sphere whose radius measures 2 cm is $\frac{4}{3}\pi(2)^3$ or $\frac{32}{3}\pi$ cm^3. The radius of a sphere whose radius measures 3 times 2 or 6 cm is $\frac{4}{3}\pi(6)^3$, or $\frac{864}{3}\pi$ cm^3. Thus the ratio between the volumes is 1:27.   ▬

EXERCISES FOR SECTION 12.5

1. Find the volume of a right rectangular prism whose base area is 30 cm^2 and whose height measures 9 cm.

2. Find the volume of a right rectangular prism whose dimensions are: length = 5 m, width = 4 m, and height = 7 m.

3. The base of a right prism is a right triangle in which the legs measure 4 and 5 dm respectively. The height of the prism measures 6 dm. Find the volume of the prism.

4. The base of a right triangular prism is an equilateral triangle whose side measures 8 cm. The height of the prism measures 16 cm. Find the volume of the prism.

5. Find the volume of a pyramid whose base area is 40 sq. cm, and whose height measures 9 cm.

6. The base of a pyramid is a right triangle whose legs measure 10 cm, and 24 cm. The height of the pyramid measures 11 cm. Find the volume of the pyramid.

7. Each edge of the base of a regular square pyramid measures 16 cm and the height of the pyramid measures 30 cm. Find the volume.

8. The volume of a pyramid is 288 cubic cm. The altitude of the pyramid measures 16 cm. Find the area of its base.

9. Find the volume of a right circular cone, if the area of its base is 124 sq in. and its height measures 15 in.

10. The radius of a cylindrical garbage can measures 28 in. Its height measures 42 in. Find the capacity of the can in liters. (Use $\pi = \frac{22}{7}$.)

11. Find the volume of a right circular cone whose slant height measures 26 cm and whose altitude measures 10 cm.

12. Find the volume of a sphere whose radius measures 6 in.

13. A conical coffee filter has a diameter of 18 cm and a height of 14 cm. What is the maximum amount of liquid, in milliliters, that the coffee filter can hold? (Use $\pi = \frac{22}{7}$.)

14. A cylindrical can of paint has a radius which measures 4.6 cm and a height which measures 14 cm.

   a) What is the volume of this can?

b) What is the (lateral) area of the label that will just cover the curved surface of the can?

c) If the paint fills $\frac{2}{3}$ of the paint can, what is the volume of the paint?

15. Find the volume of each of the following:

a)

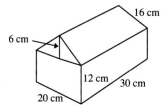

b)

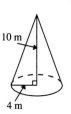

c)

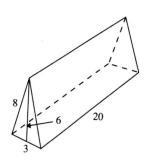

d)

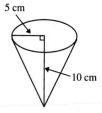

e)

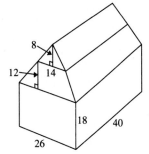

f)

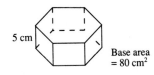

g)   **h)**

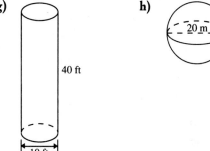

16. A beer mug has a base area of 44 cm². The height of the mug measures 7.5 cm. To what depth should the mug be filled so that it will contain 250 cm³ of beer?

PROBLEM-SOLVING EXERCISES

17. A contractor is building a new walkway in a shopping mall. The walkway is to be 30 feet long and 15 feet wide. If the average depth of the walkway is to be 4 inches, how many cubic feet of cement will be needed for the job?

18. The contractor mentioned in the previous exercise is also excavating for the foundation of a loading platform that will be 81 feet long, 21 feet wide and 6 feet deep. How many cubic yards of earth must be removed?

19. The cylindrical water storage tank of a camp has a diameter of 36 feet and a height of 18 feet. How many gallons of water can be stored in this tank? (*Hint:* One cubic foot contains approximately 7.5 gallons.)

20. A pyramid has a square base 8 cm on each side and a height which measures 10 cm. A cone has a radius which measures 5 cm and a height which measures 10 cm. Which figure has the greater volume?

21. What is the capacity of the following box?

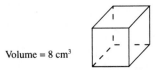

Volume = 8 cm³

22. Two cubes have edges whose lengths measure 5 cm and 10 cm respectively. What is the ratio of their volumes?

23. What volume of cement is needed to make a nuclear containment region in the form of a right circular cylinder whose dimensions are shown below?

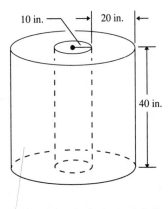

10 in. → | 20 in. |←

40 in.

24. What is the capacity of a spherical balloon whose radius measures 45 cm?

25. The radius of an 88 cm long drainage pipe measures 4 cm. How much water is contained in this pipe when it is fully loaded?

26. An aluminum baking pan measures 12 cm × 12 cm × 4 cm. What is the capacity of the pan (in liters)?

27. A manufacturer is consider packaging canned applesauce in cases containing either No. $2\frac{1}{2}$ cans or No. 2 cans. Each case will hold 24 cans of either size. How much greater is the volume when No. $2\frac{1}{2}$ cans are used? (*Hint:* The height and inside diameter of a No. $2\frac{1}{2}$ can are 11.9 cm and 9.9 cm respectively. Also, the height and inside diameter of a No. 2 can are 11.6 cm and 8.3 cm respectively.)

28. What is the capacity of each of the following:

a)

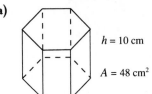

$h = 10$ cm

$A = 48$ cm²

b)

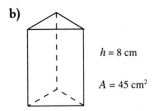

$h = 8$ cm

$A = 45$ cm²

c)

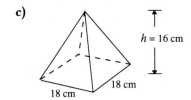

$h = 16$ cm

18 cm

18 cm

29. What is the capacity (in liters) of a swimming pool whose dimensions are: length 120 meters, width 40 meters, and depth 2 meters?

30. What is the capacity (in liters) of the swimming pool shown below?

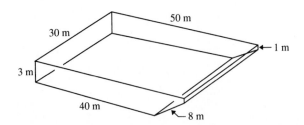

50 m

30 m

3 m

1 m

40 m

8 m

Brain-Teaser Problems

**31. A right circular cylinder is inscribed in a cube whose edge measures 20 meters, as shown below. Find the volume of the cylinder.

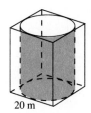

20 m

**32. A sphere is inscribed in a cylinder as shown below. What is the ratio of the volume of the sphere to the volume of the cylinder?

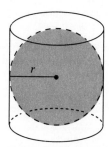

**33. Miguel wishes to pour 1000 ml of a chemical into a special can whose radius measures 7.6 cm and whose height measures 17 cm. To what depth will 1 L of this chemical be poured? Round your answer to the nearest tenth of a centimeter.

**34. The following two cylinders have the same lateral area. Do they also have the same volume?

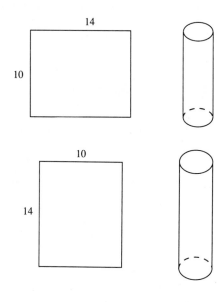

**TYPICAL CLASSROOM
QUESTIONS**

1. A student wonders whether a planar figure has a surface area. How do you respond?
2. What, if any, is the difference between the slant height of a pyramid and the height (altitude) of a pyramid?
3. What are the advantages in using the metric system as opposed to the British system; i.e., is the cost of changing from the British system worth it?
4. A student is holding a can of tuna fish and a can of soda. The dimensions of these cans are:

Tuna fish	Soda
Radius = 3 cm Height = 2 cm	Radius = 2 cm Height = 4.5 cm

The student claims that since both cans have the same volume, then they have the same (total) surface area. Do you agree?

5. A student recalls seeing the following road sign on numerous highways in Canada. Is there anything wrong with the information on this sign?

```
┌─────────────┐
│             │
│    SPEED    │
│    LIMIT    │
│             │
│   100 KM    │
│   60 MPH    │
│             │
└─────────────┘
```

STUDY GUIDE

The following is a chapter outline in capsule form. You should now be able to demonstrate your knowledge of the ideas mentioned by giving definitions or specific examples. Page references are given in parentheses.

The two standard systems of measurement in use today are the **British System** (used in the U.S.) and the **metric system** used throughout most of the civilized world. (p. 692)

The **standard units** in these systems are: for length, yardstick or foot as opposed to the meter; for weight, the pound as opposed to the gram; for volume, the gallon as opposed to the liter. (p. 692)

The following standard prefixes (which are powers of 10) are added to the various metric units to indicate multiples or submultiples of the basic units.

Prefix	Symbol	Meaning
kilo-	k	one thousand times
hecto-	h	one hundred times
deka-	da	ten times
deci-	d	one tenth of
centi-	c	one hundredth of
milli-	m	one thousandth of

Some metric units of length and their abbreviations are:

Metric unit	Commonly used abbreviation	How many meters?
Kilometer	km	1000
Hectometer	hm	100
Dekameter	dam	10
Meter	m	1
Decimeter	dm	1/10 or 0.1
Centimeter	cm	1/100 or 0.01
Millimeter	mm	1/1000 or 0.001

Some metric units of weight and their abbreviations are:

Unit of weight	Commonly used abbreviation	How many grams?
Kilogram	kg	1000
Hectogram	hg	100
Dekagram	dag	10
Gram	gm	1
Decigram	dg	1/10 or 0.1
Centigram	cg	1/100 or 0.01
Milligram	mg	1/1000 or 0.001

Some metric units of volume and their abbreviations are:

Unit of volume	Commonly used abbreviation	How many liters?
Kiloliter	kL	1000
Hectoliter	hL	100
Dekaliter	daL	10
Liter	L	1
Deciliter	dL	1/10 or 0.1
Centiliter	cL	1/100 or 0.01
Milliliter	mL	1/1000 or 0.001

We can measure temperature in the **Fahrenheit scale** where water freezes at 0° and boils at 212°, or in the **Celsius scale** where water freezes at 0° and boils at 100° (p. 698)

If we select any two points A and B on a real number line where A corresponds to a and B corresponds to b, then the **distance** from A to B, denoted as AB, is the real number obtained as the non-negative difference between a and b. (p. 701)

The distance from 0 to 1 on the number line is called the **unit distance**. (p. 701)

Triangular inequality   For any three distinct points A, B, and C, the distance between A and B plus the distance between B and C is greater than or equal to the distance between A and C, that is, $AB + BC \geq AC$. (p. 701)

The sum of the lengths of the sides of a polygon is called the **perimeter** of the polygon. (p. 701)

The perimeter of a circle is called its **circumference**. (p. 702)

A **sector** of a circle is a pie-shaped region of the circle determined by the central angle. (p. 709)

Rule of Pythagoras   In any right triangle, the sum of the areas of the squares on the legs is equal to the area of the square on the hypotenuse. (p. 711)

Pythagorean Theorem   In a right triangle, if the legs have lengths a and b, and if the hypotenuse has length c, then $a^2 + b^2 = c^2$. (p. 711)

When three integers are so related so that the sum of the squares of two of them equals the square of the third, then the set of three integers is called a **Pythagorean triple**. (p. 713) The converse of the Pythagorean theorem is also true.

The **lateral area** of a three-dimensional figure having bases is the sum of the area of its lateral faces, that is, the lateral area is the total surface area minus the area of its bases. (p. 716)

The (total) **surface area** is the sum of the lateral area and the area of its bases. (p. 716)

In any right regular pyramid, the height L of its triangular face is called its **slant height**. (p. 720)

A **great circle** of a sphere is a circle whose radius is equal to the radius of the sphere. (p. 722)

Volume is a measure of the amount of space that a figure occupies. (p. 724)

The volume of a cube that is one unit on each edge is **1 cubic unit.** In the British system, the standard unit of volume is the **cubic foot**. In the metric system, the standard unit of volume is the **cubic centimeter**. (p. 725)

Cavalieri's principle   Two three-dimensional solids will have the same volume if they are contained between two parallel planes where every plane parallel to the two given planes cuts cross-sections of the solids with equal areas. (p. 729)

Units of **capacity** are used in everyday measurements to specify the quantity (volume) that can be placed in cans or containers. (p. 731)

KEY TERMS

The following list presents the key terms introduced in this chapter.

12.1 yard
      metric system
      foot-pound system
      British system
      meter
      gram
      liter
      degrees Celsius
      degrees Fahrenheit

12.2 distance
      unit distance
      triangular inequality
      perimeter
      circumference
      pi (π)

      area
      apothem

12.3 rule of Pythagoras
      Pythagorean theorem
      Pythagorean triples

12.4 surface area
      lateral area
      slant height
      great circle

12.5 volume
      cubic centimeter
      cubic foot
      Cavalieri's principle
      capacity

FORMULAS TO REMEMBER

The following list summarizes all the formulas given in this chapter.
To convert from the metric system to the British system, or vice versa, we can use the following information:

	To convert from	to	multiply by
Length	inches	millimeters	25
	inches	centimeters	2.54
	feet	centimeters	30.48
	feet	meters	0.3
	yards	meters	0.914
	miles	kilometers	1.6
	millimeters	inches	0.04
	centimeters	inches	0.4
	meters	feet	3.28
	meters	yards	1.1
	kilometers	miles	0.62
Weight	ounces	grams	28.3
	pounds	kilograms	0.45
	grams	ounces	0.035
	kilograms	pounds	2.2
Liquid measure	ounces	milliliters	29.76
	pints	liters	0.476
	quarts	liters (liquid)	0.95
	gallons	liters	3.81
	milliliters	ounces	0.034
	liters	pints	2.1
	liters	quarts (liquid)	1.05
	liters	gallons	0.26
Dry measure	liters	dry quarts	0.91
	dry quarts	liters	1.1

To convert from degrees Fahrenheit (F°) to degrees Celsius (C°) use the formula $C = \dfrac{F - 32}{1.8}$. To convert from degrees Celsius (C°) to degrees Fahrenheit (F°), use the formula $F = 1.8C + 32$.

Two-Dimensional Figures: Area

Figure	Formula	Comment
Triangle	$A = \frac{1}{2}bh$	b = base of triangle h = height (altitude) of triangle to that base
Rectangle	$A = lw$	l = length of rectangle w = width of rectangle

Two-Dimensional Figures: Area (cont'd.)

Figure	Formula	Comment
Square	$A = s^2$	s = side of square
Parallelogram	$A = bh$	b = base of parallelogram h = height of parallelogram
Trapezoid	$A = \frac{1}{2}h(a + b)$	a and b are lengths of parallel sides and h is height of trapezoid
Regular polygon	$A = \frac{1}{2}ap$	a = apothem of polygon p = perimeter of polygon
Circle	$A = \pi r^2$	r = radius of circle
Sector of circle	$A = \dfrac{\theta \pi r^2}{360}$	θ is the measure of the central angle forming the sector and r is the radius of the circle containing the sector

When working with three-dimensional figures, the following symbols apply.

A = area of base	L = slant height
e = edge of cube	p = perimeter of base
h = height	r = radius of circular base or of sphere
l = length	w = width

Figure	Lateral area	Surface area	Volume
Right prism	ph	$2A + ph$	Ah
Right rectangular prism	$2lh + 2wh$	$2lh + 2wh + 2lw$	lwh
Cube	$4e^2$	$6e^2$	e^3
Right circular cylinder	$2\pi rh$	$2\pi r^2 + 2\pi rh$	$\pi r^2 h$
Right regular pyramid	$\frac{1}{2}pL$	$A + \frac{1}{2}pL$	$\frac{1}{3}Ah$
Right circular cone	$\pi r\sqrt{h^2 + r^2}$ or πrL	$\pi r^2 + \pi r\sqrt{h^2 + r^2}$ or $\pi r^2 + \pi rL$	$\frac{1}{3}\pi r^2 h$
Sphere		$4\pi r^2$	$\frac{4}{3}\pi r^3$

Units of volume and capacity

Volume	1 cm^3	1000 cm^3	1 m^3
Capacity	1 mL	1000 mL = 1 L	1 kL

CHAPTER REVIEW EXERCISES

1. If the circumference of a circle is doubled, then the diameter of the circle
   a) increases by 2
   b) is doubled

   c) is multiplied by 4

   d) remains the same

   e) none of these.

2. The circumference of a circle is 12π. What is the radius of the circle?

3. The lengths of the two legs of a right triangle are 3 and 5. Find, in radical form, the length of the hypotenuse.

4. Convert 85°F to degrees Celsius.

5. Consider a 2-liter bottle of soda. Does it contain more or less than a 64 ounce bottle of the same soda?

6. A certain liquor sells for $12.95 per quart. Find the cost of one liter.

7. A chemical tank contains 7 kiloliters of a chemical. Find the volume, in cubic meters, of the tank.

8. Convert 185 kg to pounds.

9. A rectangular room measures 18 meters by 96 centimeters. Find the area of the room in square feet.

10. The posted speed limit in a certain village is 30 mph. What is the speed limit in the metric system?

For questions 11–14 refer to trapezoid $ABCD$ shown below, where $\overleftrightarrow{AB} \parallel \overleftrightarrow{DC}$, $\overleftrightarrow{AD} \perp \overleftrightarrow{AB}$, and $\overleftrightarrow{DB} \perp \overleftrightarrow{BC}$, $m(\overline{AB}) = 8$, $m(\overline{AD}) = 8$, and $m(\overline{DC}) = 16$.

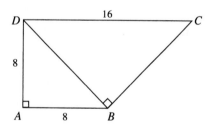

11. Find $m(\overline{DB})$ in radical form.

12. Find the area of $\triangle ABD$.

13. Find the area of trapezoid $ABCD$.

14. Find the area of $\triangle DBC$.

15. Find the total surface area and volume of each figure below:

   a)

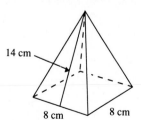

   b)

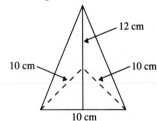

16. The volume of the pyramid shown below is 507 cm³. If the prism and the pyramid have the same base and the same height, what is the volume of the prism?

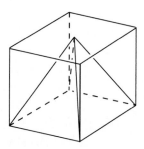

17. A certain can has a diameter of 16 cm and a height of 14 cm. The can is packed inside a cube that measures 16.5 cm on each edge. Find the volume of the part of the cube not filled with the can. (Round your answer to the nearest tenth.)

18. Find the capacity of the following three-dimensional figure.

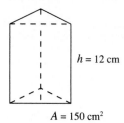

$h = 12$ cm

$A = 150$ cm²

19. Which of the following has the greater volume? How much greater is it?
Pyramid: square base 10 cm on each side, and a height of 16 cm.
Cone: whose base radius is 6 cm, and whose height is 16 cm.

20. What happens to the lateral area of a cone when the measure of the radius and the measure of its slant height are each doubled?

21. The area of a sphere is 196π square feet. Find the measure of the diameter of the sphere.

22. Find the volume of a right prism whose base is a regular hexagon with each side measuring 9 cm and whose altitude measures 7 cm.

23. Find the area of the shaded region in the diagram below.

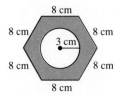

8 cm
8 cm   8 cm
      3 cm
8 cm   8 cm
      8 cm

24. The area of a circle is 80 sq cm. Find the area of a sector whose central angle measure is 45°.

25. The area of the sector of a circle whose central angle measures 40° is 12π. Find the radius of the circle.

26. Find the area of a triangle with vertices at $A(2, 3)$, $B(8, 11)$, and $C(0, 7)$.

27. Find the area of a quadrilateral whose vertices are at $(-2, 3)$, $(3, 7)$, $(8, 6)$, and $(12, 4)$.

28. Find the capacity of a fishtank that measures 12 cm in height, 18 cm in length, and 10 cm in width.

29. Seth pours 100 mL of a liquid into a right cylindrical can whose radius is 2 cm and whose height measures 8 cm. Will all the liquid fit in?

30. Solve for x. (*Hint:* Use the Pythagorean theorem.)

SUGGESTED FURTHER READING

Brougher, J., "Discovery Activities With Area and Perimeter," in *The Arithmetic Teacher* **20** (May 1973), 382–385.

Hart, K., "Which Comes First—Length, Area or Volume?" in *The Arithmetic Teacher* **31** (May 1984), 16–18, 26–27.

Hawking, V., "The Pythagorean Theorem Revisited: Weighing the Results," in *The Arithmetic Teacher* **32** (December 1984), 36–37.

Hirstein, J., C. Lamb, and A. Osborne. "Student Misconceptions About Area Measure," in *The Arithmetic Teacher* **25** (March 1978), 19–26.

Loomis, E., *The Pythagorean Propositions*. Washington, D.C.; National Council of Teachers of Mathematics, 1972.

Tolman, M., "The Steps of Metric Conversion," in *The Arithmetic Teacher* **30** (November 1982), 32–33.

Urion, D., "Using the Cuisenaire Rods to Discover Approximations of Pi," in *The Arithmetic Teacher* **27** (December 1979), 17.

CHAPTER 13

Similar and Congruent Figures: Constructions

CHAPTER OBJECTIVES

☐ **To determine** when polygons and triangles are congruent. We list various congruence properties. (*Section 13.1*)

☐ **To learn** how we prove some congruence theorems. (*Section 13.2*)

☐ **To discuss** similar polygons and similar triangles, and the properties they satisfy. (*Section 13.3*)

☐ **To point out** how we can use a compass and a straightedge to construct many geometric figures. (*Section 13.4*)

☐ **To introduce** a new way of studying geometry by way of translations, rotations, reflections, etc. This is transformation geometry. (*Section 13.5*)

☐ **To indicate** what tesselations of the plane are, and how they can be applied. (*Section 13.6*)

☐ **To examine** how the LOGO computer graphics program can be used to draw similar and congruent triangles. (*Section 13.7*)

In its March 1989 *Curriculum and Evaluation Standards For School Mathematics* (p. 167), The National Council of Teachers of Mathematics recommends that the mathematics curriculum should include the study of geometry of two and three dimensions from an algebraic point of view so that all students can

☐ deduce properties of figures using transformations and coordinates,

☐ identify congruent and similar figures using transformations,

☐ analyze properties of Euclidean transformations.

One of the most important connections in all of mathematics is that between geometry and algebra. Recently, the study of geometry through the use of transformations—the geometric counterpart of functions—has changed the subject from static to dynamic, providing in the process great additional power that can be used, for example, to describe and produce figures on a video screen. Viewed as an algebraic system, transformations also provide college-oriented students with valuable experiences with properties of function composition and group structure.

The interplay between geometry and algebra strengthens students' ability to formulate and analyze problems from situations both within and outside mathematics. Transformations serve as powerful problem-solving tools and permit students to develop a broad concept of congruence and similarity that applies to all figures. The derivation of congruence properties through isometries (distance-preserving transformations) and of similarity properties through composites of dilations (ratio-preserving transformations) and isometries provides a connection with, and a reinforcement of, synthetic methods.

Transformations are also often used to represent physical motions, such as slides, flips, turns, and stretches. It is for this reason that in this chapter we study and analyze transformation geometry.

Introduction

We live in a modern industrialized society. Often it is necessary to make copies of an item so that each copy will have the same size and shape as the original. For example, when the U.S. Mint makes coins, each dime must be exactly the same size and shape as all the other dimes. In industry a machine may stamp out many duplicates of a piece of metal, each copy having the same size and shape as the original. All of these are examples of what the mathematician calls congruent figures.

Of course, it may turn out that one figure is an enlarged version or a reduced version of another figure. In this case we may have similar figures. In this chapter we discuss some of the properties of congruent and similar figures. Straightedge and compass constructions will play a crucial role in our development.

HISTORICAL NOTE

As mentioned earlier, Euclid of Alexandria is often considered to be the "father of geometry." Although many of the Euclidean geometric facts contained in *The Elements* were already known, Euclid's use of definitions, postulates, and axioms with statements to be proved (theorems), was unique.

The ancient Greeks also used straightedge and compass constructions in their studies of geometrical figures. They considered the straight line and the circle as the basic geometrical figures. Over the years, mathematicians have attempted to prove or disprove many geometrical construction problems using only a straightedge and compass. For example, can we trisect an angle with just these tools? In the 19th century, using the results of the works of the French mathematician Évariste Galois, it was finally proved that this construction, along with certain others, cannot be done using a compass and a straightedge.

13.1

CONGRUENT POLYGONS AND CONGRUENT TRIANGLES

How are we to determine whether two polygons have the same size and shape? One way is to place one polygon on top of the other. If the figures coincide exactly, that is, if they can be turned in such a way that the sides of one polygon fit *exactly* upon the sides of the other polygon and also the

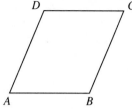
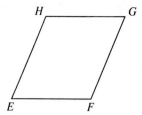

Figure 13.1

congruent polygons

angles of one polygon fit *exactly* upon the angles of the other, then we have **congruent polygons.** If two polygons are congruent, then we symbolize this as polygon $ABCD \cong$ polygon $EFGH$, where $\cong$ stands for "is congruent to." For example, polygon $ABCD$ of Fig. 13.1 is congruent to polygon $EFGH$ if we make

vertex A correspond to vertex E

vertex B correspond to vertex F

vertex C correspond to vertex G

vertex D correspond to vertex H

side $\overline{AB}$ correspond to side $\overline{EF}$

side $\overline{BC}$ correspond to side $\overline{FG}$

side $\overline{CD}$ correspond to side $\overline{GH}$

side $\overline{DA}$ correspond to side $\overline{HE}$

corresponding angles

In the above one-to-one correspondence we refer to the vertices that correspond as **corresponding angles.** Angle E will fit exactly on angle A so that vertex A corresponds to vertex E. Angles A and E are thus corresponding angles and angle $A \cong$ angle E.

corresponding sides

Similarly, since side $\overline{EF}$ will fit exactly on side $\overline{AB}$, that is, $\overline{AB} \cong \overline{EF}$, we call these sides **corresponding sides.** Also side $\overline{BC} \cong \overline{FG}$, so that $\overline{BC}$ and $\overline{FG}$ are corresponding sides; $\overline{CD} \cong \overline{GH}$, so $\overline{CD}$ and $\overline{GH}$ are corresponding sides; and $\overline{DA} \cong \overline{HE}$, so $\overline{DA}$ and $\overline{HE}$ are corresponding sides.

Observe that in the previous example all the pairs of corresponding sides and corresponding angles are congruent. We then have the following.

Definition 13.1 Congruent Polygons Two polygons are **congruent** if there is a one-to-one correspondence between their vertices where (a) all pairs of corresponding sides are congruent and (b) all pairs of corresponding angles are congruent.

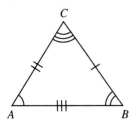 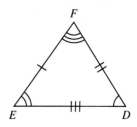

Figure 13.2

corresponding
parts

Comment   The pairs of congruent angles and the pairs of congruent sides are called **corresponding parts**, so that if two polygons are congruent, then their corresponding parts must be congruent.

Now consider the two triangles shown in Fig. 13.2. We have

congruent triangles

> **Definition 13.2   Congruent Triangles**   Suppose that triangle *ABC* and triangle *DEF* are such that under the correspondence, ∠*A* corresponds to ∠*D*, ∠*B* corresponds to ∠*E*, and ∠*C* corresponds to ∠*F*, and where all the corresponding sides and corresponding angles are congruent as shown in Fig. 13.2, then △*ABC* is congruent to △*DEF*, and we write this fact as △*ABC* ≅ △*DEF*.

Using Definition 13.2, for these two triangles to be congruent we would have to establish the following: (No matter how the triangles are positioned.)

Corresponding congruent angles	Corresponding congruent sides
∠*A* ≅ ∠*D*	$\overline{AB} \cong \overline{ED}$
∠*B* ≅ ∠*E*	$\overline{BC} \cong \overline{EF}$
∠*C* ≅ ∠*F*	$\overline{AC} \cong \overline{DF}$

It turns out, however, that it is possible for us to prove that two triangles are congruent by proving that fewer than three pairs of sides and three pairs of angles are congruent. To accomplish this let us do the following. For the triangle *ABC* shown in Fig. 13.3, we note that side *AB* = 4 cm, side *AC* = 3 cm and the included angle *A* has a measure of 60°. (Angle *A* is **included** between side $\overline{AB}$ and side $\overline{AC}$ as the two segments are on the sides of the angle.)

Now copy $\overline{AB}$ onto a working line so that the length of $\overline{DE}$ will be 4 cm (see Fig. 13.4). In Section 13.4 we will indicate how these constructions can be done accurately. Then, using a compass, copy ∠*A* where the vertex will be at point *D*. (We can also use a protractor to draw

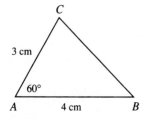

Figure 13.3

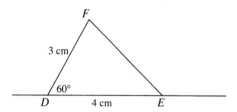

Figure 13.4

an angle of 60° whose vertex is at point D.) Next, copy $\overline{AC}$ onto the side of $\angle D$ which was last drawn—that is, draw a line segment which measures 3 cm and which starts at point D and ends at point F. Finally draw $\overline{FE}$ to complete the triangle.

If we measure sides $\overline{CB}$ and $\overline{FE}$, we find that their measures are equal. Also, if we measure angle C and angle F we find that their measures are equal. The same is true for the measures of angles B and E. Furthermore, if we cut out $\triangle DEF$ and place it on top of $\triangle ABC$, or vice versa, the two triangles will coincide. Thus it would appear that the two triangles are congruent. If the above procedure would be repeated with different sets of measurements for the two sides and the included angle it would appear again that we have congruent triangles. On the basis of these observations we state the following side-angle-side property.

SAS congruence property

> **Property 1   Side-Angle-Side (SAS) Congruence Property**
> If two sides and the included angle of one triangle are congruent respectively to two sides and the included angle of another triangle, then the two triangles are congruent. [SAS ≅ SAS] (Fig. 13.5.)
>
>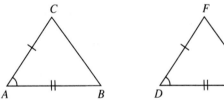
>
> Figure 13.5

Comment   The SAS congruence property tells us that to prove that two triangles are congruent, we need only verify that two sides and the included angle of one triangle are congruent respectively to two sides and the included angle of another triangle.

Problem-Solving Example

EXAMPLE 1

In isosceles triangle ABC, with $\overline{AC} \cong \overline{BC}$ and $\overline{CD}$ the bisector of $\angle C$, prove that the base angles of the triangle are congruent. (Fig. 13.6.)

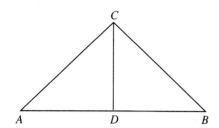

Figure 13.6

SOLUTION

Understanding the Problem
We are told that △ABC is isosceles. This means that two sides are congruent. In our case, $\overline{AC} \cong \overline{BC}$ as specified. We wish to prove that the angles opposite these congruent sides (the base angles) are congruent.

A Plan to Solve the Problem
We will use the fact that $\overline{CD}$ is the bisector of ∠C, together with the fact that $\overline{AC} \cong \overline{BC}$, to show that △ACD and △BCD are congruent. Hence, angles A and B would be corresponding angles of congruent triangles which would then have to be congruent. To accomplish this, we note that since $\overline{CD}$ is the bisector of angle C, then ∠ACD ≅ ∠BCD. Also, we have $\overline{CD} \cong \overline{CD}$ and $\overline{AC} \cong \overline{BC}$, so that by the SAS congruence property △ACD ≅ △BCD. Thus ∠A and ∠B, which represent corresponding angles of these congruent triangles, must be congruent.

Checking Our Solution
We can check our solution by measuring angles A and B. They both should contain the same measure. Also, if we cut out the triangles and place one upon the other, they should coincide.   ▪

We can prove that the converse of this result is also true, namely that "if two angles of a triangle are congruent, then the triangle must be an isosceles triangle." This will be left as an exercise.

Now let us consider the triangle ABC shown in Fig. 13.7. In this diagram, $m(\angle A) = 50$, $m(\angle C) = 70$, and the included side $\overline{AC}$ measures 3 cm.

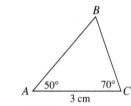

Figure 13.7

Let us copy $\overline{AC}$ onto a working line so that the length of $\overline{DE}$ will be 3 cm (see Fig. 13.8). Using a compass, copy angle A where the vertex will be at point D (again we can also use a protractor to draw an angle at 50° whose vertex is at point D). Similarly, copy angle C where the vertex will be at point E. To complete the triangle, we extend the sides of these angles until they intersect at point F.

If we measure sides $\overline{AB}$ and $\overline{DF}$ we find their lengths are equal. Also if we measure sides $\overline{BC}$ and $\overline{FE}$, again their lengths are equal. Also, $m(\angle B)$ will equal $m(\angle F)$. Moreover, if we cut out △DEF and place it on top of

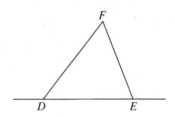

Figure 13.8

$\triangle ABC$, or vice versa, the two triangles will coincide. Thus it would appear that the two triangles are congruent. If the above procedure would be repeated with different sets of measurements for the two angles and the included side, it would again appear that we have congruent triangles. On the basis of these observations, we state the following angle-side-angle property.

ASA congruence property

Property 2 Angle-Side-Angle (ASA) Congruence Property
If two angles and the included side of one triangle are congruent respectively to two angles and the included side of another triangle, then the triangles are congruent. [ASA ≅ ASA] (Fig. 13.9.)

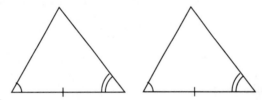

Figure 13.9

EXAMPLE 2

In Fig. 13.10 point C bisects $\overline{BD}$ and $\angle ABC$ and $\angle EDC$ are right angles. Prove that triangle ABC and triangle CDE are congruent.

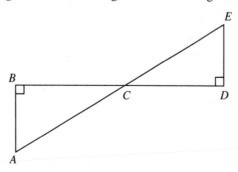

Figure 13.10

SOLUTION

Since point C bisects $\overline{BD}$, we must have that $\overline{BC} \cong \overline{CD}$. Also $\angle ABC$ and $\angle EDC$ are right angles so that $\angle ABC \cong \angle EDC$. (Why?) Finally $\angle ACB$ and $\angle ECD$ are vertical angles which must be congruent. (Why?) Thus $\angle ACB \cong \angle ECD$. Using the ASA congruence property, triangles ABC and CDE must be congruent. ◼

Now let us consider the triangle ABC shown in Fig. 13.11. In this diagram, the three sides $\overline{AB}$, $\overline{BC}$, and $\overline{CA}$ measure 5, 6, and 7 cm respectively. Now copy $\overline{AC}$ onto a working line so that the length of $\overline{DE}$ will be 7 cm (see Fig. 13.12).

Using point D as a center, draw an arc of a circle whose radius is 5 cm in length. Then, using point E as a center, draw an arc of a circle whose radius is 6 cm in length. This arc intersects the first arc at a point F. We now draw sides $\overline{DF}$ and $\overline{FE}$ to complete the triangle. If we measure $\angle A$ and $\angle D$ we will find that their measures are equal. The same will be true for $\angle B$ and $\angle F$, that is $\angle B \cong \angle F$. Also $\angle C \cong \angle E$. Moreover, if we cut out $\triangle DEF$ and place it on top of $\triangle ABC$, or vice versa, the two triangles will coincide. Thus it would appear that the two triangles are congruent.

If the above procedure would be repeated with different sets of measurements for all three sides, it would again appear that we have congruent triangles. On the basis of these observations, we state the following side-side-side property.

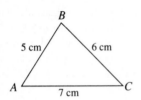

Figure 13.11

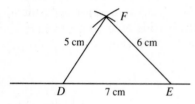

Figure 13.12

SSS congruence property

Property 3   Side-Side-Side (SSS) Congruence Property   If three sides of one triangle are congruent respectively to three sides of another triangle (see Fig. 13.13), then the triangles are congruent. [SSS $\cong$ SSS]

Figure 13.13

EXAMPLE 3

In Fig. 13.14, $\overline{BD}$ is a median that is drawn to the base of isosceles triangle ABC where $\overline{AB} \cong \overline{BC}$. Prove that $\triangle ABD \cong \triangle CBD$.

SOLUTION

We are told that $\overline{BD}$ is a median drawn to the base of isosceles triangle ABC.

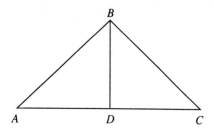

Figure 13.14

Thus $\overline{AD} \cong \overline{DC}$. Also, we are told that $\overline{AB} \cong \overline{BC}$. We know that $\overline{BD} \cong \overline{BD}$, so by the SSS congruence property, $\triangle ABD \cong \triangle CBD$. ■

There is a fourth property which can be used to prove that two triangles are congruent. We have

AAS congruence property

Property 4 **Angle-Angle-Side (AAS) Congruence Property**
If two angles and a side opposite one of these angles in a triangle are congruent to two angles and the corresponding side of another triangle (see Fig. 13.15), then the two triangles are congruent. [AAS ≅ AAS]

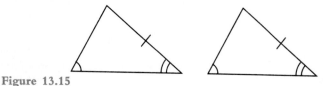

Figure 13.15

We can summarize our discussion to this point in the following:

Methods of Proving Triangle Congruent

1. SAS   Congruence property
2. ASA   Congruence property
3. SSS   Congruence property
4. AAS   Congruence property

Until now, we have not considered whether there are angle-angle-angle (AAA) or side-side-angle (SSA) congruence properties.

Consider Fig. 13.16, in which all pairs of corresponding angles are congruent. The triangles are not congruent because the corresponding sides of triangle ABC are not congruent to the corresponding sides of

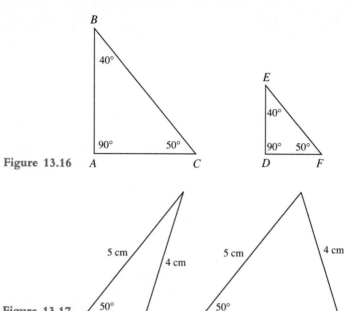

Figure 13.16

Figure 13.17

triangle *DEF*. Thus we *cannot* say that there is an angle-angle-angle (AAA) congruence property. In a later section we will indicate that these triangles are similar.

Consider Fig. 13.17. In this case we note that two sides and the nonincluded angle of one triangle are congruent respectively to two sides and the nonincluded angle of the other triangle. However, because not all pairs of corresponding sides are congruent and not all pairs of corresponding angles are congruent, we *cannot* say that the two triangles must always be congruent.

EXERCISES FOR SECTION 13.1

1. Determine whether there is sufficient information to prove the indicated statement. Justify your answer.

a) Is △*ABC* ≅ △*DEF*?

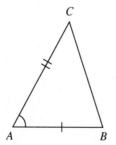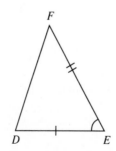

b) Is △*ABC* ≅ △*DEC*?

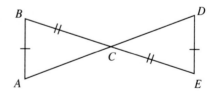

c) Is $\triangle ABC \cong \triangle DBC$?

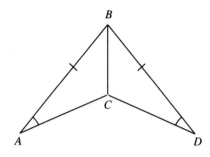

d) Is $\triangle ABD \cong \triangle BCD$?

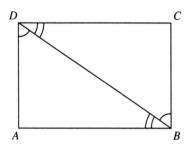

e) Is $\triangle ABC \cong \triangle CDE$?

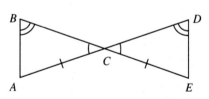

f) Is $\triangle ABC \cong \triangle ADC$?

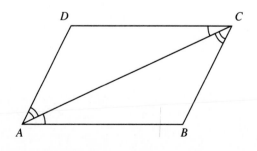

g) Is $\triangle ABC \cong \triangle EDC$?

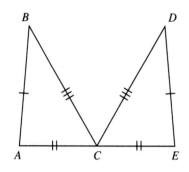

h) Is $\triangle ABC \cong \triangle ADC$?

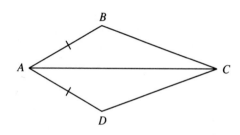

i) Is $\triangle ABC \cong \triangle DFE$?

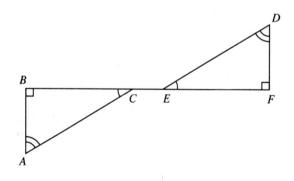

2. Determine whether the following pairs of triangles are necessarily congruent.

a)

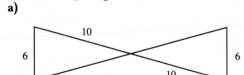

b)

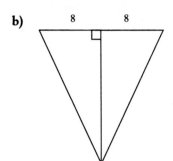

c)

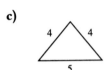

3. Name the pair of corresponding sides that would have to be proved congruent for the following triangles to be congruent by the SSS congruence principle.

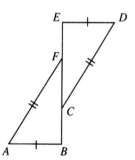

4. Name the pair of corresponding sides or corresponding angles that would have to be proved congruent for the following triangles to be congruent by the ASA congruence principle.

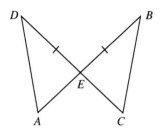

5. Name the pair of corresponding sides or corresponding angles that would have to be proved congruent for the following triangles to be congruent by the SAS congruence principle.

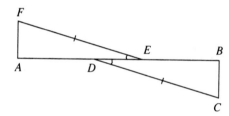

PROBLEM-SOLVING EXERCISES

6. Prove that if two angles of a triangle are congruent, then the triangle is isosceles.

13.2

SOME CONGRUENCE THEOREMS

In this section we indicate how the four congruence properties for triangles discussed in the previous section can be applied to deduce various properties of quadrilaterals.

EXAMPLE 1

Problem-Solving Example

A parallelogram is a quadrilateral in which one pair of opposite sides is both parallel and congruent. Prove that the second pair of opposite sides must also be congruent (see Fig. 13.18).

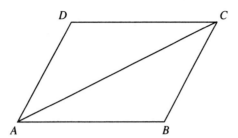

Figure 13.18   *A*   *B*

SOLUTION

Understanding the Problem
We are given that *ABCD* is a parallelogram in which one pair of opposite sides is both parallel and congruent. In Fig. 13.18, sides $\overline{AB}$ and $\overline{DC}$ are both parallel and congruent. Thus $\overline{AB} \parallel \overline{DC}$ and $\overline{AB} \cong \overline{DC}$. We wish to prove that $\overline{AD} \cong \overline{BC}$.

A Plan to Solve the Problem
Let us draw diagonal *AC* as shown in Fig. 13.18. Then we will prove that $\overline{AD}$ and $\overline{BC}$ are both corresponding parts of congruent triangles. Hence they must be congruent. We know that $\overline{DC} \parallel \overline{AB}$. Therefore $\angle DCA$ and $\angle CAB$ both are congruent because they are alternate interior angles of parallel lines. Also, $\overline{AC} \cong \overline{AC}$ and $\overline{AB} \cong \overline{DC}$. Thus by the SAS congruence property, $\triangle ADC \cong \triangle ABC$. The corresponding sides $\overline{AD}$ and $\overline{BC}$ of these triangles must be congruent.

Checking Our Solution
When listing the properties of a parallelogram, many books actually state that "a parallelogram is a quadrilateral in which *both* pairs of opposite sides are both parallel and congruent." ◾

EXAMPLE 2

Prove that the diagonals of a rectangle are congruent.

SOLUTION

In Fig. 13.19 we have rectangle *ABCD* where we must show that diagonal *AC* and diagonal *BD* are congruent. Since *ABCD* is a rectangle, it must

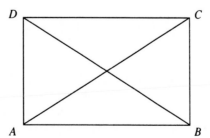

Figure 13.19   *A*   *B*

have all the properties of a parallelogram as well as four right angles. Thus sides $\overline{AD}$ and $\overline{BC}$ are both parallel and congruent. Also sides $\overline{DC}$ and $\overline{AB}$ are both parallel and congruent. Angles DAB and CBA are both right angles that are congruent, so we now have $\overline{AB} \cong \overline{DC}$, $\overline{AD} \cong \overline{BC}$ and $\angle DAB \cong \angle CBA$. Therefore, by the SAS congruence principle, $\triangle ADB = \triangle BCA$, so diagonal $\overline{AC}$ and diagonal $\overline{BD}$ are both corresponding parts of congruent triangles. Hence, they must be congruent. ▬

PROBLEM SOLVING EXERCISES FOR SECTION 13.2

1. Prove that if both pairs of opposite sides of a quadrilateral $ABCD$ (sides that do not have a common endpoint) are congruent, then $\triangle ABC \cong \triangle CDA$.

2. Prove that if both pairs of opposite angles of a quadrilateral are congruent, then the quadrilateral is a parallelogram.

3. A rhombus is a parallelogram which has two congruent consecutive sides. Prove each of the following:

   a) If all sides of a quadrilateral are congruent, then the quadrilateral is a rhombus.

   b) The diagonals of a rhombus bisect its angles.

   c) The diagonals of a rhombus are perpendicular to each other.

4. A rectangle is a parallelogram one of whose angles is a right angle. Prove that all the angles of a rectangle are right angles.

5. Prove that a diagonal of a parallelogram divides the parallelogram into two congruent triangles.

6. Prove that the diagonals of a parallelogram bisect each other.

7. Prove that the adjacent angles of a parallelogram are supplementary.

8. Prove that a rhombus that has a right angle is a square.

9. Prove that if the diagonals of a rhombus are congruent, then the rhombus is a square.

10. Prove that if the two consecutive angles of a quadrilateral are congruent, then the quadrilateral is a rectangle.

11. Prove that in a parallelogram the distances to a diagonal from two opposite vertices are equal.

▶ **Brain-Teaser Problems** ◀

**12. An isosceles trapezoid is a trapezoid in which the non-parallel sides are congruent. Prove that the

   a) diagonals of an isosceles trapezoid are congruent.

   b) base angles of an isosceles trapezoid are congruent.

**13. Prove that if the successive midpoints of the sides of a parallelogram are joined, then the figure formed is a parallelogram.

**14. Prove that the diagonals of a regular pentagon are congruent.

13.3

SIMILAR POLYGONS AND SIMILAR TRIANGLES

Consider Fig. 13.20. We notice that both polygons have the "same shape" but not the "same size." If we analyze the polygons we see that the corresponding angles are congruent. Moreover, each of the sides of polygon $ABCD$ is twice the size of its corresponding side in polygon

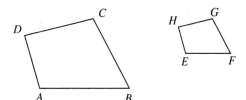

Figure 13.20

EFGH, that is, the ratio of the measures of the corresponding sides is 2 : 1. Such polygons are said to be similar. We indicate that polygon *ABCD* is similar to polygon *EFGH* by writing polygon *ABCD* ~ polygon *EFGH*.

More generally, we have the following.

similar polygons

> **Definition 13.3   Similar Polygons**   Two polygons are similar if there is a one-to-one correspondence between their vertices where (a) all pairs of corresponding angles are congruent and (b) the ratios of the measures of all pairs of corresponding sides are equal.

In the previous example, if polygon *ABCD* is similar to polygon *EFGH*, then we must have both of the following:

Congruent corresponding angles	Equal ratios between the measures of the corresponding sides
$\angle A \cong \angle E$	$\dfrac{AB}{EF} = \dfrac{BC}{FG} = \dfrac{CD}{GH} = \dfrac{DA}{HE}$
$\angle B \cong \angle F$	
$\angle C \cong \angle G$	
$\angle D \cong \angle H$	

Comment   We wish to emphasize the fact that for two polygons to be similar, *both* of the following conditions must be satisfied.

a) All pairs of corresponding angles must be congruent.

b) The ratios of the measures of the corresponding sides must be equal.

In Fig. 13.21 the ratios of the measures of the sides of polygons *ABCD* and *EFGH* are equal. Yet the polygons are not similar because their corresponding angles are not congruent.

Also in Fig. 13.22 the corresponding angles of polygons *ABCD* and *EFGH* are congruent. However, the polygons are not similar since the ratios of the measures of their corresponding sides are not equal.

What about triangles? Since triangles are polygons, we can prove that two triangles are similar by proving that they satisfy the conditions required for polygons to be similar, as given in Definition 13.3. However,

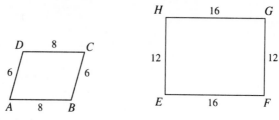

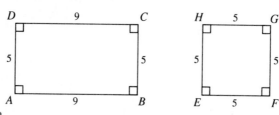

Figure 13.21

Figure 13.22

there are shorter methods for proving triangles similar. First we have a definition.

similar triangles

> **Definition 13.4   Similar Triangles**   If $\triangle ABC$ and $\triangle DEF$ are two triangles where angles A and D are congruent corresponding angles, angles B and E are congruent corresponding angles, angles C and F are congruent corresponding angles, and the ratios of the measures of the corresponding sides are equal, then $\triangle ABC$ is similar to $\triangle DEF$ and we write $\triangle ABC \sim \triangle DEF$.

proportional

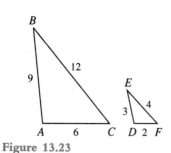

Figure 13.23

Comment   If the ratios of the measures of the corresponding sides are all equal, we often say that the corresponding sides are **proportional**.

In Fig. 13.23 side $\overline{DE}$ = 3 units, side $\overline{EF}$ = 4 units, and side $\overline{DF}$ = 2 units. Now measure sides $\overline{AB}$, $\overline{BC}$, and $\overline{AC}$. You should get 9, 12, and 6 units, respectively. Note that side $\overline{AB}$ is 3 times side $\overline{DE}$. Similarly, side $\overline{BC}$ is 3 times side $\overline{EF}$, and side $\overline{AC}$ is 3 times side $\overline{DF}$. Each side of $\triangle ABC$ is 3 times its corresponding side in $\triangle DEF$. We express this fact by saying that all three sides are **proportional**. In this example we have

$$\frac{m(\overline{AB})}{m(\overline{DE})} = \frac{m(\overline{BC})}{m(\overline{EF})} = \frac{m(\overline{AC})}{m(\overline{DF})}$$

$$\frac{9}{3} = \frac{12}{4} = \frac{6}{2} = 3$$

This leads us to the following property of similar triangles.

> **Property 1** If two triangles are similar, then the corresponding sides are proportional.

Measure angles A and D with a protractor. You should find that $m(\angle A) = m(\angle D)$. Similarly, if you measure the other angles, you will find that $m(\angle B) = m(\angle E)$ and $m(\angle C) = m(\angle F)$. This leads us to the following property.

> **Property 2** If two triangles are similar, then the corresponding angles are equal in measure. The converse of this statement is also true.

There are many other properties of similar triangles that we can prove. We summarize some of these properties in the following:

> **Properties of Similar Triangles** Two triangles are similar if and only if at least one of the following are true.
>
> 1. **AAA similarity property** Three angles of one triangle are congruent to three angles of another triangle.
> 2. **AA similarity property** Two angles of one triangle are congruent to two angles of another triangle.
> 3. **SAS similarity property** Two pairs of corresponding sides are proportional and their included angles are congruent.
> 4. **SSS similarity property** All three pairs of corresponding sides are proportional.

EXAMPLE 1

In the similar triangles shown in Fig. 13.24, find the measure of the lengths of the unmarked sides.

SOLUTION

Since the triangles are similar, we know by Property 1 that the sides are proportional. Thus

$$\frac{m(\overline{AB})}{m(\overline{DE})} = \frac{m(\overline{BC})}{m(\overline{EF})}$$

$$\frac{m(\overline{AB})}{3} = \frac{8}{4}$$

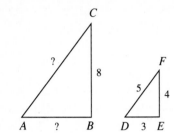

C
?
8
F
5
4
A
?
B
D
3
E
Figure 13.24

Multiplying both sides by 3 gives

$$3\frac{m(\overline{AB})}{3} = 3\cdot\frac{8}{4}$$

$$m(\overline{AB}) = 3\cdot\frac{8}{4}$$

$$= 3\cdot 2 = 6$$

Similarly, we have

$$\frac{m(\overline{AC})}{m(\overline{DF})} = \frac{m(\overline{CB})}{m(\overline{FE})}$$

$$\frac{m(\overline{AC})}{5} = \frac{8}{4}$$

Multiplying both sides by 5 gives

$$5\frac{m(\overline{AC})}{5} = 5\cdot\frac{8}{4}$$

$$m(\overline{AC}) = 5\cdot\frac{8}{4}$$

$$= 5\cdot 2 = 10$$

EXAMPLE 2

In the similar triangles shown in Fig. 13.25, find the measure of the unmarked angles.

SOLUTION

Since the sum of the angles of a triangle is 180°, we know that

$$m(\angle D) + m(\angle E) + m(\angle F) = 180°$$

$$57° + 91° + m(\angle F) = 180°$$

$$148° + m(\angle F) = 180°$$

Thus

$$m(\angle F) = 32°$$

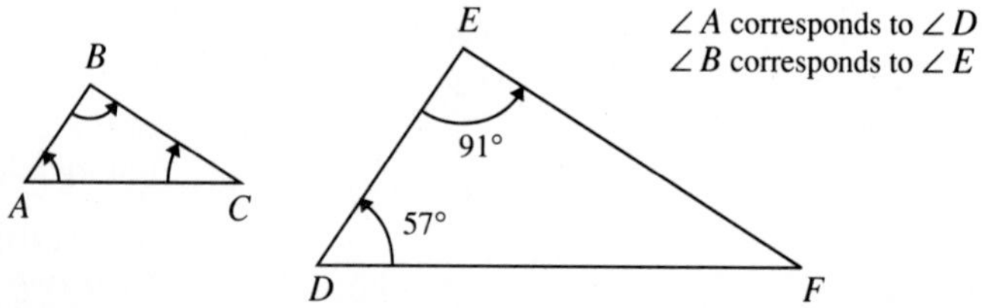

B
A
C
E
91°
57°
D
F
∠A corresponds to ∠D
∠B corresponds to ∠E
Figure 13.25

By property 2 the angles of $\triangle ABC$ must be equal in measure to those of $\triangle DEF$. Thus

$$m(\angle A) = m(\angle D) = 57°, \; m(\angle B) = m(\angle E) = 91°, \quad \text{and}$$
$$m(\angle C) = m(\angle F) = 32°$$

EXAMPLE 3

If a lamp post 30 ft high casts a shadow of 40 ft, how high is a pole next to it if the pole's shadow is 10 ft long?

SOLUTION

First we draw a diagram (see Fig. 13.26). We will assume that the lamppost and the pole stand vertically and that the sun strikes each at the same angle. These angles are marked with an "x". In the figure, each triangle has two equal angles, the right angle and the angle marked x.

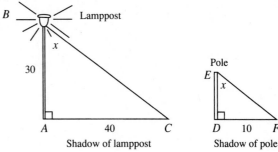

Figure 13.26

Thus the third angles are equal. (Why?) Since the triangles have their corresponding angles equal, the triangles are similar. It follows that their sides are proportional. Thus we have

$$\frac{m(\overline{DE})}{m(\overline{AB})} = \frac{m(\overline{DF})}{m(\overline{AC})}$$

$$\frac{m(\overline{DE})}{30} = \frac{10}{40}$$

Multiplying both sidess by 30, we get

$$m(\overline{DE}) = 30 \cdot \frac{10}{40} = 7\frac{1}{2} \text{ ft}$$

There are many other interesting and useful properties of congruent and similar triangles, some of which will be discussed later.

EXERCISES FOR SECTION 13.3

In Exercises 1-6, the pairs of triangles or rectangles are similar. Find the sides or angles labeled with a question mark.

1.

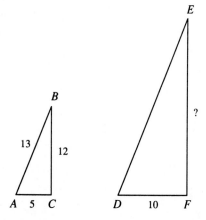

2.

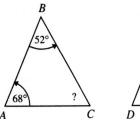

3.

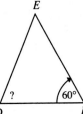

4.

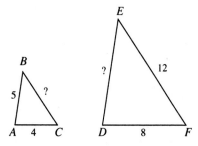

5.

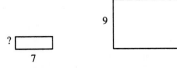

6.

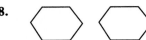

The idea of congruent or similar triangles can be extended to any geometric figures. With this idea in mind, state whether each of the pairs of figures given in Exercises 7–15 appear to be congruent or similar.

7.

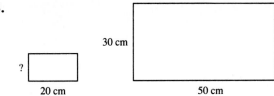

8.

9.

10.

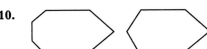

11. ⎯⎯⎯⎯ ⎯⎯⎯⎯

12.

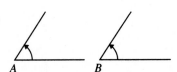

13.

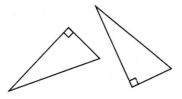

14.

15.

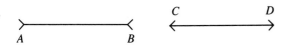

16. Are all equilateral triangles congruent? Explain.

17. Are all equilateral triangles similar? Explain.

18. Are all right triangles similar? Explain.

19. Are all isosceles right triangles similar? Explain.

20. Are all isosceles right triangles congruent? Explain.

21. Consider the figures shown below. Are the figures similar to each other?

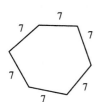
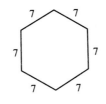

22. Can a quadrilateral be similar to a hexagon? Explain.

23. Consider the diagram below. Is parallelogram *ABCD* similar to rectangle *MNOP*? Explain.

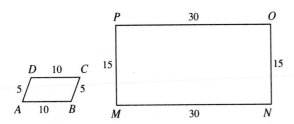

24. The following pairs of polygons are similar. Find the length of every side in each polygon.

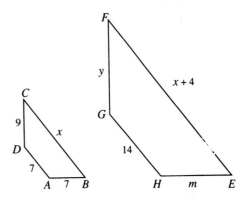

25. A picture 18 cm long and 12 cm wide is to be enlarged so that its width will be 15 cm. How long will the enlarged picture be?

26. Trudy has a wallet-size picture of her baby that is $2\frac{1}{2}$ cm wide by $4\frac{1}{4}$ cm long. She wishes to enlarge it for a wall poster that will be 42.5 cm long. How wide will the enlargement be?

27. In right triangles *ABC* and *DEF*, $m(\angle A) = m(\angle D)$ as shown.

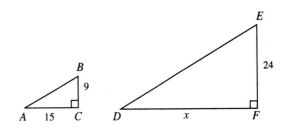

a) Is triangle *ABC* similar to triangle *DEF*?

b) Find *x*.

28. A certain flagpole casts a shadow 7 m long. At the same time a nearby boy who is $1\frac{1}{2}$ m tall casts a shadow 4 m long. Find the height of the flagpole.

29. A statue casts a shadow 20 ft long. At the same time an observer $4\frac{1}{2}$ ft tall casts a shadow 9 ft long. How tall is the statue?

30. In the accompanying diagram △ABC and △DEC are similar. Find $\overline{AB}$ and $\overline{DE}$.

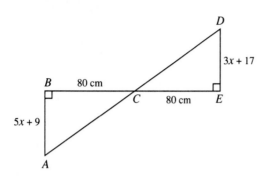

31. Consider △ABC and △ADE. These triangles are similar. Can you explain why?

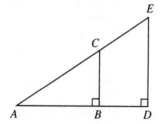

32. In △ABC shown below, where $\overline{DE} \parallel \overline{AB}$, find $\overline{AD}$.

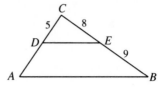

33. In △ABC below, where $\overline{DE} \parallel \overline{AB}$, find $\overline{AB}$.

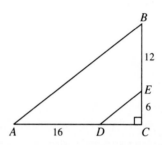

34. If the ratio of the measures of the sides of two similar triangles is 2 : 1, how do the areas of the two triangles compare?

Brain-Teaser Problems

**35. Are all rhombuses similar? Explain.

13.4

SOME BASIC STRAIGHTEDGE AND COMPASS CONSTRUCTIONS

As we indicated earlier, the ancient Greeks studied geometry and constructed geometric figures using a straightedge and a compass. In this section we indicate how we can perform such basic compass-and-straightedge constructions.

CONSTRUCTION 1

To Construct a Circle Given its Center and Radius

Given A line segment $\overline{AB}$ and a fixed point O.

Objective To construct a circle whose center is at point O and whose radius has the same measure as that of segment $\overline{AB}$ (see Fig. 13.27).

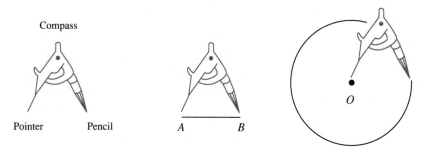

Compass

Pointer   Pencil A B

O

Figure 13.27

Procedure Open the compass and place it on the segment $\overline{AB}$ so that the steel point is at point A and the pencil point is at point B. Without changing the opening of the compass, place the steel point at O. Holding the pointer at O, move the other end of the compass to draw the circle.

Explanation The construction makes the radius of the circle have the same measure as that of segment $\overline{AB}$.

Comment   For any fixed point O and any real positive number r, we can always construct a circle whose center is at O and whose radius is r. The previous construction indicates that a circle can be thought of as the set of all points in a plane which are at a fixed distance (called the **radius**) from a given point (called the **center**). A circle whose center is at O is called circle O.

radius
center

arc

When constructing circles, we think of an **arc** as any part of the circle that can be drawn without lifting the pencil (see Fig. 13.28). An arc is either part of the circle or the entire circle.

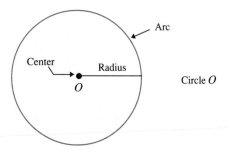

Center   Arc

Radius

O Circle O

Figure 13.28

CONSTRUCTION 2

To Construct a Line Segment Congruent (Equal in Length) to a Given Line Segment

Given Line segment $\overline{AB}$.

Objective To construct a line segment $\overline{CD}$ congruent to segment $\overline{AB}$.

Procedure On line segment $\overline{AB}$ place the compass so that the steel point is at A and the pencil point is at B (see Fig. 13.29). Now, on any line l, choose a point C. Then without changing the setting on the compass, place the steel point at C and construct an arc that intersects the line l. Label the point of intersection D. Then $\overline{AB} \cong \overline{CD}$.

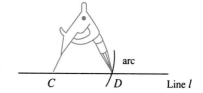

Figure 13.29

Explanation The construction makes $\overline{AB} \cong \overline{CD}$, since $\overline{AB}$ and $\overline{CD}$ are radii of congruent circles.

CONSTRUCTION 3

To Construct an Angle Congruent to a Given Angle

Given Angle ABC and a point D.

Objective To construct at point D an angle congruent to $\angle ABC$.

Procedure Through point D construct any line $\overleftrightarrow{PQ}$ (see Fig. 13.30). Using B as the center of a circle, construct an arc that intersects $\overrightarrow{BC}$ and

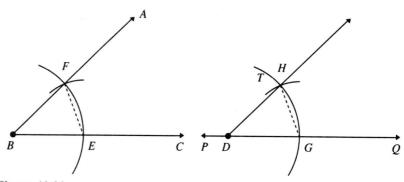

Figure 13.30

$\overrightarrow{BA}$ at points E and F respectively. Without changing the setting of the compass and using D as a center, construct arc $\overline{GH}$ which intersects $\overrightarrow{DQ}$ at G. Now construct $\overline{EF}$. Without changing the setting of the compass and using G as a center, construct an arc which intersects $\overline{GT}$ at H. Finally, construct $\overline{DH}$. We then have $\angle HDQ \cong \angle ABC$.

Explanation When we draw $\overline{GH}$, the construction makes $\overline{DH} \cong \overline{BF}$, $\overline{GH} \cong \overline{EF}$, and $\overline{BE} \cong \overline{DG}$. By the SSS congruence principle, we must have $\triangle BFE = \triangle DHG$. Thus, since the corresponding parts of congruent triangles are congruent, we must have $\angle HDQ \cong \angle ABC$.

CONSTRUCTION 4

To Construct the Perpendicular Bisector of a Given Line Segment

Given Line segment $\overline{AB}$.

Objective To construct a line $\overleftrightarrow{CD}$ such that $\overleftrightarrow{CD} \perp \overline{AB}$ and $\overleftrightarrow{CD}$ intersects $\overline{AB}$ at its midpoint.

Procedure Open the compass so that the distance between the steel point and the pencil point (this distance is called the radius) is more than one-half the length of $\overline{AB}$. Then using point A as a center, construct one arc above $\overline{AB}$ and one arc below $\overline{AB}$ (see Fig. 13.31). Also, using the same radius but this time with point B as a center, construct another pair of arcs, one above $\overline{AB}$ and one below $\overline{AB}$. Let C be the point of intersection of the arcs on one side of $\overline{AB}$ the and let D be the intersection of the arcs on other side of $\overline{AB}$. Construct line $\overleftrightarrow{CD}$. Then $\overleftrightarrow{CD}$ is the perpendicular bisector of $\overline{AB}$.

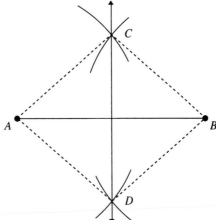

Figure 13.31

Explanation When $\overline{CA}$, $\overline{CB}$, $\overline{DA}$, and $\overline{DB}$ are drawn, they all represent radii of equal circles. Since all radii of equal circles are congruent, the construction makes $\overline{CA} \cong \overline{CB}$ and $\overline{DA} \cong \overline{DB}$. It can be shown that any two points equidistant from the ends of a line segment must fall on the perpendicular bisector of that line segment. Therefore, since we have two points that are equidistant from the ends of the line segment, $\overleftrightarrow{CD}$ is the perpendicular bisector of $\overline{AB}$.

CONSTRUCTION 5

To Bisect a Given Angle

Given $\angle ABC$.

Objective To bisect $\angle ABC$.

Procedure Place the steel point of the compass at point B (see Fig. 13.32). Using B as a center and any convenient radius, construct an arc that intersects sides $\overrightarrow{BA}$ and $\overrightarrow{BC}$. Label the points of intersection P and Q respectively. Using points P and Q as centers and with equal radii of sufficient length, construct arcs that intersect at point R. Construct $\overrightarrow{BR}$. Then $\overrightarrow{BR}$ bisects $\angle ABC$. This is because $\angle ABR \cong \angle CBR$.

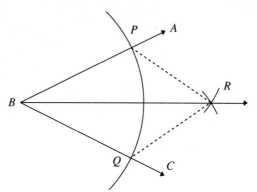

Figure 13.32

Explanation When $\overline{RP}$ and $\overline{RQ}$ are drawn, the construction makes $\overline{BP} \cong \overline{BQ}$ and $\overline{PR} \cong \overline{QR}$. Since $\overline{BR} \cong \overline{BR}$, we apply the SSS congruence property and conclude that $\triangle BPR \cong \triangle BQR$. Therefore, $\angle ABR \cong \angle CBR$.

CONSTRUCTION 6

To Construct a Line Perpendicular to a Given Line and Passing Through a Given Point on the Line

Given Point P on line $\overleftrightarrow{AB}$.

Objective To construct a line perpendicular to line $\overleftrightarrow{AB}$ and which passes through point P on line $\overleftrightarrow{AB}$.

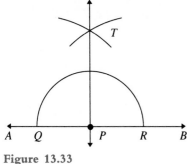

Figure 13.33

Procedure Place the steel point of the compass at point P (see Fig. 13.33). Using point P as a center and any convenient radius, construct an arc that intersects $\overleftrightarrow{AB}$ at points Q and R. Using points Q and R as centers and with a radius greater in length than the one used before, construct arcs that intersect at point T. Now construct $\overleftrightarrow{TP}$. This line will be perpendicular to $\overleftrightarrow{AB}$ at point P.

Explanation We know that angle APB is a straight angle. The construction bisects this straight angle. Thus, $\angle APT$ and $\angle BPT$ are right angles. Therefore, $\overleftrightarrow{TP}$ is perpendicular to $\overleftrightarrow{AB}$ at point P, since we have two straight lines which intersect at right angles. The lines must be perpendicular to each other.

CONSTRUCTION 7

To Construct a Line Perpendicular to a Given Line which Passes Through a Specified Point not on the Given Line

Given Point P that is not on line $\overleftrightarrow{AB}$.

Objective To construct a line perpendicular to $\overleftrightarrow{AB}$ which passes through point P.

Procedure Place the steel point of the compass at point P (see Fig. 13.34). Using point P as center and any convenient radius, construct an arc which intersects $\overleftrightarrow{AB}$ at points Q and R. Then, using points Q and R as centers and with a radius greater in length than one-half $\overline{QR}$, construct arcs which intersect at point T. Construct $\overleftrightarrow{TP}$. This line is perpendicular to $\overleftrightarrow{AB}$.

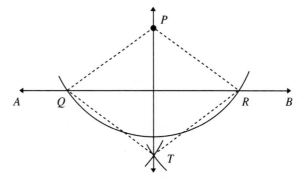

Figure 13.34

Explanation When $\overline{PQ}$, $\overline{PR}$, $\overline{TQ}$ and $\overline{TR}$ are drawn, the construction makes $\overline{PQ} \cong \overline{PR}$ and $\overline{TQ} \cong \overline{TR}$. Thus $\overleftrightarrow{PT}$ is the perpendicular bisector of $\overline{QR}$. This is because if points Q and R are equidistant from the ends of a line segment then they must determine the perpendicular bisector of the line segment.

CONSTRUCTION 8

To Construct a Line Parallel to a Given Line Through a Specified Point That is Not on the Given Line.

Given Line $\overleftrightarrow{AB}$ and a point P not on line $\overleftrightarrow{AB}$.

Objective To construct a line parallel to $\overleftrightarrow{AB}$ which passes through point P.

Procedure Through point P construct any transversal which intersects line $\overleftrightarrow{AB}$ at point C (see Fig. 13.35). Using Construction 3 given earlier, and making sure that the vertex is at point P, construct $\angle DPN$ so that, $\angle DPN \cong \angle PCB$. We notice that $\angle DPN$ and $\angle PCB$ are corresponding angles. Thus line $\overleftrightarrow{MN}$ or line $\overleftrightarrow{PN}$ passes through point P and is parallel to line $\overleftrightarrow{AB}$.

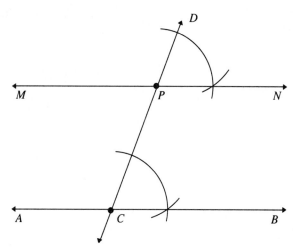

Figure 13.35

Explanation By the construction, we have $\angle DPN \cong \angle PCB$. Line $\overleftrightarrow{MN}$ must be parallel to line $\overleftrightarrow{AB}$ because if two lines are cut by a transversal and if the corresponding angles formed are congruent, then the lines are parallel.

CONSTRUCTION 9

To Divide a Given Line Segment Into any Number of Congruent Parts.

Given Line segment $\overline{AB}$.

Objective To divide $\overline{AB}$ into any specified number of parts. (In our construction we will divide the given line segment into three congruent parts.)

Procedure Construct $\overrightarrow{AP}$, which makes any convenient angle with line segment $\overline{AB}$, (see Fig. 13.36). Placing the steel point of the compass at point A, lay off any convenient length, $\overline{AC}$, three times. Thus $\overline{AC} \cong \overline{CD} \cong \overline{DE}$. Now construct $\overline{BE}$. Using Construction 8 and point D, construct $\overleftrightarrow{DQ} \parallel \overleftrightarrow{BE}$. Again, by means of Construction 8 but now using point C, construct $\overleftrightarrow{CR} \parallel \overleftrightarrow{BE}$. We then have that line segment $\overline{AB}$ is divided into the three congruent parts $\overline{AR}$, $\overline{RQ}$, and $\overline{QB}$.

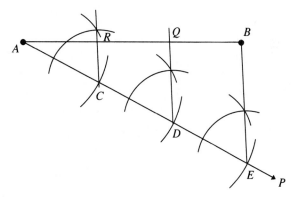

Figure 13.36

Explanation By the construction we know that $\overline{AC} \cong \overline{CD} \cong \overline{DE}$ and that $\overleftrightarrow{CR} \parallel \overleftrightarrow{DQ} \parallel \overleftrightarrow{BE}$. It can be shown that if three (or more) parallel lines cut off segments of equal length on one transversal, then they cut off equal lengths on any transversal. Thus $\overline{AR} \cong \overline{RQ} = \overline{QB}$.

CONSTRUCTION 10

To Locate the Center of a Circle.

Given A circle.

Objective To find the center of the circle.

Procedure In the circle draw a chord $\overline{AB}$ and then construct its perpendicular bisector $\overleftrightarrow{MN}$ (see Fig. 13.37). Construct a second chord $\overline{BC}$ and its perpendicular bisector $\overleftrightarrow{QR}$. The point of intersection of lines $\overleftrightarrow{MN}$ and $\overleftrightarrow{QR}$ (call this point O) is the center of the circle.

Explanation The center of the given circle must lie on $\overleftrightarrow{MN}$, the perpendicular bisector of chord $\overline{AB}$, as the perpendicular bisector of a chord in a

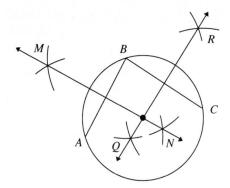

Figure 13.37

circle must pass through the center of the circle. Similarly, the center of the circle must lie on line $\overleftrightarrow{QR}$, the perpendicular bisector of chord $\overline{BC}$. These two lines intersect at point O, which is the center of the circle.

CONSTRUCTION 11

To Construct a Triangle Similar to a Given Triangle on a Given Line as a Base

Given $\triangle ABC$ and a line segment $\overline{PQ}$.

Objective To construct a triangle similar to $\triangle ABC$ on line segment $\overline{PQ}$ where $\overline{PQ}$ will correspond to side $\overline{AB}$ of $\triangle ABC$ (see Fig. 13.38).

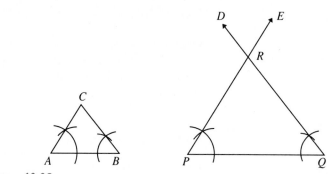

Figure 13.38

Procedure Using Construction 3 and point P as a vertex, construct $\angle QPE$ congruent to $\angle BAC$. Again using Construction 3 but now with point Q as a vertex, construct $\angle PQR$ congruent to $\angle ABC$. Rays $\overrightarrow{PE}$ and $\overrightarrow{QD}$ intersect at a point. Call this point R. The required triangle is then $\triangle PQR$.

Explanation By the construction, $\angle P \cong \angle A$ and $\angle Q \cong \angle B$. Since two angles of one triangle are congruent respectively to two angles of the other triangle, by the AA similarity property, the triangles are similar.

There are some interesting constructions that can be performed involving circles and polygons. We can have circumscribed circles and inscribed circles. A **circumscribed circle** contains the points of the polygon as points on the circle. On the other hand, an **inscribed circle** touches each side of the polygon in exactly one point. In Fig. 13.39(a) we have a triangle circumscribed by a circle; in Fig. 13.39(b) we have a circle inscribed within the triangle.

circumscribed circle
inscribed circle

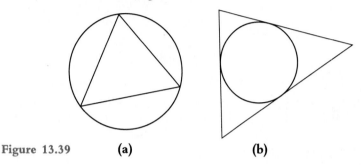

Figure 13.39   **(a)**   **(b)**

CONSTRUCTION 12

To Construct a Circle Circumscribed About a Triangle

Given $\triangle ABC$.

Objective To circumscribe a circle about $\triangle ABC$.

Procedure Construct $\overleftrightarrow{PQ}$, the perpendicular bisector of $\overline{BC}$ (see Fig. 13.40). Also construct $\overleftrightarrow{RT}$, the perpendicular bisector of $\overline{AC}$. Both of these perpendicular bisectors intersect at a point. Call this point of intersection O. Using point O as a center, construct a circle whose radius has length $\overline{OA}$. The circle so constructed is the required circle.

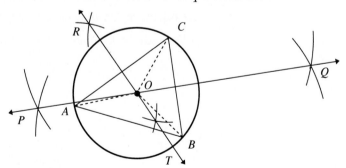

Figure 13.40

Explanation If we draw $\overline{OA}$, $\overline{OC}$, and $\overline{OB}$ then since any point on the perpendicular bisector of a line segment is equidistant from the ends of the segment, then with $\overleftrightarrow{RT}$ as the perpendicular bisector of $\overline{AC}$, we must have $OA = OC$. By a similar reasoning, since $\overleftrightarrow{PQ}$ is the perpendicular bisector of

$\overline{BC}$, we must have $OC = OB$. Thus $OA = OB = OC$, so we have a circle whose center is at point O, whose radius has length OA, and which passes through points A, B, and C. Then, by definition, circle O circumscribes $\triangle ABC$.

CONSTRUCTION 13

To Inscribe a Circle Within a Given Triangle

Given $\triangle ABC$.

Objective To inscribe a circle in $\triangle ABC$.

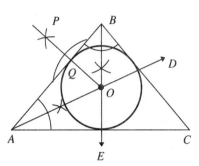

Figure 13.41

Procedure Construct $\overrightarrow{AD}$, the bisector of $\angle A$, and $\overrightarrow{BE}$, the bisector of $\angle B$ (see Fig. 13.41). These angle bisectors intersect at a point. Call this point of intersection O. Using point O as a center, construct $\overleftrightarrow{OP}$ perpendicular to $\overline{AB}$. Line $\overleftrightarrow{OP}$ intersects $\overline{AB}$ at point Q. Using O as the center and a radius whose length is the length of segment $\overline{OQ}$, construct the required circle O.

Explanation We know that any point on the bisector of an angle must be equidistant from the sides of the angle. Thus, since $\overrightarrow{AD}$ is the bisector of $\angle A$, point O must be equidistant from both $\overline{AB}$ and $\overline{AC}$. Also, it must be equidistant from $\overline{BA}$ and $\overline{BC}$, so that it is equidistant from $\overline{AB}$, $\overline{BC}$, and $\overline{AC}$. A circle whose center is at O and whose radius has length OQ (the distance from point O to $\overline{AB}$) will touch each side of the triangle in exactly one point. Thus circle O is inscribed in $\triangle ABC$.

CONSTRUCTION 14

To Inscribe a Square in a Given Circle

Given Circle O.

Objective To inscribe a square within circle O.

Procedure In circle O, construct any diameter $\overline{AB}$ (see Fig. 13.42).

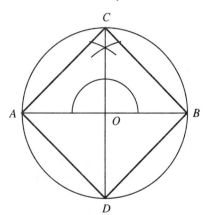

Figure 13.42

Construct diameter $\overline{CD}$ perpendicular to diameter $\overline{AB}$ at point O. Construct $\overline{AC}$, $\overline{CB}$, $\overline{BD}$, and $\overline{DA}$. The resulting quadrilateral $ABCD$ is a square.

Explanation By the construction, all of the central angles are right angles which are congruent. Thus, $\overset{\frown}{AC} \cong \overset{\frown}{CB} \cong \overset{\frown}{BD} \cong \overset{\frown}{DA}$, so $ABCD$ is a square as the chords of these arcs form a regular inscribed polygon.

CONSTRUCTION 15

To Inscribe a Regular Hexagon in a Given Circle

Given Circle O.

Objective To inscribe a regular hexagon in circle O.

Procedure In circle O construct any radius $\overline{OA}$ (see Fig. 13.43). Using point A as a center and a radius of length $\overline{OA}$, construct an arc which intersects the circle at point B. Then using point B as a center, construct an arc which has the same length as radius $\overline{OA}$. This arc will intersect the circle at a point which we call C. Similarly, we obtain points D, E, and F on the circle. If we draw $\overline{AB}$, $\overline{BC}$, $\overline{CD}$, $\overline{DE}$, $\overline{EF}$, and $\overline{FA}$, we obtain regular hexagon $ABCDEF$ inscribed in circle O.

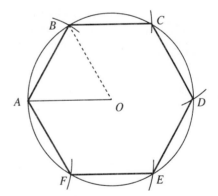

Figure 13.43

Explanation If we draw $\overline{OB}$, we find that $\triangle AOB$ is an equilateral triangle as all three of its sides are congruent, since $\overline{AB} \cong \overline{OA} \cong \overline{OB}$. The measure of central angle AOB is $60°$, so that $m(\overset{\frown}{AB}) = 60°$. We then have 6 congruent arcs. The chords of these arcs then form a regular hexagon.

Comment The ancient Greeks also attempted the following straightedge and compass construction. If we are given a circle, can we construct a square of equal area? Try it and see what happens. Although the ancient Greeks were unsuccessful in their endeavors, modern mathematicians have proved that this construction is impossible using only a straightedge and compass.

Many of the constructions discussed until now have many interesting applications, even for younger children. In the accompanying student page from *Addison-Wesley Mathematics*, 1987, grade 7, p. 155, we note that students are instructed that by following the detailed steps, an egg-shaped region will be created.

THINK MATH

Shape Perception

Follow the steps below to draw the shape of an egg.

1. Draw a circle with $\overline{AB} \perp \overline{CD}$.
2. Extend chords $\overline{AC}$ and $\overline{BC}$ as shown.
3. Draw $\widehat{BF}$ with center at A. Draw $\widehat{AE}$ with center at B.
4. Draw $\widehat{EF}$ with center at C.
5. Shade in the egg-shaped region.

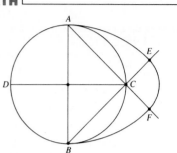

EXERCISES FOR SECTION 13.4

1. Construct a median from vertex A for the following triangle. (A **median** of a triangle is a line segment which joins any vertex of the triangle to the midpoint of the opposite side.)

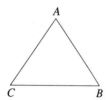

2. Construct the angle bisector of angle A in the following triangle.

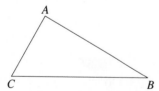

3. Construct an altitude from vertex A for the following triangle. (An **altitude** of a triangle is a line segment

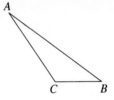

drawn from any vertex of the triangle perpendicular to and ending in the opposite side, extended if necessary.)

4. Construct an angle whose measure is equal to the sum of the measures of the following two angles.

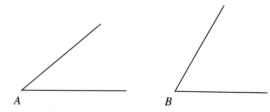

5. Construct the triangle whose three sides are given below.

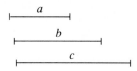

6. Construct the triangle whose two sides and included angle are as follows.

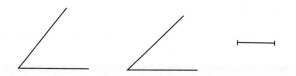

7. Construct the triangle whose two angles and included side are as follows.

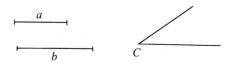

8. Construct an equilateral triangle.

9. Inscribe an equilateral triangle in the following circle.

10. Circumscribe a square about the following circle.

11. Construct a trapezoid that has two right angles.

12. Construct two lines, each perpendicular to the following line $\overleftrightarrow{AB}$, one passing through A, and the other

passing through B. How are the two constructed lines related? Justify your answer.

13. Is it always possible to inscribe a circle in a quadrilateral? Explain your answer.

14. Consider the circle shown below, in which we have drawn serveral angles. Find a relationship between angles 1, 2, and 3. Explain your answer.

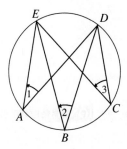

15. Which of the following can be constructed so as to locate a point equidistant from the vertices of a triangle?

a) the perpendicular bisectors of the sides

b) the angle bisectors

c) the altitudes

d) the medians

 Brain-Teaser Problems

**16. Construct a regular pentagon in a circle. Then indicate how we can construct the following:

a)

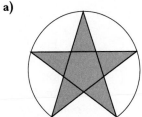

b)

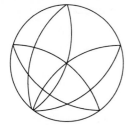

c)

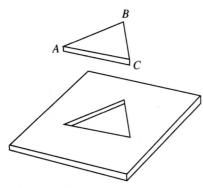

d)

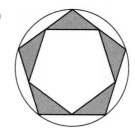

**17. Construct a regular decagon. (*Hint:* First construct a regular pentagon in a circle and then construct the perpendicular bisectors of the sides of the pentagon.)

13.5

TRANSFORMATION GEOMETRY

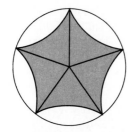

Figure 13.44

In this section we examine some interesting properties of geometric figures that arise when a figure is transformed in a certain way into another figure. For example, suppose we cut an equilateral triangle out of a block of wood, as shown in Fig. 13.44. How many ways can we put the triangle back into the wooden block? One way of putting the triangle into the block is shown here.

Original position   Final position

However, this new position is merely a change or transformation of the vertices of the original triangle. We note that under this "transformation" some points move about and change their position in the plane, whereas some of the points in the plane remain fixed. (Can you find which points remain fixed?) Nevertheless, after this transformation is performed the plane appears full and complete; i.e., there are no missing points just as the block of wood appears full after the triangle is placed back into it.

We can generalize this idea to form the definition of a transformation in the plane.

transformation

> **Definition 13.5**   A **transformation** T is a one-to-one correspondence between the points in a plane that indicates a change in position or a fixed position for each point in the plane. Under a transformation, each point P is associated with a unique point P' called the **image** of P.

image

Although there are many types of transformations that can take place in a plane, in this section we will analyze only several special transformations; i.e., those that follow a definite pattern or rule.

Translation

Imagine that a car is towed from one block to another. In this case the car has been moved a certain distance d in a certain direction along a line. This type of transformation is called a "slide" or a "shift," or a "**translation.**" To further understand this, consider $\triangle ABC$ shown in Fig. 13.45. We notice that $\triangle ABC$ is moved 5 cm in the direction indicated by the arrow.

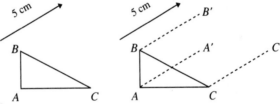

Figure 13.45

What is the image of $\triangle ABC$ under this translation? We can find the image by drawing segments 5 cm long parallel to that arrow which shows the direction of the shift. In Fig. 13.46 we see that $AA' = BB' = CC' = 5$ cm, and also $AA' \parallel BB' \parallel CC'$. When we connect the images of A, B, and C, we obtain $\triangle A'\,B'\,C'$.

Such a transformation is called a translation.

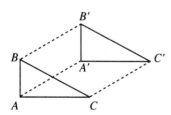

Figure 13.46

> **Definition 13.6**   A **translation** is a transformation of the plane that shifts every point in the plane the same distance in the same direction to its image. No twisting or turning is involved.

translation

Comment   Under a translation, if one point moves then all points move. That is, no points remain fixed.

isometry

In the previous example we note that under the transformation, distance is preserved. Any transformation that preserves distance (that is, in which the distance between the images of any two points is the same as the distance between the two original points) is called an **isometry**.

A translation always preserves parallelism between lines, distance, angle measure, collinearity, and midpoints of lines. An isometry also preserves congruence. Can you see why?

Translations can easily be studied in terms of coordinate geometry. Consider the translation pictured in Fig. 13.47, where $\overline{A'B'}$ is the image of $\overline{AB}$. We note that the translation actually moves every point on $\overline{AB}$ six units to the right and five units down. Symbolically we can then say that under this translation, the image of every point (x, y) is $(x + 6, y - 5)$.

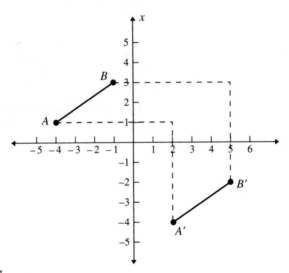

Figure 13.47

More generally, any translation that slides any point (x, y) "a" units horizontally and "b" units vertically is denoted as

$$T_{a, b} (x, y) = (x + a, y + b)$$

EXAMPLE 1

A translation maps $P(7, -2)$ onto $P'(4, 6)$. Under the same translation find the image of $A(2, 0)$.

SOLUTION

If we plot points P and P' on graph paper (see Fig. 13.48), we note that the translation moves point P three units to the left and eight units up. We can denote this translation as $T_{-3, 8} (x, y) = (x - 3, y + 8)$, so that under the same translation the image of $A(2, 0)$ is $A'(2 - 3, 0 + 8)$ or $A' (-1, 8)$. Thus the image of $A(2, 0)$ under this translation is $A' (-1, 8)$.

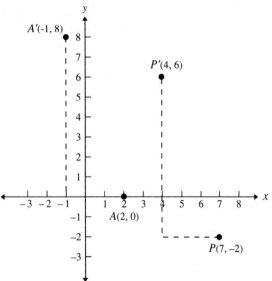

Figure 13.48

Line Reflections
line of reflection

Consider $\triangle ABC$, below. Let us fold the page along line l, which is called a **line of reflection**. When this is done we will obtain $\triangle A'\,B'\,C$ as the image of $\triangle ABC$. This triangle will fit exactly on top of $\triangle ABC$.

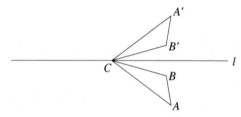

We note that point A corresponds to A' and that B corresponds to B'. However, under this reflection point C, which is on the line of reflection, remains invariant. Such a point is called a **fixed point**.

fixed point

If we draw line segments connecting some of the points with their images under this transformation, we notice that the line of reflection is the perpendicular bisector of these line segments. Based on these observations we have the following definition.

reflection

Definition 13.7   A reflection in a line l is a transformation of the plane such that

a) for any point on line l, the image of P is P,

b) for any point not on line l, the image of P is P' and line l is the perpendicular bisector of the segment PP'.

Comment   Under a line reflection, the image of a segment is another segment. Using a compass and a straightedge, we can construct the line of reflection l by finding the perpendicular bisector of PP'.

In terms of coordinate geometry, if the reflection line l is the y-axis, then the image any point $P(x, y)$ will be $P(-x, y)$. This is often denoted as $r_{y\text{-axis}}(x, y) = (-x, y)$.

EXAMPLE 2

The vertices of $\triangle ABC$ are $A(3, 8)$, $B(7, 9)$, and $C(5, -3)$. Find the image of $\triangle ABC$ under a reflection in the y-axis.

SOLUTION

We first plot $\triangle ABC$ (see Fig. 13.49). We then note that under this line reflection we have the following:

Point	Image under reflection in y-axis
$A(3, 8)$	$A'(-3, 8)$
$B(7, 9)$	$B'(-7, 9)$
$C(5, -3)$	$C'(-5, -3)$

These can be seen in the diagram.

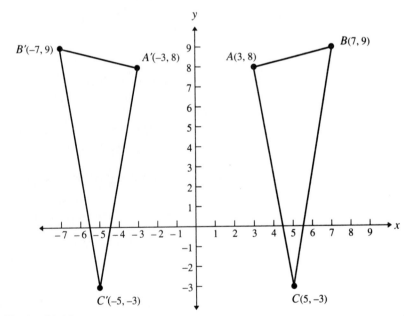

Figure 13.49

EXAMPLE 3

For the vertices of $\triangle ABC$ given in Example 2, find the image under a reflection in the x-axis.

SOLUTION

We first plot $\triangle ABC$ (see Fig. 13.50). From the diagram we notice that under this line reflection, we have the following.

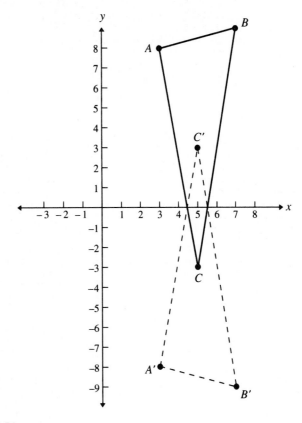

Figure 13.50

Point	Image under reflection in x-axis
$A(3, 8)$	$A'\,(3, -8)$
$B(7, 9)$	$B'\,(7, -9)$
$C(5, -3)$	$C'\,(5, 3)$

On the basis of this example we can say that under a reflection in the x-axis the image of any point $P(x, y)$ will be $P(x, -y)$. This is often denoted as $r_{x\text{-axis}}\,(x, y) = (x, -y)$. ▪

EXAMPLE 4

Find the image of $\overline{AB}$ where the coordinates of A and B are $A(3, 5)$ and $B(8, 6)$ when this segment is reflected in the line whose equation is $y = x$.

SOLUTION

We first plot $\overline{AB}$ (see Fig. 13.51). We note that in this case the image of $\overline{AB}$ is $\overline{A'B'}$ where we have the following:

Point	Image under reflection in $y = x$
$A(3, 5)$	$A'(5, 3)$
$B(8, 6)$	$B'(6, 8)$

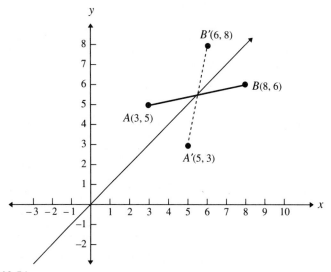

Figure 13.51

Based upon this example we can say that under a reflection in the line $y = x$, the image of a point $P(x, y)$ will be $P'(y, x)$. This is often denoted as $r_{y=x}(x, y) = (y, x)$.

The reader should verify that under a line reflection we have the following (some of these were already illustrated in the previous examples):

a) Distance is preserved; i.e., each segment and its image are equal in length.

b) Angle measure is preserved; i.e., each angle and its image are equal in measure.

c) Parallelism is preserved; i.e., if two lines are parallel, then their images will be parallel lines.

d) Collinearity is preserved; i.e., if three or more points lie on a straight line, then their images will also lie on a straight line.

Line Symmetry

Consider the rectangle shown in Fig. 13.52. If we draw the vertical line *m* we notice that for every point *P* of the figure not on the line, there is another point on the figure such that line *l* is the perpendicular bisector of *PP'*. Line *m* is called a vertical line of symmetry. Similarly, line *l* is a horizontal line of symmetry. We say that rectangle *ABCD* has both horizontal and vertical symmetry and that each line is called an axis of symmetry.

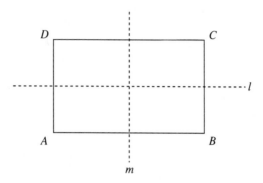

Figure 13.52

More generally we have the following.

line symmetry

axis of symmetry

> **Definition 13.8** **Line symmetry** occurs in a figure when the figure is its own image under a reflection in a line. Such a line is called the **axis of symmetry**.

reflectional symmetries

Line symmetries, which are sometimes called **reflectional symmetries**, occur frequently in nature and in industry, as can be seen in the following figures.

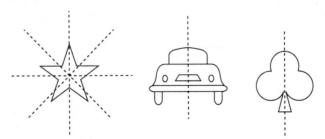

Young children are often asked to identify line symmetries that occur in nature, as can be seen in the following student page from *Addison-Wesley Mathematics*, 1987, Grade 7, p. 150.

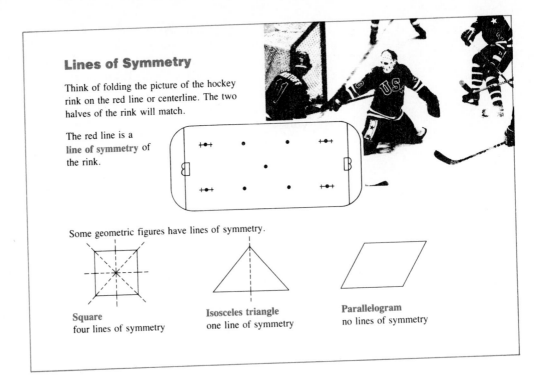

Lines of Symmetry

Think of folding the picture of the hockey rink on the red line or centerline. The two halves of the rink will match.

The red line is a **line of symmetry** of the rink.

Some geometric figures have lines of symmetry.

Square
four lines of symmetry

Isosceles triangle
one line of symmetry

Parallelogram
no lines of symmetry

Point Symmetry

Figure 13.53

Now consider the playing card shown in Fig. 13.53. We notice that every point in the figure moves to its image through a point of reflection located in the "center" of the figure. Such a point of reflection is called a point of symmetry and the resulting figure is said to have point symmetry. We have the following:

> **Definition 13.9**   **Point symmetry** occurs in a figure when the figure is its own image under a reflection in a point.

Is it possible for a figure to have both line symmetry and point symmetry? In Fig. 13.54 we have four lines of symmetry and one point of symmetry.

On the other hand, the parallelogram shown in Fig. 13.55 has only point symmetry but does not have line symmetry. The point of symmetry is point E, where both diagonals meet. In this case, the image of A is C, the image of B is D, the image of C is A, and the image of D is B, etc.

Young children are often asked to count the number of lines of symmetry that can found in familiar everyday things. This can be seen in

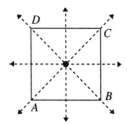

Figure 13.54

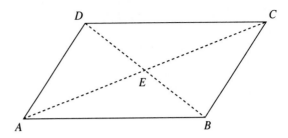

Figure 13.55

Symmetric Figures

The picture on this greeting card suggests the idea of a **symmetric figure**. When the card is closed, the two halves of the figure fit exactly on each other. The fold line of the card is the **line of symmetry** of the figure.

Here are three familiar types of triangles and their lines of symmetry.

Equilateral triangle
3 lines of symmetry

Isosceles triangle
1 line of symmetry

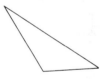

Scalene triangle
0 lines of symmetry

the accompanying student page from *Addison-Wesley Mathematics*, 1987, Grade 6, p. 266. How many of the familiar types of figures shown have point symmetry?

In coordinate geometry, the most common type of point reflection is a reflection in the origin. If we consider the triangle *ABC* shown in Fig. 13.56, where the vertices are *A*(5, 9), *B*(9, 3) and *C*(3, 2), we notice that these vertices are reflected in the origin. We obtain the following images for △*A′ B′ C′*.

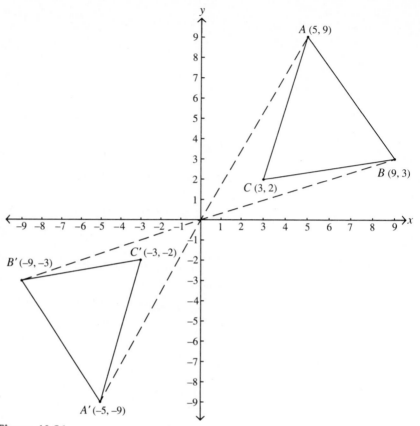

Figure 13.56

Point	Image under reflection in the origin
$A(5, 9)$	$A'(-5, -9)$
$B(9, 3)$	$B'(-9, -3$
$C(3, 2)$	$C'(-3, -2)$

Based on this, we can conclude that under a reflection in the origin, the image of any point $P(x, y)$ is $P'(-x, -y)$. We symbolize a reflection in the origin as $R_{origin}(x, y) = (-x, -y)$. The reader should verify that under a point reflection, all of the properties listed previously for a line reflection are valid. These include preservation of distance, preservation of angle measure, parallelism, and collinearity.

Rotations

Consider what happens as the pointer of the stop watch shown at the top of the next page is moved. We notice that every point on the pointer moves through an arc, so that the position of every point is changed. Except for the fixed point in the center of the watch, each point is moved

by the same number of degrees. Such a transformation is called a rotation. We have

rotation
center of rotation

> **Definition 13.10**   A **rotation** is a transformation of the plane about a fixed point P, called the **center of rotation**, and through an angle which measures x degrees such that
> (a) the image of the fixed point P is P
> (b) for any other point, the image of A is A' where $m(\angle APA') = x$ and $\overline{PX} = \overline{PX'}$.

Comment   By virtue of Definition 13.10, all of the properties listed previously for a line reflection are also valid for rotations.

Consider the regular hexagon shown in Fig. 13.57. We notice that if we rotate the hexagon 60°, then it is its own image. Similarly, if a regular pentagon is rotated 72° again we notice that it is its own image. Such figures have rotational symmetry. We have

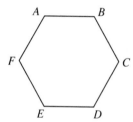

Figure 13.57

rotational symmetry

> **Definition 13.11   Rotational symmetry** occurs in a figure if the figure is its own image under a rotation of x degrees and if only the center remains fixed.

Dilations

Imagine that we have taken pictures and wish to obtain prints from the negative. A photograph is actually an enlargement of a negative. The ratio of the distances between points in the negative compared to the distances between these images in the photograph remain constant. The same phenomenon occurs in a reduction. We have

> **Definition 13.12**   Let C be any positive number. Then a **dilation** of C is a transformation such that
> (a)   the image of point O, the center of the dilation, is O;
> (b)   for any other point, the image of P is P' where OP and OP' name the same ray and $OP' = C \cdot \overline{OP}$. C is called the **constant of dilation.**

Although angle measure, parallelism, and collinearity are preserved under a dilation, distance is not. Thus, under any dilation, a figure and its image are only similar figures. In view of the fact that angle measure is preserved and that every side of one figure is C times every side of a second figure, similarity between figures can be thought of in terms of transformations. Compare this with our discussion of similar polygons given earlier.

In coordinate geometry, if the center of a dilation is the origin, then the image of $P(x, y)$ under a dilation of a positive number c is $P'(cx, cy)$. Symbollically, $D_c(x, y) = (cx, cy)$.

EXAMPLE 5

Find the image of $\triangle ABC$ under a dilation of 3, where the vertices are $A(1, 2)$, $B(6, 5)$, and $C(3, 7)$.

SOLUTION

Under a dilation of 3, we have

Point	Image under dilation of 3
$A(1, 2)$	A' $(3, 6)$
$B(6, 5)$	B' $(18, 15)$
$C(3, 7)$	C' $(9, 21)$

Thus the image of $\triangle ABC$ is $\triangle A'B'C'$, whose coordinates are $A'(3, 6)$, $B'(18, 15)$, and $C'(9, 21)$. ■

The last type of transformation we discuss is a combination of a translation and a reflection. Such a transformation is called a glide reflection. We have

glide reflection

Definition 13.13   A **glide reflection** is a transformation of the plane that represents the composition (in either order) of a line reflection and a translation that is parallel to the line of reflection. It is the result of a slide and a flip.

The pattern of a person's footsteps (see Fig. 13.58) as the person strolls down a street represents a glide reflection. As the person walks, we can reflect footstep 1 in line l to footstep 2, and then translate this image in a direction parallel to the line of reflection. The same pattern occurs from footstep 2 to footstep 3, and so on.

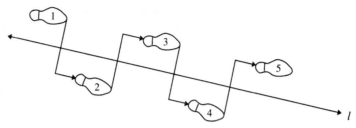

Figure 13.58

Transformations serve as powerful problem-solving tools and permit students to develop a broad concept of congruence and similarity that applies to all figures. The derivation of congruence properties through isometries (distance-preserving transformations) and of similarity properties through composites of dilation (ratio-preserving transformations) and isometries provides a connection with, and a reinforcement of, synthetic methods. Transformations often can be used to represent physical motions, such as slides, flips, turns, and stretches. As we shall see in Section 13.7, you can use the LOGO computer software to explore properties of translations, line reflections, rotations, and dilations, as well as compositions of these transformations. This can be seen in Fig. 13.59, where the LOGO turtle can be used to show the effect on the plane of the composites of two transformations. Such graphic experiences not only help students develop an understanding of the effects of various transformations but also contribute to the development of their skills in visualizing congruent and similar figures.

Even the midpoint formula discussed previously in terms of a coordinate approach can also be proved using a dilation with scale factor 2 (or $\frac{1}{2}$) and with center at the triangle vertex that is common to the two sides whose midpoints are connected.

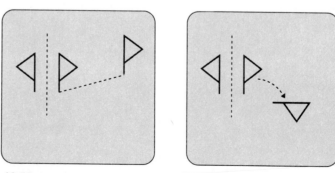

Figure 13.59

EXERCISES FOR SECTION 13.5

1. Find the image of $\triangle ABC$ under a line reflection in line l.

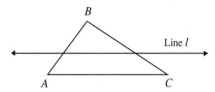

2. Find the image of quadrilateral $ABCD$ after a line reflection in line l.

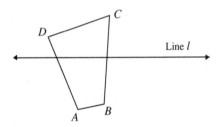

3. Which of the following words has line symmetry? If such symmetry exists, draw the line of symmetry.
a) WOW   **b)** COOK
b) CHOKE   **d)** CODE

4. Find the number of lines of symmetry that each of the following figures has.

a) Heart

b) Octagon

c) Rhombus

d) Equilateral triangle

e) Isosceles trapezoid

5. A translation maps $P(-4, 7)$ onto $P'(8, 3)$. Find the image C' of $C(3, 5)$ under the same translation.

6. Do the following figures have line symmetry, point symmetry, or rotational symmetry, or any combination of these?

a)

b)

For questions 7–13 find the image of (3, 2) under the indicated transformation.

7. A reflection in the x-axis.

8. A reflection in the y-axis.

9. A reflection in the line $y = x$.

10. A reflection through the origin.

11. A translation $T_{4, -7}$

12. A dilation of 7, center at origin.

13. A clockwise rotation of 90° about the origin.

14. Given $\triangle ABC$, whose vertices have coordinates $A(2, 3)$, $B(0, 6)$, and $C(2, 6)$:
a) State the coordinates of $\triangle A'B'C'$, the image of $\triangle ABC$ after a reflection in the y-axis.
b) State the coordinates of $\triangle A''B''C''$, the image of $\triangle A'B'C'$ after a reflection in the line $y = x$.
c) State the coordinates of $\triangle A'''B'''C'''$, the image of $\triangle A''B''C''$ after a rotation of 90° clockwise about the origin.

15. Which of the following has point symmetry?
a) A   **b)** B   **c)** N   **d)** T

16. Which of the following symbols has 90° rotational symmetry?
a) X   **b)** H   **c)** S   **d)** 8

17. Which of the following transformations is not an isometry?
a) line reflection   **b)** translation   **c)** dilation
d) rotation

18. Figure (B) is the image of Fig. (A) under which single transformation?

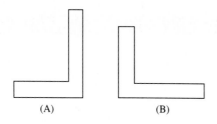

(A)   (B)

a) line reflection   **b)** translation

c) rotation   **d)** glide-reflection

For questions 19–22 refer to the following square.

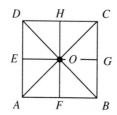

19. Under a reflection in line $\overleftrightarrow{HF}$, find the image of C.

20. Under a reflection through point O, find the image of A.

21. Under a counterclockwise rotation of 90°, find the image of B.

22. Under the translation where A is the image of H, find the image of C.

23. Draw all the lines of symmetry for each of the following.

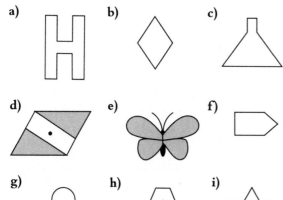

a) **b)** **c)**

d) **e)** **f)**

g) **h)** **i)**

24. How many lines of symmetry does each of the following polygons have?

a) **b)** **c)**

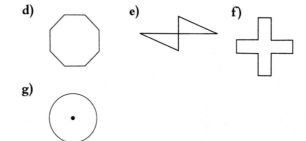

d) **e)** **f)**

g)

25. In each diagram below, quadrilateral $A'B'C'D'$ is the image of quadrilateral $ABCD$ under a transformation in the plane. Identify the type of transformation as a dilation, a translation, a rotation, or a line reflection.

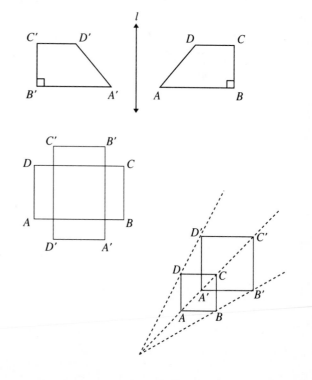

26. Identify the transformation that maps parallelogram $ABCD$ onto rectangle $A'B'C'D'$.

a)

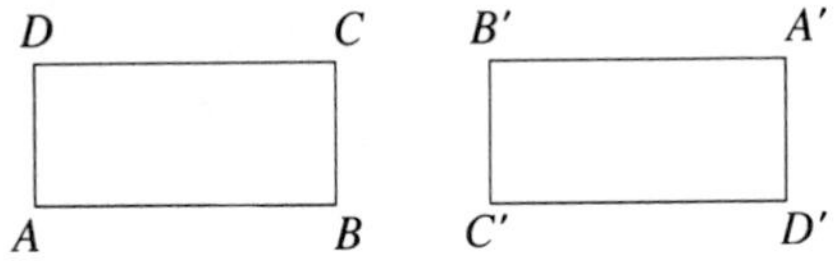

b)

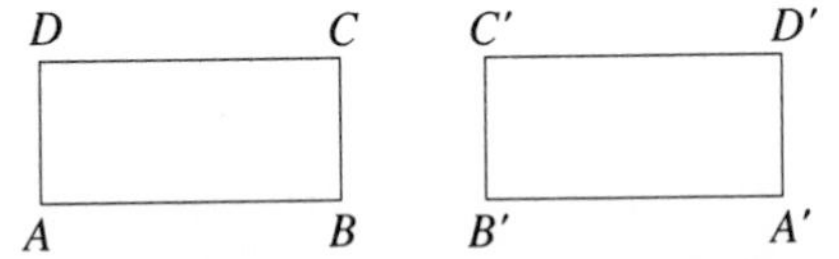

Brain-Teaser Problems

27. $\triangle ABC$ has vertices $A(-5, 7)$, $B(-5, 3)$ and $C(4, 7)$.

a) State the coordinates of $\triangle A'B'C'$ after a reflection of $\triangle ABC$ in the line $y = -x$.

b) State the coordinates of $\triangle A''B''C''$, the image of $\triangle A'B'C'$, after the translation $T_{3,\,4}$

c) Which single transformation maps $\triangle ABC$ onto $\triangle A''B''C''$?

(i) line reflection (ii) glide reflection

(iii) rotation (iv) point reflection.

13.6

TESSELATIONS OF THE PLANE

Let us examine the arrangement of the equilateral triangles shown in Fig. 13.60. We notice that these repeated equilateral triangles cover the entire plane, yet none of the triangles overlap and there are no gaps. This is what we mean by a tesselation. We have

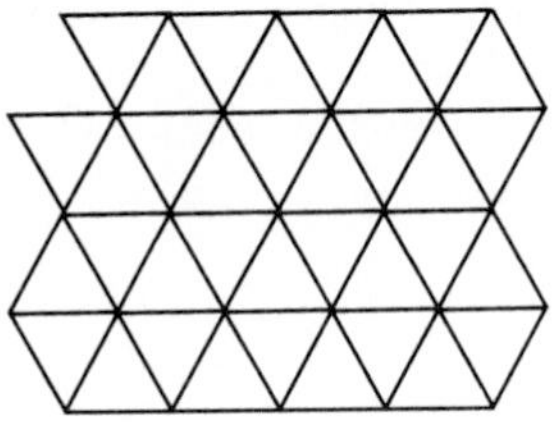

Figure 13.60

> **Definition 13.14** A **tesselation** of the plane is the filling of the entire plane by repeating a figure as many times as needed in such a way that no figures overlap and there are no gaps. The figures have only sides in common.

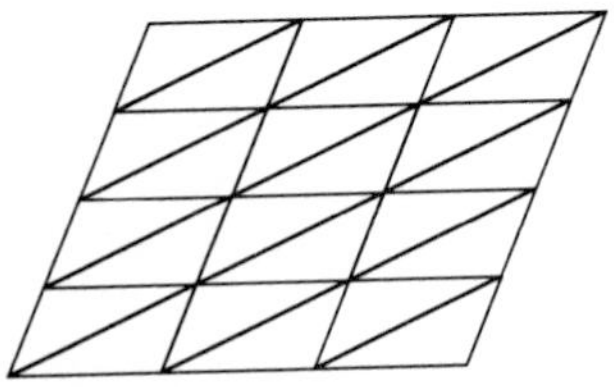

Figure 13.61

Comment Many rooms have mosaic tiles as the flooring. Exactly how they are tiled illustrates the concept of tesselations.

Which polygonal shapes can be used to tile a floor, that is, to form a tesselation? In Fig. 13.60 we note that equilateral triangles can always be used to form a tesselation. Observe that at each vertex we have six equilateral triangles. Since each interior angle is 60°, then the exterior angle at each vertex measures 120°.

Must the triangle be equilateral to form a tesselation? In Fig. 13.61 we have a tesselation with obtuse scalene triangles. In Fig. 13.62 we have a tesselation of the plane with scalene right triangles. It thus should be obvious that any triangle can be used to tesselate a plane.

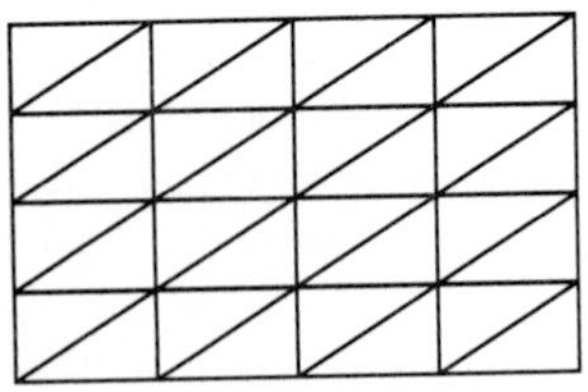

Figure 13.62

What about quadrilaterals? Will any type of quadrilateral tesselate the plane? In Fig. 13.63 we indicate two ways in which squares can be used to tesselate the plane. Parallelograms and trapezoids can also be used to tesselate the plane, as shown in Fig. 13.64.

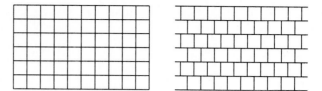

Figure 13.63

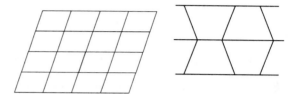

Figure 13.64

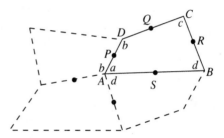

Figure 13.65

As a matter of fact, the following procedure can be used to tesselate the plane with any arbitrary convex quadrilateral. Assume that we are given any quadrilateral, such as the one shown in Fig. 13.65. Successive rotations of the quadrilateral about the midpoints P, Q, R, and S of its sides will generate four congruent quadrilaterals around the common vertex A shown in the diagram. It is suggested that the reader trace the quadrilateral and then actually rotate the quadrilateral $180°$ around the midpoint of any side and trace the images to be convinced that the above procedure does indeed work. As a matter of fact, the above procedure can be used even for nonconvex quadrilaterals. Notice that the sum of the measures of the angles around vertex A is $a + b + c + d$. This actually represents the sum of the measures of the interior angles of the quadrilateral. We already know that this sum is $360°$.

What about regular polygons, regular hexagons, or regular n-gons? Can they form tesselations of the plane by themselves? You will recall from the discussion in Chapter 10 that for any regular polygon of n sides the measure of

Each vertex or interior angle is	Each central angle is	Each exterior angle is
$\dfrac{(n-2)\cdot 180°}{n}$	$\dfrac{360°}{n}$	$\dfrac{360°}{n}$

so that depending on the number of sides (the value of n), the following holds:

Regular polygon of n sides	Measure of interior angle
Triangle $(n = 3)$	60°
Square $(n = 4)$	90°
Pentagon $(n = 5)$	108°
Hexagon $(n = 6)$	120°
Heptagon $(n = 7)$	$\dfrac{900°}{7}$
Octagon $(n = 8)$	135°
Nonagon $(n = 9)$	140°
Decagon $(n = 10)$	144°

It turns out that in order for a regular polygon to form a tesselation of the plane, its vertex must be a divisor of 360°, as a whole number of copies of the polygon must meet at a vertex to form a 360° angle. For a regular pentagon, each vertex angle measures 108°. Since 108° is *not* a divisor of 360°, we can conclude that regular pentagons cannot be used to tesselate the plane; they will not fit together without gaps or overlapping. This can be clearly seen in Fig. 13.66.

Since each vertex angle of a regular hexagon measures 60°, which is a divisor of 360°, we know that regular hexagons can tesselate a plane. In Fig. 13.67 we present one such tesselation.

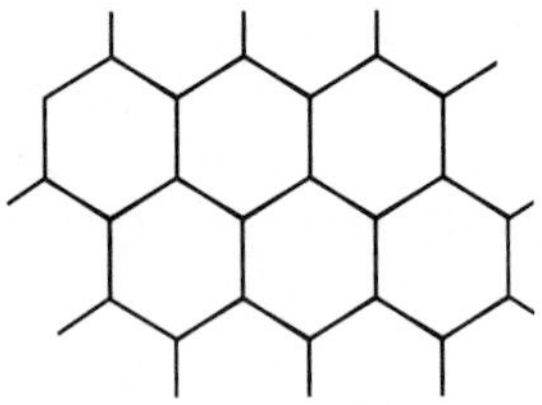

No regular polygon which has more than six sides can tesselate the plane. However, we can combine different regular polygons whose sides have the same length to form tesselations of the plane. When this is done, many interesting patterns can be obtained. One such pattern is shown in Fig. 13.68. Such patterns are often used for tiling a floor, for designing wall covering, or more generally in artistic work. M.C. Escher used tesselations of the plane in his artistic designs. For more details on how this was done, see the Suggested Further Reading list at the end of this chapter. Specifically, read the article by B. Zurstadt.

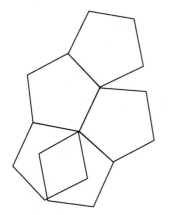

Figure 13.66

Figure 13.67

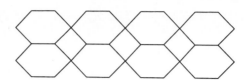

Figure 13.68

EXERCISES FOR SECTION 13.6

1. On a square lattice, draw a tesselation of each of the following triangles.

a)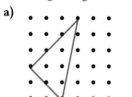

b)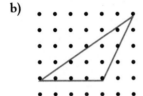

2. On a square lattice, draw a tesselation of each of the following quadrilaterals:

a)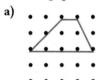

b)

c)

d)

3. A **pentomino** is a polygon composed of five congruent, nonoverlapping squares. Show that it is possible to tesselate the plane with the following pentominos.

a)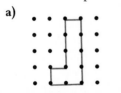

b)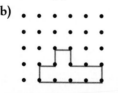

4. Show how the following acute isosceles triangle can tesselate the plane.

5. The **dual of a tesselation** is the tesselation found by connecting the centers of polygons that share a common side. The dual tesselation of the equilateral triangle tesselation is shown below.

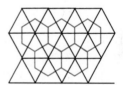

Find the dual tesselation of the following tesselations:

a)   **b)**

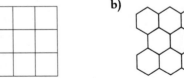

6. Try to find ways of tesselating the plane by using only
    a) equilateral triangles, squares, and regular hexagons
    b) regular octagons and squares

*13.7

USING LOGO TO DRAW SIMILAR AND CONGRUENT FIGURES

We can use the LOGO program to help us construct triangles using parts of a triangle. Before reading further, the reader is urged to review the material on LOGO given earlier, as well as the detailed discussion given later in Section 14.7.

To begin, we will always assume that the turtle is in the HOME position. The following LOGO program can be used to construct triangles when we are given information for an SAS situation.

```
TO SAS :SIDE1 :ANGLE :SIDE2
   FD :SIDE1
   RT  180 — :ANGLE
   FD :SIDE2
   HOME
END
```

EXAMPLE 1

Using the above SAS program, determine the output when the following LOGO program is executed.

    SAS 40 70 45

SOLUTION

When the above is executed, the shape shown in Fig. 13.69 will be drawn by the turtle.

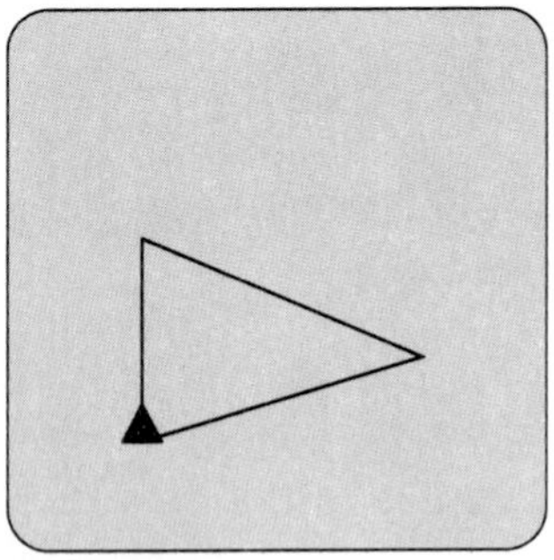

When given information for an ASA situation or an AAS situation, the following LOGO programs can be used.

Figure 13.69

TO ASA :A1 :SIDE :A2
   FD 120
   BK 120
   LT :A1
   FD :SIDE
   RT (180 — :A2)
   FD 120
   HOME
END
	TO AAS :A1 :A2 :SIDE
	   ASA :A1 :SIDE :180 — (:A1 + :A2)
	END

EXAMPLE 2

Using the above ASA program, determine the output when the following LOGO program is executed.

ASA 50 70 60

SOLUTION

When the above is executed, the shape shown in Fig. 13.70 will be drawn by the turtle.

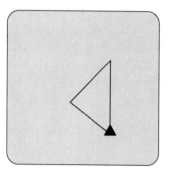

Figure 13.70

EXAMPLE 3

What does the following LOGO program produce?

```
TO SIMILAR.TRIANGLES :SIDE1 :ANGLE :SIDE2 :C
  BACK :SIDE1
  RIGHT :ANGLE
  FORWARD :SIDE2
  HOME
  BACK :C * :SIDE1
  RIGHT :ANGLE
  FORWARD :C * SIDE2
  HOME
END
```

SOLUTION

When executed, the above program produces similar triangles whose sides are *C* times as much as before.

EXAMPLE 4

What does the following LOGO procedure do?

```
TO ANGLE.BISECT :ANGLE
  HT
  RT 90
  FD 60
  BK 60
  LT :ANGLE
  FD 60
  BK 60
  RT :ANGLE/2
  FD 60
  BK 120
  PU
  HOME
  PD
END
```

SOLUTION   The above LOGO program draws the bisector of any arbitrary angle.

EXERCISES FOR SECTION 13.7

For Exercises 1–6, use the LOGO programs given in this section to determine the output when the following LOGO programs are executed.

1. SAS 70 100 70

2. SAS 40 80 50

3. ASA 110 40 20

4. AAS 60 80 50

5. ANGLE.BISECT 150

6. ANGLE.BISECT 40

7. SIMILAR.TRIANGLES 10 50 30 3

8. Write a LOGO procedure to construct triangles using the SSS congruence property.

*9. Write a LOGO procedure to draw a circle with variable center O and variable radius r.

10. We can use LOGO to help us study transformation geometry. The following LOGO program utilizes a procedure, which we have called TRIANGLE, to first draw a triangle with two sides of lengths 20 and 40 with an included angle that measures 100°. Then we use the turtle's SETHEADING (SETH), to tell the turtle the direction of the translation. We have the following:

```
   TO TRIANGLE
     PD
```

```
   FD 20
   MAKE "X XCOR
   MAKE "Y YCOR
   BK 20
   RT 100
   FD 40
   SETXY :X :Y
   END
```

```
   TO TRANSLATE :DIRECTION :DISTANCE
   HT
   TRIANGLE
   PU
   HOME
   SETH :DIRECTION
   FD :DISTANCE
   SETH 0
   PD
   TRIANGLE
   END
```

Using the above program, determine the output when the following LOGO program is executed.

```
   TRANSLATE 30 20
```

11. Write a LOGO computer program to draw a triangle and then to rotate it a specified number of degrees.

TYPICAL CLASSROOM QUESTIONS

1. A student claims that, when given two right triangles, one need only prove that the two legs of one right triangle are congruent to the two legs of the other triangle for the triangles to be congruent. Do you agree?

2. A student claims that the following triangles are congruent by the SAS congruence property. Do you agree?

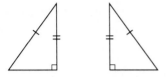

3. One student claims that the two right triangles shown here are congruent, since the hypotenuse and a leg of one of them are congruent to the hypotenuse and leg of the other triangle. A second student says that this is impossible as this represents an SSA situation (when we include the two right angles) and that there is no such thing as an SSA congruence property. Who is right? Explain your answer.

4. Bill and Heather each drew a triangle in which two sides and an angle measured, respectively, 5 cm, 8 cm and 70°. It turns out that the triangles are not congruent. Can you explain what could have happened?

STUDY GUIDE

The following is a chapter outline in capsule form. You should now be able to demonstrate your knowledge of the ideas mentioned by giving definitions or specific examples. Page references are given in parentheses.

Two **polygons are congruent** if there is a one-to-one correspondence between their vertices where all pairs of corresponding angles are congruent and all pairs of corresponding sides are congruent. When two polygons are congruent, their **corresponding parts** are congruent. (p. 747)

Two **triangles are congruent** if they satisfy any of the following conditions:

a) Side, Angle, Side $\cong$ Side, Angle, Side (SAS property)

b) Side, Side, Side $\cong$ Side, Side, Side (SSS property)

c) Angle, Side, Angle $\cong$ Angle, Side, Angle (ASA property)

d) Angle, Angle, Side $\cong$ Angle, Angle, Side (AAS property) (pp. 749–753)

Two **polygons are similar** if there is a one-to-one correspondence between their vertices where all pairs of corresponding angles are congruent and the ratios of the measures of all corresponding sides are equal. (p. 759)

Two **triangles are similar** if and only if at least one of the following are true:

a) Three angles of one triangle are congruent to three angles of another triangle (AAA similarity property)

b) Two angles of one triangle are congruent to two angles of another triangle (AA similarity property)

c) Two pairs of corresponding sides are proportional and their included angles are congruent (SAS similarity property)

d) All three pairs of corresponding sides are proportional (SSS similarity property) (p. 761)

If two triangles are similar, then the **corresponding sides are proportional**. Also, if two triangles are similar, then the corresponding angles are equal in measure. (p. 761)

The following **constructions** using a compass and straightedge were discussed.

1. Constructing a circle with a given center and a specified radius. (p. 766)

2. Constructing a line segment congruent to a given line segment. (p. 768)
3. Constructing an angle congruent to a given angle. (p. 768)
4. Constructing the perpendicular bisector of a given line segment. (p. 769)
5. Constructing the bisector of a given angle. (p. 770)
6. Constructing a perpendicular through a given point on a line. (p. 770)
7. Constructing a perpendicular from a given point to a line. (p. 771)
8. Constructing a line parallel to a given line through a point not on the line. (p. 772)
9. Dividing a given line segment into any number of congruent parts. (p. 773)
10. Locating the center of a circle. (p. 773)
11. Constructing a triangle similar to a given triangle. (p. 774)
12. Circumscribing a circle about a triangle. (p. 775)
13. Inscribing a circle within a given triangle. (p. 776)
14. Inscribing a square in a given circle. (p. 776)
15. Inscribing a regular hexagon in a given circle. (p. 777)

A **transformation** is a one-to-one correspondence between the points in a plane that indicates a change in position or a fixed position for each point in the plane. Under a transformation, each point P is associated with a unique point P', called the **image** of P. Any transformation that preserves distance is called an **isometry**. (p. 781)

A **translation** is a transformation of the plane that shifts every point in the plane the same distance in the same direction to its image. (p. 781)

A **reflection in a line** l is a transformation of the plane such that:

a) for any point on line l, the image of P is P.

b) For any point not on line l, the image of P is P' and line l is the perpendicular bisector of the segment $\overline{PP'}$ (p. 783)

Line symmetry (or **reflectional symmetry**) occurs in a figure when the figure is its own image under a reflection in a line which is called the **axis of symmetry**. (p. 787)

Point symmetry occurs in a figure when the figure is its own image under a reflection in a point. (p. 788)

A **rotation** is a transformation of the plane about a fixed point P, called the **center of rotation**, and through an angle which measures x degrees such that:

a) The image of the fixed point P is P.

b) For any other point, the image of A is A' where $m\,(\angle APA') = x$ and $\overline{PX} = \overline{PX'}$. (p. 791)

Rotational symmetry occurs in a figure if the figure is its own image under a rotation of x degrees and if only the center remains fixed. (p. 791)

A **dilation** of any positive number C is a transformation such that:

a) the image of point O, the center of the dilation, is O.

b) For any other point, the image of P is P' where $\overline{OP}$ and $\overline{OP'}$ name the same ray and $\overline{OP'} = C \cdot \overline{OP}$. C is called the **constant of dilation.** (p. 791)

A **glide reflection** is a transformation of the plane that represents the composition of a line reflection and a translation that is parallel to the line of reflection. It is the result of a slide and a flip. (p. 792)

A **tesselation of the plane** is the filling of the entire plane by repeating a figure as many times as needed in such a way that no figures overlap and there are no gaps. The figures have only sides in common. (p. 796)

The only polygons that tesselate the plane are triangles, (convex) quadrilaterals, and a regular hexagon. (p. 797)

The computer **LOGO** graphics program can be used to construct triangles using parts of a triangle. (p. 800)

KEY TERMS

The following list presents the key terms introduced in this chapter.

13.1 **congruent polygons**
corresponding angles
corresponding sides
congruent triangles
SAS congruence property
ASA congruence property
SSS congruence property
AAS congruence property

13.3 **similar polygons**
similar triangles
proportional

13.5 **transformation**

image
translation
isometry
slide or shift
line reflection
line (reflectional)
symmetry
axis of symmetry
point symmetry
rotations
rotational symmetry
dilation
glide reflection

FORMULAS TO REMEMBER

The following list summarizes all of the formulas discussed in this chapter.

Methods of Proving Triangles

Congruent	Similar
SAS congruence property	AAA similarity property
ASA congruence property	AA similarity
SSS congruence property	SAS similarity property
AAS congruence property	SSS similarity property

A translation that slides any point a units horizontally and b units vertically is denoted as $T_{a, b}(x, y) = (x + a, y + b)$.

Under a line reflection in the y-axis $r_{y\text{-axis}}(x, y) = (-x, y)$

Under a line reflection in the x-axis $r_{x\text{-axis}}(x, y) = (x, -y)$

Under a line reflection in the line $y = x$ $r_{y=x}(x, y) = (y, x)$

Under a point reflection in the origin $R_{\text{origin}}(x, y) = (-x, -y)$

Under a dilation by a positive number c $D_c(x, y) = (cx, cy)$

CHAPTER REVIEW EXERCISES

1. Which figure has $60°$ rotational symmetry?

   a) square   **b)** regular octagon   **c)** equilateral triangle   **d)** regular hexagon.

2. If $A(2, 7)$ is reflected in the line $y = 5$, what are the coordinates of A'?

3. A transformation maps $P(x, y)$ onto $P'(x + 3, y - 2)$. Find the coordinates of Q, whose image under the same transformation is $Q'(6, 2)$.

4. Which letter has horizontal but *not* vertical line symmetry?

   a) X   **b)** O   **c)** V   **d)** E

5. What kind of symmetry does the word TOOT have?

   a) vertical line symmetry only

   b) horizontal line symmetry only

   c) both vertical and horizontal line symmetry

   d) neither horizontal nor vertical line symmetry

6. Find the image of $(3, -2)$ under the dilation D_2.

7. Which transformation does *not* preserve distance?

   a) dilation   **b)** rotation   **c)** line reflection   **d)** point reflection

For questions 8–10 use the following information. $\triangle ABC$ has vertices at $A(-1, -2)$, $B(0, -4)$, and $C(3, -1)$.

8. State the coordinates of $\triangle A'B'C'$, the image of $\triangle ABC$, after a reflection in the origin.

9. State the coordinates of $\triangle A''B''C''$, the image of $\triangle ABC$ after a translation $T_{5, -3}$.

10. State the coordinates of $\triangle A'''B'''C'''$, the image of $\triangle A'B'C'$, after a reflection in the line $y = x$.

11. Which of the following has point symmetry?

   a)

   b)

   c)

   d)

12. How many pairs of congruent triangles can you find in the following picture?

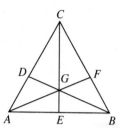

13. In the accompanying figure, triangle *ABC* is similar to triangle *DEF*. If $m(\overline{AC}) = 6$, $m(\overline{AB}) = 7$, $m(\overline{DE}) = 28$, $\angle B \cong \angle E$, and $\angle C \cong \angle F$, find $m(\overline{DF})$.

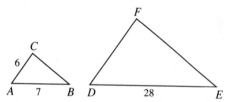

14. The lengths of the sides of triangle *ABC* are 5, 6, and 7. Triangle *RST* is similar to △*ABC*. The longest side of △*RST* is 21. Find the length of the *shortest* side of △*RST*.

15. Consider the following triangles, which are similar. Find *x*.

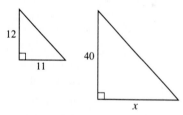

16. A tree 10 meters in height casts a shadow 25 meters long. At the same time a person casts a shadow 5 meters long. What is the number of meters in the height of the person?

17. Which *one* of the following statements can be used to prove that $\overrightarrow{BD}$ bisects $\angle ABC$?

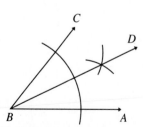

a) An angle has one and only one bisector.

b) The SAS congruence principle.

c) The SSS congruence principle.

18. Which *two* of the following statements can be used to prove that $\overleftrightarrow{CD}$ is perpendicular to $\overleftrightarrow{AB}$ at point D on line $\overleftrightarrow{AB}$?

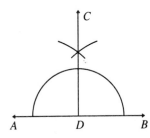

a) Two points equidistant from the ends of a line segment, determine the perpendicular bisector of the line segment.

b) When a straight line is bisected, two right angles are formed.

c) The ASA congruence property.

d) Two right triangles are congruent if the legs of one triangle are congruent to the legs of the other triangle.

19. When constructing one angle congruent to a given angle, which *two* of the following can be used to prove that angle A is congruent to angle A'?

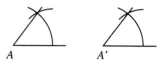

a) Corresponding parts of congruent triangles are congruent.

b) The ASA congruence property.

c) The SSS congruence property.

d) The SAS congruence property.

20. An advertisement poster that is 9 inches long and $5\frac{1}{2}$ inches wide is to be reduced by a photocopying machine so that it will be only $4\frac{1}{2}$ inches long. How wide will the reduced poster be?

21. In the figure shown here, $\overline{AB}$ is the length of a swamp and $\overline{CD}$ is a line segment where $m(\angle ABE) \cong m(\angle DCE)$. If $AE = 150$ yd, $ED = 40$ yd, and $CD = 48$ yd, find AB the length of the swamp.

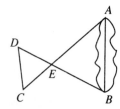

22. For the triangles shown below, specify why $\triangle ABC \cong \triangle A'B'C'$ and then find $\overline{BC}$ and $\overline{B'C'}$.

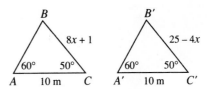

23. For the triangles shown below, specify why $\triangle ABC \sim \triangle A'B'C'$ and then find $\overline{BC}$ and $\overline{B'C'}$.

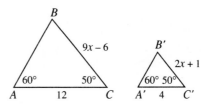

SUGGESTED FURTHER READING

Edwards, R., "Discoveries in Geometry by Folding and Cutting," in *The Arithmetic Teacher* **24** (March 1977), 196–198.

Horak, V., and W. Horak, "Using Geometry Tiles as a Manipulative for Developing Basic Concepts," in *The Arithmetic Teacher* **30** (April 1983), 8–15.

Johnson, M., "Generating Patterns for Transformations," in *The Arithmetic Teacher* **24** (March 1977), 191–195.

Maletsky, E., "Activities: Fun With Flips," in *The Mathematics Teacher* **66** (October 1973), 531–534.

Sanok, G., "Living in a World of Transformations," in *The Arithmetic Teacher* **25** (April 1978), 36–40.

Van de Walle, J., and C. Thompson, "Cut and Paste for Geometrical Thinking," in *The Arithmetic Teacher* **31** (September 1983), 8–13.

Zurstadt, B., "Tesselations and the Art of M.C. Escher," in *The Arithmetic Teacher* **31** (January 1984), 54–55.

CHAPTER 14

Computers and Their Uses

NCTM GUIDELINES

In its March 1989 *Curriculum And Evaluation Standards For School Mathematics* (p. 176), The National Council of Teachers of Mathematics recommends that the mathematics curriculum include topics so that students can

☐ investigate problem situations that arise in connection with computer validation and the application of algorithms.

Computer technology today wields an ever-increasing influence on how mathematics is created and used. Computers are essentially finite, discrete machines, and thus topics from discrete mathematics are essential to solving problems using computer methods.

Mathematics instruction should stress the role of recurrence formulas as important tools for solving enumeration problems, since they can be translated easily into computer programs to obtain solutions. The development and analysis of algorithms lie at the heart of computer methods of solving problems. Thus a consistent effort should be made throughout the mathematics curriculum to provide opportunities for students to construct mathematics from an algorithmic point of view.

It is for this reason that in this chapter we will emphasize how we can write BASIC computer programs to obtain solutions for recurrent situations.

Introduction

We live in a computer age. The computer is a very important work machine. At home, as well as at the office or in school, personal computers are appearing in greater numbers and are being used for a variety of purposes such as word processing, record keeping, accounting, and other workaday tasks. Additionally, computer games have become very popular. Although a good deal of the initial home computer use was generated by games, the widespread availability of personal computers today and the supporting software allow the user to complete office or school work at home.

Computers have been on the market for only a little more than 40 years; nevertheless, in this short time they have become an integral part of our society and our lives. Computers are not electronic beasts as some people claim but are rather very efficient servants of humans (when used properly). As is true of learning to drive a car, operating a computer (mainframe or personal) is an easy task, once you learn how to navigate the keyboard, how to negotiate the disc operating system (DOS), what each applications program can do, and which key gets it to do those things. Computer manufacturers have tried to make computers more "user friendly." However, the newcomer to computers can look forward to a long period of study and trial-and-error.

Our objective in this chapter is to help you become computer literate and to give you an overview of what a computer is and what it is not. After presenting some historical facts about computers, we will discuss how a computer works.

To communicate with a computer, we must use one of the many computer languages available. In this chapter we concentrate on a very popular conversational language called BASIC. This language consists of short, easy-to-learn commands that are quite similar to everyday English. Thus many people can learn to use this language quickly, since no prior computing background knowledge is needed. One can then write computer programs for almost any personal computer. This explains the popularity of the BASIC language.

In this chapter we discuss in detail the BASIC computer language.

14.1

A BRIEF HISTORY OF COMPUTERS

abacus (counting board)

Ever since people learned how to count, they have been looking for ways to make calculations easier. One of the earliest devices invented for this purpose was the **abacus**, or **counting board** (see Fig. 14.1).

Computations using the abacus are performed by moving the beads back and forth along the rods. Although the abacus can be used to perform

Figure 14.1 An abacus

many calculations quickly, it requires a great deal of skill to operate properly. For example, if we add 5 and 8, we get 3 in the "ones" column and must "carry" a 1 to the "tens" column. The abacus cannot do this mechanically. The user must move a bead on the next (tens) rod by hand. This may be one reason why the abacus was not accepted by Western merchants who often had to add large columns of numbers.

The problems encountered in using the abacus led to the invention of other calculating devices in the seventeenth century. One such invention was Napier's bones, which were used to perform multiplication. See the discussion on page 158. The first mechanical adding machine was invented by Blaise Pascal. His adding machine was similar to many modern-day

Pascal's adding machine. In 1642 the French philosopher Blaise Pascal, 19 years old and tired of totaling up figures for his tax-collecting father, invented this fancy machine for adding and subtracting. Its cylinders and gears were housed in a small box. The wheels on top of this box corresponded to units, 10s, 100s, and so on. Each wheel could register the digits 0 through 9. *Courtesy of IBM.*

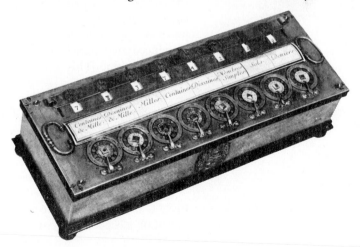

inexpensive desk calculators. The user had to enter each number on a dial by hand and then pull a handle to register the number. This had to be repeated for each number entered. This was a slow and time-consuming process, and various improvements were made on it in the years that followed.

About 150 years later, the Englishman Charles Babbage (1791–1871) invented his "difference engine," which was an automatic calculator capable of doing calculations with numbers of up to 20 decimal places. Although Babbage obtained the financial backing of the British government, his project was not completely successful because the technology of the time had not advanced sufficiently to produce the parts needed for his machine.

In 1833, Babbage began to work on the "analytical engine," which would have the capacity to read data from punched cards, and was to be powered by steam. It also was to have a "memory unit" and a unit for doing arithmetic operations. The results were to be printed out. These ideas are all part of the structure of our modern-day computers. Unfortunately, Babbage did not succeed because neither the funds nor the technology to complete the project was available.

The first major advance in computers came about as a direct result of the 1890 United States Census. It had taken the U.S. Census Bureau almost nine years to tabulate the results of the 1880 census. The population of the United States had grown considerably in the years from 1880 to 1890, and it was rather obvious that considerably more time would be needed to process the 1890 results. At the time, Herman Hollerith (1860–1927) was working in the U.S. Patent Office. Hollerith knew that Joseph Marie Jacquard had invented a weaving loom that used punched cards. In 1804, Jacquard had built a loom capable of producing the most complicated designs and controlled by means of punched cards (see the photograph on p. 000). "Instructions" to the machine were punched on a card, which then wove the appropriate design. Hollerith was convinced that punched cards could be used to enter numbers into an adding machine. This would make the tallying of the census figures much easier.

An early keypunch machine.
Courtesy of IBM.

automatic data-processing machine

Several years later, Hollerith did indeed invent such a machine. He invented the first **automatic data-processing machine**. In 1896, Hollerith started the Tabulating Machine Corporation. This company was later to become the International Business Machines Corporation, commonly known as IBM. With the help of Hollerith's machine the 1890 census was completed in three years.

In 1971 a miniature computer (as opposed to the original 30-ton ENIAC computer of 1946) utilizing a microprocessor was invented. This invention has opened the way for computers that are much smaller but just as efficient.

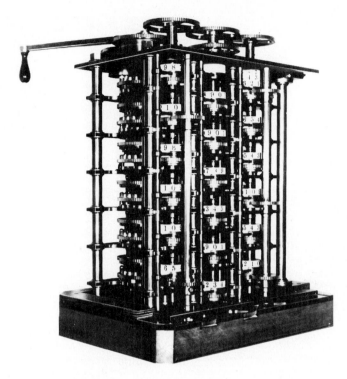

Babbage's multiplier. The computing element of Babbage's complex machine for multiplying was a series of toothed wheels on shafts. They worked like the wheels of a modern mileage indicator. *Courtesy of IBM.*

microprocessor

The **microprocessor** is actually a computer on a silicon chip, since it contains the entire processing unit of a computer. A tiny microprocessor is at the heart of the personal computer. The first personal computer, the Altair 880C, appeared on the market shortly after the microprocessor was designed.

fifth-generation computers

Japanese scientists today are feverishly trying to develop **fifth-generation computers** using a parallel processing technology. Such artificial-intelligence computers would use logical rules rather than arithmetic operations to act on information. Current predictions are that such machines would work about 2000 times faster than today's most advanced computers and would be capable of making 1 billion inferences per second.

advanced mainframe supercomputer

The United States and Japan are currently in a technological race to be the first country to develop an **advanced mainframe supercomputer** that would run 2000 times as fast as our present-day super computer, which runs about 500 million operations per second in a short burst. Today, supercomputers are used in designing aircraft, in geological expeditions for oil, and even in designing circuits for other computers. Currently, the CRAY X-MP computer built by the Cray Research Company is one of the fastest and most powerful supercomputers in the world.

Suspect Arrested

NEW YORK: The Federal Bureau of Investigation announced today the arrest of a suspect in the recent burglary of a Brooklyn bank. Extensive computer traces of fingerprints and criminal records by the National Crime and Information Center of the FBI in Washington led to the arrest. The name of the suspect was not disclosed pending further investigation.

THE BULLETIN, March 11, 1988

Computer Goof

BERGENVILLE—Bank officials were at a loss to explain how a $100,000 mistake went unnoticed for several days. According to Al Carlton, President of County Savings Bank, an unidentified depositor closed his savings account last week. The computer inadvertently made out a check in the amount of $100,000 instead of $1000. The mistake went unnoticed until a routine audit disclosed the mistake. In the meantime, the check had been cashed. The unidentified depositor has since moved out of town without leaving a forwarding address.

THE DAILY, August 20, 1989

Computers are becoming more a part of our lives with each passing day. When used properly, they can be extremely helpful in such areas as criminal investigations. This is shown by the first newspaper article above. When used improperly, they can produce great monetary losses as illustrated by the second newspaper article. Computers can also be used in a variety of other ways both in the scientific field and in the general business field.

Since a computer is only a huge piece of metal, how does the computer do it? Can a computer think? Will computers replace people?

Computers have been on the market for about 35 years. In this short period of time they have already become a necessity for many businesses, schools, hospitals, and government agencies. This is because of the computer's wide-ranging capabilities, as we shall see shortly. Even small companies today are finding it harder and harder to compete in business unless they have access to a computer. Typically, many businesses and offices have desktop microcomputers installed on or near the executive's desk. Information stored within these computers can be "brought up" and displayed on a computer screen by pushing a few buttons. Stored information can also be updated instantly.

In the future, we can expect increased use of the computer. It is even possible that every home will actually have its own terminal hooked up to a large computer or at least have a microcomputer.

Today, a large high-speed computer is capable of doing far more work than most users actually need. Moreover, such computers are costly, and often a company cannot afford to buy or rent such a machine. It is particularly costly and wasteful if the machine is left unused for large periods of time. Therefore many companies do not buy or rent their own computers. Instead they buy time on another computer. This is called **time-sharing**. In time-sharing, a company has a *terminal* that looks like a large typewriter. The terminal is connected (by telephone or other means) to a computer that may be many miles away from the terminal. The user types programs on the terminal and receives results back the same way. The user pays only for the time that the computer is used or the time that he or she wants it available for use. Because of the computer's tremendous capacity, many different terminals can be hooked up to the same computer. With such an arrangement the computer can work on several programs at the same time.

time-sharing

> When used effectively, computers can be great servants as they perform tasks at lightning speeds. Nevertheless, as the newspaper article indicates, some people program the computer to do the wrong thing. Thus they can make the computer an accomplice to their embezzlement schemes.

Computer Crime up Again

WASHINGTON—Government officials announced yesterday the establishment of a special task force to combat the increase in computer crime. Under the scheme, some shady employees were bilking banks out of millions of dollars by programming the computer to register loans to various customers when such transactions never actually occurred. The employees would then pocket the money. When the customers complained, the computers were then programmed to transfer the loan to a second customer, and so on.

The task force will thoroughly investigate the security system that is being used by the banks and will recommend some restrictions on who has access to the programming of such transactions on a computer.

COMPUTER NEWS, February 13, 1985

14.2

HOW A COMPUTER WORKS

Although a computer can perform difficult and time-consuming calculations at lightning speeds, we must realize that it is not capable of doing its own thinking. In this chapter we discuss only the type of computer called **digital**. Most of the computers produced in the United States today are of this type. There is another type of computer called an **analog computer**,

digital computer
analog computer

which we will not discuss at all. Such computers are widely used in science.

program

Before a computer can begin performing functions, it must be told exactly what has to be done. This is accomplished by writing a **program**. A program is a set of instructions telling the computer exactly what has to be done and in what order. This is the job of the **computer programmer** who actually writes the program.

computer programmer

Depending upon the task that is to be done, programs can be written in many different languages, each suited to a particular need. Great care must be exercised when writing computer programs. With the slightest mistake, even a minor spelling mistake, the machine will not be able to proceed. The machine will then send you a **syntax error** message, meaning that you have made a programming error. This will occur no matter what programming language is used. The program then has to be **debugged** to find the error. Often it is a difficult task to find the error.

syntax error

debugged

high-level languages

Computing languages can generally be divided into two main categories: **high-level languages** and **low-level languages**. High-level languages, such as BASIC, FORTRAN, PILOT, LOGO, and Pascal, use commands and concepts in a manner that is comparable to everyday human language and thought. No extensive background knowledge of the computer or of programming is needed to use these languages.

low-level languages

On the other hand, the low-level languages, that is assembly language and machine language, require that the user have some background knowledge of the computer. Generally speaking, they take longer to learn. However, the reward is a detailed knowledge of what the computer is actually doing.

Some of the more commonly used programming languages are the following:

1. **BASIC**, which represents the words Beginner's All-purpose Symbolic Instruction Code, was invented by John Kemeny at Dartmouth College. BASIC is used widely by business and personal computer systems because of its simplicity. No prior programming ability is needed to quickly learn and easily use this language. In this chapter we will discuss some details of BASIC.

2. **PL/1**, which represents the words Programming Language One, is a general-purpose language that can be used by both experienced and beginning programmers. It is used primarily when working with the large mainframe computer rather than with the personal microcomputer.

3. **COBOL**, which represents the words Common Business Oriented Language, is a business-oriented programming language. As with PL/1, it is used primarily when working with the large mainframe computers.

4. **FORTRAN**, which represents the words <u>Fo</u>rmula <u>Tra</u>nslator, is used primarily in scientific-oriented or mathematical research. Its combination of mathematical simplicity and power accounts for its popularity in solving many scientific and business problems. FORTRAN's weakness lies in its ability to handle input and output, for example, in generating reports or manipulating text.

5. **Pascal** was developed to teach programming as a clear, systematic approach to problem solving. Statements in Pascal are put together much like statements in English.

6. **Logo**, a recently created language, introduces programming to children in an intuitive way. A turtle (a small triangle that moves around the screen) is used to draw different geometric figures. The language is designed to introduce programming concepts in a problem-solving manner.

7. **PILOT** was designed for teachers. It enables the teacher to generate computer-aided instruction lessons, including graphics, for classroom use.

Today there are well over 175 different programming languages in use, and new languages are constantly being developed to suit some particular need.

input unit

How does a computer work? All computers must have an **input unit**. The input mechanism enters the data and instructions into the machine. "Input" into the machine can be accomplished by using punched cards, paper tapes, console typewriters, discs, magnetic tapes, or optical scanners such as those used in many supermarkets. Input might even be at a terminal in an office miles away from the computer. If a punched card is used, it is placed into a card reader, and the machine will "read" the information from the card by noting the presence or absence of holes in certain positions. This information is punched on the card using one of the many possible progamming languages. The information on the card is then transferred by means of electrical impulses into a **compiler**.

compiler

Although we perform all our arithmetical calculations in the decimal system, computers perform these calculations in the binary system (see Chapter 3). With the modern-day computer, it is not necessary for the programmer to convert decimal numbers into binary system numbers. All of this is done by the compiler or coder. The compiler converts numbers and instructions into binary numbers so that the machine can understand them. Before the compiler became part of the computer, programmers had to do all of the translation themselves; that is, they had to type in instructions and data that were already written in the binary system.

control unit

After the input information has been translated into a language that the machine can understand, the information is passed on (by way of electrical signals) to the **control unit**. The control unit receives and interprets the instructions that it receives from the input unit. Then the control unit sends these signals to the various other units, called the **arithmetic unit**, the **memory unit**, and the **output unit**. The control unit determines which calculations are necessary for a given problem and in which order these calculations must be performed in order to solve the problem. The control unit also keeps track of the proper sequencing of the mathematical computations performed in the arithmetic unit. The control

central processing unit (CPU)

unit with the processing unit make up the **central processing unit (CPU)**.

arithmetic unit

The **arithmetic unit** performs all the calculations that are needed to solve a given problem. All computations that are performed here are done in the binary system.

memory unit

The **memory unit** stores all the data, whether a number, an instruction for performing a calculation, or the results of the calculation itself. Information can be sorted in several ways. Many computers store information by using magnetic cores. These tiny doughnut-shaped pieces of metal, which are called *bits*, are no larger than a pinhead. The memory unit of a typical machine has thousands of such cores. These cores can be magnetized in one of two directions. When magnetized in one direction, the number 1 is represented, and when magnetized in the other direction the number 0 is represented. With improvements in technology the size of these magnetic cores is constantly decreasing.

As we mentioned earlier, computers use the binary system, in which only the digits 0 and 1 are used. Each 0 or 1 in the binary system is called

bit

a **bit**. By themselves, single bits cannot store all of the numbers, letters, and special characters that a computer must process. Instead, the bits are put together in groups usually containing six or eight bits. Such groups are

bytes

called **bytes**.

The storage capacity of a computer is often expressed in terms of the letter K. A **kilobyte** is K bytes, that is, 1024 bytes. Most microcomputers have between 4K and 64K bytes. Minicomputers have anywhere from 64K bytes to 1 megabyte (millions of bytes), and the large mainframe computers have from 512K bytes up to 16 megabytes and even more.

chips

Many third-generation computers store information using cores grouped into small **chips** that are no larger than one-eighth of an inch on each side. There are 256 cores on a typical chip. Such storage ability greatly increases the capabilities of the machine. The more storage places a memory unit has, the more information the computer can store. The size of these magnetic cores, which are usually grouped into small *chips*, has been constantly decreasing, thereby increasing the memory capabilities of the machine.

magnetic drums
discs

Some computers store information by using **magnetic drums** or **discs**. Such drums are usually about one foot in diameter. Information is stored in these drums by magnetizing certain spots on the drums or discs.

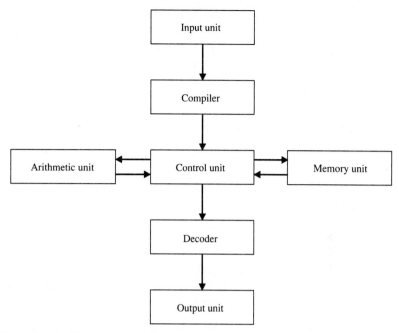

Figure 14.2 The parts of a modern computer

output unit

After the computer solves the problem, the control unit sends the solution to the **output unit**. Before reaching the output unit, the solution is decoded from machine language back into the programming language being used. The output unit may give the answer by printing the result on paper, by punching holes in a card, by displaying it visually on a video screen, or by plotting a graph. These all depend on how the machine has been programmed.

hardware

In Fig. 14.2 we show the parts of a computer and how they interact with each other. The physical parts of a computer are referred to as the **hardware**. This includes the machine itself, the terminals, the typewriters, card readers and printers, magnetic tapes and discs, etc. On the other hand, the programming techniques and the actual programs are referred to as the **software**. In recent years there has been remarkable progress in both the hardware and software areas of the computer industry.

software

EXERCISES FOR SECTION 14.2

1. Why is machine language referred to as a low-level language?

2. When using programming languages, when is debugging necessary?

3. What is the difference between a high-level and a low-level language?

Each of Exercises 4–8 gives an alternative programming language. In each case, state what the abbreviation stands for, and then discuss when the language might be used. (Consult the library if necessary.)

4. RPG   **5.** ALGOL   **6.** APL

7. LISP   **8.** SNOBOL

9. When would a syntax error message appear on a computer monitor?

10. How does the control unit or central processing unit (CPU) get its input?

11. Which part of the computer is in charge of arithmetic, logic, decision-making, and the like?

12. Name several ways in which a computer can receive information or instructions.

13. What is the significance of having a computer with internal storage capabilities?

14. Why might the CPU be called a *microprocessor*?

15. Which part of the computer can be called the "brain" of the computer? Why?

16. How does the computer let a human see the results of its calculations?

17. What do card readers, disc drives, even telephone hook-ups (modems) all have in common?

18. What is the difference between a digital and an analog computer? (Consult the library if necessary.)

14.3

USING PERSONAL COMPUTERS

microcomputers

More and more people are purchasing personal computers these days than ever before. Such **microcomputers**, as they are called, have microprocessors for their CPU (central processing unit) and usually have memory of 1024K or less. People use these computers for a multitude of functions. Some of these are the following:

a) Business accounting

b) Home accounting

c) Writing programs to sell or use

d) Playing games

e) Education (e.g., spelling, math, vocabulary)

f) Helping learn more about computers

g) Learn programming

h) Word processing

i) Filing/record keeping

j) Technical calculations

k) Telecommunications linking to other computer information systems.

Recent surveys show that the most frequent application for computers at home is word-processing, and not game-playing. A personal computer combined with a word processor allows the user to compose documents on a screen. A document can be reorganized, revised, and corrected as the user moves along. More sophisticated word processing programs designed for business and professional use even allow the user to combine several documents into one or to produce fancy printing and layouts. Some word-processing programs even automatically check for spelling or typing errors against a dictionary of words stored by the program.

hardware

All personal computer systems (no matter which brand) consist of certain basic components called **hardware**. Some computer systems may have more components than others, but the most important parts are the following:

microprocessor

1. **Microprocessor.** The microprocessor carries out sequences of instructions (called programs) stored in an area of the computer's main memory.

main memory

2. **Main memory.** This is where a computer stores programs while it is running them. Whenever only a portion of the main memory (that is running a program) is being used, then the remaining portion is available for storing information entered at the keyboard or other information that the computer is working on.

keyboard

3. **The keyboard.** The keyboard allows the user to send information to the computer. The user can type text or push certain control characters.

Additionally, to make the computer useful, various input/output devices must be connected to the computer to complete the system. These

peripherals

are called the **peripherals** of the system and include the following:

computer monitor

4. **A computer monitor or display device.** A monitor enables the computer to convey information to the user either in words or numbers (text) or in pictures (graphics) on a screen.

disc drive

5. **A disc drive.** A disc drive reads and writes information on a magnetic disc in much the same way that a tape recorder can record and play back music. Information saved on a disc can be recalled and loaded back into main memory. Otherwise, when a computer is turned off, everything in main memory is lost.

flexible (floppy) or hard discs

6. **Flexible (floppy) or hard discs.** A disc is similar to tape used with a tape recorder. Some discs are completely blank, and the user stores any information created on them. Others have prerecorded programs on them. These are usually purchased in a computer supply store.

operating system

Depending upon the computer's microprocessor, a computer needs a master control program that synchronizes the execution of computer programs. This is known as the computer's **operating system**. Different computers use different operating systems. Often a computer that has been designed for use with one operating system can be made to run on a different operating system. This can be accomplished by purchasing a special circuit board. It is important to know in advance the type of operating system that a computer has, since not all of the thousands of commercially available programs run on all operating systems.

printer

Regardless of the brand of computer used, one usually needs a **printer** to transfer information from the computer to paper. Often, in addition to hardware incompatability, there is at least partial incompatability between a printer and the programs being used. The computer program simply does not understand the printer's codes.

computer graphics

Printers can be used to generate graphics. **Computer graphics** can include drawings, maps, photo-images, graphs, and shapes with varying details. To accomplish this, a printer must be able to produce tiny dots on the paper within close tolerances. These tiny dots are created when the print head fires one pin at a time.

dot-matrix

A computer printer can be of the **dot-matrix** type. A printer of this type has a print head consisting of one or more vertical rows of tiny pins that strike an inked ribbon against the paper as the print head moves back and forth. Such printers can create letters of any shape or graphics such as charts and maps of any kind.

daisy-wheel

Computer printers can also be of the **daisy-wheel** type. In this type of printer a wheel spins until the desired letter is in position. A hammer then strikes it against the ribbon, which in turn strikes the paper. Generally speaking, the characters produced by a daisy-wheel printer are of much better quality than those of the dot-matrix printer, though the daisy-wheel printer cannot produce graphics.

laser printers

Today there are even **laser printers**. High quality type and graphics are etched via a laser beam onto a rotating drum. Toner then coats the drum and is fused onto paper as it passes under the drum. The graphics possibilities and the large selection of typefaces available make laser printers a popular option for the desk-top publisher.

If you determine that you need a personal computer, then you must decide in advance what you will use it for. In turn, this will help you decide what type of computer to buy, what type of printer and/or peripherals to look for, and what software or commercially available programs are needed.

EXERCISES FOR SECTION 14.3

1. What is the function of a microprocessor?

2. What is the difference between a dot-matrix computer printer and a daisy-wheel computer printer?

3. Why is it necessary to have an operating system for a personal computer?

4. Personal computers are often used for data base management and for electronic spreadsheets. Explain how personal computers accomplish this. (Use a library to obtain additional information if necessary.)

5. A **modem** is a device that enables a user to "hook up" with another computer through a telephone connection. Explain the advantages of using a modem.

6. Computer "hackers" are individuals who use their personal computers to illegally obtain information from another computer's memory. Can you explain how this is accomplished and what can be done to prevent it?

14.4

PROGRAMMING A COMPUTER

computer program

As we mentioned earlier, if you want a computer to do a job for you, it must be given detailed, step-by-step instructions. If one step is left out, then the machine cannot do the job properly. These instructions are contained in the **computer program**, which is fed into the machine.

A computer program can be written in many different languages as mentioned earlier in this chapter. As was also mentioned then, we will be talking specifically about BASIC.

The BASIC (Beginner's All-purpose Symbolic Instruction Code) language was developed by John Kemeny at Dartmouth College during the 1960s.[1] BASIC is easy to learn because it is similar in many respects to ordinary English and mathematics. It should be pointed out that our discussion is not intended to be a complete and detailed analysis of the BASIC language but is merely intended to give you a feeling for the kind of detail that is necessary to get a program to run on a machine. A more complete discussion can be found in any manual on BASIC.

Flowcharts

flowchart

Often the number of steps involved in writing a program is lengthy and quite complicated. In such cases it is usually advisable to first draw a **flowchart**. This is a diagram indicating the logical sequence of steps to be followed by the computer; that is, flowcharts show us what is to be done

TABLE 14.1

Symbols commonly used when drawing flowcharts

Symbol	When used
⬭ or ◯	to indicate the beginning or end of a program
▱	to indicate input or output of data
▭	to indicate the processing of the program
◇	to indicate that a decision must be made and to show the branching to different alternatives depending on the decision made
← or ↓ or →	to indicate the direction to go in the flowchart to find the next step

---

[1] Recently published are new "structured" forms of BASIC such as *TRUE BASIC* by Kemeny and Kurtz.

and in what order. They also indicate when decisions have to be made. Flowcharts can help us analyze programs since they provide a visual insight into what is happening.

When drawing a flowchart, it is standard to use circles (or ovals) to indicate the beginning or end of a program and rectangles to indicate the processing of a program. Input/output is usually indicated by using the parallelogram symbol. We also use the diamond symbol to indicate that a decision must be made. These symbols are illustrated in Table 14.1.

Let us construct flowcharts for several different situations.

EXAMPLE 1

Construct a flowchart to compute the area A of a triangle whose base B is 8 cm and whose height H is 12 cm.

SOLUTION

This is a rather simple program since no decisions must be made. The flowchart is shown in Fig. 14.3.

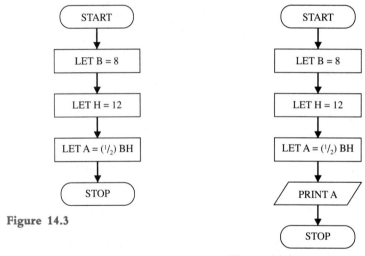

Figure 14.3

Figure 14.4

A program written from this flowchart will tell the computer to find the area by multiplying one-half of the base, 8, by the height, 12, obtaining 48. However, since the computer cannot talk to us, how are we to be told the answer? Obviously, we must tell the computer to print out the answer that it obtains. The flowchart for this problem would now be as shown in Fig. 14.4. ■

Comment When using flowcharts, we follow the arrows from step to step.

EXAMPLE 2

Consumer price index. The Consumer Affairs Department of New York City keeps accurate records on the prices of different items. It then publishes a weekly cost-of-living index. It usually has its shoppers purchase the same items on a weekly basis in local supermarkets. It then computes the average cost of these items. Assume that the shoppers have purchased 25 different items. Write a flowchart to help the department find the average cost of these items.

SOLUTION

To calculate the mean (average), we must first tell the computer what the prices are. This is accomplished by a READ statement, such as READ A_1, A_2, A_3, ..., A_{25}, where the A_i values are the prices of the items. This READ instruction gets the numbers into the computer. Once the prices have been entered, we have the computer add them and then divide the sum by 25. Finally, we want the computer to print out the result. The flowchart that accomplishes these things is shown in Fig. 14.5. ■

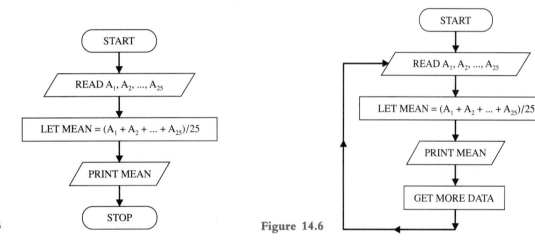

Figure 14.5

Figure 14.6

EXAMPLE 3

In the preceding example, suppose the department would like to reuse the program and compare the results for several weeks. Write a flowchart to help the department find the average price for several weeks.

SOLUTION

looping

In this case the same program can be used over and over again for each week. The only thing that will be different is the data for the different weeks. We indicate that the computer is to do the same thing by **looping** it back to the READ statement to start again. The flowchart that accomplishes this is shown in Fig. 14.6. When the computer runs out of data it will stop automatically. ■

Let us now draw a flowchart for a situation in which a decision is involved.

EXAMPLE 4

Write a flowchart to print the square roots of the first 25 (natural) numbers.

SOLUTION

In this case the flowchart will involve a loop and a decision symbol. It is shown in Fig. 14.7. Let us analyze this flowchart carefully. The first step tells the computer that $N = 1$ and then that $A = \sqrt{N} = \sqrt{1} = 1$. The computer prints this information. The computer must now decide if $N > 25$ or not. If the answer is yes, then the program is done, and the computer stops. If the answer is no, then the machine increases the value of N by 1. In BASIC computer language we write $N = N + 1$. This is not to be interpreted as an algebraic equation. Instead, it is an instruction to the computer that the new value of N, wherever it appears from now on, is to be the old value with one added to it. With this change in mind the computer now loops back to find the value of A. Since N is now 2, the value of A is $\sqrt{2}$, or 1.414. The same procedure is followed until the value of N reaches 25 when the program ends and the computer stops. ■

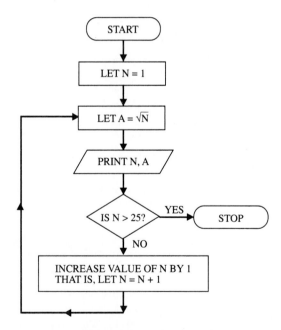

Figure 14.7

Comment When using the diamond symbol to indicate that a decision is to be made, we must tell the computer what to do with each alternative, that is, how to proceed if the answer to the question is yes or if the answer is no.

In Section 14.5, when we actually write computer programs in BASIC, we suggest that you always draw a flowchart appropriate for the problem so that you can actually see how a logical thought or process becomes an instruction to be executed by the computer.

EXERCISES FOR SECTION 14.4

1. Write a flowchart to find the area of a trapezoid whose bases are 10 cm and 16 cm and whose height is 8 cm. (*Hint: $A = \frac{1}{2}$ height $\times$ (base 1 + base 2).*)

2. Write a flowchart to find the average of the numbers 23, 79, 68, 41, 83, and 72.

3. Write a flowchart to find the median of the numbers 23, 79, 68, 41, 83, and 72.

4. Write a flowchart to find the mode of the numbers 23, 79, 68, 41, 83, and 72.

5. Write a flowchart to find the average deviation of the numbers 23, 79, 68, 41, 83, and 72.

6. Write a flowchart to find the standard deviation of the numbers 23, 79, 68, 41, 83, and 72.

7. Write a flowchart to convert an angle measured in radians to an angle measured in degrees.

8. Write a flowchart to convert the measure of a liquid from gallons to liters.

9. Write a flowchart to convert the weight of a person from pounds to grams.

10. Write a flowchart to determine the cost of sending a telegram of 33 words if the cost for the first 8 words is 86 cents and the cost for each additional word is 7 cents.

11. Write a flowchart to find the square root of the integers from 10 to 25.

12. Write a flowchart to find the cube root of the integers from 15 to 25.

13. The State Lottery Commission pays one particular vendor 8 cents for each lottery ticket that she sells. Additionally, if she sells more than 1000 lottery tickets for any one drawing, she is given an extra 3 cents for every lottery ticket over 1000 that she sells. Assuming that she sells more than 1000 tickets in a week, write a flowchart to determine the number of dollars D in her weekly income in terms of the number N of tickets sold.

14. Write a flowchart to determine the number of passengers N on an airplane if there are D double seats and T triple seats, each of which is occupied.

15. A cashier earns $8 an hour for the first 30 hours per week worked and $13 for each hour over 30 hours worked per week. Write a flowchart that the company can use to compute the weekly earnings E of its cashiers if a cashier works H hours per week.

In each of the Exercises 16–19, tell what the flowchart does.

16.

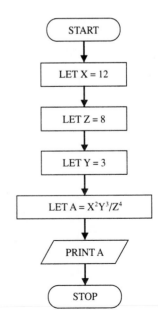

17.

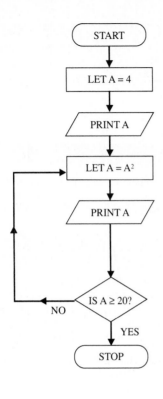

18.

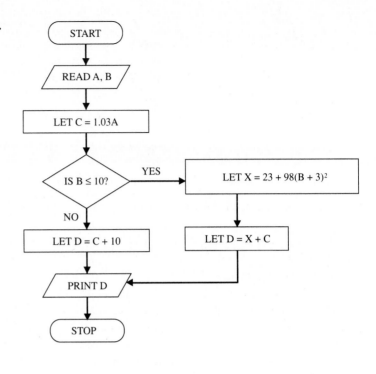

19.

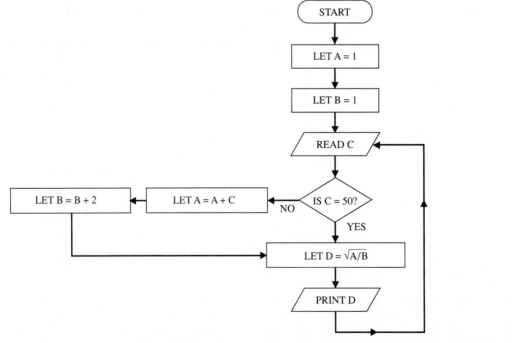

**20. Write a flowchart to determine the maximum finance charge that can be charged by banks and oil companies on any outstanding indebtedness as shown in the table to the right:

**21. Write a flowchart to convert the number $1101101_{(2)}$ written in base 2 to a number in base 10.

State	Average daily balance	Monthly rate of interest
Ohio	Less than $400	$1\frac{1}{2}\%$
	$400 and over	1%
Minnesota	All	1%
New York	Less than $500	$1\frac{1}{2}\%$
	$500 and over	1%
Arizona	All	$\frac{5}{6}\%$

14.5

SOME SAMPLE BASIC PROGRAMS

In this section we will actually write some sample BASIC programs. It should be pointed out that, depending on the capabilities and design of the computer machines at different schools, the actual programs may have to be changed slightly to conform to a machine's specifications before they will actually run. However, the programs we give should work on the vast majority of the computers in use today.

Let us consider the Abel Office Equipment Company, which rents photocopying machines for a flat rental fee of $100 a month plus a charge of 4 cents for each copy made. Since each customer pays the same rental fee of $100 and the same 4 cents for each copy made, the company is interested in writing a BASIC program that would determine the amount of money to bill each customer depending on the number of copies made. How can such a program be written?

As we indicated in the last section, it is usually advisable to first draw a flowchart that indicates the logical sequence to be followed by the computer. It is important to remember that a program will run *only* if the commands of the programming language are used.

Since personal computers are gaining in popularity, let us pause for a moment to discuss how we input information into the computer. The first thing we do is turn on the computer and the monitor. When this is done, a flashing square, flashing rectangle, or flashing line will appear on the monitor. This flashing square is called a **cursor**. At this point you should begin typing your program much as you would do on any typewriter. The cursor will move and will appear where the next typed item will appear on the monitor. Try this with the programs given in this section. As a statement is typed, it will appear on the monitor. However, it is not entered into the computer's memory until the return key or enter key is pressed. Thus if a typing mistake is discovered before the return key is

cursor

pressed, just move the cursor to the appropriate position and make the necessary corrections. If a mistake is discovered after the return key has been pressed, then we proceed as follows: As we shall see shortly, each step of a program has a line number. We can correct an error on a line that has already been entered into the computer's memory by retyping the same line, making any necessary corrections and using the same line number as the original line that had an error. The computer then replaces the line that has an error with the corrected version.

syntax error

If you attempt to run a program and you have made an error in programming, then the computer will inform you that you have made a **syntax error**. Usually, this means that you made a mistake in typing or that you left something out. Be careful. Make any necessary corrections as indicated above, or else the program will not run or you will not obtain the desired results.

In what follows, we give some sample BASIC programs. It is suggested that if you have access to a computer, you actually use it. Type and then run the programs given. Such hands-on experience is very valuable.

EXAMPLE 1

Suppose one customer of the Abel Office Equipment Company made 1505 copies on the rented photocopier during a particular month. Write a BASIC program to determine the amount of money that the company should bill the customer.

SOLUTION

Let N = the number of copies made during the month and let C = the charge for these N copies. A flowchart and a BASIC program that can be used to determine the amount of money A that the customer should be billed are shown below.

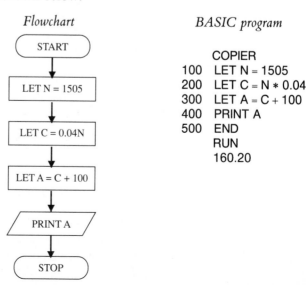

Flowchart

START

LET N = 1505

LET C = 0.04N

LET A = C + 100

PRINT A

STOP

BASIC program

```
      COPIER
100   LET N = 1505
200   LET C = N * 0.04
300   LET A = C + 100
400   PRINT A
500   END
      RUN
      160.20
```

Although the above BASIC progam will accomplish the job, there are many steps that should be added so that the program is really useful. As we proceed with our discussion of this program, we will add many extra steps so that by the time we are done we will have a "useful" program. In each case we will indicate why the extra step (instruction to the computer) was added.

Let us now analyze our simple program. We notice that this program has been named COPIER. Each program that is run on the computer should have a name, which can be no longer than six characters. Although we are free to choose any name we want for any program, it is best to select a name that will identify the program being run. In our case we have selected the six-letter word COPIER as the name of the program for obvious reasons. A program *must* have a name if one wishes to save it and reuse it at a later date.

Notice that each line in the program has a number. We can use any numbers from 1 to 99999 as the line numbers, provided that they are chosen in numerical order with respect to the order of the steps and that each line number is different. Most progammers skip numbers between lines to allow for the insertion of other lines between two existing lines without having to change all the line numbers in the program. Skipping numbers also makes corrections a rather simple process. For example, in our case, if the company decides to charge 6 cents a copy instead of 4 cents, we can simply insert the following new line 250:

```
        COPIER
100     LET N = 1505
200     LET C = N * 0.04
250     LET C = N * 0.06
300     LET A = C + 100
400     PRINT A
500     END
        RUN
        190.30
```

The computer will now use this new line 250 to replace the previous value of C that was obtained when line 200 was used.

Line 100 contains a LET statement. This is a very important instruction, since it tells the computer to replace N by 1505. Similarly, line 200 tells the computer to replace C by the value obtained when N is multiplied by 0.04. Line 300 tells the computer that A is to be replaced by the value obtained for C + 100. In BASIC an instruction like N = N + 1 is also perfectly meaningful, since it tells the computer that N now has the value N + 1.

Line 300, 300 LET A = C + 100, contains two types of characters: a variable and a constant. A **constant** is a number that never changes, whereas a **variable** may change in value as the problem proceeds. In BASIC a variable name can consist of either a single letter or a single letter

constant

variable

followed by a single digit. In our example, N, C, and A are one-character variable names. Examples of two-character BASIC names are X6, A7, B3, etc.

In BASIC, all mathematical calculations are performed much like ordinary algebraic or arithmetic calculations. The following symbols are used in BASIC.

BASIC symbol	Meaning	Example of BASIC expression	Similar algebraic expression
+	Addition	A + B	$a + b$
−	Subtraction	A − B	$a - b$
=	Equal	A = B	$a = b$
*	Multiplication	A * B	ab
/	Division	A / B	$\frac{a}{b}$ or $a \div b$
↑	Powers	A ↑ 3	a^3
( )	Grouping symbol	(A + B)/3	$\frac{a + b}{3}$

In BASIC, each symbol must be indicated. Nothing is taken for granted. Thus although we may write *ab* in ordinary algebra to stand for *a* times *b*, in BASIC we *must* write A*B. The symbol AB does not mean A times B.

Generally speaking, when the computer must perform several calculations, powers are evaluated first, then multiplications and divisions (from left to right), and finally addition and subtraction (again from left to right). Parentheses are used to group or to change the order of operations in a problem. Thus the statement A + B/3 tells the computer to first divide B by 3 and then to add the results to A, as opposed to the statement (A + B)/3, which tells the computer first to add A and B together and then to divide the sum by 3.

EXAMPLE 2

Which of the following are correct BASIC statements? If incorrect, explain why.

a) 100   LET A = B + 400
b) 300   LET X34 = B + 75
c) LET T = 5
d) 400   LET A + B = 31
e) 500   LET N = N + 1

SOLUTION

a) Correct

b) Incorrect; the BASIC variable has three characters. In BASIC, at most two character variables are permitted.

c) Incorrect; there is no line number.

d) Incorrect; we cannot have two variables to the left of the equal sign.

e) Correct.   ▬

EXAMPLE 3

Translate each of the following mathematical equations or formulas into BASIC statements.

a) $y = 3x + 2$

b) $a = \dfrac{2b + c}{3}$

c) $a = \dfrac{b^2}{3}$

d) $u = \dfrac{x_1 + x_2 + x_3 + x_4}{4}$

e) $y = \dfrac{(x + 2)^3}{7x}$

f) $y = \sqrt{x + 1}$ or $y = (x + 1)^{1/2}$

g) $x = \dfrac{-b + \sqrt{b^2 - 4ac}}{2a}$

h) $v = \dfrac{4}{3}\pi r^3$ (Use $\pi = 3.14159$)

SOLUTION

The BASIC statements corresponding to each of the mathematical equations or formulas are as follows.

a) 100   LET Y = 3 * X + 2
b) 120   LET A = (2 * B + C)/3
c) 130   LET A = (B ↑ 2)/3
d) 140   LET U = (X1 + X2 + X3 + X4)/4
e) 150   LET Y = ((X + 2) ↑ 3)/(7 * X)
      160   LET Y = (X + 1) ↑ (1/2) or
f) 161   LET Y = (X + 1) ↑ .5
g) 170   LET X = (− B + (B ↑ 2 − 4 * A * C) ↑ .5)/(2 * A)
h) 180   LET V = (4 * 3.14159 * R ↑ 3)/3   ▬

EXAMPLE 4

What is wrong with each of the following BASIC statements? Can you suggest a correction?

a) 100   LET A = 2(B + 7)
b) 110   A = 2
c) 400   LET A = (X + 5) ↑ 1/2

SOLUTION

a) There is no multiplication symbol. A possible correction is as follows.

   101   LET A = 2 * (B + 7)

b) The LET statement has been left out. The correction is as follows.

   111   LET A = 2

c) If the square root is intended, then parentheses symbols must be used. A possible correction is as follows.

401 LET A = (X + 5) ↑ (1/2)

As it stands, statement 400 tells the computer to raise $X + 5$ to the first power and divide the result by 2. In other words, evaluate $(x + 5)/2$. ▪

Let us now return to line 400 of our original problem (Example 1). It is

400 PRINT A

When the computer determines that the cost is \$160.20, it will simply print 160.20. We could change line 400 to read as follows:

401 PRINT N, C, A

This would cause the computer to print the following:

1505   60.20   160.20

The commas in the PRINT statement tell the computer to skip 15 spaces before printing the next numbers or words. By using this type of PRINT statement we are now able to have the original data printed out along with the result.

It is also possible to use a PRINT statement to have the computer print out words. We simply enclose the message to be printed within quotation marks followed by a semicolon. The semicolon tells the computer what to print next and to disregard the predetermined **fields**. Thus in our case we could replace line 400 by

fields

402 PRINT "TOTAL COST TO CUSTOMER IS"; A

The computer output for this would then be

TOTAL COST TO CUSTOMER IS 160.20

Suppose the Abel Office Equipment Corporation wants to use this program to calculate the total cost for several of its customers. With the program currently available it would have to reenter a new program that contains different data for each customer. How can we use this same program and change only the data? This can be accomplished by using READ and DATA statements as shown in the following example.

EXAMPLE 5

Write a BASIC program that would determine the total cost to a customer of the Abel Office Equipment Corporation who made 1505 photocopies during the month and that can be used to compute the costs to be charged to other customers.

SOLUTION

The BASIC program accomplishing this is as follows.

```
        COPIER
100   PRINT "CUSTOMER", "COPIES USED", "TOTAL COST"
200   PRINT
300   READ M, N
400   LET C = N * 0.04
500   LET A = C + 100
600   PRINT M, N, A
700   DATA 1, 1505
800   END
      RUN
```

READ statement

DATA statement

The **READ statement** tells the computer to find the values of M and N in the **DATA statement**. We always list the variables to be read after the READ statement and the values of these variables in the DATA statement. The numbers in the DATA statement must be separated by commas, and the number of data terms must be a multiple of the number of variables used. DATA statements are generally placed right before the END statement.

The BASIC program above will result in the following printout:

CUSTOMER	COPIES USED	TOTAL COST
1	1505	160.20

Notice that line 100 tells the computer to print headings, whereas line 200, which contains only the word PRINT, causes the computer to skip a line. Line 800 is the END statement. Every program written in BASIC must have an END statement that tells the computer that the program has been completed.

Note also the use of the RUN statement. We never assign a line number to a RUN statement. A RUN statement is always placed after an END statement and tells the computer to begin executing the program.

All the programs that we have discussed so far were relatively simple. None of them required the computer to make any decisions or to repeat the same type of calculation several times. The computer can be programmed to perform the same type of operation many times by using **GO TO statement** a **GO TO statement**, as shown in the following example.

EXAMPLE 6

Write a BASIC program that would allow the Abel Office Equipment Corporation to determine the total cost to customer 1 who made 1505 photocopies during the month, customer 2 who made 1227 copies, and customer 3 who made 1807 copies.

SOLUTION

The BASIC program accomplishing this is as follows.

```
          COPIER
100   READ M, N
200   LET C = N * 0.04
300   LET A = C + 100
350   PRINT "CUSTOMER NUMBER"; M
375   PRINT "NUMBER OF COPIES USED"; N
400   PRINT "TOTAL COST $"; A
425   PRINT
450   PRINT
475   PRINT
600   PRINT
700   GO TO 100
800   DATA 1, 1505, 2, 1227, 3, 1807
900   END
          RUN
```

Notice that in line 700 we have added a GO TO statement. This causes the computer to go to the line number indicated. After the computer determines the total charge for customer 1, we want the computer to go to the READ statement, read new values for M and N, and determine the total cost for these values. Thus we insert the GO TO 100 statement right after the PRINT statement and before the DATA statement. The computer goes to line 100, computes the total cost for customer 2, and then goes through the same procedure for customer 3. The computer is now in a **loop**.

loop

When all the data in line 800 are used up, the computer will stop and tell us "out of data in line 100." This means that there are no more numbers in the data list to read.

The previous program will cause the computer to print out the following results:

```
CUSTOMER NUMBER 1
NUMBER OF COPIES USED 1505
TOTAL COST $160.20


CUSTOMER NUMBER 2
NUMBER OF COPIES USED 1227
TOTAL COST $149.08


CUSTOMER NUMBER 3
NUMBER OF COPIES USED 1807
TOTAL COST $172.28


OUT OF DATA IN LINE 100
```

EXAMPLE 7

Write a BASIC program to compute the area of three different circles, one with a radius of 7, one with a radius of 9, and one with a radius of 10.6. (Remember that the area of a circle is given by $A = \pi r^2$ or $A = 3.14159r^2$, where r is the radius of the circle and where we have used 3.14159 as the value of π.)

SOLUTION

The BASIC program that will accomplish this is as follows.

```
        AREA
100     READ R
125     LET A = 3.14159 * R ↑ 2
150     PRINT "IF RADIUS OF CIRCLE IS"; R
175     PRINT "AREA OF CIRCLE IS"; A
200     PRINT
300     PRINT
400     PRINT
500     PRINT
600     GO TO 100
700     DATA 7, 9, 10.6
800     END
        RUN
```

When the computer executes this program, it will print out the following.

```
IF RADIUS OF CIRCLE IS 7
AREA OF CIRCLE IS 153.93791


IF RADIUS OF CIRCLE IS 9
AREA OF CIRCLE IS 254.46879


IF RADIUS OF CIRCLE IS 10.6
AREA OF CIRCLE IS 352.9890524


OUT OF DATA IN LINE 100
```

EXAMPLE 8

Write a BASIC program to compute the squares and cubes of the first five numbers.

SOLUTION

As indicated earlier, it is advisable to first draw a flowchart to picture the logical steps that are necessary to execute the program. Using the symbols given in Section 14.4, we have the flowchart shown in Fig. 14.8. A BASIC program based on this flowchart is as follows.

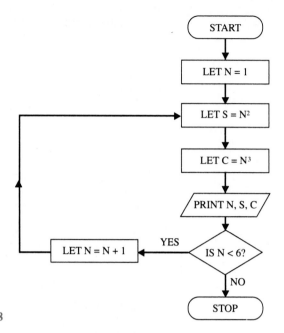

Figure 14.8

```
        SQUARE
100   PRINT
200   PRINT
300   LET N = 1
400   LET S = N ↑ 2
500   LET C = N ↑ 3
525   PRINT "IF NUMBER IS"; N
550   PRINT "SQUARE IS"; S
575   PRINT "CUBE IS"; C
600   PRINT
625   PRINT
650   PRINT
700   LET N = N + 1
800   IF N < 6 THEN 400
900   END
      RUN
```

IF THEN statement

Notice that in line 800 we have used an **IF THEN statement**. Such a statement tells the computer to decide whether the relationship given is true or false. If the relation given is true, the computer will jump to the line number given in the statement. If the relation is false, the computer proceeds to the next BASIC statement in sequence.

When the computer executes this program, the following will be printed out:

```
IF NUMBER IS 1
SQUARE IS 1
CUBE IS 1


IF NUMBER IS 2
SQUARE IS 4
CUBE IS 8


IF NUMBER IS 3
SQUARE IS 9
CUBE IS 27


IF NUMBER IS 4
SQUARE IS 16
CUBE IS 64


IF NUMBER IS 5
SQUARE IS 25
CUBE IS 125
```

For Example 8 a BASIC program can also be written that will have the computer print out the results in the following format:

NUMBER	SQUARE OF NUMBER	CUBE OF NUMBER
1	1	1
2	4	8
3	9	27
4	16	64
5	25	125

The following list summarizes the various relational symbols that can be used in **BASIC IF THEN** statements.

TABLE 14.2

Some BASIC symbols and their meanings

BASIC symbol	Meaning	BASIC symbol	Meaning
=	is equal to	< =	is less than or equal to
<	is less than	> =	is greater than or equal to
>	is greater than	< >	is not equal to

EXAMPLE 9

The Cal Finance Company charges different interest rates on outstanding monthly balances depending on the amount of money involved as shown below:

Outstanding monthly balance	Annual interest rate
Up to $200.00	18%
From $200.01 to $500.0C	15%
Above $500.00	12%

Write a BASIC program to determine the finance charge for five accounts whose outstanding monthly balances are $58.17, $423.17, $312.98, $1400.16, and $817.64.

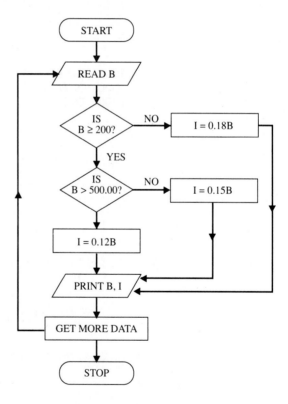

Figure 14.9

SOLUTION

It is best to first draw a flowchart for the problem. Let B = the outstanding balance and let I = the finance charge. Then a flowchart for the problem is as shown in Fig. 14.9 above. Using this flowchart, we set up the following BASIC program:

```
        CHARGE
100   PRINT
200   PRINT
300   READ B
400   IF B > 200.00 THEN 700
500   LET I = B * 0.18
600   GO TO 1100
700   IF B > 500,00 THEN 1000
800   LET I = B * 0.15
900   GO TO 1100
1000  LET I = B * 0.12
1100  PRINT = "IF OUTSTANDING BALANCE IS $"; B
1125  PRINT "FINANCE CHARGE IS $"; I
1130  PRINT
1150  PRINT
1175  PRINT
1180  PRINT
1200  GO TO 300
1300  DATA 58.17, 423.17, 312.98, 1400.16, 817.64
1400  END
        RUN
```

When this program is executed, the computer printout will be as follows:

```
IF OUTSTANDING BALANCE IS $58.17
FINANCE CHARGE IS $10.47


IF OUTSTANDING BALANCE IS $423.17
FINANCE CHARGE IS $63.48


IF OUTSTANDING BALANCE IS $312.98
FINANCE CHARGE IS $46.95


IF OUTSTANDING BALANCE IS $1400.16


IF OUTSTANDING BALANCE IS $817.64
FINANCE CHARGE IS $98.12


OUT OF DATA IN LINE 300
```

EXERCISES FOR SECTION 14.5

Which of the variable names given in Exercises 1–6 are not acceptable in BASIC?

1. A23   **2.** KKK   **3.** B12

4. 10X   **5.** B4   **6.** JFK

In Exercises 7–11, write each of the given algebraic statements as equivalent BASIC statements.

7. $D = RT$

8. $y = x^2 - 5x + 3$

9. $y = z\,(7x - 3)$

10. $F = \frac{9}{5}C + 32$

11. $A = \dfrac{B - C}{D + E}$

In Exercises 12–16, what is the value of A in each BASIC statement? (Use X = 10, Y = 12, and Z = 2.)

12. 20   LET A = 3 ∗ (X + Y)

13. 30   LET A = Z ↑ 3

14. 40   LET A = (X + Y + 1)/Z

15. 50   LET A = Z ↑ 2 + X ↑ 2

16. 60   LET A = (Z + X) ↑ 2

17. Is the following a correct BASIC statement? Explain your answer.

     10   LET A12 = X – 3

18. Is the following a correct BASIC statement? Explain your answer.

     100   PRINT "THE ANSWER IS A

19. Is the following a correct BASIC statement? Explain your answer.

     200   READ A, B, C, D
     250   DATA 8, 9, 20, 35, 76

In Exercises 20–22, find at least one error in each BASIC program.

20.   EXMPLE
     10   LET A = 10
     20   LET B = 20
     30   LET N = (A ∗ (B – 5)
     40   PRINT A, B, N
     50   END
        RUN

21.   MEAN
     10   LET A = 5
     20   LET B = 15
     30   LET AV = A + B/2
     40   PRINT "THE MEAN OF A AND B IS"
     50   PRINT AV
     60   END
        RUN

22.   EXMPLE
     10   READ B2
     20   READ MN
     30   LET A = MN + B2
     40   PRINT A
     50   DATA 20, 30
     60   END
        RUN

In Exercises 23–25, explain what the computer will print out when it executes the indicated BASIC programs.

23.   EXMPLE
     10   LET A = 5
     20   LET B = 75
     30   LET C = 8
     40   LET M = (A ∗ B) ↑ 2 ∗ C
     50   PRINT M
     60   END
        RUN

24.   EXMPLE
     10   LET A = 5
     20   LET B = 3 ↑ A
     30   LET M = B – A
     40   PRINT "THE VALUE OF M IS"; M
     50   END
        RUN

25.   EXMPLE
     100   READ A, B
     120   IF A > B THEN 220
     150   PRINT B "IS BIGGER THAN"; A
     200   GO TO 100
     220   PRINT A, "IS BIGGER THAN"; B
     250   GO TO 100
     280   DATA 220, – 75, 570, 320, – 5, 50
     300   END
        RUN

26. Write a BASIC program for computing the area of several rectangles whose bases and heights are as follows.

Base, in cm	Height, in cm
53	23
17	55
61.3	18.2
847.7	62.73
7298.3	509.67

27. Write a BASIC program to compute the area of a square.

28. Write a BASIC program to find the sum of the first 25 integers.

29. Write a BASIC program to find the product of the integers 20 through 30.

30. Write a BASIC program to compute the compound interest on a bank deposit of $2000 that earns annual interest of 8%, compounded annually for eight years.

31. In a math course, three tests are given, plus a final exam. The final is counted as two tests. The grade in the course is the average of all the tests (with the final counted twice). For example, if a student's three test scores are 85, 61, and 92 and his or her final exam is 74, then the grade is

$$\frac{85 + 61 + 92 + 2(74)}{5}$$

which equals 81.2. Write a BASIC program to compute a student's grade in this course.

32. Write a BASIC program to calculate the value of 9!.

33. Write a BASIC program to find the sum of the cubes of the integers from 10 to 20 inclusive.

34. Write a BASIC program to compute the value of the hypotenuse c shown below: (*Hint:* Remember that for the right triangle shown, $c = \sqrt{a^2 + b^2}$.)

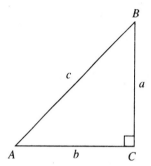

A first-degree equation of the form $ax + b = c$ has as its solution

$$x = \frac{c - b}{a}$$

Write a BASIC program that can be used to solve each of the equations given in Exercises 35–39.

*35. $7x + 5 = 26$ ***36.** $0.4x + 9 = 17$ ***37.** $5x - 4 = 19$

*38. $\frac{2}{3}x + 8 = 22$ ***39.** $\frac{5}{7}x - 9 = 50$

A quadratic equation of the form $ax^2 + bx + c = 0$ has as one of its solutions

$$x = \frac{-b + \sqrt{b^2 - 4ac}}{2a}$$

Write a BASIC program to solve each of the equations given in Exercises 40–43.

*40. $x^2 - 9x + 18 = 0$ ***41.** $x^2 + 5x + 6 = 0$

*42. $x^2 - x - 6 = 0$ ***43.** $x^2 - 10x + 24 = 0$

14.6

PROGRAMMING IN LOGO

turtle

LOGO is a computer language that enables us to draw a variety of geometric figures and shapes. This "computer graphics" program utilizes a small triangle called the **turtle** which appears on the screen. The turtle moves around, thereby enabling the user to draw a great variety of figures.

prompt
cursor

Home position

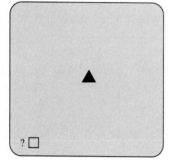

Figure 14.10

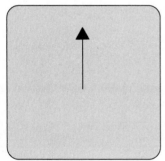

Figure 14.11

We can think of the turtle as a mechanical robot that methodically follows our commands.

After we load the computer with the LOGO program, a question mark called a **prompt** and a flashing **cursor** will appear on the screen. This tells us that the computer is awaiting instructions. The computer will accept instructions in the nodraw, draw, and edit mode.

If we type DRAW and press the ⃞RETURN⃞ key, then we enter the draw mode. The turtle will now appear in the center of the screen as shown in Fig. 14.10. This is the turtle's **HOME position**. The turtle points toward the top.

Note that Fig. 14.10 shows a question mark followed by a rectangular cursor. This typical split-screen mode enables us to use the bottom of the screen for user input and the computer's output. The balance of the screen is used for drawing geometric figures.

The following control characters will prove helpful in managing the screen.

Control character	What it does
CTRL-F	Shows full graphics screen
CTRL-T	Shows full text screen
CTRL-S	Shows split graphics text/screen

There are several versions of LOGO currently in use and the commands used in each are slightly different. It is therefore suggested that the reader have access to a computer and actually type in the given LOGO commands while reading this material. In our discussion, we will present LOGO commands in either Terrapin LOGO or Apple LOGO. In many cases, the commands are the same. The summary of LOGO commands at the end of this section presents a list of these commands in both Terrapin LOGO and Apple LOGO.

The LOGO commands **FORWARD** and **BACK** are used to make the turtle draw lines. The commands **RIGHT** and **LEFT** are used to make the turtle turn. If we type the graphics command **FORWARD** 20 and press ⃞RETURN⃞, the turtle will move forward 20 steps in the direction it is pointing. (See Fig. 14.11.) We usually abbreviate this as FD 20. Similarly, the **BACK** 40 command sends the turtle back 40 steps.

Generally speaking, the LOGO commands **FORWARD** and **BACK** must be followed by a blank space and a numerical input.

Comment   Instructing the turtle to move forward or backward too great a number of steps will cause the turtle to "wrap around" the screen. Enter **FORWARD** 275 and see what happens.

The commands **RIGHT** (abbreviated RT) and **LEFT** (abbreviated LT) followed by a blank space and a numerical input turns the turtle in its place the specified number of degrees to the right or left of its current heading.

If we want to move the turtle but without leaving a trail, then we use the command **PENUP** abbreviated as PU. The command **PENDOWN** abbreviated as PD makes the turtle leave a trail again. Similarly, the command **HIDETURTLE** makes the turtle disappear and the command **SHOWTURTLE** makes the turtle reappear.

EXAMPLE 1

SOLUTION

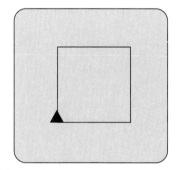

Figure 14.12

Write LOGO commands to draw a square whose lengths measure 20.

The following sequence of LOGO commands can be used to accomplish this.

```
FD 20
RT 90
FD 20
RT 90
FD 20
RT 90
FD 20
RT 90
```

When executed, the above commands produce the square shown in Fig. 14.12.

In the previous example, we notice that the sequence of commands contains the instructions FD 20 and RT 90 repeated four times. If we wish, we can use the LOGO **REPEAT** command to repeat a sequence of instructions. In our example, we could type the following:

```
REPEAT 4 [FD 20 RT 90]
```

When using the **REPEAT** command we must indicate which instructions are to be repeated and how many times they are to be repeated. The instructions inside the brackets are repeated the number of times specified by the number in front of the brackets.

Comment   In the previous example, had we not included the last instruction RT 90, the final position of the turtle would have been as shown in Fig. 14.13.

We can always return the turtle to its initial or "home" position on the screen by using the **HOME** command, that is, **HOME** returns the turtle to its original position in the center of the screen pointing toward the top.

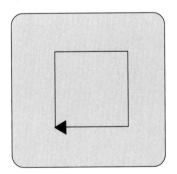

Figure 14.13

state transparent
state change
invariant

Comment In the previous example, the set of commands sends the turtle around a perfectly closed path and the turtle returns to its initial position and heading. We then say that the set of commands is **state transparent** and that the closed path is **state change invariant**.

After we are finished with a figure, we can type **DRAW**, which clears the screen and returns the turtle to its initial position and direction in the center of the screen. (In Apple LOGO, the command **CLEARSCREEN** accomplishes this.)

EXAMPLE 2

Write LOGO commands to draw a dashed horizontal line.

SOLUTION

The following LOGO commands accomplish this.

```
RT
REPEAT 4 [FD 10 PU FD 10 PD]
FD 10
```

After these commands are executed, the following will be displayed.

— — — — ▶

Figure 14.14

EXAMPLE 3

Write LOGO commands to draw an equilateral triangle each of whose sides measures 25.

SOLUTION

We know that each exterior angle of the triangle measures 120° (see Fig. 14.15). The turtle will have to turn through the number of degrees in the exterior angle of the triangle. Thus we must instruct the turtle to repeatedly move first 25 steps and then turn 120°. This must be repeated three times. We accomplish this by typing

```
REPEAT 3 [FD 25 RT 120]
```

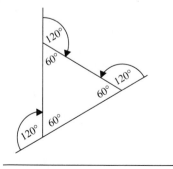

Figure 14.15

After these commands are executed, the following will be displayed.

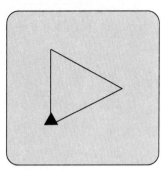

Figure 14.16

EXAMPLE 4

Write LOGO commands to draw a regular hexagon each of whose sides measures 25.

SOLUTION

In this case, each exterior angle of the hexagon will contain 60°, so the turtle will have to repeatedly move 25 steps and then turn 60°. This can be accomplished by typing

    REPEAT 6 [FD 25 RT 60]

When executed, the following will be displayed.

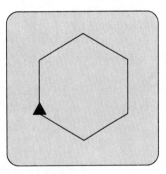

Figure 14.17

Defining Logo Procedures

procedure

If we wish to use a figure or set of instructions again at a later point and do not wish to retype the entire sequence of commands, we can store these commands in the computer's memory by creating a **procedure** which is nothing more than a set of instructions to the computer to be used at a later time and which has been given a specific name.

To create a procedure, we proceed as follows: First, we type **TO** and the name of the procedure we wish to define. The name must be a sequence of symbols with no spaces. We then press $\boxed{\text{RETURN}}$. This causes the computer to enter the edit mode. We then type the list of commands that make up the procedure. Finally, we type **END** followed by the Control C command. We press the C-key while holding down the ⌷Control⌷ key. For example, we can define a procedure for drawing the square given in Example 1 as follows:

```
TO SQUARE1
    FD 20
    RT 90
    FD 20
    RT 90
    FD 20
    RT 90
    FD 20
    RT 90
END
CTRL-C
```

The first line causes the computer to enter the edit mode. The procedure is called SQUARE1. The lines that follow together with the END statement make up the procedure. (END is the last statement in a procedure.) The CTRL-C command tells the computer to remember the procedure by the name SQUARE1. The computer now stores these instructions in its memory. The computer can reuse and execute this procedure as a LOGO command simply by typing its name in the draw mode.

EXAMPLE 5

Problem-Solving Example
Use a LOGO procedure to draw the diagram in Fig. 14.18.

SOLUTION

Understanding the Problem
We must write a LOGO procedure to draw the diagram shown in Fig. 14.18. If we analyze this diagram, we see that it consists of an equilateral triangle on top of a square.

A Plan to Solve the Problem
We already know how to write a LOGO set of instructions to create an equilateral triangle (Example 3) and how to create a square in LOGO (Example 1). Thus we must now find a new procedure for combining two other procedures. Let us call our new procedure "House," for obvious reasons. We first draw the square. From Example 1 we already know that the procedure

```
TO SQUARE1
    REPEAT 4 [FD 25 RT 90]
END
CTRL-C
```

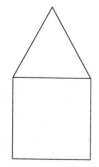

Figure 14.18

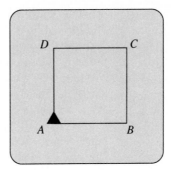

Figure 14.19

accomplishes this. However, after executing this, the turtle returns to its initial position A as shown in Fig. 14.19.

We must now move the turtle to position D, the upper left corner of the square, before drawing the triangle. This is accomplished by typing FD 25. Then we must turn the triangle 30° to the right so that it is oriented in the proper direction before drawing the triangle. RT 30 accomplishes this. Now we are ready to draw the triangle. From Example 3, we know that the procedure

```
TO TRIANGLE
    REPEAT 3 [FD 25 RT 120]
END
CTRL-C
```

accomplishes this. Thus we can combine these two procedures to obtain the complete procedure for drawing "House," which is

```
TO HOUSE
   SQUARE1
   FD 25
   RT 30
   TRIANGLE
   HIDE TURTLE
END
```

Checking Our Solution
Although other techniques can be found for drawing "House," we can check our procedure by executing it. When HOUSE is run, the first thing that is drawn is the square, after which the turtle moves from the lower left corner to the upper left corner and changes its orientation. Then the turtle calls on the triangle procedure to draw the triangle. Finally, HOUSE hides the turtle.

Comment In this example, you may wonder why we need to insert the two intermediate steps FD 25 and RT 30 after drawing the square. The

Figure 14.20

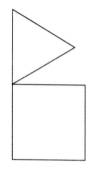

Figure 14.21

reader should verify that both of these are needed. Drawing the square followed by the triangle (without the two extra instructions) produces the shape shown in Fig. 14.20. Can you see why? Also, if we draw the square and move the turtle from the lower left corner to the upper left corner by typing FD 25 — but forget to reorient the turtle—then we get the shape in Fig. 14.21. Can you see why?

Example 5 indicates how we can use one procedure within another procedure. If we change our mind and want to stop while creating a procedure, we type **CTRL-G**. In effect this cancels the procedure and leaves us in the edit mode. By typing DRAW, we can return to the draw mode.

The following is a useful list of editing commands.

LOGO Editing Command	What It Does
ESC or DELETE	Removes preceding characters.
DRAW	Clears the graphics screen and returns
CLEARSCREEN	The turtle to its HOME position in the draw mode.
EDIT	Enters the edit mode.
TO (procedure)	Enters edit mode and begins definition of the specified procedure.
END	Ends the definition of a procedure.
EDIT (procedure)	Enters edit mode and recalls the specified procedure from the workspace. The specified procedure can now be edited and redefined.
← or →	Moves cursor to left or right.
CTRL-A	Moves cursor to the start of current line.
CTRL-E	Moves cursor to the end of current line.
CTRL-N	Moves cursor to next line.
CTRL-P	Moves cursor to previous line.
CTRL-X	Erases to end of current line.

Using Procedures with Variables

Until now, all of our procedures used fixed distances and fixed angles. Thus, in Example 1, the procedure SQUARE1 specified that the length of the side of the square be 25. However, we might want to draw smaller or larger squares. We would like to be able to write a procedure that can be used to draw a square of any size. This can be accomplished in LOGO by using a variable as input rather than a fixed number. We use a colon followed by the variable which can be any alphanumeric string. The value of the variable quantity is input when the procedure is executed. In our case, we can use SIDE as the variable. We place the name of the variable on the first line in the title, but this is not part of the name. The following procedure draws a square whose side measures any length.

```
TO SQUARE :SIDE
    REPEAT 4 [FD :SIDE RT 90]
END
```

If we want the turtle to draw a square whose side measures 50, we type SQUARE 50. We do not type SQUARE :50 as 50 is not a variable.

Procedures can have more than one input. The following RECTANGLE will draw rectangles of different sizes.

```
TO RECTANGLE :HEIGHT :WIDTH
    FD :HEIGHT   RT 90
    FD :WIDTH    RT 90
    FD :HEIGHT   RT 90
    FD :WIDTH    RT 90
END
```

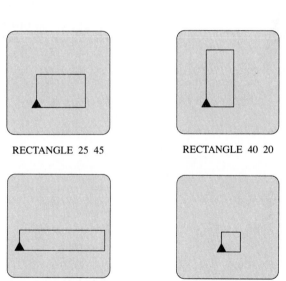

RECTANGLE 25 45   RECTANGLE 40 20

RECTANGLE 10 95   RECTANGLE 10 10

RECTANGLE 10 0

The LOGO program can easily be used to picture points on a coordinate system. This is because each point on the screen is associated with an ordered pair of numbers (x, y). The turtle's HOME position is the origin $(0, 0)$. The LOGO command SETX a moves the turtle horizontally to the point whose x-coordinate is a. Similarly, the LOGO command SETY b moves the turtle vertically to a point whose y-coordinate is b. The LOGO command SETXY a b combines the SETX a and SETY b commands. It moves the turtle to the point whose coordinates are (a, b).

In Section 11.7 we indicated how we can use LOGO in coordinate geometry to draw different geometrical figures given in coordinate form, how LOGO can be used to find the distance between points, the midpoint of the line segment joining two points, and other applications.

There are other interesting commands and activities that LOGO can execute. The interested reader can consult the many books on LOGO that are available. For the benefit of the reader, we present the following summary of LOGO commands. All the commands are the same in Terrapin LOGO and Apple LOGO unless otherwise specified.

Summary of Logo Commands

LOGO command	What it does
FORWARD (FD)	Moves the turtle forward (in the direction the turtle is facing) the number of positive units that are specified.
BACK (BK)	Moves the turtle backwards the number of positive units that are specified.
RIGHT (RT)	Turns the turtle to the right the number of positive degrees that are specified.
LEFT (LT)	Turns the turtle to the left the number of positive degrees specified.
PENUP (PU)	In the graphics mode, it enables the turtle to move without leaving a track.
PENDOWN (PD)	In the graphics mode, it causes the turtle to leave a track.
HIDETURTLE (HT)	It causes the turtle to disappear.
SHOWTURTLE (ST)	It causes the turtle to reappear.
HOME	It causes the turtle to return to the center of the screen pointing up. If the pen is down, a track is left connecting the turtle's present position to the home position.
DRAW (CLEARSCREEN in Apple LOGO)	It clears the screen and sends the turtle HOME.
CLEARSCREEN	It clears the screen.

LOGO command	What it does
SETX a	It moves the turtle horizontally to the point whose *x*-coordinate is *a*.
SETY b	It moves the turtle vertically to the point whose *y*-coordinate is *b*.
SETXY a b (SETPOS (a, b) in Apple LOGO)	It moves the turtle to the point whose coordinates are (*a*, *b*).
XCOR	It indicates the turtle's *x*-coordinate.
YCOR	It indicates the turtle's *y*-coordinate.
REPEAT n [list]	It accepts a number and a list as input and then executes the instructions in the list n times.
TO (EDIT (ED) in Apple LOGO)	Uses the name of a procedure as input and causes LOGO to enter the edit mode.
DRAW (CLEARSCREEN (CS) in Apple LOGO)	It sends the turtle home and clears the graphics screen.
NODRAW (ND) (TEXTSCREEN (CTRL-T) in Apple LOGO)	It exits the graphics mode, clears the screen, and places the cursor in the upper left corner.

EXERCISES FOR SECTION 14.6

1. The following LOGO commands contain errors. Find each error and indicate how it can be corrected.

   a) SET X 50   **b)** BK25

   c) SETXY 15, 30   **d)** DRAW TRIANGLE

   e) REPEAT [SQUARE1 RT 45]

2. Determine what the turtle will do after executing the following: (Check your answers by actually running the instructions on the computer.)

   a) REPEAT 6 [SQUARE1 RT 45]

   b) FD 80
   RT 90
   FD 40
   RT 90
   FD 40
   RT 90
   FD 40

PROBLEM-SOLVING EXERCISES

3. Write a LOGO procedure for drawing an equilateral triangle, each of whose sides measures 40, and then to draw a perpendicular bisector to one of these sides.

4. Write a LOGO procedure to draw two horizontal parallel lines intersected by a transversal inclined 40° to the horizontal.

5. Write LOGO procedures for drawing each of the following:

   a)   **b)**

   c)

d)

e)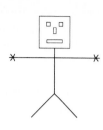

IIII ► Brain-Teaser Problems ◄ IIII

**6. Refer back to Example 5. Write a LOGO program which draws the indicated figure but without retracing any segment.

**7. What happens if we type SQUARE with no additional input, that is, if we enter TO SQUARE?

f)

g)

TYPICAL CLASSROOM QUESTIONS

1. A student claims that computer languages are obsolete. Do you agree?
2. A student wonders why someone would want to write a computer program using a low-level programming language. How do you respond?
3. A student asks: "Why study programming languages, flowcharts, or programs in general, considering that there are so many software programs currently on the market?" What is your response?
4. Why do you need DOS (disc operating system) if you already have a microprocessor?
5. A student believes that most hand-held calculators are not good examples of personal computers since they cannot be programmed by the user. Do you agree?

STUDY GUIDE

The following is a chapter outline in capsule form. You should now be able to demonstrate your knowledge of the ideas mentioned by giving definitions or specific examples. Page references are given in parentheses.

The **abacus** or **counting board** was one of the earliest devices invented for making computations easier. (p. 813)

Computer professionals classify computers as belonging to particular generations. **First-generation computers** used vacuum tubes and performed calculations in a few milliseconds. **Second-generation computers** were built with transistors instead of vacuum tubes and performed calculations in a few microseconds. **Third-generation computers** use groups of transistors and integrated circuits and operate at a speed of a billionth of a second. **Fourth-generation computers** use microprocessors and very large-scale integrated circuits and are capable of processing 100 million to 1 billion instructions per second. **Fifth-generation computers** will use a parallel-processing technology. Such artificial intelligence computers would work about 2000 times faster than today's most advanced computers and would use logical rules rather than arithmetic operations to act on information. (p. 815)

A **microprocessor** is actually a computer on a silicon chip since it contains the entire processing unit of a computer. (p. 815)

In **time-sharing**, a company has a terminal upon which the user both types programs and receives information. The user pays only for the time that the computer is used. (p. 817)

Most of the computers produced in the United States today are **digital computers** as opposed to **analog computers**. (p. 817)

A **program** is a set of instructions telling the computer exactly what has to be done and in what order. The **computer programmer** actually writes the program. (p. 818)

A **syntax error** is a message from the computer indicating that a programming error has been made. The program then has to be **debugged.** (p. 818)

High-level computer languages, such as BASIC, FORTRAN, PILOT, LOGO, and Pascal, use commands and concepts in a manner that is comparable to everyday human language and thought. (p. 818)

Low-level, or **assembly** and **machine computer**, languages require the user to have some background knowledge of the computer. (p. 818)

The **input unit** of the computer enters the data and instructions into the machine. (p. 819)

The **control unit** receives and interprets the instructions that it receives from the input unit. (p. 819)

The **arithmetic unit** performs all the calculations that are needed to solve a problem. (p. 820)

The **memory unit** stores all the data or the results of the calculation itself. (p. 820)

The physical parts of a computer are called its **hardware**. (p. 821)

The programming techniques and the actual programs are called its **software**. (p. 831)

The most important parts of any personal computer are its **microprocessor, main memory unit**, and **keyboard**. Additionally, the **peripherals** of the system include a **computer monitor**, a **disc drive**, and a **printer**. (p. 823)

A master control program that synchronizes the execution of computer programs is known as the computer's **operating system.** (p. 823)

Computer printers may be of the **dot-matrix**, **daisy-wheel**, or **laser** type. (p. 824)

A **flowchart** is a diagram indicating the logical sequence of steps to be followed by the computer. (p. 825)

The flashing square, flashing rectangle, or flashing line that appears when a computer is turned on is called a **cursor**. (p.831)

LOGO is a computer graphics program that enables the user to draw a variety of geometric figures and shapes. The program utilizes a small triangle, called the **turtle**, which appears on the screen. (p. 845)

In the DRAW mode, we can instruct the turtle to draw a variety of geometric figures. We use the commands FORWARD, BACK, RIGHT, LEFT, PENUP, PENDOWN, HIDETURTLE, SHOWTURTLE, etc., to accomplish this. (p. 846)

The turtle's HOME position is the center of the screen. (p. 846)

Commands are **state transparent** if they send the turtle around a perfectly closed path and the turtle returns to its original position. The closed path is **state change invariant.** (p. 848)

In LOGO, a **procedure** is a set of instructions to the computer to be used at a later time and which has been given a specific name. (p. 852)

Procedures which contain **variables** can also be used. (p. 852)

A summary list of LOGO commands and what they do appears on p. 854.

KEY TERMS

Terms

The following list presents the key terms introduced in this chapter.

14.1 **abacus (counting board)**
      microprocessor
      fifth-generation computers
      advanced mainframe
          supercomputer

14.2 **digital computer**
      analog computer
      program
      computer programmer
      syntax error
      debugging
      low-level languages
      high-level languages
      input unit
      compiler
      CPU (Central Processing Unit)
      arithmetic unit
      memory unit
      output unit
      bits
      chips
      magnetic drums
      discs

      hardware
      software

14.3 **microprocessor**
      main memory
      keyboard
      peripherals
      computer monitor
      disc drive
      floppy or hard discs
      operating systems
      printer
      dot-matrix printer
      daisy-wheel printer
      laser printer
      modem

14.4 **computer program**
      flowcharts
      looping

14.5 **cursor**
      syntax error
      BASIC constant

BASIC variable	14.6	turtle
fields		prompt
READ statements		cursor
DATA statements		HOME position
GO TO statements		procedure
loop		state transparent
IF THEN statement		state change invariant

Manual for Quick Reference

The following lists of symbols or key words summarizes the BASIC statements and symbols or flowchart symbols discussed in this chapter.

	Flowchart symbols	BASIC statements	
⬭ or ◯	start or end of program	LET	tells the computer that a variable has a particular value.
		PRINT	tells the computer to print out the results that it obtained.
		READ	tells the computer to obtain data from the DATA statement in sequential order.
▱	input or output of data	DATA	stores the data to be used as input information.
		GO TO	tells the computer to go out of sequence and go to the line number indicated.
▭	processing of program	IF THEN	tells the computer to make a decision and to proceed according to the answer to the decision made.
		END	tells the computer that the program is done. It is always the last statement in the program.
◇	decision symbol	RUN	tells the computer to start executing the program.
←↓→	direction to go in flowchart		

BASIC operations	BASIC decision symbols
+ Addition	= is equal to
− Subtraction	< is less than
* Multiplication	> is greater than
/ Division	< = is less than or equal to
↑ Exponents (powers)	> = is greater than or equal to
( ) Grouping symbol	< > is not equal to
= Equality	

1. If a computer sends you a message that you have made a programming error, then this is called a

   a) syntax error   **b)** debugging error   **c)** simulation error
   d) data base error   **e)** none of these

2. A set of instructions telling the computer exactly what has to be done and in what order is known as a

   a) compiler   **b)** decoder   **c)** program   **d)** translator
   e) none of these

3. A computer language that uses commands and concepts in a manner that is comparable to everyday language and thought is called

   a) assembly language   **b)** machine language
   c) low-level language   **d)** high-level language
   e) none of these

4. Which of the following computer languages is used primarily in scientific oriented or mathematical research?

   a) Pascal   **b)** BASIC   **c)** COBOL   **d)** FORTRAN
   e) none of these

5. A computer language designed for teachers and used to generate computer-aided instruction lessons is

   a) LOGO   **b)** PILOT   **c)** PL/1   **d)** FORTRAN
   e) none of these

6. The part of the computer that receives and interprets the instructions that it receives from the input unit is called the

   a) control unit   **b)** memory unit   **c)** arithmetic unit
   d) peripheral unit   **e)** none of these

7. The physical parts of a computer are referred to as the

   a) hardware   **b)** software   **c)** peripherals
   d) hard discs   **e)** none of these

8. A personal computer is an example of a

   a) mainframe computer   **b)** supercomputer
   c) first-generation computer   **d)** microcomputer
   e) none of these

9. Which part of a personal computer carries out sequences of instructions stored in an area of the computer's memory?

   a) main memory   **b)** computer monitor
   c) microprocessor   **d)** keyboard   **e)** none of these

10. A computer programmer can send information to the computer with a

    a) monitor   **b)** keyboard   **c)** microprocessor

d) decoder   **e)** none of these

11. A computer's master control program that synchronizes the execution of the computer program is called the

    a) operating system   **b)** disc drive   **c)** main memory

    d) peripheral   **e)** none of these

12. A computer printer that has a print head consisting of one or more vertical rows of tiny pins is called

    a) thermal   **b)** dot-matrix   **c)** daisy-wheel

    d) continuous roller-feed   **e)** none of these

13. When a computer is turned off, everything in main memory is

    a) temporarily lost but will reappear when the computer is turned on again   **b)** partially lost   **c)** completely lost

    d) automatically transferred to a blank disc in the disc drive

    e) none of these

14. A person who actually writes computer programs is called a

    a) systems analyst   **b)** keypunch operator

    c) computer programmer   **d)** compositor   **e)** none of these

15. Which of the following computer parts is in charge of performing a process?

    a) keyboard   **b)** screen or monitor   **c)** printer   **d)** CPU

    e) none of these

16. When using flowcharts, the □ symbol is used to indicate

    a) the beginning or end of a program

    b) input or output of data

    c) the processing of the program

    d) that a decision must be made

    e) none of these

17. What is the BASIC symbol for less than or equal to?

18. Rewrite the following BASIC statement into an ordinary algebraic expression:

    20   LET A = B * C / D ↑ (1/5)

19. Translate the following into a BASIC statement:
    $$y = 2x^3z^4$$

20. What will be printed when the following BASIC program is run?

    ```
        EXMPLE
    10  LET A = 7.6
    15  LET B = 11.6
    18  LET C = A/(B – A)
    25  PRINT A, B, C
    30  END
        RUN
    ```

21. Find at least one error in the following BASIC program.

```
    EXMPLE
10  LET A1 = 10
20  LET A2 = 6
30  PRINT A1 ↑ A2
40  END
    RUN
```

22. What does the following computer instruction mean?

```
20  LET A = A + 5
```

23. A computer program to be saved for later use should have a name that is no longer than _____ characters.

24. When writing computer programs, any numbers from 1 to _____ can be used as line numbers.

25. In BASIC we write $a^2 b^5$ as _____ .

26. What will be printed when the following program is run?

```
    EXMPLE
10  READ M, N, P, Q
20  LET A = (M – Q)/(N + P) ↑ 2
30  PRINT A
40  DATA 7, 8, 12, 6
50  END
    RUN
```

27. Is the following a correct BASIC statement? If correct, explain why.

```
20  LET X15 = Y – 3
```

28. Translate the following into a BASIC statement:

$$y = -a + \sqrt[3]{7m^2y^5}$$

29. *True or false?* In BASIC, AB stands for A times B.

30. What does the statement A – B/2 tell the computer to do?

31. In BASIC a variable name can consist of either a single letter or a single digit followed by a _____ .

32. Find at least one error in the following BASIC program.

```
    EXMPLE
10  LET X = 7
20  LET Y = 10
30  LET A = (X + 6)/(Y – 8) ↑ 2
40  PRINT "A EQUALS; A
50  END
    RUN
```

33. What does the following BASIC program accomplish?

```
    EXMPLE
10  LET A = 1
20  PRINT A
30  LET A = A + 1
40  IF A > 100 THEN 60
50  GO TO 20
60  END
    RUN
```

34. What does the following BASIC program accomplish?

```
    EXMPLE
10  LET A = 100
20  PRINT A
30  IF A < 1 THEN 60
40  LET A = A – 1
50  GO TO 20
60  END
    RUN
```

35. What does the following BASIC program accomplish?

```
    EXMPLE
10  LET A = 1
20  PRINT "I AM A SMART COMPUTER"
30  LET A = A + 1
40  IF A > 10 THEN 60
50  GO TO 20
60  END
    RUN
```

36. What does the following BASIC program accomplish?

```
    EXMPLE
10  PRINT "WHO IS PRESIDENT OF THE USA?"
20  PRINT "1. NIXON 2. BUSH 3. CARTER 4. REAGAN"
30  PRINT "THE NUMBER OF THE CORRECT CHOICE IS"; N
40  IF N = 2 THEN 70
50  PRINT "INCORRECT, TRY AGAIN."
60  GO TO 10
70  PRINT "CORRECT."
80  END
    RUN
```

37. Write a LOGO procedure to draw the following diagrams:

a)

b)

38. What does the following flowchart accomplish?

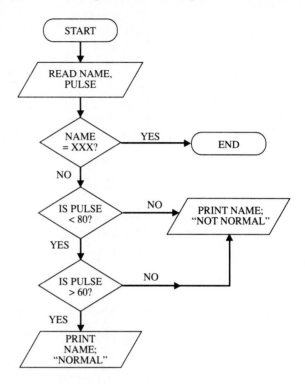

39. The following LOGO command contains an error. Find it and indicate how it can be corrected.

FD 20

40. What will the LOGO turtle draw when the following set of instructions are executed?

FD 60
LT 90
FD 40
LT 90
FD 20
LT 90
FD 40
LT 90
FD 15
LT 90
FD 5
RT 90
FD 5

SUGGESTED FURTHER READING

Bratlien, M., "Computer Development in Educational Administration," in *T.H.E. (Technical Horizons in Education) Journal* **16**, No. 10 (June 1989), 46–56.

Computers and Computation (Readings from *Scientific American*). San Francisco: W.H. Freeman, 1971. Contains many interesting articles on the history, uses, and future of the computer. Articles 23–26 discuss the applications of the computer to technology, organization, education, and science.

Eames, C., and R. Eames, *A Computer Perspective*. Cambridge, Mass.: Harvard University Press, 1973. Gives a pictorial history of the development of computers.

Hawkes, N., *The Computer Revolution*. New York: World of Science Library, Dutton, 1972. Contains detailed discussions on how the computer is applied. Specifically, Chapter 2 discusses computers in business, Chapter 3 computers in science, Chapter 4 the computer and the arts, and Chapter 8 the future.

Kemeny, J.G., *Man and the Computer*. New York: Scribner, 1972.

Reichardt, J., *The Computer in Art*. New York: Van Nostrand, Reinhold, 1971.

Rosen, S., "Electronic Computers: A Historical Survey," in *Computing Surveys* **1**(1): March 1969.

Springer, C.H., *et al.*, *The Mathematics for Management Series*. Homewood, Ill.: Richard D. Irwin, 1966. Volume 3 discusses several computer applications.

Appendices

PROPOSITIONS AND TRUTH TABLES

When doing the exercises of Section 2.4, you probably found that in some (especially those with three hypotheses) the number of possible diagrams became very large. Perhaps in some cases you failed to obtain the correct answer simply because you did label the standard diagram correctly. Fortunately, we have available another method of testing validity called **truth tables**. This method is purely mechanical, as we shall see shortly. Nothing is left to chance.

This new technique also has the advantage of working for statements for which the standard diagram does not apply. For example, we are unable to draw a standard diagram for the statement "Sherry will have either fish or meat for dinner."

We will start our discussion with simple sentences. Examples of these are:

1. All humans breathe oxygen.

2. 1 + 1 = 2.

3. *Hamlet* was written by John Davidson.

4. Ronald Reagan is the king of Iran.

5. How are you?

6. Crack is a popular type of hair spray.

7. Shut up!

8. The word "drug" is a four-letter word.

9. $x + 3 = 5$.

10. Right on!

In the above examples, sentences (1), (2) and (8), are definitely true. Sentences (3), (4), and (6) are false. Sentences (5), (7), (9), and (10) are neither true nor false. In sentence (9) if we replace x by 2, then it becomes a true sentence. If we replace x by any other value, then it becomes a false sentence. We will be concerned only with true or false sentences.

proposition

statement

> **Definition A-1**   Any sentence that is either true or false is called a **proposition** or **statement**. Propositions are denoted by the lower case letters p, q, r, ...

truth value

> **Definition A-2**   If a proposition is a true statement, then we say its **truth value** is true, denoted by T. If a proposition is a false statement, then we say its **truth value** is false, denoted by F.

The examples given above are simple statements. Each expresses but one idea. If we were to use only simple sentences in everyday speech and thought, then what we could express would be extremely limited. (Try for just one hour to express your ideas using only simple sentences.) For this reason we will also deal with compound statements.

compound statements

> **Definition A-3**   Simple statements joined together in different ways are called **compound statements**.

One way of combining statements is by means of the word "and." For example, if we have the simple statements

1. Bruce failed math,

and

2. Bruce passed folk dancing,

then we can form the compound statement "Bruce failed math and passed folk dancing." Such a statement is called a *conjunction*.

conjunction

> **Definition A-4** A **conjunction** consists of two or more statements joined together by means of the word "and." We use the symbol "∧" to stand for the word "and."

If p stands for "Bruce failed math" and q stands for "Bruce passed folk dancing," then the statement "Bruce failed math and passed folk dancing" can be symbolized by $p \wedge q$.

As another example, if we let p = "all dogs wear glasses" and q = "flowers are intelligent," then the symbol $p \wedge q$ stands for "all dogs wear glasses and flowers are intelligent." Notice that the two simple statements forming the conjunction are not related. There is no rule that specifies that the statements must be related in any way.

It is necessary for us to have a method of determining the truth value for a conjunction, depending on the truth values of its components (that is, the simple statements out of which it is formed). We will make up a table (similar to the multiplication and addition tables learned in elementary school). This table will show all the different combinations of truth values for p and q and the resulting value for $p \wedge q$. Such a table is called a **truth table**.

truth table

Conjunction table

p	q	$p \wedge q$
T	T	T
T	F	F
F	T	F
F	F	F

Look at the first line of this table. It says that if p is true and q is true, then $p \wedge q$ is true. This seems reasonable, and it agrees with everyday usage. The second line says that if p is true and q is false, then $p \wedge q$ is false. The third line says that if p is false and q is true, then $p \wedge q$ is false. Finally, the last line says that when p is false and q is false, we conclude that $p \wedge q$ is false. These also agree with everyday usage. Thus the conjunction of two statements is true whenever each of the statements individually is true. In any other case it is not true.

Now, if we are given any conjunction, we do not have to consider its meaning to decide if it is true or false. We can just look at the table and determine *mechanically* its truth value, depending on the truth or falsity of the individual parts. We will see in Section A-2 how this is done.

If we join together simple statements by the word "or," we have what is known as a **disjunction**.

disjunction

> **Definition A-5**   A **disjunction** consists of two or more statements joined together by the word "or." We use the symbol "∨" to stand for the word "or."

If p stands for "Joe will get an A in his math course" and q stands for "Joe will get an A in his English course," then the statement "Joe will get an A in his math course or an A in his English course" can be symbolized by $p \vee q$. In this example, it is quite possible that Joe will get an A in both courses, so that both components of the disjunction may be true. This is referred to as the **inclusive disjunction**.

inclusive disjunction

As another example, let p = "Bill Murray will be elected president of the United States in 1996" and q = "Jane Smith will be elected president of the United States in 1996." Then the symbol $p \vee q$ stands for "Bill Murray will be elected president of the United States in 1996 or Jane Smith will be elected president of the United States in 1996." In this case it is obvious that both cannot be true. At most, one of the statements is true. It may turn out that neither is true. If both components of a disjunction cannot be true at the same time, then this is referred to as the **exclusive disjunction**.

exclusive disjunction

In our discussion we will use only the inclusive disjunction. Again, this means the disjunction $p \vee q$ is true if p is true, or if q is true, or if both p and q are true.

It is easy to see how to construct the truth table for disjunction:

**Disjunction table
(inclusive case)**

p	q	$p \vee q$
T	T	T
T	F	T
F	T	T
F	F	F

Look at the first line of this table. It says that if p is true and q is true, then $p \vee q$ is true. This conforms to the inclusive use of the disjunction. The second and third lines say that $p \vee q$ is true if either of the components (p or q) is true. The fourth line says that a disjunction is false if both components are false.

Suppose we are given the statement "it is raining." From this we can form another statement, "it is not raining," by inserting the word "not." This is referred to as the **negation** of the original statement. Alternative ways of writing this are "it is false that it is raning" and "it is not true that it is raining."

negation

> **Definition A-6** The **negation** of statement p is the statement "p is not true" denoted as $\sim p$ (read as "not p"). Often, to avoid awkward English, we form the negation by simply inserting "not" in the appropriate place.

EXAMPLE 1

a) If p is "Sharon is a genius," then $\sim p$ is "Sharon is not a genius."
b) If p is "$2 + 2 = 4$," then $\sim p$ is "$2 + 2$ is not equal to 4."
c) If p is "I was a fool to take this course," then $\sim p$ is "I was not a fool to take this course."
d) If p is "I take a bath once a month," then $\sim p$ is "I do not take a bath once a month."

The truth table for the negation is rather obvious. It is

Negation table

p	$\sim p$
T	F
F	T

In everyday language, conjunctions, disjunctions, and negations are often combined in the same sentence. Sentences of this kind can be symbolized as illustrated in the following examples.

EXAMPLE 2

Symbolize the following.

a) My cat is stuck in the tree, and the firemen are not coming to rescue it.
b) My cat is not stuck in the tree, and the firemen are not coming to rescue it.

SOLUTION

Let $p =$ "my cat is stuck in the tree," and let $q =$ "the firemen are coming to rescue it." Then we can symbolize statement (a) as $p \wedge (\sim q)$. Using the same notation, we can symbolize statement (b) as $(\sim p) \wedge (\sim q)$.

EXAMPLE 3

If p stands for "my car rattles" and q stands for "my mouse squeaks," then express in words each of the following symbolic expressions.

a) $(\sim p) \wedge q$

b) $(\sim p) \wedge (\sim q)$

c) $(\sim p) \vee q$

SOLUTION

a) My car does not rattle and my mouse squeaks.

b) My car does not rattle and my mouse does not squeak.

c) Either my car does not rattle or my mouse squeaks.

What would you say is the negation of "all violets are blue"? Here are some answers suggested by students recently.

1. All violets are not blue.

2. No violets are blue.

3. All violets are green.

4. Some violets are not blue.

Let us analyze each of these answers: Answer (1) says "all violets are not blue." This has more than one meaning. Two possible interpretations are:

a) "Anything that is a violet is not blue," or to put it another way, "no violets are blue."

b) "It is not true that each and every violet is blue," or to put it another way, "some violets are not blue."

We know that both white violets and blue violets exist. Thus the statements "all violets are blue" and "no violets are blue" are both false. But the negation table tells us that the negation of a false statement must be true. Thus "no violets are blue" cannot be the negation of "all violets are blue."

On the other hand, *"some violets are not blue" is a correct negation of "all violets are blue."*

We have seen that answer (2) is incorrect. Answer (4) is a correct negation.

Finally, look at answer (3). This statement "all violets are green" is false. So is the given statement "all violets are blue." Therefore the negation table shows us that this answer cannot be the negation we are seeking. Answer (4) is the only correct negation.

Similarly, the negation of "all teachers are rich" is "some teachers are not rich."

Now consider the statement "some violets are blue." What is its negation? The first answer that comes to mind is "some violets are not blue." Is this correct? Both of the statements "some violets are blue" and "some violets are not blue" are true statements. Hence one cannot be the negation of the other; the negation table requires that the negation of a true statement must be false.

"Some violets are blue" means that there is at least one violet that is blue. If this is false, then there can be no violets that are blue. Thus *the negation of "some violets are blue" is "no violets are blue."*

Similarly, the negation of "some women are tall" is "no women are tall."

Now consider the statement "some violets are not blue." This means that there is at least one violet that is not blue. To put it another way, it is possible to find a violet that is not blue. The negation would then say that it is *not* possible to find a violet that is not blue. Another way of saying this is "all violets are blue." Thus *the negation of "some violets are not blue" is "all violets are blue."*

Similarly, the negation of "some cigarettes are not menthol flavored" is "all cigarettes are menthol flavored."

Now consider the statement "no violets are blue." This says that it is *not* possible to find a violet that is blue. Then the negation says it *is* possible to find a violet that is blue, or that "some violets are blue." Thus *the negation of "no violets are blue" is "some violets are blue."*

Similarly, the negation of "no moon people are green" is "some moon people are green."

The results of the above discussions are summarized for the reader's convenience in the following chart:

Original statement	Negation
All violets are blue.	Some violets are not blue.
Some violets are blue.	No violets are blue.
Some violets are not blue.	All violets are blue.
No violets are blue.	Some violets are blue.

An important statement that occurs frequently is the **implication** or **conditional**. These are statements such as the following.

1. If Mary likes Pete, then she is insane.

2. If I eat my spinach, then I will be strong.

3. If I were a cat, then I would bark.

4. If I were a bell, then I would ring.

5. If I were you, I'd run.

The implication can be defined in the following way.

implication

conditional

> **Definition A-7**   An **implication** or **conditional** is any statement of the form "if p, then q." We symbolize this as $p \rightarrow q$. This is read as "p implies q" and means that if p is true, then q must be true.

hypothesis

conclusion

> **Definition A-8**   The p statement of the conditional "$p \rightarrow q$" is called the **hypothesis**, and the q statement is called the **conclusion**.

EXAMPLE 4

If p stands for "Leon passes the Math 5 exam" and q stands for "I will eat my hat," then the implication "if Leon passes the Math 5 exam, then I will eat my hat" can be symbolized as $p \rightarrow q$. The hypothesis is "Leon passes the Math 5 exam." The conclusion is "I will eat my hat." ■

EXAMPLE 5

a) Let q stand for "you are out of Schlitz" and let r stand for "you are out of beer." The implication "if you are out of Schlitz, you are out of beer" can be symbolized as $q \rightarrow r$. The hypothesis is "you are out of Schlitz," and the conclusion is "you are out of beer." What is $r \rightarrow q$?

b) Let p stand for "it is raining" and q stand for "the streets are wet." The implication "if it is raining, then the streets are wet" can be symbolized as $p \rightarrow q$. What does the symbol $q \rightarrow q$ represent? ■

Christina's father has made the following promise to her: If she gets A's in all her courses this semester, then he will buy her a new car. Four different things can happen.

1. Hypothesis true: She gets A's in all her courses.
Conclusion true: Her father buys her a new car.

2. Hypothesis true: She gets A's in all her courses.
Conclusion false: Her father does not buy her a new car.

3. Hypothesis false: She does not get A's in all her courses.
Conclusion true: Her father buys her a new car.

4. Hypothesis false: She does not get A's in all her courses.
Conclusion false: Her father does not buy her a new car.

In case (1) her father certainly kept his promise. Thus the implication "if she gets A's in all her courses this semester, then he will buy her a new car" is true. *The hypothesis and conclusion are true, and this makes the implication true.*

In case (2) her father definitely did not keep his promise. Thus the implication "if she gets A's in all her courses this semester, then he will buy her a new car" is false. *The hypothesis is true, but since the conclusion is false, this makes the implication false.*

In case (3) and (4), Christina does not live up to her end of the deal. Therefore her father's promise is never put to the test. Whether he buys her a car or not, he cannot be said to have broken his promise. Thus we cannot call his implication false. Since all statements are either true or false, we then classify his implication as true. This leads us to the following truth table.

Implication table

p	q	$p \rightarrow q$
T	T	T
T	F	F
F	T	T
F	F	T

The first two lines of the implication table seem to agree with everyday usage. You may not yet be convinced of the third and fourth lines. This is because in everyday speech we do not make implications that have false hypotheses. To prove to yourself that they are reasonable, consider the following discussion overheard in the student cafeteria.

Eric: My uncle is a famous movie producer.
José: If your uncle is a famous movie producer, then I am the king of France.

José's comment indicates his strong disbelief in Eric's claim that his uncle is a famous movie producer. José is sure that Eric's statement is false. José knows that his own statement "I am the king of France" is false. He definitely intends his own implication to be true. Thus José is really saying that "false implies false" results in a true statement. This corresponds to line 4 of the implication table. This is an example of an implication with a false hypothesis being used in everyday conversation. Can you find an example from everyday usage that illustrates line 3 of the implication table?

Variations of the Conditional

Let us look at the implication (or conditional) "if it is raining, then the streets are wet." Now consider the following variations (changes).

Original statement: If it is raining, then the streets are wet.

1. *Converse:*   If the streets are wet, then it is raining.
2. *Inverse:*   If it is not raining, then the streets are not wet.
3. *Contrapositive:*   If the streets are not wet, then it is not raining.

converse

inverse

contrapositive

If we let p stand for "it is raining" and q stand for "the streets are wet," then the original statement can be symbolized as $p \rightarrow q$.

The **converse** (statement 1) is formed by interchanging the hypothesis ("it is raining") and the conclusion ("the streets are wet"). Thus the converse is symbolized as $q \rightarrow p$.

In part (a) of Example 5 we asked you to find $r \rightarrow q$. This was just the converse of the given implication $q \rightarrow r$. Similarly, in part (b) of Example 5, $q \rightarrow p$ is the converse of the given implication $p \rightarrow q$.

The **inverse** (statement 2) is formed by inserting the word "not" in the hypothesis ("it is raining") and the word "not" in the conclusion ("the streets are wet"). Thus we have "if it is not raining, then the streets are not wet." So the inverse is $(\sim p) \rightarrow (\sim q)$.

The **contrapositive** (statement 3) is formed by switching around the hypothesis and the conclusion *and* then inserting the word "not" in both the hypothesis and the conclusion. Thus we symbolize the contrapositive of $p \rightarrow q$ as $(\sim q) \rightarrow (\sim p)$.

Comment   The contrapositive of an implication is really obtained by first taking the converse of the given statement and then taking the inverse of the result. Try it for our original statement.

Now it is obvious that the original statement "if it is raining, then the streets are wet" is true. Must the converse also be true? Obviously not. It is possible that the street cleaners have just washed the streets. Thus if the streets are wet, it does not necessarily mean that it is raining. In other words, the converse is not necessarily true. (It may be either true or false.)

What can we say about the inverse? Must it be true? Again your answer should be "no." If it is not raining, it does not automatically follow that the streets are not wet. The street cleaners may have just washed the street. Obviously, the inverse may be false.

How about the contrapositive? Everyone would agree that if the streets are not wet, then it can't be raining. Thus the contrapositive must be true.

Summarizing   If the original implication is true, then *only* the contrapositive *must* be true. The converse and inverse may or may not be true. In the next section, when we discuss truth tables in more detail, we will *prove* this.

As another example, consider the implication "if John studies hard, then he will pass this course." We have the following.

Original statement: If John studies hard, then he will pass this course.

Converse: If John passes this course, then he will have studied hard.

Inverse: If John does not study hard, then he will not pass this course.

Contrapositive: If John does not pass this course, then he will not have studied hard.

Look at the original statement. The hypothesis is "John studies hard." In forming the converse we rephrased this as "he will have studied hard." This change in the English was done merely to avoid an awkward sentence. (Had we not made this change, the converse would have read,"if he will pass this course, then John studies hard." Sounds peculiar, doesn't it?) This change does not affect the statement itself. Now look at the inverse and contrapositive. We have made similar changes. What would the inverse and contrapositive be without these adjustments?

Comment   When asked for the converse of "if John studies hard, then he will pass this course," some students answer, "John will pass this course if he studies hard." This is wrong because it says the same thing as the original statement.

It may be helpful to put these results into a table.

		Symbolic form	Truth value of this statement, assuming original statement is true
Original statement	If p, then q.	$p \rightarrow q$	True
Converse	If q, then p.	$q \rightarrow p$	May be true or false
Inverse	If $\sim p$, then $\sim q$.	$(\sim p) \rightarrow (\sim q)$	May be true or false
Contrapositive	If $\sim q$, then $\sim p$.	$(\sim q) \rightarrow (\sim p)$	*Must* be true

Biconditional or Equivalence

Professor Burns has told her student John Williams: "I will give you an A in this course if and only if you get at least 91 on the final." Let p stand for "I will give you an A," and let q stand for "you get at least 91 on the final." Professor Burns' promise can be rewritten as p *if and only if q*. She is really saying two things:

1. If you get at least 91 on the final, then I will give you an A. Symbolically, $q \rightarrow p$.

2. In order to get an A, you need at least a 91 (even 90 is not good enough). In other words, if you get an A, you must have at least a 91 on the final. Symbolically, $p \rightarrow q$.

Professor Burns' statement then boils down to the following: "$p \rightarrow q$ and $q \rightarrow p$." Such a statement is referred to as a **biconditional** or **equivalence**.

biconditional

equivalence

> **Definition A-9   A biconditional** or **equivalence** is any statement of the form "p if and only if q." We symbolize this as $p \leftrightarrow q$. Read this as "p is equivalent to q."

EXAMPLE 6

"Gwendolyn swims if and only if it is summer." Let p denote "Gwendolyn swims" and q "it is summer." This statement can be rewritten as $p \leftrightarrow q$.

The truth table for the biconditional is as follows:

p	q	$p \leftrightarrow q$
T	T	T
T	F	F
F	T	F
F	F	T

Biconditional table

Note that the biconditional is true only when both parts (p and q) have the *same* truth value.

To understand this truth table, consider the example "I cry if and only if I am sad." Let p be "I cry" and q "I am sad." If I am crying and I am sad, then both p and q are true. Clearly, the resulting biconditional is then true. This illustrates line 1 of the truth table. If I am sad but I am not crying, or if I am crying but not sad, then the biconditional is obviously false. This explains lines 2 and 3 of the truth table. Think about line 4. Can you justify it?

In the rest of the appendices we will make frequent use of the truth tables for conjunction, disjunction, implication, negation, and biconditional. Therefore for handy reference, we summarize them here.

Conjunction table

p	q	$p \wedge q$
T	T	T
T	F	F
F	T	F
F	F	F

Disjunction table

p	q	$p \vee q$
T	T	T
T	F	T
F	T	T
F	F	F

Implication table

p	q	$p \rightarrow q$
T	T	T
T	F	F
F	T	T
F	F	T

Negation table

p	$\sim p$
T	F
F	T

Biconditional table

p	q	$p \leftrightarrow q$
T	T	T
T	F	F
F	T	F
F	F	T

EXERCISES FOR A-1

1. Determine which of the following expressions are propositions and which are not.
   a) Gosh!
   b) You have to be a genius to operate those new compact disc players.
   c) Do you have a buck?
   d) People who are nearsighted cannot use binoculars.
   e) Excuse me!
   f) Credit card users are always being ripped off.
   g) Can you lend me your wheels?
   h) Kerosene heaters are so safe that everybody should own one.

2. Let p stand for "I love music" and let q stand for "I attend rock concerts." Express in words each of the following symbolic expressions:
   a) $p \wedge q$
   b) $\sim q$
   c) $p \vee q$
   d) $(\sim p) \wedge q$
   e) $(\sim p) \wedge (\sim q)$
   f) $p \leftrightarrow (\sim q)$
   g) $\sim (p \vee q)$
   h) $(\sim p) \vee (q)$
   i) $(\sim p) \vee (\sim q)$
   j) $\sim (p \wedge q)$

3. Let p stand for "I am a salesman" and let q stand for "I fly frequently between New York and California." Express in symbolic form each of the following sentences.
   a) If I am a salesman, then I fly frequently between New York and California.
   b) I am a salesman, but I do not fly frequently between New York and California.
   c) I am not a salesman, and I do not fly frequently between New York and California.
   d) It is not true that I am a salesman and that I fly frequently between New York and California.
   e) Although I fly frequently between New York and California, I am not a salesman.
   f) If I do not fly frequently between New York and California, then I am not a salesman.

4. Write the negation of each of the following statements:
   a) Some airlines have a better safety record than others.
   b) All instant coffees raise the blood cholesterol level of humans.
   c) Some cardiologists do not carry extensive medical malpractice insurance.
   d) No president of the United States has ever died of cancer while in office.

5. If p stands for "I am afraid of heights" and q stands for "I have flown in an airplane," then express in words each of the following expressions:
   a) $p \rightarrow q$
   b) $q \leftrightarrow p$
   c) $p \rightarrow (\sim q)$
   d) $(\sim p) \rightarrow q$
   e) $(\sim p) \leftrightarrow (\sim q)$
   f) $(\sim q) \rightarrow (\sim p)$

6. Write the inverse, converse, and contrapositive of each of the following implications:
   a) If an airplane crashes into the ocean, then the seats will float.
   b) If you suffer from migraine headaches, then you use a lot of aspirin.
   c) If the consumer price index rises by more than 4 percent, then college tuition costs will increase moderately.

7. Assume that the following implication is true: "If there is a water shortage, then people will conserve water." Which of the following statements must be true? Explain.
   a) If there is no water shortage, then people will not conserve water.
   b) If people are not conserving water, then there is no water shortage.
   c) If people are conserving water, then there is a water shortage.
   d) People will conserve water if there is a water shortage.

8. Mack was told by the parole board of his prison that he would be released on probation after a year *only if* he would be a model prisoner. By the end of the year,

Mack was rated as a model prisoner but still was not released on probation. He appealed to the governor, claiming that the parole board lied. Is Mack's appeal justified? Why or why not?

9. The New Dorp Insurance Company will promote its sales representatives to vice-presidents *only if* they generate at least $500,000 of sales during a year. For the calendar year of 1990, Maureen O'Hara generated more than $500,000 of sales and was not promoted. She has accused the company of sex discrimination in not promoting her. Is her claim valid? Explain.

10. Consider the following statistical statement: "If your luggage is fastened securely on all overseas flights, then it will usually arrive safely at its destination."

a) Write another English statement that you know is true based upon this sentence.

b) Write another English statement that you know is false based upon this sentence.

11. Let p stand for "Joan has good recommendations," let q stand for "Joan has a high college grade point average," and let r stand for "Joan was accepted to medical school." Express in words each of the following symbolic expressions.

a) $p \wedge (q \to r)$

b) $p \vee (q \wedge r)$

c) $(\sim p) \vee [(\sim q) \wedge (\sim r)]$

d) $p \vee [q \to (\sim r)]$

e) $(\sim p) \leftrightarrow (r \wedge q)$

f) $[(\sim q) \vee (\sim r)] \wedge p$

A-2

TAUTOLOGIES AND SELF-CONTRADICTIONS

In everyday language, as well as in mathematics, we usually make statements that combine conjunctions, negations, disjunctions, implications, and biconditionals in different forms. Take, for example, the following statement: "If it rains this evening, I will either go to the movies or go bowling." By means of truth tables we can determine when such statements are true or false. These truth tables will involve combinations of $\wedge$, $\vee$, $\sim$, $\to$ and $\leftrightarrow$. Let us now look at some truth tables and analyze them.

EXAMPLE 1   Determine the truth table for $(\sim p) \vee q$.

SOLUTION   Two letters are involved, p and q. So we have a column for each of these.

Again looking at the given expression, we notice that the negation of p occurs as one of the parts. So we add another column, $\sim p$. We then have the following:

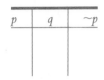

p	q	$\sim p$

Now we need a column for $(\sim p) \vee q$. This gives us the following:

p	q	$\sim p$	$(\sim p) \vee q$

Comment   We arrive at the last column by working our way across. We start *first* with the simple letters and *then* add the necessary $\sim$, $\wedge$, $\vee$, $\rightarrow$ and $\leftrightarrow$ where needed, in the order in which they occur. The parentheses in the above example tell us that we must *first* take the negation of p and *then* the disjunction of this with q.

Comment   Note that in this example we do not need a column for $p \vee q$, since this is not part of the original expression. We need a column *only* for $(\sim p) \vee q$.

Getting back to this example, we now complete the table, using the basic truth tables given on p. A-12. We work from left to right, filling in the blanks.

TABLE 1.A			
p	q	$(\sim p)$	$(\sim p) \vee q$
T	T	F	
T	F	F	
F	T	T	
F	F	T	

In the first two columns we have written all possible combinations of T and F (there are exactly four). The third column is obtained from the negation table. To get the final column, we go to the disjunction table and apply it to the disjunction of $(\sim p)$ and q. Notice that to do this, we cannot use the *headings* of the disjunction table. We just work from the *entries* as follows. We look at the first row in Table 1.A. The entries for $(\sim p)$ and q are F and T *in that order*. In the disjunction table we find the entries F and T *in that order*. They appear on the third row. The result for this row is T. So we enter T in the first row of Table 1.A.

Now we look at the second row of Table 1.A. The entries for (~p) and q are F and F in that order. In the disjunction table, we find the entries F and F in that order. These are on the fourth row and their result is F. So we enter F on the second row of Table 1.A. We now look at the third row of Table 1.A. The entries for (~p) and q are T and T, in that order. In the disjunction table these entries are on the first row and their result is T. So we enter T in the third row of Table 1.A. Finally, on the fourth row of Table 1.A the entries for (~p) and q are T and F in that order. We look for T and F in that order in the disjunction table, and find them on the second row. The result is T, so we enter T on the fourth row of Table 1.A.

The final table then looks like this:

p	q	$(\sim p)$	$(\sim p) \vee q$
T	T	F	T
T	F	F	F
F	T	T	T
F	F	T	T

The final column of the table is circled. This means:

1. If p and q are both true, then the whole statement is true.

2. If p is true and q is false, then the whole statement is false.

3. If p is false and q is true, then the whole statement is true.

4. If p is false and q is false, then the whole statement is true.

The truth value of the entire statement may be true or false depending on the truth values of p and q.

EXAMPLE 2

SOLUTION

Determine the truth table for $(p \wedge q) \rightarrow (p \vee q)$.

The parentheses tell us that we first take $p \wedge q$. Then we take $p \vee q$. Finally we connect $(p \wedge q)$ with $(p \vee q)$ by means of $\rightarrow$. Again two letters, p, and q, are involved. So we need a column for each of these. Looking at the expression, we see that we also need columns for $p \wedge q$ and $p \vee q$. Finally, we need a column for the whole expression [which connects $(p \wedge q)$ with $(p \vee q)$ by means of $\rightarrow$]. The truth table is as follows:

p	q	$p \wedge q$	$p \vee q$	$(p \wedge q) \rightarrow (p \vee q)$
T	T	T	T	T
T	F	F	T	T
F	T	F	T	T
F	F	F	F	T

As in the previous example, we must consider all possible combinations of truth values for the letters p and q. This gives us the first two columns. The entries in the third and fourth columns are obtained from the conjunction and disjunction tables, respectively.

The final column is obtained by applying the implication table to the entries in the $(p \wedge q)$ and $(p \vee q)$ columns. This is because the last column states that the third and fourth columns are connected by means of implication. For example, the entries in the second row of the $(p \wedge q)$ and $(p \vee q)$ columns are F and T *in that order*. So we go to the implication table and look for the row containing F and T in that order. It is in the third row. The result is T, so we enter T in the final column of our chart. In a similar manner we complete the final column.

Again we circle the final column. Notice that in this example all the entries in the final column are T. This means that $(p \wedge q) \rightarrow (p \vee q)$ is true regardless of the truth values of p and q. In other words, the statement $(p \wedge q) \rightarrow (p \vee q)$ is *always* true. Such a statement is called a **tautology**.

tautology

> **Definition A-10** Any statement that is always true is called a **tautology**. This means that in the final column of its truth table there are only T's.

Example 1 is not a tautology. Why not?

EXAMPLE 3

Construct the truth table for $(p \rightarrow q) \wedge [p \wedge (\sim q)]$.

SOLUTION

Proceeding in the same manner as we did in Example 2 we make columns for p, q, $\sim q$, $(p \rightarrow q)$, $p \wedge (\sim q)$, and finally for $(p \rightarrow q) \wedge [p \wedge (\sim q)]$. We then have the following truth table:

p	q	$\sim q$	$p \rightarrow q$	$p \wedge (\sim q)$	$(p \rightarrow q) \wedge [p \wedge (\sim q)]$
T	T	F	T	F	F
T	F	T	F	T	F
F	T	F	T	F	F
F	F	T	T	F	F

The final column of this table consists only of F's. This statement is *never* true. Such a statement is called a **self-contradiction**.

self-contradiction

> **Definition A-11** Any statement that is always false is called a **self-contradiction**. This means that in the final column of its truth table there are only F's.

To better understand the idea of a self-contradiction, consider the following: "I have read *Hamlet*, and I have not read *Hamlet*." Clearly, this statement cannot be true under any circumstances. We can examine it symbolically by letting p stand for "I have read *Hamlet*." Symbolized, this statement is $p \land (\sim p)$. Its truth table is:

p	$\sim p$	$p \land (\sim p)$
T	F	F
F	T	F

Since we have only F's in the final column, it is a self-contradiction.

EXAMPLE 4

SOLUTION

Determine the truth table for $[(p \to q) \land (q \to r)] \to (p \to r)$.

In this case we need columns for $p, q, r, (p \to q), (q \to r), (p \to q) \land (q \to r),$ $(p \to r)$, and finally for the whole statement $[(p \to q) \land (q \to r)] \to (p \to r)$. The truth table for this is as follows:

p	q	r	$(p \to q)$	$(q \to r)$	$(p \to q) \land (q \to r)$	$p \to r$	$[(p \to q) \land (q \to r)] \to (p \to r)$
T	T	T	T	T	T	T	T
T	T	F	T	F	F	F	T
T	F	T	F	T	F	T	T
T	F	F	F	T	F	F	T
F	T	T	T	T	T	T	T
F	T	F	T	F	F	T	T
F	F	T	T	T	T	T	T
F	F	F	T	T	T	T	T

The table has eight lines, since there are eight possible combinations of T and F for the three letters. If there were four letters, how many lines would we need for the truth table? Notice that this expression is a tautology, since we have only T's in the final column.

EXAMPLE 5

Show by means of truth tables that if an implication is true, then its converse does not necessarily have to be true.

SOLUTION

Let the implication be $(p \rightarrow q)$. Then its converse is $(q \rightarrow p)$. We compare their truth tables.

p	q	$p \rightarrow q$
T	T	T
T	F	F
F	T	T
F	F	T

p	q	$q \rightarrow p$
T	T	T
T	F	T
F	T	F
F	F	T

Looking at line 3 of each table, we see that if p is false and q is true, then $(p \rightarrow q)$ is true, whereas $(q \rightarrow p)$ is false. Compare the other lines of the truth tables; $(p \rightarrow q)$ and $(q \rightarrow p)$ may have different or the same truth values depending on the truth values of p and q. ▪

EXAMPLE 6

Show by means of truth tables that if the implication $p \rightarrow q$ is true, then its contrapositive $(\sim q) \rightarrow (\sim p)$ must be true.

SOLUTION

In this case we need columns for p, q, $(\sim p)$, $(\sim q)$, $p \rightarrow q$, and finally a column for $(\sim q) \rightarrow (\sim p)$. The truth table for this is the following:

p	q	$\sim p$	$\sim q$	$p \rightarrow q$	$(\sim q) \rightarrow (\sim p)$
T	T	F	F	T	T
T	F	F	T	F	F
F	T	T	F	T	T
F	F	T	T	T	T

Notice that the entries in the column for $(\sim q) \rightarrow (\sim p)$ are identical to the entries for $p \rightarrow q$. This means that $p \rightarrow q$ and $(\sim q) \rightarrow (\sim p)$ are equivalent statements and that, when one is true, the other is true. ▪

More generally, we say that

equivalent statements

> **Definition A-12** Two statements are said to be **equivalent** if the final columns of their truth tables are identical (assuming, of course, that in both tables, the truth values of p and q are written in the same order.)

Thus to determine whether two statements are equivalent, we first write the truth tables for each statement. Then we compare the final columns of each table. If the entries are identical, then the statements are equivalent. Otherwise, they are not equivalent.

EXERCISES FOR A-2

Construct a truth table for each of the statements in Exercises 1–20, and then determine whether the statements are tautologies, self-contradictions, or neither.

1. $\sim(p \rightarrow q)$ 2. $\sim(p \vee q)$

3. $(p \vee q) \rightarrow (p \wedge q)$ 4. $(p \wedge q) \rightarrow p$

5. $\sim[(p \vee q) \rightarrow (q \vee p)]$ 6. $(p \wedge q) \rightarrow (\sim r)$

7. $(\sim p) \rightarrow (q \vee r)$ 8. $[\sim(p \wedge q)] \vee [(\sim p) \wedge (\sim q)]$

9. $(p \rightarrow q) \wedge (\sim s)$ 10. $(p \wedge q) \rightarrow (\sim r)$

11. $[(p \rightarrow q) \wedge (\sim r)] \rightarrow r$ 12. $(p \vee q) \leftrightarrow [(\sim q) \wedge r]$

13. $\sim[(\sim p) \rightarrow ((\sim q) \vee r)]$ 14. $[(p \vee q) \wedge (\sim r)] \leftrightarrow r$

15. $[(p \wedge (\sim q)) \rightarrow r] \rightarrow (\sim r)$

16. $[(\sim q) \vee p)] \wedge [(\sim s) \rightarrow (\sim r)]$

17. $(p \rightarrow q) \vee [s \rightarrow (\sim r)]$ 18. $[(\sim p) \wedge s] \rightarrow (r \vee q)$

19. $[(p \wedge q) \rightarrow (\sim r)] \leftrightarrow (\sim p)$

20. $[(q \wedge (\sim r)) \vee p] \rightarrow (\sim p)$

21. Show by means of truth tables that if the implication $p \rightarrow q$ is true, then its inverse $(\sim p) \rightarrow (\sim q)$ may be false. (You will appreciate this exercise more if you reread the discussion of this on p. A-10 before attempting this exercise.)

22. If an expression involves four different letters, how many lines are needed for the truth table?

23. If an expression involves five different letters, how many lines are needed for the truth table?

24. If an expression involves n different letters, how many lines are needed for the truth table?

Assuming that p is true and q is false, find the truth value of each of the statements given in Exercises 25–33.

25. $\sim(p \rightarrow q)$ 26. $\sim[p \rightarrow (\sim q)]$

27. $\sim[p \wedge (\sim q)]$ 28. $(p \wedge q) \rightarrow (\sim q)$

29. $[(\sim p) \wedge q] \vee (\sim q)$ 30. $(p \wedge q) \vee (\sim q)$

31. $(p \rightarrow q) \leftrightarrow (\sim p)$

32. $\sim[(p \vee q) \rightarrow (q \rightarrow p)]$

33. $(\sim p) \wedge [(\sim q) \vee p]$

Consider the truth tables in Exercises 34 and 35. Find compound statements to replace the question marks.

34.

p	q	?	?	?
T	T	F	F	F
T	F	F	F	F
F	T	F	T	T
F	F	T	F	T

35.

p	q	?	?	?
T	T	T	F	F
T	F	F	T	T
F	T	T	T	T
F	F	T	F	T

Find the truth values for each of the statements given in Exercises 36–39.

36. If $2 + 2 = 4$, then $5 + 2 = 8$.

37. Either the nation's health food craze is a fraud or America's 1985 national budget had a huge surplus.

38. If Abraham Lincoln was shot while president of the United States and John Kennedy's brother was assassinated, then the name of this chaper is "Logic."

39. Cigarette smoking is dangerous to your health, but the American Cancer Society has found a cure for cancer.

40. Determine which of the following pairs of statements are equivalent.

   a) $\sim(p \vee q)$ and $(\sim p) \vee (\sim q)$

   b) $p \wedge (q \wedge r)$ and $(p \wedge q) \vee r$

   c) $\sim(p \vee q)$ and $p \rightarrow q$

   d) $p \wedge (q \vee r)$ and $(p \wedge q) \vee (p \wedge r)$

   e) $(p \rightarrow q) \wedge p$ and q

   f) $p \rightarrow (\sim q)$ and $(\sim p) \vee (\sim q)$

41. The symbol $p \veebar q$ means that *either p or q is true but not both*. This is the **exclusive disjunction** discussed in Section A-1. Write the truth table for $p \veebar q$.

42. The symbol $p \downarrow q$ means that *p and q must both be false*. This is called the **joint denial** of p and q. Write the truth table for $p \downarrow q$.

43. Construct the truth table for $\sim(p \downarrow q) \wedge [(\sim p) \veebar q]$.

A-3

APPLICATION TO ARGUMENTS

Truth tables provide a second method of testing the validity of arguments. The best way to see how this method works is to actually try it on some examples.

EXAMPLE 1

Test the validity of the following argument: "If Bigmouth wins the election, then I will leave this state. I am not leaving this state. Therefore Bigmouth will not win the election."

SOLUTION

Let p stand for "Bigmouth wins the election" and let q stand for "I will leave this state." We can rewrite each sentence as follows:

	Verbally	Symbolically
Hypotheses:	If Bigmouth wins the election, then I will leave this state.	$p \rightarrow q$
	I am not leaving this state.	$\sim q$
Conclusion:	Bigmouth will not win the election.	$\sim p$

Remember that an argument is valid if the conclusion follows logically from the hypotheses. In other words, it is valid if the hypotheses imply the conclusion. In our example we must determine whether *the hypotheses $(p \rightarrow q)$ and $(\sim q)$ together imply the conclusion $(\sim p)$.* That is, we are asked to determine whether $[(p \rightarrow q) \wedge (\sim q)] \rightarrow (\sim p)$ is always true. (Remember, $\wedge$ stands for "and." We are asking if the conclusion follows from *both* of the hypotheses and not from one or the other alone. Therefore we connect them by "and.") This gives us the truth table shown below. Since the last column has only T's, the expression is always true. Hence whether the hypotheses are true or false, the conclusion *always* follows from them. Therefore the argument is valid.

p	q	$\sim p$	$\sim q$	$p \rightarrow q$	$(p \rightarrow q) \wedge (\sim q)$	$[(p \rightarrow q) \wedge (\sim q)] \rightarrow (\sim p)$
T	T	F	F	T	F	T
T	F	F	T	F	F	T
F	T	T	F	T	F	T
F	F	T	T	T	T	T

EXAMPLE 2

Test the validity of the following argument: "If the teacher talks too long, Arthur gets a headache. Arthur has a headache. Therefore the teacher is talking too long."

SOLUTION

Let *r* stand for "the teacher talks too long" and let *s* stand for "Arthur gets a headache." We can symbolize each sentence of the argument as shown below.

	Verbally	*Symbolically*
Hypotheses:	If the teacher talks too long, Arthur gets a headache.	$r \rightarrow s$
	Arthur has a headache.	s
Conclusion:	The teacher is talking too long.	r

We must now determine whether $(r \rightarrow s)$ and *s* together imply *r*. We want to know if $[(r \rightarrow s) \wedge s] \rightarrow r$ is always true. The truth table is as follows:

r	s	$r \rightarrow s$	$(r \rightarrow s) \wedge s$	$[(r \rightarrow s) \wedge s] \rightarrow r$
T	T	T	T	T
T	F	F	F	T
F	T	T	T	F
F	F	T	F	T

The final F of line 3 shows us that if *r* is false and *s* is true, then the conclusion does *not* follow from the hypotheses. A deductive argument is valid only if the conclusion *always* follows from the hypotheses. Hence this argument is *invalid*.

Comment   In Example 1 we had all T's in the truth table, so the expression $[(p \rightarrow q) \wedge (\sim q)] \rightarrow (\sim p)$ was a tautology, and the argument was valid. In Example 2, since we had one F, the statement was not a tautology, and the argument was invalid. *If an argument is valid, its truth table must be a tautology.*

EXAMPLE 3

Test the validity of the following argument. "If Dave sings, the cat howls. Either the baby cries or the cat howls. The baby is not crying. Therefore Dave is not singing."

SOLUTION

Let *p* stand for "Dave sings," *q* for "the cat howls," and *r* for "the baby cries." We have:

	Verbally	*Symbolically*
Hypotheses:	If Dave sings, the cat howls.	$p \rightarrow q$
	Either the baby cries or the cat howls.	$r \vee q$
	The baby is not crying.	$\sim r$
Conclusion:	Dave is not singing.	$\sim p$

The argument is symbolized as $[(p \to q) \wedge (r \vee q) \wedge (\sim r)] \to (\sim p)$. Its truth table is as follows:

p	q	r	$\sim p$	$\sim r$	$p \to q$	$r \vee q$	$(p \to q) \wedge (r \vee q)$	$(p \to q) \wedge (r \vee q) \wedge (\sim r)$	$[(p \to q) \wedge (r \vee q) \wedge (\sim r)] \to (\sim p)$
T	T	T	F	F	T	T	T	F	T
T	T	F	F	T	T	T	T	T	F
T	F	T	F	F	F	T	F	F	T
T	F	F	F	T	F	F	F	F	T
F	T	T	T	F	T	T	T	F	T
F	T	F	T	T	T	T	T	T	T
F	F	T	T	F	T	T	T	F	T
F	F	F	T	T	T	F	F	F	T

Since the final column contains one F, this statement is not a tautology. Hence the argument is invalid. ▪

direct reasoning

An alternate method for testing the validity of an argument involves **direct reasoning** and the form of the argument. For example, consider the following:

EXAMPLE 4

Test the validity of the argument: If the weather is nice, then I will go swimming. The weather is nice. Therefore, I will go swimming.

SOLUTION

Let p stand for "The weather is nice" and let q stand for "I will go swimming." Then the argument can be symbolized as

$$\begin{array}{ll} \textit{Hypotheses:} & p \to q \\ & \underline{p} \\ \textit{Conclusion:} & q \end{array}$$

law of detachment (or modus ponens)

There is a general **law of detachment** (or **modus ponens**) which states that if an argument is of the form "if p, then q "and "p is true," then "q must also be true." Using this law, we can immediately determine that the conclusion is valid. ▪

chain rule

Another form of an argument involves the **chain rule**, which can be stated as follows: "If p, then q and if q, then r" are true, then "if p, then r" is true. We illustrate this rule with an example.

EXAMPLE 5

Test the validity of the following argument: "If the players on the team are healthy, then we will win the playoffs. If we win the playoffs, our school will be proud of us. Therefore, if the players on the team are healthy, then our school will be proud of us."

SOLUTION:

Let p stand for "The players on the team are healthy," q stand for "We will win the playoffs," and r stand for "Our school will be proud of us." Then the argument can be symbolized as

$$\text{Hypotheses:} \quad \begin{array}{c} p \to q \\ \underline{q \to r} \end{array}$$
$$\text{Conclusion:} \quad p \to r$$

The chain rule immediately tells us that the conclusion is valid.   ▬

indirect reasoning

modus tolens

Another form of reasoning involves **indirect reasoning** and the form of the argument. The rule, which is known as **modus tolens**, can be stated as follows: If we have a conditional accepted as true, and we know that the conclusion is false, then the hypothesis must be false.

We illustrate this rule with an example:

EXAMPLE 6

Test the validity of the following argument: "If my grade point average (GPA) is above 3.5, then I will graduate with honors. I am not graduating with honors. Therefore, my GPA is not above 3.5."

SOLUTION

Let p stand for "My grade point average (GPA) is above 3.5," and let q stand for "I will graduate with honors." The argument can be symbolized as

$$\text{Hypothesis:} \quad \begin{array}{c} p \to q \\ \underline{\sim q} \end{array}$$
$$\text{Conclusion:} \quad \sim p$$

The law of modus tolens tells us that the conclusion is valid.   ▬

There are many other rules of logic that we can use to determine the validity of arguments. One can use truth tables to show that these laws are indeed valid. For the convenience of the reader, we summarize some of the frequently used laws.

Law of logic	Symbolic forms	
1. Law of detachment (modus ponens)	*Hyp:* $\quad p \rightarrow q$ $\qquad\quad p$ $\overline{\qquad\qquad}$ *Concl:* $\quad q$	$[(p \rightarrow q) \wedge p] \rightarrow q$
2. Chain rule (law of the syllogism)	*Hyp:* $\quad p \rightarrow q$ $\qquad\quad q \rightarrow r$ $\overline{\qquad\qquad}$ *Concl:* $\; p \rightarrow r$	$[(p \rightarrow q) \wedge (q \rightarrow r)] \rightarrow (p \rightarrow r)$
3. Law of modus tolens	*Hyp:* $\quad p \rightarrow q$ $\qquad\quad {\sim}q$ $\overline{\qquad\qquad}$ *Concl:* $\quad {\sim}p$	$[(p \rightarrow q) \wedge ({\sim}q)] \rightarrow ({\sim}p)$
4. Law of the contrapositive	*Hyp:* $\quad p \rightarrow q$ *Concl:* $\; ({\sim}q) \rightarrow ({\sim}p)$	$[(p \rightarrow q)] \leftrightarrow [({\sim}q) \rightarrow ({\sim}p)]$
5. Law of disjunctive inference	*Hyp:* $\quad p \vee q$ $\qquad\quad {\sim}p$ $\overline{\qquad\qquad}$ *Concl:* $\quad q$ or *Hyp:* $\quad p \vee q$ $\qquad\quad {\sim}q$ $\overline{\qquad\qquad}$ *Concl:* $\quad p$	$[(p \vee q) \wedge ({\sim}p)] \rightarrow q$ $[(p \vee q) \wedge ({\sim}q)] \rightarrow p$
6. De Morgan's laws	*Hyp:* $\quad {\sim}(p \wedge q)$ *Concl:* $({\sim}p) \vee ({\sim}q)$ or *Hyp:* $\quad {\sim}(p \vee q)$ *Concl:* $({\sim}p) \wedge ({\sim}q)$	${\sim}(p \wedge q) \leftrightarrow ({\sim}p) \vee ({\sim}q)$ ${\sim}(p \vee q) \leftrightarrow ({\sim}p) \wedge ({\sim}q)$
7. Law of simplification	*Hyp:* $\quad p \wedge q$ *Concl:* p or *Hyp:* $\quad p \wedge q$ *Concl:* q	$(p \wedge q) \rightarrow p$ $(p \wedge q) \rightarrow q$
8. Law of double negation	*Hyp:* $\quad {\sim}({\sim}p)$ *Concl:* p	$[{\sim}({\sim}p)] \leftrightarrow p$
9. Law of disjunctive addition	*Hyp:* $\quad p$ *Concl:* $p \vee q$	$p \rightarrow (p \vee q)$

Determine whether the argument forms given in Exercises 1–6 are valid or invalid.

1. Hypotheses: $p \rightarrow q$
$\dfrac{\sim q}{}$

Conclusion: p

2. Hypotheses: $p \vee q$
$\dfrac{\sim p}{}$

Conclusion: $\sim q$

3. Hypotheses: $p \rightarrow q$
$(\sim q) \wedge r$
$\dfrac{\sim p}{}$

Conclusion: $\sim q$

4. Hypotheses: $p \wedge q$
$q \rightarrow r$
$\dfrac{r}{}$

Conclusion: $\sim p$

5. Hypotheses: $p \rightarrow r$
$q \vee r$
$\dfrac{(\sim q) \rightarrow (\sim p)}{}$

Conclusion: $(\sim p) \rightarrow (\sim r)$

6. Hypotheses: $\sim(p \wedge q)$
$r \rightarrow (\sim p)$
$\dfrac{q \vee r}{}$

Conclusion: $p \rightarrow r$

Translate each of the arguments given in Exercises 7–20 into symbolic form and then test its validity.

7. If Felicia exercises too much, she gets leg cramps. Felicia has leg cramps. Therefore Felicia has exercised too much.

8. Either Tracy will go on to medical school or she will become a lawyer. Tracy is not a lawyer. Therefore Tracy has gone on to medical school.

9. If Roger wins the lottery, then he will be rich. Roger is not rich. Therefore Roger has not won the lottery.

10. If Richard goes to England, then his girlfriend will date someone else. If his girlfriend dates someone else, then Richard's parents will be very upset. Therefore if Richard goes to England, then his parents will be very upset.

11. If Jennifer eats too much red meat, then her cholesterol level will be elevated. If her cholesterol level is elevated, then she will suffer from clogged arteries. Jennifer's cholesterol level is not elevated. Therefore if Jennifer eats too much red meat, then she will not suffer from clogged arteries.

12. If college tuition costs are raised, then students will either take a loan or be forced to drop out of college. If students take a loan, then they will not be forced to drop out of college. Therefore college tuition costs will not be raised.

13. If you're out of Schlitz, then you're out of beer. If you're out of beer, then you won't enjoy the game. Either you're out of beer or you will enjoy the game. Therefore if you're out of Schlitz, then you will enjoy the game.

14. If Cleon is hungry, then he will have a snack at McDonald's or at Burger King. If Cleon has a snack at Burger King, then he is not hungry. Cleon is hungry. Therefore Cleon will have a snack at McDonald's.

15. Paul has been told by the dean to improve his grade performance or be dropped from the college team. Paul does not improve his grade performance. Therefore Paul will be dropped from the college team.

16. If nuclear disarmament is not started quickly, then the world will become unsafe to live in. If nuclear disarmament is started quickly, then our children will enjoy healthy lives. The world will not become unsafe to live in. Therefore our children will not enjoy healthy lives.

17. For the museum to remain open, admission fees must be raised or new benefactors must be found. If new benefactors have not been found, then the admission fees will not be raised. Therefore the museum will not remain open.

Brain-Teaser Problems

**18. If you use laundry detergent, make sure it is biodegradable. If the laundry detergent is biodegradable, then chemical action will break it down into simpler compounds and our lakes will not be harmed. Therefore if our lakes are harmed, then you are using laundry detergent that is not biodegradable.

**19. If you do not report all of your income, then you will be audited by the I.R.S. If you are audited by the I.R.S., then you will need an accountant and be fined a steep penalty. Therefore if you were not fined a steep penalty, then you did report all of your income.

**20. If you sit in front of a computer monitor for too many hours, then your back may hurt or your eyesight will be temporarily blurred. Therefore if your back does not hurt, then you do not sit in front of a computer monitor for too many hours.

A-4

GROUPS

In Section 5.5 we pointed out that the mod 4 clock (or modulo 4 arithmetic, which is the same thing) has the following important properties.

1. The binary operation $\oplus$ is closed.

2. $\oplus$ is associative.

3. 0 is an identity for $\oplus$.

4. Every number on the clock has an inverse for $\oplus$.

Clearly, any other clock besides the mod 4 clock has these four properties also. Many other systems found in widely varying branches of mathematics also have these properties. Such systems are called **groups**. Because they occur so often, mathematicians devote a good deal of attention to them. We will first give a formal definition of a group and then illustrate it with several examples.

group

> **Definition A-13** A **group** is a set of elements G, together with a binary operation "$\circ$", with the following properties.
>
> *Property 1.* "$\circ$" is closed.
> *Property 2.* "$\circ$" is associative.
> *Property 3.* There is an identity element in G for "$\circ$". If we call this identity element i, then this means that for any element a in G we have $a \circ i = a$ and $i \circ a = a$. In other words, i is the "do-nothing" element for "$\circ$". In the mod 4 clock, 0 was the identity for the operation $\oplus$.
> *Property 4.* Every element in G has an inverse for "$\circ$". This means that for any element a, we can find another element which operating on a with "$\circ$" gives i. For the mod 4 clock we actually listed the inverse for each element on p. 288.

Comment The operation "$\circ$" may vary from one situation to another, as we shall see. It may sometimes be ordinary addition or multiplication. Sometimes it will be the turning of a clock hand as in clock arithmetic. In other situations it will be a totally different operation.

The best way to understand groups is to look at some examples.

EXAMPLE 1

Let G = {integers} and let "$\circ$" stand for ordinary addition. This system is a group. Let us see why.

In Chapter 4 we saw that addition of integers is closed and associative. We also saw that 0 is the identity element. So the first three properties are satisfied.

Let us verify Property 4. Consider the integer 3. Its inverse is -3, since $3 + (-3) = 0$, which is the identity. Similarly the inverse of -11 is $+11$, since $(-11) + (+11) = 0$. It is clear that *every* element has an inverse. Thus Property 4 is satisfied.

Since all four properties are satisfied, it follows that this system is a group.

EXAMPLE 2

Let $G = \{\text{integers}\}$ and let "$\circ$" be ordinary multiplication. Let us see if this system is a group.

Again we know from our work in Chapter 4 that multiplication of integers is closed and associative. We also know that 1 is the identity for multiplication. So Properties 1, 2, and 3 are satisfied. What about Property 4? Consider the integer 3. Does it have an inverse for multiplication? We are asking if there is an *integer* such that

$$3 \cdot (\text{integer}) = 1.$$

HISTORICAL NOTE

The term "group" was first used by the brilliant young French mathematician Évariste Galois in 1830. Although he was a mathematical genius, his abilities were not recognized by his teachers. In fact, he was twice denied admission to the famous École Polytechnique, *the* school for mathematicians and scientists in Paris. Twice he submitted papers containing his important discoveries to the French Academy, and each time they were lost.

At the age of 20 he became involved in a quarrel over a woman and was challenged to a duel. He spent the entire night before the duel writing down his ideas. The next morning he was killed. It is interesting to think about what he might have contributed to mathematics had he lived a normal life span.

Galois studied groups in order to solve certain problems in algebra. His discoveries greatly expanded the field of algebra. Furthermore, his ideas have also been applied to physics. They have been particularly valuable in the study of quantum mechanics.

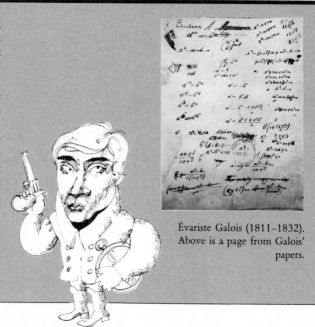

Évariste Galois (1811–1832). Above is a page from Galois' papers.

The only number which when multiplied by 3 gives 1 is $\frac{1}{3}$. However, $\frac{1}{3}$ is not an integer. Thus *there is no element in G that is an inverse for 3*. Property 4, which says that *every* element must have an inverse, is *not* true in this case. So this system is *not* a group.

EXAMPLE 3

In Example 2 we saw that the set of integers with the operation of multiplication did not form a group. The problem was that not every element had an inverse. The only numbers that could be inverses were rational numbers like $\frac{1}{3}$.

If we change G from the integers to the rational numbers, then we *do* have numbers like $\frac{1}{3}$. Thus if we let G = {rational numbers} and let "∘" be ordinary multiplication, it looks as if we have a group. Unfortunately, this is not the case; 0 has no inverse. If you doubt this, try to find a number which when multiplied by 0 will give you 1. It can't be done! However, if we let G = {rational numbers, without 0} and let "∘" be multiplication, then we *do* have a group.

EXAMPLE 4

Let G = { – 1, 1} and let "∘" be ordinary multiplication. We will verify that this is a group.

Property 1.

$$1 \circ 1 = 1$$
$$1 \circ (-1) = -1$$
$$(-1) \circ 1 = -1$$
$$(-1) \circ (-1) = +1$$

These results are summarized in the following table:

∘	– 1	1
– 1	1	– 1
1	– 1	1

All possible ways of multiplying elements of G result in some element of G. Thus ∘ is a closed operation.

Property 2. Since ∘ is just ordinary multiplication, we already know that the associative law holds for ∘.

Property 3. 1 is the identity.

Property 4. The inverse of 1 is 1, since $1 \circ 1 = 1$. The inverse of – 1 is – 1, since $(-1) \circ (-1) = 1$.

Therefore this system is a group.

EXAMPLE 5

Let $G = \{1, -1\}$ and let "$\circ$" be ordinary addition. Then this system is *not* a group. For one thing, "$\circ$" is not a closed operation, since $1 + 1$ is 2, and 2 is not an element of G. Moreover, there is no identity. Why? ■

EXAMPLE 6

Consider a set G whose elements are a, b, and c. Let the operation "$\circ$" be given by Table 2.A. Does this system form a group?

TABLE 2.A			
$\circ$	a	b	c

SOLUTION

We must verify that the four properties of a group hold.

Property 1.   Since all the elements in the table are elements of G, "$\circ$" is a closed operation.

Property 2.   The associative law holds. We will verify it for one case. Readers should verify it for a few others to convince themselves.

$$
\begin{array}{c|c}
a \circ (b \circ c) & (a \circ b) \circ c \\
= a \circ a & = b \circ c \\
= a & = a
\end{array}
$$

Property 3.   We see from the table that a is the identity, since a applied to any element results in the same element.

Property 4.   Every element has an inverse.
The inverse of a is a because $a \circ a$ = the identity which is a.
The inverse of b is c because $b \circ c$ = the identity which is a.
The inverse of c is b because $c \circ b$ = the identity which is a.

Since all four properties are satisfied, this system forms a group. ■

Some groups have an additional property called the *commutative* property. This is defined as follows.

Abelian group

> **Definition A-14**   A group is called an **Abelian group** if the commutative property holds. This means that if a and b are any elements of G, then $a \circ b = b \circ a$.

All the groups we have discussed so far are commutative.

HISTORICAL NOTE

Abelian groups are named after the Norwegian mathematician Niels Henrik Abel. A gifted mathematician, Abel unfortunately died of consumption before he was 27 years old. Despite his illness, personal hardships, and many disappointments in his career, Abel managed to make a solid contribution to mathematics.

Niels Henrik Abel
(1802–1829).

More Examples of Groups

In the remainder of this section we will examine some interesting groups that arise when we move around geometric shapes such as triangles, squares, etc. (A background in geometry is not needed. You only have to know what triangles, squares, and rectangles are.)

EXAMPLE 7

Figure A.1

Let us look at an **equilateral triangle**. This is just a triangle with three equal sides and three equal angles as shown (Fig. A.1).

Suppose we cut such a triangle out of a wooden block. We ask the following question: How many ways can we put the triangle back into the wooden block without turning the triangle over? (We suggest that the reader cut such a triangle out of a piece of paper or cardboard and refer to it as he or she reads along.) The triangle and block are shown in Fig. A.2.

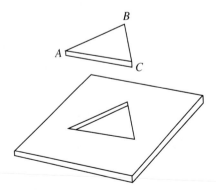

Figure A.2

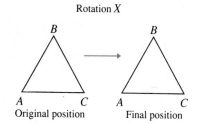
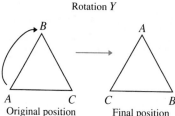
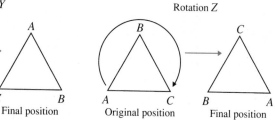

Figure A.3

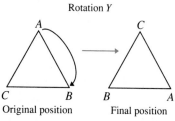

Figure A.4

One way of putting the triangle back into the block is to put it back exactly as it was taken out. This we will call rotation X. (See Fig. A.3).

Another way of putting the triangle back into the block is to rotate it one-third of the way around (120°). This we call rotation Y.

The only other way of putting the triangle back into the block is to rotate it two-thirds of the way around (240°). This we will call rotation Z.

These illustrations show the rotation performed on the triangles starting in the original positions only. However, we may perform the rotation from any starting position that fits into the block. One such possibility is shown in the rotation Y of Fig. A.4.

Let G be the set containing these three rotations, that is, $G = \{X, Y, Z\}$. Now we define an operation "$\circ$" on G in the following way: $Y \circ Z$ means "first apply rotation Y and then apply rotation Z to the result." If we start with the triangle in the original position, then $Y \circ Z$ is as illustrated in Fig. A.5. $Y \circ Z$ leaves the triangle in the original position. This is the same as rotation X. Thus $Y \circ Z = X$.

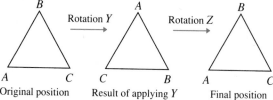

Figure A.5

Similarly, we define $X \circ Z$ as first applying X and then Z. If we start in the original position, then the result is as shown in Fig. A.6. Thus $X \circ Z = Z$.

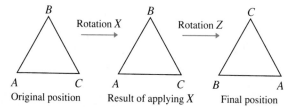

Figure A.6

In the same way we define ∘ for other elements of G. We can summarize all possibilities by the following table:

∘	X	Y	Z
X	X	Y	Z
Y	Y	Z	X
Z	Z	X	Y

Now we ask: Is this system a group? We must verify the four group properties.

Property 1. From the table we see that ∘ is a closed operation.
Property 2.   It is easy to verify that the associative law holds. Try it.
Property 3. The identity is X.
Property 4. The inverse of X is X.
            The inverse of Y is Z.
            The inverse of Z is Y.

Hence this system is a group. It is even a commutative or Abelian group.

EXAMPLE 8

symmetries of the triangle

We consider the same situation as in the last example. However, we now allow the triangle to be turned over as well. We still have the three rotations as in the preceding example, but we rename them *symmetries X, Y,* and *Z*. In addition, we have three new ways of putting the triangle back into the block. These are shown in Fig. A.7 and are called symmetries *P, Q,* and *R*. In each case we flip the triangle over around the dotted line.

The operation "∘" is defined as in Example 7. Thus $X \circ P$ means "first apply X and then apply P." See Fig. A.8.

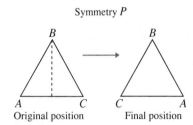
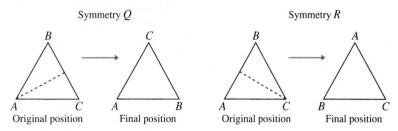

Figure A.7

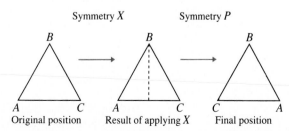

Figure A.8

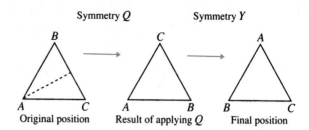

Figure A.9   Original position   Result of applying Q Final position

Similarly, $Q \circ Y$ means "first apply Q and then apply Y." See Fig. A.9. All possible results are summarized in the following table:

∘	X	Y	Z	P	Q	R
X	X	Y	Z	P	Q	R
Y	Y	Z	X	R	P	Q
Z	Z	X	Y	Q	R	P
P	P	Q	R	X	Y	Z
Q	Q	R	P	Z	X	Y
R	R	P	Q	Y	Z	X

This system also forms a group called the **symmetries of a triangle**. It is *not* a commutative group. (See p. A-30.)[1]

EXAMPLE 9

symmetries

symmetries of the
square

Suppose we now have a square cut out of a block of wood, as in the previous two examples. Let us find all possible ways of replacing the square in the block of wood. Flipping over is allowed. There are eight possible ways of doing this, as shown in Fig. A.10. These are called **symmetries**.

We define "∘" as we did for the triangle. For example, $r \circ v$ means "first apply r and then apply v to the result." The table for ∘ is shown below. This system forms a group called the **symmetries of the square**. It is clear from the table that ∘ is a closed operation.

∘	p	q	r	s	t	u	v	w
p	p	q	r	s	t	u	v	w
q	q	r	s	p	w	v	t	u
r	r	s	p	q	u	t	w	v
s	s	p	q	r	v	w	u	t
t	t	v	u	w	p	r	q	s
u	u	w	t	v	r	p	s	q
v	v	u	w	t	s	q	p	r
w	w	t	v	u	q	s	r	p

---

1. The smallest group that is not commutative has six elements; that is, a group with fewer than six elements *must* be commutative.

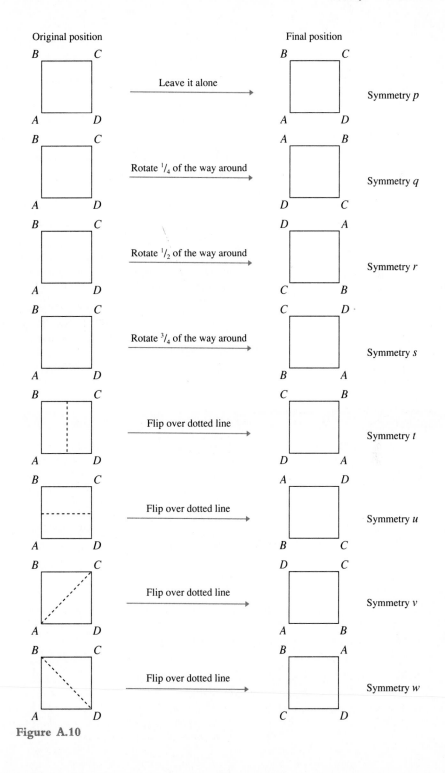

Figure A.10

The associative law holds. Since there are 512 possible combinations, we will check just one of them:

$$t \circ (q \circ r) \qquad\qquad (t \circ q) \circ r$$
$$= t \circ s \qquad\qquad\quad = v \circ r$$
$$= w \qquad\qquad\qquad\quad = w$$

The identity element is obviously p. Every element has an inverse. For example, the inverse of s is q.

It can be shown that the identity for a group is unique. This means that there cannot be more than one identity. As an illustration, if we look at the group of symmetries of the square (Fig. A.10) we notice that the identity is p. There is no other identity. Now if we were to study *any* other group, we would immediately know that there is only one identity. We would not have to prove it.

This process is typical of mathematical activity. Mathematicians try to discover general properties and then apply them to specific situations as they arise. Of course, in establishing general concepts they are usually motivated by specific examples. (Refer back to the discussion of inductive and deductive reasoning in Chapter 2.)

EXERCISES FOR A-4

Determine whether each of the sets described in Exercises 1–11 forms a group under the specified operation.

1. The set of odd integers with the operation of addition.

2. The set of odd integers with the operation of multiplication.

3. The set of even integers with the operation of multiplication.

4. The set of negative integers with the operation of addition.

5. The set of negative integers with the operation of multiplication.

6. Mod 4 arithmetic, that is, 0, 1, 2, 3 (mod 4), with the operation of multiplication.

7. Mod 4 arithmetic, that is, 0, 1, 2, 3 (mod 4), without zero with the operation of multiplication.

8. The set of multiples of 5 with the operation of addition.

9. The set of multiples of 5 with the operation of multiplication.

10. The set of real numbers with the operation of addition.

11. The set of real numbers with the operation of multiplication.

In each of Exercises 12–15 an operation "$\circ$" is given by the table shown. Determine whether each is a group.

12.

$\circ$	a	b
a	a	b
b	b	a

13.

$\circ$	c	d
c	c	d
d	e	c

14.

$\circ$	d	e	f
d	d	e	g
e	e	d	f
f	f	e	d

15.

$\circ$	d	e	f
d	d	d	d
e	d	e	f
f	d	e	f

16. Which of the groups given in Exercises 1–15 are Abelian (or commutative) groups?

17. Let $G = \{a, b, c\}$ and let "∘" be the operation given by the following table:

∘	a	b	c
a	a	b	c
b	b	a	c
c	c	b	a

a) Find the identity element.

b) Find the inverse of each element.

c) Is G an Abelian group?

18. Let $G = \{0, 5, 8, 9\}$ and let "∘" be defined by the following table:

∘	0	5	8	9
0	0	0	0	0
5	0	5	0	8
8	0	8	5	9
9	0	8	9	8

Does this system form a group? Explain your answer.

19. Let $G = \{\alpha, \beta, \gamma\}$ and let "∘" be defined by the following table:

∘	α	β	γ
α	α	β	γ
β	β	γ	α
γ	γ	α	β

Does this system form a group?

20. Let $G = \{1, 2, 3, 4, 5, 6\}$ and let "∘" be defined by the following table:

∘	1	2	3	4	5	6
1	1	1	1	1	1	1
2	1	2	3	4	5	6
3	1	3	5	1	3	5
4	1	4	1	4	1	4
5	1	5	3	1	5	3
6	1	6	5	4	3	2

a) Is ∘ a closed operation?

b) Is there an identity? If yes, find it.

c) Is there an inverse for 3? If yes, find it.

d) Is there an inverse for 6? If yes, find it.

e) Is ∘ commutative?

f) Does this system form a group?

21. Let $G = \{\alpha, \beta, \gamma, \Delta\}$ and let "∘" be given the following table:

∘	α	β	γ	Δ
α	α	β	γ	Δ
β	β	α	Δ	γ
γ	γ	Δ	α	β
Δ	Δ	γ	β	α

a) Is ∘ a closed operation?

b) Is ∘ a commutative operation?

c) Is there an identity element? If yes, find it.

d) Find the inverse of each element.

e) Does this system form a group?

22. Let $G = \{x, y, z\}$ and let "∘" be given the following table:

∘	x	y	z
x	x	y	z
y	x	z	y
z	x	y	z

a) Find $(x \circ y) \circ (z \circ y)$.

b) Find $(x \circ y) \circ z$ and $x \circ (y \circ z)$.

c) Is the set closed under the operation of "∘"? Explain.

d) Does this set form a group?

23. Let $G = \{1, 2, 3, 4, 5\}$ and let "∘" be the operation of addition modulo 6. Does this system form a group? Explain.

24. Let $G = \{1, 2, 3, 4, 5, 6\}$ and let "∘" be the operation of multiplication modulo 8. Does this system form a group? Explain.

25. **a)** Verify all cases of the associative law for Example 7.

b) In Example 9, verify the associative law for three different cases.

26. In Example 8, find the inverse of each element.

27. a) Find all the symmetries (possible ways of putting it back into the wood block) for any rectangle that is not a square. See Fig. A.11. (*Hint:* There are four of them.)

b) Show that this system is a group. It is called the **Klein 4 group**.

Figure A.11

28. An isosceles triangle is a triangle with two equal sides, as in Fig. A.12 where side *a* = side *b*. (The third side does not necessarily have to equal the other two sides.)

a) Find all the symmetries of this isosceles triangle.

b) Do these symmetries form a group?

Figure A.12

29. A regular pentagon has five equal sides, as shown in Fig. A.13.

a) Find all the symmetries of a regular pentagon.

b) Do these symmetries form a group?

$a = b = c = d = e$

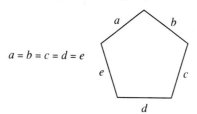

Figure A.13

30. Private Bond is standing at attention. Sergeant Stone comes along and gives him orders such as "right turn," "left turn," "about face," or "as you were."

Let

> *r* stand for right turn,
> *l* stand for left turn,
> *a* stand for about face, and
> *s* stand for as you were.

Let "∘" represent any combination of these orders. For example, *l* ∘ *r* would mean "first make a left turn and then a right turn." Your result is, of course, the starting position. So *l* ∘ *r* = *s*.

a) Make up a table for ∘.

b) Is ∘ closed?

c) Is ∘ commutative?

d) Is there an identity element? If so, find it.

e) Find the inverse of each element.

f) Find *l* ∘ (*s* ∘ *a*) and (*l* ∘ *s*) ∘ *a*.

g) Does this system form a group?

31. Show by example that the group of Example 8 is not commutative.

Brain-Teaser Problems

**32. Let $G = \{$all integers$\}$ and let "∘" be defined as follows: If *a* and *b* are in G, then $a \circ b = (a \cdot b) - (a + b)$. For example, if *a* and *b* are 6 and 7, then $a \circ b = (6 \cdot 7) - (6 + 7) = 42 - 13 = 29$. Does this system form a group?

**33. Let $G = \{$all rational numbers$\}$ and let "∘" be defined as follows: If *a* and *b* are in G, then $a \circ b = (a \cdot b) - \frac{a}{b}$. For example, if *a* and *b* are 3 and 2, then $a \circ b = (3 \cdot 2) - \frac{3}{2}$ or $4\frac{1}{2}$. Does this system form a group? Explain.

**34. Consider the following operations on $G = \{$integers$\}$.

i) □ is defined as $a \,\square\, b = a + 2b$.

ii) ⊙ is defined as $a \odot b = a$.

iii) △ is defined as $a \,\triangle\, b = a(a + b)$.

iv) ∗ is defined as $a \ast b = a + b - ab$.

For each of the above, answer the following questions.

a) Is the operation associative?

b) Is the operation commutative?

c) Is there an identity? If so, what is it?

d) Does the system form a group?

**35. Let G = {rational numbers between 0 and 1 inclusive} and let "$\circ$" be defined as $x \circ y = x + y - xy$, where x and y are any elements in G.

a) Is this system a group?

b) Is this system an Abelian group?

36. Let G = {integers} and let "$\circ$" be multiplication modulo m, where m is a composite number. Does this system form a group?

KEY TERMS

The following list presents the key terms introduced in these appendixes.

A-1 **proposition (statement)**
     truth value
     compound statement
     conjunction
     disjunction
     negation
     implication (conditional)
     converse
     inverse
     contrapositive
     variations of
        the conditional
     equivalence
     biconditional

A-2 **tautology**
     self-contradiction
     equivalent statement

A-3 **direct reasoning**
     law of detachment
        (modus ponens)
     chain rule
     indirect reasoning
        (modus tolens)

A-4 **group**
     Abelian group
     symmetries of a triangle
     symmetries of a square
     Klein-4 group

Tables

TABLE A.1
The exponential function

x	e^x	x	e^x	x	e^x	x	e^x	x	e^x
0.00	1.00000	0.50	1.64872	1.00	2.71828	1.50	4.48169	2.00	7.38906
0.01	1.01005	0.51	1.66529	1.01	2.74560	1.51	4.52673	2.01	7.46332
0.02	1.02020	0.52	1.68203	1.02	2.77319	1.52	4.57223	2.02	7.53832
0.03	1.03045	0.53	1.69893	1.03	2.80107	1.53	4.61818	2.03	7.61409
0.04	1.04081	0.54	1.71601	1.04	2.82922	1.54	4.66459	2.04	7.69061
0.05	1.05127	0.55	1.73325	1.05	2.85765	1.55	4.71147	2.05	7.76790
0.06	1.06184	0.56	1.75067	1.06	2.88637	1.56	4.75882	2.06	7.84597
0.07	1.07251	0.57	1.76827	1.07	2.91538	1.57	4.80665	2.07	7.92482
0.08	1.08329	0.58	1.78604	1.08	2.94468	1.58	4.85496	2.08	8.00447
0.09	1.09417	0.59	1.80399	1.09	2.97427	1.59	4.90375	2.09	8.08491
0.10	1.10517	0.60	1.82212	1.10	3.00417	1.60	4.95303	2.10	8.16617
0.11	1.11628	0.61	1.84043	1.11	3.03436	1.61	5.00281	2.11	8.24824
0.12	1.12750	0.62	1.85893	1.12	3.06485	1.62	5.05309	2.12	8.33114
0.13	1.13883	0.63	1.87761	1.13	3.09566	1.63	5.10387	2.13	8.41487
0.14	1.15027	0.64	1.89648	1.14	3.12677	1.64	5.15517	2.14	8.49944
0.15	1.16183	0.65	1.91554	1.15	3.15819	1.65	5.20698	2.15	8.58486
0.16	1.17351	0.66	1.93479	1.16	3.18993	1.66	5.25931	2.16	8.67114
0.17	1.18530	0.67	1.95424	1.17	3.22199	1.67	5.31217	2.17	8.75828
0.18	1.19722	0.68	1.97388	1.18	3.25437	1.68	5.36556	2.18	8.84631
0.19	1.20925	0.69	1.99372	1.19	3.28708	1.69	5.41948	2.19	8.93521
0.20	1.22140	0.70	2.01375	1.20	3.32012	1.70	5.47395	2.20	9.02501
0.21	1.23368	0.71	2.03399	1.21	3.35348	1.71	5.52896	2.21	9.11572
0.22	1.24608	0.72	2.05443	1.22	3.38719	1.72	5.58453	2.22	9.20733
0.23	1.25860	0.73	2.07508	1.23	3.42123	1.73	5.64065	2.23	9.29987
0.24	1.27125	0.74	2.09594	1.24	3.45561	1.74	5.69734	2.24	9.39333
0.25	1.28403	0.75	2.11700	1.25	3.49034	1.75	5.75460	2.25	9.48774
0.26	1.29693	0.76	2.13828	1.26	3.52542	1.76	5.81244	2.26	9.58309
0.27	1.30996	0.77	2.15977	1.27	3.56085	1.77	5.87085	2.27	9.67940
0.28	1.32313	0.78	2.18147	1.28	3.59664	1.78	5.92986	2.28	9.77668
0.29	1.33643	0.79	2.20340	1.29	3.63279	1.79	5.98945	2.29	9.87494
0.30	1.34986	0.80	2.22554	1.30	3.66930	1.80	6.04965	2.30	9.97418
0.31	1.36343	0.81	2.24791	1.31	3.70617	1.81	6.11045	2.31	10.07442
0.32	1.37713	0.82	2.27050	1.32	3.74342	1.82	6.17186	2.32	10.17567
0.33	1.39097	0.83	2.29332	1.33	3.78104	1.83	6.23389	2.33	10.27794
0.34	1.40495	0.84	2.31637	1.34	3.81904	1.84	6.29654	2.34	10.38124
0.35	1.41907	0.85	2.33965	1.35	3.85743	1.85	6.35982	2.35	10.48557
0.36	1.43333	0.86	2.36316	1.36	3.89619	1.86	6.42374	2.36	10.59095
0.37	1.44773	0.87	2.38691	1.37	3.93535	1.87	6.48830	2.37	10.69739
0.38	1.46228	0.88	2.41090	1.38	3.97490	1.88	6.55350	2.38	10.80490
0.39	1.47698	0.89	2.43513	1.39	4.01485	1.89	6.61937	2.39	10.91349
0.40	1.49182	0.90	2.45960	1.40	4.05520	1.90	6.68589	2.40	11.02318
0.41	1.50682	0.91	2.48432	1.41	4.09596	1.91	6.75309	2.41	11.13396
0.42	1.52196	0.92	2.50929	1.42	4.13712	1.92	6.82096	2.42	11.24586
0.43	1.53726	0.93	2.53451	1.43	4.17870	1.93	6.88951	2.43	11.35888
0.44	1.55271	0.94	2.55998	1.44	4.22070	1.94	6.95875	2.44	11.47304
0.45	1.56831	0.95	2.58571	1.45	4.26311	1.95	7.02869	2.45	11.58835
0.46	1.58407	0.96	2.61170	1.46	4.30596	1.96	7.09933	2.46	11.70481
0.47	1.59999	0.97	2.63794	1.47	4.34924	1.97	7.17068	2.47	11.82245
0.48	1.61607	0.98	2.66446	1.48	4.39295	1.98	7.24274	2.48	11.94126
0.49	1.63232	0.99	2.69123	1.49	4.43710	1.99	7.31553	2.49	12.06128

(continued)

TABLE A.1
The exponential function (*continued*)

x	e^x	x	e^x	x	e^x	x	e^x	x	e^x
2.50	12.18249	3.00	20.08554	3.50	33.11545	4.00	54.59815	4.50	90.01713
2.51	12.30493	3.01	20.28740	3.51	33.44827	4.01	55.14687	4.51	90.92182
2.52	12.42860	3.02	20.49129	3.52	33.78443	4.02	55.70110	4.52	91.83560
2.53	12.55351	3.03	20.69723	3.53	34.12397	4.03	56.26091	4.53	92.75856
2.54	12.67967	3.04	20.90524	3.54	34.46692	4.04	56.82634	4.54	93.69080
2.55	12.80710	3.05	21.11534	3.55	34.81332	4.05	57.39745	4.55	94.63240
2.56	12.93582	3.06	21.32756	3.56	35.16320	4.06	57.97431	4.56	95.58347
2.57	13.06582	3.07	21.54190	3.57	35.51659	4.07	58.55696	4.57	96.54411
2.58	13.19714	3.08	21.75840	3.58	35.87354	4.08	59.14547	4.58	97.51439
2.59	13.32977	3.09	21.97708	3.59	36.23408	4.09	59.73989	4.59	98.49443
2.60	13.46374	3.10	22.19795	3.60	36.59823	4.10	60.34029	4.60	99.48431
2.61	13.59905	3.11	22.42104	3.61	36.96605	4.11	60.94671	4.61	100.48415
2.62	13.73572	3.12	22.64638	3.62	37.33757	4.12	61.55924	4.62	101.49403
2.63	13.87377	3.13	22.87398	3.63	37.71282	4.13	62.17792	4.63	102.51406
2.64	14.01320	3.14	23.10387	3.64	38.09184	4.14	62.80282	4.64	103.54435
2.65	14.15404	3.15	23.33606	3.65	38.47467	4.15	63.43400	4.65	104.58498
2.66	14.29629	3.16	23.57060	3.66	38.86134	4.16	64.07152	4.66	105.63608
2.67	14.43997	3.17	23.80748	3.67	39.25191	4.17	64.71545	4.67	106.69774
2.68	14.58509	3.18	24.04675	3.68	39.64639	4.18	65.36585	4.68	107.77007
2.69	14.73168	3.19	24.28843	3.69	40.04485	4.19	66.02279	4.69	108.85318
2.70	14.87973	3.20	24.53253	3.70	40.44730	4.20	66.68633	4.70	109.94717
2.71	15.02928	3.21	24.77909	3.71	40.85381	4.21	67.35654	4.71	111.05216
2.72	15.18032	3.22	25.02812	3.72	41.26439	4.22	68.03348	4.72	112.16825
2.73	15.33289	3.23	25.27966	3.73	41.67911	4.23	68.71723	4.73	113.29556
2.74	15.48698	3.24	25.53372	3.74	42.09799	4.24	69.40785	4.74	114.43420
2.75	15.64263	3.25	25.79034	3.75	42.52108	4.25	70.10541	4.75	115.58428
2.76	15.79984	3.26	26.04954	3.76	42.94843	4.26	70.80998	4.76	116.74592
2.77	15.95863	3.27	26.31134	3.77	43.38006	4.27	71.52163	4.77	117.91924
2.78	16.11902	3.28	26.57577	3.78	43.81604	4.28	72.24044	4.78	119.10435
2.79	16.28102	3.29	26.84286	3.79	44.25640	4.29	72.96647	4.79	120.30136
2.80	16.44465	3.30	27.11264	3.80	44.70118	4.30	73.69979	4.80	121.51041
2.81	16.60992	3.31	27.38512	3.81	45.15044	4.31	74.44049	4.81	122.73161
2.82	16.77685	3.32	27.66035	3.82	45.60421	4.32	75.18863	4.82	123.96509
2.83	16.94546	3.33	27.93834	3.83	46.06254	4.33	75.94429	4.83	125.21096
2.84	17.11577	3.34	28.21913	3.84	46.52547	4.34	76.70754	4.84	126.46935
2.85	17.28778	3.35	28.50273	3.85	46.99306	4.35	77.47846	4.85	127.74039
2.86	17.46153	3.36	28.78919	3.86	47.46535	4.36	78.25713	4.86	129.02420
2.87	17.63702	3.37	29.07853	3.87	47.94238	4.37	79.04363	4.87	130.32091
2.88	17.81427	3.38	29.37077	3.88	48.42421	4.38	79.83803	4.88	131.63066
2.89	17.99331	3.39	29.66595	3.89	48.91089	4.39	80.64042	4.89	132.95357
2.90	18.17414	3.40	29.96410	3.90	49.40245	4.40	81.45087	4.90	134.28978
2.91	18.35680	3.41	30.26524	3.91	49.89895	4.41	82.26946	4.91	135.63941
2.92	18.54129	3.42	30.56941	3.92	50.40044	4.42	83.09628	4.92	137.00261
2.93	18.72763	3.43	30.87664	3.93	50.90698	4.43	83.93141	4.93	138.37951
2.94	18.91585	3.44	31.18696	3.94	51.41860	4.44	84.77494	4.94	139.77024
2.95	19.10595	3.45	31.50039	3.95	51.93537	4.45	85.62694	4.95	141.17496
2.96	19.29797	3.46	31.81698	3.96	52.45732	4.46	86.48751	4.96	142.59379
2.97	19.49192	3.47	32.13674	3.97	52.98453	4.47	87.35672	4.97	144.02688
2.98	19.68782	3.48	32.45972	3.98	53.51703	4.48	88.23467	4.98	145.47438
2.99	19.88568	3.49	32.78595	3.99	54.05489	4.49	89.12144	4.99	146.93642

x	e^x	x	e^x	x	e^x	x	e^x
5.00	148.41316	7.00	1096.63309	9.00	8103.08295	11.00	59874.13477
5.10	164.02190	7.10	1211.96703	9.10	8955.29187	11.10	66171.15430
5.20	181.27224	7.20	1339.43076	9.20	9897.12830	11.20	73130.43652
5.30	200.33680	7.30	1480.29985	9.30	10938.01868	11.30	80821.63379
5.40	221.40641	7.40	1635.98439	9.40	12088.38409	11.40	89321.72168
5.50	244.69192	7.50	1808.04231	9.50	13359.72522	11.50	98715.75879
5.60	270.42640	7.60	1998.19582	9.60	14764.78015	11.60	109097.78906
5.70	298.86740	7.70	2208.34796	9.70	16317.60608	11.70	120571.70605
5.80	330.29955	7.80	2440.60187	9.80	18033.74414	11.80	133252.34570
5.90	365.03746	7.90	2697.28226	9.90	19930.36987	11.90	147266.62109
6.00	403.42877	8.00	2980.95779	10.00	22026.46313		
6.10	445.85775	8.10	3294.46777	10.10	24343.00708		
6.20	492.74903	8.20	3640.95004	10.20	26903.18408		
6.30	544.57188	8.30	4023.87219	10.30	29732.61743		
6.40	601.84502	8.40	4447.06665	10.40	32859.62500		
6.50	665.14159	8.50	4914.76886	10.50	36315.49854		
6.60	735.09516	8.60	5431.65906	10.60	40134.83350		
6.70	812.40582	8.70	6002.91180	10.70	44355.85205		
6.80	897.84725	8.80	6634.24371	10.80	49020.79883		
6.90	992.27469	8.90	7331.97339	10.90	54176.36230		

TABLE A.2
Mortgage amortization program

Mortgage Amount	$130,000
Fixed Interest Rate	9.5%
Number of Years	15
Monthly Payments	$1357.50

Payment Number	Date	Principal	Interest	Balance	Payment Number	Date	Principal	Interest	Balance
1	7/1/86	$328.32	$1,029.18	$129,671.68	31	1/1/89	415.95	941.55	118,515.52
2	8/1/86	330.92	1,026.58	129,340.76	32	2/1/89	419.24	938.26	118,096.28
3	9/1/86	333.54	1,023.96	129,007.22	33	3/1/89	422.56	934.94	117,673.72
4	10/1/86	336.18	1,021.32	128,671.04	34	4/1/89	425.91	931.59	117,247.81
5	11/1/86	338.84	1,018.66	128,332.20	35	5/1/89	429.28	928.22	116,818.53
6	12/1/86	341.53	1,015.97	127,990.67	36	6/1/89	432.68	924.82	116,385.85
7	1/1/87	344.23	1,013.27	127,646.44	37	7/1/89	436.10	921.40	115,949.75
8	2/1/87	346.96	1,010.54	127,299.48	38	8/1/89	439.55	917.95	115,510.20
9	3/1/87	349.70	1,007.80	126,949.78	39	9/1/89	443.03	914.47	115,067.17
10	4/1/87	352.47	1,005.03	126,597.31	40	10/1/89	446.54	910.96	114,620.63
11	5/1/87	355.26	1,002.24	126,242.05	41	11/1/89	450.08	907.42	114,170.55
12	6/1/87	358.07	999.43	125,883.98	42	12/1/89	453.64	903.86	113,716.91
13	7/1/87	360.91	996.59	125,523.07	43	1/1/90	457.23	900.27	113,259.68
14	8/1/87	363.77	993.73	125,159.30	44	2/1/90	460.85	896.65	112,798.83
15	9/1/87	366.65	990.85	124,792.65	45	3/1/90	464.50	893.00	112,334.33
16	10/1/87	369.55	987.95	124,423.10	46	4/1/90	468.18	889.32	111,866.15
17	11/1/87	372.47	985.03	124,050.63	47	5/1/90	471.88	885.62	111,394.27
18	12/1/87	375.42	982.08	123,675.21	48	6/1/90	475.62	881.88	110,918.65
19	1/1/88	378.39	979.11	123,296.82	49	7/1/90	479.38	878.12	110,439.27
20	2/1/88	381.39	976.11	122,915.43	50	8/1/90	483.18	874.32	109,956.09
21	3/1/88	384.41	973.09	122,531.02	51	9/1/90	487.00	870.50	109,469.09
22	4/1/88	387.45	970.05	122,143.57	52	10/1/90	490.86	866.64	108,978.33
23	5/1/88	390.52	966.98	121,753.05	53	11/1/90	494.75	862.75	108,483.48
24	6/1/88	393.61	963.89	121,359.32	54	12/1/90	498.66	858.84	107,984.82
25	7/1/88	396.73	960.77	120,962.59	55	1/1/91	502.61	854.89	107,482.21
26	8/1/88	399.87	957.63	120,562.72	56	2/1/91	506.59	850.91	106,975.62
27	9/1/88	403.03	954.47	120,159.69	57	3/1/91	510.60	846.90	106,465.02
28	10/1/88	406.22	951.28	119,753.47	58	4/1/91	514.64	842.86	105,950.30
29	11/1/88	409.44	948.06	119,344.03	59	5/1/91	518.72	838.78	105,431.66
30	12/1/88	412.68	944.82	118,931.35	60	6/1/91	522.82	834.68	104,908.84

Payment Number	Date	Principal	Interest	Balance	Payment Number	Date	Principal	Interest	Balance
61	7/1/91	526.96	830.54	104,381.88	100	10/1/94	716.70	640.80	80,224.76
62	8/1/91	531.13	826.37	103,850.75	101	11/1/94	722.38	635.12	79,502.38
63	9/1/91	535.34	822.16	103,315.41	102	12/1/94	728.10	629.40	78,774.28
64	10/1/91	539.58	817.92	102,775.83	103	1/1/95	733.86	623.64	78,040.42
65	11/1/91	543.85	813.65	102,231.98	104	2/1/95	739.67	617.83	77,300.75
66	12/1/91	548.15	809.35	101,683.83	105	3/1/95	745.53	611.97	76,555.22
67	1/1/92	552.49	805.01	101,131.34	106	4/1/95	751.43	606.07	75,803.79
68	2/1/92	556.87	800.63	100,574.47	107	5/1/95	757.38	600.12	75,046.41
69	3/1/92	561.28	796.22	100,013.19	108	6/1/95	763.37	594.13	74,283.04
70	4/1/92	565.72	791.78	99,447.47	109	7/1/95	769.42	588.08	73,513.62
71	5/1/92	570.20	787.30	98,877.27	110	8/1/95	775.51	581.99	72,738.11
72	6/1/92	574.71	782.79	98,302.56	111	9/1/95	781.65	575.85	71,956.46
73	7/1/92	579.26	778.24	97,723.30	112	10/1/95	787.83	569.67	71,168.63
74	8/1/92	583.85	773.65	97,139.45	113	11/1/95	794.07	563.43	70,374.56
75	9/1/92	588.47	769.03	96,550.98	114	12/1/95	800.36	557.14	69,574.20
76	10/1/92	593.13	764.37	95,957.85	115	1/1/96	806.69	550.81	68,767.51
77	11/1/92	597.82	759.68	95,360.03	116	2/1/96	813.08	544.42	67,954.43
78	12/1/92	602.56	754.94	94,757.47	117	3/1/96	819.52	537.98	67,134.91
79	1/1/93	607.33	750.17	94,150.14	118	4/1/96	826.01	531.49	66,308.90
80	2/1/93	612.13	745.37	93,538.01	119	5/1/96	832.54	524.96	65,476.36
81	3/1/93	616.98	740.52	92,921.03	120	6/1/96	839.14	518.36	64,637.22
82	4/1/93	621.87	735.63	92,299.16	121	7/1/96	845.78	511.72	63,791.44
83	5/1/93	626.79	730.71	91,672.37	122	8/1/96	852.47	505.03	62,938.97
84	6/1/93	631.75	725.75	91,040.62	123	9/1/96	859.22	498.28	62,079.75
85	7/1/93	636.75	720.75	90,403.87	124	10/1/96	866.03	491.47	61,213.72
86	8/1/93	641.79	715.71	89,762.08	125	11/1/96	872.88	484.62	60,340.84
87	9/1/93	646.87	710.63	89,115.21	126	12/1/96	879.79	477.71	59,461.05
88	10/1/93	651.99	705.51	88,463.22	127	1/1/97	886.76	470.74	58,574.29
89	11/1/93	657.16	700.34	87,806.06	128	2/1/97	893.78	463.72	57,680.51
90	12/1/93	662.36	695.14	87,143.70	129	3/1/97	900.85	456.65	56,779.66
91	1/1/94	667.60	689.90	86,475.96	130	4/1/97	907.98	449.52	55,871.68
92	2/1/94	672.89	684.61	85,803.21	131	5/1/97	915.17	442.33	54,956.51
93	3/1/94	678.21	679.29	85,125.00	132	6/1/97	922.42	435.08	54,034.09
94	4/1/94	683.58	673.92	84,441.42	133	7/1/97	929.72	427.78	53,104.37
95	5/1/94	689.00	668.50	83,752.42	134	8/1/97	937.08	420.42	52,167.29
96	6/1/94	694.45	663.05	83,057.97	135	9/1/97	944.50	413.00	51,222.79
97	7/1/94	699.95	657.55	82,358.02	136	10/1/97	951.98	405.52	50,270.81
98	8/1/94	705.49	652.01	81,652.53	137	11/1/97	959.51	397.99	49,311.30
99	9/1/94	711.07	646.43	80,941.46	138	12/1/97	967.11	390.39	48,344.19

(continued)

TABLE A.2 Mortgage amortization program (*continued*)

Payment Number	Date	Principal	Interest	Balance
139	1/1/98	974.77	382.73	47,369.42
140	2/1/98	982.48	375.02	46,386.94
141	3/1/98	990.26	367.24	45,396.68
142	4/1/98	998.10	359.40	44,398.58
143	5/1/98	1,006.00	351.50	43,392.58
144	6/1/98	1,013.97	343.53	42,378.61
145	7/1/98	1,021.99	335.51	41,356.62
146	8/1/98	1,030.08	327.42	40,326.54
147	9/1/98	1,038.24	319.26	39,288.30
148	10/1/98	1,046.46	311.04	38,241.84
149	11/1/98	1,054.74	302.76	37,187.10
150	12/1/98	1,063.09	294.41	36,124.01
151	1/1/99	1,071.51	285.99	35,052.50
152	2/1/99	1,079.99	277.51	33,972.51
153	3/1/99	1,088.54	268.96	32,883.97
154	4/1/99	1,097.16	260.34	31,786.81
155	5/1/99	1,105.84	251.66	30,680.97
156	6/1/99	1,114.60	242.90	29,566.37
157	7/1/99	1,123.42	234.08	28,442.95
158	8/1/99	1,132.32	225.18	27,310.63
159	9/1/99	1,141.28	216.22	26,169.35
160	10/1/99	1,150.32	207.18	25,019.03
161	11/1/99	1,159.42	198.08	23,859.61
162	12/1/99	1,168.60	188.90	22,691.01
163	1/1/00	1,177.85	179.65	21,513.16
164	2/1/00	1,187.18	170.32	20,325.98
165	3/1/00	1,196.58	160.92	19,129.40
166	4/1/00	1,206.05	151.45	17,923.35
167	5/1/00	1,215.60	141.90	16,707.75
168	6/1/00	1,225.22	132.28	15,482.53
169	7/1/00	1,234.92	122.58	14,247.61
170	8/1/00	1,244.70	112.80	13,002.91
171	9/1/00	1,254.55	102.95	11,748.36
172	10/1/00	1,264.48	93.02	10,483.88
173	11/1/00	1,274.49	83.01	9,209.39
174	12/1/00	1,284.58	72.92	7,924.81
175	1/1/01	1,294.75	62.75	6,630.06
176	2/1/01	1,305.00	52.50	5,325.06
177	3/1/01	1,315.33	42.17	4,009.73
178	4/1/01	1,325.75	31.75	2,683.98
179	5/1/01	1,336.24	21.26	1,347.74
180	6/1/01	1,346.82	10.68	0.92

TABLE A.3
Amortization payments table

n	$\frac{1}{4}\%$	$\frac{1}{2}\%$	$\frac{3}{4}\%$	1%	$1\frac{1}{4}\%$	$1\frac{1}{2}\%$	$1\frac{3}{4}\%$	2%	$2\frac{1}{2}\%$	3%
1	1.002500	1.005000	1.007500	1.010000	1.012500	1.015000	1.017500	1.020000	1.025000	1.030000
2	0.501876	0.503753	0.505632	0.507512	0.509394	0.511278	0.513163	0.515050	0.518827	0.522611
3	0.335002	0.336672	0.338346	0.340022	0.341701	0.343383	0.345067	0.346755	0.350137	0.353530
4	0.251565	0.253133	0.254705	0.256281	0.257861	0.259445	0.261032	0.262624	0.265818	0.269027
5	0.201503	0.203010	0.204522	0.206040	0.207562	0.209089	0.210621	0.212158	0.215247	0.218355
6	0.168128	0.169595	0.171069	0.172548	0.174034	0.175525	0.177023	0.178526	0.181550	0.184598
7	0.144289	0.145729	0.147175	0.148628	0.150089	0.151556	0.153031	0.154512	0.157495	0.160506
8	0.126410	0.127829	0.129256	0.130690	0.132133	0.133584	0.135043	0.136510	0.139467	0.142456
9	0.112505	0.113907	0.115319	0.116740	0.118171	0.119610	0.121058	0.122515	0.125457	0.128434
10	0.101380	0.102771	0.104171	0.105582	0.107003	0.108434	0.109875	0.111327	0.114259	0.117231
11	0.092278	0.093659	0.095051	0.096454	0.097868	0.099294	0.100730	0.102178	0.105106	0.108077
12	0.084694	0.086066	0.087451	0.088849	0.090258	0.091680	0.093114	0.094560	0.097487	0.100462
13	0.078276	0.079642	0.081022	0.082415	0.083821	0.085240	0.086673	0.088118	0.091048	0.094030
14	0.072775	0.074136	0.075511	0.076901	0.078305	0.079723	0.081156	0.082602	0.085537	0.088526
15	0.068008	0.069364	0.070736	0.072124	0.073526	0.074944	0.076377	0.077825	0.080766	0.083767
16	0.063836	0.065189	0.066559	0.067945	0.069347	0.070765	0.072200	0.073650	0.076599	0.079611
17	0.060156	0.061506	0.062873	0.064258	0.065660	0.067080	0.068516	0.069970	0.072928	0.075953
18	0.056884	0.058232	0.059598	0.060982	0.062385	0.063806	0.065245	0.066702	0.069670	0.072709
19	0.053957	0.055303	0.056667	0.058052	0.059455	0.060878	0.062321	0.063782	0.066761	0.069814
20	0.051323	0.052666	0.054031	0.055415	0.056820	0.058246	0.059691	0.061157	0.064147	0.067216
21	0.048939	0.050282	0.051645	0.053031	0.054437	0.055865	0.057315	0.058785	0.061787	0.064872
22	0.046773	0.048114	0.049477	0.050864	0.052272	0.053703	0.055156	0.056631	0.059647	0.062747
23	0.044795	0.046135	0.047498	0.048886	0.050297	0.051731	0.053188	0.054668	0.057696	0.060814
24	0.042981	0.044321	0.045685	0.047073	0.048487	0.049924	0.051386	0.052871	0.055913	0.059047
25	0.041313	0.042652	0.044016	0.045407	0.046822	0.048263	0.049730	0.051220	0.054276	0.057428
26	0.039773	0.041112	0.042477	0.043869	0.045287	0.046732	0.048203	0.049699	0.052769	0.055938
27	0.038347	0.039686	0.041052	0.042446	0.043867	0.045315	0.046791	0.048293	0.051377	0.054564
28	0.037023	0.038362	0.039729	0.041124	0.042549	0.044001	0.045482	0.046990	0.050088	0.053293
29	0.035791	0.037129	0.038497	0.039895	0.041322	0.042779	0.044264	0.045778	0.048891	0.052115
30	0.034641	0.035979	0.037348	0.038748	0.040079	0.041639	0.043130	0.044650	0.047778	0.051019
31	0.033565	0.034903	0.036274	0.037676	0.039109	0.040574	0.042070	0.043596	0.046739	0.049999
32	0.032556	0.033895	0.035266	0.036671	0.038108	0.039577	0.041078	0.042611	0.045768	0.049047
33	0.031608	0.032947	0.034320	0.035727	0.037168	0.038641	0.040148	0.041687	0.044859	0.048156
34	0.030716	0.032056	0.033431	0.034840	0.036284	0.037762	0.039274	0.040819	0.044007	0.047322
35	0.029875	0.031215	0.032592	0.034004	0.035451	0.036934	0.038451	0.040002	0.043206	0.046539

(continued)

TABLE A.3 Amortization payments table (continued)

n	$\frac{1}{4}\%$	$\frac{1}{2}\%$	$\frac{3}{4}\%$	1%	$1\frac{1}{4}\%$	$1\frac{1}{2}\%$	$1\frac{3}{4}\%$	2%	$2\frac{1}{2}\%$	3%
36	0.029081	0.030422	0.031800	0.033214	0.034665	0.036152	0.037675	0.039233	0.042452	0.045804
37	0.028330	0.029671	0.031051	0.032468	0.033923	0.035414	0.036943	0.038507	0.041741	0.045112
38	0.027618	0.028960	0.030342	0.031761	0.033220	0.034716	0.036250	0.037821	0.041070	0.044459
39	0.026943	0.028286	0.029669	0.031092	0.032554	0.034055	0.035594	0.037171	0.040436	0.043844
40	0.026302	0.027646	0.029030	0.030456	0.031921	0.033427	0.034972	0.036556	0.039836	0.043262
41	0.025692	0.027036	0.028423	0.029851	0.031321	0.032831	0.034382	0.035972	0.039268	0.042712
42	0.025111	0.026456	0.027845	0.029276	0.030749	0.032264	0.033821	0.035417	0.038729	0.042192
43	0.024557	0.025903	0.027293	0.028727	0.030205	0.031725	0.033287	0.034890	0.038217	0.041698
44	0.024029	0.025375	0.026768	0.028204	0.029686	0.031210	0.032778	0.034388	0.037730	0.041230
45	0.023523	0.024871	0.026265	0.027705	0.029190	0.030720	0.032293	0.033910	0.037268	0.040785
46	0.023040	0.024389	0.025785	0.027228	0.028717	0.030251	0.031830	0.033453	0.036827	0.040363
47	0.022578	0.023927	0.025325	0.026771	0.028264	0.029803	0.031388	0.033018	0.036407	0.039961
48	0.022134	0.023485	0.024885	0.026334	0.027831	0.029375	0.030966	0.032602	0.036006	0.039578
49	0.021709	0.023061	0.024463	0.025915	0.027416	0.028965	0.030561	0.032204	0.035623	0.039213
50	0.021301	0.022654	0.024058	0.025513	0.027018	0.028572	0.030174	0.031823	0.035258	0.038865
51	0.020909	0.022263	0.023669	0.025127	0.026636	0.028195	0.029803	0.031459	0.034909	0.038534
52	0.020532	0.021887	0.023295	0.024756	0.026269	0.027833	0.029447	0.031109	0.034574	0.038217
53	0.020169	0.021525	0.022935	0.024400	0.025917	0.027485	0.029105	0.030774	0.034254	0.037915
54	0.019820	0.021177	0.022589	0.024057	0.025578	0.027151	0.028777	0.030452	0.033948	0.037626
55	0.019483	0.020841	0.022256	0.023726	0.025251	0.026830	0.028461	0.030143	0.033654	0.037349
56	0.019159	0.020518	0.021935	0.023408	0.024937	0.026521	0.028158	0.029847	0.033372	0.037084
57	0.018845	0.020206	0.021625	0.023102	0.024635	0.026223	0.027866	0.029561	0.033102	0.036831
58	0.018543	0.019905	0.021326	0.022806	0.024343	0.025937	0.027585	0.029287	0.032842	0.036588
59	0.018251	0.019614	0.021037	0.022520	0.024062	0.025660	0.027314	0.029022	0.032593	0.036356
60	0.017969	0.019333	0.020758	0.022244	0.023790	0.025393	0.027053	0.028768	0.032353	0.036133
61	0.017696	0.019061	0.020489	0.021978	0.023528	0.025136	0.026802	0.028523	0.032123	0.035919
62	0.017431	0.018798	0.020228	0.021720	0.023274	0.024888	0.026559	0.028286	0.031901	0.035714
63	0.017176	0.018543	0.019976	0.021471	0.023029	0.024647	0.026325	0.028058	0.031688	0.035517
64	0.016928	0.018297	0.019731	0.021230	0.022792	0.024415	0.026098	0.027839	0.031482	0.035328
65	0.016688	0.018058	0.019495	0.020997	0.022563	0.024191	0.025880	0.027626	0.031285	0.035146

66	0.034971	0.031094	0.027421	0.025668	0.023974	0.022341	0.020771	0.019265	0.017826	0.016455
67	0.034803	0.030910	0.027223	0.025464	0.023764	0.022126	0.020551	0.019043	0.017602	0.016229
68	0.034642	0.030733	0.027032	0.025266	0.023560	0.021917	0.020339	0.018827	0.017384	0.016010
69	0.034486	0.030562	0.026847	0.025075	0.023363	0.021715	0.020133	0.018618	0.017172	0.015797
70	0.034337	0.030397	0.026668	0.024889	0.023172	0.021519	0.019933	0.018415	0.016967	0.015590
71	0.034193	0.030238	0.026494	0.024710	0.022987	0.021329	0.019739	0.018217	0.016767	0.015389
72	0.034054	0.030084	0.026327	0.024536	0.022808	0.021145	0.019550	0.018026	0.016573	0.015194
73	0.033921	0.029936	0.026165	0.024367	0.022634	0.020966	0.019367	0.017839	0.016384	0.015004
74	0.033792	0.029792	0.026007	0.024204	0.022465	0.020792	0.019189	0.017658	0.016201	0.014819
75	0.033668	0.029654	0.025855	0.024046	0.022301	0.020623	0.019016	0.017482	0.016022	0.014639
76	0.033548	0.029520	0.025708	0.023892	0.022141	0.020459	0.018848	0.017310	0.015848	0.014464
77	0.033433	0.029390	0.025564	0.023743	0.021987	0.020300	0.018684	0.017143	0.015679	0.014293
78	0.033322	0.029265	0.025426	0.023598	0.021836	0.020144	0.018525	0.016981	0.015514	0.014127
79	0.033215	0.029143	0.025291	0.023457	0.021690	0.019993	0.018370	0.016822	0.015354	0.013965
80	0.033112	0.029026	0.025161	0.023321	0.021548	0.019847	0.018219	0.016668	0.015197	0.013807
81	0.033012	0.028912	0.025034	0.023188	0.021410	0.019704	0.018072	0.016518	0.015044	0.013653
82	0.032916	0.028803	0.024911	0.023059	0.021276	0.019564	0.017929	0.016371	0.014896	0.013503
83	0.032823	0.028696	0.024792	0.022934	0.021145	0.019429	0.017789	0.016228	0.014750	0.013356
84	0.032733	0.028593	0.024676	0.022812	0.021018	0.019297	0.017653	0.016089	0.014609	0.013213
85	0.032647	0.028493	0.024563	0.022694	0.020894	0.019168	0.017520	0.015953	0.014470	0.013074
86	0.032563	0.028396	0.024454	0.022578	0.020773	0.019043	0.017391	0.015820	0.014335	0.012937
87	0.032482	0.028303	0.024347	0.022466	0.020656	0.018920	0.017264	0.015691	0.014203	0.012804
88	0.032404	0.028212	0.024244	0.022357	0.020541	0.018801	0.017141	0.015564	0.014074	0.012674
89	0.032328	0.028124	0.024144	0.022251	0.020430	0.018685	0.017021	0.015441	0.013948	0.012546
90	0.032256	0.028038	0.024046	0.022148	0.020321	0.018571	0.016903	0.015320	0.013825	0.012422
91	0.032185	0.027955	0.023951	0.022047	0.020215	0.018461	0.016788	0.015202	0.013705	0.012300
92	0.032117	0.027875	0.023859	0.021949	0.020112	0.018353	0.016676	0.015087	0.013587	0.012181
93	0.032051	0.027797	0.023769	0.021853	0.020011	0.018247	0.016567	0.014974	0.013472	0.012064
94	0.031987	0.027721	0.023681	0.021760	0.019913	0.018144	0.016460	0.014864	0.013360	0.011950
95	0.031926	0.027648	0.023596	0.021669	0.019817	0.018044	0.016355	0.014756	0.013249	0.011839
96	0.031866	0.027577	0.023513	0.021581	0.019723	0.017945	0.016253	0.014650	0.013141	0.011730
97	0.031809	0.027507	0.023432	0.021495	0.019632	0.017849	0.016153	0.014547	0.013036	0.011623
98	0.031753	0.027440	0.023354	0.021411	0.019543	0.017756	0.016055	0.014446	0.012932	0.011518
99	0.031699	0.027375	0.023277	0.021329	0.019456	0.017664	0.015959	0.014347	0.012831	0.011415
100	0.031647	0.027312	0.023203	0.021249	0.019371	0.017574	0.015866	0.014250	0.012732	0.011314

(continued)

36	0.085345	0.080994	0.076715	0.072513	0.068395	0.064366	0.060434	0.056606	0.052887	0.049284
37	0.084924	0.080545	0.076237	0.072005	0.067857	0.063800	0.059840	0.055984	0.052240	0.048613
38	0.084539	0.080132	0.075795	0.071535	0.067358	0.063272	0.059284	0.055402	0.051632	0.047982
39	0.084185	0.079751	0.075387	0.071099	0.066894	0.062780	0.058765	0.054856	0.051061	0.047388
40	0.083860	0.079400	0.075009	0.070694	0.066462	0.062320	0.058278	0.054343	0.050523	0.046827
41	0.083561	0.079077	0.074660	0.070318	0.066059	0.061891	0.057822	0.053862	0.050017	0.046298
42	0.083287	0.078778	0.074336	0.069968	0.065683	0.061489	0.057395	0.053409	0.049540	0.045798
43	0.083034	0.078502	0.074036	0.069644	0.065333	0.061113	0.056993	0.052982	0.049090	0.045325
44	0.082802	0.078247	0.073758	0.069341	0.065006	0.060761	0.056616	0.052581	0.048665	0.044878
45	0.082587	0.078011	0.073500	0.069060	0.064700	0.060431	0.056262	0.052202	0.048262	0.044453
46	0.082390	0.077794	0.073260	0.068797	0.064415	0.060122	0.055928	0.051845	0.047882	0.044051
47	0.082208	0.077592	0.073037	0.068553	0.064148	0.059831	0.055614	0.051507	0.047522	0.043669
48	0.082040	0.077405	0.072831	0.068325	0.063898	0.059559	0.055318	0.051189	0.047181	0.043306
49	0.081886	0.077232	0.072639	0.068112	0.063664	0.059302	0.055040	0.050887	0.046857	0.042962
50	0.081743	0.077072	0.072460	0.067914	0.063444	0.059061	0.054777	0.050602	0.046550	0.042634
51	0.081611	0.076924	0.072294	0.067729	0.063239	0.058835	0.054529	0.050332	0.046259	0.042322
52	0.081490	0.076787	0.072139	0.067556	0.063046	0.058622	0.054294	0.050077	0.045982	0.042024
53	0.081377	0.076659	0.071995	0.067394	0.062866	0.058421	0.054073	0.049835	0.045719	0.041741
54	0.081274	0.076541	0.071861	0.067243	0.062696	0.058232	0.053864	0.049605	0.045469	0.041471
55	0.081178	0.076432	0.071736	0.067101	0.062537	0.058055	0.053667	0.049388	0.045231	0.041213
56	0.081090	0.076330	0.071620	0.066969	0.062388	0.057887	0.053480	0.049181	0.045005	0.040967
57	0.081008	0.076236	0.071512	0.066846	0.062247	0.057729	0.053303	0.048985	0.044789	0.040732
58	0.080932	0.076148	0.071411	0.066730	0.062116	0.057580	0.053136	0.048799	0.044584	0.040508
59	0.080862	0.076067	0.071317	0.066622	0.061992	0.057440	0.052978	0.048622	0.044388	0.040294
60	0.080798	0.075991	0.071229	0.066520	0.061876	0.057307	0.052828	0.048454	0.044202	0.040089
61	0.080738	0.075921	0.071147	0.066426	0.061766	0.057182	0.052686	0.048295	0.044024	0.039892
62	0.080683	0.075856	0.071071	0.066337	0.061664	0.057064	0.052552	0.048143	0.043854	0.039705
63	0.080632	0.075796	0.071000	0.066254	0.061567	0.056953	0.052424	0.047998	0.043692	0.039525
64	0.080585	0.075740	0.070934	0.066176	0.061476	0.056847	0.052304	0.047861	0.043538	0.039353
65	0.080541	0.075688	0.070872	0.066103	0.061391	0.056748	0.052189	0.047730	0.043390	0.039188
66	0.080501	0.075639	0.070814	0.066034	0.061310	0.056654	0.052081	0.047606	0.043249	0.039030
67	0.080464	0.075594	0.070760	0.065970	0.061235	0.056565	0.051978	0.047488	0.043115	0.038879
68	0.080429	0.075553	0.070710	0.065910	0.061163	0.056482	0.051880	0.047375	0.042986	0.038734
69	0.080397	0.075514	0.070663	0.065854	0.061096	0.056402	0.051787	0.047267	0.042863	0.038595
70	0.080368	0.075478	0.070620	0.065801	0.061033	0.056328	0.051699	0.047165	0.042745	0.038461
71	0.080340	0.075444	0.070579	0.065752	0.060974	0.056257	0.051616	0.047068	0.042633	0.038333
72	0.080315	0.075413	0.070541	0.065705	0.060918	0.056190	0.051536	0.046975	0.042525	0.038210
73	0.080292	0.075384	0.070505	0.065662	0.060865	0.056127	0.051461	0.046886	0.042422	0.038092
74	0.080270	0.075357	0.070472	0.065621	0.060815	0.056067	0.051390	0.046802	0.042323	0.037978

(continued)

TABLE A.3 Amortization payments table (*continued*)

n	3½%	4%	4½%	5%	5½%	6%	6½%	7%	7½%	8%
1	1.035000	1.040000	1.045000	1.050000	1.055000	1.060000	1.065000	1.070000	1.075000	1.080000
2	0.526401	0.530196	0.533998	0.537805	0.541618	0.545437	0.549262	0.553092	0.556928	0.560769
3	0.356934	0.360349	0.363773	0.367209	0.370654	0.374110	0.377576	0.381052	0.384538	0.388034
4	0.272251	0.275490	0.278744	0.282012	0.285294	0.288591	0.291903	0.295228	0.298568	0.301921
5	0.221481	0.224627	0.227792	0.230975	0.234176	0.237396	0.240635	0.243891	0.247165	0.250456
6	0.187668	0.190762	0.193878	0.197017	0.200179	0.203363	0.206568	0.209796	0.213045	0.216315
7	0.163544	0.166610	0.169701	0.172820	0.175964	0.179135	0.182331	0.185553	0.188800	0.192072
8	0.145477	0.148528	0.151610	0.154722	0.157864	0.161036	0.164237	0.167468	0.170727	0.174015
9	0.131446	0.134493	0.137574	0.140690	0.143839	0.147022	0.150238	0.153486	0.156767	0.160080
10	0.120241	0.123291	0.126379	0.129505	0.132668	0.135868	0.139105	0.142378	0.145686	0.149029
11	0.111092	0.114149	0.117248	0.120389	0.123571	0.126793	0.130055	0.133357	0.136697	0.140076
12	0.103484	0.106552	0.109666	0.112825	0.116029	0.119277	0.122568	0.125902	0.129278	0.132695
13	0.097062	0.100144	0.103275	0.106456	0.109684	0.112960	0.116283	0.119651	0.123064	0.126522
14	0.091571	0.094669	0.097820	0.101024	0.104279	0.107585	0.110940	0.114345	0.117797	0.121297
15	0.086825	0.089941	0.903114	0.096342	0.099626	0.102963	0.106353	0.109795	0.113287	0.116830
16	0.082685	0.085820	0.089015	0.092270	0.095583	0.098952	0.102378	0.105858	0.109391	0.112977
17	0.079043	0.082199	0.085418	0.088699	0.092042	0.095445	0.098906	0.102425	0.106000	0.109629
18	0.075817	0.078993	0.082237	0.085546	0.088920	0.092357	0.095855	0.099413	0.103029	0.106702
19	0.072940	0.076139	0.079407	0.082745	0.086150	0.089621	0.093156	0.096753	0.100411	0.104128
20	0.070361	0.073582	0.076876	0.080243	0.083679	0.087185	0.090756	0.094393	0.098092	0.101852
21	0.068037	0.071280	0.074601	0.077996	0.081465	0.085005	0.088613	0.092289	0.096029	0.099832
22	0.065932	0.069199	0.072546	0.075971	0.079471	0.083046	0.086691	0.090406	0.094187	0.098032
23	0.064019	0.067309	0.070682	0.074137	0.077670	0.081278	0.084961	0.088714	0.092535	0.096422
24	0.062273	0.065587	0.068987	0.072471	0.076036	0.079679	0.083398	0.087189	0.091050	0.094978
25	0.060674	0.064012	0.067439	0.070952	0.074549	0.078227	0.081981	0.085811	0.089711	0.093679
26	0.059205	0.062567	0.066021	0.069564	0.073193	0.076904	0.080695	0.084561	0.088500	0.092507
27	0.057852	0.061239	0.064719	0.068292	0.071952	0.075697	0.079523	0.083426	0.087402	0.091448
28	0.056603	0.060013	0.063521	0.067123	0.070814	0.074593	0.078453	0.082392	0.086405	0.090489
29	0.055445	0.058880	0.062415	0.066046	0.069769	0.073580	0.077474	0.081449	0.085498	0.089619
30	0.054371	0.057830	0.061392	0.065051	0.068805	0.072649	0.076577	0.080586	0.084671	0.088827
31	0.053372	0.056855	0.060443	0.064132	0.067917	0.071792	0.075754	0.079797	0.083916	0.088107
32	0.052442	0.055949	0.059563	0.063280	0.067095	0.071002	0.074997	0.079073	0.083226	0.087451
33	0.051572	0.055104	0.058745	0.062490	0.066335	0.070273	0.074299	0.078408	0.082594	0.086852
34	0.050760	0.054315	0.057982	0.061755	0.065630	0.069598	0.073656	0.077797	0.082015	0.086304
35	0.049998	0.053577	0.057270	0.061072	0.064975	0.068974	0.073062	0.077234	0.081483	0.085803

TABLE A.3   Amortization payments table (continued)

n	3½%	4%	4½%	5%	5½%	6%	6½%	7%	7½%	8%
75	0.037869	0.042229	0.046721	0.051322	0.056010	0.060769	0.065583	0.070441	0.075332	0.080250
76	0.037765	0.042139	0.046644	0.051257	0.055956	0.060725	0.065547	0.070412	0.075304	0.080231
77	0.037664	0.042052	0.046571	0.051196	0.055906	0.060683	0.065513	0.070385	0.075287	0.082214
78	0.037567	0.041969	0.046501	0.051138	0.055858	0.060644	0.065482	0.070359	0.075267	0.080198
79	0.037474	0.041890	0.046434	0.051082	0.055812	0.060607	0.065452	0.070336	0.075248	0.080183
80	0.037385	0.041814	0.046371	0.051030	0.055769	0.060573	0.065424	0.070314	0.075231	0.080170
81	0.037299	0.041741	0.046310	0.050980	0.055729	0.060540	0.065398	0.070293	0.075215	0.080157
82	0.037216	0.041671	0.046252	0.050932	0.055690	0.060509	0.065374	0.070274	0.075200	0.080146
83	0.037137	0.041605	0.046197	0.050887	0.055654	0.060480	0.065351	0.070256	0.075186	0.080135
84	0.037060	0.041541	0.046144	0.050844	0.055619	0.060453	0.065329	0.070239	0.075173	0.080125
85	0.036987	0.041479	0.046093	0.050803	0.055587	0.060427	0.065309	0.070223	0.075161	0.080116
86	0.036916	0.041420	0.046045	0.050764	0.055556	0.060402	0.065290	0.070209	0.075150	0.080107
87	0.036848	0.041364	0.045999	0.050727	0.055527	0.060380	0.065272	0.070195	0.075139	0.080099
88	0.036782	0.041310	0.045955	0.050692	0.055499	0.060358	0.065256	0.070182	0.075129	0.090092
89	0.036719	0.041258	0.045913	0.050659	0.055473	0.060338	0.065240	0.070170	0.075120	0.080085
90	0.036658	0.041208	0.045873	0.050627	0.055448	0.060318	0.065225	0.070159	0.075112	0.080079
91	0.036599	0.041160	0.045835	0.050597	0.055424	0.060300	0.065212	0.070149	0.075104	0.080073
92	0.036543	0.041114	0.045798	0.050568	0.055402	0.060283	0.065199	0.070139	0.075097	0.080067
93	0.036488	0.041070	0.045763	0.050541	0.055381	0.060267	0.065186	0.070130	0.075090	0.080062
94	0.036436	0.041028	0.045730	0.050515	0.055361	0.060252	0.065175	0.070121	0.075084	0.080058
95	0.036385	0.040987	0.045698	0.050490	0.055342	0.060238	0.065164	0.070113	0.075078	0.080053
96	0.036337	0.040949	0.045667	0.050466	0.055324	0.060224	0.065154	0.070106	0.075072	0.080050
97	0.036290	0.040911	0.045638	0.050444	0.055307	0.060211	0.065145	0.070097	0.075067	0.080046
98	0.036245	0.040875	0.045610	0.050423	0.055291	0.060199	0.065136	0.070092	0.075063	0.080042
99	0.036201	0.040841	0.045584	0.050402	0.055276	0.060188	0.065128	0.070086	0.075058	0.080039
100	0.036159	0.040808	0.045558	0.050383	0.055261	0.060177	0.065120	0.070081	0.075054	0.080036

TABLE A.4   Annual percentage rates

Annual percentage rate / Number of Payments	6	12	18	24	30	36	42	48	60
10.00%	2.94	5.50	8.10	10.75	13.43	16.16	18.93	21.74	27.48
10.25%	3.01	5.64	8.31	11.02	13.78	16.58	19.43	22.32	28.22
10.50%	3.08	5.78	8.52	11.30	14.13	17.01	19.93	22.90	28.96
10.75%	3.16	5.92	8.73	11.58	14.48	17.43	20.43	23.48	29.71
11.00%	3.23	6.06	8.93	11.86	14.83	17.86	20.93	24.06	30.45
11.25%	3.31	6.20	9.14	12.14	15.19	18.29	21.44	24.64	31.20
11.50%	3.38	6.34	9.35	12.42	15.54	18.71	21.94	25.23	31.96
11.75%	3.45	6.48	9.56	12.70	15.89	19.14	22.45	25.81	32.71
12.00%	3.53	6.62	9.77	12.98	16.24	19.57	22.96	26.40	33.47
12.25%	3.60	6.76	9.98	13.26	16.60	20.00	23.47	26.99	34.23
12.50%	3.68	6.90	10.19	13.54	16.95	20.43	23.98	27.58	34.99
12.75%	3.75	7.04	10.40	13.82	17.31	20.87	24.49	28.18	35.77
13.00%	3.83	7.18	10.61	14.10	17.66	21.30	25.00	28.77	36.52
13.25%	3.90	7.32	10.82	14.38	18.02	21.73	25.51	29.37	37.29
13.50%	3.97	7.46	11.03	14.66	18.38	22.17	26.03	29.97	38.06
13.75%	4.05	7.60	11.24	14.95	18.74	22.60	26.55	30.57	38.83
14.00%	4.12	7.74	11.45	15.23	19.10	23.04	27.06	31.17	39.61
14.25%	4.20	7.89	11.66	15.51	19.45	23.48	27.58	31.77	40.39
14.50%	4.27	8.03	11.87	15.80	19.81	23.92	28.10	32.37	41.17
14.75%	4.35	8.17	12.08	16.08	20.17	24.35	28.62	32.98	41.95
15.00%	4.42	8.31	12.29	16.37	20.54	24.80	29.15	33.59	42.74
15.25%	4.49	8.45	12.50	16.65	20.90	25.24	29.67	34.20	43.53
15.50%	4.57	8.59	12.72	16.94	21.26	25.68	30.19	34.81	44.32
15.75%	4.64	8.74	12.93	17.22	21.62	26.12	30.72	35.42	45.11
16.00%	4.72	8.88	13.14	17.51	21.99	26.57	31.25	36.03	45.91
16.25%	4.79	9.02	13.35	17.80	22.35	27.01	31.78	36.65	46.71
16.50%	4.87	9.16	13.57	18.09	22.72	27.46	32.31	37.27	47.51
16.75%	4.94	9.30	13.78	18.37	23.08	27.90	32.84	37.88	48.31
17.00%	5.02	9.45	13.99	18.66	23.45	28.35	33.37	38.50	49.12
17.25%	5.09	9.59	14.21	18.95	23.81	28.80	33.90	39.13	49.92
17.50%	5.17	9.73	14.42	19.24	24.18	29.25	34.44	39.75	50.73
17.75%	5.24	9.87	14.64	19.53	24.55	29.70	34.97	40.37	51.55
18.00%	5.32	10.02	14.85	19.82	24.92	30.15	35.51	41.00	52.36
20.00%	5.91	11.16	16.52	22.15	27.89	33.79	39.85	46.07	58.96
25.00%	7.42	14.05	20.95	28.09	35.49	43.14	51.03	59.15	76.11
30.00%	8.93	16.98	25.41	34.19	43.33	52.83	62.66	72.83	94.12
35.00%	10.45	19.96	29.96	40.44	51.41	62.85	74.74	87.06	112.94
40.00%	11.99	22.97	34.59	46.85	59.73	73.20	87.24	101.82	132.51

Answer To Selected Exercises

CHAPTER 1

Section 1.2, pp. 17–19

1. $2^9 \cdot 5^9 = (2 \cdot 5)^9 = 10^9 = 1{,}000{,}000{,}000$
$2^n \cdot 5^n = (2 \cdot 5)^n = 10^n$

3. The result is always 6174.

5. a) The square numbers between 1 and 100 inclusive are 1, 4, 9, 16, 25, 36, 49, 64, 81, and 100.

b) If we examine the pattern for the first few square numbers, we note that, for example, the square number $25 = 5^2$. Thus the next square number is 6^2, or 36.

7. a) 2 and 1   **b)** 64 and 128   **c)** 8 and 7   **d)** $\frac{1}{2}$ and $\frac{1}{4}$
e) $\frac{1}{3}$ and $\frac{1}{9}$ **f)** 81 and 243. These are powers of 3
g) 27 and 32. Add 5 to any term.
h) 50 and 72. These are the values of $2x^2$ where x is a natural number.
i) 53 and 75. These are the values of $2x^2 + 3$ where x is a natural number.

j) T and O. The letters represent the digits ten, nine, eight, . . . in reverse order.

9. 6   **11.** 12 seconds

13. a) The next three ratios are $\frac{11}{7}$, $\frac{18}{11}$, and $\frac{29}{18}$.   **b)** The next three ratios are $\frac{99}{70}$, $\frac{239}{169}$, and $\frac{577}{408}$.

15. There are ten triangles. These are *AIB, BHC, CGD, DFE, AJC, BKD, CLE, AND, AOE, BME.*

17. The page numbers are 97 and 98.

Section 1.3, pp. 24–25

1. 8   **3.**

8	1	6
3	5	7
4	9	2

5.

17	24	1	8	15
23	5	7	14	16
4	6	13	20	22
10	12	19	21	3
11	18	25	2	9

7.

6	2	34	33	35	1
25	11	27	10	8	30
19	23	16	15	20	18
13	14	22	21	17	24
12	29	9	28	26	7
36	32	3	4	5	31

9.

32	41	50	3	12	21	30
40	49	9	11	20	29	31
48	8	10	19	28	37	39
7	16	18	27	36	38	47
15	17	26	35	44	46	6
23	25	34	43	45	5	14
24	33	42	51	4	13	22

13. a) 3.3   **b)**

1.4	0.9	1.0
0.7	1.1	1.5
1.2	1.3	0.8

15. $\dfrac{n(n^2 + 1)}{2}$

Section 1.4, pp. 31–32

1. $12^3 - 48 = 1680$ **3.** 855   **5.** 829   **7.** 0.020011911

9. Most calculators will display an error message. Others will blink or display 0.

11. 16.37   **13.** 0.00   **15.** 5804.87   **17.** 707.32   **19.** 2945.50

21. $7 \times 729 = 5103$ **23.** 1   **25.** 8ELLS

27. The same three-digit number that you started with.

Typical Classroom Questions, pp. 32–33

1. Most calculators will display an error message. This is because 0^{10} is an indeterminate number.

2. Most calculators are programmed to display 0 together with an error message when an operation that cannot be legitimately performed is attempted.

3. Not all calculators are programmed to round answers.

Chapter Review Exercises, pp. 34–37

1. $\frac{49}{50}$ **2.** 20, 22, and 26

3. a)
```
      78
   +  87
   ─────
     165
   + 561
   ─────
     726
   + 627
   ─────
    1353
   +3531
   ─────
    4884
4 additions
```
b)
```
     148
   + 841
   ─────
     989
1 addition
```
c)
```
     379
   + 973
   ─────
    1352
  + 2531
  ──────
    3883
2 additions
```
4. 29, 37, and 46

5. a) 6   12   18   24   30   36   **b)** The 50th multiple of 50, or 2500

6.

$\frac{7}{5}$	$\frac{9}{10}$	$\frac{1}{1}$
$\frac{7}{10}$	$\frac{11}{10}$	$\frac{3}{2}$
$\frac{6}{5}$	$\frac{13}{10}$	$\frac{4}{5}$

7. Since you took 3 eggs, you have only 3 eggs. However, there are 9 eggs left over.

8. 1, 5, and –1   **9. a)** $5 + 12345 \times 8$ **b)** 98765

10. a) $9 \times 54321 - 1$ **b)** 488888   **c)** 788, 888, 888

11.

Sum	Alternate form
125	5^3
216	6^3

12. 20, 12, and 10

13.

Problem	Answer
1×1	1
11×11	121
111×111	12321
1111×1111	1234321
11111×11111	123454321

14. Choice (a)   **15.** Choice (b)

16. E, U, and F   **17.** $\frac{75}{46}$, $\frac{121}{75}$, and $\frac{196}{121}$

18.

4.5	2.5	5.3
4.9	4.1	3.3
2.9	5.7	3.7

19. $\frac{454}{321}$, $\frac{1096}{775}$, and $\frac{2646}{1871}$

CHAPTER 2

Section 2.1, pp. 49–52

1. The set of the months of the year that begin with the letter J.

3. The set of all prime numbers between 2 and 19 inclusive.

5. The set of the days of the week beginning with the letter T.

7. The set of some computers on the market today.   **9.** {M, I, S, P}

11. {Truman, Eisenhower, Kennedy, Johnson, Nixon, Ford, Carter, Reagan, Bush}   **13.** {14, 16, 18}

15. {Florida, Indiana, Virginia, Texas, Alabama, Mississippi, Louisiana, North Carolina, Georgia, South Carolina, Nevada}

17. ϕ **19.** Not well-defined   **21.** Not well-defined   **23.** Well-defined

25. Finite nonempty set   **27.** Finite nonempty set   **29.** Null set   **31.** Finite nonempty set

33. Null set   **35.** False   **37.** False   **39.** False   **41.** False   **43.** Yes

45. Equivalent and equal   **47.** Neither   **49.** Neither   **51.** Equivalent but not equal

53. Neither   **55.** 2   **57.** 1   **59.** 10

61. a) {The regional telephone companies created by the divestiture of AT&T}
   b) {famous female tennis players}   **c)** {popular computer software packages}   **d)** {imported cars}
   e) {next-day delivery service companies)   **f)** {fish}   **g)** {space programs}
   h) {popular soft drinks sold in the U.S.}

63. a) {9}, {11}, and {12}   **b)** {9, 11}, {9, 12} and {11, 12}   **c)** {9, 11, 12}   **d)** { }

65. a) True   **b)** True   **c)** True   **d)** True   **e)** False
   f) False   **g)** True   **h)** False   **i)** True

67. 2   **69.**

Number of elements in set	6	10	100	n
Number of possible subsets	64	1024	2^{100}	2^n

71. Yes   **73.** $n(n-1)(n-2) \cdots 1$ or $n!$

75. Draw lines from the center of the circle to the square.

Section 2.2, pp. 58–60

1. a) {a, b, c, d, e, f, g, i}   **b)** {f, g}   **c)** {b, c, e, h, i}   **d)** {b, c, e, f, g, h, i}   **e)** {a, d}
   f) {b, c, e, i}   **g)** ϕ **h)** {a, d, g}
   i) {(a, b), (a, f), (a, i), (d, b), (d, f), (d, i), (f, b), (f, f), (f, i), (g, b), (g, f), (g, i)}
   j) {(b, a), (b, d), (b, f), (b, g), (f, a), (f, d), (f, f), (f, g), (i, a), (i, d), (i, f), (i, g)}
   k) {b, c, e, f, i,}   **l)** ϕ **m)** {h}   **n)** {a, c, d, e, g, h}

3. a) A is a subset of B **b)** B is a subset of A **c)** B is a subset of A **d)** A is a subset of B

5. $A = \phi$ **7. a)** B   **b)** ϕ **c)** B   **d)** C   **e)** C   **f)** D   **g)** B   **h)** B   **i)** U

9. a) 234   **b)** 125   **c)** 48   **d)** 140   **11. a)** 2   **b)** 3   **c)** 6

13. {(finished basement, solar heat), (finished basement, oil heat),
   (finished basement, gas heat), (unfinished basement, solar heat),
   (unfinished basement, oil heat), (unfinished basement, gas heat)}

Section 2.3, pp. 70–74

1. a) 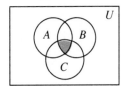   **b)** 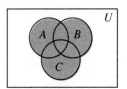   **c)**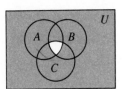

d) 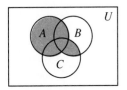   **e)** 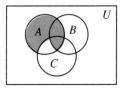   **f)**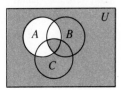

g) 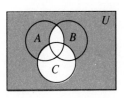   **h)**   **i)**

3. a) 235   **b)** 22   **c)** 177   **d)** **235**   **e)** 121   **f)** 215

5. Region 2 = $A' \cap B' \cap C$ Region 3 = $A' \cap B' \cap C$ Region 4 = $A' \cap B \cap C'$
Region 5 = $A \cap B \cap C'$ Region 6 = $A \cap B \cap C$ Region 7 = $A \cap B' \cap C$
Region 8 = $A \cap B' \cap C'$

7. a) $A' \cap B \cap C'$ **b)** $A' \cap B \cap C$ **c)** $A \cap B'$ **d)** $A \cap C$

9. a) 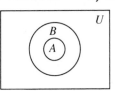   **b)** 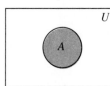   **c)**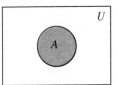

d) 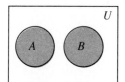   **e)** 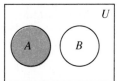   **f)**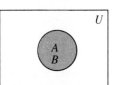

g) 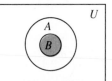   **h)** 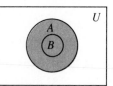   **i)**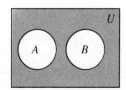

11. a) 102 **b)** 189 **c)** 79 **13. a)** 21 **b)** 19

15. a) 29 **b)** 39 **c)** 27 **d)** 18 **e)** 0

17. a) 159 **b)** 107 **c)** 177 **d)** 86 **e)** 58 **f)** 27

19. a) Any committee that consists of at least four of these people or three of these people if Ann is one of the members also.

   b) Any committee that consists of at most two of these people or any committee of three people if Ann is *not* one of the members.

   c) Any three-person committee of which Ann is a member.

   d) No.

21. Yes

23. Minimal winning: Any coalition consisting of the "Big Five" and four others.
Losing: Any coalition consisting of six or fewer members that does not include any of the "Big Five" countries.
Blocking: Any coalition consisting of at least one of the "Big Five" countries.

25. The numbers are inconsistent. Their sum is only 1986 when it should be 2000.

27. a) 1420 **b)** 620, since 3600 – 2800 = 800 and 1420 – 800 = 620

Section 2.4, pp. 84–90

1. Inductive **3.** Inductive **5.** The one that offers the semiannual raise.

7. a) 25. The numbers represent the squares of the natural numbers.

   b) 8. We have a sequence of three even numbers with the first number of the previous group always deleted.

   c) 21. Any number is obtained by adding the preceding two numbers in the sequence.

   d) 1. We have a sequence of 1's and a sequence of multiples of 3 combined together.

   e) 17. These are the prime numbers.

   f) T. The sequence represents the first letters of the digits one, two, three, . . .

   g) 50. Each term in the sequence is obtained by adding the next odd number 3, 5, 7, . . . to the previous term.

   h) 3. The sequence represents the digits arranged alphabetically: Eight, Five, Four, Nine, One, Seven, Six, . . .

   i) $\frac{6}{9}$

8. a) 8 **b)** 14 **c)** 22

   d) If there are n circles, the plane is divided into a maximum of $n^2 - n + 2$ regions.

9.

Number of points on the circle	5	6	7	8
Number of regions	16	31	57	96

11. $5^3 = 15^2 - 10^2$ and $6^3 = 21^2 - 15^2$

13. a) Row 6   1   6   15   20   15   6   1   **b)** $1 + 1 = 2$ or $2'$
       Row 7   1   7   21   35   35   21   7   1

   c) $1 + 2 + 1 = 4$ or 2^2 **d)** $1 + 3 + 3 + 1 = 8$ or 2^3 **e)** $1 + 4 + 6 + 4 + 1 = 16$ or 2^4 **f)** 2^n

15. Valid   **17.** Invalid   **19.** Invalid   **21.** Invalid   **23.** Invalid   **25.** Valid

26. The amount of money spent does not necessarily equal the sum of the balances.

31. Bill Holland is going to England; Pat Canada is going to Holland;
Debbie English is going to Canada.

32. The blind person wore a white hat.   **34.** No   **39.** Mr. Gusher did it.

40. Pointing to one particular road, she would ask, "Would a member of the other tribe tell me to take this road?"

42. This is the famous "Liar's Paradox."

Typical Classroom Questions, pp. 90–91

1. The symbol "$\subset$" stands for "is a proper subset of " and the symbol "$\in$" stands for "is an element of." They are not the same. There is a difference.

2. Using the clue given, the answer is no. Thus the null set is assumed to be a subset of every set.

3. Yes; $A \times B = \{(1, 3), (1, 1), (3, 3), (3, 1)\}$ and $B \times A = \{(3, 1), (3, 3), (1, 1), (1, 3)\}$

4. a) Otherwise the same element will be counted more than once.
   b) Let $A = \{a, b, c, d, e\}$ and $B = \{m, n, o\}$. Then $A \cup B = \{a, b, c, d, e, m, n, o\}$, so that $n(A \cup B) = 8$ and $5 + 3 = 8$.
   c) Let $A = \{a, b, c, d, e, f, g, h\}$ and $B = \{m, n, o, p, q, r, s\}$. Then $A \cup B = \{a, b, c, d, e, f, g, h, m, n, o, p, q, r, s\}$, so that $n(A \cup B) = 15$ and $8 + 7 = 15$.
   d) Let $A = \{a, b, c, d, e, f\}$ and $B = \phi$. Then $A \cup B = \{a, b, c, d, e, f\}$, so that $n(A \cup B) = 6$ and $6 + 0 = 6$.

5. Inductive reasoning is used in mathematics to discover new truths, whereas deductive reasoning is used to prove these truths.

Chapter Review Exercises, pp. 94–98

   1. $2^5 = 32$.   Choice (d)   **2.** Choice (a)   **3.** Choice (b)   **4.** Choice (b)   **5.** Choice (a)

   6. Choice (b)   **7.** Choice (d)   **8.** Choice (d)   **9.** Choice (e)   **10.** Choice (d)

11. Choice (d)   **12.** Choice (b)   **13.** Choice (c)   **14.** Choice (a)   **15.** Choice (b)

16. Choice (a)   **17.** Choice (c)   **18.** Choice (a)   **19.** Choice (a)   **20.** Choice (c)   **21.** 530

22. Choice (c)   **23.** Choice (c)   **24.** Choice (a)   **25.** Choice (c)   **26.** Choice (b)   **27.** 7

28. $(A \cup B')' = A' \cap B$ **29.** $5 \times 3 = 15$ ways   **30.** 45 female freshman business majors

31. Choice (c)   **32.** Choice (b)   **33.** Choice (b)   **34.** Choice (b)   **35.** Choice (b)

CHAPTER 3

Section 3.1, pp. 104–107

1. a) 336   **b)** 22,135   **c)** 1247   **d)** 12,434   **e)** 1119   **f)** 11,229

3. a) ; 5775

b) ; 34,978   **c)** ; 210

d) ; 7988

5. a) … **b)** … **c)** …

d) … **e)** … **f)** …

g) … **h)** …

7. a) … **b)** … **c)** … **d)** … **e)** … **f)** …

9. One dot · moved up one space

Section 3.2, p. 112

1. a) LIX   **b)** XCIV   **c)** LXIX   **d)** MCCXXXIV   **3.** MDCLX

Section 3.3, p. 120

1. $111100_{(two)}$ **3.** $2258_{(nine)}$ **5.** $2130_{(four)}$ **7.** $2567_{(eight)}$ **9.** $105_{(six)}$ **11.** $52551_{(seven)}$

13. $221020202_{(three)}$ **15.** $2261_{(nine)}$ **17.** $451_{(six)}$ **19.** $14t_{(twelve)}$ **21.** $b = 9$ **23.** $b = 9$

25. Otherwise there would be only one digit.   **27.** Base 7   **29.** Base 8   **31.** $A = 0$; $M = 1$; $D = 2$

33. Yes. For example $32_{(five)} = 17_{(ten)}$, which is an odd number, assuming that 32 is interpreted as a group of *numerals*. On the other hand, if 32 is assumed to be an even *number* in base 10, then even means divisible exactly by 2 with no remainder so that $32_{(ten)}$ written in any base will still be even. Division by 2 in any other base will leave a remainder of zero.

Section 3.4, pp. 125–126

1. a) $12213_{(four)}$ **b)** $1203_{(five)}$ **c)** $11210_{(three)}$ **d)** $652_{(eight)}$ **e)** $666_{(nine)}$ **f)** $1252_{(seven)}$
   g) $1442_{(six)}$ **h)** $235_{(twelve)}$ **i)** $116_{(sixteen)}$ **j)** $2123_{(five)}$ **k)** $1010100_{(two)}$ **l)** $364_{(seven)}$
   m) $10000001_{(two)}$ **n)** $1e2_{(twelve)}$ **o)** $1163_{(eight)}$ **p)** $27e4_{(twelve)}$

3. $217_{(ten)} = 11011001_{(two)} = 331_{(eight)}$. When regrouped, 11011001 becomes 11 011 001 as powers of 2

$$\underbrace{11}_{3}\ \underbrace{011}_{3}\ \underbrace{001}_{1}$$

or 331 as powers of 8. Also $301_{(ten)} = 100101101_{(two)} = 455_{(eight)}$.   **7.** $230_{(five)}$

9. Arlene = \$49,682, Tom = \$28,343, and Bill \$62,511. Therefore, Bill.

Section 3.5, pp. 133–134

1. a) Good combination   **b)** Good combination   **c)** Bad combination   **d)** Good combination
   e) Good combination

Section 3.6, pp. 149–151

1. a) Commutative law of addition   **b)** Associative law of addition
   c) Distributive law of multiplication   **d)** Law of closure for addition
   e) Associative law of addition   **f)** Commutative law for addition
   g) Commutative law for multiplication   **h)** Associative law of multiplication
   i) Distributive law of multiplication   **j)** Law of closure for multiplication

3. a) No   **b)** Yes   **c)** Yes   **d)** Yes   **e)** Yes   **f)** No   **g)** Yes

5. a) Yes   **b)** Yes   **c)** Yes   **7.** \$437   **9. a)** 1900   **b)** 9300   **c)** 1134   **11.** Yes; 1

13. No, although $5 \div 1 = 5$, $1 \div 5 = \frac{1}{5}$, and $5 \div 1 \neq 1 \div 5$.   **15.** As a placeholder

17.

Other answers are possible.

19. When we divide both sides by $(b - a)$, we are dividing by 0.

Section 3.7, pp. 161–162

1. a) 1019   **b)** 1983   **c)** 26630   **d)** 17080

3. a) 1855   **b)** 666   **c)** 2714   **d)**   **e)**

7. a) 424   **b)** 585   **c)** 23,936   **d)** 44,536   **e)** 36,423   **f)** 41,472   **g)** 222,385

9. a) $23\overline{)35029}$ 1523   **b)** $14\overline{)13510}$ 965   **c)** $26\overline{)16146}$ 621   **d)** $18\overline{)9414}$ 523   **e)** $29\overline{)18590}$ 641 remainder 1

Section 3.8, pp. 165–166

1. a) $(7 \times 10^1) + (8 \times 10^0) + (1 \times 10^{-1})$

   b) $(3 \times 10^2) + (1 \times 10^1) + (6 \times 10^0) + (0 \times 10^{-1}) + (1 \times 10^{-2})$

   c) $(4 \times 10^2) + (1 \times 10^1) + (2 \times 10^0) + (3 \times 10^{-1}) + (7 \times 10^{-2})$

   d) $(5 \times 10^1) + (1 \times 10^0) + (0 \times 10^{-1}) + (0 \times 10^{-2}) + (1 \times 10^{-3})$

   e) $(6 \times 10^2) + (1 \times 10^1) + (9 \times 10^0) + (8 \times 10^{-1}) + (2 \times 10^{-2}) + (3 \times 10^{-3})$

   f) $(3 \times 10^3) + (4 \times 10^2) + (7 \times 10^1) + (2 \times 10^0) + (1 \times 10^{-1}) + (3 \times 10^{-2})$

   g) $(4 \times 10^3) + (6 \times 10^2) + (0 \times 10^1) + (9 \times 10^0) + (1 \times 10^{-1}) + (8 \times 10^{-1}) + (8 \times 10^{-2}) + (2 \times 10^{-3})$

   h) $(3 \times 10^3) + (2 \times 10^2) + (4 \times 10^1) + (7 \times 10^0) + (1 \times 10^{-1}) + (9 \times 10^{-2}) + (3 \times 10^{-3})$

   i) $(4 \times 10^2) + (5 \times 10^1) + (3 \times 10^0) + (0 \times 10^{-1}) + (2 \times 10^{-2}) + (5 \times 10^{-3}) + (8 \times 10^{-4})$

3. -2 **5.** 5   **7.** 3   **9.** -5 **11.** -10 **13.** 907 kilograms   **15.** 30,000,000,000 cm/sec

17. 5,000,000,000 years   **19.** 0.0000054 milliliters   **21.** 3,022,387 square miles

23. 9.5×10^{12} km   **25.** 7.5×10^{-4} cm   **27.** 6×10^{23} atoms   **29.** 3.15576×10^7 seconds

31. 2×10^9 miles

Typical Classroom Questions, pp. 166–167

1. Neither, as 89 is written as LXXXIX and 91 is written as XCI.

3. No, it is just coincidental. Try other numbers.   **4.** No, as $5 - 0 = 5$, $0 - 5 = -5$, and $5 - 0 \neq 0 - 5$

Chapter Review Exercises, pp. 170–172

1. Choice (b)   **2.** Choice (b)   **3.** Choice (a)   **4.** Choice (b)   **5.** Choice (a)   **6.** Choice (a)

7. Choice (d)   **8.** Choice (a)   **9.** Choice (b)   **10.** Choice (b)   **11.** Choice (c)

12. Choice (a)   **13.** $t5756_{(\text{twelve})}$ **14.** $67_{(\text{nine})}$ **15.** $31_{(\text{four})}$ **16.** $470_{(\text{eight})}$

17. Choice (d)   **18.** Choice (a)   **19.** 4,230,000   **20.** Choice (a)

21. $(4 \times 10^2) + (5 \times 10^1) + (1 \times 10^0) + (6 \times 10^{-1}) + (2 \times 10^{-2}) + (3 \times 10^{-3})$ **22.** 1.43×10^{11}

23. Base Twelve $1t\overline{)11270}$ 726   **24.** $B = 16$ **25.** $155_{(\text{six})}$ **26.** $101110_{(\text{two})}$ **27.** Choice (a)

28. 6936   **29.** 1699   **30.** 489

CHAPTER 4

Section 4.1, pp. 186–188

1. a) $+24$ **b)** -11 **c)** $+5$ **d)** $+1$ **e)** -5 **f)** -1 **g)** -13 **h)** $+8$
i) -1 **j)** -24 **k)** $+24$ **l)** -24 **m)** -7 **n)** 0 **o)** $+14$ **p)** -9
q) -2 **r)** $+4$ **s)** 0 **t)** undefined

3. 0

5. Let x, y, and z be any integers. Then

Name of law	Symbolically
Closure for addition	$x + y$ is an integer
Closure for multiplication	xy is an integer
Commutative law for multiplicaiton	$xy = yx$
Associative law for addition	$x + (y + z) = (x + y) + z$
Associative law for multiplication	$x(yz) = (xy)z$

7. Yes

9. a) Commutative law of addition   **b)** Distributive law of multiplication

c) Associative law of addition   **d)** Law of closure for multiplication

e) Associative law of multiplication   **f)** Distributive law of multiplication

g) Multiplication property of zero or law of closure for multiplication

h) Additive inverse property or law of closure for addition

i) Commutative law of multiplication

11. $(-1) \cdot x = -(1 \cdot x) = -x$ **13.** 2414 **15. a)** $W \subset I$ **b)** $N \subset W$ **c)** $N \subset I$

17. a) 11 **b)** 8 **c)** 7 **d)** 0 **e)** 0 **f)** 4 **g)** 3 **h)** 5 **i)** 0

19. a) Let $a = 3$ and $b = -2$, so that $|3| > |-2|$; then $3 + (-2) = 1 = |3| - |-2| = 3 - 2 = +1$.
b) Let $a = 2$ and $b = -3$, so that $|-3| > |2|$; then $2 + (-3) = -1 = -(|-3| - |2|) = -(3 - 2) = -1$.

21. a) $+80$. Each entry is multiplied by -2 to obtain the next integer.
b) -10. We subtract 6 from each entry to obtain the next integer.
c) $+324$. Each entry is multiplied by -3 to obtain the next integer.
d) -10. We subtract 4 from each entry to obtain the next integer.

23. a) True
b) False, let $x = 5$ and $y = -3$, then $|5 - (-3)| = |8| \neq |5| - |-3|$
   and $8 \neq 2$
c) True

25. Let $2n$ be an even integer and $2m + 1$ an odd integer. Then their sum is $2n + 2m + 1 = 2(m + n) + 1$. Since m and n are integers, then $m + n$ is an integer. Therefore, $2(m + n) + 1$ is an odd integer.

Section 4.2, pp. 191–192

1. Yes

3.

	$f(1)$	$f(0)$	$f(-3)$	$f(a)$	$f(x + h)$
a)	1	-3	-15	$4a - 3$	$4x + 4h + 3$
b)	5	2	-7	$3a + 2$	$3x + 3h + 2$
c)	4	3	12	$a^2 + 3$	$x^2 + 2xh + h^2 + 3$
d)	3	0	27	$3a^2$	$3x^2 + 6xh + 3h^2$
e)	8	14	20	$(2 - a)(7 + a)$	$(2 - x - h)(7 + x + h)$
f)	14	6	-6	$a^2 + 7a + 6$	$x^2 + 2xh + h^2 + 7x + 7h + 6$
g)	17	5	-43	$2a^3 + 3a^2 + 7a + 5$	$2(x + h)^3 + 3(x + h)^2 + 7(x + h) + 5$

5. a) Yes

  b) $y = 0.06x$ when $x \le 25{,}000$
   $y = 0.06(25{,}000) + .08(x - 25{,}000)$ when $x > 25{,}000$ or
   $y = 0.08x - 500$

  c) January: $0.06(24{,}228) = \$1453.68$
   February: $0.06(17{,}368) = \$1042.08$
   March: $0.08(26{,}014) - 500 = \$1581.12$
   April: $0.08(28{,}132) - 500 = \$1750.56$
   May: $0.08(29{,}485) - 500 = \$1858.80$
   June: $0.08(38{,}692) - 500 = \$2595.36$

7.

Domain	Range
a) All real numbers	All positive real numbers
b) All real numbers greater than or equal to $\frac{-2}{7}$	All non-negative numbers
c) All real numbers except $\frac{-1}{2}$	All real numbers except 2
d) All real numbers	All non-negative numbers

Section 4.3, pp. 202–204

1. a) $x = 3$ **b)** $x = -4$ **c)** $x = 2$ **d)** $x = 2$ **e)** $x = 10$ **f)** $x = -6$ **g)** $x = 10$
  h) $x = -2$ **i)** $x = 21$ **j)** $x = \frac{4}{7}$ **k)** $x = 6$ **l)** $x = \frac{-65}{4}$ **m)** $x = 1$ **n)** $x = 2$
  o) $x = 6$ **p)** $x = 6$ **q)** $x = \dfrac{c + 5}{b}$ **r)** $x = 15$ **s)** $\dfrac{a - 6}{b} = x$ **t)** $x = \dfrac{9b}{2}$
  u) $x = 2a$ **v)** $x = 4$ **w)** $x = 2$ **x)** $x = \frac{-51}{7}$ **y)** $x = 5$ **z)** $x = -3$

3. a $\rightarrow$ viii;   b $\rightarrow$ ix;   c $\rightarrow$ vi;   d $\rightarrow$ iii;   e $\rightarrow$ v;   f $\rightarrow$ ii;   g $\rightarrow$ iv;   h $\rightarrow$ i.

5. Percent decrease is $33\frac{1}{3}\%$.   **7.** Seven \$10 bills, ten \$5 bills, and forty \$1 bills

9. Monday = 2; Tuesday = 4; Wednesday = 4   **11.** He must pay \$45,733.94.

13. Secretary is 22 years and president is 66 years.   **15.** Stephanie at least 14 and Mary at least 84.

17. 23,000 gallons   **19.** 24,000 miles   **21.** Width = 4 feet and length = 12 feet.

Section 4.4, pp. 207–208

1. $x = 5$; $y = 3$ **3.** $x = -3$; $y = 1$ **5.** $x = 4$; $y = 3$ **7.** $x = 3$; $y = 2$

9. $x = 3$; $y = -2$ **11.** $x = \frac{29}{87} = \frac{1}{3}$; $y = \frac{5}{10} = \frac{1}{2}$ **13.** No solution

15. Fifteen \$10 bills and ten \$5 bills   **17.** Ball costs \$4 and a bat costs \$12

19. Prelaw = 1500 applications and Premedical = 4500 applications   **21.** 1200 males and 1000 females

23. 0.48 cups of orange juice and 2.78 cups of milk

Section 4.6, pp. 224–227

1. 4×3 **3.** 4×2 **5.** 1×1 **7.** 3×3

9. Those matrices given in Exercises 5, 6, and 7 are square matrices.

11. $x = 9$ **13.** $x = 8$; $y = -5$ **14.** $x = 5$; $y = 0$; $z = \frac{10}{3}$

15. Not possible, since they are not of the same dimensions.

17. $\begin{pmatrix} 3 & 7 \\ -11 & 13 \end{pmatrix}$ **19.** $\begin{pmatrix} 4 & -1 & 4 \\ 13 & 5 & 11 \end{pmatrix}$ **21.** Cannot be done   **23.** $\begin{pmatrix} 3 & 4 & 14 \\ 9 & -2 & -2 \\ 1 & 15 & -13 \end{pmatrix}$

25. $\begin{pmatrix} 5 & 3 & 2 \\ 1 & 4 & 7 \\ 0 & 2 & 9 \end{pmatrix}$ **27.** $\begin{pmatrix} 4 & 7 \\ x & y \end{pmatrix}$ **29.** $\begin{pmatrix} -55 & 39 \\ -18 & 12 \end{pmatrix}$ **31.** $\begin{pmatrix} -54 & 47 \\ -66 & 60 \end{pmatrix}$ **33.** (-133)

35. $\begin{pmatrix} 1 & 70 & 7 \\ 178 & 46 & 69 \end{pmatrix}$ **37.** $\begin{pmatrix} 0 & -12 & -30 \\ -1 & -7 & -4 \\ -30 & -48 & 42 \end{pmatrix}$ **39.** $\begin{pmatrix} 39 & 41 \\ 5 & 39 \end{pmatrix}$ **41.** $\begin{pmatrix} 9 & -4 & 49 \\ -6 & -31 & 9 \\ -5 & -32 & 27 \end{pmatrix}$

43. $x = 15$; $y = 6$

45. In either case our answer is: **47. a)**

$\begin{pmatrix} 5 & -5 & 9 \\ 3 & 7 & 10 \\ 6 & 10 & 16 \end{pmatrix}$

	Engine tune-up	Transmission tune-up	Exhaust sys. repair	Charge air cond. sys.	New tires
City A	+ 14	+ 9	+ 13	+ 2	+ 7
City B	+ 13	+ 11	+ 12	+ 1	0
City C	+ 4	- 3	+ 5	- 3	+ 7

b) Engine tune-up in city A

c) Transmission tune-up in city C

49. If $A = \begin{pmatrix} 1 & 1 \\ 0 & -1 \end{pmatrix}$ then $A^2 = \begin{pmatrix} 1 & 0 \\ 0 & 1 \end{pmatrix}$

51. If $x = w$ and $z = -y$, then $A \cdot B = B \cdot A$ as

$$\begin{pmatrix} x & y \\ -y & x \end{pmatrix} \cdot \begin{pmatrix} 1 & 1 \\ -1 & 1 \end{pmatrix} = \begin{pmatrix} 1 & 1 \\ -1 & 1 \end{pmatrix} \begin{pmatrix} x & y \\ -y & x \end{pmatrix} = \begin{pmatrix} x-y & x+y \\ -y-x & -y+x \end{pmatrix}$$

53. If $A = \begin{pmatrix} 1 & 0 \\ 1 & 0 \end{pmatrix}$ then $A \cdot A = A$

Section 4.7, pp. 242–245

1. a) $(7 \quad 8 \quad 4 \quad 6 \quad 9)$ **b)** $\begin{pmatrix} 3.21 \\ 2.69 \\ 4.92 \\ 6.52 \\ 5.02 \end{pmatrix}$ **c)** Total cost is \$147.97   **3.** $\begin{pmatrix} 153 \\ 135 \end{pmatrix}$

5. \$272.64   **7.** Multiply each row by -3.   **9.** Multiply each row by $\frac{2}{3}$.

11. New row 3 equals 3 times row 2 added to original row 3; new row 1 equals original row 1 added to -2 times row 2. Row 2 remains unchanged.

13. Interchange rows 1 and 3. Row 2 equals original row 2 added to 2 times row 1; row 3 equals original row 3 added to -5 times row 1. Interchange rows 2 and 3. Multiply row 2 by $\frac{1}{3}$. Row 3 equals original row 3 added to -7 times row 2. Multiply row 3 by $\frac{3}{41}$. Row 2 equals original row 2 added to $\frac{2}{3}$ times row 3; row 1 equals original row 1 added to -2 times row 3.

15. $\begin{pmatrix} 7 & 3 & | & 11 \\ 5 & -2 & | & 19 \end{pmatrix}$ **17.** $\begin{pmatrix} 2 & -3 & | & 5 \\ 7 & 12 & | & 19 \end{pmatrix}$ **19.** $\begin{pmatrix} 2 & 3 & -5 & | & 10 \\ 3 & -7 & 8 & | & -15 \end{pmatrix}$

21. $\begin{pmatrix} 3 & -5 & 8 & | & 12 \\ 2 & 3 & 0 & | & 12 \end{pmatrix}$ **23.** $\begin{pmatrix} 1 & 0 & 0 & | & 7 \\ 0 & 1 & -3 & | & 10 \\ 1 & 0 & -8 & | & 23 \end{pmatrix}$ **25.** $\begin{pmatrix} 2 & 3 & 5 & -8 & | & 7 \\ 3 & -2 & -4 & 7 & | & 0 \\ 4 & 7 & -3 & -4 & | & -3 \\ 2 & 0 & 3 & -1 & | & 1 \end{pmatrix}$

27. $A = \begin{pmatrix} 5 & 3 \\ 2 & -5 \end{pmatrix}$ $A^{-1} = \begin{pmatrix} \frac{5}{31} & \frac{3}{31} \\ \frac{2}{31} & \frac{-5}{31} \end{pmatrix}$ $x = 2;\ y = 1$

29. $A = \begin{pmatrix} 8 & 5 \\ 4 & -6 \end{pmatrix}$ $A^{-1} = \begin{pmatrix} \frac{-6}{-68} & \frac{-5}{-68} \\ \frac{-4}{-68} & \frac{8}{-68} \end{pmatrix}$ $x = -1;\ y = -4$

31. $A = \begin{pmatrix} 6 & 8 \\ 3 & -5 \end{pmatrix}$ $A^{-1} = \begin{pmatrix} \frac{-5}{-54} & \frac{-8}{-54} \\ \frac{-3}{-54} & \frac{6}{-54} \end{pmatrix}$ $x = 8;\ y = 0$

33. $A = \begin{pmatrix} 7 & -3 \\ 1 & 2 \end{pmatrix}$ $A^{-1} = \begin{pmatrix} \frac{2}{17} & \frac{3}{17} \\ \frac{-1}{17} & \frac{7}{17} \end{pmatrix}$ $x = 1;\ y = -3$

35. $A = \begin{pmatrix} 3 & -1 \\ 6 & 2 \end{pmatrix}$ $A^{-1} = \begin{pmatrix} \frac{2}{12} & \frac{1}{12} \\ \frac{-6}{12} & \frac{3}{12} \end{pmatrix}$ $x = 3;\ y = 2$

37. $A = \begin{pmatrix} 2 & -7 \\ 3 & 4 \end{pmatrix}$ $A^{-1} = \begin{pmatrix} \frac{4}{29} & \frac{7}{29} \\ \frac{-3}{29} & \frac{2}{29} \end{pmatrix}$ $x = -1;\ y = -4$

39. WVOAE-NE-FO-AOAIP-FJAOY   **41.** SINK-THE-SHIP

Typical Classroom Questions, p. 246

1. No. If $x = -4$ and $y = -3$, then $x < y$ but $x^2 > y^2$.

2. No. If $x = -4$ and $y = +3$, then $|x + y| = |-4 + 3| = |-1| = 1 \neq |-4| + |+3| = 7$.

3. No   **4.** Yes

Chapter Review Exercises, pp. 249–253

1. Choice (b)   **2.** Choice (a)   **3.** Choice (a)   **4.** Choice (b)   **5.** Choice (b)   **6.** Choice (b)

7. Choice (b)   **8.** 2782 years   **9.** $\frac{18}{7}$ **10.** Choice (b)   **11.** Choice (d)   **12.** $x > -\frac{1}{11}$

13. $x \leq -8$ **14.** Choice (c)   **15.** Helper's hourly wage is $3.00.   **16.** 3 nickles, 17 quarters

17. 5.45 hours   **18.** Faster bricklayer needs 9 hours. Slower bricklayer needs 18 hours.

19. $1000 invested at 6%. $4000 invested at 8%.

20. $\begin{pmatrix} 1 & 7 \\ 6 & 9 \\ 3 & -2 \end{pmatrix}$ **21.** $x = 3;\ y = \frac{13}{2}$ **22.** $\begin{pmatrix} \frac{9}{57} & \frac{7}{57} \\ \frac{3}{57} & \frac{-4}{57} \end{pmatrix}$ **23.** $\begin{pmatrix} 4 & 3 & | & 17 \\ 2 & -9 & | & 12 \end{pmatrix}$

24. $\begin{pmatrix} -27 & 39 & -26 \\ 21 & -26 & -21 \\ -16 & -4 & 31 \end{pmatrix}$ **25.** $\begin{aligned} 7x + 12y &= 5 \\ 3x - 4y &= 11 \end{aligned}$ **26.** There is none because $ad - bc = 1(7) - 7(1) = 0$.

27. $\begin{pmatrix} -2 & 36 \\ -108 & 22 \end{pmatrix}$ **28. a)** $A^{-1} = \begin{pmatrix} \frac{5}{38} & \frac{-6}{38} \\ \frac{3}{38} & \frac{4}{38} \end{pmatrix}$ **b)** $(A^{-1})^{-1} = A$

29. $A(B + C) = \begin{pmatrix} -122 & 106 \\ 7 & 80 \end{pmatrix}$ $A \cdot B + A \cdot C = \begin{pmatrix} -122 & 106 \\ 7 & 80 \end{pmatrix}$

In both cases our answer is $\begin{pmatrix} -122 & 106 \\ 7 & 80 \end{pmatrix}$

30. Plumber = \$90; helper = \$70   **31.** 95

32. Dr. Jones earned \$197,400 from those operations and Dr. Smith earned \$165,800 from these operations.

33. YBA — INQXVTNUI — NE — NO — YBA — QFIAXF

34. a) $\begin{pmatrix} 16 & 20 \\ 0 & 2 \\ 0 & 3 \\ 7 & 11 \\ 8 & 8 \\ 466 & 702 \\ 566 & 735 \\ 456 & 660 \\ 5365 & 6961 \end{pmatrix}$ **b)** 9102 in 1978 as opposed to 6884 in 1974

35. Total income for period is \$3535 + \$2370 + \$2765 + \$3235 = \$11,905.

CHAPTER 5

Section 5.1, pp. 265–267

1. a) The divisors of 56 are 1, 2, 4, 7, 8, 14, 28, and 56.
   b) The divisors of 86 are 1, 2, 43, and 86.
   c) The divisors of 98 are 1, 2, 7, 14, 49, and 98.
   d) The divisors of 62 are 1, 2, 31, and 62.
   e) The divisors of 132 are 1, 2, 3, 6, 11, 12, 22, 44, 66, and 132.
   f) The divisors of 160 are 1, 2, 4, 5, 8, 10, 16, 20, 32, 40, 80, and 160.
   g) The divisors of 149 are 1 and 149.
   h) The divisors of 482 are 1, 2, 241, and 482.
   i) The divisors of 376 are 1, 2, 4, 8, 47, 94, 188, and 376.
   j) The divisors of 558 are 1, 2, 3, 6, 9, 18, 31, 62, 93, 186, 279, and 558.

3.

Number	Divisible by				
	2	3	4	5	6
324	Yes	Yes	Yes	No	Yes
436	Yes	No	Yes	No	No
864	Yes	Yes	Yes	No	Yes
685	No	No	No	Yes	No
293	No	No	No	No	No
456	Yes	Yes	Yes	No	Yes
890	Yes	No	No	Yes	No
3402	Yes	Yes	No	No	Yes
5678	Yes	No	No	No	No
1396	Yes	No	Yes	No	No

5. Only 864 and 456 are divisible by 8.   **7.** 189,000 is one such number.

9. A number is divisible by 50 if its last 2 digits are both zeros or if its last two digits form the integer 50.

11. 220 and 284.

13. a)

$$
\begin{aligned}
1 &= 1^3 = 1 \\
3 + 5 &= 2^3 = 8 \\
7 + 9 + 11 &= 3^3 = 27 \\
13 + 15 + 17 + 19 &= 4^3 = 64 \\
21 + 23 + 25 + 27 + 29 &= 5^3 = 125 \\
31 + 33 + 35 + 37 + 39 + 41 &= 6^3 = 216 \\
43 + 45 + 47 + 49 + 51 + 53 + 55 &= 7^3 = 343 \\
57 + 59 + 61 + 63 + 65 + 67 + 69 + 71 &= 8^3 = 512 \\
73 + 75 + 77 + 79 + 81 + 83 + 85 + 87 + 89 &= 9^3 = 729
\end{aligned}
$$

15.

```
.               .              .
. .            . .            . .
. . .          . . .          . . .
. . . .        . . . .        . . . .
. . . . .      . . . . .      . . . . .
. . . . . .    . . . . . .    . . . . . .
   21         . . . . . . .   . . . . . . .
                  28         . . . . . . . .
                                  36
```

17. a) 35   **b)** 455   **c)** 2925

  d) If the numbers are consecutive, then the product will be divisible by 6.

  e) If the numbers are consecutive, then the product will be divisible by 6.

19. a) When the digits of *any* three-digit number are rewritten in the same order to form a six-digit number and the result divided by 13, there will never be any remainder.

b) Let the number be represented by *abcabc*. Then the number

$$abcabc = a \times 10^5 + b \times 10^4 + c \times 10^3 + a \times 10^2 + b \times 10 + c$$
$$= a(10^5 + 10^2) + b(10^4 + 10) + c(10^3 + 1)$$
$$= 10^2(1001a) + 10(1001b) + 10^0(1001c)$$
$$= 1001(100a + 10b + c)$$

The coefficient 1001 is divisible by both 13 and 7 as $\frac{1001}{13} = 77$ and $\frac{1001}{7} = 143$

21. True

Section 5.2, pp. 271–273

1. 377, 610, 987, 1597, 2584, 4181, 6755, and 10946.

3. The remainders form the pattern 1, 1, 2, 3, 1, 0, 1, 1, 2, 3, 1, 0, 1, 1, 2, 3, 1, 0, ...

5. To cell 5:   13 possible paths
    To cell 6:   21 possible paths
    To cell 7:   34 possible paths

7. The way we obtain the numbers that make up a Pascal triangle is reminiscent of the Fibonacci numbers.

9. $6 = 110_{(2)}$ The number of 1's form a Fibonacci
       $28 = 11100_{(2)}$ sequence pattern. The number of 0's
      $496 = 111110000_{(2)}$ appearing is a multiple of 2 (after
     $8128 = 1111111000000_{(2)}$ the first 0).

11. 129   **13.** 8   **15.** 390,625   **17.** Geometric   **19.** Arithmetic

21. Not a wise decision as 2^{30} cents = 1073741820 cents or \$10,737,418.20, which is greater than \$25,000.

Section 5.3, pp. 279–280

1. 2, 3, 5, 7, 11, 13, 17, 19, 23, 29, 31, 37, 41, 43, 47, 53, 59, 61, and 67   **3.** 8, 9, and 10

5. 2, 3, 5, 7, 11, 13, 17, 19, 23, 29, 31, 37, 41, 43, 47, 53, 59, 61, 67, 71, 73, 79, 83, 89, and 97

7. Never in a 6, but it may end in a 5.

9. 11 can be written as $4 \cdot 2 + 3$; 19 can be written as $4 \cdot 4 + 3$; and 23 can be written as $4 \cdot 5 + 3$.

11. a) If $n = 2$ then $2! + 1 = 3$ is a prime. Also, if $n = 3$, then $3! + 1 = 7$ is a prime.

　　b) If $n = 4$, then $4! + 1 = 25$ is a composite number. Also, if $n = 6$, then $6! + 1 = 721$ is a composite number.

13. 3, 5 and 7

15. a) 2, 3, 5, 7, 11, 13, 17, 19, 23, 29, 31, 37, 41, 43 and 47. There are 15 of them.

　　b) These indicated in part (a) and also 53, 59, 61, 67, 71, 73, 79, 83, 89 and 97. There are 25 of them.

17. a)

Prime Number	Prime Number + 1	Prime Number – 1
5	6	4
7	8	6
11	12	10
13	14	12
17	18	16
19	20	18

b)

	Prime Number + 1	Prime Number – 1
Remainders {	0	4
	2	0
	0	4
	2	0
	0	4
	2	0

c) When any prime number + 1 is divided by 6, the remainder is 0 or 2 if the prime number is larger than 3. When any prime number – 1 is divided by 6, the remainder will always be 0 or 4 when the prime number is larger than 3.

19. $10 = 5 + 5$; $12 = 5 + 7$; $14 = 7 + 7$; $16 = 5 + 11$; $18 = 7 + 11$; $20 = 7 + 13$; $22 = 11 + 11$; $24 = 11 + 13$; $26 = 7 + 19$; $28 = 11 + 17$; $30 = 11 + 19$; $32 = 13 + 19$; $34 = 17 + 17$; $36 = 17 + 19$.

21. a) $2 = 1^2 + 1$; $17 = 4^2 + 1$; and $37 = 6^2 + 1$.   **b)** $143 = 12^2 - 1$ and $323 = 18^2 - 1$.

Section 5.4, pp. 285–286

1. a) GCF (15, 18) = 3   **b)** GFC (14, 72) = 2   **c)** GCF (18, 24, 60) = 6
   LCM (15, 18) = 90   LCM (14, 72) = 1008   LCM (18, 24, 60) = 360

d) GCF (72, 88) = 8   **e)** GCF (144, 200) = 8   **f)** GCF (96, 156, 175) = 1
   LCM (72, 88) = 1584   LCM (144, 200) = 3600   LCM (96, 156, 175) = 218,400

3. a) LCM (144, 220) = $2^4 \cdot 3^2 \cdot 5 \cdot 11 = 7920$

b) LCM (44, 68, 84) = $2^2 \cdot 3 \cdot 7 \cdot 11 \cdot 17 = 15,708$

c) LCM (104, 220, 360) = $2^3 \cdot 3^2 \cdot 5 \cdot 11 \cdot 13 = 51,480$

5. a)

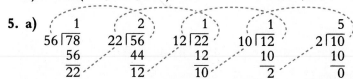

The last nonzero remainder of 2 represents the greatest common factor of 56 and 78.

b)

$$
\begin{array}{r}
6 \\
12\overline{)75} \\
72 \\
\hline
3
\end{array}
\qquad
\begin{array}{r}
4 \\
3\overline{)12} \\
12 \\
\hline
0
\end{array}
$$

The last nonzero remainder of 3 represents the greatest common factor of 12 and 75.

c)

$$
\begin{array}{r}
6 \\
18\overline{)120} \\
108 \\
\hline
12
\end{array}
\qquad
\begin{array}{r}
1 \\
12\overline{)18} \\
12 \\
\hline
6
\end{array}
\qquad
\begin{array}{r}
2 \\
6\overline{)12} \\
12 \\
\hline
0
\end{array}
$$

The last nonzero remainder of 6 represents the greatest common factor of 18 and 120.

7. After 56 minutes they will meet each other.

9. a) GCF (3456, 5678) = 2   **b)** GCF (9682, 8594) = 2   **11.** $\frac{17}{209}$

Section 5.5, pp. 294–296

1. a)

$\oplus$	0	1	2	3	4	5	6
0	0	1	2	3	4	5	6
1	1	2	3	4	5	6	0
2	2	3	4	5	6	0	1
3	3	4	5	6	0	1	2
4	4	5	6	0	1	2	3
5	5	6	0	1	2	3	4
6	6	0	1	2	3	4	5

b)

$\oplus$	0	1	2	3	4	5	6	7
0	0	1	2	3	4	5	6	7
1	1	2	3	4	5	6	7	0
2	2	3	4	5	6	7	0	1
3	3	4	5	6	7	0	1	2
4	4	5	6	7	0	1	2	3
5	5	6	7	0	1	2	3	4
6	6	7	0	1	2	3	4	5
7	7	0	1	2	3	4	5	6

c)

$\oplus$	0	1
0	0	1
1	1	0

d)

$\oplus$	0	1	2	3	4
0	0	1	2	3	4
1	1	2	3	4	0
2	2	3	4	0	1
3	3	4	0	1	2
4	4	0	1	2	3

3. a) 1   **b)** 0   **c)** 6   **d)** 8   **e)** 2   **f)** 1   **g)** 0   **h)** 9   **i)** 2   **j)** 2   **k)** 0   **l)** 7

5. a) mod 6   **b)** mod 7   **c)** mod 5   **d)** mod 7   **e)** mod 12   **f)** mod 8

7. The inverse of 0 is 0; the inverse of 1 is 8; the inverse of 2 is 7; the inverse of 3 is 6; the inverse of 4 is 5; the inverse of 5 is 4; the inverse of 6 is 3; the inverse of 7 is 2; the inverse of 8 is 1.

9. a) 9   **b)** 7   **c)** 4   **d)** 15   **e)** 2   **f)** 3   **g)** 5   **h)** 5

11. a) True   **b)** True   **c)** True   **d)** True   **e)** False
f) False   **g)** True   **h)** True   **i)** True   **j)** True

13. a) 5   **b)** 11   **c)** 10   **d)** 5   **e)** 2   **f)** 10   **g)** 14   **h)** 4   **i)** 20   **j)** 25

15. Thursday   **17.** The programmer has 89 discs.   **21.** No

Section 5.6, pp. 300–301

1. 1191 **3.** 289 **5.** 895 **7.** 15,708 **9.** 13,289 **11.** 12,695,822 **13.** 865

15. 13,617 **17.** 58 **19.** 6472 **21.** 33,995 **23.** 5,810,454

27. a) $1041_{(eight)}$ **b)** $1523_{(eight)}$ **c)** $53,122_{(eight)}$

Typical Classroom Questions, pp. 301–302

1. She merely interchanged two digits. The sum of the digits will be the same.

2. The remainders are the same. **3.** Yes, the sum of the digits must be exactly divisible by 9. **4.** No

6. Because the product of 1×8 equals 2×4. More generally, if the numbers to be multiplied are represented as ab and cd, then $ab = 10a + b$ and $cd = 10c + d$ so that $ab \times cd = (10a + b)(10c + d) = 100ac + 10ad + 10bc + bd$ and $ba \times dc = (10b + a)(10d + c) = 100bd + 10ad + 10bc + ac$. Upon simplification, we get $ab \times cd = ba \times dc$ if and only if $ac = bd$. This represents the reversed number products.

7. Yes **8.** Yes

Chapter Review Exercises, pp. 304–306

1. The answer is 999999. **2.** The divisors of 1492 are 1, 2, 4, 373, 746, and 1492. **3.** Choice (b)

4. Choice (a) **5.** Choice (a) **6.** Choice (a) **7.** Choice (d) **8.** Choice (d) **9.** Choice (c)

10. GCF (124, 160) = 16 **11.** GCF (108, 144) = $2^2 \cdot 3^2 = 36$

12. The last nonzero remainder of 2 represents the greatest common factor of 82 and 96.

13. GCF (824, 960) = $2^3 = 8$ **14.** LCM (124, 160) = $2^5 \cdot 5 \cdot 31 = 4960$ **15.** GCF (88, 120, 160) = $2^3 = 8$

16. LCM (28, 36, 48) = $2^4 \cdot 3^2 \cdot 7 = 1008$ **17.** The teacher has 76 papers.

18. a) 895 **b)** 289 **c)** 253,272 **19.** Choice (d) **20.** Monday **21.** Leslie has 92 coins.

22. a) 1209 **b)** 1209 **c)** The answers are the same, as these represent reversed number products.

23. Yes, as 2024 is divisible by 4. **24.** Choice (b) **25.** Choice (b)

26. a)

Number of divisors that number has	Numbers
0	
1	1
2	2, 3, 5, 7, 11, 13, 17, 19, 23, 29, 31, 37
3	4, 9, 25
4	6, 8, 10, 14, 15, 21, 22, 26, 27, 33, 34, 35, 38, 39
5	16
6	12, 18, 20, 28, 32
7	
8 or more	24, 30, 36, 40

b) These are the prime numbers between 2 and 40 inclusive.

CHAPTER 6

Section 6.1, pp. 321–322

1. a) $\frac{35}{36}$ **b)** $\frac{-13}{18}$ **c)** $\frac{1}{6}$ **d)** $\frac{1}{9}$ **e)** 2   **f)** -1 **g)** 5   **h)** $\frac{-6}{5}$

3. a) $\frac{24}{27}$ **b)** $\frac{12}{39}$ **c)** $\frac{15}{21}$ **d)** $\frac{12}{33}$

5. a) $7\frac{3}{5} = \frac{38}{5}$ **b)** $2\frac{3}{7} = \frac{17}{7}$ **c)** $-3\frac{2}{9} = \frac{-29}{9}$ **d)** $-8\frac{4}{7} = \frac{-60}{7}$

7. a) $\frac{5}{40}$ **b)** $\frac{16}{20}$ **c)** $\frac{25}{30}$ **d)** $14\frac{1}{3} < 14\frac{6}{16}$ **e)** $\frac{3}{4} < \frac{4}{5}$ **f)** $\frac{9}{15} = \frac{18}{30}$

9. George purchased more   **11. a)** $\frac{5}{11}$ **b)** $\frac{1}{3}$ **c)** $\frac{14}{17}$

13. a) Definition of addition of rational numbers   **b)** Commutative law of multiplication

c) Commutative law of addition   **d)** Definition of addition of rational numbers

15. a) $\frac{1}{3} = \frac{1}{6} + \frac{1}{6}$ **b)** $\frac{1}{4} = \frac{1}{8} + \frac{1}{8}$ **c)** $\frac{1}{n} = \frac{1}{2n} + \frac{1}{2n}$

17. a) $\frac{-a}{b} = \frac{a}{-b}$ is true because $(-a)(-b) = +ab = ab$ by the definition of equal rational numbers and by the rules for multiplying signed numbers.

b) Same procedure as in part (a)

19. a) The missing fraction is $7\frac{2}{5}$. Each successive term is $1\frac{3}{5}$ more than the previous term.

b) The missing fraction is $\frac{7}{1}$ or 7.

Section 6.2, pp. 331–332

1. a) $\frac{2}{3}$ **b)** $\frac{25}{12}$ **c)** $\frac{12}{17}$ **d)** $\frac{-104}{187}$ **e)** 1   **f)** $\frac{28}{15}$ **g)** 2   **h)** $\frac{7}{54}$ **i)** $\frac{-25}{12}$ **j)** 1

3. a) $\frac{18}{11}$ **b)** $\frac{39}{16}$ **c)** 9   **d)** $\frac{20}{21}$

5. a) $\frac{7}{4}$ **b)** 4   **c)** $\frac{4}{13}$ **d)** 1   **e)** $\frac{20}{9}$ **f)** $\frac{21}{2}$ **g)** $\frac{56}{45}$

7. a) $x > \frac{12}{5}$ **b)** $x \le \frac{-32}{3}$ **c)** $x < \frac{-35}{24}$ **d)** $x > \frac{-8}{5}$

e) $x \le \frac{-329}{468}$ **f)** $x \le \frac{-67}{22}$ **g)** $x \le \frac{-1881}{910}$ **h)** $x \ge \frac{49929}{90420}$

11. 17 Hangers   **13.** $32\frac{5}{8}$ yards   **15.** He has completed 24 credits until now.

Section 6.3, pp. 339–340

1. $\frac{16}{9}$ **3.** $\frac{3}{4}$ **5.** $\frac{7}{16}$ **7.** 16 cars   **9.** $\frac{3}{5}$ **11.** The one containing 10 bars for $2.25

13. 15 gallons of white paint and 10 gallons of blue paint

15. Dried apricots 160 pieces; dried apples 140 pieces

17. $\frac{8}{7} = \frac{15}{14}$ is not valid.   **19.** $\frac{7}{1} = \frac{14}{2}$ is valid.   **21.** $\frac{18}{4} = \frac{27}{6}$ is valid.   **23.** $x = 40$ **25.** $x = 13.5$

27. $x = 4$ **29.** 65 km/hr **31.** Approximately 20.54 gallons **33.** \$8.25 **35.** \$2460

37. 144 miles **39.** Yes

Section 6.4, p. 344

1. a) $\frac{1}{256}$ **b)** $\frac{8}{27}$ **c)** $\frac{2}{81}$ **d)** 1 **e)** $\frac{729}{125}$ **f)** $\frac{2^{20}}{3^{20}}$ **g)** $\frac{49}{25}$ **h)** $\frac{5}{64}$ **i)** $\frac{17}{72}$ **j)** 8

k) 64 **l)** 40

3. a) $(\frac{1}{3})^5$ is the larger. **b)** $(\frac{2}{3})^2$ is the larger. **c)** $(\frac{4}{5})^{10}$ is the larger.

Typical Classroom Questions, pp. 344

1. No

2. a) You are dividing by zero. **b)** $\frac{6+3}{3} \neq \frac{6}{3} + 3 \cdot$ However, $\frac{6+3}{3} = \frac{6}{3} + \frac{3}{3} = 2 + 1 = 3$

c) $\frac{16}{8} = \frac{16}{4+4} \cdot$ However, $\frac{16}{4+4} \neq \frac{16}{4} + \frac{16}{4}$

3. No **4.** Yes

Chapter Review Exercises, pp. 348–349

1. $\frac{299}{36}$ **2.** $\frac{-391}{24}$ **3.** $\frac{108}{133}$ **4.** $\frac{245}{52}$ **5.** $x = \frac{56}{5}$ **6.** $\frac{729}{64}$ **7.** $\frac{315}{92}$ **8.** $\frac{819}{922}$

9. a) $\frac{4}{5} = \frac{20}{25}$ **b)** $\frac{5}{6} \neq \frac{2}{3}$ **c)** $3\frac{5}{4} = 4\frac{1}{4}$ **10.** $\frac{-41}{168}$ **11.** $3\frac{3}{4}$

12. $\frac{3x + 5}{5x^2}$ **13.** $\frac{3^{10}}{2^{14}}$ **14.** 8 **15.** $\frac{x^4 y^4}{(y^2 + x^2)^2}$ **16.** No **17.** \$4.55 **18.** 64

19. Approximately 5.74 cups of oil **20.** \$1175 **21.** Bill is faster.

22. The 18 ounce jar is a better buy. **23.** 24 cars **24.** Approximately 23.33 minutes **25.** $\frac{1}{21}$

26. $\frac{6}{11} < \frac{5}{8} < \frac{2}{3}$ **27.** $x \geq \frac{21}{25}$ **28.** $x \geq -35$ **29.** $x \leq \frac{260}{61}$ **30.** $x \geq \frac{-1505}{2196}$

CHAPTER 7

Section 7.1, pp. 364–366

1. a) Terminating **b)** Nonterminating but repeating **c)** Terminating **d)** Terminating

e) Nonterminating and nonrepeating **f)** Nonterminating and nonrepeating **g)** Terminating

3. a) $0.83 = \frac{83}{100}$ **b)** $0.2 = \frac{2}{10} = \frac{1}{5}$ **c)** $58.321 = \frac{58321}{1000}$ **d)** $0.00000029 = \frac{29}{100,000,000}$

5. a) $\frac{28}{99}$ **b)** $\frac{89}{99}$ **c)** $\frac{19}{99}$ **d)** $\frac{356}{999}$ **e)** $\frac{847}{999}$ **f)** $\frac{518}{99}$ **g)** $\frac{746}{99}$ **h)** $\frac{51616}{9900}$

7. a) 12% **b)** 56.7% **c)** 1% **d)** 0.2% **e)** 510% **f)** 623% **g)** 101% **h)** 100%

9. 6.65   **11.** 47.396   **13.** 80   **15.** $4.12   **17.** 20.479 miles/gallon

19. Gross sales were $526,000.   **21.** 5.36%   **23.** $169   **25.** 8.33%   **27.** 1.26% had virus

29. $323.53   **31.** $33\frac{1}{3}\%$ **33.** $28,700

35. The prime factorization of the denominator contains primes other than 2 or 5.

Section 7.2, pp. 373–374

1. $4320   **3.** 32.42%   **5.** 0.3889 years   **7.** 7.251%   **9.** $14,265.58   **11.** $11,860.29

13. $3272.73   **15.** Julia, as she will have $2180.92 and Miguel will have $2180.83

17. a) $1082.50   **b)** $1084.20   **c)** $1085.09   **d)** $1085.69   **e)** $1086.00

Section 7.3, pp. 380–381

1. $2150   **3.** 10 months

5. The second method where interest is 2% since the total amount paid is $656.68 as opposed to the first method where the total amount paid is $724.07

7. $568.86   **9.** $351.81   **11.** $731.39   **13.** $356.59

15. a) $89.70   **b)** APR is approximately 14.50%.   **17.** $583.33

Section 7.4, pp. 395–397

1. 8 feet   **3. a)** *I* **b)** *I* **c)** ϕ **d)** *R* **e)** *R* **f)** *W* **g)** *R* **h)** *Q* **i)** *I*

5.

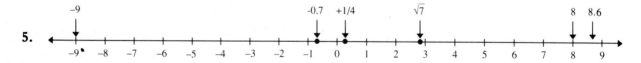

7. a)

c)

e)

g)

b)

d)

f)

h)

9. a) Multiply both sides of the equation by $1/x$ assuming $x \neq 0$. Then use the associative law of multiplication, the multiplicative inverse property, and the multiplicative identity property to prove that $a = b$.

b) Division by 0 is not permissible.

11. The rational number 2 is between $\sqrt{3}$ and $\sqrt{5}$.

13. a) 50   **b)** 8   **c)** 21   **d)** 51   **e)** -20 **f)** 34   **g)** 89   **h)** 131   **i)** $\frac{1}{2}$ **j)** 85

k) 144   **l)** 324   **m)** -10 **n)** 63   **o)** 2142

23. a) $(5\sqrt{3})(4\sqrt{3}) = 20\sqrt{9} = 60$. Product is rational   **b)** $\dfrac{5\sqrt{3}}{4\sqrt{3}} = \dfrac{5}{4}$. Quotient is rational

c) $5\sqrt{3} + 4\sqrt{3} = 9\sqrt{3}$.   Sum is irrational

25. Line segment AB measures $\sqrt{5}$ inches long

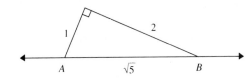

27. If $u = 5$ and $v = 4$, then $\{40, 9, 43\}$ is a primitive Pythagorean triple.
If $u = 7$ and $v = 6$, then $\{84, 13, 85\}$ is a primitive Pythagorean triple.
If $u = 8$ and $v = 5$, then $\{80, 39, 89\}$ is a primitive Pythagorean triple.

29. 3.001

Section 7.5, p. 402

1. a) 64   **b)** 4096   **c)** -32 **d)** $\frac{1}{2}$ **e)** 8   **f)** 15,625   **g)** 1   **h)** 1024   **i)** 16
j) 4096   **k)** $\frac{1}{343}$ **l)** 18   **m)** 10,077,696

3. 320   **5. a)** $12\sqrt{2}$ **b)** $3\sqrt{2}$ **c)** $\frac{2}{3}$ **d)** $\frac{4\sqrt{2}}{5}$

7. a) $7\sqrt{2}$ **b)** $4x\sqrt{3}$ **c)** $3\sqrt[3]{3}$ **d)** $5\sqrt{5}$ **e)** $-\sqrt{7}$

9. a) 1.68179283   **b)** 1.82263466   **c)** 6.04605679   **d)** 3.20427951

11. a) 2.24   **b)** 3.96   **c)** 0.17

Typical Classroom Questions, p. 403

1. Not necessarily. $\frac{1}{3}$ and $\frac{2}{3}$ are repeating decimals. However, their sum is a whole number.

2. Not necessarily. If we add $3\sqrt{2}$ and $-3\sqrt{2}$ our answer is 0.

3. Not possible. The maximum cut possible is 100%, in which case you are working for nothing.

4. No. True only if x is nonnegative, or else we must compute x^2 first.

5. No. $\sqrt{-3}$ is an imaginary or complex number.   **6.** Student 1 is correct.

Chapter Review Exercises, pp. 406–408

1. 88.89%   **2.** 53.2%   **3.** 0.0275   **4.** 16.2   **5.** 120

6. a) 2.75   **b)** 3.38   **c)** 302.82   **d)** 0.04   **e)** 2.34   **f)** 6970.43

7. $35.03   **8.** $0.191919\ldots = \frac{19}{99}$ **9.** True   **10.** Choice (a)   **11.** 56   **12.** $\frac{1}{2}$ **13.** $\frac{8}{5}$

14. $24   **15.** Approximately 81.48% passed.   **16.** $9\frac{1}{2}$% annual interest rate   **17.** 0.75   **18.** $6\sqrt{2}$

19. $18\sqrt{3}$ **20.** -14 **21.** $1687.50   **22.** $1750   **23.** 57.14%   **24.** $1000   **25.** 9.417%

26. $5545.24   **27.** $7971.98   **28.** $1524.72   **29.** $3800   **30.** $10,331.11   **31.** $54.37

32. $2679.95

CHAPTER 8

Section 8.1, pp. 419–420

1. 72 different ways   **3.** 720 different ways   **5.** 5040 different ways   **7.** 1,000,00   **9.** 72

11. 720   **13. a)** 24   **b)** 120   **c)** 720

15.

	Child 1	Child 2	Child 3	Child 4	Family consists of
				Boy	Boy, boy, boy, boy
			Boy	Girl	Boy, boy, boy, girl
		Boy	Girl	Boy	Boy, boy, girl, boy
				Girl	Boy, boy, girl, girl
	Boy		Boy	Boy	Boy, girl, boy, boy
		Girl		Girl	Boy, girl, boy, girl
			Girl	Boy	Boy, girl, girl, boy
Start				Girl	Boy, girl, girl, girl
			Boy	Boy	Girl, boy, boy, boy
		Boy		Girl	Girl, boy, boy, girl
			Girl	Boy	Girl, boy, girl, boy
	Girl			Girl	Girl, boy, girl, girl
		Girl	Boy	Boy	Girl, girl, boy, boy
				Girl	Girl, girl, boy, girl
			Girl	Boy	Girl, girl, girl, boy
				Girl	Girl, girl, girl, girl

17. 5028

Section 8.2, pp. 430–432

1. a) 20 **b)** 42 **c)** 1 **d)** $\frac{1}{7}$ **e)** 20,160 **f)** 5040 **g)** 360 **h)** 6,652,800 **i)** 720
j) 1 **k)** 3024 **l)** 1 **m)** 35 **n)** 56 **o)** 6 **p)** 720 **q)** 1 **r)** 8 **s)** 8
t) 10 **u)** 10 **v)** 1 **w)** 1 **x)** 126 **y)** impossible **z)** 1

3. $_{10}P_4 = 5040$ **5.** $_{20}P_{10} = \dfrac{20!}{10!}$ **7.** $_{12}P_4 = 11{,}880$

9. a) $_8C_4 \cdot _9C_3 = 5880$ **b)** $_8C_4 \cdot _9C_3 + _8C_5 \cdot _9C_2 + _8C_6 \cdot _9C_1 + _8C_7 \cdot _9C_0 = 8156$

11. a) $_7P_7 = 5040$ **b)** $_8P_8 = 40{,}320$ **13.** $_{11}C_4 \cdot _8C_5 \cdot _5C_2 = 184{,}800$ **15.** $_{10}C_3 \cdot _9C_2 = 20{,}160$

17. a) 1 **b)** 2 **c)** 3 **d)** 5 **e)** They form a Fibonacci sequence.

19. a) $_7C_1 \cdot _4C_1 \cdot _3C_1 \cdot _2C_1 = 168$ **b)** 847 possible committees

Section 8.3, pp. 443–445

1. a) 0 **b)** $\frac{6}{36} = \frac{1}{6}$ **c)** $\frac{1}{6}$ **d)** $\frac{1}{2}$ **e)** $\frac{1}{36}$ **3.** $\frac{1}{4}$ **5. a)** $\frac{109}{418}$ **b)** $\frac{203}{418}$ **c)** $\frac{235}{418}$
7. Choice (a) and choice (b) **9. a)** $\frac{37}{1000}$ **b)** $\frac{411}{1000}$ **c)** $\frac{425}{1000}$ **d)** $\frac{207}{1000}$ **11.** $\frac{1}{10}$

13. There are 100 numbers listed in columns 1 and 2. Send letters to those 100 owners whose license plate numbers appear on these lists.

15. Those owners whose serial numbers are 6917, 2798, 1517, 3944, 6046, 1860, 7119, 5774, 3886, 5686, 1866, 3632, 6768, 4756, 6075, 5532, 1859, 8314, 7698, 7646, 4583, 6095, 6656, 8976, 3283, 3793, 3997, 7408, 7622, and 2657.

17. Those restaurants whose license numbers are 141, 248, 187, 058, 176, 298, 136, 047, 263, 287, 153, 147, 222, 086, 205, 254, 258, 253, 081, and 300.

19. a) $\frac{688}{4800}$ **b)** Greater

Section 8.4, pp. 450–452

1. Not mutually exclusive **3.** Not mutually exclusive **5.** Not mutually exclusive **7.** $\frac{19}{32}$
9. 0.92 **11.** 0.63 **13.** $\frac{6}{7}$ **15.** 0.35 **17.** $\frac{454}{5040}$ **19.** 0.56

Section 8.5, pp. 457–459

1. $\frac{19}{27}$ **3.** $\frac{31}{82}$ **5.** 0.0171 **7.** $\frac{2}{3}$ **9.** 0.4011 **11.** 0.0987

Section 8.6, pp. 466–468

1. 12:40 or 3:10 **3.** 9:6 or 3:2 **5.** 4:5

7. Television = (70000)(0.37) = \$25,900
Radio = (37000)(0.56) = \$20,720
Magazine = (45000)(0.49) = \$22,050
Distributing free samples = (50000)(0.42) = \$21,000

9. $\$-421$ **11.** $\$-88$ **13.** $\$2.78$ **15. a)** 0   **b)** 1   **17. a)** $\frac{1}{2}$ **b)** $\frac{1}{2}$ **c)** 0

Typical Classroom Questions, pp. 468–469

1. No, the two possibilities are not equally likely.   **2.** Yes, since order counts.

3. No. Each birth is independent of the previous births.   **4.** $\dfrac{1}{2^{48}}$

5. The events are not mutually exclusive.   **6.** No   **7.** No   **8.** No   **9.** No

Chapter Review Exercises, pp. 472–475

1. Choice (d)   **2.** Choice (d)   **3.** Choice (a)   **4.** Choice (b)   **5.** Choice (d)   **6.** $_7C_3 \cdot _8C_3 = 1960$

7. Choice (d)   **8.** $\frac{251}{900}$ **9.** $\frac{123}{422}$ **10.** $\frac{123}{251}$ **11.** $\frac{21}{26}$ **12. a)** $\frac{1}{4}$ **b)** $\frac{1}{4}$ **c)** $\frac{1}{2}$ **13.** $\frac{1}{6}$

14. 132,600   **15.** 676,000,000   **16.** 120   **17.** $\frac{9}{26}$ **18.** $_{12}C_5 \cdot _{18}C_6 = 14,702,688$

19. $_{16}C_2 \cdot _{10}C_2 = 5400$ **20.** $_{12}P_3 = 1320$

21. $_6P_6 = 720$ if order counts, or $_6C_6 = 1$ if order does not count.   **22.** $_{40}C_6 = 3,838,380$ **23.** 1920

24. 90   **25.** $_{10}P_{10} = 3,628,800$ **26.** $\$3234.33$ **27.** 0.38   **28.** 105:20 or 21:4   **29.** $\frac{8}{17}$

30. $_{28}C_{22} \cdot _{25}C_{16} = (376,740)(2,042,975)$

CHAPTER 9

Section 9.2, pp. 489–491

1. Mean = $\$1519.17$ Median = $\$1495$ Mode = none

3. Mean = $\$13,080$ Median = $\$7000$ Mode = $\$7000$

5. $\$26$ a share   **7.** Each will be increased by 10%.   **9.** The mean is affected by extreme scores.

11. a) It is increased by 3.   **b)** It is decreased by 4.   **c)** It is multiplied by 7.   **d)** It is divided by 5.

13. 67.5th percentile   **15.** It remains the same.   **17. a)** $\Sigma x^2 = 928$ **b)** $(\Sigma x)^2 = 88^2 = 7744$

Section 9.3, pp. 497–498

1. Range = 20 $\mu = 19.6$ Standard deviation ≈ 5.589

3. Range = $\$27 - \$19 = \$8$ $\mu = 23.375$ Standard deviation $\approx \$2.595$

5. μ (mean) = 797.667   Standard deviation ≈ 67.915798

7. 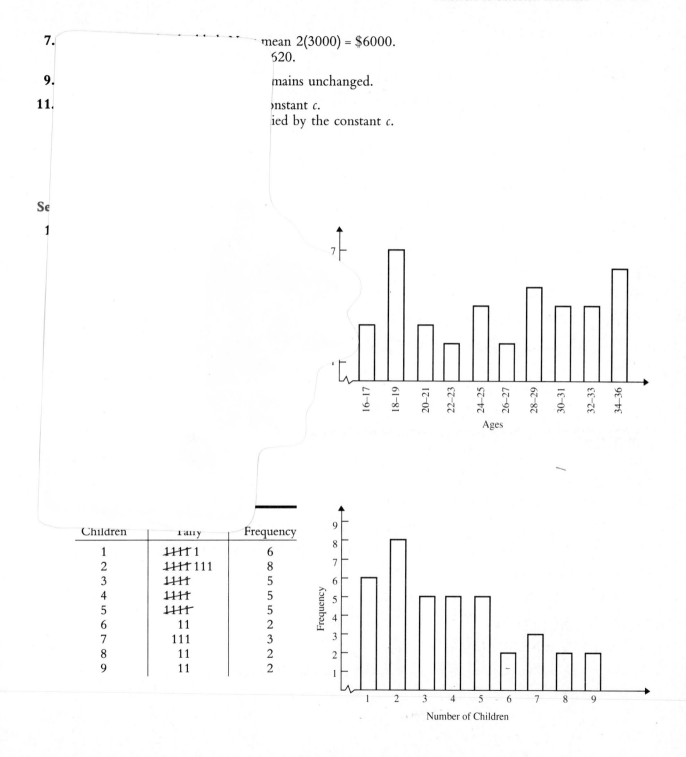 mean 2(3000) = $6000.
620.

9. mains unchanged.

11. onstant c.
ied by the constant c.

Se

1

Children	Tally	Frequency
1	~~1111~~ 1	6
2	~~1111~~ 111	8
3	~~1111~~	5
4	~~1111~~	5
5	~~1111~~	5
6	11	2
7	111	3
8	11	2
9	11	2

5. $\frac{103}{823} = 0.1252 = 12.52\%$

$\frac{203}{823} = 0.2467 = 24.67\%$

$\frac{91}{823} = 0.1106 = 11.06\%$

$\frac{127}{823} = 0.1543 = 15.43\%$

$\frac{106}{823} = 0.1288 = 12.88\%$

$\frac{82}{823} = 0.0996 = 9.96\%$

$\frac{62}{823} = 0.0753 = 7.53\%$

$\frac{49}{823} = 0.0595 = 5.95\%$

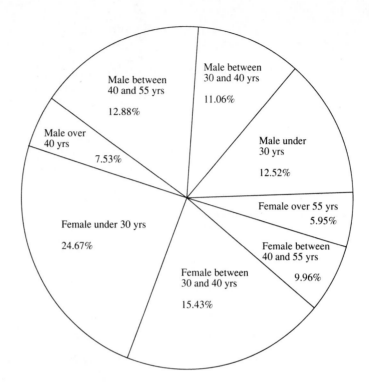

7. a) 400　　**b)** 500　　**c)** From 300 to 700 or by 400

9.

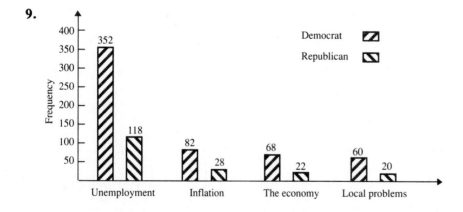

11.

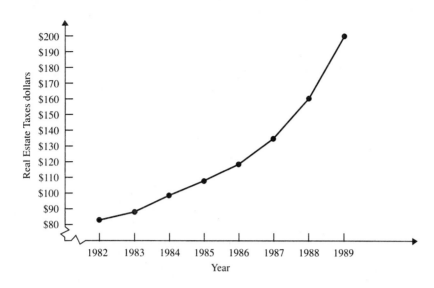

13.

Stem	Leaves
31	.4 .7 .7
32	.9
33	.2 .9
34	.7 .5
35	.9 .3 .4 .6
36	.2 .1 .1 .1 .4
37	.7 .6 .6 .3
38	.2 .1 .3 .6 .8
39	.7 .5 .0
40	.2

15.

Stem	Leaves
1	
1	28 32 23 31 27 33 39
1	49 45
1	73 75 61
1	86 88 85 87 93 83 86
2	13 01 12 10 15 19 03
2	26 25
2	
2	72 63
2	

Section 9.5, pp. 529–531

1. Only (a)

3. a) 0.4973   **b)** 0.3186   **c)** 0.0853   **d)** 0.0239   **e)** 0.0029   **f)** 0.9222
g) 0.9706   **h)** 0.9806

5. a) $z = 1$ **b)** $z = 3$ **c)** $z = -2$ **d)** $z = 0$

7. a) The highest z-scores to the lowest, or B, C, D, E, and A.
   b) Those whose z-scores are positive, or B, C, and D.
   c) Those whose z-scores are negative, or A and E.

9. 0.0045   **11.** 0.1056

13. a) 3.44th percentile.   **b)** 10.2th percentile   **c)** 70.88th percentile   **d)** 32.64th percentile

15. $\mu = 118.0728$

Section 9.6, pp. 543–547

1. a)

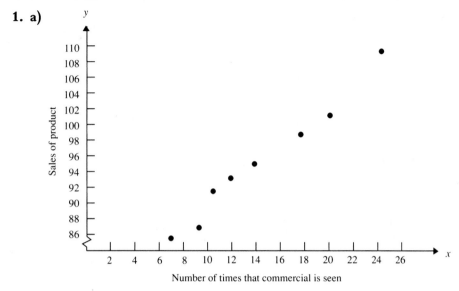

b) 0.9876　　**c)** Regression equation is $y = 1.354x + 75.534$　　**d)** When $x = 222$, $y = 105.322$.

3. a)

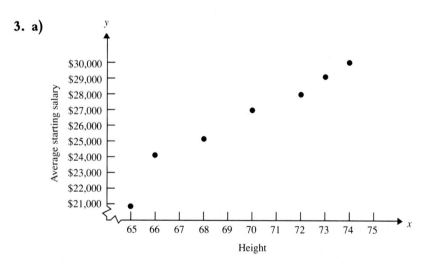

b) 0.977　　**c)** Regression equation is $y = 879.377x - 35,019.455$

d) When $x = 69$, $y = \$25,657.56$

5. a) 0.9955   **b)** Regression equation is $y = 4.35x + 32.072$ **c)** 77.747

7. a) 0.9668   **b)** Regression equation is $y = 2.502x + 73.06$ **c)** 90.574

9. a) -0.9522 **b)** Regression equation is $y = -11.173x + 609.8$ **c)** 576.281

11. a) Regression equation is $y = -1334.016x + 9479.446$ **b)** 3476.374

Typical Classroom Questions, pp. 549–550

1. The second student, since there are different numbers of employees in the different titles.

2. The one from company B. It has a smaller standard deviation.

3. All the subtractions mentioned are not called "working days."

4. No. Bill had a higher z-score.

Chapter Review Exercises, pp. 554–558

1. Choice (d)   **2.** 0.9871   **3.** $y = 2.188x + 7.5699$ **4.** 27.2619   **5.** Choice (c)

6. a) $\Sigma x^2 = 1668$ **b)** $(\Sigma x)^2 = 7744$ **7.** $z = 1.13$ **8.** Choice (b)   **9.** Choice (c)

10. Choice (b)   **11.** 74th percentile   **12.** Choice (d)   **13.** Choice (a)   **14.** Choice (b)

15. Choice (a)   **16.** 0.9324   **17. a)** 45   **b)** 115

18. Probably the mode, as it would then satisfy the most number of people.

19. Since it is truly in the middle, with 50% above the median and 50% below.

20.

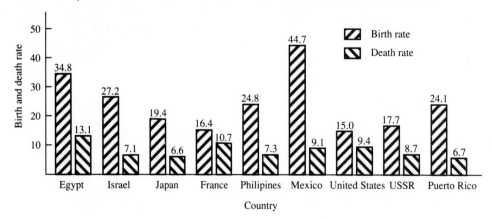

21.

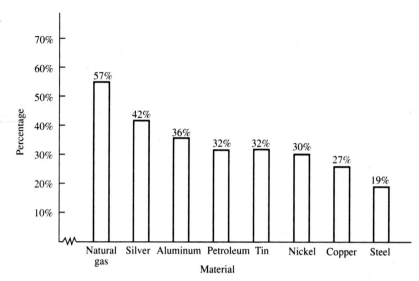

22. Yes, based on the graph.   **23.** 50,000   **24.** $y = 2721.429x + 10647.14$ **25.** \$22,893.57

CHAPTER 10

Section 10.1, pp. 570–572

1. $\overline{BC}$ **3.** $\overline{AC}$ **5.** $\overline{BC}$ **7.** $\overline{AD}$ **9.** Point B **11.** $\overline{CD}$ **13.** Point D **15.** $\overrightarrow{EA}$

17. All points on line segment $\overline{BC}$ or line segment $\overline{DE}$.

19. All points on line segment $\overline{BC}$ or line segment $\overline{CD}$.   **21.** Point C

23. All points on the sides of quadrilateral $ABCD$.   **25.** Point B **27.** 3   **29.** Yes

31. An infinite number   **33.** Yes   **37.** No; Yes.   **39.** 4

Section 10.2, pp. 583–584

1.

3.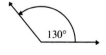

5.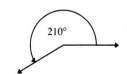

7.

9.

11. *a* and *d*, *b* and *c*, *e* and *h*, and *f* and *g* are vertical angles. *a* and *b*, *b* and *d*, *d* and *c*, *c* and *a*, *e* and *f*, *f* and *h*, *h* and *g*, and *g* and *e* are adjacent angles.

13. No vertical angles; *s* and *r*, and *r* and *q* are adjacent angles.

15. No vertical angles; *e* and *d*, *d* and *c*, *c* and *b*, and *b* and *a* are adjacent angles.

17. $\frac{7\pi}{6}$ radians   **19.** $\frac{-\pi}{4}$ **21.** -4π **23.** $\frac{-19\pi}{6}$ **25.** $\frac{-\pi}{3}$ **27.** $\frac{80\pi}{9}$ **29.** $90°$ **31.** $165°$

33. $-432°$ **35.** $900°$ **37.** $\overrightarrow{AB}$ **39.** Point *A*   **41. a)** $30°$ **b)** $140°$ **c)** $60°$ **d)** $50°$

43. The angle measures $108°$ and its supplement measures $72°$.

45. The smaller angle measures $20°$ and the larger angle measures $70°$.

47. The measure of the angle is $70°$ and its supplement measures $110°$.   **49.** No   **51.** $127°$

Section 10.3, pp. 592–595

1. Closed   **3.** Closed   **5.** Not closed   **7.** Polygon   **9.** Polygon   **11.** Polygon

13. It can be done. It is an acute triangle.   **15.** 34 cm   **17.** 15   **19.** $\sqrt{369}$ **21.** $\sqrt{91}$

23. The distance from the top of the ladder to the ground is approximately 22 feet.

25. $a = b$

27. No   **29.** It can't be done   **31.** 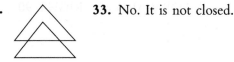   **33.** No. It is not closed.

35. a) False   **b)** False   **c)** False   **d)** True   **e)** False   **f)** True   **g)** False

37. a) A heptagon has 7 sides. $900°$ **b)** An octagon has 8 sides. $1080°$
   c) A nonagon has 9 sides. $1260°$ **d)** A decagon has 10 sides. $1440°$

39. a) $n = 7$ **b)** $n = 11$ **c)** $n = 14$ **d)** $n = 17$

41. The angles measure $60°$, $75°$, $90°$, and $135°$.   **43.** $120°$

45. In Figure 10.67 there are 55 squares and in Figure 10.68 there are 18 squares.

47. a) The first part of the sentence is true. The second part is false.   **b)** False

49. a) Concave   **b)** Convex   **c)** Concave

Section 10.5, pp. 611–613

1. a)   **b)**   **c)**

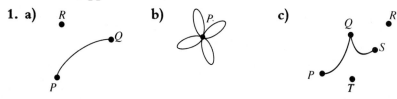

d) 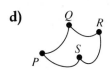 **e)**  **f)**

3. Can be drawn   **5.** Cannot be drawn   **7.** Can be drawn   **9.** Cannot be drawn

11. Cannot be drawn   **13.** Yes   **15.** Yes   **17.** Yes   **19.** Connected, $V = 3$, $E = 3$, and $F = 2$.

21. Connected, $V = 1$, $E = 2$, and $F = 3$.   **23.** Connected, $V = 5$, $E = 6$, and $F = 3$.

25. Connected, $V = 2$, $E = 2$, and $F = 2$.   **27.** Connected, $V = 8$, $E = 7$, and $F = 1$.

Section 10.6, p. 615

1. You get two interlocking strips.

Section 10.7, pp. 618–619

1. a) LEFT   **b)** RIGHT   **c)** LEFT   **d)** LEFT

5. a) FORWARD 60   RIGHT 90
FORWARD 20   RIGHT 90
FORWARD 60   RIGHT 90
FORWARD 20

b) FORWARD 30   LEFT 90
FORWARD 20   RIGHT 90
FORWARD 20   RIGHT 90
FORWARD 50   RIGHT 90
FORWARD 50   RIGHT 90
FORWARD 20

Typical Classroom Questions, pp. 619–620

1. No   **2.** No   **3.** Any convex polygon   **4.** Yes   **5.** Yes   **6.** Only if they are coplanar

7. No   **8.** No

Chapter Review Exercises, pp. 624–627

1 Other leg is 5.   **2.** Each equal angle measures 15°.   **3.** $3x - 4$ **4.** $\frac{5\pi}{12}$ radians   **5.** 105°

6. The angles measure 40°, 80°, and 60°. The largest angle measures 80°.

7. The length of the hypotenuse is $\sqrt{34}$.

8.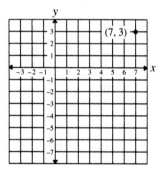

9. Yes   **10.** 18 sides   **11.** 5 sides   **12.** The polygon has 5 sides.

13. Each base angle measures 35°.   **14.** 85°   **15.** $x = 20$ **16.** $x = 25$ **17.** $x = 15$ **18.** $x = 8$

19. The angles are 40°, 60°, 80°, and 180°. The smallest angle measures 40°.   **20.** Choice (b)

21. Point D **22.** All points on segment $\overline{BG}$ or $\overline{FC}$

23. All points on the sides of quadrilateral $ABCD$ **24.** Points D and G

25. The third angle must be a right angle, or measure 90°.   **26.** Choice (d)   **27.** $x = 30°$

28. $x = 5°$ **29.** 110°

CHAPTER 11

Section 11.1, pp. 634–635

1. (2, 1)   **3.** (5, −3)   **5.** (−2, 0)   **7.** (0, −2)

9.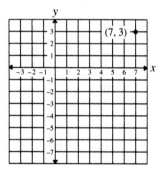

11.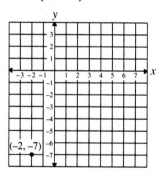

13.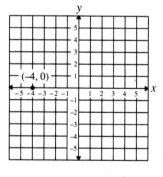

15.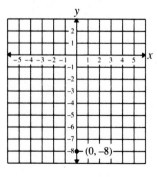

17.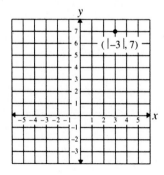

19.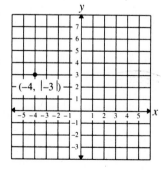

21. IV   **23.** II   **25.**

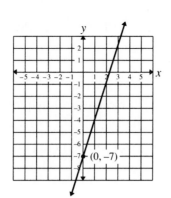

27. $y = 0$ **29.** $(0, 0)$

Section 11.2, pp. 648–650

1. a) Distance = $\sqrt{17}$ Midpoint = $\left(\dfrac{7}{2}, 7\right)$ **b)** Distance = $\sqrt{17}$ Midpoint = $\left(4, \dfrac{1}{2}\right)$

c) Distance = $\sqrt{130}$ Midpoint = $\left(\dfrac{-3}{2}, \dfrac{3}{2}\right)$ **d)** Distance = $2\sqrt{13}$ Midpoint = $(2, 0)$

e) Distance = $\sqrt{106}$ Midpoint = $\left(\dfrac{-1}{2}, \dfrac{1}{2}\right)$ **f)** Distance = $\sqrt{26}$ Midpoint = $\left(\dfrac{-9}{2}, \dfrac{-7}{2}\right)$

g) Distance = $\sqrt{10}$ Midpoint = $\left(\dfrac{-1}{2}, \dfrac{-3}{2}\right)$ **h)** Distance = $3\sqrt{2}$ Midpoint = $\left(\dfrac{7}{2}, \dfrac{7}{2}\right)$

3. Since distance $\overline{AB}$ = distance $\overline{AC} = \sqrt{17}$ we have an isosceles triangle.

5. Using the quadratic formula, $x = 5 \pm \sqrt{33}$.   **7.** $3x^2 - 46x + 3y^2 - 56y + 219 = 0$

9. Coordinates of M_1 = midpoint of $\overline{BC}$ = $(-1, 3)$
Coordinates of M_2 = midpoint of $\overline{AC}$ = $(3, 4)$
Coordinates of M_3 = midpoint of $\overline{AB}$ = $(2, 9)$
Distance $\overline{AM_1}$ = $7\sqrt{2}$
Distance $\overline{BM_2}$ = $\sqrt{41}$
Distance $\overline{CM_3}$ = $5\sqrt{5}$

11. a) Center $(4, 1)$ radius = $\sqrt{49} = 7$ **b)** Center $(-4, 6)$ radius = $\sqrt{65}$
c) Center $(-2, -9)$ radius = $\sqrt{12}$ **d)** Center $(0, -2)$ radius = $\sqrt{16} = 4$

13. a) Point $P(-4, 3)$ lies on the circle.   **b)** Point $P(3, 2)$ lies on the circle.
c) Point $P(2, -7)$ does not lie on the circle.   **d)** Point $P(-3, -2)$ does not lie on the circle.

15. Distance $\overline{AB} = \sqrt{52}$

Distance $\overline{BC} = \sqrt{104}$

Distance $\overline{AC} = \sqrt{52}$

Since $(\overline{AB})^2 + (\overline{AC})^2 = (\overline{BC})^2$, $\triangle ABC$ is a right triangle with hypotenuse $\overline{BC}$.

Coordinates of $M = \left(\dfrac{3+5}{2}, \dfrac{8+(-2)}{2}\right) = (4, 3)$

Distance $\overline{AM} =$ distance $\overline{BM} =$ distance $\overline{CM} = \sqrt{26}$

17. Coordinates of $M_1 =$ median of $\overline{BC} = (7, 7)$.

Coordinates of $M_2 =$ median of $\overline{AC} = (4, 6)$.

Coordinates of $M_3 =$ median of $\overline{AB} = (3, 2)$.

The three medians $\overline{AM_1}$, $\overline{BM_2}$, and $\overline{CM_3}$ intersect at $(5, 5)$. These are the coordinates of the centroid.

19. a) Midpoint of $\overline{AC} = (11, 5)$

Midpoint of $\overline{BD} = (11, 5)$

b) Length of diagonal $\overline{AC} = 10$

Length of diagonal $\overline{BD} = 10$

c) Length of $\overline{AB} =$ length of $\overline{CD} = \sqrt{90}$

Length of $\overline{BC} =$ length of $\overline{AD} = \sqrt{10}$

Since both pairs of opposite sides are congruent, the quadrilateral is a parallelogram.

d) $(\overline{AB})^2 + (\overline{BC})^2 = (\overline{AC})^2$ and $(\overline{AB})^2 + (\overline{AD})^2 = (\overline{BD})^2$ so that angles A and B are right angles. A parallellogram with right angles is a rectangle.

21. Distance $\overline{AB} +$ distance $\overline{BC} =$ distance $\overline{AC}$. Thus points A, B, and C are collinear.

23. Since the length of diagonal $\overline{AC} =$ length of diagonal $\overline{BD} = a\sqrt{2}$, diagonals of a square are congruent.

25. Midpoint of $\overline{PS} = (d, e) =$ coordinates of D.

Midpoint of $\overline{SR} = (d + b, e + c) =$ coordinates of C.

Midpoint of $\overline{RQ} = (b + a, c) =$ coordinates of B.

Midpoint of $\overline{PQ} = (a, 0) =$ coordinates of A.

Length of $\overline{DC} =$ length of $\overline{AB} = \sqrt{b^2 + c^2}$

Length of $\overline{DA} =$ length of $\overline{CB} = \sqrt{(d-a)^2 + e^2}$.

Since both pairs of opposite sides are congruent, the quadrilateral is a parallelogram.

27. Coordinates of point $E = (b, c)$.
Coordinates of point $D = (b + a, c)$.

Length of median $\overline{BE} = \sqrt{(2a - b)^2 + c^2}$.

Length of median $\overline{AD} = \sqrt{(b + a)^2 + c^2}$.
Since the medians are congruent, their lengths are equal. So $a = 2b$.
Thus the coordinates of $\triangle ABC$ are $A(0, 0)$, $C(2b, 2c)$ and $B(4b, 0)$

Using the distance formula, the length of $\overline{AC}$ = length of $\overline{BC} = \sqrt{4b^2 + 4c^2}$. Thus $\triangle ABC$ is isosceles.

29. a) Distance = $\sqrt{108}$
Midpoint = $(3, 1, 4)$

b) Distance = $\sqrt{36} = 6$
Midpoint = $(3, -5, 2)$

Section 11.3, p. 655

1. Graph of $y = 3x + 7$

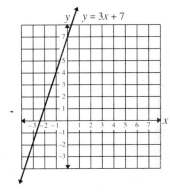

3. Graph of $y = -3x + 7$

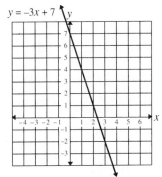

5. Graph of $y = -3x$

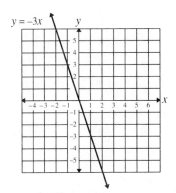

7. Graph of $5y = -15$

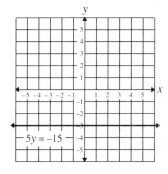

9. Graph of $5x + 3y = 15$

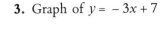
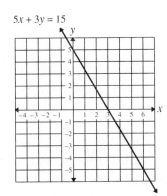

11. Graph of $y = \dfrac{-x}{3} - 4$

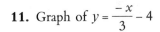
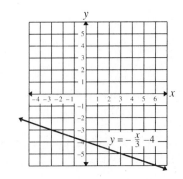

13. Graph of $|x - 2| = 9$

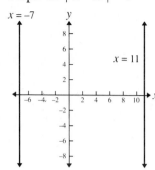

15. Graph of $|x - y| = 3$

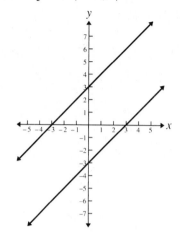

17. Graph of $|y| - |x| = 3$

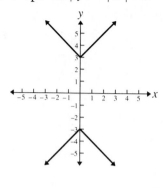

19. a) $x = 3$ **b)** $y = 3$

Section 11.4, p. 665–666

1. a) $\frac{200}{1000} = \frac{1}{5}$ **b)** No slope   **c)** 0

3. a) slope = 3 y = intercept = -1 **b)** slope = $\frac{1}{3}$ y-intercept = 4   **c)** slope = $\frac{3}{5}$ y-intercept = 3
   d) slope = $\frac{8}{5}$ y-intercept = -8 **e)** slope = 1 y-intercept = 0   **f)** slope = 0 y-intercept = 7
   g) no slope   no y-intercept

5. a) x-intercept = 3 y-intercept = -4 **b)** x-intercept = -3 y-intercept = $\frac{3}{2}$
   c) x-intercept = 0 y-intercept = 0   **d)** x-intercept = $\frac{5}{2}$ y-intercept = -5
   e) x-intercept $x = 3$ y-intercept none   graph is vertical
   f) x-intercept none y-intercept $y = \frac{-14}{3}$ graph is horizontal

7. $y = 4x - 14$ **9.** $y = 3x + 0$ or $y = 3x$

11. a) Slope = $\frac{1}{2}$ **b)** Slope = $\dfrac{-2}{x - 7}$ **c)** $x = +3$ **d)** $y = -6x + 18$

13. Slope of $\overline{AB} = \frac{-3}{2}$ Slope of $\overline{BC} = \frac{2}{3}$ Slope of $\overline{CD} = \frac{-3}{2}$ Slope of $\overline{AD} = \frac{2}{3}$

Since $\overline{AB}$ and $\overline{CD}$ have the same slope, they are parallel to each other. Also slope $\overline{BC}$ = slope $\overline{AD}$. So $\overline{BC} \| \overline{AD}$ and $ABCD$ is a parallelogram. Also slope $\overline{AB}$ is negative reciprocal of slope $\overline{BC}$, so that $\angle B$ is a right angle. Thus $ABCD$ is a rectangle.

15. The orthocenter of the triangle is $\left(\dfrac{-31}{7}, \dfrac{118}{7} \right)$

Section 11.5, p. 670

1. Graph of $x > 3$

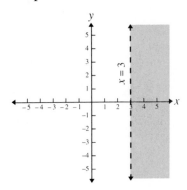

3. Graph of $y \geq 5$

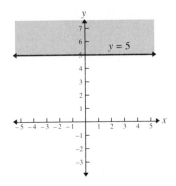

5. Graph of $x \geq 0$

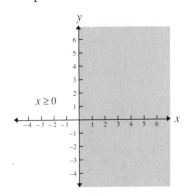

7. Graph of $y > 3x$

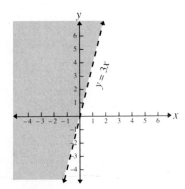

9. Graph of $2y - 3x > 12$

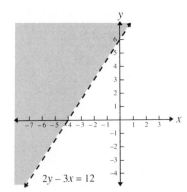

11. Graph of $2x + 3y > 6$

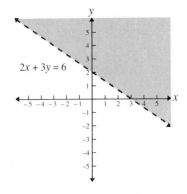

13. Graph of $y - x \leq -4$

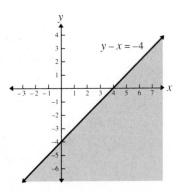

15. Graph of $x \leq -2y$

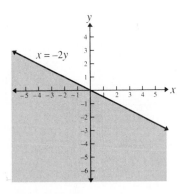

17. Graph of $2x + y - 3 \geq 0$

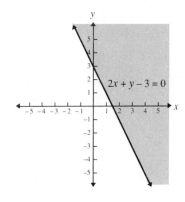

19. Graph of $5x - 4y \leq 20$ **21.** $6y \geq 5x - 12$ **23.** $y \geq x$ **25.** $2y \leq 3x + 4$

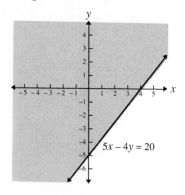

Section 11.6, p. 676

1. $x = 3,\ y = 12$ **3.** $x = 0,\ y = 1$ **5.** $x = 2,\ y = -1$ **7.** $x = 1,\ y = 2$ **9.** $x = 5,\ y = 5$

11. $x = -6,\ y = 3$ **13.** $x = -3,\ y = -2$ **15.** Equations are inconsistent.

17. System is dependent.   **19.** System is dependent.

21.

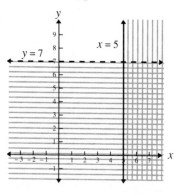

23.

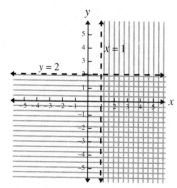

25.

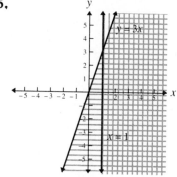

27.

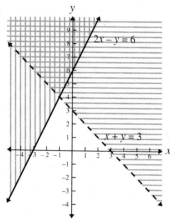

29.

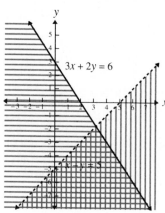

31.

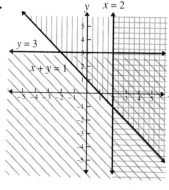

33.

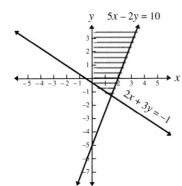

35.

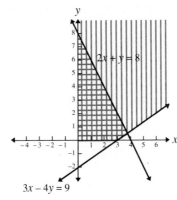

Section 11.7, p. 680

3. a) PENUP
SETXY   20   60
PENDOWN
SETXY   30   70
PENUP
END

b) TO MIDPOINT 20 60 30 70
SETXY $(20 + 30)/2$ $(60 + 70)/2$
END

c) TO DISTANCE   20 60 30 70
PRINT SQRT $(30 - 20) * (30 - 20) + (70 - 60) * (70 - 60)$
END

Typical Classroom Questions, p. 680

1. No, undefined slope is not the same as zero slope.

2. When graphing inequalities, we shade regions (not specific points) that satisfy the inequalities.

3. Yes. Pick a test point.   **4.** No. A line has no midpoint. Only a line segment has a midpoint.

5. No; No; A line parallel to the y-axis has only an x-intercept. A line parallel to the x-axis has only a y-intercept.

6. No. The radius of a circle cannot be negative.

7. No. The square root of a sum is not equal to the sum of the square roots of the individual numbers.

Chapter Review Exercises, pp. 684–687

1. Length $= 2\sqrt{5}$ **2.** Slope $= 9$ **3.** $(6, 1)$ **4.** Choice (b)   **5.** Choice (b)   **6.** Choice (a)

7. Choice (d)   **8.** $(x - 1)^2 + (y + 5)^2 = 7$ represents the equation of a circle whose center is at $(1, -5)$.

9. Coordinates of $M =$ midpoint of $\overline{AB} = (0, 16)$.   Coordinates of $N =$ midpoint of $\overline{BC} = (4, 19)$.

    Slope of $\overline{MN} = \frac{3}{4}$ Slope of $\overline{AC} = \frac{3}{4}$ Since $\overline{MN}$ and $\overline{AC}$ have the same slope, $\overline{MN} \,\|\, \overline{AC}$.

10. Choice (b)   **11.** Choice (d)   **12.** (7, 3)

13. The three medians $\overline{AM_1}$, $\overline{BM_2}$, and $\overline{CM_3}$ intersect at $\left(\dfrac{-1}{3}, \dfrac{8}{3}\right)$. These are the coordinates of the centroid.

14. $2y = x$ **15.** $h = 3$ **16.** $y = 7$

17. a) Length of $\overline{OS} = 5 =$ length of radius   **b)** Equation of circle $= x^2 + y^2 = 25$

   c) Slope of $\overleftrightarrow{OS} = \dfrac{-4}{3}$. Slope of $\overleftrightarrow{AB} = \dfrac{3}{-4}$ since it is perpendicular to $\overrightarrow{OS}$.   **d)** $4y + 3x = 7$

   e) $\left(0, \dfrac{7}{4}\right)$ is on $\overleftrightarrow{AB}$. Other answers are possible.

18. Midpoint of $\overline{BC} = (4, -3) =$ coordinates of D. Thus D is bisector of $\overline{BC}$.

Slope of $\overline{BC} = 1$. Slope of $\overline{AD} = -1$

Since slope of $\overline{BC}$ is the negative reciprocal of slope of $\overline{AD}$, $\overline{AD}$ is perpendicular to side $\overline{BC}$. Thus, $\overline{AD}$ is the perpendicular bisector of $\overline{BC}$.

19. $k = 15$ **20. a)** Slope of $\overline{AB} = \dfrac{1}{3}$ **b)** $k = 3$ **c)** $y = x$ **d)** Coordinates of E are (5,5)

21. $x = 2$, $y = 5$ **22.** $x = 1$, $y = -4$

23. a)

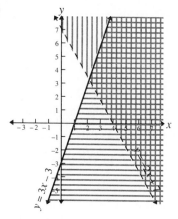

b) $x = 10$, $y = 5$ is one possible answer. Other answers are possible.

24. a)

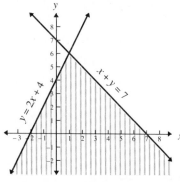

b) $x = 0$, $y = 0$ is one possible answer. Other answers are possible.

25. Slope $\overline{AB} = \frac{3-5}{2-4} = 1 = $ Slope $\overline{CD} = \frac{5-0}{7-2} = 1$. Thus $\overline{AB} \parallel CD$.

Slope $AC = \frac{0-5}{2-4} = \frac{5}{2} \neq $ Slope $\overline{BD} = \frac{5-3}{7-2} = \frac{2}{5}$.

Thus $\overline{AC}$ is not parallel to $\overline{BD}$.

Length of $\overline{AC} = \sqrt{(0-5)^2 + (2-4)^2} = \sqrt{29}$

Length of $\overline{BD} = \sqrt{(5-3)^2 + (7-2)^2} = \sqrt{29}$

Thus $ABCD$ is an isosceles trapezoid.

CHAPTER 12

Section 12.1, p. 700

1. 8.226 meters   **3.** 7.35 liquid quarts   **5.** 17,280,000 cg   **7.** 365.76 cm

9. If we convert from ml to ounces and then to gallons, we get 0.4675 gallons. If we convert from ml to liters and then to gallons, we get 0.4576 gallons.

11. 275,000 gm   **13.** 400.4 yards   **15.** 20,421.2 mm   **17.** 118.8 lb.   **19.** 14.56 dry quarts

21. 125.952 feet   **23.** 389.4 liters   **25.** 70,000 cg   **27.** 56 km/hour

29. 6′5″ = 195.58 cm   **31.** 1200 mg = 0.042 inches   **33.** About 36 cents   **35.** $-9.4°F$
195 pounds = 87.75 kg
38 inches = 96.52 cm

37. 291mm or 29.1cm   **39.** 1647.464 gallons per month.

Section 12.2, pp. 708–711

1. 30   **3.** 30π **5.** 40   **7.** 72   **9.** 56   **11.** 192   **13.** 196   **15.** $\pi b^2 - \pi a^2$ **17.** $xy + wz$

19. $7a^2$ **21.** $34.5\, \pi r^2$ **23.** $ab - \pi r^2 - x^2$ **25.** $64\pi - 48\sqrt{3}$. The base of each triangle is 8.

27. $100\pi - 25\sqrt{3}$ **29.** 26   **31.** 58   **33.** 37.5

Section 12.3, pp. 714–715

1. a) $x = 5$ **b)** $x = 10$ **c)** $x = \sqrt{58}$ **d)** $x = \sqrt{3}$ **e)** $x = 7\sqrt{2}$ **f)** $x = 8$

3. The diagonal is $25\sqrt{2}$ **5.** Skateboard will not fit in box, even if placed diagonally.

7. $x^2 + \left(\dfrac{x^2 - 1}{2}\right)^2 = \left(\dfrac{x^2 + 1}{2}\right)^2$

$x^2 + \dfrac{x^4 - 2x^2 + 1}{4} = \dfrac{4x^2 + x^4 - 2x^2 + 1}{4} = \dfrac{x^4 + 2x^2 + 1}{4} = \left(\dfrac{x^2 + 1}{2}\right)^2$

$\left(\dfrac{x^2 + 1}{2}\right)^2 = \left(\dfrac{x^2 + 1}{2}\right)^2$

Section 12.4, pp. 723–724

1. Lateral area = 324 cm^2 **3.** Lateral area = 576   **5.** Lateral area = 192π square inches
Surface area = 486 cm^2 Surface area = $(72\sqrt{3} + 576)$ cm^2 Surface area = 480π square inches

7. $h = 12.5$ Slant height is 25

9. a) Surface area = 312 cm^2 **b)** Surface area = 252 cm^2 **c)** Surface area = $(192π)$ cm^2

11. The surface area is 9 times as much as it was originally.   **13.** 2112 square inches

15. $(2500π + 50π \sqrt{3400})$ square feet

17. The second can needs more metal to manufacture since its surface area is 150π cm^2 larger.

19. The surface area of sphere equals the lateral area of the cylinder.

Section 12.5, pp. 732–735

1. Volume = 270 cm^3 **3.** Area of base = 10 dm^2 Volume = 60 dm^3 **5.** Volume = 120 cm^3

7. Volume = 2560 cm^3 **9.** 620 cubic inches   **11.** 1920π

13. Volume = 1188 cm^3 Capacity = 1188 ml

15. a) 9000 cm^3 **b)** $\frac{160}{3}π$ m^3 **c)** 180   **d)** $\frac{250}{3}π$ cm^3 **e)** 30560   **f)** 400 cm^3
g) radius = 5   volume = 1000π   **h)** radius = 10   volume = 1000π m^3

17. 1800 cubic feet   **19.** Volume = 18,329.14286 cubic feet ≈ 2443.89 gallons   **21.** Capacity = 8 ml

23. 32,000π cubic inches   **25.** Volume = capacity ≈ 4425 ml

27. No. 2½ cans: Volume is 6997.914π cm^3 **29.** Volume = 9,600,000 L
No. 2 cans: Volume is 4794.744π cm^3
The difference in volume is $(2203.17π)$ cm^3

31. 2000π m^3 **33.** 5.5 cm

Typical Classroom Questions, pp. 735–736

1. Yes, for a planar figure, surface area is the same as regular area.

2. The slant height equals the square root of the square of the radius plus the square of the altitude.

3. The metric system uses multiples of 10.

4. No. The surface area of tuna fish can = $2π (3^2) + 2π (3)(2) = 30π$.
The surface area of soda can = $2π(2^2) + 2π (2)(4.5) = 26π$.

5. Yes. 100 km = 100(0.62) = 62 miles, not 60 miles.

Chapter Review Exercises, pp. 740–743

1. Choice (b)   **2.** $r = 6$ **3.** The hypotenuse is $\sqrt{34}$.   **4.** 29.44°

5. A 2-liter bottle contains more than 64 ounces.   **6.** $13.60   **7.** 7 m³   **8.** 407 pounds

9. 188.928 square feet   **10.** 48 km   **11.** $8\sqrt{2}$ **12.** 32   **13.** 96   **14.** 64

15. a) Area = 288   Volume = $\frac{896}{3}$ cm³
   b) Area of base = $25\sqrt{3}$ Slant height = 13   Area = $(25\sqrt{3} + 195)$ cm²   Volume = $100\sqrt{3}$ cm³

16. 507   **17.** Volume of can = 2816   Volume of cube = 4492.125   **18.** Volume = capacity = 1800 ml
       Volume of part not filled = 1676.125 cm³

19. The cone has greater volume. The difference is 603.43 – 533.33 = 70.1.

20. Lateral area is four times as great.   **21.** Radius = 7 feet   Diameter = 14 feet

22. Base area = $\frac{243}{2}\sqrt{3}$ Volume = $(850.5\sqrt{3})$ cm³   **23.** $96\sqrt{3} - 9\pi$ **24.** 10 square cm   **25.** $6\sqrt{3}$

26. 20   **27.** 28.5   **28.** 2160 ml

29. Volume = capacity = 100.57 ml
   Since the volume is 100.57 ml, the 100 ml will fit in.

30. $\overline{DC} = 9$ $\overline{AC} = 16$ Since $\overline{AC} = \overline{AD} + \overline{DC}$, then $\overline{AD} = 7$.

CHAPTER 13

Section 13.1, pp. 754–756

1. a) Yes, by the SAS congruence property.   **b)** No   **c)** No
   d) Yes, by the ASA congruence property. $\overline{DB} \cong \overline{DB}$ **e)** Yes, by the AAS congruence property.
   f) Yes, by the ASA congruence property.   **g)** Yes, by the SSS congruence property.
   h) No   **i)** No

3. $\overline{EC}$ and $\overline{FB}$ **5.** $\overline{AE}$ and $\overline{DB}$

Section 13.3, pp. 764–766

1. $\overline{EF} = 24$ **3.** $\overline{DE} = 10$ **5.** 12 cm   **7.** Similar   **9.** Similar   **11.** Congruent

13. Congruent   **15.** Neither   **17.** Yes   **19.** Yes   **21.** No, the angles are not congruent.

23. No, the angles are not congruent.   **25.** 22.5 cm

27. a) Yes, by the AA similarity property.   **b)** $x = 40$ **29.** 10 feet

31. They have angle A in common, and they both have right angles.   **33.** $\overline{CD} = 8$ $\overline{DE} = 10$ $\overline{AB} = 30$

35. No. The angles may be different.

Section 13.4, pp. 778–780

1. Use Construction 4 to bisect $\overline{BC}$, then join vertex A to midpoint $\overline{BC}$.   **3.** Use Construction 7.

5. Use Construction 2.   **7.** Use Constructions 2 and 3.   **9.** Use Construction 15.

11. Use Construction 6.   **13.** Not necessarily   **15.** Choice (a)

Section 13.5, pp. 794–796

1.

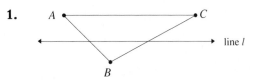

3. a) Vertical line symmetry W Ọ W
   b) Vertical line symmetry CO ┊ OK
   c) No line symmetry
   d) No line symmetry

5. The x-coordinate is moved 12 spaces to the right and the y-coordinate of the point is moved 4 spaces down. The image of (3, 5) is (15, 1).

7. (3, −2)   **9.** (2, 3)   **11.** (7, −5)   **13.** (2, −3)   **17.** Choice (c)   **19.** Point D **21.** Point C

23. a) one horizontal and 1 vertical   **b)** one horizontal and 1 vertical   **c)** one vertical   **d)** none
   e) one vertical   **f)** one horizontal   **g)** one vertical   **h)** one vertical
   i) one vertical and 1 horizontal

25. (1) line reflection   (2) rotation   (3) dilation

27. a) $A'(−7, 5)$, $B'(−3, 5)$, $C'(−7, −4)$ **b)** $A''(−4, 9)$, $B''(0, 9)$, $C''(−4, 0)$ **c)** Choice (ii)

Section 13.7, pp. 802

1.

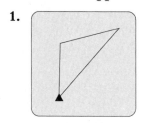

3.

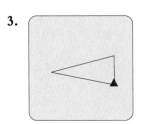

5. The program draws the bisector of a 150° angle.

7. The program draws a triangle similar to the given triangle whose two sides are 10 and 30 and whose included angle measures 50°. The sides of the new triangle will be 3 times as much as the sides of the original triangle.

Typical Classroom Questions, pp. 802–803

1. Yes.   **2.** No. The angle is not included between the two sides.   **3.** The first student.

4. The angle drawn by one of them may not be an included angle that was drawn by the other student.

Chapter Review Exercises, pp. 806–809

1. Choice (d)   **2.** (2, 3)   **3.** (9, 0)   **4.** Choice (d)   **5.** Choice (a)   **6.** (6, −4)

7. Choice (a)   **8.** $A'(1, 2)$, $B'(0, 4)$, $C'(−3, 1)$ **9.** $A''(4, −5)$, $B''(5, −7)$, $C''(8, −4)$

10. $A'''(2, 1)$, $B'''(4, 0)$, $C'''(1, −3)$ **11.** Choice (d)

12. With the necessary information, we could conceivably prove the following triangles congruent:
    (a) $\triangle ACF$ and $\triangle BCD$ **(b)** $\triangle AGD$ and $\triangle BGF$ **(c)** $\triangle ACE$ and $\triangle BCE$
    (d) $\triangle AGE$ and $\triangle BGE$ **(e)** $\triangle ABD$ and $\triangle BFA$ **(f)** $\triangle CDG$ and $\triangle CGF$
    (g) $\triangle AGC$ and $\triangle BGC$

13. $\overline{DF} = 24$ **14.** $x = 15$ **15.** $\frac{110}{3}$ or $36.6\overline{7}$ **16.** 2 meters   **17.** Choice (c)

18. Choices (a) and (b)   **19.** Choices (a) and (c)   **20.** 2.75 inches   **21.** $AB = 180$ yards

22. The triangles are congruent because of the ASA congruence property. $\overline{BC} = \overline{B'C'} = 17$

23. The triangles are similar because of the AA similarity property. $\overline{BC} = 21$ and $\overline{B'C'} = 7$

CHAPTER 14

Section 14.2, pp. 821–822

1. Because machine languages require that the user have some background knowledge of how the computer works, its capabilities, and its limitations.

3. High-level languages use commands and concepts in a manner comparable to everyday human language and thought. Low-level languages require that the user have some background knowledge of the computer. Prior programming knowledge is needed.

5. ALGOL stands for *Algorithmic Language* and is used primarily in Europe for scientific programming.

7. LISP stands for *List Processor* and was designed for the processing of non-numeric data (for example, symbols, words, characters). It is often used with programs dealing with artificial intelligence.

9. When a programming error has been made.   **11.** The control unit.

13. It means that the computer can store the information and instructions necessary to process the program so that the programmer can do something else while the program is being run. The operation of the computer need not be supervised.

15. The control unit.

17. They are all mechanisms for entering data and instructions into the computer.

Section 14.3, p. 824

1. It carries out sequences of instructions stored in the computer's main memory.

3. A personal computer must have an operating system as a master control program to synchronize the execution of computer programs.

5. The user can be many miles away from the computer.

Section 14.4, pp. 829–831

1.

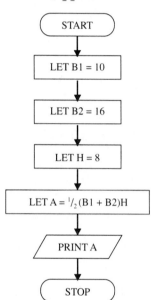

3–15. Answers similar to those given for Exercise 1.

17. It prints out each of the integers from 4 to 20 inclusive as well as their squares. It then stops.

19. Starting with values of $A = B = 1$, it reads a value for C. It then computes a value for D and prints the result. It then reads a new value for C, after which it computes a new value for D.

Section 14.5, pp. 843–845

1. Not acceptable   **3.** Not acceptable   **5.** Acceptable   **7.** 100   LET D = R∗T

9. 110   LET Y = Z∗ (7∗X – 3)   **11.** 140 LET A = (B – C)/(D + E)   **13.** $A = Z^3 = 2^3 = 8$

15. $A = Z^2 + X^2 = 10^2 + 2^2 = 104$ **17.** No, the BASIC variable is wrong. It has more than 2 characters.

19. No, there are 4 variables in the READ statement and 5 values in the DATA statement.

21. Mistake in Line 30.   **23.** The computer will print out 1,125,000, which represents the value of M.

25. 220 IS BIGGER THAN − 75   570 IS BIGGER THAN 320   50 IS BIGGER THAN − 5

30. $3701.86   **33.** 42,075   **35.** $x = 3$ **37.** $x = 4.6$ **39.** $x = 82.6$ **41.** $x = -2$ **43.** 6

Section 14.6, pp. 855–856

1. a) Should be   SETX 50   **b)** Should be   BK 25   **c)** Should be   SETXY 15 30
d) Does not specify how the triangle is to be drawn.
e) Does not specify how many times the instruction is to be repeated.

Typical Classroom Questions, p. 856

1. No. Especially not to the programmer.

2. The reward is a detailed knowledge of what the computer is actually doing.

3. Somebody has to write the software programs.

4. A computer's DOS represents a master control program that synchronizes the execution of computer programs.

5. No. They can be programmed.

Chapter Review Exercises, pp. 860–864

1. Choice (a)   **2.** Choice (c)   **3.** Choice (d)   **4.** Choice (d)   **5.** Choice (b)   **6.** Choice (a)

7. Choice (a)   **8.** Choice (d)   **9.** Choice (c)   **10.** Choice (b)   **11.** Choice (a)

12. Choice (b)   **13.** Choice (c)   **14.** Choice (c)   **15.** Choice (d)   **16.** Choice (c)   **17.** < =

18. $A = \dfrac{bc}{\sqrt[5]{d}}$ **19.** 100   LET Y = 2 * (X ↑ 3) * (Z ↑ 4)   **20.** 7.6   11.6   1.9

21. Error in Line 30   **22.** Replace a by $a + 5$, or add 5 to the previous value of a.   **23.** Six

24. 99999   **25.** (A ↑ 2) * (B ↑ 5)   **26.** 0.0025   **27.** No, variable name cannot be 3 characters long.

28. 100   LET Y = (− A) + (7 * (M ↑ 2) * (Y ↑ 5)) ↑ (1/3)

29. False. In BASIC, the symbol AB is meaningless.

30. First to divide the value of B by 2 and then to subtract the result from A.

31. A single digit.   **32.** Mistake in Line 40, missing end of quotation marks.

33. Prints the integers in order from 1 to 100 inclusive.

34. Prints the integers in reverse order from 100 to 1 inclusive, starting from 100.

35. Prints I AM A SMART COMPUTER 10 times.

36. Asks the user WHO IS THE PRESIDENT OF THE USA? If the user inputs the correct choice (from among those given) it prints CORRECT; otherwise, it prints INCORRECT, TRY AGAIN. The user must input that N = 2 is the correct choice.

37. Prints the name and pulse of a person and whether the pulse is NORMAL or NOT NORMAL, depending on whether pulse is less than 80 or greater than 60.

38. Should be   FD   20

40.

APPENDICES

Appendix A.1, pp. A-13–A-14

1. a) Not a proposition   **b)** Proposition   **c)** Not a proposition   **d)** Proposition
   e) Not a proposition   **f)** Proposition   **g)** Not a proposition   **h)** Proposition

3. a) $p \rightarrow q$ **b)** $p \wedge (\sim q)$ **c)** $(\sim p) \wedge (\sim q)$ **d)** $\sim(p \wedge q)$ **e)** $q \wedge (\sim p)$ **f)** $(\sim q) \rightarrow (\sim p)$

5. a) If I am afraid of heights then I have flown in an airplane.
   b) I have flown in an airplane if and only if I am afraid of heights.
   c) If I am afraid of heights then I have not flown in an airplane.
   d) If I am not afraid of heights then I have flown in an airplane.
   e) I am not afraid of heights if and only if I have not flown in an airplane.
   f) If I have not flown in an airplane then I am not afraid of heights.

7. Choices (b) and (d)   **9.** No

11. a) Joan has good recommendations, and if she has a high college grade point average then she was accepted to medical school.
   b) Either Joan has good recommendations or she has a high college grade point average and she was accepted to medical school.
   c) Either Joan does not have good recommendations or she does not have a high college grade point average and has not been accepted to medical school.
   d) Either Joan has good recommendations or if she does have a high college grade point average then she was not accepted to medical school.

e) Joan does not have good recommendations if and only if she was accepted to medical school and she has a high college grade point average.

f) Either Joan does not have a high college grade point average or was not accepted to medical school, and has good recommendations.

Appendix A.2, p. A-20

1. Neither　　**3.** Neither　　**5.** Self-contradiction　　**7.** Neither　　**9.** Neither　　**11.** Neither

13. Neither　　**15.** Neither　　**17.** Neither　　**19.** Neither

21.

p	q	$\sim p$	$\sim q$	$p \to q$	$(\sim p) \to (\sim q)$
T	T	F	F	T	T
T	F	F	T	F	T
F	T	T	F	T	F
F	F	T	T	T	T

These don't match.

23. 32　　**25.** True　　**27.** False　　**29.** True　　**31.** True　　**33.** False

35.

p	q	$p \to q$	$[p \wedge (\sim q)] \vee [(\sim p) \wedge q]$	$\sim(p \wedge q)$
T	T	T	F	F
T	F	F	T	T
F	T	T	T	T
F	F	T	F	T

37. True $\vee$ True gives True　　**39.** True $\wedge$ False gives False

41.

p	q	$p \veebar q$
T	T	F
T	F	T
F	T	T
F	F	F

43.

p	q	$\sim p$	$p \downarrow q$	$\sim(p \downarrow q)$	$(\sim p) \veebar q$	$\sim(p \downarrow q) \wedge [(\sim p) \veebar q]$
T	T	F	F	T	T	T
T	F	F	F	T	F	F
F	T	T	F	T	F	F
F	F	T	T	F	T	F

Appendix A 3, p. A-26

1. Invalid   **3.** Valid   **5.** Invalid

7. *Hypotheses:* $p \rightarrow q$
    q Invalid

    Conclusion: p

9. *Hypotheses:* $p \rightarrow q$
    $\sim q$ Valid

    Conclusion: $\sim p$

11. *Hypotheses:* $p \rightarrow q$
    $q \rightarrow r$ Valid
    $\sim q$

    Conclusion: $p \rightarrow (\sim r)$

13. *Hypotheses:* $p \rightarrow q$
    $q \rightarrow (\sim r)$ Invalid
    $q \vee r$

    Conclusion: $p \rightarrow r$

15. *Hypotheses:* $p \vee q$
    $\sim p$ Valid

    Conclusion: q

17. *Hypotheses:* $p \rightarrow (q \vee r)$
    $(\sim r) \rightarrow (\sim q)$ Invalid

    Conclusion: $\sim p$

19. *Hypotheses:* $\sim p \rightarrow q$
    $q \rightarrow (r \wedge s)$ Valid

    Conclusion: $(\sim s) \rightarrow p$

Appendix A.4, pp. A-36–A-39

1. No. Closure is not maintained.   **3.** No. No identity element   **5.** No. No identity element

7. No.   **9.** No. Not every element has an inverse. Also no identity

11. No. 0 has no inverse   **13.** No. (Not closed)   **15.** Yes

17. a) a **b)** The inverse of a is a; the inverse of b is b; the inverse of c is c.   **c)** No   **19.** Yes

21. a) Yes   **b)** Yes   **c)** Yes, α
    d) The inverse of α is α; the inverse of β is β; the inverse of γ is γ; the inverse of $\triangle$ is $\triangle$.   **e)** Yes

23. No. There is no identity.

25. b) $r \circ (s \circ t) = (r \circ s) \circ t$ $q \circ (u \circ v) = (q \circ u) \circ v$ $v \circ (w \circ r) = (v \circ w) \circ r$
    $r \circ v = q \circ t$ $q \circ s = v \circ v$ $v \circ v = r \circ r$
    $w = w$ $p = p$ $p = p$

27. Let X, Y, Z, and W be the following symmetries:

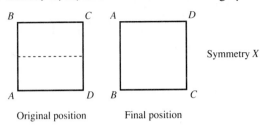

Symmetry X

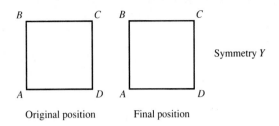

Symmetry Y

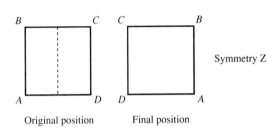

Symmetry Z

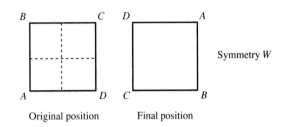

Symmetry W

∘	X	Y	Z	W
X	Y	X	W	Z
Y	X	Y	Z	W
Z	W	Z	Y	X
W	Z	W	X	Y

This forms an Abelian group.

29. b) Yes

31. $Z \circ P$, which is Q, is not equal to $P \circ Z$, which is R.

33. No. The associative law does not hold.

35. a) No   **b)** No

Index